# Dilapidations:

## The Modern Law and Practice

2013–14

# Dilapidations:

## The Modern Law and Practice

2013–14

**Nicholas Dowding QC, MA (Cantab), Hon RICS, Kirk Reynolds QC, MA, (Cantab), Hon RICS and Alison Oakes BA (Hons) (Dunelm), Barrister**

**SWEET & MAXWELL**

Published in 2013 by Sweet & Maxwell, 100 Avenue Road, London NW3 3PF part of
Thomson Reuters (Professional) UK Limited (Registered in England & Wales, Company No
1679046.
Registered Office and address for service: Aldgate House, 33 Aldgate High Street, London
EC3N 1DL)

For further information on our products and services, visit *www.sweetandmaxwell.co.uk*

Typeset by Letterpart Limited, Caterham on the Hill, Surrey CR3 5XL

Printed and bound in Great Britain by CPI Group (UK) Ltd, Croyden, CR0 4YY.

No natural forests were destroyed to make this product; only farmed timber was used and
re-planted.

A CIP catalogue record of this book is available for the British Library.

ISBN: 978-0-41402-499-1

Thomson Reuters and the Thomson Reuters logo are trademarks of Thomson Reuters.

Sweet & Maxwell ® is a registered trademark of Thomson Reuters (Professional) UK
Limited.

Crown copyright material is reproduced with the permission of the Controller of HMSO and
the Queen's Printer for Scotland.

This book is affectionately dedicated to the memory of Christopher Priday, QC, MA (Oxon), Head of Falcon Chambers 1986–1992.

## Acknowledgements

The Pre-Action Protocol for Terminal Dilapidations Claims for Damages in relation to the Physical State of Commercial Property at the Termination of Tenancy reproduced herein is the copyright of the Property Litigation Association and is reproduced with their kind permission.

# Foreword to the First Edition by the President of the Royal Institution of Chartered Surveyors

Dilapidations is an area of law, whether involving commercial or residential property, that is of great importance to the modern Chartered Surveyor and his clients. An abundance of examples that affect any individual or company spring to mind, including advice needed when granting a lease, acquiring a freehold or leasehold investment, setting up in business, buying a flat, facing an emergency, such as burst pipes or an invasion of dry rot from the neighbouring property, or finally, receiving that awful farewell present of a Schedule of Dilapidations upon departure from the leased premises. On all such occasions, a Chartered Surveyor as well as his lawyer will be able to help and give advice.

The problems which arise, and the solutions which are required are essentially practical. Yet the Law of Dilapidations is ancient in origin, arcane in content and obscure in application. It is a subject which, therefore, cries out to be de-mystified. In this book, the authors have sought to put the Law and Practice of Dilapidations into its modern and practical context.

The book contains a comprehensive discussion of all the relevant legal principles, together with many examples of how those principles may apply to every day problems which arise in real life. The problems which occur as a result of new building methods and new building materials are specifically addressed and old cases concerned with "oil-based paints" and "main timbers" are put into the context of buildings composed entirely of glass and steel.

This book is written by authors highly qualified to write on such subjects and they have particularly recognised that the text offers much for the Chartered Surveyor, as valuer and general property advisor, as well as the more specialist building surveyors. The specific contributions from a valuation surveyor (with worked examples) and from a tax lawyer are particularly welcome. It is published at a time when the awareness of the vast number of skills that Chartered Surveyors possess is now being more widely recognised by the community at large and the business sector in particular. It will greatly assist Surveyors in providing up to date practical advice in a modern and understandable context. An invaluable guide to Continuous Professional Development and readable by newcomers to the profession as well as old-stagers anxious to bring themselves up to date. A welcome addition to serious coverage of an important property specialist activity dispelling the mystique that surrounds dilapidations.

July 5, 1994
Clive Lewis FRICS FSVA
President of the Royal Institution of Chartered Surveyors

# Preface to the Fifth Edition

In *R v Ion*[1] counsel contended – and the judges did not dispute – that there is "no doubt a rule that a writer on law is not to be considered an authority in his lifetime" (although the footnote records that the rule seemed "more honoured in the breach than the observance"). In *On Law and Justice*[2] Professor Paul Freund noted that:

> " In England until recently it was a tradition that authors were not to be cited as authority in judicial opinions. On one occasion the Lord Chief Justice, despite the tradition, could not refrain from citing Prof. Holdsworth's History of English Law, but when he did so he was careful to refer to Prof. Holdsworth as one 'who happily is not an authority'. The reporter of decisions, in puzzling over the passage, concludes that it may have been a slip of the pen, and so when it was published it read 'Professor Holdsworth who unhappily is not an authority!'"

It is in this context that we record with mixed feelings a passage from the judgment of H.H. Judge Cooke in *Indiana Investments v Taylor*,[3] in which, having quoted with approval a passage from the Third Edition of this work, he went on to say that "the learned authors are still alive and in practice but their work is at this point, a convenient summary of known authority". We are pleased to report that we are indeed still alive and in practice, from which it would appear to follow (to jurisprudential purists, at least) that this Fifth Edition, like its predecessors, sadly cannot properly be regarded as authority for anything at all. Nonetheless, we hope that it may continue to offer the odd useful insight or two on the modern law and practice of dilapidations, which has developed considerably since the First Edition of this work was published in 1995.

We have tried, as always, to cover the sort of legal and practical problems which confront the modern practitioner, and to answer as best we can those questions which, in our experience, seem to arise time and time again in practice. To take but a few examples: we have included a new Ch.37 containing a detailed treatment of the Pre Action Protocol for Claims for Damages in Relation to the Physical State of Commercial Property at the Termination of a Tenancy (the Dilapidations Protocol), which came into force on January 1, 2012; we have largely rewritten our treatment of damages for terminal disrepair, which has been divided into two new chapters (Ch.29 dealing with the common law, and Ch.30 with s.18(1) of the Landlord and Tenant Act 1927); and we have rewritten Ch.13 on mechanical and electrical services and plant (which now includes, among

---

[1] (1852) 2 Den. CC 475.
[2] Harvard University Press, 1963.
[3] [2004] 3 E.G.L.R. 63.

other things, a discussion of the problems caused by the fact that the use of recycled R22 refrigerant gas in air conditioning systems will become unlawful at the end of 2014) to reflect the increasing prominence and importance of such items in most modern schedules of dilapidations. We have included a large number of new dilapidations cases, both from this jurisdiction and from the Commonwealth.

As always, the finished work reflects far more than our own unaided efforts. Those who have helped us are too numerous to name individually, but they include, as always, our friends and colleagues at Falcon Chambers and in the legal and surveying professions more generally. Special thanks are due to the excellent team at Malcolm Hollis (among them Vivien King and Stephen Lemon), who have kindly commented on various drafts and provided us with the benefit of their very considerable practical experience; to Anthony Tanney and Mark Sefton of Falcon Chambers, who assisted us considerably with, respectively, Ch.24 and Chs 29 and 30; and to Nicholas Taggart of Landmark Chambers, who made a number of enormously valuable suggestions in relation to Chs 29 and 37. We are also grateful, as always, to Nicholas Eden FRICS FCIArb, a partner in Kinney & Green, Chartered Surveyors, for contributing the worked examples in Ch.31.

We need hardly say that any errors which remain are, of course, ours alone.

This Edition, like its predecessors, is dedicated to the memory of Christopher Priday QC, Head of Falcon Chambers from 1986 to 1992, who inspired the writing of this work, and whose learning and deep understanding of the law of dilapidations remains reflected in many parts of this Fifth Edition.

We have tried to state the law as at July 1, 2013.

Nicholas Dowding QC
Kirk Reynolds QC
Alison Oakes

# TABLE OF CONTENTS

## 2.  THE DURATION OF THE OBLIGATION

## 3.  WHO CAN SUE AND BE SUED

## 8. THE SECOND QUESTION: IS THE SUBJECT-MATTER OF THE COVENANT IN A DAMAGED OR DETERIORATED CONDITION?

## 9. THE THIRD QUESTION: IS THE NATURE OF THE DAMAGE SUCH AS TO BRING THE CONDITION OF THE SUBJECT-MATTER BELOW THE STANDARD CONTEMPLATED BY THE REPAIRING COVENANT?

## 10. THE FOURTH QUESTION: WHAT WORK IS REQUIRED IN ORDER TO PUT THE SUBJECT-MATTER OF THE REPAIRING COVENANT BACK INTO THE CONTEMPLATED CONDITION?

## 11. THE FIFTH QUESTION: IS THAT WORK NONETHELESS OF SUCH A NATURE THAT THE PARTIES DID NOT CONTEMPLATE IT WOULD BE THE LIABILITY OF THE COVENANTING PARTY?

## 12. THE APPLICATION OF THE REPAIRING COVENANT IN RELATION TO COMMONLY ENCOUNTERED DEFECTS

## 13. MECHANICAL AND ELECTRICAL SERVICES AND PLANT

## 14. FORMS OF EXPRESS COVENANT

## 19. THE LANDLORD'S IMPLIED OBLIGATIONS TOWARDS THE TENANT AT COMMON LAW

## 20. THE LANDLORD'S IMPLIED OBLIGATIONS TOWARDS THE TENANT UNDER STATUTE

## 23. CONSIDERATIONS AFFECTING THE PERFORMANCE OF TENANTS' OBLIGATIONS TO REPAIR

## 24. SUB-LEASES

## 25. FIXTURES

## 26. THE LANDLORD'S REMEDIES FOR BREACH OF COVENANT ON THE PART OF THE TENANT

## 27. FORFEITURE

## 29. DAMAGES AT THE END OF THE TERM (1): THE COMMON LAW MEASURE OF DAMAGES FOR BREACH OF THE COVENANT TO REPAIR

## 30. DAMAGES AT THE END OF THE TERM (2): S.18(1) OF THE LANDLORD AND TENANT ACT 1927

## 31. VALUATIONS UNDER THE FIRST LIMB OF S.18(1) OF THE LANDLORD AND TENANT ACT 1927: WORKED EXAMPLES

## 32. DAMAGES AT THE END OF THE TERM (3): BREACHES OF COVENANT OTHER THAN THE COVENANT TO REPAIR

## 33. THE TENANT'S REMEDIES FOR BREACH OF COVENANT ON THE PART OF THE LANDLORD

## 36. DILAPIDATIONS CLAIMS IN PRACTICE

CONTENTS xlix

# TABLE OF CASES

li

# TABLE OF STATUTES

# TABLE OF STATUTORY INSTRUMENTS

CHAPTER 1

# THE EXISTENCE OF THE OBLIGATION

## EXPRESS TERMS

### Express terms

An obligation to repair on the part of landlord or tenant usually arises as an express term of the contract between them. Where the letting is effected by a written tenancy agreement or a formal lease under seal, the ascertainment of the repairing liabilities is a question of construction of the document in question.[1] In the case of an oral letting, the question whether or not there is a repairing obligation depends upon what the parties have said. Oral tenancies are far more common in the context of rack rented residential property, and in some cases the factual question of precisely what has been agreed can give rise to substantial difficulties.[2] Where the tenant holds over either under statute or under an implied periodic tenancy arising from payment and acceptance of rent, he will generally do so on the same terms as to repair as those contained in the expired tenancy.[3]

**1–01**

### Section 11 of the Landlord and Tenant Act 1985

Where s.11 of the Landlord and Tenant Act 1985 applies[4] (so that the tenancy contains the landlord's repairing covenant implied by that section) any covenant by the tenant to repair the premises (including a covenant to pay money on account of repairs by the landlord) is of no effect in so far as it relates to the matters covered by the landlord's obligation.[5]

**1–02**

---

[1] For a discussion of the principles applicable to the construction of repairing and other covenants imposing liability for dilapidations, see Ch.4, below.
[2] See for example the facts of *Maggs v Marsh* [2006] B.L.R. 395.
[3] See Ch.2, paras 2–07 to 2–12, below.
[4] See para.20–17 et seq., below.
[5] See para.20–43, below.

## IMPLIED TERMS[6]

## Types of implied term

**1–03**    The express terms of the contract between the parties may be supplemented or modified by terms which are not expressed but implied. The two most important categories of implied terms are those implied in fact and those implied in law. The former arise out of the specific facts of the particular contract and depend solely upon the presumed intention of the parties. It follows that what may be an implied term of one contract will not necessarily be an implied term of another. The latter category comprises terms that are imposed by law as a legal incident of a particular type of contract. For this reason they will be referred to in this Chapter as terms imposed by law. What follows in this section is a general discussion of each category; implied terms in both categories specifically relating to dilapidations are dealt with in Chs 19, 20 and 21, below.

## Terms implied in fact

**1–04**    The starting point for deciding whether a term should be implied into a contract is the speech of Lord Hoffmann, giving the advice of the Privy Council, in *A-G of Belize v Belize Telecom*, in which he said:[7]

> "**16** Before discussing in greater detail the reasoning of the Court of Appeal, the Board will make some general observations about the process of implication. The court has no power to improve upon the instrument which it is called upon to construe, whether it be a contract, a statute or articles of association. It cannot introduce terms to make it fairer or more reasonable. It is concerned only to discover what the instrument means. However, that meaning is not necessarily or always what the authors or parties to the document would have intended. It is the meaning which the instrument would convey to a reasonable person having all the background knowledge which would reasonably be available to the audience to whom the instrument is addressed: see *Investors Compensation Scheme Ltd v West Bromwich Building Society* [1998] 1 W.L.R. 896, 912–913. It is this objective meaning which is conventionally called the intention of the parties, or the intention of Parliament, or the intention of whatever person or body was or is deemed to have been the author of the instrument.
>
> **17** The question of implication arises when the instrument does not expressly provide for what is to happen when some event occurs. The most usual inference in such a case is that nothing is to happen. If the parties had intended something to happen, the instrument would have said so. Otherwise, the express provisions of the instrument are to continue to operate undisturbed. If the event has caused loss to one or other of the parties, the loss lies where it falls.
>
> **18** In some cases, however, the reasonable addressee would understand the instrument to mean something else. He would consider that the only meaning consistent with the other provisions of the instrument, read against the relevant background, is that something is to happen. The event in question is to affect the rights of the parties. The instrument may not have expressly said so, but this is what it must mean. In such a case, it is said that the court implies a term as to what will happen if the event in question occurs. But the implication of the term is not an addition to the instrument. It only spells out what the instrument means.
>
> **19** The proposition that the implication of a term is an exercise in the construction of the instrument as a whole is not only a matter of logic (since a court has no power to alter what the

---

[6] For a more definitive treatment, see Lewison, *The Interpretation of Contracts*, 5th edn (London: Sweet & Maxwell, 2011), Ch.6 and *Chitty on Contracts*, edited by H.G. Beale, 30th edn (London: Sweet & Maxwell, 2011), Ch.13.

[7] [2009] 1 W.L.R. 1988.

instrument means) but also well supported by authority. In *Trollope & Colls Ltd v North West Metropolitan Regional Hospital Board* [1973] 1 W.L.R. 601, 609 Lord Pearson, with whom Lord Guest and Lord Diplock agreed, said:

'the court does not make a contract for the parties. The court will not even improve the contract which the parties have made for themselves, however desirable the improvement might be. The court's function is to interpret and apply the contract which the parties have made for themselves. If the express terms are perfectly clear and free from ambiguity, there is no choice to be made between different possible meanings: the clear terms must be applied even if the court thinks some other terms would have been more suitable. An unexpressed term can be implied if and only if the court finds that the parties must have intended that term to form part of their contract: it is not enough for the court to find that such a term would have been adopted by the parties as reasonable men if it had been suggested to them: it must have been a term that went without saying, a term necessary to give business efficacy to the contract, a term which, though tacit, formed part of the contract which the parties made for themselves.'

**20** More recently, in *Equitable Life Assurance Society v Hyman* [2002] 1 A.C. 408, 459, Lord Steyn said: 'If a term is to be implied, it could only be a term implied from the language of [the instrument] read in its commercial setting.'

**21** It follows that in every case in which it is said that some provision ought to be implied in an instrument, the question for the court is whether such a provision would spell out in express words what the instrument, read against the relevant background, would reasonably be understood to mean. It will be noticed from Lord Pearson's speech that this question can be reformulated in various ways which a court may find helpful in providing an answer—the implied term must 'go without saying', it must be 'necessary to give business efficacy to the contract' and so on—but these are not in the Board's opinion to be treated as different or additional tests. There is only one question: is that what the instrument, read as a whole against the relevant background, would reasonably be understood to mean?

**22** There are dangers in treating these alternative formulations of the question as if they had a life of their own. Take, for example, the question of whether the implied term is 'necessary to give business efficacy' to the contract. That formulation serves to underline two important points. The first, conveyed by the use of the word 'business', is that in considering what the instrument would have meant to a reasonable person who had knowledge of the relevant background, one assumes the notional reader will take into account the practical consequences of deciding that it means one thing or the other. In the case of an instrument such as a commercial contract, he will consider whether a different construction would frustrate the apparent business purpose of the parties. That was the basis upon which *Equitable Life Assurance Society v Hyman* [2002] 1 A.C. 408 was decided. The second, conveyed by the use of the word 'necessary', is that it is not enough for a court to consider that the implied term expresses what it would have been reasonable for the parties to agree to. It must be satisfied that it is what the contract actually means.

**23** The danger lies, however, in detaching the phrase 'necessary to give business efficacy' from the basic process of construction of the instrument. It is frequently the case that a contract may work perfectly well in the sense that both parties can perform their express obligations, but the consequences would contradict what a reasonable person would understand the contract to mean. Lord Steyn made this point in the *Equitable Life* case, at p.459, when he said that in that case an implication was necessary 'to give effect to the reasonable expectations of the parties'.

**24** The same point had been made many years earlier by Bowen L.J. in his well-known formulation in *The Moorcock* (1889) 14 PD 64, 68:

'In business transactions such as this, what the law desires to effect by the implication is to give such business efficacy to the transaction as must have been intended at all events by both parties who are business men.'

**25** Likewise, the requirement that the implied term must 'go without saying' is no more than another way of saying that, although the instrument does not expressly say so, that is what a reasonable person would understand it to mean. Any attempt to make more of this requirement runs the risk of diverting attention from the objectivity which informs the whole process of construction into speculation about what the actual parties to the contract or authors (or supposed authors) of the instrument would have thought about the proposed implication. The imaginary conversation with an officious bystander in *Shirlaw v Southern Foundries (1926) Ltd* [1939] 2 K.B. 206, 227 is celebrated throughout the common law world. Like the phrase 'necessary to give business efficacy', it vividly emphasises the need for the court to be satisfied that the proposed implication spells out what the contact would reasonably be understood to mean. But it carries the danger of barren argument over how the actual parties would have reacted to the proposed amendment. That, in the Board's opinion, is irrelevant. Likewise, it is not necessary that the need for the implied term should be obvious in the sense of being immediately apparent, even upon a superficial consideration of the terms of the contract and the relevant background. The need for an implied term not infrequently arises when the draftsman of a complicated instrument has omitted to make express provision for some event because he has not fully thought through the contingencies which might arise, even though it is obvious after a careful consideration of the express terms and the background that only one answer would be consistent with the rest of the instrument. In such circumstances, the fact that the actual parties might have said to the officious bystander 'Could you please explain that again?' does not matter.

**26** In *BP Refinery (Westernport) Pty Ltd v Shire of Hastings* (1977) 180 C.L.R. 266, 282–283 Lord Simon of Glaisdale, giving the advice of the majority of the Board, said that it was '[not] necessary to review exhaustively the authorities on the implication of a term in a contract' but that the following conditions ('which may overlap') must be satisfied:

'(1) it must be reasonable and equitable; (2) it must be necessary to give business efficacy to the contract, so that no term will be implied if the contract is effective without it; (3) it must be so obvious that 'it goes without saying' (4) it must be capable of clear expression; (5) it must not contradict any express term of the contract.'

**27** The Board considers that this list is best regarded, not as series of independent tests which must each be surmounted, but rather as a collection of different ways in which judges have tried to express the central idea that the proposed implied term must spell out what the contract actually means, or in which they have explained why they did not think that it did so. The Board has already discussed the significance of 'necessary to give business efficacy' and 'goes without saying'. As for the other formulations, the fact that the proposed implied term would be inequitable or unreasonable, or contradict what the parties have expressly said, or is incapable of clear expression, are all good reasons for saying that a reasonable man would not have understood that to be what the instrument meant."

In *Crema v Cenkos Securities*,[8] Aikens L.J. summarised the principles to be derived from *A-G of Belize v Belize Telecom* as follows:

"The principles are: (1) A court cannot improve the instrument it has to construe to make it fairer or more reasonable. It is concerned only to discover what the instrument means. (2) The meaning is that which the instrument would convey to the legal anthropomorphism called 'the reasonable person', or the 'reasonable addressee'. That 'person' will have all the background knowledge which would reasonably be available to the audience to whom the instrument is addressed. The objective meaning of the instrument is what is conventionally called the intention of 'the parties' or the intention of whoever is the deemed author of the instrument. (3) The question of implication of terms only arises when the instrument does not expressly provide for what is to happen when some particular (often unforeseen) event occurs. (4) The default position is that nothing is to be implied in the instrument. In that case, if that particular event has caused loss, then the loss lies where it falls. (5) However, if the 'reasonable addressee' would understand the instrument, against the other terms and the relevant background, to mean something more, i.e. that something *is* to happen in that particular event which is not expressly dealt with in the instrument's terms, then it is said that the court implies a term as to what will happen if the event in question occurs. (5) Nevertheless, that process does not add another term to the instrument; it only spells out what the instrument means. It is

8 [2010] EWCA Civ 1444 at [38].

an exercise in the construction of the instrument as a whole. In the case of all written instruments, this obviously means that term is there from the outset, i.e. from the moment the contract was agreed ..."

The above approach has been applied or referred to in a number of subsequent cases.[9] It has been said that it applies equally irrespective of whether the contract is wholly written, wholly oral or partly oral and partly in writing.[10]

The implication of a term is therefore properly to be regarded as part of the overall process of interpreting the contract. The central question is whether the proposed implied term properly reflects what the contract, read as a whole against the relevant background, would reasonably be understood to mean. Lord Simon's list of conditions in *BP Refinery (Westernport) Ltd v Shire of Hastings*,[11] which was referred to and commented on by Lord Hoffmann in the above passage, cannot any longer (for the reasons given by Lord Hoffmann) be taken as a definitive list of the conditions which must be satisfied in order for a term to be implied. Nonetheless, it is thought that it sets out useful guidelines, in the sense that, as Lord Hoffmann explained in the above passage, if one or more of the five requirements is not satisfied in relation to a proposed implied term, that will be a good reason for saying that a reasonable man would not have understood that to be what the instrument meant.

**1–05**

Three further points of a general nature can be made.

**1–06**

First, in most cases, the correct view is likely to be that no term is to be implied, because if the parties had intended to provide for the matter in question, they would have done so expressly. Thus, for example, at common law no term will generally be implied into a lease entitling the landlord to enter and repair,[12] because the parties are presumed, by having provided for the grant of exclusive possession to the tenant without any express reservation of a right of entry in favour of the landlord, to have intended the landlord to be excluded from the premises for all purposes. The presumption against implying terms is particularly strong where the contract is detailed and has obviously been drafted with care.[13] Thus, in *Duke of Westminster v Guild*,[14] Slade L.J. said:

"[C]lause 2 of the lease contains a number of careful and elaborate provisions defining the tenant's contractual obligations in regard to repair and maintenance. If it had been intended that other contractual obligations relating to repair should be placed on the landlords themselves, one would prima facie have expected this particular lease to say so."

---

[9] See for example *Town Quay Developments Ltd v Eastleigh Borough Council* [2010] 2 P. & C.R. 19; *Chantry Estates (South East) Ltd v Anderson* [2010] EWCA Civ 316; *KG Bominflot Bunkergesellschaft für Mineraloele mbH & Co v Petroplus Marketing AG* [2010] EWCA Civ 1145; and *Societe Generale, London Branch v Geys* [2011] EWCA Civ 307.

[10] *Crema v Cenkos Securities*, above, per Aikens L.J. at [41]. Hughes L.J. and the Chancellor did not find it necessary to consider the point.

[11] (1978) 52 A.L.J.R. 20.

[12] See para.19–02, below.

[13] *Duke of Westminster v Guild* [1985] Q.B. 688; *Gordon v Selico Co Ltd* [1986] 1 E.G.L.R. 71; *Hafton Properties Ltd v Camp* [1994] 1 E.G.L.R. 67; *Adami v Lincoln Grange Management Ltd* [1998] 1 E.G.L.R. 58.

[14] Above.

**1–07**   So also in *Gordon v Selico Co Ltd*[15] the Court of Appeal refused to imply terms relating to repair into a lease for much the same reasons. Slade L.J. said:

> "Where a written tenancy agreement relating to a flat, forming part of a larger building in multiple occupation, manifestly does not embody the complete agreement between the parties the court may well be willing to supplement the written document by implying terms placing obligations on one party or the other. Such a case was *Liverpool City Council v. Irwin*[16] ... The repair and maintenance scheme provided by this lease is a very cumbersome one and we agree with the learned judge that, even if the lessors and their agents were duly to carry out their obligations, the scheme might not always suffice to give the lessees necessary and timely protection ... Nevertheless, on a reading of the lease, we feel little doubt that it was intended, by all parties, to provide a comprehensive code in regard to repair and maintenance of the block. We are by no means satisfied that the implication of any further terms in this respect is necessary to give the lease business efficacy, or that the lessor, assuming it to have been a reasonable person, would have 'agreed without hesitation' to the insertion of the suggested implied additional terms relating to the repair and maintenance of the block."

Second, Lord Simon's fourth requirement emphasises that it must be possible to say not only that a term ought to be implied but also what that term is. The fact that the proposed term is incapable of clear expression is another reason why arguments based upon implied terms frequently fail in practice. The suggested term may simply be too vague or ambiguous,[17] or there may be a number of different possible formulations of it.[18] Either of these will generally be fatal.

Last, as appears from Lord Simon's fifth requirement, a term cannot be implied if its effect is to contradict an express term in the contract. The reason for this is that if the parties have expressly dealt with the point in one way, there is no room for supposing that they intended to deal with it in any other. An example from the law of dilapidations is *Duke of Westminster v Guild*.[19] In that case the demised premises were served by a drain which was situated partly under the demised land and partly under the landlord's adjoining land. The drain became defective and in need of extensive work. The lease contained a tenant's covenant to repair the demised premises. Clause 2(IV) of the lease contained a covenant on the part of the tenant to pay a fair proportion of the cost of repairing a number of items (including drains) belonging to or used by the demised premises jointly with adjoining occupiers. There was no express covenant by the landlord to repair the drain. The tenant argued, among other things, that a covenant on the part of the landlord to repair the items falling within cl. 2(IV) (including the drain) ought to be implied. One of the grounds on which this was rejected by the Court of Appeal was that it would be inconsistent with the tenant's repairing covenant, since a number of items in cl.2(IV) were part of the demised premises and therefore expressly subject to the tenant's repairing obligation.

A further example is *Janet Reger International v Tiree*,[20] in which a lease imposed a full repairing obligation on the tenant and conferred on the landlord the right (but not the obligation) to make alterations and improvements, Mr

---

[15] [1986] 2 E.G.L.R. 71.

[16] [1977] A.C. 239. See para.19–08, below.

[17] See *Shell UK Ltd v Lostock Garages Ltd* [1976] 1 W.L.R. 1187.

[18] See *Trollope & Colls Ltd v North-West Metropolitan Regional Hospital Board* [1973] 1 W.L.R. 601.

[19] [1985] Q.B. 688.

[20] [2006] 3 E.G.L.R. 131.

Terence Mowschenson QC (sitting as a deputy judge of the Chancery Division) refused to imply an obligation on the part of the landlord to remedy defects in the structure that caused damage to those parts of the demised premises that the tenant was obliged to maintain. One of his reasons was that the suggested term would contradict an express term of the lease by turning a right into an obligation and transfer work falling within the tenant's repairing covenant to the landlord's repairing covenant.

The principles relating specifically to the implication of repairing covenants into leases are discussed in Chs 19 to 21, below.

## Terms imposed by law

Terms are sometimes imposed by law as a legal incident of a particular type of contract. An example is the covenant to repair the structure and exterior that is implied into certain kinds of short leases of dwelling-houses by s.11 of the Landlord and Tenant Act 1985[21]; or the implied obligation on all tenants to use the demised premises in a tenant-like manner.[22] Some of these, like the former, are imposed by statute and cannot be excluded by agreement; others, like the latter, are imposed at common law only in the event of the contract being silent on the point, and give way to an express term dealing with the same subject matter.

**1–08**

### COLLATERAL CONTRACTS[23]

#### Introductory

Although the repairing obligations will normally be found in the express terms of the contract itself, they may be supplemented or their operation affected by the existence of a collateral contract between the parties. However, not every casual remark will give rise to a collateral contract. The statement relied upon must have been intended by the parties to have contractual effect. In *The Inntrepreneur Pub Company (GL) v East Crown Ltd*[24] Lightman J. summarised the relevant legal principles regarding the recognition of pre-contractual promises or assurances as collateral contracts as follows:

**1–09**

(1)  A pre-contractual statement will only be treated as having contractual effect if the evidence shows that the parties intended this to be the case. Intention is a question of fact to be decided by looking at the totality of the evidence.

(2)  The test is the ordinary objective test for the formation of a contract: what is relevant is not the subjective thought of one party but what a reasonable outside observer would infer from all the circumstances.

---

[21] See paras 20–17 to 20–21, below.
[22] See para.21–02 et seq., below.
[23] For a detailed treatment of collateral contracts, see *Chitty on Contracts*, edited by H.G. Beale, 30th edn (London: Sweet & Maxwell, 2011), para.12–003 et seq.
[24] [2002] 2 Lloyd's Rep. 611.

(3)    In deciding the question of intention, one important consideration will be whether the statement is followed by further negotiations and a written contract not containing any term corresponding to the statement. In such a case it will be harder to infer that the statement was intended to have contractual effect because the prima facie assumption will be that the written contract contains all the terms the parties wanted to be binding between them.

(4)    A further important factor will be the lapse of time between the statement and the making of the formal contract. The longer the interval, the greater the presumption must be that the parties did not intend the statement to have contractual effect in relation to a subsequent deal.

(5)    A representation of fact is much more likely to have contractual effect than a statement of future fact or a future forecast.[25]

In addition to bringing himself within the above principles, a party seeking to rely on a collateral obligation must have given consideration for it, although entering into the main contract will usually be sufficient consideration.[26] An "entire agreement" clause[27] will, if otherwise effective and apt as a matter of construction to cover collateral contracts of the sort alleged, prevent one party from setting up a collateral contract.[28] If a statement does not take effect as a collateral contract, then (unless it gives rise to an estoppel[29]) it will generally be of no effect by virtue of the parol evidence rule.[30]

Where a collateral contract is established, the principles applicable to its operation are much the same as those for the main contract. However, the position regarding the enforcement of collateral contracts by and against successors in title is not wholly straightforward.[31] This will not matter where the agreement is intended to be personal to the original parties, and indeed, this fact is very often in practice the reason why a written collateral contract (such as a side letter) is used. Nonetheless, when collateral matters are agreed, consideration should always be given to what is to happen if either party assigns its interest. If successors are intended to be affected, then in the absence of special circumstances, it is good practice for the parties' respective rights and obligations to be contained in the lease itself and not in a collateral document.

There are generally two types of collateral contract arising in relation to leases: the first is where one party (usually the landlord) agrees not to enforce a particular obligation of the other; and the second is where one party (again, usually the landlord) agrees to undertake some obligation over and above those imposed by the lease. These are considered below.

---

[25] These principles were applied by the Court of Appeal in *Business Environment Bow Lane v Deanwater Estates* [2007] 2 E.G.L.R. 51 at [46], [47] and [60].

[26] For an example, see *Shanklin Pier v Detel Products Ltd* [1951] 2 K.B. 854.

[27] For example one which provides that the entire agreement between the parties is to be found in the document containing the clause, and not elsewhere.

[28] *The Inntrepreneur Pub Company (GL) v East Crown Ltd*, above; *Ravennavi Spa v New Century Shipbuilding Co* [2007] 2 Lloyds Rep 24. It has been held that an entire agreement clause does not fall foul of s.3 of the Misrepresentation Act 1967: *McGrath v Shah* (1987) 57 P. & C.R. 452.

[29] See para.1–14, below.

[30] See para.4–18, below.

[31] See paras 3–24 to 3–28, below.

## (a)   Agreement not to rely on strict rights

An example of a collateral contract of this type is *Brikom Investments Ltd v Carr*.[32] In that case landlords of a number of blocks of flats offered to sell to sitting tenants long leases of their flats. At the time of the offer the roofs of the blocks were in need of repair, and the landlords made oral representations both to the tenants' association and to individual tenants that they would repair the roofs at their own expense. One such representation was made to Mrs Carr, and she subsequently entered into a long lease on the faith of it. The lease contained a covenant by the landlords to repair the main structure of the blocks including the roofs, and also a covenant by Mrs Carr to pay a service charge in respect of the expenditure incurred by the landlords in complying with their covenant. The landlords subsequently repaired the roofs and claimed a proportion of the cost from, among others, Mrs Carr by way of service charge. The Court of Appeal held that they were not entitled to do so. All three members of the Court held that there was a collateral contract between the landlords and Mrs Carr, the effect of which was that the former had agreed, in consideration of the latter entering into the lease, not to seek any contribution to the cost of the roof from her. Roskill L.J. said:

1–10

> "When two parties are about to enter into an agreement for lease, a lease which imposes on the lessee a very burdensome obligation in respect to repairs, I can see no reason why one party cannot say to the other; 'In relation to those outstanding matters, whatever may be our legal position under the terms of the lease, we will not as landlords enforce that obligation against you'. I see no reason why effect should not be given to such a position."

However, a claim to a collateral contract of this type failed in *Business Environment Bow Lane v Deanwater Estates*.[33] In that case, the landlord had given the tenant a written assurance during the course of negotiations for a new lease that it would not serve a terminal schedule of dilapidations. After the assurance was given, the parties continued to negotiate and then entered into a new lease containing contrary provisions. At first instance Briggs J. held that the landlord was bound by the assurance. The Court of Appeal allowed the landlord's appeal on the ground that the evidence did not show sufficiently clearly that the parties intended to make any contract other than that arising from the grant of the lease.

## (b)   Agreement to undertake additional obligations

The commonest form of collateral contract in this category is where the landlord agrees to undertake works to the premises over and above those which he is liable to do under the terms of the lease itself. Such a contract may be express,[34] or it may arise out of oral assurances given in the course of negotiations. Thus, in *De*

1–11

---

[32] [1979] Q.B. 467.
[33] [2007] 2 E.G.L.R. 51.
[34] For an example, see *Lotteryking Ltd v AMEC Properties Ltd* [1995] 2 E.G.L.R. 13, in which the landlord undertook to use reasonable endeavours to rectify certain defects within six months. Similarly, in *System Floors Ltd v Ruralpride Ltd* [1995] 1 E.G.L.R. 48, the landlord agreed to accept surrenders within three months of a rent review date on certain terms.

*Lassalle v Guildford*,[35] a person who intended to take a lease of a house refused to do so until he was given an assurance by the proposed lessor that the drains were in good condition. The assurance was given, but the lease was entered into without any reference to the condition of the drains. When the drains proved not to be in good order the landlord was held liable, not under the terms of the lease, but under a collateral contract for which taking of the lease was the consideration.[36] Likewise, in *Mann v Nunn*[37] the tenant agreed to take a lease of the landlord's premises if the landlord would first carry out certain repairs, and the landlord agreed. A written lease was entered into which contained no reference to the landlord's promise. The court held that the landlord was nonetheless liable to do the work under a contract collateral to the main lease.

## VARIATION OR RELEASE OF THE OBLIGATION

## A question of construction

1–12   The parties to a lease containing obligations relevant to dilapidations may agree to vary or release some or all of those obligations. One question which may arise in such cases is the date from which the variation or release takes effect, and what happens in relation to existing or past breaches. The answer in any particular case will depend on the proper construction of the agreement. As always, the question will be what a reasonable person, having all the background knowledge which would have been available to the parties, would have understood them to be using the language in the agreement to mean.[38]

In *Perriam Ltd v Wayne*,[39] the landlord of a mill, in anticipation of a sale of its reversion, entered into a deed of variation with the tenant on April 24, 2007 extending the lease, and containing the following provisions:

> "3.4 The landlord has agreed to release the tenant from its obligations under the lease as and from 17 November 2007.
> 3.5 It has been agreed that the tenant's repairing obligations shall be varied as is provided herein.
> ....
> 4.2 The obligations of the tenant in the lease shall be varied so that there is no continuing obligation to repair, keep in repair or replace the external windows in the premises.
> ...
> 5.2 The landlord releases the [guarantor] from its obligations under the lease as and from 17 November 2007 save as to any antecedent breach."

At the date of the deed, the windows required either complete replacement or part replacement and part extensive repair. The landlord argued that the deed on its true construction only operated to release the tenant from liability in respect of the windows from the date of the deed, so that the tenant (and therefore its

---

[35] [1901] 2 K.B. 215.

[36] Contrast *Kennard v Ashman* (1894) 10 T.L.R. 213, (affirmed 10 T.L.R. 447) (statement by landlord that house was well built held not to amount to a collateral contract).

[37] (1874) 30 L.T. 526. See also *Walker Property Investments (Brighton) v Walker* (1947) 177 L.T. 204.

[38] See Ch.4, below.

[39] [2011] EWHC 403 (Q.B.).

guarantor) remained liable for antecedent breaches. That argument succeeded at first instance. Coulson J., allowing the tenant's appeal, held that, on the proper construction of the deed in the light of the relevant factual background, the release of the tenant's repairing obligation was intended to have immediate effect from the date of the deed, and that the deed operated as a waiver or release of the tenant's existing liability in respect of the windows.

In *Baroque Investments Ltd v Heis*[40] four leases of office premises were granted for terms expiring on March 30, 2014. Each lease contained a covenant to keep the premises in repair and yield them up in repair at the expiration or sooner determination of the term. Two licences to alter were subsequently entered into, each of which contained a covenant on the part of the tenant "Before the end of the Lease … to dismantle and remove the Works and reinstate the Premises …". On November 13, 2009 the leases were surrendered on terms which included the following:

> "[The landlord] and [the tenant] respectively release each other from the rights and obligations contained in the Lease and from all liability in respect of any breach of those rights and obligations whether arising on or after, but not before, the date of this Surrender."

It was common ground that the obligation to yield up the premises in repair had been released by the surrenders. However, the landlord contended that the tenant's liability to reinstate had not been so released. The Chancellor found in favour of the tenant, saying:

> "The licences gave to the tenant the full period of the term created by the leases within which to carry out the requisite reinstatement. Accordingly, as at 13th November 2009, there was no breach of the obligation to reinstate. If the works were not carried out before 30th March 2014 then the tenant would have been in breach but that would have been after, not before, the date of the surrenders. In my view the inescapable consequence is that that potential liability was released by the surrenders."

## ESTOPPEL

### Estoppel in the law of dilapidations

A detailed consideration of the law relating to estoppel is outside the scope of this work. However, common to all types of estoppel is that one party so conducts itself as to make it inequitable for it to insist on its strict legal rights.[41] This may operate to affect liability for dilapidations in two principal ways: first, it may work defensively to prevent one party from enforcing against the other his strict rights under the lease; and second, where the parties have arranged their affairs on the basis of a particular state of affairs (such as that one of them is liable to repair), then even if that state of affairs does not represent the true position, one or other of them may be estopped from departing from that basis where it would be inequitable to allow him to do so.

1–13

---

[40] [2012] EWHC 2886 (Ch.).
[41] See generally *Halsbury's Laws*, 4th edn, Vol.16(2), para.951 et seq.

### (a)   As a defence to liability

**1–14**     An estoppel of this sort generally arises where one party has made to the other some express or implied promise that he will not enforce his strict legal rights, or otherwise so conducts himself that he leads the other party so to believe, and the other party, in reliance upon this, alters his position to his detriment. In such a case the party making the representation may be estopped from subsequently seeking to rely on his strict rights where it would be inequitable for him to do so.

Thus, in *Hughes v Metropolitan Railway Co Ltd*[42] the landlord served upon the tenant a notice to repair, to which the tenant responded by offering to sell his interest to the landlord. Negotiations followed, in the course of which the tenant was led to believe that he would not be required to comply with the notice whilst the negotiations continued. In reliance upon this, the tenant took no steps to do the repairs. Negotiations broke down, and the landlord sought to forfeit the lease by reason of the tenant's failure to comply with the notice. It was held that the effect of the negotiations was to suspend the notice, Lord Cairns L.C. saying:

> "[I]t is the first principle upon which all Courts of Equity proceed, that if parties who have entered into definite and distinct terms involving legal results—certain penalties or legal forfeiture—afterwards by their own act or with their own consent enter upon a course of negotiation which has the effect of leading one of the parties to suppose that the strict rights arising under the contract will not be enforced, or will be kept in suspense, or held in abeyance, the person who otherwise might have enforced those rights will not be allowed to enforce them where it would be inequitable having regard to the dealings which have thus taken place between the parties."

In *Brikom Investments Ltd v Carr*[43] (the relevant facts of which are set out in para.1–10 above) Lord Denning M.R. held that the landlords were estopped from claiming the cost of repairs to the roof by way of service charges.

In *London Borough of Havering v Smith*[44] an intending purchaser of a long lease acquired under the "right to buy" provisions in the Housing Act 1985 made enquiries of the landlord regarding proposed external work, and was assured that she would not be charged more than the sum set out in a notice under s.125 of the Act served on the then tenant. She then completed her purchase on the faith of such assurances. The landlord was held to be estopped by representation from claiming any greater amount than the amount in the notice together with the statutory allowance for inflation.

### (b)   Imposition of liability

**1–15**     Estoppel may also operate positively to impose liability where none exists in strict law. The following two examples from the law of dilapidations illustrate how this may happen.

In *Brikom Investments Ltd v Seaford*[45] the landlords were not liable under the covenants implied by statute into certain leases of residential premises (because

---

[42] (1877) 2 App. Cas. 439.
[43] [1979] Q.B. 467.
[44] [2012] UKUT 295 (LC).
[45] [1981] 1 W.L.R. 863.

the terms created by the tenancies exceeded seven years).[46] Nonetheless fair rents had been registered, and demanded and accepted, by the landlords on the basis that they were liable under the statutory provisions. If the landlords had not been responsible for repairs the fair rents would have been lower. The Court of Appeal held that so long as the increased rent was claimed by the landlords, they were estopped from denying liability under the implied covenants.[47] In order to be released from this liability by estoppel, the landlords would have to apply to have the registration of fair rents corrected so as to reflect the true position with regard to repairs.

In *Industrial Properties (Barton Hill) Ltd v Associated Electrical Industries Ltd*,[48] a company, which had no title to grant any legal interest in factory premises, granted to another company a lease containing full tenant's repairing obligations. The tenant remained in possession, paying the rent, for the full term of the lease, but at its expiry yielded up the factory in a state of substantial disrepair. In a claim by the "landlords" for dilapidations, the tenant, which had discovered the want of title, alleged that the landlords had no title to sue. The Court of Appeal held that the tenants were estopped from disputing their landlords' title, and thus their right to sue, because they had been let into possession by the landlords, and had without interruption enjoyed possession throughout the term.[49] A contrary result had been arrived at by the Court of Appeal in *Harrison v Wells*,[50] which proceeded on the basis that the estoppel ceased once the tenant had gone out of possession. This was based on a misunderstanding of certain old authorities and was held in the *Industrial Properties* case to have been decided per incuriam.

The common feature of these cases is that although in reality there was no liability under the repairing covenants, the circumstances were such that it was inequitable to allow the true state of affairs to be relied on. Cases of this type are to be contrasted with *Dunn v Bradford Metropolitan District Council*,[51] in which a secure tenancy had come to an end by virtue of the tenants' failure to comply with the terms of a suspended possession order. The tenants remained in possession, paying a certain amount of rent, until they left voluntarily some years later. They then commenced proceedings against the landlord for failure to repair in the period following the termination of their tenancies. The Court of Appeal held that the landlord was not estopped from denying that the tenants had a tenancy during the relevant period even though both parties had acted in the belief that the original tenancy had not ended.

---

[46] See paras 20–17 to 20–21, below.
[47] Cf. *Murphy v Hurly* [1922] 1 A.C. 369, considered in para.1–17, below.
[48] [1977] Q.B. 580.
[49] Likewise a person may be estopped from denying that he has become liable under a lease as assignee: *Rodenhurst Estates Ltd v Barnes* [1936] 2 All E.R. 3; *Brown & Root Technology Ltd v Sun Alliance & London Insurance Co Ltd* [2001] Ch. 733.
[50] [1967] 1 Q.B. 263.
[51] [2002] 3 E.G.L.R. 104.

## Distinction between collateral contract and estoppel

**1–16**     In some cases it may be difficult to determine whether a claim is properly analysed as a collateral contract[52] or an estoppel. Thus, in *Business Environment Bow Lane v Deanwater Estates*[53] Briggs J. stated:

> "In a case where the detriment or alteration of position consists of party A's execution of the written agreement that party B promises not fully to enforce, the doctrines of promissory estoppel and collateral contract become almost indistinguishable, as indeed they were in both [*City & Westminster Properties (1934) v Mudd*[54] ] and [*Brikom Investments Ltd v Carr*[55] ]."

It was common ground in the Court of Appeal that the defence of promissory estoppel added nothing to the defence of collateral contract.[56]

## THE EFFECT OF CARRYING OUT REPAIRS WITHOUT LIABILITY

## Carrying out repairs without liability

**1–17**     In practice, one party may carry out repairs which are not, or may not be, his liability under the lease. It may then be argued that he has, by implication, agreed to undertake repairs of that description in the future, or that he is estopped from denying that he is not liable for such repairs.[57] Whilst each case will depend on its own facts, it will generally be necessary, in order for such an argument to succeed, to show something more than the mere carrying out of repairs in the past.

In *Board of Governors of the London Hospital v Jacobs (No.1)*[58] the landlords let a house in 1931 on a written weekly tenancy agreement in which the tenant agreed to keep the premises in good and tenantable repair, fair wear and tear excepted. For well over 20 years the landlords did substantially the whole of the repairs. The Court of Appeal rejected the contention that the landlords had thereby become liable to repair. Lord Evershed M.R. said:

> "With all respect to the learned judge, I am quite unable to accept his view that [the evidence] compelled or entitled him to draw the inference that at some time, unspecified, there had been a change in the terms of the bargain. It is not uncommon that landlords (particularly good landlords) may do, both in their own interests and in the interests of their tenants, things which they are not bound to do ... The fact that the landlords elected to do the works which they did, assuming that the works were not covered in any case by the fair wear and tear exception, does not prove that there has been a transfer of the burden from the statutory tenant to the landlords."

---

[52] See para.1–09 et seq., above.
[53] [2007] 2 E.G.L.R. 51.
[54] [1959] Ch. 129.
[55] [1979] Q.B. 467.
[56] [2007] 2 E.G.L.R. 51 at [3].
[57] Estoppel is dealt with in paras 1–13 to 1–15, above.
[58] [1956] 2 All E.R. 603.

In *Credit Suisse v Beegas Nominees Ltd*[59] it was argued on behalf of the tenant that the landlord was estopped (by convention[60]) from denying that he was and remained liable under the terms of an underlease to remedy defects causing the ingress of water. Lindsay J., having found for the tenant on other grounds, rejected the estoppel claim. He said:

> "I do not find the facts necessary to establish a convention as to [the] construction or effect [of the underlease]. In the context that a landlord may indicate a willingness to do works outside his strict obligation and in a context, as here, in which the landlord believes he may have a good case to get others to do works or to recover the expense of works from others, merely to point to a landlord's apparent willingness to do works or have them done is not, of itself, material sufficient to show a convention as to the effect of the underlease."

In *Demetriou v Robert Andrews (Estate Agencies) Ltd*[61] various landlords had for a period not disputed their liability to carry out repairs (although no repairs had in fact been done). They did so in the mistaken belief that the tenant was a Rent Act tenant and that they were liable under statute to keep the structure and exterior in repair.[62] The judge at first instance held, basing himself on the landlords' conduct, that the tenancy contained an implied term obliging the landlords to repair the structure and exterior. The Court of Appeal allowed the landlord's appeal.[63]

In *Delgable v Perinpanathan*[64] the issue was whether liability for the repair of a roof was that of the head tenant or the sub-tenant. Lloyd L.J. (with whom Keene and Pill L.JJ. agreed) referred to the fact that the head tenant had done work to the roof in the past in the following terms:

> "It is, I think, a point of marginal importance to note that the [head tenant] did, at some point, have some work done to the roof, at a point in time when perhaps she or her advisers had not focused upon the question of whether it was her obligation to pay for it. I take that not as any kind of evidential indication that she was obliged to repair the roof, but, at least, as indicating that there was no problem for her about gaining access to the roof for the purposes of repairs if she did need to gain that access."

The above cases may be contrasted with *Murphy v Hurly*,[65] in which the demised land consisted of holdings in Ireland which ran down to the foreshore and were exposed to the Atlantic. Following the grant of the tenancy, the landlords constructed a protective sea wall. After the wall was built, the landlords continuously made repairs to the wall; the rent was twice fixed by the Irish Land Commission on the express basis that the landlords were liable to keep the wall in

---

[59] [1994] 4 All E.R. 803.
[60] An estoppel by convention arises where parties to a legal relationship have acted on the agreed assumption that a particular state of fact or law is to be accepted between them as true, and it would be unfair to allow one of them to resile to the detriment of the other: see generally Spencer Bower, *Estoppel by Representation*, 4th edn (London: LexisNexis, 2004), Ch.VIII and *Halsbury's Laws*, 4th edn (London: LexisNexis), Vol.16(2) at para.1005 et seq.
[61] (1990) 62 P. & C.R. 536.
[62] Under s.32 of the Housing Act 1961 (the then equivalent of s.11 of the Landlord and Tenant Act 1985).
[63] See para.19–06, below, in which this case is further considered.
[64] [2006] 1 E.G.L.R. 78. See further para.7–11 below, in which this case is further considered.
[65] [1922] 1 A.C. 369.

repair; and on one occasion the tenants recovered from the landlords damages for disrepair to the wall resulting in damage to the holdings. The House of Lords rejected the landlords' contention that they were not liable to keep the wall in repair.

## ABUSE OF PROCESS

### Abuse of process

**1–18**     A party may be precluded from bringing or defending a claim for dilapidations by virtue of the principles relating to abuse of process.

As a general principle of civil litigation, a claimant must bring all his claims at the same time. A subsequent claim which could have been brought in earlier proceedings may be struck out as an abuse of process.[66] The principle was explained by Wigram V.C. in *Henderson v Henderson*[67] as follows:

> "In trying this question I believe I state the rule of the Court correctly when I say that, where a given matter becomes the subject of litigation in, and of adjudication by, a court of competent jurisdiction, the Court requires the parties to that litigation to bring forward their whole case, and will not (except under special circumstances) permit the same parties to open the same subject of litigation in respect of a matter which might have been brought forward as part of the subject in contest, but which was not brought forward, only because they have, from negligence, inadvertence, or even accident, omitted part of their case. The plea of res judicata applies, except in special cases, not only to points upon which the Court was actually required by the parties to form an opinion and pronounce a judgment, but to every point which properly belonged to the subject of litigation, and which the parties, exercising reasonable diligence, might have brought forward at the time."

The principle extends not only to the re-opening of a matter already decided in proceedings between the same parties, but also to:

> "issues or facts which are so clearly part of the subject-matter of the litigation and so clearly could have been raised that it would be an abuse of the process of the court to allow a new proceeding to be started in respect of them.[68]"

The rule was authoritatively considered by the House of Lords in *Johnson v Gore-Wood & Co.*,[69] in which Lord Bingham said:

> "The underlying public interest is the same: that there should be finality in litigation and that a party should not be twice vexed in the same matter. This public interest is reinforced by the current emphasis on efficiency and economy in the conduct of litigation, in the interests of the parties and the public as a whole. The bringing of a claim or the raising of a defence in later proceedings may, without more, amount to abuse if the court is satisfied (the onus being on the party alleging abuse) that the claim or defence should have been raised in the earlier proceedings if it was to be raised at all. I would not accept that it is necessary, before abuse may be found, to identify any additional element such as a collateral attack on a previous decision or some dishonesty, but where those elements are present the later proceedings will

---

[66] For a full treatment of the applicable principles, see the *White Book* (London: Sweet & Maxwell), Vol.1, para.3.4.3.

[67] (1843) 3 Hare 100.

[68] *Greenhalgh v Mallard* [1947] 2 All E.R. 255 at 257.

[69] [2002] 2 A.C. 1.

be much more obviously abusive, and there will rarely be a finding of abuse unless the later proceeding involves what the court regards as unjust harassment of a party. It is, however, wrong to hold that because a matter could have been raised in early proceedings it should have been, so as to render the raising of it in later proceedings necessarily abusive. That is to adopt too dogmatic an approach to what should in my opinion be a broad, merits-based judgment which takes account of the public and private interests involved and also takes account of all the facts of the case, focusing attention on the crucial question whether, in all the circumstances, a party is misusing or abusing the process of the court by seeking to raise before it the issue which could have been raised before."

The principle was relied on in a dilapidations context in *Henley v Bloom*,[70] in which the landlord brought possession proceedings against a residential tenant who had complained about damp problems in his flat for some years. The claim was settled on terms that the tenant would give up possession and the landlord would pay him £16,000 in instalments once he had vacated, and £4,000 towards his costs. The consent order contained recitals that the payments were to be in full and final settlement of any claim that the tenant might have arising from his improvements to the flat, and that he would give up the flat in good tenantable repair and condition. The tenant vacated the flat, but before doing so commissioned an expert to report on the disrepair and damp. He did not raise the question of disrepair with the landlord until after she had carried out significant works of refurbishment to the flat. The tenant then commenced proceedings claiming damages for disrepair. The judge at first instance struck out the claim as an abuse and because it would be impossible to have a fair trial.

The Court of Appeal allowed the tenant's appeal on both points. As to the abuse point, the tenant could easily have raised or brought the disrepair claim during the possession proceedings, but the central issue was not whether he could, but whether he should, have raised the disrepair claim during the negotiations. If the court was not satisfied that a claimant's attempt to raise his claim was actually abusive in the light of his previous failure to raise it, the claim could not be barred from proceeding, however desirable it might have been for him to have raised it earlier. The claim was not an abuse for two reasons: (i) the two claims involved different issues, since the possession claim did not involve the question of whether the flat was out of repair, let alone whether any disrepair was the landlord's liability or had resulted in loss to the tenant; and (ii) if the possession claim had proceeded to trial, the subsequent disrepair claim would not have been an abuse even if the possession claim had succeeded. So the landlord's real argument was that the disrepair claim represented a challenge to the integrity of the compromise of the possession claim. But that ran into an obvious difficulty, namely that the parties had spelt out in the consent order that their agreement covered any claim by the tenant in respect of his improvements, but no other claim. It followed that by bringing the disrepair claim after the possession claim had been settled, the tenant was not abusing the process of the court. However, if the court hearing the disrepair claim was satisfied that costs had been unnecessarily increased as a result of the claim being brought after the possession claim had been settled, rather than being raised in the settlement negotiations which culminated in the consent order, then it might be appropriate to reflect that fact in an appropriate manner in any costs order made in the disrepair claim. On

---

[70] [2010] EWCA Civ 202.

the fair trial point, the landlord had failed to establish that there could not be a fair trial of the disrepair claim. Although she would probably be at a disadvantage, it would not be a very substantial or extraordinary disadvantage, and it was a disadvantage for which the court could make allowances.

See further para.20–48, below (dealing with issue estoppel in the context of s.11 of the Landlord and Tenant Act 1985).

CHAPTER 2

# THE DURATION OF THE OBLIGATION

## INTRODUCTORY

### The duration of liability

Questions may arise in practice as to liability for dilapidations occurring in periods other than during the original term of the lease (for example, prior to the grant of the lease, during a period of holding over or following the grant of a new tenancy). This Chapter is concerned with the extent to which a party who has undertaken liability for dilapidations is liable to remedy defects which occur in such periods.

2–01

## THE GENERAL RULE

### Liability limited to the period between the grant of the lease and its termination

The general rule is that obligations imposing liability for dilapidations, like other leasehold covenants, apply only during the period over which the lease subsists. It follows that the covenanting party is not liable to remedy defects other than those which exist during the term of the lease, nor can he be liable for the consequences of failing to remedy such defects. Thus, a tenant who takes a full repairing lease does not become retrospectively liable in relation to previous defects which were remedied prior to the grant of the lease. In the absence of express provision to the contrary, this applies even where the term of the lease is backdated to a date prior to the date on which the lease is executed.[1]

2–02

However, the position is different where the relevant defect continues in existence after the lease is granted. Whilst the fact that a particular defect is in existence at the date of the lease may be relevant to whether or not the covenanting party is liable in respect of it,[2] obligations imposing liability for dilapidations do not generally distinguish between defects which arose before and after the grant of the lease. In principle, therefore, once the lease has been granted, the party assuming the obligation becomes liable to remedy any defects which exist at the date of grant (assuming that the language of the obligation and the nature of the defect are such that he would otherwise be liable to do so). An

---

[1] *Shaw v Kay* (1847) 1 Exch. 412; *Jervis v Tomkinson* (1856) 1 H. & N. 195 at 206; *Cadogan (Earl) v Guinness* [1936] 1 Ch. 515; *Bradshaw v Pawley* [1980] 1 W.L.R. 10.
[2] See paras 9–21 to 9–23 and 11–23, below.

example may help to clarify this. Suppose that prior to the grant of the lease, the roof is in disrepair and leaks. A tenant taking a full repairing lease would ordinarily become liable to carry out the necessary repairs, even though the disrepair already existed at the date of the lease. However, he would not be liable for the consequences of any failure to repair the roof prior to the date of the lease, because he was not then under an obligation to repair.

## TERMINATION

### Expiry by effluxion of time, notice to quit or break notice

2–03    Where the lease ends by effluxion of time, or by service of a notice to quit or break notice by either party, both parties' contractual obligations regarding dilapidations come to an end. Where the repairing liability was that of the tenant, he is not liable for new defects which occur after the expiry of the term. However, he remains liable for damages in respect of any breaches of his repairing obligations which were committed during or at the end of the term. The same is true where the repairing liability under the lease was that of the landlord.

### Forfeiture

2–04    Where the lease is forfeited, the term ends on the date of service of the claim form seeking possession.[3] The obligation must be performed up to and including that date, but no liability arises in relation to defects occurring thereafter.[4] Where the tenant obtains relief, the lease is restored retrospectively as if it had never been forfeited, so that the tenant is deemed to have continued liable on the covenants for the intervening period.[5]

### Surrender

2–05    The effect of a surrender is to put an end to the lease and its covenants with effect from the date of the surrender. Neither party is therefore liable in respect of breaches of covenant occurring after that date. In addition, the terms of the surrender may expressly or by necessary implication release the parties, or one of them, from liability for breaches of covenant occurring prior to the surrender.[6] Where this is not the case, however, the parties remain liable for all breaches of covenant committed prior to the surrender.[7]

---

[3] See para.27–76, below.
[4] *Associated Deliveries Ltd v Harrison* (1984) 50 P. & C.R. 91. See further Ch.27, below.
[5] See para.27–83, below, and cf. *Lambeth LBC v Rogers*, [2000] 1 E.G.L.R. 28.
[6] See further para.1–12, above.
[7] *Dalton v Pickard* [1926] 2 K.B. 545; *Richmond v Savill* [1926] 2 K.B. 530. Note that the position is different in relation to covenants which only come into effect at the end of the lease: see para.2–06, below.

In *Baroque Investments Ltd v Heis*[8] four leases of office premises were granted for terms expiring on March 30, 2014. Each lease contained a covenant to keep the premises in repair and yield them up in repair at the expiration or sooner determination of the term. Two licences to alter were subsequently entered into, each of which contained a covenant on the part of the tenant "Before the end of the Lease ... to dismantle and remove the Works and reinstate the Premises ...". On November 13, 2009 the leases were surrendered on terms which included the following:

"[The landlord] and [the tenant] respectively release each other from the rights and obligations contained in the Lease and from all liability in respect of any breach of those rights and obligations whether arising on or after, but not before, the date of this Surrender."

It was common ground that the obligation to yield up the premises in repair had been released by the surrenders. However, the landlord contended that the tenant's liability to reinstate had not been so released. The Chancellor found in favour of the tenant, saying:

"The licences gave to the tenant the full period of the term created by the leases within which to carry out the requisite reinstatement. Accordingly, as at 13th November 2009, there was no breach of the obligation to reinstate. If the works were not carried out before 30th March 2014 then the tenant would have been in breach but that would have been after, not before, the date of the surrenders. In my view the inescapable consequence is that that potential liability was released by the surrenders."

## Obligations which apply at the end of the term or in the last year of the term

It is a question of construction to what extent, if at all, a covenant which is expressed to come into operation at the end of the term (for example, to deliver up in repair at the end of the term) or in the last year of the term (for example, to decorate in the last year of the term) applies at all where the lease is determined prematurely by forfeiture or by service of a break notice.

**2–06**

It is usual in modern leases for such covenants to be expressed to apply "at the end or sooner determination of the term" or "in the last year of the term howsoever determined", so as to make it clear that they come into effect even if the term ends before the original agreed term date. However, where the covenant is expressed to apply "at the expiration of the term" or "in the last year of the term" without more, the position may be less clear.

In *Bevan v Chambers*,[9] a lease of a farm was granted for 21 years with a tenant's right to break at the end of the 7th and 14th years. The landlord covenanted to pay compensation for certain crops "at the end of the said term". The tenant determined the term at the end of the 14th year under the break clause. The Court of Appeal held that the landlord was liable to pay the agreed compensation, the relevant words being construed as meaning the end of the term

---

[8] [2012] EWHC 2886 (Ch.).
[9] (1896) 12 T.L.R. 417.

brought about by the break notice. By contrast, in *Dickinson v St Aubyn*[10] a flat was let for seven years from September 29, 1937, on terms which included (a) a tenant's covenant to paint in "the last quarter of the said term", (b) a tenant's covenant to yield up "at the end or sooner determination of the tenancy", and (c) a tenant's option to determine at the end of the 5th year. The tenant exercised the option and the lease duly ended on September 29, 1942. The Court of Appeal held that the words "the last quarter of the term" referred to the last quarter of the term of seven years and not to the last quarter of the period of five years for which the lease had actually subsisted. The court relied primarily on the contrast between the words "the last quarter of the said term" in the painting covenant, and the words "the end or sooner determination of the tenancy" in the covenant to yield up, as showing that the parties intended the former to refer only to the original term of seven years.[11]

A different approach may apply where the lease is surrendered. In such a case "the entire relation of landlord and tenant is dissolved"[12] and with it the tenant's liability on the covenant (even where it refers to "the end or sooner determination" of the term or similar words).[13] In Ex p. *Sir W Hart Dyke, Re Morrish*[14] a lease of a farm contained covenants by both parties which were expressed to take effect at the expiration or sooner determination of the term. The tenant's trustee in bankruptcy disclaimed the lease during the term. The Court of Appeal, treating the case as one of a statutory surrender, held that neither party could claim the benefit of the covenants. Jessel M.R. said in the course of his judgment:

> "[The surrender] puts an end to the lease, not merely to the term, but to the lease itself. On the one hand, therefore, it deprives the landlord of the future benefit of all those clauses of the lease which give him a benefit; and, on the other hand, it deprives the tenant of the future benefit of all those clauses of the lease which give him a benefit. The result, therefore, is that in the present case neither party can claim the benefit of those provisions of the lease which arise only at the end or sooner determination of the lease."

This was followed by Plowman J. in *Re ABC Engineering Co Ltd (No.3)*[15] (a case of express surrender). A lease contained a covenant to yield up at the expiration or sooner determination of the term with full vacant possession. The liquidator of the tenant company agreed with the landlord to surrender the lease without prejudice to the landlord's rights in respect of any antecedent breach of covenant. The judge held that the covenant to yield up did not survive the surrender because any breach could not be regarded as an antecedent breach, and went on to hold that the matter was in any event concluded by *Re Morrish*.[16] In *Baroque Investments Ltd v Heis*[17] a covenant to reinstate "Before the end of the Lease …" was held to have been released by a surrender in which both parties

---

[10] [1944] 1 K.B. 454.

[11] See also *Kirklinton v Wood* [1917] 1 K.B. 332, considered in Ch.16, below.

[12] Ex p. *Glegg, Re Latham* (1881) 19 Ch. D. 7 per Lush L.J. at 17.

[13] But note that liability for accrued breaches prior to the surrender is unaffected (unless the parties agree they should be released): see para.2–05, above.

[14] (1882) 22 Ch. D. 410.

[15] [1970] 1 W.L.R. 702.

[16] See also Ex p. *Glegg, Re Latham*, above.

[17] [2012] EWHC 2886 (Ch.).

respectively released each other from all liability "in respect of any breach ... whether arising on or after, but not before, the date of this Surrender."[18]

## WHERE THE TENANT HOLDS OVER UNDER STATUTE

### Statutory continuation

A number of statutes confer security of tenure by restricting what would otherwise be the landlord's right to possession at the end of the original term. Such statutes commonly provide, expressly or impliedly, for the terms of the original tenancy to continue to bind the tenant for the period during which he remains in possession by virtue of the statute. Thus, a tenant who becomes a statutory tenant under the Rent Act 1977 on the termination of a protected tenancy must observe and is entitled to the benefit of all the terms and conditions of the original contract of tenancy so far as consistent with the provisions of the Act[19]; a statutory periodic tenancy arising under the Housing Act 1988 contains (subject to the provisions of the Act, which include giving the parties an opportunity to seek a modification) the same terms as those of the fixed-term tenancy which preceded it (other than terms providing for determination by the landlord or the tenant)[20]; and Pt II of the Landlord and Tenant Act 1954 operates by continuing the tenancy on the same terms.[21] In all these cases, terms as to repair or decoration which bound the parties during the original tenancy will be carried over into the new or continuation tenancy.[22]

**2–07**

## Obligations framed by reference to the expiry of the original term

Problems may arise where the relevant obligation is framed by reference to the determination of the original term. In such cases, it will be a question of construction whether the obligation can be read as including the determination of the new or continuation tenancy (i.e. as an obligation which arises on the termination of the tenant's right of occupation as opposed to the original term granted), or whether it means the date on which the original tenancy ended or would have ended but for the statute.

**2–08**

In *Ward v Hicks*[23] a covenant to redecorate "on the expiration or determination of the said term" was held to be carried over into a statutory tenancy under the Rent Acts. In *Boyer v Warbey (No.1)*[24] (another Rent Act case) the tenant covenanted that she would "on her ... quitting the said premises at the end of the term hereby granted ... pay to [the landlord] immediately after the expiration or sooner determination of the tenancy whenever it shall happen" a fixed sum in lieu

---

[18] See further on this case para.2–05, above.
[19] Rent Act 1977 s.3(1).
[20] Housing Act 1988 s.5(3).
[21] Landlord and Tenant Act 1954 s.24.
[22] See, for example, *Hewitt v Rowlands* (1924) 93 L.J.K.B. 1080 (landlord's repairing covenant carried over into statutory tenancy under the Rent Acts).
[23] [1952] C.L.Y. 3023, County Court.
[24] [1953] 1 Q.B. 234, CA.

of repairs. The Court of Appeal held, by a majority, that the obligation applied at the end of the statutory tenancy, "at the end of the term", meaning "at the end of the tenancy". However, in *Langford Property Co Ltd v Saunders*[25] a covenant to carry out decorative work "in the last month before the determination of the tenancy" was held to refer to the last month of the original term and not to be incorporated into the statutory tenancy.[26]

The problem most commonly occurs in practice in relation to business leases within Pt II of the Landlord and Tenant Act 1954 which contain covenants by the tenant to yield up the premises in repair at the end of the term (or words to that effect). On one view, references to "the term" are (in the absence of words showing a contrary intention) to be read as being to the original term only, so that the covenant comes into effect, if at all, on the last day of the original term[27] and is not carried over into a continuation tenancy[28] (although there would be nothing to stop the parties from expressly defining the term as including any period of statutory continuation under the 1954 Act[29]). It is thought, however, that in the absence of contrary words or special circumstances, the covenant is likely to be read as intended to come into operation at the end of the tenant's rights of occupation under the tenancy, so that the relevant date would be the end of the continuation tenancy.[30]

## Obligations requiring to be performed periodically

2–09     Leases often contain obligations relevant to dilapidations which require to be performed periodically, either on specified dates or at specified intervals following a given date. A common example is a covenant to decorate the exterior of the premises every five years. The extent to which such obligations are carried over where the tenant holds over under statute is a question of construction in each case. One possible conclusion will be that the covenant was only intended to operate during the original contractual term and not thereafter. Thus, in *Willison v Cheverell Estates*[31] a lease granted for 20 years from September 29, 1980 contained (i) provision for rent review on specified dates, namely, September 29, 1985, 1990 and 1995, and (ii) a break clause entitling the landlord to determine

---

[25] [1947] L.J.N.C.C.R. 113.

[26] It is thought that this case is to be regarded with some caution, given the two decisions to the opposite effect referred to above.

[27] Although damages would be assessed on the basis that the tenancy would continue under the 1954 Act: see Ch.30, below.

[28] Cf. *City of London Corp v Fell* [1994] A.C. 458. A covenant to keep in repair and any other continuing obligation imposing liability for dilapidations would, of course, be carried over into the continuation tenancy.

[29] See *GMS Syndicate Ltd v Gary Elliott Ltd* [1982] Ch. 1; *Herbert Duncan v Cluttons* [1994] 1 A.C. 458. In *Felnex Central Properties Ltd v Montague Burton Properties Ltd* [1981] 2 E.G.L.R. 73 (the facts of which are set out in para.2–12, below) references in the definition of "the term" to "any statutory continuation" of the term granted and in the repairing covenant to "any extension of the term hereby granted under the provisions of the Landlord and Tenant Act 1954" were held to be to a statutory continuation of the original term under s.24(1) of the 1954 Act and not to a new tenancy granted under that Act.

[30] Cf. the cases considered above, and see also para.2–06 above.

[31] [1996] 1 E.G.L.R. 116.

the term for redevelopment on giving not less than six months' notice expiring not before September 29, 1985. The landlord served a break notice determining the term on May 18, 1990, after which date the tenancy continued under the Landlord and Tenant Act 1954. The Court of Appeal held that the rent review provisions ceased to be operative on the expiry of the break notice, the effect of the definition of the term in the lease being that there was no longer anything on which the review clause could operate.

As always, the correct conclusion in each case will depend on the specific facts. It is to be noted that one of the principal reasons for the decision in *Willison* was the particular provisions of the rent review clause relating to the hypothetical term. No such difficulty arises in relation to, for example, a covenant to decorate at specified intervals, and it is thought that absent contra-indications in the lease or the surrounding circumstances, the court might well be prepared to hold that such an obligation survives into a continuation tenancy under the 1954 Act.

## WHERE THE TENANT IS GRANTED A NEW TENANCY

### New tenancy by express grant

Where the tenant is granted a new tenancy on the coming to an end of a previous tenancy, the repairing obligations under the latter will cease to have effect as regards liability for disrepair after the grant of the new tenancy, and the position from then on will be governed by the terms of the new tenancy. The ascertainment of those terms will depend on the principles considered in Ch.1, above. Where the new tenancy is in writing, it is common to find an express provision which has the effect of incorporating the repairing obligations in the old tenancy into the new tenancy by reference.

One question which may arise is whether the tenant's repairing obligations under the new tenancy are to be construed solely by reference to the state of the premises at the date of the new tenancy and the length of the new term, or whether regard may properly be had to the state of the premises at the date of grant of the old tenancy and the length of the previous term.[32] The answer will obviously depend on the detailed facts, but it is thought that in the straightforward case of an agreed renewal of the tenancy on the same terms, the latter is likely to be the correct analysis. However, the facts may point to a different conclusion.[33]

2–10

### Release of pre-existing liability

Another question which sometimes arises when a tenancy which contains repairing obligations ends and is then renewed by agreement is whether the effect of the grant of the new tenancy is to release either party from a pre-existing liability for disrepair. Whilst each case will turn on its own facts, it is thought that

2–11

---

[32] See paras 9–21 to 9–23 and 11–23, below.

[33] Cf. *Johnson v Churchwardens and Overseers of the Parish of St Peter, Hereford* (1836) 11 E.R. 883 (considered in *Felnex Central Properties Ltd v Montague Burton Properties Ltd* [1981] 2 E.G.L.R. 73 at 75L–76A).

absent an express provision to that effect or a necessary implication arising from the particular circumstances, the answer will generally be that any such liability is not released.

## Where the tenant holds over under an implied periodic tenancy

**2–12**     Where following the expiry of a fixed term tenancy, the tenant holds over under an implied periodic tenancy arising by virtue of the payment and acceptance of rent,[34] the general principle is that he holds on the terms of the old tenancy so far as not inconsistent with a periodic tenancy.[35] In *Felnex Central Properties Ltd v Montague Burton Properties Ltd*[36] Slade J. explained the principle as follows:

> "What the court is doing in such cases, I think, is to impute an agreement to the parties. The relevant rule is no more than a presumption and accordingly is rebuttable, where the facts show sufficiently clearly that the parties' intentions were of a different nature. However, where a tenant holds over after the expiration of the term granted by a lease, and the facts do not exclude an implied agreement to hold on the terms of the original lease, then the court will imply that he holds subject to all the covenants in the lease which regulate his relationship with the landlord in his capacity as tenant and are applicable to the new situation."

The effect of the general principle will usually be that any repairing obligations in the expired tenancy will be carried over into the implied periodic tenancy. *Felnex Central Properties Ltd v Montague Burton Properties Ltd*[37] is a good example of this. In that case, a lease of business premises granted for three years contained obligations on the part of the tenants to keep the premises in good and substantial repair and condition, to yield them up in that state at the end of the term and to decorate the premises during the last year of the term. The expression "the term" was defined as "the term of years hereby created together with any statutory continuation thereof". The relevant obligations were subject to a proviso that if the tenants should not obtain an extension of the term under the provisions of the Landlord and Tenant Act 1954, the obligations were to be void and of no effect and the tenant was to yield up the premises at the expiration of the term in no worse a condition than they were in at the commencement of the term. The tenants served on the landlord a request for a new tenancy under s.26 of the 1954 Act but made no application to the court, so that the tenancy ended on its contractual term date. The tenants then held over under an implied periodic tenancy arising by payment and acceptance of rent. Slade J. held that the new tenancy contained both the same repairing and decorating obligations as the old tenancy and the proviso.

---

[34] For the principles applicable to whether a new tenancy has arisen by implication from payment and acceptance of rent, see *Woodfall: Landlord and Tenant* (London: Sweet & Maxwell) Vol.1, para.1.021.4.

[35] *Lowther v Clifford* [1927] 1 K.B. 130.

[36] [1981] 2 E.G.L.R. 73.

[37] [1981] 2 E.G.L.R. 73.

By contrast, in *Johnson v Churchwardens and Overseers of the Parish of St Peter, Hereford*[38] it was held on special facts that the repairing obligations in a lease granted for 21 years were not carried over into an implied annual tenancy.

## TERMINATION OF SECURE AND ASSURED TENANCIES UNDER THE HOUSING ACTS 1985 AND 1988

### Termination of secure tenancies

Where a possession order is made against a secure tenant on or after May 20, 2009, the tenancy ends on the date on which the order is executed.[39] The parties' respective repairing obligations therefore continue up to that date.

**2–13**

Where a suspended possession order was made on conditions prior to May 20, 2009, the tenancy ended at the time the conditions were broken.[40] If the landlord nonetheless allowed the tenant to remain in possession after that date, he became what was called a "tolerated trespasser". In such a case, neither party could enforce the repairing obligations in the former tenancy, nor did the tenant have any rights under the Defective Premises Act 1972[41] (although the tenant had a sufficient interest to bring an action against the landlord in nuisance).[42] The tenancy could be revived by a further order of the court postponing the date for possession (or rescinding or discharging the possession order),[43] in which case the tenancy was treated for all purposes as if it had continued throughout what would otherwise have been the limbo period, such that either party could acquire retrospective repairing liabilities.[44] However, by virtue of Sch.11 of the Housing and Regeneration Act 2008, a former tenant in occupation as a tolerated trespasser now acquires a new replacement tenancy. The possession order by virtue of which the original tenancy ended is to be treated, so far as practicable, as if it applies to the new tenancy.[45] The new tenancy has effect on the same terms and conditions, subject to modification in specified circumstances, as those applicable to the original tenancy immediately before it ended.[46] Subject to any such modification, therefore, any repairing obligations will be carried over into the new replacement tenancy. The court may order that the new tenancy and the original tenancy are to be treated as the same tenancy and a tenancy which continued uninterrupted throughout the termination period for the purposes of

---

[38] (1836) 11 E.R. 883 (considered in *Felnex Central Properties v Montague Burton Properties* [1981] 2 E.G.L.R. 73 at 75L–76A).

[39] Housing Act 1985 s.82 (1A), (2) (substituted by the Housing and Regeneration Act 2008 s.299 Sch. 11 with effect from May 20, 2009).

[40] *Thompson v Elmbridge BC* [1987] 1 W.L.R. 1425; *Burrows v Brent LBC* [1996] 1 W.L.R. 1448; *Harlow DC v Hall* [2006] 1 W.L.R. 2116; *White v Knowsley Housing Trust* [2009] A.C. 636; *Austin v Southwark LBC* [2011] 1 A.C. 355.

[41] *Burrows v Brent LBC*, above, per Lord Browne-Wilkinson at 1455; *Pemberton v Southwark LBC* [2000] 2 E.G.L.R. 33.

[42] *Pemberton v Southwark LBC*, above.

[43] *Burrows v Brent LBC*, above; *Marshall v Bradford MDC*, above.

[44] *Greenwich LBC v Regan*, above; *Marshall v Bradford MDC*, above; *Lambeth LBC v Rogers* [2000] 1 E.G.L.R. 28.

[45] Housing and Regeneration Act 2008 s.299 Sch.11 para.20.

[46] Housing and Regeneration Act 2008 s.299 Sch.11 para.18.

(among other things) (i) a claim by the ex-tenant or the ex-landlord for breach of a term or condition of the original tenancy in respect of which proceedings were brought on or after May 20, 2009 or in respect of which proceedings were brought but not finally determined before that date, and (ii) a claim by the ex-tenant against the ex-landlord for breach of statutory duty in respect of which proceedings are or were so brought.[47]

## Termination of assured tenancies

2–14    An assured tenancy under the Housing Act 1988 ends on the date on which a possession order is executed.[48] Any repairing obligations will therefore continue until such time.

## WHERE THE TENANT HOLDS OVER AS A TRESPASSER

## The general principle

2–15    The general principle where the tenant remains in possession as a trespasser after the expiry of his lease is that neither he nor his former landlord are liable under any repairing or other obligation contained in the expired lease in respect of any period after the expiry of the lease. Depending on the circumstances, however, there may be a claim in nuisance.[49]

---

[47] Housing and Regeneration Act 2008 s.299 Sch.11 para.21.

[48] *White v Knowsley Housing Trust* [2009] A.C. 636; Housing Act 1988 s.5(1A) (substituted by the Housing and Regeneration Act 2008 s.299 Sch.11 with effect from May 20, 2009.

[49] *Foster v Warblington UDC* [1906] 1 K.B. 648; *Hunter v Canary Wharf* [1997] A.C. 655; *Pemberton v Southwark LBC* [2000] 2 E.G.L.R. 33.

CHAPTER 3

# WHO CAN SUE AND BE SUED[1]

INTRODUCTORY

## The relevant party

By the time a dilapidations question arises, the respective interests of the original
parties to the lease may have changed hands, quite often more than once. In such
a case it will be necessary to consider who is entitled to enforce the relevant
covenants, and who is liable under them. In addition, where the party entitled to
the lease or the reversion at the time the question arises is insolvent or cannot be
found, it will also be necessary to consider whether there is anyone else in the
chain of title who can be made liable.

3–01

Since the coming into force on January 1, 1996 of the Landlord and Tenant
(Covenants) Act 1995 (which will be referred to as "the 1995 Act"), it is
necessary to distinguish between new tenancies to which that Act applies and
other tenancies.[2] In this Chapter tenancies to which the 1995 Act applies will be
referred to as "new tenancies", and other tenancies as "old tenancies". The
following are considered, in relation both to old and new tenancies:

(1)    the position of the original parties;
(2)    the position of successors in title;
(3)    collateral contracts and covenants in licences;
(4)    the position of sureties;
(5)    assignments of rights of action under repairing covenants;
(6)    the practical choice of claimant and defendant.

The position regarding sub-tenants is dealt with in Ch.24, below.

---

[1] For an authoritative treatment of leasehold covenants, see Harpum, C., Bridge, S. and Dixon, M.,
*Megarry & Wade: The Law of Real Property*, 8th edn (London: Sweet & Maxwell, 2012) Ch.20;
Fancourt, T.M., *Enforceability of Leasehold Covenants*, 2nd edn (London: Sweet & Maxwell, 2006).
[2] The detailed provisions of the 1995 Act are outside the scope of this work and reference should be
made to the Act itself.

## Distinction between "old tenancies" and "new tenancies"

3–02    A tenancy is a "new tenancy" within the meaning of the 1995 Act if it was granted after January 1, 1996 otherwise than in pursuance of an agreement entered into before that date, or an order of the court made before that date.[3] A tenancy granted on or after January 1, 1996 pursuant to an option granted before that date is to be regarded as granted in pursuance of an agreement entered into before that date, and accordingly is not a new tenancy, whether or not the option was actually exercised before that date.[4] All other tenancies are old tenancies. In broad terms, therefore, the test for deciding whether a tenancy is a new tenancy or an old tenancy is whether it was granted before or after January 1, 1996.

## OLD TENANCIES: THE ORIGINAL PARTIES

## The original parties under an old tenancy

3–03    The position at common law, which it was the object of the 1995 Act to reform for the future, is as follows. A lease or tenancy agreement creates both a contract and an estate. By virtue of privity of contract, it binds each of the contracting parties (the original landlord and the original tenant) throughout the whole of the term. No assignment either of the term or of the reversion will of itself release the original landlord or the original tenant from the burden of his covenants.[5] This is subject to any express provision to the contrary in the lease but it is uncommon to find any such provision.[6]

## The liability of the original tenant under an old tenancy

### (a)    Liability

3–04    Absent an express provision to the contrary, an original tenant under an old tenancy who has assigned his lease remains liable for breach of the repairing and other covenants in the lease for the remainder of the term. So, for example, a claim for terminal dilapidations may be made against him following the expiry of the lease. However, in the absence of express provision, he is not liable for breaches committed by an assignee during a continuation tenancy under Pt II of the Landlord and Tenant Act 1954.[7]

---

[3] Landlord and Tenant (Covenants) Act 1995 s.1(3).

[4] See above, s.1(6). An option includes a right of first refusal: see above, s.1(7).

[5] *Thames Manufacturing Co Ltd v Perrotts (Nichol & Peyton) Ltd* (1984) 50 P. & C.R. 1 (original tenant); *Stuart v Joy* [1904] 1 K.B. 362 (original landlord).

[6] Although see *Avonridge Property Company Ltd v Mashru* [2005] 1 W.L.R. 3956 (in which the lease contained a provision that the original landlord was not to be liable after it has disposed of its interest in the property).

[7] *City of London Corp v Fell* [1994] 1 A.C. 458.

## (b)    Defences to liability

In *Allied London Investments Ltd v Hambro Life Assurance Plc*,[8] Walton J. was:    **3–05**

> "[P]erfectly clear that when he is sued ... on the covenants contained in the original lease, the original tenant's only possible defences are either: (1) that he has performed the covenants; or (2) that the relevant assignee has performed the covenants; or (3) that there has been some operation conducted upon the lease—for example, surrender of the whole—which has put a complete end to the liability ... Short of one of these defences, there is no defence."

It is therefore no defence for a tenant under an old tenancy to show that:

(1)    the assignee has subsequently surrendered part of the demised premises[9] (although the original tenant is released from future performance of the covenants where the assignee surrenders the whole of the premises[10]);

(2)    the landlord has released a surety for the assignee against whom the tenant would have had a right of indemnity[11];

(3)    the lease has subsequently been varied by agreement between the landlord and the assignee without reference to the original tenant[12];

(4)    the landlord has alternative remedies against other assignees or sureties in the chain of title[13];

(5)    the assignee in possession is insolvent and the lease has been disclaimed by his trustee in bankruptcy or liquidator[14];

(6)    the assignee in possession has entered into a voluntary arrangement under the Insolvency Act 1986[15];

(7)    there has been an assignment of the reversion.[16]

However, the original tenant may be released where the landlord releases the assignee. The relevant question in such a case will be whether, as a matter of construction of the bargain between the landlord and the assignee, having regard to the surrounding circumstances and taking into account the express words and any terms which can properly be implied, the agreement precludes the landlord from enforcing his rights against the original tenant.[17] If the bargain amounts to a discharge of the relevant obligation sought to be enforced against the original tenant, the latter will be released from performance of that obligation because it

---

[8] [1984] 1 E.G.L.R. 16.

[9] *Baynton v Morgan* (1888) 22 Q.B.D. 74.

[10] *Allied London Investments Ltd v Hambro Life Assurance Plc* [1984] 1 E.G.L.R. 16.

[11] *Allied London Investments Ltd v Hambro Life Assurance Plc*, above.

[12] *Friends Provident Life Office v British Railways Board* [1996] 1 All E.R. 336. However, the liability of the original tenant cannot be increased or varied by the agreement between the landlord and the assignee: see para.3–06, below.

[13] *Norwich Union Life Insurance Society v Low Profile Fashions Ltd* [1992] 1 E.G.L.R. 86; *Milverton Group Ltd v Warner World Ltd* [1995] 2 E.G.L.R. 28.

[14] *Hindcastle Ltd v Barbara Attenborough Associates* [1997] A.C. 70.

[15] *Johnson v Davies* [1999] Ch. 117 (but note that a voluntary arrangement may as a matter of construction have the effect of releasing the original tenant: see below).

[16] *Arlesford Trading Co Ltd v Servansingh* [1971] 1 W.L.R. 1080. For the rights of the assignee of the reversion, see para.3–16, below.

[17] *Johnson v Davies*, above; *Watts v Aldington* [1999] L. & T.R. 578 (note); *Sun Life Assurance Society Plc v Tantofex (Engineers) Ltd* [1999] L. & T.R. 568.

will be deemed to have been performed.[18] However, a mere release of the assignee without performance or deemed performance of the obligation will not of itself release the original tenant.[19] The test is the same where the deal between the landlord and the assignee is contained in a voluntary arrangement under the Insolvency Act 1986, which is to be treated as a consensual arrangement for the purposes of deciding whether third parties are released.[20]

## (c)  Subsequent variations

**3–06**   At common law the obligations of the original tenant cannot be varied or increased by an agreement made subsequently between the landlord and an assignee.[21] Thus, for example, the original tenant would not be liable for damages for breach by an assignee of an additional or more onerous repairing obligation undertaken by the assignee after the assignment, but he would remain liable for any failure by the assignee to perform the original terms of the lease.[22] However, if the lease itself provides for some variation in the future of the obligations to be performed by the tenant, the original tenant may be bound to perform the obligations as so varied, even though the variations happen after the original tenant has assigned on.[23] That situation occurs most frequently, however, in rent review cases where the lease sets out a formula by which the reviewed rent is to be calculated, but the same principle applies in relation to repairing covenants.

The 1995 Act provides that a former tenant who has assigned the tenancy but who remains bound by any tenant covenant[24] is not liable under the covenant to pay any amount in respect of the covenant to the extent that the amount is referable to any relevant variations[25] of the tenant covenants of the tenancy, and neither is his guarantor.[26] This applies both to old and new tenancies.[27] However, it does not apply to any variation effected before January 1, 1996, which continues to be governed by the common law as set out above.[28]

---

[18] *Sun Life Assurance Society Plc v Tantofex (Engineers) Ltd*, above; *Deanplan v Mahmoud* [1993] Ch. 151.

[19] *Sun Life Assurance Society Plc v Tantofex (Engineers) Ltd*, above (in which it was held that a landlord, who had granted a licence to an assignee to assign on and had at the same time released him from a direct covenant to pay the rent and perform the covenants which he had given when he took the assignment, had not thereby released the original tenant).

[20] *Johnson v Davies*, above.

[21] *Friends' Provident Life Office Ltd v British Railways Board*, above.

[22] See above.

[23] *Friends Provident Life Office v British Railways Board*, above, per Sir Christopher Slade.

[24] See para.3–19, below.

[25] This means a variation which the landlord has, at the time it occurs, an absolute right to refuse to allow, or where he would have had such a right but for a variation of the tenant covenants at or after the assignment: Landlord and Tenant (Covenants) Act 1995 s.18(4). In determining whether he has or would have such a right at any particular time, regard must be had to all the circumstances, including the effect of any provision made by or under any enactment: 1995 Act s.18(5).

[26] 1995 Act s.18.

[27] 1995 Act s.1(2).

[28] 1995 Act s.18(6).

### (d)   Liability for fixed charges

At common law, the original tenant is liable for sums due to the landlord from the
assignee (including damages), even though he was unaware of the assignee's
default. The 1995 Act reforms this by restricting the liability of the original tenant
and his guarantor for fixed charges due from an assignee.[29] A fixed charge means
rent, any service charge or any amount payable under a tenant covenant of the
tenancy providing for payment of a liquidated sum in the event of a failure to
comply with any such covenant.[30] The relevant provisions apply to all tenancies,
whenever granted.[31] Neither a former tenant who has assigned the tenancy, nor
his guarantor, are liable to pay any amount in respect of any fixed charge unless,
within the period of six months beginning with the date on which the fixed charge
becomes due, the landlord serves[32] on him a notice in the prescribed form[33]
informing him (a) that the charge is now due, and (b) that in respect of the charge
the landlord intends to recover from him such amount as is specified in the notice
and (where payable) interest calculated on such basis as is so specified.[34] The
same is the case in relation to a former tenant who has under an authorised
guarantee agreement guaranteed the performance by his assignee of any tenant
covenant under the tenancy.[35] Where the rent is subject to a rent review but the
actual amount has not been determined, the fixed charge that becomes due on
each payment date after the rent review is the rent at the level before the review
date; the additional rent does not become "due" until the reviewed rent is agreed
or determined and is then a new and separate fixed charge.[36] The sums for which
the former tenant, or his guarantor, are liable cannot (subject to certain
exceptions) exceed the amount in the notice.[37] The inclusion in the notice of
items to which the landlord is not entitled does not invalidate it in regard to items
to which he is entitled.[38] A person who pays in full the amount which he has been
required to pay, plus any interest payable, is entitled to an overriding lease.[39]

3–07

---

[29]   1995 Act s.17.

[30]   1995 Act s.17(6). It may therefore be a fixed charge would include sums due from the assignee in
respect of the cost of works carried out by the landlord under a covenant entitling him to enter and
carry out works which the tenant has failed to carry out in breach of covenant (see Ch.28, below).

[31]   1995 Act s.1(2). A fixed charge which became due before January 1, 1996 is treated for the
purposes of the Act as having become due on that date: 1995 Act s.17(5). The restrictions do not apply
to proceedings which were instituted against the original tenant or his guarantor before that date: 1995
Act s.17(5).

[32]   The Landlord and Tenant Act 1927 s.23 applies to the service of the notice: 1995 Act s.27(5).
Where a notice was sent by recorded delivery to the tenant's last known place of abode, and was
returned by the post office undelivered, it was held that the notice had been validly served in
accordance with the section: *Commercial Union Life Assurance Co Ltd v Moustafa* [1999] 2 E.G.L.R.
44. See further para.27–26, below.

[33]   The form of notice is prescribed by the Landlord and Tenant (Covenants) Act 1995 (Notices)
Regulations 1995 (SI 1995/2964). A notice which is not in the prescribed form or in a form
substantially to the like effect is not effective: Landlord and Tenant (Covenants) Act 1995 s.27(4).

[34]   1995 Act s.17(1) and (2). The same is the case in relation to a former tenant which has

[35]   1995 Act s.17(1) and (2).

[36]   *Scottish & Newcastle Plc v Raguz (No.2)* [2008] 1 W.L.R. 2494.

[37]   Landlord and Tenant (Covenants) Act 1995 s.17(4).

[38]   *Commercial Union Life Assurance Co Ltd v Moustafa*, above (in which a notice was not
invalidated by an error as to the way interest was calculated under the lease).

[39]   Landlord and Tenant (Covenants) Act 1995 ss.19 and 20.

The landlord need not serve a s.17 notice on the original tenant before making a claim against the original tenant's guarantor.[40]

### (e)  Rights of the original tenant when sued

**3–08**     The steps open to an original tenant under an old tenancy against whom a claim for dilapidations is made after he has parted with the lease are limited. He has no right to possession of the premises, so that he cannot enter the premises and carry out the works. Generally, the most he can hope to do is to take steps to obtain recompense in one form or another from persons further down the chain. It is usual for an assignment to contain an express covenant or indemnity on the part of the assignor. The extent to which an express covenant extends to breaches in existence at the date of the assignment as well as to those occurring thereafter is a question of construction.[41] In the absence of an express covenant or indemnity, the original tenant has a statutorily implied covenant for indemnity against the assignee.[42] He also has the following further rights of indemnity:

(1)     there is an implied obligation at common law by the assignee in possession to indemnify the original tenant against breaches committed by the assignee during the time he holds the lease.[43] This arises independently of any contract.[44] It is not excluded by a provision in the assignment excluding the statutorily implied covenant referred to above.[45] It extends to continuing breaches of the covenant to repair which were in existence at the date of the assignment[46];

(2)     there is an implied right of indemnity against the surety of the assignee in possession.[47]

Section 17 of the 1995 Act[48] does not apply as between the original tenant and an assignee or surety against whom he has a right of indemnity, so that no notice

---

[40] *Cheverell Estates Ltd v Harris* [1998] 1 E.G.L.R. 27.
[41] See *Gooch v Clutterbuck* [1899] 2 Q.B. 148 (covenant in assignment of lease of old premises, which were out of repair at the time, that the assignee "will henceforth pay the rent by the said lease reserved, and observe and perform the lessee's covenants therein contained, and from the payment and performance thereof respectively will keep indemnified [the assignor]" held to include continuing breaches of the covenant to repair in existence at the date of the assignment).
[42] Law of Property Act 1925 s.77(1)(c) and Sch.2 Pt IX (which applies where the conveyance is for valuable consideration); Land Registration Act 1925 s.24(1)(b).
[43] *Moule v Garrett* (1872) L.R. 7 Ex. 101. See also *Electricity Supply Nominees Ltd v Thorn EMI Ltd* (1991) 63 P. & C.R. 143.
[44] *Re Healing Research Trustee Co Ltd* [1992] 2 All E.R. 481.
[45] *Re Healing Research Trustee Co Ltd*, above.
[46] *Middlegate Properties Ltd v Bilbao* (1972) 24 P. & C.R. 329.
[47] *Selous Street Properties Ltd v Oronel Fabrics Ltd* [1984] 1 E.G.L.R. 50; *Becton Dickinson UK Ltd v Zwebner* [1989] Q.B. 208; *Re A Debtor (No.21 of 1995)* [1995] N.P.C. 170. This is by virtue of the principle that as between the original tenant and the assignee in possession, the liability of the latter is primary or ultimate: see above. It may be that the original tenant would also be entitled to be indemnified by a subsequent assignee (or his surety) who has himself assigned on but who remains liable to the landlord under a direct covenant. The decision in *Selous Street Properties Ltd v Oronel Fabrics Ltd* supports this to some extent, but the position has not yet been settled beyond doubt.
[48] See para.3–07, above.

under that section need be served by the original tenant before making a claim for indemnity or contribution.[49] However, it is not wholly clear to what extent the original tenant is entitled to recover sums paid by him to the landlord which he was not liable to pay because no s.17 notice had been served on him. It has been held at first instance that he cannot recover such sums under a covenant of indemnity.[50] However, a different conclusion was reached in relation to the statutorily implied covenant of indemnity under s.24(1)(b) of the Land Registration Act 1925 in circumstances in which payment of the charges by the assignor was in both parties' interests to enable an assignment to go ahead and future liabilities to be stemmed.[51]

It has been held that the original tenant has no right to compel his assignee either to assign to the original tenant the benefit of the assignee's covenant of indemnity with a subsequent assignee, or to bring proceedings against the subsequent assignee for an order that the assignee pay rent to the landlord.[52]

The difficulty with the original tenant's rights of indemnity is that they depend for their efficacy upon the persons liable to indemnify being solvent. In practice, however, it is generally the very fact that those persons are insolvent that causes the landlord to proceed against the original tenant in the first place. In such a case the only remaining step open to the original tenant (apart from seeking to prove in the bankruptcy or liquidation) is to seek to acquire the residue of the lease (if it still exists) from the assignee's liquidator or trustee in bankruptcy, either by agreement or by applying for a vesting order,[53] in the hope that it is of some value and can be sold or otherwise put to good use. In addition, where the original tenant pays pursuant to a s.17 notice,[54] he is entitled to an overriding lease.

## The liability of the original landlord under an old tenancy

The principles governing the continuing liability of the original landlord who has assigned his reversion are similar to those relating to the liability of the original tenant. Thus, the landlord remains liable on his covenants for the whole term notwithstanding any assignment of the reversion.[55] It may be that the original landlord's continuing liability can be enforced against him by an assignee of the term.[56]

3–09

The extent to which the original landlord is entitled to be indemnified by a successor in title against subsequent breaches of the landlord's covenants under

---

[49] *Fresh (Retail) Ltd v Emsden* [1999] 5 C.L. 455; *M W Kellogg Ltd v Tobin* [1999] L. & T. R. 513.
[50] *MW Kellogg Ltd v Tobin*, above (in which the claim was brought under an express covenant of indemnity in the assignment and the covenant implied by s.77(1) and Sch.2 to the Law of Property Act 1925).
[51] *Scottish & Newcastle Plc v Raguz (No.2)* [2008] 1 W.L.R. 2494.
[52] *RPH Ltd v Mirror Group (Holdings) Ltd* [1993] 1 E.G.L.R. 74.
[53] Insolvency Act 1986 ss.181(3) (company) and 320(3) (individual). Both of these apply only where the lease has been disclaimed, by the liquidator under s.178 (where the assignee is a company) or by the trustee in bankruptcy under s.320 (where the assignee is an individual).
[54] See para.3–07, above.
[55] *Stuart v Joy & Nantes* [1904] 1 K.B. 362; *Wright v Dean* [1948] Ch. 686.
[56] See *Celsteel Ltd v Alton House Holdings Ltd (No.2)* [1986] 1 W.L.R. 666 at 672, (affirmed [1987] 1 W.L.R. 291 at 296).

the lease is less clear. The statutorily implied covenants do not appear to extend to this situation. It is probable, however, that there would be an implied right of indemnity at common law from the landlord in whom the reversion is vested when the breach occurs.[57]

## SUCCESSORS IN TITLE UNDER OLD TENANCIES

### Introductory

**3–10**
The general rule in relation to old tenancies is that successors in title to the original parties are liable to perform all covenants in the lease that "touch and concern land". Conversely, they are entitled to the benefit of all such covenants on the part of the other party. Any other covenants are personal to the original parties, and neither the benefit nor the burden will run on an assignment of their interest. However, these principles apply only where the assignment of the term or the reversion is effective to transfer the legal estate to the assignee.

A lease can only validly be assigned by deed.[58] Any other form of "assignment" will not generally suffice to transfer either the legal estate in the lease, or the liability under its covenants. This remains so even though the "assignee" has entered into possession and paid rent.[59] In addition, where the lease is registered, the legal estate does not pass until the assignment is registered at HM Land Registry.[60] Likewise, the reversion can only validly be assigned by deed,[61] and where the title is registered, the transfer must be registered for the legal estate to pass.[62] However, the circumstances may be such that the parties are estopped as against each other from denying that a valid assignment has taken place.[63]

The parties will usually be defined in the lease in a manner which is apt to include successors in title. However, the fact that this has not been done does not prevent the transfer of rights and liabilities under covenants which touch and concern land (unless the lease makes it clear that the benefit or burden of the covenant in question is personal to the relevant party). By statute, a covenant which touches and concerns land is deemed to be made (i) (unless a contrary intention is expressed) by the party giving the covenant on behalf of himself and his successors in title and the persons deriving title under him or them,[64] and (ii)

---

[57] It is thought that the principle in *Moule v Garrett* (see para.3–08, above) is wide enough to include the case of an original landlord who is sued by the tenant in respect of breaches of covenant committed by a successor landlord.

[58] Law of Property Act 1925 s.52(1); *Crago v Julian* [1992] 1 W.L.R. 372; *London Borough of Croydon v Buston* [1991] 24 H.L.R. 36. This is the case even where the tenancy was made under hand or orally.

[59] *Cox v Bishop* (1857) 8 De G.M. & G. 815; *Brown & Root Technology Ltd v Sun Alliance & London Insurance Co Ltd* [2001] Ch. 733.

[60] Land Registration Act 1925 s.22(1); Land Registration Act 2002 s.27(1); *Brown & Root Technology Ltd v Sun Alliance & London Insurance Co Ltd*, above.

[61] Law of Property Act 1925 s.52.

[62] See fn.60, above.

[63] See *Rodenhurst Estates Ltd v Barnes* [1936] 2 All E.R. 3. An argument based on estoppel failed in *Brown & Root Technology Ltd v Sun Alliance & London Insurance Co Ltd*, above.

[64] Law of Property Act 1925 s.79.

with the covenantee and his successors in title and the persons deriving title under him or them.[65] "Successors in title" includes the owners and occupiers for the time being of the land.[66]

Where the lease is held on trust, the person liable under the tenant's covenants to repair is the trustee (in whom the legal estate is vested), not the beneficiary. Thus, in *Ramage v Womack*[67] a lease contained a covenant to repair on the part of the tenant, and a declaration that the tenant held the premises in trust for a third party. The third party occupied the premises and paid the rent. It was held that the third party was not liable for breach of the repairing covenant.

## Covenants which touch and concern the land: old tenancies

There is no general definition of what is meant by "touching and concerning the land". Nevertheless, the following has been stated to be a satisfactory working test for determining whether, in any given case, a covenant touches and concerns the land so as to run with the reversion:

3–11

(1)   the covenant benefits only the reversioner for the time being, and if separated from the reversion ceases to be of benefit to the covenantee;

(2)   the covenant affects the nature, quality, mode of use or value of the land of the reversioner;

(3)   the covenant is not expressed to be personal (i.e. neither being given only to a specific reversioner nor in respect of the obligations only of a specific tenant);

(4)   the fact that a covenant is to pay a sum of money will not prevent it from touching and concerning the land so long as the three foregoing conditions are satisfied and the covenant is connected with something to be done on, to or in relation to the land.[68]

The following covenants of relevance to the law of dilapidations have been held to touch and concern the land:

(1)   to repair the demised premises[69];

(2)   to leave the demised premises in repair[70];

---

[65] 1925 Act s.78.

[66] 1925 Act ss.78(1) and 79(1).

[67] [1900] 1 Q.B. 116.

[68] *P&A Swift Investments Ltd v Combined English Stores Ltd* [1989] A.C. 632, per Lord Oliver. Proposition (3) needs to be qualified by reference to the decision of the Court of Appeal in *System Floors Ltd v Ruralpride Ltd* [1995] 1 E.G.L.R. 48, in which it was stated that a covenant could "touch and concern" land even if its benefit was intended to be enjoyed only by the original tenant. Moreover, in *Harbour Estates Ltd v HSBC Bank Plc* [2005] 1 E.G.L.R. 107 Lindsay J. held that a break clause personal to the original tenant but capable of being assigned to specified assignees "touched and concerned" the land.

[69] *Matures v Westwood* (1598) Cro. Eliz. 599; *Windsor's Dean and Chapter Case* (1601) 5 Co. Rep. 24; *Martyn v Clue* (1852) 18 Q.B. 661; *Amsprop Trading Ltd v Harris Distribution Ltd* [1997] 1 W.L.R. 1025.

[70] *Martyn v Clue*, above; *Amsprop Trading Ltd v Harris Distribution Ltd*, above.

(3)   to permit the landlord to enter the premises and give notice of all wants of repair found[71];
(4)   to remedy defects notified by the landlord within three months after such notice (or immediately in the case of emergency) and in default to permit the landlord to enter the premises and carry out the works, and to pay the landlord's costs of the works on demand[72];
(5)   to repair, renew and replace tenant's fixtures and machinery affixed to the demised premises[73];
(6)   to expend a certain sum on repairs each year or to pay to the landlord the difference between that sum and the sum actually expended[74];
(7)   to pay £40 towards the cost of redecoration on quitting the demised premises[75];
(8)   to build upon the demised premises[76];
(9)   to insure against fire[77];
(10)  a covenant by a surety that the tenant will perform the covenants in the lease[78];
(11)  a covenant by a surety to accept a new lease of the demised premises on similar terms to those in the tenant's lease in the event of the tenant going into liquidation.[79]

3–12   The following covenants of relevance to the law of dilapidations have been held not to touch and concern land:

(1)   to replace chattels which might become worn out, damaged, destroyed or otherwise rendered useless[80];
(2)   to keep and deliver up in repair utensils and moveable chattels used in the business.[81]

In many cases the landlord will covenant to repair property which is not part of the demised premises, such as the common parts of the building of which the premises form part. As a general principle, such covenants run where repairs to the property in question directly benefit the demised premises.[82] Thus, in *Lyle v Smith*[83] a covenant to repair a sea-wall, which was not part of the demised premises, but which was necessary for their protection from the sea, was held to

---

[71] *Amsprop Trading Ltd v Harris Distribution Ltd*, above.
[72] Ibid.
[73] *Williams v Earle* (1868) L.R. 3 Q.B. 739.
[74] *Moss Empires Ltd v Olympia (Liverpool) Ltd* [1939] A.C. 544.
[75] *Boyer v Warbey (No.1)* [1953] 1 Q.B. 234.
[76] *Spencer's Case* (1583) 5 Co. Rep. 16a; *City of London v Nash* (1747) 3 Atk. 512.
[77] *Vernon v Smith* (1821) 5 B. & Ald. 1.
[78] *P&A Swift Investments Ltd v Combined English Stores Group Ltd* [1989] A.C. 632.
[79] *Coronation Street Industrial Properties Ltd v Ingall Industries Ltd* [1989] 1 W.L.R. 304.
[80] *Gorton v Gregory* (1862) 3 B. & S. 90. It would apparently have been different had the covenant been limited to the replacing, etc. of fixtures.
[81] *Williams v Earle*, above.
[82] *Sampson v Easterby* (1829) B. & C. 505 (affirmed (1830) 6 Bing. 644); *Lyle v Smith* [1909] 2 Ir. R. 58.
[83] [1909] 2 Ir. R. 58.

touch and concern land. The ordinary case of a landlord's covenant to repair property ancillary to the demised premises, such as the structure and exterior, or the means of access, would clearly fall within this.

However, where the condition of the property in question does not benefit the demised premises in this way, the position is more uncertain. The leading case (albeit now of doubtful authority) is *Dewar v Goodman*,[84] in which a head lease of a number of buildings contained a covenant to repair on the part of the head tenant. The head tenant granted a sub-lease of two of the buildings, and covenanted with the sub-tenant to perform the covenants in the head lease so far as they related to premises not comprised in the sub-lease. The head lease was assigned, and the assignee committed breaches of the repairing covenant in the head lease, as a result of which the head lease was forfeited. The House of Lords held that the covenant in the sub-lease to perform the covenants in the head lease did not run, being collateral to the thing demised, so that the assignee of the head lease was not liable to the sub-tenant for breach. The decision is a surprising one, given that the performance of the sub-lessor's covenant was "manifestly of value to the underlessee for the time being and to no one else",[85] and failure to perform exposed the sub-tenant to forfeiture. The decision is perhaps reconcilable with the other authorities on the ground that performance of the covenant did not benefit the demised premises but only the sub-tenant's estate in those premises.[86] If this is right, there are important implications in the comparatively common case of a demise of a flat in an estate of several blocks, or a unit on an industrial estate. It may be that a landlord's covenant to repair the remainder of the estate will not survive an assignment of the reversion save and insofar as it relates to those parts of the estate which directly benefit the demise in the sense discussed above. However, in *Kumar v Dunning*[87] it was said that *Dewar v Goodman* was irreconcilable with the decision of the House of Lords in *Dyson v Forster*,[88] and that the latter decision was to be preferred. It is probable, therefore, that *Dewar v Goodman* is no longer good law, either for this reason, or following the decision of the House of Lords in *P&A Swift Investments Ltd v Combined English Stores Ltd.*[89]

## The liability of successors in title of the original tenant under an old tenancy

### (a)    The liability of the assignee

An assignee of the term is liable by virtue of privity of estate to perform all the covenants in the lease that touch and concern the land.[90] However, he is only liable for breaches occurring while the term is vested in him, and not for breaches

3–13

---

[84] [1909] A.C. 72. See the contrasting approach in *Kumar v Dunning* [1987] 2 All E.R. 801.
[85] *Kumar v Dunning* [1987] 2 All E.R. 801, per Sir Nicolas Browne-Wilkinson V.C.
[86] See *Kumar v Dunning*, above, per Sir Nicolas Browne-Wilkinson V.C.
[87] See *Kumar v Dunning*, above.
[88] [1909] A.C. 98.
[89] [1989] A.C. 632.
[90] *Spencer's Case* (1583) 5 Co. Rep. 16a.

committed either before or after that time.[91] The practical application of this rule in the context of the law of dilapidations is frequently complicated by the fact that there may be breaches of the repairing covenant which began during the assignor's time and continued after the date of the assignment. In general terms, the assignee is not liable for breaches committed by his predecessor which have been made good prior to the assignment, but he is liable to make good any such breaches which continue after he becomes the tenant.[92] He therefore "takes over" the state of repair as he finds it when he becomes tenant. He remains liable for breaches occurring during his time notwithstanding the fact that he subsequently assigns on.[93]

### (b)    Where the assignee has given a direct covenant

**3–14**    In many cases the assignee will enter into a direct covenant with the landlord to perform the covenants for the remainder of the term. Such covenants are frequently to be found in licences to assign, and it is the practice of many landlords to insist upon them as a condition of consenting to the assignment. The effect of such a covenant is to put the assignee into the same position as the original tenant with regard to the period after the assignment to him. The landlord will therefore be in the happy position of having two (or perhaps more) parties against whom he can claim in the event of the last assignee in the chain being unable to satisfy the claim. Whether a direct covenant makes the assignee liable for the remainder of the term notwithstanding a further assignment, or whether he is liable only for such time as the term remains vested in him, depends on the proper construction of the covenant.[94] A direct covenant may on its proper construction extend to the period of a continuation tenancy under Pt II of the Landlord and Tenant Act 1954.[95]

For the principles relating to the transmission of the benefit and burden of covenants in licences, see paras 3–28 to 3–30, below.

---

[91] *Chancellor v Poole* (1781) 2 Doug. K.B. 764. Accordingly, a landlord may not levy distress in relation to rent falling due and unpaid before the assignment: *Wharfland Ltd v South London Co-operative Building Company Ltd* [1995] 2 E.G.L.R. 21.

[92] *Granada Theatres Ltd v Freehold Investment (Leytonstone) Ltd* [1959] Ch. 592.

[93] *Harley v King* (1835) 2 Cr. M. & R. 18. See also *City & Metropolitan Properties Ltd v Greycroft Ltd* [1987] 1 W.L.R. 1085, per Mr John Mowbray QC.

[94] See *J Lyons & Co Ltd v Knowles* [1943] K.B. 366, in which an assignee who covenanted to pay the rent "during the residue of the term" was held liable for the remainder of the term notwithstanding further assignment, and *Estates Gazette Ltd v Benjamin Restaurants Ltd* [1994] 1 W.L.R. 1528 in which a covenant by an assignee "to pay the rents reserved by the Lease at the time and in manner therein provided for" (the rent under the lease being payable, "during the said term hereby granted") was held to have the same effect.

[95] *GMS Syndicate Ltd v Gary Elliott Ltd* [1981] 1 W.L.R. 478.

## The liability of successors in title of the original landlord under an old tenancy

The rules governing the liability of assignees of the landlord's reversion are generally the same as those relating to assignees of the term. The landlord for the time being is liable under all covenants which touch and concern the land,[96] and the incidents of that liability would appear to be much the same as those discussed above in relation to successors in title of the tenant. In particular, a successor in title to the original landlord is not liable in respect of breaches committed by his predecessor in title.[97] This does not mean, however, that the tenant's only remedy is to sue the previous landlord. First, the new landlord is liable for such breaches to the extent that they continue after the date of the assignment. Accordingly, if he fails to remedy them, he is liable for any resulting loss to the tenant. Second, where the tenant is entitled to damages for disrepair against the previous landlord, he may set off such claim against the new landlord's claim for rent arrears which have been assigned to him by the previous landlord (or which have passed to him under s.141 of the Law of Property Act 1925).[98] However, a claim for unliquidated damages against a previous landlord may not be set-off against a claim by a successor in title for rent arrears falling due after the transfer of the reversion,[99] unless the lease specifically provides otherwise.[100] It has also been held in the county court that a tenant is entitled to bring an independent claim against the new landlord for damages for breaches of the repairing obligations committed by his predecessor.[101] Whilst the judge's reasons are not fully reported, it is thought that this is likewise incorrect as a matter of principle.

3–15

Where the demised premises consist of or include a dwelling, and the interest of the landlord is assigned, the new landlord has a statutory duty to give written notice of the assignment, and of his name and address, to the tenant not later than the next day on which rent is payable under the tenancy or, if that is within two months of the assignment, the end of that period of two months.[102] The old landlord remains liable to the tenant in respect of any breach of covenant, condition or agreement under the tenancy occurring in the period between the date of the assignment and the earlier of (i) the date on which written notice of the assignment and of the new landlord's name and address is given by the new landlord, and (ii) the date on which written notice of the assignment and the new landlord's name and last known address is given by the old landlord, as if he were still the landlord.[103] Where the new landlord is also liable to the tenant in respect of any breach occurring before notice is given, then he and the old landlord are

---

[96] Law of Property Act 1925 s.142.
[97] *Duncliffe v Caerfelin Properties Ltd* [1989] 2 E.G.L.R. 38.
[98] *Muscat v Smith* [2004] 1 W.L.R. 2853.
[99] *Edlington Properties v J.H. Fenner & Co* [2006] 1 W.L.R. 1583.
[100] Ibid.
[101] *Panton v St Mary's Estates* [2002] C.L. 427.
[102] Landlord and Tenant Act 1985 s.3(1). Note that the new landlord may also be required under s.3A of the Act to inform the tenant of his possible right under Pt I of the Landlord and Tenant Act 1987 to acquire the landlord's interest.
[103] 1985 Act s.3(3A) and (3B).

jointly and severally liable in respect of it.[104] It follows that where a landlord of residential premises assigns his reversion he should either give the requisite notice himself or ensure that the new landlord does so. Failure to do so will result in continued liability for breach of the landlord's repairing and other covenants until notice is given.

## The rights of successors in title of the original tenant under an old tenancy

**3–16**   The rights of assignees of the term are to all intents and purposes the same as those of assignees of the reversion. The benefit of such of the landlord's covenants as touch and concern the land pass to the assignee of the term.[105] However, there is one important difference, in that there is no equivalent of s.141 of the Law of Property Act 1925.[106] Accordingly, if at the date of the assignment the landlord is in breach of his repairing covenant, the right to sue for damage caused by breaches committed up to the date of the assignment remains with the assignor and does not pass to the assignee.[107] However, to the extent that the breaches continue after the date of the assignment, the right to sue for any resulting damage is that of the assignee not the assignor.

An example may help to clarify the above. Suppose that the landlord of a block of flats fails to repair the roof, and that damage is thereby caused both to the interior of the flat and the tenant's property inside. The tenant then assigns his lease before the necessary repairs are done, and the roof continues to leak until the landlord eventually repairs it some years later. The tenant would, notwithstanding the assignment, retain the right to sue the landlord in respect of damage suffered by him prior to the assignment. This would no doubt include the cost of repairing or replacing the damaged effects, and general damages representing discomfort and inconvenience suffered by reason of the leaking roof.[108] Depending on the facts, it might also include the amount of a reduction in the sale price caused by the disrepair.[109] The assignee would be entitled to sue for damage caused to him in the period between the date of the assignment and the date on which the repairs were ultimately carried out. It is possible, however, that in certain circumstances he would have to give credit for having bought cheap because of the disrepair.[110]

---

[104] 1985 Act s.3(3A).
[105] *Spencer's Case* (1583) 5 Co. Rep. 16a.
[106] See para.3–17, below.
[107] *City & Metropolitan Properties Ltd v Greycroft Ltd* [1987] 1 W.L.R. 1085.
[108] See Ch.32, below.
[109] See Ch.32, below.
[110] *City & Metropolitan Properties Ltd v Greycroft Ltd*, above.

# The rights of successors in title of the original landlord under an old tenancy

Assignees of the reversion are entitled by virtue of s.141 of the Law of Property Act 1925 to enforce all covenants in the lease that touch and concern the land. The right to sue for all breaches occurring after the date of the assignment therefore passes to the assignee. The assignee also acquires, and the assignor loses, the right to sue for breaches committed prior to the date of the assignment.[111] Thus, in *Re King*[112] the covenant to repair and reinstate was broken prior to the reversion being assigned, and the breaches continued after the assignment. The Court of Appeal held that the right to sue for all breaches, whether occurring before or after the assignment, had passed to the assignee. This is a common trap for the unwary, and a landlord under an old tenancy contemplating a sale of his interest at a time when there are outstanding breaches of the repairing covenant which affect the value of his reversion should take into account the fact that, unless the operation of the section is expressly excluded,[113] he will lose the right to sue for those breaches following completion of the sale.

**3–17**

It is generally thought that the right to enforce the original tenant's continuing liability throughout the term for breaches committed by a successor[114] also passes to the assignee of the reversion under s.141 without the need for an express assignment.[115] However, the point does not appear to have been expressly decided. [116]

It is important to emphasise that the above rules apply only to the transfer of the reversion to an existing lease, and not to a transfer of the landlord's interest after the lease has ended. A situation sometimes occurring in practice is a sale of the landlord's interest after the lease has ended, the tenant having failed in breach of covenant to yield the premises up in a proper state of repair. In such a case the

---

[111] *Re King* [1963] Ch. 459; *London & County (A&D) Ltd v Wilfred Sportsman Ltd* [1971] Ch. 764; *Arlesford Trading Co Ltd v Servansingh* [1971] 1 W.L.R. 1080. This remains the case even though there has never been privity of estate between the assignee of the reversion and the tenant in breach: *Arlesford Trading Co Ltd v Servansingh*, above. It was suggested in *Electricity Supply Nominees Ltd v Thorn EMI Retail Ltd* (1991) 63 P. & C.R. 143 that (by virtue of the words "by conveyance or otherwise" in s.141(3) of the 1925 Act) the same is the case where the reversion is transferred other than by assignment, e.g. where the reversion to a sub-tenancy continuing under Pt II of the Landlord and Tenant Act 1954 becomes vested in the head landlord following the expiry of the head lease. However, the point was not decided.

[112] [1963] Ch. 459.

[113] It is probable, though not absolutely certain, that the operation of s.141 can be excluded by agreement: see *Re King*, above, per Upjohn L.J. at 488.

[114] See para.3–04, above.

[115] See *Arlesford Trading Co Ltd v Servansingh* [1971] 1 W.L.R. 1080 at 1082G–H (although the breaches in that case had been committed by the original tenant himself); *Centrovincial Estates Ltd v Bulk Storage Ltd* (1983) 46 P. & C.R. 393 at 394; *W H Smith Ltd v Wyndham Investments Ltd* (1994) 70 P. & C.R. 21; *Milverton Group Ltd v Warner World Ltd* [1995] 2 E.G.L.R. 28; *Burford Midland Properties Ltd v Marley Extrusions Ltd* [1995] 1 B.C.L.C. 102 at 105.

[116] See the discussion in Harpum, C., Bridge, S. and Dixon, M., *Megarry & Wade: The Law of Real Property*, 8th edn (London: Sweet & Maxwell, 2012), para.20–016.

right to sue the tenant for the breaches remains with the assignor,[117] although he can, if he wishes, expressly assign it to the transferee.[118]

## Statutory obligations

**3–18**  The extent to which successors in title to the original parties take the benefit and burden of repairing and other obligations implied by statute depends upon the construction of the statute in question. However, in the absence of any clear indication to the contrary, it is thought that the implied obligation will generally run with the term and the reversion in the same way as an express obligation, and the rules applicable will be the same as those discussed above.

## NEW TENANCIES

### Meaning of "landlord covenants" and "tenant covenants"

**3–19**  The 1995 Act applies to a landlord covenant and a tenant covenant of a tenancy, whether or not it touches and concerns the land, and whether the covenant is express, implied or imposed by law.[119] A covenant includes a term, condition or obligation, and includes a covenant contained in a collateral agreement.[120] A landlord covenant is a covenant falling to be complied with by the landlord of a tenancy, and a tenant covenant is a covenant falling to be complied with by the tenant of premises demised by the tenancy.[121] The Act therefore applies to all covenants in leases or collateral agreements, whether they touch and concern the land or not. However, it has been held that a personal covenant given by the original landlord, the burden of which will not pass to a successor in title, is not a landlord covenant within the meaning of the Act.[122] Moreover, nothing in the Act affects certain covenants imposed under housing legislation.[123]

### The liability of the original tenant under a new tenancy

**3–20**  An original tenant who assigns his tenancy is released from the tenant covenants[124] of the tenancy, and ceases to be entitled to the benefit of the landlord covenants,[125] as from the date of the assignment.[126] The same applies to the original tenant's guarantor,[127] and also an assignee who has entered into a direct

---

[117] *Re Lyne-Stephens and Scott-Miller's Contract* [1920] 1 Ch. 472.
[118] See paras 3–34 to 3–38, below.
[119] Landlord and Tenant (Covenants) Act 1995 s.2(1).
[120] 1995 Act s.28(1). A collateral agreement means any agreement collateral to the tenancy, whether made before or after its creation: 1995 Act.
[121] 1995 Act s.28(1).
[122] *BHP Petroleum Great Britain Ltd v Chesterfield Properties Ltd* [2002] Ch. 12.
[123] Landlord and Tenant (Covenants) Act 1995 s.2(2).
[124] See para.3–19, above.
[125] See para.3–19, above.
[126] Landlord and Tenant (Covenants) Act 1995 s.5(1).
[127] 1995 Act s.24(2). See further para.3–33, below.

covenant to perform the covenants for the remainder of the term (and his guarantor). However, no release occurs in the case of an excluded assignment, i.e. an assignment in breach of the covenants of the tenancy or by operation of law.[128] The release of the original tenant does not affect (a) his liability arising from a breach of covenant occurring before the release,[129] and (b) his rights arising from a breach of a landlord's covenant occurring before the release.[130] A tenant who assigns part is released to the extent that the covenants fall to be complied with in relation to that part.[131] However, assignments of part are almost invariably prohibited in modern leases, and are rarely encountered in practice.

The 1995 Act contains anti-avoidance provisions which are framed in wide terms.[132] However, these do not apply to an agreement to the extent that it is an authorised guarantee agreement,[133] i.e. an agreement under which the tenant guarantees the performance by the assignee of the tenant covenants and which is entered into pursuant to a covenant against assignment which permits the landlord lawfully to impose as a condition of his consent the making of an authorised guarantee agreement. An agreement cannot be an authorised guarantee agreement to the extent that it purports to impose on the tenant any obligation to guarantee performance by any person other than the assignee, or to impose on the tenant any liability after the assignee has himself been released from liability under the tenant covenants by operation of the 1995 Act.[134] In summary, therefore:

(1) an authorised guarantee agreement can only be required on an assignment where the covenant restricting assignment so permits;
(2) the tenant cannot be compelled thereby to guarantee performance by anybody other than the immediate assignee (and cannot, therefore, be made to guarantee, for example, that each subsequent assignee should perform the tenant covenants); and
(3) the guarantee will only last until the next assignment.[135]

At the next assignment, of course, the landlord may require the first assignee to enter into an authorised guarantee agreement in respect of the next assignee (and so on in relation to subsequent assignments), but the original tenant's obligations will be released when the first assignee completes the assignment.

In order to enable landlords to rely upon suitably drafted provisions in the covenant against assignment included in new tenancies, the 1995 Act amends

---

[128] 1995 Act s.11. A release occurs on the next assignment, if any, which is not an excluded assignment: 1995 Act.
[129] 1995 Act s.24(1).
[130] 1995 Act s.24(4).
[131] 1995 Act s.5(3) (see also the definition in s.28).
[132] 1995 Act s.25.
[133] 1995 Act s.25(3).
[134] 1995 Act s.16(4).
[135] See further para.3–32, below.

s.19(1) of the Landlord and Tenant Act 1927 in such a way as to prevent the tenant from arguing that a requirement to enter into an authorised guarantee agreement is unreasonable.[136]

## The liability of the original landlord under a new tenancy

**3–21**    The 1995 Act does not provide for the automatic release of the landlord on an assignment of the reversion. Instead, it merely entitles the landlord to apply to be released from the landlord covenants.[137] However, the landlord cannot apply to be released from a personal covenant, the burden of which will not pass to his successor in title, because such a covenant is not a landlord covenant for the purposes of the Act.[138] The procedure for seeking a release is set out in s.8 of the Act, and involves the landlord serving a notice on the tenant requesting to be released and (if the tenant objects to his being released) the county court declaring that it is reasonable for the covenant to be released.

In addition to the s.8 procedure, the original landlord's obligations may validly be released by agreement (whether contained in the lease itself or made later) or waiver.[139]

## The rights and liabilities of successors in title of the original tenant

**3–22**    The 1995 Act provides that the benefit of all landlord covenants and the burden of all tenant covenants of a tenancy are annexed and incident to the whole, and to each and every part, of the premises demised by the tenancy.[140] As from the date of the assignment, the assignee (a) becomes bound by the tenant covenants[141] of the tenancy except to the extent that immediately before the assignment they did not bind the assignor,[142] or they fall to be complied with in relation to any demised premises not comprised in the assignment,[143] and (b) becomes entitled to the benefit of all landlord covenants[144] except to the extent that they fall to be complied with in relation to any such premises.[145] However, these provisions do not make a covenant "which (in whatever terms) is expressed to be personal to any person" enforceable by or (as the case may be) against any other person.[146] For these purposes, a covenant is expressed to be personal if the language of the tenancy, read in its context, expresses or otherwise conveys that the covenant is not to be annexed to the tenancy or the reversion, and that intention can be

---

[136]  1995 Act s.22.

[137]  1995 Act s.6.

[138]  *BHP Petroleum Great Britain Ltd v Chesterfield Properties Ltd* [2002] Ch. 12.

[139]  *Avonridge Property Company Ltd v Mashru* [2005] 1 W.L.R. 3956 (in which the lease provided that the original landlord was not to be liable after it had disposed of its interest in the property).

[140]  Landlord and Tenant (Covenants) Act 1995 s.3(1).

[141]  See para.3–19, above.

[142]  Any waiver or release which is expressed in whatever terms to be personal to the assignor is disregarded: Landlord and Tenant (Covenants) Act 1995 s.3(4).

[143]  For the meaning of this expression, see Landlord and Tenant (Covenants) Act 1995 s.28.

[144]  See para.3–19, above.

[145]  Landlord and Tenant (Covenants) Act 1995 s.3(2).

[146]  1995 Act s.3(6)(a).

expressed expressly or implicitly.[147] It follows that an assignee of the term is not bound by a tenant covenant the burden of which is (in the above sense) personal. Nor does the Act make a covenant enforceable against any person if it would not be enforceable against him by reason of its not having been registered under the Land Registration Act 2002 or the Land Charges Act 1972.[148]

An assignee who becomes bound by a tenant covenant does not become liable in relation to any time falling before the assignment, nor does he acquire any rights under a landlord covenant in relation to such a time.[149] However, such rights may be expressly assigned to him.[150]

## The rights and liabilities of successors in title of the original landlord

The 1995 Act provides that the benefit of all tenant covenants of a tenancy, and the burden of all landlord covenants, are annexed and incident to the whole, and to each and every part, of the reversion in the premises demised by the tenancy, and pass on an assignment of the reversion in the whole or any part of those premises.[151] As from the date of the assignment the assignee becomes (a) bound by the landlord covenants[152] except to the extent that immediately before the assignment they did not bind the assignor,[153] or they fall to be complied with in relation to any demised premises not comprised in the assignment,[154] and (b) entitled to the benefit of the tenant covenants[155] of the tenancy except to the extent that they fall to be complied with in relation to any such premises.[156] However, nothing in these provisions operates to make a covenant which "(in whatever terms) is expressed to be personal to any person" enforceable by or (as the case may be) against any other person.[157] Nor does the Act make a covenant enforceable against any person if it would not be enforceable against him by reason of its not having been registered under the Land Registration Act 2002 or the Land Charges Act 1972.[158] The benefit of a right of re-entry under the tenancy is likewise annexed and incident to the whole and each and every part of the reversion, and passes on an assignment of the whole or any part of the reversion.[159]

An assignee of the reversion who becomes entitled to the benefit of a tenant covenant by virtue of the 1995 Act does not by virtue of the Act have any rights

**3–23**

---

[147] *First Penthouse Ltd v Channel Hotels & Properties (UK) Ltd* [2004] 1 E.G.L.R. 16.
[148] Landlord and Tenant (Covenants) Act 1995 s.3(6)(b).
[149] 1995 Act s.23(1).
[150] 1995 Act s.23(2).
[151] 1995 Act s.3(1).
[152] See para.3–19, above.
[153] Any waiver or release which is expressed in whatever terms to be personal to the assignor is disregarded: Landlord and Tenant (Covenants) Act 1995 s.3(4).
[154] For the meaning of this expression, see Landlord and Tenant (Covenants) Act 1995 s.28.
[155] See para.3–19, above.
[156] Landlord and Tenant (Covenants) Act 1995 s.3.
[157] 1995 Act s.3(6)(a). For the meaning of this expression, see para.3–22, above.
[158] 1995 Act s.3(6)(b).
[159] 1995 Act s.4.

under the covenant in relation to any time falling before the assignment.[160] This is
the reverse of the legal position relating to old tenancies.[161] The right to sue for
breaches in existence at the date of the assignment therefore remains with the
assignor (but it may be expressly assigned to the assignee[162]). However, the right
of forfeiture is exercisable in relation to a breach occurring before the assignment
as well as one occurring after, unless by reason of any waiver or release it was not
so exercisable before the assignment.[163]

## COLLATERAL UNDERTAKINGS AND COVENANTS IN LICENCES

### Introductory

3–24    In most cases, the obligations that are relevant to a dilapidations claim are to be
found in the lease itself. Where that is so, the extent to which the benefit and
burden of the obligations run with the term and reversion is governed by the
above rules. In some cases, however, relevant provisions may be contained in a
side arrangement or licence. The commonest examples in the dilapidations
context are a collateral contract by the landlord to repair in return for the tenant
entering into the lease;[164] an agreement by the landlord to waive some liability
which the tenant would otherwise have, such as a liability to pay a service charge
in respect of certain works;[165] and a tenant's obligation to reinstate alterations at
the end of the term which is entered into as part of a licence for alterations. The
extent to which the benefit and burden of obligations of this sort run with the term
and the reversion is not yet fully established.

### Collateral contract by landlord to repair

3–25    The extent to which a landlord's covenant to repair contained in a lease binds his
successors in title and can be enforced by assignees of the term has already been
considered in relation to both old tenancies and new tenancies.[166] In considering
the position in relation to a collateral contract to repair, it is also necessary to
distinguish between the two categories of tenancy.

### (a)    Old tenancies

3–26    In order to decide whether the burden of a collateral contract to repair (assuming
it to be otherwise enforceable[167]) runs with the reversion so as to bind the
landlord's successors in title, it is first necessary to ask whether, as a matter of
construction, such contract imposes an obligation on the original landlord alone,

---

[160] 1995 Act s.23(1).
[161] See para.3–17, above.
[162] Landlord and Tenant (Covenants) Act 1995 s.23(2).
[163] 1995 Act s.23(3).
[164] See para.1–11, above.
[165] See para.1–10 above.
[166] See paras 3–15, 3–16, 3–22 and 3–23, above.
[167] See paras 1–09 to 1–11, above.

or on the landlord and his successors in title. If the contract was intended to bind only the original landlord, the burden will not bind his successors in title.[168] If the contract on its proper construction shows that the parties intended successors in title to be bound, the obligation will be enforceable against such successors under s.142 of the Law of Property Act 1925 provided that it touches and concerns the land.[169] This is so notwithstanding the fact that the obligation is contained in an independent document not under seal (such as a side letter).[170] Section 142 applies even where the benefit of the contract is personal to the tenant.[171] Since an obligation to repair touches and concerns land,[172] the burden of a collateral contract to repair will run under this section.

Where the landlord's interest is unregistered, a successor in title to the original landlord will be bound by the contract in the same way as he will be by the other terms of the lease. Where the landlord's interest is registered, and the tenant is in actual occupation, it is thought that the tenant's rights under a collateral contract would bind a successor in title by virtue of para.2 Sch.3 to the Land Registration Act 2002.[173]

The benefit of a collateral contract to repair entered into by the landlord with the tenant will not pass to that tenant's successors in title where, as a matter of construction, the benefit of the contract is personal to the tenant. Where that is not the case, it may be that the benefit of the contract will pass to subsequent assignees by virtue of the principle in *Spencer's Case*.[174] Alternatively, depending on the facts, the contract may be enforceable under the Contracts (Rights of Third Parties) Act 1999.[175]

### (b)   New tenancies

The covenants to which the 1995 Act applies include covenants contained in a collateral agreement.[176] Accordingly, the burden of a collateral contract to repair will pass to the new landlord in accordance with s.3 of the 1995 Act upon an assignment of the reversion,[177] and the benefit will pass to a successor in title of the tenant on an assignment of the term. However, by virtue of s.3(6)(a) of the Act, a collateral contract "which (in whatever terms) is expressed to be personal to any person"[178] is not enforceable by or (as the case may be) against any other person.

**3–27**

---

[168] *System Floors Ltd v Ruralpride Ltd* [1995] 1 E.G.L.R. 48.

[169] Ibid.

[170] Ibid., (applying *Weg Motors Ltd v Hales* [1962] Ch. 49). See also *Lotteryking Ltd v AMEC Properties Ltd* [1995] 2 E.G.L.R. 13.

[171] *System Floors Ltd v Ruralpride Ltd*, above.

[172] See para.3–11, above.

[173] Cf. *Gladesmore Investments Ltd v Carradine Heating Ltd* [1994] 1 E.G.L.R. 28. It is possible that where the lease falls within para.1 Sch.3, the contract will bind the successor in title by virtue of that paragraph as well as para.2.

[174] (1583) 5 Co. Rep. 16a. See para.3–16, above, and para.3–29, below.

[175] See para.24–12, below.

[176] See para.3–19, above.

[177] See para.3–23, above.

[178] For the meaning of this expression, see para.3–22, above.

## Undertaking by landlord not to enforce covenants

3–28     An undertaking by the landlord not to enforce a particular obligation by the tenant (such as a liability to repair or to pay service charge) may amount to a collateral contract, in which case the position would be the same in principle as that set out above. However, where the tenancy is an old tenancy, it is not clear to what extent such an undertaking would constitute "an obligation under a condition or of a covenant" within s.142 of the Law of Property Act 1925 such that the burden would pass to a new landlord under that section.[179]

Alternatively, an undertaking of this sort may, depending on the facts, take effect as a waiver or a promissory estoppel,[180] in which case it appears that it may be taken advantage of by successors in title to the tenant to whom the undertaking was given, unless the undertaking was intended to be personal.[181] It is not clear to what extent the burden of the undertaking binds successors in title to the original landlord, but it has been suggested that it does, at least where it amounts to a promissory estoppel.[182]

## Tenant's covenant to reinstate alterations

### (a)   Old tenancies

3–29     A tenant's covenant to reinstate alterations at the end of the term clearly touches and concerns land.[183] Where the covenant is contained in the lease, the benefit and burden will therefore run under the principles already considered.[184] Where, as is usually the case, such covenant is entered into after the grant of the lease and is contained in a separate document (such as a licence), the position is less clear.

It is often assumed in practice that the benefit and burden of a tenant's covenant to reinstate contained in a licence to carry out alterations pass automatically on an assignment of the reversion or the term (as the case may be). However, it is not clear to what extent this is correct as a matter of law, at least as regards the benefit. On the face of it, the benefit will not pass under s.141 of the Law of Property Act 1925, because that section only applies to covenants contained in the lease itself.[185] The safest course would therefore be either for the benefit of the covenant to be expressly assigned to the new landlord on the assignment, or for the licence to be drafted in such a way that the obligation to reinstate takes effect as a variation of the lease (in which case there seems no

---

[179] *System Floors Ltd v Ruralpride Ltd*, above, at 51D–E.

[180] See para.1–14 et seq., above.

[181] *Brikom Investments Ltd v Carr* [1979] Q.B. 467. The relevant facts are set out in para.1–10, above.

[182] See above, per Lord Denning M.R. Sed quaere: see the judgments of the other two members of the Court. See also *PW & Co v Milton Gate Investments* [2004] Ch. 142 at [187] to [201].

[183] See para.3–11, above.

[184] See paras 3–10 to 3–17, above.

[185] *Cole v Kelly* [1920] 2 K.B. 106; *P&A Swift Investments Ltd v Combined English Stores Group Plc* [1989] A.C. 632 at 639. See the discussion in *Megarry & Wade: The Law of Real Property*, edited by Harpum, C., Bridge S. and Dixon, M. (London: Sweet & Maxwell, 2012), 8th edn, para.20–019.

reason in principle why the benefit would not then pass under s.141) or so as to attract the operation of the Contracts (Rights of Third Parties) Act 1999.[186]

Nor is it clear to what extent the burden of a covenant to reinstate will be enforceable against the tenant's successors in title. In practice, however, the covenant will generally be entered into by the tenant as part of the terms on which he is permitted to carry out alterations, and the assignee will have the use and benefit of such alterations whilst he remains the tenant. In these circumstances, it can be said to be unfair and contrary to principle if the obligation to reinstate at the end of the term is not enforceable against the assignee. Given this, it is thought that the court would be receptive to an argument that on taking the assignment, the assignee becomes subject to the burden of the obligation to reinstate by virtue of the principle in *Spencer's Case*,[187] in the same way as he would if the covenant were contained in the lease itself. Although *Spencer's Case* was concerned with covenants in leases, it is not thought that there is anything in the judgments which would preclude the same principle from applying to tenant's covenants in licences which touch and concern the demised land.[188] Alternatively, where the entry by the tenant into a covenant to reinstate was one of the terms on which consent for the alterations was given, it might be argued that an assignee, having enjoyed the continuing benefit of the alterations, must also accept the burden of having to reinstate them.[189]

### (b)    New tenancies

Since the 1995 Act applies to covenants contained in a collateral agreement as well as covenants in the lease,[190] it would seem to follow that both the benefit and burden of a tenant's covenant to reinstate in a licence would pass in accordance with s.3 of the Act upon an assignment of the reversion and the term.[191] However, nothing in the Act operates to make a covenant which "(in whatever terms) is expressed to be personal to any person" enforceable by or (as the case may be) against any other person.[192]

**3–30**

---

[186] See para.24–12, below.

[187] (1583) 5 Co. Rep. 16a. See para.3–13, above.

[188] For a further discussion of this argument, see "Improvements and Reinstatement—Take it or Leave it?", a lecture given by J. Seitler QC and C. Shea on June 7, 2010 as part of the 35th series of Blundell Lectures.

[189] In *Tito v Waddell (No.2)* [1977] Ch. 106 Megarry V.C. held that there exists what he called the "pure principle of benefit and burden", i.e. that any party deriving a benefit from a deed must also accept any burden in the same deed. However, in *Rhone v Stephens* [1994] A.C. 310 the House of Lords was not prepared to recognise that principle, holding that a condition attached to the exercise of right can only be enforced if it is relevant to the exercise of the right. In the light of this, the argument in the text would only succeed if the court could be persuaded to regard the obligation to reinstate as reciprocal to the right to enjoy the alterations. See further *Amsprop Trading Ltd v Harris Distribution Ltd* [1997] 1 W.L.R. 1025, and *Waltham Forest LBC v Roberts* [2005] H.L.R. 2.

[190] See para.3–24, above.

[191] See paras 3–27 and 3–28, above.

[192] 1995 Act s.3(6)(a). See further para.3–27, above.

## Deeds of variation

**3–31**   The original parties to the lease, or their successors in title, may enter into a deed varying the lease. It is thought that, in general terms, the benefit and burden of any such variations will run with the term and the reversion under the principles discussed above.

## SURETIES

## The liability of the surety

**3–32**   In many cases a surety will be a party to the lease (or licence to assign) so as to guarantee the performance by the tenant (or assignee) of his obligations under the lease (although it is uncommon to find a surety of the landlord's obligations). The surety's liability depends on the proper construction of the surety covenant. Generally, the surety will covenant that the tenant or assignee will pay the rent and perform the covenants and that in default the surety will do so. In such a case whether the surety is liable will generally turn upon whether the tenant or assignee is also liable. The surety is entitled to raise by way of defence to the claim against him not only any defence that the tenant would have had but also any set-off that would have been available to the tenant.[193]

The duration of the surety's liability is likewise a question of construction of the covenant. Liability may extend for the whole of the term, or for such time as the lease remains vested in a particular tenant, or for any other period which may be stipulated. In the absence of express words to the contrary, liability under a surety covenant will not extend into a period of statutory continuation under Pt II of the Landlord and Tenant Act 1954.[194]

The benefit of a surety covenant contained in the lease runs with the reversion and will therefore pass automatically to a successor in title to the landlord with whom the covenant was made.[195] It is thought that the same would be true of a surety covenant contained in a licence to assign. A surety has an implied right of indemnity against the tenant in default.[196] A surety of the original tenant has an implied right of indemnity against the surety of the assignee in default.[197]

---

[193] For the nature of set-off, see para.33–41, below.
[194] *Junction Estates Ltd v Cope* (1974) 27 P. & C.R. 482; *A. Plesser & Co Ltd v Davis* [1983] 2 E.G.L.R. 70.
[195] *P&A Swift Investments Ltd v Combined English Stores Ltd* [1989] A.C. 643.
[196] *Moule v Garrett* (1872) L.R. 7 Ex. 101.
[197] *Selous Street Investments Ltd v Oronel Fabrics Ltd* [1984] 1 E.G.L.R. 50.

## Release of the surety[198]

The surety will be released if the lease is varied without his consent in a manner **3–33**
which might prejudice him.[199] For example, if the lease contains an absolute
covenant against alterations, and the tenant (with the landlord's licence but
without the surety's consent) carries out alterations to the demised buildings, the
surety might well be released because the burden of repairing those buildings
might be greater than that of repairing the buildings originally demised.[200]
Potential prejudice is sufficient.[201] In order for the rule to apply, however, what
must be varied is the particular contract which the surety has guaranteed, so that
a personal concession to a subsequent assignee which does not operate to vary the
assignor's liability will not operate to release the assignor's surety.[202] Nor will the
grant of a consent which is expressly contemplated by the lease release the surety,
because it is part of the bargain into which he entered.[203]

If the surety consents to a variation, he is bound.[204] The surety will be held to
have consented where he takes an active part in the transaction (as where, for
example, he arranges for it to happen[205]) or where he allows the creditor to think
he has consented.[206] It is probable that consent will only be effective for these
purposes if it is communicated to the creditor.[207] A surety will also be released if
the liability of the principal comes to an end. A surety will therefore be released if
the landlord agrees to release the principal from liability.[208] However, the surety
will not be released where the tenant becomes insolvent and the lease is
disclaimed by a liquidator or trustee in bankruptcy.[209]

The position where the tenancy is a new tenancy to which the 1995 Act applies
is considered below.[210]

---

[198] The first two sentences of this paragraph were approved and applied in *Topland Portfolio No.1 v Smiths News Trading* [2013] EWHC 1445 (Ch.) at [42].
[199] *Holme v Brunskill* (1878) 3 Q.B.D. 495; *Howard de Walden Estates Ltd v Pasta Place Ltd* [1995] 1 E.G.L.R. 79; *Metropolitan Properties Co (Regis) Ltd v Bartholomew* [1996] 1 E.G.L.R. 82; *Lloyds TSB Bank Plc v Hayward* [2005] EWCA Civ 466. Failure to take steps to enforce the covenants in the lease against the tenant does not constitute a variation within the principle: *Eurodis Electron Plc v Unicomp Inc* [2004] EWHC 979 (Ch.).
[200] See *Selous Street Properties Ltd v Oronel Fabrics Ltd*, above.
[201] *Lloyds TSB Bank Plc v Hayward*, above, at [5].
[202] *Metropolitan Properties Co (Regis) Ltd v Bartholomew*, above.
[203] *Selous Street Properties v Oronel Fabrics*, above, at 58C–59B; *Metropolitan Properties (Regis) v Bartholomew*, above, at 83G–J.
[204] *Apus Properties Ltd v Douglas Farrow Co Ltd* [1989] 2 E.G.L.R. 265.
[205] *Apus Properties v Douglas Farrow* above at 271G–K.
[206] *Meritz Fire & Marine Insurance Co. v Jan de Nul NV* [2010] EWHC 3262 at [87–88] (the point did not arise on appeal: [2011] EWCA Civ 827).
[207] *Wittmann UK v Willdav Engineering SA* [2007] EWCA Civ 824 at [27].
[208] See, however, *Collin Estates Ltd v Buckley* [1992] 2 E.G.L.R. 78, in which on the proper construction of the surety covenant (which was widely drafted), the surety was held not to have been released when the tenant agreed to compromise the landlord's claim against him by agreeing to pay a sum of money. The surety was held liable to make good the tenant's failure to abide by the agreement.
[209] *Hindcastle v Barbara Attenborough Associates Ltd* [1997] A.C. 70, overruling *Stacey v Hill* [1901] 1 K.B. 660; *Shaw v Doleman* [2009] 2 P. & C. R. 12.
[210] See para.3–34, below.

## Where the tenancy is a new tenancy

3–34 Where the tenancy is a new tenancy to which the 1995 Act applies, and the tenant assigns, the surety will be released to the extent that the tenant is himself released.[211]

The extent to which a surety under such a tenancy may validly enter into, or agree to enter into, further guarantees may be summarised as follows: (i) an existing or contracting guarantor of a tenant cannot validly be required to commit himself in advance to guarantee the liability of a future assignee; (ii) subject to (iii) and (iv), a guarantor of an assignor cannot validly guarantee the liability of the assignor's assignee; (iii) such a guarantor can validly do so by being party to an authorised guarantee agreement[212] which otherwise complies with s.16 of the 1995 Act; and (iv) such a guarantor can in any event validly guarantee the liability of an assignee on a further assignment.[213]

# ASSIGNMENTS OF RIGHTS OF ACTION UNDER REPAIRING COVENANTS

## Introductory

3–35 Where the reversion to an old tenancy (i.e. an old tenancy within the meaning of the 1995 Act[214]) is assigned, it will not generally be necessary for the new landlord to take an express assignment of any right of action that the previous landlord had against the tenant under the repairing covenants, because the new landlord acquires the right to sue for pre-assignment breaches.[215] However, the position is different (i) in the case of a new tenancy within the meaning of the 1995 Act,[216] and (ii) where the reversion is transferred after the lease has ended (in which case the only person able to sue the former tenant for breaches of the covenant to repair at the end of the lease will be the person who was the landlord at the time the lease ended).[217] In these cases it will be necessary for the right of action to be assigned expressly if it is to be validly transferred. This section deals with the extent to which assignments of rights of action under repairing covenants are valid, how such assignments are effected and the damages for which the assignee of the cause of action is entitled to sue.

## Whether the assignment is valid

3–36 The general rule is that a bare right of action cannot be assigned, so that any purported assignment is void.[218] However, this is subject to a well-established exception where the assignment is incidental and subsidiary to a transfer of

---

[211] Landlord and Tenant (Covenants) Act 1995 s.24(3). See para.3–20, above.
[212] See para.3–20, above.
[213] See *K/S Victoria Street v House of Fraser (Stores Management)* [2011] EWCA Civ 904.
[214] See para.3–02, above.
[215] See para.3–17, above.
[216] See para.3–23, above.
[217] See para.3–17, above.
[218] *Trendtex Trading Corp Ltd v Credit Suisse* [1982] A.C. 679.

property. In *Williams v Protheroe*[219] a contract for the sale of a reversion on an existing lease[220] provided for an express assignment to the purchaser of a right to sue the tenant for arrears of rent and dilapidations. The argument that the assignment was void was rejected on the ground that the purchase of the premises conferred on the purchaser an interest sufficient to validate the assignment. Nothing seems to have turned on the fact that the sale was of the reversion to an existing lease, as opposed to a lease which had ended. In *Dawson v Great Northern & City Railway Co Ltd*[221] it was held that the vendor had validly assigned to the purchaser a right to claim compensation for injurious affection to part of the land which had been suffered when the land was owned by the vendor. In so deciding, the Court of Appeal approved and applied *Williams v Protheroe*, Stirling L.J. saying:

"[W]e think that great weight must be given to the circumstance that this assignment is incidental and subsidiary to that conveyance, and is part of a bona fide transaction the object of which was to transfer to the Plaintiff the property of Blake with all the incidents which attach to it in his hands. Such a transaction seems to be very far removed from being a transfer of a mere right of litigation."

In *Ellis v Torrington*[222] the premises in question were the subject of a head lease, a sub-lease and a sub-underlease. All three contained covenants to repair. The sub-underlease was assigned to the defendant. The claimant had been a tenant of the defendant under a tenancy containing less onerous covenants than any of the superior leases. When the leases expired, the premises were out of repair and the defendant was threatening to sue the claimant on his obligations under the tenancy. The claimant subsequently acquired the freehold of the premises and, some months later, took an assignment from the former sub-tenant of the right to sue the defendant upon his repairing covenants in the sub-underlease. Since the claimant could have brought an action for disrepair against the head tenant, who would have sued the sub-tenant who would in turn have sued the defendant, this was in effect a shortcut enabling the claimant to sue the defendant directly. The assignment was held to be valid. Bankes L.J. said in the course of his judgment:

"In my opinion, Sargant J. was perfectly right when he said that the rights of action for breaches of covenant by the [defendant] were sufficiently connected with the enjoyment of the property to escape being bare rights of action ... [T]he [claimant] is seeking to enforce a right incidental to property, a right to a sum of money which theoretically is part of the property he has bought. I see nothing material in the fact that, owing to the various dealings with this property, he has had to take the assignment from an underlessee."

Scrutton L.J. said:

---

[219] (1829) 2 M. & P. 779.
[220] This case was decided before the enactment of s.141 of the Law of Property Act 1925 or any statutory predecessor.
[221] [1905] 1 K.B. 260.
[222] [1920] 1 K.B. 399.

"So in this case when the [claimant], who had bought the freehold, took also an assignment of the right to recover damages for dilapidations against the first lessee, he was not buying in order merely to get a cause of action; he was buying property and a cause of action as ancillary thereto."

**3–37**   It appears from the above cases that an assignment of a cause of action for dilapidations by a vendor to a purchaser of the dilapidated property has probably always been valid. Even if this has not always been so, the approach of the modern authorities dealing with the circumstances in which causes of action can be assigned is considerably more liberal than was formerly the case. Under the modern law, an assignment will be valid if the assignee has "a genuine and substantial commercial interest" in enforcing the cause of action.[223] Given this, it is thought that an argument that a right of action for dilapidations cannot validly be assigned by a vendor to a purchaser of the property the subject of the claim would not now succeed, even if it might have done formerly. Even if this is incorrect, there is nothing to prevent the vendor suing in his own name and agreeing to pay over to the purchaser any damages recovered, in return for an indemnity as to costs. Further, any liquidator of the vendor would be able validly to assign a claim for dilapidations.[224]

The reported cases deal only with assignments of claims against the person who was the tenant at the end of the lease. It is probable, however, that an assignment to a purchaser of a claim against some other person in the chain, such as the original tenant or a surety, would be equally valid.

## Formalities of an assignment

**3–38**   An assignment of a right of action for damages for dilapidations must be in writing.[225] Written notice of the assignment must be given to the proposed defendant.[226] The assignment is effectual in law to transfer the right of action to the transferee as from the date of the notice.[227]

In *P&O Property Holdings Ltd v Secretary of State for the Environment*[228] the landlord contracted in November 1995 (during the term of a sub-underlease) to sell its reversionary interest (an underlease) to another company in the same group. The contract provided that the reversion was sold "subject to and with the benefit of the Tenancy document" (this being a reference to the sub-underlease). The sub-underlease expired in March 1997, following which the landlord brought proceedings for damages for disrepair against the sub-undertenant. The contract for sale was completed by a transfer in October 1998. It was held that the right of action against the sub-undertenant had passed to the transferee because (i) the

---

[223] See *Trendtex Trading Corp Ltd v Credit Suisse*, above; *Brownton Ltd v Edward Moore Inbucom Ltd* [1985] 3 All E.R. 499; and *Massai Aviation Services v A-G of the Bahamas* [2007] UKPC 12 per Baroness Hale at [21].

[224] Insolvency Act 1986 s.167 and Sch.4 para.6; *Guy v Churchill* [1889] 40 Ch. D. 481; *Ramsey v Hartley* [1977] 1 W.L.R. 686.

[225] Law of Property Act 1925 s.136(1).

[226] 1925 Act s.136(1).

[227] 1925 Act s.136(1).

[228] Unreported decision of H.H. Judge Thornton QC (Technology and Construction Court) dated February 7, 2000.

claim was an incident of the underlease which directly affected it; (ii) the claim was not collateral to that interest; and (iii) the contract was expressly made subject to and with the benefit of the sub-underlease.

## Black holes

The general principle is that the assignee of a cause of action can be in no better position that the assignor, so that the damages for which he is entitled to sue are limited to those which could have been recovered by his assignor. This will be relevant in a dilapidations context where (as sometimes happens in practice) the lease ends, the tenant vacates and the landlord then sells his interest to a third party together with the benefit of his right of action against the outgoing tenant for damages for disrepair. If the price he obtains represents the market value of the premises in repair or something close to it, the outgoing tenant may argue that the landlord/assignor has himself suffered no loss by reason of the disrepair, and therefore that the assignee (being in no better position) is not entitled to substantial damages. In other words, what would otherwise have been a perfectly valid claim by the landlord/assignor has fallen into a legal "black hole".

**3–39**

However, the cases show that the courts are very reluctant to accept this sort of argument. In *Technotrade Ltd v Larkstore Ltd*[229] the general principle was held in the Court of Appeal to be that the assignee can recover the same damages (but no greater amount) as the assignor could have recovered if there had been no assignment and if the land had not been transferred to the assignee. Accordingly, in the situation considered above, the assignee will be able to sue for whatever damages the landlord/assignor could have obtained if it had neither sold its interest nor assigned its cause of action, and the tenant will not be able to rely on the transfer of the land at full value as affording it a complete defence.[230]

*Technotrade* was followed and applied in *Bizspace (NE) Ltd v Baird Corporatewear Ltd*[231] in which the tenant sold its business and assets to a company which went into occupation of the premises pursuant to a licence, one of the terms of which was that its occupation was to be subject to the same terms as the tenant's lease and that the company would indemnify the tenant in respect of any breach of those terms. The tenant then assigned its rights to the landlord who brought proceedings against the company for terminal dilapidations. The correct principle was held to be that:

> "[T]he court should strive to ensure that a wrongdoer does not escape liability merely because the cause of action lies in the hands of someone other than the person who suffered the loss."

The fact of the assignment did not therefore diminish what would otherwise have been the company's liability.

---

[229] [2006] 1 W.L.R. 2926.
[230] However (depending on the facts) the price obtained may nonetheless be compelling evidence of the value of the premises in repair. See for example *Mather v Barclays Bank* [1987] 2 E.G.L.R. 254 and see generally Ch.30, para.30–36, below.
[231] [2007] 1 E.G.L.R. 55.

In *Pegasus v Ernst & Young*,[232] Mann J., having reviewed the authorities, said that they demonstrated the following:

"(a)   The courts have not applied the sort of remorseless logic, or appeal to metaphysics, that I have referred to above.

(b)   On the contrary, the courts have sought to apply the law as to causation of loss in a manner which reflects justice and reality, in particular where the application of pure logic would, unfairly, lead to the 'disappearance' of a loss which would, absent an assignment, have been plainly recoverable.

(c)   Where a wrong has been committed in relation to property, and loss is capable of arising as a result, the fact of an assignment whether gratuitous (*GUS Property Management Ltd v Littlewoods Mail Order Stores Ltd*[233]), for part value (*GUS* again) or for full value (*Linden Gardens Trust Ltd v Lenesta Sludge Disposals Ltd*[234] and *Technotrade*) does not mean that it thenceforth has to be acknowledged that the assignor no longer can be said to have suffered loss. Whatever the metaphysician may say, the law says that the loss flowing can and should still be treated as a loss of the assignor which the assignee can recover. Black holes are to be (as all black holes should be) avoided where possible."

## THE CHOICE OF CLAIMANT AND DEFENDANT

### Where more than one party is liable

3–40     There may, and commonly will, be more than one person who is liable on the repairing covenants. Where this is the case, there is no obligation on the claimant to choose any particular one in preference to others. The claimant's remedies are cumulative, and it is no defence that he has alternative remedies against others in the chain.[235] However, it is generally not good practice to join numerous parties unless there is some good reason to do so (for example, there is doubt as to the solvency of the person ultimately liable). The presence of numerous parties in an action increases the costs which the claimant may have to pay if he is unsuccessful, and may complicate settlement negotiations considerably. For these reasons, if there is one party who is clearly liable and that party is known to be solvent, then it is better to join that party alone.

Judgment may be obtained against any party who is liable, but the claimant cannot recover more than once. Liabilities as between individual defendants are adjusted by means of the rights of indemnity discussed above, and the court's power under the Civil Liability (Contribution) Act 1978 to award indemnity or contribution as between co-defendants.

---

[232]   [2012] EWHC 738 (Ch.) at [30].
[233]   [1982] S.C. (H.L.) 157.
[234]   (1992) 57 B.L.R. 57.
[235]   *Norwich Union Life Insurance Society Ltd v Low Profile Fashions Ltd* [1992] 1 E.G.L.R. 86.

CHAPTER 4

# THE CONSTRUCTION OF REPAIRING AND OTHER COVENANTS IMPOSING LIABILITY FOR DILAPIDATIONS

## INTRODUCTORY

Construction is the process by which an outside observer—typically the court—discovers what are the rights and obligations of the parties to the agreement which is being construed. The object of the process is to ascertain what those parties intended their rights and obligations to be. However, the word "intention" is used in a special sense because, for reasons of practicality and policy, the court of construction limits the material which may be made available to it. Thus, generally speaking, it is not the subsequent protestations of the parties which will be considered, but the hard evidence of what words they used in forming their bargain, in what circumstances, at what time, and to what end. To this objective material the court will then apply its understanding of the English language, of the ways in which people deal with each other and of the commercial object of such dealings, and will deduce from this the rights and obligations which were intended to be created. This Chapter summarises the general principles applicable to the construction of contracts, and then considers the particular ways in which the courts have approached the construction of repairing and other covenants relevant to dilapidations.

**4–01**

## GENERAL PRINCIPLES OF INTERPRETATION OF CONTRACTS[1]

### The modern approach to construction

In *Investors Compensation Scheme Ltd v West Bromwich Building Society*[2] Lord Hoffmann referred to:

**4–02**

> "[T]he fundamental change which has overtaken this branch of the law ... The result has been, subject to one important exception, to assimilate the way in which such documents are interpreted by judges to the commonsense principles by which any serious utterance would be interpreted in ordinary life. Almost all the old intellectual baggage of 'legal' interpretation has been discarded."

He went on to summarise the modern principles as follows:

---

[1] For a definitive treatment, see Lewison, *The Interpretation of Contracts*, 5th edn (London: Sweet & Maxwell, 2011).

[2] [1998] 1 W.L.R. 896.

"(1)    Interpretation is the ascertainment of the meaning which the document would convey to a reasonable person having all the background knowledge which would reasonably have been available to the parties in the situation in which they were at the time of the contract.

(2)    The background was famously referred to by Lord Wilberforce as the 'matrix of fact', but this phrase is, if anything, an understated description of what the background may include. Subject to the requirement that it should have been reasonably available to the parties and to the exception to be mentioned next, it includes absolutely anything which would have affected the way in which the language of the document would have been understood by a reasonable man.

(3)    The law excludes from the admissible background the previous negotiations of the parties and their declarations of subjective intent. They are admissible only in an action for rectification. The law makes this distinction for reasons of practical policy and, in this respect only, legal interpretation differs from the way we would interpret utterances in ordinary life. The boundaries of this exception are in some respects unclear. But this is not the occasion in which to explore them.

(4)    The meaning which a document (or any other utterance) would convey to a reasonable man is not the same thing as the meaning of its words. The meaning of words is a matter of dictionaries and grammars; the meaning of the document is what the parties using those words against the relevant background would reasonably have been understood to mean. The background may not merely enable the reasonable man to choose between the possible meanings of words which are ambiguous but even (as occasionally happens in ordinary life) to conclude that the parties must, for whatever reason, have used the wrong words or syntax: see *Mannai Investments Co. Limited v. Eagle Star Life Assurance Co. Limited* [1997] A.C. 749.

(5)    The 'rule' that words must be given their 'natural and ordinary meaning' reflects the common sense proposition that we do not easily accept that people have made linguistic mistakes, particularly in formal documents. On the other hand, if one would nevertheless conclude from the background that something must have gone wrong with the language, the law does not require judges to attribute to the parties an intention which they plainly could not have had."

## The objective nature of the process of interpretation

**4–03**    Lord Hoffmann's first principle emphasises that the intentions of the parties to the contract are to be ascertained by interpreting the words of the contract objectively, i.e. as they would be understood by a reasonable man with the same knowledge of the background as the parties might reasonably be supposed to have had. The parties are not entitled to say what they intended except by the words of their contract, and their contract cannot be interpreted by reference to subjective evidence of what they thought it meant or wanted it to mean. The only intention that is relevant is that appearing from an objective interpretation of the words used in the contract. Thus, in *BCCI v Ali (No.1)*[3] Lord Binham said:

"To ascertain the intention of the parties the court reads the terms of the contract as a whole, giving the words used their ordinary and natural meaning in the context of the agreement, the parties' relationship and all the relevant facts surrounding the transaction so far as known to the parties. To ascertain the parties' intentions the court does not of course inquire into the parties' subjective states of mind but makes an objective judgment based on the materials already identified."

In *Sirius International Insurance Co v FAI General Insurance Ltd*,[4] Lord Steyn said:

---

[3] [2001] 1 A.C. 251.
[4] [2004] 1 W.L.R. 3251.

"The aim of the inquiry is not to probe the real intentions of the parties but to ascertain the contextual meaning of the relevant contractual language. The inquiry is objective: the question is what a reasonable person, circumstanced as the actual parties were, would have understood the parties to have meant by the use of specific language. The answer to that question is to be gathered from the text under consideration and its relevant contextual scene."

In *Chartbrook Ltd v Persimmon Homes Ltd*,[5] the question was agreed to be "what a reasonable person, having all the background knowledge which would have been available to the parties, would have understood them to be using the language in the contract to mean".

In *A-G of Belize v Belize Telecom*[6] Lord Hoffmann said:

"The court ... is concerned only to discover what the instrument means. However, that meaning is not necessarily or always what the authors or parties to the document would have intended. It is the meaning which the instrument would convey to a reasonable person having all the background knowledge which would reasonably be available to the audience to whom the instrument is addressed: see *Investors Compensation Scheme Ltd v West Bromwich Building Society* [1998] 1 W.L.R. 896, 912–913. It is this objective meaning which is conventionally called the intention of the parties, or the intention of Parliament, or the intention of whatever person or body was or is deemed to have been the author of the instrument."

## The words used

The primary source for understanding what the parties meant is their language interpreted in accordance with conventional usage.[7] The general rule is that the words used are to be given their grammatical and ordinary meaning as English words, unless the context otherwise requires. In *Post Office v Aquarius Properties Ltd*[8] Hoffmann J., when considering the meaning of "repair", said:

4–04

"[T]he whole law on the subject may be summed up in the proposition that 'repair' is an ordinary English word ... in the end ... the question is whether the ordinary speaker of English would consider that the word 'repair' as used in the covenant was appropriate to describe the work which has to be done. The cases do no more than illustrate specific contexts in which judges, as ordinary speakers of English, have thought that it was or was not appropriate to do so."

He returned to the same theme in *Norwich Union Life Insurance Society Ltd v British Railways Board*,[9] making the point in doing so that it is not always easy to explain precisely why a particular provision means what it does:

"The use of ordinary language to convey meaning often involves subtle discriminations which for most people are intuitive rather than capable of lucid explanation. An explanation of why ordinary English words in a particular context convey a given meaning is frequently more likely to confuse than to enlighten. Perhaps this is what judges mean when they say that questions of construction are often matters of impression ... I come back to what seems to me to be the plain question: what as a matter of ordinary English do the words mean?"

---

5 [2009] 1 A.C. 1101 at [14].
6 [2009] 1 W.L.R. 1988.
7 *BCCI v Ali* [2002] 1 A.C. 251 per Lord Hoffmann at 269.
8 [1985] 2 E.G.L.R. 105 (affirmed on other grounds [1987] 1 All E.R. 1055).
9 [1986] 1 E.G.L.R. 136.

Likewise, in *Melanesian Mission Trust Board v Australian Mutual Provident Society*,[10] Lord Hope said:

> "The approach which must be taken to the construction of a clause in a formal document of this kind is well settled. The intention of the parties is to be discovered from the words used in the document. Where ordinary words have been used they must be taken to have been used according to the ordinary meaning of these words. If their meaning is clear and unambiguous, effect must be given to them because that is what the parties are taken to have agreed to by their contract. Various rules may be invoked to assist interpretation in the event that there is an ambiguity. But it is not the function of the court, when construing a document, to search for an ambiguity. Nor should the rules which exist to resolve ambiguities be invoked in order to create an ambiguity which, according to the ordinary meaning of the words, is not there. So the starting point is to examine the words used in order to see whether they are clear and unambiguous. It is of course legitimate to look at the document as a whole and to examine the context in which these words have been used, as the context may effect the meaning of the words. But unless the context shows that the ordinary meaning cannot be given to them or that there is an ambiguity, the ordinary meaning of the words which have been used in the document must prevail."

Where the meaning of the words in context is clear, the court must give effect to it even though the result may appear harsh. Hoffmann J. explained the reason for this in *MFI Properties Ltd v BICC Group Pension Trust Ltd*:[11]

> "[T]here will … be cases in which the language used by the parties shows beyond doubt that they intended [a provision] for which, to a third party who knows nothing of the negotiations, no commercial purpose can be discerned. In such circumstances the court has no option but to assume that it was a quid pro quo for some other concession in the course of negotiations. The court cannot reject it as absurd merely because it is counterfactual and has no outward commercial justification. On the other hand, if the language is capable of more than one meaning, I think the court is entitled to select the meaning which accords with the apparent commercial purpose of the clause rather than one which appears commercially irrational."

Similarly, in *Jumbo King Ltd v Faithful Properties Ltd*[12] he said:

> "If the ordinary meaning of the words make sense in relation to the rest of the document and the factual background, then the court will give effect to that language even though the consequences may appear hard for one side or the other. The court is not privy to the negotiation of the agreement—evidence of such negotiations is inadmissible—and has no way of knowing whether a clause which appears to have an onerous effect was a quid pro quo for some other concession. Or one of the parties may simply have made a bad bargain. The only escape from the language is an action for rectification, in which the previous negotiations can be examined. But the overriding objective in construction is to give effect to what a reasonable person rather than a pedantic lawyer would have understood the parties to mean. Therefore, if in spite of linguistic problems the meaning is clear, it is that meaning which must prevail."

He made the same point in *Chartbrook Ltd v Persimmon Homes Ltd*:[13]

---

[10] [1997] 2 E.G.L.R. 128.
[11] [1986] 1 All E.R. 974.
[12] (1999) H.K.C.F.A.R. 279 (cited with approval by the Court of Appeal in *Holding & Barnes Plc v Hill House Hammond Ltd* [2002] 2 P. & C.R. 11).
[13] [2009] 1 A.C. 1101.

"20. It is of course true that the fact that a contract may appear to be unduly favourable to one of the parties is not a sufficient reason for supposing that it does not mean what it says. The reasonable addressee of the instrument has not been privy to the negotiations and cannot tell whether a provision favourable to one side was not in exchange for some concession elsewhere or simply a bad bargain."

## The admissible background

As appears from the above discussion, the words used in the contract are to be interpreted in the light of the background against which the contract was made. Lord Hoffmann's fourth and fifth principles in *Investors Compensation Scheme*[14] emphasise the importance of the background in the construction process. Not only may it enable the court to choose between different possible meanings, but it may indicate that the parties have used the wrong words altogether.

In *Reardon-Smith Line v Hanson-Tangen*[15] Lord Wilberforce said:

4–05

"No contracts are made in a vacuum: there is always a setting in which they have to be placed. The nature of what is legitimate to have regard to is usually described as 'the surrounding circumstances' but this phrase is imprecise: it can be illustrated but hardly defined. In a commercial contract it is certainly right that the court should know the commercial purpose of the contract and this in turn presupposes knowledge of the genesis of the transaction, the background, the context, the market in which the parties are operating ... what the court must do must be to place itself in thought in the same factual matrix as that in which the parties were."

In *Mannai Investment Co Ltd v Eagle Star Life Assurance Co Ltd*[16] Lord Hoffmann said:

"In the case of commercial contracts, the restriction on the use of background has been quietly dropped. There are certain kinds of evidence, such as previous negotiations and express declarations of intent, which for practical reasons which it is unnecessary to analyse, are inadmissible in aid of construction. They can be used only in an action for rectification. But apart from these exceptions, commercial contracts are construed in the light of all the background which could reasonably have been expected to have been available to the parties in order to ascertain what would objectively have been understood to be their intention: *Prenn v. Simmonds* [1971] 1 W.L.R. 1381, 1383. The fact that the words are capable of a literal application is no obstacle to evidence which demonstrates what a reasonable person with knowledge of the background would have understood the parties to mean, even if this compels one to say that they used the wrong words. In this area, we no longer confuse the meaning of words with the question of what meaning the use of the words was intended to convey."

In *BCCI v Ali*[17] Lord Hoffmann reformulated his second principle in *Investors Compensation Scheme*[18] as follows:

4–06

"I should say in passing that when, in *Investors Compensation Scheme Limited v. West Bromwich Building Society*, I said that the admissible background included 'absolutely anything which would have affected the way in which the language of the document would have been understood by a reasonable man', I did not think it necessary to emphasise that I meant anything which a reasonable man would have regarded as relevant. I was merely saying

---

[14] See para.4–02, above.
[15] [1976] 1 W.L.R. 989.
[16] [1997] A.C. 749.
[17] [2001] 1 A.C. 251.
[18] See para.4–02, above.

that there is no conceptual limit to what can be regarded as background. It is not, for example, confined to the factual background but can include the state of the law (as in cases in which one takes into account that the parties are unlikely to have intended to agree to something unlawful or legally ineffective) or proved common assumptions which were in fact quite mistaken. But the primary source for understanding what the parties meant is their language interpreted in accordance with conventional usage: '... we do not easily accept that people have made linguistic mistakes particularly in formal documents.' I was certainly not encouraging a trawl through 'background' which could not have made a reasonable person think that the parties must have departed from conventional usage."

As this passage shows, the material of primary importance is the words used. The background may help in the interpretation of those words but it cannot override their meaning. Mummery L.J. made this clear in *Jones v Commerzbank AG*[19] in the following passage:

"I agree with [counsel] that the Deputy Judge paid insufficient attention to the actual language of the documents. He placed far too much reliance on what, in the surrounding circumstances, would have been the sensible commercial agreement between the parties. In the result he constructed from the context alone a contract that the parties in their respective situations might have made. In doing so he has not construed the language of the two letters in which the terms of the contract were in fact formally expressed. Of course, the context of a contract matters as an aid to construction, but it should not be used to construct a contract which does not properly reflect the language employed in formal contractual documents."

The admissible background in the case of repairing and other covenants relevant to dilapidations will depend on the circumstances, but may include the physical nature and layout of the premises; their age; their method of construction; their state and condition at the date of the lease; and the date of the lease.[20] An example of the last mentioned of these is *Walker v Hatton*,[21] in which it was held that covenants in a sub-lease granted in 1830 might be interpreted quite differently from identical covenants in a head lease granted in 1828 because of the difference in date.

Where the lease was granted as part of a wider transaction which included the grant of other leases, the court may look at those other leases as part of the background.[22] It may also look at an antecedent agreement for lease pursuant to which the lease was executed.[23] However, a previous draft of the lease is not admissible,[24] unless it constitutes the parties' final consensus, as when a draft lease is attached to an agreement for lease.[25]

The same principles apply even though the agreement being construed is a settlement agreement and the negotiations which led up to it were without prejudice: objective facts communicated between the parties in the course of such negotiations are admissible in order to construe the agreement.[26]

---

[19] [2003] EWCA Civ 1663.
[20] See Chs 9 and 11, below.
[21] (1842) 10 M. & W. 249. See para.24–07, below.
[22] *Holding & Barnes Plc v Hill House Hammond Ltd* [2002] 2 P. & C.R. 11 (considered further in para.7–29, below).
[23] *Ladbroke Group Plc v Bristol City Council* [1988] 1 E.G.L.R. 126; *KPMG v Network Rail Infrastructure Ltd* [2008] 1 P. & C.R. 11.
[24] *Lola Cars International Ltd v Dunn* [2004] EWHC 2616 (Ch.).
[25] *KPMG v Network Rail Infrastructure Ltd*, above.
[26] *Oceanbulk Shipping & Trading SA v TMT Asia Ltd* [2011] 1 A.C. 662.

## Evidence of negotiations

Evidence of negotiations leading up to the making of the contract cannot be looked at in order to construe the contract. In *Prenn v Simmonds*[27] Lord Wilberforce explained the reason for this rule:

> "[E]vidence of negotiations, or of the parties' intentions, and *a fortiori* of [one party's] intentions, ought not to be received, and evidence should be restricted to evidence of the factual background known to the parties at, or before the date of contract, including evidence of the 'genesis' and objectively the 'aim' of the transaction ... the reason for not admitting evidence of these exchanges is not a technical one or even mainly one of convenience ... It is simply that such evidence is unhelpful. By the nature of things, where negotiations are difficult, the parties' positions, with each passing letter, are changing and until the final agreement, though converging, still divergent. It is only the final document which records a consensus."

**4-07**

The principle that evidence of negotiations is not admissible as an aid to construction was reaffirmed by the House of Lords in *Chartbrook Ltd v Persimmon Homes Ltd*.[28] After an extensive review of the authorities and competing arguments, Lord Hoffmann stressed that, in addition to the issue of relevancy, the rule has pragmatic benefits and said:

> "The conclusion I would reach is that there is no clearly established case for departing from the exclusionary rule. The rule may well mean, as Lord Nicholls has argued, that parties are sometimes held bound by a contract in terms which, upon a full investigation of the course of negotiations, a reasonable observer would not have taken them to have intended. But a system which sometimes allows this to happen may be justified in the more general interest of economy and predictability in obtaining advice and adjudicating disputes. It is, after all, usually possible to avoid surprises by carefully reading the documents before signing them and there are the safety nets of rectification and estoppel by convention."

In *Scottish Widows Fund & Life Insurance Society v BGC International*,[29] pre-contractual negotiations were relied on as establishing the common object of the transaction. Arden L.J. said in her judgment:

> "32.  I accept that the objective fact of the common aim of the parties in entering into the Relevant lease and the supplemental agreement would be part of the background admissible on interpretation. [Counsel] submits that part of the aim of the transaction between the parties in this case was that the responsibility under the Barings lease would be transferred to BGC at the end of the initial period (that is, the clause 2(b) period) at the latest. This would be achieved by the alignment of the rents payable under the Barings lease and the Relevant lease at the end of the initial period, which would trigger the obligation to take an assignment of the Relevant lease under clause 6 of the supplemental agreement. [Counsel] submits that pre-contractual negotiations can be prayed in aid of the objective fact of the aim of a transaction.
>
> 33.  This is a difficult area: see generally, for instance, my judgment in *Square MilePartnership v Fitzmaurice McCall Ltd* [2007] 2 BCLC 23 at paragraphs 59 to 63. The judge rightly held that negotiations could not be used to support detailed points of interpretation (judgment, paragraph 17(vii)). Pre-contractual negotiations rarely descend into detail on every point; the negotiations are unlikely to throw any light on the detailed points of interpretation that generally arise after execution.

---

[27] [1971] 1 W.L.R. 1381.
[28] [2009] 1 A.C. 1101,
[29] [2012] EWCA Civ 607.

34.   However this does not necessarily mean that the pre-contractual negotiations should be accepted as evidence even as to the general object of the transaction. Statements made in the course of negotiations are often no more than statements of a negotiating stance at that point in time, thus shedding more heat than light on issues as to interpretation of the final deal. The reaction of one of the witnesses in this case to a statement made in the course of negotiating the sub-sub-underlease vividly illustrates this point. At being shown a statement that SW would not agree to any outlay beyond £10m, he said that he did not know whether SW meant that. He added: 'They would say that, wouldn't they?'

35.   These factors mean that judges should exercise considerable caution before treating as admissible communications in the course of pre-contractual negotiations relied on as evidencing the parties' objective aim in completing the transaction. Parties could agree in the course of negotiations that, come what may, the aim of their transaction will be to do X, but in that situation their communications are likely to be enforceable as a collateral contract."

As Lord Hoffmann pointed out in *Investors Compensation Scheme*, however, evidence of prior negotiations is always admissible in action for rectification. It is also admissible where the question is whether a collateral contract or estoppel has arisen.

## Use of the wrong words

**4–08**   Where a reasonable person having all the background knowledge available to the parties would conclude that something has gone wrong with the language, the mistake may be corrected as a matter of construction without the need to establish the requirements which need to be satisfied in a rectification action. This is sometimes (inaccurately) referred to as "common law rectification". It is not a separate principle but simply one aspect of the overall process by which the court interprets the document to decide what the parties must have intended.[30] In *East v Pantiles (Plant Hire) Ltd*[31] Brightman L.J. said that for a mistake to be corrected as a matter of construction, the following two conditions must be satisfied:

"[F]irst, there must be a clear mistake on the face of the instrument; secondly, it must be clear what correction ought to be made in order to cure the mistake. If those conditions are satisfied, then the correction is made as a matter of construction."

This statement was approved in *Chartbrook Ltd v Persimmon Homes Ltd*,[32] in which Lord Hoffmann said:

"23.   Subject to two qualifications, both of which are explained by Carnwath LJ in his admirable judgment in *KPMG LLP v Network Rail Infrastructure Ltd* [2007] Bus LR 1336, I would accept this statement, which is in my opinion no more than an expression of the common sense view that we do not readily accept that people have made mistakes in formal documents. The first qualification is that 'correction of mistakes by construction' is not a separate branch of the law, a summary version of an action for rectification. As Carnwath LJ said (at p.1351, para 50): 'Both in the judgment, and in the arguments before us, there was a tendency to deal separately with correction of mistakes and construing the paragraph 'as it stands', as though they were

---

[30] *KPMG v Network Rail Infrastructure* [2008] 1 P. & C.R. 11.
[31] [1982] 2 E.G.L.R. 111.
[32] [2009] 1 A.C. 1101 at [23–24].

> distinct exercises. In my view, they are simply aspects of the single task of interpreting the agreement in its context, in order to get as close as possible to the meaning which the parties intended.
>
> 24. The second qualification concerns the words 'on the face of the instrument'. I agree with Carnwath LJ (at pp 1350–1351) that in deciding whether there is a clear mistake, the court is not confined to reading the document without regard to its background or context. As the exercise is part of the single task of interpretation, the background and context must always be taken into consideration.
>
> 25. What is clear from these cases is that there is not, so to speak, a limit to the amount of red ink or verbal rearrangement or correction which the court is allowed. All that is required is that it should be clear that something has gone wrong with the language and that it should be clear what a reasonable person would have understood the parties to have meant.'"

As Lord Hoffmann pointed out in the same case, the principle does not depend for its operation on "how much use of red ink is involved". He said:

> "When the language used in an instrument gives rise to difficulties of construction, the process of interpretation does not require one to formulate some alternative form of words which approximates as closely as possible to that of the parties. It is to decide what a reasonable person would have understood the parties to have meant by using the language which they did. The fact that the court might have to express that meaning in language quite different from that used by the parties ('12th January' instead of '13th January' in *Mannai Investment Co Ltd v Eagle Star Life Assurance Co Ltd* [1997] AC 749; 'any claim sounding in rescission (whether for undue influence or otherwise)' instead of 'any claim (whether sounding in rescission for undue influence or otherwise)' in *Investors Compensation Scheme Ltd v West Bromwich Building Society* [1998] 1 WLR 896) is no reason for not giving effect to what they appear to have meant."

In *Pink Floyd Music v EMI Records*[33] Lord Neuberger M.R., having reviewed a number of authorities, endorsed the observations of Chadwick L.J. in *City Alliance v Oxford Forecasting Services*[34] that the court cannot introduce words into a contract unless:

> "satisfied (i) that the words actually used produce a result which is so commercially nonsensical that the parties could not have intended it and (ii) that they did intend some other commercial purpose which can be identified with confidence."

In *Campbell v Daejan Properties*[35] Jackson L.J. treated Lord Neuberger's approach and that of Lord Hoffmann in *Chartbrook* as "similar in their effect, although differently worded". In *Scottish Widows Fund & Life Insurance Society v BGC International*,[36] Arden L.J. said of the principle:

> "21. Accordingly, there are circumstances in which the court may, if it finds from the face of the document interpreted with the admissible background, that the parties have mistakenly included, or omitted, words in a document, interpret the document so that it has the meaning which, according to the document read with the admissible background, the parties clearly intended. As the subsequent case of *Chartbrook* makes clear, however, there are limitations. In particular:
>
> i) It must be clear from the document interpreted with the admissible background that the parties have made a mistake and what that mistake is;

---

[33] [2010] EWCA Civ 1429.
[34] [2001] 1 All E.R. Com 233.
[35] [2012] EWCA Civ 5103 at [45].
[36] [2012] EWCA Civ 607.

     ii)     It must be clear, from the rest of the agreement interpreted with the admissible background what the parties intended to agree,

     iii)    The mistake must be one of language or syntax."

The principle has generally been applied in two classes of case: first, cases in which the relevant provision makes no sense as it stands (because it is meaningless and/or words have been omitted);[37] and second, cases where the literal application of the provision produces absurd, irrational or obviously unintended consequences.[38]

**4–09**    Three examples may be given of the operation (or non-operation) of the principle in a dilapidations context.

In *Dayani v Bromley LBC (No.1)*[39] the last nine words of a repairing covenant ("up to a maximum value of eight weeks rent") were "unintelligible" and "meaningless". The court struck them out and construed the covenant as though it omitted the words in question.

In *Holding & Barnes Plc v Hill House Hammond*[40] a lease of an entire building obliged the landlord:

> "to keep the foundations and the roof in good and tenantable repair and condition and to keep the structure of the Building (other than those parts comprised in the property) in good and tenantable repair and condition."

It was agreed that the expressions "building" and "property" meant the same thing. Read literally, therefore, the second part of the clause was a nonsense: it obliged the landlord to keep the structure of the property (other than those parts comprised in the property) in good and tenantable repair and condition. The lease was one of seven leases which had been granted between the same parties on the same day as part of the sale of an insurance services business. Five were of parts of a building, and two (including the lease in question) were of a whole building. It was common ground that in construing the lease, it was permissible to have regard to the other six leases. Taking that material into account, the Court of Appeal held that the words in parenthesis had obviously been inserted in error and were to be ignored, so that the clause was to be read as imposing on the landlord a straightforward obligation to keep the structure and exterior of the property in good and tenantable repair and condition.

In *Campbell v Daejan Properties*[41] a lease of a third and fourth floor maisonette in a converted townhouse on six floors obliged the tenant (among other things) to pay to the landlord on demand two-fifths of the expense incurred by the landlord in performing its covenant in clause 3(iii). Clause 3(iii) obliged

---

[37] See for example *Holding & Barnes Plc v Hill House Hammond* [2002] 2 P. & C.R. 11; *"The Starsin"* [2004] 1 A.C. 715; and *KPMG v Network Rail Infrastructure*, above.

[38] See for example *Wilson v Wilson* (1854) 5 H.L. Cas. 40; *Littman v Aspen Oil (Broking)* [2006] 2 P. & C.R. 2; *Chartbrook v Persimmon Homes Ltd* [2009] 1 W.L.R. 1101. Contrast *JIS (1974) v MCP Investment Nominees* [2003] EWCA Civ 721, in which the Court of Appeal declined to hold that a tenant's break clause contained an obvious mistake even though "when one analyses the lease and the underlease in more detail, one can see that the clause is practically inoperable."

[39] [1999] 3 E.G.L.R. 144.

[40] Above.

[41] [2013] 1 P. & C. R. 14.

the landlord to keep the outside walls and roof of "the premises" in repair and to paint the exterior of "the premises" once every seven years and, except in cases of emergency, before carrying out any work to obtain at least two estimates and submit them to the tenant for approval. On a literal reading of the lease, the expression "the premises" meant the demised maisonette only. The expression used in the lease to denote the whole building was "the house". On the face of it, therefore, (i) clause 3(iii) obliged the landlord to repair and maintain the outside walls and roof of the maisonette only; (ii) clause 3(iii) did not impose on the landlord any repairing obligation in respect of the other roofs of the house or the external walls below third floor level; and (iii) the tenant was obliged to pay 40 per cent of the costs incurred by the landlord in carrying out the works required by clause 3(iii). At first instance, Roth J. held that something had clearly gone wrong with the language, and that the reference in clause 3(iii) to "the premises" was to be construed as being to "the house". The Court of Appeal allowed the landlord's appeal. The service charge provisions in the lease imposed a "profusion of different obligations on the lessee". There was:

> "... no obvious pattern in the various service charge provisions which leads to the conclusion that the parties must have intended the lessee to pay 40% of the repair costs of all roofs and all outside walls. Indeed such an obligation would be surprisingly onerous since the floor area of the maisonette represents only 29.2% of the total floor area of the house. Furthermore the lessee of the maisonette derives no benefit from the flat roofs above the basement and the ground floor extensions."

It was not clear that the parties had made a mistake in the drafting of clause 3(iii). Whilst the wording of that clause was "certainly capable of improvement", it did not produce a result which was commercially nonsensical. It was therefore to be construed in accordance with its actual wording without substituting the word "house" for "premises".

### Business common sense

In deciding what meaning a reasonable person with all the background knowledge available to the parties would give the words, regard must be had the extent to which the various competing interpretations accord with business common sense. Thus, in *Antaios Campania Naviera v Salen Rederiana*[42] Lord Diplock said in a well-known passage:

**4–10**

> "...I take this opportunity of restating that, if a detailed semantic and syntactical analysis of words in a commercial contract is going to lead to a conclusion that flouts business common sense, it must be made to yield to business common sense.[43]"

Similarly, in *Mannai Investment Co Ltd v Eagle Star Life Assurance Co Ltd*[44] Lord Steyn said in his speech:

---

[42] [1985] A.C. 191.
[43] This passage was referred to with approval by Lord Hoffmann in *Investors Compensation Scheme v West Bromwich Building Society* [1998] 1 W.L.R. 896. See para.4–02, above.
[44] [1997] A.C. 749.

"In determining the language of a commercial contract, and unilateral contractual notices, the law … generally favours a commercially sensible construction. The reason for this approach is that a commercial construction is more likely to give effect to the intention of the parties. Words are therefore interpreted in the way in which a reasonable commercial person would understand them. And the standard of the reasonable commercial person is hostile to technical interpretations and undue emphasis on niceties of language."

This does not mean, however, that where the parties have used unambiguous language, the court is free to depart from it simply because the result appears contrary to business common sense. Where the words are clear, the court must apply them.[45] As Neuberger L.J. put it in *Skanska Rashleigh Weatherfoil Ltd v Somerfield Stores Ltd*:[46]

"21.    As already mentioned, the interpretation of the provision in the commercial contract is not to be assessed purely by reference to the words the parties have used within the four corners of the contract, but must be construed also by reference to the factual circumstances of commercial common sense. However, it seems to me right to emphasise that the surrounding circumstances and commercial common sense do not represent a licence to the court to re–write a contract merely because its terms seem somewhat unexpected, a little unreasonable, or not commercially very wise. The contract will contain the words the parties have chosen to use in order to identify their contractual rights and obligations. At least between them, they have control over the words they use and what they agree, and in that respect the words of the written contract are different from the surrounding circumstances or commercial common sense which the parties cannot control, at least to the same extent.

22.    Particularly in these circumstances, it seems to me that the court must be careful before departing from the natural meaning of the provision in the contract merely because it may conflict with its notions of commercial common sense of what the parties may must or should have thought or intended. Judges are not always the most commercially-minded, let alone the most commercially experienced, of people, and should, I think, avoid arrogating to themselves overconfidently the role of arbiter of commercial reasonableness or likelihood. Of course, in many cases, the commercial common sense of a particular interpretation, either because of the peculiar circumstances of the case or because of more general considerations, is clear. Furthermore, sometimes it is plainly justified to depart from the primary meaning of words and given them what might, on the face of it, appear to be a strained meaning, for instance where the primary meaning of the words leads to a plainly ridiculous or unreasonable result."

However, where the words are reasonably capable of more than one meaning, the court is entitled to select the meaning which most closely accords with business common sense. In *Wickman Machine Tools Ltd v LA Schuler AG*,[47] Lord Reid said:

"No doubt some words used by lawyers do have a rigid inflexible meaning. But we must remember that we are seeking to discover intention as disclosed by the contract as a whole … The fact that a particular construction leads to a very unreasonable result must be a relevant consideration. The more unreasonable the result, the more unlikely it is that the parties can have intended it, and if they do intend it the more necessary it is that they shall make that intention abundantly clear. [The meaning argued for by Schuler] is so unreasonable that it must make me search for some other possible meaning of the contract. If none can be found then Wickman must suffer the consequences. But only if that is the only possible construction."

---

[45] *Rainy Sky SA v Kookmin Bank* [2011] 1 W.L.R. 2900 at [23].
[46] [2006] EWCA Civ 1732.
[47] [1976] 3 W.L.R. 683.

In *Co-operative Wholesale Society Ltd v National Westminster Bank Plc*,[48] Hoffmann L.J. said (referring to the above passage from *Antaios Campania Naviera v Salen Rederiana*):

> "This robust declaration does not, however, mean that one can rewrite the language which the parties have used in order to make the contract conform to business common sense. But language is a very flexible instrument and, if it is capable of more than one construction, one chooses that which seems most likely to give effect to the commercial purpose of the agreement."

In *Rainy Sky SA v Kookmin Bank*[49] Lord Clarke (with whom Lords Phillips, Mance, Kerr and Wilson agreed) said:

> "21.  The language used by the parties will often have more than one potential meaning. I would accept the submission made on behalf of the appellants that the exercise of construction is essentially one unitary exercise in which the court must consider the language used and ascertain what a reasonable person, that is a person who has all the background knowledge which would reasonably have been available to the parties in the situation in which they were at the time of the contract, would have understood the parties to have meant. In doing so, the court must have regard to all the relevant surrounding circumstances. If there are two possible constructions, the court is entitled to prefer the construction which is consistent with business common sense and to reject the other.
>
> ...
>
> ... the correct approach ... is in essence that, where a term of a contract is open to more than one interpretation, it is generally appropriate to adopt the interpretation which is most consistent with business common sense."

Lord Clarke further expressed agreement with the following passage from the speech of Lord Steyn in *Society of Lloyd's v Robinson*[50]:

> "Loyalty to the text of a commercial contract, instrument, or document read in its contextual setting is the paramount principle of interpretation. But in the process of interpreting the meaning of the language of a commercial document the court ought generally to favour a commercially sensible construction. The reason for this approach is that a commercial construction is likely to give effect to the intention of the parties. Words ought therefore to be interpreted in the way in which a reasonable commercial person would construe them. And the reasonable commercial person can safely be assumed to be unimpressed with technical interpretations and undue emphasis on niceties of language."

A similar approach was applied by Lindsay J. to the construction of repairing obligations in *Credit Suisse v Beegas Nominees Ltd*[51] as follows:

> "I am invited by [counsel for the landlord] to proceed on the basis of giving commercial effect to [the covenant to repair] ... I ... approach the underlease having in mind that the arrangements likely to have been intended to have been made by business people will be business-like arrangements. But I do not see the notion as going further than that; it does not enable me to give other than a natural meaning to the words used, although, doubtless, where two natural meanings equally beckon I should, in this context, prefer the more business-like."

---

[48] [1995] 1 E.G.L.R. 97.
[49] [2011] 1 W.L.R. 2900.
[50] [1991] 1 W.L.R. 756.
[51] [1994] 4 All E.R. 803 and (more fully) [1994] 1 E.G.L.R. 76.

## Some relevant presumptions of construction

**4–11**     The courts have developed a number of presumptions or canons of construction to assist in the process of ascertaining the intention of the parties to the contract.[52] Those rules which are of particular relevance to the law of dilapidations are considered below. It is important to appreciate, however, that although often described as "rules", these are no more than guides or pointers to the proper construction of the contract. They are not decisive, and in many cases they may be of little or no weight.

### (a)     The document must be read as a whole[53]

**4–12**     Since the particular word, phrase or sentence which is being construed is only part of the complete agreement between the parties, it would be wrong to look at it in isolation. The document as a whole may give important information as to the context of the agreement; it may indicate directly (through recitals) or indirectly (by disclosing the whole transaction) what is the aim of the agreement; it may use words in some places in such a way as to illuminate the meaning of the same words elsewhere; it may use different words in other places so as to indicate that the words being construed are used in a different and contrasting sense; it may show that the agreement has been carefully and precisely constructed; or it may show that it has been carelessly drafted, and therefore that less reliance can be placed on a careful analysis of its scheme as a whole.

An example of this principle in operation in a dilapidations context is *Ibrahim v Dovecorn Reversions Ltd*,[54] in which the demise expressly excluded "the main walls and structure" of the building. Those words were ambiguous as to whether "main" qualified not only "walls" but also "structure". However, the landlord had covenanted to repair the "main structure". Rimer J. held that, construing the lease as a whole, the exclusion was of the main walls and the main structure.[55]

### (b)     Presumption against redundant drafting[56]

**4–13**     If possible, every word used should be given some meaning. Consequently, a series of words with similar meanings will generally be construed so as to give each word an individual meaning or emphasis. However, the courts recognise that the parties will often spell out unnecessarily what is obvious; will use overlapping or repetitive expressions through mental laziness or from abundant caution; and may be deliberately repetitive in order to emphasise a point. Thus, in *Beaufort Developments (NI) Ltd v Gilbert-Ash (NI) Ltd*[57] Lord Hoffmann said:

---

[52] For a definitive treatment, see Lewison, *The Interpretation of Contracts*, 5th edn (London: Sweet & Maxwell, 2011).

[53] For a full discussion of the principle, see Lewison, *The Interpretation of Contracts*, 5th edn (London: Sweet & Maxwell, 2011), para.7.06.

[54] [2001] 2 E.G.L.R. 46.

[55] See further paras 7–40 and 7–51, below.

[56] For a full discussion of the presumption, see Lewison, *The Interpretation of Contracts*, 5th edn (London: Sweet & Maxwell, 2011), para.7.03.

[57] [1999] 1 A.C. 266.

"I think, my Lords, that the argument from redundancy is seldom an entirely secure one. The fact is that even in legal documents (or, some might say, especially in legal documents) people often use superfluous words. Sometimes the draftsmanship is clumsy; more often the cause is a lawyer's desire to be certain that every conceivable point has been covered. One only has to read the covenants in a traditional lease to realise that draftsmen lack inhibition about using too many words."

He made the same point in *Tea Trade Properties Ltd v CIN Properties Ltd*[58]:

"I have never found the presumption against superfluous drafting particularly useful in the construction of leases. The draftsmen traditionally employ linguistic overkill and try to obliterate the conceptual target by using a number of words or phrases expressing more or less the same idea. I cannot, therefore, rely upon the language alone but must, as it seems to me, construe the words also by reference to the commercial effect which would be produced by one construction or the other."

Accordingly, where the circumstances warrant it, different provisions or words will be construed as meaning much the same thing, and the court will not invent artificial differences between them when it is satisfied the parties did not intend this.[59]

Given the relative prolixity with which repairing covenants are often drafted, the presumption against redundant drafting is of particular relevance to the law of dilapidations. Its application in the specific context of repairing covenants is considered below.[60]

### (c)  *Exressio unius est exclusio alterius*[61]

Where the contract expressly mentions something but omits to mention something else that the draftsman might reasonably have been expected to mention had he intended to include it, the omission may be taken as deliberate. Suppose, for example, that an office block has wooden window frames in both the individual offices and the common parts, and that the landlord covenants to repair and decorate "... the exterior of the Building (including the frames of the windows in the common parts of the Building)". The express inclusion of the window frames in the common parts, and the exclusion of any reference to those in the offices, might well be relied on as showing that the parties intended the former but not the latter to be included within the ambit of the landlord's obligation.

However, the proper construction of the contract as a whole may show that a contrast between one part of the contract and another is not indicative of the parties' true intentions. For example, in *Norwich Union Life Insurance Society Ltd v British Railways Board*[62] it was argued that a covenant to keep the premises "in good and substantial repair and condition and when necessary to rebuild,

4–14

---

[58] [1990] 1 E.G.L.R. 155.
[59] See para.4–19 et seq. below, in which the proper approach to the different expressions found in repairing covenants is considered.
[60] See paras 4–19 to 4–22, below.
[61] For a full discussion of the principle, see Lewison, *The Interpretation of Contracts*, 5th edn (London: Sweet & Maxwell, 2011), para.7.13.
[62] [1987] 2 E.G.L.R. 137. See further on this case para.4–21, below.

reconstruct or replace the same" was not to be interpreted as imposing on the tenant a liability to rebuild the whole of the premises when necessary. Reliance was placed on a contrast with the insurance covenant, which was said to show that when the draftsman intended to impose an obligation to erect an entirely new building, he used express words to say so. Hoffmann J. held that the words of the repairing covenant were clear and that no real assistance was to be gained from the suggested contrast.[63]

## (d)    Contra proferentem[64]

**4–15**      The general effect of the *contra proferentem* principle is that where the meaning of the contract is unclear, the relevant words will be interpreted against the person who put them forward or for whose benefit they were inserted. The principle is formulated in the cases in different and sometimes conflicting ways, and its precise ambit is not clear. It has been described in one case as "of uncertain application and little utility in the case of commercially negotiated agreements",[65] and in many others as a principle "of last resort".[66]

An example of the use of the principle in a dilapidations context is the Australian case of *Justelle Nominees Pty v Martin (No.3)*,[67] in which the tenant of a hotel covenanted to:

> "maintain, replace, repair and keep the Leased Premises and every part thereof and all additions thereto and all the Lessor's fixtures therein and the doors, windows, roof, and guttering thereof and all furnishings, equipment, locks, keys and fittings thereof in good clean and substantial repair and condition"

and the landlord covenanted to:

> "maintain the Leased Premises and building of which the Leased Premises form part in a sound structural condition and ...repair all items of damage in respect of the Leased Premises which are not specifically the responsibility of the Lessee to repair under this Lease"

Blaxell J. held that the lease was to be construed *contra proferentem* against the landlord, so that the landlord's covenant was to be construed as a limitation on that of the tenant. Accordingly, the landlord was required to do all that was necessary to maintain the premises in a sound structural condition and to repair all items of damage which were not specifically the responsibility of the tenant under the lease, and the tenant was obliged to carry out all other repairs.

---

[63] See further paras 4–25 to 4–26, below.
[64] For a full discussion of the principle, see Lewison, *The Interpretation of Contracts*, 5th edn (London: Sweet & Maxwell, 2011), para.7.08.
[65] *CDV Software Entertainment AG v Gamecock Media Europe Ltd* [2009] EWHC 2965.
[66] See, for example, *The Olympic Brilliance* [1982] 2 Lloyd's Rep. 205; *Sinochem International Oil (London) Co Ltd v Mobil Sales & Supply Corporation* [2000] 1 Lloyd's Rep. 339; and *Landlord Protect Ltd v St Anselm Development Co Ltd* [2008] EWHC 1582 (Ch.).
[67] [2009] WASC 264.

## (e) Ejusdem generis[68]

Where a list of particular items, all of which have some common characteristic, is followed by general words, those general words are generally to be construed ejusdem generis with the preceding words, i.e. as limited to the same sort of things as the particular items, and not as including things of a different nature. In *Sun Fire Office v Hart*[69] Lord Watson said:

> "It is a well known canon of construction, that where a particular enumeration is followed by such words as 'or other', the latter expression ought, if not enlarged by the context, be limited to matters ejusdem generis with those specifically enumerated."

An example of a case where the principle might be applied is the covenant often found in leases to contribute to the cost of things used by the tenant in common with others. For example, the tenant may covenant to pay to the landlord a fair proportion of the cost incurred by the landlord in repairing:

> "[A]ll party walls boundary fences access ways staircases and passages of the Building and all other parts of the Building used by the Lessee in common with other lessees"

The ejusdem generis principle might be used to support an argument that the lessee is not liable to contribute to the cost of repairing communal central heating plant which, although on one view a "part of the Building ... used ... in common", is not a part of the same character as the things specifically mentioned, which are all physical parts of the building itself rather than fixtures or installations.

Two examples of the ejusdem generis principle in the context of dilapidations are:

(i) *Saner v Bilton (No.1)*,[70] in which a covenant to yield up all doors, locks, keys, etc., wainscots, hearths, stoves, marbles, and other chimney pieces, etc. and all other buildings, erections, improvements, fixtures and things on the demised premises was construed as limited to things in the nature of landlord's fixtures and not as extending to trade machinery affixed by the tenant;

(ii) *Marlborough Park Services v Rowe*,[71] in which the issue was whether certain floor joists formed part of the "main structures" of a block of flats for the purposes of the landlord's repairing obligations. One of the landlord's arguments was that the expression was subject to an implied qualification to the effect that it did not include items wholly within the envelope of one flat and exclusively serving that flat. In rejecting that argument, Neuberger L.J. (with whom Sedley and Tuckey L.J.J. agreed) relied on the fact that the lease also contained a landlord's covenant to repair gas pipes, etc. "in under or serving the Property other than those

---

[68] For a full discussion of the ejusdem generis rule, see Lewison, *The Interpretation of Contracts*, 5th edn (London: Sweet & Maxwell, 2011), at para.7.13.
[69] (1889) 14 App. Cas. 98.
[70] (1878) 7 Ch. D. 815.
[71] [2006] 2 E.G.L.R. 27.

serving only one flat in the Property", saying that it was "particularly difficult to imply [the relevant words] to the ambit of 'main structures' in [the landlord's repairing covenant] if the parties have omitted them from that provision, but have expressly included them in [the covenant to repair gas pipes, etc.]".[72]

However, the particular language used may show that the parties intended the general words to be read in a general sense (for example, the general words may be followed by expressions such as "whether or not similar to the foregoing" or "without prejudice to the generality of the foregoing".[73] In *Sun Fire Office v Hart*[74] Lord Watson went on to say:

"The canon is attended with no difficulty, except in its application. Whether it applies at all, and if so, what effect should be given to it, must in every case depend upon the precise terms, subject-matter, and context of the clause under construction."

## The autonomy of words

**4–17** The courts have consistently emphasised that each contract must be construed in its own right, and that judicial decisions on the meaning of a word or words in one particular agreement are no sure guide to the meaning even of the identical word or words in another.[75] As Scrutton L.J. said in *Westacott v Hahn*:[76]

"A flood of authorities in and since the seventeenth century were poured out upon the Court, in which somewhat similar words to this covenant had received a construction from the Courts. In my view, however, the first thing to be done is to endeavour to ascertain from the words the parties have used in this case their actual intention. If they have used words which by a settled course of authority have acquired a technical meaning, the Court will give effect to those authorities; but, unless this is so, it appears to me very unprofitable to consider what Courts have thought that other words in other documents meant and to see which reported case has the least differences from the present."

The same point was made by Robert Walker J. in *Welsh v Greenwich LBC*[77] in the context of repairing covenants:

"[T]he language of repairing covenants, and the commercial and social contexts in which they occur, are very variable. A decision on the language of one clause is never decisive, and may sometimes not even be helpful, as to the meaning of another clause, even though it uses some of the same words."

However, this must not be taken too far. A judicial decision on one set of words in a particular contract is at least an indication as to how the court might approach the same words in another. Furthermore, as the above passage

---

[72] At [11].
[73] *Chandris v Isdbrandtsen-Moller Inc* [1951] 1 K.B. 240.
[74] (1889) 14 App. Cas. 98.
[75] *Anstruther-Gough-Calthorpe v McOscar* [1924] 1 K.B. 716, per Atkin L.J. at 731; *Safeway Food Stores Ltd v Banderway Ltd* [1983] 2 E.G.L.R. 116; *Equity & Law Life Assurance Society Ltd v Bodfield Ltd* (1987) 54 P. & C.R. 290.
[76] [1918] 1 K.B. 495.
[77] [2000] 3 E.G.L.R. 41.

recognises, where words have, through judicial interpretation, acquired a recognised meaning, parties who use them may justifiably be assumed to have intended them to have that same meaning. Some judges would go further, believing commercial parties generally to be better served by the courts adopting a consistent approach to the meaning of similar provisions in contracts, at least in the absence of clear indications in the particular contract being construed that the parties intended some different meaning.[78] Nonetheless, in *Credit Suisse v Beegas Nominees Ltd*[79] Lindsay J. rejected an argument based on the desirability of consistency in the authorities dealing with repairing covenants in the following terms:

> "[Counsel for the landlord] invites me, in connection with terms commonly referred to in the authorities, to give a construction consistent with that derivable from those authorities because inconsistency is undesirable, he says, in standard forms of commercial contracts. Plainly I should accept guidance from authorities, but I do not regard this lease as a standard form of contract.[80] Although certain words recur in the authorities dealing with different repairing covenants and although some guidance can thus be derived from other cases, there is a world of difference between the case before me and cases where the courts properly strive for consistency as to the construction of, say, the printed standard form of the New York Produce Exchange."

## The parol evidence rule[81]

The "parol evidence rule" is a logical extension of the objective approach discussed above.[82] Where the parties have reduced their contract into writing, the document is presumed to represent the entirety of their agreement, and extrinsic evidence is not admissible to supplement, vary or contradict it.[83] Thus, in *Goldfoot v Welch*[84] the question was whether the outside walls of the demised premises were included in the demise. Eve J., having concluded that on the proper construction of the lease the walls had been demised, refused to admit evidence of an alleged conversation tendered for the purpose of showing that the landlord had orally reserved the walls. However, the rule in its strict form would clearly be capable of producing substantial injustice, and there are therefore a number of established exceptions. The most important of these are that extrinsic evidence is admissible to establish:

4–18

(1)   some vitiating element in the contract, such as that it was entered into under a mutual mistake, or by virtue of a misrepresentation made by one party to the other;

---

[78] See the dissenting judgment of Browne-Wilkinson L.J. in *Mecca Leisure Ltd v Renown Holdings Ltd* (1984) 49 P. & C.R. 12 and also his subsequent judgment in *British Gas Corp v Universities Superannuation Scheme Ltd* [1986] 1 All E.R. 978.

[79] [1994] 4 All E.R. 803 and (more fully) [1994] 1 E.G.L.R. 76.

[80] The repairing covenant is set out at para.4–28, below.

[81] For a full discussion of the rule, see Lewison, *The Interpretation of Contracts*, 5th edn (London: Sweet & Maxwell, 2011), para.3.11.

[82] See para.4–03, above.

[83] For a definitive treatment, see Lewison, *The Interpretation of Contracts*, 4th edn (London: Sweet & Maxwell, 2007) at para.3.10.

[84] [1914] 1 Ch. 213.

(2) that the contract as written down does not represent the true agreement between the parties, so that one party is entitled to rectification;

(3) that the contract as written down does not represent the entirety of what was agreed[85] (although there is a presumption that the written contract contains all the terms agreed[86]);

(4) a collateral contract[87];

(5) that a particular term ought to be implied into the contract[88];

(6) an estoppel.[89]

## THE APPROACH OF THE COURT TO THE INTERPRETATION OF REPAIRING AND OTHER COVENANTS RELATING TO THE CONDITION OF BUILDINGS

### The precise words used

**4–19**    As a matter of general principle, there is no reason why the construction of repairing and other covenants relevant to dilapidations should not be approached in the same way as any other type of contract. There is, however, one particular feature of what may be called the general covenant to repair which gives rise to difficulty. The traditional form of covenant used for many years, and still much used in modern times, is generally drafted in what has been called a "torrential" style[90]; that is to say, it contains a number of associated concepts and expressions, some or all of which may be thought to mean more or less the same thing.

The traditional formula generally has one or both of two separate features. First, there will be an obligation to carry out the operation of repair drafted in terms which include a number of similar concepts. Examples of this are:

> "[W]ell, sufficiently and substantially [to] repair, uphold, sustain, maintain, glaze, pave … amend and keep all and singular the said [premises].[91]
>
> [W]ell and substantially to repair uphold support maintain cleanse … the demised premises.[92]
>
> [W]ell and sufficiently to repair renew rebuild uphold sustain maintain pave purge scour cleanse glaze empty amend and keep the premises … with all needful and necessary amendments whatsoever."[93]

The second feature is a separate obligation (but usually drafted as part of the same covenant) to keep the premises in a particular state, often defined in terms

---

[85] See, for example, *Wallis v Littell* (1861) 11 C.B.N.S. 369 (in which the purchaser of a lease was held to be entitled to adduce evidence that the written agreement for the assignment was subject to a condition that it should be void if the landlord refused consent to the assignment).

[86] *Gillespie Bros v Cheney, Eggar & Co* [1896] 2 Q.B. 59.

[87] See para.1–09 et seq., above.

[88] See para.1–03 et seq., above.

[89] See para.1–13 et seq., above.

[90] *Norwich Union Life Assurance Society Ltd v British Railways Board* [1987] 2 E.G.L.R. 137, per Hoffmann J.

[91] *Lister v Lane* [1893] 2 Q.B. 212.

[92] *Brew Bros v Snax (Ross) Ltd* [1970] 1 Q.B. 612.

[93] *Ravenseft Properties Ltd v Davstone (Holdings) Ltd* [1980] Q.B. 12.

such as "in good tenantable repair"[94]; "in good tenantable repair and condition"[95]; or "in thorough repair and good condition".[96]

A strict application of the principle that every word used in a contract must, if possible, be given meaning[97] would result in each of these various expressions and concepts being construed so as to mean something different. However, there are a number of statements in the authorities to the effect that the precise words used in a repairing covenant may not matter. The question is to what extent these statements can be taken at face value.

## The apparent conflict of approach

In *Lurcott v Wakeley*[98] the relevant covenant was "well and substantially [to] repair and keep in thorough repair and good condition". The judgments in the Court of Appeal show a marked contrast between the approach of Fletcher Moulton L.J. on the one hand and Cozens-Hardy M.R. and Buckley L.J. on the other. The former analysed the covenant as though it imposed three covenants, to each of which effect should be given. He said:

4–20

> "I think it is our duty to give full meaning to each word of the covenant. It is quite true that there may be pairs of covenants in which the words used are so nearly synonymous in meaning that the scope of the two covenants will greatly overlap. It is even possible that there may be words so absolutely identical in meaning that they may make the two covenants identical. But to my mind the speculation as to the extent to which the two covenants overlap—as to whether there is anything covered by the one which is not covered by the other—is an idle speculation likely to mislead the court. The sole duty of the court is to give proper and full effect to each word used, and the question whether this leads to more or less overlapping is of no legal importance. I therefore look upon these as three separate covenants: there is a covenant to repair, there is a covenant to keep in thorough repair, and there is a covenant to keep in good condition.[99]"

By contrast, the judgments of Cozens-Hardy M.R. and Buckley L.J. proceeded implicitly on the basis that what had to be construed was simply a general obligation to repair.

A similar contrast may be found in the judgments of the Court of Appeal in *Anstruther-Gough-Calthorpe v McOscar*,[100] in which the tenant covenanted that he would:

> "[W]ell and sufficiently repair support uphold maintain paint pave empty scour cleanse amend and keep the three several messuages and buildings ... with all and all manner of needful and necessary reparations and amendments whatsoever."

Atkin L.J. said in the course of his judgment:

---

[94] *Proudfoot v Hart* (1890) 25 Q.B.D. 42.
[95] *Pembery v Lamdin* [1940] 2 All E.R. 434.
[96] *Lurcott v Wakeley* [1911] 1 K.B. 905.
[97] See para.4–13, above.
[98] [1911] 1 K.B. 905.
[99] The approach of Fletcher Moulton L.J. has subsequently been applied in *Smedley v Chumley & Hawkes Ltd* (1982) 44 P. & C.R. 50 and in *Credit Suisse v Beegas Nominees Ltd* [1994] 4 All E.R. 803 and (more fully) [1994] 1 E.G.L.R. 76. See para.4–30, below.
[100] [1924] 1 K.B. 716.

"I see no reason for construing the words of covenants in leases dealing with repair in any other way than one would construe any covenant. Effect should be given if possible to every word used by the parties. It does not appear to be useful to refer to such covenants as the usual covenants to repair, or general repairing covenants, and then consider only what is the meaning of 'repair': it appears to me still less useful to take a number of terms which may be found in different leases, treat them as synonymous, and so impute to all of them a special meaning attached by authority to one of them."

This is to be contrasted with the following passage from the judgment of Scrutton L.J.:

"In my view the matter can be dealt with as if the covenant was one to keep and yield up at the end of the term in repair. I do not think there is any substantial difference in construction between 'repair', which must mean 'repair reasonably or properly' and 'keep in good repair' or 'sufficient repair' or 'tenantable repair' or most of the various phrases cited to us."

This was a view which Bankes L.J. stated even more trenchantly in his judgment:

"I attach no importance to the particular form of words used in the covenant. The effect is the same in my opinion whatever words the parties used, provided they plainly express the intention that the premises are to be repaired, kept in repair and yielded up in repair."

Further judicial support for the view that the precise words do not matter is to be found in the following passage from the judgment of Lord Esher M.R. in *Lister v Lane*[101]:

"However large the words of the covenant may be, a covenant to repair a house is not a covenant to give a different thing from that which the tenant took when he entered into the covenant.[102]"

**4–21**     The same apparent difference of approach can be found in some of the more modern authorities. Thus, in *Halliard Property Co Ltd v Nicholas Clarke Investments Ltd*,[103] French J. commented of a lease that "it contained a repairing covenant in (if I may say so) typically verbose and repetitive form".

Likewise, in *Norwich Union Life Assurance Society Ltd v British Railways Board*[104] Hoffmann J. said of construing repairing covenants:

"Now I accept that in the construction of covenants such as this one cannot, for the reasons I have already given,[105] insist upon giving each word in a series a distinct meaning. Draftsmen frequently use many words either because it is traditional to do so or out of a sense of caution so that nothing which could conceivably fall within the general concept which they have in mind should be left out."

---

[101] [1893] 2 Q.B. 212.
[102] In *Norwich Union Life Assurance Society Ltd v British Railways Board* [1987] 2 E.G.L.R. 137 Hoffmann J. said of this passage that, strictly construed, it was "either tautologous ('a repairing covenant is a repairing covenant') or false". However, he went on to say that "in the context of the case one can easily see what the learned Master of the Rolls had in mind".
[103] [1984] 1 E.G.L.R. 45.
[104] [1987] 2 E.G.L.R. 137.
[105] i.e. that a "torrential style of drafting has been traditional for many years": see para.4–19, above.

However, in *Credit Suisse v Beegas Nominees Ltd*[106] Lindsay J. rejected the landlord's argument that the court should not look at the eight verbs in the repairing covenant[107] and see each one as intended to add to the meaning ascribable to the others. Having analysed *Norwich Union* he said:

> "*Norwich Union* is not and could not be authority for a proposition that [the] normal rule does not apply to repairing covenants. Even where there is a torrent, each stream of which it is comprised can be expected to have added to the flow."

In *Welsh v Greenwich LBC*[108] Robert Walker J. said in the course of his judgment:

> "When a lease or tenancy agreement is drafted in [a torrential style], it leaves the court with little need or scope for finding a different meaning or shade for every word used (although with that may be compared what Lindsay J. said [in the passage quoted above])."

In the New Zealand case of *Weatherhead v Deka New Zealand Ltd*[109] (the facts of which are set out at para.11–24, below) the tenant covenanted:

> "well and sufficiently [to] repair maintain amend cleanse and keep the demised premises in good and substantial repair and condition when where and so often as need shall be having regard to the condition thereof at the commencement of the term reasonable wear and tear only excepted."

The landlord contended that the covenant was to be broken down into six separate obligations. Thomas J., giving the judgment of the Court of Appeal, said:

> "This fractured approach to the construction of the covenant does not have great appeal to us. Certainly the words 'repair', 'maintain' and 'amend' may have different meanings and import different obligations. Certainly, too, none can be disregarded. But the sense of the covenant can be better discerned when it is read as a whole. For present purposes, the lessee's obligation is to repair, maintain and keep the premises in good and substantial repair and condition having regard to the condition of the premises at the commencement of the lease. Once the obligation is framed in these terms the significance of the qualification that regard is to be had to the condition of the building at the outset of the lease is plain to see."

## A reconciliation of the authorities

It is thought that those judicial statements which appear to deny the application to repairing covenants of the normal rule that each word used must, if possible, be given effect are not to be read as laying down any such principle. The passages from the judgments of the majority of the Court of Appeal in *Lurcott v Wakeley*[110] and *Anstruther-Gough-Calthorpe v McOscar*[111] are explicable on the basis that in neither case was it necessary to decide whether the different words used bore different meanings, because in both cases the majority were clearly of the view

**4–22**

---

[106] [1994] 4 All E.R. 803 and (more fully) [1994] 1 E.G.L.R. 76.
[107] The covenant is set out at para.4–28, below.
[108] [2000] 3 E.G.L.R. 41.
[109] [2000] 1 N.Z.L.R. 23
[110] [1911] 2 K.B. 905.
[111] [1924] 1 K.B. 716.

that on the particular facts the tenant was liable even if the words all meant the same thing. The dicta of French J. in *Halliard Property Co Ltd v Nicholas Clarke Investments Ltd*[112] and of Hoffmann J. in *Norwich Union Life Assurance Society Ltd v British Railways Board*[113] were intended to do no more than draw attention to the fact that in many cases it may not be possible to give a separate meaning to each word of the covenant. It is noteworthy that the actual decision in *Norwich Union* was that the additional words to be found in the covenant in question did have the effect of extending its meaning.[114]

In principle, it cannot be correct simply to classify the covenant as "a repairing covenant" and then to conclude that it must therefore have the precisely same legal effect as any other such covenant. If possible, effect must be given to each part of the covenant. In applying this, however, it is the "good sense of the agreement"[115] that must be found. The covenant "must not be strained, but reasonably construed, on the principle of 'give and take'."[116] In some, perhaps many, cases the right conclusion will be that the various expressions used in the covenant were intended to mean much the same thing. In others, it will be possible to construe different words as having either separate and distinct meanings or meanings which overlap but are not the same. Each case will turn on the particular wording of the covenant construed in the context of the lease as a whole and the relevant surrounding circumstances.

## Expressions qualifying the obligation to keep in repair

**4–23**     In some cases, the obligation will simply be to repair or keep in repair. However, it is more common to find that the obligation is to keep in "good" or "substantial" or "tenantable" repair or something similar. The extent to which such expressions add anything to the obligation to repair is considered in para.9–03 et seq., below.

## Additional operations

**4–24**     As noted above, repairing covenants are often drafted in a "torrential" style,[117] commonly requiring the covenantor not only to repair or keep in repair but also to undertake a variety of other associated operations. An example can be taken from *Anstruther-Gough-Calthorpe v McOscar*,[118] in which the tenant covenanted:

> "[W]ell and sufficiently repair support uphold maintain paint pave empty scour cleanse amend and keep [the demised premises] ... by and with all manner of needful and necessary reparations and amendments whatsoever."

---

[112] [1984] 1 E.G.L.R. 45.

[113] [1987] 2 E.G.L.R. 137.

[114] See para.4–25, below.

[115] *Nicholson v White* (1842) 4 Man. & G. 95, per Tindall C.J. at 98, cited with approval by Sachs L.J. in *Brew Bros Ltd v Snax (Ross) Ltd* [1970] Q.B. 612 at 641.

[116] *Scales v Laurence* (1860) 2 F. & F. 289.

[117] *Norwich Union Life Insurance Society Ltd v British Railways Board* [1987] 2 E.G.L.R. 137, per Hoffmann J. See para.4–19, above.

[118] [1924] 1 K.B. 716.

The extent to which extended wording of this kind imposes obligations over and above, or different to, the obligation to repair is a question of construction in each case. It is thought that the correct approach in general terms is set out in the following passage from the judgment of Blackburne J. in *Mason v TotalFinaElf UK Ltd*[119] as follows:

"In setting out [my] views, I have reminded myself that, although certain words or phrases, when used in repairing covenants, have come to have certain meanings, the question, at the end of the day, is what the particular words mean that appear in the particular lease with which the court is concerned, when construed against the other obligations contained in the lease, having regard to the general nature of the premises and any other material circumstances as they existed at the time when the lease was granted. I have also reminded myself that where, as here, the draftsman has employed a variety of closely related expressions ('uphold support maintain amend repair decorate and keep in good condition ...'), while I should not expect to give each word used a meaning distinct from the others, I should not assume that the draftsman was merely using different words to express the same concept. In short, I should endeavour, where the context allows, to give each word its proper meaning without striving to give each word a wholly distinct meaning."

In some cases, the right conclusion may be that the word in question adds very little, if anything, to the obligation to repair. For example, since an obligation to repair may require the covenantor to do more than merely reproduce what was there before,[120] the inclusion in the covenant of the word "amend" may not add anything to "repair". Thus, in *Jackson v JH Watson Property Investments*[121] the landlord covenanted:

"[W]ell and substantially to repair ... and maintain ... the exterior of the estate ... and the entrance ways paths and staircases main walls party walls roof foundations and all structural parts thereof ... with all necessary reparations and amendments whatsoever."

H.H. Judge Behrens rejected the tenant's argument the effect of the word "amendments" was that the covenant imposed a liability going beyond repair, saying that:

"[T]he context of the word 'amendments' is to my mind a reference to what has to be repaired and does not create a separate obligation different from the obligation to repair."

A further example is the inclusion in the covenant of the verb "renew". This is considered in paras 4–27 to 4–28, below.

In some cases, however, the relevant wording may impose a duty which overlaps with, but is not necessarily the same as, the obligation to repair. Examples are obligations to maintain,[122] to paint,[123] or to support.[124] In other cases, the wording may be argued to illuminate what the parties meant by the

---

[119] [2003] 3 E.G.L.R. 91.
[120] See for example para.11–36, below.
[121] [2008] 1 E.G.L.R. 33.
[122] See para.14–37, below.
[123] See Ch.15, below.
[124] See *Jacey Property Co v De Sousa* [2003] EWCA Civ 510, in which "support" in the context of a covenant to "maintain and repair the remainder of the Building and the nearby premises so as to provide support and shelter for the demised premises" was held to refer to physical support and not to support in any wider, non-physical, sense.

covenant when read as a whole. For example, where the issue concerns the extent to which the covenantor is liable for underpinning a substantial part of the premises,[125] the inclusion in the covenant of an obligation to "support" or "uphold" might enable the court to conclude that the parties intended such underpinning to be within the scope of the obligation taken as a whole. No hard and fast rule can be laid down: the right answer in any particular case will depend on the detailed facts.

## Obligations to rebuild reconstruct and replace

**4–25**  An obligation to repair will not ordinarily be construed as obliging the covenantor to rebuild the entire premises.[126] However, there is no reason why an express liability to rebuild cannot be imposed. If the words used are sufficiently clear, then they will be given effect, even if the obligation thereby imposed goes beyond ordinary notions of repair and extends to complete rebuilding or reconstructing. Nonetheless, such a covenant would be unusual, and if the language is not entirely clear, the covenant should not readily be assumed to impose unusual obligations.[127]

Thus, in *Norwich Union Life Assurance Co Ltd v British Railways Board*[128] a lease for a term of 150 years contained a tenant's covenant in the following terms:

> "To keep the demised premises in good and substantial repair and condition and when necessary to rebuild, reconstruct or replace the same and in such repair and condition to yield up the same at the expiration or sooner determination of the said lease."

An arbitrator appointed to determine a rent review held that the covenant imposed a more onerous obligation than the ordinary form of repairing covenant appearing in leases of comparable properties. He said:

> "While a covenant to repair would include the renewal or restoration of subordinate parts at various times when this became necessary during the continuance of the lease, it would not extend to rebuilding the whole. However, the words 'rebuild, reconstruct or replace' ... extend the lessees' liability, in my opinion, far beyond that contemplated in a covenant to keep the demised premises in good and substantial repair. To my mind, those words mean exactly what they say and place on the lessees an obligation to rebuild, reconstruct, and replace the demised premises in their entirety should this become necessary, and in a lease of 150 years' duration it is not inconceivable that it might indeed become necessary at some point in this time span no matter what the standard of construction of the original building might have been."

The landlord appealed against the arbitrator's decision, contending that the covenant imposed no greater obligation than the ordinary repairing covenant, the words "rebuild, reconstruct or replace" being confined to the rebuilding, reconstruction or replacement of subsidiary parts. Hoffmann J. rejected this

---

[125] See para.12–03, below.
[126] See Ch.11, below.
[127] *Norwich Union Life Assurance Society Ltd v British Railways Board* [1987] 2 E.G.L.R. 137, per Hoffmann J.
[128] Above.

argument, holding that on the proper construction of the covenant a liability beyond the ordinary meaning of "repair" had been imposed, and therefore that the arbitrator had been right.

A similar view was taken in *New England Properties Ltd v Portsmouth New Shops Ltd*,[129] in which leases of first floor offices forming part of a development contained covenants by the landlord to:

> "[K]eep and maintain or procure to be kept and maintained [the development] and in particular without prejudice to the generality of the foregoing its exterior and its structure … in good and substantial repair and condition and decoration and to renew or replace the same or any part or parts thereof whenever such renewal or replacement shall be necessary."

Mr T. Cullen QC, sitting as a deputy judge of the Chancery Division, held that the words "renew or replace" should be given their literal meaning.

Nonetheless, an obligation to rebuild will be construed narrowly, because it is a potentially onerous obligation. Thus, in *Gibson Investments Ltd v Chesterton Plc*[130] the tenant covenanted "at all times during the continuance of the term to keep in good and substantial repair and when appropriate to rebuild the whole of the demised premises and every part thereof … notwithstanding that any want of repair may be due to an inherent or latent defect in the demised premises or to normal wear and tear or deterioration or otherwise and if at any time … it shall be necessary for the purpose of complying with this covenant to rebuild the building or any part thereof forming part of the demised premises then the tenant shall … carry out such rebuilding". Neuberger J. said:

> "The covenant in the present case goes further than a normal repairing covenant … That the effect of these words enlarges the covenant beyond the normal repairing covenant is borne out by the decision of Hoffmann J. in *Norwich Union Life Insurance Society v. British Railways Board*. However, in my view the words I have just quoted should not be given any greater effect than they naturally bear. They give rise to what is, on the face of it at least, an onerous obligation, and they should therefore be given a relatively narrow meaning rather than a relatively wide meaning."

Express obligations to rebuild or replace which are included as part of the covenant to repair are often qualified by the words "if necessary" or something to that effect.[131] The effect of this will generally be to make it clear that the obligation only comes into effect where rebuilding or replacement is required in order to keep the premises in repair, i.e. where the standard of repair contemplated by the covenant[132] can only be achieved by rebuilding or replacement and not by lesser work. Thus, in the Scottish case of *Westbury Estates v The Royal Bank of Scotland*[133] the lease obliged the tenant to keep the demised premises in good and substantial repair and condition, and further provided that "…the Tenants' obligations shall extend to the maintenance, repair,

**4–26**

---

129 [1993] 1 E.G.L.R. 94.
130 [2002] 2 P. & C.R. 494.
131 See for example *Norwich Union Life Assurance Co Ltd v British Railways Board*, *New England Properties Ltd v Portsmouth New Shops Ltd* and *Gibson Investments Ltd v Chesterton Plc*, all of which are considered in para.4–25, above.
132 See Ch. 9, below.
133 [2006] CSOH 177 at [33].

renewal and if necessary replacement of all services within and external to but serving the Let Subjects". It was said that "In the context of the earlier words of the clause, 'if necessary' must mean 'if necessary so as to keep the subjects in good and substantial repair and condition'."

The point at which replacement will have become necessary is a matter of fact and degree. In the Australian case of *Greetings Oxford Koala Hotel Pty Ltd v Oxford Square Investments Pty Ltd*,[134] a lease of a hotel in a high-rise building contained a landlord's covenant to provide certain services, including "maintenance of lifts ... and replacement where required". Young J. construed "replacement when required" as meaning:

> "[W]hen the reasonable observer would be of the opinion that the stage had been reached that for the proper servicing of the building the lifts had reached such a stage that further patching was a waste of time, that it was appropriate for the lessor to replace the lifts."

## The inclusion of the verb "renew" as one of the verbs in the covenant

4–27    The verbs to be found in repairing covenants frequently include an obligation to renew in addition to the obligation to repair. The question sometimes arises as to whether the inclusion of this word obliges the covenantor to carry out works which go beyond what would ordinarily be required under a covenant simply to repair or keep in repair.

In *Collins v Flynn*,[135] the tenant covenanted "... well and substantially to repair, amend, renew, uphold, support, maintain ... [the demised premises]." It was argued that the inclusion of the word "renew" imported a liability going beyond the ordinary meaning of "repair", and obliged the tenant to construct new foundations. The judge rejected this contention, his reasoning being as follows:

> "Whilst I am most anxious to give effect to every word of the covenant, as Atkin L.J. insisted in *Anstruther-Gough-Calthorpe v. McOscar*,[136] yet every repair does involve a degree of renewal (except, perhaps, tightening a loose screw, as counsel for the tenant suggested). This was the opinion of Buckley L.J. in *Lurcott v. Wakely*[137] and I feel that I can give a separate meaning to the word 'renew' only by holding that it includes rebuilding the whole property demised; and I think that if this were intended, much stronger and more specific words would have to be used. However, this is of no importance, since I regard the word 'repair' as apt to cover the renewal of a part of the premises, and therefore, so far as the words of the covenant are concerned, I regard the obligation of the defendant lessee as being similar to that in the cases cited where only the word 'repair' is used."

In other words, since the operation of repair can include the renewal of subsidiary parts, the word "renew" added nothing to the meaning of repair. However, if one applies the rule that each expression used in the covenant should, if possible, be given effect, then this reasoning ought to have led the judge to precisely the opposite conclusion.

---

[134] (1989) 18 N.S.W.L.R. 33.
[135] [1963] 2 All E.R. 1068.
[136] [1924] 1 K.B. 716.
[137] [1911] 1 K.B. 905.

A different conclusion on different words was reached by Lindsay J. in *Credit* **4–28**
*Suisse v Beegas Nominees Ltd.*[138] That case concerned a lease of office premises
which contained the following landlord's covenant:

> "[T]o maintain repair amend renew cleanse repaint and redecorate and otherwise keep in good
> and tenantable condition:
> 1.     The structure of the building and in particular the roof foundations and walls thereof…
>        Provided that the landlord shall not be liable to the tenant for any defect or want of repair
> hereinbefore mentioned unless the landlord has had notice thereof."

The entirety of the cladding to the building required to be removed and
replaced with a new and redesigned system. The judge's primary holding was that
this fell within the obligation to keep the premises in good and tenantable
condition.[139] However, he went on to consider whether such work fell within the
remainder of the covenant. He said:

> "As Fletcher Moulton L.J. emphasises in *Lurcott v Wakely* [1911] 1 K.B. 905 at 915, the duty of
> the court is to give a proper and full effect to each word used in repairing covenants. Atkin L.J.
> endorsed this approach in *Anstruther-Gough-Calthorpe v McOscar* [1924] 1 K.B. 716 at 731.
> I see the verbs 'amend' and 'renew' as capable of going outside the verb 'repair', especially
> where, as here, the use of the phrase 'defects *or* wants of repair' [judge's emphasis] in the
> proviso to the principal covenant shows that some meaning beyond repair is contemplated."

Having held that the work went beyond "repair", he continued as follows:

> "However, I would think it right to describe such remedial work as a 'renewal' and within the
> obligation to 'repair amend renew' in the [covenant], again bearing in mind that the proviso,
> by its reference to 'defects or want of repair' indicates a possibility of liability beyond mere
> repair. In a covenant which appears to go beyond mere repair and which, in so doing, refers to
> renewal, 'renewal' can be taken to embrace reconstruction even of the entirety of the subject
> matter of the covenant—see Buckley L.J. in: [*Lurcott v Wakely*[140]]. I do not see it as a
> necessary part of a renewal (in contrast with a restoration) that the new should be exactly as
> was the old, particularly where the old had proved defective. The fact that the new cladding
> will be to a different design does not, in my view, deny it the description of being a renewal.
> On this basis, whether I am right or wrong as to the total recladding being outside 'repair', I
> find it within the obligation to 'amend, renew'. I am conscious of the argument that if 'renew'
> is to be given a separate meaning beyond 'repair' then there is probably no stopping point
> short of its ability to require the rebuilding of the whole subject matter of the covenant—see
> *Collins v Flynn*. However, the landlord in a case such as the present would be likely to have
> wished that and the tenant, whilst recognising the size of the potential burden on him,[141] could
> well have thought, in relation to a new architect-designed building thought to have been
> completed to a high specification, that the likelihood of the burden actually turning into a
> present liability during the 25 years of the underlease was so remote as to be discounted. Thus
> if the word 'renew', in a context plainly going beyond repair, can properly extend, as I believe
> it can, as far as total replacement of the subject matter to which it relates, then I see no good
> reason why it should not here do so. If it is asserted that clear words would be needed for such
> a conclusion I would say that in a context, as here, where 'defects' are within the covenant as
> alternatives to 'repairs', the words 'amend' and 'renew' are clear enough."

It is clear from the above that the wording of the proviso to the covenant
played a substantial part in the judge's reasoning. But where there is no separate

---

[138] [1994] 4 All E.R. 803 and (more fully) [1994] 1 E.G.L.R. 76.
[139] See para.4–27, below.
[140] [1911] 2 K.B. 905.
[141] i.e. the potential service charge burden.

context indicating that something more than repair is contemplated, then it is thought that "renew" is likely to be construed as it was in *Collins v Flynn*,[142] i.e. as adding nothing to the obligation to repair. Thus, in *Ultraworth Ltd v General Accident Fire & Life Assurance Co Ltd*[143] Judge Havery QC said of a covenant "well and substantially to repair cleanse and keep in good and substantial repair and condition the demised premises" that:

> "I do not consider that the presence or absence of a reference to renewal makes any significant difference in this case: the covenant is an ordinary covenant to repair the whole premises, of which the [air-conditioning] system in question is a part, albeit an important part."

Likewise, in *Janet Reger International v Tiree*,[144] which concerned a covenant on the part of the landlord to "use reasonable endeavours to maintain, repair and renew the structure", Mr Terence Mowschenson QC (sitting as a deputy judge of the Chancery Division) thought (citing *Collins v Flynn* and paras 4–25 and 4–26 of the Third Edition of this work) that: "The expression 'renew' adds little to the expression 'repair'".

In the Scottish case of *Co-operative Insurance Society Ltd v Fife Council*,[145] a 25-year lease of an office building expressly included within the demise "the whole of the external walls and roofs within which the said offices and others are contained". The tenant covenanted "to repair and keep in good and substantial repair and maintained, renewed and cleansed in every respect all to the satisfaction of the Landlords" the demised premises. The landlord argued, relying on the inclusion of the word "renewed" and the description of the demised premises as including the whole of the exterior, that the tenant was liable not only for "ordinary repairs", for which a tenant would ordinarily be liable under Scots common law but also for "extraordinary repairs", for which a landlord would ordinarily be liable.[146] Lord Glennie said:

> "That wording does not, in my opinion, go beyond the common law position. There is in fact no express obligation to renew—so even if [counsel] is correct as to the potential significance of such an obligation, it is not there in this lease. On the contrary, in my view, the description 'maintained, renewed and cleansed' is subordinate to the general purpose of the clause, descriptive of the good and substantial repair in which the subjects are to be kept. As part of the obligation to repair, and in particular the obligation to keep in good and substantial repair, which obligation I accept may go further than the bare obligation to repair (see per Lord Mackay of Drumadoon in *West Castle Properties Ltd v Scottish Ministers* 2004 SCLR 899 at para.[21]), the tenants may be obliged to renew certain elements in the structure, or in the machinery which forms part of the building, but that is as part of the repairing obligation and goes not further than that repairing obligation."

---

[142] [1963] 2 All E.R. 1068.

[143] [2000] 2 E.G.L.R. 115.

[144] [2006] 3 E.G.L.R. 131.

[145] [2011] CSOH 76.

[146] The distinction between "ordinary repairs" and "extraordinary repairs" does not exist in English law. Scots law does not lay down any universally applicable formula for distinguishing between them, but the main considerations to be taken into account are (i) the origin of the damage, and in particular whether it was caused by a fortuitous event outside the control of either party or the decay through lapse of time (which would point to its being an "extraordinary repair") as opposed to the ordinary effects of bad weather; (ii) the extent and seriousness of the damage and the likely cost of repairs; and (iii) the nature of the damage and the necessary repair, and in particular whether it amounts to total reconstruction: see Lord Glennie's Opinion at [18].

## Obligations to keep in good or tenantable condition

Covenants to repair sometimes include, in addition to an obligation to repair and keep in repair, a further obligation to keep the premises in good or tenantable condition. As a matter of language such an obligation may be distinguished from the obligation to repair on the ground that the emphasis is on the state in which the premises are to be kept rather than the operation to be performed upon them. Such a covenant may thus be argued to require whatever work is necessary to keep the premises in the specified state, whether or not that work is "repair" strictly so-called. Fletcher Moulton L.J. pointed this out in *Lurcott v Wakeley*[147] when considering a covenant to "well and substantially repair … and keep in thorough repair and good condition" the demised premises, which he treated as imposing three separate covenants:

4–29

> "If [the lessee] chooses to undertake to keep in good condition an old house, he is bound to do it, whatever be the means necessary for him to employ in so doing … the covenant to keep in good condition … is entirely free from any consideration of the means that have to be employed by the lessee to do the work. The duty undertaken is expressed in clear language and must be performed … I think that to keep in thorough repair does not in any way confine the duty of the person who is liable under the covenant to the doing of what are ordinarily called repairs. A house is spoken of as being in thorough repair when it is a house to which no repairs have to be done. But it is a description of a state and not of a mode by which that state has been arrived at, and therefore, in my own mind I draw no wide distinction between keeping in thorough repair and keeping in good condition; they both appear to me to describe the condition of the house. What a surveyor would call in good condition and what a surveyor would call in thorough repair may differ somewhat, but they would be something very like, the one to the other. As I have said, the legal obligation is to keep the house in that state, and I confess that I do not think that from the legal point of view there is much difference between the nature of the two obligations … [The covenant to repair] is a duty to perform an operation. No doubt, if you thoroughly repair, it will put the house in a good condition and in a state of thorough repair. But it is plain that the word 'repair' refers to the operation to which the defendants bind themselves to have recourse."

This approach distinguishes between, on the one hand, keeping the premises in a particular state, namely thorough repair and good condition, and on the other, performing the operation of repair.[148] This distinction formed no part of the reasoning of either Cozens-Hardy M.R. or Buckley L.J. in the same case, both of whom proceeded on the implicit assumption that the three limbs of the covenant all meant much the same thing. It was, however, cited and applied by the Court of Appeal in *Smedley v Chumley & Hawke Ltd*,[149] which concerned a covenant to "keep the main walls and roof" of a restaurant "in good structural repair and condition throughout the term and to promptly make good all defects due to faulty materials or workmanship in the construction of the premises".[150]

---

[147] [1911] 1 K.B. 905.

[148] It is to be noted, however, that Fletcher-Moulton L.J. did not think there was any real difference between a state of thorough repair and a state of good condition.

[149] (1981) 44 P. & C.R. 50. This case is considered further in para.11–21, below.

[150] See also *Bowman v Stanford* [1950] 2 S.A. (E.D.L.D.) (obligation "to keep in repair" different from an obligation "to repair", since "repair" in the former denotes a state whether resulting from repairing or from renewing).

In *Credit Suisse v Beegas Nominees Ltd*[151] Lindsay J. treated the relevant part of the covenant in that case[152] as imposing a separate obligation to keep the subject matter in good and tenantable condition, which gave rise to a liability going beyond repair. He said:

> "As Fletcher Moulton L.J. emphasises in *Lurcott v Wakely* [1911] 1 K.B. 905 at 915, the duty of the court is to give a proper and full effect to each word used in repairing covenants. Atkin L.J. endorsed this approach in *Anstruther-Gough-Calthorpe v McOscar* [1924] 1 K.B. 716 at 731 ... [H]aving regard to that phrase in the proviso,[153] I see the words 'otherwise to keep in good and tenantable condition' as having a potential going beyond repairs strictly so-called (by which I mean works of a kind which would fall within a covenant merely 'to repair').[154]"

He held that the complete removal of the cladding system of an office building and its replacement with a new and redesigned system was not within the landlord's liability "to repair" but was within the obligation to keep in good and tenantable condition.

**4–30**  In *Welsh v Greenwich LBC*[155] the Court of Appeal construed a landlord's obligation in a local authority letting "to maintain the dwelling in good condition and repair except for such items as are the responsibility of the tenant" as imposing a liability conceptually different from repair. Robert Walker L.J. said in his judgment that:

> "[T]he reference to 'good condition' in [the clause] is intended to mark a separate concept and to make a significant addition to what is conveyed by the word 'repair'."

Latham L.J. regarded "good condition" as:

> "[I]ntended to be treated as a separate concept from the word 'repair', even though there may be overlap. As far as the phrase 'good condition' is concerned, it seems to me to concentrate the mind on the state of the dwelling, whereas 'repair' is looking at the matter more from the perspective of the need to do particular repairing work.
> ...this is a contract between a local authority, as the provider of social housing, and a tenant in circumstances where one would not expect the tenant to be taking legal advice. I therefore consider that such a term [i.e. 'good condition'] should be approached on the basis that one should, so far as possible, give to it the meaning which the ordinary person in the street would accept as being the sensible construction of the phrase."

The landlord's argument that, having regard to the terms of the tenancy as a whole (which included an obligation on the part of the tenant to "carry out those minor repairs which are the tenant's responsibility and to keep the dwelling clean, in good condition and to prevent damage"), the words "good condition" meant "good structural condition" was rejected.

In *Fluor Daniel Properties Ltd v Shortlands Investments Ltd*[156] Blackburne J. had to consider a covenant which required the landlord to "uphold maintain

---

[151] [1994] 4 All E.R. 803 and (more fully) [1994] 1 E.G.L.R. 78.
[152] The covenant is set out in para.4–28, above.
[153] See para.4–28, above.
[154] It was said in *Welsh v Greenwich LBC* [2000] 3 E.G.L.R. 41 that the inclusion in the covenant of the word "otherwise" formed a significant part of the judge's reasoning.
[155] [2000] 3 E.G.L.R. 41.
[156] [2001] 2 E.G.L.R. 103.

repair amend renew cleanse and redecorate and otherwise keep in good and substantial condition and as the case may be in good working order and repair" various parts of a multi-occupied office building and its plant. He held (following *Credit Suisse v Beegas Nominees Ltd*[157]) that such a covenant "extends to the doing of works that go beyond repair strictly so-called". However, he accepted the tenant's submission that (i) the obligations presupposed that the item in question suffered from some defect (i.e. some physical damage or deterioration, or, in the case of plant, some malfunctioning) such that repair, amendment or renewal is reasonably necessary, and (ii) the condition of the item in question had to be such as to be no longer reasonably acceptable, having regard to the age, character and locality of the premises, to a reasonably minded tenant of the class likely to take a lease of the building. He expressed the same views in relation to a similarly worded covenant in *Mason v TotalFinaElf UK Ltd*.[158]

In the Scottish case of *Westbury Estates v The Royal Bank of Scotland*[159] Lord Reed said in his judgment:

"Like Fletcher Moulton LJ in *Lurcott v. Wakely* and the Court of Appeal in *Smedley v. Chumley & Hawke Ltd*, I am doubtful whether the words 'and condition', in the phrase 'good and substantial repair and condition', introduce a different concept from that of 'good and substantial repair': cases in which a contrary view has been taken, such as *Crédit Suisse v. Beegas Nominees Ltd* and *Welsh v. Greenwich LBC*, appear to me to depend on their particular circumstances (notably, the specific terms of the provision in the former case, and the context of the lease in the latter case). That issue does not however appear to me to be of critical importance to the question with which I am concerned: on either view, the obligation is concerned with the physical condition of the subjects, including the items in question, and requires that the physical condition of the subjects be maintained to a given standard. In order for the obligation to be triggered, the physical condition of the subjects must therefore fall short of the requisite standard."

In *Carmel Southend v Strachan & Henshaw*,[160] in which the relevant covenant was "to repair and keep in good and substantial repair and condition the demised premises", H.H. Judge Coulson QC set out in his judgment a summary of the relevant principles which included the following:

"An obligation to keep in good and substantial repair *and condition* [emphasis added] is different and more extensive than an obligation merely to repair: see *Welsh v. Greenwich LBC*. This may be wide enough to require the tenant put the property into that condition even if it had never been in such condition before: see *Credit Suisse v. Beegas Nominees*. However, on that point, I accept [counsel's] submission, on behalf of [the tenant], that arguments about the difference, if any, made by the inclusion of the word 'condition' in covenants of this type have tended to arise in circumstances where there is a challenge by the tenant to the scope of the works proposed or carried out by the landlord; where the tenant suggests that such works are so extensive that they have gone beyond mere repair."

Although the above cases were concerned with whether an obligation to keep in good condition imposes a liability going beyond repair, such obligation may in some circumstances may be construed as imposing a liability less than repair.

---

[157] [1994] 4 All E.R. 803 and (more fully) [1994] 1 E.G.L.R. 78.
[158] [2003] 3 E.G.L.R. 91.
[159] [2006] CSOH 177. This case is further considered in para.13–06, below, where the relevant covenant is set out.
[160] [2007] 2 E.G.L.R. 15.

Thus, in *Firstcross Ltd v Teasdale*[161] McNair J. construed a tenant's obligation in a tenancy of a furnished flat for a term of three months or less to "keep the flat and the said fixtures fittings appurtenances and items at all times in good and tenantable condition throughout the said term (allowing only for reasonable use thereof and damage by accidental fire)" as imposing on the tenant no more than an obligation to use the flat in a tenant-like manner.[162]

Accordingly, depending on the precise words used and the relevant context, a covenant which imposes or includes an obligation to keep premises in good condition may be held to impose a different liability (either more or less extensive) than a covenant to repair or keep in repair. Such covenants are further considered in Chs 9 and 11, below.

## Obligations to remedy defects in the construction or design of the premises

**4–31**
As a general rule, a covenant to repair will not be construed as requiring the covenantor to remedy defects in the design or construction of the premises before those defects have caused any physical damage.[163] However, there is no reason why the parties cannot, if they choose, expressly impose a duty to remedy such defects, although an obligation of this kind is not one which a tenant under a commercial lease might reasonably be expected to undertake, and clear words are needed before it will be held to have been imposed.[164] The position is different once the design or construction defect has resulted in physical damage to the subject matter of the repairing covenant. The covenantor may then be liable both to remedy the damage and to eliminate the defect which gave rise to it.[165] The position may also be different where the covenant imposes or includes an obligation to keep in good condition.[166]

## The impact of other parts of the lease

**4–32**
Most leases generally contain a number of provisions dealing with the carrying out of work, in addition to the repairing covenant itself. These commonly include: a covenant against alterations and additions; service charge provisions; and provisions dealing with rebuilding or reinstatement in the event of destruction or damage by insured risks. By virtue of the principle that a contract must be construed as a whole,[167] these will be of relevance in construing the repairing covenant. However, the extent to which they will affect what would otherwise be its ordinary meaning will depend on the circumstances of each particular lease. The right conclusion will often be that of Lindsay J. in *Credit Suisse v Beegas*

---

[161] [1983] 1 E.G.L.R. 87.
[162] See further para.21–03, below.
[163] See paras 8–01 to 8–04, below.
[164] *Post Office v Aquarius Properties Ltd* [1987] 1 All E.R. 1055, per Slade L.J. at 1066a.
[165] See Ch.10, below.
[166] See paras 4–29 to 4–30, above, and paras 8–12 et seq. and 11–46, below.
[167] See para.4–12, above.

*Nominees Ltd*,[168] where he said in relation to an argument that the meaning of the covenant to repair was affected by the wording of the landlord's right of entry:

> "The lease is over 45 pages of single-spaced typescript and I am far from confident that its draughtsmanship is of a quality such that one can derive very much from this sort of exercise, which requires a contrast to be made between references, for example, on page 12, with those some 30 pages or so later."

Thus, in *Norwich Union Life Insurance Society Ltd v British Railways Board*[169] Hoffmann J. held that a suggested contrast between the wording of the covenant to repair and the insurance provisions did not lead to any difference in what would otherwise be the ordinary meaning of the former. Similarly, in *Roper v Prudential Assurance Co Ltd*[170] Mr Evans-Lombe QC, sitting as a deputy judge of the Queen's Bench Division, held that the presence elsewhere in the lease of the word "replace" did not require the word "repair" in the repairing covenant to be given a special meaning.

## The construction of landlord's covenants

Landlord's covenants to repair are often framed in the same or similar terms as tenant's covenants. In principle, similar words will have a similar effect whether they appear in a landlord's or a tenant's covenant.[171] However, there may be cases where the surrounding circumstances will compel a landlord's covenant to be construed differently from a tenant's covenant expressed in the same terms. The difference in the respective interests of landlord and tenant may, depending on the facts, be a relevant factor in deciding whether particular work is work of repair within the covenant.[172] Thus, a landlord's covenant to repair the only lift in a 10-storey block of flats intended to be occupied by retired people may be construed as imposing an obligation to carry out more extensive work than would identical words in a tenant's covenant in an office building. Further examples are the cases dealing with the extent to which a repairing covenant may require the installation of a damp proof course[173]: thus, in *Eyre v McCracken*[174] a tenant was held not liable to install a damp proof course, whereas the contrary conclusion was reached in relation to a landlord in *Elmcroft Developments Ltd v Tankersley-Sawyer*.[175]

In many cases the landlord will be able to recover the cost of complying with his covenant by way of service charge. In such a case, his covenant to repair is not only an obligation but also a right, since it enables him to keep his property in

4–33

---

[168] [1994] 4 All E.R. 803 and (more fully) [1994] 1 E.G.L.R. 76.

[169] [1987] 2 E.G.L.R. 137.

[170] [1992] 1 E.G.L.R. 5.

[171] *Torrens v Walker* [1906] 2 Ch. 166; *Pembery v Lamdin* [1940] 2 All E.R. 434; *Credit Suisse v Beegas Nominees Ltd*, [1994] 4 All E.R. 803 and (more fully) [1994] 1 E.G.L.R. 76.

[172] See, for example, *R. (on the application of Sinclair Gardens Investments (Kensington) Ltd) v Lands Tribunal* [2006] 3 All E.R. 650 per Neuberger L.J. at [64].

[173] See further Ch.12, below.

[174] (2000) 80 P. & C.R. 220.

[175] [1984] 1 E.G.L.R. 47.

repair at the expense of the tenants.[176] The fact that the cost of work carried out by the landlord will be recoverable from the tenant by way of service charge must be borne in mind but is not of sufficient force to affect the ordinary meaning of words.[177] Nonetheless, in deciding whether particular work constitutes repair, it is relevant to consider at whose expense the proposed remedial work is to be done.[178] It follows that where there are several different ways of remedying a particular defect, the fact that one scheme will result in the tenants paying a greater service charge than another may be relevant in considering either whether that scheme falls within the landlord's obligation at all, or if it does, whether the cost is recoverable by way of service charge.[179]

## Conditions precedent to the performance of landlord's covenants

4–34    The performance of landlord's covenants is sometimes made subject to a condition precedent. One form of condition which is sometimes found is a provision that the landlord is not to be liable in respect of a defect until he has had notice of it.[180] Where the subject-matter of the covenant is not within the landlord's possession or control this will be implied in any event,[181] but where the landlord has retained possession or control of the relevant subject-matter, his liability would not depend on notice in the absence of a provision along these lines.[182] An entitlement to notice as a pre-condition of liability may be waived.[183]

Long leases of residential property sometimes contain provisions to the effect that performance of the landlord's covenant to repair is subject to payment by the tenant of service charges. The question in such cases is whether payment of service charges is a condition precedent to liability to repair, or whether the relevant words are intended to do no more than emphasise that the tenant will be liable to contribute to the cost of repairs by way of service charge. A provision of this type was considered by the Court of Appeal in *Yorkbrook Investments Ltd v Batten*.[184] A long lease of a flat in a multi-occupied block contained obligations on the part of the lessor to repair and obligations on the part of the tenant to contribute to the cost of such works through the service charge. The lessor's obligations were introduced by the following words:

"The lessor hereby further covenants with the lessee that subject to the lessee paying the Maintenance Contribution pursuant to the obligations under clause 4 hereof the lessor will…"

---

[176] *Plough Investments Ltd v Manchester City Council* [1989] 1 E.G.L.R. 244; *Credit Suisse v Beegas Nominees Ltd* [1994] 4 All E.R. 803 and (more fully) [1994] 1 E.G.L.R. 76.
[177] *Credit Suisse v Beegas Nominees Ltd* [1994] 4 All E.R. 803 and (more fully) [1994] 1 E.G.L.R. 76.
[178] *Holding & Management Ltd v Property Holding & Investment Trust Ltd* [1990] 1 E.G.L.R. 65 (not reported on this point at [1989] 1 W.L.R. 1313). The relevant passage is set out in para.11–13, below.
[179] See further paras 10–06 to 10–10, below.
[180] See, for example, the form of covenant in *Credit Suisse v Beegas Nominees Ltd*, above.
[181] See para.22–03, below.
[182] See para.22–16, below.
[183] *Princes House v Distinctive Clubs* [2007] 2 E.G.L.R. 75.
[184] [1985] 2 E.G.L.R. 100.

It was argued on behalf of the lessor that this introduced a condition precedent to its liability, with the result (so it was argued) that:

> "[I]f at any time the tenant is in breach of that condition he is for such period as he is in breach debarred from claiming damages in respect of a breach by the (lessor) of the covenants within that clause."

The Court of Appeal held that payment of the maintenance contribution was not a condition precedent to the liability of the lessor to perform its covenant. One of its principal reasons for reaching that conclusion was that if the contrary were the case, the landlord would cease to be liable to provide any services even where the tenant's failure to pay was not culpable.

In *Bluestorm Ltd v Portvale Holdings Ltd*[185] the tenant of a number of flats in a 12-storey block claimed damages from the landlord for disrepair. The reason why the relevant works had not been done was because of the failure of the tenant (when the previous landlord) to carry them out and then (on becoming tenant) to pay for them. The lease contained the following landlord's covenant:

**4–35**

> "That the Lessor will (subject to the receipt by the Lessor of the Maintenance Contribution from the Tenant) throughout the term hereby granted provide and carry out or procure the provision and carrying out of the purposes particulars of which are set out in the Sixth Schedule."

The landlord argued, seeking to distinguish *Yorkbrook*, that it was not liable to perform its covenants because the tenant had failed to pay its service charges. The Court of Appeal dismissed the tenant's appeal on another ground, so that it did not strictly have to consider that argument. Nonetheless, both Buxton L.J. and Sir Martin Nourse would have been prepared to distinguish *Yorkbrook* had the point arisen for decision. Buxton L.J. thought that the wording "would plainly seem to mean that the lessor is under no liability if the tenant does not pay". He went on to say:

> "[Counsel for the tenant] suggested that a construction such as was rejected by the court in *Yorkbrook* would lead to the wholly unreasonable results that no parties could have intended: for instance, if a tenant was one day late with is payment by accident, or alternatively was temporarily unable to pay, his lights or heat might be arbitrarily cut off by the landlord. I see the force of that contention, but the difficulty may have arisen … from the court in *Yorkbrook* being asked to construe the proviso as a condition precedent. One can understand the court's reluctance to accept that view of these words. If they were so construed, then they would have the all or nothing (if I may use the expression, he did not, 'blockbuster') effect that [counsel] suggested. But I doubt whether it is an acceptable alternative to that extreme case to say at the other extreme that the clause must necessarily therefore have, and be given, no meaning at all. I think that it may well be an acceptable approach to a provision such as that under consideration to say that it deprives the non-payer of the right to complain of the landlord's breach when there is a direct connection between the non-payment and the breach. Thus, some, but not all, and probably not very many, defaults in payment would disqualify action by the tenant. Applying that view of it, the single tenant with a genuine grievance in *Yorkbrook* would not be so disqualified. On the other hand a tenant such as [the tenant in that case], refusing to pay for the reasons that it did, would be."

Sir Martin Nourse agreed:

---

[185] [2004] 2 E.G.L.R. 38.

"Clearly, [the words] were not intended to bring [the landlord's liability] altogether to an end in the event of the tenant's failure or neglect to pay a single instalment of the maintenance contribution. At the other extreme, it would offend all conventional principles of construction to give them no effect at all...

...The lessor is under a continuing obligation to provide and carry out, or procure the provision and carrying out, of the purposes specified. The tenant is under a continuing obligation to pay the maintenance charge which is the product thereof. The purpose of the words 'subject to the receipt by the lessor of the maintenance contribution from the tenant' is to forge a particular link between the one obligation and the other and to provide that the tenant is not to be able to claim the benefit of the lessor's obligation if and so long as he does not discharge the burden of his own.

It may be—I express no view—that the lessor would not be able to disclaim liability under his obligation where a tenant was substantially in arrears with his maintenance contribution but nevertheless recognised his obligation to pay it. That is not this case. Here ... [the tenant] evinced the clear intention that neither he nor his companies would pay a penny more towards the costs of the building, either as leaseholders or as freeholders."

In *Earle v Charalambous*[186] the landlord's repairing obligation in a long lease of a flat was expressed to be "subject to contribution and payment by the lessee as hereinbefore provided". Carnwath L.J. commented (without referring to authority) that the precise effect of the qualification was "open to debate".

It is not easy to see any distinction of substance between the relevant wording in *Yorkbrook* and that in *Bluestorm*. In both cases, the words on their ordinary and natural meaning made the performance of the landlord's obligations conditional upon the tenant paying service charges. To this extent, it is thought that the reasoning in *Bluestorm* is to be preferred. As was recognised in both cases, however, the problem is that if the words are read literally the tenant loses the right to enforce the landlord's covenants the moment he fails to pay and irrespective of the reasons for that failure. The solution suggested in *Bluestorm* (that only certain types of failure have the effect of releasing the landlord from liability to perform) has much to commend it in terms of fairness. It may be thought, however, that it is not easy to extract from the words used.

---

[186] [2007] H.L.R. 8.

# CHAPTER 5

# THE VARIETY OF OBLIGATIONS IMPOSING LIABILITY FOR DILAPIDATIONS

## INTRODUCTORY

Obligations imposing liability to remedy defects in the demised premises or the property of which they form part take a number of forms. By far the most common is a general obligation to repair or keep in repair, which may be expressed in a number of different ways. It is with obligations of this sort that this work is principally concerned. However, modern leases invariably contain other obligations of relevance to liability for dilapidations (for example, a covenant to decorate at periodic intervals), and other such obligations may sometimes be found in side letters or licences (for example, a covenant to reinstate permitted alterations). This Chapter summarises the various different forms of obligations to be found in practice and cross-references them to those parts of the text in which they are considered in detail.

**5–01**

## THE GENERAL COVENANT TO REPAIR

A general obligation to repair or keep in repair is to be found, in one form or another, in virtually all leases of commercial property and in most residential leases. It may be a straightforward obligation "to repair and keep in repair"; or the word "repair" may be qualified in some way (for example, "good and substantial repair"); or the obligation may take a more verbose form (for example, "to well and sufficiently repair support uphold maintain paint pave empty scour cleanse amend and keep the three several messuages and buildings … with all and all manner of needful and necessary reparations and amendments whatsoever …"[1]). The meaning and operation of the general covenant is considered in Chs 6 to 11, below (much of which is also relevant to the other forms of obligation referred to below). The application of the general covenant to repair to a variety of defects commonly encountered in buildings (such as subsidence and damp) is considered in Ch.12, below, and its application in relation to mechanical and electrical services and plants is dealt with in Ch.13, below.

**5–02**

The extent to which the use of particular qualifying words and additional expressions may affect or extend the meaning of the general covenant is dealt with in Ch.4, para.4–23 et seq., above, and in Ch.9, para.9–03 et seq., below.

---

[1] The form of covenant in *Anstruther-Gough-Calthorpe v McOscar* [1924] 1 K.B. 716, considered in para.4–20, above.

Depending on the circumstances, the general covenant may also impose an obligation not to destroy the subject matter of the covenant. This aspect is discussed in Ch.18, below, in which application of the general covenant to the after-effects of a fire or other disaster is also considered.

## THE COVENANT TO YIELD UP

5–03    Covenants to yield up usually operate by reference to the general covenant to repair (and sometimes by reference to other covenants imposing liability for dilapidations as well). They require separate treatment because they operate only at the end of, rather than during, the term. They are dealt with in Ch.14, below.

## OTHER OBLIGATIONS IMPOSING LIABILITY FOR DILAPIDATIONS

5–04    The general obligation to repair imposes a continuing duty to repair throughout the term. Variations on this are sometimes encountered, for example, an obligation to repair framed by reference to a schedule of condition; an obligation to put into a specified state of repair; an obligation to repair to the satisfaction of the landlord's surveyor; an obligation to expend a specified amount on repairs; an obligation to build and repair; and a repairing obligation subject to a precondition that the landlord should have carried out repairs or should have supplied certain materials (which is only rarely encountered these days). These forms of obligation are dealt with in Ch.14, below, which also deals with related forms of covenant, such as covenants to maintain and covenants to keep in good condition.

## COVENANTS TO REPAIR ON NOTICE AND IN DEFAULT TO PAY THE COST INCURRED BY THE LANDLORD IN CARRYING OUT THE WORKS

5–05    This form of covenant is virtually always to be found in modern commercial leases, and has assumed considerable importance following the decision of the Court of Appeal in *Jervis v Harris*.[2] It is considered in Chs 14 and 28, below.

## COVENANTS TO DECORATE

5–06    A limited obligation to paint is implicit in the general covenant to repair. Both this aspect of the covenant and express covenants to decorate are considered in Ch.15, below. The measure of damages for breach of a covenant to decorate is dealt with in paras 32–13 to 32–14, below.

---

[2] [1996] Ch. 195.

## COVENANTS TO REINSTATE ALTERATIONS

Obligations to reinstate alterations are sometimes found in the lease itself but more usually in a subsequent licence to alter. The form and effect of such obligations is considered in Ch.16, below. The measure of damages for breach is dealt with in Ch.32, paras 32–09 to 32–12, below. Enforceability of such obligations by and against successors in title to the original parties is covered in Ch.3, paras 3–29 to 3–30, above.

**5–07**

## COVENANTS TO COMPLY WITH STATUTES

Certain types of work (for example, in relation to fire precautions or health and safety) may fall outside the general covenant to repair or related covenants, but may be required under a covenant to comply with statutes. Such covenants are considered in summary form in Ch.17, below.

**5–08**

## COVENANTS TO REBUILD OR REINSTATE FOLLOWING A FIRE OR OTHER DISASTER

Most covenants to insure impose on the party insuring an express or implied obligation to reinstate the insured property following damage or destruction by fire or other insured event. Such covenants are not strictly part of the law of dilapidations, but are dealt with in Ch.18 below.

**5–09**

## COVENANTS RELATING TO PLANT, MACHINERY AND SERVICES

Special considerations apply to covenants relating to the condition of plant, machinery and services. These are dealt with in Ch.13, below.

**5–10**

## COVENANTS TO COMPLY WITH THE HEAD LEASE

Sub-leases often contain covenants on the part of either or both parties to comply with the repairing or other terms of the head lease or some of them. Such covenants are considered in Ch.24, below.

**5–11**

## COVENANTS RELATING TO FIXTURES

Fixtures are dealt with in Ch.25, below.

**5–12**

## IMPLIED OBLIGATIONS

Not all obligations relating to dilapidations take the form of express covenants. Some are left to be implied, particularly in relation to residential lettings. The general principles relating to implied terms have already been considered in Ch.1,

**5–13**

paras 1–03 to 1–08, above. Landlord's repairing and other obligations implied at common law and by statute are dealt with respectively in Chs 19 and 20, below. Implied obligations and duties of the tenant to the landlord, including the law of waste, are considered in Ch.21, below.

CHAPTER 6

# INTRODUCTION TO THE FIVE-PART ANALYSIS OF LIABILITY UNDER THE GENERAL COVENANT TO REPAIR

## THE FIVE-STAGE ANALYSIS

### Introductory

This Chapter and the following five chapters concern the general covenant to repair and keep in repair, to which reference has already been made above.[1] It introduces one of the central parts of this work, which is an analysis of liability under such covenants broken down into various separate stages. Much of it is of relevance to other types of covenant as well as the general covenant, but care may be needed in applying it to other types of obligation.

Such an analysis is necessary because, by reason of the great variety of ways in which practical problems concerning liability under the general covenant have come before the courts, the decided cases contain statements of principle framed in different ways, and with different emphasis. Fundamental to each case is one basic question: "Has there been a breach of the covenant?", but in seeking to answer this question in the context in which the cases have come before them, the courts have expressed the approach to be taken in a number of different ways. Some cases have fixed on the meaning of "repair", contrasting it with other concepts such as "renewal" or "improvement"; some on the nature and character of the works necessary to remedy the defect complained of, asking whether as a matter of fact and degree those works can properly be described as "repair" within the ambit of the covenant; some on the standard to which the covenant contemplated that the premises should be maintained; and some have contrasted "repair" with "disrepair", focusing on whether there is damage requiring to be remedied. Consequently, it is impossible to resolve by reference to any single statement of principle in the cases the question of liability under the general covenant to repair. This is, of course, not surprising given the many different factual situations in which that question falls to be answered in practice.

It is, however, possible to break down the question of liability into a number of separate questions, and to examine in relation to each question certain statements of principle derived from the cases. The next five chapters contain a five-stage analysis of liability, which is intended to eliminate the confusion which might characterise a more generalised approach to liability, and to elucidate, if not necessarily to solve, problems occurring in practice as to when liability exists. By

6–01

6–02

---

[1] See para.5–02, above.

setting out a series of questions to be asked and answered in a particular order, it is also intended to make sure that the practitioner does not inadvertently overlook any relevant matter.

However, it is necessary to emphasise two points. First, the five-part approach is intended to apply to the form of general covenant to repair and keep in repair commonly encountered in leases, so that care will need to be taken when considering other forms of obligation. Second, even the general covenant may include particular wording (for example, an obligation to rebuild or an obligation to keep in good condition[2]), or there may be particular background circumstances of relevance to the construction of the covenant, which will require a modified or different approach.

## The five-stage approach

6–03     The suggested five-stage approach requires the following questions to be asked and answered, in the following order.

### (1) What is the physical subject-matter of the covenant?

6–04     This part of the approach is directed to the inquiry that logically must come first, namely, the identification of the physical premises which the party giving the covenant has bound himself to repair. It is of relevance not only to the general covenant but also to all covenants imposing liability for dilapidations.

### (2) Is the subject-matter in a damaged or deteriorated condition?

6–05     Before any question of repair arises it must first be asked whether the premises are in disrepair. This involves asking whether there has been a deterioration from some previous physical state. If the answer is no, there has been no breach of covenant notwithstanding the fact that the premises may be unsuitable for occupation or use for some other reason.

### (3) Is the nature of the damage or deterioration such as to bring the condition of the subject-matter below the standard contemplated by the covenant?

6–06     Not every occasion of physical damage or deterioration will give rise to a liability under the covenant. It is necessary to ask whether such damage or deterioration results in the premises not being in the state and condition that the parties contemplated they should be in. This involves identifying the standard imposed by the covenant and comparing it with the actual state of the premises. Again, if the answer is no, there has been no breach.

---

[2] See generally para.4–25 et seq., above.

### (4) What work is required in order to put the subject-matter of the covenant into the contemplated condition?

Once it has been ascertained that the state of the premises falls below that required by the covenant, the next stage is to identify what work is required to put them into the required state. | **6–07**

### (5) Is that work nonetheless of such a nature that the parties did not contemplate that it would be the liability of the covenanting party?

The nature of the work identified as necessary may be such that it goes outside what the parties intended the covenantor to have to carry out. This "fact and degree test" is variously formulated in the authorities, which are discussed in Ch.11, below. | **6–08**

It should be noted that the five stages will not necessarily be entirely self-contained in every case. Depending on the facts, similar considerations may apply at more than one stage. In particular, the second, third, fourth and fifth stages may well overlap each other. | **6–09**

## Practical application of the analysis

In practice the answer to most of the five questions may be obvious, and the practitioner will be able to go straight to that part of the approach which is appropriate to the particular issues with which he is dealing, without having to consider the intervening stages in any detail. The approach has been designed with this in mind. It may, for example, be clear to what premises the covenant applies; that those premises are in disrepair to such an extent that they are not in the contemplated state; and precisely what remedial work is necessary. The only issue will then be as to whether that work is the liability of the covenanting party, and the practitioner can proceed straight to Ch.11, where the fifth question is discussed in detail. | **6–10**

# CHAPTER 7

# THE FIRST QUESTION: WHAT IS THE SUBJECT-MATTER OF THE COVENANT?

## INTRODUCTORY

The first logical step in any analysis of the obligation imposed by a repairing covenant is to identify the physical property which the party assuming the obligation has bound himself to repair. This may be the whole or a specified part or parts of the demised premises themselves; the building or buildings of which they form part; or adjacent or contiguous property. Identifying the property to which the repairing obligation is intended to apply is a question of construction of the covenant itself in the context of the lease as a whole and the relevant surrounding circumstances.[1] Ideally, the draftsman will have familiarised himself with the building and its constituent parts, clarified with his client or his client's surveyor precisely what parts are to form the subject matter of the obligation, and drafted the repairing covenant accordingly. In such a case, identifying the property to which the obligation is intended to apply is an easy task. In many cases, however, the draftsman will have used relatively general expressions, such as "structure" or "interior", which may give rise to difficulties when applied to specific parts of the building in dispute (for example, windows and window frames). In other cases, he may have used a standard precedent, which is unsuitable for use in relation to the particular building in question.[2] In such cases, identifying the intended subject matter may be considerably harder. This Chapter is concerned with the various ways in which repairing covenants commonly define their subject-matter.

**7–01**

---

[1] For the general principles applicable to the interpretation of contracts, see Ch.4, above. For a definitive treatment of the law relating to the identification of the subject matter of the contract, see Lewison, *The Interpretation of Contracts*, 5th edn (London: Sweet & Maxwell, 2011) Ch.11.

[2] A notorious example is the covenant in *Plough Investments Ltd v Manchester City Council* [1989] 1 E.G.L.R. 244, under which the landlord agreed to repair the "main timbers" of a steel-framed building, which Scott J. construed as a reference to the steel frame.

THE DEMISED PREMISES

## The subject matter of the obligation

**7–02**    It is common for the subject matter of the obligation to be framed simply as "the demised premises" or some similar formulation comprehending the totality of the premises let under the lease. Ascertaining the extent of the demised property is a matter of construction of the lease as a whole to see precisely what has been demised and what has been retained.

## Identifying the demised premises

**7–03**    The lease will normally contain some more or less general description of the demised premises. The words used will indicate, with a greater or lesser degree of precision, what is intended to be demised. Commonly, this will be any of the following:

(a)    a defined parcel of land;

(b)    a defined parcel of land with a description of the building erected on it;

(c)    a named or identified building with no express mention of the land on which it stands;

(d)    a specified part of a building, such as a floor of an office block or a flat in a block;

(e)    any of the foregoing, but elaborated with a statement that, for example, future buildings and additions, or landlord's or tenant's fixtures which come into existence from time to time, are to be included.

In accordance with established principles of construction,[3] the description of the demised premises in the lease must be read in the light of the document as a whole.[4] In *Strachey v Ramage*[5] Rimer L.J. said:

> "It is a statement of the obvious that the crucial provision in the conveyance was the parcels clause, since it was there that the parties identified the land being conveyed. It is, however, fundamental that the parcels clause in a conveyance should not be considered in isolation from the remainder of the document. It is a general, and basic, principle of the construction of documents that questions of interpretation should be answered by considering the document as a whole, since only then can the provision giving rise to the question be seen in its proper context. There can be no reason for this principle not to be equally applicable in relation to the interpretation of a conveyance for the purpose of identifying the limits of the land conveyed by it."

So, for example, the exceptions and reservations, the covenants dealing with the physical subject matter of the demise, such as those relating to repair, user and alterations, and any service charge provisions may all help to identify what was intended to be demised.

---

[3] See para.4–12, above.

[4] *Drake v Fripp* [2011] EWCA Civ 1279; *Brown v Pretot* [2011] EWCA Civ 1421.

[5] [2008] 2 P. & C.R. 8 at [29].

The description of the demised premises in the lease must also be read in the light of the objective facts reasonably available to the parties at the date of the lease.[6] So where the demised premises are described as "all those premises known as ...", extrinsic evidence is admissible to identify the premises so known.[7] As Danckwerts L.J. said in *Levermore v Jobey*[8]:

7–04

> "[I]t would be quite useless and wrong to construe a lease without reference to the premises with which the lease was dealing. A lease is not intended to be either a mental exercise or an essay in literature; it is a practical document dealing with a practical situation. Therefore it is right to look and see what is the property with which the document is dealing."

In *Pennock v Hodgson*,[9] Mummery L.J. said:

> "Looking at evidence of the actual and known physical condition of the relevant land at the date of the conveyance and having the attached plan in your hand on the spot when you do this are permitted as an exercise in construing the conveyance against the background of its surrounding circumstances. They include knowledge of the objective facts reasonably available to the parties at the relevant date. Although, in a sense, that approach takes the court outside the terms of the conveyance, it is part and parcel of the process of contextual construction."

Where the terms of the lease are clear and unambiguous, it is not permissible to have regard to extrinsic evidence to contradict them.[10] However, where the lease is unclear or ambiguous or inconsistent, regard must be had to the physical features on the ground at the time of the demise to enable a sensible conclusion to be reached as to what was intended to be demised. So where a conveyance did not clearly define the boundaries of the land to be conveyed, it was held that account had to be taken of the topographical features of the land at the time of the conveyance to determine the location of the boundary.[11] In an appropriate case, the admissible material to which regard may be had includes the way the land was used at the date of the transaction.[12] However, even where the title documents are unclear, it is wrong in principle to discard them entirely and rely on the physical features of the land alone.[13]

The exercise is an objective one. The question (in a vendor and purchaser context) has been said to be: what would the reasonable layman think he was buying?[14] Direct evidence of what the parties subjectively intended to demise is not admissible. The effect of the lease is not determined by evidence of what the parties to it believed it meant, but what, against the relevant objective factual

---

[6] *Pennock v Hodgson* [2010] EWCA Civ 873 at [13]; *Drake v Fripp* [2011] EWCA Civ 1279; *Dixon v Hodgson* [2011] EWCA Civ 1612; *Cameron v Boggiano* [2012] EWCA Civ 157; *Taylor v Lambert* [2012] EWCA Civ 3; *Wood v Hudson Industrial Services Ltd* [2012] EWCA Civ 599.

[7] *Freeguard v Rogers* [1999] 1 W.L.R. 375.

[8] [1956] 1 W.L.R. 697.

[9] See above.

[10] *Horn v Phillips* [2003] EWCA Civ 1877 at [9-13]; *Pennock v Hodgson*, above, at [12]; *Cameron v Boggiano* [2012] EWCA Civ 157 at [57]; *Taylor v Lambert* [2012] EWCA Civ 3 at [34].

[11] *Pennock v Hodgson*, above; *Cameron v Boggiano*, above; *Akhtar v Brewster* [2012] EWHC 3251 (Ch).

[12] *Wood v Hudson Industrial Services Ltd* [2012] EWCA Civ 599.

[13] *Dixon v Hodgson* [2011] EWCA Civ 1612; *Cameron v Boggiano* [2012] EWCA Civ 157 at [53].

[14] *Toplis v Green* [1992] E.G.C.S. 20; *Targett and Targett v Ferguson and Diver*, above.

background, they would reasonably have understood it to mean.[15] In *Hamble Parish Council v Haggard*[16] Millett J. said:

> "Neither the conveyance itself nor the plan attached to it enables the churchyard to be identified. Extrinsic evidence is therefore admissible to identify it. Such evidence does not include evidence of the parties' intentions and accordingly evidence of what was shown on the sale plan is not admissible for this purpose. The admissible evidence is restricted to evidence of the layout of the land and the use to which it was put and other similar evidence of the surrounding circumstances at the date of the conveyance. I have to put myself into the shoes of the notional judge visiting the site in 1984 with the conveyance in one hand and gazing about him in order to try to identify on the ground those features which would enable him to ascertain the extent of the churchyard and the whereabouts of the retained land lying between the churchyard and the green strip."

However it appears that, within limits, the court may look at the subsequent conduct of parties to a lease or conveyance in order to identify the subject matter of the intended grant.[17] In *Ali v Lane*[18] Carnwath L.J. (with whom Kay and Waller L.JJ. agreed), having referred to the much criticised decision of the Privy Council in *Watcham v Attorney General of East Africa Protectorate*[19] (in which it was held that evidence of use under an ambiguous instrument was admissible to show the sense in which parties used the relevant words), said as follows:

> "*Watcham* remains good law within the narrow limits of what it decided. In the context of a conveyance of land, where the information contained in the conveyance is unclear or ambiguous, it is permissible to have regard to extraneous evidence, including evidence of subsequent conduct, subject always to that evidence being of probative value in determining what the parties intended."

He went on to say that, in principle, reference to the intentions of the parties means the parties to the original conveyance and not their successors, unless perhaps there had been a long period of acceptance of a specific boundary by successive owners on both sides of it.

## Plans

7–05    The lease may or may not include a plan of the demised premises. If it does, then as a general rule, the plan can only be looked at as an aid to construing what has been demised if it is referred to in the lease. However, it has been held that, even in the absence of any such reference, a plan may nonetheless be looked at if (a) the words of description themselves are not clear, and (b) the plan physically forms part of the deed (for example, it is bound up with it, or drawn on it).[20]

The plan may be made definitive of the demise, as where (for example) the demised premises are said to be "more particularly delineated on the plan and thereon edged red". In such a case the verbal description gives way in the event

---

[15] *Pennock v Hodgson*, above, at [13].
[16] [1992] 4 All E.R. 147.
[17] *Ali v Lane* [2007] 1 P. & C.R. 26; *Haycocks v Nelville* [2007] 1 E.G.L.R. 78 at [30] and [31]; *Bradford v Keith James*, above, at [29]; *Akhtar v Brewster* [2012] EWHC 3251 (Ch).
[18] Above.
[19] [1919] A.C. 533.
[20] *Leachman v L&K Richardson Ltd* [1969] 1 W.L.R. 1129.

of any inconsistency between the two.[21] Where the parcels clause of a lease described the demised premises as "delineated on the plan annexed to these presents", it was held that the plan was intended to define the boundaries.[22] Where a plan which is intended as a defining document is unclear, it will be necessary to have regard to such inferences as may be drawn from topographical features which existed when the instrument was executed or other admissible extrinsic evidence.[23] In *Cameron v Boggiano*,[24] Rimer L.J., having referred to the deficiencies of the plan in question, said:

"... the court can, and in my view must, have regard to all admissible evidence with a view to elucidating the true sense of the transfer. Such evidence will not of course include the parties' prior negotiations or their expressed subjective intentions as to the land to be transferred. It will, however, include a consideration of the topography of the relevant land at the time of the transfer. Recourse can be had to such evidence not for the purpose of contradicting Plan A but for the purpose of elucidating the true sense of its uncertain elements, in particular the line of the northern boundary. The court's interpretation is ultimately guided by the answer that the reasonable man, armed with the relevant material, would give to the relevant question."

Alternatively, the plan may be stated to be "for the purposes of identification only". In that case, the words prevail over the plan.[25] A plan so described is intended to do no more than identify the position and situation of the land: it is specifically not intended to identify its precise boundaries.[26] Nonetheless, it may be looked at to elucidate the verbal description, although not to contradict it.[27] So, for example, in *Ravengate Estates v Horizon Housing Group*,[28] plans described as being "for the purposes of identification only" were taken into account by the Court of Appeal in deciding that the demise included certain disputed airspace.[29] However, the plan must be treated as subordinate where the description in the lease is clear and unambiguous, and it must be disregarded in the event of any

---

[21] *Eastwood v Ashton* [1915] A.C. 900; *Wallington v Townsend* [1939] 2 All E.R. 225; *Neilson v Poole* (1969) 20 P. & C.R. 909; *Kensington Pension Developments Ltd v Royal Garden Hotel (Oddenino's) Ltd* [1990] 2 E.G.L.R. 117; *Targett and Targett v Ferguson and Diver* (1996) 72 P. & C.R. 106; *Strachey v Ramage* [2008] 2 P. & C.R. 8 at [32]; *Network Rail Infrastructure v Freemont* [2013] EWHC 1733 (Ch).

[22] *Network Rail Infrastructure v Freemont*, above.

[23] *Jackson v Bishop* (1984) 48 P. & C.R. 57; *Cook v JD Wetherspoon* [2006] 2 P. & C.R. 18; *Bradford v Keith James* [2008] EWCA Civ 837; *Dixon v Hodgson* [2011] EWCA Civ 1612; *Cameron v Boggiano* [2012] EWCA Civ 157; *Taylor v Lambert* [2012] EWCA Civ 3.

[24] Above.

[25] *Webb v Nightingale* (1957) 169 E.G. 330; *Strachey v Ramage* [2008] 2 P. & C.R. 8 at [31].

[26] *Strachey v Ramage*, above, at [31].

[27] *Wigginton & Milner Ltd v Winster Engineering Ltd* [1978] 1 W.L.R. 1462; *Scott v Martin* [1987] 1 W.L.R. 841; *Hatfield v Moss* [1988] 2 E.G.L.R. 58; *Affleck v Shorefield Holidays Ltd* [1997] E.G.C.S. 159; *Targett and Targett v Ferguson and Diver*, above; *Ravengate Estates Ltd v Horizon Housing Group Ltd* [2007] EWCA Civ 1368; *Strachey v Ramage*, above, at [31–33]; *Akhtar v Brewster* [2012] EWHC 3251 (Ch).

[28] [2007] EWCA Civ 1368.

[29] See further on this case para.7–07, below.

inconsistency.[30] Where there is an inconsistency between the plan and the topographical features on the ground at the time of the lease, the latter may be held to prevail.[31]

In *Neilson v Poole*[32] the premises intended to be conveyed were described as being "for the purposes of identification only more particularly delineated on the plan drawn hereon". Megarry J. held that the use of the two forms of expression tended to be mutually stultifying but certainly did not give the plan any predominance over the parcels. In *Druce v Druce*[33] Arden L.J. said that where both expressions are used:

> "[I]t is a question of interpretation of the conveyance whether the plan prevails over the verbal description in the conveyance itself. Thus, it seems to me that in most cases the likely construction is that the verbal description is to prevail. It is because the combination that I have given is absolutely clear by the inclusion of the word 'only' that the plan is for the sole purpose of enabling the parties or the court to identify the property."

Where the lease is registered, the boundary as shown on the land registry plan is a general boundary unless it is shown on the register as determined under s.60 of the Land Registration Act 2002.[34] A general boundary does not determine the exact line of the boundary,[35] so that the register is not definitive of whether the boundary includes (for example) the whole or part of an outside wall.

## Subsoil

7–06    The extent to which the lease includes the subsoil or strata below the surface of the demised land is a matter of construction. The starting point is the maxim *cuius est solum, eius est usque ad coelum et ad inferos*, meaning that the owner of land is presumed to own everything up to the sky and down to the centre of the earth. In *Grigsby v Melville*[36] (in which it was held that that a conveyance of "All that dwelling-house ..." included a cellar immediately beneath the house even though it could be reached only from the former owner's adjoining house) James L.J. described it as a "fundamental proposition" that:

> " ... a conveyance of land includes, unless the conveyance is to be construed to the contrary, everything beneath the surface of the land conveyed and the space directly above ... "

The presumption was recently considered by the Supreme Court in *Bocardo SA v Star Energy UK Onshore*,[37] in which it was said that it "still has value in

---

[30] *Hatfield v Moss* [1988] 2 E.G.L.R. 58.
[31] *Webb v Nightingale* (1957) 169 E.G. 330; *Wilson v Greene* [1971] 1 W.L.R. 635; *Alan Wibberley Building Ltd v Insley* [1999] 1 W.L.R. 894; *Strachey v Ramage*, above; *Brown v Pretot* [2011] EWCA Civ 1421.
[32] (1969) 20 P. & C.R. 909.
[33] [2004] 1 P. & C.R. 26.
[34] Land Registration Act 2002 s.60(1).
[35] 2002 Act s.60(2).
[36] [1974] 1 W.L.R. 80.
[37] [2011] 1 A.C. 380.

English law as encapsulating, in simple language, a proposition of law which has commanded universal acceptance".[38] Lord Hope of Craigshead said:

> "27. The better view, as the Court of Appeal recognised [2009] 3 WLR 1010, [2010] Ch. 100, para 59, is to hold that the owner of the surface is the owner of the strata beneath it, including the minerals that are to be found there, unless there has been an alienation of them by a conveyance, at common law or by statute to someone else. That was the view which the Court of Appeal took in *Mitchell v Mosley* [1914] 1 Ch 438. Much has happened since then, as the use of technology has penetrated deeper and deeper into the earth's surface. But I see no reason why its view should not still be regarded as good law. There must obviously be some stopping point, as one reaches the point at which physical features such as pressure and temperature render the concept of the strata belonging to anybody so absurd as to be not worth arguing about. But the wells that are at issue in this case, extending from about 800 feet to 2,800 feet below the surface, are far from being so deep as to reach the point of absurdity. Indeed the fact that the strata can be worked upon at those depths points to the opposite conclusion."

It follows that the owner of the surface prima facie owns the subsoil at least down to the point at which the circumstances are such that the question of ownership is academic.

The presumption has been applied to leases as well as freehold conveyances.[39] However, the fact that the landlord is the freehold owner of the subsoil by virtue of the above presumption or otherwise does not of itself mean that the subsoil will necessarily be included in a lease of the surface. The question is one of construction as to whether the subsoil was intended to be demised. Where the demise comprises part or all of the ground floor of a multi-occupied building, the correct conclusion may well be that the subsoil is not included. Thus, in *Lejonvarn v Cromwell Mansions Management Co Ltd*,[40] a building had been converted from a single dwelling into three flats, each of which was let on long leases. The lease of the ground floor flat demised:

> "all that the ground-floor and basement and cellar flat ... numbered 1 and being on the ground floor and basement and cellar of the building and including one–half part in depth of the structure between the ceilings of the flat and floors of the flat above it, and the internal and external walls of the flat up to the same level, together with the land being the garden as is shown coloured pink on a plan hereto annexed"

The tenant of the ground floor flat contended that the demise included the subsoil beneath the flat and garden, such that the landlord could not unreasonably withhold its consent to proposed alterations involving excavations below the flat. Mr J. Jarvis QC (sitting as a deputy judge of the High Court) held that as a matter of construction of the lease as a whole, the demise of the flat was limited to the built-out areas and did not include the subsoil. He further declined to apply the presumption, saying:

---

[38] [2011] 1 A.C. 380 at [26].
[39] *Kelsen v Imperial Tobacco Co (of Great Britain & Ireland) Ltd* [1957] 2 Q.B. 334 at 339–340, 345; *Haines v Florensa* [1990] 1 E.G.L.R. 73 at 75C; *Ravengate Estates Ltd v Horizon Housing Group Ltd* [2007] EWCA Civ 1368 at [8]; *Lejonvarn v Cromwell Mansions Management Co Ltd* [2011] EWHC 3838 (Ch.) at [27].
[40] See above.

"33.    The leases that I am looking at are, as I have indicated, three in number, and they form really a carefully devised structure of rights and obligations. It would seem to me that there is in this context a world of difference between being able to develop upwards and therefore be of no real consequence to the remaining tenants of the property and to start digging under and into the foundations. It seems to me that this is very different from the case of a freehold owner of a property who would naturally have all the rights below ground. It seems to me that a structure such as this does not naturally lend itself to being in the same category of case where the presumption of *usque ad* is at all appropriate. I decline to apply any such presumption on the particular facts of this scheme...

34.    There is a further reason why I would not apply the presumption in this case. The presumption is, in any event, not to apply where it is either expressly excluded – an unlikely event in a lease such as this, as conceded by [counsel] – or it is an exclusion that can be inferred from all the circumstances. It seems to me that the very careful drafting of this lease so as to define the flat to mean only, as I have found, the built out part of the flat, and the other clauses that have indicated to me that the foundations were to be retained by the freeholder and maintained by them, make it clear beyond peradventure that there was to be an exclusion of the rights as against the leaseholder of the first floor flat. Therefore, on that additional ground, I find that the presumption does not apply."

## Airspace

7–07    The *usque ad coelum et ad inferos* presumption[41] cannot be applied literally in the case of airspace, because of the development of powered flight. The correct principle as regards airspace is that the rights of the owner of the surface extend only to such height as is necessary for the ordinary use and enjoyment of his land and the structures upon it.[42]

In *Kelsen v Imperial Tobacco Co (of Great Britain & Ireland) Ltd*,[43] the demise consisted of a single storey ground floor shop with a flat roof on top, bounded on its two front sides by streets and at the back by higher buildings. The owner of one of the building erected an advertising sign which projected some eight inches into the airspace above the shop. McNair J held that prima facie the lease of the shop included the airspace above and that nothing in the lease showed an intention to the contrary.

In *Straudley Investments Ltd v Barpress*[44] it was held that a lease of three adjoining terraced buildings on its proper construction included the roof. Nicholls L.J. said in the course of his judgment that he could see no escape from the conclusion that:

"... the demise was of the whole of the building or buildings ... including, as part of that building or those buildings, the roof of the relevant two storey area and the roof of the rest of the building or buildings and, in the normal way, the air space above those roofs."

In *Davies v Yadegar*[45] a house had been divided into two flats. The lease of the top floor flat expressly included the roof and roof space. It was held that the

---

[41] See para.7–06, above.
[42] *Bernstein v Skyviews & General Ltd* [1978] Q.B. 479; *Bocardo SA v Star Energy UK Onshore Ltd* [2011] 1 A.C. 380 at [20, 26].
[43] See above.
[44] [1987] 1 E.G.L.R. 69. This case is more fully considered at para.7–09, below.
[45] [1990] 1 E.G.L.R. 71.

demise included the airspace above the roof, so as to entitle the tenant to alter the roof profile by constructing dormer windows. Woolf L.J. said:

> "On a demise of this sort of premises which includes the roof space and the roof, the demise includes the airspace above the roof and, accordingly, there is no trespass involved in carrying out an alteration which alters the profile of the roof so as to protrude further into the airspace above the existing roof. [Counsel] submits to the contrary that the airspace above the roof is not included in the demise and he does so because he submits a different principle applies where one is dealing with a property which is divided into flats. He submits that, in a case where a property is so divided, all that is in fact included in the demise is the actual area occupied by the flat. The demise is restricted laterally by the extent of the flat. He accepts, and clearly rightly accepts, that, if this were not a demise of a flat but a demise of the whole building, it would have included the air space above the roof, but he submits a different situation exists because this was merely a demise of a flat.
>
> I can well see that, in a different situation where one is considering a block of flats containing a number of different premises occupied by different tenants where no tenant has included in his demise the roof, a position different from that which I have indicated could exist. However, in the situation that we are dealing with here of what was once a single residential unit which has been divided into two flats, [counsel's] submission, in my view, has no application. The roof space and the roof were included in the demise and the logical intent would be that the airspace above should be included in that demise. Were the position otherwise, one can easily see that all sorts of absurd results would follow: if the tenant of the upper flat wished to alter his chimney he would not be in a position to do so; if he wished to erect an aerial on the roof he would not be in a position to do so; if he wished to change the flue on the roof because of changes in building practices he would not be in a position to do so without the consent of the lessor, and the lessor would have a completely unfettered discretion to refuse that consent. Such a result would, in my view, be wholly contrary to the intent of section 19(2) of the 1927 Act, which, read together with the clause dealing with the alterations in this lease, was intended to make the requirement of consent subject to the proviso that it should not be unreasonably withheld."

In *Haines v Florensa*[46] a lease of an upper floor maisonette demised "ALL THAT upper maisonette ... which said maisonette shall be deemed to extend from and include the top surface of the ceiling of the lower maisonette and extend to and include the roof ...". It was held that the demise included the airspace above the roof, such that the tenant was entitled to raise the roof as part of a proposed loft conversion.

In *Ravengate Estates Ltd v Horizon Housing Group Ltd*,[47] a lease of six flats demised:

> "The rear section of the ground floor, the rear section of the first floor and the whole of the second and third floors of 225 Streatham High Road London SW16 as is for the purposes of identification only edged red on the attached plan."

It was held that on the proper construction of the lease, having regard in particular to the attached plans, the demise included the air space above the flat roof of the second floor and the area occupied by the second and third floor balconies. Mann J., with whom Mummery and Jacob L.JJ. agreed, said:

---

[46] [1990] 1 E.G.L.R. 73.
[47] [2007] EWCA Civ 1368.

"That conclusion is reached on the basis of the true construction of the lease. It is therefore not necessary to consider the various authorities placed before us as to the extent to which air space is and is not carried with a grant of land, though for my part had it been necessary to do so I would have found in favour of the application of the presumption that a grant normally carries the airspace."

In *Dorrington Belgravia v McGlashan*,[48] the demise of an upper floor maisonette was held to include the roof and such of the air space above the roof as was reasonably necessary for the use and enjoyment of the maisonette and the fixtures, fittings and other features of it. H.H. Judge Dight said of the airspace:

"It is part of the relevant factual matrix in this case that there are features of the roof, such as the upstands and lenses which form part of skylights, which protrude beyond the flat surface of the roof. There are tanks and other items on the roof serving the maisonette and the one beneath it, in respect of which the lower maisonette has the rights excepted and reserved in clause 1 of the Lease. Chief among those facts are the presence and intended function of the skylights. It is reasonable to assume in my judgement that the parties intended the tenants to have the benefit of the skylights and if the tenants did not have ownership of a reasonable amount of air space above the skylights the intention behind the structure and design of the terrace would be defeated."

In *Rosebery Ltd v Rocklee Ltd*[49] the tenant of a flat on the sixth floor of a block of flats (Flat 15) was granted a supplemental underlease of the empty roof space outside Flat 15 and above Flat 12. The demise was described as "the terrace adjoining the premises as the same is more particularly delineated on the plan". The tenant subsequently built an extension on the roof space, for which it obtained the landlord's consent. The tenant's contention that the demise included the whole of the airspace above the extension was rejected. Mr N. Strauss QC (sitting as a deputy judge of the Chancery Division) said:

"In my opinion, the authorities do not support the proposition advanced by [counsel] that there is a presumption in any lease of, or including, a roof that it extends upwards to the full height of the airspace available to the lessor. [*Davies v Yadegar*[50]] was a case in which the demise included the entire top floor and the entire roof. The passage emphasised in the judgment of Woolf LJ above suggests that, where the demise is of the roof of a small part of the building, in circumstances in which its use could affect tenants on other floors, no such presumption applies. I agree with Lewison's *Interpretation of Contracts* (4th edn), in paras 11 and 12,[51] that there are no clear presumptions relating to divisions of individual parts of a building.[52]"

The judge held that the issue was to be approached "unhampered by any presumption", and that the question was "what a reasonable third party, equipped with the relevant background knowledge available to both parties, would

---

[48] [2009] 1 E.G.L.R. 27

[49] [2011] L. & T.R. 21.

[50] See above.

[51] The relevant passage is now in the 5th edn, para.11–12.

[52] In *Lejonvarn v Cromwell Mansions Management Co Ltd* [2011] EWHC 3838 (Ch.) the judge (Mr J. Jarvis QC sitting as a deputy judge of the High Court), having quoted this passage, suggested at [31]: "It may be that the judgment of Mr Strauss, [43], is misquoted because I doubt that he intended to say that the authorities did not support the proposition that there could be a presumption *usque ad* where there is a demise of the roof space. The authorities, it seems to me, leave the question open as to whether it would be appropriate to apply the presumption in the case of leases. I note that Mr Strauss went on to approach the issue unhampered by any presumption."

conclude". He held that (i) on the proper construction of the supplemental underlease, the demise included the airspace only up to the height of Flat 15, and (ii) on the proper construction of the agreement by virtue of which the extension was constructed, the demise included the roof of the extension, such that no one was entitled to use it save for maintenance.

## Roofs

The extent to which the demised premises will include the whole or any part of the roof is a matter of construction in every case. Where the words of demise do not point to a clear conclusion either way, it will be necessary to look at the remainder of the lease, and in particular, the covenants relating to repair and alteration and any service charge provisions, and to the objective factual background known to both parties, to decide what was intended.

Where the demise includes the roof, it may also, depending on the facts, include the airspace over the roof.[53]

In considering the decided cases, it is necessary to distinguish between cases involving leases of entire buildings and cases concerned with leases of parts of buildings.

### (a) Where the lease comprises an entire building

7–08

7–09

Where the lease is of an entire building, the correct inference will generally be that the roof is included in the demise. Thus, in *Straudley Investments Ltd v Barpress*[54] the demise consisted of three adjoining terraced buildings. The parcels clause demised "ALL THAT piece or parcel of ground with the messuages and buildings erected thereon situate and being [Nos. 67—81 Mortimer Street]". The tenant covenanted to "repair support and uphold the said messuages buildings and premises ... ". The Court of Appeal held that the roof was included in the demise. O'Connor L.J. regarded it as "quite unarguable that [the] lease does not demise the roof of the buildings and the exterior walls". Nicholls L.J. said in the course of his judgment:

"The factual position now ... is that the building or buildings ... form part of a terraced block. On those simple facts, for my part I can see no escape from the conclusion that the demise was of the whole of the building or buildings ... including, as part of that building or those buildings, the roof of the relevant two storey area and the roof of the rest of the building or buildings and, in the normal way, the air space above those roofs. If that construction were not correct, one of the conclusions which would inevitably follow in this case is that the lessee's repairing obligations would not extend to the roof of the building or buildings. Plainly that could not have been intended in the case of this lease. I add that this lease, being a long lease of a whole building or whole buildings, is quite different from a lease or tenancy of a top floor flat of a building which has been divided horizontally into flats.[55]"

---

[53] See para.7–07, above.
[54] [1987] 1 E.G.L.R. 69.
[55] See also *Tennant Radiant Heat Ltd v Warrington Development Corp* [1988] 1 E.G.L.R. 41, considered in para.7–10, below.

## (b)   Where the lease comprises an individual part of a multi-occupied building

**7–10**   Where the demised premises comprise part only of a building, the extent to which the roof will be included in the demise will depend on the detailed facts.

In *Cockburn v Smith*[56] a flat on the top floor of a large block was demised, the premises being described in the lease as "all that suite of rooms known as …". At least one other flat was also on the top floor of, and thus directly under the common roof of, the block. One of the questions which arose was whether the demise included the roof over the flat. The Court of Appeal held that it did not. Bankes L.J. said in the course of his judgment:

> "In the present case the [tenant] took only part of the building; the top flat, part of a building let in flats. What she took is quite clear from the words of the agreement of tenancy. It was a suite of rooms… The contention that because the rooms include the walls therefore they include the roof also is one which I cannot assent to. On the construction of this document, and assuming that there were other tenants holding on similar terms, it is clear that the [landlords] did not demise the roof to any one, but kept it in their own control entirely, and therefore it does not make much difference whether we are considering the roof of the [tenant's] flat, or the roof of the adjoining flat, which I assume was occupied by another tenant on similar terms, and the roof of which was also retained by the [landlords] in their own occupation and control."

Sargant L.J. said:

> "The first thing to be considered is the subject matter of the demise. That is part of a building which in its entirety contains four tiers of flats some of which are placed side by side … A common roof extends over those flats which are laterally contiguous; therefore there is no real ground for contending that because one of the flats was a top flat therefore the demise of that flat included the portion of the roof which covered it and with it the flats below. The roof after that demise remained in the occupation of the landlords as it had been before the demise."

Scrutton L.J. did not expressly consider the point, although it is implicit in his judgment that he agreed with the other two that the roof had not been demised.

The fact that the roof extends over the demised premises and adjoining premises (as was the case in *Cockburn v Smith*) may be material from which it can properly be inferred that the parties did not intend the demise to include that part of the roof which is over the demised premises. However, that will not always be the case. In *Tennant Radiant Heat Ltd v Warrington Development Corp.*[57] the demised premises comprised a self-contained warehouse unit forming part of a single storey steel-framed building divided into 22 units. The unit was divided off from the adjoining units by blockwork walls, which were built into the steel frame to the full height from floor to roof. The roof was a single continuous deck covering all 22 units, surrounded by a parapet, with rain water outlets just inside the parapet. There was no access to the roof from any of the units. The lease of the unit demised "all those premises situate and known as 6 Chetham Court, Winwick Quay, Warrington …". The lease contained a covenant on the part of the tenant to repair the demised premises and all buildings erected

---

[56] [1924] 2 K.B. 119.
[57] [1988] 1 E.G.L.R. 41.

thereon, but there was no landlord's covenant to repair the roof,[58] nor was there any covenant by the tenant to contribute to the landlord's costs of repairing the roof. However, the tenant's covenants referred expressly in two places to the roof of the demised premises. It was held that the part of the roof which was over the unit, together with the rain water outlet in such part, was included in the demise.

Where the demised premises comprise the entirety of the top floor of a building, the question whether the roof is included in the demise will again depend on the facts. In *Delgable v Perinpanathan*[59] the lease defined the demised premises as "First, Second and Third Floors, 153 Praed Street, London W2 and the stairway providing access thereto". The tenant covenanted to repair the demised premises. Paragraph 1.4 of the third schedule contained a covenant on the part of the tenant to pay a fair proportion of the expenses from time to time payable for repairing, etc. "all walls fences gutters sewers rains and any other things the use of which is common to the Premises and to other property adjoining or near thereto". The Court of Appeal held that the demise did not include the roof. Paragraph 1.4 showed that what the parties intended was that matters outside the first, second and third floors as such, the use of which was common to the premises and to other properties, such as the ground floor and basement, which would include the roof, were not included in the demise.

7–11

A different conclusion was reached on different facts in *Dorrington Belgravia v McGlashan*.[60] In that case, the demised premises consisted of an upper maisonette in a building comprising two maisonettes which formed part of a terrace of similar buildings. The demised premises were described as "ALL THAT maisonette number 3 Mertoun Terrace, 70 Seymour Place in the county of London ... which said maisonette and the appurtenances belonging thereto are situate on the first second and third floors and are delineated on the floor plan annexed hereto and thereon colour blue ...". The lease excepted and reserved to the landlord power to enter the demised premises "for the purpose of inspecting repairing the outside wood and iron work and the exterior walls and roof of the demised premises", and further contained a covenant on the part of the landlord to "maintain, cleanse, repair and where necessary renew in a good and workmanlike manner the main structure and roof of the demised premises". The roof of the terrace was a continuous flat structure with no divisions relating to the individual maisonettes beneath it. It consisted of pre-cast concrete slabs into which skylights, circular in shape and approximately one yard in diameter, had been set. The roof also contained various antennae, flues and small structures or housings containing the water tanks and down pipes for the maisonettes immediately beneath them. There was no access to the roof from the inside of the maisonettes. The skylights form part of the original design and construction of the building. The internal spaces in the maisonette illuminated by the natural light entering via the skylights would have been very substantially less attractive and suitable for domestic or residential use if the skylights did not exist.

H.H. Judge Dight held that on the proper construction of the lease, the demise included the roof immediately above the maisonette. His reasons were as follows:

---

[58] It was held that none was to be implied: see Ch.19, below.
[59] [2006] 1 E.G.L.R. 78.
[60] [2009] 1 E.G.L.R. 27.

"Weighing the various arguments it seems to me that they favour the tenants and that, albeit not expressly provided for, the Lease will only operate as it was clearly intended to do if the roof formed part of the premises demised by it. Four things lead me to that conclusion: first, it is clear from the structure and design of the maisonette that the roof with its skylights was always intended to be an integral part of the maisonette itself; secondly, the express reference in the phrase in the exceptions and reservations "the exterior walls and roof of the demised premises to the roof is a strong indication that they are to be treated in the same way as the exterior walls which is plainly that they are part of the demised premises; thirdly, the landlord's repairing obligation contains the similar expression "main structure and roof of the demised premises" again treating the roof in the same way and placing it in the same category as the walls and structure of the building; fourthly, the fact that the interior of the roof is the ceiling of the maisonette and the Lease indicates that the interior and exterior of the maisonette are demised is a strong piece of support for the earlier three reasons."

## (c)   Roof space

**7–12**     The question whether adjoining roof space was included in the demise arose in *Hatfield v Moss*.[61] In that case a second-floor flat was adjacent to a large roof space, which the lessee had converted to provide storage and a playroom. The lease demised "ALL THAT tenement or flat … on the second floor of and being Number 6 flat in the house and which is for the purpose of identification shown edged red on the plan hereto annexed … together with … all exterior walls and windows of the demised premises and the main roof of the house". The plan referred to appeared to place the roof space outside the red edging. At the date of grant of the lease the only access to the roof space was from the flat, although a trap had been cut into it from the flat below in connection with the installation of water tanks at some date. No rights of access to the roof were retained in the lease. The Court of Appeal held that the roof space was included in the demise by virtue of the express reference to the main roof of the house. Since the parcels clause was explicit, it was not permissible to look at the plan. It was proper to take into account the circumstances at the date of grant of the lease when the flat was the only means of access to the roof space, and it seemed unlikely that the landlord would have wanted to reserve the roof space in such circumstances.

A lease of a flat with a false ceiling may include the void above the ceiling.[62]

## Divisions between individual parts of buildings

**7–13**     Ascertaining the extent of the demise in the case of lettings of individual parts of multi-occupied buildings frequently causes difficulties in practice. This is partly because there is often no obvious physical division between the premises being demised and adjoining premises. For example, the joists supporting the floor of one flat will usually serve to hold in place the ceiling of the flat below, and it is not immediately obvious to which flat, if either, they belong. Difficulties also arise because, particularly in a number of older leases, the draftsman has not properly directed his mind to what is being demised, but has used general expressions such as "flat No.3", or "the offices on the fourth floor".

---

[61] [1988] 2 E.G.L.R. 58.
[62] See *Graystone Property Investments Ltd v Margulies* (1984) 47 P. & C.R. 472, considered in paras 7–16 and 7–17, below.

There are no clear presumptions relating to divisions between individual parts of buildings.[63] However, the decided cases afford some guidance and are considered below.

### (a)    Outside walls

A lease of part of a building divided vertically or horizontally will generally be presumed, in the absence of indications to the contrary, to include the whole of the external walls enclosing the demised part.[64] In *Hope Brothers Ltd v Cowan*[65] Joyce J. said:

> "I am of opinion that, unless there be an exception or a reservation or something in the context to exclude it, prima facie where there is demise of a floor or a room or an office bounded in part by an outside wall, in that case the premises demised comprise both sides of the wall."

In *Sturge v Hackett*[66] Diplock L.J. said:

> "It is ... well settled law that, in the absence of provisions to the contrary in a lease, a demise of part of a building divided horizontally or vertically includes the external walls enclosing the part so demised."

Thus, in *Goldfoot v Welch*[67] a demise of "all those rooms situate on the first and second floors" of business premises was held to include the external walls bounding the floors, with the result that the landlord was restrained from affixing advertisements to them. Likewise, in *Delegable v Perinpanathan*,[68] in which the demised premises were defined as "First, Second and Third Floors, 153 Praed Street, London W2 and the stairway providing access thereto", the Court of Appeal was content to accept that the demise included the external walls at first, second and third floor level, Lloyd L.J. (with whom Keene and Pill L.JJ. agreed) said that:

> "[I]n the absence of a more careful and exact definition of what is or is not demised, it would pose certain difficulties for the [tenant] if the external walls were not comprised in the demise because it might be a trespass to do anything, even superficially, to the interior of those walls, for example to put up a picture or clock or whatever one might wish to do involving putting a nail or other fixing device into the wall."

In many cases, however, the correct conclusion will be that the external walls were intended to be retained by the landlord, the demise including only the inside surface of such walls. Thus, in *Graystone Property Investments Ltd v Margulies*[69] Griffiths L.J. described the following as "clear indications" that the external walls

**7–14**

---

[63] Lewison, *The Interpretation of Contracts*, 5th edn (London: Sweet & Maxwell, 2011), para.11.12, approved in *Rosebery Ltd v Rocklee* [2011] L. & T.R. 21 at [43].
[64] *Carlisle Cafe Co Ltd v Muse Brothers & Co Ltd* (1897) 67 L.J. (Ch.) 53; *Hope Brothers Ltd v Cowan* [1913] 2 Ch. 312; *Goldfoot v Welch* [1914] 1 Ch. 213; *Re Webb* [1951] Ch. 808; *Sturge v Hackett* [1962] 1 W.L.R. 1257.
[65] Above.
[66] Above.
[67] Above.
[68] [2006] 1 E.G.L.R. 78.
[69] (1984) 47 P. & C.R. 472.

of a flat were not included in the demise: (1) the edging on the lease plan ran within the walls in question; (2) the landlord was liable to repair all external walls and the tenant was liable for the windows and balconies of the flats; and (3) there was a specific proviso that the tenant was to keep the walls of the flat in repair except the brick or concrete structure forming any part of any external wall. The other two Lords Justices agreed.

### (b)   Other vertical divisions

**7–15**    There is relatively little judicial guidance in relation to internal boundary walls. In *Phelps v City of London Corp*[70] the lease contained a reservation of "the way or passage and basement under the same leading from Aldermanbury to property belonging to the lessors and coloured blue on the said plan". The question arose as to what part of the floor, walls and ceiling of the passage was included in the reservation. The plan showed one-half of the north wall of the passage coloured blue. Peterson J., relying principally on the plan, held that one-half of the north wall was included. In the course of his judgment he said:

> "In the case of an external wall the demise of a room includes the whole of the wall, while in the case of a partition wall it seems to be clear that some part of the wall is included in the demise. It is, therefore, not surprising that in this lease one half of the north wall of the passage and basement should be expressly excepted or reserved as part of the passage or basement, by way of making it clear that it belongs to the lessor as the owner of the passage or basement and that no part of the south wall is excepted or reserved. In my judgment, the property in one half of the north wall of the passage and basement has been reserved ... and is not included in the demise."

The position may therefore be that, in the absence of indications to the contrary, the demise will be presumed to include one-half of any internal boundary walls.

### (c)   Horizontal divisions

**7–16**    The question of how far the demise extends horizontally frequently arises in practice in the context of who is liable to repair items such as floor joists or structural floor slabs. Where no express indication is given, the prima facie position appears to be that a demise of one floor extends at least to the underneath of the structure supporting the floor above it. In *Sturge v Hackett*[71] Diplock L.J. said that the flat in question "must have extended to at least the underside of the floor joists to which the ceiling was attached". On the facts of the case, however, it was not necessary to decide whether it extended "halfway through the thickness of the floor joists or to the top side of them".

In *Graystone Property Investments Ltd v Margulies*[72] the demise consisted of a first-floor flat in a converted Victorian house. On conversion, some (but not all) of the ceilings had been lowered to give the rooms more acceptable proportions. The effect of this had been to leave a number of voids (one as much as 6ft in

[70] [1916] 2 Ch. 255.
[71] [1962] 3 All E.R. 166.
[72] (1984) 47 P. & C.R. 472.

depth) between the new ceilings and the place where the old had been. The existence of the false ceilings was obvious from inside the flats because of the differing heights of the ceilings in the various rooms. The Court of Appeal held that the voids were included in the demise of the flat. Griffiths L.J., who gave the principal judgment, said:

> "[Counsel] submitted that the general rule is that the upper boundary of a flat is the lower boundary of the flat immediately above … It may, I think, be rather too strong to state this proposition as a general rule, but I have no doubt that it is the general expectation of anyone who takes the lease of a flat that he acquires the space between the floor of his flat and the underneath of the floor of the flat above. This no doubt arises from the almost invariable conveyancing practice of so drafting leases, and we have been referred to various conveyancing precedents which illustrate this practice … I therefore accept that where there is to be what I consider to be an exceptional departure from the general conveyancing practice, clear words are required to give effect to the landlords' intention … I can find nothing in the wording of this underlease to take it out of the ordinary expectation that the demise entitles the tenant to occupy all that space between the floor of his flat and the underneath of the floor of the flat above."

In reaching his conclusion on the facts, Griffiths L.J. expressed himself as being struck with the "extreme improbability" of the landlords wishing to retain ownership of the voids. It is clear that all three members of the court were influenced by the fact that the existence of the voids was apparent from within the flat, Stephenson L.J. saying that:

> "If there had been no part of [the flat] without a false ceiling, I should have been less certain of the right answer … But the absence of a false ceiling in what is called the living room, and perhaps in the kitchen, would have confirmed for this lessee, if confirmation were needed, what Griffiths L.J. has called the ordinary expectation of those who rent leasehold flats, and the so-called voids above the false ceilings were, I agree, included in the premises demised."

Griffiths L.J.'s observation that the general expectation of anyone taking a lease of a flat is that he acquires "the space between the floor of his flat and the underneath of the floor of the flat above" may be said to support the proposition that, absent indications to the contrary, the demise of a flat includes the floor, the ceiling and the structure supporting the floor above. However, that case was concerned with a roof space, and it is not clear to what extent Griffiths L.J. meant to go this far. Nonetheless, such a conclusion would avoid the practical difficulties that might result where the demise includes only half of the relevant structure but the entirety of it requires replacement. In that event, since the upper floor tenant (or the landlord) would presumably be liable for the other half, there would be concurrent liabilities in relation to different parts of the same item. This seems an unlikely intention to attribute to the parties in the ordinary case.

7–17

In many cases the right conclusion will be that the structure above the ceiling was intended to be retained by the landlord. Thus, in *London Underground v Shell International Petroleum*[73] the demised premises consisted of parts of a ground floor and basement, of which the upper limit was "the underside of the structural slab floor of the first floor". The structural slab floor of the first floor was supported by steel girders which were in turn supported by six concrete columns on the ground floor. The columns were expressly excluded from the

---

[73] [1998] E.G.C.S. 97.

demise. The ground floor ceiling was suspended from the slab by hangers. The landlord argued that the girders were included in the demise because they were located below the upper limit as described in the lease. It was held that the girders were not included in the demise. The words "the underside of the ... floor" were capable of extending to supporting members beneath, and should be so interpreted. Indications that this was the intention were held to include (among others) (a) the exclusion of the columns from the demise; and (b) the lack of any reservation of a right of support from the girders for the benefit of the landlord.

Where the demised premises consist of several floors of a building then, unless the lease otherwise provides or the context requires a different conclusion, the entirety of the structure between the floors is likely to be included in the demise. In *Phelps v City of London Corp*[74] Peterson J. held that the concrete floor dividing the passage from the basement was included in the reservation. His reasoning was as follows:

> "The floor is part of the passage and the ceiling is part of the basement; and I do not see any
> difference in law between the horizontal division between an upper and a lower room and the
> vertical division between two adjoining rooms."

*Cresswell v Duke of Westminster*[75] concerned somewhat unusual facts. The demised premises comprised a terraced house on three floors, part of which extended across a passageway leading to mews behind. The roof of the passage consisted of barrelled bricks, above which were rolled steel joists, then wooden joists and finally the floor of the first floor premises. The part of the house above the tunnel was described in the lease as "the rooms and premises on and above the first floor of the building erected over the land shown by yellow colour on the said plan". The court held that the demise included all the structure forming the roof of the tunnel and above the airspace in the tunnel.

## Projections

7–18    As a general rule, anything which is part of, or is fixed to, the outside walls will, in the absence of indications to the contrary, be included in the demise. In *Sturge v Hackett*[76] the question was whether an external decorative cornice fixed to the outside wall of a flat on the first floor of a converted mansion was included. Having held that the wall itself was included in the demise, Diplock L.J. went on to consider whether the cornice was included, saying:

> "The relevant test is not whether the decorative cornice is part of a wall as such, nor whether it
> is structurally necessary in order to enclose the demised premises or to render them
> weatherproof. The relevant test is whether it is, or is fixed to, a part of the external structure of
> the building which actually encloses the demised premises. Sunblinds, external shutters and
> many other external fixtures would not be described in ordinary parlance as a part of the wall,
> but undoubtedly are included in a demise of a flat. In the present case, the decorative cornice
> was fixed to the external wall and to a part of the external wall which enclosed the [demised]
> flat ... and no other flat ... The fact that the cornice fixed to the external wall fulfilled no

---

[74] [1916] 2 Ch. 255. See para.7–15, above.
[75] [1985] 2 E.G.L.R. 151.
[76] [1962] 3 All E.R. 166.

structural function but only a purely decorative one is, in our view, irrelevant. It was, or was fixed to, a part of the external structure of [the building] which actually enclosed the [demised] flat …, and subject to any provisions in the lease to the contrary was part of the premises demised to him."

He went on to hold that none of the following covenants in the lease displaced the presumption: (1) a tenant's internal repairing covenant; (2) a tenant's covenant to clean windows and chimneys; (3) a tenant's covenant not to exhibit name plates or notices; (4) a tenant's covenant not to affix to the flat or on the roof of the building an external wireless or television aerial without the landlord's consent; (5) a landlord's covenant to take all reasonable steps to prevent birds from nesting or congregating under the eaves above certain windows of the flat; (6) a landlord's external repairing covenant.

The footings and eaves of a building will generally be included in a lease of it, even though they project beyond the edge of the wall.[77]

## Land occupied but not part of the demise

Where the tenant occupies land in connection with the demised premises which is not part of the landlord's property, then he is presumed to occupy the other land as an accretion or addition to the demised premises.[78] The covenants of the lease will then apply to that other land as if it were part of the demised premises.[79] By virtue of this principle, the tenant may become liable under the repairing covenants in relation to land which is not technically part of the demise but which he occupies as part of the demised property. The same will apply where the tenant occupies land belonging to the landlord as if it formed part of the demise.[80] Alternatively the court may be prepared to imply a contract between the parties whereby the tenant is liable to repair the other land. Thus, in *White v Wakley*[81] the tenant of a farm covenanted to repair the buildings to be erected thereon. During the term, with the permission of the landlord, he built a house on waste ground adjoining the farm and occupied it as part of the farm. It was held that he was liable to repair the house by virtue of an implied contract to that effect.

7–19

## Alterations and additions during the term

As a general rule, anything which is attached to the land becomes part of it (*quicquid plantatur solo, solo cedit*).[82] When the land is subject to a lease, the thing so attached becomes part of the demise. The general principle was stated by Lord Fraser in *Ponsford v HMS Aerosols Ltd*[83] as follows:

7–20

---

[77] *Truckell v Stock* [1957] 1 W.L.R. 161.
[78] *Smirk v Lyndale Developments Ltd* [1975] Ch. 317; *Kensington Pension Developments Ltd v Royal Garden Hotel (Oddenino's) Ltd* [1990] 2 E.G.L.R. 117.
[79] *Kensington Pension Developments Ltd v Royal Garden Hotel (Oddenino's) Ltd*, above.
[80] *J F Perrott & Co Ltd v Cohen* [1951] 1 K.B. 705.
[81] (1858) 26 Beav. 17.
[82] See para.25–08, below.
[83] [1979] A.C. 63.

"There is no dispute that 'the demised premises', which originally meant the factory described in clause one of the lease, now means the factory as rebuilt after the fire, including the improvements made at the expense of the tenants, with the approval of the landlord ... The premises would have included the improvements without express provision to that effect, on the principle that anything made part of the premises by the tenants enures to the landlord."

Likewise, in *Legal & General Assurance Society Ltd v Expeditors International (UK) Ltd*[84] Lewison J. said:

"... in my judgment the premises will include anything which in law has become part of the premises by annexation."

In the ordinary case, therefore, a reference to "the demised premises" will include new buildings constructed during the term, alterations and additions to existing buildings carried out during the term and fixtures installed during the term (even if they are tenant's fixtures[85]).

In the context of the law of dilapidations, the question frequently arises as to what extent alterations or additions to the demised premises become subject to the covenant to repair. As always, the answer will depend upon the facts of each case and the proper construction of the lease in question. However, the rule laid down in a number of old authorities is that the general covenant to repair the demised premises (i.e. a covenant to repair the demised premises without any qualification on the meaning of that expression) will extend to all subsequent alterations or additions carried out during the term, but a covenant specifically framed by reference to the premises as they were at the time of the demise will not. Thus, in *Dowse v Earle*,[86] it was said:

"If a man took a lease of a messuage and land, and covenants to leave the demised premises in good repair at the end of the term, and he erects another messuage on part of the land, besides that which was there before, he shall be bound to keep and leave the messuage, by himself, so newly erected, in repair, as well as the other.[87]"

In *Cornish v Cleife*[88] Channell B. stated the rule as follows:

"The authorities cited in the textbooks establish these rules, that where there is a general covenant to repair, and keep and leave in repair, the inference is that the lessee undertakes to repair newly erected buildings. On the other hand, where the covenant is to repair, and keep and leave in repair the demised buildings, no such liability arises."

Bigham J. relied on the same principle in *Smith v Mills*[89]:

---

[84] [2007] 1 P. & C. R. 5 at [32] (on appeal: [2007] 2 P. & C. R. 10).
[85] In *Legal & General Assurance Society Ltd v Expeditors International (UK) Ltd*, above, Lewison J. said: "A fixture installed by the tenant for the purposes of his trade become part of the premises as soon as it is installed, although the tenant retains a right to sever the fixture on termination of the tenancy". See further Ch.25, below.
[86] (1689) 3 Lev. 265.
[87] This passage does not appear in the report at 2 Vent. 126.
[88] (1864) H. & C. 446.
[89] (1899) 16 T.L.R. 59.

"[T]he rule laid down in [the authorities] was that where there was a general covenant to repair that must refer both to buildings erected at the date of and subsequent to the demise; but where the covenant to repair in its terms applied to certain specified buildings, it must not be extended beyond those buildings."

Likewise, in *Rose v Spicer*[90] Fletcher Moulton L.J. said:

"Whenever erected [the additions] became on erection part of the freehold to which they were annexed, and it is elementary law that a general covenant to repair and maintain such as we have here would apply to them. If a lessee whose lease contains such a covenant erects a house on the land leased to him he is just as much bound to maintain it and keep it in repair as if it had been built before the lease was granted.[91]"

The effect of these authorities is that a covenant to repair will be construed as applying to subsequent alterations and additions, unless there is something in the language used to show that a different result was intended. Thus, where the original demised premises are burnt down, and the tenant erects new premises, then the covenant to repair will apply to those premises in the same way as it did to the original premises.[92] This presumption will often be reinforced by other indications in the lease. It is common, for example, for the demised premises to be expressly defined so as to comprise whatever is on the demised land from time to time. Tenants contemplating carrying out improvements should therefore bear in mind that they may become liable to repair, and deliver up in repair, whatever they put up.

**7–21**

However, even where the covenant to repair does not apply to new buildings as such, it may be construed as applying to alterations and additions to those buildings which are in existence at the time of the demise. This was presumably what Sankey J. had in mind in *Field v Curnick*[93] when he said:

"[A] general covenant to repair includes not merely buildings existing when the demise is made, but all those which may be erected during the term ... If, however, the covenant to repair is only one to keep in repair the demised premises it applies to those existing at the date of the lease only unless the new buildings are made part of the old ones."

Similarly, in *Cornish v Cleife*[94] Bramwell B., whilst agreeing that the covenant did not extend to the new buildings in question, was not prepared to hold that it would not extend to any new building, saying:

"[T]he covenant to repair does not extend to the newly erected houses. I emphasise the word 'houses', because I think that if an addition had been made to an old house by putting up a lean-to, a barn, or a stable, it would have been a part of the house within the meaning of the covenant. But in my opinion the covenant does not apply to a separate and independent dwelling house, erected subsequently to the date of the lease ... in my judgment, the word 'buildings' refers to what in popular parlance may be said to be a part of the house."

---

[90] [1911] 2 K.B. 234.
[91] The actual decision was reversed on appeal by the House of Lords ([1912] A.C. 623) but this passage remains good law: *Field v Curnick* [1926] 2 K.B. 374, per Sankey J.
[92] *Greens v Southcott* (1879) 6 Nfld. L.R. 176.
[93] [1926] 2 K.B. 374.
[94] (1864) H. & C. 446.

7–22    The following are examples of cases in which it has been held that the covenant to repair did not extend to subsequent changes in the original demised premises.

(a)    *Doe d. Trustees of Worcester School v Rowlands*,[95] in which a warehouse, stable and garden ground were demised, the lessee covenanting to repair "the demised buildings" and if necessary "to rebuild the warehouse". Since the grant of the lease several cottages and other buildings had been built. Coleridge J. held that the covenant was limited to the buildings which were on the premises at the time of the letting.

(b)    *Cornish v Cleife*,[96] in which the demise consisted of "all those three tenements or dwelling houses, and a field or plot of ground … adjoining thereto …". The tenant covenanted to repair "the said tenements or dwelling houses, field or plot of ground and premises, and every part thereof, as well in houses, buildings, walls … as in all other needful and necessary reparations whatsoever … and at the end [of the term] … the said premises so well and sufficiently repaired … peaceably to leave and yield up." It was held that the covenant did not extend to houses subsequently built in the adjoining field during the term, it being said that the words following on from "as well in …" were not intended to extend the covenant but to explain what had gone before.

(c)    *Hyman v Rose*,[97] in which a piece of land "together with the chapel or place of public religious worship with its offices and premises now erecting and building thereon by the … lessees" was let. The tenant covenanted to keep in repair "the said demised chapel offices buildings and premises and all the wall fences pavements … and all other appurtenances thereto belonging …", and to yield up at the end of the term "the premises with the appurtenances … with all landlord's fixtures and all improvements". During the term the tenant removed a dwarf wall surmounted by ornamental iron railings. The Court of Appeal held that this amounted to a breach of the covenant.[98] The House of Lords allowed the tenant's appeal, one of the grounds being that the items had not been shown to have been in existence at the date of the demise, and were not therefore subject to the covenant.

7–23    Examples of cases in which the covenant has been held to apply to subsequent changes in the demised premises are:

(a)    *Sunderland v Newton*,[99] in which the demised premises included a mill and steam engine. During the tenancy the tenant (a) removed the engine and substituted a new engine of greater power, and (b) carried out additions to the original building, the effect of which was to increase it both upwards and outwards. Assignees of the tenant proposed to remove both the new

[95] (1841) 9 C. & P. 734.
[96] (1864) H. & C. 446.
[97] [1912] A.C. 623.
[98] On the ground that a covenant to repair involves a duty not to destroy. See paras 18–02 et seq., below.
[99] (1830) 3 Sim. 450.

engine and the new part of the building. The court granted the landlord an interlocutory injunction restraining them, on the ground that both the new engine and the building as altered were within the tenant's covenant to repair.

(b)  *Hudson v Williams*,[100] where the demise comprised "all that piece or parcel of land ... together with the messuage or tenement and all other erections and buildings erected and built, or which may at any time during the term ... be erected and built, on the said piece or parcel of land or any part thereof ... and also that one acre of land lying at the back of the garden belonging to the said messuage ...". The tenant covenanted to repair "the said messuage or tenement and erections and buildings erected and built, or to be erected and built, upon the said ground hereby demised, or any part thereof, ... and the said messuage or tenement and premises ... at the end of the said term peaceably deliver up ...". During the term a number of houses were built upon the demised land, including the one acre field. The tenant's contention that the covenant did not extend to new buildings on the one acre field was rejected by the court, it being said that the words "ground hereby demised" included the field.

## Buildings erected pursuant to a covenant to build

Whether the covenant to repair extends to buildings put up pursuant to a covenant to build is a question of construction to be decided in accordance with the principles already discussed.[101] Where the demise consists of a piece of unbuilt land on which the tenant agrees to build, the lease will usually contain an express covenant to repair the buildings once erected. However, problems may arise in practice where the tenant puts up not only the buildings covenanted to be erected but additional buildings as well. The question will then be whether the covenant to repair extends to the extra buildings.

**7–24**

In *Dowse v Earle*,[102] in which the demise consisted of three houses, the tenant covenanted: (a) to pull them down and erect three others; (b) to repair all the houses so agreed to be built; and (c) to deliver up at the end of the term the said demised premises and houses thereon to be erected.[103] The tenant in fact built five houses.[104] The court held that the covenant to yield up applied to all the houses, not just those put up in pursuance of the obligation, that view apparently being based on the absence of the words "agreed to be built" in the covenant to yield up. The same result was reached in *Field v Curnick*,[105] where the demise comprised a piece of ground "together with the messuages or tenements and all other erections and buildings which at the time hereafter during the said term shall be built upon the same piece of ground or any part thereof." The tenant

---

[100]  (1878) 39 L.T. 632.

[101]  See paras 7–20 to 7–23, above.

[102]  (1689) 3 Lev. 265.

[103]  The actual words used in the covenant were "ac dicta dimissa premissa ac domos superinde fore erect."

[104]  Or four, according to the report in 2 Vent. 126.

[105]  [1926] 2 K.B. 374.

covenanted to build two houses, and further covenanted to repair and keep "the said premises respectively with the appurtenances in such good and substantial repair as is necessary for occupation at a rack rent ...". He subsequently erected six houses. Sankey J. held that the covenant to repair applied to all six.

A different result was reached in *Smith v Mills*.[106] In that case the demise consisted of "all that messuage or tenement and garden erected and formed on the said piece of ground", and the tenant covenanted (a) to erect certain fences, a washhouse and two "messuages or tenements" on the land; (b) to repair "the said messuage or tenement and premises hereby demised and the said fences and new erections and new messuages or tenements to be erected as aforesaid ..."; and (c) to deliver up at the end of the term "the said demised premises, fences, new erections, and new tenements ...". The tenant duly complied with (a) and also erected a factory. Bigham J. held that (b) did not apply to the factory. He also held that the presence in the lease of a covenant entitling the landlord to enter "upon the said demised premises or any part thereof to examine the condition thereof and to give [the lessees] notice in writing of any defects and that [the lessees] will within three calendar months after the delivery of every such notice make good the defects specified therein" made no difference. He was not prepared to decide whether (c) would include the factory when the lease eventually came to an end.

7–25 In special circumstances the covenant to repair may be construed as applying only to buildings erected pursuant to the obligation to build and not to buildings existing at the date of the lease. In *Lant v Norris*[107] the tenant covenanted (a) to lay out the sum of £200 within 15 years in erecting and rebuilding certain houses on the demised land; (b) to repair the said messuages or tenements so to be erected, with all such other houses, edifices, etc. as should at any time or times thereafter be erected; and (c) to yield up at the end of the term the said demised premises, with all such other houses, etc. It appears that (a) was never performed. It was held that (b) on its true construction only applied to the new buildings to be put up in pursuance of the obligation, and not to buildings existing at the date of the demise. It also appears to have been held, however, that (c) would be apt to include all the buildings on the demised land whenever erected.

Where the covenant to repair applies on its true construction to buildings covenanted to be erected, it is also likely to be held to apply to the buildings in the course of erection. Thus, in *Bennett v Herring*[108] a lease of a piece of land with two partly completed buildings on it was granted. The tenant covenanted to complete the buildings within two months and to repair, etc. "the said messuages or tenements and premises ...". Construction of the buildings began but did not proceed beyond the point where they were "in carcase only, but roofed in". The roofs became dilapidated. The tenant's argument that the covenant to repair did not apply until the buildings have been completed was rejected by all four judges who tried the case.

---

[106] (1899) 16 T.L.R. 59.
[107] (1757) 1 Burr. 287.
[108] (1857) 3 C.B. (N.S.) 370.

## Where the lease contains a covenant to contribute towards the cost of things used in common[109]

It is common for leases to contain both a tenant's covenant to repair the demised premises, and a tenant's covenant to contribute to the cost of repairing things used in common. In an appropriate case, the inclusion of the latter obligation may be held to have the effect that the things in question are not part of the demise and therefore not subject to the tenant's covenant to repair.[110] However, difficulties may arise where one of the things in question has been made part of the demise. Which of the two covenants will prevail will depend upon the proper construction of the lease. In *Brew Bros Ltd v Snax (Ross) Ltd*[111] the tenant was held liable, under a covenant to repair the demised premises, for repairs to outside drains used in common with others, notwithstanding that his obligation to contribute to the cost of things used in common required him to pay a proportion only.

7–26

### Fixtures

Fixtures, whenever attached, form part of the demised property. Fixtures in existence at the date of the lease will generally therefore be subject to the covenant to repair, and fixtures attached subsequently may become so subject under the principles discussed above.[112] The law relating to fixtures, and the circumstances in which fixtures are, or become, subject to the repairing covenant, are considered in Ch.25, below.

7–27

### PARTICULAR PARTS OF THE DEMISED PREMISES AND PARTS OF THE BUILDING NOT INCLUDED IN THE DEMISE

### Introductory

Where the demised property comprises the entirety of an industrial or commercial building, a modern lease will generally place the responsibility for the repair of the whole upon the tenant. In other cases, however, the repairing obligations will frequently be divided in some way between landlord and tenant. This is particularly likely to be so in the case of (a) leases of parts of multi-occupied buildings (such as flats or floors in an office block), where it is common for the landlord to be responsible for repairing those parts of the building retained by him, and (b) those parts of the demised premises for which it is appropriate that the landlord rather than the tenant should assume responsibility. An example of the latter is the relatively common case of the landlord assuming responsibility for the outside walls of an office building even though these may form part of the individual demises to the occupying tenants. Such parts may be defined inclusively (for example, the obligation may be to repair "the structure"), or

7–28

---

[109] See further para.7–54, below.
[110] *Delgable v Perinpanathan* [2006] 1 E.G.L.R. 78. See para.7–11, above.
[111] [1970] 1 Q.B. 612.
[112] See paras 7–20 to 7–23, above.

exclusively (for example, the landlord may be liable to repair "the building", that expression being defined to exclude premises demised to tenants).

A well drafted lease of part of a multi-occupied building will define precisely what parts fall within the parties' respective obligations. Ideally, the draftsman will have inspected the building, and taken advice from the landlord's surveyor, architect or engineer as to how it is constructed and how the repairing obligations ought to be divided up. In such a case, the lease will provide expressly for liability in relation to such problematical areas as cladding, floor and ceiling structures and windows. In other cases, however, the draftsman may use expressions which are either inappropriate or too general to enable the division of liability to be easily identified. It will then be necessary to construe the covenant carefully in the context of the lease as a whole and the building itself to see precisely who is liable for what. This section considers the correct approach to the identification of the subject-matter of the covenant where that subject-matter constitutes part only of a larger whole.

## Where there is a lacuna or overlap in the scheme of repairing obligations in relation to a multi-occupied building

**7–29**     The general scheme of repairing covenants in relation to multi-occupied buildings is usually designed to ensure that the whole building is covered. Sometimes, however, some part may have been omitted, so that neither party is liable to repair it. Where the issue is whether this has happened, it can be argued that, as a general presumption, the parties are unlikely to have intended there to be any lacuna in the scheme of repairing obligations (at least in relation to those parts of the building which are necessary for the proper enjoyment of the demised premises by the tenant), so that the lease should, where possible, be construed in such a way as to avoid any gap.

The relevant authorities point in different directions. In *Credit Suisse v Beegas Nominees Ltd*[113] it was argued by the tenant that the construction of the landlord's covenant to repair the structure of an office building should be approached on the basis that it was not to be expected that the parties should have left a gap in their obligations such that work needing to be done should transpire to be an obligation of neither party. Such a gap, it was argued, was uncommercial. Lindsay J. found this "far from obvious", because "parties can overlook some needs or even deliberately shy away from some problems". By contrast, in *Holding & Barnes v Hill House Hammond Ltd* at first instance,[114] Neuberger J. thought that:

> "[W]here two parties have entered into a lease, which imposes obligations to repair on each of them, then the court should lean in favour of a construction which results in there being a complete code so far as repair is concerned."

In the Court of Appeal (where the judge's decision on the correct construction of the provisions in question was reversed)[115] Clarke L.J. thought that there was:

---

[113] [1994] 4 All E.R. 803 and (more fully) [1994] 1 E.G.L.R. 76.
[114] [2000] L. & T.R. 428.
[115] [2002] 2 P. & C.R. 11.

"[S]ome (albeit limited) force in the point that it is unlikely that the parties intended that neither party should have repairing obligations with regard to the exterior of the property, which would be the effect of [the landlord's construction]."

The other two Lords Justices did not mention the point (although Peter Gibson L.J. ended his judgment by saying that he agreed with the reasons given by the other two).

The weight of authority is therefore marginally in favour of the existence of a presumption along the above lines, albeit not a particularly strong one. However, any such presumption must be limited to cases where both parties have entered into repairing obligations. Where, as is sometimes the case, the landlord gives no covenant to repair at all, and the tenant covenants to repair only part of the premises (such as "the interior") it is not possible to make the landlord liable, as a matter of construction, to repair the rest of the premises. This can only be done (if at all) by satisfying the stringent tests for the implication of a term.[116]

A stronger case can be made out for the existence of a presumption against an intention to create overlapping obligations, i.e. obligations on both parties to do the same work to the same part of the building. In such a case, each party would have a remedy against the other for failure to do the work, and the practical result would be to stultify both obligations. It is therefore thought that mutual repairing covenants should, if possible, be construed so as to avoid any such overlap. Take for example, a tenant's covenant to repair a flat which expressly includes "the window frames (both inside and outside)". This might enable a landlord's covenant in the same lease to repair "the exterior of the building containing the flat" to be construed as excluding the outside window frames of the flat, even though these might otherwise be encompassed in the expression "the exterior".[117] The existence of such a presumption is supported by two cases. In *Toff v McDowell*[118] Evans-Lombe J. accepted a submission that a lease of a flat should be construed so as to avoid shared liability, in particular for repairs, unless such a construction was forced on the court by the express words used in the lease. In *Petersson v Pitt Place Ltd*[119] the Court of Appeal held that the lease in question ought to be construed so as to avoid the "deeply impractical result" that both landlord and tenant were liable to each other to repair the same subject matter unless it was "literally impossible to do so".[120]

Where the premises are residential premises to which Pt IV of the Landlord and Tenant Act 1987 applies, the court has power in certain circumstances to make an order varying the lease or leases in question.[121] In an appropriate case the court may be able to put right difficulties resulting from lacunae or overlaps in the scheme of repairing obligations in the exercise of this power.

7–30

---

[116] See paras 1–03 to 1–08 above, and para.19–04 et seq., below.

[117] A passage in the First Edition of this work in similar terms to the paragraph in the text was quoted with approval by the Court of Appeal in *Petersson v Pitt Place Ltd* [2001] 82 P. & C.R. 21.

[118] (1995) 69 P. & C.R. 535.

[119] (2001) 82 P. & C.R. 21.

[120] See further on this case para.7–39, below.

[121] Landlord and Tenant Act 1987 Pt IV (as amended by the Housing Act 1988 Sch.13 and the Leasehold Reform, Housing and Urban Development Act 1993 s.86).

## Where the repairing obligation expressly excludes certain parts of the premises or certain types of work

7–31    In some cases the repairing obligation of one or other party will expressly exclude specified parts of the premises or particular works. For example, the landlord may covenant to repair "the structure and exterior of the Building (other than those parts thereof which are the liability of the Tenant hereunder)". The precise ambit of the exception is a question of construction in each case.

In *Granada Theatres Ltd v Freehold Investments (Leytonstone) Ltd*[122] the tenant's covenant to repair was subject to an exception in the case of "structural repairs of a substantial nature to the main walls roofs foundations or main drains of the demised premises". The landlord covenanted to repair the main structure walls, roof and drains of the demised building "except so far as the lessee is liable under the lessee's covenants hereinbefore contained". The covenants were construed as meaning that the landlord was liable for structural repairs of a substantial nature to the main walls, roof, foundations and main drains of the premises and the tenant was liable for anything not falling within that description.[123]

In *Holding & Barnes v Hill House Hammond Ltd*[124] seven leases were granted between the same parties on the same day as part of the sale of an insurance services business. Five of the leases were of parts of a building, and two (including the lease in question) were of a whole building. The lease in question obliged the landlord "to keep the structure of the Building (other than those parts comprised in the property) in good and tenantable repair and condition". It was common ground that the expressions "building" and "property" meant the same thing. Read literally, therefore, the clause obliged the landlord to keep the structure of the property (other than those parts comprised in the property) in good and tenantable repair and condition. It was common ground that the relevant matrix of fact which was to be taken into account in construing the lease included the other six leases. The Court of Appeal held that, viewed against that background, the words in parentheses were to be ignored, so that the clause was to be read as imposing on the landlord an obligation to keep the structure and exterior of the property in good and tenantable repair and condition.

### The identity of the whole

7–32    Questions may sometimes arise as to what is the whole to which the specified part is intended to relate. The answer will usually be clear from the context. For example, the obligation may be to repair the outside walls of "the building" or the structure of "the block"; what comprises "the building" or "the block" will generally be clear, either from an express definition in the lease, or from a consideration of all relevant circumstances. Sometimes, however, difficulties may

---

[122] [1958] 1 W.L.R. 84 (Vaisey J.) and [1959] Ch. 592, CA. See also *Samuels v Abbints Investment Ltd* (1963) 188 E.G. 689.
[123] See also the Australian case of *Justelle Nominees Pty v Martin (No.3)* [2009] WASC 264, considered in para.4–15, above.
[124] [2002] 2 P. & C.R. 11.

be caused by the fact that the unit is not a separately identifiable entity but is itself part of a larger whole. For example, the landlord of a block of flats let on long leases may covenant to repair the structure, not of the block, but of "the flat". In such a case the question will be precisely what is intended to be covered by the obligation.

Where the specified part relates to "the demised premises" or some other expression meaning what has been demised, then it will generally not be construed as extending to any part of the building outside the demise. Thus in *Peters v Prince of Wales Theatre (Birmingham) Ltd*[125] a lease of a shop and six rooms in a building contained a landlord's covenant to keep the "exterior of the demised premises" in good and tenantable condition. A sprinkler system in a room immediately above the demised premises burst. The Court of Appeal held that the covenant was limited to the exterior of the demised premises and did not therefore extend to the room in question. Goddard L.J. said:

> "[The covenant], in our opinion, must be taken as meaning every exterior part of the demised premises—in other words, as excluding that which is not demised. The sprinklers ... were not part of the exterior of the demised premises, and there is no suggestion that any part of the premises demised were out of repair."

Sometimes, the lease will define the whole in a manner which does not focus so much on what has been demised or retained as on the physical unit occupied by the tenant. An example is s.11 of the Landlord and Tenant Act 1985,[126] which imposes upon the landlord under "a lease of a dwelling house" an implied obligation to keep in repair "the structure and exterior of the dwelling house", and to keep in repair and proper working order "the installations in the dwelling house" for the supply of certain services.[127] It was held in *Campden Hill Towers Ltd v Gardner*[128] that the implied obligation is not limited to what has been demised but extends to anything which in the ordinary use of words would be regarded as part of the structure or the exterior of the dwelling-house, regarded as a separate unit.[129] On the facts of that case it applied to the outside wall or walls of the demised flat; the outside of inner party walls of the flat; the outer side of horizontal divisions between the flat and flats above and below; and the structural framework and beams directly supporting floors, ceilings and walls of the flat. This was followed in *Douglas-Scott v Scorgie*,[130] in which the roof above a top floor flat was held to be part of its structure and exterior, notwithstanding the fact that it did not form part of the demise. Slade L.J. said in the course of his judgment:

> "Following [*Campden Hill Towers Ltd v Gardner*] the crucial question to which the assistant recorder should have directed his mind was, in my opinion, whether the roof of the premises would, in the ordinary use of words, be regarded as part of the structure or exterior of the ... top floor flat, when that flat is regarded as a separate part of the [block]. ... I can see no reason

---

[125] [1943] K.B. 73. See also *Rapid Results College v Angell* [1985] 1 E.G.L.R. 530, considered at para.7–41, below.
[126] The section is discussed in paras 20–17 to 20–48, below.
[127] Landlord and Tenant Act 1985 s.11(1).
[128] [1977] Q.B. 823.
[129] See para.20–24, below.
[130] [1984] 1 W.L.R. 716.

in principle why the roof above [a top floor flat] should not be capable in some circumstances of falling within the scope of [the obligation]. ... To take the simplest case by way of example, if the ceiling and roof of a particular top floor dwelling all formed part of one flat, inseparable, structural unit, it would seem to me prima facie that in the ordinary use of words, the roof and ceiling would be regarded as part of the structure or exterior of that dwelling, as much as its outside walls, inner party walls and so forth. On the other hand, I do not think one can go so far as to say that the roof, or part of the roof, which lies above any so-called top floor flat necessarily will fall within [the obligation]. Borderline cases, for example, might arise where one found a void space or an uninhabited loft between the flat and the roof. Everything must depend on the particular facts of the case."

## Expressions commonly used to define the subject matter

### (a)   Building

**7–33**    The meaning of "building" in any particular case will depend on the context.[131] In *Paddington Corp v A-G*[132] the Earl of Halsbury said:

"The subject-matter to be dealt with is to be looked at in order to see what the word 'building' means in relation to that particular subject-matter. It is impossible to give any definite meaning to it in the loose language which is used in some cases. Anything which is in the nature of a building might be within one covenant and the same erection might not be a building with reference to another covenant."

In the absence of any definition in the lease, a useful starting point will be the ordinary meaning of the expression.[133] In normal parlance, "building" is naturally used to describe a significantly wider range of structures than simply "an inclosure of brick or stonework, covered in by a roof".[134]

The question arose on somewhat unusual facts in *Pattrick v Marley Estates Management*.[135] The demised premises included certain cloisters (called "the Chapel Cloisters") comprising a permanent man-made structure consisting of concrete, stone or brick walls, a concrete slab roof, a flight of stone or concrete stairs and an inner store room, which were all that remained of a chapel called Syon Abbey which had been demolished prior to the grant of the lease. The tenant covenanted to repair the demised premises other than the parts comprised and referred to in the landlord's covenant. The landlord covenanted to repair the "main structure ... of the houses and the buildings". The judge at first instance found that the Chapel Cloisters were not "buildings" and thus fell within the tenant's repairing obligation. The Court of Appeal allowed the landlord's appeal, holding that the Chapel Cloisters did constitute a "building". Sir Andrew-Morritt V.C. (with whom Mummery and Arden L.JJ. agreed) said:

"22.    The fact that the cloisters had previously formed part of Syon Abbey, which was undoubtedly a building until it was partially demolished, is in my view irrelevant. Was

---

[131] *R. (on the application of Ghai) v Newcastle City Council* [2010] EWCA Civ 59 at [24].
[132] [1906] 1 A.C. 1 at 3.
[133] *R. (on the application of Ghai) v Newcastle City Council*, above, per Lord Neuberger M.R. at [24].
[134] Ibid., per Lord Neuberger M.R. at [24] (commenting on an obiter passage in the judgment of Lord Esher M.R. in *Moir v Williams* [1892] 1 Q.B. 264.)
[135] [2007] EWCA Civ 1176.

it, as it stood [at the date of grant of the lease], after demolition of the chapel superstructure, a building for the purposes of clause 6(d)(i)?

23. It then had a floor, roof, three walls and a colonnade forming the fourth. They were all man-made. As the colonnade was open to the elements the uses to which the enclosed space might usefully be put were necessarily limited. If such a structure is not a building within the normal meaning of the word it is hard to know what it is."

### (b)    Structure[136]

The use of the expression "structure" to identify the subject-matter of a repairing covenant often raises difficult questions. In one sense, "a structure" is a synonym for "a building" or "a construction". In this primary sense, it refers to an edifice in its own right rather than a part of some larger entity. However, in repairing covenants, it is generally used not in this sense, but in the secondary sense of "the structure" of a building, i.e. a subsidiary part of the whole. So used, it is capable of a number of different shades of meaning. At one end of the scale, the expression would comprehend virtually all the constituent physical parts of a building and exclude only purely decorative items, such as paper and paintwork. At the other extreme, the expression would be limited only to those parts of a building which are essential to its physical integrity, i.e. without which it could not properly be described as a building at all. Used in this sense, it may include no more than the foundations, load bearing walls and roof. It is in this latter sense that one may talk of a building being "structurally sound", meaning that it is unlikely to fall down or disintegrate, but not necessarily that it is free from any defect whatsoever. The precise shade of meaning to be given in any particular case will obviously depend upon the context.

7–34

In *Horlick v Scully*[137] a lease of a mansion house and grounds, including various ornamental lakes and ponds, contained a tenant's covenant to keep "all pleasure grounds" in good and proper order and condition, and a landlord's covenant to carry out all structural repairs. The lakes became silted up with accumulated mud so as to injure the amenities and the fishing. Eve J. held that clearing out the mud from the lakes was not a structural repair for which the landlord was liable. In so holding, he did not attempt any discussion or definition of the meaning of the expression.

In *Blundell v Obsdale Ltd*[138] a house was let containing a tenant's repairing covenant which expressly excluded liability for "structural repairs to the foundations roof main walls and drains". Harman J. said in the course of his judgment:

"[I]t seems to me that the [tenant] is liable for all repairs to the demised property except for repairs which involve the structure [of the roof, etc.]. This, however, is rather to state than to solve the problem."

He did not attempt any definition of "structural repairs", but treated the question whether a particular item did or did not fall within the exception as one of fact in each case. He held that the following were not within the exception:

---

[136] See further heading (c), below.
[137] [1927] 2 Ch. 150.
[138] (1958) 171 E.G. 491.

(a) repairs to a balustrade forming the boundary of a balcony at first floor level. His reasoning was that it was not a wall at all, still less a main wall, and in any event, the repairs were not structural because the balustrade was not part of the structure but was simply a "piece of decoration";

(b) redressing and soldering a flat roof made of lead laid on boards;

(c) repairs to a dormer roof, consisting of cutting out a split in the felt, covering the felt with roofing compound and painting over with bitumastic paint.

However, stripping off the lead covering of a roof over the first floor, renewing two boards underneath and renewing the covering in asphalt was held to amount to a "structural repair" for which the tenant was not liable.

7–35    The meaning of "structural repairs" was considered later the same year in *Granada Theatres Ltd v Freehold Investments (Leytonstone) Ltd*.[139] In that case a cinema had been let on a lease containing a tenant's covenant to repair the demised premises. The covenant provided that "nothing in this clause ... shall render [the tenant] liable for structural repairs of a substantial nature to the main walls roof foundations or main drains of the demised building". The walls of the building (which were of 9in brick) had been rendered in cement. The rendering was defective and falling away, taking with it parts of the adjoining brickwork. The remedial work consisted of removing the rendering, making good the brickwork and applying new rendering. Furthermore, at least 350 to 500 slates out of approximately 12,000 on the roof required replacement. Both Vaisey J. at first instance and the Court of Appeal held that this work amounted to "structural repairs of a substantial nature", so that the tenant was not liable. In the course of his judgment Vaisey J. said:

> "It appears, rather surprisingly, that the expression 'structural repairs' has never been judicially defined, a fact to which attention is drawn in *Woodfall on Landlord and Tenant*, 25th edition, page 770, paragraph 1732, and counsel in the present case have accepted that statement as correct. The writer of the textbook submits on the same page that 'structural repairs' are those which involve interference with, or alteration to, the framework of the building, and I would myself say that 'structural repairs' means repairs of, or to, a structure. It is sometimes said that repairs must be either structural or decorative, and if that is the simple criterion we are, in this case, certainly not dealing with decorative repairs ... Again, what is a 'structure'? And what ought to be regarded as part of a 'structure'? We are dealing here with (a) the roof, and (b) one of the main walls of a cinema, and surely those are parts of the structure of the building."

In the Court of Appeal Jenkins L.J. (with whose judgment on this point the other two members of the Court agreed) expressed himself as content to adopt the above passage.

It is not wholly clear what the judge meant by "repairs of, or to, a structure". On one view, if the word "structure" was used in its primary sense of "a building", then the words would be wide enough to include virtually all work of repair to the building, or perhaps all work other than purely decorative work. That this is what the judge may have meant is supported by his reference to repairs being divided into structural and decorative repairs. However, if he did mean this, then his definition is quite different from that in the textbook which he quotes in his judgment without apparent disagreement. It is thought that he did not intend

---

[139] [1959] Ch. 592, CA.

to go this far, and that his words are to be read as meaning "repairs of, or to, the structure", i.e. the structure of a building. In other words, he used the expression "structure" to identify particular substantial parts of a building rather than its entirety (or its entirety other than its decorative components).

In *Pearlman v Keepers and Governors of Harrow School*[140] (which concerned the question whether the installation of a central heating system was "an improvement made by the execution of works amounting to structural alteration, extension or addition" for the purposes of the Housing Act 1974), Eveleigh L.J. approved the following passage from the judgment of His Honour Judge White in *Pickering v Phillimore*[141]:

> "A house is a complex unity, particularly a modern house. 'Structural' implies concern with the 'constituent or material' parts of that unity. What are the 'constituent' or 'material' parts? In my judgment in any ordinary sense they involve more than simply the load bearing elements, for example, the four walls, the roof and the foundations. The constituent parts are more complex than that. [He then suggested a definition of 'structural' as being] appertaining to the basic fabric and parts of the house as distinguished from its decorations and fittings."

In the Scottish case of *Hastie v City of Edinburgh District Council*[142] it was held in the Sherriff's Court that windows were not part of the "structure" of a house for the purposes of a landlord's covenant to keep in repair the structure and exterior of the house (including drains, gutters and external pipes). Sherrif Ireland QC said:

> "The structure of a house is that part of it which gives it stability, shape and identity as a house. The essentials seem to me to be foundations, walls and roof. If these are present, then there is a house, and any person shown it would describe it as a house, whatever shortcomings it might have as a house. In relation to a particular house, there may be other elements which form part of the structure. For example, in a two-storey house, the staircase and the upper floor may be part of the structure, since they give stability, shape and identity to *that* house (i.e. a two-storey house), and without them the house is not recognisable as a two-storey house. There is no reason why the elements comprising the structure of a house should be the same in every house, since s.8 of the Act [143] refers to the structure of *the* house—i.e. the particular identifiable house which is the subject of the lease. On the other hand the phrase 'the structure of the house' (on the assumption that 'structure' and 'house' are not identical terms) implies that there are parts of the house which are not parts of the structure of the house. Windows seem to me to fall into this category. They are parts of the house, since they are annexed to the house in such a way as to become part of the heritage. Nevertheless they are not essential to give stability, shape and identity to the house as a house. Foundation, walls and roof, and no more, would be a very uncomfortable place to live in, but I should describe the assembly of parts as a house, albeit a house without windows. The structure is complete, although the windows have to be put in. In the ordinary use of language, if one of the windows of the house is broken and has to be repaired, one talks of repairing the window. It would not occur to anyone to say that the structure was being repaired, although the expression would be quite appropriate if the repairs were being done to the foundation, walls and roof, and probably to the staircase in a house with more than one storey."[144]

---

[140] [1979] Q.B. 56.

[141] Unreported May 10, 1976, County Court.

[142] (1981) SLT (Sh. Ct.) 61.

[143] This is a reference to the Housing (Scotland) Act 1966, under which a covenant on the part of the landlord to keep in repair the structure and exterior of the house (including drains, gutters and external pipes) was implied into short leases of houses.

[144] Note that the judge's test, particularly the suggestion that something is not part of the structure of a house if the building can properly be described as a house without it, may well be too narrow in the

**7–36**     In *Irvine's Estate v Moran*[145] the question was whether various items were part of the "structure" for the purposes of the landlord's repairing covenant implied by s.11 of the Landlord and Tenant Act 1985 into leases of dwelling houses for less than seven years.[146] Mr Recorder Thayne Forbes QC (sitting as a deputy judge of the Queen's Bench Division) said:

> "... I have come to the view that the structure of the dwellinghouse consists of those elements of the overall dwelling house which give it its essential appearance, stability and shape. The expression does not extend to the many and various ways in which the dwellinghouse will be fitted out, equipped, decorated and generally made to be habitable. I am not persuaded by [counsel for the landlord] that one should limit the expression "the structure of the dwellinghouse to those aspects of the dwellinghouse which are load bearing in the sense that that sort of expression is used by professional consulting engineers and the like; but what I do feel is, as regards the words "structure of the dwellinghouse", that in order to be part of the structure of the dwellinghouse a particular element must be a material or significant element in the overall construction. To some extent, in every case there will be a degree of fact to be gone into to decide whether or not something is or is not part of the structure of the dwellinghouse. It is not easy to think of an overall explanation of the meaning of those words which will be applicable in every case and I deliberately decline to attempt such a definition. I am content for the purposes of this case to say that I accept [counsel's] submission that "structure of the dwellinghouse" has a more limited meaning than the overall building itself and that it is addressed to those essential elements of the dwellinghouse which are material to its overall construction. That I think is as far as I am able to go."

He went on to hold that for the purposes of s.11 of the 1985 Act the structure and exterior extended to windows (including frames, sash cords and window furniture (but not non-essential furniture))[147] and external doors, but did not include plaster, internal door furniture, window glass damaged by the tenant and decorations. His reasoning as regards plaster was that it was "more in the nature of a decorative finish and is not part of the essential material elements which go to make up the structure of the dwellinghouse".

The passage quoted above was cited with apparent approval in *Ibrahim v Dovecorn Reversions*.[148] In *Marlborough Park Services v Rowe*[149] Neuberger L.J., having quoted it, said:

> "[17]     Although I accept, as I have emphasised, that words such as 'structure' or 'main structures' must take their meaning from the particular document, lease or statute in which they are found, and from the surrounding circumstances, and although it can be said that any attempt to define them will, to an extent, raise as many questions as it answers, it seems to me that that is a good working definition to bear in mind, albeit not one to apply slavishly."

---

light of the other authorities considered in this section. See, however, *Hannon v Hillingdon Homes Ltd* [2012] EWHC 1437 (QB), in which *Hastie* was cited with approval by H.H. Judge Thornton QC (sitting as a judge of the High Court) at [28].

[145] [1991] 1 E.G.L.R. 261.

[146] S.11 is considered in para.20–17 et seq., below.

[147] See also *Sheffield City Council v Oliver* (Lands Tribunal) LRZ/146/2007, in which windows were held to be part of the structure and exterior for the purposes of s.11.

[148] [2001] 2 E.G.L.R. 46.

[149] [2006] 2 E.G.L.R. 27.

In *Grand v Gill*[150] the Court of Appeal accepted the judge's observations in *Irvine's Estate v Moran* as providing a good working definition, but disagreed with his conclusion that the plaster was not to be regarded as part of the structure. Rimer L.J. said:

> "25.   For myself, whilst I would accept and adopt Mr Recorder Thayne Forbes's observations as to the meaning of 'the structure ... of the dwellinghouse' as providing for present purposes, as Neuberger LJ put it, a good working definition, I am respectfully unconvinced by his holding that the plaster finish to an internal wall or ceiling is to be regarded as in the nature of a decorative finish rather than as forming part of the 'structure'. In the days when lath and plaster ceiling and internal partition walls were more common than now, the plaster was, I should have thought, an essential part of the creation and shaping of the ceiling or partition wall, which serve to give a dwellinghouse its essential appearance and shape. I would also regard plasterwork generally, including that applied to external walls, as being ordinarily in the nature of a smooth constructional finish to walls and ceilings, to which the decoration can then be applied, rather than a decorative finish in itself. I would therefore hold that it is part of the 'structure'. I would accordingly accept that the wall and ceiling plaster in Ms Grand's flat formed part of the 'structure' of the flat for the repair of which Mr Gill was responsible."

Lloyd L.J. said:

> "33.   Like Rimer LJ, I would respectfully differ from Mr Recorder Thayne Forbes on this point, not as regards the ... passage ... in which he sought to identify a principle on which to decide the point, but rather as regards his application of that principle to the particular case of plaster ... As Rimer LJ says, in the case of the use of plaster in ways which are now perhaps historic rather than current (but of which examples are certainly still to be found) such as lath and plaster construction, the plaster is clearly part of the structure. The expert's second report suggests ... that this technique may have been used in parts of the premises relevant to this case.
>
> 34.   I would not limit my reasoning, however, to cases where the wall or ceiling is of lath and plaster or similar construction. I agree that plaster as applied to even a solid wall or ceiling is not 'in the nature of a decorative finish', as Mr Recorder Thayne Forbes said, and that it is to be regarded as a part of the wall or ceiling upon or to which a decorative finish, of whatever kind, may be applied. Accordingly I would hold, as a general proposition, that plaster forming part of or applied to walls and ceilings is part of the structure of the relevant premises."

Reference should also be made to para.20–24 et seq., below, in which the meaning of "structure and exterior" in s.11 of the 1985 Act is further considered.

In *Marlborough Park Services v Rowe*[151] the question was whether the floor   **7–37** joists supporting the first floor of a ground and first floor maisonette formed part of the "main structures" of a block of flats for the purposes of the landlord's repairing covenant. The Court of Appeal held that the joists were both part of the structure and part of the "main structures".

In *Langham Estate Management Ltd v Hardy*,[152] a high-class residential property was let at a high rent on terms which (among other things) obliged the landlords to "put and keep in repair and maintain the structure and the exterior of the property". It was held that internal doors were not part of the structure.

---

[150] [2011] 27 E.G. 78.
[151] [2006] 2 E.G.L.R. 27.
[152] [2008] 3 E.G.L.R. 125. See further on this case para.24–04, above.

In *Hannon v Hillingdon Homes Ltd*[153] a tenancy of a council house obliged the landlord to keep in repair the structure and exterior of the property. It was held that bannisters on the open side of a staircase which connected the first and second floors were part of the structure. They were an integral part of the staircase, which was itself part of the structure of the house.

In the Australian case of *Reilly v Liangis Property Ltd*,[154] the tenant of a motel covenanted to "maintain renew repair and keep the whole of the demised premises in good and substantial repair working order and condition damage by reasonable wear and tear only excepted. However nothing herein contained shall impose any obligations upon the Lessee to do any work of a structural nature except such as may be occasioned by the act neglect or default of the Lessee or by its use or occupancy of the demised premises". Floor tiles became detached from the floor as a result of deterioration of the adhesive, probably due to inadequate allowance being made for thermal expansion. The possible remedial work consisted of re-laying the tiles with more adhesive, re-laying them with proper expansion and proper adhesive or removing the tiles. Young J. held that none of these involved interfering with the structure of the building, with the result that the work was the liability of the tenant. He said:

> "What [the covenant] contemplates is that the tenants have the use of the building, but that the wholeness of the building is a matter for the landlord alone. Anything that interferes with the stability of the whole or involves interference with structural members is something for the landlord. Other work is work for the tenants."

In the Australian case of *Alamdo Holdings Property Ltd v Australian Window Furnishings (NSW) Property Ltd*,[155] the demised premises consisted of two large factory buildings and seven adjacent bitumen areas. The tenant covenanted to: "maintain replace repair and keep the whole of the Demised Premises in good and substantial repair order and condition damage by reasonable wear and tear only excepted Provided that this covenant shall not impose on the Lessee any obligation in respect of any structural maintenance replacement or repair except when the same is rendered necessary by any act or omission or default on the part of the Lessee or by the Lessee's use or occupancy of the Demised Premises". At the end of the lease, three of the bitumen areas were beyond reasonable wear and tear. At first instance, Barrett J. held[156] that the bitumen areas were a structure and the necessary works were structural repairs. He said:

> "They were put on the land by a process of construction. Their character, as consisting of a skin or coating of asphalt placed upon a prepared land surface to which a basecoat of aggregate or blue metal had first been added, makes them similar to, although lesser in degree than, the 'low attractive brick fence' considered in *Durkin v Commonwealth Savings Bank of Australia*[157] where a fence 'in which the bricks are cemented to a cement base and to one another as mortar' was held to be a 'permanent domestic improvement of a structural nature'."

---

[153] [2012] EWHC 1437 (Q.B.).
[154] [2000] NSWSC 47.
[155] [2006] NSWCA 224.
[156] [2004] NSWSC 487.
[157] Unreported decision of the Full Court of the Supreme Court of South Australia dated November 30, 1990.

The judge's conclusion was upheld by the New South Wales Court of Appeal.

Helpful though the cases are (particularly the judge's "good working definition" in *Irvine's Estate v Moran* as approved by the Court of Appeal in *Grand v Gill*), the question of what constitutes the structure in any particular case will ultimately depend upon the proper construction of the lease in question. In many cases, the lease will itself provide some guidance as to what is meant. Where that is not the case, the correct approach will be to seek to identify those parts of the building that, having regard to the language and scheme of the lease as a whole, the objective background facts known to both parties at the date of the lease and the guidance given by the above cases, the parties must be taken to have regarded as comprising the structure. In the case of a separate, self-contained building, these will include, at the very least, all those parts of it which have to do with its stability and protection from the elements. On this basis, the structure of a traditionally built building will extend on any view to the roof, foundations and load-bearing walls. Depending upon the circumstances, it is likely to include other items as well. What comprises the structure of a modern office building will again depend upon the circumstances, but on any view it is likely to include the steel frame and roof. The walls will generally comprise concrete or other infills in the steel frame with prefabricated cladding on the outside. The usual function of the infills and cladding is to keep out the elements but not generally to carry loads (other than wind loads). It is thought that in the ordinary case they would nonetheless form part of the structure, as would the concrete floors. It is perhaps unlikely that raised floors would be included, but again, the answer depends on the circumstances.

7–38

The problem has a further dimension where the question is not what is the structure of a separate self-contained building, but what is the structure of some lesser unit within it (for example, a flat). In such a case it will be necessary to inquire first what is the specified unit: is it limited to what has been demised, or is it capable of extending further?[158] Once this has been done, the question will then be the same as above, namely, what in all the circumstances and as matter of the ordinary use of words can properly be said to form part of its "structure"? Depending on the facts, it may be that this will be limited to things which are physically contiguous in some way, notwithstanding the fact that the unit derives both protection and support from other parts of the building. For example, the foundations of the building will not usually be part of the "structure" of a fifth-floor flat.

### (c)   Main structure

The use of the expression "main structure" will generally indicate a more restrictive meaning than "structure" alone.[159] As always, however, the question is one of construction in every case.

7–39

---

[158] See para.7–32, above.
[159] See *Toff v McDowell* (1995) 69 P. & C.R. 535 at 541; *Ibrahim v Dovecorn Reversions Ltd* [2001] 2 E.G.L.R. 46 at 49D.

In *Samuels v Abbints Investments Ltd*[160] the landlord of a flat covenanted to "keep the main structure of the block in tenantable repair", the tenant being responsible for "the internal and external walls ... but excluding the outside brick, steel or concrete work". Ungoed-Thomas J. construed this as meaning that the landlord was liable for the outside bricks of the external walls of the flat and the tenant was liable for the inside part of the walls.[161] The landlord was accordingly held liable when saturation of the outside bricks resulted in an outbreak of dry rot in the flat.

In *Toff v McDowell*[162] a lease of a basement flat included in the demise one-half part in depth of the structure between the ceiling of the flat and the floor of the flat above it, the internal and external walls up to the same level, and the land and structure of the building below the flat including the foundations. The tenant covenanted to repair the demised premises other than those parts for which the landlord was responsible, and the landlord agreed to repair the "main structure and in particular the roof chimney stacks gutters and rainwater pipes of the building". Evans Lombe J. held that floor separating the flat from the flat above was not part of the "main structure" within the landlord's obligation but instead was the shared responsibility of the tenants of the two flats.[163]

In *Marlborough Park Services v Rowe*[164] a long lease of a ground and first floor maisonette described the demise as "including the ceilings and floors thereof and the joists and beams on which the floors are laid together with all the floors ....". The tenant covenanted to keep in repair the demised premises other than those parts referred to in cl.5. By clause 5(a)(i)(a), the landlord covenanted to maintain, renew and decorate "the roof and main structures of the Property". The Court of Appeal held that the timber floor joists of the ground floor ceiling and the floor of the first floor of the maisonette were part of the "main structures of the Property". Neuberger L.J. said:

> "In my view, the joists in this case are part of the "main structure". As the judge found on the evidence, the joists play a significant part in keeping the building stable and sound in that they provide a degree of support for walls. Their failure would directly impinge upon the effectiveness of walls of the building and, therefore, ultimately upon the integrity of the building. They would be regarded by any ordinary person as an essential part of the building, both in terms of its usability and in terms of its structural soundness. Although they are not "main" to the same degree as the external walls or the roofs, they are certainly more "main" than, say, the floorboards or even completely non–load–bearing internal partition walls. The fact that they have a structural function renders them likely to come within the ambit of the "main structures", not only as a matter of language but also in practical terms. Because of their structural function described by [the engineer], the landlord, the management company and the tenants of units in Marlborough Park would be more likely to have expected the maintenance of the floor joists to be the responsibility of the management company under clause 5(a)(i)(a), rather than of the individual tenants under clause 3(i)(m). This point is reinforced by the fact

---

[160] (1963) 188 E.G. 689.

[161] The evidence showed that there was a recognised distinction between the two parts of the wall.

[162] (1995) 69 P. & C.R. 535.

[163] See, however, *Marlborough Park Services v Rowe* [2006] 2 E.G.L.R. 27 at [22], in which Sedley L.J. expressed doubts as to the correctness of one of the arguments accepted by Evans-Lombe J. in *Toff*, namely, that the effect of the word "in particular" was to restrict the meaning of "main structure" to the particularised elements.

[164] [2006] 2 E.G.L.R. 27.

that the work in question would be tolerably substantial and would, as I have mentioned, be to the benefit, normally, not merely to the one tenant of one unit but to the tenants of a number of units."

In *Pattrick v Marley Estates Management*[165] the demise included part of a substantial grade II* mansion house with a number of Georgian sash windows carried by dressed stone frames into the main walls. The Court of Appeal held that on the proper construction of the lease in question, the windows did not form part of the "main structure".[166]

In *Luckhurst v Manyfield*[167] the demised premises comprised a flat forming part of a converted house. The landlord covenanted to repair (among other things) "the main structure and in particular the foundations external walls roof gutters and rain water pipes of the property". The solid floors of the basement contained a damp proof membrane. H.H. Judge Bowsher held that the damp-proof membrane and whatever was under it were part of the main structure for the purposes of the landlord's obligation.

A number of cases have concerned whether a landlord's obligation to repair the main structure extends to a roof terrace above the demised flat. In *Petersson v Pitt Place (Epsom) Ltd*[168] the Court of Appeal held that on the proper construction of the leases in question, the landlord was not liable to repair the roof terraces in question. The terraces formed part of the demised premises which the tenants were liable to repair. It followed that if the landlord was also liable for repairs, there would be overlapping obligations.[169] Laws L.J. said:

> "It is plain and obvious that there is a very great deal of force in [the submission] ... that as a matter of common sense these terraces fall within the main structure of the building. It seems to me however that the consequences of a conclusion which allows for shared or overlapping repairing obligations are so impractical that such a conclusion must be avoided unless it simply cannot be done on the language. I do not consider that the language here brings us to such a pass as that. It is clear that the lease could and should have been drafted a great deal more clearly than it was ... But in performing the duty of construing this lease, the imperative of avoiding if at all possible overlapping obligations has driven me to the conclusion that [the landlord's] submissions ought to be accepted. They may be accepted as a matter of language. I do not say that it is the plainest or most obvious sense to be given to [the relevant words]; but in so far as it is possible to construe 'main structure' as not including these roof terraces I, for the reasons I have given, would do so."

A different decision was arrived at in *Hallisey v Petmoor Developments Ltd*,[170] in which Patten J. held that on the proper construction of the lease, the roof terrace in question (i.e. both the underlying structure and the surface) was within the landlord's obligation to maintain and keep in good and substantial repair and

**7–40**

---

[165] [2007] EWCA Civ 1176.

[166] Although they were held to be part of the "exterior" for the purposes of the landlord's obligation to decorate: see para.7–33, below.

[167] Unreported decision of H.H. Judge Bowsher, QC dated July 30, 1992 (noted in the *Handbook of Dilapidations* at DC256).

[168] [2001] 82 P. & C.R. 21.

[169] See paras 7–29 to 7–30, above.

[170] [2000] E.G.C.S. 124. The decision was said to be correct by Neuberger L.J. in *Marlborough Park Services v Rowe* [2006] 2 E.G.L.R. 27 at [14].

condition "the main structure of the building including the principal internal structures and the exterior walls and the foundations and the roof of the Building". He said:

> "[T]he eighth floor roof terrace was constructed with layers of asphalt and external tiles in order to provide the necessary weather proofing for the porous concrete slab beneath. It seems to me that the 'main structure' of the building ought properly to be construed so as to include not only the bare concrete shell but also whatever additional surfaces were created by the lessor in order to make that shell a complete and effective structure for the purpose of maintaining the physical integrity of the flats within the development. To construe 'the main structure' as including both the concrete slab and the asphalt and tiles above it is entirely consistent with the inclusion ... in that structure of the exterior walls, foundations and roofs all of which serve the same purpose.
> Conversely, if the asphalt and tiles are not part of the 'main structure' then one has to assume that the landlord deliberately ceded control and responsibility for the repair and maintenance of part of the exterior fabric of the building to one of the tenants rather than retain the right to maintain the fabric of the building (and the value of its reversion) with the benefit of a full indemnity under the service charge provisions. In so doing there could be no guarantee that the tenant would carry out these obligations and their enforcement might ultimately require legal action by the landlord.
> This seems to me to be an unlikely scenario and is not required by the lease."

In *Ibrahim v Dovecorn Reversions Ltd*,[171] the demise expressly excluded "the main walls and structure" of the building. The landlord covenanted to repair the "main structure." Rimer J. held that, construing the lease as a whole, "main" qualified both "walls" and "structure". Having reviewed the above authorities, he held that the roof terrace in question was part of the "main structure" and therefore excluded from the demise. In his view:

> "[T]he more natural interpretation of the leases is that the reference to 'main structure' ... includes the whole of the roof terrace (save only its surface area, which I hold is demised to the lessee)."

## (d)  Exterior

**7–41**    Prima facie, the "exterior" will include all external parts of the building or unit, i.e. the roof and the structure supporting it, chimneys, external cladding, all outside gutters and pipes, outside walls and external doors. It will generally also include windows and window frames.[172] Thus, in *Ball v Plummer*[173] the landlord of a public house covenanted to do "outside repairs". It was held that this included windows, "the windows being part of the skin of the house".[174]

It was argued in *Holding & Barnes v Hill House Hammond Ltd*[175] at first instance that the expressions "structure and exterior" were to be read as covering much the same thing. Disagreeing, Neuberger J. said that it was arguable, for instance, that "the outside of the windows or doors are not part of the 'structure',

---

[171] [2001] 2 E.G.L.R 46. The decision was said to be correct by Neuberger L.J. in *Marlborough Park Services v Rowe* [2006] 2 E.G.L.R. 27 at [14].

[172] *Sheffield City Council v Oliver* (Lands Tribunal) LRZ/146/2007.

[173] (1879) 23 S.J. 656.

[174] See also para.7–50, below.

[175] [2000] L. & T.R. 428. Note that Neuberger J.'s decision was reversed by the Court of Appeal, who did not comment on this part of his judgment: [2002] 2 P. & C.R. 11.

however, they are undoubtedly part of the 'exterior'." A distinction along much the same lines was drawn by the Court of Appeal in *Pattrick v Marley Estates Management*,[176] in which Georgian sash windows carried by dressed stone frames into the main walls of a substantial grade II\* mansion house were held to be part of the "exterior" but not of "the main structure".

In the Scottish case of *Hastie v City of Edinburgh District Council*,[177] it was held in the Sherriff's Court that windows were part of the "exterior" of a house for the purposes of a landlord's covenant to keep in repair the structure and exterior of the house (including drains, gutters and external pipes). Sherriff Ireland QC said:

> "In my opinion, the exterior of the house is the part of the house which lies between what is outside the house and what is inside the house. It is the part of the house which you can see if you look at it from the outside.
> If either of these definitions is correct, then a window is part of the exterior of the house."

In *Rapid Results College Ltd v Angell*,[178] the demised premises comprised offices on the second floor of a three-storey building. The landlord covenanted to repair "the external walls and structure and in particular the roof ... of the building", the expression "the building" meaning the totality of the building containing the demised premises. The tenant covenanted to pay a service charge equal to 50 per cent of:

> "[T]he following expenses and outgoings incurred by the landlords in respect of the premises being the offices on the First and Second Floors forming part of the building and shown bounded by the red line on the said plan annexed hereto (hereinafter called 'the first and second floor offices'): ... 4. Maintenance of the exterior."

The question was whether the landlords were entitled to levy a service charge in respect of the cost of taking down and rebuilding the parapet wall on the flat roof of the building. The Court of Appeal construed the words "maintenance of the exterior" as meaning "maintenance of the exterior of the first and second floor offices", and held that the roof and parapet wall did not form part of the exterior of the offices. The reasoning of Nicholls L.J. was as follows:

> "The difficulty I feel with [the landlord's argument] is that ... the roof and parapet wall extend over not only the part of the building edged in red on the lease plan but also the part of the building edged in brown on the plan. Thus at best only part of the roof and parapet wall would be within item 4, because only part of the roof and parapet wall are contiguous to the part of the second floor which is edged in red. Hence, even if one were to accept that the roof and parapet wall are capable of being 'the exterior', the end result would be the unattractive one that part, but only part, of the single flat roof and of the one continuous perimeter parapet wall would be within item 4. I find it impossible to believe that such a result was, or is to be taken as having been, the intention of the parties. Furthermore, construing item 4 as contended would have the result that although occupying one third of the building, the tenants under this short lease would be responsible for half the costs of the maintenance of the roof and parapet wall. It may be said that this is not inappropriate, because the tenants occupy the top floor of the building immediately below the roof; but I do not think that this result is so obviously right that it prompts the conclusion that this must be what the parties to the lease intended."

---

[176] [2007] EWCA Civ 1176.
[177] (1981) SLT (Sh. Ct.) 61.
[178] [1986] 1 E.G.L.R. 53.

In *Fincar SRL v 109/113 Mount Street Management Co Ltd*[179] a sub-tenant of part of a building which included a basement and vaults covenanted to:

"[K]eep the exterior of the Building in a proper state of structural and decorative repair in accordance with the terms of [the superior lease] ... and in particular ... to carry out ... (i) ... repair of the exterior walls the roof gutters foundations and generally of the exterior and structure of the Building."

The relevant part of the superior lease contained a covenant to:

"[K]eep the demised buildings (both inside and outside) in a proper state of structural and decorative repair and as and when reasonably necessary ... rebuild in a proper and workmanlike manner ... the whole or such part of the demised buildings as may require to be rebuilt ..."

The vaults had been incorporated into the basement in order to create usable space, and the relevant works included applying a waterproof rendering ("tanking") to the inside surfaces of the exterior walls of the enlarged area (save that in two areas polythene secured by battens or a stud and plasterboard false wall had been used). The Court of Appeal held (by a majority) that, having regard to the wording of the superior lease, the tanking was part of the exterior of the building within the meaning of the covenant in the sub-lease, but that liability did not extend to the temporary expedients adopted in relation to the two non-tanked sections.

**7–42**     In the ordinary case, all walls which enclose the premises will be included in the expression "exterior" whether or not they are actually exposed to the air. In *Green v Eales*[180] the premises at the time of the demise consisted of a terraced building, and the landlord covenanted to repair "all the external parts of the demised premises ... except the glass and lead of the windows thereof". The adjoining house was subsequently pulled down by the local authority acting under statutory powers, and what had formerly been an inner party wall thereupon became an exposed and unsupported outside wall. It subsided and required taking down and rebuilding. Lord Denman C.J., giving judgment of the court, said:

"The ... question in this case, is whether the wall between [the demised premises] and [the adjoining premises] was an external part of the premises within the covenant in the lease. We are of the opinion that it was. We think that it was so even before [the adjoining premises were] pulled down, but certainly afterwards. The external parts of premises are those which form the enclosure of them, and beyond which no part of them extends; and it is immaterial whether those parts are exposed to the atmosphere, or rest upon and adjoin some other building which forms no part of the premises let.[181]"

In *Pembery v Lamdin*[182] part of the demised premises consisted of a basement, the walls of which were below ground and in contact with the earth. Likewise, in

---

[179] [1999] L. & T.R. 161.

[180] [1841] 2 Q.B. 255.

[181] Note, however, that in *Fincar SRL v 109/113 Mount Street Management Co Ltd* [1999] L. & T.R. 161, Beldam L.J. regarded this passage as "helpful only to determine what parts of the premises are to be regarded as external parts".

[182] [1940] 2 All E.R. 434.

*Luckhurst v Manyfield*,[183] it was held by the Official Referee that the external walls of a flat included the exterior brick walls that were below ground.

It is not clear to what extent the "exterior" of a steel framed office building includes any part of the steel frame as opposed to the curtain walling or cladding. The question was raised but not answered in *Plough Investments Ltd v Manchester City Council*.[184] It was held in that case that even if the exterior of the building was limited to the surface cladding, nonetheless if damage was caused to the condition of surface cladding by rust on the external sections of the steel frames, then the covenant to repair on its proper construction required the covenantor to deal with the rust.

**7–43**

The lease may on its proper construction provide for a division of responsibility in relation to different sides of the external walls. Thus, in *Samuels v Abbints Investments Ltd*[185] a lease of a flat contained a landlord's covenant to keep the main structure of the block in tenantable repair. The tenant was responsible for "the internal and external walls … but excluding the outside brick, steel or concrete work". The evidence showed that there was a recognisable distinction between the outside brickwork of the external walls and the internal part of the walls. Ungoed-Thomas J. held that the landlord was liable for the outside bricks of the external walls, and the tenant was responsible for the internal part of the walls.

The extent to which expressions such as "exterior" or "external parts" apply only to the demised building itself as opposed to any other part of the demised premises (for example, land) is a question of construction in each case. In *McAuliffe v Moloney*[186] a covenant to keep "the external parts" of premises in repair was held not to apply to a gate or gateway. However, essential means of access may be included.[187]

The repairing covenant implied by s.11 of the Landlord and Tenant Act 1985 extends to the "exterior" of the dwelling-house, and reference should also be made to the cases decided under that section.[188]

### (e)   Interior

It is relatively common for a tenant's repairing (or decorating[189]) covenant to be limited to "the interior of the demised premises", or some similar formulation such as "the internal parts of the premises".[190] Construing such a covenant

**7–44**

---

[183] Unreported decision of H.H. Judge Bowsher QC dated July 30, 1992 (noted in the *Handbook of Dilapidations* at DC256).
[184] [1989] 1 E.G.L.R. 244.
[185] (1963) 188 E.G. 689.
[186] [1971] I.R. 200.
[187] See the cases on the meaning of "exterior" in s.11 of the Landlord and Tenant Act 1985, discussed in para.20–24 et seq., below.
[188] See para.20–27, below.
[189] See Ch.15, below.
[190] See the Australian case of *Gerraty v McGavin* (1914) 18 C.L.R. 152 (covenant to keep in repair "the internal part of the premises" in a lease of premises comprising a hotel, a bakehouse and other buildings, and saleyards held not to apply to the internal dividing fences of the saleyards).

involves, firstly, a consideration of what comprises "the demised premises",[191] and then a consideration of what subsidiary part of them is their "interior". Prima facie, the expression is used by way of antithesis to "exterior". So used, it would normally extend to all internal parts of the demised premises whether visible or not, and whether structural or not.[192] Thus it would include, among other things, the totality of all walls lying within the demised premises, whether load-bearing or not.[193] The context may indicate, however, that the expression is limited to the surfaces of such walls. Likewise, the expression would prima facie include all floors and floor structure lying within the demise and not constituting a horizontal boundary between the demise and other premises.

In *Langham Estate Management Ltd v Hardy*,[194] the tenant of a high-class residential property let at a high rent covenanted "to keep the interior of the property and all fixtures and fittings clean and in as good a condition and state of repair as at the start of the letting, fair wear and tear and accidental damage by landlords' insured risks only excepted". It was held that the covenant on its proper construction applied only to the interior of the buildings on the property, and not to everything inside the boundary fence, with the result that the tenant was not liable to remove moss from the driveway.

A common difficulty in practice is to what extent a reference to the interior of premises is apt to include the windows. For example, the landlord may covenant to repair the exterior of the demised premises and the tenant the interior. Prima facie the landlord will be liable for the external part of the windows and the tenant for the internal part. However, this may give rise to difficulties where the same part of the window (for example the frame) has an external and an internal surface. There is no easy answer to problems of this sort, and the correct construction in any particular case will depend on the intention of the parties to be derived from a consideration of the lease as a whole. Recourse may need to be had to one or other of the various presumptions considered above.

## (f)   Main walls

**7–45**   The use of the adjective "main" indicates that the parties only intended to include within the ambit of the obligation the principal walls of the building, as opposed to all walls. In *Holiday Fellowship Ltd v Hereford*[195] Harman J. at first instance defined "main walls" as "those which support the structure of the building or have directly to do with its stability". This definition received implicit approval in the Court of Appeal from Romer and Ormrod L.JJ., the latter of whom, having quoted the judge's definition, added:

---

[191]   See para.7–02, et seq., above.

[192]   It is a common fallacy that an "internal repairing covenant" extends only to non-structural items. Whilst this may be the case on the proper construction of a particular lease, prima facie there is nothing in the word "interior", as used in contradistinction to "exterior", that excludes structural items which are part of the interior of the building.

[193]   But note that some internal walls may be excluded if the lease contains a landlord's covenant to repair the structure or main walls of the building: see paras 7–33 to 7–39, above, and 7–45 to 7–47, below.

[194]   [2008] 3 E.G.L.R. 125. See further on this case para.21–04, above.

[195]   [1959] 1 W.L.R. 211. The decision of Harman J. at first instance is not reported but the passage which follows is quoted in the judgments of Romer and Ormerod L.JJ. in the Court of Appeal.

"[A]nd I suppose that in addition [the main walls] go further than that in that they are a necessary part of the building, as they enclose, or help to enclose, the area on which the building or structure, or whatever it is, is erected."

These passages indicate that "main walls" have two characteristics: they support the structure of the building or have to do with its integrity, and they enclose it. Whilst this represents the prima facie meaning of the expression, the context may show that something else is intended. For example, the outside walls of a modern office building will often comprise concrete or other infill in a steel frame with external prefabricated cladding panels. The infill does not generally carry loads (except wind loads), but it is thought that it would nonetheless be part of the "main walls" of the building. Whether the cladding would likewise be included depends on the facts, but in the absence of any indication either way, it may be that the cladding does not form part of the wall.

A problem frequently arising in practice is the extent to which references in a repairing covenant to "walls" or "main walls" are apt to include window frames and glass. The answer appears to be that, in the absence of any contrary indication in the lease or the surrounding circumstances, windows properly so called are not included, although the position may well be different if the so-called "windows" are in effect the wall itself. Thus, in *Holiday Fellowship Ltd v Hereford*[196] the demise consisted of a dwelling-house with windows of the ordinary type set into the walls in the usual way. The landlord covenanted to repair the main walls of the demised premises, these being expressly excepted from the tenant's repairing obligation. The Court of Appeal held that the landlord was not liable to repair either the wooden window surrounds or the glass. Lord Evershed M.R. said:

**7–46**

"We are not concerned with any question of repair to the brick or stone structures containing the actual windows. For the purposes of this case … I take 'windows' to mean, and to be confined to, the glass panels and the wooden framework and the apparatus in which the glass is placed; and the question is whether, for the purposes of this lease, 'main walls' ought to be treated as including the windows as I have defined them … I should unhesitatingly say, in ordinary language, that the windows, as I have defined them are distinct from the walls. No doubt they are in the walls. Walls may have eyes as well as ears. But I would say that they are, as physical things, distinct from the walls in which they are inserted … to my mind, it is plain that … the windows in the walls would be treated as something different from the walls themselves."

Romer L.J. added:

"I ventured to suggest in the course of argument that it would not be a misuse of language to describe, for example, the walls and roof of the old Crystal Palace as being made of glass, and if they were regarded as a series of windows the latter would form the walls, because the whole structure was glass. On the other hand, if you have a small house with ordinary windows, it does not appear to me to be possible to say that the windows form part of the walls of the house, still less that they form part of the 'main walls' of the house."

Ormerod L.J. said:

---

[196] Above.

"In most buildings it is necessary to have means of ingress and egress, and, of course, some means of admitting light; therefore the walls form the setting for the necessary doors and windows which certainly a dwelling house and a very large number of other buildings must have. But to say that those doors and windows, inserted in those settings, are part of the main walls of the building seems to me to be going very much further than the ordinary use of language would require or allow. It is, as Romer L.J. has said, a matter of degree. There may be cases where the walls are built so much of glass that it would be impossible to say whether they are walls or windows. In the sense that they admit light they are windows, and in the sense that they enclose the premises they are walls. But in the case of a house of this kind, an ordinary house with walls and the normal amount of windows, that position of course cannot apply."

**7–47**     As appears from the above, although a reference to walls will not generally include windows, the position may be different where the facts are such that the windows are in effect the walls, and vice versa. Thus, in *Boswell v Crucible Steel Co of America*[197] the walls of the demised building were largely made of glass. Bankes L.J. thought that the county court judge "was wrong in holding that these windows were not part of the walls of the house", and Atkin L.J. referred to the glass as "representing the walls of the house, so that without them there would be nothing that could reasonably be described as a warehouse at all".[198] A further example (given by Romer L.J. in *Holiday Fellowship*) is the "old Crystal Palace".[199] A more contemporary one might be a modern high tech office block constructed with very extensive external glass set in a concrete or steel frame. In both these cases it can properly be said as a matter of ordinary English that the windows form part of the walls, so that the prima facie rule would not apply.

A further question is to what extent a reference to "walls" or "main walls" will include things fastened on to the outside of the wall, such as drainpipes or gas supply pipes. The approach of the Court of Appeal in *Holiday Fellowship* would seem to suggest that such things are not included. In the ordinary use of language, they are additions or appendages to the wall, rather than part of the wall itself. However, it may well be comparatively easy to show by reference to the context that the parties intended items of this kind to be included in the obligation.[200] The same is true of internal plaster, which is probably not, strictly speaking, part of a wall.[201] Again, however, the context may show that the parties nonetheless intended to treat it as such. Furthermore, the covenantor will be liable to make good any damage done to plaster caused in the course of carrying out repairs to the wall to which it has been applied.[202]

It has been held that a balustrade forming the boundary of a balcony to a first floor front room is not a main wall within the meaning of a covenant excluding liability for structural repairs to the foundations, roof, main walls and drains.[203]

---

[197] [1925] 1 K.B. 119.
[198] See further on this case, para.7–56, below.
[199] The Crystal Palace, moved from its site in Hyde Park to Anerley Hill following the Great Exhibition of 1851, was destroyed by fire in 1937, some 22 years before *Holiday Fellowship* was decided.
[200] See paras 7–29 to 7–30, above.
[201] See para.20–26, below.
[202] See para.22–47 et seq., below.
[203] *Blundell v Obsdale Ltd* (1958) 171 E.G. 491.

### (g)  Main timbers

The "timbers" of a building are ordinarily those parts of it which are made of **7–48**
wood, such as rafters, purlins, beams and joists. On this basis, the "main timbers"
of a building would ordinarily refer to its principal wooden parts. In this sense,
the expression is more appropriate for a traditionally constructed building than a
modern commercial building, whose supporting structure consists of steel and
concrete. However, the expression has been held to include iron beams[204] and a
steel frame.[205]

### (h)  Roof

It is thought that prima facie a reference to a roof will include both the external **7–49**
covering of the roof and the supporting structure, such as rafters and beams. The
extent to which it would include items such as chimney stacks, parapet walls
downpipes and guttering is a question of construction in each case.

In *Masterton Licensing Trust v Finco*[206] (a New Zealand case) a downpipe and
guttering were treated as being part of the roof for the purposes of a covenant on
the part of the landlord to "keep and maintain in good and tenantable
weatherproof wear and condition the roof and outer walls" of the demised shop.

In *Taylor v Webb*[207] the landlord covenanted to repair "outside walls and
roofs". At some stage there had been an addition to the original building, in that a
passage had been built over the roof of the rear ground floor premises which led
to an upper storey behind. The passage was lit from above by means of glass
skylights, which appear to have formed a very substantial part of the passage. Du
Parcq J. held that these were within the landlord's obligation. He said:

> "I have no doubt that the skylights are part of the building, and I also think that they are part of
> the roofs, and that was the intention of the parties. If they were not, it would mean that over
> that part of the building there would be no roofs."

However, as Lord Evershed M.R. pointed out in *Holiday Fellowship Ltd v
Hereford*,[208] it does not follow from this that skylights are always part of the roofs
in which they are set. The question in every case depends upon the proper
construction of the lease.

### (i)  Windows

The meaning of "window" in any particular context will depend on the words **7–50**
used, interpreted in the light of the relevant background circumstances. However,
a helpful general discussion is to be found in the judgment of Edwards-Stuart J.
in *Twinmar Holdings v Klarius*,[209] in which one of the questions arising was

---

[204] *Manchester Bonded Warehouse Ltd v Carr* (1880) 5 C.P.D. 507.
[205] *Plough Investments v Manchester City Council* [1989] 1 E.G.L.R. 244.
[206] [1957] N.Z.L.R. 1137. See further on this case para.22–23, below.
[207] [1961] 2 K.B. 283 (not appealed on this point).
[208] [1959] 1 W.L.R. 211.
[209] [2013] EWHC 944 (TCC) at [31–34].

whether roof lights in a warehouse building were "windows" within the meaning of a covenant "When necessary to replace and renew and to keep clean all windows in the Premises". In holding that they were not, the judge said:

"31. In the context of a lease, I consider that the essential characteristics of a window are that it is a glazed panel in a frame that is set into the external envelope of a building (although sometimes there can be internal windows to allow the passage of light within a building), the purpose of which is to let in light and, usually, to enable those in the building to see out. However, sometimes windows are specially treated, for reasons of either privacy or security, to prevent someone outside the building from seeing in. But in my view this does not mean that it is no longer a window: it is just a particular type of window. Further, it is reasonably clear that a window does not have to be in a vertical plane: opening glazed roof lights (such as the 'Velux' type window) are in my view properly described as windows. Whilst many windows are capable of being opened, this is not an essential characteristic of a window.

32. For the purposes of this case I leave out of consideration the modern glazed curtain wall, or similar structures, where glass panels may be mounted on a metal frame. These are not windows in the sense of being glazed panels set into a frame, but whether they are to be regarded as windows or part of a curtain wall is a question that would have to be decided by reference to the terms of the relevant lease if and when the point arises.

33. It seems to me axiomatic that windows are typically made of glass. I accept that there may be rare examples of windows that are not made of glass, but made of some other transparent material such as Perspex, but for it to be a window I regard it as essential that the glass substitute effectively behaves like glass in terms of the transmission of light (unless for reasons of security or privacy it has been deliberately 'frosted').

34. For these reasons I do not consider that roof lights of the type installed on this building are windows. Apart from anything else, they are not glazed (either with glass or a glass equivalent) and have no frame."

The judge's view that it is not an essential characteristic of a window that it should be capable of being opened accords with *Easton v Isted*,[210] in which Joyce J. said at first instance:

"A window is not less a window because it is not capable of being opened, nor is it less a window because it is not fixed in a vertical plane. I think the glazed top of a conservatory was just as much a window as the fixed portions of the vertical side."

That case concerned whether skylights in a conservatory that had been converted into a passage by bricking up the vertical glazed side were "windows" for the purposes of an agreement made at the time of erecting the conservatory, under which the plaintiff agreed to pay 1s. a year "as an acknowledgment for allowing the windows in my conservatory adjoining to open on to and overlook" the defendant's property. The judge's conclusion that the skylights were windows within the meaning of the agreement was upheld by the Court of Appeal in short order.[211]

The judge's view that a window does not have to be in a vertical plane accords with *Ayling v Wade*,[212] in which the tenant had covenanted to repair "the interior of the premises including all … windows", and the question was whether "windows" included the glass in a skylight on the flat roof of part of the premises. Danckwerts L.J. recorded counsel's concession that it did not in the following terms:

---

[210] [1903] 1 Ch. 405.
[211] [1903] 1 Ch. 405.
[212] [1961] 2 Q.B. 228.

"Apparently, it is accepted that a window does not include a skylight in the present case, a matter on which I think I should have felt some difficulty."

### (j)  Balconies

The premises demised by a flat lease may expressly include balconies. Usually, it will be clear to what part of the building this is intended to refer. However, in two cases the question has arisen as to whether a reference to balconies was apt to include a roof terrace. In *Petersson v Pitt Place Ltd*[213] the landlord covenanted to repair "the main structure of the buildings upon the Estate including the external walls foundations balconies and the roof thereof with its gutters and rainwater pipes". The Court of Appeal held that on the proper construction of the lease in question the reference to "balconies" did not include roof terraces.[214] Similarly, in *Ibrahim v Dovecorn Reversions Ltd*,[215] the demise included "any balcony outside of and forming part of the Demised Premises and for its sole and exclusive use (but expressly excepting and excluding the main walls and structure of the Building)". Rimer J. said:

**7–51**

> "I have so far referred to the [roof terrace in issue] as a terrace, although I accept that it might also be referred to in conversation as a 'balcony'. In my view, however, a 'balcony' more usually means an overhanging ballustraded platform, projecting from the wall of a building. There are such balconies in this building and I consider that it is to structures of this type that [the relevant provision] is more naturally referring, not to the type of roof terrace with which this case is concerned.[216]"

### (k)  Staircases, landings and passages

Expressions such as these will very largely be self-explanatory, although difficulties can sometimes be caused by the draftsman using language which is inappropriate to the physical nature and layout of the building. The answer to such difficulties will generally be found by seeking to identify those parts of the building to which the parties must have been intending to refer. Thus, in *Elmcroft Developments Ltd v Tankersley-Sawyer*[217] a basement flat was demised together with "the use in common with the lessor ... of the entrance hall, staircase, landings, passageways and lift in and about the building for the purpose of obtaining access to the demised premises and garden". The lease contained a landlord's covenant to "keep the said entrance hall, stairs, passages ... well lighted". The question was whether this obligation extended to external areas at the front and rear of the building, which afforded the only means of entry to the flat. The Court of Appeal upheld the decision of the county court judge, who had held that the expression "passages" was not limited to internal passages, but included the areas in question.

**7–52**

---

[213] [2001] 82 P. & C.R. 21.
[214] See further on this case para.7–39, above.
[215] [2001] 2 E.G.L.R. 46.
[216] See further on this case para.7–40, above.
[217] [1984] 1 E.G.L.R. 47.

In *Billson v Tristrem*[218] a lease of a basement flat was drafted in such a way that on the literal reading of the words the tenant was not liable to contribute towards the landlord's costs of maintaining those common parts of the building which she was not entitled to use. The Court of Appeal held that the obvious intention of the parties was that the obligation should relate to the common parts throughout the building, and construed the lease accordingly.

### (l)   Partitions

**7–53**     Precisely what amounts to a partition in any particular case will depend on the proper construction of the lease in question. In *City of London v Black*[219] the tenant covenanted to yield up (among other things) "partitions". H.H. Judge Lamb QC, having emphasised that the question of what was a partition was one of fact, went on to say:

> "... if a judicial view without the assistance of experts is likely to be of any assistance in the preparation for trial, I am inclined to think that a partition is a structure, of whatever material it is made, which divides one portion of the premises from another and which has no structural purpose. In a word, it is a non-bearing internal wall."

### (m)   Party walls, party structures and things used in common

**7–54**     A party wall is a legal term of art meaning a wall which separates land or buildings in different ownership. A reference in a repairing or other covenant to party walls or party structures is likely to be given the same meaning as under the general law, unless the context shows that some different meaning was intended.

In *Twyman v Charrington*[220] the demised premises consisted of the ground floor and basement of a building on basement, ground, first and second floors. The tenant covenanted to contribute to the cost of repairs to, among other things, "all ... mutual or party walls and fences mutual or party structures and other items which may belong to or be used for the demised premises in common with other premises near or adjoining thereto ...". The landlord carried out repairs to the roof of the building. The tenant contended that the roof did not fall within the list of items for which a service charge was payable. His argument was rejected by the Court of Appeal. Woolf L.J. held that the intention was that:

> "[S]tructures which are immediately adjoining the demised premises shall be regarded as party structures, and those parts which are used for their common benefit which are not immediately contiguous should be regarded as mutual, and I would so regard the roof."

Sir John Megaw said:

> "I think that the word 'mutual' ... really has the meaning of 'in common', and a 'mutual structure' includes in this case the roof because that structure provides a service, a benefit, an advantage, to the demised premises as well as to the rest of the building, even though it is not physically adjacent to the demised premises, being separated from it by the other floors of the building."

---

[218] [2000] L. & T.R. 220.
[219] (1960) 175 E.G. 51.
[220] [1994] 1 E.G.L.R. 243.

Both members of the Court held in the alternative that the roof was an "other item" within the concluding part of the covenant.

In *Daejan Properties Ltd v Bloom*[221] a sub-lease of a basement garage built below the forecourt of a block of flats contained a covenant by the sub-tenant to pay:

> "[A] reasonable proportion attributable to the demised premises in common with the owners or occupiers of any adjoining or contiguous premises of the charges for rebuilding, repairing and cleansing all walls, fence walls, fences, drains, ways and other conveniences belonging or which shall belong to the said premises hereby demised or such adjoining or contiguous premises and which shall be used or be capable of being used by the lessee in common with the owners or occupiers of such adjoining or contiguous premises."

The basement garage was separated from the forecourt by metal girders, a reinforced concrete slab and an asphalt membrane. The Court of Appeal held that these items were "conveniences" within the meaning of the covenant and therefore that the sub-tenant was liable to contribute to the cost of repairing them.

In *Delegable v Perinpanathan*[222] a lease of the first, second and third floors of a building contained a tenant's covenant to pay a fair proportion of the expenses from time to time payable for repairing, etc. "all walls fences gutters sewers rains and any other things the use of which is common to the Premises and to other property adjoining or near thereto". It was held that the reference to "other things etc." was apt to include the roof.

### (n)  Fixtures

Fixtures are considered in Ch.25, below.  **7–55**

### (o)  Landlord's fixtures

Covenants to repair or to yield up in repair sometimes expressly include  **7–56**
"landlord's fixtures". This expression may be used to mean all fixtures other than tenant's fixtures, including those affixed by the tenant during the term which he has no right to remove;[223] or it may also be used in the more limited sense of fixtures on the property at the time of the letting, which therefore form part of the original demised premises. Either way, it is likely to be construed as not including things which form an integral part of the building as opposed to things that can reasonably be described as "fixtures".[224]

In *Boswell v Crucible Steel Co of America*[225] the tenant covenanted to "keep the inside of the demised premises including all landlord's fixtures in good repair". The demised premises, as originally built, consisted of a ground floor warehouse and office building about 11ft high. On the two frontages facing streets there were brick walls to a height of 3ft 6in supporting plate glass windows 7ft 6in high. On one frontage the windows occupied in width 29ft out of

---

221 [2000] E.G.C.S. 85.
222 [2006] 1 E.G.L.R. 78. See further para.7–11, above.
223 See para.25–24 et seq., below.
224 See para.25–24 et seq., below.
225 [1925] 1 K.B. 119.

33ft, and on the other, 23ft out of 25ft. In other words, the walls of the building consisted to a large extent of glass. The windows could not be opened. The question arose as to who was liable to replace seven broken windows. It was argued that the glass constituted a landlord's fixture, so that the tenant was liable to do the work. The Court of Appeal held that the windows were not landlord's fixtures on the ground that they formed part of the original structure of the building. Bankes L.J. said in the course of his judgment:

> "It is impossible to say that windows such as these, forming part of the original structure of the house, are landlord's fixtures. The county court judge was wrong in holding that these windows were not part of the walls of the house."

Scrutton L.J. said:

> "The meaning of the term 'tenant's fixtures' is well understood, but I have always had difficulty in understanding what is meant by 'landlord's fixtures'. But at all events it seems to me clear that that expression cannot include a thing which forms part of the original structure of the building. It must be regarded as confined to things which have been brought into the house and affixed to the freehold after the structure is completed. If these windows could be treated as landlord's fixtures, the whole house would be a landlord's fixture."

Atkin L.J. added:

> "A fixture, as that term is used in connection with a house, means something which has been affixed to the freehold as accessory to the house. It does not include things which were made part of the house itself in the course of its construction. And the expression 'landlord's fixtures', as I understand it, covers all those chattels which have been so affixed by way of addition to the original structure, and were so affixed either by the landlord, or if by the tenant, under circumstances in which they were not removable by him. As these windows were part of the original structure, representing the walls of the house, so that without them there would be nothing that could be described as a warehouse at all, they cannot come under the head of landlord's fixtures. If they could, every brick used in the building would be a landlord's fixture."

It is thought that if the article in question is an integral part of the building, then it will not generally matter whether it was part of the original structure (as it was in *Boswell v Crucible Steel*), or whether it was added subsequently. In neither case will it be a "fixture" in the ordinary sense of the word.

CHAPTER 8

## THE SECOND QUESTION: IS THE SUBJECT-MATTER OF THE
## COVENANT IN A DAMAGED OR DETERIORATED CONDITION?

### THE REQUIREMENT OF DISREPAIR

Inherent in the concept of repairing something is the notion of "mending" it **8–01**
because it is in some way in a worse state than it was. It follows that, generally
speaking, no question of a breach of covenant to repair[1] can arise unless there is
in existence relevant damage (or "disrepair"), that is to say, a deterioration of the
subject matter from some previous physical condition. That this is a necessary
and separate ingredient of a breach of covenant to repair is suggested by the
dictum of Atkin L.J. in *Anstruther-Gough-Calthorpe v McOscar*[2] to the effect
that repair:

> "[C]onnotes the idea of making good damage so as to leave the subject so far as possible as
> though it had not been damaged."

The existence of the principle has been confirmed by two separate decisions of
the Court of Appeal. In *Quick v Taff-Ely Borough Council*[3] a dwelling-house was
let on a tenancy to which s.11 of the Landlord and Tenant Act 1985 applied, so
that the landlords were liable to keep in repair the structure and exterior of the
house.[4] Very severe condensation occurred, due principally to cold bridging from
uninsulated window lintels, sweating from single glazed metal window frames
set in wooden surrounds, and the inadequacy of the central heating system. The
effect of this is graphically described in the judgment of Dillon L.J.:

> "[T]here was severe condensation on the walls, windows and metal surfaces in all rooms of the
> house. Water had frequently to be wiped off the walls; paper peeled off the walls and ceilings,
> woodwork rotted, particularly inside and behind the fitted cupboards in the kitchen. Fungus or
> mould growth appeared in places and particularly in the two back bedrooms there was a
> persistent and offensive smell of damp. Among the places where there was mould growth were
> the wooden sills and surrounds of the windows in the bedrooms and some of these have
> become rotten … I would conclude that, by modern standards, the house was in winter, when,
> of course, the condensation was at its worst, virtually unfit for human habitation."

The house had been built in accordance with the regulations in force and the
standards accepted at the time, when problems caused by cold bridging were not

---

[1] The position may be different in relation to an obligation to keep in good condition: see paras 8–12
to 8–14, below.
[2] [1924] 1 K.B. 716.
[3] [1986] Q.B. 809.
[4] See para.20–17 et seq., below.

realised. There was no damage to the metal windows or lintels, which were in more or less the same state as when the house was built. The work necessary to alleviate the condensation included the replacement of the existing metal window frames with frames of a less conductive material (such as wood or UPVC) and providing the lintels with insulation facings. The county court judge held that the landlord was liable to carry out the work. The Court of Appeal allowed the landlord's appeal on the ground that there was insufficient evidence of any damage to the subject matter of the covenant,[5] and there was therefore no "disrepair" which required to be remedied. The tenant's argument that anything defective or inherently inefficient for living in or ineffective to provide the conditions of ordinary habitation is in disrepair was rejected by Dillon L.J. in the following terms:

"In my judgment, the key factor in the present case is that disrepair is related to the physical condition of whatever has to be repaired, and not to questions of lack of amenity or inefficiency ... Where decorative repair is in question one must look for damage to the decorations, but where, as here, the obligation is merely to keep the structure and exterior of the house in repair, the covenant will only come into operation where there has been damage to the structure and exterior which requires to be made good."

Lawton L.J. said:

"[T]he landlord need not do anything until there exists a condition which calls for repair. As a matter of the ordinary usage of English that which requires repair is in a condition worse than it was at some earlier time ... It follows that, on the evidence in this case, the trial judge should first have identified the parts of the structure and exterior of the house which were out of repair and then gone on to decide whether, in order to remedy the defects, it was reasonably necessary to [carry out the works] ... In my judgment, there must be disrepair before any question arises whether it would be reasonable to remedy a design fault when doing the repair."

**8–02** *Quick v Taff-Ely Borough Council* was followed and applied in *Post Office v Aquarius Properties Ltd.*[6] That case concerned a lease of an office building which contained a tenant's covenant to "keep in good repair and condition the demised premises and every part thereof". The building had been constructed in the mid-1960s. Subsequently the water table in the area had risen and, due to the defective construction of the "kicker" joint between the walls and floor, the basement became ankle deep in water. The joint was in the same condition as it had been when constructed, and there was no evidence that the water had resulted in any damage to any part of the building. Ralph Gibson L.J. said:

"I see no escape from the conclusion that if, on the evidence, the premises demised are and at all times have been in the same physical condition ... as they were when constructed, no want of repair has been proved for which the tenants could be liable under the covenant."

Accordingly:

"The questions considered by the learned judge as to whether, as a matter of degree, any of the schemes of work qualified as 'repair', as contrasted with works of alteration, do not arise."

---

[5] i.e. the structure and exterior of the house.
[6] [1987] 1 All E.R. 1055.

Slade L.J. added that "… a state of disrepair, in my judgment, connotes a deterioration from some previous physical condition."

The principle established in *Quick* has been approved, albeit in passing, by the House of Lords. In *Southwark LBC v Mills*[7] (in which the question was whether a local authority tenant had any remedy against his landlord in nuisance or under the covenant for quiet enjoyment for interference caused by inadequate sound proofing). Lord Hoffmann (with whom Lords Slynn, Steyn and Clyde agreed) said in his speech:

> "Keeping in repair means remedying disrepair. The landlord is obliged only to restore the house to its previous good condition. He does not have to make it a better house than it originally was: see *Quick v. Taff-Ely Borough Council*."

The consequence of the principle in *Quick* is that if there has been no relevant damage or deterioration, then the fact that the building suffers from defects in design or construction or a lack of amenity, or that it is in some way inefficient, or that it is in some other way unsuitable or incapable of beneficial occupation for its intended use, is irrelevant so far as liability under the covenant to repair is concerned. It was argued in *Post Office v Aquarius Properties Ltd* that the rule does not apply to problems caused by defective workmanship, reliance being placed on the fact that the condensation in *Quick v Taff-Ely Borough Council* was not so caused. The Court of Appeal rejected this argument, holding that the principle is of general application. Ralph Gibson L.J. said:

> "[T]he reasoning of the Court in *Quick's* case is equally applicable whether the original defect resulted from error in design, or in workmanship, or from deliberate parsimony or any other cause."

The principle in *Quick* has been applied, or referred to, in a number of subsequent cases.[8] In *Southwark London Borough Council v McIntosh*[9] (which concerned a claim for damages for breach of the landlord's covenant implied by s.11 of the Landlord and Tenant Act 1985) the premises included a cupboard containing hot pipes used by the tenant used for drying clothes, which led to condensation and consequent damp problems both in the cupboard and elsewhere in the flat. In allowing the landlord's appeal against a finding of liability at first instance, Lightman J. said in his judgment:

**8–03**

> "It is established by the decision of the Court of Appeal in *Quick* … and succeeding cases that 'disrepair' is established for the purposes of section 11 if, and only if, there is established to be physical damage to the structure or exterior of the premises that does not arise by reason of the tenant's default. A landlord is not liable under the covenant merely because there is the most serious damp in the demised premises. In a case such as the present, where the occasion for complaint is damp, the tenant must establish either that the damp arises from a breach of the

---

[7] [2001] 1 A.C. 1.
[8] *McNerny v Lambeth London Borough Council* (1989) 21 H.L.R. 188; *Fluor Daniel Properties v Shortlands* [2001] 2 E.G.L.R. 103; *Southwark London Borough Council v McIntosh* [2002] 1 E.G.L.R. 25; *Lee v Leeds City Council* [2002] 1 W.L.R. 1488; *Janet Reger International v Tiree* [2006] 3 E.G.L.R. 131; *Jackson v J H Watson Property Investment* [2008] 1 E.G.L.R. 33; *Brunskill v Mulcahy* [2009] EWCA Civ 686; *Grand v Gill* [2011] EWCA Civ 554; *Hammersmatch Properties (Welwyn) v Saint-Gobain Ceramics & Plastics* [2013] EWHC 1161 (TCC) at [53].
[9] [2002] 1 E.G.L.R. 25. See further on this case para.20–23, below.

covenant (i.e. physical damage to the structure or exterior of the premises) or that the damp has itself caused damage to the structure or exterior and that this damage, in turn, has caused the damp of which complaint is made."

He went on to hold on the facts that the tenant's claim had not been made out.[10]

In *Lee v Leeds City Council*,[11] the facts were very similar to those in *Quick v Taff Ely Borough Council*. Two council houses suffered from excessive condensation and mould due to their construction, insulation, ventilation and heating, as a result of which they were virtually uninhabitable. It was argued that *Quick* had been decided per incuriam because the court's attention had not been drawn to *Proudfoot v Hart*,[12] and in particular to the meaning which Lord Esher M.R. and Lopes L.J. gave to the expression "good tenantable repair".[13] It was argued in the alternative that s.3 of the Human Rights Act 1998 required the covenant implied by s.11 of the Landlord and Tenant Act 1985 to be given a different interpretation to that in *Quick*, and in particular to be interpreted as obliging the landlord to remedy the causes of internal condensation. The Court of Appeal rejected both arguments.

In *Janet Reger International v Tiree*[14] the demised premises comprised a basement and ground floor shop. The landlord covenanted to "use reasonable endeavours to maintain, repair and renew the structure". The basement suffered from damp, which was caused by the fact that the damp-proof membrane in the floor slab stopped short of the walls, so that there was no continuous damp-proof protection between the floor and the walls. This was the result of defective construction. The remedial work consisted of the removal of the existing floor screed and the installation of an applied linked horizontal and vertical damp-proof coating and a three-coat Sika wall render. It was common ground that the damp-proof membrane formed part of the structure. There was no evidence that the damp had resulted in any deterioration in the brickwork of the basement walls, and if there was any such deterioration, it was not such as required the bricks to be repaired or replaced. Mr Terence Mowschenson QC (sitting as a deputy judge of the Chancery Division), citing *Quick* and *Post Office*, held that the landlord was not liable for the remedial works.

**8–04**  Although the above cases all concerned damp, the principle is not confined to such cases. In *Secretary of State for the Environment v Euston Centre Investments Ltd (No.2)*,[15] an arbitrator appointed to determine a rent review had fixed the rent on the assumption that the tenant had been obliged under his repairing covenant to remove all asbestos in the building prior to the review date. Chadwick J. held that no such obligation would arise unless there was damage to, or deterioration in the physical condition of, the asbestos. He thought that for these purposes there

---

[10] See further on damp *Ball v Plymouth City Council* [2004] EWHC 134 (QB), in which the tenant failed to establish that the relevant damp resulted from penetration through defective external walls as opposed to design defects.
[11] [2002] 1 W.L.R. 1488.
[12] (1890) 25 Q.B.D. 42.
[13] See para.9–06, below.
[14] [2006] 3 E.G.L.R. 131.
[15] [1994] N.P.C. 130

was no difference in principle between an inherent defect which gives rise to some hazard to health or safety, and an inherent defect which results in lack of efficiency or amenity.[16]

In the Scottish case of *Westbury Estates v The Royal Bank of Scotland*[17] it was held that the tenant was not liable for the cost of replacing mechanical and electrical items which were neither defective nor malfunctioning simply on the ground that they were at or approaching the end of their economic life.[18]

In *Alker v Collingwood Housing Association*[19] the landlord covenanted to keep the demised property (a house) in good condition and to repair and maintain, among other parts, external doors. The house had a front door with a ribbed glass panel which was not safety glass but ordinary annealed glass. The tenant suffered serious injuries when she accidentally put her hand through the panel. The tenant claimed damages against the landlord under s.4 of the Defective Premises Act 1972.[20] That claim could only succeed if the state of the glass panel amounted to a breach of the landlord's repairing obligation (or would have done so if he had had notice of it).[21] The Court of Appeal held that it did not. The glass panel was not in disrepair and there had been no failure to maintain it. Laws L.J. (with whom Carnwath and Moore-Bick L.JJ. agreed) said in his judgment:

> "No doubt, the two concepts [i.e. repair and maintain] overlap. Neither of them, however, can, in my judgment, possibly be said to encompass or to include a duty or obligation to make safe. Moreover, a duty to keep 'in good condition', the words used here, even if it encompasses a duty to put into good condition, again cannot encompass a duty to put in safe condition."

In *Drysdale v Hedges*[22] the landlord of a terraced house covenanted to provide and maintain the structure and exterior of the property in good repair. The claimant tenant was injured when she slipped on the stone front steps leading to the premises. The steps were slippery from a combination of paint and wet, and the wall at the side of the steps was not sufficiently high and/or was not fitted with a guardrail or handrail to stop someone falling down to basement level. The paint had been applied by the landlord, and its effect had been to increase the slipperiness of the steps. It was held that neither the low and unguarded wall nor the presence of the paint on the steps amounted to disrepair in breach of the landlord's covenant.

---

[16] This case is further considered in para.12–39, below.

[17] [2006] CSOH 177.

[18] This case is further considered in para.13–05, below.

[19] [2007] 2 E.G.L.R. 43.

[20] The 1972 Act is considered in Ch.20, below. Note that the tenant was precluded from claiming under the covenant itself because the landlord did not have actual notice of any disrepair to the door or panel. See para.22–03, et seq., below.

[21] See para.20–56, below.

[22] [2012] 162 N.L.J. 1056. Cf. *Brunskill v Mulcahy* [2009] EWCA Civ 686, in which it was held, dismissing the tenant's application for permission to appeal against the dismissal of his claim for damages under s.11 of the Landlord and Tenant Act 1985 (see para.20–17 et seq., below) arising out of a fall attributed by him to moss or slime on the front outer steps to his ground floor flat, that the removal of moss which had been on the step for an indeterminate amount of time was not a matter of repair.

A number of other examples may be given: a house may have very steep stairs with no railings or a hidden step;[23] a commercial building may have insufficient floor to ceiling heights or insufficient floor loadings; the premises may be constructed throughout of high alumina cement concrete; or the roof may be laid to insufficient falls. In none of these cases can the covenantor under a covenant to repair be compelled to rectify the state of affairs or part of the building in question. It is important to note, however, that the position is otherwise where that state of affairs has itself resulted in physical damage, or where the part in question is itself damaged. The covenantor is then prima facie liable under his covenant to remedy that damage, and his liability may extend to remedying the cause of the damage.[24] In *Lee v Leeds City Council*[25] Chadwick L.J. summarised the position as follows:

"The cases show that, where there is a need to repair damage to the structure, the due performance of the obligation to repair may require the landlord to remedy the design defect which is the cause of the damage. They do not support the proposition that the obligation to repair will require the landlord to remedy a design defect which has not been the cause of damage to the structure; notwithstanding that the defect may make the premises unsuitable for occupation or unfit for human habitation.[26]"

The requirement for damage does not necessarily apply in the case of covenants to keep the premises in good condition. This is considered further below.[27]

## The relevant time for comparison

8–05   The question whether there is relevant damage or deterioration is to be answered by comparing the condition of the subject matter at the relevant time with its condition at the time of its construction and not (if different) its condition when the lease was granted. Thus, in *Post Office v Aquarius Properties Ltd*[28] Ralph Gibson L.J. said that no want of repair will be proved if the premises "are and at all times have been in the same physical condition ... as they were when constructed". Likewise, in *Gibson Investments Ltd v Chesterton Plc*[29] Neuberger J. said that the relevant comparison is between "the condition now and the condition at the date of construction". This approach can be justified on the basis that "disrepair" is a state to be assessed objectively, and whether or not there has been damage or deterioration cannot depend upon the accident of when the lease

---

[23] Examples given by Laws L.J. in *Alker v Collingwood Housing Association* [2007] 2 E.G.L.R. 43 at [14].
[24] See para.11–38, below.
[25] [2002] 1 W.L.R. 1488.
[26] See further Chadwick L.J.'s judgment in *Dunn v Bradford Metropolitan District Council* [2002] 3 E.G.L.R. 104.
[27] See paras 8–12 to 8–14, below.
[28] [1987] 1 All E.R. 1055. See the passage from Ralph Gibson L.J.'s judgment set out in para.8–02, above.
[29] [2002] 2 P. & C.R. 494.

happened to be granted.[30] There is the further point that even where a covenant to repair does not expressly oblige the covenantor to "put" the premises into repair, nonetheless it will be construed as though it did, since an obligation to keep premises in repair involves a duty to put them into repair in so far as they are out of it.[31] This principle would appear to be inconsistent with the relevant date for assessing disrepair being the date of the lease.

It follows that if, by the time the question arises, the condition of the building has deteriorated from its condition when built, there will exist "disrepair", the remedying of which may (depending upon the answers to the last three stages of the five-part approach) fall within the ambit of the repairing covenant.

## What amounts to "damage or deterioration" within the principle

The existence or otherwise of disrepair depends on the physical state of the subject matter. If that state is in a worse condition than it was when new,[32] disrepair will exist. Thus, plaster which is so saturated that it requires complete renewal is in disrepair.[33] But troughs in galvanised steel roof sheeting which have suffered no deterioration are not in disrepair.[34]

**8–06**

Damage or deterioration is not necessarily to be equated with a failure in function. It is possible for a part of the building not to perform its intended function and yet not be in disrepair. For example, a badly designed window may be in perfect physical condition and yet not keep out the rain. Thus, in *Stent v Monmouth District Council*[35] Stocker L.J. said:

> "[I]f the only defect in the door was that it did not perform its primary function of keeping out the rain, and the door was otherwise undamaged and in a condition which it or its predecessors had been at the time of the letting, then it seems to me, on the authorities of *Quick* and *Aquarius*, that this cannot amount to a defect for the purpose of a repairing covenant even though, as it seems to me in layman's terms, that a door which does not keep out the rain is a defective door and one which is in need of some form of repair or modification or replacement."

Conversely, a part of the building may be damaged or deteriorated and yet continue to perform its function. For example, the pointing on an external wall may be in poor state of repair and still keep out the weather. Thus, in the Australian case of *Alcatel Australia v Scarcella*,[36] the tenant of an office building was held liable to remove and re-anodise or replace corroded aluminium window frames, notwithstanding the fact that the frames remained functional.

---

[30] Note, however, that the state of the premises when the lease is granted may be relevant to the third and fifth questions in the analysis: see Chs 9 and 11, below.
[31] See para.9–21, below.
[32] See para.8–05, above.
[33] *Staves v Leeds City Council* [1992] 2 E.G.L.R. 37.
[34] *Postel Properties Ltd v Boots the Chemist* [1996] 2 E.G.L.R. 60.
[35] [1987] 1 E.G.L.R. 59.
[36] [2001] NSWSC 154. See further para.9–15, below.

**8-07**  Corrosion or rusting will generally amount to disrepair.[37] In *Re Mayor and Corp of London*[38] an underground railway station was constructed with walls, columns, girders and arches which supported Smithfield Meat Market. The station was then let on leases containing a covenant by the tenant to "well and sufficiently maintain, uphold, support, and keep in good, substantial, and tenantable repair" the girders supporting the meat market. Some of the girders had corroded and become weakened. The tenant contended that its liability was confined to keeping the girders in such a condition as would enable them safely to support the meat market. Eve J. rejected this, holding the tenant liable to keep the girders in substantially the same condition as they were in at the date of the tenancy.[39]

In *Sheldon v West Bromwich Corp*[40] (in which the landlord was under an implied statutory obligation to repair the structure and exterior of the demised flat[41]) a water tank corroded and burst, causing damage to the premises. The tank was within the landlord's repairing liability. The evidence was that six weeks before the bursting, the landlord's plumber had visited and had inspected the tank. There was present some discoloration which had been there for some years past, but no "weeping", that is to say, no droplets of water were apparent on the outside of the tank. The expert evidence was that discoloration was a sign of corrosion, but that until "weeping" appeared there was never, or hardly ever, any immediate risk of the tank bursting. The Court of Appeal, reversing the decision of the trial judge that because there was no "weeping" the landlords had no actual knowledge of the need to replace or reline the tank, held that the tank was in disrepair such as to put the landlords on inquiry that repairs were needed. In the course of his judgment, Stephenson L.J. said:

> "The question in this case is, I think, a narrow one ... was the condition of this tank as regards discoloration on [the date of the inspection] such a condition of disrepair as to put the landlord upon inquiry as to whether works of repair were needed—in other words, as to require repair, not immediately, not the next day, but within a reasonable time, and within a reasonable time short of six weeks which elapsed before this tank in fact burst ... I have come to the conclusion that ... the landlords ... ought, by their plumber who carried out this inspection of the tank ... to have realised that this tank required repair before [the date of the burst]. This was an old tank. The evidence of the [landlord's expert] was that [the tank] must have been as old as the house, which was nearly forty years old, that he would expect the life of one of these tanks to be fifty to sixty years but that some tanks would start to corrode after twenty years ... What the argument for the [landlords] amounts to is that there is no obligation, in accordance with the statutory covenant, upon a landlord to carry out any repairs to a discoloured tank unless a hole has actually been made so that weeping has begun ... I have come to the conclusion that the absence of weeping is not fatal to the Plaintiffs' case. In my judgment the time for which discoloration had existed in this aged tank did mean that it required to be

---

[37] See *Re Mayor and Corp of London* [1910] 2 Ch. 314; *Sheldon v West Bromwich Corp* (1973) 25 P. & C.R. 360; *Plough Investments Ltd v Manchester City Council* [1989] 2 E.G.L.R. 244; *Postel Properties Ltd v Boots the Chemist* [1996] 2 E.G.L.R. 60; *Minja Properties Ltd v Cussins Property Group Plc* [1998] 2 E.G.L.R. 52; *Alcatel Australia v Scarcella* [2001] NSWSC 154; *Gibson Investments Ltd v Chesterton Plc* [2002] 2 P. & C.R. 494. See further para.12–21 et seq., below.

[38] [1910] 2 Ch. 314. See further on this case para.9–29, below.

[39] Note, however, that his decision may well have turned on, or at any rate been influenced by, the inclusion of the word "maintain" in the covenant: see the Scottish case of *Westbury Estates v The Royal Bank of Scotland* [2006] CSOH 177 at [20]; *Twinmar Holdings v Klarius UK* [2013] EWHC 944 (TCC) at [12].

[40] (1973) 25 P. & C.R. 360.

[41] See para.20–17 et seq., below.

repaired by the landlords as soon as they had knowledge of the state of discoloration and, possibly, decay in the metal which it had reached by [the date of inspection] ... they were bound to take action although there was no weeping and to put this tank in repair, either by re-lining it or replacing it."

In *Minja Properties Ltd v Cussins Property Group Plc*[42] Harman J. held that metal window frames, which had become corroded by rust, were out of repair for the purposes of a landlord's covenant to "maintain and keep in good and tenantable repair the ... window frames (excluding glass)". He said:

"The evidence at one point suggested that rusting is a mere discoloration of the surface of the window frame. As I understand the factual position, and I believe I am entitled to find this as a fact, rusting is not a mere discoloration of the surface. It involves an actual erosion of the structure of the iron which is rusted, the change of the ferrous metal into iron oxide which can be rubbed off and which leaves behind the metal itself thinner and lighter for the part that has oxidised. If the process goes on long enough, rusting can and does produce actual holes in a piece of steel. That being so, it is clear that rusting affects the substance of the window frame itself."

Other cases will turn on their own facts.

8–08

In *Windever v Liverpool City Council*,[43] the kitchen and living room floors of a dwelling-house had become significantly off-level due to settlement. They were not hazardous but their condition amounted to more than just a minor nuisance and interfered with the tenant's daily use of the rooms. It was held in the Liverpool County Court that what had to be considered was whether an item was or was not, in the ordinary sense, in disrepair, i.e. whether it had deteriorated to such an extent that it no longer performed the function that it was designed to perform. Applying that test, the floors were in disrepair for the purposes of the landlord's implied repairing obligation under s.11 of the Landlord and Tenant Act 1985.[44]

In *Twinmar Holdings v Klarius*,[45] one of the questions was whether GRP polyester roof lights in a warehouse building were in disrepair. They were not leaking, but the surfaces had become abraded to a substantial degree. This had resulted in wind driven dirt particles becoming trapped, with a consequent reduction of translucence. Edwards-Stuart J. rejected the tenant's surveyor's view that a roof light was not in disrepair until it leaked. He held the correct approach to be as follows:

"In my judgment, a roof light ceases to be in good condition within the meaning of the covenant once there has been a visible and a significant reduction in its translucence. By 'significant'I mean a reduction in translucence such that the light coming through the rooflights has to be augmented by artificial lighting in weather conditions that would not have required additional lighting when the roof lights were new."

---

[42] [1998] 2 E.G.L.R. 52.
[43] [1994] C.L. 299.
[44] See para.20–17 et seq., below.
[45] [2013] EWHC 944 (TCC) at [16–30].

In an appropriate case, the requirement of physical damage or deterioration may be satisfied where the subject-matter in question requires cleaning.[46] Thus, in *Greg v Planque*[47] it was held that cleaning a flue amounted to "executing repairs" within the meaning of a provision in the lease which entitled the landlord to enter the demised premises to execute repairs and alterations. Greer L.J. said in the course of his judgment:

> "I have had some hesitation in coming to the conclusion that the word 'repair' is wide enough to include the cleaning of the flue, but as between these parties I feel bound to treat the word as covering the maintenance of the flue in the condition in which it ought to be to carry out the purposes for which it was placed where it was."

Blockages in gutters or downpipes have been held to constitute disrepair in several cases. Thus, in *Bishop v Consolidated London Properties Ltd*[48] an external gutter, which was within the landlord's covenant to repair, was blocked by a dead pigeon, and overflowed, causing damage to the demised premises. The report does not disclose that there was anything else wrong with the gutter. Du Parcq J. nonetheless held the landlord liable for breach of the covenant to repair. In *Melles & Co v Holme*[49] a gutter which had been blocked by ash discharged from chimneys was treated as being in disrepair. In *Masterton Licensing Trust v Finco*[50] (a New Zealand case), the partial or substantial blockage of a downpipe on the roof by pigeon debris was held to be disrepair for the purposes of a proviso that the landlord should not be liable "for any damage caused by any failure ... to keep and maintain [the roof and outer walls] in good and tenantable repair".

### The subject-matter of the disrepair

**8–09**    The requisite damage or deterioration must be to the subject-matter of the covenant.[51] Thus, where decorative repair is in question, what is relevant is damage to the decorations, but where the obligation is to keep the structure and exterior in repair, the covenant will only come into operation if there has been damage to the structure and exterior which requires to be made good.[52]

In applying this approach, it is only those parts of the subject-matter which are said to be in disrepair which are relevant. Thus, where the subject-matter comprises the whole of a block of flats, the fact that the rear external wall is defective and in need of repointing would not of itself justify the conclusion that the other walls are in disrepair as well. However, this must be approached in a common-sense way having regard to the facts of each individual case. In many cases it will be correct to look at a particular part of the subject-matter as a single entity, and to ask whether, so regarded, it is in a damaged or deteriorated

---

[46] *Greg v Planque* [1936] 1 K.B. 669; *Twinmar Holdings v Klarius* [2013] EWHC 944 (TCC) at [56–61].
[47] Above.
[48] (1933) 102 L.J.K.B. 257.
[49] [1918] 2 K.B. 100.
[50] [1957] N.Z.L.R. 1137.
[51] *Quick v Taff-Ely Borough Council* [1986] Q.B. 809.
[52] See above; *Staves v Leeds City Council* [1992] 2 E.G.L.R. 37.

condition. An example might be a roof over a block of flats. If it comprises a number of individual flat roof areas, some of which are damaged and some of which are not, the right view may be that only the former are in disrepair. If, however, the roof comprises a single continuous flat roof, of which by far the greater part is in a deteriorated condition, then the fact some areas are undamaged would not of itself prevent complete replacement from being repair.[53]

In *Reston v Hudson*,[54] many of the wooden windows in a block of flats were defective and required replacing. The landlord reasonably came to the conclusion that it would be cheaper and more appropriate to replace all the windows in the block at the same time. It was held that the cost of such work fell within the landlord's repairing covenant and was recoverable by way of service charge.[55]

## Anticipated future damage

It follows from the general principle considered above that if no part of the subject-matter of the covenant is damaged or deteriorated, then no work is required under the covenant, notwithstanding the fact that future damage may be inevitable. For example, the structural beams in a building may have been constructed of high alumina cement concrete; it may be clear that the beams will eventually fail and need replacing; but they may, for the moment, be in perfect condition; and they may remain in that state for some years. They are not in disrepair and the covenantor is not liable to replace them.[56] In *Twinmar Holdings v Klarius*[57] (in which the tenant of a warehouse building covenanted to keep it in good and substantial repair) Edwards-Stuart J. stated the general principle as follows:

**8–10**

> ".... there will be no breach of covenant unless and until the building is actually out of repair: it is not sufficient that the building will become out of repair at some future time if that time will be after the expiry of the lease. But if that time will arrive during the term of the lease, then if the tenant does not take the steps necessary to prevent the deterioration coming about, he will do so at his own risk."

It was argued in *Mason v TotalFinaElf UK Ltd*[58] that "mere preventative work" (i.e. work undertaken to avoid the occurrence of damage from a future but reasonably anticipated state of disrepair) was within the scope of a covenant "well and substantially [to] uphold support maintain amend repair decorate and keep in good condition the demised premises". Blackburne J. rejected that argument, holding that the covenant on its proper construction did not extend to the carrying out of purely preventative work when no state of disrepair existed.

However, once defects begin to occur, the fact that part of the relevant item is undamaged will not necessarily prevent replacement of the entirety from

---

[53] Cf. *Postel Properties v Boots the Chemist* [1996] 2 E.G.L.R. 60.
[54] [1990] 2 E.G.L.R. 51.
[55] Although the judge does not appear in terms to have considered the question whether replacement of even those windows which were not defective nonetheless constituted repair.
[56] See further paras 10–15 to 10–18 and 12–24, below.
[57] [2013] EWHC 944 (TCC) at [15].
[58] [2003] 3 E.G.L.R. 91.

amounting to repair.[59] Thus, in *Postel Properties Ltd v Boots the Chemist*[60] it was held that a phased programme of roof replacement was within the landlord's obligation "with all due diligence to keep the ... roofs ... in good and substantial repair and condition". Ian Kennedy J. said:

> "It was [the landlord's surveyor's] conclusion, after walking the roof and making her own survey, that the point had been reached at which a phased replacement of the roof covering was more economic than continuing with patch repairs. It has to be remembered that at this time the covering was within five years of attaining the maximum expected life, a life expectancy which was not improved by the presence of various items of plant on the roofs. I am quite unpersuaded that decision was premature. It has to be remembered that she had to look five years ahead, and it was highly undesirable that roof covering should be left to threaten an emergency in which large sections failed at the one time."

The extent to which a covenant to repair requires the carrying out of preventative works is further considered in Ch.10, below.

## The consequences of there being a state of disrepair

**8–11**     It is important for present purposes to distinguish between a defect in design or workmanship in the construction of the building, and physical damage or deterioration caused by such a defect. As has been said, the former on its own does not constitute "disrepair", and the remedying of it does not fall within the ambit of the repairing covenant; however, if it results in physical damage to the subject-matter of the covenant, then such damage may constitute "disrepair" which the covenantor is liable to remedy. In remedying it, he may also be liable to eradicate the design or construction defect as well, if this is what a sensible, practical man would do.[61] In this regard, the facts of *Quick v Taff-Ely Borough Council*[62] and *Post Office v Aquarius Properties Ltd*[63] were somewhat unusual in that, in the first, the minimal amount of damage which had occurred to the subject-matter of the covenant (the structure and exterior of the house) did not justify eradicating the cause of it, and in the second, there was no evidence that the flooding in the basement had caused any damage to the building, and the Court of Appeal specifically left open the question of what the position would be if subsequent flooding were to cause such damage.

The circumstances in which the remedying of the physical damage may be held to require the remedying of the "inherent defect" which caused it are considered in questions four and five of the five-part approach.[64]

---

[59] See para.8–09, above.
[60] [1996] 2 E.G.L.R. 60.
[61] See para.11–38, below.
[62] [1986] Q.B. 809.
[63] [1987] 1 All E.R. 1055.
[64] See Chs 10 and 11, below.

## WHERE THE OBLIGATION IS TO KEEP IN GOOD CONDITION

A covenant which imposes or includes a liability to keep in good condition, or good tenantable condition, may be construed as imposing a liability which is conceptually different from an obligation to repair or keep in repair.[65] Where this is the case, it is unclear to what extent the requirement that the covenant only comes into effect once damage or deterioration has occurred still applies. On the face of it, what has to be kept in good condition is the physical subject-matter of the covenant. If that subject-matter is undamaged, then it is in good condition and no work is required under the covenant. However, the relevant authorities suggest that a more flexible approach may be appropriate in some cases.

**8–12**

In *Credit Suisse v Beegas Nominees Ltd*[66] a lease of an office building obliged the landlord (in summary[67]) to repair and otherwise keep in good and tenantable condition the structure of the building, subject to a proviso that the landlord should not be liable to the tenant for any "defect or want of repair" unless he had notice. Lindsay J., having construed the covenant as imposing a separate obligation to keep the subject matter in good and tenantable condition which imposed a liability going beyond repair,[68] said:

> "[W]hilst I accept the inevitability of the conclusion of the Court of Appeal in *Aquarius* that one cannot have an existing obligation to repair unless and until there is a disrepair, that reasoning does not apply to a covenant to keep (and put) into good and tenantable condition. One cannot sensibly proceed from 'No disrepair, ergo no need to repair' to 'no disrepair, ergo no need to put or keep in the required condition' ... all that is needed, in general terms, to trigger a need for activity under an obligation to keep in (and put into) a given condition is that the subject matter is out of that condition."

The judge went on to identify the condition in question as being:

> "[S]uch condition as, having regard to the age, character and locality of the property, would make it reasonably fit for the occupation of a reasonably minded tenant of the class likely to take it ... although one cannot lower the nature of that condition by reference to deterioration in the expectations of the hypothetical tenant consequential upon a deterioration in the class of tenants after the date of the lease."

He went on to hold on the facts that the premises were not in the required condition because they were not watertight (although he found that in any event there had in fact been physical deterioration in the subject-matter).

On the judge's approach, the covenant was broken once the condition of the premises fell short of such condition as, having regard to the age, character and locality of the premises, would make them reasonably fit for the occupation of a reasonably minded tenant of the class likely to take them, even though there may then have been no physical damage or deterioration in the subject matter. It is thought, however, that the judge's construction turned to a significant extent on the wording of the proviso (and in particular the reference to "defects or want of

---

[65] See paras 4–30 to 4–31 above and paras 9–41 to 9–42, below.
[66] [1994] 4 All E.R. 803 and (more fully) [1994] 1 E.G.L.R. 76. This case is further considered in paras 4–29 and 4–30, below, and paras 9–41 and 11–46 below.
[67] The relevant part of the covenant is set out in full in para.4–28, above.
[68] See paras 4–29 and 4–30, above.

repair", which the judge thought indicated "a potential going beyond repairs strictly so-called"[69]), so that it is not clear to what extent his approach is of more general application.[70]

8–13    In *Welsh v Greenwich LBC*[71] a local authority letting contained a landlord's covenant "to maintain the dwelling in good condition and repair except for such items as are the responsibility of the tenant". The flat suffered from severe black-spot mould growth and damp, which was caused by condensation which was the result of a lack of insulation. It had been conceded in the court below that the condensation was not the result of disrepair, and that the landlord's failure to do anything about it was not a breach of the landlord's statutorily implied obligation to keep in repair,[72] and the appeal proceeded on the same basis.[73] However, the Court of Appeal held that (i) the obligation to maintain the dwelling in good condition imposed a liability conceptually different to that of the obligation to keep in good repair,[74] and (ii) the landlord was in breach of that obligation by failing to provide thermal insulation or dry lining for the walls. In other words, the landlord was liable under the covenant to carry out works for which he would not have been liable had the covenant been merely to repair or keep in repair.[75]

The Court of Appeal rejected the landlord's argument that a distinction was to be drawn between the physical make-up of the building and the amenity or efficiency of the dwelling. Robert Walker L.J. regarded the contrast between the two as "an intelligible contrast, but only ... towards the extreme ends of the contrast". He went on to say:

> "Where there is severe black spot mould growth ... that cannot, in my judgment, be regarded as merely a matter of amenity dissociated from the physical condition of the flat, even if there was, as counsel agreed, no damage to the structure."

This passage suggests that even though there need not necessarily be disrepair, nonetheless some form of physical manifestation in the subject-matter of the covenant is required before the covenantor is liable. In principle, this must be correct, since if it were not, it is difficult to see where the covenantor's liability ends: for example, it might be said that he is liable to carry out strengthening work to a building designed and built with inadequate floor loadings.

8–14    To a considerable extent, *Welsh v Greenwich LBC* turned on its own special facts. As Latham L.J. pointed out in his judgment, it concerned a "contract between a local authority, as the provider of social housing, and a tenant in circumstances

---

[69]  The relevant part of the covenant is set out in para.4–28, above.
[70]  See the view of Lord Reed in *Westbury Estates v The Royal Bank of Scotland* [2006] CSOH 177, quoted in para.8–14, below.
[71]  [2000] 3 E.G.L.R. 41.
[72]  Under s.11 of the Landlord and Tenant Act 1985, considered in Ch.23, below.
[73]  This concession was no doubt made as a result of the decision in *Quick v Taff-Ely* [1986] Q.B. 809 (see para.8–01, above). In the Court of Appeal the tenant sought leave to argue that the landlord was in breach of the covenant to keep in repair implied by s.11 of the 1985 Act and to challenge the decision in *Quick*, but permission was refused.
[74]  See paras 4–29 to 4–30, above.
[75]  This case is further considered in para.4–30, above.

where one would not expect the tenant to be taking legal advice", so that the obligation to maintain in good condition should, so far as possible, be given "the meaning which the ordinary person on the street would accept as being the sensible construction of the phrase". Where the relevant circumstances are different, an obligation to keep in good condition may be construed as meaning that no work will be required until a state of "disrepair" exists. Thus, in *Fluor Daniel Properties Ltd v Shortlands Investments Ltd*[76] the landlord covenanted to "uphold maintain repair amend renew cleanse and redecorate and otherwise keep in good and substantial condition and as the case may be in good working order and repair" various parts of a multi-occupied office building and its plant. Whilst accepting that this "extends to works that go beyond repair strictly so-called", the judge accepted the submission "that the obligations in the clause presuppose that the item in question suffers from some defect (i.e. some physical damage or deterioration, or, in the case of plant, some malfunctioning) such that repair, amendment or renewal is reasonably necessary". The same point arose in *Mason v TotalFinaElf UK Ltd*,[77] which concerned a covenant "well and substantially [to] uphold support maintain amend repair decorate and keep in good condition the demised premises". Blackburne J. held that the covenant on its proper construction did not extend to the carrying out of purely preventative work when no state of disrepair existed.

In the Scottish case of *Westbury Estates v The Royal Bank of Scotland*[78] Lord Reed was:

"[D]oubtful whether the words 'and condition', in the phrase 'good and substantial repair and condition', introduce a different concept from that of 'good and substantial repair': cases in which a contrary view has been taken, such as *Crédit Suisse v. Beegas Nominees Ltd* and *Welsh v. Greenwich LBC*, appear to me to depend on their particular circumstances (notably, the specific terms of the provision in the former case, and the context of the lease in the latter case). That issue does not however appear to me to be of critical importance to the question with which I am concerned: on either view, the obligation is concerned with the physical condition of the subjects, including the items in question, and requires that the physical condition of the subjects be maintained to a given standard. In order for the obligation to be triggered, the physical condition of the subjects must therefore fall short of the requisite standard."

In *Alker v Collingwood Housing Association*,[79] in which the landlord covenanted to keep the demised property (a house) in good condition and to repair and maintain specified parts, it was held that the obligation to keep in good condition, even if it encompassed an obligation to put into good condition, did not encompass a duty to put the front door of the premises into safe condition by replacing a glass panel made of ordinary annealed glass with a panel made of safety glass where the panel was not in disrepair and there had been no failure to maintain it.

---

[76] [2001] 2 E.G.L.R. 103.
[77] [2003] 3 E.G.L.R. 91.
[78] [2006] CSOH 177. This case is further considered in para.13–06, below, where the relevant covenant is set out.
[79] [2007] 2 E.G.L.R. 43.

# CHAPTER 9

# THE THIRD QUESTION: IS THE NATURE OF THE DAMAGE SUCH AS TO BRING THE CONDITION OF THE SUBJECT-MATTER BELOW THE STANDARD CONTEMPLATED BY THE REPAIRING COVENANT?

## INTRODUCTORY

The fact that the subject-matter of a repairing covenant is in a damaged or deteriorated condition does not of itself mean that the covenantor is liable without more to carry out whatever work is necessary to remedy the damage. The authorities indicate that he will only be so liable if the condition of the premises falls below the standard of repair required by the covenant. The question of the standard of repair is also relevant to the further question of what remedial work is required,[1] because the covenantor's liability will not generally extend beyond restoring the premises to that standard. The practical questions which arise at this stage will generally centre around whether a particular identified defect in the subject-matter of the covenant requires to be remedied, or whether it can safely be left unattended to without any breach of covenant being committed, and the extent of any work required. For example, to what extent does the covenant require that surface cracks in an external render be made good? Does any work need to be carried out to a steel-framed building suffering from the early stages of "Regent Street Disease"?[2] Is it enough to patch-repair a roof or must it be replaced in its entirety? The answer to questions of this sort will depend upon the correct analysis of the standard of repair intended to be imposed by the covenant. This will vary according to the precise words used in the lease, and the surrounding circumstances, such as the age, character and locality of the building. This Chapter is concerned with identifying the relevant standard and the circumstances in which it will or will not have been complied with.

**9–01**

---

[1] See Ch.10, below.
[2] See para.12–21.

## THE STANDARD OF REPAIR IMPOSED BY THE GENERAL COVENANT TO REPAIR

### Introductory

**9–02**    The appropriate standard of repair is in all cases a question of construction of the relevant covenant, and it is not possible to lay down any hard and fast rule. The obligation to repair may, for example, be limited by reference to the state of the premises at a particular time as evidenced by a schedule of condition[3]; it may be qualified by the exclusion of "fair wear and tear"[4]; it may require the premises to be kept only "wind and watertight"[5]; or it may require the premises to be repaired to the satisfaction of the landlord's surveyor.[6] Each of these will import a different standard. However, there is a reasonable measure of agreement in the authorities as to the standard of repair required by the "general" covenant, that is to say, an obligation to repair or keep in repair with or without the addition of qualifying expressions such as "good", "tenantable" or "habitable". This section is concerned with the standard of repair under the general covenant as so defined. Covenants to keep in good, etc. condition are discussed separately in para.9–41, et seq., below.

### Qualifying expressions

**9–03**    The general obligation to repair is commonly qualified by expressions such as "good", "substantial", "tenantable" or "habitable". Some examples from the cases are as follows:

> "…[To] put into habitable repair the said premises … and … deliver up the same … in such a state of habitable repair;[7]
> …[to] keep [the premises] and … deliver up the same in good repair …[8];
> …during the said term [to] keep the said premises in good tenantable repair, and so leave the same at the expiration thereof."[9]

The general principle that every word in a contract must, if possible, be given a separate meaning has already been considered,[10] as has the extent to which that principle applies to repairing covenants.[11] Since the question is one of construction in each case, no fixed rule can be laid down. In general terms, however, the courts have not treated qualifying expressions of this sort as affecting the standard of repair in any appreciable way. In *Anstruther-Gough-Calthorpe v McOscar*[12] Scrutton L.J. said:

---

[3] This sort of covenant is considered in Ch.14, below.
[4] See para.9–32, below.
[5] See para.21–10, below.
[6] See para.14–20, below.
[7] *Belcher v Mackintosh* (1839) 2 Moo. & R. 186.
[8] *Payne v Haine* (1847) 16 M. & W. 541.
[9] *Proudfoot v Hart* (1890) 25 Q.B.D. 42.
[10] See para.4–13, above.
[11] See para.4–20 et seq., above.
[12] [1924] 1 K.B. 716.

"In my view the matter can be dealt with as if the covenant was one to keep and yield up at the end of the term in repair. I do not think there is any substantial difference in construction between 'repair', which must mean 'repair reasonably or properly' and 'keep in good repair' or 'sufficient repair' or 'tenantable repair' or most of the various phrases cited to us."

Nor does there appear to be any relevant difference in meaning between the various qualifying expressions commonly used. In *Belcher v Mackintosh*[13] Alderson B. is reported as having said that:

"It is difficult to suggest any material difference between the term 'habitable repair' used in this agreement, and the more common expression 'tenantable repair'."[14]

In *Proudfoot v Hart*[15] Lord Esher M.R. expressed the view that "good repair" is "much the same thing as tenantable repair". In *Anstruther-Gough-Calthorpe v McOscar*[16] Atkin L.J. said that:

"...I should have thought that the original and proper sense of 'tenantable' was fit to be tenanted, that is, occupied, and that the word meant no more than, if it meant as much as, 'habitable'."

In *Truscott v Diamond Rock Boring Co Ltd*,[17] a lease of a house obliged the tenant "to do necessary repairs". Jessel M.R. said:

"The word 'necessary' is not material, for it only expresses that repairs are required. If repairs are wanted at all they are necessary, and if they are not wanted a tenant under an agreement to repair would not be bound to do anything; the agreement, therefore, is in substance simply an agreement that the tenant shall repair ... It imposes on the tenant the burden of doing all repairs which are required; and that includes all the repairs which but for the agreement the landlord would be obliged to do."

Brett L.J. held that the covenant obliged the tenant to carry out "all repairs as would be necessary to enable the landlord to hand over the property to a new tenant in substantial and tenantable repair". Holker L.J. said that the tenant was bound to do "all repairs".

It follows that in the ordinary case, the standard of repair imposed by the general covenant is unlikely to vary much according to the precise adjectives used in relation to "repair".[18] However, it can be said that the use of words such

---

[13] Above.
[14] This passage was cited by Lord Esher in *Proudfoot v Hart*, above, and by Lord Atkin in *Summers v Salford Corp* [1943] A.C. 283. It is taken from the report at (1839) 2 Moo. & R. 186. However, in (1839) 9 C. & P. 720, Alderson B. is reported as having said that: "The term 'tenantable repair' may have a somewhat different meaning to the term 'habitable repair' but in either case the repair must have reference to the state of the premises at the time of the making of the agreement."
[15] Above.
[16] [1924] 1 K.B. 716.
[17] (1882) 20 Ch. D. 251, per Jessel M.R.
[18] See further the cases considered in para.9–04, below. The position may be different in Scotland: see *West Castle Properties Ltd v Scottish Ministers* [2004] S.C.L.R. 899 at [21]. Contrasting views have been taken in two Australian decisions: in *Clowes v Bentley Property Ltd* [1970] W.A.R. 24 it was held that "good substantial and tenantable repair and condition" meant no more than "good tenantable repair"; however, in *Alcatel Australia Ltd v Scarcella* [1998] N.S.W. Conv. R. 56, 495 (upheld on appeal at (1998) 44 NSWLR 349) it was said that the use of the conjunction "and" in the phrase "good and substantial repair" suggested that not only must the state of repair be good, it must

as "habitable" or "tenantable" emphasises the relevance of the extent to which the defects adversely affect the ability to occupy or let the premises, and that words such as "good" or "substantial" reinforce the general principle that a covenant to repair does not require the premises to be kept in perfect repair.[19]

## Substantial not perfect repair

**9–04**   A covenant simply to repair does not require the premises to be kept in perfect repair. It will generally be satisfied by keeping the premises in substantial repair.[20] Provided that the premises are in that state, the covenantor need not attend to every defect, however minor. In *Harris v Jones*[21] Tindall C.J. directed the jury that the question for them was:

> "[W]hether the covenants had been really and substantially complied with? For that, in cases of this nature, it was hardly to be expected that a strict and literal performance of so general a covenant (unless where the language pointed to any particular matter) could be proved. The words at the end of the latter member of the covenant (as to yielding up the premises in good and substantial repair and condition) were to be taken as giving a clue to the meaning of the general words."

In *Stanley v Towgood*[22] the same judge said:

> "I agree that in all these cases the question is whether the premises have been kept in substantial repair, as opposed to claims for fancied injuries, such as a mere crack in a pane of glass, or the like."

Similarly, in *Perry v Chotzner*[23] it was said:

> "It is a monstrous thing to say that because a person puts nails into the walls of a house he must take them out and fill up the holes, or commit a breach of the covenant of a repairing lease."

In *Commercial Union Life Assurance Co Ltd v Label Ink Ltd*[24] H.H. Judge Rich, QC (sitting as a deputy High Court judge) said of a covenant at all material times to keep the demised premises in good and substantial repair and condition that "good and substantial repair does not, in my judgment, mean pristine

---

also be substantial, so that a covenant to "keep in good and substantial repair" imposed greater obligations than a covenant to keep in "good tenantable repair".

[19] See para.9–04, below.

[20] *Harris v Jones* (1832) 1 Moo. & R. 173; *Langham Estate Management Ltd v Hardy* [2008] 3 E.G.L.R. 125 at [75] (in which the equivalent passage in the Third Edition of this work was approved). See also *Royal Trust Co v R.* [1924] Exch. C.R. 121 (Canada).

[21] Above.

[22] (1836) 3 Bing. N.C. 4.

[23] (1893) 9 T.L.R. 477.

[24] [2001] L. & T.R. 29. It is to be borne in mind when reading this case that the question of disrepair arose in the context of whether or not the tenant had complied with a condition precedent in a break option, and that the judge's construction of the condition precedent was subsequently disapproved by the Court of Appeal in *Fitzroy House Epworth Street (No.1) v The Financial Times* [2006] 2 E.G.L.R. 13.

condition or even perfect repair".[25] Having referred to *Proudfoot v Hart*, he went on to say that "although 'substantial' is not the same word as 'tenantable', it necessarily falls short of perfection", so that (among other things) minor scratches and dents to the front elevation did not amount to a breach of covenant.

In *Simmons v Dresden*[26] the tenant covenanted "from time to time and at all times during the said term well and substantially to repair renew cleanse and keep in good and substantial repair and condition and maintain the demised premises ...". H.H. Judge Richard Seymour, QC said:

"I accept that, taken in isolation, the word 'repair' connotes, as Atkin LJ said in *Anstruther-Gough-Calthorpe v. McOscar*, 'the idea of making good damage so as to leave the subject so far as possible as though it had not been damaged'. The basic concept is thus that, so far as is physically possible, something the state of which has been altered as a result of physical harm or wear and tear is to be restored to its original state. However, in clause 2(5) the standard to be achieved by repair, renewal or cleansing was expressly qualified. What was required was that the tenants 'well and substantially' repair, and so forth, and keep in 'good and substantial' repair. The force of 'substantially' and 'substantial', in my judgment, was to require that in its essentials, but not necessarily in each and every minute detail, the premises were to be repaired, renewed, cleansed and kept. I do not think that that is a standard which in practical terms is different from the standard of 'such repair as, having regard to the age, character, and locality of the house, would make it reasonably fit for the occupation of a reasonably minded tenant of the class who would be likely to take it' which [counsel] submitted was the appropriate standard. What that standard requires in any given case must be a question of fact and degree."

In *Riverside Property Investments v Blackhawk Automotive*[27] Judge Coulson QC said:

"A covenant 'well and substantially' to repair does not require the tenant to put the property into perfect repair (see *Proudfoot v Hart*[28]) or into a 'pristine condition' (see *Commercial Union Life Assurance Co Limited v Label Ink Limited*)."

He said the same thing in *Carmel Southend v Strachan & Henshaw*[29] in relation to a covenant "to keep in good and substantial repair".

In *Langham Estate Management Ltd v Hardy*,[30] H.H. Judge Hazel Marshall QC (citing para.9–03 of the Third Edition of this work) agreed with counsel's submission that the principle that a covenant to "repair" does not require the premises to be kept in perfect repair but only "substantial" repair was of general application, and added that:

"Even the wider covenant to "maintain and/or "keep in proper working order" does not mean that the landlord is automatically in breach if any fault develops, nor requires the emergence of every minor fault or maladjustment to be dealt with as though it required attention as an emergency."

---

[25] This part of H.H. Judge Rich, QC's judgment was cited and applied by H.H. Judge Coulson in *Riverside Property Investments v Blackhawk Automotive* [2005] 1 E.G.L.R. 114 at [54] and *Carmel Southend v Strachan & Henshaw* [2007] 3 E.G.L.R. 15 at [7].
[26] [2004] EWHC 993 (TCC).
[27] [2005] 1 E.G.L.R. 114 at [54].
[28] (1890) 25 Q.B. 42. See further below.
[29] [2007] 3 E.G.L.R. 15 at [8].
[30] [2008] 3 E.G.L.R. 125 at [75].

The effect of the above is that not every defect in the subject matter of the covenant will necessarily amount to a breach. Thus, for example, whether a cracked shop window is a breach of the covenant to repair is a question of fact depending on whether the damage is of a substantial character as distinguished from a mere fanciful injury[31]; cracks in the brickwork of a building which is over 60 years old, which were present when the lease was granted, did not constitute breaches of a covenant to repair[32]; and cracks in plaster may be insufficiently serious to amount to a breach of covenant.[33]

It should be noted, however, that identical words in different leases will not always mean the same thing in each.[34] The question is always one of the proper construction of the particular covenant in the particular circumstances of the case. Moreover, a covenant to keep in good condition does not necessarily import the same standard as a covenant to repair.[35]

## The standard of repair under the general covenant

9–05    As a general principle, the standard of repair under the general covenant is such repair as, having regard to the age, character and locality of the premises, would make them reasonably fit for the occupation of a reasonably-minded tenant of the class who would be likely to take them. This test applies to functional items (for example, an air handling plant) as well as to the building fabric itself.[36]

In *Belcher v Mackintosh*[37] Alderson B. is reported as having directed the jury that covenants to put premises into "habitable repair" or "tenantable repair" imported:

> "[S]uch a state as to repair that the premises might be used and dwelt in not only with safety, but with reasonable comfort, by the class of persons by whom, and for the sort of purposes for which, they were to be occupied."[38]

This passage has been approved in the House of Lords.[39]

The leading case is *Proudfoot v Hart*,[40] which concerned a lease of a house in Kentish Town for a term of three years from November 12, 1885. The tenant agreed to keep the premises in "good tenantable repair", and to leave them in that state at the end of the term. The question was what standard of repair this involved, and in particular the extent to which the tenant was liable to paper, paint

---

[31] *Julian v McMurray* (1924) 24 S.R. (N.S.W.) 402.
[32] *Plough Investments Ltd v Manchester City Council* [1989] 1 E.G.L.R. 244.
[33] *Hallet v Camden LBC, Legal Action*, August 1994, p.17.
[34] See *Walker v Hatton* (1842) 10 M. & W. 249, considered in para.9–24, below.
[35] See paras 9–41 to 9–42, below, where this is considered.
[36] *Land Securities Plc v Westminster City Council (No.2)* [1995] 1 E.G.L.R. 245; *Fluor Daniel Properties Ltd v Shortlands Investments Ltd* [2001] 2 E.G.L.R. 103.
[37] (1839) 2 Moo. & R. 186.
[38] The report at (1839) 9 C. & P. 720 does not contain this passage. It does, however, contain the following: "The tenant here is not to make a new house, but regard being had to the state in which it was at the time of the agreement, and also to the situation and class of persons who are likely to inhabit it, he is to put it into a condition fit for a tenant to inhabit."
[39] *Summers v Salford Corp* [1943] A.C. 283, per Lord Atkin at 289.
[40] (1890) 25 Q.B.D. 42.

and whitewash, and to replace a rotten kitchen floor with a new one. Lord Esher M.R. propounded the test in the following terms:

"Lopes L.J. has drawn up a definition of the term 'tenantable repair' with which I entirely agree. It is this: 'Good tenantable repair' is such repair as, having regard to the age, character and locality of the house, would make it reasonably fit for the occupation of a reasonably minded tenant of the class who would be likely to take it. The age of the house must be taken into account, because nobody could reasonably expect that a house 200 years old should be in the same condition of repair as a house lately built; the character of the house must be taken into account, because the same class of repairs as would be necessary to a palace would be wholly unnecessary to a cottage; and the locality of the house must be taken into account, because the state of repair necessary for a house in Grosvenor Square would be wholly different from the state of repair necessary for a house in Spitalfields. The house need not be put into the same condition as when the tenant took it; it need not be put into perfect repair; it need only be put into such a state of repair as renders it reasonably fit for the occupation of a reasonably minded tenant of the class who would be likely to take it."

Lord Esher's observations in relation to the rotten floor afford an illustration of the operation of the test in practice. He said:

"The question is, what is the state of the floor when the tenant is called upon to fulfil his covenant? If it has become perfectly rotten he must put down a new floor, but if he can make it good in the sense [that it would satisfy a reasonably-minded tenant] he is not bound to put down a new floor. He may satisfy his obligation under the covenant by repairing it. If he leaves the floor out of repair when the tenancy ends, and the landlord comes in, the landlord may do the repairs himself and charge the costs as damages against the tenant; but he is only entitled to charge him with the necessary cost of a floor which would satisfy a reasonable man taking the premises."

The approach in *Proudfoot v Hart* was formulated in relation to a covenant to keep in "good tenantable repair". It may be asked to what extent it can be regarded as being of universal application to a general covenant to repair which does not specifically use those adjectives, or whether on the contrary the use of the word "tenantable" connotes a standard by reference to a hypothetical tenant, so that different considerations might apply where the covenant does not use that word. However, the test has been quoted with approval in a number of subsequent cases in which the relevant covenant did not contain the word "tenantable".[41] Moreover, *Proudfoot v Hart* was considered in detail in *Anstruther-Gough-Calthorpe v McOscar*[42] (where the covenant did not include the word "tenantable"), and none of the members of the Court of Appeal appear to have suggested this as a possible ground of distinction.[43] It is therefore thought that the *Proudfoot* approach represents the proper standard of repair under the general covenant in the ordinary case.

**9–06**

---

[41] See *Lurcott v Wakely* [1911] 1 K.B. 905, per Fletcher Moulton L.J. at 920–921; *Elmcroft Developments Ltd v Tankersley-Sawyer* [1984] 1 E.G.L.R. 47, per Ackner L.J.; *Land Securities Plc v Westminster City Council (No.2)* [1995] 1 E.G.L.R. 245; *Fluor Daniel Properties Ltd v Shortlands Investments Ltd* [2001] 2 E.G.L.R. 103; *Mason v TotalFinaElf UK Ltd* [2003] 3 E.G.L.R. 91; *Fairgate International v Citibank International* [2005] 2 E.G.L.R. 48 at [16]; *Pgf II S.A. v Royal & Sun Alliance Insurance Plc* [2010] EWHC 1459 (TCC) at [48-50]; *Hammersmatch Properties (Welwyn) v Saint-Gobain Ceramics & Plastics* [2013] EWHC 1161 (TCC) at [53].

[42] [1924] 1 K.B. 716.

[43] Indeed, Scrutton L.J. thought that there was no substantial difference in construction between "repair" and "keep in good repair" or "tenantable repair": see the passage cited in para.9–03, above.

## The relevant date

**9–07**  Over the course of the lease the character and locality of the premises may change, with the result that the class of tenants likely to take them may alter. Or the market may change, so that the original purpose for which the building was let and constructed has become obsolete. For example, what was let as the newly constructed headquarters building of a large local company may, by the end of the lease 30 years later, have become subdivided into small and shoddy office suites with occupiers of a corresponding nature. In such cases, the *Proudfoot* test will be likely to produce different answers according to whether it is applied at the beginning or the end of the lease.

The general principle is that the standard of repair is to be assessed by reference to the circumstances at the date on which the lease is granted, so that a deterioration in the class of tenants likely to occupy the building does not produce a corresponding deterioration in the standard of repair.[44] The leading case is *Anstruther-Gough-Calthorpe v McOscar*,[45] which concerned a 95-year lease granted in 1825 of three newly erected houses in Gray's Inn Road, at that time a fashionable and prosperous area. The tenant covenanted to "well and sufficiently repair support uphold maintain paint pave empty scour cleanse amend and keep [the demised premises] … by and with all manner of needful and necessary reparations and amendments whatsoever" and to yield them up in that state. The lease expired in 1920, the character of the locality and the premises having by then undergone a considerable deterioration. The then landlord brought an action for damages for breach of the repairing covenant against the then tenant. It was common ground that the measure of damages was the cost of the necessary repair, but the parties differed as to what was necessary. The tenant contended, relying on *Proudfoot v Hart*,[46] that his obligation was limited to carrying out such repairs as would make the premises reasonably fit to satisfy the requirements of reasonably-minded tenants of the class likely to take the premises at the end of the term. The arbitrator appointed to assess the damages found as a fact that such persons would take only the houses separately, or part of a house, for short terms, and that their requirements would not include many repairs which in his opinion were necessary for the repair and maintenance of the property.[47] The arbitrator assessed damages on alternative footings, depending upon whether the tenant's contention was right. On the footing that it was not, he awarded the landlord £586, which was the cost of putting the premises:

> "(a) [I]nto such condition as I should have expected to find them in had they been managed by a reasonably minded owner, having full regard to the age of the buildings, the locality, the class of tenant likely to occupy them, and the maintenance of the property in such a way that

---

[44] *Morgan v Hardy* (1887) 35 W.R. 588, per Lord Esher M.R. (affirmed (1888) 13 App. Cas. 351); *Anstruther-Gough-Calthorpe v McOscar* [1924] 1 K.B. 716; *Fluor Daniel Properties v Shortlands Investments* [2001] 2 E.G.L.R. 103; *Twinmar Holdings v Klarius* [2013] EWHC 944 (TCC0 at [8-13]; *Hammersmatch Properties (Welwyn) v Saint-Gobain Ceramics & Plastics* [2013] EWHC 1161 (TCC) at [53].

[45] Above.

[46] (1890) 25 Q.B.D. 42.

[47] Bankes L.J. summarised such tenants as being: "content so long as the rain does not penetrate the walls or the sanitary inspector does not interfere on the ground that a nuisance exists on the premises".

only an average amount of annual repair would be necessary in the future; or

(b) in such a state of repair as would satisfy the requirements of reasonably minded person who would be prepared to take on lease the houses either singly or as a block upon similar repairing covenants to those contained in the expired lease and on such conditions as to rent as would presume the premises being put at the commencement of the term free of expense to the lessee in such a state of good and sufficient repair as would render only an average amount of annual expenditure necessary during the term."

On the footing that the tenant's contention was correct, he awarded £220, which was the cost of such repairs as:

"[W]ould satisfy the literal requirements of reasonably minded tenants of the class now likely to occupy the premises who would not accept any repairing obligations, with such additions as would be necessary to avoid the receipt of notices from the local authorities. Such repairs would not include many repairs necessary for the maintenance of the structures in accordance with (a) and (b) above, the neglect of which, however, would not (i) interfere with the immediate comfort of the occupiers and so come within their requirements, or (ii) cause danger to health and so come within the purview of the local authorities."

The Court of Appeal rejected the tenant's contention. *Proudfoot v Hart* was distinguished on the ground that the tenancy in that case was for a three-year term and there would have been no difference between the class of tenants likely to take the premises at the beginning and end of the term. All three members of the court were prepared to accept the arbitrator's formulation in (a) as being correct. Bankes L.J. said in relation to *Proudfoot v Hart*:

9–08

"If the rule contended for by the [tenant] exists it must apply to cases where the status of the house to be repaired has appreciated as well as to cases where it has depreciated, and it must descend to such depths of degradation as to meet the case where what had at the commencement of the tenancy been a high-class residence is at the end of the tenancy occupied in tenements by a class of tenants who look upon an outer door or an area gate as an unnecessary obstruction, and who therefore require neither the one nor the other. If the rule in *Proudfoot v. Hart* is of universal application it would have to be applied in such a case as that just mentioned, and apparently also even if the condition of things at the end of the tenancy had been largely, if not entirely, brought about by a failure to perform the covenant to repair. In my opinion the case of *Proudfoot v. Hart* lays down no rule of universal application. The language used by the Lords Justices is quite appropriate to the facts of that case and must, I think, be read as applicable to those facts and to similar facts only ... In construing the covenant in the present case, or any other covenant, it is material to see what the subject matter was which the parties had in their contemplation when the covenant was entered into ... Here there is no doubt as to the subject matter, it was the three houses described in the lease, and the obligation undertaken was the repair of those houses. How can the extent of such an obligation be measured by the requirements of the class of tenants who happen to be occupying the premises ninety five years afterwards? *Proudfoot v. Hart* did not, in my opinion, lay down any such rule. When the facts of that case are looked into it is manifest that the Lords Justices who decided the case had no such question in their minds. What they were dealing with, and all they were dealing with, was a three years' agreement for a tenancy, in which the class of tenants at the end of the tenancy was, in their view, no doubt the same as the class of tenants at the commencement. Upon that assumption, and upon that assumption only, is the rule laid down by Lopes L.J. and accepted by the Master of the Rolls, in my opinion, explicable or intelligible."

He went on to set out what he regarded as the correct approach:

"The arbitrator ... has rendered a real service by laying down so clearly the lines on which he proceeded. In his mind apparently heads (a) and (b) [set out above] mean the same thing, or at any rate, lead to the same result. To most people, head (a) will, I think, prove the more useful guide; and provided the age of the buildings is regarded as the dominant feature, and the locality and class of tenant is only taken into account in relation to, or as a consequence of, the age of the buildings then I consider the rule laid down by the arbitrator a good working rule of general application. Had it been applied to the facts in *Proudfoot v. Hart* it would have produced the same result as the rule framed by Lopes L.J. for those facts."

**9–09** Scrutton L.J. was likewise prepared to accept head (a) of the arbitrator's first award as the correct approach. He said:

"The question in dispute seems to be whether, as the purposes for which such a subject matter would ordinarily be used may vary from time to time, the standard of repair is to vary from time to time, or remains as it was when the subject matter was demised. For instance, where a fashionable mansion let for a long term of years has fallen to the position of a tenement house for the poorer classes, is the standard of repair to become less onerous than when the house is let? To take an illustration of Bankes L.J., if the sub-tenants of a tenement house do not want a front door, is the tenant to be excused from keeping a properly repaired front door on the premises? ... In *Proudfoot v. Hart* the lease was for three years only, and the covenant was to keep in good tenantable repair. There was no suggestion of any change in character of the house or its probable tenants between the beginning and the end of the term ... I do not think there was any intention of suggesting that a deterioration in the class of tenants would lower the standard of repairs ... Therefore, in my view, we are bound to look to the character of the house and its ordinary uses at the time of the demise. It must then be put in repair and kept in repair. An improvement of its tenants or its neighbourhood will not increase the standard of repair, nor will their deterioration lower that standard. It follows in this case that the principle put forward by the tenant was erroneous, and that the statement by the arbitrator in [head (a)] is accurate, but must be limited to conditions at the time of the demise."

Atkin L.J. said:

"To apply [the *Proudfoot* test] to a repairing covenant taken upon a ninety five years' term seems to me to expose both landlord and tenant to possibilities of the most astonishing variation of obligation and rights. The obligation is a continuing obligation, and therefore would presumably vary with the requirements of the hypothetical possible tenant during each moment of the tenancy. The neighbourhood might deteriorate, or it might appreciate, or it might during the term several times alternate between the two extremes. In this decade it might be lettable as a dwelling house, in that only for a shop, or in the next for a factory ... Unguided I should have thought that the original and proper sense of 'tenantable' was fit to be tenanted, that is, occupied, and that the word meant no more than, if it meant as much as, 'habitable'. But *Proudfoot v. Hart* binds me to hold that in a three years agreement it has reference to the reasonable requirements of a tenant of the class who would be likely to take it. Accepting that construction I have no doubt that the requirements of such a tenant are deemed to continue the same throughout the term, or if not, are to be estimated by the requirements of such a tenant as would be likely to take the premises at the commencement of the term...

Once one is extricated from the clutch of the hypothetical tenant I do not think there is much difficulty in construing the covenant in this case ... Speaking generally, I have not seen a better statement of the duties of a tenant under such a covenant as this than the statement in the present case by the arbitrator of the principles on which he proceeded in arriving at the higher sum ... It is true that he refers to the class of tenant likely to occupy [the premises] as being one of the matters a prudent owner would have regard to, but I gather from the whole report that he does not regard this consideration as involving a fluctuating standard. I would myself prefer to eliminate the possible tenant, and would be content with ... [such repair as is] needful and necessary for the maintenance of the structure so that it may be expected to last for its normal life if properly kept in repair."

**9–10** On one view the standard of repair laid down in *Anstruther's* case is different to the approach in *Proudfoot v Hart*. The former is by reference to how the reasonably-minded owner would have managed the premises (see head (a) of the arbitrator's higher award), whereas the latter (as explained in *Anstruther*) proceeds on the footing of what would make the premises reasonably fit for the occupation of a reasonably minded tenant at the beginning of the term. However, it is thought that there is no difference in substance between the two formulations, the emphasis in both being on what is reasonable measured by reference to the age and character of the premises at the date of the lease. The judgments of Bankes and Scrutton L.JJ. in *Anstruther* seem to have proceeded on the footing that, once the *Proudfoot* approach is applied at the date of the lease, the two approaches were to all intents and purposes the same. Atkin L.J. was clearly less happy with the notion of the standard of repair being measured by reference to the reasonable requirements of a hypothetical tenant, but his doubts are not reflected in the subsequent authorities.

*Anstruther* was considered and applied in the Scottish case of *West Castle Properties v Scottish Ministers*,[48] in which the tenant's covenants included the following:

> "The Tenant HEREBY ACCEPTS by his execution hereof, the premises ... as in good and tenantable condition and repair and BINDS HIMSELF at his sole expense during the currency of this Lease, to keep wind and water tight, and well and substantially to repair, maintain, renew, restore, cleanse and keep in the like good tenantable condition and repair the whole premises."

It was held by the Outer House of the Court of Session that that the covenant required the tenant to:

> "[52] ... [C]arry out any works which a prudent owner of the premises would have carried out, in order to maintain the premises so that they could be expected to last for their normal life. In seeking to define the extent of the obligations on the [tenants] in terms of [the covenant], some regard also requires to be had to the requirements of the class of tenants that would be likely to occupy the premises, with those requirements being determined as at the commencement of the term of the Lease. However, as the judgments in *Anstruther-Gough-Calthorpe* (per Banks L.J at p. 728, Scrutton L.J at p. 729 and Atkin L.J. at p. 734) make clear, those requirements, whatever they may be established to be, should not be looked at in isolation.
>
> ...
>
> [63] In my opinion, the extent of the obligations on the [tenants] ... does not fall to be determined by looking solely at what a reasonably-minded owner would have done or by looking solely at the condition that a reasonably-minded tenant would have required. In my opinion, it is important to have regard to all of the factors I have mentioned in answering this Question, before determining whether as a matter of fact the [tenants] have fulfilled their obligations."[49]

The approach in *Anstruther* is an application of the ordinary principle that a contract is to be construed by reference to the circumstances existing at the date

---

[48] [2004] S.C.L.R. 899. For further cases in which the approach in *Anstruther-Gough-Calthorpe v McOscar* was applied, see *Gemmell v Goldsworthy* [1942] S.A.S.R. 55 (in which Cleland J. said that it was "the best guide to the practical effect and construction" of a tenant's covenant well and substantially to repair, keep in good order and substantial repair, and yield up at the end of the term in good order and substantial repair), and *Fleming v Breenan* [1940] I.R. 499.

[49] It must be borne in mind as regards this passage that, as the judge pointed out at [43], the common law of Scotland as regards repairs is not the same as that of England. However, the judge was relying primarily on English authorities, and it is thought that his comments are consistent with the position in England.

of the contract and to what was in the contemplation of the parties at that time.[50] Such circumstances cannot as a general rule include matters occurring subsequently which the parties could not have had in mind when they made their contract. The result is that, unless the lease contemplates a varying standard of repair,[51] the appropriate standard of repair is to be ascertained by reference to the circumstances existing at the date of the lease. It is to be noted, however, that this is concerned only with establishing the existence and extent of any breaches of the covenant to repair. Changes in the character or locality of the premises, or the type of tenants likely to take them, occurring between the date of the lease and its expiry date may be highly material when assessing the amount of damages payable at the end of the term.[52]

An example of the application of the *Anstruther* approach in practice is *Mason v TotalFinaElf UK Ltd*,[53] in which a petrol filling station and associated buildings (then on a trunk road) had been let to an oil company for 35 years in 1964. By the end of the lease, the premises were no longer on a trunk road, and economic circumstances were such that no major oil company would have been interested in taking them. Blackburne J. held that the court should approach the standard of repair:

> "[B]y asking itself, doing the best that it can, what, given the age and character of the premises (a converted inter-war dwelling house already 30 or so years old at the time) and their locality (a semi-rural position with a fairly small road frontage, but on a trunk road leading from Crawley to East Grinstead), a reasonably minded oil company would reasonably require, at the time the lease was granted, to render the premises reasonably fit for use as a place from which to run the business of a petrol filling station and attached shop, together with car sales and, at the rear of the site, facilities for motor vehicle repairs."[54]

## Variations in the standard of repair

**9–11**    There may be cases where it is implicit in the lease itself, or is clear from the surrounding circumstances, that the tenant is required to keep the premises in repair to a standard appropriate to the nature of the premises from time to time. In such a case, the principle in *Anstruther* will not apply. An example might be a lease of an old warehouse building which expressly entitles the tenant, if he so desires and is able to obtain the requisite permissions, to demolish the premises and erect a new office building on the site. The standard of repair may well be different in relation to the office building than in relation to the former warehouse. Similarly, in appropriate circumstances, it may be proper to infer

---

[50] In *Ladbroke Hotels Ltd v Sandhu* [1995] 2 E.G.L.R. 92 Robert Walker J. treated *Anstruther-Gough-Calthorpe v McOscar* as establishing the general proposition that the standard of repair required by a repairing covenant is to be determined by the parties' expectations at the time the lease is granted. The judge relied on that decision to support his view that the expected commercial life of a building is not relevant when considering the appropriate standard of repair. See further para.9–27, below.

[51] See para.9–11, below.

[52] See Chs 29 to 32, below.

[53] [2003] 3 E.G.L.R. 91.

[54] See further on this case para.9–19 below.

from a licence to carry out alterations an intention to vary the standard of repair to that appropriate for the premises as so altered.

The covenant itself may make it clear that the standard of repair is not fixed at the date of the lease. For example, it may require the premises to be kept in such state of repair as may be appropriate from time to time for a modern high class office building in the City of London. Even here, however, the covenant will not be construed as being unlimited in its operation. Thus, in *Gooderham & Worts Ltd v Canadian Broadcasting Corp*[55] a lease of land, premises, plant and equipment comprising a radio station, studio and offices contained a covenant by the tenant "to keep the whole of the premises modern and up to date and in good repair and operating condition". Describing the terms of the covenant as "unusual and of very wide scope", the Privy Council construed it as imposing an obligation to keep the whole of the demised premises modern and up to date, in so far as the thing demised is capable of being kept modern and up to date. However, even on this wide basis it did not require the tenant to acquire additional land if the existing site of the station was inadequate for the accommodation of the plant necessary for a modern station, nor did it extend to the substitution for the existing five-kilowatt station of an installation involving the use of higher power.

## Standard of repair unaffected by tenant's breaches of covenant

As appears above, the standard of repair will generally be an objective standard fixed at the date of the lease. The tenant cannot rely on his own breaches of covenant in order to lower the standard.[56] In *Ladbroke Hotels v Sandhu*[57] Robert Walker J. said:

> "If a tenant disregards his repairing obligations and, as a result, the premises become run-down and commercially unattractive, it hardly lies in the tenant's mouth to rely upon that fact as lowering the standard of repair required under the tenant's repairing covenant."

9–12

## The age of the premises

The age of the building is of particular importance in ascertaining the required standard of repair. An old building still has to be kept in repair, but only to a standard appropriate to a building of its age. In *Stanley v Towgood*[58] Tindall C.J. said:

> "The misdirection complained of is that the jury were told it was of no consequence for them to consider whether the house were completely new, or old, at the time of the demise. If such really had been the direction given to the jury, I should have thought there ought to be another trial."

9–13

---

[55] [1947] A.C. 66.
[56] *Ladbroke Hotels v Sandhu* [1995] 2 E.G.L.R. 92 at 95; *Carmel Southend v Strachan & Henshaw* [2007] 3 E.G.L.R. 15 at [9].
[57] Above.
[58] (1836) 3 Bing. N.C. 4.

Similarly, in *Mantz v Goring*[59] he said:

"The covenant is to keep the premises in good and tenantable repair, reasonable wear and tear excepted. Every one knows what such a covenant means, and the tenant must fulfil it according to the nature of the premises: for it is established by *Stanley v. Towgood*[60] and other cases that the same nicety of repair is not exacted for an old building as for a new one."

In *Payne v Haine*[61] Parke B. is reported as having intervened in argument, in response to a submission that "good repair" related to state of the premises at the date of the lease, in the following terms:

"It has been decided in several cases that, so far as the [tenant] is concerned, that expression [i.e. 'good repair'] has relation only to the age of the building. Good repair is different in old and new premises…"

Lord Esher M.R. made the same point in *Proudfoot v Hart*[62]:

"[T]he question whether the house was, or was not, in tenantable repair when the tenancy began is immaterial; but the age of the house is very material with respect to the obligation both to keep and to leave it in tenantable repair. It is obvious that the obligation is very different when the house is fifty years older than it was when the tenancy began."

**9–14**    In *Lurcott v Wakely*[63] Fletcher Moulton L.J. explained the relationship between the standard of repair and the age of the subject-matter, in the context of a covenant to keep the demised premises in good condition:

"In the year 1881 these premises were old. Nearly thirty years have passed since then, and there is no doubt that although they had not then suffered from age as much as was the case at the termination of the lease, even then they were old premises. Now what is the meaning of keeping old premises in good condition? I can see no difficulty in deciding the meaning of that. It means that, considering they are old premises, they must be in good condition as such premises. Let me take a parallel to which I referred in argument. Suppose the case of a ship. A man who covenants to keep the 'Mauretania' in good condition must, of course, keep her in the perfection of condition by reason of the fact that she is a vessel of her class and new.[64] Suppose a man covenants for a year to keep in good condition a tramp that has been at sea for fifteen years, he must perform the covenant just as much as the man who covenanted to keep the 'Mauretania' in good condition. But the keeping in good condition in the second case will mean something very different from that which it meant in the former case: it will mean in good condition for a vessel of that age and nature."

Likewise, in *Anstruther-Gough-Calthorpe v McOscar*[65] Bankes L.J. emphasised that the age of the premises is the most important factor in determining the standard of repair:

---

[59] (1838) 4 Bing. N.C. 451.
[60] (1836) 3 Bing. N.C. 4.
[61] (1847) 16 M. & W. 541.
[62] (1890) 25 Q.B.D. 42.
[63] [1911] 1 K.B. 905.
[64] *Lurcott v Wakely* was decided in 1911. The *Mauretania* was launched in 1907. In her day she was the largest and most modern of the transatlantic passenger liners. She held the Blue Riband of the Atlantic for 22 years, before being sold to be broken up in March 1935.
[65] [1924] 1 K.B. 716.

"[P]rovided the age of the buildings is regarded as the dominant feature, and the locality and class of tenant is only taken into account in relation to, or as a consequence of, the age of the buildings then I consider the rule laid down by the arbitrator a good working rule of general application."

Atkin L.J. said:

"Time must be taken into account; an old article is not to be made new; but so far as repair can make good, or protect against the ravages of time and the elements, it must be undertaken."

It follows that a defect which might constitute a breach of a repairing covenant in relation to a new building may not be a breach where the building is old. Thus, in *Plough Investments Ltd v Manchester City Council*[66] Scott J. said in relation to cracks in the curtain walling of a steel-framed building constructed in about 1925:

"Nor, in my opinion, would [the obligation to repair] include the removal and replacement of every cracked brick or block, no matter how small the crack. There were cracks when the leases were granted. A building of this sort, over 60 years old, is bound, in my view, to have some cracks in the bricks or blocks."

Similarly, the covenant will not generally be construed so as to require the covenanting party to bring premises which were constructed some time ago up to latter day standards of construction or specification. Thus, in *Pgf II S.A. v Royal & Sun Alliance Insurance Plc*[67] (which concerned an office building in the heart of London's financial centre which had been built to a high specification in 1973 and let for 35 years from June 1973) H.H. Judge Toulmin, QC said:

"The lease is dated 1973. The building is in the heart of the City of London close to the Lloyds Building. It was in 1973 and is now, a prestige block in the heart of the financial area. The standard of repair is that which is required to put such a 1973 building in repair. The tenant is not required to improve a 1973 building to the standard of 2008."[68]

In *Sunlife Europe Properties v Tiger Aspect Holdings*[69] (which concerned the correct approach to the assessment of damages in a terminal dilapidations claim in relation to a 1970's office and retail building), Edwards-Stuart J. identified the relevant legal principles as including the following:

"(2) The tenant is obliged to return the premises in good and tenantable condition and with the M&E systems in satisfactory working order: he is not required to deliver up the premises with new equipment or with equipment that has any particular remaining life expectancy. The standard to which the building is to be repaired or kept in repair is to be judged by reference to the condition of its fabric, equipment and fittings at the time of the demise, not the condition that would be expected of an equivalent building at the expiry of the lease."

---

[66] [1989] 1 E.G.L.R. 244.
[67] [2010] EWHC 1459 (TCC) at [51].
[68] This passage was cited by Edwards-Stuart J. in *Sunlife Europe Properties v Tiger Aspect Holdings* [2013] EWHC 463 (TCC) at [29].
[69] Above.

## The ageing process

**9–15**
The age of the building is primarily to be considered as at the date of the lease,[70] the question being what standard is appropriate in relation to a building of that age. However, the building will, of course, continue to get older as the term progresses. The tenant is not required to return the premises to the landlord at the end of the term in the same condition in which they were let. His obligation is to keep the premises in a state appropriate to their age from time to time. Thus, in *Mason v TotalFinaElf UK Ltd*[71] Blackburne J. said:

> "[T]he covenant does not require that the tenant return the premises at the end of the lease in as good condition as they were at the start. The tenant's obligation is to keep the premises in a proper state having regard, among other matters, to their age at any particular time."

In the Scottish case of *West Castle Properties v Scottish Ministers*[72] it was said that:

> "[55] It is clear from the guidance to be gained from *Proudfoot v. Hart* and subsequent authorities that maintaining the premises 'in good and tenantable condition and repair' did not require the premises to be kept in perfect repair or in as new a condition as they had been in at the commencement of the Lease. Whilst the premises became older, as the Lease ran its course, the passage of time did not alter the nature of the obligations on the tenants. Nevertheless, in fulfilling those obligations, the tenants were entitled to take account of the increasing age of the building. As Lord Esher M.R indicated in *Proudfoot v. Hart* at p. 52, 'the age of the house is very material with respect to the obligation both to keep it and leave it in tenantable repair'. Accordingly, in assessing whether or not the [tenants] had complied with their obligations, as at the expiry of the Lease, allowance can be made for the age of the premises and the age of their various component parts...
>
> [56] In my opinion, however, the [covenant] did not require the [tenant] to restore the premises to an 'as new' condition at the end of the Lease, by, for example, stripping out parts of the premises, such as roofs, windows, lifts, boilers and electrical equipment, which were perfectly serviceable and had periods of useful life left, merely to ensure that those component parts (once replaced) had, as at the expiry of the Lease, the same individual life expectancies as their predecessor parts had enjoyed at the commencement of the Lease.
>
> ...
>
> [77] ... the nature of these obligations did not alter whilst the Lease ran its course. On the contrary, it was known at the outset of the Lease that these obligations would apply throughout the Lease and thus would be applied to premises that were of increasing age. In seeking to determine whether the [tenants] have complied with the obligations on them, it could not be left out of account that the premises were 25 years older at the expiry of the Lease than they had been when the Lease began. To that extent, the [tenants] are correct that the premises have aged and that some features of their condition may have been affected by the passage of time. The [tenants] are correct that the Lease did not place them under an obligation to reverse the natural ageing process of the lease. That is conceded on behalf of the pursuers. Beyond that it is a question of fact, whether the condition of any parts of the premises has led to the premises not being in 'good tenantable condition and repair' at the expiry of the Lease."[73]

---

[70] See paras 9–07 to 9–10, above.

[71] [2003] 3 E.G.L.R. 91.

[72] [2004] S.C.L.R. 899. The relevant part of the covenant is set out in para.9–10, above.

[73] It is necessary to bear in mind as regards this passage that, as the judge pointed out at [43], the common law of Scotland as regards repairs is not the same as that of England. However, the judge was relying primarily on English authorities, and it is thought that his comments are consistent with the position in England.

It goes without saying, however, that the tenant cannot reduce the relevant standard by relying on the fact that the premises have prematurely "aged" by reason of his own default in carrying out repairs as and when necessary.[74]

In the Australian case of *Alcatel Australia v Scarcella*[75], a newly constructed office building was let in 1969 for a term of just over 50 years. The tenant covenanted well and substantially to repair and keep in good and substantial repair the premises. The anodised aluminium window frames had become corroded. Both parties agreed that the corrosion was a defect requiring repair. Regular maintenance over the previous 30 years of the term would have substantially reduced the rate of corrosion. It was held in the New South Wales Supreme Court that the tenant's obligation was to put the frames in as good a condition as if they had been properly maintained. The landlord's expert evidence was that reinstatement of the anodised coating was needed, of a kind that required disassembling of the windows and treatment off-site, but a practical and more economical alternative would be to replace the entire window framing structure of the building. The court accepted that evidence and held that the tenant was liable accordingly.

## The character and locality of the premises

The character of the premises and the locality in which they are situated must both be taken into account when considering the standard of repair.[76] Lord Esher M.R. gave the reason in *Proudfoot v Hart*[77]:

9–16

> "[T]he same class of repairs as would be necessary to a palace would be wholly unnecessary to a cottage; and ... the state of repair necessary for a house in Grosvenor Square would be wholly different from the state of repair necessary for a house in Spitalfields."

The relevant question is what would ordinarily be expected of premises of the character and in the locality in question (viewed as at the date of the lease[78]). In *Gibson Investments Ltd v Chesterton Plc*[79] Neuberger J. said:

> "'Good and substantial repair' means more than just that the building must be capable of occupation. It means in this case that the building must be in a state of repair which is appropriate for a high class office building in a prime office location in Birmingham."

Regard must therefore be had to what would generally be expected of buildings of the same class and type as the premises. In *Saner v Bilton (No.1)*[80] Fry J. said in relation to a covenant to "keep the main walls and main timbers of [the demised premises] in good repair and condition" that:

---

[74] See para.9–12 above.
[75] [2001] NSWSC 154.
[76] See paras 9–05 to 9–06, above.
[77] (1890) 25 Q.B.D. 42.
[78] See para.9–07 et seq., above.
[79] [2002] 2 P. & C.R. 494.
[80] (1878) 7 Ch. D. 815.

"[T]he question, what is 'good repair and condition', is to be viewed having regard to the class to which the demised tenement belongs, and not with regard to that tenement itself alone. If it were not so, I should be landed in this absurdity. Assuming that the main walls and main timbers were in bad repair when the lessee took the warehouse, and assuming that the 'good repair' is to be construed with regard to the particular subject matter, good repair would mean bad, and the covenant to keep in good repair would be satisfied by keeping the tenement in bad repair. Not only is that opposed to common sense, but, if authority were necessary, it is opposed to the decision in *Payne v. Haine*,[81] where it was held with regard to a house in bad condition, that a covenant to keep it in good condition required that it should be put into good condition, which would not be the case if the covenant were read with reference to the condition of the demised tenement itself."

**9–17**  The fact that the premises have been defectively designed or constructed may also be relevant when deciding upon the appropriate standard of repair. In *Lee v Leeds City Council*[82] it was argued that there was to be implied into tenancies of council houses an obligation on the part of the landlord to remedy design defects which had resulted in excessive condensation and mould but which did not themselves constitute disrepair for the purposes of the landlord's implied repairing obligation under s.11 of the Landlord and Tenant Act 1985.[83] This was said to be a necessary correlative obligation to the tenant's limited obligations in respect of internal decorative repair. In rejecting that argument, Chadwick L.J. said:

"If the premises suffer from condensation and mould by reason of some inherent design defect, then the tenant cannot be required to do more by way of decoration than is reasonable in those circumstances. To hold that the landlord is obliged to put the premises into a state in which they are free from condensation so that the tenant can decorate them would be to impose on the landlord an obligation which goes far beyond anything that can properly be regarded as correlative to the tenant's obligations."

In other words, what might otherwise have been the tenant's liability under the covenant was qualified by reference to the state of the property resulting from the design defect. The tenant was only liable to do what was reasonable in the circumstances.

## The reasonably-minded tenant

**9–18**  The *Proudfoot* approach requires the court to ask itself what, having regard to age, character and locality of the premises, would make them reasonably fit for the occupation of a reasonably-minded tenant of the class likely to take them.

The emphasis on the likely requirements of a reasonably-minded tenant has not found universal approval.[84] Such a person is a hypothetical tenant, not the actual tenant. It might be objected that what he would require by way of repairs would vary according to market conditions or the level of rent he is being asked to pay or what terms he is being asked to accept. However, this overlooks the fact that the test focuses not on what the reasonably-minded tenant would accept or

---

[81] (1847) 16 M. & W. 541.
[82] [2002] 1 W.L.R. 1488.
[83] See para.20–17 et seq., below.
[84] See *Anstruther-Gough-Calthorpe v McOscar* [1924] 1 K.B. 716 per Atkin L.J., and see paras 9–07 to 9–10, above.

require by way of bargain, but on what, viewing the matter objectively, would make the premises reasonably fit for his occupation. The standard of repair is an objective one, which does not depend on what, in the particular circumstances at the relevant time, a particular incoming tenant would accept.[85] Thus, in *Commercial Union Life Assurance v Label Ink*[86] H.H. Judge Rich, QC said that the standard of repair was:

"[T]hat of an intending occupier of an industrial warehouse building, with modern construction, who judges repair reasonably by reference to his intended use of the premises."

Likewise, in *Hammersmatch Properties (Welwyn) v Saint-Gobain Ceramics & Plastics*,[87] Ramsey J. identified the relevant question as being "what a reasonably minded tenant would require to render the premises reasonably fit for use as a place from which to run its business".

The condition contemplated by the covenant is not therefore altered by the fact that at the relevant date there happens to be a high demand for premises of that type, or the fact that with a suitable adjustment in rent, it may be possible to persuade a tenant to take the premises in a different, and worse, condition. This is shown by *Jaquin v Holland*,[88] in which the cost of the remedial works was either £91 13s 6d (the tenant's surveyor's estimate) or £102 16s (the landlord's surveyor's estimate). The diminution in the value of the reversion was £50. The landlord had carried out works to the value of £19 10s and had then relet the premises. The registrar at first instance awarded damages of £19 10s. The Court of Appeal allowed the landlord's appeal, holding that the relevant remedial works were those costing £91 13s 6d or £102 16s, so that (in accordance with s.18(1) of the Landlord and Tenant Act 1927) the proper amount of damages was £50.[89] Ormerod L.J. said:

"Counsel for the landlord ... contended that there was no evidence to justify the registrar in coming to the conclusion that £19 10s was the proper figure: it was true that that was the amount which had actually been spent by the landlord in doing such repairs as she considered necessary to make the house presentable, and that she was then able to let the house at the same figure, but that was not the proper way to apply the test [in *Proudfoot v Hart*]. The test was not whether the house could be let in all the circumstances and whatever the pressure for houses might be in that particular area at any particular time. The real test to apply was the test of the amount that was necessary to put the house into a proper condition for letting in accordance with the terms of the covenant, so that it would be taken by a reasonable man wanting a home in reasonable condition, having regard to the nature and type of house involved...

All that I need say is that I accept that view. It is not correct, in a case of this kind, to take

[85] *Westbury Estates v Royal Bank of Scotland* [2006] CSOH 177 at [37] (discussed more fully at para.13–06, below); *Carmel Southend v Strachan & Henshaw* [2007] 3 E.G.L.R. 15 at [11]; *Hammersmatch Properties (Welwyn) v Saint-Gobain Ceramics & Plastics* [2013] EWHC 1161 (TCC) at [53]. The equivalent sentence in the Third Edition of this work was approved by H.H. Judge Coulson, QC in *Carmel Southend v Strachan & Henshaw*, above, at [11].
[86] [2001] L. & T.R. 29. Note that the question of disrepair arose in the context of whether or not the tenant had complied with a condition precedent in a break option, and the judge's construction of the condition precedent was subsequently disapproved by the Court of Appeal in *Fitzroy House Epworth Street (No.1) v The Financial Times* [2006] 2 E.G.L.R. 13.
[87] [2013] EWHC 1161 (TCC) at [53].
[88] [1960] 1 W.L.R. 258.
[89] See Ch.30, below.

the circumstances of letting and say that, because any house can be let almost in any condition at the present time, then there is no obligation on a tenant to perform his covenant to repair. The rule in *Proudfoot v Hart* is a guide as to the extent of repair which may be necessary in order to comply with a covenant of this kind. But it is a guide that calls for that useful individual, the reasonable man, acting in reasonable circumstances."

As the above makes clear, , the fact that the landlord has done certain works in order to achieve a reletting does not mean that those works correspond to what is required in order to comply with the standard of repair. In an appropriate case, however, the stance taken by an actual incoming tenant may, depending on the facts, constitute evidence of what work is required to meet the standard.[90]

**9–19**   In *Mason v TotalFinaElf UK Ltd*[91] a petrol filling station had been let in 1964 for 35 years to Total Oil Products (GB) Limited. The landlord argued that since the original tenant was a major oil company, the appropriate standard of repair was that of a major oil company even though the evidence showed that no such company would have been interested in taking the premises at the end of the lease. Blackburne J. said of this:

> "I agree ... that the class of reasonably minded tenant likely at the commencement of the term to take the premises refers to the quality of reasonably minded tenant that would have done so, having regard to the then age, character and locality of the premises, and therefore that the standard of repair etc. is what would make the premises reasonably fit for the occupation of such a tenant. On the face of it, since Total was the tenant that took the lease, the class of tenant was a person or organisation such as Total. But ... there is no satisfactory evidence of Total's standing or requirements at that time relative to those of other oil companies. In this connection, I remind myself that, since 1964, Total has undergone many changes including, not least, two mergers with other oil companies ... the present day defendant is very different from the Total of 1964. Nor is there any evidence of the condition of the premises at the time the lease was granted ... there is much force, therefore, in [counsel's] observation that the court should not be drawn into a speculative inquiry into what a major oil company, assuming that Total was such a company, would then have expected of the premises in the way of the standard of repair."

It appears from this that the nature and quality of the original tenant will be material when identifying the class of tenant likely to have taken the premises at the date of the lease, but that the court will be reluctant to make detailed assumptions about these matters without evidence. If no such evidence is available, the court will have to do the best it can on what it has. In *Mason* Blackburne J. held that the court should approach the question of the likely hypothetical tenant:

> "[B]y asking itself, doing the best that it can, what ... a reasonably minded oil company would reasonably require, at the time the lease was granted, to render the premises reasonably fit for use as a place from which to run the businesses of a petrol filling station and attached shop, together with car sales and, at the rear of the site, facilities for motor vehicle repairs."

To the same effect is the following passage from the judgment of Ramsey J. in *Hammersmatch Properties (Welwyn) v Saint-Gobain Ceramics & Plastics*:[92]

---

[90] *Latimer v Carney* [2006] 3 E.G.L.R. 13; *Carmel Southend v Strachan & Henshaw*, above, at [11].
[91] [2003] 3 E.G.L.R. 91.
[92] [2013] EWHC 1161 (TCC).

"In the present case I must therefore take into account the age, character and locality of the Norton Building which was a purpose-built manufacturing building which was about 50 years old at the date of the lease. It is necessary to consider what a reasonably minded tenant of the relevant user class would reasonably require in December 1984 to render the building fit for occupation for the purposes contemplated by the lease, being an industrial building with ancillary offices (West wing and first floor of East wing) and offices on the 2nd and 3rd floors of the East wing and a wholesale warehouse or repository on the ground floor of the East Wing."

In *West Castle Properties v Scottish Ministers*[93] (a Scottish case) the premises had been newly built at the date of the lease (1977) and let to the tenant for 25 years. It was contended on behalf of the landlord that the reasonably minded tenant was to be assumed to be taking a lease on the same terms (apart from rent) as the actual lease (i.e. a 25-year lease containing full repairing obligations).[94] The consequence was argued to be that the covenant was to be construed as requiring the premises to be yielded up in such condition as would make them reasonably fit for the requirements of such a person, i.e. the requisite condition at the end of the lease was such that any new tenant commencing a 25-year lease on that date would have faced virtually the same prospects of requiring to repair and maintain the premises as the original tenant had faced when the actual lease commenced, so that:

"[T]he programmes and timescale for repair, renovation, renewal and replacement of component parts and equipment, insofar as they could be foreseen, should be the same as those the [tenants'] predecessor had faced back in 1977."

That argument was rejected by the Outer House of the Court of Session in the following terms:

"[39] None of the authorities to which I have referred define the class of tenants in such a narrow way as the [landlords] now seek to do, by limiting its membership to those commercial tenants prepared to take the premises on a lease of precisely the same terms and of precisely the same duration of the original lease. In my opinion, it is a question of fact how the class of reasonably-minded tenants, likely to have taken a particular set of premises at a particular time, is defined or constituted. In particular, looking back to 1977, which is the date on which the [landlords] focus, it is a question of fact whether the members of the class at that time would fall to be limited to potential tenants, who would be interested in a 25 year lease of the premises. The class may have been limited to those prepared to take a 25 year lease. It may not have been. Likewise, it is a question of fact whether 25 years ago commercial tenants would have been likely to have leased the premises on the same, as opposed to similar, terms as those to be found in the Lease."

As the judge pointed out,[95] the common law of Scotland as regards repairs is not the same as that of England (although most of the cases cited to the court were English authorities), so that this passage must be approached with some caution. Nonetheless, it is thought that the judge's decision was correct. The approach contended for by the landlords overlooked the fact that the premises

---

[93] [2004] S.C.L.R. 899. The relevant part of the covenant is set out in para.9–10, above.

[94] Reliance was placed on a suggestion in para.9–06 of the Second Edition of this work (2000). That same paragraph (which was not included in the Third Edition) was referred to by H.H. Judge Coulson, QC in *Riverside Property Investments v Blackhawk Automotive* [2005] 1 E.G.L.R. 114 at [54] and in *Carmel Southend v Strachan & Henshaw* [2007] 3 E.G.L.R. 15 at [11].

[95] [2004] S.C.L.R. 899 at [43].

were necessarily 25 years older at the end of the lease than they were at the beginning, and its effect, if correct, was to require the tenant at the end of the lease to reproduce the condition and lifespan of the premises at the start of the lease. That seems wrong in principle.[96]

## The user provisions in the lease

**9–20**  In considering the appropriate standard of repair, regard must be had to the uses to which the premises were permitted to be put under the lease.[97] Thus, for example, where the lease permits the demised premises to be used only as a warehouse, it would not ordinarily be right, when identifying the requisite standard of repair contemplated by the parties, to take into account what a reasonably minded tenant might have required, at the date of the lease, to occupy them as offices.

## Disrepair at the date of the lease

**9–21**  The standard of repair required by a covenant to repair is an objective one. Insofar as the premises are out of repair at the date of the lease, the covenanting party is obliged to put them into repair.[98] That is so even though the covenantor does not expressly covenant to do anything more than "keep" the premises in repair, since they cannot be kept in the required state unless they are first put into it.[99]

Thus, in *Stanley v Towgood*,[100] which concerned a tenant's covenant to keep and leave the premises in good and tenantable order and repair, Tindall C.J. said in the course of his judgment:

> "The misdirection complained of is that the jury were told it was of no consequence for them to consider whether the house were completely new, or old, at the time of the demise. If such had really been the direction given to the jury, I should have thought there ought to be another trial; but the [trial judge] does not report to us that such was the direction given, and the counsel are not agreed as to the precise words: it is probable, therefore, that there has been some little misunderstanding, and that the language, if employed, was only used in illustration or explanation of the proposition that, under a covenant to keep and leave premises in repair, the state of repair at the time of the demise is not to be taken into consideration."

---

[96] Although where the premises were newly constructed at the date of the lease, that fact will be relevant both to the standard of repair and the work which the covenantor is obliged to undertake: see paras 9–21 and 11–21, below.

[97] *Simmons v Dresden* [2004] EWHC 993 (TCC) at [34] and [48]; *Hammersmatch Properties (Welwyn) v Saint-Gobain Ceramics & Plastics* [2013] EWHC 1161 (TCC) at [53].

[98] *Payne v Haine* (1847) 16 M. & W. 541; *Truscott v Diamond Rock Boring Co.* (1881) 20 Ch. D. 251 at 256; *Proudfoot v Hart* (1890) 25 Q.B.D. 42; *Saner v Bilton (No.1)* (1878) 7 Ch.D. 815; *Chatfield v Elmstone Resthouse Ltd* [1975] 2 N.Z.L.R. 269 (New Zealand); *Langham Estate Management Ltd v Hardy* [2008] 3 E.G.L.R. 125 at [59]. In *Credit Suisse v Beegas Nominees Ltd* [1994] 4 All E.R. 803 and (more fully) [1994] 1 E.G.L.R. 76 Lindsay J. said of this principle that it has "been acted upon, by now, in probably hundreds of cases and still survives".

[99] See the cases in the preceding footnote.

[100] (1836) 3 Bing. N.C. 4.

In *Payne v Haine*[101] it was argued that a covenant to keep premises in "good repair, order and condition" was performed by keeping them substantially in the same condition in which they were at the date of the lease. At the trial Platt B. had accepted this contention, and directed the jury that it was enough if the tenant left the premises in as good a state as he found them. A new trial was ordered on the grounds of misdirection. Parke B. said:

9–22

> "If, at the time of the demise, the premises were old and in bad repair, the lessee was bound to put them in good repair as old premises; for he cannot 'keep' them in good repair without putting them into it. He might have contracted to keep them in the state in which they were at the time of the demise. This is a contract to keep the premises in good repair, as old premises; but that cannot justify the keeping them in bad repair because they happened to be in that state when the [tenant] took them. The cases all show that the age and class of the premises let, with their general condition as to repair, may be estimated, in order to measure the extent of the repairs to be done. Thus, a house in Spitalfields may be repaired with materials inferior to those requisite for repairing a mansion in Grosvenor Square, but this lessee cannot say he will do no repairs, or leave the premises in bad repair, because they were old and out of repair when he took them. He was to keep them in good repair, and in that state, with reference to their age and class, he was to deliver them up at the end of the term."

Rolfe B. added:

> "The term 'good repair' is to be construed with reference to the subject matter, and must differ, as that may be a palace or a cottage; but to 'keep in good repair' presupposes the putting into it, and means that during the whole term the premises shall be in good repair."

Similarly, in *Proudfoot v Hart*[102] Lord Esher M.R. dealt with the condition of the premises at the date of demise as follows:

> "What is the true construction of a tenant's contract to keep and deliver up premises in 'tenantable repair'? Now, it is not an express term of that contract that the premises should be put into tenantable repair, and it may therefore be argued that, where it is conceded, as it is in this case, that the premises were out of tenantable repair when the tenancy began, the tenant is not bound to put them into tenantable repair, but is only bound to keep them in the same repair as they were in when he became the tenant of them. But it has been decided—and, I think, rightly decided—that, where the premises are not in repair when the tenant takes them, he must put them into repair in order to discharge his obligation under a contract to keep and deliver them up in repair. If the premises are out of repair at any time during the tenancy the landlord is entitled to say to the tenant 'You have now broken your contract to keep them in repair'; and if they were out of repair at the end of the tenancy he is entitled to say 'You have broken your contract to deliver them up in repair'. I am of opinion that under a contract to keep the premises in tenantable repair and leave them in tenantable repair, the obligation of the tenant, if the premises are not in tenantable repair when the tenancy begins, is to put them into, keep them in, and deliver them up in tenantable repair ... The result of the cases seems to be this: the question whether the house was, or was not, in tenantable repair when the tenancy began is immaterial."

Whilst the above cases were concerned with tenant's covenants, it appears that the same rule applies to a landlord's covenant.[103]

---

[101] (1847) 16 M. & W. 541.
[102] (1890) 25 Q.B.D. 42.
[103] *Saner v Bilton (No.1)* (1878) 7 Ch. D. 815; *Uniproducts (Manchester) Ltd v Rose Furnishers Ltd* [1956] 1 W.L.R. 45, per Glyn-Jones J. at 49.

## The general condition of the premises at the date of the lease

**9–23**  The general condition of the premises at the date of the lease may be relevant in identifying the appropriate standard of repair. Thus, in *Burdett v Withers*[104] the tenant of certain farms covenanted to keep the demised premises in good and sufficient repair. At the trial of the landlord's action for damages for breach of this covenant, the tenant sought to cross-examine the landlord's witnesses as to the state of the premises at the time of the demise. Alderson B. stopped this line of questioning, and directed the jury that they were to assess damages in the sum which it would cost to put the premises into tenantable repair, without reference to the state in which the tenant had found them. Lord Denman C.J., in a short judgment, ordered a new trial, saying:

> "It is very material, with a view both to the event of the suit, and to the amount of damages, to show what the previous state of the premises was."

In *Mantz v Goring*,[105] which was an action for breach of a covenant to keep a house in tenantable repair, reasonable wear and tear excepted, the tenant wished to ask one of his witnesses whether some of the defects did not exist prior to the date of the lease. Coltman J. held that he was entitled to show generally in what state of repair the premises were at the commencement of the term, but that he was not entitled to go into matters of detail. The jury found for the landlord. Tindall C.J. refused to disturb their finding, saying that:

> "[T]he learned judge allowed the [tenant] to go into evidence of the general state of repairs at [the date of the lease]: I think that was sufficient, and that in effect, the [tenant] had all that he asked for."

Both *Stanley v Towgood*[106] and *Burdett v Withers*[107] were considered in detail in *Payne v Haine*,[108] in which Parke B. said in the course of his judgment:

> "The cases all show that the age and class of the premises let, with their general condition as to repair, may be estimated, in order to measure the extent of the repairs to be done."

Alderson B. said:

> "The marginal note of *Burdett v Withers* may be incorrect,[109] but the judgment is quite right, and shows that a lessee who has contracted to keep demised premises in good repair, is entitled to prove what their general state of repair was at the time of the demise, so as to measure the amount of damages for want of repairs by reference to that state. *Stanley v Towgood* had seemed to show that, though the age of a house at the time of its demise must be considered in estimating the amount of repair on which a lessor can insist, yet any inquiry into its state of

---

[104] (1837) 7 Ad. & E. 136.
[105] (1838) 4 Bing. N.C. 451.
[106] (1836) 3 Bing. N.C. 4.
[107] (1837) 7 Ad. & E. 136.
[108] (1847) 16 M. & W. 541.
[109] This is perhaps a reference to the note at the beginning of the report of *Burdett v Withers* to the following effect: "…. the tenant is entitled to prove at the trial what the state of the premises was at the time of the demise." Alderson B. no doubt thought that this stated the ratio decidendi of *Burdett v Withers* too widely. It is thought that if this is what he meant, then he was correct.

repair at the time of entry would be misplaced. However, as some want of repair then existed, and the case was left to the jury as to the amount of damages, which they found under £20, the Court would not interfere."

Both Parke B. and Alderson B. therefore seem to have accepted that the general state of the premises at the date of the lease might be relevant in determining the standard of repair required by the covenant.

Perhaps the clearest statement is that of Parke B. in the subsequent case of *Walker v Hatton*.[110] A lease for 21 years was granted on May 10, 1828, containing a tenant's covenant to repair. A sub-lease of the same premises was subsequently granted on June 15, 1830, for the term of the head lease less 10 days containing a tenant's covenant to repair framed in the same terms. The sub-tenant failed to repair. The head landlord sued the tenant and recovered damages and costs. The tenant then sued the sub-tenant, and the question arose as to whether the damages payable by the latter should include the head landlord's costs of the proceedings which the tenant had been ordered to pay, and the tenant's own costs of defending the action brought against him. It was held that the sub-tenant was not so liable. Parke B. based his judgment on the fact that the covenants in the two leases were different in their operation so that the costs in question were not the necessary consequence of the sub-tenant's breaches. He said:

**9–24**

"Although the covenants contained in the sub-lease are, with the exception of that relating to painting, the same in language with those contained in the original lease, yet they are different in substance; the periods at which the leases were granted being different. It is now perfectly well settled, that a general covenant to repair must be construed to have reference to the condition of the premises at the time when the covenant begins to operate; and as the one lease was granted in 1828, and the other in 1830, allowing an interval of two years, it is clear that the covenants would not have the same effect, but would vary substantially in their operation."

In *Pontifex v Foord*[111] Pollock B. said in the course of his judgment:

"It is common knowledge that, where there is a covenant to repair such as those contained in this lease and sub-lease, and a surveyor is called in to make an estimate of the damages arising from non-fulfilment of the covenant, the first question he goes into is as to the character and age of the house when the tenancy commenced."

To much the same effect is the following passage from the judgment of H.H. Judge Richard Seymour, QC in *Simmons v Dresden*[112] said:

"In reaching a conclusion as to whether the requisite standard had been met in respect of a particular matter it is plainly relevant to take into account the standard of repair and decoration at the date of the demise and also the uses to which the premises were permitted to be, and had been, put. To that extent I accept the submission of [counsel] as to the significance of the user covenant."

[110] (1842) 10 M. & W. 249. See also *Woolcock v Dew* (1858) 1 F. & F. 337; *Scott v Brown* (1904) 69 J.P. 89.
[111] (1884) 12 Q.B.D. 152.
[112] [2004] EWHC 993 (TCC).

In *Fitzpatrick v Exel Holdings*,[113] the question was whether a sub-undertenant's liablity under its repairing obligations in a sub-underlease were less extensive that that of the sub-tenant's liability to the head tenant by reason of differences in the dates on which the underlease and sub-underlease were granted and the length of the terms. In deciding that the repairing obligations were not identical in nature and extent, Mr Recorder Michael Black QC (sitting as a judge of the Technology and Construction Court) treated *Walker v Hatton* as authority for the proposition that "if two leases are in the same terms but are of different dates, the repairing covenants in the leases do not impose the same obligation because one must also have regard to the starting point of those obligations, namely the condition of the premises before the commencement of the lease" (although he emphasised that the question is ultimately one of construction).[114]

**9–25**    It is thought that the principal relevance of the general state of the premises at the date of the demise is that in many, perhaps most, cases it will afford evidence of the appropriate standard of repair.[115] In the ordinary case, where the landlord lets the premises on the open market, and the tenant takes them for his own occupation, it may be relatively easy to equate the general state of the premises at the date of the letting with what the parties are likely to have intended should be the appropriate standard of repair under the repairing covenant. Thus, in the absence of evidence either way, the court may be prepared to infer that the premises were in tenantable repair at the date of the lease.[116] In such cases the covenantor's obligation to remedy subsequent defects will be measured by reference to the general state of the premises at the date of the lease, and not any higher standard. It follows that the fact that the premises were newly constructed at the date of the letting may be highly relevant when identifying the appropriate standard of repair. It may enable the court to hold that the relevant standard is that appropriate to a new building, albeit taking into account the ageing process during the term.[117] Thus, in *Twinmar Holdings v Klarius*,[118] the tenant of a newly built warehouse let for 25 years covenanted to keep the whole of the premises in good and substantial repair and condition. One of the questions concerned the extent to which he was liable to repair the GRP polyester roof lights. In holding that he was, Edwards-Stuart J. said:

> "... I consider that the condition of the roof lights must be, so far as maintenance and repair can do it, the condition in which they were at the commencement of the lease. In other words, they must be capable of letting in about the same amount of light and must be structurally sound and weatherproof."

Nonetheless, the general state of the premises at the date of the lease, whilst relevant, cannot be conclusive as to the required standard. First, the obligation to

---

[113] Unreported decision of Mr Recorder Michael Black QC, sitting as a judge of the Technology and Construction Court, dated July 16, 2008.
[114] See further on this case para.24–07, below.
[115] *Woolcock v Dew* (1858) 1 F. & F. 337; *Scott v Brown* (1904) 69 J.P. 89; *Re Mayor and Corp of London* [1910] 2 Ch. 314; *Vicro Investments Ltd v Adams Brands Ltd* [1963] 2 O.R. 583; *Credit Suisse v Beegas Nominees Ltd* [1994] 4 All E.R. 803 and (more fully) [1994] 1 E.G.L.R. 76.
[116] *Brown v Trumper* (1858) 26 Beav. 11.
[117] See para.9–15, above.
[118] [2013] EWHC 944 (TCC) at [13-14].

keep in repair obliges the covenantor to put the premises into repair if they are not in repair.[119] It follows that the obligation to repair or keep in repair is not an obligation to keep the premises in the same state they were in at the date of the lease. Whilst that state may afford evidence as to the general standard contemplated by the parties, it does not relieve the covenantor from the obligation to remedy specific disrepair existing at that date. Second, there may be cases where the condition of the premises at the date of the lease affords no assistance at all as to the contemplated standard of repair. Suppose, for example, that for a number of years prior to the grant of a lease of a suite of offices, the premises have been alternately vacant or occupied by short-term licensees. The landlord then decides to let them on a 21-year lease containing a tenant's repairing covenant, with a six-month rent-free period to reflect the undoubted fact that substantial work is necessary. In circumstances such as these it is highly unlikely that the state of repair at the date of the lease would afford any guide at all to the state contemplated by the parties, which would have to be determined by reference to the criteria discussed above.

Where there are defects at the date of the lease of which the tenant is unaware, the correct conclusion may be that what is relevant is not the actual condition of the premises at that date but what the tenant believed, or can reasonably be taken as having believed, was their then condition (their "putative" condition). Thus, in *Credit Suisse v Beegas Nominees Ltd*[120] Lindsay J. said in the course of his judgment:

**9–26**

> "Of course, in most circumstances the hypothetical required condition and the actual condition as at the date of the lease will coincide. If there is no reason to regard the actual tenant as other than a reasonably minded member of the class likely to take the building of the kind in question and if he has inspected before he takes the lease it can reasonably be inferred, if the circumstances add nothing, that the building reached the standard that the hypothetical tenant would have thought fit for his occupation. But so far as concerns good and tenantable condition I cannot see it as relevant minutely to examine into whether, on the very day of the lease, [the building] was or was not watertight and if it was not, why it was not. If, as I think it is, the relevant standard of condition is what I shall call the putative condition, namely the condition that the tenant of the class I have described would require, then what is important is not so much the state of fact as at the date of the demise but what the tenant in particular then thought was the fact or, in the absence of direct evidence as to that, what it can reasonably be inferred the tenant is likely then to have thought in relation to the condition of the building.[121]"

Lindsay J.'s distinction between the actual state of the premises at the date of the lease and their putative condition was applied by Robert Walker J. in *Ladbroke Hotels Limited v Sandhu*.[122] In deciding what condition was to be assumed for rent review purposes, an arbitrator had declined to take into account the fact that the premises had been badly built (and therefore did not have a life expectation of 60 years), because this was not known to the parties when the lease was granted. Robert Walker J. held that he had not made an error of law. He

---

[119] See paras 9–21 to 9–22, above.

[120] [1994] 4 All E.R. 803 and (more fully) [1994] 1 E.G.L.R. 26. See para.8–12 above.

[121] See also *Smedley v Chumley & Hawke Ltd* (1982) 44 P. & C.R. 50, discussed in para.11–21, below.

[122] [1995] 2 E.G.L.R. 92. The facts are set out in para.9–27, below.

regarded it as implicit in Lindsay J.'s judgment in *Credit Suisse* that the actual condition at the time of the grant of the lease was irrelevant, and went on to say:

> "The fact that both freehold and leasehold interest may change hands more than once during the term … may be a further reason for an objective assessment of what is supposed to have been in the contemplation of the original lessor and lessee."

## The expected commercial life of the premises

9–27    The premises may be such that they will reach the end of their useful commercial life whilst still being perfectly capable of being repaired. An example might be a large purpose-built cinema which can no longer be profitably run and which is incapable of any other use. The building fabric may, if kept in proper repair, be capable of lasting for many more years, but no owner would regard it as commercially worthwhile to spend more than a minimal amount on repairs. One question arising in such cases is whether the expected commercial life of the premises is relevant when ascertaining the standard of repair.

It was held in *Ladbroke Hotels Ltd v Sandhu*[123] that it is not. In that case a hotel built in the late 1960s was let in 1970 on a 99-year lease which included a tenant's repairing covenant. The reviewed rent under the lease was to be assessed on the assumption that the covenant had been complied with. An arbitrator was appointed to fix the reviewed rent. One issue before him was what work the tenant was obliged to carry out. In the arbitration the tenant's engineer produced two reports. In the first ("Pyle no.1"), he set out his view that the estimated life of the original structure, if properly constructed, would have been at least 60 years. However, a tower forming part of the hotel had been so badly constructed that there were doubts as to its stability, and the recommended repairs would cost in the order of £500,000. In a second report ("Pyle no.2"), he recommended works costing just over £60,000 on the basis of his instructions that the hotel had an expected commercial life of no more than 15 years. The arbitrator held that it was not relevant to assess the remaining commercial life of the hotel, and he therefore fixed the rent on the basis that the work in Pyle no.1 had been carried out. Robert Walker J. held that he was correct to do so.

It follows that whilst what Robert Walker J. called the "structural life" of the building (that is to say, its expected lifespan as a structure) may be relevant, the fact that it may become incapable of beneficial use commercially cannot be taken into account, even where this means that in reality no one would do the repairs in question. That fact, however, may have an important bearing on the amount of damages recoverable.[124]

---

[123] [1995] 2 E.G.L.R. 92.
[124] See Chs 29 to 32, below.

## The cause or origin of the defect

As a general rule, where the premises suffer from a defect, the question whether **9–28**
that defect brings them below the contemplated standard does not depend on the
cause or origin of the defect.[125] In *Gibson Investments Ltd v Chesterton Plc*[126]
Neuberger J. said:

> "The covenant in this case specifically provides that the tenant is liable, even though any want
> of repair is due to inherent or latent defect in the demised premises or normal wear and tear or
> deterioration or otherwise. This makes it clear that the origin or reason for the relevant defect
> is not relevant, but it should be said that that is normally the case even without a provision to
> that effect."

Thus, defects which are the result of the tenant's deliberate act,[127] natural
disasters,[128] bad design or construction,[129] or fair wear and tear[130] may all require
to be remedied under the general repairing covenant. What is relevant is whether
the defect brings the premises below the standard identified above. If it does, the
tenant will be obliged to carry out the necessary remedial work unless that work
goes beyond repair as a matter of fact and degree.[131]

## The intended function of the part of the premises in disrepair

Where the damage or deterioration is such that the part of the premises in **9–29**
question has ceased to perform its intended function, its condition will generally
have fallen below the contemplated standard of repair. An example is *Windever v
Liverpool City Council*,[132] in which the kitchen and living room floors in a
dwelling had become significantly off-level due to settlement such that, although
their condition was not hazardous, it interfered with the tenant's daily use of the
rooms. It was held in the Liverpool County Court that the floors were in disrepair
for the purposes of s.11 of the Landlord and Tenant Act 1985[133] because they had
deteriorated to the extent where they no longer performed the function they were
designed to perform. However, the converse is not always true. The premises may
be below the requisite standard even though the part in question continues to
perform its intended function. Thus, a roof may be below the contemplated
standard of repair even though it is not letting in water. Similarly, electric wiring
may be below the requisite standard notwithstanding the fact that it conducts
current adequately and is not dangerous.

The same is true of parts of the premises which are intended to perform a
structural function. Thus, in *Re Mayor and Corp of London*[134] an underground

---

[125] Cf. *Passley v Wandsworth LBC* (1998) 30 H.L.R. 165 per Hobhouse L.J. at 171.
[126] [2002] 2 P. & C.R. 494.
[127] See para.18–02 to 18–03, below.
[128] See para.18–08 et seq., below.
[129] See para.11–28 et seq., below.
[130] *Clowes v Bentley Property Ltd* [1970] W.A.R. 24 (Australia).
[131] See Ch.11, below.
[132] [1994] C.L. 299. See further on this case para.8–08, above.
[133] See Ch.23, below.
[134] [1910] 2 Ch. 314.

railway station was constructed with walls, columns, girders and arches which supported Smithfield Meat Market. The station was then let on leases containing a covenant by the tenant:

"[W]ell and sufficiently [to] maintain, uphold, support, and keep in good, substantial, and tenantable repair, order, and condition ... the premises hereby demised, including the retaining and other walls, piers, pillars, supports, and roof, forming a part of the same."

Some of the girders supporting the meat market had corroded and become weakened since they were originally constructed. The tenant contended that its liability was confined to keeping the girders in such a condition as would enable them safely to support the meat market. Eve J. rejected this, holding the tenant liable to keep the girders in substantially the same condition as they were in at the date of the tenancy.[135] He said:

"I think that in the face of this covenant, plain and explicit in terms, it is not open to the company successfully to contend that the measure of their obligation is the safety and the absolute safety of the superstructure, but that the true measure of their obligation has to be ascertained with reference to that which constituted this part of the demised premises at the time when the tenancy commenced. For reasons which no doubt seemed good and sufficient the parties to the lease agreed upon a certain standard of efficiency, and I do not think it is open to either of them to depart from that standard; the liability of the lessees to support the superstructure is to be ascertained, and at the same time limited by the condition of affairs subsisting at the date of the lease."

## Alterations before the grant of the lease

**9–30** Where the premises have been altered before the grant of the lease, the relevant standard of repair will generally be that applicable to the premises as altered. The tenant is not liable to restore the premises to their original state.[136]

## Where there is a landlord's covenant to put the premises into repair before the grant of the lease

**9–31** Where the landlord covenants to put the premises into repair before the grant of the lease, the standard to which the repairs must be carried out will depend on the proper construction of the covenant, regard being had to the relevant surrounding circumstances. It will be relevant to consider the use which the parties contemplate will be made of the premises. If, to the knowledge of the landlord, that use requires a particular standard of repair, the landlord may be liable to repair to a higher standard than might otherwise be the case. However, in the absence of such knowledge, the standard of repair will be that ordinarily applicable.[137]

---

[135] Although it is possible that his decision turned on, or at any rate was influenced by, the inclusion of the word "maintain" in the covenant: see the Scottish case of *Westbury Estates v The Royal Bank of Scotland* [2006] CSOH 177 at [20].

[136] *Bailey v John Paynter (Mayfield) Property Ltd* [1966] 1 N.S.W.L.R. 596 (Australia).

[137] *McClure v Little* (1868) 19 L.T. 287.

## THE EXCLUSION OF FAIR WEAR AND TEAR

### Introductory

Repairing covenants in short lettings[138] are often qualified by an exclusion of "fair wear and tear" or some similar formulation. Where the exclusion appears, the extent to which it governs all parts of the repairing obligations is a question of construction. Thus, for example, in *City of London v Black*[139] an exclusion of fair wear and tear was held to apply only to the concluding part of the covenant, which obliged the tenant to yield up a list of specified items at the end of the term whole and undefaced, and not to the preceding part, which obliged the tenant to repair and yield up the premises in repair. By contrast, in *Bunyip Buildings Pty Ltd v Gestetner Pty Ltd*[140] a lease contained a covenant to keep the premises in tenantable repair and condition (damage by fire and tempest excepted), and a covenant to yield up the premises at the expiration of the lease "reasonable wear and tear excepted". It was held that the two covenants must be read together, so that the tenant's obligation to keep the premises in good and tenantable repair and condition was subject to the fair wear and tear exclusion.[141]

9–32

### The meaning of "fair wear and tear"

The expression "fair wear and tear" has been said to be "... a very old English idiom ... common in leases and tenancy agreements for two or three centuries".[142] "Reasonable wear and tear"[143] has been defined as follows:

9–33

> "The meaning is that the tenant ... is bound to keep the house in good repair and condition, but is not liable for what is due to reasonable wear and tear. That is to say, his obligation to keep in good repair is subject to that exception. If any want of repair is alleged and proved in fact, it lies on the tenant to show that it comes within the exception. Reasonable wear and tear means the reasonable use of the house by the tenant and the ordinary operation of natural forces ..."[144]

The qualification therefore exempts the tenant from liability for defects occurring as the result of (1) his reasonable use of the premises, and (2) the ordinary operation of natural forces. It is necessary to consider these separately.

---

[138] Usually furnished residential lettings.
[139] (1960) 175 E.G. 51. To much the same effect are the decisions in *Dwellings Developments v Drake* (1954) 163 EG 192, and *South London & Streatham Estates v Large* [1957] EGD 236.
[140] [1969] S.A.S.R. 87.
[141] This case may perhaps be contrasted with *Cugg Property Ltd v Gibo Property Ltd* [2001] NSWSC 297, in which the New South Wales Supreme Court declined to read a covenant to comply with statutes and notices as impliedly qualified by the covenants to repair and yield up in repair. See further para.17–03, below.
[142] *Taylor v Webb* [1937] 2 K.B. 283, per Scott L.J. at 302.
[143] It is thought that this means the same as fair wear and tear.
[144] *Haskell v Marlow* [1928] 2 K.B. 45, per Talbot J. at 58–59, approved by the House of Lords in *Regis Property Co Ltd v Dudley* [1959] A.C. 370.

## Reasonable use

**9–34** Defects caused by the reasonable use of the premises by the tenant for the purposes contemplated by the lease are within the exception. Thus, in *Royal Trust Co. v R.*[145] (a Canadian case) the tenant covenanted to repair and leave the premises in repair "reasonable wear and tear" excepted. Audette J. held that "wear and tear" was to be considered in the light of the purpose for which the premises were let and the nature of the use to which it might be put. So, for example, worn floors in an office building resulting from being constantly walked on by the tenant's staff would be within the ambit of "fair wear and tear".

However, defects caused by use which is unreasonable in extent or which is not contemplated by the lease do not fall within the exception, and neither does destruction caused as a result of some unforeseen catastrophe, even one which occurs in the course of reasonable use of the premises. Thus, in *Manchester Bonded Warehouse Ltd v Carr*[146] the tenant of a warehouse covenanted to repair, maintain and keep the inside of the premises in good and tenantable repair and condition, damage by fire, storm or tempest, or other inevitable accident, and reasonable wear and tear only excepted. One floor of the building was overloaded with flour, as a result of which the entire building collapsed. The court held that the tenant could not rely upon the exclusion. Lord Coleridge C.J. said:

> "It ... remains to consider whether reasonable wear and tear can include destruction by reasonable use. These words, no doubt, include destruction to some extent, *e.g.*, destruction of surface by ordinary friction, but we do not think they include total destruction by a catastrophe which was never contemplated by either party. It follows that the defendant is liable under his express covenant to make good the cost of putting the inside of the floors demised to him and the fixtures therein in good and tenantable repair."

## The ordinary operation of natural forces

**9–35** Defects caused by the normal action of natural forces are within the exclusion. In *Gutteridge v Munyard*[147] Tindall C.J. stated the effect of the exclusion in the following words:

> "What the natural operation of time flowing on effects, and all that the elements bring about in diminishing the value, constitute a loss which, so far as it results from time and nature, falls upon the landlord. But the tenant is to take care that the premises do not suffer more than the operation of time and nature would effect; he is bound by reasonable applications of labour to keep the house as nearly as possible in the same condition as when it was demised."

The above passage has been quoted with approval in the Court of Appeal.[148]

In *Miller v Burt*[149] the tenant covenanted to keep the premises in the same state of repair as they then were, "fair wear and tear and damage by fire, storm or tempest only excepted", and to yield them up in such repair at the end of the term.

---

[145] [1924] Ex CR 121.
[146] (1880) 5 C.P.D. 507.
[147] (1834) 1 Moo. & R. 334. See para.11–15, below, as to the reliability of the report of this case.
[148] *Brown v Davies* [1958] 1 Q.B. 117.
[149] (1918) 63 S.J. 117.

The tenancy ended, and an arbitrator was appointed to determine whether the tenant had committed any breaches of covenant. He stated a special case under s.19 of the Arbitration Act 1889. The court agreed upon the following formula for his guidance:

"The tenant is responsible for repairs necessary to maintain the premises in the same state as when he took them. If, however, wind and weather have a greater effect on the premises, having regard to their character, than if the premises had been sound, the tenant is not bound so to repair as to meet the extra effect of the dilapidations so caused."

In *Terrell v Murray*[150] the tenant of a house covenanted to deliver it up at the end of the term in as good repair and condition as it was in at the date of the lease, reasonable wear and tear excepted. It was held that he was not liable to paint the outside woodwork of a house, to repoint the brickwork and to repair parts of the kitchen floor which had become affected by dry rot. Bruce J. said in the course of his judgment that:

"The meaning of the covenant ... was that the tenant was bound at the end of the tenancy to deliver up the premises in as good condition as they were in at the beginning subject to the following exception, that was to say, dilapidations caused by the friction of the air, dilapidations caused by exposure, and dilapidations caused by ordinary use."

The exclusion covers the ordinary operation of time and nature.[151] It does not apply where the defect is the result of some unforeseen natural or other disaster, such as lightning, an exceptionally violent storm, flooding, fire or an earthquake.[152]

## Defects caused by the landlord's failure to repair[153]

Whilst the position is not clear-cut, it may be that the fair wear and tear exception will extend to damage caused to the demised premises by the landlord's failure to repair adjoining premises. Thus, in *Citron v Cohen*[154] the tenant covenanted to repair the interior of the demised premises "reasonable wear and tear excepted". Damage was caused to the interior when an outside water-pipe burst. The pipe belonged to the landlord, who had had notice of its defective state but had failed to repair it. Sankey J. held that the tenant was not liable to repair the damage. It appears that in so holding he was relying at least to some extent on the fact that reasonable wear and tear were excluded from the tenant's covenant.

**9–36**

---

[150] (1901) 17 T.L.R. 570.
[151] See, for example, *Bartram v Rempel* [1949] 2 W.W.R. 1183 (Canada) (tenant who covenanted to repair "reasonable wear and tear, and damage by fire and tempest excepted" held not liable to repair a fence which was falling down because its posts were rotting).
[152] *Taylor v Webb* [1937] 2 K.B. 283, per Scott L.J. at 302.
[153] See further para.23–05, below.
[154] (1920) 36 T.L.R. 560.

## Consequential damage

**9–37**    Defects caused by ordinary wear and tear, if left unremedied, may lead to other more substantial defects which would not have occurred had the original defect been remedied. For example, a slate on the roof may slip slightly, allowing water to penetrate into the interior of the building. The slipped slate is the result of fair wear and tear, and the tenant is not liable to do anything about it. However, the water penetration causes the roof timbers to rot and the top floor ceilings to collapse. The question is the extent to which the tenant is liable to repair those defects.

After some initial confusion in the authorities, it is now clear following the decision of the House of Lords in *Regis Property Co Ltd v Dudley*[155] that it is only those defects which are the direct result of fair wear and tear that are excluded from the scope of the repairing obligation. The tenant is liable for all other defects, even those which are indirectly caused by fair wear and tear in the sense discussed above.[156] It had previously been held by the Court of Appeal in *Taylor v Webb*[157] that the tenant is relieved not only from the immediate effects of wear and tear, but also from any obligation to take steps to avert any consequential damage.[158] That decision was distinguished by a different Court of Appeal in *Brown v Davies*,[159] and in so far as it purported to lay down any general principle, it was overruled by the House of Lords in *Regis Property Co Ltd v Dudley*. The House approved the following passage from the judgment of Talbot J. in the earlier case of *Haskell v Marlow*[160] (which had itself been overruled by the Court of Appeal in *Taylor v Webb*):

> "The exception of want of repair due to wear and tear must be construed as limited to what is directly due to wear and tear, reasonable conduct on the part of the tenant being assumed. It does not mean that if there is a defect originally proceeding from reasonable wear and tear the tenant is released from his obligation to keep in good repair and condition everything which it may be possible to trace to that defect. He is bound to do such repairs as may be required to prevent the consequences flowing originally from wear and tear producing others which wear and tear would not directly produce ... For example, if a tile falls off the roof, the tenant is not liable for the immediate consequences; but, if he does nothing and in the result more and more water gets in, the roof and walls decay and ultimately the top floor or the whole house becomes uninhabitable, he cannot say that it is due to reasonable wear and tear, and that therefore he is not liable under his obligation to keep the house in good repair and condition. In such a case the want of repair is not in truth caused by wear and tear. Far the greater part of it is caused by the failure of the tenant to prevent what was originally caused by wear and tear from producing results altogether beyond what was so caused. On the other hand, take the gradual wearing away of a stone floor or a staircase by ordinary use. This may in time produce

---

[155] [1959] A.C. 370.

[156] See for example *Lane v B-Line Express Ltd* [1976] 4 W.W.R. 432 (Canada) (tenant liable for damage to warehouse wall resulting from protective loading dock bumpers becoming so damaged that trucks using the dock could strike the walls).

[157] [1937] 2 K.B. 283.

[158] In that case, the landlord had covenanted to repair the outside walls and roof, "fair wear and tear excepted". The Court of Appeal held that he was not liable for serious disrepair caused to the interior of the demised premises by water penetration resulting from defects in the roofs and skylights which he had done nothing about over a substantial period of time.

[159] [1958] 1 Q.B. 117.

[160] [1928] 2 K.B. 45.

a considerable defect in condition, but the whole of the defect is caused by reasonable wear and tear, and the tenant is not liable in respect of it."

In the House of Lords Lord Denning said in his speech:

"I have never understood that in an ordinary house a 'fair wear and tear' exception reduced the burden of repairs to practically nothing at all. It exempts a tenant from liability for repairs that are decorative and for remedying parts that wear out or come adrift in the course of reasonable use, but it does not exempt him from anything else. If further damage is likely to flow from the wear and tear, he must do such repairs as are necessary to stop that further damage. If a slate falls off through wear and tear and in consequence the roof is likely to let through water, the tenant is not responsible for the slate coming off but he ought to put in another one to prevent further damage."

In the Australian case of *Cugg Property Ltd v Gibo Property Ltd*,[161] the demised **9–38** premises consisted of an office building erected over a railway tunnel. Part of the building was built over a concrete slab forming the ceiling to the tunnel. The slab was included in the demise. The tenant's repairing covenants were subject to a fair wear and tear exception and also a proviso that the obligation was limited to the condition of the premises at the commencement of the lease. The steel reinforcement of the slab had corroded with consequent loss of concrete cover. The landlord argued, by reference to the principle in *Regis Property Co. v Dudley*, that the tenant ought to have put a protective barrier under the slab which would have prevented moisture penetration and therefore further corrosion. Hodgson C.J. found on the facts that the slab was in substantially the same condition as it was in at the commencement of the lease, the requisite works being essentially the same. A protective barrier would probably greatly have reduced any ongoing corrosion, but most of the relevant damage had already been done by the date of the lease, and the barrier would have made little difference to the problem. Any deterioration since the date of the lease was within the fair wear and tear exception.

In the Australian case of *Alamdo Holdings Property Ltd v Australian Window Furnishings (NSW) Property Ltd*[162], the demised premises consisted of two large factory buildings and seven adjacent bitumen areas. The tenant covenanted to:

"maintain replace repair and keep the whole of the Demised Premises in good and substantial repair order and condition damage by reasonable wear and tear only excepted Provided that this covenant shall not impose on the Lessee any obligation in respect of any structural maintenance replacement or repair except when the same is rendered necessary by any act or omission or default on the part of the Lessee or by the Lessee's use or occupancy of the Demised Premises."

At the end of the lease, the bitumen areas had deteriorated. It was common ground that the state of three of the areas went beyond reasonable wear and tear, but the tenant relied on the reasonable wear and tear exception in relation to the condition of the other four. The relevant deterioration had begun in the form of cracking but became more pronounced when the cracking was not treated so that water ran in underneath the asphalt skin and undermined both it and the basecourse, which led to greater cracking in the form of "crocodile cracking" and

---

[161] [2001] NSWSC 297.
[162] [2006] NSWCA 224.

potholes. The landlord contended, relying on *Regis Property Co. v Dudley*, that the defects amounted to consequential damage which the tenant ought to have repaired. That argument was rejected by Barrett J. at first instance.[163] He said:

> "The evidence is that the pavement was at the end of its useful and expected life. It had, over time, got to a state where 'crocodile cracking' occurred. This is symptomatic of decomposition or deterioration inherent in asphalt paving and to be expected in the ordinary course. It leads on to rutting and potholing. The expert evidence shows, in my view, that the process by which this pavement fell into a holed and rutted state was no more and no less than a working out of the forces of nature upon the material concerned. Even allowing for the fullest effect of the principles stated [in *Regis Property Co. v Dudley*], it cannot be the case that, despite an exception for reasonable wear and tear, a tenant must continually scan an asphalt pavement for the first signs of any crack and then immediately act to repair it in case it becomes larger or lets water through into the basecourse. That would set at nought the exception for reasonable wear and tear. The pavement must, in my view, be seen as a whole and subject to the ordinary processes of deterioration to which such a pavement, viewed as a whole, is susceptible."

The judge's decision was upheld by the majority of the New South Wales Court of Appeal. Hodgson J.A. said:

> "In my opinion, the principle in *Haskell* does not preclude this result. That principle applies where the ordinary operation of natural forces results in a condition which could be regarded as something to be dealt with by ordinary maintenance, and which would, if not attended to, cause damage going substantially beyond what could reasonably be considered reasonable wear and tear. In such cases, a tenant who has covenanted to maintain and repair, reasonable wear and tear excepted, will be required to carry out normal maintenance so as to prevent this kind of damage, even though the initial condition could fall within the term "reasonable wear and tear". I do not think the existence of surface cracking and a small amount of potholes which could in time lead to further deterioration meant that the existence of such features demonstrates either a failure to maintain or a condition that exceeds reasonable wear and tear."

Agreeing McCellan C.J. (who no doubt had in mind Talbot J.'s example of the roof tile in *Haskell v Marlow*[164]) said:

> "To my mind there is a significant difference between a road pavement which involves the integrated construction of sub-base with a surface seal and a building where the roof forms a separate component of the entirety. In the ordinary course surface cracks will appear in the road surface which will allow penetration and ultimately failure of the road which when it was constructed had a predictable and finite life depending on the nature and quality of both the sub-base and the seal."

The opposite conclusion was reached in the Australian case of *Reilly v Liangis Property Ltd*,[165] in which floor tiles had become detached from the floor due to a deterioration of the adhesive, probably due to inadequate allowance for thermal expansion. The result was that there was a ridge in the middle of the floor. Young J. held, following *Regis Property Co. v Dudley* that although the original problem came through reasonable wear and tear, its manifestation was one that the tenant was liable to repair.

The practical result of the decision in *Regis Property Co. v Dudley* is to limit the value of the fair wear and tear exception, in some cases substantially. The

---

[163] [2004] NSWSC 487.
[164] See above.
[165] [2000] NSWSC 47. The facts are set out at para.7–37, above.

practical result in many cases will be that the tenant must repair a defect occurring through fair wear and tear, even though he is not liable to do so, in order to prevent it causing consequential damage, which he will then be liable to repair. Obvious areas where this is likely to apply are the external parts of the premises, such as the roof, gutters and downpipes, and external walls where a failure to remedy defects occurring through fair wear and tear may lead to internal damage by water penetration. The exclusion remains of practical importance, however, in relation to decorative items and parts of the premises where the need for remedial work arises as a direct result of the natural operation of time and the elements or the reasonable use of the premises by the tenant.

## Burden of proof

Once a defect is established which would otherwise fall within the tenant's repairing covenant, the burden of proving that liability for the defect falls within the fair wear and tear exception is on the tenant.[166] It was held in the Canadian case of *Stellarbridge Management Inc v Magna International (Canada) Inc*[167] that the same is true in relation to the amount by which any damages claimed should be reduced by reason of the exception. In that case, the tenant of a new industrial building covenanted to repair and maintain the premises during the term subject to reasonable wear and tear, to surrender the premises at the end of the lease in a good state of repair and maintenance "subject to the exceptions herein provided", and to restore the interior premises "to its former condition" immediately prior to the installation of fixtures, alterations or changes to the interior, reasonable wear and tear excepted. The judge at first instance awarded damages to the landlord for breach but reduced the amount by 35 per cent to reflect the reasonable wear and tear exception. The reduction was overturned by the Court of Appeal for Ontario on the ground that there was no evidence given at the trial to support a 35 per cent discount or any discount. The court held that it is for a tenant who relies on a reasonable wear and tear exception to prove not only that the relevant defect falls within the exception, but also the extent of the reduction in damages claimed in reliance on the exception.

**9–39**

## No implied obligation on landlord to repair defects caused by fair wear and tear

The fair wear and tear exception operates to exclude liability for damage caused by fair wear and tear from the tenant's repairing covenant. It does not of itself impose on the landlord any implied duty to repair such damage.[168] However, the question is one of construction in each case, and the lease when construed as a whole may show that such an obligation was intended to be imposed.

**9–40**

[166] *Brown v Davis* [1958] 1 Q.B. 117, per Lord Evershed M.R. at 127; *Haskell v Marlow* [1928] 2 K.B. 45 as approved by the House of Lords in *Regis Property Co Ltd v Dudley* [1959] A.C. 370; *Lintott Property Developments v Bower* [2005] AER (D) 454. See also *Henderson v Harvison* [1916] Q.W.N. 6.
[167] (2004) 71 OR (3d) 263.
[168] *Collins v Winter* [1924] N.Z.L.R. 449 (New Zealand); *Arden v Pullen* (1842) 10 M. & W. 321.

COVENANTS TO KEEP THE PREMISES IN GOOD CONDITION

## The relevant standard to which the subject matter must be kept

**9–41**     A covenant to keep in good or tenantable condition may be held to impose a liability to carry out work going beyond what might ordinarily be called "repairs".[169] Even where this is the case, it is thought that the standard imposed by such a covenant is to be judged by much the same factors as apply to a covenant to repair. In deciding whether the premises are in good or tenantable condition, it will therefore be necessary to look at their age, character and locality, and whether they are fit for the occupation of a reasonably-minded tenant of the class likely to take them.[170] Thus, in *Lurcott v Wakely*[171] Fletcher Moulton L.J. said of a covenant to keep the demised premises in good condition:

> "In the year 1881 these premises were old … Now what is the meaning of keeping old premises in good condition? I can see no difficulty in deciding the meaning of that. It means that, considering they are old premises, they must be kept in good condition as such premises … the words 'keep in good condition' will have a different meaning according to the nature and age of the house."

Likewise, in *Credit Suisse v Beegas Nominees Ltd*[172] Lindsay J. said in the course of his judgment:

> "[T]he expression ['good and tenantable condition'] refers to such condition as, having regard to the age, character and locality of the property, would make it reasonably fit for the occupation of a reasonably minded tenant of the class who would be likely to take it … though one cannot lower the nature of that condition by reference to deterioration in the expectations of the hypothetical tenant consequential upon a deterioration in the class of tenants after the date of the lease."

Similarly, in *Mason v TotalFinaElf UK Ltd*[173] Blackburne J., having held that an obligation "well and substantially [to] uphold support maintain amend repair decorate and keep in good condition the demised premises" extended to the doing of works that "went beyond repair strictly so-called", recorded it as common ground that the appropriate standard was such as, having regard to the age, character and locality of the premises at the start of the lease, would make them fit for the occupation of a reasonably-minded tenant of the class who would be likely, at that time, to take them.

**9–42**     However, the question will always depend upon the proper construction to be given to the covenant in the context of the circumstances in which it was entered into, and there may be cases in which a covenant to keep in "good" or "tenantable" condition will impose a different standard than a covenant to repair. Thus, in *Firstcross Ltd v Teasdale*[174] a tenancy of a furnished flat for a term of three months or less contained a covenant by the tenant to:

---

[169] See paras 4–29 et seq. and 8–12 to 8–14, above, and para.11–46, below.
[170] See para.9–05 et seq., above.
[171] [1911] 1 K.B. 905.
[172] [1994] 4 All E.R. 803 and (more fully) [1994] 1 E.G.L.R. 76.
[173] [2003] 3 E.G.L.R. 91.
[174] [1983] 1 E.G.L.R. 87. See further on this case para.21–04, below.

> "[K]eep the flat and the said fixtures fittings appurtenances and items at all times in good and tenantable condition throughout the said term (allowing only for reasonable use thereof and damage by accidental fire)"

McNeill J. rejected an argument that the covenant meant the same as a general covenant to keep in repair, and that it imposed on the tenant an obligation to put the flat into tenantable repair and decoration. He held that a distinction is to be drawn in law between a phrase such as "good habitable repair" and "good tenantable condition", and that the sense of the tenant's obligation was limited to using the premises in a tenant-like manner.[175]

---

[175] For the meaning of this, see para.21–03, below.

# CHAPTER 10

**THE FOURTH QUESTION: WHAT WORK IS REQUIRED IN ORDER TO PUT THE SUBJECT-MATTER OF THE REPAIRING COVENANT BACK INTO THE CONTEMPLATED CONDITION?**

## INTRODUCTORY

### A question of expert evidence not law

Once it has been established that the subject-matter of the repairing covenant[1] is damaged or deteriorated[2] and that its condition is thereby below that which the parties contemplated it would be kept in,[3] the next logical stage is to identify what work is required to put it back into the contemplated condition. This is primarily a matter for the professional judgment of the surveyor. It is for him to identify the standard of repair appropriate to the particular premises (having regard to the principles set out in Ch.9 above), and to apply that standard in deciding what work is required. The matters which are relevant at this stage of the inquiry are considered below, although in practice there is likely to be a considerable overlap between this stage and the third and fifth stages of the five-part approach.

**10–01**

## THE REQUISITE WORK

### The chosen method must be reasonable

As a general principle, once there is shown to exist a defect which is required to be remedied under the repairing covenant, the covenanting party must adopt such method of repair as a reasonable surveyor might advise is appropriate in all the circumstances. Thus, in *Gibson Investments Ltd v Chesterton Plc*[4] Neuberger J. said:

**10–02**

> "Once it is established that there is disrepair requiring to be remedied, performance of the obligation requires the covenantor to undertake such remedial work as is prudent, i.e. such methods and mode of repair as a sensible person would adopt."

He continued:

---

[1] See Ch.7, above.
[2] See Ch.8, above.
[3] See Ch.9, above.
[4] [2002] 2 P. & C.R. 494.

> "[T]he work [the paying party] selects must be such as a competent, careful surveyor or other appropriate professional person would advise as being appropriate."

## The work must not be futile

**10–03**    The covenantor is not obliged or entitled to carry out work which would be futile. As a general principle, where one proposed method of remedy would involve the continual redoing of the same work time after time, whereas another would cure the problem once and for all, and the latter is the sensible and practical course, the court is likely to hold that the former is not a proper performance of the covenant. In *Gibson Investments Ltd v Chesterton Plc*[5] Neuberger J. said:

> "The person responsible for carrying out repair work should ensure the work he carries out is not futile. In some circumstances, therefore, performance of the covenant is not achieved if the work proposed will not remedy the covenant[6] once and for all."

Thus, in *Elmcroft Developments Ltd v Tankersley-Sawyer*[7] a basement flat suffered from extensive damp penetration which had caused the plaster on the walls to perish. It was argued on behalf of the landlords that their covenant to repair was limited to carrying out patching up repairs to the plaster as and when it became perished, and did not extend to inserting a damp-proof course which would, on the expert evidence, have cured the problem. Rejecting this argument, Ackner L.J. said:

> "The patching work would have to go on and on and on, because, as the plaster absorbed (as it would) the rising damp, it would have to be renewed, and the cost to the appellants in constantly being involved with this sort of work, one would have thought, would have outweighed easily the cost in doing the job properly. I have no hesitation in rejecting the submission that the appellants' obligation was repetitively to carry out futile work instead of doing the job properly once and for all."

In *Stent v Monmouth District Council*[8] the demised premises consisted of a house which had been built in 1953 with a wooden front door. The house stood on an elevated and exposed site facing into the direction of the prevailing south-west wind, and water frequently penetrated through or under the door. Over the years the landlord sought to fulfil its repairing obligations in a variety of ways, which included cutting out rotten parts of the door and frame, and replacing the door from time to time with one of similar construction and design. Eventually in 1983 the landlord installed a weatherproof aluminium self-sealing door, since when there were no further problems. The tenant sought damages for breach of the landlord's obligation, on the footing that such work ought to have been carried out much earlier. The Court of Appeal upheld his claim. Stocker L.J. said in the course of his judgment:

---

[5] [2002] 2 P. & C.R. 494.

[6] It is thought that "covenant" must be a typographical error and that what the judge must have meant was "problem".

[7] [1984] 1 E.G.L.R. 47.

[8] (1987) 54 P. & C.R. 193.

"Accordingly, in my view ... the repair carried out in 1983 by the installation of a purpose-built, self-sealing aluminium door was one of the methods which could have been adopted much earlier, and which in my view should have been adopted. Of course, it does not follow that the self-sealing door is the only sensible way in which that object could be achieved. There may well have been others, but in my view the obligation under the covenant in this case was one which called upon the appellants to carry out repairs which not only effected the repair of the manifestly damaged parts but also achieved the object of rendering it unnecessary in the future for the continual repair of this door. Accordingly, some such steps as were in fact taken in 1983 should in my view have been carried out at any rate by 1979 and perhaps earlier, there being no suggestion either before the trial judge or before this court that the steps adopted were not ones which were for any reasons impracticable at that date."

Sir John Arnold P. said:

"[O]n the true construction of the covenant to repair there is required to be done, not only the making good of the immediate occasion of disrepair, but also, if this is what a sensible, practical man would do, the elimination of the cause of that disrepair through the making good of an inherent design defect at least where the making good of that defect does not involve a substantial rebuilding of the whole ... it is plain that if all that was done to the door which stood in need of repair was to patch it or even to renew it and to leave, when so doing, the causes of the damage, which was the absence of any agent to defeat the collection of the rotting water beneath the door, then one was not doing that which the sensible, practical man would have advised as a sensible way of dealing with the problem. Accordingly, on the true construction of this covenant, ... the appellant council had the obligation of making good the design defect which caused the collection of water which occasioned the rotting."

It has been suggested that the judgments in *Stent* do not go so far as to say that the landlord was *obliged* to provide a modern substitute.[9] However, it is thought that the effect of the judgments is that, whilst the landlord may not have been obliged to deal with the problem in the precise way it eventually did, nonetheless it was obliged to do something to prevent the past problems from recurring again in the future, and that, on the facts, merely replacing the defective door with one of a similar type would not have been enough.

**10–04**

The above cases should be contrasted with *Creska v Hammersmith LBC*,[10] in which work which involved repairing an underfloor heating system was held not to be futile in the above sense, albeit that it would have been more economic and less disruptive to instal electric night storage heaters.

The above principle does not mean that a method of repair involving a permanent solution will always be preferred to one which involves work of a more temporary nature.[11] The principle will only come into play where the latter is not work which the "sensible, practical man" would do. Where either solution could equally reasonably be adopted by a sensible person, the fact that one is more long lasting than the other will not prevent either from constituting a performance of the covenant.

---

[9] See *Creska v Hammersmith LBC* [1998] 3 E.G.L.R. 35 per Evans L.J. (giving the judgment of the court) at 38D–E.

[10] See para.10–13, below, in which the relevant facts are set out.

[11] See, for example, *Murray v Birmingham City Council* [1987] 2 E.G.L.R. 53, *Riverside Property Investments v Blackhawk Automotive* [2005] 1 E.G.L.R. 114 and *Carmel Southend v Strachan & Henshaw* [2007] 3 E.G.L.R. 15, in all of which the court rejected the tenant's argument that the landlord was obliged to replace a roof as opposed to carry out patching repairs. See further para.10–06, below, and para.12–07 et seq., below.

## Work which is desirable or convenient but not necessary

**10–05**   As a general rule, the work which the covenantor is required or entitled to carry out is limited to that which is reasonably necessary to remedy the defect in the subject-matter. This may include ancillary work rendered necessary by the carrying out of repairs, such as, for example, making good damage caused in the course of the work.[12] However, it does not generally extend to work which is merely desirable or convenient but not otherwise necessary.

Thus, in *Secretary of State for the Environment v Euston Centre Investments Ltd (No.2)*,[13] Chadwick J. held that the tenant was only liable to remove damaged or deteriorated asbestos if the only practicable or, in a realistic sense, possible way of effecting the repair which the tenant was thus obliged to undertake was to remove all the asbestos and make good in some other material. The fact that it would have been convenient to remove the asbestos along with other works of repair was not enough. Likewise, in *London Borough of Camden v Civil Aviation Authority*[14] the Court of Appeal held that remedial works to a building which contained beams made of high alumina cement (HAC) concrete were not repairs for the purposes of s.19 of the General Rate Act 1967 because the work was not necessary. Eveleigh L.J. said:

> "[I]t was not work that positively had to be done. The condition of the building was not such that, as a result of the ... HAC beams, it could not be used as offices. The condition of those members was such that a prudent landlord might well, at some time, decide, for the continuing and ultimate stability and duration of the building, to carry out such work as those investigations indicated was desirable—at some time, and a time of his choosing."

A fortiori, the covenantor is not entitled or obliged to carry out work which is unnecessary and achieves no useful purpose. In *Postel Properties Ltd v Boots the Chemist*[15] the lease of a unit in a shopping centre contained a landlord's covenant "with all due diligence to keep the ... roofs ... in good and substantial repair and condition". The landlord carried out works of replacement of the flat roof covering, including priming the entire upper surface of the underlying galvanised steel sheeting which had been exposed by the removal of the old covering. Ian Kennedy J. held that priming the ridges was within the covenant, because this was necessary to allow the new covering to be stuck to the sheeting, but that priming the troughs (which showed no evidence of deterioration) achieved no useful purpose and was not within the covenant.

---

[12] See para.22–47 et seq., below.
[13] [1994] N.P.C. 130.
[14] [1981] 1 E.G.L.R. 113.
[15] [1996] 2 E.G.L.R. 60. This case is further considered in para.12–12, below.

# WHERE THERE ARE SEVERAL POSSIBLE WAYS OF REMEDYING THE DEFECT

## Different methods of repair

The nature of the defect may often be such that there is more than one way of remedying it. Thus, in *Stent v Monmouth District Council*[16] Stocker L.J. said in the course of his judgment:

10–06

> "Accordingly, in my view ... the repair [actually carried out] ... was one of the methods which could have been adopted ... Of course, it does not follow that [it] is the only sensible way in which that object could be achieved. There may well have been others ..."

A common example is a leaking roof. One surveyor may decide that it is at the end of its useful life and there is no point carrying on patching it up any further. The sensible solution would be to strip off the old covering and put on a new one. Another surveyor may take the view that further patching repairs will be sufficient for the time being, and that the state of the roof does not as yet justify complete renewal. The question then arises as to what work the covenanting party is liable to carry out.

Any method of repair which does not restore the premises to the condition contemplated by the covenant can be ruled out. Subject to this, the general principle is that where there are several possible methods of repair, each of which would comply with the required standard, the choice between them is one for the covenanting party to make.[17] This applies equally where the choice is between two ways of putting right an immediate problem once and for all, and where it is between a temporary method of alleviating the symptoms of a chronic problem and a more radical cure of the underlying problem.[18] It follows that where the covenanting party is the tenant, it is for him to decide which method of repair to adopt. Provided he chooses one which complies with the appropriate standard of repair, then he has performed his covenant notwithstanding the fact that, had the choice been up to the landlord, another and more expensive solution would have been adopted.[19] In *Riverside Property Investments v Blackhawk Automotive*,[20] H.H. Judge Coulson, QC said:

10–07

---

[16] (1987) 54 P. & C.R. 193.

[17] *Fox v Jolly* [1916] 1 A.C. 1; *Post Office v Aquarius Properties Ltd* [1985] 2 E.G.L.R. 105 (affirmed on different grounds [1987] 1 All E.R. 1055); *Plough Investments Ltd v Manchester City Council* [1989] 1 E.G.L.R. 244; *McDougall v Easington District Council* (1989) 58 P. & C.R. 201; *Ultraworth Ltd v General Accident, Fire & Life Assurance Co Ltd* [2000] 2 E.G.L.R. 115; *Gibson Investments Ltd v Chesterton Plc*, above; *Riverside Property Investments v Blackhawk Automotive* [2005] 1 E.G.L.R. 114 at [54]; *Carmel Southend v Strachan & Henshaw* [2007] 3 E.G.L.R. 15 at [9]; *Langham Estate Management Ltd v Hardy* [2008] 3 E.G.L.R. 125 at [72]; *PGF II SA v Royal & Sun Alliance Insurance Plc* [2011] 1 P & CR 11 at [52]..

[18] *McDougall v Easington District Council*, above.

[19] The equivalent part of the text in previous editions of this work was approved by H.H. Judge Coulson QC in *Carmel Southend v Strachan & Henshaw* [2007] 3 E.G.L.R. 15 at [9(a)] and by H.H. Judge Toulmin QC in *PGF II SA v Royal & Sun Alliance Insurance Plc* [2011] 1 P & CR 11 at [52].

[20] [2005] 1 E.G.L.R. 114.

> "[I]f there are two ways in which the covenant might properly be performed, the tenant is entitled to choose which method to utilise. Since the tenant is almost certainly going to choose the least expensive option, it cannot be criticised for so doing: see [*Ultraworth v. General Accident, Fire & Life Assurance Co. Limited*[21]]. That position is not different to the situation concerning a claim for defects under a building contract where proper remedial works can be carried out in one of two ways. All other things being equal, the cheapest option will be appropriate: see the judgment of Judge Hicks QC in *George Fischer Holdings Ltd v. Multi Design Consultants Ltd* (1968) 61 Con LR 85."

In the Scottish case of *West Castle Properties v Scottish Ministers*[22] it was said by the Outer House of the Court of Session that:

> "[58] If, under reference to the Schedule of Dilapidations, what the [landlords] are seeking to recover are the full costs of replacing individual component parts of the premises, the [tenants] will only be liable to meet those costs, if it can be established by the [landlords] that there was no other reasonable way for the [tenants] to have complied with their obligations under the Lease, short of the replacement of the individual parts in question. If there were alternative and less onerous courses of action, by which the [tenants] could have complied with their obligations, then the [tenants] would have been entitled to have opted for them and the [landlords'] claims against the [tenants] will fall to be restricted accordingly.[23]"

An example of this principle in a rent review context is *Land Securities Plc v Westminster City Council (No.2)*,[24] in which the rent review provisions in a lease of Westminster City Hall required the arbitrator to assume that the tenant had complied with its covenants, including its repairing obligations. The building contained certain air handling plant. The landlord argued that the rent should be fixed on the basis that prior to the review date the plant had been replaced by the tenant pursuant to its repairing obligation. The arbitrator proceeded on the basis that whether the rent should be fixed on this basis depended on whether complete replacement of the plant was the only way in which the building could have been put into proper repair. He held on the evidence that the plant remained capable of repair so as to bring it back to near its maximum efficiency, although it would have a maximum extended life of five years only. Consequently, it would have been working satisfactorily on the review date, although close to the end of its useful life. Jonathan Parker J. held that he had not gone wrong in law.

Likewise, where the covenanting party is the landlord, it is he who is entitled to decide how to carry out the requisite repair.[25] Thus, in *Murray v Birmingham City Council*,[26] a house built in 1908 was let on a weekly tenancy, and the landlord was under an implied statutory obligation to keep in repair the structure and exterior.[27] The roof had given trouble over the years and the landlord had dealt with each occasion of disrepair by carrying out localised repairs to the area in question. The tenant contended that the roof had reached the stage where

---

[21] [2000] 2 E.G.L.R. 115.

[22] [2004] S.C.L.R. 899.

[23] It must be borne in mind as regards this passage that, as the judge pointed out at [43], the common law of Scotland as regards repairs is not the same as that of England. However, the judge was relying primarily on English authorities, and it is thought that his comments are consistent with the position in England.

[24] [1995] 1 E.G.L.R. 245.

[25] *Plough Investments Ltd v Manchester City Council*, above.

[26] [1987] 2 E.G.L.R. 53.

[27] See para.20–17 et seq., below.

complete replacement was the only way of complying with the landlord's obligation. The assistant recorder who tried the action found that "… at all material times the roof was capable of being repaired and the covenant carried out by replacing the slates which had slipped by renailing them". The Court of Appeal dismissed the tenant's appeal. Slade L.J. said:

> "[I]n any case where the landlord, or the tenant for that matter, is under an obligation to keep in repair an old roof, the stage may come where the only practicable way of performing that covenant is to replace the roof altogether … [there was] no evidence to suggest that a piecemeal repair of the roof in 1976 right up to 1982 was not a perfectly practicable proposition. I, for my part, am quite unable to accept the submission that, merely because there had been some half a dozen, no doubt troublesome, incidents of disrepair occurring during those six years, it necessarily followed from that that the roof was incapable of repair by any way other than replacement."

Similarly, in *Dame Margaret Hungerford Charity Trustees v Beazeley*[28] the landlords continued to carry out running repairs to the roof of the demised premises as and when they were notified of a problem with it, although they were aware that it had become highly desirable that the roof should be completely replaced. The judge at first instance found that no breach of covenant had occurred, and his decision was upheld in the Court of Appeal.

## Where the cost of the works is recoverable by way of service charge[29]

The principle that it is for the covenantor to choose the method of repair is to some extent qualified where the covenantor is the landlord and the cost of the work is recoverable by way of service charge. Whilst each case depends on the proper construction of the lease in question, two inter-related general principles apply as regards the recovery of the cost of the work. The first is that the landlord is not obliged to adopt the solution that will result in the lowest cost to the tenant. The second is that the landlord's decision as to what method to adopt must be reasonable in all the circumstances.[30]

10–08

In *Plough Investments Ltd v Manchester City Council*[31] Scott J. said:

> "The landlord's … repairing obligation is, although nominally an obligation, in a sense also a right. If it were simply an obligation, then, presumably, the three tenants of the building could choose to release the landlord, in whole or in part, from that obligation. But the provision is not, in my view, simply or even mainly for the benefit of the tenants. It is also a provision for the benefit of the landlord. It enables the landlord to keep its building in repair at the tenants' expense. If the repairing obligation had been imposed on the tenant, the tenant would have been entitled to decide on the manner in which it would be discharged. Provided remedial works were sufficient to discharge the obligation, the landlord could not require a different

---

[28] [1993] 2 E.G.L.R. 144.
[29] A full treatment of the law relating to service charges is outside the scope of this work, and reference should be made to specialist works on the subject. In particular a statutory code applies in relation to service charges claimed in respect of residential premises: see the Landlord and Tenant Act 1985.
[30] *Plough Investments Ltd v Manchester City Council* [1989] 1 E.G.L.R. 244; *Fluor Daniel Properties Ltd v Shortlands Investments Ltd* [2001] 2 E.G.L.R. 103.
[31] Above.

type of repair to be effected. Under these leases, however, the relevant decisions regarding repairs to the exterior are to be taken by the landlord. If reasonable remedial works are proposed by the landlord in order to remedy a state of disrepair for the purposes of its … obligations, the tenants are not, in my judgment, entitled to insist that cheaper remedial works be undertaken. [Counsel] accepted that the landlord's decisions had to be reasonable ones. The tenants, after all, have to pay for the … repairs. But I accept [counsel's] point that the tenants are not entitled to require the landlord to adopt simply a minimum standard of repair. Provided proposed works of repair are such as an owner who had to bear the cost himself might reasonably decide upon and provided the works constitute 'repairs' … the tenant is not, in my judgment, entitled to insist upon more limited works or cheaper works being preferred. I agree with [counsel] that the landlord cannot be limited to a minimum standard of repair only.[32]"

**10–09**     The judge's formulation of the test by reference to an owner who had to bear the cost of the works himself is open to criticism on the ground that it fails to give sufficient weight to the fact that (i) the tenant is paying for the work, and (ii) the tenant has a more limited interest than that of an owner. It is also arguably inconsistent with the following passage in the judgment of Nicholls L.J. in *Holding & Management Ltd v Property Holding & Investment Trust Ltd*[33]:

"A prudent building owner bearing the costs himself might well have decided to adopt such a scheme despite its expense. But what is in question is whether owners of 75 year leases in the building could fairly be expected to pay for such a scheme under an obligation to 'repair'."

In *Scottish Mutual Assurance Plc v Jardine Public Relations Ltd*,[34] offices on the second floor of a three storey office and retail building with a flat roof were let for 3 years. The defendant landlord covenanted to use its best endeavours to provide certain services, which included "maintaining repairing and (if necessary) renewing … and otherwise keeping in good and substantial condition (as appropriate) … the structure of the Building and in particular the roofs …". The plaintiff tenant covenanted to pay a fair proportion of the sums "reasonably and properly expended incurred or expected to be so expended or incurred by the landlord in relation to the Property computed upon the basis of providing an indemnity to the Landlord in respect of the services …." The roof was in disrepair. At the relevant time two options were open to the landlord, one comprising piecemeal repairs and providing a short term solution, and the other involving re-covering the roof. The landlord opted for the latter. Mr David Blunt QC (sitting as a judge of the Technology and Construction Court) held that whilst the work was repair within the landlord's obligation, the cost was not recoverable by way of service charge. His reasons included the following:

"I merely remind myself that the effect of every lease will depend upon its own terms, and note that in *Plough Investments* the leases were long leases, that in each case the tenants had enjoyed the benefit of the landlord's covenant for in excess of 10 years, and that when the legal proceedings were begun there were apparently 7–8 years still to run. By contrast in the present case the lease was for 3 years only and was admitted on the pleadings to be outwith the provisions of the Landlord and Tenant Act 1954 Part II—something which must have been agreed between the parties from the outset. Vis a vis the Defendant the Plaintiff's obligation so

---

[32] See also *Credit Suisse v Beegas Nominees Ltd* [1994] 4 All E.R. 803 at 818f–h and (a fuller report) [1994] 1 E.G.L.R. 76 at 85 F–H; *Postel Properties Ltd v Boots the Chemist* [1996] 2 E.G.L.R. 60.
[33] [1990] 1 E.G.L.R. 65 at 69A–B (not reported on this point at [1989] 1 W.L.R. 1313). The facts are set out in para.12–18, below.
[34] [1999] E.G.C.S. 43.

far as the provision of services were concerned were limited in time to the period of the (short) term. In those circumstances I have no doubt and find as a fact that the Plaintiff would not have been in breach of the its' obligation to the Defendant if it had opted for the more limited repairs suggested by [the tenant's expert]. But it seems to me that one can go further than that. In my judgment, in the context of this short lease, the provisions relating to service charges were inter alia to enable the landlord to comply with his repairing obligations (partly) at the tenant's expense. Those obligations were to use his best endeavours to provide the services of inter alia '*maintaining and repairing etc. the structure of the building including the roofs*' during the short (i.e. three year) period of the term. In my judgment this lease does not entitle the landlord to charge to the tenant the cost of carrying out works suitable for the performance of his obligations over a period of twenty or more years when such works are not necessary for the fulfilment of those obligations over the actual period to which they relate.In the present case, of course, the Defendant is only one of a number of tenants. The leases relating to these other tenancies were not before me, but there was evidence that they were for 25 year terms expiring on the 24 December 2002. In those circumstances it might well be that the three other tenants would be unable to resist contributing fully to repairs of a long-term nature, but it does not follow from that that the Defendant is bound to be treated in the same way.

In my judgment, vis a vis the Defendant, the totality of the amounts expended by the Plaintiff on the works to the roof was not "*reasonably and properly expended or incurred* " because those works went significantly beyond what was required for the performance of the Plaintiffs obligations to the Defendant in respect of the condition of the premises, because considerable monies had been very recently expended upon short-term repairs and there was no evidence that these had been ineffective, and because there was no evidence of any continuing leakage and there was therefore no pressing need to commence long-term repairs prior to the end of the Defendant's term (which end was imminent)."

In *Fluor Daniel Properties Ltd v Shortlands Investments Ltd*[35] Blackburne J. had to decide whether certain works (consisting principally of the renewal of the air conditioning system) to an office building fell within the landlord's repairing obligation (which included an obligation to keep in good condition), such that the costs would be recoverable by way of service charge. The judge said:

"I see no reason why the principle identified by Scott J. in *Plough Investments Limited v. Manchester City Council* should not apply. The obligations have been cast upon the landlord. It is for the landlord to decide how to discharge them. Provided it acts reasonably, it is for the landlord to decide how it goes about the matter. The tenant cannot complain simply because the landlord could have adopted another cheaper method of repair."

Having contrasted Scott J.'s formulation of the standard of work that the landlord should be free to carry out at the tenant's expense with what Nicholls L.J. had had to say in the above passage from *Holding & Management Ltd v Property Holding & Investments Trust Plc*,[36] he went on to say that the standard adopted:

"[M]ust be such as the tenants, given the length of their leases, could fairly be expected to pay for. The landlord cannot, because he has an interest in the matter, overlook the limited interest of the tenants who are having to pay by carrying out works that are calculated to serve an interest extending beyond that of the tenants. If the landlord wished to carry out repairs that go beyond those for which the tenants, given their more limited interest, can fairly be expected to pay for, then, subject always to the terms of the lease or leases, the landlord must bear the additional cost himself."

[35] [2001] 2 E.G.L.R. 103.
[36] [1990] 1 E.G.L.R. 65.

**10–10**     The result of these authorities is that whilst the landlord is not obliged to select the cheapest method of repair available, nonetheless his choice of work is not unfettered. If he wishes to recover the cost of the work by way of service charge, he must act reasonably and have proper regard to the interest of the tenant, and in particular the length of the tenant's lease. It is thought that this must mean the length of lease as originally granted and not that remaining at the date when the issue arises. The relevant question will be whether, in all the circumstances including the length of term granted, the parties to the lease can fairly be taken to have contemplated that the tenant should be liable to pay for the relevant work or whether it goes significantly beyond what is reasonably necessary to perform the landlord's obligations over the period of the lease.

The effect of the distinction between the landlord's obligation under his covenant to repair and his right to recover the cost of repairs under the service charge provisions may be summarised as follows. His obligation is only to carry out such work as will comply with the appropriate standard of repair.[37] He cannot be compelled to carry out any more extensive work. If, however, he does carry out more extensive work, the fact that he could have elected to carry out a more limited scheme will not prevent him from recovering the cost of the work actually done, provided that such work falls within his obligation and is reasonable in the sense discussed above.[38] If he goes further and carries out work which (i) is so extensive as to fall outside his obligation, but (ii) nonetheless has the effect of remedying the relevant defect, it is a question of construction as to whether he is nonetheless entitled to the amount that it would reasonably have cost to remedy the defect or whether he is not entitled to anything.[39]

## REPLACEMENT AS AGAINST PATCH REPAIR

### Introductory

**10–11**     A question which frequently arises in practice is whether a particular item of building fabric or plant can be patch-repaired or whether it must be replaced in its entirety. No difficulty will arise where the item has been substantially destroyed, or removed in its entirety: in such a case, no course other than replacement will generally be possible. Where this is not the case, however, complex questions may arise in practice as to whether the condition of the item is such that the covenantor is obliged or entitled to replace it. Something will obviously turn on the wording of the covenant in question.[40] In general terms, however, the covenanting party will only be liable to replace an item if patch-repair is not

---

[37] See Ch.9, above.
[38] Cf. *McDougall v Easington District Council* (1989) 58 P. & C.R. 201 per Mustill L.J. at 206.
[39] See *Scott v Brown* (1904) 69 J.P. 89; *Moore v Todd* (1903) 68 J.P. 43; *Crane Road Properties v Hundalani* [2006] EWHC 2066 (Ch.).
[40] See paras 4–25 to 4–31, above.

reasonably or sensibly possible,[41] the burden of proof on that issue being on the party who asserts that replacement is necessary.[42]

The practical application of this principle in relation to commonly encountered defects in buildings is considered in Ch.12, below, and the position as regards mechanical and electrical services and plant is dealt with in Ch.13, below.

## Replacement with something different

Once the point has been reached at which complete replacement of a particular item is required in order to comply with the covenant, difficult questions may arise as to the extent to which the covenantor is obliged (or if not obliged, entitled) to replace it with something other than what was there before. Such questions often arise in practice in relation to items of mechanical and electrical plant that are obsolete and beyond repair.

**10–12**

The answer in any particular case will depend on the detailed facts. However, it is possible to make various points of a general nature.

First, the covenant will not ordinarily oblige or entitle the covenantor in every case to replace the item in question with an exact replica. He may, depending on the facts, be obliged or entitled to instal something which differs from the original, so as, for example, to comply with legislation or regulations, comply with good practice, take advantage of more modern design or technology, prevent the original defect from recurring, or because that is what a sensible and practical surveyor would advise.[43]

Second, however, there may come a point at which the replacement item differs so substantially from what was there before that it can no longer be regarded as a performance of the covenant at all, but as something outside that contemplated by the covenant. That may be so even though it performs the same function as the original item, and in that limited sense at least, remedies the defect.

In *Morcom v Campbell-Johnson*,[44] the question was whether expenditure on certain works carried out by the landlords of a block of flats entitled them to an increase in the controlled rents payable by the tenants because it was "expenditure on the improvement of the dwelling house (not including expenditure on decoration or repairs)", within the meaning of s.2(1)(a) of the Increase of Rent and Mortgage Interest (Restrictions) Act 1920. The relevant works were as follows:

(1)   To the drainage system: as originally constructed there was a system of separate pipes for refuse from the water closets and foul water from wash-hand basins and baths (a "two-pipe system"). After 60 years the

---

[41] *Riverside Property Investments v Blackhawk Automotive* [2005] 1 E.G.L.R. 114 at [54]; *Carmel Southend v Strachan & Henshaw* [2007] 3 E.G.L.R. 15 at [9]; *Hammersmatch Properties (Welwyn) v Saint-Gobain Ceramics & Plastics* [2013] EWHC 1161 (TCC) at [53].

[42] *Hammersmatch Properties (Welwyn) v Saint-Gobain Ceramics & Plastics*, above, at [53].

[43] See paras 11–30 to 11–40, below, and see also Chs 12 and 13 (especially paras 13–08 to 13–09), below.

[44] [1956] 1 Q.B. 106.

two-pipe system had come to the end of its life and the landlords took advice as to how it should be replaced. They were advised that rather than repairing the two-pipe system piece-by-piece, the better and cheaper way was to install a one-pipe system;

(2)  To the cold-water supply: when the flats were built, each had its own storage cistern in the flat. That system had worn out and the advice given to the landlords was that the best way to make the system good was to have one larger tank in the building instead of the individual tanks.

In both instances the landlords acted on the advice given and claimed that, as a result, the works were "improvement ... (not ... repairs)". Rejecting this argument, Denning L.J. said:

"It seems to me that the test, so far as one can give any test in these matters, is this: if the work which is done is the provision of something new for the benefit of the occupier, that is, properly speaking, an improvement; but if it is only the replacement of something already there, which has become dilapidated or worn out, then, albeit that it is a replacement by its modern equivalent, it comes within the category of repairs and not improvements. Applying this test, it seems to me that the drainage system in these flats is the same now as the system which existed before. All that has happened is that, instead of there being two pipes to carry the water and refuse away, there is one pipe. That is simply the replacement of the older two-pipes system by its modern equivalent of one pipe. It comes, I think, properly within the category of repairs and not that of improvement. So, also with the cold-water system. There were six individual tanks before, one in each flat. Those have been replaced by one bulk storage tank in the roof of the block. That, again, is simply the replacement of something which existed before by a more suitable modern substitute. In both cases, as the surveyor said, it was a cheaper way of doing it than it would have been simply to restore the old system as it was. It seems to me that in both those instances the work done properly comes within the category of repairs and not that of improvements.
So far as the tenants are concerned, the position in the flats for them from the practical point of view is no different from what it was before. The water closets, the baths and the cold water system all operate just as they did before. ... In a sense, of course, the work benefits them in the same way as any repairs must benefit the people who live in a house when it gets old and dilapidated, because they are better off when it is repaired and made good. But that is the extent of the benefit to them. There is no provision of anything new for their benefit, but only the replacement of the old parts by a modern equivalent."

Agreeing, Hodson L.J. said:

"[I]t is obvious that all repairs, if well done, will, in the majority of cases, involve some improvement, particularly in the case of old property where modern methods have been introduced—modern systems of plumbing, improved systems of drainage and so forth—where it would be foolish to replace them in their ancient condition in order to carry out the repair."

Morris L.J. said:

"A consideration of the evidence leads me to the view that here it was in substance work of repair that was being done, although that repair involved some degree of improvement and although the modern substitute might be better than that which had gone before."

**10–13**  A different conclusion was arrived at on the facts in *Creska v Hammersmith and Fulham LBC*.[45] In that case, an office building was constructed with an

---

[45] [1998] 3 E.G.L.R. 35. For a further development in the same litigation, see para.28–43, below.

underfloor heating system which consisted of electric power running in cables embedded in concrete floors. The tenant covenanted "well and substantially to repair and maintain and in all respects keep in good and substantial repair and condition the interior of the Premises … including … all electrical heating … installations therein". The heating system was defective and in particular some cables were broken or their insulation was damaged. The evidence was that electric underfloor heating was virtually unheard of in modern office buildings, because other forms of heating were much more effective in economic terms, and that the remedial work would be expensive. The tenant proposed to perform its obligation by installing modern electric night storage wall heaters. The judge at first instance held that this amounted to a proper performance of the obligation. The Court of Appeal allowed the landlord's appeal, holding that the tenant was bound to repair the existing system and was not entitled to perform its obligation by providing alternative heating. Evans L.J. said:

"This is not a case where it is impossible or even impracticable to maintain the existing under-floor storage heating system in good working condition, nor where doing so would be 'futile' in the sense that the repair would be short-lived and commercially unsound. Nor in our judgment can it be said that individual storage heaters are the same "electrical heating … installation" in a different guise. It seems to us that they are two different methods achieving the same result, notwithstanding that the same techniques are employed. We therefore hold that the case is as straightforward as [counsel] submits. The council undertook to maintain the existing under-floor installation in good repair. It is defective and needs repair and the repairs, although expensive, can be carried out. The fact that repairs carried out now would incorporate some improvements in design, particularly the use of flexible connectors where appropriate, does not mean that they cease to be works of repair which the party liable under the repairing covenant is bound to perform. Morcom v. Campbell-Johnson [46] is direct authority for this. On the evidence, the existing installation (as distinct from the failure to incorporate flexible connections) cannot properly be regarded as a design defect in the original structure at the date of the lease, but even if it was, the case is not one where attempts to repair it would be futile or where the only "sensible and practical" course is to substitute some other system. We therefore hold that the council is not entitled to discharge its obligations under the repairing covenant by substituting individual storage heaters for the under-floor system, and the question whether they would be entitled or bound to do so, if repairs to the existing installation were no longer practicable, does not arise."

It is clear from the above passage that the result would or might have been different if it had been impossible or impracticable to repair the existing system, or doing so would have been futile, such that the only sensible and practical course would have been to substitute some other system. Where that is not the case, the broad distinction suggested by the above passage is between, on the one hand, providing the same thing under a different guise, and on the other, a different method of achieving the same result.

The point arose in a different context in *Gibson v Chesterton (No.2)*,[47] in which the issue was whether the relevant works fell within an express disregard of improvements in a rent-review clause contained in a lease of an office building.[48] The tenant proposed to replace the existing two-pipe air conditioning system with a four-pipe system. It was agreed that this was work within the tenant's repairing obligation (which included a performance specification).

---

[46] See above.
[47] [2003] EWHC 1255.
[48] See para.35–11, below.

However, the original system had perimeter fan coil units, and the tenant proposed to put the new units in the ceiling, thereby freeing up additional (valuable) space on the office floors. It was agreed that the relevant covenant could be complied with by replacing the system at the perimeter. H.H. Judge Rich, QC held that the relocation was an improvement. He said in his judgment:

> "17. It is agreed, that in the present case the necessary repairs to the air-conditioning system could be undertaken by replacing the system at the perimeter. The relocation, however, is neither necessary to such repair, nor is it ...merely an alternative way of doing the repair. It both accomplishes the replacement of the air-conditioning system in the sense of providing a substitute system, and at the same time alters the building in a way which adds to its letting value. It is an alteration which could in theory, although, no doubt uneconomically, have been carried out even if the perimeter air-conditioning system was not in disrepair. It is not, however, an obligation under [the tenant's covenant] if the perimeter system would comply with the performance specification.
>
> 18. Mr Justice Forbes in *Ravenseft Properties v Davstone (Holdings)*[49], in a judgment which is usually treated as a leading authority in distinguishing repairs from improvements, treated the question as one of degree, and in part, of necessity. It may be that the use of a four pipe system was rendered necessary by the performance specification. But even if it were not actually necessary, nonetheless, if, as appears, it is the modern method of proving an air-conditioning system to modern standards, it would, as a matter of degree, be regarded as repair of a two pipe air-conditioning system which needed replacing. In the same way a modern electric lift replacing a worn out hydraulic lift, although better than that which it replaces, is merely a means of repair. If, however, a tenant takes advantage of the need to replace an out of date lift with one extending to floors not previously served, such additional provision is not prevented from being an improvement by reason of the need for repair or replacement of the original lift in order to serve the floors originally served. Both [counsel] agree about this. The cost or extent of the variation from mere replacement, as well as the effect may be taken into account in identifying whether particular works are, as a matter of degree, to be classified as repairs or improvements.
>
> 19. When, however, the works, whilst overcoming a state of disrepair, create something which is recognisably different from what would result from merely remedying such state, and the difference has a significant effect upon letting value, the creation of the difference is, in my judgment, the carrying out of an improvement. In such case the works may involve both repair, in the example of the lifts to the original floor level, and improvement in its extension to further levels. If, however, as here, the replacement of the air-conditioning system in, or about its present location is repair, its replacement elsewhere so as to make such repair unnecessary, must either amount to improvement, or else be classified in its entirety as itself repair.
>
> 20. In my judgment, the relocation of the piping is, as a matter of degree, an improvement which the tenant can carry out instead of replacing the air-conditioning system in or about the present location. It needs consent under clause 3(15) of the lease, as well as approval of the specification under clause 3(5)(a). The replacement would be a matter of obligation under [the tenant's covenant], and therefore on rent review is to be assumed to be done. Its relocation is not, however, a matter of obligation, nor could the landlord require it. It is therefore, if written consent is obtained, an improvement to be disregarded on rent review in accordance with clause 6(c)(ii), but to be disregarded, on the assumption that a perimeter system had been installed, as was the obligation under [the tenant's covenant]."

The distinction drawn by the judge is therefore between, on the one hand, the provision of essentially the same thing, albeit by modern methods and to modern standards, and on the other, the provision of something recognisably different from that which would result merely from remedying the relevant defect. The former is within the covenant, but the latter is not, even though it in fact obviates the need for repair.

---

[49] [1980] Q.B. 12.

The same point arose in *Sunlife Europe Properties v Tiger Aspect Holdings*,[50] which concerned a claim for terminal dilapidations in relation to a 1970's office and retail building. Edwards-Stuart J. identified the legal principles applicable to the outgoing tenant's liability under the relevant covenants as including the following:

**10–14**

> "(2) The tenant is obliged to return the premises in good and tenantable condition and with the M&E systems in satisfactory working order: he is not required to deliver up the premises with new equipment or with equipment that has any particular remaining life expectancy. The standard to which the building is to be repaired or kept in repair is to be judged by reference to the condition of its fabric, equipment and fittings at the time of the demise, not the condition that would be expected of an equivalent building at the expiry of the lease.
>
> (3) In a case such as the present, where there are covenants against making alterations to the premises, the tenant is not entitled, let alone obliged, to deliver up the premises in a condition that involves any material alteration to the building or the fixtures as demised: the fact that the landlord can consent to any such alteration does not affect the basic obligation.
>
> (4) Accordingly, where the requirement to put and keep the premises and fixtures in good and tenantable condition involves the replacement of plant that is beyond economic repair, the tenant is required to replace it on a like for like or nearest equivalent basis: he is not required to upgrade it in order to bring it into line with current standards (unless required to do so by law or to comply with any necessary regulations). However, as with most obligations in commercial contracts, this obligation must be interpreted in a manner that accords with commercial common sense."

The judge's reference to the covenant against alterations requires discussion. The covenants in *Sunlife* were in fairly standard form. They included an absolute prohibition against making any "structural alteration or addition" to the premises or to any fixtures or fittings or other items; a covenant not to make any other alteration or addition without the landlord's consent, not to be unreasonably withheld; and a covenant not to fix any machinery to the outside of the premises without the landlord's approval. It was submitted on behalf of the tenant (and accepted by the judge in his point (3) above) that the tenant was not obliged to carry out any remedial works which involved "any material alteration" to what was demised. The judge's acceptance of a limitation on the tenant's obligation by reference to the covenants against alterations is puzzling. The cases do not suggest that work which might otherwise be described as an alteration is, for that reason alone, outside the ambit of the covenant to repair. Thus, for example, repairing a flat roof by overcladding it,[51] or replacing a two pipe fan coil air conditioning system with a four pipe system[52], can be repair even though they involve an element of alteration. As a general principle, the covenant to repair and the covenant against alterations must be read together in a sensible way so as to give proper effect to each.[53] So where a state of disrepair can only be remedied by the carrying out of works which would otherwise be prohibited by the covenant against alterations if they were done voluntarily, such works (assuming that they would otherwise be required by the repairing obligation) cannot sensibly be prohibited by the restriction on alterations: either they are not to be regarded as

---

[50] [2013] EWHC 463 (TCC) at [46].
[51] See para.12–14, above.
[52] *Gibson v Chesterton (No.2)* [2003] EWHC 1255.
[53] Cf. *Goldmile Properties v Lechouritis* [2003] 1 E.G.L.R. 60.

"alterations" for that purpose at all,[54] or they constitute an implied exception to the restriction. It is difficult to see why that should not also be the case where the only sensible and practical way of remedying the state of disrepair is by the carrying out works which go beyond merely replacing the original item with an exact replica, even if, at least theoretically, the obligation could be performed by works which do not involve any element of alteration. It is perhaps to reflect this that the judge commented, at the end of his point (4) that "as with most obligations in commercial contracts, this obligation must be interpreted in a manner that accords with commercial common sense".

The judge's reference in his point (4) to replacement on a "like for like or nearest equivalent basis" makes it clear that this is subject to the work being lawful. It is thought that, consistently with *Creska v Hammersmith and Fulham LBC*,[55] it must also be subject to the work not being impossible, impracticable or futile. In addition, it appears to have been accepted on behalf of the tenant that the tenant would not be bound to replace items that were obsolete and beyond repair with precisely similar items regardless of cost.[56] In principle, that seems correct. It would be odd if the covenantor can be made liable to reproduce the original item with a like for like equivalent, even where that would cost substantially more than an alternative, and equally good if not better, solution, and is something which no one would ever do in practice.

It is thought that whilst each case will turn on its own facts, the effect of the above cases, in general terms, is that (all other things being equal) replacement of a particular item with something other than an exact replica will remain repair so long as in substance what is being done is the provision of the same sort of item as existed before. However, there will come a point when the change is sufficiently substantial that the provision of the new item cannot be said to be a performance of the covenant, even though it fulfils essentially the same function as the original. Thus, for example, it may be that the replacement of an old oil-fired boiler with a gas boiler would remain repair, whereas replacing a central boiler and radiators on each floor with separate self-contained systems on each floor would not be.

## WORK NECESSARY TO REMEDY ANTICIPATED FUTURE DAMAGE

### Introductory

**10–15**  Where no damage or deterioration to the subject-matter of the covenant has occurred, the covenantor is not required to carry out any work.[57] Conversely, where the subject-matter of the covenant has been damaged, the fact that the remedial work includes an element aimed at preventing damage which has not yet occurred prevent the work from being repair. However, where no relevant damage has occurred, work which is purely anticipatory is not within the covenant.

---

[54] Cf. *Bickmore v Dimmer* [1903] 1 Ch. 158.
[55] Above.
[56] See at [31].
[57] See Ch.8, above.

## Work aimed at preventing future disrepair

A number of situations occurring in practice may involve not only work to parts **10–16** of the subject-matter of the covenant that are damaged but also work aimed at preventing future disrepair. For example, it may be appropriate at periodic intervals to carry out localised repairs to the external woodwork of a dwelling-house and at the same time to repaint it in its entirety in order to maintain its protection against the weather. A further example is where damage has occurred to part of the subject-matter and is highly likely to occur to the remainder within the foreseeable future. In such a case it may be better, in practical terms, to carry out all the work at the same time, even to the (as yet) undamaged parts. For example, a building may be constructed with concrete beams contaminated by some corrosive substance. Although damage to the entirety of the beams will inevitably occur sooner or later, the process of deterioration will not occur at a uniform rate in relation to each beam. At a particular point in time, some may already have failed; others may have begun to crack; and the remainder may still be in perfect condition. Depending on the extent and seriousness of the problem, the sensible and practical course may be to replace all the beams now rather than do it piecemeal.

The relevant authorities make it clear that work does not cease to be repair merely because it includes an element of preventative measures aimed at preventing future disrepair. In *London & North Eastern Railway Co Ltd v Berriman*[58] a railwayman whose duties were to carry out routine oiling and cleaning of mechanisms on the railway track was held to be engaged in "repairing" it, within the meaning of the relevant statute relating to employer's liability.[59] Similarly, in *Day v Harland & Wolff Ltd*[60] Pearson J. held that anti-fouling a ship was work of repair within the Shipbuilding Regulations 1931. He said:

> "[V]ery broadly speaking, I think that to repair is to remedy defects, but it can also properly include an element of the 'stitch in time which saves nine'. Work does not cease to be repair work because it is done to a large extent in anticipation of forthcoming defects or in rectification of incipient defects, rather than the rectification of defects which have already become serious. Some element of anticipation is included."

In *Holding & Management Ltd v Property Holding & Investment Trust Plc*,[61] Nicholls L.J., after discussing the various factors relevant to the question whether particular work constitutes repair, said:

---

[58] [1946] A.C. 278.

[59] On the face of it, this suggests that work can still be repair even though the subject matter is not damaged. However, there is some suggestion in the report that the man's duties also extended to carrying out works which obviously were "repairs", such as tightening a nut that had worked loose, and looking out for necessary repairs, such as nuts which were damaged and needed to be replaced, and that it was impractical in the context of the employer's statutory duty to distinguish between those different areas of activity.

[60] [1953] 2 All E.R. 387. See further para.10–18, below.

[61] [1989] 1 W.L.R. 1313.

"[W]here a design or construction fault has led to part of the building falling into a state of disrepair, and the proposed remedial works extend to other parts of the building, an important consideration will be the likelihood of similar disrepair arising in other parts of the building if the remedial work is not undertaken there also, and how soon such further disrepair is likely to arise."

**10–17**     The same issue arose in *McDougall v Easington District Council*.[62] That case concerned a council house which suffered from fundamental flaws in its design or construction, as a result of which it was not watertight. The council had in the past carried out temporary works to make the house wind and watertight. Ultimately the council carried out very extensive works which involved, among other things, removing and replacing the roof. One of the issues was whether that work amounted to repair within the meaning of the council's implied obligation to keep the structure and exterior in repair.[63] It was argued that it did not because the house was not leaking at the relevant time. The Court of Appeal rejected that argument. Mustill L.J. said in the course of his judgment:

"[That contention assumes] that prophylactic measures taken to prevent the occurrence of deterioration in the future of a kind which has already had to be repaired in the past is incapable of amounting to a repair … I do not regard this as the ordinary understanding of the word. Moreover in his judgment in *Ravenseft Properties Limited v. Davstone (Holdings) Limited*,[64] a judgment which has already received the express or tacit approval of this court on more than one occasion, Forbes J. held that the removal of the whole of the stone cladding on the face of a building and its replacement by new cladding which incorporated expansion joints which had not previously been there, in order to prevent further dangerous falls of stone, was capable of amounting to repair. There was no suggestion that it made any difference that not all the stones had fallen off or were just about to do so. It seems to me that the repairs in that case consisted of putting right a situation which had caused trouble in the past and was likely to do so in the future. So also here."

In *Postel Properties Ltd v Boots the Chemist*[65] the landlord decided, on the advice of its management surveyors, to replace the roof of a shopping centre in sections in order of priority. Ian Kennedy J. held that the totality of the replacement work fell within the landlord's covenant "with all due diligence to keep the … roofs … of the demised premises in the Shopping Centre in good and substantial repair and condition". He said of the inspection by the landlord's surveyor:

"It was her conclusion, after walking the roof and making her own survey, that the point had been reached at which a phased replacement of the roof covering was more economic than continuing with patch repairs. It has to be remembered that at this time the covering was within five years of attaining the maximum expected life, a life expectancy which was not improved by the presence of various items of plant on the roofs. I am quite unpersuaded that decision was premature. It has to be remembered that she had to look five years ahead, and it was highly undesirable that the roof covering should be left to threaten an emergency in which large sections failed at the one time."

It does not follow, however, that in every case the covenantor will be obliged or entitled to remedy damage in advance of it occurring. First, there must be some

---

[62] (1989) 58 P. & C.R. 201.
[63] See para.20–17 et seq., below.
[64] [1980] Q.B. 12.
[65] [1996] 2 E.G.L.R. 60.

damage or deterioration to the subject-matter before remedial work can amount to repair.[66] Second, it must be reasonable in all the circumstances to carry out preventative as well as remedial work. The question is one of fact and degree in every case.

## Purely preventative work

As a general rule, the covenantor is not liable to carry out work which is purely preventative in the sense that no relevant damage has yet occurred. This follows from the general principle that no work is required under the covenant until the subject-matter has suffered deterioration or damage.[67] In *Mason v TotalFinaElf UK Ltd*[68] it was argued on behalf of the landlord that "mere preventative work" (i.e. work undertaken to avoid the occurrence of damage from a future but reasonably anticipated state of disrepair) was within the scope of a covenant to repair. Blackburne J. rejected that argument, holding that the covenant on its proper construction did not extend to the carrying out of purely preventative work when no state of disrepair existed. He commented on *Day v Harland & Wolff Ltd*[69] in the following terms:

> "It seems reasonably clear that, having concluded that the anti-fouling paint is 'part of the ship', and having found that, to some extent, the paint was already defective (i.e. a part of the ship was out of repair) Pearson J. was doing no more than saying that, as well as remedying the defective paintwork, it was permissible repair—the matter being one of fact and degree—to repaint those parts that were not yet defective. In the same way, repairing defective paintwork (where the repairing covenant extends to repainting those parts of a building that are ordinarily painted) does not cease to be repair merely because, in the process, the opportunity is taken to repaint those parts of the structure (for example a window frame) where the paintwork is not yet defective even though other parts of it are. I do not consider that that decision is authority for the proposition that work that is purely anticipatory—i.e. where no damage or deterioration in the condition of the subject matter of the covenant has occurred (or has yet occurred to an extent sufficient to constitute a breach of the covenant)—can be called for, or the reasonable cost of it recovered."

He then considered the decision in *Sheldon v West Bromwich Corp*,[70] and said of it that:

> "I do not consider that decision as authority for the proposition that merely because a piece of equipment is old and there must inevitably come a time when the equipment must be replaced, preventative works can be required to prevent the consequences of the equipment failing even though, in the meantime, it continues to perform its function."

10–18

---

[66] See Ch.8, above.
[67] See Ch.8, above.
[68] [2003] 3 E.G.L.R. 91.
[69] [1953] 2 All E.R. 387. See para.10–16, above.
[70] (1973) 25 P. & C.R. 360. The facts are set out in para.8–07, above.

## MATERIALS AND WORKMANSHIP

### The standard of materials

**10–19**     Once the remedial work has been identified, the appropriate standard of materials to be used depends on the standard of repair contemplated by the covenant, which in turn depends on the matters considered in Ch.9, above.

As a general rule, the materials employed in the work must be of such quality that on completion of the work, the premises are up to the standard required by the covenant. As has been seen, that standard varies according to such matters as the age, character and locality of the premises, and what would make them reasonably fit for the occupation of a reasonably-minded tenant of the class likely to have taken them at the date of the lease.[71] It follows that no hard-and-fast rule can be laid down as to what is in any particular case an acceptable repair. For example, it may be permissible to retile the roof of a Victorian factory building with asbestos tiles; conversely, Welsh slate may be the only acceptable method of repair in relation to a town house in Belgravia. The question is one of fact in each case.

### The standard of workmanship

**10–20**     The position in relation to the required standard of workmanship is the same as that in relation to materials, namely, that the workmanship must be of such quality that, on completion of the work, the premises are up to the standard required by the covenant. In general terms, therefore, the work must be done to a reasonable standard, having regard to the age, character and locality of the premises and what would make them reasonably fit for the occupation of a reasonably minded tenant of the class likely to have taken them at the date of the lease.[72]

Precisely what will be required in any given case is a question of fact. For example, minor imperfections in a newly applied plaster finish may be of no consequence in relation to the ground floor of a terraced house now used as a grocer's shop; but the same may be unacceptable in relation to a newly constructed office building in the City of London.

In *Bilgili v Paddington Churches Housing Association*,[73] the landlord replaced old Crittall windows in the demised premises with modern UPVC windows. The Crittall window that was removed from the kitchen had a spinner vent, but the replacement window was fixed, had no means of opening and no form of ventilation was set into it. The county court judge allowed the tenant's appeal from the finding of the district judge that the landlords were not in breach of their repairing covenant. Sedley L.J. declined to grant the landlords permission to appeal to the Court of Appeal: it was "as plain as a pikestaff" that a kitchen window which was acknowledged to require ventilation, and so had a spinner

---

[71] See para.9–05 et seq., above.
[72] See generally Ch.9, above.
[73] [2010] EWCA Civ 1341.

vent in it, had not been properly repaired if it was replaced with a sealed window that had neither a means of opening nor any form of ventilation.

## Good building practice and current regulations

The covenantor must carry out the work in such a way as a reasonable surveyor might advise.[74] He must act in accordance with good building practice, and comply with such regulations as may be applicable.[75] For example, he may be required when rebuilding a wall which was originally constructed without proper footings or a damp-proof course, to construct proper concrete foundations and damp-proof courses.[76]

    10–21

Even when the building regulations do not apply, the court may nonetheless proceed on the assumption that they represent good practice.[77] Thus, in *Postel Properties Ltd v Boots the Chemist*[78] an increase in the insulation layer of fibreboard underneath the top layer of asphalt to a thickness which conformed with building regulations was held not to take the work of replacing the roof of a shopping centre outside the ambit of the landlord's covenant.

However, the fact that the effect of regulations is that the work can only be lawfully carried out in a certain way will not mean that the work constitutes repair if as a matter of fact and degree it goes beyond repair.[79]

## Matching

A common problem in practice is that of matching new work and materials with those already there. For example, six tiles in a WC may be cracked and require replacing, but the remainder may be in acceptable condition. It may not be possible to replace the six defective tiles with tiles of exactly the same shade or size, but even if it is, the new tiles will gleam, leaving the remainder of the wall looking dull. The same problem occurs in practice in relation to suspended ceilings, carpet tiles and light fittings.

    10–22

The answer to this sort of difficulty will depend on the standard of repair contemplated by the covenant. In some cases, that standard will be sufficiently high for the covenantor to be obliged to replace non-defective parts of the original material in order to achieve an acceptable match.[80] For example, where the premises consist of a substantial private residence in a high-class area, the requisite standard of repair may require that bathroom tiling is of the same size, colour and shade throughout, so that it may not be sufficient to replace a single cracked tile with one that does not match the remainder: instead, it will be

---

[74] Cf. para.10–02, above.
[75] *Lurcott v Wakely* [1911] 2 K.B. 905; *Halliard Property Co Ltd v Nicholas Clarke Investments Ltd* [1984] 1 E.G.L.R. 45; *Ravenseft Properties Ltd v Davstone (Holdings) Ltd* [1980] Q.B. 12. See further paras 11–35 to 11–36, below.
[76] *Lurcott v Wakely*, above.
[77] *Postel Properties Ltd v Boots the Chemist* [1996] 2 E.G.L.R. 60 at 62L.
[78] Above. This case is further considered in para.12–12, below.
[79] See Ch.11, below and see in particular para.11–35, below.
[80] See *Johnson v Gooch* (1848) 11 L.T. (O.S.) 315, considered in para.15–04, below.

necessary to replace all of them so as to achieve the same effect as the original. Thus, in *Sunlife Europe Properties v Tiger Aspect Holdings*,[81] (which concerned a claim for terminal dilapidations in relation to a combined office and retail building built in the early 1970s) Edwards-Stuart J. agreed with the landlord's expert that it would not be acceptable to "create a patchwork effect by fitting some new tiles into a ceiling that contained a substantial proportion of existing tiles".[82] In other cases, the fact that the new material does not match the old will not matter. So, for example, where the premises are a factory used for heavy industry, and the cracked tiles are in a WC on the shop floor, it may be acceptable simply to replace those tiles that are cracked, even if an exact match cannot be achieved with what is already there.

Problems of matching may also occur in relation to cleaning. Where areas need cleaning, the covenantor will generally be liable to carry out the cleaning in such a way as to produce a reasonably uniform appearance. Thus, in *Shortlands Investments Ltd v Cargill Plc*[83] the landlord recovered the cost of cleaning stained or discoloured ceiling tiles. The Official Referee said in the course of his judgment: "To clean some tiles and not to clean others would produce an appalling patchwork effect. All the tiles had to be cleaned and coated."

In the same way, a covenant to decorate at periodic intervals will ordinarily require the covenantor to decorate in such a way as to achieve an acceptable match. Thus, in *Commercial Union Life Assurance Co Ltd v Label Ink Ltd*[84] (which concerned a warehouse building) H.H. Judge Rich QC (sitting as a deputy High Court judge) said:

> "The first matter complained of is that the painted block work at a low level has been painted in a non-matching shade in breach of the redecoration clause. I accept that it should have been repainted in a matching colour or the whole block work should have been painted in one colour in the fifth year in a workmanlike manner."

In *Vukelic v The Major and Burgesses of Hammersmith & Fulham*[85] the defendant council was liable to carry out works to remedy damage to the claimant tenant's shop resulting from an admitted nuisance for which the defendant was responsible. In considering the extent of consequential redecoration which would be required, HHJ Seymour QC said:

> "The need to redecorate in such circumstances is not a need to perform Mrs Vukelic's obligations under the Lease, but a need to remedy the effects of the nuisance for which the Council is liable. If the need to redecorate arises in this way, then the decoration should be undertaken utilising good quality materials and a good standard of workmanship. It is not, in my judgment, demonstrating a good standard of workmanship to hang a couple of strips of non-matching wallpaper on a wall where the other paper would not otherwise need

---

[81] [2013] EWHC 463 (TCC) at [109].
[82] Although he went on to hold that sufficient undamaged tiles could have been recovered so that, at least on some of the ceilings, the damaged tiles could have been replaced by undamaged tiles taken from other ceilings: see para.10–23, below.
[83] [1995] 1 E.G.L.R. 51.
[84] [2001] L. & T.R. 29. Note that the question of disrepair arose in the context of whether or not the tenant had complied with a condition precedent in a break option, and that the judge's construction of the condition precedent was subsequently disapproved by the Court of Appeal in *Fitzroy House Epworth Street (No.1) v The Financial Times* [2006] 2 E.G.L.R. 13.
[85] [2003] EWHC 188 (TCC).

replacement, or to patch a hole in wallpaper caused by removal of a light switch by sticking a random piece of non-matching wallpaper over the hole. It makes no difference, as it seems to me, that the non-matching wallpaper and the original wallpaper is then painted the same colour if the non-matching wallpaper remains, as it seemed to me on my view it did, obtrusive. What is manifestly required, in my judgment, is complete replacement of all the wallpaper in the restaurant area—there was not that much of it—with a uniform paper."

Covenants to decorate are further considered in Ch.15, below.

## Cannibalising

It may happen in practice that items or installations which form part of the overall subject matter of the covenant are defective in some areas but not in others. Take, for example, a ten storey office block with suspended ceilings on every floor. At the end of the term, the majority of the ceiling tiles may be damaged or discoloured to the point where the only feasible way of restoring the building to the standard contemplated by the covenant is to replace all ten ceilings. In practice, however, a significant number of tiles on each floor may be undamaged, and it may be possible to collect these together and use them to restore, say, two of the ceilings to an acceptable standard, leaving only the remaining eight to be replaced. The same may be true of mechanical and electrical installations. For example, it may be possible to repair defective fan coil units or boilers, which would otherwise need replacing, by using parts from other defective units, thereby reducing the total number of units requiring replacement.

10–23

In principle, there is no reason why the covenantor cannot re-use non-defective items in this way, provided obviously that the end result complies with the standard of repair required by the covenant. The fact that a particular item requires to be replaced does not of itself mean that the covenanting party must necessarily provide and install a brand new item. If it is possible to achieve the appropriate standard of repair by re-using an existing item, then that will be a sufficient performance of the covenant. Thus, in *Sunlife Europe Properties v Tiger Aspect Holdings*[86] (which concerned a claim for terminal dilapidations in relation to a combined office and retail building built in the early 1970s) Edwards-Stuart J., having agreed with the landlord's expert that it would not be acceptable to fit new tiles into suspended ceilings that contained a substantial proportion of existing tiles, went on to hold:

"I consider that sufficient undamaged tiles could have been recovered so that, at least on some of the ceilings, the damaged tiles could have been replaced by undamaged tiles taken from other ceilings, even allowing for damage caused by the partitions and a certain amount of damage and breakage caused during taking down. Doing the best I can, I consider that the ceilings on two of the larger floors could probably have been made good using recovered tiles, leaving new tiles to be used on the other floors."

As always, however, each individual case will depend on its own detailed facts. So, for example, if the building were a high class headquarters office building in a prime area, and the effect of re-using ceiling tiles was to produce a significant difference in appearance between ceilings on different floors (some

---

[86] [2013] EWHC 463 (TCC) at [109].

comprising re-used tiles and others having been replaced with new), it may be, depending on the precise circumstances, that the requisite standard of repair would not be achieved.

CHAPTER 11

# THE FIFTH QUESTION: IS THAT WORK NONETHELESS OF SUCH A NATURE THAT THE PARTIES DID NOT CONTEMPLATE IT WOULD BE THE LIABILITY OF THE COVENANTING PARTY?

INTRODUCTORY

## The remedial work may go beyond repair

It might be thought that if the subject-matter of the covenant[1] is in a damaged or deteriorated condition[2] such that it falls below the standard contemplated by the covenant,[3] and that certain work is necessary in order to put it back into the contemplated condition,[4] then it could be concluded without more that the covenanting party would be liable in respect of that work. However, the authorities show that this is not the position. The courts have not generally treated a covenant to repair as a warranty that the premises will always be in a state of "repair" regardless of what work may be required to achieve that state.[5] On the contrary, the authorities proceed on the footing that what the covenanting party has bound himself to do is to carry out the operation called repair, and there may come a point when the nature of the defect is such that the necessary remedial work cannot properly be called "repair" at all, but amounts to something different and more extensive. Put another way, the work which is required is such that the parties are not to be taken to have contemplated that the covenanting party would be liable to carry it out.

**11–01**

This Chapter is concerned with the various tests and expressions which have been used by the courts to identify precisely when the above point has been reached. There is, perhaps not surprisingly, a large body of case law on the subject, which has given rise to a number of different formulations of the correct approach. Ultimately, however, the question will be seen to be one of fact and degree. An alternative formulation of the fifth question might be: "Looked at generally as a matter of fact and degree, is the relevant work of 'repair' within the meaning of the covenant?"

---

[1] See Ch.7, above.

[2] See Ch.8, above.

[3] See Ch.9, above.

[4] See Ch.10, above.

[5] The position in relation to a covenant to keep in good condition may be different: see paras 4–29 and 4–30, above, and para.11–46, below.

THE DOCTRINE OF INHERENT DEFECT

## The doctrine of inherent defect

**11–02** There was formerly believed in some circles to exist a "doctrine of inherent defect" applicable to covenants to repair in leases. This was to the effect:

> "[T]hat where wants of reparation arise which are caused by some inherent defect in the premises demised, the results of the inherent defect can never fall within the ambit of a covenant to repair.[6]"

By "inherent defect" was meant an omission of something in the original design but not a defect in the quality of workmanship or materials.[7] According to the doctrine, remedying the results of bad design could never be within a covenant to repair. An alternative formulation was that the covenantor is not bound to carry out works which in fact remedy an inherent defect.[8] The doctrine had its origin in the following passage from the judgment of Lord Esher M.R. in *Lister v Lane*[9]:

> "If a tenant takes a house which is of such a kind that by its own inherent nature it will in the course of time fall into a particular condition, the effects of that result are not within the tenant's covenant to repair."

**11–03** However, in *Ravenseft Properties Ltd v Davstone (Holdings) Ltd*,[10] Forbes J. held, after an extensive examination of the authorities, that there was no such doctrine. That case concerned a 16-storey block of maisonettes constructed with a reinforced concrete frame with stone cladding. Expansion joints had been omitted from the cladding when the building was put up, because at that time the necessity for expansion joints was not realised. Principally as a result of this omission, but also because of defective workmanship in failing properly to tie in the stones, the cladding started to bow away from the concrete frame of the building. Parts of it became dangerous, and had to be taken down and then retied to the building with the inclusion of expansion joints. The landlord carried out the work and then claimed the costs from the tenants under a service charge provision. The tenants relied on the doctrine of inherent defect. They argued that since the damage was caused by an inherent defect (namely, the lack of expansion joints), the remedial work could not constitute repair. Alternatively they contended that they were not bound to pay for inserting the expansion joints, since that was work which remedied an inherent defect.

Forbes J. found in favour of the landlord. He was, he said, "unable to accept [counsel's] contention that a doctrine such as he enunciates has any place in the law of landlord and tenant".[11] Instead the correct test was that:

---

[6] See *Ravenseft Properties Ltd v Davstone (Holdings) Ltd* [1980] Q.B. 12 at 18.
[7] Ibid., at 21.
[8] Ibid.
[9] [1893] 2 Q.B. 212.
[10] Above.
[11] Ibid., at 21.

"[I]t is always a question of degree whether that which the tenant is being asked to do can properly be described as repair, or whether on the contrary it would involve giving back to the landlord a wholly different thing from that which he demised."

He held that on a proper application of the fact and degree approach, the relevant work was repair.

The only subsequent case in which the doctrine of inherent defect appears to have been argued is *Halliard Property Co Ltd v Nicholas Clarke Investments Ltd*,[12] in which French J. followed and applied *Ravenseft*. *Ravenseft* has since been referred to and approved in a number of subsequent decisions of the Court of Appeal,[13] and it must now be taken to be the law that the "doctrine of inherent defect" does not exist as a separate principle of the law of dilapidations.

Accordingly, the mere fact that the property suffers from an inherent defect does not of itself mean that the eradication of that defect, or of damage resulting from it, cannot be a repair. However, where the inherent defect has resulted in physical damage to the subject-matter of the covenant,[14] the covenantor may be liable to eradicate the inherent defect itself as well as remedying the damage it has caused.[15] Thus, a landlord who has covenanted to keep the main walls of a flat in repair may be liable to insert a damp-proof course as well as remedying the defective plaster caused by the lack of a damp-proof course.[16] It does not follow, however, that the eradication of an inherent defect will always be within the scope of a covenant to repair. First, the inherent defect may not have resulted in any physical damage to the subject-matter of the covenant, in which case no action under the covenant is called for.[17] Second, it may be reasonable and practicable to remedy the damage without remedying the inherent defect. Third, the necessary remedial work may go beyond repair as a matter of fact and degree.[18]

## THE TEST OF FACT AND DEGREE

The correct approach to the question whether the covenantor is liable to carry out the requisite work is to ask whether, looked at as a matter of fact and degree, that work can fairly be called "repair" within the meaning of the covenant. The classic formulation is that of Sachs L.J. in *Brew Bros Ltd v Snax (Ross) Ltd*[19]:

**11–04**

---

[12] [1984] 1 E.G.L.R. 45. For the facts, see para.11–34, below.

[13] *Elmcroft Developments Ltd v Tankersley-Sawyer* [1984] 1 E.G.L.R. 47 (in which *Ravenseft* was "clearly approved", according to Dillon L.J. in *Quick v Taff-Ely Borough Council* [1986] Q.B. 809 at 821); *Quick v Taff-Ely Borough Council* [1986] Q.B. 809; *Stent v Monmouth District Council* (1987) 54 P. & C.R. 193; *Post Office v Aquarius Properties Ltd* [1987] 1 All E.R. 1055; *McDougall v Easington District Council* (1989) 58 P. & C.R. 201.

[14] See Ch.8, above.

[15] See para.11–38, below.

[16] *Elmcroft Developments Ltd v Tankersley-Sawyer*, above. See further para.12–27 et seq., below.

[17] See Ch.8, above. It is noteworthy that in both *Quick v Taff-Ely Borough Council*, above, and *Post Office v Aquarius Properties Ltd*, above, the premises suffered from design defects but in neither case was a state of "disrepair" held to exist.

[18] See para.11–04 et seq., below.

[19] [1970] 1 Q.B. 612.

"It seems to me that the correct approach is to look at the particular building, to look at the state which it is in at the date of the lease, to look at the precise terms of the lease, and then come to a conclusion as to whether, on a fair interpretation of those terms in relation to that state, the requisite work can fairly be termed repair. However large the covenant it must not be looked at *in vacuo* ... Quite clearly this approach involves in every instance a question of degree."

He relied upon a passage from the judgment of Lord Evershed M.R. in *Wates v Rowland*[20] in which, after setting out two examples of work which would, and would not, be within the covenant, the Master of the Rolls said:

"Between the two extremes, it seems to me to be largely a matter of degree, which in the ordinary case the county court judge could decide as a matter of fact, applying a common-sense man-of-the-world view."

The numerous authorities on the meaning of "repair" contain a number of different formulations of what is the appropriate test. It is thought that these are not to be regarded as definitions of general application, but simply as different formulations by the judges, in relation to the particular facts which they had to consider, of the basic test of fact and degree. Thus, in *Brew Bros* Sachs L.J. said:

"In the course of their submissions counsel referred to a number of varying phrases which had been used by judges in an endeavour to express the distinction between the end-product of work which constituted repair and that of work which did not. They included 'improvement,' 'important improvement,' 'different in substance,' 'different in nature,' 'a new and different thing,' and just 'something different.' They likewise referred to another set of phrases seeking to define the distinctive quality of the fault to be rectified, such as 'inherent nature' (frequently used since *Lister v. Lane*[21]), 'radical defect in the structure,' 'inherent defect' and 'inherent vice'. Each of these two sets of phrases in turn was discussed in what tended to become an exercise in semantics. Moreover, it is really not much use looking for individual phrases which necessarily deal with only one of the infinitely variable sets of circumstances that can arise ... For my part I doubt whether there is any definition—certainly not any general definition—which satisfactorily covers the above distinctions: nor will I attempt to provide one. Things which can be easily recognised are not always susceptible of simple definition."

**11–05**   In *Post Office v Aquarius Properties Ltd*[22] Hoffmann J. at first instance said that he had derived most assistance from the judgment of Sachs L.J. in *Brew Bros* which:

"[S]ays, in effect, that the whole law on the subject may be summed up in the proposition that 'repair' is an ordinary English word. It also contains a timely warning against attempting to impose the crudities of judicial exegesis upon the subtle and often intuitive discriminations of ordinary speech. All words take meaning from context, and it is, of course, necessary to have regard to the language of the particular covenant and the lease as a whole, the commercial relationship between the parties, the state of the premises at the time of the demise and any other surrounding circumstances which may colour the way in which the word is used. In the end, however, the question is whether the ordinary speaker of English would consider that the word 'repair' as used in the covenant was appropriate to describe the work which has to be done. The cases do no more than illustrate specific contexts in which judges, as ordinary speakers of English, have thought that it was or was not appropriate to do so."

---

[20] [1952] 2 Q.B. 12.
[21] [1893] 2 Q.B. 212.
[22] [1985] 2 E.G.L.R. 105 (affirmed on other grounds [1987] 1 All E.R. 1055: see para.8–02, above).

It follows that the various antitheses in the cases between "repair" on the one hand, and "improvement", "giving back a new and different thing" or "renewal" on the other, should not be treated as being distinct tests as opposed to aspects of the same test. Nonetheless, distinctions of this kind may be of considerable assistance in applying the fact and degree test. Many such concepts border upon repair but are distinguishable from it in different ways.[23] Thus, to contrast "repair" with "substantially a rebuilding of the whole subject-matter of the covenant"[24] may be helpful in relation to a particular set of factual circumstances. Where the facts are different, the relevant distinction may be between repair and "structural alterations and improvements".[25] In other circumstances, it may be helpful to ask whether the effect of the work would be to give back to the lessor a wholly different thing from that which he demised.[26] All these may be useful in any given situation, but none on its own can give a definitive answer in all cases. This is emphasised in the following passage from the judgment of Hoffmann J. in *Post Office v Aquarius Properties Ltd*[27]:

"[Counsel for the landlords] formulated a number of propositions ... the most important [of which] was that the test for whether or not the work which needed to be done was repair was whether it would give the landlord a wholly different thing from that which he had before. In this case, he said, the landlord would still have essentially the same building and therefore the work was repair. This proposition, in my view, illustrates the wisdom of Sachs L.J.'s warning,[28] because it does not make allowance for the range of distinctions embodied in ordinary words ... it does express what is usually implied in the distinction between repair and rebuilding or reconstruction, but these are not the only concepts which border upon repair. There are also words like 'improvement', 'alteration' and 'addition' which are distinguishable from repair in different ways. For example, one usually thinks of an improvement as a fairly substantial and identifiable addition to or change in a building but involving a subsidiary part rather than the building as a whole. Nevertheless, 'improvement' is different from repair. It is often said that whether or not something is repair is a question of degree, but the question of degree which has to be answered is not always necessarily the same. There are various criteria for distinguishing the word 'repair' from its near neighbours. These differences can be seen operating in *Brew Bros.*, in which the majority of the court thought that the works taken as a whole were so extensive as to amount to a reconstruction rather than a repair. Harman L.J. did not accept that the totality was reconstruction, but thought that one part of the work, namely the construction of new foundations, was an improvement. *Wright v. Lawson*[29] is also an example of an addition or improvement, the construction of a new bay window, which could not be described as a rebuilding or reconstruction of the premises as a whole."

The above passage clearly demonstrates the limitations upon the use of any one single antithesis as a comprehensive expression of the distinction between repair and work of a different nature.

---

[23] *Post Office v Aquarius Properties Ltd*, above.
[24] *Lurcott v Wakely* [1911] 1 K.B. 905, per Buckley L.J.
[25] *Post Office v Aquarius Properties Ltd* (at first instance), above.
[26] *Ravenseft Properties Ltd v Davstone (Holdings) Ltd* [1980] Q.B. 12.
[27] [1985] 2 E.G.L.R. 105 (affirmed on other grounds [1987] 1 All E.R. 1055: see para.8–02, above).
[28] See *Brew Bros Ltd v Snax (Ross) Ltd*, fn.19 above.
[29] (1903) 19 T.L.R. 510.

## Repair and renewal

**11–06**    The antithesis between "repair" and "renewal" is of high authority, being referred to in each of the judgments of the Court of Appeal in *Lurcott v Wakely*.[30] However, in each of those judgments it is recognised that the antithesis is not complete. Every repair will nearly always involve some element of renewal, however minor. Buckley L.J. made this point at the beginning of his judgment:

> "'Repair' and 'renew' are not words expressive of a clear contrast. Repair always involves renewal; renewal of a part; of a subordinate part."

Fletcher Moulton L.J. made the same point:

> "Many, and in fact most, repairs imply that some portion of the total fabric is renewed, that new is put in place of old. Therefore you have from time to time as things need repair to put new for old."

Applying this reasoning, it was held in *Collins v Flynn*[31] that the express inclusion in a general repairing covenant of an obligation "to renew" was to be understood in the above sense, and added nothing to the obligation "to repair".[32]

**11–07**    However, there is a distinction between the renewal of subsidiary parts, and the renewal of the whole, or substantially the whole, of the subject-matter of the covenant. In *Lurcott v Wakely* Buckley L.J. went on to say in his judgment:

> "Repair is restoration by renewal or replacement of subsidiary parts of a whole. Renewal, as distinguished from repair, is reconstruction of the entirety, meaning by the entirety not necessarily the whole but substantially the whole subject-matter under discussion. I agree that if repair of the whole subject-matter has become impossible a covenant to repair does not carry an obligation to renew or replace. That has been affirmed by *Lister v. Lane*[33] and *Wright v. Lawson*.[34] But if that which I have said is accurate, it follows that the question of repair is in every case one of degree, and the test is whether the act to be done is one which in substance is the renewal or replacement of defective parts, or the renewal or replacement of substantially the whole."

Fletcher Moulton L.J. said:

> "For my own part, when the word 'repair' is applied to a complex matter like a house, I have no doubt that the repair includes the replacement of parts. Of course, if a house had tumbled down, or was down, the word 'repair' could not be used to cover rebuilding. It would not be apt to describe such an operation."

That this is, in effect, a test of fact and degree is shown by that part of Buckley L.J.'s formulation which refers to the renewal or replacement of "substantially the whole" of the subject matter of the covenant. The question of the substantiality of the works required is itself a matter of degree, as Buckley L.J. recognised when he said "the question of repair is in every case one of degree".

---

[30] [1911] 1 K.B. 905.
[31] [1963] 2 All E.R. 1068.
[32] See further paras 4–27 to 4–28, above.
[33] [1893] 2 Q.B. 212.
[34] (1903) 19 T.L.R. 510.

It is therefore thought that there is no conflict between the "repair or renewal" test and the test of fact and degree. This further appears from the following passage from the judgment of Phillimore L.J. in *Brew Bros Ltd v Snax (Ross) Ltd*[35]:

> "I agree with the Judge, who concluded after reviewing the authorities and particularly the observations of Lord Esher M.R. in *Lister v. Lane* and those of Buckley L.J. in *Lurcott v. Wakely*, that the vital question in each case is whether the total work to be done can properly be described as repair since it involves no more than renewal or replacement of defective parts, or whether it is in effect renewal or replacement of substantially the whole. It is, as Megaw J. held, a question of degree in each case."

## REPAIR AND IMPROVEMENT

The antithesis between "repair" and "improvement" appears from time to time in the cases on repair.[36] It is also commonly used in practice in the course of negotiations between surveyors settling dilapidations claims to distinguish between repairs and works going beyond repairs. Like the other formulations discussed above, it can on occasion be a helpful way of expressing the distinction. However, the reasoning of Buckley L.J. in *Lurcott v Wakely*[37] in relation to the distinction between repair and renewal applies with equal force to the distinction between repair and improvement. Many repairs will involve an element of improvement, if only in the sense that an old item has been replaced with a new. It is therefore thought that the repair/improvement dichotomy is not a test in itself but an aspect of the wider fact and degree test discussed above.    **11–08**

It is common for rent review clauses to contain a disregard of tenant's improvements coupled with an express or implied assumption that the tenant's repairing obligations have been performed as at the review date. In such cases it will be necessary to consider the difference between repair and improvement for the purposes of deciding to what extent particular work carried out by the tenant falls to be valued or disregarded.[38]

## Repair and work which results in a different thing

The antithesis between works of repair and those which give the landlord or tenant "a different thing" from which he let or took derives from the decision of the Court of Appeal in *Lister v Lane*.[39] There Lord Esher M.R. said:    **11–09**

> "However large the words of the covenant may be, a covenant to repair a house is not a covenant to give a different thing from that which the tenant took when he entered into the covenant. He has to repair that thing which he took; he is not obliged to make a new and different thing, and moreover, the result of the nature and condition of the house itself, the result of time upon that state of things, is not a breach of the covenant to repair."

---

[35] [1970] 1 Q.B. 612.
[36] See, for example, *Soward v Legatt* (1836) 7 C. & P. 613; *Post Office v Aquarius Properties Ltd* [1985] 2 E.G.L.R. 105 (affirmed on different grounds [1987] 1 All E.R. 1055).
[37] [1911] 1 K.B. 905. See para.11–07, above.
[38] See para.35–11.
[39] [1893] 2 Q.B. 212.

In the same case Kay L.J., discussing the nature of the work for which the landlord was seeking to make the tenant liable, said:

"Would that be repairing or upholding or maintaining the house? To my mind it would not; it would be making an entirely new or different house."

In *Pembery v Lamdin*,[40] in which the tenant claimed that the landlord was obliged under his general repairing covenant to make waterproof a cellar which was damp due to the absence of damp-proof course or other waterproofing, Slesser L.J. said:

"[I]f the counterclaim here made by Mrs Lamdin be correct, she is entitled to receive at the hands of this landlord a different thing from that which she took when she entered into the covenant. She took this old house with a cellar without any waterproof protection, and she is asking the landlord so to repair that house as to give her a cellar which has a waterproof protection and is dry. That is not a right which she can possibly maintain, because the obligation of the landlord is to repair that which is demised, and not to give her something much drier in its nature than that which was demised."

A similar formulation is to be found in the judgment of Cozens-Hardy M.R. in *Lurcott v Wakely*[41]:

"That being so, it seems to me that we are driven to ask in this particular case, and in every case of this kind, is what has happened of such a nature that it can fairly be said that the character of the subject-matter of the demise, or part of the demise, in question has been changed? Is it something which goes to the whole, or substantially the whole, or is it simply an injury to a portion, a subsidiary portion, to use Buckley L.J.'s phrase, of the demised property?"

**11–10** The same emphasis on the effect which the required works would have upon the subject-matter of the covenant was expressed by Lynskey J. in *Sotheby v Grundy*,[42] where he said of the proposed work of underpinning a house:

"That, in my view, would, in effect, be asking the tenant to give the landlord something different in kind from that which had been demised. The premises demised here were premises with insecure foundations. What the tenant would have had to do would be to put in a new foundation which would alter the nature and extent of the property demised, turning a building which, as originally constructed, would not last more than some 80 odd years into a building that would last for probably another 100 years."

Phillimore L.J. in *Brew Bros Ltd v Snax (Ross) Ltd*[43] put it in much the same way:

"It is well established that a tenant is not liable to produce a different thing from that which he took when he entered into the lease or to remedy the results of bad design. On what basis, then, where a house is doomed at the time he leases it, is he to be required substantially to rebuild it so as to hand back to his landlord something which is in fact quite different from what he took?"

---

[40] [1940] 2 All E.R. 434.
[41] [1911] 2 K.B. 905.
[42] [1947] 2 All E.R. 761.
[43] [1970] 1 Q.B. 612.

In *McDougall v Easington District Council*[44] Mustill L.J. identified three tests for whether the relevant work amounts to repair, of which one was:

> "Whether the effect of the alterations was to produce a building of a wholly different character from that which had been let."

Recent judicial formulations to the same effect include those of Harman J. in *Minja Properties Ltd v Cussins Property Group Ltd*[45] as follows:

**11–11**

> "The matter thus turns upon the question; is the repair proposed so radical and extravagant as to amount to creating a new thing in place of what was there and not a mere replacement, such as a new pipe or a new window or a new slate would be, for the former window that was there?"

And of Pill L.J. in *Eyre v McCracken*[46]:

> "In my judgment, to require the tenant to insert a damp proof course and ancillary work would be to require him to give back to the landlord a different thing from that demised to him in 1976.[47]"

And of Neuberger J. in *Gibson Investments Ltd v Chesterton Plc (No.1)*[48]:

> "[T]he cases establish ... that the work will not be repair if it involves giving something back to the landlord wholly different from that which he demised."

It should be noted that the reference in the above cases to "a different thing" does not mean that the work will only cease to be repair where it results in the whole subject-matter of the covenant becoming different.[49] It is sufficient if a substantial part of the premises is made different.[50]

As before, it is thought that the above formulations are simply another way of expressing the fact and degree test. This is indicated by the following passage from the judgment of Forbes J. in *Ravenseft Properties Ltd v Davstone (Holdings) Ltd*[51]:

> "The true test, as the cases show, is that it is always a question of degree whether that which the tenant is being asked to do can properly be described as repair, or whether on the contrary it would involve giving back to the landlord a wholly different thing from that which he demised."

---

[44] (1989) 58 P. & C.R. 201. See further para.11–13, below.
[45] [1998] 2 E.G.L.R. 52. See further para.12–37, below.
[46] (2000) 80 P. & C.R. 220.
[47] See further para.12–33, below.
[48] [2002] 2 P. & C.R. 32.
[49] *Post Office v Aquarius Properties Ltd* [1987] 1 All E.R. 1055, per Ralph Gibson L.J. at 1064g.
[50] See,e.g. *Wright v Lawson* (1903) 19 T.L.R. 203 (affirmed 19 T.L.R. 510) (bay window); *Pembery v Lamdin* [1940] 2 All E.R. 434 (cellar walls); *Halliard Property Co Ltd v Nicholas Clarke Investments Ltd* [1984] 1 E.G.L.R. 45 (back addition); *Eyre v McCracken*, above (basement walls).
[51] [1980] Q.B. 12. See also *Sotheby v Grundy*, above (the relevant passage is set out in para.11–18, below).

## Repair and work which is outside the contemplation of the parties

**11–12**     A number of the cases on the meaning of repair emphasise that what the court is seeking to do is to ascertain what the parties must, as reasonable people, have intended. Such cases focus on the extent to which the parties are likely to have contemplated that particular work would be the tenant's liability. Thus in *Brew Bros Ltd v Snax (Ross) Ltd*[52] Sachs L.J. cited with approval the formulation of Tindal C.J. in an earlier case[53]:

> "In the upshot 'it is the "good sense of the agreement" that has to be ascertained'—a phrase conveniently quoted from the 1842 judgment of Tindal C.J."

A similar emphasis on a common sense construction is to be found in the opening words of Lord Esher M.R.'s judgment in *Lister v Lane*[54]:

> "However large the words of the covenant may be, a covenant to repair a house is not a covenant to give a different thing from that which the tenant took when he entered into the covenant."

The same idea is suggested by Cozens-Hardy M.R. in *Lurcott v Wakely*,[55] in which he said of *Torrens v Walker*[56]:

> "I think that decision was quite right on the facts and that the change of circumstances in that case was one which could not have been in the contemplation of the parties when the covenant was entered into, and that the covenant must be construed with reference to that limitation."

He said much the same thing of *Lister v Lane*[57]:

> "I see no reason to quarrel with their decision that the change of circumstances which had arisen could not have been in the contemplation of the parties and that it would not be reasonable to construe the covenant to repair as applicable to that change of circumstance."

The above approach is most explicitly articulated in the judgment of Phillimore L.J. in *Brew Bros Ltd v Snax (Ross) Ltd*,[58] where he said:

> "In my judgment, the work which these tenants were required to perform and to pay for went far beyond what any reasonable person would have contemplated under the word 'repair' … Suppose some busybody had said to these parties when signing the contract: 'You realise, of course, that it might be necessary within 18 months to spend between £8,000 and £9,000 to render this building safe. If that had happened, would you both regard that as repair?' I suspect that even a landlord (unless utterly unreasonable) would have replied: 'Of course not'."

These passages emphasise that the words of a repairing covenant must be construed with reference to the limitation that they are not to extend the liability of the covenantor beyond what a reasonable person would have contemplated as

---

[52] [1970] 1 Q.B. 612.
[53] *White v Nicholson* (1842) 4 Man. & G. 95 at 98.
[54] [1893] 2 Q.B. 212.
[55] [1911] 2 K.B. 905.
[56] [1906] 2 Ch. 166.
[57] [1893] 2 Q.B. 212.
[58] [1970] 1 Q.B. 612.

coming within an obligation to repair. However, whether particular works do or do not come within the obligation remains a matter of fact and degree.

## Different tests for deciding whether the works are repairs

In some cases an attempt has been made to bring together the various aspects of the fact and degree test. Thus, in *McDougall v Easington District Council*[59] Mustill L.J. said:

> "[I do not] think it necessary to attempt a complete reconciliation of the whole body of authority by means of a single statement of principle: for I believe that whatever particular formula one selects from the various judgments, the result in the present instance must be the same. It is sufficient to say that, in my opinion, three different tests may be discerned, which may be applied separately or concurrently as the circumstances of the individual case may demand, but all to be approached in the light of the nature and age of the premises, their condition when the tenant went into occupation, and the other express terms of the tenancy:
> (i)    Whether the alterations went to the whole or substantially the whole of the structure or only to a subsidiary part;
> (ii)   Whether the effect of the alterations was to produce a building of a wholly different character from that which had been let;
> (iii)  What was the cost of the works in relation to the previous value of the building, and what was their effect on the value and lifespan of the building."

In *Holding & Management Ltd v Property Holding & Investment Trust Ltd*[60] (a service charge case), Nicholls L.J. held that the proper approach was as follows:

> "[T]he exercise involves considering the context in which the word 'repair' appears in a particular lease and also the defect and remedial works proposed. Accordingly, the circumstances to be taken into account in a particular case under one or other of these heads will include some or all of the following: the nature of the building; the terms of the lease; the state of the building at the date of the lease; the nature and extent of the defect sought to be remedied; the nature, extent and cost of the proposed remedial works, at whose expense the proposed remedial works are to be done; the value of the building and its expected lifespan[61]; the effect of the works on such value and lifespan; current building practice; the likelihood of a recurrence if one remedy rather than another is adopted; and the comparative cost of alternative remedial works and their impact on the use and enjoyment of the building by the occupants. The weight to be attached to these circumstances will vary from case to case.
> This is not a comprehensive list. In some cases there will be other matters properly to be taken into account. For example, as in the present case, where a design or construction fault has led to part of the building falling into a state of disrepair, and the proposed remedial works extend to other parts of the building, an important consideration will be the likelihood of similar disrepair arising in other parts of the building if the remedial work is not undertaken there also, and how soon such further disrepair is likely to arise."

In the next section various factors relevant to the fact and degree test are discussed.

11–13

---

[59] (1989) 58 P. & C.R. 201.
[60] [1990] 1 E.G.L.R. 65 (not reported on this point at [1989] 1 W.L.R. 1313.).
[61] In *Ladbroke Hotels Ltd v Sandhu* [1995] 2 E.G.L.R. 92 Robert Walker J. treated this as a reference to the expected structural life of the building, not its expected commercial life. See further para.9–27, above.

PARTICULAR FACTORS RELEVANT TO THE FACT AND DEGREE TEST

## The nature of the building

**11–14**   In construing the covenant, regard must be had to the nature of the particular building.[62] This will include its age, character, locality and the way it was designed and constructed.

## Old premises

**11–15**   A number of the authorities dealing with repair were concerned with old premises, where the defect complained of was the inevitable result either of the way the premises were designed and built, or simply the passage of time. Dicta in some of these cases suggest that this factor is conclusive, or at least highly indicative, that the work is not repair. Thus, in *Gutteridge v Munyard*[63] the premises consisted of a house between 200 and 300 years old which was in a "very dilapidated state, the walls with cracks in them, and out of the perpendicular; the floors sunk; many of the timbers rotten; the tilings and woodwork of the sashes broken, etc." Tindal C.J. is reported to have said in directing the jury:

> "Where a very old building is demised, and the lessee enters into a covenant to repair, it is not meant that the old building is to be restored in a renewed form at the end of the term, or of greater value than it was at the commencement of the term. What the natural operation of time flowing on effects, and all that the elements bring about in diminishing the value, constitute a loss which, so far as it results from time and nature, falls on the landlord."

However, *Gutteridge v Munyard* must be approached with caution. First, there is a "remarkable discrepancy"[64] between the two reports of it.[65] The above passage only appears in one report.[66] Second, one of the covenants in that case contained the words "reasonable use and wear thereof in the meantime only excepted". This goes some way towards explaining Tindal C.J.'s direction to the jury.

**11–16**   The leading case on old premises is *Lister v Lane*.[67] A house in Lambeth was built on boggy soil on a platform of timber. In the course of time the timber rotted and one of the walls of the house bulged out. After the lease had ended it was condemned as a dangerous structure and pulled down. The landlord contended that the tenant should have repaired the wall during the lease (which was for seven years). This could only have been done by means of underpinning, i.e. digging down through 17ft of mud to the gravel underneath and then building up

---

[62] *Brew Bros Ltd v Snax (Ross) Ltd* [1970] 1 Q.B. 612, per Sachs L.J. (see para.11–04, above); *Holding & Management Ltd v Property Holding & Investment Trust Ltd* [1990] 1 E.G.L.R. 65 (not reported on this point at [1989] 1 W.L.R. 1313), per Nicholls L.J.

[63] (1834) 1 Moo. & R. 334.

[64] Per Cozens-Hardy L.J. in *Lurcott v Wakely* [1911] 1 K.B. 905. See below.

[65] (1834) Moo. & R. 334 and 7 C. & P. 127.

[66] (1834) 1 Moo. & R. 334.

[67] [1893] 2 Q.B. 212.

from that to the brickwork of the house. The Court of Appeal held that the tenant was not liable. Both Lord Esher M.R. and Kay L.J. relied heavily on the nature of the house in arriving at their decision. Lord Esher M.R. relied upon the following extract from *Smith's Landlord and Tenant*:[68]

"[W]hen there is a general covenant to repair, the age and general condition of the house at the commencement of the tenancy are to be taken into consideration in considering whether the covenant has been broken; and a tenant who enters upon an old house is not bound to leave it in the same state as if it were a new one."

He said in a well-known passage:

"[I]f a tenant takes a house which is of such a kind that by its own inherent nature it will in course of time fall into a particular condition, the effects of that result are not within the tenant's covenant to repair."

He went on to say that:

"[T]he builder placed a platform of timber on this muddy soil, and built the house upon it. That is the nature of this house. Whatever happens by natural causes to such a house in the course of time—the effects of natural causes upon such a house in the course of time—are 'results from time and nature which fall upon the landlord', and they are not a breach of the covenant to repair. They are matters which must be taken into account in considering whether the covenant to repair has been broken, and, when they are the results of time and nature operating on such a house, they are not a breach of the covenant and the tenant is not bound to do anything with regard to them."

Kay L.J. said:

"[R]egard must be had to the character of the house to which the covenant applies ... the lessee ... is not liable under his covenant for damage which accrued from such a radical defect in the original structure."

The above passages must be read in the light of the facts with which the court was dealing. The remedial work in question involved substantially reconstructing the entire house. The decision of the court was that this went beyond the covenant.

The same conclusion, i.e. that work involving the substantial reconstruction of old premises goes beyond the covenant, has been reached in a number of subsequent cases. Thus, in *Torrens v Walker*,[69] the front and back walls of a house were taken down by the local authority as being dangerous structures. The building was about 200 years old. The tenant brought proceedings against the landlord, who had covenanted to keep the outside of the premises in good and substantial repair. Warrington J. found the following facts:

**11–17**

"[T]he building in question ... was absolutely worn out and had come to the end of its time. Its condition was not due to any neglect on the part of the lessor, but to the effect of time and the elements on the materials used. It was found on the survey that the front wall was beyond repair; nothing could be done to make it safe without rebuilding. The bricks had come to such a state that they could not be used again, and the mortar was perished to such an extent that the

---

[68] 3rd edn, p.302.
[69] [1906] 2 Ch. 166.

whole of the wall above the first floor, *i.e.* the whole front wall of the demised premises, really consisted of nothing but a heap of dry bricks. The back wall, being of much smaller extent, was not in such bad condition, parts of it might have been preserved, but I find as a fact that the whole of the back wall above the level of the second floor would have had to be rebuilt, and it is very probable that when the work was begun it would be found necessary to rebuild both walls lower down, even below the level of the first floor. I find therefore as a fact that ... repairing the building, in the ordinary sense, was impossible. Nothing could be done but rebuild. It was not merely that rebuilding was the course which a prudent owner would have adopted as the best but it was the only practicable course to make the building stand."

He went on to hold that the landlord was not liable.

**11–18**  A similar case is *Sotheby v Grundy*,[70] in which the main walls of a house were built in 1861, contrary to the Metropolitan Building Act 1855, without, or on defective, footings and on made-up ground. In 1944 the walls were bulged, fractured and overhanging and were demolished by the local authority under statutory powers. The evidence showed that the only way this could have been avoided was by underpinning, which would have involved shoring up, removing the foundations and constructing new foundations. Lynskey J. held that the tenant was not liable. Having quoted Lord Esher in *Lister v Lane*,[71] he said:

"That raises the question whether it can be said that this was a building which, by its own inherent nature would, in the course of time, fall into a particular condition. I am sure that is so, but the matter does not end there, because ... it seems to me that it must be a question of degree in each case. It may be that the inherent nature of a building may result in its partial collapse. One can visualise the floor of a building collapsing, owing to defective joists having been put in. I do not think *Lister v. Lane* would be applicable to such a case. In those circumstances, in my opinion, the damage would fall within the ambit of the covenant to repair, but, as I say, it must be a question of degree in each particular case ... [The necessary work in the present case] would, in effect, be asking the tenant to give the landlord something different in kind from that which had been demised. The premises demised here were premises with insecure foundations. What the tenant would have had to do would be to put in a new foundation which would alter the nature and extent of the property demised, turning a building which, as originally constructed, would not last more than some 80 odd years into a building that would last for probably another 100 years.

In my view, that does not come within the purview of the repairing covenant in question here. If the landlord desired to obtain such rights, he ought to have made it clear in the lease, so that the tenant would know that he was undertaking an obligation, not merely to repair, maintain and support the existing building demised, but also to make good original defects in the premises as erected. The expenses claimed were incurred because of the inherent nature of the defect in the premises and do not come within the terms of the covenant contained in the lease."

It is apparent from the beginning of this passage that the mere fact that an old building will "by its own inherent nature" fall into a particular condition does not mean that the work necessary to remedy such condition cannot be repair. Instead, as the judge makes clear, the matter is one of fact and degree in each case.

*Lister v Lane* was relied on again in *Pembery v Lamdin*.[72] In that case a shop and underground basement were demised by a lease containing a covenant by the landlord to "keep the external part of the demised premises (other than the shop front) in good and tenantable repair and condition". The premises were at least

---

[70] [1947] 2 All E.R. 761.
[71] [1893] 2 Q.B. 212.
[72] [1940] 2 All E.R. 434.

100 years old, and had been built without any form of waterproofing for the basement. Water was penetrating into the basement and the walls were saturated. The tenant contended that the landlord was liable to carry out works to remedy this. The works included asphalting the walls, building a new 4.5in wall inside to keep the asphalt in position, and laying a new concrete floor about 4in thick to prevent water coming under the walls. The Court of Appeal held that the landlord was not liable. Slesser L.J. said:

"The first question which arises in this case is what was the nature of the obligation to repair. In order to ascertain that, it is first necessary to consider the nature of the premises which had to be repaired under the covenant. I think that, for the purposes of this case, the principle, which has never been doubted, is to be found stated in a short passage in a judgment of Lord Esher M.R. in *Lister v. Lane* ... if the counterclaim here made by Mrs Lamdin be correct, she is entitled to receive at the hands of this landlord a 'different thing' from that which she took when she entered into the covenant. She took this old house with a cellar without any waterproof protection, and she is asking the landlord so to repair that house as to give her a cellar which has a waterproof protection and is dry. That is not a right which she can possibly maintain, because the obligation of the landlord is to repair that which is demised, and not to give her something much drier in its nature than that which was demised ... [the premises] have to be kept in repair in the condition of the house when it was demised, according to the character of the house."

Lord Esher's judgment in *Lister v Lane* was also relied on in *Collins v Flynn*.[73] A **11–19** house was built on inadequate foundations. Part of the rear main wall was supported by a girder which was in turn carried by a pier. Settlement caused by the inadequate foundations resulted in the pier sinking and consequential movement and fractures in the rear wall. The requisite remedial work involved rebuilding the pier and rear and side wall with newly designed foundations and footings. Sir Brett Cloutman, the Official Referee, held that the tenant was not liable.[74] He held that the work was:

"[M]anifestly a most important improvement, which if executed by the tenant, would involve him in rendering up the premises in different condition from that in which they were demised, and on the authority of Lord Esher M.R. in *Lister v. Lane*, I do not think that the tenant is under any such obligation."

Some of the statements of principle in the above cases, particularly those of Tindall C.J. in *Gutteridge v Munyard*[75] and Lord Esher M.R. in *Lister v Lane*,[76] appear to indicate that as a matter of law the remedying of defects caused by the inevitable effect of time and weather on an old building are not within the ambit of a covenant to repair. It is clear, however, from *Lurcott v Wakely*[77] (in which the relevant authorities were considered by the Court of Appeal) that there is no such principle. In that case Cozens-Hardy M.R. said of *Gutteridge v Munyard*:

---

[73] [1963] 2 All E.R. 1068.
[74] It should be noted that in *Ravenseft Properties Ltd v Davstone (Holdings) Ltd* [1980] Q.B. 12, Forbes J. held that Sir Brett Cloutman in *Collins v Flynn* had misdirected himself on the ratio decidendi of *Sotheby v Grundy*, [1947] 2 All E.R. 761, and therefore that the case was "of doubtful authority".
[75] (1834) 1 Moo. & R. 334. See para.11–15, above.
[76] [1893] 2 Q.B. 212. See para.11–16, above.
[77] [1911] 1 K.B. 905.

"I certainly am not prepared to assent to the view that 'what the natural operation of time flowing on effects, and all that the elements bring about in diminishing the value, constitute a loss which, so far as it results from time and nature, falls upon the landlord.' That is obviously too wide. If he only meant to say that, given an old house which in the course of the term, though still a habitable house, is rendered worse by mere lapse of time and the effects of wind and weather, the loss falls on the landlord, I should not object to the statement; but if it is be made use of as [counsel] sought to make use of it, as meaning that the tenant is not liable for anything which can be said to be due to the lapse of time and the elements, I respectfully do not assent to it, and it seems to me to be plainly inconsistent with the subsequent authorities.
... when I come to what I should have thought was everyday experience in cases of this kind, when I come to consider what is to happen when by reason of the elements acting on an old building, say, a chimney stack is blown down, is it possible for the tenant to say he is not liable to put that up because the collapse was due merely to age and the elements? I am astonished to hear that such a contention can be raised. So, if a tenant under a repairing lease finds that a floor has become so rotten that it cannot be patched up, that it is in such a condition that it cannot bear the weight of human beings or of furniture upon it, can it be said that the tenant is exempt from the liability of replacing that floor, and repairing it in the only way in which it can be repaired in order to make the house habitable, merely because the state of the floor is due to time and the elements? I am entirely unable to follow that argument. *Proudfoot v. Hart*[78] seems to lay down a perfectly sound and intelligible proposition on this point, namely, that in such a case it is the duty of the tenant, if he cannot patch up the floor so as to make it a floor, to replace that which is no longer a floor by something which is a floor."

He explained *Lister v Lane*[79] and *Torrens v Walker*[80] as being cases where:

"[T]he change of circumstances which had arisen could not have been in the contemplation of the parties and that it would not be reasonable to construe the covenant to repair as applicable to that change of circumstances."

He went on to express the proper question as being:

"[W]hether what has happened is of such a nature that it can fairly be said that the character of the subject matter of the demise, or part of the demise, has been changed."

**11–20**    In the same case, Buckley L.J. said of *Gutteridge v Munyard*[81]:

"Every decay which is the subject of repair is effected by the operation of the lapse of time and the elements diminishing the value. Decay always results from time and nature. Of course the Chief Justice did not mean his words to be understood as meaning that all decay is to be borne by the landlord. They are words which follow upon a sentence in which he was speaking of a building of a particular character, namely, a very old building, and was negativing the argument that the old building was, under the operation of a covenant to repair, to be converted into a new one."

He dealt with the dictum of Lord Esher M.R. in *Lister v Lane*[82] in the following terms:

"Now every house is of such a kind that by its own inherent nature it will in the course of time fall into a particular condition. Lord Esher did not, of course, mean that decay is in every case not within the tenant's covenant to repair. The context shows that he did not mean that."

---

[78] (1890) 25 Q.B.D. 42.
[79] [1893] 2 Q.B. 212. See para.11–16 above.
[80] [1906] 2 Ch. 166. See para.11–17 above.
[81] (1834) 1 Moo. & R. 334. See para.11–15, above.
[82] [1893] 2 Q.B. 212. See para.11–16, above.

He explained the cases on the following footing:

"If repair be understood in the sense which I suggest, the authorities are not, I think, difficult. In *Gutteridge v. Munyard*[83] the building was a very old building, and the finding of the jury under the directions of Tindal C.J. only involved that the tenants had substantially kept the building such as it was in repair, although they had not improved it. *Lister v. Lane*[84] and *Wright v. Lawson*[85] were cases in which the buildings could not by any repair be brought into their original condition. In *Lister v. Lane* the only thing that could be done was, not to replace the old timber platform, but to support the house entirely anew by walls carried down another 17 feet to the subjacent gravel. That would not be repairing such a house as was there in question, namely, a house whose foundations were timbers lying on oozy soil, but providing a new house in the sense that its foundations would be on the gravel. In *Wright v. Lawson* the bay window could not be replaced, supported as it must have been before by cantilevers, but could be reproduced only by that which would be a new structure, namely, a bay window supported by vertical supports from the ground.

*Torrens v. Walker* was a case in which the covenant was to keep the outside of the premises in repair. The house was triangular in form at the junction of two streets. The pulling down amounted to a demolition of substantially the whole subject matter of the covenant. In these circumstances the finding of the learned judge was justified, that repairing the building, or, as I prefer to say, repairing the subject matter of the covenant, namely, the outside of the premises, was impossible, and that nothing could be done but rebuild. The learned judge found in that case that the act to be done was not one of renewal or replacement of a subsidiary part, but substantially a rebuilding of the whole subject matter of the covenant. All the cases, to my mind, come only to this, that the question is one of degree."

Likewise, in the New Zealand case of *Weatherhead v Deka New Zealand Ltd*,[86] the Court of Appeal of New Zealand, in upholding the arbitrators' conclusion that major works to an old structure which was fundamentally unsound were not within the tenant's repairing obligations under the lease, treated the question as one of fact and degree.

The true explanation of the cases on old buildings is therefore not that the work went beyond repair because the defect was the inevitable result of time and weather upon an old building, but that as a matter of fact and degree, the work was too extensive to amount to repair. There is therefore no separate rule relating to old buildings. The question is one of fact and degree in every case, and the age of the premises and the inevitability or otherwise of the defect are simply factors to be taken into account.

## New buildings

One of the formulations of the fact and degree test in the cases is whether the necessary work would involve giving back to the landlord something different in character.[87] This involves comparing the premises in the state in which they were when demised and the state in which they will be on completion of the remedial work.[88] However, the position is not necessarily the same where the premises are newly built. In that event, depending on the facts, the relevant comparison may be

**11–21**

---

[83] (1834) 1 Moo. & R. 334. See para.11–15, above.
[84] [1893] 2 Q.B. 212. See para.11–16, above.
[85] (1903) 19 T.L.R. 510. The facts are set out in para.11–33, below.
[86] [2000] 1 N.Z.L.R. 23. The facts are set out in para.11–24, below.
[87] See paras 11–09 to 11–11, above.
[88] See paras 11–09 to 11–11 above.

between the state in which the parties contemplated the premises were at the date of the lease and their state after completion of the work.

The above is suggested by the decision of the Court of Appeal in *Smedley v Chumley & Hawke Ltd.*[89] That case concerned a restaurant and other buildings built in 1971. The restaurant was built very near to the River Bure. It was a timber-framed building constructed on a concrete raft. The raft was supported at the river end on piles sunk into the river bank. There were no piles at the other end. It was let on December 31, 1971, for 21 years. The landlords covenanted:

> "To keep the main walls and roof in good structural repair and condition throughout the term and to promptly make good all defects due to faulty materials or workmanship in the construction of the premises."

By about 1976 the end of the raft furthest from the river was sinking into the ground so that the raft was tilting, with consequential damage to the structure of the walls and roof. The remedial work consisted of jacking up the building and the raft, driving in additional piles to support the raft, placing joists upon the piles and then lowering the building and the raft down on to the joists. The Court of Appeal held that the work was the liability of the landlords under their covenant. Cumming Bruce L.J., who gave the leading judgment, said:

> "The argument [for the landlords] is put in two ways. There is a long line of authority to the effect that where a tenant is liable to keep in repair, he is not liable to do work that has the effect of giving the landlord a different and better house than the house that was let. Counsel for the landlords ... relied upon *Lister v. Lane,*[90] *Pembery v. Lamdin,*[91] *Sotheby v. Grundy*[92] and *Brew Bros. Limited v. Snax (Ross) Limited.*[93]
>
> I make two observations upon those cases. It is important to distinguish the obligations where the lessor has let to the lessee an old house which has gradually deteriorated, through the inevitable effect of the passage of time, from the extent of the obligations imposed in connection with a lease of premises recently constructed. Many of the old cases are concerned with the former situation and do not assist in the analysis of the latter situation. Secondly, in order to discover whether there is an obligation to do work made necessary in order to correct the effect of defects in design, it is necessary to examine carefully the whole lease and to decide the intention to be collected therefrom, and in this lease the intention was to place upon the landlords an unqualified obligation to keep the walls and roof in good structural condition.
>
> Then it was contended that the work required to make the walls and roof safe was such that it involved an improvement to the premises and rendered the premises different premises from the parcels demised. Those parcels were, it is said, premises with defective foundations, so designed that the base on which the walls were built were bound to tilt over in four, or five years ... It was contended on behalf of the landlords that the test whether the effect of the works was to render the premises something different from the premises conveyed is to be applied by comparing the physical state of the premises as they were at the date of the lease with their physical state after the work had been done.
>
> I prefer to compare the premises contemplated by the parties at the date of the lease with the premises as changed by the works actually done ... the only difference [after the works] was that the structure of walls and roof were stable and safe upon foundations made structurally stable ... [The] emphasis upon structure [in the covenant] is significant, because the structural condition of walls and roof is likely to depend on their foundations. So here I would hold that

---

[89]  (1981) 44 P. & C.R. 50.
[90]  [1893] 2 Q.B. 212.
[91]  [1940] 2 All E.R. 434.
[92]  [1947] 2 All E.R. 761.
[93]  [1970] 1 Q.B. 612.

after the works were done the difference to the premises was that the walls and roof were in the condition that both parties contemplated as their necessary condition at the date of the lease."

The above approach was applied by Lindsay J. in *Credit Suisse v Beegas Nominees Ltd*[94] in relation to a covenant to repair and otherwise keep the structure of a newly constructed office and residential building in good and tenantable condition.[95] He held that the condition in question was not the actual condition at the date of the lease but the condition which a reasonably-minded tenant of the class likely to take the building at the date of the lease would have required (the "putative condition").[96]     **11–22**

On the face of it, this approach is quite different from the approach discussed above in relation to old buildings. Where what is let is a new or nearly new building, the parties will virtually always contemplate that it will be structurally sound. It would follow that any work necessary to make it structurally sound would be within the covenant, no matter how extensive. However, it is thought that *Smedley v Chumley & Hawke Ltd*[97] is not to be read as going this far. First, the property had been built by the landlords, so that there is nothing surprising or unfair in their covenant being construed as, in effect, a warranty that they had built it properly. Second, the covenant was widely drafted. The obligation was to keep the premises in good structural condition as well as repair. The reference to faulty materials or workmanship in the construction of the premises supports the view that the parties had in mind the condition of the building as it ought to have been as opposed to whatever its actual condition may have been. All this suggests that the parties intended the landlord to take full responsibility for the structural condition of the building. It is to be noted that in *Ladbroke Hotels Ltd v Sandhu*[98] Robert Walker J. suggested that the Court of Appeal in *Smedley* construed the covenant as imposing liability for the relevant work in order to avoid a harsh result in circumstances where the landlord was personally responsible for the defective state of the building.

## The condition of the premises at the date of the lease

As appears above, the state of the building when the lease is granted is a relevant factor when applying the fact and degree test.[99] It will be of greater or lesser weight depending on the circumstances. In general terms, however, if at the date of the lease the building is in a reasonable state, it may be easier to conclude that work becoming necessary during the term was intended by the parties to be the tenant's liability than if the premises were already suffering from the defect in     **11–23**

---

[94] [1994] 4 All E.R. 803 and (more fully) [1994] 1 E.G.L.R. 76.
[95] The covenant is set out in para.4–28, above.
[96] See further para.9–26, above.
[97] (1981) 44 P. & C.R. 50.
[98] [1995] 2 E.G.L.R. 92.
[99] See *Brew Bros Ltd v Snax (Ross) Ltd* [1970] 1 Q.B. 612, per Sachs L.J.; *Holding & Management Ltd v Property Holding & Investment Trust Ltd* [1990] 1 E.G.L.R. 65 (not reported on this point at [1989] 1 W.L.R. 1313); *Plough Investments Ltd v Manchester City Council* [1989] 1 E.G.L.R. 244; *Eyre v McCracken* (2000) 80 P. & C.R. 220; *Gibson Investments Ltd v Chesterton Plc (No.1)* [2002] 2 P. & C.R. 32.

question. The converse is equally true. For example, the Court of Appeal in *Brew Bros Ltd v Snax (Ross) Ltd*,[100] in holding that the remedial work went beyond repair,[101] appears to have been influenced to a considerable extent by the fact that the remedial work was already necessary at the date of the demise. Nothing the tenant could have done on becoming tenant would have prevented the subsequent filling of the flank wall which was the cause of all the trouble. Similarly, in *Eyre v McCracken*[102] the Court of Appeal, in holding that the tenant was not liable to install a damp-proof course, took into account the fact that there was no damp-proof course when the property was built or demised.

It is necessary to emphasise, however, that the condition of the building when the lease was granted is only one aspect of the fact and degree test. The fact that the defect existed at the date of the lease is not conclusive in favour of the view that to remedy it would go beyond repair. Moreover, there will be cases in which the relevant consideration will not be the actual condition of the building at the date of the lease but its "putative" condition (i.e. the condition which the parties contemplated that it was in).[103]

**11–24**     In some cases the lease may expressly require regard to be had to the condition of the premises at the date of the demise.[104] Thus, in the New Zealand case of *Weatherhead v Deka New Zealand Ltd*,[105] a lease of retail premises granted in 1980 for 40 years obliged the tenant to repair and keep the premises in good and substantial repair and condition "having regard to the condition thereof at the commencement of the term reasonable wear and tear only excepted". The demised building included a two storey brick structure, originally built as a stand-alone warehouse in 1914, which had become a serious earthquake risk by reason of deterioration of the structural concrete bands running through the walls, the consequent rusting of the steel reinforcing and the erosion of the mortar. The deterioration had commenced when the structure was built in 1914. Very substantial deterioration would already have taken place when the lease was granted in 1980, both in terms of the decay to the concrete and the loosening of the mortar. The structure was fundamentally unsound and could only be made sound by undertaking major works. The cost of repairing the structure would come close to the cost of replacing it with a new building. The Court of Appeal upheld the conclusion of the arbitrators appointed to determine the matter that the work was outside the covenant. Thomas J., giving the judgment of the court, said:

> "Approaching the issue as a question of degree, therefore, there was ample evidence to support the arbitrators' findings of fact. The inherent defects in the building at the commencement of the lease, the structural character of the work required, and the nature and extent of the work necessary to remedy those defects are all matters pointing strongly to the conclusion that the words in [the repairing covenant] giving rise to the lessee's obligation were not appropriate to

---

[100] [1970] 1 Q.B. 612.
[101] The facts are set out in para.11–29, below.
[102] Above.
[103] See paras 11–21 to 11–22, above.
[104] Covenants to repair by reference to the condition of the premises at the date of the lease are considered in para.14–13 et seq., below.
[105] [2000] 1 N.Z.L.R. 23.

describe the work required. Indeed, it does not seem to us that the arbitrators were wide of the mark in stating that, if the work was carried out by a lessee, it would effectively give the lessors a 'windfall'"

## The prospective life of the premises

It is relevant to consider what effect the works will have on the prospective life of the premises.[106] If the work will result in that life being substantially extended then it may be held to go beyond repair. Thus, in *McDougall v Easington District Council*,[107] Mustill L.J. said:

> "The outcome [of the works] was a house with a substantially longer life and worth nearly twice as much as before. Acknowledging that repairs, properly so called, inevitably involve an element of renewal or improvement, I still think it clear that the learned recorder was right to hold that these could not be described as repairs. They gave the building new life in a different form."

**11–25**

## The length of the lease

The longer the lease, the easier it will be to conclude that substantial work is within the ambit of the covenant to repair. Thus, in *Gibson Investments Ltd v Chesterton Plc*[108] Neuberger J. said:

> "In construing the covenant one relevant factor is the length of the lease, and the present lease is one for a relatively long term of 33 years."

**11–26**

In *Norwich Union Life Assurance Society Ltd v British Railways Board*[109] Hoffmann J. took into account the length of the lease in construing the covenant as imposing on the tenant a liability going beyond repair. He said in the course of his judgment:

> "This is ... a lease for a term of 150 years, and it seems to me that in such a case it is not as inconceivable as it would have been in *Lister v Lane* that the tenant should have accepted an obligation to rebuild the premises when they come to the end of their natural life."

Equally, the fact that the lease is short may be a relevant factor in deciding that the tenant is not liable for particular work.[110] In *Fitzpatrick v Exel Holdings*[111] Mr Recorder Michael Black QC (sitting as a judge of the Technology and Construction Court) said:

---

[106] *McDougall v Easington District Council* (1989) 58 P. & C.R. 201; *Holding & Management Ltd v Property Holding & Investment Trust Ltd* [1990] 1 E.G.L.R. 65 (not reported on this point at [1989] 1 W.L.R. 1313).
[107] Above.
[108] [2002] 2 P. & C.R. 32.
[109] [1987] 2 E.G.L.R. 137.
[110] *Eyre v McCracken* [2000] 80 P. & C.R. 220. (residential lease for seven-and-a-quarter years); *Fitzpatrick v Exel Holdings* (unreported decision of Mr Recorder Michael Black QC, sitting as a judge of the Technology and Construction Court, July 16, 2008) (commercial sub-underlease for 18 months).
[111] See above. The facts are set out in para.24–07, below.

"It was held to be significant in *Gibson* that the term was a long one. It must be equally significant if the term were a very short one, such as in the present case. Having said that however, I think it is misleading to look at the term in the present case of 18 months and the rent of £129,500 per annum and say, "How can a tenant who is to pay a total of less than £200,000 throughout the entire term have agreed to be potentially liable for more than twice that sum by way of dilapidations? That is to use hindsight as an aid to construction, particularly in the absence of evidence as to market rents at the date of the lease, the state of the premises at that time and the reasonably foreseeable costs of repair."

It has been said that once disrepair is proved, the weight that can properly be given to the length of the lease is not large.[112] However, greater weight may be given to the length of the term in cases where the landlord's costs of repair are recoverable from the tenant by way of service charge.[113]

## The interest of the covenantor

**11–27**   The interest held by the covenantor is a relevant factor in deciding whether particular work is work of repair.[114] Thus, it has been said that for the purposes of deciding whether particular work is within the covenant, there is a "relevant difference between the limited interest of a tenant and the interest of a landlord".[115] Thus, for example, in *Eyre v McCracken*[116] it was held that a tenant under a lease granted for seven-and-a-quarter years was not liable as a matter of fact and degree to install a damp proof course where none had existed before. This is to be contrasted with *Elmcroft Developments Ltd v Tankersley-Sawyer*,[117] in which the contrary conclusion was reached in the case of a landlord.[118]

## The nature of the defect sought to be remedied

**11–28**   In applying the fact and degree test, regard must be had to the nature of the defect to be remedied. However, the fact that the defect is "inherent", in the sense that it is the result of the way the building was designed or constructed, will not prevent the remedial work from constituting repair provided that it can properly be so described as a matter of fact and degree.[119] The cause or origin of the defect will not generally be relevant.[120]

---

[112]   *Post Office v Aquarius Properties Ltd* [1987] 1 All E.R. 1055, per Ralph Gibson L.J.

[113]   See *Holding & Management Ltd v Property Holding & Investment Trust Ltd* [1990] 1 E.G.L.R. 65 per Nicholls L.J. (not reported on this point at [1989] 1 W.L.R. 1313); *Scottish Mutual Assurance Plc v Jardine Public Relations Ltd* [1999] E.G.C.S. 43; *Fluor Daniel Properties Ltd v Shortlands Investments Ltd* [2001] 2 E.G.L.R. 103. See further paras 10–08 to 10–10, above.

[114]   *Eyre v McCracken* [1999] 80 P. & C.R. 220.

[115]   Above.

[116]   Above.

[117]   [1984] 1 E.G.L.R. 47.

[118]   See further on these cases paras 12–31 to 12–34, below.

[119]   See paras 11–02 to 11–03, above.

[120]   See para.9–28, above.

## The nature of the remedial work

For the purposes of deciding whether the work can properly be described as repair as a matter of fact and degree,[121] the work must, as a general rule, be looked at as a whole and not as a series of separate operations. Thus, in *Brew Bros Ltd v Snax (Ross) Ltd*,[122] a building constructed in about 1937 was let on June 24, 1965, for 14 years on a lease containing a tenant's repairing covenant. Seepage from drains, which had been defective for many years, together with the removal of a large tree in the pavement outside the property, caused the foundations to move and the flank wall to tilt towards neighbouring premises. The owners of those premises brought an action against the landlords and the tenant claiming that the condition of the wall constituted a nuisance. The landlords contended that the tenant was responsible for the necessary remedial work, which comprised the repair of the foundations; the rebuilding of the wall; and the repair of the drains. One of the questions before the Court of Appeal was whether these operations had to be looked at together or separately. Harman L.J. held that the latter was the right approach, and went on to hold the tenant liable for the repair of the drain and the rebuilding of the wall, but not for the work to the foundations. Sachs and Phillimore L.JJ., however, took the contrary view and held that the work had to be looked at as a whole, and that, so regarded, it was not repair. Likewise, in *Postel Properties Ltd v Boots the Chemist*,[123] Ian Kennedy J. said in the course of his judgment:

11–29

> "Whether I look at each item individually or, as I believe I should, at the replacement of the roof covering as a whole, I reach the same conclusion."

It is thought that the above approach (that of the majority in *Brew Bros*) will generally only be appropriate in relation to work which (like the work in that case and in *Postel*), stems from the same defect and which is intended to remedy that defect. It is less clear whether it would be right to apply it where the work consists of a large number of items all of which are unconnected with each other. For example, a terminal schedule of dilapidations may contain 100 items of alleged repair relating to various different parts of the building, including the replacement of a small quantity of cracked or slipped slates. It is thought that the latter item would constitute repair on any view, and nonetheless so because it is included in amongst numerous other items. It may be, however, that where a substantial number of items of work are needed, all of which when viewed individually amount to repair, but which together will change the character of the building, then the right approach will be to look at the items as a whole.

### (a)  *Work which involves renewal of part*

The necessary remedial work may, and frequently will, involve the complete renewal of subsidiary parts of the subject matter of the covenant. Viewed in

11–30

---

[121]  See para.11–04 et seq., above.
[122]  [1970] 1 Q.B. 612.
[123]  [1996] 2 E.G.L.R. 60.

isolation, those parts will not have been repaired but replaced in their entirety. However, there has never been any doubt that a covenant to repair may require the renewal of a whole part, such as a floor, a door or a window.[124] At some point on the scale between this and complete replacement of the entirety of the subject matter, the work will cease to be repair. When that point is reached is a question of fact and degree.

The leading case is *Lurcott v Wakely*.[125] A house was demised in 1881 for 28 years from March 25, 1881, on a lease containing a tenant's covenant to "well and substantially repair ... and keep in thorough repair and good condition" the premises. The house was at least 200 years old. One of the outside walls got into a dangerous condition and in 1909 the local authority served a statutory notice requiring it to be taken down to the level of the ground floor. The landlord did the work. Subsequently, in compliance with a further statutory notice, he pulled down the rest of it and rebuilt it with concrete foundations and damp courses in accordance with the requirements of the London Building Act 1894. He then sought to recover the cost from the tenant by way of damages for breach of the tenant's covenant to repair.

At first instance the Official Referee found that the condition of the wall was caused by old age and lapse of time, and it could not have been repaired without rebuilding it. He held that the tenant was liable. His decision was upheld in the Court of Appeal. Buckley L.J. said in a well-known passage:

> "'Repair' and 'renew' are not words expressive of a clear contrast. Repair always involves renewal; renewal of a part; of a subordinate part. A skylight leaks; repair is effected by hacking out the putties, putting in new ones, and renewing the paint. A roof falls out of repair, the necessary work is to replace the decayed timbers by sound wood; to substitute sound tiles or slates for those which are cracked, broken, or missing; to make good the flashings, and the like. Part of a garden wall tumbles down, repair is effected by building it up again with new mortar, and, so far as necessary, new bricks or stone. Renewal, as distinguished from repair, is reconstruction of the entirety, meaning by the entirety not necessarily the whole but substantially the whole subject matter under discussion. I agree that if repair of the whole subject matter has become impossible a covenant to repair does not carry an obligation to renew or replace. That has been affirmed by *Lister v Lane*[126] and *Wright v Lawson*.[127] But if that which I have said is accurate, it follows that the question of repair is in every case one of degree, and the test is whether the act to be done is one which in substance is the renewal or replacement of defective parts, or the renewal or replacement of substantially the whole.
> ... All the cases, to my mind, come only to this, that the question is one of degree, and what we have to look to in the present case is to see whether the Official Referee in his findings of fact has treated the front wall of this house as being a subsidiary part of a larger structure, or has regarded the necessary operations as amounting to substantially a re-erection of the house ... here [the house] requires a new wall. When it has got its new wall it will not be a new house; it will be the old house put into repair in the sense that there has been renewed or replaced a worn-out subordinate part of the whole."

**11–31** Cozens-Hardy M.R. said:

> "[I]n many cases repair necessarily involves, not repair strictly so called, but renewal. If an earthenware pipe breaks, you can only repair it by renewing it. Or again, if window frames become rotten and decayed, you cannot repair them except by renewing; and many other

---

[124] *Post Office v Aquarius Properties Ltd* [1987] 1 All E.R. 1055, per Ralph Gibson L.J. at 1064f.
[125] [1911] 1 K.B. 905.
[126] [1893] 2 Q.B. 212.
[127] (1903) 19 T.L.R. 510.

instances might be given.

> … it seems to me that we are driven to ask in this particular case, and in every case of this kind, is what has happened of such a nature that it can fairly be said that the character of the subject-matter of the demise, or part of the demise, in question has been changed? Is it something which goes to the whole, or substantially the whole, or is it simply an injury to a portion, to a subsidiary portion, to use Buckley L.J.'s phrase, of the demised property? … this portion of the wall, 24 feet in front, is merely a subsidiary portion of the demised premises, the restoration of this wall leaving the rest of the building, which goes back more than 100 feet, untouched. The restoration of this wall will not change the character or nature of the building, and I am unable to say that the question differs in any way from that which we should have had to consider if by reason of the elements and lapse of time, say, some rafters in the roof had become rotten, and a corner of the roof gave way so that water came in."

Fletcher Moulton L.J.'s judgment was to the same effect:

> "For my own part, when the word 'repair' is applied to a complex matter like a house, I have no doubt that the repair includes the replacement of parts. Of course, if a house had tumbled down, or was down, the word 'repair' could not be used to cover rebuilding. It would not be apt to describe such an operation. But, so long as the house exists as a structure, the question whether repair means replacement, or, to use the phrase so common in marine cases, substituting new for old, does not seem to me to be at all material. Many, and in fact most, repairs imply that some portion of the total fabric is renewed, that new is put in place of old. Therefore you have from time to time as things need repair to put new for old. If you properly repair as you go along the consequence will be that you will always get a house which will be in repair and usable as a house, but you will not get a house that does not suffer from age, nor a house which when old is the same as it was when it was new."

The decision in *Lurcott v Wakely* should be contrasted with that in *Brew Bros Ltd v Snax (Ross) Ltd*,[128] which concerned liability for the repair of foundations, the rebuilding of a flank wall and the repair of drains.[129] Harman L.J. held that the rebuilding of the flank wall amounted to repair on the ground that:

> "The wall was, though large, a subsidiary portion of the building. After its repair it was just the same kind of wall as it was before, and the fact that the lower courses of bricks were, owing to modern building regulations, 13.5 inches instead of nine inches in thickness is not such an alteration in the character of the wall as to make it a new thing."

However, Sachs and Phillimore L.JJ. held that, looked at as a matter of degree, the entirety of the work (i.e. the repair of the foundations, the rebuilding of the flank wall and the repair of the drains) was not within the tenant's covenant. The latter analysed the "vital question" as being:

> "[W]hether the total work to be done can properly be described as repair since it involves no more than renewal or replacement of defective parts, or whether it is in effect renewal or replacement of substantially the whole. It is … a question of degree in each case."

Examples of a complete replacement of part of the subject-matter of the covenant being held to constitute repair are to be found in *Elite Investments Ltd v TI Bainbridge (Silencers) Ltd (No.2)*[130] (in which a covenant to repair an industrial building was held to require the replacement of the roof); *Roper v Prudential*

**11–32**

---

[128] [1970] 1 Q.B. 612.

[129] See further on this case para.11–29, above.

[130] [1986] 2 E.G.L.R. 43. This case should be contrasted with *Riverside Property Investments v Blackhawk Automotive* [2005] 1 E.G.L.R. 114 and *Carmel Southend v Strachan & Henshaw* [2007] 3

*Assurance Co Ltd*[131] (in which an obligation to repair maintain and keep in good and substantial repair order and condition a farmhouse, cottages and farm buildings was held to cover replacing the electrical wiring of the farmhouse); and *Minja Properties Ltd v Cussins Property Group Plc*[132] (where a landlord's covenant to maintain and keep in good and tenantable repair various parts of an office building, including the window frames, was held to extend to the replacement of defective metal-framed windows with double-glazed units). In the last case, Harman J. said that the authorities:

> "[E]stablish that it is beyond question that renewing a part of a building by replacing it is within the obligation of a covenant to repair that thing; though you are not, to use a different word, 'patching up' and leaving there the original thing with some bits added to it, but taking out the original thing and putting in a new one, that is 'repair', so long, always, as one is dealing with only part of the whole structure."

It was argued in *Post Office v Aquarius Properties Ltd*[133] that Hoffmann J. at first instance (who had held that the remedial work went beyond repair[134]) had misapplied the fact and degree test by failing to give proper weight to the fact that the work was to a subordinate part of the building only. In rejecting that criticism, Ralph Gibson L.J. (with whom Sir Roger Ormrod agreed) said:

> "The relationship of the part on which work is required to the whole of the subject matter of the demise is ... a question of proportion and degree. At one end of the scale there has never been any doubt that a party liable under a covenant to repair may have to renew in effect a whole part such as a floor, or a door, or a window ... I do not accept, however, that it is only open to the court to hold that work involves giving back a wholly different thing if it is possible to say that the whole subject matter of the demise, or a whole building within the subject matter of the demise, will by the work be made different."

It should be noted that the covenant may on its proper construction impose a liability which goes beyond repair and extends to complete replacement of the entirety of the subject matter.[135] In such a case, no question will arise as to whether such work is repair as a matter of fact and degree, because it will be covered by the express obligation to replace.

### (b)  Work which involves replacement with something different

**11–33**    Where the point has been reached at which the covenantor is obliged to replace a particular item of building fabric or plant in its entirety, the extent to which he is required or entitled to do more than merely replace it with an exact replica of the original is likewise a question of fact and degree. The relevant considerations are discussed elsewhere.[136]

---

E.G.L.R. 15, in both of which it was held that patch repairs were sufficient to comply with the tenant's obligations in relation to the roof. See further para.12–07 et seq., below.

[131]   [1992] 1 E.G.L.R. 5.
[132]   [1998] 2 E.G.L.R. 52.
[133]   [1987] 1 All E.R. 1055.
[134]   The facts are set out in para.11–34, below.
[135]   See paras 4–25 to 4–28 above, and para.11–44 to 11–45, below.
[136]   See Ch.10, paras 10–12 to 10–14, above, and Ch.13, paras 13–07 to 13–08, below.

## (c)    Work which involves structural alterations or additions

The remedial work may involve major structural alterations or additions to the original building, the effect of which may be to produce something different in kind from what existed before. In such a case, the work may be held to go beyond repair. Thus, in *Pembery v Lamdin*[137] it was held that the works necessary to waterproof a basement, which included asphalting the walls, building a new 4.5in wall inside to keep the asphalt in position, and laying a new concrete floor about 4in thick to prevent water coming under the walls, went beyond repair. The same conclusion was reached in *Post Office v Aquarius Properties Ltd*,[138] which concerned an office building built in the mid-1960s. The "kicker" joint between the walls and the floor of the basement had been defectively constructed with the result that when the level of the water-table rose, the basement was ankle-deep in water. Various waterproofing schemes were before the court. Common to all was the making of a substantial structural addition to the basement in the form of a new concrete slab with reinforcement to the upper side, and the construction of inner concrete skins against the existing walls. Hoffmann J. held that the work was not repair within the tenant's covenant. He concluded:

11–34

> "[D]eploying my ordinary understanding of language, I do not think it would be appropriate to describe any of the three schemes of treatment as work of repair. In my judgment, they involve structural alterations and improvements to the basement.[139]"

In *Halliard Property Co Ltd v Nicholas Clarke Investments Ltd*[140] the demised premises consisted of a single-storey building forming part of a terrace built in about 1910. In about 1953 a "jerry-built" structure was put up at the rear. What had been an open yard was enclosed by a new brick wall and was roofed over by a corrugated asbestos roof supported on planks resting on the brick wall. The wall was only 4.5in thick. It was supported by two 9in brick piers on either side of a doorway leading out into a lane, but otherwise was not supported either at the top or at the sides or at any point along its length. It was not keyed in where it abutted the premises, and the planks which supported the corrugated roof were not attached to the top of the wall. The premises were let for 14 years from 1979 on a full tenant's repairing covenant. In 1982 the wall collapsed. The landlords contended that the tenant was liable to rebuild the structure. This would have involved excavating the foundations to a depth of at least 2ft 6in; concreting them to a level of 6in below ground level; erecting brickwork incorporating a damp-proof course in two skins, with intervening cavity bonding at all positions where abutting adjoining structures, up to a height of 9ft; constructing a timber wall plate on the inside leaf to receive the roof structure on purlins at right angles to the line of corrugation. French J. held that, although the case was "borderline",

---

[137] [1940] 2 All E.R. 434.
[138] [1985] 2 E.G.L.R. 105 (affirmed on different grounds [1987] 1 All E.R. 1055: see Ch.8, above).
[139] In the Court of Appeal ([1987] 1 All E.R. 1055), where the judge's decision was upheld on another ground (see Ch.8, above), Ralph Gibson L.J. rejected the tenant's criticism that the judge had misunderstood or misapplied the appropriate test.
[140] [1984] 1 E.G.L.R. 45.

the work went beyond repair. Applying the dictum of Forbes J. in *Ravenseft Properties Ltd v Davstone (Holdings) Ltd*,[141] he said:

> "While ... that which would be handed back on the expiry of the demise would include the intact 'two thirds in area' front part of the premises, it would involve handing back to [the landlords], so far as the utility room was concerned, an edifice entirely different from the unstable and jerry-built structure of which the [tenant] took possession at the start of the lease."

Further examples of cases where remedial work involving major structural alterations or additions was held to be outside the tenant's repairing obligations are to be found in the cases dealing with old premises considered in paras 11–15 to 11–20, above.

### (d) Work which is necessary to comply with legislation or regulations[142]

**11–35**  Legislation or regulations may impinge upon the remedying of a particular defect by making it unlawful to carry out the work other than in a certain way. This does not of itself mean that such work is repair. Thus, in *Wright v Lawson*[143] a house and shop in the King's Road had a bay window on the first floor. It had become defective and dangerous, and the local authority required the tenant to take it down. The tenant did so, and then built a new window set back in the main wall of the house. The landlord contended that the tenant was liable under his covenant to repair to restore the premises to their original condition. The only way a new bay window could lawfully have been put up was by supporting it with two columns from the ground. This was a wholly different method to that which had existed before. It was held that the tenant was not liable.

However, where compliance with the requirements of legislation or regulations would not prevent the work from being repair as a matter of fact and degree, then the covenantor is liable to do the work in such a way as to comply. Thus, in *Lurcott v Wakely*[144] a wall was built with no proper footings and no damp-proof course. It became defective, and was rebuilt in accordance with the requirements of a notice under the London Building Act 1894, with concrete foundations and damp-proof courses. It could not lawfully have been rebuilt in any other way. The Court of Appeal held the tenant liable for the whole of the cost of the works. Cozens-Hardy M.R. said:

> "It seems to me that we should be narrowing in a most dangerous way the limit and extent of these covenants if we did not hold that the defendants were liable under covenants framed as these are to make good the cost of repairing this wall in the only sense in which it can be repaired, namely, by rebuilding according to the requirements of the county council."

---

[141] [1980] Q.B. 12.
[142] See further para.10–21, above.
[143] (1903) 19 T.L.R. 203 (Kekewich J.) and 510, CA.
[144] [1911] 1 K.B. 905.

In *Halliard Property Co Ltd v Nicholas Clarke Investments Ltd*[145] there was a conflict of opinion between the expert witnesses as to the remedial work necessary. French J. decided that reinstatement:

> "[M]ust mean proper reinstatement, must mean lawful reinstatement. It would be wrong to assume that, in breach of building regulations, codes of practice, byelaws and so forth, some builder would do, or be expected to do, that which was done back in the 1940s or 1950s, when the utility room was constructed."

In *Craighead v Homes for Islington Ltd*,[146] the replacement of life expired single glazed Crittall windows with double glazed Crittall windows, in circumstances where that was (absent intervention by English Heritage) the only lawful way of effecting the remedial works in accordance with the applicable building regulations, was held to be work of repair within the ambit of a provision entitling the landlord to recover the cost of "repair maintenance and renewal" of the premises.

### (e) Work which is necessary to comply with good practice[147]

It may not be unlawful to carry out work in a particular way in the sense that it is in breach of some statute or regulation. However, it may be contrary to good practice, in that no sensible person would do the job in that particular way.[148] This occurred in *Ravenseft Properties Ltd v Davstone (Holdings) Ltd*,[149] in which defective cladding was reinstated with expansion joints which were not present in the original building. No responsible engineer doing the job properly would have allowed the cladding to be put back up without expansion joints. Forbes J. held that the totality of the work was repair. He said:     **11–36**

> "It is quite clear to me from the evidence of ... the two expert engineers who gave evidence, and the only evidence I have on this point, that no competent professional engineer would have permitted this remedial work to be done without the inclusion of these expansion joints. By this time it was proper engineering practice to see that such expansion joints were included, and it would have been dangerous not to include them. In no realistic way, therefore, could it be said that there was any other possible way of reinstating this cladding other than by providing the expansion joints which were, in fact, provided. It seems to me to matter not whether that state of affairs is caused by the necessary sanction of statutory notices or by realistic fact that as a matter of professional expertise no responsible engineer would have allowed a rebuilding which did not include such expansion joints to be carried out."

It follows that work which is necessary to comply with good practice will generally be within the covenant to repair, provided that it does not so change the nature of the work as to take it outside the concept of repair altogether.

---

[145] [1984] 1 E.G.L.R. 45. The facts are set out at para.11–34, above.
[146] [2010] UKUT 47 (LC). The facts are set out at para.12–37, below.
[147] See further para.10–21, above.
[148] Note that even where the relevant regulations do not apply to the work, the court may nonetheless proceed on the assumption that they represent good practice: *Postel Properties Ltd v Boots the Chemist* [1996] 2 E.G.L.R. 60 at 62L.
[149] [1980] Q.B. 12. The facts are set out at para.11–03, above.

### (f)  Work which involves the use of a different design or more modern materials or methods

**11–37**  In many cases, particularly where the relevant premises are no longer modern, the most appropriate way of remedying the defect may not be to replicate the original construction in its entirety but to employ a more up-to-date design or to use modern materials and methods. Whether this prevents the work from being repair is a question of fact and degree in every case. Where the change is necessary or desirable to comply with good practice or to take advantage of developments in design, materials or methods, then, depending obviously on the precise facts in each case, the work is likely to remain repair. Thus, for example, a change from Welsh slate to asbestos tile, or from metal to plastic downpipes, would not ordinarily result in the work going beyond repair. In *Elite Investments Ltd v TI Bainbridge (Silencers) Ltd*[150] a roof made of corrugated galvanised steel sheeting was replaced with polyvinyl chloride coated corrugated steel sheeting. In holding that the work constituted repair, H.H. Judge Paul Baker QC, sitting as a judge of the High Court, said:

> "As I see that, it is not the roof that is going to be very different. It is a new material, but that is just taking advantage of better materials that are now on the market. It does not really alter the basic structure of the building and, after all, this is quite a simple building ... the roof will not be largely changed simply because it has got a roof looking similar to the existing roof but made of modern materials. Further, it seems largely irrelevant, because the old material is available and costs the same.[151]"

Further examples are *Postel Properties Ltd v Boots the Chemist*[152] (in which the replacement of the flat roof coverings of a shopping centre with thicker insulation and a higher specification cap sheet was held to be within the landlord's covenant to keep the roofs in good and substantial repair and condition); *Minja Properties Ltd v Cussins Property Group Ltd*[153] (in which an injunction was granted allowing the landlord access to replace defective single-glazed windows with double-glazed units, such work being held to be work of repair within the landlord's covenant to maintain and keep the window frames in good and tenantable repair); and *Creska v Hammersmith and Fulham LBC*[154] (in which remedial work to an underfloor heating system, which involved incorporating a more modern design, was held to be within the tenant's obligation well and substantially to repair and maintain and in all respects keep in good and substantial repair and condition the electrical heating installations in an office building). In the last, Evans L.J., giving the judgment of the Court of Appeal, said:

> "The fact that repairs carried out now would incorporate some improvements in design, particularly the use of flexible connectors where appropriate, does not mean that they cease to be works of repair that the party liable under the repairing covenant is bound to perform."

---

[150] [1986] 2 E.G.L.R. 43. See para.12–11, below.
[151] See further Ch.12, below.
[152] [1996] 2 E.G.L.R. 60.
[153] [1998] 2 E.G.L.R. 52. See para.12–37, below.
[154] [1998] 3 E.G.L.R. 35. See para.10–04, above.

The fact that taking advantage of modern technology or construction methods will not result in a significant increase in cost may be a relevant factor in favour of the work being within the covenant.[155]

The question whether replacement with the modern equivalent of what was there before goes beyond repair often arises in practice in the context of service plant and equipment, such as lifts and boilers. This is considered in Ch.13, below.

### (g)   Work which is necessary to prevent the defect from recurring

A defect in design or construction does not of itself constitute "disrepair", so that no work is required under a covenant to repair until the defect results in damage to the subject matter of the covenant.[156] However, when such damage does occur, the obligation to repair may (depending on the facts) involve not only remedying the damage in question but also eliminating the design or construction defect. Thus, in *Quick v Taff-Ely Borough Council*[157] Dillon L.J. said in the course of his judgment:

**11–38**

> "If there is … damage caused by an unsuspected inherent defect, then it may be necessary to cure the defect, and thus to some extent improve without wholly renewing the property as the only practicable way of making good the damage to the subject matter of the repairing covenant."

Lawton L.J. summarised both the problem and the correct approach as follows:

> "Broadly speaking [the decisions on the meaning of repair] come to this: a tenant must take the house as he finds it; neither a landlord nor a tenant is bound to provide the other with a better house than there was to start with; but, because almost all repair work requires some degree of renewal, problems of degree arise as to whether after the repair there is a house which is different from that which was let.
> …in putting right what has gone wrong, it may be necessary to abandon the use of the defective materials or to use a different and better method of construction.
> When something like this happens, does the landlord or the tenant have a better building? In one sense he does: he gets a building without the design defect which caused the damage; but the repair could only have been done in a sensible way by getting rid of the design defect."

Thus, it has been held that the installation of ties and expansion joints when replacing defective stone cladding was work of repair[158]; that a landlord who had covenanted to keep the main walls of a flat in repair was obliged not only to replace damp plaster but also to insert a damp-proof course so as to eliminate the cause of the damp[159]; and that the installation of cathodic protection following the removal and repair of cracked external stonework and brickwork caused by

---

[155] See for example the approach of Harman J. in *Minja Properties Ltd v Cussins Property Group Ltd*, above.

[156] See Ch. 8, above.

[157] [1986] Q.B. 809.

[158] *Ravenseft Properties Ltd v Davstone (Holdings) Ltd* [1980] Q.B. 12. See further paras 11–02 to 11–03, above, and para.12–18, below.

[159] *Elmcroft Developments Ltd v Tankersley-Sawyer* [1984] 1 E.G.L.R. 47. The contrary conclusion was reached in *Eyre v McCracken* [1999] 80 P. & C.R. 20 (where the covenantor was a tenant under a short lease). See further paras 12–31 to 12–34, below.

rusting steels was a repair even though it was a "wholly new item in the building".[160] Likewise, where a landlord covenanted to keep a wooden door in repair, and the door became rotten and in need of replacement, it was held that the landlord was obliged not only to remedy the immediate disrepair (the rot in the original door) but also to eliminate the cause of that disrepair (the absence of any method of stopping water collecting beneath the door and causing rot) by, for example, the installation of a modern self-sealing aluminium door (which is what the landlord had in fact done, albeit belatedly), because that was what a "sensible, practical man" would have done.[161]

**11–39**   However, it does not follow that where a design or construction defect has resulted in damage, the covenant will always require not only the remedying of that damage but also the elimination of the defect giving rise to it. This will depend in part on the extent to which remedying the damage can reasonably be said to require eliminating the design defect. Thus, in *Quick v Taff-Ely Borough Council*[162] condensation in a house caused by the lack of any effective cold bridging resulted in, among other things, rot in part of the wooden surrounds to some of the windows, and perished plaster. There was no evidence of any other physical damage to the structure and exterior of the house. To eradicate the condensation would have involved, among other things, the replacement of the existing metal window frames with frames of a different material and providing the lintels with insulation facings. The Court of Appeal held that the landlords were not liable for the work because the rot in the wooden window surrounds and defective plaster did not justify the extensive works contended for—it could be sufficiently cured by replacing the defective lengths of wood. Lawton L.J. said:

> "[T]he trial judge should first have identified the parts of the structure and exterior of the house which were out of repair and then have gone on to decide whether, in order to remedy the defect, it was reasonably necessary to replace the concrete lintels over the windows, which caused 'cold bridging', and the single glazed metal windows, both of which were among the causes, probably the major causes, of excessive condensation in the house."

He went on to hold that there was no evidence that the works in question were reasonably necessary to remedy the rot and perished plaster. Neill L.J. made the position clear:

> "On the evidence it seems clear that the council were in breach of ... covenant but only in respect of: (a) some parts of the wooden surrounds of some of the windows; and (b) some plaster damage. There was no evidence, however, to indicate any damage to or want of repair in the metal windows themselves or the concrete lintels or, indeed, any other part of the 'structure and exterior'.
> The authorities to which we were referred establish that, in some cases, the only realistic way of effecting the relevant repairs is to carry out some additional work which will go somewhat further than putting the property back into its former condition and will indeed result in some improvement.
> But this case does not fall into that category. The repair work consisting of the replacement of the defective parts of the wooden windows and the replacement of the areas of plaster did not require as a realistic way of effecting those repairs the replacement of the metal windows by wooden framed windows or windows with P.V.C. frames."

---

[160] *Gibson Investments Ltd v Chesterton Plc* [2002] 2 P. & C.R. 32. See further para.12–23, below.
[161] *Stent v Monmouth District Council* (1984) 19 H.L.R. 269. See paras 10–03 and 10–04, above.
[162] [1986] Q.B. 809. See para.8–01, above.

It is therefore necessary to ask whether the remedying of the design fault is "reasonably necessary" in order to remedy the damage (per Lawton L.J.), or "the only realistic way" of effecting the repairs (per Neill L.J.), or whether this is what the "sensible practical man" would do.[163] So viewed, the question is one of fact and expert evidence. There comes a point where the design defect is so bound up with the damage it has caused that it is neither sensible nor practical to remedy the one without also eradicating the other. Precisely when this point has been reached depends on the facts.

**11–40**

Even where the eradication of the design defect is the only sensible way of doing the work, however, it will not necessarily follow that the work will constitute repair. It may be so extensive that, on a proper application of the fact and degree test, it goes beyond what can properly be described as repair. Thus, in *Gibson Investments Ltd v Chesterton Plc (No.1)*[164] Neuberger J. said:

> "Where it is contended that the repair work should extend to eradicating the problem rather than being limited to prophylactic measures, the cases establish, first, that the work will not be repair if it involves giving something back to the landlord wholly different from that which he demised ..., but, secondly, that there will be circumstances in which such work can be repair even though it involves adding something to the premises which was not there originally."

## The cost of the works

In applying the fact and degree test, the cost of the work may be a relevant consideration.[165] The relevant comparison will generally be between the cost of the work and the cost of a new building. Thus, in *Brew Bros Ltd v Snax (Ross) Ltd*[166] the cost of making the flank wall safe was in the order of £8,000; the value of the premises, if in good repair, would have been between £7,500 and £9,500; and the cost of a new building on the same site, of the same size and general specification as the premises, would have been between £9,000 and £10,000. In the Court of Appeal Phillimore L.J. took these figures into account in coming to his conclusion that the tenant was not liable. He said:

**11–41**

> "The essence of the tenants' case here is that these landlords less than 18 months after letting the premises were requiring work to remedy defects which existed at the date of the lease at a cost which would be about equal to that of rebuilding the premises as new. After all, the judge had found that the estimate of just under £8,000 to make the premises safe was acceptable, but had added that he was satisfied that the flank wall would have to be pulled down and rebuilt on new foundations. This must surely have added largely to the £8,000 figure.
> ... Suppose some busybody had said to these parties when signing the contract: You realise, of course, that it might be necessary within 18 months to spend between £8,000 and £9,000 to render this building safe. If that happened, would you both regard that as repair? I suspect that even a landlord (unless utterly unreasonable) would have replied: 'Of course not'."

---

[163] Per Sir John Arnold P. in *Stent v Monmouth District Council*, above. The relevant passage is set out in para.10–03, above.

[164] [2002] 2 P. & C.R. 32.

[165] *Brew Bros Ltd v Snax (Ross) Ltd* [1970] 1 Q.B. 612; *Ravenseft Properties Ltd v Davstone (Holdings) Ltd* [1980] Q.B. 12; *McDougall v Easington District Council* (1989) 21 H.L.R. 310; *Holding & Management Ltd v Property Holding & Investment Trust Ltd* [1990] 1 E.G.L.R. 65 (not reported on this point at [1989] 1 W.L.R. 1313); *Minja Properties Ltd v Cussins Property Group Plc* [1998] 2 E.G.L.R. 52; *Weatherhead v Deka New Zealand Ltd* [2000] 1 N.Z.L.R. 23.

[166] [1970] 1 Q.B. 612. The facts are set out at para.11–29, above.

Forbes J. carried out a similar exercise in *Ravenseft Properties Ltd v Davstone (Holdings) Ltd*[167] in relation to the question whether inserting ties and expansion joints when replacing the defective stone cladding of a block of maisonettes was repair. He said:

> "In deciding [the question of fact and degree] the proportion which the cost of the disputed work bears to the value or cost of the whole premises may sometimes be helpful as a guide ... that part of the remedial work relating solely to the insertion of expansion joints ... would have [cost] in the region of £5,000. The total cost of the remedial works was around £55,000, the balance of £50,000 being for refixing the stones and other ancillary works which was not, as I find, necessary to cure any defect of design, but to remedy what was originally defective workmanship. For comparison, the cost of building a structure of this kind in 1973 would have been in the region of £3 million, or rather more. I find myself wholly unable to accept that the cost of inserting these joints could possibly be regarded as a substantial part of the cost of repairs, much less a substantial part of the value or cost of the building."

**11–42**   In *Halliard Property Co Ltd v Nicholas Clarke Investments Ltd*[168] the cost of the remedial work would have been in the order of £3,000 excluding VAT and professional fees. The cost of rebuilding the demised premises in their entirety would have been about £10,000. The value of the landlord's interest in the existing premises subject to the lease (a rent review was coming up) was £12,000 to £14,000. French J., taking this into account, decided that the work went beyond repair.

In *Elite Investments Ltd v TI Bainbridge (Silencers) Ltd (No.2)*[169] Judge Paul Baker QC, sitting as a judge of the High Court, held that, where the value of the building is very much less than the cost of a new one, it is the latter figure which is relevant for the purposes of the comparison. That case concerned the question whether a new roof was a repair.[170] The judge said:

> "[W]hen you get a situation where the value is very much less than the cost of a new building it is the cost, not the value, which is relevant for determining whether one has gone beyond repairs. That is the case I have got here. The cost of putting this new building up has been estimated, I think, at about £30 a foot, so we are getting near to £1m to re-erect a completely new building, which is very much beyond the figure which I put on the value of it as repaired, *i.e.* £140,000. When assessing the size of repairs which are going to cost money, then what you look at, as a guide to whether you are going over the top and you are really giving back to the landlord a complete new building, is what the new building will actually cost. The value of the resulting building has no bearing, in my judgment, on the construction of the covenant itself."

He dismissed counsel's submission that the work was not repair because, among other things, the cost was totally disproportionate to the value of the building in repair. His reasoning was:

> "What has to be compared in this connection in determining whether you have got repair or not, is not the value of the resulting building with the new roof but what it will cost you to do away with the building altogether and build a new one, or substantially build a new one."

---

[167] [1980] Q.B. 12. The facts are set out at para.11–03, above.
[168] [1984] 1 E.G.L.R. 45. The facts are set out at para.11–34, above.
[169] [1986] 2 E.G.L.R. 43.
[170] The facts are set out in para.11–37 above, and see also para.12–11, below.

In an appropriate case, however, the relevant comparator may be the previous **11–43**
value of the building[171]; or the value of the building after the works have been
completed[172]; or the rental value of the premises.[173] Thus, in *Post Office v
Aquarius Properties Ltd*[174] the cheapest waterproofing scheme would have cost
£86,000 and the most expensive £175,000. On the assumption that the basement
was waterproofed, the annual rent would have been in the region of £50,000 to
£60,000. The capital value of the building was about £687,000 and the cost of
rebuilding it would have been "a good deal more". In coming to his conclusion
that the work was not repair, Hoffmann J. said:

> "I think I am entitled to take into account the probable cost of the work, which at the lower end
> of the range of figures mentioned in the evidence is about £100,000. This is twice the likely
> annual market rent for the whole building with waterproof basement and over 15 per cent. of
> its capital value. I was not given a separate figure for the capital value of the basement but it
> must be a small fraction of the whole."

However, in the Court of Appeal[175] (where Hoffmann J.'s conclusion was
affirmed on a different point) Ralph Gibson L.J. agreed with counsel for the
landlord that, assuming the necessary damage or deterioration to be proved, the
weight that could properly be given to the cost of the scheme was not large.

In *Gibson Investments Ltd v Chesterton Plc (No.1)*[176] (which concerned
substantial works to a steel framed office building) Neuberger J., in rejecting an
argument based on the cost of the works, said:

> "[T]he cost of the work, namely around £1 million, in the context of a building of this size held
> under a lease for a term of 33 years, does not appear to me to bring into question whether the
> second scheme can fairly be characterised as repair."

The above cases are all examples of the comparative cost approach being used
to help decide the question whether the remedial work was repair. It should be
emphasised, however, that it is not a scientific exercise but one of a number of
possible relevant factors. It can never be conclusive, and it may be more helpful
in some cases than others. The fact that the work is comparatively cheap is not
conclusive in favour of it being repair any more than the fact that it costs a lot
necessarily means it is not repair.

---

[171] *McDougall v Easington District Council* (1989) 58 P. & C.R. 201.

[172] *McDougall v Easington District Council*, above; *Holding & Management Ltd v Property Holding
& Investment Trust Ltd* [1990] 1 E.G.L.R. 65 (not reported on this point at [1989] 1 W.L.R. 1313).

[173] *Post Office v Aquarius Properties Ltd* [1985] 2 E.G.L.R. 105 (affirmed on different grounds:
[1987] 1 All E. R. 1055).

[174] *Post Office v Aquarius Properties Ltd*, above.

[175] [1987] 1 All E.R. 1055.

[176] [2002] 2 P. & C.R. 32. The facts are set out in para.12–23, below.

## EXPRESS WORDS

### Covenants to rebuild or replace

**11–44**    The fact and degree test considered above will generally only be appropriate in relation to a covenant to repair in the ordinary form. The words of the covenant may show that the covenantor is liable for work going beyond repair, and if so, then the words will prevail. Thus, for example, the covenant may make it clear that complete replacement of the whole is required where necessary.[177] The circumstances in which the covenant will be construed as imposing a liability going beyond repair are considered in Ch.4, paras 4–25 and 4–26, above.

### The inclusion in the covenant of "renew"

**11–45**    Depending on the words used and the context, an obligation to renew may be interpreted either as adding little to the obligation to repair, or as going further and imposing a more extensive liability. Reference should be made to the discussion in Ch.4, paras 4–25 and 4–26, above.

### Covenants to keep in good condition

**11–46**    The extent to which the inclusion of a separate obligation to keep the subject-matter in good or tenantable condition may oblige the covenantor to carry out works going beyond repair properly so-called has already been considered.[178] The question is one of construction in every case. Where the right conclusion is that a wider liability was intended, it will be necessary to consider what limitations there may be on such liability.

In *Credit Suisse v Beegas Nominees Ltd*[179] Lindsay J. held (on the particular wording of the relevant covenant[180]) that an obligation on the part of the landlord to keep the structure of the building "in good and tenantable condition" gave rise to a liability extending beyond repair. He said:

> "Of course, as with covenants to repair, questions as to the age and nature and class of the subject matter to be put and kept in the specified condition have to be borne in mind ... So cases on 'repair' cannot be wholly discarded but, as I see it, it is no necessary escape from liability under a covenant to put and keep in a specified condition that the work needed in order that condition should be achieved is not a repair strictly so called. Nor do I see it as important on this part of the landlord's covenant that the work required to achieve the given condition is of a particular great cost. I can see that may well affect and has been frequently taken to affect whether the work is one of 'repair' but I do not see it as material to an obligation to put and keep in a given condition. I have not understood any authority cited to me as disabling me from giving to the words of the covenant '*otherwise* to keep in good and tenantable condition' the meaning which *Proudfoot v Hart* ascribes to similar phrases, nor as

---

[177] *Norwich Union Life Assurance Co Ltd v British Railways Board* [1987] 2 E.G.L.R. 137; *New England Properties Ltd v Portsmouth New Shops Ltd* [1993] 1 E.G.L.R. 94.

[178] See paras 4–29 to 4–30, 8–12 to 8–14, and 9–41 to 9–42, above.

[179] [1994] 4 All E.R. 803 and (more fully) [1994] 1 E.G.L.R. 76. This case is further considered in para.4–28 and 9–26, above and para.12–19, below.

[180] The relevant part of the covenant is set out at para.4–28, above.

obliging me to attach to these words all the qualifications which have been held to circumscribe or affect an obligation to 'repair'.

It may perhaps be (but it is, as I mention below, unnecessary for me to decide) that a proper limitation on the obligation to put and keep in tenantable condition is that the landlord cannot be required to provide the tenant with something 'of a wholly different character to that which had been let': see *McDougall v Easington District Council*.[181] I thus say nothing as to that."

The above passage suggests that something akin to the fact and degree test applies to a covenant to keep in good condition in much the same way as it does to a covenant to keep in repair. It is thought that in principle this must be correct. In the ordinary case, the parties are unlikely to have intended the covenantor to be liable to carry out whatever works may be necessary to keep the premises in good condition, even if those works extend to a complete demolition and rebuilding of the whole premises. The difficulty in identifying any limitation, however, lies in the fact that (unlike an obligation to repair, which requires the carrying out of an operation) a covenant to keep in good condition requires the covenantor to keep the premises in the requisite state without regard to the means by which this is achieved. Accordingly, it will not be appropriate to ask whether the remedial work can fairly be described as "repair" because ex hypothesi the covenant has been interpreted as imposing a liability extending beyond repair. However, it is thought that the test suggested by Lindsay J. (which is one of the ways in which the fact and degree test has been expressed in relation to covenants to repair[182]) will generally be the correct limitation in the ordinary case, so that what must be asked is whether the works are so extensive that either they result in a new and different thing from that which was demised,[183] or they go beyond what the parties can reasonably be supposed to have contemplated as the covenantor's liability.[184]

[181] (1989) 58 P. & C.R. 201.
[182] See paras 11–09 to 11–11, above.
[183] See paras 11–09 to 11–11, above.
[184] See para.11–12, above.

CHAPTER 12

# THE APPLICATION OF THE REPAIRING COVENANT IN RELATION TO COMMONLY ENCOUNTERED DEFECTS

## INTRODUCTORY

The suggested five-part approach set out in Chs 7 to 11 is concerned with the general principles applicable to whether or not particular work falls within an obligation to repair. This Chapter is concerned with the operation of the repairing covenant in relation to some of the problems commonly encountered in practice in relation to particular parts of buildings or defects, namely subsidence,[1] defective roofs,[2] defective cladding,[3] rusting steel frames,[4] defective concrete,[5] rising and penetrating damp,[6] defective windows,[7] asbestos[8] and contamination of the building or land.[9] The discussion under each head is not intended to be comprehensive but to focus on the sorts of difficulties generally met in practice, and (in the main) on the application of the covenant to repair as opposed to other covenants imposing liability for dilapidations (although much of the discussion may be of relevance to these as well). Mechanical and electrical services are considered in Ch.13, below.

**12–01**

## SUBSIDENCE

### Introductory

Serious subsidence often manifests itself by damage to the inside as well as the outside of the building. The remedial works usually include some form of underpinning. In practice, there is scope for genuine disagreement between experts at almost every stage. The extent to which subsidence has taken, or is taking, place may itself be unclear. In most cases the damage caused by subsidence tends to be gradual, so that extensive monitoring may be needed to ascertain the existence and the degree of movement. Once movement is identified, the causes may often be unclear, and there may be more than one

**12–02**

---

[1] See para.12–02 et seq., below.
[2] See para.12–06 et seq., below.
[3] See para.12–16 et seq., below.
[4] See para.12–21 et seq., below.
[5] See para.12–26 et seq., below.
[6] See para.12–27 et seq., below.
[7] See para.12–36 et seq., below.
[8] See para.12–38 et seq., below.
[9] See para.12–39 et seq., below.

cause. Soil samples may need to be taken and other investigations carried out. There may be a number of different possible schemes of remedial work, some of which may be more extensive and expensive than others. The choice between the various schemes may depend on the correct view as to the cause and likely progress of movement. There may be third parties, such as insurers or the owner of adjoining land, involved.

Once subsidence has been identified, the necessary works will generally fall into two main categories: underpinning or other work necessary to prevent further subsidence; and works necessary to remedy consequential damage to the interior of the building, such as uneven floors, cracked plaster and doors that no longer open and close. The question will be the extent to which the covenantor is liable for work falling within either of these categories.

## Underpinning

12–03    The main question arising under repairing covenants in relation to underpinning is generally whether, as a matter of fact and degree, the work is too extensive to amount to repair.[10] In most of the decided cases, underpinning has been held to fall outside a tenant's liability to repair. These include the following:

(1)    *Lister v Lane*,[11] in which a house was built on a timber platform. The timber rotted, and one of the walls bulged out. The wall could only have been repaired by digging down through 17ft of mud to the gravel underneath and then building up from that to the brickwork of the house. It was held that the tenant was not liable for the work.

(2)    *Sotheby v Grundy*,[12] in which the main walls of a house were built without, or on defective, footings and on made-up ground. The walls became bulged, fractured and overhanging. The only way of remedying this was by shoring up, removing the foundations, and constructing new foundations. The tenant was held not liable for the work.

(3)    *Collins v Flynn*,[13] where part of the rear main wall of a house was supported by a girder which was in turn carried by a pier. Settlement caused by inadequate foundations resulted in the pier sinking and consequential movement and fractures in the rear wall. The requisite remedial work involved rebuilding the pier and rear and side wall with newly designed foundations and footings. Again, this was held to be outside the tenant's liability.[14]

(4)    *Brew Bros Ltd v Snax (Ross) Ltd*,[15] where seepage from drains, which had been defective for many years, together with the removal of a large tree in the pavement outside the property, caused the foundations of the building to

---

[10]    See Ch.11, above.

[11]    [1893] 2 Q.B. 212. See further para.11–16, above.

[12]    [1947] 2 All E.R. 761. See further para.11–18, above.

[13]    [1963] 2 All E.R. 1068. See further para.11–19, above.

[14]    It should be noted that in *Ravenseft Properties Ltd v Davstone (Holdings) Ltd* [1980] Q.B. 12, Forbes J. held that Sir Brett Cloutman in *Collins v Flynn* had misdirected himself on the ratio decidendi of *Sotheby v Grundy*, above, and therefore that the case was "of doubtful authority".

[15]    [1970] 1 Q.B. 612. See further para.11–29, above.

move and the flank wall to tilt. The remedial work comprised the repair of the foundations, the rebuilding of the wall and the repair of the drains. The Court of Appeal held that the tenant was not liable for the work to the foundations, and (by a majority) that he was not liable for the remaining work either.

The same conclusion has been reached in relation to the meaning of "work of repair or maintenance" under legislation relating to VAT. In *ACT Construction Ltd v Commissioners for Customs & Excise*[16] a number of houses had been built in the 1930s with shallow foundations. Subsidence damage had occurred in the drought of 1976. A specialist company underpinned the houses by constructing additional foundations. This was done by placing a large concrete beam underneath the original shallow foundations with pillars sunk in the ground to support it. In the Court of Appeal the argument proceeded on the basis that "repair" and "maintenance" were used in antithesis to one another, and it was conceded that the work did not amount to work of repair. The Court held that it did not amount to work of maintenance. Brandon L.J. gave his reasons as follows:

> "[T]he work done was not done to any existing part of the building; it was entirely new work. It involved a radical and fundamental alteration to the construction of the building as it had been before. It involved an extension of the building in a downward direction. Such work in my view is not capable of coming within the expression 'maintenance' in the ordinary and natural meaning of that word."

In the House of Lords[17] it was held that "repair or maintenance" was a single composite phrase, and that the work did not fall within it. Lord Roskill, with whom the other Law Lords agreed, quoted with approval the above passage from the judgment of Brandon L.J. in the Court of Appeal.

*Lister v Lane*[18] and *ACT Construction Ltd v Commissioners of Customs & Excise*[19] involved underpinning the entirety of the foundations of the house, and the other cases mentioned above concerned underpinning a substantial part of the premises. However, where the underpinning is to a subsidiary part of the premises, then it may, depending on the detailed facts, be held to constitute repair. Thus, in *Rich Investments Ltd v Camgate Litho Ltd*[20] a brick wall enclosing a fire escape suffered subsidence damage, and the tenant was held liable for underpinning the wall and stitching damaged brickwork. Likewise, in *Alexander v Lambeth LBC*[21] it was held in the county court that underpinning part of a ground floor flat with concrete was work of repair which the landlord was obliged to carry out under its covenant to keep the structure and exterior in repair.

In *Woods v Cooper*[22] a house was built in 1923 to the requirements of the original lessee, who covenanted to "repair, renew, uphold and support" the

**12–04**

---

[16] [1981] 1 W.L.R. 49, CA (affirmed on different grounds [1982] 1 W.L.R. 1542, HL).
[17] [1982] 1 W.L.R. 1542.
[18] [1893] 2 Q.B. 212. See para.12–03, above.
[19] Above.
[20] [1989] E.G.C.S. 132.
[21] [2000] C.L.Y. 3931.
[22] [1934] E.G.D. 193.

premises. By 1932 serious cracks in a wall had occurred, and "considerable underpinning" was required. The tenant argued that the work was not repair because the foundations as constructed were inadequate and the work would involve giving back to the landlord something which was not there before. Talbot J. held that it had not been proved on the evidence that the foundations were inadequate, but further held that in any event the work was within the covenant. He is reported as having said at the end of his judgment:

> "It had been argued that what was required to be done was not a repair, but to contend that underpinning was not a repairing, supporting or amending was not consistent with common sense."

*Woods v Cooper* is not fully reported, and it is not clear how extensive either the damage or the remedial work was. For that reason, it is not a particularly satisfactory authority.

In *Smedley v Chumley & Hawke Ltd*[23] a timber-framed restaurant building had been constructed on a concrete raft which was supported at one end on piles sunk into the river bank. There were no piles at the other end. That end began to sink into the ground and the raft tilted. The remedial work consisted of jacking up the building and the raft, driving in additional piles to support the raft, placing joists upon the piles and then lowering the building and the raft down on to the joists. The landlords had covenanted to "keep the main walls and roof in good structural repair and condition throughout the term and to promptly make good all defects due to faulty materials or workmanship in the construction of the premises". The Court of Appeal held that the landlords were liable for the remedial works. A key feature of the decision on the facts was that the premises had been newly built by the landlords and let on terms which imposed liability for structural defects. Against this background, the conclusion that the landlords were nonetheless not liable for the relevant defects would have been a harsh one.[24]

The above cases show that whether and to what extent the covenanting party is liable for underpinning will depend on the detailed facts. There is no principle to the effect that underpinning can never constitute repair. In the ordinary case, however, it is thought that underpinning the entirety of the premises will not generally fall within a tenant's covenant to repair. However, (i) the position may be different where only a part of the premises is affected, and (ii) there may be particular wording or background circumstances which point to a contrary intention. Where the covenanting party is the landlord, the court may be readier to hold that necessary underpinning to the whole of the premises falls within the covenant, particularly where the premises were newly built by the landlord.

---

[23] (1981) 44 P. & C.R. 50. See further on this case para.11–21, above.

[24] See Robert Walker J.'s comments in *Ladbroke Hotels Ltd v Sandhu* [1995] 2 E.G.L.R. 92.

## Consequential damage

The remedying of damage caused to the premises as a result of settlement will ordinarily fall within the covenant to repair unless the relevant work is so extensive that it cannot be described as repair as a matter of fact and degree.[25] One question which may arise in practice is whether the covenantor is liable to remedy such damage in circumstances where he is not liable to carry out the necessary underpinning work (because it is not repair). Where this would achieve no useful purpose (because unless the underlying movement is dealt with, the work will need re-doing at periodic intervals) the right conclusion may be that the covenantor is not required to do it. Depending on the facts, such an approach can be supported by reference to the principles that (a) a covenant to repair does not require the carrying out of futile work,[26] and (b) the remedial work must be looked at as a whole and not as a series of separate operations.[27] However, each case will turn on its own facts, and there may be cases where the covenant on its proper construction will require damage resulting from settlement to be remedied even though the work necessary to remedy the settlement itself is outside the covenant.

12–05

## ROOFS

## Introductory

The problem to which roofs generally give rise in practice is the extent to which the covenanting party is liable for complete replacement. It is common, for example, to find in terminal schedules of dilapidation a requirement for the tenant to strip and replace the roof covering. This will usually be fiercely contested by the tenant's surveyor on the ground that the roof has not yet reached the point where it requires replacement, and in the alternative, that replacement goes beyond repair. Whether the tenant is liable for complete replacement will depend on the factors discussed below.

12–06

## Where there are several available repair options

No work is required under the covenant until the roof is physically defective[28] in such a way as to bring it below the standard contemplated by the covenant.[29] Once there is relevant damage or deterioration, the question will be whether it is so extensive that complete replacement is the only feasible option. Where the roof is no longer reasonably capable of further patch repair, the position will generally be relatively straightforward. In many cases, however, there may be other options, such as continued patch repairs, or over-sheeting, or a proprietary

12–07

---

[25] See para.11–04 et seq., above.
[26] See para.10–03, above.
[27] See para.11–29, above.
[28] See paras 8–01 to 8–04, above.
[29] See Ch.9, above.

process, such as "turnerising", and the question will be which option is the covenanting party obliged, or entitled, to adopt.

### (a) Whether the lesser work complies with the requisite standard of repair

**12–08**    The first logical question where there is more than one proposed method of remedying the defect is whether each such method will comply with the requisite standard of repair, i.e. whether it will restore the roof to the state contemplated by the covenant.[30] If not, then the method in question can be disregarded. As always, the question depends on the detailed facts.

In some cases, the standard of repair appropriate to the particular premises may preclude anything less than complete replacement. Thus, in *Sun Life Assurance Plc v Racal Tracs Ltd*[31] a light industrial unit and ancillary offices and storage was let for use for the purpose of "the business as designers and manufacturers of electronic equipment". The roof (which consisted of asbestos tiles) suffered from leaks. The tenant had dealt with this during the term by "turnerising" it (i.e. applying a nylon membrane and black bitumen) but the roof was leaking again by the end of the lease. The tenant's surveyor contended that turnerising would be appropriate. The landlord's surveyor's evidence was that turnerising was "low-quality, short-term and cheap treatment", and that the only two options were stripping and renewing the covering or (the more cost effective option) oversheeting it with a profiled metal sheet. Mr Recorder Black (sitting as a deputy judge of the Queen's Bench Division) found in favour of the landlord. He regarded the premises as "somewhat more than … an industrial shed that was not required to be totally watertight". Having referred to the appropriate standard of repair and to the fact that there was no evidence that the tenant's solution would work, he said:

> "I am thus faced with [the landlord's surveyor's] recommendation, which it is common ground will provide an adequate repair, and [the tenant's surveyor's] recommendation, which *might* provide an adequate repair. There is no evidence before me that it would be possible to apply [the tenant's surveyor's] solution to the roof …, it being outside his experience to say whether it is possible.
>
> I am, therefore, left with no alternative but to hold that [the landlord's surveyor's] suggestion that the roof … should be entirely overclad with profiled sheet steel is the appropriate method of repair."

In other cases, however, the facts may be such that the appropriate standard of repair can be achieved either by complete replacement or by lesser works.

### (b) The choice between methods

**12–09**    Where any one of several methods would comply with the standard of repair, the choice between them is for the covenanting party to make.[32]

---

[30] For a full discussion of the standard of repair, see Ch.9, above.

[31] [2000] 1 E.G.L.R. 138. Note that the case went to the Court of Appeal on another point ([2001] 1 W.L.R. 1562) but no appeal was brought against the judge's decision on the repair issue.

[32] See paras 10–06 to 10–07, above.

As Ian Kennedy J. pointed out in *Postel Properties Ltd v Boots the Chemist*[33] (which concerned the replacement of the flat roof coverings of a large shopping centre), the decision whether or not to replace a roof can involve matters of fine judgment:

> "Clearly it is a matter for experience and judgment when the time has come to renew a roof. The cost of replacement must be balanced against the likely increasing cost of patch repairs. A consideration is that patch repairs are expensive in terms of the preliminary elements in the overall cost. With an enormous building such as this centre, the work of replacement has to be phased over four or more years, to spread the cost and minimise disturbance to the tenants' businesses."

As a general rule, provided that the decision arrived at produces a result which accords with the requisite standard, the covenant has been performed, albeit that another method might also have constituted performance. The cases contain a number of examples of the application of this principle in practice. In *Murray v Birmingham City Council*[34] a roof of a house had given trouble over the years and the landlord had dealt with each occasion of disrepair by carrying out localised repairs to the area in question. The roof remained capable of being repaired by replacing the slates which had slipped by renailing them. The Court of Appeal rejected the tenant's argument that the landlord was liable to replace the roof in its entirety. In *Dame Margaret Hungerford Charity Trustees v Beazeley*[35] the landlords continued to carry out running repairs to the roof of the demised premises as and when they were notified of a problem with it, notwithstanding the fact that they were aware that it was highly desirable for the roof to be completely replaced. The trial judge's view that they were not in breach of covenant by failing to replace the roof was upheld in the Court of Appeal. In *Commercial Union Life Assurance Co Ltd v Label Ink Ltd*[36] H.H. Judge Rich QC (sitting as a deputy High Court judge) held that cleaning and sealing leaking valley gutters was an appropriate method of repair. He said:

> "I accept that for a roof of this kind, which has leaked after only some five years from original erection, a five-year repair is adequate even if replacement sheets might last longer."

He regarded the landlord's surveyor as having failed to take into account:

> "[T]he true meaning of [the covenant]. His complaints were against a standard of perfection; what a pristine building should look like, not what was required by a covenant to keep, what had been a pristine building, in good and substantial repair."

In *Riverside Property Investments v Blackhawk Automotive*[37] the demised premises consisted of a steel-framed light industrial unit with a pitched roof constructed of some 600 corrugated asbestos cement sheets attached by hook

---

[33] [1996] 2 E.G.L.R. 60.
[34] [1987] 2 E.G.L.R. 53.
[35] [1993] 2 E.G.L.R. 144.
[36] [2001] L. & T.R. 29. Note that the question of disrepair arose in the context of whether or not the tenant had complied with a condition precedent in a break option, and that the judge's construction of the condition precedent was subsequently disapproved by the Court of Appeal in *Fitzroy House Epworth Street (No.1) v The Financial Times* [2006] 2 E.G.L.R. 13.
[37] [2005] 1 E.G.L.R. 114.

bolts to steel purlins fixed to the top of the steel frame, and GRP roof lights. The tenant covenanted "well and substantially to repair, uphold, cleanse, support, maintain, amend and keep and when necessary rebuild, reconstruct, renew or replace the demised premises and every part thereof" and to yield them up at the end of the term in good and substantial repair and condition in accordance with its covenants. Prior to the expiry of the lease, the tenant carried out works to the roof consisting of the replacement of 122 defective sheets with new fibre cement roof sheets fixed with topfix fasteners and all the GRP roof lights. As soon as the lease ended, the landlord stripped off the roof and replaced with a new Kingspan roof. H.H. Judge Coulson QC held that (i) immediately prior to the commencement of the tenant's works, the roof remained capable of being put into the covenanted condition by the carrying of works falling short of the complete replacement of the existing covering; (ii) the works actually carried out by the tenant were sufficient to put the roof into substantial repair; and (iii) the landlord was not therefore entitled to the cost of the new roof by way of damages.

A similar conclusion was arrived at by the same judge in *Carmel Southend v Strachan & Henshaw*,[38] in which the demised premises likewise consisted of a steel-framed industrial unit with corrugated asbestos cement sheeting fixed by hook bolts, and GRP roof lights. The tenant covenanted "to repair and keep in good and substantial repair and condition the demised premises" and to yield them up in that state at the end of the term. The roof leaked during the tenancy, and remained in disrepair at the end of the lease, with defective roof lights and seals, areas of rainwater ingress and isolated cracked roof sheets. The tenant sublet the premises to a third party who remained in occupation following the expiry of the lease in December 2004. In July 2005, the landlord relet the premises to the sub-tenant on the basis that the landlord would pay for the overcladding of the roof with new profile metal sheeting. That work was carried out, and the landlord claimed the cost from the tenant by way of damages for disrepair. The tenant contended that the roof remained capable of being patch repaired by the replacement of the roof lights and a small number of roof sheets. The judge found in favour of the tenant. The patch repairs were neither futile nor impracticable. They were reasonably and sensibly possible and were therefore the appropriate way of performing the covenant, albeit that the overcladding works actually carried out could also be described as repair.

To the same effect is the decision of Edwards-Stuart J. in *Sunlife Europe Properties v Tiger Aspect Holdings*,[39] which concerned the roof of a 1970s office and retail building. No work had been carried out to the roof during the term. The landlord contended that the roof required to be repaired by applying a multi-layered liquid plastics roof covering. The tenant argued that the roof could be effectively patch-repaired at a much lesser cost. The judge found in favour of the tenant. He said:

> "I am not persuaded that a tenant of the type that could reasonably be anticipated to take a lease of this building would be concerned by the existence of patch repairs on the roof ... I do not consider that if it was tidily patched it would have been a factor that would have adversely

---

[38] [2007] 3 E.G.L.R. 15.
[39] [2013] EWHC 463 (TCC) at [33–35].

affected the judgment of the appropriate type of tenant. I find that such a tenant would have been concerned with its weatherproofing properties, rather than its appearance."

However, the judge increased the tenant's proposed cost to reflect further works that would have been necessary to deal with hidden defects that would almost certainly have appeared if a patch repairs scheme had been implemented.

These cases should be contrasted with two cases going the other way. In *Manor House Drive Ltd v Shahbazian*,[40] the roof above a maisonette leaked. The landlord was advised by a surveyor that the zinc layer below a canvas and bitumen covering was defective and required replacing with new zinc; that, if done, this would last for about 25 to 30 years; and that temporary treatment would be a waste of money and be likely to remain effective for no more than a few months. On this advice, the landlord installed a new zinc roof and claimed the cost from the tenants by way of service charge. The tenants called evidence to the effect that instead of a new zinc roof, first aid repairs could have been done by putting on a heavy coat of bitumen or aquaseal. Although this would not last as long as the new roof, the cost of periodic treatment would amount over 20 years to about £300 as against £400 for the new roof. The new roof was not therefore necessary. The Court of Appeal rejected the tenants' argument. The work was a reasonable and proper way of maintaining the roof, and patching up was not reasonable. In *Princes House v Distinctive Clubs*[41] the landlords covenanted to use all reasonable endeavours to repair (among other things) the roof of a block. The roof was defective and required replacement. The judge at first instance held that the landlords were entitled to carry out patch repairs whilst working up a scheme for the replacement, but that once such a scheme had been set up, they were in breach of covenant by failing to replace the roof thereafter. His decision was upheld on appeal.[42]

It should be noted that the fact that replacing the roof amounts to a performance of a landlord's repairing covenant does not necessarily mean that the cost will be recoverable from the tenant by way of service charge: that depends on the proper construction of the service charge provisions.[43]

**12–10**

## Complete replacement

Once it has been determined that complete replacement of the old roof is necessary to restore the building to the state contemplated by the covenant, the question will be whether, as a matter of fact and degree, that work is the liability of the covenanting party.[44] Where the roof is a subsidiary part of the subject-matter of the covenant (i.e. where the covenant is to repair other parts of the building as well as the roof) then complete replacement is likely to be held to

**12–11**

---

[40] (1965) 195 E.G. 283.
[41] [2007] EWCA Civ 374.
[42] [2007] 2 E.G.L.R. 75.
[43] See *Scottish Mutual Assurance Plc v Jardine Public Relations Ltd* [1999] E.G.C.S. 43, considered below. See also paras 10–08 to 10–10, above.
[44] See Ch.11, above.

be within the covenant.[45] The fact that the work involves a new method of design or construction will not necessarily prevent it being repair provided that the change can be justified by reference to the need to comply with legislation or regulations,[46] or there is otherwise some good reason for not duplicating the original.[47] Suppose, for example, that the old roof was a flat roof which suffered from incorrect falls caused by a badly designed or poorly constructed underlying structure. No sensible surveyor would recommend the laying of a new roof covering without at the same time doing whatever is necessary to the underlying structure to ensure that the new covering will be laid to correct falls. It is thought that this would not prevent the whole of the work from amounting to repair. The same reasoning could no doubt be used to justify putting on solar reflective paint when the old roof covering had none.

The installation of a new roof using more modern materials and methods of construction was held to be within the tenant's liability in *Elite Investments Ltd v TI Bainbridge (Silencers) Ltd*.[48] That case involved an industrial building that had been constructed in 1940 as a factory for the assembly of aircraft. It had a concrete floor and a steel frame supporting a lattice metal roof truss. The pitched roof was covered with corrugated galvanised steel sheeting with a row of windows about halfway up each side. The building was subsequently divided into three units, and a rubberised or bitumastic coating was applied to the roof. One unit was let for 20 years from January 1, 1972, and a second unit was let on June 15, 1977, for a term expiring on October 8, 1984. Both leases contained covenants on the part of the tenant to repair the demised premises including the roof. In the course of time the galvanising wore off and the roof sheets became severely corroded. This process had already started to occur when the rubberised coating was put on. The roof would still have been repairable when the leases were granted, but by October 1984 it was beyond patching and needed complete replacement. The proposed new material was polyvinyl-chloride-coated corrugated steel sheeting, which was lighter than the original galvanised steel, and virtually maintenance-free. It was also proposed to install a new form of polyester insulation, different from the original material. It would have been possible to replace the roof with galvanised steel similar to the original but this, together with the necessary bituminous coating, would have cost about the same as the new material. The second unit was unlettable in its then state. After the work had been done it would have been worth about £140,000. It would have cost nearly £1 million to put up a new unit of similar size.

It was argued on behalf of the tenants that the work was not repair. H.H. Judge Paul Baker QC, sitting as a judge of the High Court, found in favour of the landlords. In answer to the submission that the proposed roof was not repair because it was completely different from what was there before, he said:

"As I see that, it is not the roof that is going to be very different. It is a new material, but that is just taking advantage of better materials that are now on the market. It does not really alter the basic structure of the building and, after all, this is quite a simple building ... the roof will not

---

[45] See paras 11–30 to 11–32, above.
[46] See para.11–35, above.
[47] See paras 11–36 to 11–40, above.
[48] [1986] 2 E.G.L.R. 43.

be largely changed simply because it has got a roof looking similar to the existing roof but made of modern materials. Further, it seems largely irrelevant, because the old material is available and costs the same."

A similar conclusion was reached on different wording in *New England* **12–12** *Properties Ltd v Portsmouth New Shops Ltd.*[49] The landlord of a retail and office building covenanted to:

"[K]eep and maintain or procure to be kept and maintained [the development] and in particular without prejudice to the generality of the foregoing its exterior and its structure ... in good and substantial repair and condition and decoration and to renew or replace the same or any part or parts thereof whenever such renewal or replacement shall be necessary."

The original roof was inadequate in a number of respects. In particular the roof trusses were not thick enough and did not have sufficient lateral restraint nor sufficient longitudinal rafter ties; the longitudinal rafter ties were not continuous; and the roof was built with a 22.5-degree pitch, which increased the risk of water penetration and lifting tiles in strong winds. The roof became damaged and was in danger of collapse. The landlord carried out a remedial scheme which involved inserting new trusses with a 30-degree pitch, with more substantial timbers forming the trusses and rafters, and a proper system of lateral and horizontal restraint. The landlord claimed the cost of the scheme from the tenants by way of service charge. It was argued by the tenants that the covenant on its proper construction was limited to renewal or replacement piece by piece, and in the alternative that covenant was limited to renewing or replacing the roof with a replica of the original and did not extend to any substantial element of radical improvement. Mr T. Cullen QC, sitting as a deputy judge of the Chancery Division, rejected both these arguments, holding that the covenant imposed an absolute obligation to renew or replace whenever necessary. In the alternative, on the assumption that the reference to renewal and replacement added nothing to repair, he held that the work amounted to repair. His reasoning was as follows:

"It seems to me that this is a borderline case ... Looking at the matter broadly and taking into account in particular the nature and extent of the defects in design and construction of the roof and the fact that, as a result, it was in imminent danger of collapse; the fact that the comparative cost of merely patching up as opposed to replacing the whole roof was not a substantial difference; the fact that it was pointless rather than impossible to replace the roof by one of similar construction with a 22 degree pitch; and the fact that, at the end of the day, one still has a roof fulfilling precisely the same function but doing so in a way which will not involve the occupiers with further disruption by recurring defects, I consider that the new roof is not such a different roof that it must be regarded as an improvement or some other class of work – alteration or addition or change, whatever one likes to call it. I do not regard it as coming under that category rather than a matter of repair."

In *Postel Properties Ltd v Boots the Chemist*[50] it was held that the complete replacement of the flat roof coverings of a large shopping centre was within a landlord's covenant "with all due diligence to keep the ... roofs of the demised premises in the Shopping Centre in good and substantial repair and condition" such that the landlord was entitled to recover the cost from the tenants of the

---

[49] [1993] 1 E.G.L.R. 94.
[50] [1996] 2 E.G.L.R. 60.

centre by way of service charge. It was further held that the recoverable cost included the cost of thicker insulation (which would have been required by the building regulations had they applied) and a higher specification cap sheet but not the cost of priming troughs in the underlying decking (which achieved no useful purpose). Ian Kennedy J. said in the course of his judgment:

> "Whether I look at each item individually or, as I believe I should, at the replacement of the roof covering as a whole, I reach the same conclusion. These are repairs which a reasonably minded building owner might undertake, and they do not amount to giving back to the landlord something different from that which existed before."

**12–13**    In *Scottish Mutual Assurance Plc v Jardine Public Relations Ltd*,[51] the roof of an office building, whilst it had not leaked in the recent past, was defective and in need of repair, and had the potential for further water penetration. The judge found that at the relevant time two options were open to the landlord, one comprising piecemeal repairs and providing a short-term solution, and the other involving re-covering the roof. The landlord opted for the latter, re-using various parts. The falls of the original roof had been defective because the supporting beams (being of inadequate strength) had deflected, and the renewed roof included firring pieces along the top of the beams so as to provide proper falls. Mr David Blunt QC (sitting as a judge of the Technology and Construction Court) held that the work was repair within a landlord's covenant to use its best endeavours to provide certain services, namely, "maintaining repairing and (if necessary) renewing ... and otherwise keeping in good and substantial condition (as appropriate) ... the structure of the Building and in particular the roofs ...". He rejected the tenant's argument that the work fell within the "renewing" part of the covenant, such that it needed to be "necessary". He said:

> "[T]he Tecton beams and wood wool slabs were re-used. They were not replaced or renewed. Other elements (*e.g.* the asphalt, flashings etc.) were renewed. Nevertheless I am satisfied that whilst parts of the roof were renewed the roof taken as a whole was not, and I find that the effect of the works which were carried out was to repair the roof and not to renew it ... neither the works required to overcome the effect of the inherent defects in the roof nor the totality of the works carried out went beyond 'repair'."

The judge went on to find that the landlord would not have been in breach of its covenant if it had carried out the more limited piecemeal repairs suggested by the tenant's surveyor, and that (on the proper construction of the service charge provisions of the lease) the cost of the long-term solution in fact adopted by the landlord was not recoverable by way of service charge because, in all the circumstances including the short length of the lease, that cost was not reasonably or properly incurred.[52]

Further examples of the replacement of an existing defective roof with a new roof being held to be repair are *Wandsworth LBC v Griffin*[53] (in which the flat roofs of buildings on a Council estate were replaced with pitched roofs) and

---

[51] [1999] E.G.C.S. 43.

[52] See further on this case para 10–09, above.

[53] [2000] 2 E.G.L.R. 105 (Lands Tribunal) (in which the Member (Norman Rose FRICS) said that it did not seem to him that "a repair ceases to be a repair if it also effects an improvement").

*Mason v TotalFinaElf UK Ltd*[54] (which involved the replacement of two flat roofs forming part of petrol filling station premises).

The above decisions should not, of course, be regarded as anything more than the application of general principles to specific factual situations. However, they show that in appropriate circumstances complete replacement of a roof with a new roof constructed of modern materials and with a different design to the existing roof may amount to repair.

## Overcladding

One method of dealing with a defective roof which is sometimes encountered in practice, particularly in relation to industrial buildings, is to overclad it with a new roof structure constructed over the top of the original. In *Carmel Southend v Strachan & Henshaw*,[55] the roof of an industrial unit comprised corrugated asbestos cement sheeting fixed by hook bolts, and GRP roof lights. It was held that overcladding the roof with new profile metal sheeting was work of repair. However, damages for breach of the tenant's covenant to repair the roof were assessed by reference to the cost of lesser patch repair works which remained reasonably and sensibly possible.

**12–14**

## Roof lights

Many industrial buildings have profiled asbestos or fibre cement or metal roofs with GRP (glass reinforced plastic) roof lights. The amount of light admitted through the roof lights may decrease over time for a variety of possible reasons, which include (i) degradation of the GRP resin by ultra-violet light, so that the GRP becomes brittle and cracks as a result of movement caused by wind, snow or hail, (ii) abrasion of the surface by wind driven dirt, which exposes the glass fibres which in turn traps the dirt particles, (iii) deterioration of fixings and sealant with age, and (iv) discolouration of the resin through age.[56] In *Twinmar Holdings v Klarius*[57] one of the questions was the extent to which the tenant of a warehouse building was obliged under a covenant to keep the premises in good and substantial repair and condition to repair roof lights which, by the end of the lease, suffered from a substantial degree of abrasion of the surface which had reduced their translucence by an amount which was not insignificant. It was held that the roof lights were in disrepair and that the tenant was liable for the requisite work, which consisted of the application of a Delglaze coating, together with associated safety measures.[58]

**12–15**

---

[54] [2003] 3 E.G.L.R. 91.
[55] [2007] 3 E.G.L.R. 15. See para.12–09, above, where this case is further considered. See further *Sun Life Assurance PLC v Racal Tacs Ltd* [2000] 1 E.G.L.R. 138 (considered in para.12–08 above).
[56] See *Twinmar Holdings v Klarius* [2013] EWHC 944 (TCC) at [19].
[57] Above.
[58] See further on this case paras 7–50, 8–08 and 9–25, above.

## CLADDING

### Introductory

**12–16**  Well-designed and well-constructed cladding seldom gives rise to problems under repairing covenants. Where, however, the cladding is defectively designed or constructed, then major work may be necessary, sometimes involving the removal and replacement of the entirety of the cladding. The question then arises as to whether such work is too extensive to constitute repair.

### Replacement of damaged panels

**12–17**  Damage to cladding caused by defective design or construction does not necessarily occur to each individual panel at the same time. The process may be gradual, and deterioration may be more advanced in some cases than others. Nonetheless, it will often be the case that damage to all the panels is inevitable within the foreseeable future. The question may then be whether the covenantor is obliged or entitled to replace all the panels, including those that are not yet damaged, or whether he must wait until damage occurs. It is thought that if a substantial number of panels are already damaged, and similar damage is likely to occur to the remainder in the future, then replacement of the entirety would not be prevented from being repair merely because some panels are undamaged.[59] However, the question is one of fact and degree and depends on what is reasonable in the particular circumstances of each individual case. If the facts are such that a reasonable surveyor might equally well advise either complete replacement or piecemeal treatment of individual panels, then either will amount to a performance of the covenant.[60]

### Whether replacement amounts to repair

**12–18**  Whether removal and replacement of the cladding constitutes repair in any given case is a question of fact and degree.[61] Thus, in *Ravenseft Properties Ltd v Davstone (Holdings) Ltd*[62] a 16-storey rectangular block of maisonettes was constructed between 1958 and 1960 of a reinforced concrete frame with stone cladding on two elevations. No expansion joints were cut into the cladding stones because the necessity for this was not realised at the time. In 1973 part of the cladding became loose and in danger of falling. This was principally because of the lack of expansion joints but also because of defective workmanship in failing properly to tie in the stones. The landlord removed the whole of the cladding on the eastern elevation, and replaced it with proper ties and expansion joints. The stones on the western elevation were not removed but two out of three stones

---

[59] See paras 10–15 et seq., above.
[60] See paras 10–06 to 10–07, above.
[61] See Ch.11, above.
[62] [1980] Q.B. 12.

were pinned to the frame by the insertion of metal dowels and expansions joints were cut. Forbes J. held that the work, looked at as a matter of fact and degree, constituted repair.

The work in *Ravenseft* involved removing only part of the cladding, and the stones which were removed were refixed rather than replaced. By contrast, in *Holding & Management Ltd v Property Holding & Investment Trust Ltd*[63] the court had to consider a scheme which involved the removal and replacement of the whole of the cladding. The building in question was a 12-storey block of flats constructed in the 1960s of reinforced concrete with a brickwork cladding. The flats were let on long leases, under which one of the parties was a maintenance trustee who covenanted to apply the maintenance fund on trust for, among other things, the purpose of keeping the structure of the building "in good repair and condition". Following the discovery in 1985 of defects in the exterior, the maintenance trustee sought advice from a firm of consulting engineers, who recommended the removal of all the brickwork down to the second floor and then recladding with stainless steel angles to support the brickwork, together with expansion joints, compression joints and weepholes. The cost of that scheme (the "McHallam scheme A") was in excess of £1m. The tenants obtained advice from another firm of engineers, who recommended a much more limited scheme, involving localised repairs to the brickwork. That scheme cost about £0.25 million (the "Tietz scheme"). Subsequently the firm instructed by the maintenance trustee produced a revised scheme costing about £0.5 million (the "McHallam scheme B"). Proceedings were commenced in which the maintenance trustee contended that it was entitled to carry out the McHallam scheme B and the lessees argued that the appropriate work was the Tietz scheme. By the third day of the trial the respective experts agreed upon a scheme which comprised the items which were common ground between the McHallam scheme B and the Tietz scheme together with additional work. That scheme involved removing only very limited areas of brickwork. It cost about £0.25 million. One of the questions before the court was whether the McHallam scheme A constituted repair such that certain costs incurred by the maintenance trustee in connection with it were payable by the lessees or out of the maintenance fund. The Court of Appeal held that the work went beyond repair. Nicholls L.J. said in the course of his judgment:

> "[The McHallam scheme A] went beyond what was sensibly needed to cure the physical defects which had arisen: falling slip bricks, cracked brickwork, sheared concrete nibs, and so forth. Doubtless it would have resulted in a much better building. The building would have had a new brickwork cladding incorporating the features which experience since the early and mid-1960s has shown are needed in buildings with a reinforced concrete frame. A prudent building owner bearing the costs himself might well have decided to adopt such a scheme, despite its expense. But what is in question is whether owners of 75 year leases in the building could fairly be expected to pay for such a scheme under an obligation to 'repair'."

It is thought that the decision must be regarded as turning on its own facts. An important point was that the maintenance trustee had abandoned McHallam scheme A in favour of McHallam scheme B by the time proceedings were commenced, and subsequently agreed an even more limited scheme. In these

---

[63] [1990] 1 E.G.L.R. 65 (not reported on this point in [1989] 1 W.L.R. 1313).

circumstances it is perhaps not surprising that the court should have concluded that McHallam scheme A went beyond what was reasonably necessary. The decision should not be seen as authority for the proposition that complete removal of cladding cannot constitute repair under any circumstances.

**12–19**    In *Credit Suisse v Beegas Nominees Ltd*[64] a newly erected office and residential building suffered from water penetration. It was agreed between the experts that the only practical solution was to dismantle the existing cladding system and replace it with a new and redesigned system at a cost of about £1.2 million. Lindsay J. held that the work did not amount to repair on the ground that:

> "The question is established to be one of degree and in my judgment the whole cladding system, whilst well short of being the whole subject matter of the covenant, is too substantial and important a portion of the whole subject matter ... for its complete removal, redesign and replacement to be regarded as an operation in respect of only a subordinate or subsidiary part."

In so holding, the judge was applying the distinction drawn by Buckley L.J. in *Lurcott v Wakely*[65] between the renewal or replacement of defective parts, and the renewal or replacement of substantially the whole.[66] However, given his finding elsewhere in his judgment that the building with a new and redesigned cladding system would not be a building of a wholly different kind from that which had been let, his conclusion that the work did not amount to repair is perhaps open to question. In the event, however, this made no difference because he held that the work fell within the landlord's obligation to keep the structure in good and tenantable condition, and in the alternative, that it fell within the landlord's obligation to "renew".[67]

The above cases suggest that work which involves the complete removal and replacement of the cladding is likely on any view to be near the borderline between repair and work going beyond repair. It is thought, however, that provided such work can be justified by reference to the state of the existing cladding, and that the resulting building will not be one of a wholly different character from that let, there is no reason in principle why it should not be held to constitute repair in an appropriate case.

## The choice of work

**12–20**    In accordance with the principles already considered,[68] where any one of several methods of repair would comply with the requisite standard of repair, the choice between them will be for the covenanting party to make. In *Pgf II SA v Royal & Sun Alliance Insurance Plc*[69] both parties' experts put forward different schemes for repairing the cladding. It was held on the facts that the cladding scheme put forward by the tenant's expert was sufficient to comply with the tenant's

---

[64] [1994] 4 All E.R. 803 and (more fully) [1994] 1 E.G.L.R. 76. See further para.4–28, above.
[65] [1911] 1 K.B. 905.
[66] See paras 11–30 to 11–32, above.
[67] For the language used in the covenant and the judge's construction of it, see para.4–28 above.
[68] See para.10–06 et seq., above.
[69] [2010] EWHC 1459 (TCC).

obligation "well and substantially … to keep in good and substantial repair and condition" the demised premises", and damages were assessed on that basis.

## STEEL FRAMES

### Introductory

Most of the authorities on the meaning of "repair" were decided in relation to traditionally constructed buildings. As a result there is relatively little authority on the application of the covenant to steel-framed buildings. Such buildings differ from traditional buildings in the important respect that the building loads are carried on the steel frame, and the outer walls or cladding are generally non-load-bearing (except wind loads). Where the covenant has been drafted in a form which is more appropriate to traditional buildings, this may give rise to difficulties in identifying the subject-matter of the covenant. For example, it may be unclear to what extent "the exterior" is apt to include the steel frame as opposed to the outer cladding.[70] Other areas of difficulty include identifying the point at which the condition of the steel frame falls below the standard contemplated by the covenant, and the extent to which substantial work involving the exposure and treatment of the steelwork goes beyond repair. The latter arises particularly in relation to buildings suffering from "Regent Street disease" (where water penetration causes the steel frame to rust and expand, which results in outward pressure on the encapsulating brick or stonework, which in turn causes it to crack and/or move outwards).

**12–21**

### The standard of repair

The existence of rust in a steel frame does not of itself mean that the covenantor is obliged to undertake remedial work.[71] Liability will only arise when the rust is such as to bring the condition of the frame below the standard contemplated by the covenant. In some cases this point will have been reached when the steel has rusted to a material degree, even though it remains quite capable of supporting the relevant building loads.[72] In an appropriate case, however, no work may be required until the rust either is such as materially affects the adequacy of the strength of the steel frame, or causes or threatens to cause damage to the external walls. Thus, in *Plough Investments Ltd v Manchester City Council*[73] a steel-framed office building constructed in 1925 was let in parts in 1973 and 1974. The steel frame was rusting, and the rusting had (by expansion) caused some cracking and displacement of bricks. Scott J. recorded the submissions of counsel in the following terms:

**12–22**

---

[70] See paras 7–41 to 7–43, above.
[71] Although its existence will usually satisfy the requirement that there must be physical damage or deterioration before a liability to repair arises: see para.8–07, above.
[72] See *Re Mayor and Corp of London* [1910] 2 Ch. 314 discussed at para.8–07, above.
[73] [1989] 1 E.G.L.R. 244.

"[Counsel for the tenant] accepted that if rust on the steel frame had caused bricks or blocks forming part of the external wall to crack, the cleaning of the rust affected steel would form a part of the repairs to be done pursuant to the fifth schedule covenant whether or not the steel frame were regarded as part of the exterior of the building. And [counsel for the landlords] did not contend that a degree of rust which did not materially affect either the external walls or the adequacy of the strength of the steel member would nonetheless require to be remedied in compliance with the fifth schedule repairing obligation."

**12–23**    In *Gibson Investments Ltd v Chesterton Plc*[74] a substantial steel-framed office building in Birmingham constructed between 1914 and 1915 was let for 35 years. The tenant covenanted:

"At all times during the continuance of the term to keep in good and substantial repair and when appropriate to rebuild the whole of the demised premises and every part thereof ... notwithstanding that any want to repair may be due to an inherent or latent defect in the demised premises or to normal wear and tear or deterioration or otherwise and if at any time ... it shall be necessary for the purpose of complying with this covenant to rebuild the building or any part thereof from time to time forming part of the demised premises then the tenant shall ... carry out such rebuilding."

The building suffered from cracking in the external stonework and brickwork which was caused or contributed to by the rusting and consequent expansion of the steel frame. There was a significant degree of cracking over all four external elevations and the cracking had accelerated over the past five or six years. It was common ground that the tenant was liable to carry out remedial works, but the issue was which of three schemes of work would amount to a compliance with the covenant. The first (which would cost £425,000) involved sealing the cracks, removing and replacing cracked stones and bricks only where it was not sensibly possible to fill in the cracks and treating any exposed rusted steel. The second (which would cost £875,000 to £1.05 million) involved removing cracked stones or bricks and opening up neighbouring stone and brickwork along the line of the steelwork thereby exposed until it was free of laminating, and making good. The third (which would cost £780,000) lay somewhere between the first and second, but involved in addition the installation of a cathodic protection system. The tenant contended that the first would satisfy its repairing obligations. The landlord rejected the first, but was content with either the second or the third. Neuberger J. held that the first scheme was not an acceptable way of performing the covenant. He said:

"First, in my judgment the first scheme, if carried out, unlike the second or third scheme, would not result in the building being in repair even at the moment that the works were completed. The continued presence of laminating rust in areas adjacent to places where the laminated rust has caused cracking would, in my view, constitute disrepair. The rusting is substantial, and the rusting which the second scheme would involve removing would be in runs which have already caused cracking. If there is a run of laminated rust which has not caused cracking there would be no need to deal with it under the second scheme. The fact that the structural frame is not currently under threat does not, in my view, call this conclusion into question. It appears to me that the fact that laminating rusting has already caused significant cracking in places means that one cannot say that the building is in repair if there are runs of laminating rusting which have caused the cracking.
    Secondly, it seems to me that it would be inappropriate not to carry out the extra remedial work involved in the second scheme over the first scheme at the same time as repairing the

---

[74] [2002] 2 P. & C.R. 32.

cracks in the stonework and brickwork. ... The effect of implementing the second or third schemes (costing about £1 million at the most) should obviate the need for any significant work to the exterior walls for the remaining eleven or so years of the lease, and possibly much longer than that. The first scheme works, if carried out, costing a little over £400,000, will probably have to be repeated some three times before the lease ends."

He went on to hold that the second scheme would constitute compliance with the covenant, and that whilst the works in the third scheme were not prevented from being repair on the ground that the introduction of cathodic protection was the installation of a wholly new item into the building, a reasonable person could take the view that they were or were not an acceptable way to repair the building. The tenant could therefore elect for the second or the third option.

Where rust in the steel frame has resulted in cracks in the outer curtain walling, the covenantor will prima facie be liable to make good that damage. However, not every crack will require to be made good, particularly where the building is old. The cracking must be such as to bring the condition of the walls below the requisite standard. Thus, in *Plough Investments Ltd v Manchester City Council*[75] Scott J. said:

"Nor, in my opinion, would [the obligation to repair] include the removal and replacement of every cracked brick or block, no matter how small the crack. There were cracks when the leases were granted. A building of this sort, over 60 years old, is bound, in my view, to have some cracks in the bricks or blocks."

## Treatment of the steel frame

Identifying the point at which treatment of the frame ceases to be repair is a matter of fact and degree.[76] The remedial scheme proposed by the landlord in *Plough Investments Ltd v Manchester City Council*[77] involved (on the assumption that all the steelwork was rusty) removing the external cladding so as to expose the steelwork; removing the rust by shotblasting; treating the steel with a rust inhibitor; enclosing the treated steel in concrete so as to compensate for the reduced strength of the member in question, or if strengthening was unnecessary, painting it; and reinstating the cladding. Scott J. said in his judgment:

12–24

"If, in the present case, the degree of rusting had so reduced the strength of the steel frame as to require the substantial reinforcement of the whole of the external steel frame in the manner contemplated by ... the remedial works proposed by the plaintiff, I would have been of the opinion that the remedial works went, as a matter of degree, beyond 'repair'. But if one section only, say the section at or around location A, required strengthening by being surrounded with reinforced concrete, I would not regard that work as going beyond repair. At some point between those two extremes a line would, in my opinion, need to be drawn."

In *Gibson Investments Ltd v Chesterton Plc*[78] (the facts of which are set out in para.12–23 above) Neuberger J. said of the second scheme:

---

[75] [1989] 1 E.G.L.R. 244.
[76] See Ch.11, above.
[77] [1989] 1 E.G.L.R. 244.
[78] [2002] 2 P. & C.R. 32.

"If the second scheme would otherwise constitute repair, I do not believe that the nature or cost of the works involved in that scheme would take it out of being repair. Removal and replacement of some of the stonework and brickwork, and the removal of the laminated rust and the application of some rust-preventing coating on the steel, followed by replacement of the stonework and brickwork, appear to me to be quite conceptually capable, to put it at its lowest, of constituting repair, particularly in the context of such a substantial building, which shows no sign of being anywhere near the end of its useful life, and which is the subject of a 33 year lease — particularly given the nature of the problem, namely that rusting is causing the cracking of the brick work and the stonework. Similarly, the cost of the work, namely around £1 million, in the context of a building of this size held under a lease for a term of 33 years, does not appear to me to bring into question whether the second scheme can fairly be characterised as repair."

## Cathodic protection

**12–25** Cathodic protection is a relatively new technique, at least when applied to buildings. It involves introducing an electrical circuit into the steel frame, the purpose of which is to prevent the steel oxidising and thereby rusting. If successful, it prevents further rusting, although it has no effect on existing rusting. In *Gibson Investments Ltd v Chesterton Plc*[79] (the facts of which are set out in para.12–23 above), the third scheme under consideration by the court involved the installation of cathodic protection. The tenant contended that this went beyond repair because "not only was it not something included in the original demise, it would not even replace an item of a different nature but intended to perform a similar function in the original demise". Neuberger J. rejected that argument "albeit with real hesitation", holding that the third scheme was capable of amounting to repair (on the principal ground that it was analogous to the damp-proof course in *Elmcroft Developments Ltd v Tankersley-Sawyer*[80]), and that it was a scheme which could properly be adopted. In relation to this last, he said:

"In my view, ... the third scheme is capable of falling on either side of the band of reasonableness. In other words, it seems to me that where, as here, there is disrepair which might be dealt with by cathodic protection, and which expert evidence suggests probably could be satisfactorily dealt with by cathodic protection, a paying party could reasonably take the view that cathodic protection was appropriate, but equally reasonably he could take the view that it was too risky because of the early stage in the history of cathodic protection."

## CONCRETE

## Actual or prospective loss of strength

**12–26** The application to defective concrete of the principles already considered generally presents no special difficulty. In some cases, however, problems in practice may arise from the fact that the concrete in question, whilst continuing to perform its structural function safely and adequately for the time being, is perceived as suffering from a risk of future failure. For example, concrete beams or slabs may be constructed of high alumina cement concrete (HAC). Such

---

[79] Above.
[80] [1984] 1 E.G.L.R. 47. See para.12–31, below.

concrete may suffer a progressive loss of strength where it is subjected to a chemical attack coupled with excessive or persistent damp conditions. Or the item may have been constructed using permanent wood wool shuttering, which may have resulted in poor compaction or inadequate or non-existent covering of embedded reinforcement bars.

The principal question in such cases will be whether the item is in disrepair.[81] It is thought that the mere presence of (for example) HAC or wood wool shuttering will not, of itself, amount to disrepair (save in exceptional circumstances[82]). If no disrepair can be shown to exist, then no work is required under the covenant. If, however, damage has occurred (for example, corrosion of the embedded reinforcement or cracking of the concrete) then the questions will be, in turn, whether that damage brings the subject-matter of the covenant below its contemplated condition[83]; what remedial work is required[84]; and whether that work is too extensive to be regarded as "repair" properly so-called.[85]

One relevant factor in answering some of these questions will be the extent to which the work is necessary to enable the building to continue being occupied. In *London Borough of Camden v Civil Aviation Authority*[86] a building constructed in the mid-1970s contained beams made of HAC. The expert evidence was that the strength of some of the beams had deteriorated and that there was a possibility of the concrete being defective to a serious degree. The Court of Appeal held that the necessary remedial works were not repairs for the purposes of s.19 of the General Rate Act 1967. One reason for this was that the works were not then necessary because the premises could still be used as offices. Eveleigh L.J. said:

> "[I]t was not work that positively had to be done. The condition of the building was not such that, as a result of the … HAC beams, it could not be used as offices. The condition of those members was such that a prudent landlord might well, at some time, decide, for the continuing and ultimate stability and duration of the building, to carry out such work as those investigations indicated was desirable—at some time, and a time of his choosing."

## DAMP

### Introductory

For present purposes, damp occurring in buildings may be broadly divided into penetrating damp, rising damp and damp resulting from condensation.[87] Penetrating damp is generally due to the defective state of some part of the building, such as the external walls, or the roof. Rising damp is usually due either to a defect in the building, such as the failure of a damp-proof course, or a design or construction fault in the building, such as the absence of a damp-proof course, or the laying of a damp-proof membrane in such a way that it is ineffective.

**12–27**

---

[81] See Ch.8, above.

[82] See para.8–10, above.

[83] See Ch.9, above.

[84] See Ch.10, above.

[85] See Ch.11, above.

[86] [1981] 1 E.G.L.R. 113.

[87] Damp may also result from leaking services, but it is not thought that any separate treatment of this is necessary.

Condensation occurs where the moisture in the air condenses on cold surfaces of the building, such as windows and wall surfaces. It is generally caused by inadequate or defective insulation, ventilation or heating (or a combination of these) together with a source of moisture in the air (such as human activity) resulting in a high relative humidity. It often produces mould growth on carpets, furniture and stored clothes.

## Penetrating damp

**12–28**   The first question in relation to penetrating damp is whether the subject matter of the covenant is in disrepair, i.e. whether it is in a damaged or deteriorated condition.[88] The mere existence of damp is not "disrepair".[89] If no disrepair exists, the covenantor will not generally be liable to carry out whatever work is necessary to prevent continuing penetration. Thus, in *Post Office v Aquarius Properties Ltd*[90] a defectively constructed "kicker" joint resulted in water penetration into the basement of an office building. The joint was in the same condition as it had been when constructed, and there was no evidence of any damage or deterioration resulting from the water penetration. The tenant was held not liable to carry out the requisite waterproofing work on the ground that there was no damage to the subject-matter of the covenant.[91]

However, once it is possible to identify damage or deterioration (whether causing or caused by the damp penetration), the covenant to repair comes into operation. The question in practice is then likely to be whether the necessary remedial work is too extensive to amount to repair.[92]

The position in relation to roofs has already been discussed.[93] Where the cause of the damp is defective pointing or guttering in the area adjacent to the damp areas, then whether the remedial work amounts to repair is unlikely to cause much difficulty in practice. However, where substantial internal waterproofing work is needed, the position may be more difficult. In two cases, waterproofing work involving the construction of additional structure within the building has been held to go beyond repair. In *Pembery v Lamdin*[94] the demised premises consisted of a shop and underground basement, which were at least 100 years old, and had been built without any form of waterproofing for the basement. Water was penetrating into the basement and the walls were saturated. The remedial works included asphalting the walls, building a new 4¹in wall inside to keep the asphalt in position, and laying a new concrete floor about 4in thick to prevent water coming under the walls. The Court of Appeal held that this went beyond repair.[95]

---

[88]   See Ch.8, above.
[89]   *Quick v Taff-Ely Borough Council* [1986] Q.B. 809; *Lee v Leeds City Council* [2002] 1 W.L.R. 1488; *Southwark LBC v McIntosh* [2002] 1 E.G.L.R. 25. See further Ch.8, above.
[90]   [1987] 1 All E.R. 1055.
[91]   See further on this case para.8–02, above.
[92]   See Ch.11, above.
[93]   See paras 12–06 to 12–15, above.
[94]   [1940] 2 All E.R. 434.
[95]   See further para.11–34, above.

In *Post Office v Aquarius Properties Ltd*[96] various waterproofing schemes were before the court. Common to all was the making of a substantial structural addition to the basement in the form of a new concrete slab with reinforcement to the upper side, and the construction of inner concrete skins against the existing walls. At first instance Hoffmann J. held that the work was not repair within the tenant's covenant. As a matter of ordinary English, the work was not repair but "structural alterations and improvements to the basement".[97] His decision was affirmed by the Court of Appeal on the different ground that there was no disrepair requiring to be remedied (so that the question whether the work went beyond repair did not arise).

## Rising damp

Rising damp may be caused by failure of the damp-proofing system of the building, or the absence of any such system.                                                12–29

### (a)    Failure of the damp-proofing system

Where the building already has a damp-proofing system when the lease is       12–30
granted, the covenantor will be generally liable to repair it if it breaks down. Thus, in *Luckhurst v Manyfield*[98] the solid floor of the basement of the demised flat contained a damp-proof membrane which had broken down, and the landlord was held liable to repair it under a covenant to repair (among other things) "the main structure and in particular the foundations external walls roof gutters and rain water pipes of the property". The work for which the covenantor is liable may include replacing the damp proofing system where this is the only sensible and practical way of effecting repairs.[99] Where substantial additional works are required as well, then (depending on their nature and extent) the work as a whole may go beyond repair as a matter of fact and degree.[100]

### (b)    Absence of a damp-proofing system

It is a commonly held misconception that a covenant to repair does not oblige the    12–31
covenantor to install a damp-proof course unless one exists already and is defective. This is too simple a view. Where rising damp is caused by the lack of a damp-proof course, the first question is whether it has resulted in disrepair, i.e. damage or deterioration in the subject-matter of the covenant.[101] The mere

---

[96] [1985] 2 E.G.L.R. 105 (affirmed on different grounds [1987] 1 All E.R. 1055: see para.8–02, above).

[97] See para.11–32, above.

[98] Unreported decision of H.H. Judge Bowsher, QC dated July 30, 1992 (noted in the *Handbook of Dilapidations* at DC256).

[99] See paras 11–30 to 11–32, above.

[100] See *Pembery v Lamdin*, above; *Post Office v Aquarius Properties Ltd*, above, discussed in para.12–28, above; and *Yanover v Romford Finance & Development Co Ltd*, below discussed in para.12–34, below.

[101] See Ch.8, above.

existence of damp is not "disrepair".[102] If there is no damage to the subject-matter of the covenant, then no question of liability to install a damp-proof course arises. If there is damage or deterioration to the subject-matter of the covenant (for example, defective brickwork or plaster[103]), then the covenantor will prima facie be liable to remedy that damage, and depending on all the circumstances his obligation may include installing a damp-proof course to prevent further damage.

In *Elmcroft Developments Ltd v Tankersley-Sawyer*[104] a landlord was held liable to install a damp-proof course. That case concerned a basement flat in a late Victorian purpose-built mansion block in a fashionable area of London. The flat was let for 60 years less three days from September 29, 1955, on a lease containing a landlord's covenant to "maintain and keep the exterior of the building and the roof, the main walls, timbers and drains thereof in good and tenantable repair and condition". As constructed, the external and party walls of the flat included what had been intended to be a damp-proof course, consisting of slates laid horizontally. However, this was ineffective because it was positioned below ground. The flat suffered from extensive rising damp which had affected the internal plaster, decorations and woodwork. The tenant contended that the landlords were liable under their covenant to install a damp-proof course in the external walls. Her contention was upheld by the county court judge and by the Court of Appeal. Ackner L.J., who gave the leading judgment, said:

> "[T]he learned judge was wholly right in the decision which he made as to the failure by the [landlords] to comply with the repairing covenant and their obligation in regard to curing the damp by using the only practical method at this price, namely, injecting silicone into the wall. [Counsel] was at one stage prepared to concede that, as the plaster became saturated (which, of course, it was) his clients had the obligation to do the necessary patching—that is removing—the perished plaster and renewing it. I am bound to say that concession made the resistance to inserting the damp-proof course a strange one. The damp proof course, once inserted, would on the expert evidence cure the damp. The patching work would have to go on and on and on, because, as the plaster absorbed (as it would) the rising damp, it would have to be renewed, and the cost to the appellants in constantly being involved with this sort of work one would have thought, would have outweighed easily the cost in doing the job properly. I have no hesitation in rejecting the submission that the [landlord's] obligation was repetitively to carry out futile work instead of doing the job properly once and for all."

As is clear from this passage, the important point is that it was not realistic to effect the relevant repairs (to the plaster) without also getting rid of the design defect (the absence of an effective damp-proof course).[105]

**12–32**   It is true that in *Elmcroft* the building had been constructed with what was intended to be a damp-proof course, so that it may be said that in this respect the case is not on all fours with cases where there has never been a damp-proof course. However, it is thought that the position is the same in relation to cases of

---

[102] *Quick v Taff-Ely Borough Council* [1986] Q.B. 809; *Lee v Leeds City Council* [2002] 1 W.L.R. 1488; *Southwark LBC v McIntosh* [2002] 1 E.G.L.R. 25; *Janet Reger International v Tiree* [2006] 3 E.G.L.R. 131; *Jackson v JH Watson Property Investment* [2008] 1 E.G.L.R. 33. See further Ch.8, above, in which these cases are considered.
[103] See Ch.8, above.
[104] [1984] 1 E.G.L.R. 47.
[105] See *Quick v Taff-Ely Borough Council* [1986] Q.B. 809 and *Stent v Monmouth District Council* (1987) 54 P. & C.R. 193, in both of which *Elmcroft* was explained in this way. See also paras 11–38 to 11–40, above.

the latter kind. In *Elmcroft* the slate layer in question was ineffective as a damp-proof course. It is difficult to see any sensible distinction between this and cases where there is no form of damp-proofing to begin with. Moreover, there is nothing in the judgment in *Elmcroft* to suggest that the decision would have been different if the building had been constructed without any form of damp-proofing.

It follows that the covenantor may be obliged under the covenant to install a damp-proof course. It must be emphasised again, however, that this is subject to the qualification that there must be physical damage or deterioration to the subject-matter of the covenant before any work can be required.[106] The lack of damp-proof course does not of itself constitute damage.[107] It is only when rising damp resulting from lack of damp-proofing has caused relevant damage to the subject matter of the covenant that the above principle will come into play. In *Elmcroft* there was damage to the plasterwork, which the Court of Appeal implicitly treated as part of the subject-matter of the landlord's covenant,[108] and it was that damage which brought the principle into operation.[109] Damage to parts of the building other than the subject-matter of the covenant will not suffice.[110]

*Elmcroft* had not been reported by April 11, 1984, when a differently constituted Court of Appeal held in *Wainwright v Leeds City Council*[111] that the insertion of a damp-proof course was not a repair. That case concerned a back-to-back terraced house, which had been built in the early part of the twentieth century without a damp-proof course. The landlord council was under an implied statutory obligation to keep in repair the structure and exterior.[112] It was contended on behalf of the tenant that the council was obliged to provide a damp-proof course so as to eradicate rising damp. At first instance the recorder held that he was bound by *Pembery v Lamdin*[113] to hold that the council was not liable. The tenant appealed and the Court of Appeal dismissed his appeal. Dunn L.J., who gave the leading judgment, said:

> "So, applying the facts of [*Pembery*] to the facts of this case, the tenant in this case took a house without a damp-proof course. What he is asking from the landlord is a house with a damp-proof course, which is a different thing to the house which was the subject of the demise. As Slesser L.J. makes clear [in *Pembery*] the obligation of the landlord does not go beyond repairing the thing which was the subject of the demise, namely in this case a house without a damp-proof course, so on the facts I find *Pembery* indistinguishable from the facts in this case, and indeed [counsel] realistically accepts that."

It is thought that *Wainwright* must be approached with caution. First, it proceeded on the footing that *Pembery v Lamdin* was indistinguishable on its facts. However, the remedial work in *Pembery* was of a quite different order. It involved the asphalting of an underground basement, the construction of a new     **12–33**

---

[106] See Ch.8, above.

[107] Cf. *Southwark LBC v McIntosh* [2002] 1 E.G.L.R. 25.

[108] It has subsequently held by the Court of Appeal in *Grand v Gill* [2011] 1 W.L.R. 2253 that plaster is part of the structure for the purposes of the landlord's repairing obligation implied by s.11 of the Landlord and Tenant Act 1985. See further para.7–36, above.

[109] Cf. *Janet Reger International v Tiree* [2006] 3 E.G.L.R. 131 at [65].

[110] See para.8–09, above.

[111] [1984] 1 E.G.L.R. 67.

[112] See para.20–17 et seq., below.

[113] [1940] 2 All E.R. 434. See para.12–28, above.

4.5in wall to keep the asphalt in place, and the laying of a new 4in thick concrete floor to prevent water coming under the walls. This is a long way from the insertion of a damp-proof course. Secondly, the principal argument for the tenant was that the obligations of a local authority landlord were wider than those of a private landlord. It is difficult to see how this can be so.[114] Thirdly, no argument appears to have been addressed to the court along the lines of the analysis in *Elmcroft*. In these circumstances, once it was accepted that *Pembery v Lamdin* was indistinguishable, then the conclusion that the insertion of a damp-proof course was outside the covenant was bound to follow.

However, *Elmcroft* was distinguished by the Court of Appeal in *Eyre v McCracken*.[115] That case concerned residential premises let for seven-and-a-quarter years. The tenant covenanted:

> "[T]o put the premises ... in good and substantial repair and condition [and to] well and substantially repair, maintain, cleanse, paint, amend and keep the said premises as so intended to be put into such repair as aforesaid."

The house had been built in the last century without a damp-proof course. At first instance the county court judge held that the tenant was liable to put a damp-proof course into the basement at a cost (together with ancillary work) of about £15,000. The Court of Appeal allowed the tenant's appeal. Pill L.J. said:

> "I have regard to the age (over 150 years) and the design of the building. It has no damp proof course. That is an original design feature common to buildings of that age. Its absence will eventually allow dampness to develop. I bear in mind the limited interest of the tenant and the poor condition of the premises at the date in 1976 when the term started. It is common ground that it would be sensible to put in a damp proof course. The issue is whether, under his repairing covenant, the tenant is required to do so in the circumstances of this case. My conclusion is that he is not. In my judgment, to require the tenant to insert the damp proof course and ancillary work would be to require him to give back to the landlord a different thing from that demised to him in 1976. The circumstances are very different from those involved in the consideration of the landlord's covenant in *Elmcroft*."

Although the grounds on which the court distinguished *Elmcroft* are not entirely clear from the report, the relevant distinction appears to lie principally in the fact that in *Eyre* the covenantor was a tenant under a relatively short lease, whereas in *Elmcroft* the covenantor was the landlord under a long lease.

In *Holding & Barnes v Hill House Hammond*,[116] the basement floors of a terraced brick-built building were almost totally rotted and broken up in large part, and the walls suffered from damp. The main cause of the latter was the lack of a damp proof course, but significant further causes were the absence of any satisfactory ventilation, and penetrating damp caused by the external wall not being properly rendered. The tenant was liable to repair to keep the premises in

---

[114] This was described by Lawton L.J. in *Quick v Taff-Ely Borough Council* [1986] Q.B. 809, as a submission based "on social rather than on legal grounds".

[115] (2000) 80 P. & C.R. 220.

[116] Unreported decision of Neuberger J. dated March 17, 2000. This was the trial of the action following the judge's determination of a preliminary issue concerning the meaning of the landlord's repairing covenant (reported at [2000] L. & T.R 428) and prior to the decision of the Court of Appeal (reported at [20002] 2 P. & C. R. 11 and considered in para.4–09, above) allowing the tenant's cross-appeal on the preliminary issue.

good internal repair, and the landlord was liable to keep the exterior in good and tenantable repair and condition. Neuberger J., having considered *Elmcroft* and *Eyre*, held that the tenant was liable to install a damp-proof course, on the ground that this was "far more intimately connected with the replacing of the floors and repairing the plaster on the interior walls than it is connected with the external rendering".[117]

In *R. (on the application of Sinclair Gardens Investments (Kensington) Ltd) v Lands Tribunal*,[118] a leasehold valuation tribunal held that the provision by the landlord of a chemical damp-proof course and associated re-plastering and rendering in certain walls of the basement flat in a converted house constituted an improvement not a repair, so that the cost was not recoverable from the tenants under the service charge provisions of their leases. The landlord sought permission to appeal from the Lands Tribunal, which refused it on the ground that the conclusions of the LVT were ones which it could reasonably have reached. The landlord applied for judicial review of the Lands Tribunal's decision. Its application failed at first instance and in the Court of Appeal. In his judgment, Neuberger L.J. (with whom Laws and Auld L.JJ. agreed) described the question whether the work fell within the landlord's covenant as "fact sensitive and nuanced". Having referred to *Pembery v Lamdin, Elmcroft Developments v Tankerlsey-Sawyer, Wainwright v Leeds City Council* and *Eyre v McCracken*, he said:

> "At the risk of going into the merits further than is appropriate, I consider that the facts of the present case have features which, when viewed in the light of these four authorities, can be said to point to opposite conclusions. There was no damp proof course in the relevant location and the building was more than 100 years old, but the leases were long leases, and, for what it is worth, the covenant was imposed on the landlord, not on the tenant, albeit that the tenants, rather than the landlord, ultimately had to pay for the cost of the repairs, through the service charge provisions."

Reference should also be made to the decision of Park J. in *Yanover v Romford Finance & Development Co Ltd*.[119] In that case a ground floor flat was let in 1963 on a lease containing an obligation on the part of the landlord to keep the exterior of the building in repair. The relevant byelaws in force in 1963 when the building was constructed required it to have an over-site layer of impervious concrete and a damp-proof membrane in the outer leaf of the external walls, and it complied with these requirements. The byelaws did not require damp-proof membranes in over-site concrete or a damp-proof course in the inner leaf of a cavity wall, and these were not provided. The building would not have complied with the Building Regulations, which came into force several years later. Damage to decorations and furniture in the flat from damp occurred in and after 1972, but prior to 1979 the greater part was due to condensation, the contribution made by rising damp being minimal. After that date, rising damp was responsible for about

**12–34**

---

[117] Note, however, that the judge's construction of the landlord's covenant was subsequently held to be incorrect by the Court of Appeal (see the preceding footnote), so that his decision on the damp proof course issue needs to be read with this in mind.

[118] [2006] 3 All E.R. 650.

[119] Unreported decision of Park J. on March 29, 1983. It is noted at (1983) 269 C.S.W. 79, but it is necessary to read the transcript for the full facts.

half the damage. The increase in rising damp was probably attributable to a change in the water-table. But for that change, the original damp-proof arrangements would have continued to be effective. The work necessary to remedy the rising damp consisted of lifting the parquet floors, inserting a bitumen damp-proof membrane with screed laid on top, and silicon injecting the walls and partitions. This was described in the evidence as a major building operation which would cause great disruption and inconvenience and would probably require the occupants to move out during some of the work. The cost at 1982 prices was between £4,000 and £8,000. Park J. held that the landlord was not liable to carry out the work.

It is not clear whether the ground for the decision was that (i) the existing damp-proofing arrangements were not in disrepair (as opposed to being unable to cope with a rise in the water-table[120]), or (ii) the work went beyond repair as a matter of fact and degree. If (i) is the correct basis, then it is thought that the decision has to be approached with caution. It was not sufficient to conclude that the damp-proof system itself was not in disrepair. In accordance with the principles already considered,[121] the judge should have asked himself whether there was damage to the subject-matter of the covenant (including, but not limited to, the damp-proof system) which required remedying. If there was, then it would have been necessary to go on and ask whether it would have been "futile" to have remedied that damage without also eliminating the cause of it.[122] The judge did not in terms carry out this exercise. However, the judge's citation from *Brew Bros Ltd v Snax (Ross) Ltd*[123] suggests that (ii) was the real basis for his decision. It is thought that the decision can be justified on this ground, having regard in particular to the condition of the premises at the date of the lease and the relatively extensive nature of the work.

## Condensation

12–35    The mere existence of damp or mould resulting from condensation is not "disrepair".[124] No work will be required under the covenant unless either (a) the condensation results from a state of disrepair (for example, the physically defective state of the insulation or heating) as opposed to a design defect (for example, inadequate ventilation), or (b) the damp has resulted in disrepair to the subject-matter of the covenant which can only sensibly be remedied by eradicating the cause of the condensation at the same time.[125] In practice, it may be very difficult to prove either of these. Thus, in *Ball v Plymouth City Council*

---

[120] In this respect the facts are similar to those in *Post Office v Aquarius Properties Ltd* [1987] 1 All E.R. 1055. See Ch.8, above.

[121] See Chs 8 and 9, above.

[122] See *Elmcroft Developments Ltd v Tankersley-Sawyer* [1984] 1 E.G.L.R. 47, per Ackner L.J. See paras 10–03 to 10–04 and 11–38 to 11–40, above.

[123] [1970] Q.B. 612.

[124] *Quick v Taff-Ely Borough Council* [1986] Q.B. 809; *Lee v Leeds City Council* [2002] 1 W.L.R. 1488; *Southwark LBC v McIntosh* [2002] 1 E.G.L.R. 25; *Grand v Gill* [2011] EWCA Civ 554. See further Ch.8, above.

[125] See the authorities referred to in the preceding footnote, and see Chs 8 and 11, above.

[126] the tenant failed to prove that the source of the moisture was defective walls. In *Quick v Taff-Ely Borough Council*[127] the tenant failed to prove that such disrepair as had occurred required the remedying of the inherent design defect which had given rise to the condensation. Even if the tenant can establish either of these, the remedial work may go beyond repair as a matter of fact and degree.[128] However, the position may be different where the relevant obligation is to keep in good condition.[129]

## DEFECTIVE WINDOWS[130]

### Whether part of the subject-matter of the covenant

Many old leases of parts of multi-occupied buildings do not make it clear to what extent the windows and window frames are included in the parties' respective repairing obligations. That question will often have to be answered by reference to whether the windows and frames are part of the "structure", the "exterior", the "main walls" or any other similar expression the draftsman has chosen to use. This is a question of construction of the lease in question, and the applicable principles are considered elsewhere.[131]

**12–36**

### Whether replacement is repair or improvement

Replacement of defective window frames with an equivalent item will generally amount to repair under the principles already considered, provided obviously that the existing frames have reached the point at which this is the appropriate course. Greater problems may arise where the opportunity is taken to upgrade what was there before by installing double glazing in place of single glazing. In *Mullaney v Maybourne Grange (Croydon) Management Co Ltd*[132] Mr Julian Jeffs QC held that the replacement of wooden-framed windows in a modern tower block of flats, which had "from the very outset been a source of trouble, leaking water, requiring painting every four years … and causing considerable trouble and expense …" with double-glazed windows was not a repair. He thought that:

**12–37**

> "[I]n the context of the replacement of the windows … what was being done here went beyond what was necessary for the purpose of effecting a repair and was by way of a long-term improvement. It was looking to the future not to the present."

A different conclusion was reached by Harman J. in *Minja Properties Ltd v Cussins Property Group Plc*,[133] which concerned steel-framed windows in an office building constructed in the late 1960s or early 1970s. The frames suffered

---

[126] [2004] EWHC 134 (QB).
[127] [1986] Q.B. 809.
[128] See Ch.9, above.
[129] *Welsh v Greenwich Borough Council* [2000] 3 E.G.L.R. 41. See paras 4–29 and 4–30, above.
[130] For the meaning of "window" in the context of a repairing covenant, see para.7–50, above.
[131] See Ch.7, above.
[132] [1986] 1 E.G.L.R. 70.
[133] [1998] 2 E.G.L.R. 52.

from corrosion because, when made and installed, they had not been adequately treated against rust. The landlord proposed to replace all the windows with aluminium-frame double-glazed windows. Harman J. held (on the landlord's application for an injunction requiring the tenant to allow access for the work) that this was within the landlord's covenant to "maintain and keep in good and tenantable repair the ... window frames (excluding glass) ...". He said:

> "The objection made is that what is proposed is aluminium frame double glazed windows. Using such common sense and such knowledge of the world as I possess, I am reasonably confident that these are frames with two channels in them to take two panes of glass with a fixed gap between them, which gap will provide a certain degree, depending on the gap, of insulation. Such a form of frame does not on the evidence seem to be very substantially different from the former single glazed steel frame that was there before.
>
> [Counsel for the tenant] did not argue for a single moment that it would not be perfectly proper to replace these steel frame single pane windows with aluminium frame single pane windows, even though aluminium frames may be—I do not say are—more expensive than steel frames would be because the metal is a more expensive material. That, he accepted, would be an improvement of degree, not in any sense radical enough to amount to renewal in the sense in which it is used in *Lurcott v. Wakely*[134] rather than repair.
>
> ...There is ample evidence for me to be convinced here that the additional cost of using frames that will take double glazing and, in due course, of installing two panes of glass where one was before, since it will fall to the landlord who has damaged the glass to replace with new glass, is of a comparatively trivial amount, a question purely of degree and quite incapable of being an alteration of a kind so as to constitute a renewal and not within a covenant to repair."

Whilst each case turns on its own facts, it is thought that the approach of Harman J. in *Minja* is to be preferred, and that, all other things being equal, replacement of defective single glazed windows with double glazing does not of itself take the work out of the general concept of repair.[135] Thus, in *Wandsworth LBC v Griffin*[136] the Lands Tribunal concluded that the replacement of single-glazed metal-frame windows in blocks of Council flats with UPVC double-glazed units was within the ambit of a landlord's covenant:

> "[T]o repair ... and maintain the exterior of the windows window frames window sashes and the glass therein to the flat and as often as may be necessary to replace the whole or part of the windows window frame sashes and window furniture (as appropriate)."

Legislation or building regulations may also impact upon whether the question whether replacement amounts to repair within the meaning of the covenant. Thus in *Craighead v Homes for Islington Ltd*[137] the relevant leases entitled the landlord to recover the cost of "the repair maintenance and renewal" of the premises. The landlord replaced life expired single glazed Crittall windows with double glazed Crittall windows. In the absence of intervention by English Heritage, the use of double glazing was the only lawful way of effecting the remedial works in accordance with the applicable building regulations. The LVT held that the cost

---

[134] See paras 11–30 to 11–32, above.
[135] See further to the same effect *Sutton (Hastoe) Housing Association v Williams* [1988] 1 E.G.L.R. 56 and *Reston v Hudson* [1990] 2 E.G.L.R. 51.
[136] [2000] 2 E.G.L.R. 105.
[137] [2010] UKUT 47 (LC).

of the work was recoverable and its conclusion was upheld by the Lands Chamber of the Upper Tribunal on appeal. Mr A. Trott FRICS said:

> "The council was under an obligation to repair, inter alia, the windows at the Spa Green Estate. The necessity to carry out such works is not disputed, nor is the standard to which they were carried out. The council could only lawfully do the works by using double glazing. This cost an extra 13% but did not significantly alter the premises in any way. In my opinion this extra expenditure was necessarily incurred and whilst as a matter of fact the double glazing was an improvement in terms of its functional efficiency compared with the single glazing previously in situ, I agree with the LVT that the cost of the double glazing work was incurred in effecting repairs and was properly and proportionately included within the service charge of all the appellants. I conclude that it was open to the LVT on the evidence to conclude that the double glazing works were works of repair."

However, where windows are to be replaced, it will not be a performance of the covenant if the replacement windows omit an essential feature of the original windows. Thus, in *Bilgili v Paddington Churches Housing Association*,[138] the landlord replaced old Crittall windows in the demised premises with modern UPVC windows. The Crittall window that was removed from the kitchen had a spinner vent, but the replacement window had no means of opening, and no form of ventilation was set into it. The county court judge allowed the tenant's appeal from the finding of the district judge that the landlords were not in breach of their repairing covenant. Sedley L.J. declined to grant the landlord's permission to appeal to the Court of Appeal: in his view, it was "as plain as a pikestaff" that a kitchen window which was acknowledged to require ventilation and so had a spinner vent in it, had not been properly repaired if it was replaced with a sealed window that had neither a means of opening nor any form of ventilation.

## ASBESTOS

### Introductory

The last 30 years or so have seen an increasing realisation of the dangers of unencapsulated asbestos in buildings. This has resulted in an understandable desire on the part of owners of buildings containing asbestos to encapsulate or, preferably, to remove it as quickly as possible. The question is to what extent this can properly be required under a covenant to repair.

**12–38**

### Asbestos removal

The mere presence of asbestos does not constitute disrepair.[139] It follows that the covenantor cannot be made to remove asbestos just because it is there. For example, it was at one time the practice for the purposes of fire prevention to spray brown asbestos onto the steel beams of a building as a cheaper alternative to encasing them in concrete. If there is nothing physically wrong with either the beams or the asbestos layer, then the covenantor cannot be required either to

**12–39**

---

138 [2010] EWCA Civ 1341.
139 See Ch.8, above.

encapsulate or to remove the asbestos. If, however, there is physical damage to the subject-matter of the covenant which requires to be remedied, then the covenant may in appropriate circumstances require the encapsulation or removal of asbestos. For example, a lift shaft may contain asbestos sheeting. If the sheeting itself is damaged, then the covenantor is obliged to repair it. It may be either unlawful, or contrary to good practice, or both, simply to repair it without either encapsulating it, or removing it and replacing it with some other material. In such a case it is thought that the work would not be prevented from being repair simply because it involves encapsulation or removal. The position may the same where the asbestos itself is not damaged, but necessary remedial work elsewhere involves interference with the asbestos.[140]

The above accords with the decision of Chadwick J. in *Secretary of State for the Environment v Euston Centre Investments Ltd*,[141] which concerned the liability of the tenant to remove asbestos used in the building when it was constructed. The judge held that such liability only arose if (a) there was damage to, or deterioration in the physical condition of, the asbestos, and (b) the only practicable or, in a realistic sense, possible way of effecting the repair which the tenant was thus obliged to undertake was by removing all the asbestos and making good in some other material. The fact that it was convenient to remove the asbestos along with other works of repair was not enough.

The above is concerned with the position under the repairing covenant. However, a covenant to comply with statutes and regulations, if the relevant lease contains one, may be highly relevant to asbestos.[142] For example, if the demised premises constitute a place of work within the meaning of the Health and Safety etc. at Work Act 1974, then it may be that a duty to encapsulate or remove asbestos arises as part of the tenant's duty under s.2 of that Act to provide a safe place of work. Liabilities may also arise under the relevant regulations.[143] These matters are outside the scope of this work, and reference should be made to specialist works on the subject.

## CONTAMINATION

### Introductory

**12–40**    The law relating to contaminated land is outside the scope of this work. It is principally contained in the Environmental Protection Act 1990, the Environment Act 1995 and various regulations, and reference should be made to the specialist works on the subject. This section is concerned only with potential liability under the covenant to repair.

---

[140] See for example *Sunlife Europe Properties v Tiger Aspect Holdings* [2013] EWHC 463 (TCC) at [191].

[141] [1994] N.P.C. 130.

[142] See Ch.17, below.

[143] See now the Control of Asbestos Regulations 2012, which came into force on April 6, 2012.

## Where the contamination is in or affects the subsoil

Where the contamination is present in, or otherwise affects, the subsoil, it will be necessary to decide to what extent the affected area forms part of the subject matter of the covenant. That may involve difficult questions of construction.[144]

**12–41**

Further questions will be whether the existence of contamination in the subsoil amounts to "disrepair",[145] and whether necessary remediation works to subsoil (involving, for example, the removal and replacement, in-situ treatment or encapsulation of contaminated soil) can properly be described as "repair" within the meaning of the covenant. In the latter regard, it might be argued that "repair" is a concept which is appropriate only to buildings or structures and not the land itself. However, whilst everything depends on the words used interpreted in the light of the relevant background, it is thought that in appropriate circumstances the court might well be persuaded to interpret an obligation to repair or keep in repair as extending to remediation work. In addition, it seems very likely that a covenant to keep the subject matter in good and substantial condition, or something similar, would be held to impose liability in respect of contaminated subsoil.[146]

In the New Zealand case of *BP Oil New Zealand v Ports of Auckland*,[147] the land became contaminated by spills and leaks resulting from the tenant's storage of petroleum products. The relevant leases contained obligations on the part of the tenant to keep all buildings and structures on the demised land in good order, condition and repair. The landlord did not suggest that the covenants created an obligation to remediate the land itself. It argued instead that the tenant was liable for consequential damage caused as a result of breaches of covenant, including contamination resulting from the tenant's failure to repair and maintain storage tanks and ancillary equipment. That argument succeeded before Rodney Hansen J., who held that the tenant was liable for contamination which was a reasonably foreseeable consequence of any breaches of the covenants to repair.

## The test of fact and degree

Even where remediation work would otherwise fall within the ambit of the covenant to repair, it will also be necessary to show that it amounts to repair as a matter of fact and degree.[148] Depending on the facts, that may be difficult where large-scale remediation work is involved, particularly where (in the case where the tenant's liability is in question) the contamination was present at the date of the lease.[149]

**12–42**

---

[144] See para.7–06, above.
[145] See Ch.8, above.
[146] See paras 4–29 to 4–30, 8–12 et seq., 9–41 and 11–46, above.
[147] [2004] 2 N.Z.L.R. 208.
[148] See Ch.11, above.
[149] See paras 9–23 to 9–26 and 11–23 to 11–24, above.

## Other relevant obligations

**12–43**  In considering the liability of one or other party in relation to contamination, it will be necessary to look not only at the repairing covenant but also at other relevant covenants in the lease. A number of modern leases contain express covenants intended to allocate liability in respect of contamination. Reference will also need to be made to the covenant to comply with statutes,[150] the user covenant (where the contamination has resulted from the tenant's use of the premises), the law relating to waste[151] and the general law relating to nuisance and negligence. It is not thought that a landlord's covenant for quiet enjoyment would be held to impose liability for contamination which was present at the date of the lease.[152]

In the New Zealand case of *BP Oil New Zealand v Ports of Auckland*[153] (the facts of which are set out in para.12–41, above), it was held that (i) no term was to be implied into the leases that the tenant would not commit waste against the reversion by causing or allowing the land to become contaminated; (ii) the repairing covenants did not exclude liability in tort for waste, with the result that the tenant was liable for injury to the land resulting from its acts or omissions, excluding damage resulting from reasonable use;[154] (iii) the tenant would be liable in negligence for contamination caused by careless acts or omissions; but (iv) the tenant was not liable in nuisance or under the rule in *Rylands v Fletcher* because those torts were directed to acts causing injury to neighbouring land as opposed to land in the defendant's own occupation.

## Rights of entry

**12–44**  The extent to which an express right of entry entitles the landlord to enter to carry out an environmental investigation survey is considered at para.22–29, below.

---

[150] See Ch.17, below.
[151] See Ch.21, below.
[152] See *Southwark LBC v Mills* [2001] 1 A.C. 1.
[153] [2004] 2 N.Z.L.R. 208. See further on this case para.12–40, above.
[154] See further on this case para.21–17, below.

CHAPTER 13

# MECHANICAL AND ELECTRICAL SERVICES AND PLANT

## INTRODUCTORY

All buildings contain a variety of mechanical and electrical items. These **13–01** commonly include: electrical wiring; electrical installations such as a service head, distribution board, fusebox, power points, etc.; cold water supply pipes and tanks; drainage pipes and sewers; gas pipes; apparatus for heating and supplying hot water; apparatus for heating the building or individual parts of it; lifts; air conditioning plant; and fire fighting apparatus and fire alarms. In addition, buildings constructed or adapted for manufacturing or other processes contain specialised plant and machinery for the purpose of the process carried on.

The principles governing the operation of repairing and other covenants in relation to mechanical and electrical services are no different to those which apply in the case of the building itself. In principle, therefore, the five-part approach to liability under repairing covenants considered in Chs 7 to 11 above applies as much where the subject-matter consists of mechanical and electrical services as it does in relation to building fabric. However, plant, services and machinery have a number of characteristics which do not apply to the building fabric and which justify treating them in a separate Chapter. Among other things:

(1)    they frequently have a much shorter useful life than the building itself. For example, a purpose-built block of flats constructed between the wars with a lift of the sort commonly installed in such buildings at that time may remain in reasonable condition for its age, but the lift may have become a virtual museum piece;

(2)    it may be impossible to find an exact or even a near replica of a particular item of plant which requires replacement;

(3)    where an exact or near replica cannot be obtained, replacement with the nearest available modern equivalent may, because of technological advances, involve a considerable degree of what might ordinarily be termed "improvement";

(4)    even if the original item is available, it may be contrary to regulations or codes of practice to install it without major changes or additions elsewhere;

(5)    although the item in question may adequately perform its intended function, the market may regard it as old-fashioned, under-specified or likely to cause problems in the future, so that in order to get the building let, it may be necessary to replace the item with something more modern.

This Chapter considers the liability imposed by repairing and other covenants in relation to mechanical and electrical services and plant.

## THE SUBJECT-MATTER OF THE COVENANT[1]

13–02    The importance of properly identifying the subject-matter of the covenant in the case of mechanical and electrical services is twofold. First, it determines whether the relevant services are subject to the covenant at all. Thus, a covenant limited to "the structure of the building" would not ordinarily include heating plant, which is not part of the structure. Second, it may assist in answering the question whether complete replacement of a particular item of plant goes beyond repair for the purposes of a covenant to repair and keep in repair: that is because, if the subject-matter comprises the whole or part of the building in addition to the plant, it may be easier to conclude that complete replacement of the plant is within the obligation to repair than it will if the relevant plant constitutes the entirety of the subject-matter.[2]

The extent to which the covenant applies to plant, services and machinery is a question of construction. It may expressly refer to the item in question. For example, it may include fixtures or landlord's fixtures,[3] or it may go further and specifically include plant and equipment[4] or some similar expression. In other cases, the lease may be silent, and the obligation may be simply be to repair "the demised premises". This would generally only be apt to include such items of plant and machinery as amount to fixtures.[5]

Note that practical difficulties may arise where the lease distinguishes between plant forming part of, or serving, only the demised premises and that relating to common parts, in circumstances where the two are in reality part and parcel of the same system.

## COVENANTS TO REPAIR AND KEEP IN REPAIR

### The requirement of disrepair

13–03    No work is required under the general covenant to repair and keep in repair until there is damage or deterioration to the relevant item of plant or equipment which is the subject-matter of the covenant,[6] which has caused it to fall below the standard contemplated by the covenant.[7] The fact that an item of plant is old-fashioned, or that it is less efficient when compared with its modern equivalent, or that the market would not regard it as suitable, is not enough to

---

[1] See generally Ch.7, above.
[2] See para.13–08, below.
[3] See Ch.25, below.
[4] In *RA & K Becker Pty Ltd v Cariste Pty Ltd* (2001) 11 B.P.R. 20, 111, a reference to "plant and equipment" in a lease of premises used as a service station was held in the New South Wales Supreme Court to include underground tanks and pipes.
[5] See Ch.25, below.
[6] See Ch.8, above.
[7] See Ch.9, above.

bring the covenant into play. As a general principle, it must be possible to identify a respect in which its physical condition has deteriorated to a point where it is below the standard to which the parties required it to be kept. Thus, in *Mason v TotalFinaElf UK Ltd*[8] Blackburne J. held that underground fuel tanks which were old but not shown to be in any way defective were not in disrepair. He said:

> "[T]he notion that [the tanks] were not [in good and substantial condition] . . . is founded simply upon their age . . . coupled with an appeal to the indisputable view that there is likely to come a time when the tanks will fail, although quite when nobody can say. In my judgment, that is insufficient to establish a breach [of covenant]."

The requirement that there must be disrepair before the covenant comes into operation will ordinarily mean that a failure in function, which is not the result of physical damage or deterioration, will not give rise to any liability under the covenant to carry out work. An example may be cited from the past. For many years in London, a company supplied to its subscribers hydraulic power through a system of pipes. An important use made of this power was to operate lifts in various blocks of flats. It ceased to be economic for the company to provide the power. It therefore decided to wind up this part of its business and to give notice terminating its supply contracts with its various subscribers, including the landlords of various blocks. This caused much argument, and it is believed litigation, between the landlords and their tenants. It is difficult to see how a landlord who had covenanted "to keep the lifts in repair" could have been obliged to replace the existing hydraulic system with a new electrically-operated one, since the existing lifts were not in disrepair. However, a landlord who had covenanted in more general terms "to ensure the operation at all times of an efficient lift service" might have been liable to install replacement lifts.

## R22

A more topical example concerns the use of the HCFC refrigerant gas R22 in air conditioning systems. R22 falls foul of European Regulation 1005/2009 (commonly known as the Ozone Depleting Substance Regulation). Its use in new equipment was banned in 2004, and since 2010 it has been unlawful to use virgin (as opposed to recycled) R22 in the maintenance of existing equipment. At the time of writing, it remains permissible to use recycled R22 when maintaining existing equipment, but even that will be unlawful after December 31, 2014. The effect, inevitably, has been that recycled R22 is becoming scarcer and more expensive. The result is that the maintenance of existing equipment will become impossible when and if recycled R22 ceases to be available, and at the latest, after December 31, 2014. In relation to air conditioning systems that use chillers as part of central plant (most commonly, induction systems, variable air volume systems, fan coil unit systems and chilled beam or ceiling systems) it may be possible to "retro-fit" the chiller with a new refrigerant gas, although problems

**13–04**

---

[8] [2003] 3 E.G.L.R. 91.

can arise with regard to refrigerant leaks, oil return and loss of cooling capacity.[9] In other cases (such as variable refrigerant flow systems) it may not be possible to "retro-fit" a new refrigerant gas, and the only viable option will be complete replacement with a compliant system.

Whilst each case will turn on its own particular circumstances, it is not thought that a system which is (lawfully) being topped up with recycled R22 would be held to be in disrepair for the purposes of a covenant to repair and keep in repair, merely by virtue of the fact that there will come a time when recycled R22 is no longer available or cannot any longer lawfully be used.[10] A more difficult question, however, is whether, once that has happened, the system is then in disrepair. It might be said that the answer is no, because there is nothing physically wrong with it. But that might be said to overlook the fact that the system lacks an important physical component required to keep it functioning, namely, refrigerant gas. A section of roof without tiles would clearly be in disrepair. A boiler with a missing heating tube would equally clearly be in disrepair, and none the less so because it is of an obsolete design and a replacement heating tube is unobtainable. It can be said that there is no difference of substance between these examples and a chiller without refrigerant. It is thought that this is the better analysis, but the position is not clear.

A further question may be whether systems which have been "retro-fitted" with a new refrigerant gas would be held to be in repair for the purposes of the covenant.[11] It is thought that the answer will depend on how successful the retro-fitting is. A retro-fitted system which operates with a reasonable degree of reliability and which provides cooling to the sort of standard which the parties at the date of the lease can reasonably be taken to have contemplated as being appropriate for the building is likely to be held to comply with the covenant. Thus, in *Fluor Daniel Properties Ltd v Shortlands Investments Ltd*,[12] the landlords covenanted to "uphold maintain repair amend renew cleanse and redecorate and otherwise keep in good and substantial condition and as the case may be in good working order and repair" various parts of a multi-occupied office building and its plant, and also "to supply... throughout the year conditioned air so as to maintain a reasonable temperature in accordance with statutory requirements". The landlords proposed to replace the chillers with new air-cooled equipment (which would render the two cooling towers redundant), on the sole ground that the chillers used the banned CFC refrigerant gas R12, and to recover the cost from the tenants of the building by way of service charge. Blackburne J. found on the evidence that it would be possible to install an alternative gas (Isceon 39TC), which would be an effective replacement with a performance comparable to R12. He held that it would be "quite unreasonable" for the landlord to replace the chillers and remove the cooling towers.

---

[9] Note that there is relatively little data available to determine how effective retro-fit solutions may be, and it is not thought that any manufacturers are willing to endorse it.

[10] Cf. paras 10–15 to 10–18, above.

[11] The problem may be compounded in practice by the fact that systems using R22 are generally over ten or more years old, not many having been produced after 2001/2. Retrofit projects are therefore often undertaken by landlords in conjunction with a refurbishment scheme rather than in isolation, which may give rise to further arguments over liability.

[12] [2001] 2 E.G.L.R. 103.

## Reliability

As plant nears the end of its life, it tends to become increasingly unreliable, and **13–05** suffer from frequent failures and breakdowns.[13] It may be possible to keep it going only by repeated patch repairs. At any one point in time, the item in question may happen coincidentally to be working as it should: but to what extent does its condition nonetheless amount to a breach of the covenant to repair and keep in repair?

Each case will, of course, turn on the proper construction of the relevant covenant and the particular circumstances relating to the item of plant in question. However, it is thought that as a general principle, a covenant to repair and keep in repair require plant to be kept in such a state that it can be kept going with a reasonable degree of reliability. Thus, in *Berryman v Hounslow LBC*[14] a covenant to keep certain lifts "in reasonable repair" was interpreted to mean "the same as keeping [them] in reasonable working order". In *Ultraworth Ltd v General Accident Fire & Life Assurance Co Ltd*,[15] it was held that a covenant to keep plant in good and substantial repair and condition would be satisfied if the system is

> "in good working order, *i.e.* ... in repair, and work[ing] substantially as well as the original system did (or as it should have done) when new. It is not necessary that it should require as little maintenance as a new system".

In *Westbury Estates v The Royal Bank of Scotland*[16] (a Scottish case) it was said that an obligation to keep in good and substantial repair and condition "might be triggered if an item of plant was unreliable and prone to breakdowns", because "the standard of 'good and substantial repair and condition' can be understood as encompassing, in relation to plant and services, a reasonable degree of reliability".

What is reasonable will depend on all the circumstances. For example, a higher standard of reliability may be demanded in relation to an air conditioning system in a high-class office building in the City of London than a basic heating installation in a warehouse.

## Published lifespan data

In deciding whether the condition of particular plant amounts to a breach of **13–06** covenant, it is important not to be over-reliant on published data as to the likely lifespan of plant of the same description, such as the tables published by the Chartered Institute of Building Services Engineers (CIBSE).[17] Plant which has exceeded the published projected lifespan for that type of item is often referred to as being at the end of its useful or economic life. This may be a helpful concept where the issue is whether it would be economic for the building owner to replace

---

[13] See further para.13–06, below.
[14] (1998) 30 H.L.R. 567.
[15] [2000] 2 E.G.L.R. 115.
[16] [2006] CSOH 177. See further below.
[17] *Maintenance Engineering and Management* (CIBSE Guide M).

the plant now rather than later. However, it is potentially misleading where the issue is whether the plant is in disrepair, since everything will depend on the physical condition of the item in question. Thus, for example, the fact that boilers generally last 25 years does not mean that a particular boiler which has been in service for over 25 years is necessarily in disrepair such that work is required. Whilst it must obviously be properly inspected, and its service history and performance carefully examined, the fact that it has already lasted beyond its projected lifespan is not conclusive as to the existence of disrepair, still less that complete replacement is necessary. In some cases, plant may last for a shorter time than its expected lifespan[18]; in others, it may last longer.[19] Much will depend on whether it has been regularly serviced and how it has been operated.[20] Consequently, where the issue is whether a particular piece of plant is in disrepair, it will not generally be enough simply to point to published tables: whilst these may be of general assistance, the issue must be resolved by reference to the condition of the actual piece of plant at the time.

The above accords with the approach of Blackburne J. in *Fluor Daniel Properties Ltd v Shortlands Investments Ltd*,[21] which concerned the proposed replacement by the landlord of substantial parts of an air conditioning system in an office building. The judge pointed out that a report prepared for the landlord had laid much emphasis on published predicted lifespans, but had not considered the available maintenance records. These records would have revealed that "the usual indicators that plant is coming to the end of its working/economic life", namely, "an increase in the frequency of breakdowns and a rise in the cost of maintenance" were not present. Accordingly, "whatever the lifespans set out in the CIBSE or other professionally prepared tables, it was evident that these items of plant had not reached the end of their working life". He concluded the relevant part of his judgment by accepting the view of the tenants' expert that the tables were no more than a starting point, and rejecting "the notion that merely because an item of plant has reached the end of its recommended lifespan, as suggested by the CIBSE or some other guidelines, it was and is reasonable for [the landlords] to want to replace it at the tenants' expense."

The same conclusion was reached in the Scottish case of *Westbury Estates v The Royal Bank of Scotland*.[22] A converted office building was demised for 25 years on terms which included the following covenant on the part of the tenant:

---

[18] An example in another context is *Postel Properties Ltd v Boots the Chemist* [1996] 2 E.G.L.R. 60, in which phased replacement of roofs began before they had reached their maximum life expectancy.
[19] See for example *Ultraworth Ltd v General Accident Fire & Life Assurance Co Ltd* [2000] 2 E.G.L.R. 115, in which the landlord's engineer relied on "standard projected lifetimes" in support of his view that substantial renewal of the systems was necessary, but the court held that reconditioning was sufficient. See further on this case para.13–06, below.
[20] Cf. *Postel Properties Ltd v Boots the Chemist* above, at 61M: "…. the maximum life that could reasonably be expected from that type of [roof] covering is 20 years, though they have been known to fail in 10–15 years. Much will depend on the quality of maintenance ….." . See also *Fluor Daniel Properties Ltd v Shortlands Investments Ltd* [2001] 2 E.G.L.R. 103.
[21] [2001] 2 E.G.L.R. 103.
[22] [2006] CSOH 177.

"[T]hroughout the whole currency of this Lease the Tenants shall at all times uphold, maintain, repair and renew the Let Subjects both externally and internally so as to keep the Let Subjects in good and substantial repair and condition, it being declared that the Tenants' obligations shall extend to all work necessary upon the Let Subjects whether structural or otherwise and whether of the nature of maintenance, repair, renewal or rebuilding and whether normally the obligation of a Landlord or of a Tenant, the Landlords having no duties, liabilities or obligations in respect of such work or the cost thereof and further that the Tenants' obligations shall extend to the maintenance, repair, renewal and if necessary replacement of all services within and external to but serving the Let Subjects (either alone or in common with other subjects) including lifts, heating installations, ventilation or air conditioning systems, drainage system and gas, electricity and water supplies and any other services."

Following the expiry of the lease, the landlord replaced the lifts, fire alarm, wiring, boiler and convector heating at a cost of over £500,000 and then sought to recover the cost from the tenant by way of damages for breach of covenant. It was not suggested that any of the relevant items were defective or malfunctioning. Instead, the landlord's case was that the age of the items either approached or exceeded the lifespans set out in the CIBSE guidelines; the items were therefore at or nearing the end of their economic life (which the landlord defined as the period of time at the end of which it is necessary to replace an item because it no longer represents the least expensive method of performing its function); and accordingly the items were not in good and substantial repair and condition within the meaning of the covenant. The Outer House of the Court of Session found in favour of the tenant. Having referred to a number of the English authorities on repair, including *Fluor Daniel Properties Ltd v Shortlands Investments Ltd*,[23] Lord Reed continued as follows:

"[35] ... [The landlords'] averment is that it is 'necessary' to replace an item when 'the item no longer represents the least expensive method of performing its function'. Whether an item of plant 'represents the least expensive method of performing its function' appears to me to be an entirely different question from whether its replacement is necessary 'so as to keep the subjects in good and substantial repair and condition.' The fact that the item is less efficient than a more modern equivalent tells one nothing about whether the item is in 'good and substantial repair and condition'.

[36] It therefore appears to me that the fact that an item is at the end of its economic life, in the particular sense in which that expression is defined in the [landlords'] averments, does not entail that the tenant is necessarily obliged under the repairing covenant to replace it. Equally, the fact that an item is of a given age, and that (as averred) the CIBSE guidelines indicate that an item of that age is at or approaching the end of its economic life (presumably, in the same sense in which that expression is defined in the [landlords'] averments), does not *ipso facto* entail that the subjects are other than in 'good and substantial repair and condition', particularly when it is also averred that the items are capable of being operated, and that the [landlords] have no knowledge of their reliability or servicing costs.

[37] The difference between an obligation to replace an item whenever it ceases to represent the least expensive method of performing its function, on the one hand, and an obligation to replace it if necessary 'so as to keep the Let Subjects in good and substantial repair and condition', on the other hand, cannot be bridged by offering to prove that the CIBSE guidelines 'are accepted generally as appropriate standards in the building services industry' and that 'tenants and landlords of commercial property rely on advice from the building services industry'. I do not doubt that it is often helpful, in applying a repairing covenant, to consider whether particular works would be undertaken by a prudent owner; but an affirmative answer to that question cannot bring the works in question within the scope of the covenant if the language of the covenant does not admit them. The intention of the parties to the lease has to be determined from the language which they have used. There is, in particular, a danger of

---

23 [2001] 2 E.G.L.R. 103.

confusing the question whether it would be economic for a prudent building owner to replace an item of plant with the question whether the plant is in such a state that the subjects cannot be said to be in good and substantial repair and condition. Equally, there is a danger of confusing the question whether an incoming tenant would regard the item as old-fashioned or under-specified or liable to cause problems at some point in the future, with the question whether the subjects are, as matters stand, in good and substantial repair and condition. I would observe that the test of the hypothetical tenant which was adopted in *Proudfoot v Hart* was concerned not with what a tenant would expect or accept (something which might depend on market conditions, rent and the other terms of the lease), but with what would make the premises reasonably fit for occupation. Even if it were proved, for example, that commercial landlords would normally replace a boiler which was 15 years old (and that incoming tenants would normally expect such a boiler to have been replaced), that would not entail that subjects with a 15 year old boiler, which remained in perfect working order and continued to perform satisfactorily, were not in 'good and substantial repair and condition'."

Although Lord Reed pointed out earlier in his judgment that the common law of Scotland in relation to repairing obligations in leases is different from that in England,[24] nonetheless it is thought that the above passage accurately represents the law in England, and that the judge's warning of the danger of confusing whether an item is in the covenanted state with whether it is at the end of its economic life, or would be regarded as outdated by an incoming tenant, is a particularly apposite one. This accords with *Sunlife Europe Properties Ltd v Tiger Aspect Holdings*,[25] in which Edwards-Stuart J. said:

"The tenant is obliged to return the premises in good and tenantable condition and with the M & E systems in satisfactory working order: he is not required to deliver up the premises with new equipment or with any particular remaining life expectancy."

Likewise, in *Hammersmatch Properties (Welwyn) Ltd v Saint Gobain Ceramics & Plastics*,[26] Ramsey J. cited *Fluor Daniel* and *Westbury* in support of the proposition that "the fact that an item has exceeded its indicative life so that it would or might be economic for a prudent owner to replace it does not mean that it is not in a good and safe working order repair and condition".

## Replacement

**13–07**   Subject to the terms of the particular lease in question, the covenanting party will generally only be liable to replace an item of plant if patch-repair is not reasonably or sensibly possible,[27] the burden of proof on that issue being on the party who asserts that replacement is necessary.[28]

The choice between replacement and continued patch repairs will often involve questions of fine judgment. Ian Kennedy J. pointed this out in *Postel*

---

[24] At [17].
[25] [2013] EWHC 463 (TCC).
[26] [2013] EWHC 1161 (TCC).
[27] *Riverside Property Investments v Blackhawk Automotive* [2005] 1 E.G.L.R. 114 at [54]; *Carmel Southend v Strachan & Henshaw* [2007] 3 E.G.L.R. 15 at [9]; *Hammersmatch Properties (Welwyn) v Saint-Gobain Ceramics & Plastics* above at [53]. See further Ch.10, para.10–11 et seq., above.
[28] *Hammersmatch Properties (Welwyn) v Saint-Gobain Ceramics & Plastics*, above, at [53].

*Properties Ltd v Boots the Chemist*,[29] when he said in relation to the decision whether or not to replace a roof of a large shopping centre:

"Clearly it is a matter for experience and judgment when the time has come to renew a roof. The cost of replacement must be balanced against the likely increasing cost of patch repairs."

The same is true of in relation to mechanical and electrical services and plant. The higher cost of a new item must be balanced against (as the case may be) likely increased maintenance costs, lower efficiency, greater unreliability or increasing unavailability of spares if the old item is kept going. If either course could be recommended by a reasonable surveyor, then both will amount to a performance of the covenant, and the choice between them is for the covenanting party to make.[30] If no reasonable surveyor would take the view that complete replacement is necessary, then a continuing programme of patch repairs will be all that can be required or justified. Conversely, if no reasonable surveyor would recommend continued patching up as being any longer reasonably or sensibly possible, then only complete replacement will amount to performance of the covenant.

Thus, in *Roper v Prudential Assurance Co Ltd*[31] complete replacement of the electrical installations of a farmhouse was held to fall within the covenant. Likewise, in *Sunlife Europe Properties v Tiger Aspect Holdings*[32] it was held that the covenant required the replacement of the boilers and electrical installations in a 1970s office and retail building. By contrast, in *Land Securities Plc v Westminster City Council (No.2)*,[33] continued patch repairs to air conditioning plant would have brought the plant near to its maximum efficiency with a maximum extended life of five years. The court held that replacement was not required under the covenant. Similarly, in *Ultraworth Ltd v General Accident Fire & Life Assurance Co Ltd*[34] Judge Havery QC held that substantial renewal of an air conditioning and heating system fell within the ambit of the tenant's covenant "well and substantially to repair cleanse and keep in good and substantial repair and condition the demised premises . . . including . . . all parts of the . . . central heating air conditioning plant", but held that reconditioning would be another reasonable way of complying with the covenant. Applying the principle that it is for the covenantor to decide how to perform the covenant,[35] he held that the tenant was not liable for anything more than reconditioning. He would not, he said, describe the maintenance of an elderly but working system as futile work. He summarised his conclusion as follows:

"The claimant is not entitled to a new system simply because the system was new at the beginning of the term. It is sufficient to comply with the repairing covenant that the system be in good working order, *i.e.* that it should be in repair, and work substantially as well as the

---

[29] [1996] 2 E.G.L.R. 60.
[30] See paras 10–05 and 10–07, above.
[31] [1992] 1 E.G.L.R. 5.
[32] [2013] EWHC 463 (TCC) at [33-35].
[33] [1995] 1 E.G.L.R. 245. This case is further considered in para.10–06, above.
[34] [2000] 2 E.G.L.R. 115.
[35] See para.10–06 and 10–07, above.

original system did (or as it should have done) when new. It is not necessary that it should require as little maintenance as a new system. Whether the covenant is complied with is a question of fact and degree."

In *Fluor Daniel Properties Ltd v Shortlands Investments Ltd*[36] the landlords covenanted to "uphold maintain repair amend renew cleanse and redecorate and otherwise keep in good and substantial condition and as the case may be in good working order" various parts of an office building, including the plant. They proposed to replace substantial parts of the air conditioning system and recover the cost under the service charge provisions of the relevant leases. Blackburne J. held on the evidence that this went beyond what was reasonably necessary. In some cases, there was nothing wrong with the relevant item, and in others, the appropriate work fell well short of complete replacement.

## Whether complete replacement goes beyond repair

**13–08**  Complete replacement of plant may (depending on the facts) be held to go beyond repair if it involves "the reconstruction of the entirety, meaning by the entirety not necessarily the whole but substantially the whole subject matter under discussion" as opposed to "restoration by renewal or replacement of subsidiary parts of a whole".[37] It is therefore important to identify whether the covenant applies to a subject-matter other than just the plant in question. Complete replacement is less likely to be held to be repair if the plant in question is the entire subject-matter of the covenant.[38]

In the Canadian case of *Brennan v Brennan Educational Supply*,[39] the tenant of commercial premises covenanted to pay "the cost for general maintenance and repairs to the plant and equipment supplying climate control"'. The plant and equipment in question consisted in large part of seven natural gas furnaces or heaters located in various places in the building, and two central air conditioning units mounted on the roof. The furnaces ranged in age from 30 years old down to 15 years old. The heating system was in good working order when the lease was granted in January 2001. The landlords replaced three of the furnaces following an annual inspection which revealed cracks in the heat exchangers, prompting the inspector (i) to call for their replacement because there was a danger of carbon monoxide poisoning and (ii) to warn that if the furnaces were not replaced, their condition would be reported to the gas authorities who would then shut them down. The replacement of the furnaces was the only means available in the circumstances to restore them to the working condition they had been in at the inception of the lease. It was held in the Saskatchewan Court of Appeal that the tenant's obligation to pay for the repair of the furnaces extended to their replacement. The furnaces were but component parts of the heating system, which was itself but a component part of the whole of "the plant and equipment supplying climate control". Had the furnaces themselves been the subject matter

---

[36] [2001] 2 E.G.L.R. 103.
[37] *Lurcott v Wakely* [1911] 2 K.B. 905, per Buckley L.J. See para.11–30 et seq., above.
[38] See the tenant's argument in *Roper v Prudential Assurance Co Ltd* [1992] 1 E.G.L.R. 5.
[39] (2006) SKCA 9.

of the covenant, there might have been something to be said for the proposition that repair did not extend to replacement. But that was not the case.

## Replacement with something different

Once the point has been reached at which a particular item of mechanical or electrical plant requires to be replaced in its entirety in order to comply with the relevant covenant, the question may arise as to what the extent the covenantor is entitled or obliged to replace it with a more up to date item, or different system, so as (for example) to take advantage of developments in design and technology, or to achieve greater efficiency. This question is considered at paras 10–12 to 10–14, above.

13–09

## Maintenance and servicing records

In any dispute involving mechanical and electrical services and plant, it will generally be important in practice to look at any available maintenance and servicing records for the item in question.[40] These will give the engineer important indications as to the quality (or lack of it) of the maintenance regime in the past. The better the maintenance regime, the more likely it will be that the item will have been serviced appropriately, and that any defects will have been properly attended to as and when necessary, and the easier it may be to conclude that the item is in a state which complies with the relevant covenant, or could be put into such state without undue expense. Conversely, a poor or non-existent maintenance regime may, when taken together with other indicators, make it more likely that more substantial work, or even complete replacement, is necessary. The maintenance records will also enable the engineer to see to what extent there have been past failures, and if so, what work has been done and whether the breakdown rate is increasing. A high or rising rate of failures may suggest that the item has reached the point in its lifecycle at which continued patch repair may be impractical or uneconomic, such that the only sensible and practical course may be to replace it.[41]

13–10

## The effect of regulations

The existence of regulations may be relevant to liability in relation to plant, services and machinery. For example, an existing electrical system may have complied with IEE regulations in force when it was installed, but it may not comply with current regulations. Once it has fallen into disrepair, it may be that

13–11

---

[40] As was done in *Fluor Daniel Properties v Shortlands Investments* [2001] 2 E.G.L.R. 103: see para.13–06, above.

[41] See *Maintenance Engineering and Management* (CIBSE Guide M), in which it is suggested (by reference to the "bathtub curve ") that plant typically has three phases in its life: a decreasing failure rate when the system is new; a constant failure rate when the system is in a settled state; and then an increasing failure rate as major components begin to fail and random failures increase with time, at which point the cost of repair begins to exceed the cost of replacement.

the necessary remedial work cannot lawfully be done unless the system is made to comply with current regulations. It is thought that in such a case the additional work necessary to ensure compliance with the regulations would ordinarily still amount to repair, because the defects cannot lawfully be remedied in any other way.[42]

## Insurers' requirements

13–12　Further questions may arise in practice where plant or machinery falls short of insurers' requirements. This fact will not, of itself, mean that the state of the relevant item amounts to a breach of the covenant to repair and keep in repair. In many cases, however, the state of affairs by virtue of which the relevant item does not comply with insurers' requirements will also amount to a breach of covenant. An example might be frayed or worn ropes in a lift. In other cases, however, the two will be different. An example might be where the insurers are only prepared to provide cover for a lift with manual doors if a lift attendant is provided. This would effectively mean that, unless an attendant is provided, the existing lift would have to be shut down even though it is otherwise perfectly serviceable. These considerations would not of themselves justify and require the replacement of the existing lift with an automatic lift under the covenant to repair, since it could not be said that the lift was in disrepair.

## COVENANTS TO KEEP IN GOOD CONDITION

13–13　The distinction between a covenant to repair and keep in repair and a covenant to keep in good condition is considered elsewhere.[43] Depending on the facts of each case, it may be that a covenant to keep in good condition would be held to impose a greater liability in relation to plant than would a covenant to repair or keep in repair.

## COVENANTS TO MAINTAIN PLANT

13–14　Covenants to maintain are considered in Ch.14, para.14–37, below, to which reference should be made. In the context of service plant, such as lifts or boilers, a covenant to maintain is likely to be held to require the covenantor not only to remedy such defects as may arise, but also to take proper steps to ensure that defects do not arise. Thus, in the Australian case of *Greetings Oxford Koala Hotel Pty Ltd v Oxford Square Investments Pty Ltd*[44] a lease of hotel premises in a high-rise building provided that the landlord would "be responsible for and shall supply to the lessee" certain facilities including "maintenance of lifts... and replacement when required". Young J. held that:

---

[42] See paras 10–21 and 11–35, above.
[43] See paras 4–29 to 4–30, 9–41 to 9–42 and 11–46, above.
[44] (1989) 18 N.S.W.L.R. 33.

"[T]he word 'maintain' carries with it the connotation that the landlord is obliged not only to attend to cases where there is a malfunction of the lift, but also to take such preventative measures as should ensure that the lifts should not malfunction and that if it comes about that despite these efforts the lifts malfunction to such an extent, then to replace the lifts with lifts that do function satisfactorily."

The above accords with *Langham Estate Management Ltd v Hardy*,[45] in which H.H. Judge Hazel Marshall QC said:

"a landlord's covenant to 'keep in proper working order' or to 'maintain' is likely to be wider in its scope than a covenant to 'repair', although even this will depend upon the true construction of the covenant in its context. This point is particularly relevant to plant, machinery, equipment and installations. 'Repair' involves remedying a state of disrepair that has arisen, and the obligation does not arise until it has. 'Keep in proper working order', and possibly merely 'maintain', may well require proactive preventative maintenance work, or carrying out adjustments or general servicing before any actual fault develops or a want of repair exists."

The covenant in *Greetings Oxford Koala Hotel Pty Ltd v Oxford Square Investments Pty Ltd*[46] expressly included an obligation to replace where necessary. The position regarding liability for complete replacement is less clear where the relevant obligation is simply "to maintain". It may be that such an obligation is capable of extending to complete replacement if required, but whether it would do so in any particular case would depend on the facts. However, in the absence of clear words, it would not include extending the relevant service. Thus, in *Greetings Oxford Koala Hotel Pty Ltd v Oxford Square Investments Pty Ltd*[47] three lifts existed at the date of the lease, but more than three would have been required to give proper service. Young J. held that the covenant did not entitle the tenant to such a lift service as a reasonable person would consider proper, but was limited to maintaining and replacing the three lifts that existed at the date of the lease.

It has been held that a covenant to maintain does not mean that the covenanting party "is automatically in breach if any fault develops, nor [require] the emergence of every minor fault or maladjustment to be dealt with as though it required attention as an emergency".[48]

## COVENANTS TO KEEP PLANT IN WORKING ORDER

A covenant to keep plant in working order is concerned with the manner in which **13–15** the relevant plant performs. It must function in such a way that it can properly be said to be in working order. If it does not so function, the covenantor is liable to do whatever is necessary to restore it to working order, even if that requires the remedying of a defect in design or construction or the carrying out works which are not repair properly so-called. Thus, in *Liverpool City Council v Irwin*[49] it was held that the covenant implied by s.11 of the Landlord and Tenant Act 1985 into

---

[45] [2008] 3 E.G.L.R. 125 at [62]. See also *Greetings Oxford Koala Hotel Pty Ltd v Oxford Square Investments Pty Ltd* (1989) N.S.W.L.R. 33, discussed in para.13–14, above.
[46] Above.
[47] Above.
[48] *Langham Estate Management Ltd v Hardy*, above.
[49] See para.20–17 et seq., below.

short leases of dwelling-houses (which obliges the landlord to keep in repair and "proper working order" various installations in the dwelling-house) imposes on the landlord an absolute duty to ensure that the installations work, including, if necessary, remedying defects in design.[50] In *O'Connor v Old Etonian Housing Association Ltd*[51] Lord Phillips M.R. (giving the judgment of the Court of Appeal) (distinguishing various cases in which it had been held that an obligation to repair does not, of itself, require the covenantor to remedy defects in design or construction[52]) said:

> "There is an obvious distinction between the duty to keep 'in repair' and the duty to keep 'in proper working order'.... An installation cannot be said to be in proper working order if, by reason of a defect in construction or design, it is incapable of working properly."

Likewise, in *Langham Estate Management Ltd v Hardy*,[53] H.H. Judge Marshall QC said that a covenant to keep in proper working order "may also require the remedying of design or construction defects, which are not wants of repair".

However, the mere presence of a design or construction defect is not enough in itself to trigger an obligation to carry out work under a covenant of this type, unless its effect is that the item in question does not work properly. This approach accords with the decision in *Fluor Daniel Properties Ltd v Shortlands Investments Ltd*,[54] in which the landlord covenanted to "uphold maintain repair amend renew cleanse and redecorate and otherwise keep in good and substantial condition and as the case may be in good working order and repair" various parts of a multi-occupied office building and its plant. Whilst accepting that this "extends to works that go beyond repair strictly so-called", Blackburne J. accepted the submission that:

> "[T]he obligations in the clause presuppose that the item in question suffers from some defect (*i.e.* some physical damage or deterioration, or, in the case of plant, some malfunctioning) such that repair, amendment or renewal is reasonably necessary."

The point at which an item ceases to be in working order for the purposes of the covenant will depend on the circumstances of each case. It has been said that a covenant to keep plant in proper working order does not mean that the covenanting party "is automatically in breach if any fault develops, nor [require] the emergence of every minor fault or maladjustment to be dealt with as though it required attention as an emergency".[55] In general terms, it is thought that the relevant item must operate in a proper, safe and reasonably reliable manner. In *Ultraworth Ltd v General Accident Fire & Life Assurance Co Ltd*,[56] it was held that a covenant to keep plant in good and substantial repair and condition would be satisfied if the system is:

---

[50] [1977] A.C. 239, per Lord Edmund-Davies. See further para.20–28, below.
[51] [2002] 1 E.G.L.R. 38. See further on this case paras 20–28 to 20–29, below.
[52] See Ch.8, above.
[53] [2008] 3 E.G.L.R. 125.
[54] [2001] 2 E.G.L.R. 103.
[55] *Langham Estate Management Ltd v Hardy* [2008] 3 E.G.L.R. 125.
[56] [2000] 2 E.G.L.R. 115.

"in good working order, *i.e.* . . . in repair, and work[ing] substantially as well as the original system did (or as it should have done) when new. It is not necessary that it should require as little maintenance as a new system".

The extent to which the use of the adjectives "good", "proper" or "satisfactory" add anything to the obligation to keep in working order is a question of construction in each case. However, a helpful discussion in a non-dilapidations context is to be found in *Veolia Water Central v London Fire & Emergency Planning Authority*,[57] which concerned the obligation imposed on a water authority by s.57(3) of the Water Industry Act 1991 to keep fire hydrants on its mains "in good working order". Edwards-Stuart J. held that on the proper construction of the section, and having regard to its purpose, a hydrant must be kept "in a condition such that (a) it is fit for the purpose of firefighting, (b) does not present a risk of contamination to the water supply and (c) is not a source of danger to members of the public or potential users". He went on to say:

"91. In the context of something being in working order, there are other adjectives that come to mind apart from 'good'. A machine could be described as in perfect working order, or proper working order or, if different, in satisfactory working order. 'Working order' is defined in the Shorter Oxford Dictionary as 'the condition in which a machine, system, etc, works satisfactorily or in a specified way'. On the basis of this definition it is clear that the adjective 'satisfactory' adds nothing. I consider also that the adjective 'proper' adds nothing to the definition of 'working order'. However, when a person speaks of a machine being in 'perfect working order', I consider that he or she would be describing a machine that ran flawlessly. A proud owner of a vintage motor car, if describing it as being in 'perfect working order', would be conveying the impression that it was working just as well as it did many decades earlier shortly after it left the factory.

92. As a matter of ordinary language, I consider that 'good' denotes a rather better condition than 'satisfactory' but a poorer condition than 'perfect'. Whether it is closer to 'satisfactory' or to 'perfect' might be a matter of debate, although I would incline to the former. Accordingly, I consider that the adjective 'good' does add something to the expression 'working order' and that the word is not simply redundant."

A covenant to keep plant and equipment in good or proper working order is likely to be held to require the covenanting party to undertake preventative work before a fault develops. Thus, in *Langham Estate Management Ltd v Hardy*[58] H.H. Judge Marshall QC said:

"a landlord's covenant to "keep in proper working order or to 'maintain' is likely to be wider in its scope than a covenant to 'repair', although even this will depend upon the true construction of the covenant in its context. This point is particularly relevant to plant, machinery, equipment and installations. 'Repair' involves remedying a state of disrepair that has arisen, and the obligation does not arise until it has. 'Keep in proper working order', and possibly merely 'maintain', may well require proactive preventative maintenance work, or carrying out adjustments or general servicing before any actual fault develops or a want of repair exists."

Thus, for example, a covenant to keep in good or proper working order an air conditioning system which uses R22 refrigerant gas may be held to oblige the covenanting party to "retro-fit" the chillers with a new refrigerant gas in advance of recycled R22 becoming unavailable or unlawful to use, or, if that is not practical or cannot be done in such a manner that the chiller will operate with a

---

[57] [2009] EWHC 3109 (Q.B.).
[58] Above.

reasonable degree of reliability, to replace the chiller, and in any event to do so once recycled R22 has become unavailable or unlawful to use.[59]

## COVENANTS TO KEEP SERVICE INSTALLATIONS UP TO DATE

**13–16**    There is no reason why parties should not agree, if they wish, that plant and services are to be kept in a modern and up-to-date condition. Such a covenant may expressly require (where necessary) the replacement of the existing installations with their modern equivalent. However, even an obligation of this kind would be unlikely to be construed as requiring unlimited work. Thus, in *Gooderham & Worts Ltd v Canadian Broadcasting Corp*[60] a lease of a radio station, studio and offices contained a covenant by the tenant "to keep the whole of the premises modern and up to date and in good repair and operating condition". The Privy Council construed the covenant as obliging the tenant to keep the whole of the demised premises modern and up to date, but only in so far as the thing demised was capable of being kept modern and up to date. On this basis it did not require the tenant to substitute for the existing 5kW station an installation involving the use of higher power.

## COVENANTS TO SUPPLY SERVICES

**13–17**    A distinction must be drawn between a covenant which relates to the physical condition of plant and services, such as a covenant to repair, and a covenant to supply services. The latter may require the covenantor to carry out whatever work is necessary to provide the service, even though that work goes beyond what would ordinarily be called repair. Thus, in *Yorkbrook Investments Ltd v Batten*[61] a landlord of a block of flats covenanted:

> "[U]nless prevented by mechanical breakdown or failure of fuel supply or other cause beyond the control of the Lessor to provide and maintain a good sufficient and constant supply of hot and cold water to the Building throughout the term hereby granted and also an adequate supply of heating in the hot water radiators (if any) in the cold season between the dates to be determined by the Surveyor and to remedy any mechanical breakdown in the hot water and central heating systems."

Heating to the block was provided by three oil-fired boilers, which broke down on numerous occasions. The principal cause was that the equipment was antiquated and unserviceable. The Court of Appeal rejected the landlords' argument that the covenant had to be construed in relation to the heating system available at the date of the lease and operated in the manner intended by its original designers, and held that the covenant had been broken. The landlords were liable to provide hot water and heating; how they achieved it was a matter for them. On the facts they should have replaced the equipment in order to perform their obligations.

---

[59] See the discussion in para.13–04 above.
[60] [1947] A.C. 66.
[61] (1986) 52 P. & C.R. 51.

In *Clarke v Lloyds TSB Bank Plc*[62] the landlord of an office building covenanted    **13–18**
to perform certain services in an efficient manner throughout the term, subject to
a proviso that the landlord was not to be liable in respect of certain failures and
interruptions. The services included (a) the "inspection maintenance repair
renewal and replacement by way of repair of... systems plant and equipment
relating to... the supply of air conditioning mechanical ventilation heating and
domestic water", and (b) the provision of air conditioning "to be functioning in
the manner in which it was designed to function". Mr Recorder Black (sitting as
a deputy judge of the Queen's Bench Division) said of the obligation:

> "In my judgment, it is wrong to approach the construction of the covenant as if it were a
> repairing covenant. It is not. It is a covenant to perform services.
>     The obligation is to perform the services in an 'efficient manner'. The claimants suggest
> that this means the lessor must do everything reasonably possible to ensure that the lessee gets
> what it contracted to get, and in particular that any failures or breakdowns are properly
> attended to. I consider that the claimants overstate the position and that the normal meaning of
> 'efficient' is to carry out an action with adequate skill.
>     ... I consider that the primary obligation is an absolute one to provide the services, but, by
> the proviso, the lessor is excused from liability for breach in certain circumstances. The
> secondary obligation is to inspect, maintain and repair. It is equally absolute, and the duty to
> inspect is inconsistent with the implication of some form of qualification that the duty to repair
> arose only on notice."

He went on to hold that the obligation had been broken for periods of time
amounting to 1,380 days, for which the tenants were entitled to damages of
£165,000.[63]

## REMOVAL OF PLANT AT THE END OF THE TERM

A covenant to yield up may require the removal at the end of the term of    **13–19**
redundant mechanical and electrical services or plant installed by the tenant
during the term. This is considered in Ch.25, para.25–46, below.

---

[62] [2002] 3 E.G.L.R. 93.
[63] See further Ch.33, below.

# CHAPTER 14

## FORMS OF EXPRESS COVENANT

### INTRODUCTORY

### Forms of covenant

Covenants imposing liability for dilapidations (whether in the form of obligations to repair or otherwise) appear in leases in a number of different forms. This Chapter is concerned with the various forms in which such covenants are generally to be found.

**14–01**

### COVENANTS TO PUT INTO REPAIR, KEEP IN REPAIR AND YIELD UP IN REPAIR

### Covenants to put into repair[1]

The general covenant to repair will sometimes include an express obligation to put the premises into repair. Given the general principle that a covenant to repair involves a duty to put the premises into repair in so far as they are out of it,[2] there would seem to be little difference in practice between the two formulations.[3] However, the inclusion of an express obligation to put into repair serves to emphasise that the standard contemplated by the covenant is not necessarily the same as the state of the premises at the date of the lease.[4] It adds weight to the argument that the parties intended specific disrepair at the date of the lease (or occurring during the lease as a result of a state of affairs at the date of the lease) to be within the tenant's obligations. Moreover, the provisions of the Leasehold Property (Repairs) Act 1938[5] do not apply to an obligation to put premises in repair that is to be performed upon the lessee taking possession of the premises or within a reasonable time thereafter.[6]

**14–02**

The covenant will usually specify a period within which the work is to be carried out. An obligation to carry out the work "forthwith" or "as soon as

---

[1] See further para.14–08, below.
[2] See para.9–21, above, and para.14–03, below.
[3] See, for example, *Chatfield v Elmstone Resthouse Ltd* [1975] 2 N.Z.L.R. 269 (New Zealand) (landlord's obligation to "keep" the roof and outer walls of the demised premises in good and watertight repair held to oblige him to "put" the roof into repair).
[4] See paras 9–21 to 9–26 et seq., above.
[5] See para.27–33, below.
[6] Leasehold Property (Repairs) Act 1938 s.3.

possible" will generally be construed as requiring performance within a reasonable time unless there are exceptional circumstances showing that immediate compliance was intended.[7] Where no period is specified, it is thought that the right construction will usually be that the work is to be done within a reasonable time of taking possession.[8]

## Covenants to repair and keep in repair

**14–03**  As a general principle, a covenant to repair or to keep in repair requires the covenantor to put the premises into repair insofar as they are out of it, even where the relevant defect exists at the date of the letting.[9]

A covenant to repair and keep in repair imposes a continuing duty to repair throughout the term.[10] It was argued in *Luxmoore v Robson*[11] that the covenant is performed by the premises being put into repair at any time before the expiry of the term, so that no right of action for breach vests in the landlord until the term has ended. The court rejected this as being supported by neither "common sense nor any principle of law".[12]

Sometimes, the covenant includes formulations such as "from time to time" or "at all times during the term hereby granted". It is not thought that these add anything (other than emphasis) to the general rule set out above.

It has been suggested that there is a difference between a covenant "to repair" and "to keep in repair", in that the former requires the carrying out of repairs, whereas the latter describes the state in which the subject-matter must be kept, irrespective of whether this is achieved by repairing or by more extensive work.[13] If this is right, then the former is a lesser obligation than the latter. However, in most of the decided cases the two covenants have been treated as meaning much the same.[14]

---

[7] See para.14–08, below.

[8] Cf. *Farimani v Gates* [1984] 2 E.G.L.R. 66 (implied term in covenant to expend insurance money in reinstating after fire that reinstatement to be carried out within a reasonable time of receiving the insurance money).

[9] *Payne v Haine* (1847) 6 M.&W. 541; *Truscott v Diamond Rock Boring Co Ltd* (1882) 20 Ch. D. 251 at 256; *Proudfoot v Hart* (1890) 25 Q.B.D. 42; *Saner v Bilton* (1878) 1 Ch D 815; *Chatfield v Elmstone Resthouse Ltd* [1975] 2 N.Z.L.R. 269 (New Zealand); *Langham Estate Management Ltd v Hardy* [2008] 3 E.G.L.R. 125 at [59]. In *Credit Suisse v Beegas Nominees Ltd* [1994] 4 All E.R. 803 and (more fully) [1994] 1 E.G.L.R. 76 Lindsay J. said of this principle that it has "been acted upon, by now, in probably hundreds of cases and still survives". See further para.9–21 et seq., above.

[10] *Coward v Gregory* (1866) 2 L.R. 2 C.P. 153; *Granada Theatres Ltd v Freehold Investment (Leytonstone) Ltd* [1959] Ch. 592; *British Telecommunications Plc v Sun Life Assurance Society Plc* [1996] Ch. 69; *Gibson Investments Ltd v Chesterton Plc* [2002] 2 P. & C.R. 32. See further paras 22–18 to 22–22, below.

[11] (1818) 1 B. & Ad. 584.

[12] *Luxmoore v Robson* per Bayley J. at 585. See also *Granada Theatres Ltd v Freehold Investment (Leytonstone) Ltd* [1959] Ch. 592, per Jenkins L.J. at 608.

[13] *Lurcott v Wakely* [1911] 2 K.B. 905, per Fletcher Moulton L.J.; *Bowman v Stanford* [1950] 2 S.A. (E.D.L.D.). See also *British Telecommunications Plc v Sun Life Assurance Society Plc*, above, per Nourse L.J. at 79 D–E.

[14] See para.4–20, et seq., above.

In *Riaz v Masaku*[15] a licence contained an obligation on the part of the licensee to keep the property in good repair and condition, both externally and internally, and to carry out all repairs necessary to maintain the property in good condition. The county court judge held that this obliged the licensee to indemnify the owner against liability to the local authority arising out of the service on the owner of a dangerous structure notice under the London Building Acts (Amendment) Act 1939. The Court of Appeal allowed the owner's appeal. The obligation obliged the licensee to keep the premises in repair. It did not impose on him an obligation to indemnify the owner against whatever liability he might be under as a result of the statutory notice.

## Covenants to yield up

Most modern leases contain a covenant on the part of the tenant to yield up the premises in repair at the expiry of the lease. This is often drafted simply as an obligation to yield up in repair (or some similar formulation). However, since the obligation will generally be to yield up "the demised premises", it is thought that it operates as an obligation to deliver up possession (i.e. vacant possession) of the demised premises as well as an obligation to deliver them up in repair.[16]    **14–04**

Even where there is no express obligation to yield up, there will generally be an implied obligation on the tenant to deliver up vacant possession of the demised premises to the landlord at the end of the term.[17]

### (a)    The obligation to deliver up in repair

The obligation to deliver up in repair takes effect on the stroke of midnight on the last day of the term. The premises must at that moment be in a state which is consistent with the performance of the covenants to repair and decorate. Where the lease is for a fixed term, the covenant takes effect on the term date. Where the tenancy is a periodic tenancy, the covenant takes effect on the expiry of the notice to quit. Where the lease is determined prior to the end of the original term, for example, by forfeiture or surrender, it is a question of construction whether the covenant comes into operation on such determination, or whether it never takes effect.[18]    **14–05**

The covenant to yield up in repair is a separate and distinct covenant from a covenant to repair on notice during the term, so that notice is not a necessary condition precedent to an action on the covenant to yield up.[19] Similarly, the covenant to yield up is a separate covenant from the covenant to repair and keep

---

[15] [2001] L. & T.R. 22.
[16] See *Woodfall: Landlord and Tenant* (London: Sweet & Maxwell), Vol.1, Ch.19, para.19.002.
[17] See *Woodfall: Landlord and Tenant* (London: Sweet & Maxwell), Vol.1, Ch.19, para.19.001.
[18] See para.2–06, above, where the effect of early termination on the covenant to yield up is discussed.
[19] *Harflet v Butcher* (1622) Cro. Jac. 644; *Wood v Day* (1817) 7 Taunt. 646. See para.14–10, below.

in repair during the term, so that an action for damages for breach of the latter during the tenancy is no bar to an action on the covenant to yield up at the end of the term.[20]

The covenant to yield up in repair does not apply to defects occurring after the end of the term.[21]

## (b) The obligation to deliver up possession

**14–06**     Absent particular wording leading to a contrary conclusion, the obligation to deliver up possession does not require the tenant to remove fixtures installed by him during the term, even if they are tenant's fixtures (i.e. fixtures which the tenant has the right in law to remove).[22] In *Legal & General Assurance Society Ltd v Expeditors International (UK) Ltd*[23] Lewison J. said:

> "… in my judgment the premises will include anything which in law has become part of the premises by annexation. A fixture installed by the tenant for the purposes of his trade becomes part of the premises as soon as it is installed, although the tenant retains a right to sever the fixture on termination of the tenancy. Whether something is a fixture depends on the degree and purpose of annexation; in each case looked at objectively. If something has become part of the premises by annexation then it is part of a thing of which vacant possession has to be given. Its presence does not amount to an impediment to vacant possession itself."

However, the tenant will generally be liable to remove chattels brought onto the premises by him or his sub-tenants or licensees during the tenancy.[24] Schedules of dilapidations frequently (and wrongly) specify as breaches of the covenant to repair items such as failure to remove desks, shelving, cupboards, partitions and carpets installed by the tenant during the term, and failure to remove rubbish. This is a misconception. Thus, in *Commercial Union Life Assurance Co Ltd v Label Ink Ltd*[25] H.H. Judge Rich QC (sitting as a deputy High Court Judge) said:

> "Item 7.5 complains of a breach of [the covenant to repair and yield up in repair] and a failure to remove certain shelves and cupboard units from the workshop. These are put forward as an unauthorised internal addition or alteration. I do not see how their presence could be classed as a disrepair."

---

[20] *Ebbetts v Conquest* (1900) 82 L.T. 560. See also *Coward v Gregory* (1866) L.R. 2 C.P. 153.

[21] *Associated Deliveries Ltd v Harrison* (1984) 50 P. & C.R. 91. See further para.23–18 et seq., below.

[22] See further para.25–43 et seq., below.

[23] [2007] 1 P. & C. R. 5 at [32] (on appeal: [2007] 2 P. & C. R. 10).

[24] Cf. *Cumberland Consolidated Holdings Ltd v Ireland* [1946] K.B. 264; *Legal & General Assurance Society Ltd v Expeditors International Ltd* [2007] 1 P. & C.R. 5 (Lewison J.) and [2007] 2 P. & C. R. 10) (Court of Appeal); *NYK Logistics (UK) Ltd v Ibrend Estates BV* [2011] 2 P. & C.R. 9 at [44]. See further *Woodfall: Landlord and Tenant*, (London: Sweet & Maxwell), Vol.1, Ch.19, para.19.003.

[25] [2001] L. & T.R. 29. Note that the question of disrepair arose in the context of whether or not the tenant had complied with a condition precedent in a break option, and that the judge's construction of the condition precedent was subsequently disapproved by the Court of Appeal in *Fitzroy House Epworth Street (No.1) v The Financial Times* [2006] 2 E.G.L.R. 13.

In so far as the items in question are chattels, failure to remove them is a breach not of the covenant to repair but of the express or implied covenant to deliver up possession. In so far as they are fixtures, there may be no obligation to remove them in the absence of a specific covenant to that effect,[26] (although the obligation to yield up may be construed in certain circumstances as requiring the removal of redundant fixtures[27]).

## Covenants to yield up in repair and carry out additional works

In some cases, the lease may oblige the tenant not only to yield up the premises in repair at the end of the term but also to carry out additional works (such as the removal of fixtures, the reinstatement of alterations or the carrying out of specified improvements). The inter-relationship of the various obligations will depend on the proper construction of the lease.

**14–07**

In *Fairgate International v Citibank International*[28] an office lease contained a tenant's covenant in the following terms:

"(8)(A)  At the expiration or sooner determination of the said term quietly to yield up the Demised Premises decorated repaired cleaned and kept in accordance with the Tenant's covenants herein contained together with all additions and improvements thereto and all fixtures and fittings which may be fixed or fastened to or upon the Demised Premises EXCEPT tenant's fixtures and fittings which the Tenant is entitled to and does remove prior to the expiration or sooner determination of the said term and to reinstate.

(B)  If so required by the Landlord prior to or upon the expiration or sooner determination of the said term at the Tenant's own expense:

(i)  to remove all or any furnishings fixtures fittings or other items of whatsoever nature that the Tenant may have installed and to make good all damage caused to the Demised Premises by such removal and restore the same to their original condition to the reasonable satisfaction of the Landlord's surveyor

(ii)  to fit out equip and lay out the Demised Premises (other than the flats on the seventh floor) in accordance with the specification set out in the Third Schedule and the said flats in accordance with the specification set out in the Fourth Schedule all materials and finishes used in such works to be of a quality and (where applicable) pattern previously approved in writing by the Landlord such approval not to be unreasonably withheld and all such works to be carried out to the reasonable satisfaction of the Landlord's surveyor."

The third and fourth schedules both contained brief specifications. The tenant accepted that an obligation created by a request under cl.(8)(B) would override an obligation under cl.(8)(A) that was inconsistent with it, but contended that cll.8(B)(i) and (ii) were mutually exclusive. Its argument was rejected both at first instance and in the Court of Appeal. The sub-clauses were to be interpreted as entitling the landlord to require the tenant to carry out work under cl.2(8)(B)(i) except to the extent, if any, that it was inconsistent with, or was rendered unnecessary by, the provisions of cl.2(8)(B)(ii).

---

[26]  See para.25–43 et seq., below.
[27]  See para.25–47, below.
[28]  [2005] 2 E.G.L.R. 48.

## OTHER FORMS OF REPAIRING COVENANT

### Covenants to put the premises into repair forthwith

**14–08**   Sometimes the lease will provide that the premises are to be put into repair, or into a specified state of repair, "forthwith" or "as soon as possible" or some similar formulation. Covenants of this type are most commonly entered into where the obligation to carry out work is part of the consideration given by the tenant for the grant of the lease. Often this will be the case where the premises are in a neglected and dilapidated condition which the landlord seeks to remedy by finding a tenant willing to put them right; or where the obligation is entered into as part of the compromise of a dilapidations claim arising under a previous lease of the premises; or where the covenant is included following unsuccessful opposition by the landlord to the grant of a new business tenancy under the Landlord and Tenant Act 1954 on the grounds of failure to comply with repairing obligations under the tenancy being renewed.[29] The provisions of the Leasehold Property (Repairs) Act 1938 will not generally apply to covenants of this type.[30]

An obligation to put premises into repair "forthwith" will be construed reasonably and is not limited to any specific time.[31] It is a question of fact whether the covenantor has done what he reasonably ought in performance of it.[32] It will generally be construed as requiring performance within a reasonable time unless there are exceptional circumstances showing that immediate compliance was intended. In *R. v Worcestershire Justices*[33] Coleridge J. said:

> "I agree that the word 'forthwith' is not to receive a strict construction like the word 'immediately', so that whatever follows, must be done immediately after that which has been done before … whatever is to be done … ought to be done without any unreasonable delay. I think the word 'forthwith' must be considered as having that meaning."

The same is likely to be held to be the case in relation to a covenant to put premises into repair "as soon as possible". In *Hydraulic Engineering Co Ltd v McHaffie Goslett & Co Ltd*[34] Bramwell L.J. said:

> "To do a thing 'as soon as possible' means to do it within a reasonable time, with an undertaking to do it in the shortest practicable time."

What is reasonable in any particular case will depend on all the circumstances.[35] Of particular importance in the context of a covenant to carry out a programme of works will be the practical steps required to be taken in order

---

[29] See para.35–05, below.
[30] See para.27–33, below.
[31] *Doe d Pittman v Sutton* (1841) 9 C. & P. 706 (covenant "forthwith" to put premises into "good and substantial repair").
[32] *Doe d Pittman v Sutton* (1841) 9 C. & P. 706 (covenant "forthwith" to put premises into "good and substantial repair").
[33] (1839) 7 Dowl. 789.
[34] [1878] 4 Q.B.D. 670.
[35] See *Measures v McFadyn* (1910) 11 C.L.R. 723 (in which the covenant was to execute, perform and carry out alterations and additions of a stated value on the demised premises "forthwith", and it was held that 21 months was not "forthwith").

to complete the works.[36] However, the tenant's financial or other personal circumstances will not generally be relevant.[37]

## Covenants to carry out repairs within a specified time

The covenant may provide for works of repair to be carried out within a specified time, such as six months. What amounts to a breach of such a covenant will depend upon the exact terms in which the covenant is framed. If it is in a form such as "to commence, diligently proceed with and complete" the works, there is a breach if they are not commenced within a reasonable time, or thereafter diligently proceeded with, or completed on the due date. If there is only a general obligation to complete by a specified date it would seem that there is no breach until that date is past. It is possible, however, that if the tenant were to make it clear before the due date that he was not proposing to do the work, or to delay starting the work for so long that there was no realistic possibility of it being completed by the due date, then the court would hold there to have been an anticipatory breach.[38] A failure to complete in time is a "once-and-for-all" breach, so that for the purposes of the law of forfeiture it is capable of waiver.[39] It is, however, a "remediable" breach, so that the right of re-entry is not exercisable until the defaulting tenant has been given a further reasonable time to complete the works.[40]

**14–09**

## Covenants to repair on notice

In modern times, the covenant to repair on notice is generally part of a composite provision entitling the landlord, if the tenant fails to comply with the notice, to enter the premises, carry out the work and recover the cost from the tenant.[41] However, leases granted in the 19th century often contained, in addition to the general covenant to repair, a covenant to repair specific defects notified by the landlord within a specified time (often three months) of notice being given, without any default provision entitling the landlord to enter and repair if the tenant failed to comply with the notice. As a general rule, the covenant to repair and the covenant to repair on notice are separate and distinct covenants.[42] Proceedings may therefore be brought for breach of the former even though no

**14–10**

---

[36] Cf. para.22–14, below.

[37] *Alghussein Establishment v Eton College,* [1988] 1 W.L.R. 587. See further on this case para.18–30, below.

[38] Cf. *Billson v Residential Apartments Ltd (No.1)* [1991] 3 All E.R. 265, per Sir Nicolas Browne-Wilkinson V.C. at 274 (not considered on appeal [1992] 1 A.C. 494).

[39] *Grescott v Green* (1699) 1 Salk. 199; *Stephens v Junior Army & Navy Stores Ltd* [1914] 2 Ch. 516. See para.27–05 et seq., below.

[40] *Expert Clothing Service & Sales Ltd v Hillgate House Ltd* [1986] Ch. 340. See para.27–23 et seq., below.

[41] See paras 14–11 to 14–12, below.

[42] *Harflet v Butcher* (1622) Cro. Jac. 644; *Wood v Day* (1817) 7 Taunt. 646; *Baylis v Le Gros* (1858) 4 C.B.N.S.537; *Doe d. Goatley v Paine* (1810) 2 Camp. 520; *Doe d. Morecraft v Meux* (1825) 4 B. & C. 606. See also *Thistle v Union Forwarding & Railway Co* (1878) 29 C. & P. 76 (Canada).

notice has been given under the latter.[43] The same applies where the lease contains a covenant to repair on notice and a covenant to yield up.[44] In an appropriate case, however, the two covenants may be construed as one single covenant, in which case a notice will be required before the tenant is in breach. Thus, in *Horsefall v Testar*[45] it was held that a covenant to repair at all times when occasion should require during the term "and at furthest within three months after notice" created a single covenant, so that no proceedings could be brought until notice had been given and had expired without the required work being done.

The notice required under the covenant is a contractual notice, which is not the same as a notice under s.146 of the Law of Property Act 1925.[46] If the tenant fails to comply with the notice, and thereby commits a breach of covenant, then a separate s.146 notice would be necessary before the landlord can forfeit for that breach. It should be noted that the giving of notice under the covenant to repair on notice will prevent forfeiture for breach of the general covenant to repair until after the expiry of the notice,[47] although it will not affect the right to forfeit for such breaches in so far as they continue after the date of service of the notice.

The facts may be such that the landlord is estopped from relying on the tenant's failure to comply with a notice to repair pursuant to the covenant. Thus, in *Hughes v The Metropolitan Railway*[48] it was held that the effect of negotiations between landlord and tenant for a surrender was to suspend the notice to repair until negotiations had been broken off.

## Covenants to pay the cost incurred by the landlord in executing repairs carried out on the tenant's default[49]

14–11    Modern commercial leases almost invariably contain a composite provision entitling the landlord to enter the demised premises, execute work which the tenant has failed to carry out in breach of his general covenant to repair, and recover the costs thereby incurred from the tenant. Typically, such clauses contain a number of separate obligations on the part of the tenant as follows:

(1)    to permit entry by the landlord to inspect the demised premises, draw up a schedule of disrepair and serve a notice requiring the tenant to remedy the disrepair within a specified period;

(2)    to comply with that notice within the specified period;

(3)    in default of compliance, to allow the landlord to enter and carry out the works himself;

---

[43] *Baylis v Le Gros*, above.
[44] *Harfelt v Butcher* (1622) Cro. Jac. 644; *Wood v Day* (1817) 1 Moore 389.
[45] (1817) 7 Taunt. 385.
[46] See para.27–12 et seq., below.
[47] This is considered in para.27–10, below.
[48] (1876) 1 C.P.D. 120; affirmed (1877) 2 App. Cas. 439. The facts are set out in para.1–14, above.
[49] See further para.28–32 et seq., below.

(4) to pay to the landlord the cost incurred by the landlord in carrying out those works. The sum is usually expressed to be recoverable by the landlord as money due, or as a debt, or sometimes as additional rent in arrears or as liquidated damages.

In *Jervis v Harris*[50] the Court of Appeal held that the Leasehold Property (Repairs) Act 1938 does not apply to a claim under the fourth component for the cost of work carried out by the landlord.[51] This has removed many of the previous limitations on the remedy. Even without the fourth component, however, such a covenant is an important weapon in the landlord's overall armoury to deal with disrepair. This is particularly so in the case of a lease which has many years to run, where the demised premises form part only of a building, and the disrepair of a single part is likely to have an adverse effect upon the letting value of the remainder. In the absence of such a clause, the landlord would have no right to enter upon the premises to remedy the disrepair,[52] and would be left with the less satisfactory course of pursuing the tenant on his general covenant to repair.

It should be noted that the landlord's right of entry to carry out the works only arises at the time and subject to the conditions provided by the clause. Those conditions must be complied with to the letter, or the subsequent entry upon the premises may be held to be a trespass. If, for example, the clause gives the tenant a period of three months to comply with the notice, the right of entry will not arise until the end of that period, and any prior entry by the landlord, however urgent the circumstances, may be unlawful. A well-drafted clause will generally seek to overcome this difficulty by providing that the tenant must commence the works forthwith upon receipt of the notice, and that the landlord may carry out the works in default if he does not.

In *Amsprop Trading Ltd v Harris Distribution Ltd*[53] a sub-lease contained covenants by the sub-tenant (i) to permit the superior landlords and the landlords to enter the premises and give notice of all wants of repair found, and (ii) within three months after such notice (or immediately in the case of emergency) to remedy the defects in the notice, in default of which the superior landlords and the landlords were entitled to enter and carry out the works and the sub-tenant was to pay the cost on demand as liquidated damages. On February 20, 1996 the head tenant served a repairs notice requiring the sub-tenant to carry out repairs within three months. On March 24, 1996 the sub-tenant surrendered the sub-lease. Soon afterwards the head landlord forfeited the head tenancy. The head landlord claimed to be entitled to enforce covenant (ii) against the sub-tenant. Neuberger J. dismissed his claim. One of the grounds on which he did so was that the sub-lease had come to an end within the three-month period, and the obligation to comply with the notice had therefore fallen away, with the result that the landlord's right to recover the cost of the work in the notice had also gone.[54] The judge said in the course of his judgment:

**14–12**

---

[50] [1996] Ch. 195.
[51] See further para.28–39, below.
[52] See para.22–30, below.
[53] [1997] 1 W.L.R. 1025.
[54] See further para.24–09, below.

> "[A] provision such as [the covenant in question], which gives the landlords substantial powers, and in particular power to carry out work at the tenant's expense, should be construed narrowly rather than widely."

The inclusion of a covenant of this type in the lease will bring s.4(4) of the Defective Premises Act 1972 into play.[55] This will not avail the tenant,[56] but it will render the landlord liable to third parties in the circumstances set out in the subsection.

It may be that if the landlord exercises his right to enter and carry out the works, he thereby waives his right to forfeit for the breaches of the repairing covenants which existed before he entered.[57]

## Covenants to repair by reference to the condition of the premises at the date of the lease

**14–13**   The lease may provide that the premises are to be kept in the state in which they were at the date of the lease. A common formulation is to limit the tenant's obligation to keeping the premises "in no worse state than that in which they are now in". The state of the premises at the date of the lease will be a matter of evidence at whatever future date the matter falls to be considered. In order to avoid the obvious evidential difficulties which might otherwise arise, the parties will often prepare a schedule of condition. When this has been done, the covenant to repair will usually incorporate an express reference to the schedule, by providing, for example, that the premises are to be kept in "the state in which they are now in as evidenced by the schedule of condition annexed hereto", or some similar formulation.

### (a)   Where no schedule of condition has been prepared

**14–14**   Where no schedule of condition has been prepared, the state of the premises at the date of the lease must be proved by evidence. The practical difficulties will depend on the availability of sufficient evidence, which in turn will be governed to some extent by the amount of time that has elapsed. The original landlord or tenant, or their respective advisers, or third parties such as a previous landlord or tenant, or neighbours, may all to some degree recollect the condition of the premises at the relevant date. All such evidence, together with supporting documents such as notes of inspection, correspondence about the state of the premises, photographs, etc. will in principle be admissible, and will be tested by the court in the ordinary way and given such weight as appropriate. In some cases it may be possible to call expert evidence from a surveyor who can express an opinion, based on an inspection, as to how the premises must have been at the date of the lease.

---

[55] See para.20–49 et seq., below.

[56] See para.20–62, below.

[57] *Doe d. Rutzen v Lewis* (1836) 5 A. & E. 277. This is further discussed in para.27–05 et seq., below.

## (b) Where a schedule of condition is referred to in the lease but has never existed or has been lost

It is not unknown for a schedule of condition to be referred to in a lease without **14–15** the parties ever having got around to preparing one. It can also happen that a schedule is referred to but has been lost or destroyed. In such a case the court has to do the best it can with whatever extrinsic evidence is available to "reconstruct" the schedule. Where it appears that the schedule was intended to do no more than evidence the actual state of repair at the date of the lease, the task will be no different to the one described above. However, where it appears that the schedule was intended to define a standard which was not directly related to the condition of the premises at that date, it may be more difficult to ascertain that standard. Once again the court must do the best it can with whatever evidence is available so as to give effect as far as possible to what the parties intended.

## (c) The evidential value of the schedule of condition

The schedule of condition, where it can be found, will generally be made **14–16** definitive of the matters set out in it. If so, it will not be open to either party to dispute the accuracy of the schedule except by claiming rectification.

It is common to find that the schedule is drafted in fairly general terms. In such a case it may not be possible to identify the required standard of repair with sufficient precision by reference to the schedule alone. For example the roof of premises may be noted to be "in generally fair condition but some slates cracked". If a dispute were to arise as to how many slates were cracked, and how badly, it is thought that extrinsic evidence would be admissible to amplify and clarify this incomplete description. However, it would not be open to either party to contradict what was stated in the schedule, such as by seeking to prove that no slates were cracked, or that the roof was not in "generally fair condition".

## (d) The works required

Difficult practical problems may arise in deciding what works must be carried out **14–17** by the tenant in order to comply with this sort of limited repairing obligation. The obligation will generally require the premises to be kept in the same state in which they were at the date of the lease. However, it may be impossible to reproduce the exact state of the premises at that time, and in practice the only way of performing the obligation may be to carry out work which results in the premises being repaired to a higher standard. For example, the schedule of condition might show that a small part of the front door of the premises was rotten at the date of the lease. By the end of the lease the rot may have spread significantly, so that the whole door needs replacing. In theory, the tenant could perform his obligation by installing a door which is in exactly the same state as was the original door at the date of the lease. In practice, however, this is likely to be either impossible or uneconomic, or both, and the only realistic way of performing the obligation will be to put in a new door. For this reason, repairing covenants framed by reference to a schedule of condition may be of less value to tenants than is commonly supposed.

It is thought, however, that the covenant must be construed in accordance with the "good sense of the agreement",[58] so that (in the above example) the tenant could not be criticised if he were able to find a second-hand door which was in about the same condition as the door when demised. Likewise, if the state of the decorations at the date of the lease is recorded in the schedule as being "generally fair", it is thought that the tenant could not be criticised if he has redecorated two years before the expiry of the lease so that, in very general terms, the state of decoration conforms to that described in the schedule of condition.

Where the covenant can only be performed in such a way as to produce a building in better repair than was the building at the date of the lease, the tenant will not generally be entitled to any discount for betterment.[59]

### (e)   Assessment of damages

**14–18**    In practice, a number of the disputes which arise in relation to covenants of this type centre on the amount of damages payable by the tenant for breach. One question which commonly arises is whether, if the state of the premises falls materially below that described in the schedule of condition but (for the reasons explained above) the relevant defects cannot in practice be remedied without improving the premises over and above the condition in the schedule, damages for breach are to be assessed on the basis of the condition described in the schedule or the work the tenant should have carried out. This is considered elsewhere.[60]

## Covenants to repair to the satisfaction of, or using materials specified by, the landlord's surveyor

**14–19**    The covenant to repair will sometimes provide that the repairs are to be done to the satisfaction of the landlord's surveyor, or that materials of a type approved by the landlord's surveyor must be used. These types of covenant give rise to a number of questions in practice.

### (a)   Whether the appointment of a surveyor is a condition precedent to the tenant's liability under the repairing covenant

**14–20**    Whether the appointment by the landlord of a surveyor is a condition precedent to the tenant's liability is a question of construction. Where the works cannot be done unless a surveyor is appointed, this will be an indication that such appointment is intended to be a condition precedent. Thus, in *Combe v Green*[61]

---

[58] *Nicholson v White* (1842) 4 Man. & G. 95, per Tindall C.J. at 98, cited with approval by Sachs L.J. in *Brew Bros Ltd v Snax (Ross) Ltd* [1970] Q.B. 612 at 641.

[59] See para.29–16 et seq., below.

[60] See para.29–15, below.

[61] (1843) 11 M. & W. 480.

the tenant covenanted to spend £100 in improving the demised premises "under the direction or with the approbation of some competent surveyor, to be named by and on the part of the landlord". It was held that the appointment of a surveyor was a condition precedent to the tenant's liability under the covenant for "until one was appointed he could not give directions as to how the money was to be expended". A similar conclusion was reached in *Hunt v Bishop*[62] in which the tenant covenanted to finish four unfinished houses on the demised land on or before a named date "under the direction and to the satisfaction of the surveyor" of the landlord. Pollock C.B. reasoned that because no surveyor had been appointed, "no direction could be given or satisfaction expressed". The appointment of a surveyor is therefore likely to be held to be a condition precedent where the tenant covenants to repair to the satisfaction of the landlord's surveyor or using materials first approved by him.

Where, however, the surveyor's role is only to supervise the carrying out of the work or to approve the workmanship, his appointment is unlikely to be held to be a condition precedent. Thus, in *Cannock v Jones*[63] specified works to be carried out pursuant to a landlord's covenant were "to be left to the superintendence" of certain persons. It was held that no condition precedent was intended.

### (b) The identity of the surveyor

In some cases, the lease will define what is meant by the landlord's surveyor. In other cases, it may simply refer to "the landlord's surveyor" or something similar. Where the lease specifies a surveyor, it is not open to the landlord to substitute a person from another discipline, however well qualified in other respects and even though he is appointed to act in a surveying role.[64] It will generally be implicit that the person appointed must be both a qualified surveyor and independent of the landlord.[65]

**14–21**

### (c) The matters which must be referred to the surveyor

The nature of the matters which must be referred to the surveyor will depend on the proper construction of the covenant. In some cases, the surveyor may be entitled to specify the work to be done and the materials to be used. In others, his involvement may be limited to ensuring that the completed work has been carried out to an appropriate standard of workmanship. In *Mason v TotalFinaElf UK Ltd*[66] a lease of a petrol filling station contained a covenant on the part of the tenant that he would:

**14–22**

---

[62] (1853) 8 Ex. 675. See also *Hunt v Remnant* (1854) 9 Ex. 635; *Re Northumberland Avenue Hotel Co Ltd, Fox & Braithwaite's Claim* (1887) 56 L.T. 833.
[63] (1849) 3 Exch. 233 (affirmed (1850) 5 Exch. 713).
[64] *Jacey Property Co v De Sousa* [2003] EWCA Civ 510 (landlord's solicitor).
[65] Cf. (in a service charge context) *Finchbourne v Rodrigues* [1976] 3 All E.R. 581.
[66] [2003] 3 E.G.L.R. 91.

> "[F]rom time to time and at all times during the said term to the satisfaction of the Lessor's Surveyor well and substantially uphold support maintain amend repair decorate and keep in good condition the demised premises."

Blackburne J. held that this entitled the landlord's surveyor to prescribe the work to be done as well as the manner in which it was to be done. He said:

> "I see no reason why [the surveyor's judgment] should be confined to manner of performance of the works to be undertaken and not apply to what the work is that has to be done. As [counsel for the landlord] pointed out, the phrase qualifies the whole of the content of the tenant's obligation, not just a part of it. In any event, as [counsel for the tenant] accepted, there is a point at which the manner in which work is to be done becomes, for all practical purposes, indistinguishable from what the work is that is to be done."

He further rejected the tenant's contention that the landlord's surveyor's requirement had to be communicated to the tenant prior to the expiry of the lease, holding that it was for the tenant to take a view on what would or should have satisfied the landlord's surveyor, if necessary consulting the landlord to find out what his surveyor might require, before it vacated the premises, and to carry out such works. Had it done so and received no response it might well be that the landlord would be in no position subsequently, through his surveyor, to require some other mode of compliance provided that what the tenant had done was fairly to be regarded as compliance with the covenant.

### (d)  Questions of law

**14–23**     Where questions of law, such as the proper interpretation of the repairing obligations in the lease, are involved, it will be a question of construction as to whether the surveyor's judgment has been made final and binding. It is thought that in the absence of clear words showing otherwise, the surveyor's judgment is likely to be held to be binding only in relation to matters within his expertise, such as, for example, what defects exist and how they ought to be remedied.[67] However, there is no rule of public policy which prevents parties from agreeing to refer to the decision of an expert questions which involve construction or other questions of law.[68] Consequently, it is open to the parties to agree if they wish that the surveyor's judgment will be binding in relation to such matters as, for example, the meaning of an expression in the lease such as "the structure".

### (e)  Limitations on the surveyor's judgment

**14–24**     The covenant may expressly provide that the surveyor is to act reasonably. For example, it may provide that the tenant is to repair to the reasonable satisfaction of the surveyor, or that the tenant is to use materials of a type and design to be approved by the surveyor, such approval not to be unreasonably withheld. The

---

[67] Cf. *Re Davstone Estates' Leases* [1969] 2 Ch. 378.

[68] *Nikko Hotels (UK) Ltd v MEPC Plc* [1991] 2 E.G.L.R. 103 (doubting an obiter dictum in *Re Davstone Estates' Leases*); *Brown v GIO Insurance* [1998] Lloyd's Rep. I.R. 201. See Kendall, Freedman & Farrell, *Expert Determination*, 4th edn (London: Sweet & Maxwell, 2008), para.11.5 et seq.

effect of this is that there will be no breach of covenant if the surveyor acts unreasonably,[69] i.e. if he comes to a decision to which no reasonable surveyor could have come in the circumstances. However, where there is room for more than one view as to what should be done or used, the view of the appointed surveyor will prevail, even where the tenant's surveyor disagrees or the court might have taken a different view had it been asked to decide the matter itself.[70] In practice, it may be difficult to persuade the court that a surveyor who has acted honestly and conscientiously (and who has not misinterpreted the lease) has come to a perverse decision in the above sense.

Sometimes the covenant will simply refer to the satisfaction or approval of the landlord's surveyor, without qualifying this in any way. Whether there is any implied limitation of reasonableness will depend on the facts of each individual case. In most cases, however, it is thought that the court will be fairly ready to interpret the covenant as meaning that the surveyor must act reasonably, or to imply a term to that effect. Thus, in *Mason v TotalFinaElf UK Ltd*,[71] which Blackburne J., having construed a tenant's covenant "... from time to time and at all times during the said term to the satisfaction of the Lessor's Surveyor well and substantially uphold support maintain amend repair decorate and keep in good condition the demised premises ..." as entitling the landlord's surveyor to prescribe the work to be done as well as the manner in which it was to be done, said:

> "The fact that the phrase is unqualified does not give the surveyor carte blanche as to what he may require. The works to be undertaken must be to make good a want of repair or absence of good condition. In stipulating what must be done the surveyor must exercise his own judgment and come to an honest view of what is required. It is plainly implicit that he must act reasonably. He will be acting unreasonably if he seeks to require work which no reasonable surveyor could have required. On the other hand, provided he reaches a decision which a reasonable surveyor could reach, it matters not that the tenant's surveyor favours another cheaper but no less reasonable decision as to what should be done."

## Covenants subject to a precondition that the landlord shall carry out repairs or supply materials

A number of old authorities deal with cases where the tenant's covenant to repair **14–25** was qualified by a stipulation that the landlord would carry out specified works of repair at the commencement of the term, or that he would provide materials or otherwise assist in the tenant's performance of his covenant. The question arising in relation to such covenants is whether on the proper construction of the lease: (a) performance by the landlord is a precondition to the tenant's liability; or (b) the landlord's undertaking is an absolute and independent covenant but not a precondition; or (c) the landlord's undertaking is both an independent covenant with a life of its own and a precondition. If it is a precondition, then no question of performance (and therefore no question of breach) by the tenant arises unless and until the landlord has fulfilled his part of the contract. If, on the other hand, it

---

[69] *Doe d. Baker v Jones* (1848) 2 Car. & Kir. 743.
[70] Cf. *Re W.* [1971] A.C. 682, per Lord Hailsham at 700: "There is a band of decisions within which no court should seek to replace the individual's judgment with its own".
[71] [2003] 3 E.G.L.R. 91.

is merely an independent covenant by the landlord, the consequences of its non-fulfilment are that the tenant has a right of action against the landlord without his own liability under his covenant being postponed or diminished. If it is both a precondition and an independent covenant, there is the double consequence that the tenant's obligation is postponed and he has a right of action in the meantime for breach of covenant against his landlord.

### (a)  Precondition that the landlord shall carry out repairs

**14–26**  The question whether a precondition that the landlord shall repair amounts to a condition precedent to the tenant's liability under his covenant is one of construction in every case. In *Slater v Stone*[72] a tenant's covenant to repair the premises "from and after" the carrying out of repairs by the landlord was held to be subject to a condition precedent that the landlord should first repair. The same conclusion was reached in *Neal v Ratcliff*,[73] in which the premises were demised:

> "[U]pon and subject to the terms that the lessees should maintain and keep in good and tenantable repair and condition the said messuage or public house, buildings and premises, the same being first put into good and tenantable repair and condition by the lessor."

The lessees also entered into a general repairing covenant and a covenant to yield up in repair, the general covenant being expressly qualified in the same manner. On the termination of the lease the lessor claimed damages for dilapidations. The lessor had done repairs to some parts of the premises but had not repaired the whole in accordance with the stipulation. The lessees had carried out no repairs at all. They were held liable at first instance for failure to repair the parts of the premises which the lessor had repaired, but not the other parts. On appeal it was held (i) that the stipulation was a condition precedent, and (ii) that the condition precedent was not divisible, and therefore the landlord was not entitled to recover damages even in respect of the non-repair of those parts of the premises which he had repaired. On the second point, Wightman J. said:

> "We do not mean to lay down that in no case may a condition precedent be divisible; cases may easily be conceived in which the covenant or agreement to which it is attached may apply to two or more subject matters, so distinct that the covenant or agreement, which is one in form, is several in fact, and the condition, in the same way, attached to each is several in fact, though one in form; and in such a case it may be clear that, by the intention of the parties … the performance as to one part may entitle to an action for the non-performance of the corresponding part of the covenant. But the burden of showing this will clearly lie on the party who insists upon it, and who seeks to make that divisible which on its face is entire … in the present instance, we see no ground for concluding this to have been the case. The defendants have taken, not two separate dwelling-houses of which one may be completely enjoyed though the other may not be in condition for proper occupation, but they have taken a dwelling-house with appurtenant outbuildings; … and it seems to us that the unrebutted presumption is, that they intended to have, and the plaintiff agreed they should have, the whole premises in tenantable repair before they were bound to repair any part."

---

[72] (1622) Cro. Jac. 645.
[73] (1850) 15 Q.B. 916.

A similar result was reached in *Coward v Gregory*,[74] where the landlord had given an express covenant "forthwith" to put the premises in repair and the tenant covenanted to keep them in repair "the lessor having first put the premises in good and tenantable repair". Performance of the landlord's covenant was held to be a condition precedent to performance of the tenant's covenant as well as an independent covenant. Erle C.J. summarised the effect of *Neal v Ratcliff* as follows:

> "It has had the effect of removing a doubt from my mind whether this was more than a ground for a cross-action; for it goes the whole length of deciding that, until the lessor has fulfilled his covenant to put the premises in repair, no liability to repair is cast upon the tenant by his covenant."

In *Pick v Leon Goodman Displays*,[75] the tenant under a 14-year lease covenanted to:

> "maintain the premises in their present state as set out in the schedule of condition ... a copy of such schedule being annexed hereto until the premises have been put into good and substantial repair and condition (by the lessor under its covenant) and thereafter to keep and maintain the demised premises and all additions thereto ... in such good and substantial repair and condition throughout the term and in such repair and condition to yield up the same at the determination of the said term."

It was held by the Court of Appeal that various defects in the roof and a failure to paint the windows were fatal to the landlord's claim for terminal dilapidations.

The principle has been extended to a case where the landlord's liability arose not under the terms of the lease itself but under a collateral contract. In *Henman v Berliner*[76] the parties agreed (a) that the prospective landlord would put the drains of the house in sound and proper condition; and (b) that the proposed tenant would accept a lease of the house with the drains in such good condition. The proposed tenant would not have entered into the lease unless the proposed landlord had so agreed to repair the drains. The lease was subsequently granted containing no covenant on the landlord to carry out repairs to the drains, but containing a full repairing covenant on the part of the tenant. In fact no works of repair to the drains had been carried out, and diphtheria broke out in the house after some years. The landlord had to carry out works of repair pursuant to an order of the local authority. The judge found that these works would not have been necessary if the landlord had done the agreed work prior to the grant of the lease. The landlord sued the tenant for the cost of works pursuant to his obligation in the lease to pay "outgoings" and to keep the premises in repair. The tenant was held not to be liable on the ground that the outgoings and repairs for which the parties contemplated the tenant would be liable related to the premises as repaired by the landlord pursuant to the prior agreement, and not in the state in which they were in fact let.

**14–27**

---

[74] (1866) L.R. 2 C.P. 153. See also *Haldane v Newcomb* (1863) 3 New. Rep. 139; *Counter v Macpherson* (1845) 5 Moo. P.C.C. 83.
[75] (1962) 181 E.G. 549.
[76] [1918] 2 K.B. 236.

A precondition as to the carrying out of works by the landlord may also amount to a cross-covenant by him to do the works. Thus, in *Cannock v Jones*[77] the lessee of a farmhouse and certain buildings agreed to do certain repairs, "the said farmhouse and buildings being previously put in repair, and kept in repair by the lessor". Upon the lessor's failure to carry out works of repair, the lessee brought an action, contending that the words quoted amounted to an independent covenant by the lessor. The court found in favour of the lessee.

## *(b)    Precondition that the landlord shall supply materials*

**14–28**     A tenant's covenant to repair which is made subject to a precondition that the landlord must supply the necessary materials is almost unheard of in modern times, when building materials are generally readily available. The relevant authorities were decided in an age when both the obtaining and the transport of materials, particularly timber, were more difficult than they are today, and the cases must be read with this in mind.

In *Thomas v Cadwallader*[78] the tenant covenanted to repair the premises, the landlord "finding allowing and assigning timber sufficient for such reparations during the said term to be cut and carried by" the tenant. The tenant, on being sued for failure to repair, pleaded that sufficient timber had not been made available in order to enable him to carry out repairs. The court held that the provision of sufficient timber was a condition precedent, so that the tenant was not liable. The reasoning was that:

> "[T]his finding of timber was a thing in its nature necessary to be done first, and therefore must be considered as a qualification of the lessee's covenant … a man cannot repair unless the timber is assigned to him for such repairs."

On similar wording it was held in *Martyn v Clue*[79] that the condition precedent was satisfied if the landlord had at all times been ready and willing to furnish timber, and it was not necessary that he should have cut it.

**14–29**     By contrast, in *Tucker v Linger*[80] the tenant agreed to keep farm buildings in repair, and the landlord undertook to find, upon notice from the tenant, materials for such repairs. It was held that the tenant's obligation to repair was not conditional upon the landlord finding the materials.

The precondition may be held to amount to a cross-obligation on the landlord. Thus, in *Westacott v Hahn*[81] the tenant of a farm covenanted:

> "([B]eing allowed all necessary material for this purpose (to be previously approved in writing by the lessors) and carting such materials free of cost a distance not exceeding five miles from the farm) well and so often as need shall require well and substantially (to) repair and maintain … the farm house."

---

[77] (1849) 3 Exch. 233; affirmed 5 Exch. 713.
[78] (1744) Willes 496.
[79] (1852) 18 Q.B. 661.
[80] (1882) 21 Ch. D. 18. See also *Anon* Bro. N.C. 42; *Browne v Walker* (1687) 1 Lut. 394; *Mucklestone v Thomas* (1739) Willes 146; *Dodd v Innis* (1772) Lofft. 56.
[81] [1918] 1 K.B. 495. See also *Miles v Tobin* (1867) 17 L.T. 432.

The question arose whether this imposed upon the lessor an obligation to supply materials necessary for the repairs. The Court of Appeal held that the words in parentheses were to be construed as a qualification of the lessee's obligation only, and did not impose any positive obligation on the lessor to make available the necessary materials. The court stressed that this result emerged from a consideration of all the relevant terms of the lease, and that the reservation by the lessor of the right of approval was a particularly important pointer against there being any positive obligation. The principle to be derived from the various decided cases was summarised thus by Pickford L.J.:

> "I think the only principle which these cases establish which is useful to the question before us is that covenant is a matter of intention, and that any words will make a covenant, whether participial or not, if it can be clearly seen that such was the intention of the parties. A particular clause, therefore, such as that in this case, may be only a qualification in the sense that the lessor's performance of his covenant may be a condition precedent to the lessee's obligation to perform his. In former days it seems to have been considered that a clause could not be both a covenant and a qualification, but I think that is not the law now."

The reference to the supply of materials may be held to amount neither to a condition precedent, nor to a cross-obligation by the landlord, but only to a licence to the tenant to take the materials he needs. Thus, in *Dean & Chapter of Bristol v Jones*[82] the tenant agreed to do repairs "having or taking in and upon the premises competent and sufficient house bote etc. for the doing thereof without committing any waste or spoil". It was held that these words amounted only to a licence to the tenant to take materials necessary for the repairs, and that his obligation to repair was not conditional on there being a sufficient supply of these materials upon the premises.

14–30

Reference should also be made to the discussion of preconditions in para.14–26 above.

## Covenants to build and repair

A covenant to build by a particular date is broken once and for all if the tenant fails to build in time. The right to forfeit for the breach will be lost if rent is accepted thereafter with knowledge of the breach.[83] A covenant to repair the buildings once erected will not come into operation because there is nothing to which it can apply. Thus, in *Stephens v Junior Army & Navy Stores Ltd*[84] the tenant covenanted to erect specific buildings within a certain time and to repair those buildings "and all other erections and buildings which now are or at any time hereafter during the said term shall be erected and built". He failed to erect any buildings by the specified date. The Court of Appeal held that no further covenant to build could be implied from the covenant to repair. That covenant presupposed the existence of buildings on the site, and if there were none, then there was nothing upon which it could operate.

14–31

---

[82] (1859) 1 E. & E. 484.
[83] See para.27–05 et seq., below.
[84] [1914] 2 Ch. 516.

A covenant to build may be made conditional on the original demised premises falling into disrepair. Thus, in *Evelyn v Raddish*[85] a lease of four houses was granted for 99 years containing a tenant's covenant to put them in good repair within two years and to take them down "as occasion may require" within the first 50 years and to erect four new houses in their place. It was held that if the four original houses were properly repaired within the first 50 years so that they were substantially as good as new houses, then the obligation to build four new houses did not arise.

The extent to which the covenant to repair applies to new buildings erected, or alterations made, during the term or pursuant to covenants to build is dealt with elsewhere.[86]

## Covenants to spend a specified amount on repairs

**14–32**  Old leases will sometimes be found to contain an obligation on the tenant not to repair to a general or specific standard or to carry out particular works, but simply to spend a particular sum on works of repair within a given time or during each year of the term. If framed in completely general terms, such an obligation in practice gives to the tenant a discretion as to what works he does, provided that those works conform to the description set out in the covenant (for example, expenditure on decorations might not count as expenditure "on repairing the demised premises") and that the requisite amount is expended. Once that duty has been performed, it is no breach of the covenant if the premises remain in disrepair because they needed more to be spent on them than was agreed.

In *Moss Empires Ltd v Olympia (Liverpool) Ltd*[87] the tenant covenanted to spend £500 per annum on repairs and decoration to the premises or in default to pay to the landlord the difference between £500 and what was spent. The House of Lords held that a claim for the recovery of the specified sum was not a claim in damages, but a claim in debt. It followed that the claim did not fall foul of s.18(1) of the Landlord and Tenant Act 1927.[88] The same was held to be the case where the specified sum was payable pursuant to an option given to the landlord to require the tenant to pay a specified sum in lieu of painting the premises in the last year of the term.[89]

OTHER FORMS OF COVENANT IMPOSING LIABILITY FOR DILAPIDATIONS

## Covenants to rebuild reconstruct or replace

**14–33**  These are dealt with in paras 4–25 to 4–26 and 11–44, above.

---

[85] (1817) Taunt. 411.
[86] See para.7–20 et seq., above.
[87] [1939] A.C. 544. See further on this case para.30–64, below.
[88] See Ch.30, below.
[89] *Plummer v Ramsey* (1934) 78 S.J. 175.

## Covenants to renew

These are dealt with in paras 4–27 to 4–28 and 11–45, above.    **14–34**

## Covenants to keep in good condition

These are dealt with in paras 4–29 to 4–30, 8–12 to 8–14, 9–41 to 9–42 and    **14–35**
11–46, above.

## Obligations to remedy defects in the construction or design of the premises

These are considered in para.4–31, above.    **14–36**

## Covenants to maintain

Whilst many covenants to repair include the word "maintain" as part of a list of    **14–37**
operations that the covenantor is bound to carry out, it is rare to find in a lease a
covenant simply to maintain without more. Consequently, there is little authority
in the context of leasehold covenants to indicate how such an obligation would be
likely to be construed.[90] However, maintenance is a flexible concept, and much
depends on the context.

In *ACT Construction Ltd v Customs & Excise Commissioners*[91] Ackner L.J.
said of the expression "maintenance" in Gp 8 of Sch.4 to the Finance Act 1972
that:

> "[W]ithout entering into the realms of definition, maintenance generally involves the following
> characteristics: firstly, an element of repetition, because the object is to keep the building in
> the condition in which it started; secondly, that the work is generally speaking foreseeable ...;
> thirdly, again generally speaking, that the work is of a minor character and habitual, although
> naturally there are exceptions as in the case of roof works; fourthly, that generally speaking in
> maintenance one does not add something substantial which is new; and, lastly, that you do not
> in ordinary maintenance make a substantial improvement to that which you maintain."

In *Day v Harland & Wolff Ltd*[92] Pearson J., in considering the meaning of
"repair" in the Shipbuilding Regulations 1931, said of "maintenance" that:

> "[It] is a vague word. It is not necessarily distinguished from 'repair'. It may in some contexts
> be the same as 'repair', and it may in some contexts have a wider meaning which includes
> repairing as well as other operations."

---

[90] Although there is ample authority in other contexts: see, for example, *Potteries Electric Traction Co Ltd v Bailey* [1931] A.C. 151 (rating); *Galashiels Gas Co Ltd v O'Donnell* [1949] A.C. 275 (employer's liability); *London Transport Executive v Betts* [1959] A.C. 213; *Hamilton v National Coal Board* [1960] A.C. 633; *John Fairfax & Sons Ltd v Australian Telecommunications Commission* [1977] 2 N.S.W.L.R. 400; *R v Hackney LBC*, Ex p. *Secretary of State for the Environment* [1989] E.G.C.S. 105 (Local Authorities (Goods and Services Act) 1970); *Mott MacDonald v Department of Transport, Environment and the Regions* [2006] 1 W.L.R. 3356 (highways).
[91] [1981] 1 W.L.R. 49 (affirmed on different grounds [1981] 1 W.L.R. 1542).
[92] [1953] 1 W.L.R. 906.

The extent to which a covenant to maintain, or the inclusion of "maintain" as one of the verbs in a general covenant to repair, is to be regarded as imposing a different liability to an obligation simply to repair or keep in repair is a question of construction in every case. It is thought, however, that in principle, there are three possible differences. First, where the remedial work is very substantial, it may be that on a proper application of the fact and degree test[93] the work would cease to be "maintenance" before it ceased to be "repair".[94] Second, the condition of the premises at the date of the lease may be of greater relevance in relation to an obligation to maintain than in the case of a covenant to repair.[95] Thus, in *Janet Reger International v Tiree*,[96] in which the landlord covenanted to "use reasonable endeavours to maintain, repair and renew the structure", Mr Terence Mowschenson QC (sitting as a deputy judge of the Chancery Division) held that "The expression 'maintain' connotes an obligation in this context to keep the structure in the same condition as when it was demised", with the result that the landlord was not liable for the necessary remedial work, because the relevant structure was in the same state as it was in when the lease was granted. Third, an obligation to maintain may require a greater degree of preventative work than would a covenant to repair. Thus, in *Langham Estate Management Ltd v Hardy*[97] H.H. Judge Hazel Marshall QC said:

> "a landlord's covenant to 'keep in proper working order or to maintain' is likely to be wider in its scope than a covenant to 'repair ', although even this will depend upon the true construction of the covenant in its context. This point is particularly relevant to plant, machinery, equipment and installations. 'Repair' involves remedying a state of disrepair that has arisen, and the obligation does not arise until it has. 'Keep in proper working order', and possibly merely 'maintain', may well require proactive preventative maintenance work, or carrying out adjustments or general servicing before any actual fault develops or a want of repair exists."

An obligation to maintain does not require the covenantor to make safe in circumstances where the item in question is not in disrepair and there has been no failure to maintain it.[98]

Covenants to maintain service plant are considered in Ch.13, para.13–14, above.

## Covenants to decorate

14–38    These are considered in Ch.15, below.

---

[93] See Ch.11.
[94] See the passage from Ackner L.J.'s judgment in *ACT Construction Ltd v Customs & Excise Commissioners* quoted above.
[95] See the passage from Ackner L.J.'s judgment in *ACT Construction Ltd v Customs & Excise Commissioners* quoted above.
[96] [2006] 3 E.G.L.R. 131.
[97] [2008] 3 E.G.L.R. 125 at [62]. See also *Greetings Oxford Koala Hotel Pty Ltd v Oxford Square Investments Pty Ltd* (1989) N.S.W.L.R. 33, discussed in para.13–13, above
[98] *Alker v Collingwood Housing Association* [2007] 2 E.G.L.R. 43 at [13] and [14]. See para.8–04, above, where this case is further considered.

## Covenants to reinstate alterations

These are dealt with in Ch.16, below.                                    **14–39**

## Covenants to comply with statutes

These are dealt with in Ch.17, below.                                    **14–40**

## Covenants to rebuild or reinstate after fire

These are considered in Ch.18, paras 18–27 et seq., below.               **14–41**

## Covenants to comply with the terms of the headlease

These are considered in Ch.24, below.                                    **14–42**

### REPAIRING OBLIGATIONS AVOIDED BY STATUTE

### Section 11 of the Landlord and Tenant Act 1985

Where s.11 of the Landlord and Tenant Act 1985 applies, so that the tenancy    **14–43**
contains the landlord's repairing covenant implied by that section, any covenant
by the tenant to repair the premises (including a covenant to pay money on
account of repairs by the landlord) is of no effect in so far as it relates to the
matters covered by the landlord's obligation.[99] Section 11 is considered in Ch.20,
below.

---

[99] Landlord and Tenant Act 1985 s.11(4). See para.20–43, below.

CHAPTER 15

# DECORATION

## INTRODUCTORY

An obligation to decorate usually arises in one of two ways: as part of the work required under a covenant to repair, or by virtue of an express covenant to decorate. Both are considered in this Chapter.

**15–01**

## THE EXTENT TO WHICH DECORATION IS REQUIRED BY THE COVENANT TO REPAIR

### Introductory

Modern leases usually contain express obligations to decorate at periodic intervals. Where there is no separate painting covenant, the question will be to what extent the general covenant to repair and keep in repair involves a duty to paint. The same question arises where the express obligation to decorate is to be performed at periodic intervals, and the premises are in poor decorative order between painting dates.

**15–02**

### The extent to which the covenant to repair obliges the covenantor to decorate

In some cases, the obligation to repair will expressly apply to the paintwork of the premises.[1] Even where that is not the case, however, a covenant to repair premises which have been painted will necessarily apply to the paintwork as well as the underlying fabric.

**15–03**

In considering the extent to which the obligation requires the covenantor to repaint, two aspects of the law relating to the general covenant must be borne in mind: first, no work is required until the subject matter of the covenant is in a damaged or deteriorated condition;[2] and second, no remedial work is required until the nature of the relevant damage or deterioration is such as to bring the subject-matter below the contemplated standard.[3] It follows that a covenant to repair does not oblige the covenantor to do any painting until the condition of the existing paintwork is defective to such an extent as to fall below the appropriate

---

[1] See for example the form of covenant in *Latimer v Carney* [2006] 3 E.G.L.R. 13.
[2] See Ch.8, above.
[3] See Ch.9, above.

standard. In *Proudfoot v Hart*[4] (which concerned a covenant to keep the premises in "good tenantable repair" and to leave them in that state at the end of the term) Lord Esher M.R. said in the course of his judgment:

> "The Official Referee appears to have said that in his view 'tenantable repair' included painting, papering and decorating. If he meant … that it included all papering, painting and decorating, I have no hesitation in saying that his construction of the term 'tenantable repair' was wrong. Again, he said that the tenant's obligation is to 'repaper with similar paper to that which was on the walls before, and repaint with similar paint to that which was on the painted portion of the premises before'. I think that view was wrong also."

In general terms, the standard contemplated by the covenant in relation to painting is the same as that in relation to repair work generally.[5] It follows that where the existing decorative condition of the premises is not such as would satisfy a reasonably-minded tenant of the class likely to take them, the covenant to repair will require remedial decorative work to be carried out. In *Proudfoot v Hart*[6] Lord Esher M.R. said with regard to decoration:

> "Take … the case of a house in Grosvenor Square having an ornamental ceiling, which is a beautiful work of art. A tenant goes in and finds such a ceiling in the house, and in course of time the gilding becomes in such a bad condition, or so much worn off, that the ceiling is no longer ornamental. I should think that a reasonable tenant taking a house in Grosvenor Square would not require a gilded ceiling at all. If that be so, on the mere covenant to leave the premises in tenantable repair, I should think that the tenant who has entered into that covenant was not bound to regild the ceiling at all."

With regard to repapering, he said:

> "[The tenant] is not bound to repaper simply because the old paper has become worn out, but I do not agree with the view that under a covenant to keep a house in tenantable repair the tenant can never be required to put up new paper. Take a house in Grosvenor Square. If when the tenancy ends, the paper on the walls is merely in a worse condition than when the tenant went in, I think the mere fact of its being in a worse condition does not impose upon the tenant any obligation to repaper under the covenant, if it is in such a condition that a reasonably minded tenant of the class who take houses in Grosvenor Square would not think the house unfit for his occupation. But suppose that the damp has caused the paper to peel off the walls, and it is lying upon the floor, so that such a tenant would think it a disgrace, I should say then that the tenant was bound, under his covenant to leave premises in tenantable repair, to put up new paper. He need not put up paper of a similar kind—which I take to mean of equal value—to the paper which was on the walls when his tenancy began. He need not put up a paper of a richer character than would satisfy a reasonable man within the definition."

Of whitewashing:

> "[O]ne knows it is impossible to keep ceilings in the same condition as when they have just been whitewashed. But if, though the ceilings have become blacker, they are still in such a condition that a reasonable man would not say 'I will not take this house because of the state of the ceilings', then I think that the tenant is not bound under his covenant to leave the house in tenantable repair to whitewash them."

Lopes L.J. commented:

---

[4] (1890) 25 Q.B.D. 42.
[5] For a discussion of the standard, see para.9–05 et seq., above.
[6] Above.

"As to papering and painting, generally speaking the tenant would not be bound to repaper or repaint. Most clearly he is not bound to repaper with similar paper to that which was on the walls when the tenancy began, or to repaint with similar paint. Most clearly, also, he is not bound to do repairs which are merely decorative. But if at the end of the lease the paper and paint are in such a condition as to cause portions of the premises to go into decay, he is bound to repaper and repaint to such an extent as will satisfy the terms of the definition which I have stated.[7] Again, if the paint through the lapse of time has worn off, or the paper has become worn out, so that their condition has become such as not to satisfy a reasonably minded tenant of the class who would be likely to take the house, then he must repaper and repaint so as to make the premises reasonably fit, within the definition, for the occupation of such a tenant."

In *Irvine v Moran*[8] one of the questions was the extent to which the landlord's implied obligation to keep in repair the structure and exterior of the dwelling-house[9] included an obligation to decorate. Mr Thayne Forbes QC, sitting as a deputy judge of the Queen's Bench Division, held that the obligation to keep in repair extended to painting and decorating the exterior of the dwelling-house, because that would "inevitably and invariably involve a degree of protection against the elements and against the processes of rot and the like". In relation to internal painting, he held that the obligation did not extend to purely decorative work but would include painting required for the purposes of repairing or keeping in repair.

## The extent of painting required[10]

It follows from the above that the obligation to repair will not require the covenantor to redecorate regardless of the state of the existing decoration. Redecoration will only be required once the condition of the existing paintwork has fallen below the standard contemplated by the covenant. The covenantor must then do such painting as will restore it to that standard. The precise extent of the painting required will depend on the facts. If the existing paintwork is only defective in parts and it is possible by patching up to restore it to the standard contemplated by the covenant, the covenantor is not obliged to repaint the entirety of the subject-matter.[11] If, on the other hand, patching up will not have this effect, then complete repainting may be required. Thus, in *Johnson v Gooch*[12] the tenant covenanted to paint the outside every fourth year, to keep the premises during the term in necessary repairs and amendments and to deliver them up in all things well and sufficiently repaired. He argued that since there was no covenant

**15–04**

---

[7] See para.9–05, above.
[8] [1991] 1 E.G.L.R. 261.
[9] See para.20–17 et seq., below.
[10] See generally *Monk v Noyes* (1824) 1 C. & P. 265; *Hopkinson v Viand* (1847) 10 L.T. (O.S.) 108; *Johnson v Gooch* (1848) 11 L.T. (O. S.) 315; *Darlington v Hamilton* (1854) Kay 550; *Scales v Laurence* (1860) 2 F. & F. 289; *Crawford v Newton* (1886) 36 W.R. 54; *Moxon v Marquis Townshend* (1886) 2 T.L.R. 717 (affirmed (1887) 3. T.L.R. 392); *Proudfoot v Hart* (1890) 25 Q.B.D. 42; *Gemmell v Goldsworthy* [1942] S.A.S.R. 55 (Australia); *Trustees of the Liverpool Friendly Society v Woolf* [1951] 158 E.G. 609; *Irvine v Moran* [1991] 1 E.G.L.R. 261; *Bunyip Buildings Pty Ltd v Gestetner Pty Ltd* [1969] S.A.S.R. 87 (Australia). Note that the cases decided in the 19th century are not always entirely consistent with each other. See also para.15–03, above.
[11] *Moxon v Marquis Townshend*, above; *Johnson v Gooch*, above (considered further in para.15–06, below). See further para.10–22, above.
[12] (1948) 11 L.T. (O.S.) 315.

to paint the inside, he could only be called upon to patch up blemishes and stains. This was rejected by Parke B., who gave his reasons as follows:

> "[The repairing] covenants might render it necessary for him to repaint the inside if the walls were so stained and blemished that they could not be put into fair and proper repair short of that general painting. If there were only a few stains, spots and blemishes on the walls in ordinary wear and tear which a skilful artist might well repair and repaint in detail and set to rights, then the defendant was not bound notwithstanding that his lease did not contain any express covenant to paint the inside."

## Where there is an express covenant to paint

**15–05** The presence in the lease of an express covenant to paint does not relieve the covenantor from such duty to paint as he may have under the repairing covenant by virtue of the principles set out above.[13] Thus, in the Australian case of *Gemmell v Goldsworthy*[14] it was held that the tenant's obligation under the covenant to repair to keep up the painting was not affected by the existence of a separate covenant to paint every two years. Cleland J. said in the course of his judgment:

> "The term to paint every two years is absolute and unconditional. It had to be done whether it was apparently necessary or not, whereas the duty under the term to repair was to 'keep up' the condition of the painting during the intervening period of two years only if and when it was necessary and proper to do so."

## Where the repairing covenant expressly includes a duty to paint

**15–06** The repairing covenant may include an express reference to painting. It may, for example, require the tenant to repair and paint the premises. In such a case, it is thought that, in the absence of any indication to the contrary, the covenantor will not generally be obliged to paint more often or to any greater extent than is reasonably necessary to keep the premises in the condition contemplated by the covenant.[15]

Thus, in *Scales v Lawrence*[16] the tenant covenanted as often as necessary, well and sufficiently to repair, uphold, sustain, paint, glaze, cleanse and scour, and keep and leave the premises in such repair, reasonable wear and tear excepted. It was held that if the tenant had repainted within a reasonable time before leaving, he was not obliged at the end of the term to repaint as opposed to cleaning the old paint. Similarly in *Moxon v Marquis Townshend*[17] the covenant to repair included an express obligation to paint. Wills J. rejected the landlord's claim that the entire premises needed repainting and repapering, and accepted the evidence of the tenant's surveyor that a little touching up was all that was required.

---

[13] *Johnson v Gooch*, above; *Gemmell v Goldsworthy*, above.
[14] Above.
[15] *Scales v Laurence*, above; *Moxon v Marquis Townshend*, above.
[16] Above.
[17] Above.

## Damage to decorations caused in the court of carrying out repairs

As a general rule, even where the covenant does not require the covenantor to decorate, he must nonetheless make good damage to decorations caused in the course of carrying out repairs for which he is liable. This principle is considered in Ch.22, para.22–47 et seq., below.

**15–07**

## Section 18 of the Landlord and Tenant Act 1927

It has been held by the Court of Appeal that a claim for damages by reason of the tenant's failure to decorate is subject to the statutory cap on damages imposed by s.18(1) of the Landlord and Tenant Act 1927 where such failure constitutes a breach of the covenant to repair, even though that same failure also constitutes a breach of a covenant in the same lease to redecorate at periodic intervals.[18] The effect in practice is thought to be that most breaches of the covenant to decorate will be caught by the subsection.

**15–08**

EXPRESS COVENANTS TO DECORATE

### Introductory

Since the covenant to repair does not usually oblige the tenant to carry out more than a limited amount of decoration,[19] modern commercial leases virtually always contain a further covenant or covenants by the tenant to paint and decorate the demised premises at specified intervals. It is common to find a requirement that the exterior is to be painted once every three years and in the last year, and the interior once every seven years and in the last year. Such a covenant obliges the covenantor to paint the premises even though no painting is necessary.[20] Some modern leases contain an alternative formulation that the tenant is to decorate as often as reasonably necessary or as often as in the opinion of the landlord is reasonably necessary but not more often than at specified intervals.

**15–09**

### What must be decorated

Express covenants to decorate will often require the covenanting party to paint or treat the "interior" or the "exterior" of the premises. The meaning of expressions such as these is considered elsewhere.[21]

Sometimes, the parts of the premises to be decorated will be those "usually so decorated" or words to that effect. One question which arises in such cases is whether "usually" is to be read as referring to what has been done in the past in

**15–10**

---

[18] *Latimer v Carney* [2006] 3 E.G.L.R. 13. See further para.30–03, below.
[19] See paras 15–03 to 15–04, above.
[20] *Gemmell v Goldsworthy* [1942] S.A.S.R. 55 (Australia); *Simmons v Dresden* [2004] EWHC 993 (TCC).
[21] See paras 7–41 to 7–44, above.

relation to the particular premises, or whether it imports an objective standard by reference to what would ordinarily be done in relation to items of the type in question. Whilst each case turns on the proper construction of the relevant provision, it is thought that the latter will ordinarily be the correct construction. Thus, in the Australian case of *Alamdo Holdings Property Ltd v Australian Window Furnishings (NSW) Property Ltd*,[22] a lease of two large factory buildings contained a covenant on the part of the tenant:

> "in the last year of the term and from time to time if necessary or reasonably required by the Lessor paint, repaint, clean or otherwise appropriately treat in a proper and workmanlike manner such part of the Demised Premises usually so treated."

The roof was of galvanised steel of a type expected to be maintenance free during its expected serviceable life. It was coated in the course of manufacture and was intended to be a paint-free product. However, it had in fact been recoated in the past with a view to extending its life beyond its normal service life. The issue between the parties was what was meant by "usually so treated". At first instance,[23] Barrett J. held that the tenant was not liable to repaint the roof in the last year of the term. The relevant criterion of what is "usual" was to be approached by reference to what is habitually done by way of painting and other treatment of the particular material in the ordinary course as that material proceeds towards the end of its useful life. The covenant did not have in mind:

> "the taking of steps of a new and different kind with a specific purpose of prolonging life beyond the conclusion it would have in the ordinary course of deterioration."

The judge's conclusion was upheld by the New South Wales Court of Appeal. Hodgson J.A. (with whom Basten J.A. and McClellan C.J. agreed) regarded the probability as being that the word "usually", like the words "proper and workmanlike manner", invokes an objective standard rather than referring to what has been done in the past at the demised premises themselves.

## Time for performance

**15–11**    Where there is a covenant to paint during a specified year, then the tenant is not be in breach until the year has ended without the painting being done. It may be, however, that if the tenant were to make it clear before the end of the year that he was not proposing to do the work, or to delay starting the work for so long that there was no realistic possibility of it being completed by the end of the year, the court would hold there to have been an anticipatory breach.[24] Furthermore, if the tenant serves a break notice to determine the lease before the end of the year, he may nonetheless be in breach if the painting remains undone at that time, because

---

[22] [2006] NSWCA 224.

[23] [2004] NSWSC 487.

[24] Cf. *Billson v Residential Apartments Ltd (No.1)* [1991] 3 All E.R. 265, per Sir Nicolas Browne-Wilkinson V.C. at 274 (not considered on appeal [1992] 1 A.C. 494).

he will have put it out of his power to perform his covenant. Thus, in *Kirklinton v Wood*[25] a lease contained the following tenant's covenant:

"And will in the year 1909, and also in the year 1916, if this lease shall so long last paint varnish and grain all the inside wood and iron work ..., with three coats of good oil and white lead paint in a proper and workmanlike manner."

The tenant determined the lease by notice expiring on March 1, 1916, no painting having been done by then. Lush J. held that the tenant was in breach. His reasoning was as follows:

"It is quite true that if the lease had not been determined there would have been no breach on the part of the executors of the lessee on the date in question, namely, March 1, 1916; but nonetheless there was an obligation on the executors of the lessee, as soon as the year 1916 commenced, to perform that covenant, and inasmuch as the executors of the lessee, by giving that notice, put it out of their power to perform the covenant after March 1, 1916 they cannot contend that they were not under an obligation to perform it during the period that intervened between January 1 and March 1. The executors, by giving the notice, shortened the period during which they had the opportunity of doing the painting and performing the covenant. It seems to me quite impossible for them, having taken that course, to say that they had the whole of the year 1916 to perform it, and that therefore there was no breach on March 1 ... The lessee's executors gave the notice, and in my opinion, the obligation having attached to as soon as the year 1916 commenced, they were bound to perform it or show some excuse for non-performance."

The judge declined to say what the position would have been if the lease had been determined by notice given by the landlord as opposed to the tenant. It is thought that the result would have been different, since the landlord would by so doing have put it out of the tenant's power to perform the covenant before the expiry of the period within which performance was required. The same might be the case if the lease were to be forfeited during the year.

A reference in a covenant to decorate to "the last year of the term" or similar **15–12** wording may be construed as meaning either (i) the last year for which the tenancy subsists, or (ii) the last year of the term originally granted (so that the tenant is not liable if the lease is determined before that date). Which of these two possible meanings will be the correct one in any given context, will depend upon the proper construction of the lease. The point is generally put beyond argument in modern leases by the use of formulations such as "whether determined by effluxion of time or otherwise" or "howsoever determined" so as to make it clear that what is meant by the last year of the tenancy whenever it ends. However, where this has not been done, then it will be necessary to ascertain the parties' intention from the lease as a whole.[26] In *Dickinson v St Aubyn*[27] a tenant's covenant to paint in "the last quarter of the said term" was interpreted by the Court of Appeal as referring to the last quarter of the term of seven years, so that no liability arose where the tenant terminated the tenancy earlier by a contractual break notice.[28]

---

[25] [1917] 1 K.B. 332.
[26] See para.2–06, above. See also *Plummer v Ramsay* (1934) 78 S.J. 175, considered in para.16–05, below.
[27] [1994] 1 K.B. 454.
[28] See further on this case para.2–06, above.

## The standard of decoration

**15–13** Whilst each case turns on the wording of the particular covenant in question, it is thought that, in principle, the standard of decoration required by a covenant to decorate is to be judged by reference to much the same factors as those applicable to the standard of repair under a covenant to repair.[29] The appropriate standard of preparation, workmanship, colours and materials will therefore depend on the age, character and locality of the building and the type of tenant likely to have taken it at the date of the lease. In the ordinary case, inadequate preparation, poor workmanship or the use of unsuitable colours or materials will not comply with the requisite standard. Such cases apart, however, (and save where the covenant otherwise so provides[30]), the tenant may use whatever colours or materials he wishes, and the landlord has no right to control his choice. It is for this reason that many modern leases provide that the tenant is to use colours and materials specified or approved by the landlord.

In most cases, a covenant to decorate will be interpreted as requiring the covenantor to paint in such a way as to achieve an acceptable match.[31] In *Commercial Union Life Assurance Co Ltd v Label Ink Ltd*[32] a lease of a warehouse building contained a covenant by the tenant to paint and treat the inside wood and metal work of the demised premises in every fifth year and in the last year. H.H. Judge Rich QC (sitting as a deputy High Court judge) said:

> "The first matter complained of is that the painted block work at a low level has been painted in a non-matching shade in breach of the redecoration clause. I accept that it should have been repainted in a matching colour or the whole block work should have been painted in one colour in the fifth year in a workmanlike manner."

In *Simmons v Dresden*[33] the tenant covenanted at periodic intervals:

> "[T]o paint, french polish or otherwise treat as the case may be all the inside … wood and ironwork usually or requiring to be painted french polished or otherwise treated of the demised premises … with two coats of best paint or best quality polish or other suitable material of the best quality in a proper and workmanlike manner and afterwards grain marble and varnish the parts (if any) usually grained marbled and varnished and also wash distemper paint as aforesaid or repaper the ceilings and walls in the usual manner and to wash down all tiles faiences glazed bricks and similar washable surfaces."

H.H. Judge Richard Seymour QC held that on the true construction of the covenant (and in particular having regard to the use of the disjunctive "or" in the expression "also wash distemper paint as aforesaid or repaper the ceilings and walls in the usual manner") the tenant had the option as to the treatment to be applied to walls (save that, by virtue of "repaper", papering was only available if

---

[29] See generally Ch.9, above.
[30] See para.15–14, below.
[31] See further para.10–22, above.
[32] [2001] L. & T.R. 29. Note that the question of disrepair arose in the context of whether or not the tenant had complied with a condition precedent in a break option, and the judge's construction of the condition precedent was subsequently disapproved by the Court of Appeal in *Fitzroy House Epworth Street (No.1) v The Financial Times* [2006] 2 E.G.L.R. 13.
[33] [2004] EWHC 993 (TCC).

a wall or ceiling had previously been papered) and was not obliged to have regard to whatever had been the decorative treatment at the date of the lease.

## Where the colours or materials are to be specified or approved by the landlord or his surveyor

Where the tenant covenants to decorate using colours and materials to be specified or approved by the landlord, it will be a question of construction as to whether the latter's right to prescribe what must be used is unqualified or whether he must act reasonably. In most cases, however, it is thought that the covenant will be interpreted as meaning that he cannot act unreasonably.[34] Where that is the case, he cannot specify, or withhold his approval to, colours or materials which no reasonable landlord in his position would require or (as the case may be) object to. The same will be true, a fortiori, where the covenant provides that the colours or materials must be specified or approved not by the landlord himself but by his surveyor.[35]

15–14

It will also be a question of construction as to whether it is a precondition of liability under such a covenant that the landlord (or his surveyor, where the lease so provides) must take the initiative in making his requirements known to the tenant at the appropriate time. Absent an express provision to this effect, however, it is thought that the better view will generally be that the tenant must approach the landlord (or his surveyor) to ascertain his requirements or seek his approval, and that if he fails to do so, he cannot rely on the landlord not having communicated his requirements, or given his approval, as a defence to liability.[36]

## Section 147 of the Law of Property Act 1925

Section 147 of the Law of Property Act 1925 contains provisions whereby in certain circumstances the tenant may be released from liability to perform a covenant in so far as it relates to internal decorative repairs. This is dealt with in Ch.27, para.27–89 et seq., below.

15–15

[34] See para.14–24, above.
[35] Cf. *Mason v TotalFinaElf UK Ltd* [2003] 3 E.G.L.R. 91. See para.14–24, above.
[36] Cf. *Mason v TotalFinaElf UK Ltd*, above. See para.14–22, above.

CHAPTER 16

## COVENANTS TO REINSTATE ALTERATIONS

### INTRODUCTORY

## Reinstatement of alterations

Dilapidations claims in practice frequently involve, in addition to a claim for disrepair, a claim for the reinstatement of alterations carried out by the tenant during the term. Sometimes the relevant obligation is to be found in the lease itself, but more often it is one of the terms included in a deed of licence in which specific consent was given to alterations or improvements requiring the landlord's approval.[1] In this Chapter, various aspects of the obligation are considered.

16–01

### OBLIGATIONS TO REINSTATE ALTERATIONS

## Absolute obligations to reinstate

In some cases, a covenant to reinstate alterations is absolute, that is to say, its operation is not dependent on notice given by the landlord. In such a case, the tenant must reinstate by the time specified in the covenant (usually the expiry date of the lease), and if he fails to do so, he is in breach of covenant.

16–02

In *Baroque Investments Ltd v Heis*[2] two licences to alter obliged the tenant "Before the end of the Lease…to dismantle and remove the Works and reinstate the Premises…". The relevant leases were surrendered on terms that each party released the other from all liability in respect of any breach of covenant "whether arising on or after, but not before, the date of this Surrender". It was held that the obligations to reinstate could be performed at any time up to the end of the term, with the result that they had been released by the surrender. The Chancellor said in his judgment:

"The licences gave to the tenant the full period of the term created by the leases within which to carry out the requisite reinstatement. Accordingly, as at [the date of the surrender], there was no breach of the obligation to reinstate. If the works were not carried out before [the end of the

---

[1] The Landlord and Tenant Act 1927 s.19(2), which implies into covenants against alterations a proviso of reasonableness, expressly stipulates that "this proviso does not preclude … in the case of an improvement which does not add to the letting value of the holding … an undertaking on the part of the tenant to reinstate the premises in the condition in which they were before the improvement was executed".

[2] [2012] EWHC 2886 (Ch.). See further on this case para.2–05, above.

lease] then the tenant would have been in breach but that would have been after, not before, the date of the surrenders. In my view the inescapable consequence is that that potential liability was released by the surrenders."

## Covenants to reinstate on notice

16–03    More commonly, a covenant to reinstate alterations will oblige the tenant to reinstate if the landlord shall so require by notice. In such a case, the giving of a valid notice is a precondition to liability. It follows that if no notice is given, or any notice is invalid because it does not say what the lease requires it to say or because it is given too late, no liability to reinstate will arise.

### (a)    Form of notice

16–04    The form of notice necessary to trigger the obligation to reinstate will depend upon the proper construction of the obligation. In the ordinary case, however, no particular form of notice will generally be required. All that will be necessary is for the landlord to make it clear that he requires the premises to be reinstated.

In *Westminster City Council v HSBC Bank Plc*[3] a number of licences to carry out alterations contained obligations to reinstate if so required by the landlord. Mr Recorder Black (sitting as a deputy judge of the Queen's Bench Division) held that various requirements to reinstate in a schedule of dilapidations constituted proper notice, even though the schedule did not in terms refer to the licences. He said:

> "The Schedule did not, as a matter of fact, refer to the licences. The appropriate test is whether, nevertheless, a reasonable recipient would have understood one of the purposes of the schedule as giving the notice necessary to invoke the reinstatement obligations.
> ... I find that a reasonable recipient in the position of the [tenant] would not have been misled as to the [landlord's] intentions. When I focus upon the fact, as I am enjoined to do by Lord Steyn's speech in [*Mannai Investment Co Ltd v Eagle Star Life Assurance Co Ltd*[4]], that a reasonable recipient is bound to have the terms of the lease in the forefront of his mind, I am confident that the schedule would be understood to be referring to reinstatement under the licences, given that the authorised alterations could only be called upon to be removed and reinstated under the licences."

A notice to reinstate will not ordinarily be invalidated by the fact that the precise details of the work will need to be agreed with or approved by the landlord at a future date. Thus, in *Fairgate International v Citibank International*[5] a lease of substantial office space contained a covenant on the part of the tenant as follows:

> "(8)(A) At the expiration or sooner determination of the said term quietly to yield up the Demised Premises decorated repaired cleaned and kept in accordance with the Tenant's covenants herein contained together with all additions and improvements thereto and all fixtures and fittings which may be fixed or fastened to or upon the Demised

---

[3] [2003] 1 E.G.L.R. 62.
[4] [1997] A.C. 749.
[5] [2005] 2 E.G.L.R. 48.

Premises EXCEPT tenant's fixtures and fittings which the Tenant is entitled to and does remove prior to the expiration or sooner determination of the said term and to reinstate.

(B)    If so required by the Landlord prior to or upon the expiration or sooner determination of the said term at the Tenant's own expense:

    (i)    to remove all or any furnishings fixtures fittings or other items of whatsoever nature that the Tenant may have installed and to make good all damage caused to the Demised Premises by such removal and restore the same to their original condition to the reasonable satisfaction of the Landlord's surveyor

    (ii)    to fit out equip and lay out the Demised Premises (other than the flats on the seventh floor) in accordance with the specification set out in the Third Schedule and the said flats in accordance with the specification set out in the Fourth Schedule all materials and finishes used in such works to be of a quality and (where applicable) pattern previously approved in writing by the Landlord such approval not to be unreasonably withheld and all such works to be carried out to the reasonable satisfaction of the Landlord's surveyor."

The third and fourth schedules both contained brief specifications. The landlord sent a letter to the tenant stating:

"In accordance with clause 2(8)(B) of the lease we hereby require you to reinstate the premises in accordance with sub-clauses 2(8)(B)(i) and 2(8)(B)(ii)."

The tenant contended that the notice was void for uncertainty because it did not tell him what he had to do (for example, it did not tell him which fixtures and fittings to remove). The Court of Appeal upheld the notice. Having held that clauses (8)(B)(i) and (ii) were not mutually exclusive,[6] Dyson L.J. (with whom Maurice Kay and Buxton L.JJ. agreed) said:

"I am persuaded by the answer given by [counsel]. He submitted that, upon receipt of the notice, the tenant would have known that it was required to comply with the third and fourth schedules. These contained no more than the barest of design briefs, the details of which would have to be worked out to the reasonable satisfaction of the landlord's surveyor. Until the detailed specifications had been agreed, the tenant would not know precisely which of the fixtures and fittings, etc, (if any) it was required to remove. It would have known that, in principle, it was being required by the notice to remove any fixtures and fittings, etc, whose removal would not be overridden by the specifications that were finally agreed. The important point is that the notice will have engendered no more uncertainty in the tenant's mind as to what was required in relation to clause 2(8)(B)(i) than in relation to clause 2(8)(A). At the date of the notice, the tenant might well have been uncertain as to what repairing obligations it was required to discharge. It was implicit in this lease that the precise scope of work required under clause 2(8)(A) and (B) might not be defined at the end of the term or when the notice was first given by Fairgate. This would become clear only when the details of the work required to be carried out in accordance with the third and fourth schedules had been finalised. In my view, therefore, the notice of 28 August 2002 was not void for uncertainty."

In the Scottish case of *L Batley Pet Products v North Lanarkshire Council*,[7] a licence to alter contained the following tenant's covenant:

"By the expiration and sooner determination of the period of the sub lease (or as soon as the license hereby granted shall become void) if so required by the mid landlord and at the cost of the sub tenant to dismantle and remove the Works and to reinstate and make good the premises and to restore it to its appearance at the date of entry under the sub lease, such reinstatement to

---

[6]  See para.14–07, above.
[7]  [2011] CSOH 209.

> be carried out on the same terms (*mutatis mutandis*) as are stipulated in this license with respect to the carrying out of the works in the first place (including as to consents, the manner of carrying out works, reinstatement, inspection, indemnity, costs and otherwise)."

No written notice to reinstate was given before the lease expired. It was held that on the proper construction of the licence a requirement to reinstate could validly be made orally.

### (b)    When notice must be given

**16–05**    Sometimes, the covenant to reinstate will specify the last date by which the landlord's notice to reinstate must be given. It is thought that time will ordinarily be of the essence in such cases, with the result that a notice given out of time will be ineffective to trigger the obligation.

In many cases, however, no date will be specified. It is thought that where this is the case, the right construction will ordinarily be that notice must be given at the latest before the expiry of the lease, when the relationship of landlord and tenant comes to an end.

A more difficult question, and one which often arises in practice, is whether, in such cases, the notice must be given sufficiently early to allow the tenant a reasonable time to carry out the works before the lease ends. The answer in each case will depend on the wording of the obligation interpreted in the light of the relevant surrounding circumstances when the lease was granted. Absent a clear indication one way or the other, there is much to be said for the view that the parties are likely to have intended the notice to be given in sufficient time to allow the tenant to complete the work before the term date of the lease. It can be said in support of this that if a notice which is given too late for the tenant to do the work is nonetheless valid, then there are only two possibilities, neither of which is very attractive: either the tenant is in breach as soon as the term ends without the work having been completed, or the tenant is entitled to remain in the premises after the term date in order to do the work. The first seems wrong in principle, given that the landlord is in complete control of when the notice is given, and it might be said that if the parties had intended the second, they would have said so expressly and provided for the terms on which the tenant is entitled to remain in occupation. It can be argued the other way, however, that a requirement that the notice be served in good time to enable the tenant to do the work before the end of the lease is potentially unfair on the landlord, particularly where the work is substantial and/or the market is in flux, because he may have to make his decision well in advance of the term date, at a time when he does not know for certain what an incoming occupier will demand when he comes to relet. It can further be said since the tenant has, for his own purposes, altered the landlord's property, it is not unfair for the landlord to have until the end of the lease to decide whether or not he wishes to have it reinstated. On this basis, if the parties themselves have not said that the notice must be given any particular time before the term date, the lease should not be interpreted as though they had.

Such authorities as there are suggest that, in the absence of express words or necessary implication, a covenant of this type is likely to be construed as entitling the landlord to give notice at any time prior to the expiry of the term. Thus, in

*Plummer v Ramsey*,[8] a lease contained a covenant by the tenant to paint in the last year of the term, and a landlord's option to require the tenant to pay a specified sum in lieu of painting. The option did not fix any time within which it had to be exercised. The tenant argued that it had to be exercised at least a year before the end of the term so as to enable the tenant to know in good time that he need not paint. Branson J. rejected this, holding that the option could be exercised at any time so long as the obligation of the tenant existed and the tenant was not in breach. On the facts a notice served a month before the end of the term was held to be valid.

To much the same effect is *Scottish Mutual Assurance Society Ltd v British Telecommunications Plc*,[9] in which a licence to alter provided that the tenant "should reinstate the property to its original design and layout at the expiry of the Lease at its own cost should the Lessor reasonably so require". On June 18, 1992 the landlord served a schedule of dilapidations, which included a requirement to reinstate. The lease expired on June 24, 1992. The tenant argued that, since after the determination of the lease the tenant would have no entitlement to remain on the premises, the words "should the Lessor reasonably so require" should be construed as relating not only to the reasonableness or otherwise of the requirement as such but also as to the reasonableness of its timing. Mr Anthony Butcher, QC (sitting as a recorder hearing Official Referee's business) found for the landlord. He held that the intention was, given a reasonable requirement by the landlord that the work should be carried out, to require the necessary work to be put in hand at the time of, but not to be completed by, the expiry of the lease, the tenant being allowed a reasonable time after the expiry of the lease to complete the works. He therefore held that the landlord's requirement was made in sufficient time. He added that he was satisfied that the period from June 18 to June 24 was an unreasonably short period for carrying out the reinstatement, so that, had he accepted the tenant's argument as to the construction of the licence, he would have held that the landlord's requirement was not made in time.[10]

The judge's view that the tenant was entitled to remain in the premises after the end of the lease in order to complete the work is consistent with the decision of the majority of the Court of Appeal (and Lord Atkinson in the House of Lords) in *Matthey v Curling*,[11] in which it was held that in the events which had happened a covenant to lay out insurance moneys in reinstating damage by fire was capable of being performed after the end of the term.[12] Lord Atkinson said in his speech:

**16–06**

> "We have not been referred to any authority establishing that in such a case as this reinstatement must take place within the term of the lease. Nor have I myself been able to find one. Until I have been referred to it, or discovered it, I fear I shall remain of opinion that in the case of an ordinary covenant to reinstate, a covenantor shall in the absence of words expressly or impliedly fixing a time for the performance of his covenant, have what is a reasonable time

---

[8] (1934) 78 S.J. 175.

[9] Unreported decision of Mr Anthony Butcher QC (sitting as a recorder hearing Official Referee's business) dated March 18, 1994.

[10] See further the Scottish case of *L Batley Pet Products v North Lanarkshire Council* [2011] CSOH 209 (considered in para.16–04, above), in which it was not in dispute between the parties that the relevant requirement to reinstate had to be given before the expiry of the lease.

[11] [1922] 2 A.C. 180.

[12] See para.18–31, below.

under all the circumstances of the case for its performance, whether, in the case of a leasehold, that time extends beyond the term or the contrary. [13]"

In *Baroque Investments Ltd v Heis*[14] (which is more fully considered elsewhere[15]) the tenant covenanted "Before the end of the Lease…to dismantle and remove the Works and reinstate the Premises…". The Chancellor accepted counsel's submission, based on *Matthey v Curling*, that, absent the words "Before the end of the Lease …", the tenant would have a reasonable time after the end of the lease to carry out the reinstatement works, the purpose of the words being to limit the time within which the tenant might carry out the works to the term of the lease.

It is thought, however, that a right on the part of the tenant to remain in possession for the purposes of complying with the notice would only arise where the tenant has done what he can to put the work in hand by the end of the term. If he has not, and has thereby demonstrated an intention not to comply with the notice in any event, it seems wrong in principle that the landlord should not be entitled to possession immediately.

Where the tenant is entitled to remain in possession, difficult questions may arise as to the terms on which he does so. These would include, for example, whether he is liable for rent or mesne profits and whether he remains bound by the other covenants of the lease. The existence of these difficulties might be said to be an argument in favour of construing the covenant as requiring the landlord to give his notice in sufficient time to enable the tenant to comply before the lease ends. Thus far, however, this solution does not seem to have commended itself to the courts.

### (c)  Whether the requirement to reinstate must be reasonable

**16–07**  The covenant may provide that the landlord's requirement to reinstate must be reasonable. Where this is the case, the notice will be invalid if the tenant can show that no reasonable landlord would have required reinstatement in the circumstances. In practice, that is likely to be difficult, at least where the landlord is acting bona fide. Where the covenant does not provide that the requirement to reinstate must be reasonable, it is thought that, in the ordinary case, no such limitation will be implied.

## Covenants to reinstate unless the landlord otherwise requires

**16–08**  A form of obligation sometimes encountered in practice is an obligation to reinstate unless the landlord otherwise requires by notice. The effect is that the tenant is obliged to reinstate unless released from his obligation by notice.

Difficult questions may arise in practice where the notice is given at a time when the tenant has already reinstated. The landlord may contend that the effect of the notice is that the work of reinstatement is to be treated as not having been

---

[13] See further on this case paras 18–24 to 18–25, below.

[14] [2012] EWHC 2886 (Ch.).

[15] See para.2–05, above.

carried out pursuant to the covenant, with the result that it amounts to a breach of the covenant against alterations, such that the landlord is entitled to damages. The tenant is likely to argue that (i) work carried out prior to the giving of notice cannot be retrospectively rendered unlawful in this way, alternatively (ii) in order to be effective the notice must be given a reasonable time before the end of the term so as to enable the tenant to know in good time that he need not reinstate.[16] The answer will depend on the proper construction of the covenant.

In practice, a tenant who is proposing to reinstate under a covenant of this type would be well-advised to ask the landlord beforehand whether and if so to what extent the landlord requires reinstatement. If the landlord were to state unequivocally that it does require the premises to be reinstated, and the tenant were then to reinstate, it is thought that it would then be too late for the landlord to serve a notice under the covenant.

## What reinstatement is required

The precise scope of the obligation imposed by a covenant to reinstate will depend on the proper construction of the covenant in question. In general terms, however, the tenant must remove whatever he has installed, make good any damage caused in the course of the removal and put back whatever was there previously. In most cases, this will not cause any difficulty. In some cases, however, it may not be possible to reproduce exactly what was there before, either because the materials are not available, or because planning permission cannot be obtained. In such cases, some assistance may be derived from the principles relating to obligations to rebuild or reinstate after fire. These are considered in Ch 18, paras 18–33 to 18–37, below.

16–09

## Partial reinstatement

Some forms of covenant to reinstate expressly entitle the landlord to specify those parts of the premises which he wishes to be reinstated, and those which he wishes to be left in their altered condition. However, the drafting of some covenants is unclear as to what extent the landlord may "pick and choose" in this way. This may be of importance in practice if some of the works increase the value of the demised premises from the landlord's point of view, whereas others decrease it. It may be a material consideration in the interpretation of such covenants whether the works of alteration are distinct, so that there is no practical difficulty or extra expense involved in partial reinstatement, or whether the subject-matter of the covenant is, in practical terms, incapable of severance. Where partial reinstatement would cause no difficulty or prejudice to the tenant, it may well be that the court would be receptive to an argument that the covenant is to be construed as entitling the landlord to require partial reinstatement only. It would seem to be to no one's advantage in such a case to insist on an "all or nothing" approach. As always, however, the answer will depend on the proper construction of the particular lease.

16–10

---

[16] Cf. the discussion in para.16–05, above.

## THE POSITION OF SUCCESSORS IN TITLE

### Successors in title

**16–11**  Often the issue as to the enforcement of covenants to reinstate will arise not between the original parties to the licence but between their successors in title. The extent to which the benefit and burden of covenants in licences run with the term and the reversion is considered in Ch.3, paras 3–29 and 3–30, above.

## DAMAGES FOR BREACH

### Damages

**16–12**  Damages for breach of a covenant to reinstate alterations are considered in Ch.32, paras 32–09 to 32–12, below.

CHAPTER 17

## COVENANTS TO COMPLY WITH STATUTES

### INTRODUCTORY

Many leases contain a covenant on the part of the tenant in one form or another to comply with the provisions of statutes, or regulations made thereunder, or notices served pursuant thereto.[1] Compliance with the statute, regulation or notice in question may involve the carrying out of works which the tenant could not be required to do under his repairing covenant. For that reason, such covenants are often relied on by landlords in terminal dilapidations claims as imposing additional liabilities on the tenant in relation to (in particular) mechanical and electrical items, asbestos and fire safety matters. In some cases, the work may form a substantial part of the overall claim. In addition, statutory and other requirements may affect the way in which works required by the repairing or other covenants must be carried out.[2]

Whilst a detailed consideration of the many statutes and regulations which may apply in any particular case is beyond the scope of this work, this Chapter considers a number of general points in relation to the interpretation and operation of such covenants.

**17–01**

### LIABILITY

#### Liability under the covenant

The extent of the liability imposed by the covenant is a question of construction in every case. It will generally be necessary to approach the matter in three stages.

The first stage will be to read the covenant carefully to ascertain what it requires the tenant to do. Some covenants are widely drafted and oblige the tenant to comply with all applicable statutes and regulations. Others are narrower and require the tenant to comply only with specified statutes. Some covenants are limited to requiring compliance with statutory notices, so that no liability arises unless and until a notice is served.

**17–02**

---

[1] For example, the Factories Act 1961; the Offices, Shops and Railway Premises Act 1963; the Health and Safety etc. Act 1974; the Housing Act 1985; the Workplace (Health, Safety and Welfare) Regulations 1992; the Disability Discrimination Act 1995 (as amended by the Disability Discrimination Act 2005); and the Regulatory Reform (Fire Safety) Order 2005.

[2] See para.17–05, below.

The second stage will be to obtain a complete and up-to-date copy of the statute or regulation in question to ascertain in what circumstances it applies, what liabilities it imposes and on whom. It may be necessary to take specialist advice (for example, from a health and safety consultant).

The third stage will be to decide to what extent the relevant requirements apply in the particular circumstances existing at the relevant time. For example, many statutory or other requirements depend for their application on the premises being used or occupied in a particular way, so that it will be necessary to investigate the facts to see to what extent the premises are so used or occupied.

In practice, the need to undertake the second and third stages is often overlooked or left by landlords until a relatively late stage in the claim. It is quite common, for example, to find schedules of dilapidations which limit themselves to reciting or referring to the covenant to comply with statutes, then setting out (in very general terms) the state of affairs alleged to amount to a breach of the covenant and finally specifying the remedial work said to be necessary, without ever properly identifying or particularising the statutory or other provisions relied on. As well as being poor practice, this often results in it being necessary to amend, or even withdraw, the relevant part of the claim at a later stage once the scope of the relevant requirements has been properly investigated. It is suggested that where the covenant to comply with statutes is to be relied on, proper consideration should be given at an early stage to identifying (i) the relevant statute or regulation; (ii) whether and to what extent it applied in the particular circumstances; (iii) what requirements it imposed; and (iv) how those requirements could reasonably have been complied with.

## Scope of the obligation

**17–03**   In principle, a covenant to comply with statutes may, and often will, require the covenanting party to carry out work which goes beyond the scope of the work required by other covenants in the lease, such as the covenant to repair. Thus, in the Australian case of *Cugg Property Ltd v Gibo Property Ltd*,[3] a lease of an office building contained (in cll.8 and 9) covenants on the part of the tenant to repair and yield up in repair, which were subject to a fair wear and tear exception and also subject to a proviso that the tenant's obligation was limited to the condition of the premises at the commencement of the lease. The tenant further covenanted (in cl.10) to:

> "comply with the terms of any present or future legislation affecting the demised premises and with any notices served upon the Lessor or the Lessee by the Board of Health, licensing, municipal or other competent authority involving the destruction of noxious weeds or animals or the carrying out of any repairs alterations or works (including works of a structural character)."

The tenant argued that cl.10 was to be read consistently with cll.8 and 9 and not as requiring the tenant to improve the premises. Hodgson C.J. held that cl.10 was not restricted in its effect by either cl.8 or cl.9. Performance of the latter

---

[3] [2001] NSWSC 297.

might involve improvement of the premises beyond their condition at the date of the lease if that was the only way the obligations could be performed.

## Where there is more than one way of performing the obligation

In some cases, there will be only one possible way in which the covenanting party's obligation to comply with a particular statute or regulation can be performed. If, for example, the relevant statutory duty can only be complied with by carrying out particular work, the covenanting party must carry out that work or he will be in breach of covenant. In other (perhaps most) cases, however, it will be possible to comply with the relevant statute or regulation in a variety of different ways. If so, the general principle will apply that where the covenant can reasonably be performed in more than one way, the choice of method is that of the covenanting party,[4] as will the allied principle that damages for breach will be assessed by reference to the method of performance most beneficial to the covenanting party.[5] This is one of several reasons why it is necessary in practice to look carefully at what the statute or regulation requires and how those requirements can reasonably be met.

17–04

## Statutory requirements in relation to the carrying out of works

As a general principle, works required by the covenant to repair must be carried out in such a way as to comply with any relevant statutory or other requirements even without a specific covenant to do so.[6] Where it applies, however, a covenant to comply with statutes may afford an additional reason why the works must be carried out in compliance with any applicable statutory and other requirements.[7]

17–05

## Claims for damages at the end of the term for failure to carry out statutory works

Most claims against tenants for damages for breach of the covenant to comply with statutes or regulations are brought as part of a terminal dilapidations claim following the expiry of the lease, and relate to works which it is said that the tenant ought to have carried out in order to comply with the statute or regulation in question.

17–06

An example often encountered in practice concerns fire safety works. Suppose, for example, that during the term the tenant was, in relation to the demised premises, the responsible person for the purposes of the Regulatory Reform (Fire Safety) Order 2005[8]; that the covenant on its proper construction

---

[4] See para.10–06 et seq., above.
[5] See *Lavarack v Woods of Colchester* [1967] 1 Q.B. 278; *Paula Lee v Robert Zehil & Co* [1983] 2 All E.R. 390; *McGregor on Damages*, 18th edn (London: Sweet & Maxwell, 2011), para.8–060 et seq. See further paras 29–14 and 29–15, below.
[6] See paras 10–21 and 11–35, above.
[7] Such as the Building Regulations (but only where Building Regulation Consent is required).
[8] See art.3 of the 2005 Order.

obliged him to comply with the requirements of that Order; that pursuant to such Order he was liable to install an external fire escape; and that he failed to do so. In such a case, the landlord's claim for terminal dilapidations may include a claim for the cost of installing a fire escape, on the footing that if the tenant had complied with his obligations during the term, the premises would have been delivered up with a fire escape in place. On the face of it, that argument is a powerful one.

However, the position is not straightforward. It can be said that, absent an express obligation in the lease to deliver up the premises at the end of the term in a physical state consistent with performance of the covenant to comply with statutes, the correct inference as a matter of construction is that the parties intended such covenant to apply only during the term and not at the end of it. On this analysis, the purpose of the covenant is to protect the landlord against possible liability to third parties resulting from breaches of the relevant statutory duty during the term, and not to confer on him a windfall benefit in the form of improved premises at the end of the term. This approach accords with the decision in *Johnsey Estates (1990) v The Secretary of State for the Environment*,[9] in which the tenant of a large building used for storage and offices (the Secretary of State) covenanted as follows:

> "4(12)   So far as any such requirements as are hereinafter mentioned are valid and binding on the Tenant or his successors in office or any Government Department or person as lessee for the time being of the demised premises to comply at all times during the said term with all statutory and other requirements for ensuring the health, safety and welfare of the persons using or employed in or about the demised premises or any part thereof. ... Provided that the user of the demised premises for the purposes authorised by sub clause (8) of this Clause shall not be deemed to be a breach of this covenant."

The landlord's claim for terminal dilapidations included the cost of carrying out various works required by statute. The judge rejected that part of the claim on the ground that the covenant had no application on the facts. His reasons were as follows:

> "Leases frequently include covenants of the type included in clause 4(12) but no reported authority concerning the construction of such a clause was cited to me in argument and so far as I am aware there is no such authority. So I must approach the construction of the clause from basic principles. Its wording does not immediately suggest that it has anything to do with the condition of the premises at the end of the term: it imposes an obligation 'at all times during the said term' and makes no reference to the end of the term. Clause 4(20) [the covenant to yield up] does not appear to me to remedy that deficiency: that covenant (at the determination of the term to yield up the demised premises) is concerned with the state of repair of the premises at the end of the term and not with their compliance with statutory criteria. The covenant says nothing about the state of the premises, being apparently concerned with the health, safety and welfare of the persons using the premises during the term. Those features in my judgment indicate what the true purpose of the covenant is, being to protect the landlord from any possible liability for breach of statutory duty during the term by providing him with an indemnity against the lessee on the basis that it is the lessee's primary duty to ensure the health, safety and welfare of the lessee's employees and visitors. The covenant

---

[9] Unreported decision of H.H. Judge Moseley QC (sitting as an Official Referee in the Technology and Construction Court) dated August 6, 1999.

therefore appears to me to have no application to a dilapidations claim. Moreover, in so far as there is any ambiguity in its construction it is to be construed contra proferentem and therefore against the landlord who relies on it."

A similar argument can be advanced where (as is often be the case in practice) the application of the relevant statutory or other requirement depends on whether, and if so how, the premises are used at the relevant time.[10] In such a case, it can be said that, because (i) (absent a positive user covenant) the tenant was not obliged to use the premises during the term at all, let alone in such a way as to bring the relevant requirement into play, and (ii) (subject to any other relevant provisions of the lease, such as a covenant against alterations) the tenant could lawfully have removed the relevant works as soon as the circumstances concerning the use of the premises became such that the relevant requirement ceased to apply (and at the latest, on vacating the premises at the end of the term), the covenant should be construed as intended to protect the landlord only against loss caused by a failure to carry out the requisite statutory works during the term, and not against damage to the value of his interest caused by the works not being in situ when the lease ends.

**17–07**

It is not clear what view a court would take. However, returning to the example at the beginning of this paragraph, the decision in *Johnsey Estates (1990) v The Secretary of State for the Environment* perhaps suggests that the landlord's claim for the cost of a new fire escape at the end of the term in circumstances where (i) no such escape was provided by him at the outset, and (ii) the absence of an escape during the term has caused him no loss, might be regarded by the court as somewhat unattractive. As always, the correct answer in any particular case will depend on the detailed facts.

## Section 18(1) of the Landlord and Tenant Act 1927

It is thought that a claim for damages for breach of a covenant to comply with statutes or regulations will not generally fall within the statutory cap on damages imposed by s.18(1) of the Landlord and Tenant Act 1927.[11] However, the position may perhaps be different if the relevant works consist of repairs, such that the landlord's real claim is that there has been a failure to repair.[12]

**17–08**

### APPORTIONMENT OF EXPENSES OF COMPLIANCE

A number of statutes contain provisions for the apportionment of the expense of works required to be executed thereunder between the person who incurred the expense and other persons, and also for the modification of leases.[13] This may

**17–09**

---

[10] As is the case in relation to, for example, the requirements of the Disability Discrimination Act 1995 (as amended by the Disability Discrimination Act 2005) and the Regulatory Reform (Fire Safety) Order 2005.

[11] See Ch.30, below.

[12] Cf. *Latimer v Carney* [2006] 3 E.G.L.R. 13, considered in paras 15–08, above, and 30–03, below.

[13] For example, the Factories Act 1961 s.170; the Offices, Shops and Railway Premises Act 1963 s.73; and the London Building Acts (Amendment) Act 1939 s.107. See further *Woodfall: Landlord and Tenant* (London: Sweet & Maxwell), Vol.1, para.12–067 et seq.

have the effect of removing the right of one party to sue under a covenant which provides for another party to be liable for the expenses in question, and of replacing it with an entitlement to seek an apportionment under the statute.[14] The existence of the covenant, however, will generally be a highly relevant factor in the exercise of the court's discretion to order an apportionment.[15]

It is to be noted that the Fire Precautions Act 1971 has been superceded by the Regulatory Reform (Fire Safety) Order 2005,[16] and the apportionment and modification provisions contained in s.28 of the former have not been reproduced in the latter. It would seem to follow that a covenant which has the effect of imposing on the tenant liability to comply with the Order is therefore enforceable according to its terms.

---

[14] *Monk v Arnold* [1902] 1 K.B. 761; *Horner v Franklin* [1905] 1 K.B. 479; *Stuckey v Hooke* [1906] 2 K.B. 20; *Monro v Lord Burghclere* [1918] 1 K.B. 291.
[15] The relevant statutory provisions expressly direct the court to make such apportionment as it considers just and equitable in the circumstances, regard being had to the terms of any contract between the parties.
[16] SI 2005/1541, in force from April 1, 2006.

## CHAPTER 18

## DESTRUCTION OF THE SUBJECT-MATTER

### INTRODUCTORY

### Additional obligations

Covenants to repair are generally concerned only with the carrying out of works **18–01** of repair. However, in two classes of case, the general covenant to repair and keep in repair imposes or may impose additional obligations which do not concern the carrying out of repairs within the usual meaning of that expression. Both concern the destruction of the subject-matter. First, the repairing covenant may, as a matter of construction, oblige the tenant not to destroy the subject-matter. Second, if the subject-matter is destroyed by fire or other disaster, then the tenant will ordinarily be obliged to rebuild or reinstate it. This Chapter is concerned with these two aspects of the general covenant to repair. It also deals with covenants to rebuild and reinstate following the occurrence of an insured risk.

### OBLIGATION NOT TO DESTROY

### A question of construction

It has been held in a number of cases that the covenant to repair has been broken **18–02** by destroying or altering the subject-matter of the covenant, either in whole or in part. Thus, in *Gange v Lockwood*[1] the tenant of certain rooms in a house opened two doorways in the walls between the house and an adjoining house. Willes J. directed the jury in the following terms:

> "[A] covenant to repair, uphold and maintain, or keep in good repair, raises a duty not to destroy the demised premises; and the pulling them down, wholly or partly, is a breach of such covenant."

The jury found that breaches had been committed.

On the same principle, the covenant to repair has been held to be broken by making a doorway through the wall of the demised house into an adjoining house;[2] removing a veranda[3]; pulling down the entirety of the demised premises[4];

---

[1] (1860) 2 F&F 115.
[2] *Doe d. Vickery v Jackson* (1817) 2 Stark 293.
[3] *Penry's Administratrix v Brown* (1818) 2 Stark. 403.
[4] *Maddock v Mallet* (1860) 12 I.C.L.R. 173.

pulling down a brick wall dividing the courtyard at the front of the premises from a yard at the side[5]; removing a lavatory[6;] removing bush timber sheep yards[7]; creating a new flat in a roof space;[8] and removing aluminium mesh sunscreens from an office building.[9] The fact that the tenant has put up a new building in place of the destroyed one and that the demised premises have thereby increased in value is no defence.[10]

18–03    In *Devonshire Reid Properties Ltd v Trenaman*[11] H.H. Judge Rich QC (sitting as a deputy judge of the Chancery Division) regarded the obligation not to destroy as a general rule of law. He said:

> "In my judgment, a covenant to repair and maintain raises a duty not to destroy wholly or partly and a proposal to do so is a breach of covenant."

However, in *Hannon v 169 Queen's Gate Ltd*[12] Mr Bernard Livesey QC (sitting as a judge of the Chancery Division) took a different view. Having referred to Judge Rich QC's formulation of the principle, he continued as follows:

> "It strikes me that the logic behind a such a principle is suspect and the principle is faintly absurd nowadays, and I am inclined not to follow *Trenaman* on this point. [Counsel] calls it a 'pedantic legalistic approach', and I agree. In any event, it seems to me, on the basis of first principle (supported also by authority: see *Woodfall* at para.13.063), that whether the implied duty not to destroy is absolute must depend on the construction of the lease and that not every alteration of the premises amounts to a breach of the covenant to repair."

Much the same view was taken by Lewison J. in *British Glass Manufacturers' Confederation v University of Sheffield*[13]:

> "[Counsel] advances [the submission that a covenant to repair carries with it a duty not to destroy the subject matter of the covenant] as a general rule of the construction of repairing covenants. . . . But, in my judgment, the principle thus expressed is not an absolute rule of law. It is a conclusion reached as a question of construction of the lease."

The correct principle is therefore that there is no rule one way or the other, and the question of whether, and if so, to what extent, a covenant to repair obliges the covenanting party not to destroy the subject-matter of the covenant is in each case a question of construction of the lease in the light of the admissible background.

---

[5] *Doe d. Wetherell v Bird* (1883) 6 C&P 734
[6] *Graham v Markets Hotel Pty Ltd* (1943) 67 C.L.R. 567 (Australia).
[7] *Re Zis* [1961] W.A.R. 120 (Australia).
[8] *Devonshire Reid Properties Ltd v Trenaman* [1997] 1 E.G.L.R. 45.
[9] *Alcatel Australia v Scarcella* [2001] NSWSC 154 (Australia).
[10] See *Maddock v Mallet*, above.
[11] [1997] 1 E.G.L.R. 45.
[12] [2000] 1 E.G.L.R. 40.
[13] [2004] 09 E.G. 146; [2004] 1 E.G.L.R. 40; [2004] L. & T. R. 14.

## Relevant considerations

In construing the covenant, regard must be had in particular to what the parties to    **18–04**
the lease are to be taken as having contemplated would be permissible. It will be
relevant to consider in particular the existence and terms of any covenant against
alterations. Thus, if, for example, the lease contains a covenant prohibiting only
structural alterations, the right view may be that the parties contemplated that
non-structural alterations would be permissible, and therefore that the making of
such alterations would not be a breach of the covenant to repair.[14] Other
indications in the lease that the parties contemplated the making of alterations
may also lead to the conclusion that the alterations so contemplated are not a
breach of the covenant to repair. Thus, in *Doe d. Dalton v Jones*[15] a
dwelling-house was let for 40 years. The tenant covenanted to repair and keep
repaired the premises "together with such buildings improvements, and additions
whatsoever, as at any time during the said term should be erected, set up or made
by him." The tenant took down part of the front of the house, and converted the
lower part of the premises into a shop and exhibition room for pictures. On the
outside, the old windows were removed, and new, larger shop windows were put
in. On the inside, a partition on the ground floor was broken through, a new door
made in it, and an old one stopped up. It was held that no breach had been
committed, because the lease contemplated that improvements and additions
would be made. Parke B. said:

> "[The lease]... contemplates 'improvements and additions', and only provides against
> non-repair, which is permissive waste. Under such a lease can it be said that a valuable house
> was to be kept in precisely the same condition for forty years?"

It will also be relevant to consider the permitted user of the premises. Thus, in
*Hyman v Rose*[16] a piece of ground and a chapel standing on it were demised for
99 years under a lease containing covenants by the tenant to complete the chapel
by a given date, and well and substantially to repair support uphold maintain pave
amend and keep it in good and substantial repair. The chapel was completed, and
was used as a chapel for 60 years. It was then sold for use as a cinema. Nothing in
the lease prohibited the use of the building as a cinema, or the making of internal
alterations to make it suitable for that use. It was adapted for use as a cinema by
the removal of a dwarf wall and iron railings separating it from the street; the
opening of a new door in the west wall; the enlarging of an existing doorway in
the east wall; and the making of various alterations in the interior, including
removing two wooden staircases and a portion of wooden gallery, constructing
two new staircases, and raising the floor level. A majority of the Court of Appeal
held that these works amounted to a breach of the covenant to repair.[17] Fletcher
Moulton L.J. said:

---

[14] See the dissenting judgment of Buckley L.J. in *Rose v Spicer* [1911] 2 K.B. 234 (approved in the House of Lords: *Hyman v Rose* [1912] A.C. 623).
[15] (1832) 4 B. & Ad. 126.
[16] [1912] A.C. 623.
[17] [1911] 2 K.B. 234.

"Had the railings or the staircases or the gallery fallen out of repair a notice to repair them must
have been obeyed by the lessees on pain of forfeiture. How can it be gravely suggested then
that their actual removal and destruction is not a substantial breach of the covenant to repair
and maintain?"

Buckley L.J. dissented, relying on (a) the reference to "improvements" in the
covenant to yield up; (b) the fact that the use as a cinema was not forbidden by
the lease so that "[f]or the purposes of use for any trade not being a forbidden
trade the lessees could, I think, reasonably arrange and equip the interior of the
building as they thought proper"; and (c) the fact that the covenant against
alterations prohibited only alterations to the west wall, from which it could be
inferred that other alterations were permitted. The House of Lords allowed the
tenant's appeal. Earl Loreburn L.C. (with whom Lords Macnaghten, Atkinson
and Shaw agreed) agreed with the judgment of Buckley L.J., and referred in his
speech to the purpose permitted by the lease as being the "governing
consideration". The removal of the wall and railings was held not to amount to a
breach on the further ground that there was no evidence that they existed at the
date of the lease.

**18–05**     In *Devonshire Reid Properties Ltd v Trenaman*[18] a building containing four flats
was let on leases containing a landlord's covenant to maintain, repair, redecorate
and renew the structure of the building and in particular the roof. The landlord
proposed to create a new flat in the roof space. H.H. Judge Rich QC (sitting as a
deputy judge of the Chancery Division) held that this would amount to a breach
of the repairing covenant. However, his decision was not followed in *Hannon v
169 Queen's Gate Ltd*.[19] In that case, the claimant tenant had a 999-year lease of
a top-floor flat in a purpose-built block of 25 flats. Following the grant of
planning permission, the landlord (a company wholly owned by the tenants of the
block) proposed to construct two flats on the roof, one of which would be
immediately above that of the claimant tenant. He contended that the proposed
construction would (among other things) be a breach of the landlord's repairing
covenant. Mr Bernard Livesey QC (sitting as a judge of the Chancery Division)
found in favour of the landlord. He said:

"In construing the covenant, regard must be had, in particular, to what the parties to the lease
are to be taken as having contemplated would be permissible. It will be relevant to consider
the existence and terms of any covenant against alterations. The defendant points out that in
the instant lease there is a covenant on the lessee to repair and a further covenant on him not to
make alterations. There is not, however, such a covenant restricting the lessor from making
alterations. On the contrary, since, in this lease, the lessor has the entitlement to execute
'necessary repairs or alterations to or upon any part of the Building' (see clause 2(j)) and to
execute 'building operations additions alterations decorations repairs or improvements to the
building' (clause 9 *supra*), it seems to me that the claimant is not able to advance his argument
on this aspect past 'first base'. The claimant says that I should not read clause 9 as giving the
defendant the power to build, make additions or alterations, but merely as limiting the lessee's
remedies should it do so. I reject this submission. At the very least, the powers are implicit."

---

[18]   [1997] 1 E.G.L.R. 45.
[19]   [2000] 1 E.G.L.R. 40.

In *Marlton v Turner*[20] it was held in the county court that the removal of 4.5m of a hedgerow in order to construct a means of access was not a breach of an obligation in an inclosure award to keep the hedgerow "in good repair and condition". Judge Langan said:

> "It seems to me, as a matter of commonsense as well as proper interpretation, that to breach the hedge by an access of the kind proposed is in no way inconsistent with the keeping of the hedge in good repair and condition. The hedge will remain, for by far the greater part of its length, in position after the proposed work just as it has done for the past two centuries and more."

In *British Glass Manufacturers' Confederation v University of Sheffield*[21] the tenant was granted a lease for 1,000 years at an annual rent of £1. The tenant covenanted (a) forthwith to erect a laboratory and office building; (b) well and substantially to repair and keep in repair and yield up in repair the laboratory and office building and all other buildings and erections which may at any time be upon the demised land; and (c) at the end of the term to yield up "the said laboratory and office building and other buildings and erections well and substantially repaired in accordance with" the repairing covenant. The lease contained no restriction on user or alterations. The tenant proposed to demolish the buildings and erect other buildings. Lewison J. held that this would not be a breach of the repairing covenant. He said:

**18–06**

> "Like all questions of construction, the question in the present case turns on what the terms of the lease, read in context, would convey to a reasonable reader. Do they lead the reasonable reader to conclude that the parties had intended that the tenant should be obliged to keep in repair for 1,000 years the very same buildings that it had first erected? Or do they lead him to conclude that the parties intended that the tenant should keep in repair the buildings on the site, whatever they happened to be? First, apart from estoppel, it is common ground that the lease contains no restriction on the use to which the property can be put. If, therefore, the tenant wished to use the existing buildings for residential use, and obtained planning permission to do so, there is nothing in the lease to stop it. In such a case, in conformity with the principle set out by Buckley LJ, and approved by the House of Lords [in *Hyman v Rose*], a right to adapt the property for that purpose would be implied. Second, the term of the lease is 1,000 years. The period of use contemplated by the parties was as long a period as separated them from Anglo-Saxon England. Apart from a handful of parish churches, there can be no buildings in the country still in use in their original form after 1,000 years. Add to that the parties' original contemplation, that the buildings to be erected were to be used for cutting-edge scientific research, and it becomes highly improbable that they expected, let alone agreed, that the buildings would remain unaltered for the term of the lease."

He regarded the landlord's strongest point as being that the covenant to yield up required the tenant to yield up the land "together with the said laboratory and office building and other buildings and erections". But:

> "The present case is a case where, in my judgment, the overall commercial context drives one to the conclusion that something has gone wrong with the language and that the word 'and' should be read as 'or'. I think, also, that I am entitled to take into account the absence of a prohibition on alterations, even though such covenants in leases had been common for a

---

[20] [1998] 3 E.G.L.R. 185.
[21] [2004] 1 E.G.L.R. 40.

century or more. In my judgment, therefore, the terms of the lease do not prohibit the demolition and reconstruction of the buildings comprised in the lease, or their use for residential purposes."

## Limitation

**18–07** Breach of a covenant to repair is a continuing breach, so that time runs afresh every day that the breach continues.[22] The same is true where the breach consists of the complete destruction of the demised buildings and their replacement by something different.[23]

## LIABILITY TO REINSTATE AFTER FIRE OR OTHER DISASTER

## Introductory

**18–08** Destruction of the premises by fire or other disaster may provide the occasion for landlord and tenant to review between themselves the future of the lease. Sometimes, they will be able to reach an agreement which will obviate the need to repair or rebuild the premises. For example, it may be the case that the premises were ripe for redevelopment anyway, and that the tenant is able to find alternative premises which are better suited to his needs; the parties may then be able to agree that the lease should be surrendered (for or without a consideration passing from one party to the other) to enable the landlord to redevelop the site. Even where the premises are to be rebuilt, most leases impose obligations on one party (usually but not always the landlord) to insure and to expend the insurance money on reinstatement. In such cases damage by fire is frequently excluded from the repairing covenant. It will not therefore usually be necessary to consider the position under the covenant to repair. However, where the parties are unable to agree on what should be done, and the position is not governed by insurance provisions, the question will be to what extent the repairing obligations oblige the tenant (or the landlord, if he is the covenanting party) to rebuild the premises.

## Liability where no express agreement

**18–09** In the absence of an express covenant, neither party is under an implied obligation to repair or rebuild the premises in the event of damage or destruction by fire or other disaster. The fact that the tenant's repairing covenant expressly excludes damage by fire will not generally be any ground for implying an obligation on the part of the landlord to make good such damage.[24] The contrary was argued in *Weigall v Waters*,[25] in which Lord Kenyon C.J., rejecting it, said:

---

[22] See para.26–18, below.
[23] *Maddock v. Mallet* (1860) 12 I.C.L.R. 173.
[24] *Weigall v Waters* (1795) 6 T.R. 488; *Bayne v Walker* (1815) 3 Dow 233; *Broom v Preston & Stabb* (1825) 1 Nfld. L.R. 427.
[25] Above.

"I do not indeed see by what covenant the landlord is bound to repair damages occasioned by fire or tempest; the exception was introduced in the lessee's covenant, for his benefit, and to exempt him from particular repair."

Neither will the landlord be liable by virtue of the ordinary covenant for quiet enjoyment.[26] However, it should be noted that under s.83 of the Fires Prevention (Metropolis) Act 1774, one party may have the right to require insurance money payable under a policy effected by the other to be laid out in reinstating. This is considered in para.18–40, below.

## Liability in tort

The above does not, however, prevent one party being liable to the other in tort where such liability would otherwise arise, i.e. by virtue of the duty not to commit waste,[27] or where the fire or other disaster is caused by the deliberate or negligent act or omission of one or other of them, or of someone for whom they are responsible.[28]   **18–10**

In certain circumstances, the right of one party to sue the other for negligence may be held to have been excluded by implied agreement between them. Thus, in *Mark Rowlands Ltd v Berni Inns Ltd*[29] the landlord covenanted to insure the demised premises and to lay out any monies received in rebuilding and reinstating. The tenant covenanted to pay to the landlord the sums expending in insuring. Damage by insured risks was excluded from the tenant's repairing and decorating covenants. The premises burnt down, allegedly because of the tenant's negligence. The landlord's insurers, having paid up on the policy, brought proceedings in the name of the landlord against the tenant for negligence. In so doing, they claimed to be exercising their right of subrogation, and hence their action could only be well-founded if they could establish that the landlord would have had a right to sue the tenant for negligence himself. The Court of Appeal held that the clear intention of the parties was that, in the event of fire, the landlord's loss was to be recouped from the insurers, and that he had no separate and additional right to bring an action against the tenant for negligence. The insurers' claim therefore failed.

However, the mere fact that the landlord agrees to insure the premises does not, of itself, lead to the conclusion that such insurance is for the tenant's benefit as well as his own, such that he has no right of action against the tenant if the

---

[26] *Brown v Quilter* (1764) Amb. 619; *Lapedus v Glavey* (1955) 99 I.L.T.R. 1 (affirmed (1965) I.L.T.R. 4).

[27] See *Rook v Worth* (1750) 1 Ves. Sen. 460. It is thought that the effect of s.86 of the Fires Prevention (Metropolis) Act 1774 is to exclude liability in waste in relation to accidental fires. See the following footnote.

[28] The Fires Prevention (Metropolis) Act 1774 s.86, which excludes liability for fires started "accidentally", is limited to fires started by mere chance or which are incapable of being traced to any cause; it does not apply to fires caused intentionally or negligently: *Filliter v Phippard* (1847) 11 Q.B. 347; *Musgrove v Pandelis* [1919] 2 K.B. 43.

[29] [1986] Q.B. 211. In *Sadlers v Clements* [1995] E.G.C.S. 197 the court declined to apply the principle in *Mark Rowlands Ltd v Berni Inns Ltd* on the ground that the defendant was not a tenant See also *Quirkco Investments Ltd v Aspray Transport Ltd* [2012] L. & T.R. 12 at [44].

premises are damaged or destroyed by the latter's negligence.[30] Thus, in *Lambert v Keymood Ltd*[31] the landlord agreed to insure, and the relevant premises were (as to one unit) damaged and (as to the other) destroyed by a fire caused by the tenant's negligence. There was no obligation on the part of the tenant to pay an insurance rent. It was held that there was nothing in the express terms of the bargain or the relevant preceding correspondence (which was held to be admissible for this purpose) to show that the landlord had agreed to insure for the tenant's benefit.

In the Scottish case of *Barras v Hamilton*,[32] the insurance rent payable by the tenant covered the landlord's cost of insuring the demised premises, and the tenant negligently started a fire which destroyed not only the demised premises but other property belonging to the landlord. The Court of Session held that the landlord was entitled to recover his uninsured losses from the tenant, with the exception of losses relating to the demised premises, which were excluded by the principle in *Mark Rowlands Ltd v Berni Inns Ltd*.

## Covenants to repair: the general rule

18–11　The general principle is that a covenant to repair obliges the covenantor to rebuild or reinstate the premises if they are destroyed or damaged by fire, even an accidental fire. The earliest reported judicial statement of this appears to be *Paradine v Jane*,[33] in which it was said that:

> "[I]f the lessee covenant to repair a house, though it be burnt by lightning, or thrown down by enemies, yet he ought to repair it."

Similarly, in *Pool v Archer*[34] Lord Kenyon C.J. said:

> "The cases cited on behalf of the [landlord] have always been considered and acted upon as law. In the year 1754 a great fire broke out in Lincoln's Inn, and consumed many of the chambers, and among the rest those rented by Mr Wilbraham; and he, after taking the opinions of his professional friends, found it necessary to rebuild them."

The Lord Chief Justice continued as follows:

> "On a general covenant like the present, there is no doubt but that the lessee is bound to rebuild in case of an accidental fire; the common opinion of mankind confirms this, for in many cases an exception of accidents by fire is cautiously introduced into the lease to protect the lessee."

18–12　Another clear statement of the principle is to be found in *Earl of Chesterfield v Duke of Bolton*,[35] in which the tenant covenanted to "repair and keep in good and

---

[30] *Lambert v Keymood Ltd* [1997] 2 E.G.L.R. 70. See further paras 18–38 and 18–39, below.
[31] See above.
[32] 1994 S.L.T. 949.
[33] (1647) Aleyn. 26. See also *Compton v Allen* (1649) Sty. 162.
[34] (1684) Skin. 210.
[35] (1738) Comyns. 627.

sufficient reparation" the demised premises. A substantial part of the premises was subsequently burned down. The argument advanced on behalf of the tenant is reported to have been as follows:

> "The covenant is, that he shall keep in repair, not that he shall rebuild, and therefore it could not be the intent of the parties to bind the [tenant] beyond the common and ordinary repair, and not to make a new house, if by accident, without the [tenant's] default, it should be burnt or demolished."

The court dealt with the argument in the following way:

> "[W]hen the [tenant] covenants that he will repair, and keep in good and sufficient reparation without any exception, this imports that he should in all events repair it; and in case it be burnt or fall down, he must rebuild it, otherwise he doth not keep it in good and sufficient reparation; and this is warranted by the cases cited, which show that the covenantor must rebuild if necessity require, as where the house is burnt by fire, etc."

The existence of the principle has been expressly or tacitly assumed in the authorities ever since.[36] It is not affected by s.86 of the Fires Prevention (Metropolis) Act 1774.[37] Once the premises have been rebuilt, the covenant to repair will apply to the new building in the same way as it did to the original one.[38]

## Other disasters

The general rule is not confined to fire but includes damage or destruction by other disasters. Thus, in *Redmond v Dainton*,[39] the reinstatement of damage caused by an enemy bomb was held to be within the scope of a covenant "to repair, uphold, support, sustain, and maintain the dwelling-house, walls and premises and every part thereof". It was argued in that case that the presence in the lease of a tenant's covenant to keep the dwelling-house insured against fire during the term, and to expend upon the demised premises all money received from the insurance in rebuilding restoring or reinstating the premises meant that by implication the tenant was not bound to rebuild if the premises were destroyed by any other cause. Darling J. rejected this contention, holding that such covenant did not absolve the tenant " . . . from his liability to perform the repairing covenant even though it necessitates the work of rebuilding."

Likewise, the principle has been held to apply to damage or destruction caused by lightning,[40] snowfall[41] and flood.[42] There is no reason in principle why it

**18–13**

---

[36] *Belfour v Weston* (1786) 1 T.R. 310; *Pym v Blackburn* (1796) 3 Ves. 34; *Bullock v Dommitt* (1796) 2 Chit. 608; *Digby v Atkinson* (1818) 4 Camp. 275; *Clarke v Glasgow Assurance Co Ltd* (1854) 1 Macq. (H.L.) 668; *Gregg v Coates* (1856) 23 Beav. 33; *Matthey v Curling* [1922] 2 A.C. 180; *Sturcke v S.W. Edwards Ltd* (1972) 23 P. & C.R. 185. See also *Combara Nominees Pty Ltd v McIlwraith-Davey Pty Ltd* (1991) 6 W.A.R. 408 (Australia).

[37] See para.18–40, below. The section expressly provides that "no contract or agreement made between landlord and tenant shall be hereby defeated or made void". It follows that it does not prevent the tenant being liable under his repairing covenant even where the fire was accidental.

[38] *Greene v Southcott* (1879) 6 Nfld. L.R. 176. See paras 7–20 to 7–23, above.

[39] [1919] 2 K.B. 256.

[40] *Paradine v Jane* (1647) Aleyn. 26.

should not also apply to damage or destruction resulting from other causes, such as earthquakes, explosions, riots or crashing aeroplanes.

## Qualifications to the general rule

**18–14**  The general rule can be excluded by express words in the lease.[43] Thus, it is common to find phrases such as "damage by insured risks excluded" in repairing covenants. Many modern leases contain comprehensive insurance provisions, the effect of which is that the repair or reinstatement of damage by fire or other disaster is paid for out of insurance money, and the tenant is not liable to repair or reinstate, unless the insurance money is withheld by reason of his act or default. Where it is the tenant who is to insure and reinstate, it is common to find an obligation that he must make up any deficiency in the insurance moneys out of his own pocket.

However, the mere fact that the lease contains provisions relating to insurance does not automatically mean that liability under the covenant to repair is excluded. Thus, in *Digby v Atkinson*[44] the lease contained a tenant's covenant to: (i) keep the demised premises in repair, and (ii) insure the premises against fire for the sum of £600. The premises burnt down, and it was argued that the tenant's liability under the repairing covenant was confined to £600. Lord Ellenborough rejected this, saying that:

> "The covenant to insure was introduced for the security of the landlord, leaving the tenant still absolutely liable on the covenant to repair."

This is not to say, however, that the proper construction of the repairing covenant will not in some cases be influenced by the insurance provisions, particularly where the parties obviously intended them to be interlocking. Depending on the context, the right conclusion may be that the parties intended the general rule not to apply. The decision in *Mark Rowlands Ltd v Berni Inns Ltd*[45] might be used to support an argument to this effect in a case where the lease contains detailed provisions relating to insurance and the application of the insurance money.

It should also be noted that the landlord's repairing covenant implied by s.11 of the Landlord and Tenant Act 1985 in the case of short leases of dwelling-houses,[46] does not require the landlord to rebuild or reinstate the premises in the case of destruction or damage by fire, or by tempest, flood or other inevitable accident.[47]

---

[41] *Hall v Campbellford Cloth Co* [1944] D.L.R. 247.
[42] *Brecknock & Abergavenny Canal Navigation Co v Pritchard* (1796) 2 B. & P. 65.
[43] *Bullock v Dommitt* (1796) 2 Chit. 608.
[44] (1818) 4 Camp. 275.
[45] [1986] Q.B. 211. See para.18–10, above.
[46] See para.20–17 et seq., below.
[47] See para.20–33, below.

## Rationale of the general rule

At first sight, the general rule seems somewhat startling, and at odds with the **18–15** "fact and degree" test of liability under a repairing covenant already discussed.[48] It may be thought to be anomalous and inconsistent that the extensive remedial works required in such cases as *Lister v Lane*[49] should be outside the covenant, yet had the whole premises burned down through no fault of the tenant, he would have been obliged to rebuild them in their entirety. It is a noteworthy feature of those cases in which the rule is laid down (as opposed to those in which it is merely assumed to exist) that (with one sole exception[50]) they were decided in the eighteenth or early nineteenth centuries, and therefore before a number of the cases establishing the modern law of repair, and in particular the "fact and degree" approach, were decided. It is therefore necessary to examine the basis of the rule with some care to see whether, and to what extent, it continues to represent the law in modern times.

One possible explanation of the rule is that it is based on the notion that "repair" connotes not so much an operation as a description of a state, and that a covenant to keep premises in repair obliges the covenantor to keep them in that state, whatever work is required to do that. If this is the true explanation of the rule, then whether it survives at all in modern times must be seriously in doubt. The view that a covenant to repair obliges the covenantor to keep the premises in a particular state whatever work that may involve is not consistent with the majority of the later authorities, all of which proceed on the more or less express basis that there may be work required which is so extensive that it is outside the ambit of the covenant altogether.[51] Many of those authorities were decided in this century, and most treat the question whether particular work is within the covenant as being primarily one of fact and degree in each case.[52] Such an approach would preclude a blanket doctrine that damage caused by fire or other disasters is within the covenant as a matter of law. Instead it would leave that question to be decided on the specific facts of each case. Moreover, such an approach would generally mean that complete rebuilding would be outside the covenant, as being, on a proper application of the fact and degree test, work going beyond what can properly be called repair.[53]

However, the more likely explanation for the rule is that the tenant's obligation to **18–16** repair the premises is an absolute one, from which he is not released by the occurrence of a catastrophe. Since that obligation can only be performed in relation to premises which exist, it follows that if the premises are destroyed or damaged the tenant must rebuild or reinstate them in order to put himself back into a position in which he can perform his contract. It is thought that this is what

---

[48] See Ch.11, above.
[49] [1893] 2 Q.B. 212.
[50] *Redmond v Dainton* [1919] 2 K.B. 256, in which it was argued only that the rule did not apply on the facts of that particular case, rather than that it did not exist at all.
[51] See Ch.11, above.
[52] An exception is the judgment of Fletcher Moulton L.J. in *Lurcott v Wakeley* [1911] 1 K.B. 905. He regarded an obligation to keep in repair as much the same as an obligation to keep in good condition, i.e. as a description of a state: see para.4–30, above.
[53] See para.11–29, above.

was meant by the passage from the judgment in *Earl of Chesterfield v Duke of Bolton* set out above.[54] It is noteworthy that reliance was placed in that case on *Paradine v Jane*,[55] which concerned a claim for rent. The defence was that the tenant had been dispossessed of the demised premises by a foreign enemy, and had therefore ceased to be liable for the rent. In rejecting this defence, the court applied the general contractual principle that a promise to do an act must be performed even though a change of circumstances has occurred in the meantime making performance more difficult or more onerous. This appears from the following passage in the judgment:

> "[W]hen the party by his own contract creates a duty or charge upon himself, he is bound to make it good, if he may, notwithstanding any accident by inevitable necessity, because he might have provided against it by his contract."

There followed the passage already set out above,[56] and then the following:

> "Rent is a duty created by the parties upon the reservation, and had there been a covenant to pay it, there had been no question but the lessee must have made it good, notwithstanding the interruption by enemies, for the law would not protect him beyond his own agreement, no more than in the case of reparations."

It is thought that the continuance of the rule in modern times can be justified on the basis that there is a difference between work which becomes necessary as a result of the ordinary effect of time, usage and weather on the building, and work which becomes necessary as a result of some sudden catastrophe.[57] In relation to work in the first category, the repairing covenant is not intended to confer on the landlord a "windfall" in the form of a new or substantially different building: hence, the fact and degree test applies to exclude work going beyond repair from the ambit of the covenant. However, where the premises cease to exist altogether as the result of some disaster for which neither party is responsible, it can be said that rebuilding or reinstating them does not give the landlord anything different in kind to that which he demised, save obviously that the materials will be new. It is not necessarily a misuse of language to describe such an operation as "repair" even though none of the original subject-matter survives. Another way of putting the same point is to say that the landlord takes the risk of defects occurring during the term of the lease which arise from the nature of the demised property and its ordinary use, and which are so substantial as to require remedial work going beyond what can properly be called "repair". It is his building and it is proper that risks of this sort should fall on him. The tenant, on the other hand, takes the risk, not only of disrepair occurring during the term, but also of unforeseen catastrophes. It is his duty under his covenant to restore to the landlord at the end of the term that which he was given, namely a building repaired and in a form undamaged by fire or other disaster. It is thought

---

[54] See para.18–12, above.
[55] (1647) Aleyn. 26.
[56] See para.18–11, above.
[57] This explanation is supported by the Irish cases of *Groome v Fodhla Printing Co* [1943] I.R. 380, per Black J. at 408, and *Lapedus v Glavey* (1965) 99 I.L.T.R. 1.

that the allocation of risks in this way is not obviously contrary to ordinary fairness or the probable intention of most landlords and tenants.

In any event, the general rule has been assumed to be part of the law of dilapidations for at least three centuries, and no doubt countless landlords, tenants and insurance companies have arranged their affairs accordingly. It is thought that in these circumstances the courts would be reluctant to overturn it at this comparatively late stage. It is therefore thought that, whatever its true explanation may be, the above principle continues to form part of the law of repair.

## Where rebuilding or reinstatement is impossible because planning permission cannot be obtained

Where the demised premises are destroyed by fire or other disaster, planning permission will generally be required before they can be rebuilt. In practice, it may not always be possible to obtain planning permission to put back what was there before. The question in such cases will be whether the covenantor is relieved by this impossibility from his obligation to rebuild, or whether he remains liable and must pay damages for breach. The answer seems to be that the covenantor will remain liable to pay damages where the lease was granted after the coming into force of the Town and Country Planning legislation, but where the lease was granted prior to that legislation, it may be that his obligation would be held to have been discharged by supervening impossibility.

**18–17**

In *Maud v Sandars*[58] a tenant covenanted to keep and deliver up the demised premises in repair. The term ended on March 25, 1942, following which the landlord sued the tenant for damages for breach of covenant. The tenant contended that the effect of certain Defence Regulations then in force (which prohibited the expenditure of more than £100 on repairs or decorations without a licence granted by the Minister) was to discharge him from liability to perform his covenant. Lewis J. rejected this. His principal reason appears to have been that the object of the regulations was to conserve building materials rather than to interfere with the rights of landlords against tenants. It appears that he would have rejected a claim by the landlord which resulted in the actual expenditure without licence of more than £100, for that would have been contrary to the object of the regulations. But he was not prepared to hold that the object or effect of the regulations was to eliminate the landlord's claim for the damage to his reversion which (it was admitted) had been caused by the tenant's failure to repair. His judgment contains the following further passage:

> "[E]ven if I am wrong in taking that view with regard to the section, a [tenant] who wishes to avail himself of it must satisfy the court that he has applied for a licence to spend more than £100 and has been unable to get one.
>
> The landlord, if [the tenant is] right, would certainly be entitled to £100, because it is not made unlawful to spend £100 worth of material; you can do that without any licence at all, but if you want to spend more than £100 in materials you have got to get a licence for it; and, in my view, it is for the [tenant] to show the court that he has been unable to obtain a licence from the Minister to the extent of anything excess of the £100."

---

[58] [1943] 2 All E.R. 783.

**18–18**    *Regal Property Trust Ltd v Muldoon*[59] concerned the same regulations. In that case an agreement for lease contained a tenant's obligation to carry out certain work by a specified date as a condition precedent to the grant of the lease. The tenant failed to do the work, alleging that his obligation had been discharged because a licence under the regulations had not been granted. Lynsey J. rejected this, and it appears from the short report of his judgment that he did so on the ground that the tenant had not applied for a licence, and it was impossible to say what would have happened had he done so.

The question of what the position would be if a licence were to be applied for and refused arose in *Eyre v Johnson*.[60] In that case a lease was granted in 1930 for 21 years containing a tenant's covenant to repair and yield up in repair, and also a right for the tenant to break the lease on six months' notice. The tenant gave the requisite notice, and applied to the minister for licences to effect repairs. These were refused and the premises were yielded up unrepaired. The tenant contended that he had been discharged from performance, and therefore from any liability to pay damages. Denning J. found against him on the primary ground that the condition of the premises had been brought about by a series of breaches of the covenant to repair, which had begun to occur at a time when there were no regulations. He went on to hold, however, that in any event the covenant had not been discharged. He said:

> "It seems to me that although illegality which completely forbids the performance of a contract may give rise to frustration in some cases, illegality as to the performance of one clause which does not amount to frustration in any sense of the word, does not carry with it the necessary consequence that the party is absolved from paying damages. Take this case. The landlord has performed all his part of the bargain. The tenant has had the premises all this time. The fact that it has become difficult, or even impossible, for the tenant to perform the covenants does not relieve him from the obligation of paying damages."

The above passage suggests that the judge was proceeding on the footing that it is not possible as a matter of law for a particular obligation in a lease, as opposed to the entire lease itself, to be discharged by illegality. If he was right about this, then an obligation to repair or reinstate would only be discharged if the circumstances are such that the entire lease has been frustrated.[61] If that was the basis of the judge's decision, then he was almost certainly wrong.[62] Nonetheless, *Eyre v Johnson* remains important as an example of a further case in which the limitations imposed on performance of the covenant by the relevant regulations were held to be no defence to an action for damages for non-performance.

**18–19**    In *Cricklewood Property & Investment Trust Ltd v Leighton's Investment Trust Ltd*[63] a building lease was granted in 1936 for a term of 99 years containing a tenant's covenant to erect a number of shops within a time limit. Temporary

---

[59] (1947) 149 E.G. 428.
[60] [1946] K.B. 481.
[61] See para.32–52, below.
[62] See *Cricklewood Property & Investment Trust Ltd v Leighton's Investment Trust Ltd* [1945] A.C. 221 at 233–234 and 244; *Sturcke v SW Edwards Ltd* (1972) 23 P. & C.R. 185 (in which Goff J. was prepared to hold that Denning J. was wrong on this point); *John Lewis Properties Plc v Viscount Chelsea* [1993] 2 E.G.L.R. 77.
[63] [1945] A.C. 221.

wartime restrictions on building made it impossible for this lawfully to be done. The tenant claimed by way of defence to the landlord's claim for rent that the lease had been frustrated. It was not therefore strictly necessary for the court to consider what effect impossibility of performance had upon the obligation to build taken alone. However, both Lord Russell and Lord Goddard appear to have assumed that the tenant would have had a good defence to an action for breach of that covenant. The former said:

> "It seems to me clear that the intention of the parties was that rent would be payable even though the sites were vacant, and that the landlord was not to be driven to sue for damages for breach of covenant to erect shops. To such an action, the wartime restrictions might well afford a defence, but that is a consequence very different and far removed from frustration [of the lease as a whole]."

The latter said:

> "If however the tenants came under an obligation to build, but were prevented from so doing by the orders, they would furnish them with a good defence, were they sued for breach of their covenant to build, but not to a claim for rent under the lease."

In *Re King*[64] a lease of a factory contained covenants on the part of the tenant to keep the demised premises in good and substantial repair and condition, to insure the demised premises and to lay out all insurance moneys received in rebuilding or reinstating and make up any deficiency out of the tenant's own money. The factory was severely damaged by fire, so that it was reduced to a shell. Owing to wartime and post-war restrictions it could not be rebuilt or repaired at that time. Subsequently the local authority compulsorily acquired all the interests in the premises, pulled down what remained of the factory and built a housing estate. The insurers had in the meantime paid up under the policy effected by the tenant pursuant to the covenant. The Court of Appeal proceeded on the assumption that the obligation had been discharged. Upjohn L.J. referred in the course of his judgment to "supervening circumstances" having made it "impossible [for the parties] to carry out their common intention of reinstating the premises" so that "that part of the contract is thereby frustrated".[65] The question whether the tenant was in breach of the obligations to repair and reinstate did not directly arise for decision.

In *Sturcke v SW Edwards Ltd*,[66] a lease granted in 1956 contained a tenant's **18–20** covenant to repair and to deliver up the premises in repair at the end of the term. The premises were damaged by fire to such an extent that they could not be repaired without planning permission. Following the fire, the landlord granted a licence to assign which contained a covenant by the assignee to carry out and complete all the repairs under the repairing covenant within six months. Planning permission for the repairs was subsequently refused. The landlord then determined the lease pursuant to a break clause, and claimed damages for breach of (a) the repairing covenant in the lease, and (b) the covenant in the licence. The

---

[64] [1963] Ch. 459.
[65] [1963] Ch. 459 at 493.
[66] (1972) 23 P.&C.R. 185.

tenant contended that the obligations had been discharged by supervening illegality, and in the alternative, that a term discharging him from liability ought to be implied.

Goff J. held that the tenant was liable for breach of the repairing covenants in the lease. He held that, whilst the principle of frustration by supervening illegality could apply to a particular obligation in a lease and was not limited to cases where the illegality affected the entire lease, the principle did not apply to the case before him because the Town and Country Planning Acts were already in force at the date of the lease. He said in the course of his judgment:

> "[The tenants] covenanted to do that which they could never lawfully do without consent, and their failure to get consent, against which they might have protected themselves, particularly in the licence when the extent of the fire was known, was not in my judgment a supervening event sufficient to absolve them."

He rejected the argument that a term was to be implied into the lease. However, he held that a term was to be implied into the licence that the obligation was to be operative only in the event of the requisite planning permission being obtained. The distinction between the lease and the licence seems to have been that the full position was known at the date of the latter.

**18–21**  *Sturcke v SW Edwards Ltd* is a clear first instance authority to the effect that, in the case of a lease entered into after the passing of the Town and Country Planning legislation, a covenant to repair will not be discharged by failure to obtain the necessary planning permission. In such cases, the covenant is to do that which, both at the time of the destruction and at the date of the lease, cannot lawfully be done without planning permission. The correct inference is therefore that the parties intended the covenanting party to take the risk of the obligation proving to be impossible to perform lawfully. It is thought that this will generally be the correct analysis, so that although an inability to obtain planning permission may afford the covenantor a defence to an action for specific performance,[67] it will not absolve him from liability to pay damages.[68]

However, a number of leases still exist which were granted before the enactment of the first Town and Country Planning legislation in 1947. Although the reasoning in *Sturcke v S.W. Edwards Ltd* does not apply to these, nonetheless the decisions in *Maud v Sandars*,[69] *Regal Property Trust Ltd v Muldoon*[70] and *Eyre v Johnson*[71] (in all of which the lease was granted before the enactment of the relevant regulations) suggest that even here performance of the covenant would not be discharged by failure to obtain planning permission. However, these cases are not easy to reconcile with the above dicta in *Cricklewood Property & Investment Trust Ltd v Leighton's Investment Trust Ltd*[72] and *Re King*.[73] *Maud v*

---

[67] See Ch.28, below.
[68] See also the Australian case of *Re De Garis and Rowe's Lease* [1924] V.L.R. 38, in which a prohibition on building except in brick or stone imposed under a byelaw made after the date of the lease but under a statute which already existed at the date of the lease was held not to discharge the landlord from an obligation to rebuild a wooden building in the event of destruction by fire.
[69] [1943] 2 All E.R. 783.
[70] (1947) 149 E.G. 428.
[71] [1946] K.B. 481.
[72] [1945] A.C. 221. See para.18–19, above.

*Sandars* and *Regal Property Trust Ltd v Muldoon* may be explained on the basis that in neither case had the tenant applied for the necessary licence, so that it was not clear on the facts whether performance was in fact illegal. As for *Eyre v Johnson*, it may be that it was wrongly decided, having proceeded on an erroneous view of the applicability of the principle of supervening illegality to individual covenants in leases.[74] Alternatively, it may be that the actual decision can be justified on the ground that the illegality was only temporary (in the sense that it only came into operation after a substantial part of the term had already expired).[75] Both the dicta in *Cricklewood* and *Re King*, and the approach of Goff J. in *Sturcke v SW Edwards Ltd*, are consistent with the view that the covenant will generally be held to be frustrated where the cause of the illegality neither exists nor is foreseen at the date of the lease. It is thought that this is the better view.

The above is supported by the decision of Mummery J. in *John Lewis Properties Plc v Viscount Chelsea*.[76] In that case leases granted in 1939 for 999 years contained covenants to pull down the buildings on the demised land and erect and complete new buildings before December 25, 1987. Part of the site was occupied by a building which was listed as Grade II in 1969. At the date of the lease, listed building consent was not required for the demolition or alteration of any of the buildings, nor was the requirement for listed building consent foreseen or foreseeable. Throughout the 1980s it was impossible for the tenant to obtain listed building consent for the demolition of the building in question. The landlord brought proceedings for forfeiture for breach of the obligations to redevelop. His claim was dismissed by Mummery J. on the ground that the covenant was impossible to perform. He added:

> "[M]y finding does not discharge [the tenant] from its obligations. The leases continue for over 930 years. Circumstances will change. There may come a time when [the tenant] no longer has a lawful excuse for non-performance of the obligation to demolish and rebuild. Statutory restrictions may be relaxed or removed; the condition of the buildings themselves may change; artistic taste and appreciation may change; all sorts of things may change."

It appears from this passage that impossibility of performance will not necessarily discharge the covenanting party from performance for all time. The scope of this doctrine is not clear.

It is therefore thought that where the lease was entered into before the enactment of the Town and Country Planning legislation, an inability to obtain planning permission may be held to absolve the covenanting party from an obligation to reinstate. In practice, however, much is likely to depend on the wording of the lease (for example, it may be clear from reading the lease as a whole that the parties intended the covenanting party to be bound come what may), and the extent to which the prohibition was foreseeable as at the date of the lease.

**18–22**

---

[73] [1963] Ch. 459. See para.18–19.
[74] See para.18–18, above.
[75] See *Sturcke v SW Edwards Ltd*(1972) 23 P.&C.R. 185, per Goff J.
[76] [1993] 2 E.G.L.R. 77.

## Where rebuilding or reinstatement is impossible because the premises have been compulsorily acquired or requisitioned

**18–23**  The covenant may become impossible to perform because the land has been compulsorily acquired or requisitioned by some authority acting lawfully under its powers. It appears that in certain circumstances this will have the effect of discharging the covenant. Thus, in *Baily v De Crespigny*[77] a landlord covenanted that neither he nor his assignees would permit building on land adjoining the demised premises. Subsequently the land was compulsorily acquired by a railway company, and a station was built on it. It was held that the landlord was not liable for breach of the covenant, one of the reasons given by the court being that, by reason of what had happened, it was impossible for the landlord to secure performance of the covenant.

In *Mills v Guardians of Poor of East London Union*[78] a lease was granted in 1859 for 21 years. In February 1866 the tenant received a notice to treat from a railway company. The lease was subsequently assigned to the company on November 21, 1870. One of the issues was whether the tenant remained liable on his covenant to repair up until the date of the assignment, or whether his liability ceased on the service of the notice to treat. The tenant argued for the latter on the ground that it thereupon became impossible for him to perform the covenant which was therefore discharged. The court held that the tenant remained liable up until the date of the assignment. In the course of his judgment Grove J. said:

> "I see nothing to exempt the [tenants] from their obligation to perform their covenants until they were turned out of possession. From that period, *viz.*, the 21st of November 1870, when the property and the possession passed to the railway company, and the [tenants] could not effect the repairs, their liability ceased."

This might be thought to support the existence of a principle to the effect that a covenant to repair will be discharged if it cannot be performed because the premises have been compulsorily acquired. However, it appears that the point in question was never argued (it having been agreed between the parties that the period between the date of the assignment and the commencement of the action was of no importance).[79] It would therefore appear that *Mills v Guardians of Poor of East London Union* does not take the question very much further.

**18–24**  The leading case in relation to covenants to repair is *Matthey v Curling*.[80] The lease in question in that case had been granted in 1898 for a term of 21 years. On January 29, 1918, the premises (which consisted of a house and grounds) were requisitioned by the military authorities, and part was thereafter used for housing German prisoners of war. On February 12, 1919, the house was destroyed by fire. The lease expired on March 25, 1919, and the military authorities formally relinquished possession on June 4, 1919. The landlord began proceedings against the tenant for, among other things, damages for breach of the covenants to repair,

---

[77] (1869) L.R. 4 Q.B. 180.
[78] (1872) L.R. 8 C.P. 79.
[79] In *Matthey v Curling* [1922] 2 A.C. 180, Lord Buckmaster said that this removed "the weight that would otherwise attach to the dictum of Grove J."
[80] [1922] A.C. 180.

and to lay out insurance moneys in reinstating. The tenant contended that performance of the covenants had become impossible and therefore that he was released. In the Court of Appeal, the majority (Bankes and Younger L.JJ.) held that the tenant remained liable on the covenants. Bankes L.J. did so on the primary ground that there was a "complete absence of evidence" that the use of the premises by the military had made performance of the covenants impossible as a matter of fact. He said:

> "[T]he [tenant] would no doubt be entitled to rely upon the defence of impossibility of performance if he could have established it...
>
> In order to arrive at a conclusion in the [tenant's] favour upon this question of impossibility of performance, which appears to me to be a question of fact rather than a question of law, I think it essential that more evidence should have been given than was given from which the inference of impossibility of performance could legitimately have been drawn. Much might depend upon the precise nature of the repairs which had to be done."

He held that the covenant to reinstate remained capable of being performed after the term ended so that no question of impossibility arose in relation to it. Younger L.J. agreed that the covenant to keep in repair had not been discharged. He appears to have been influenced to a large extent by the fact that the tenant had remained in occupation of part of the premises and treated the lease as subsisting in the expectation that he would receive compensation. He said:

> "From [the facts] I can deduce no other conclusion than this, that the [tenant] deliberately elected... to maintain in its integrity position as tenant of the holding, looking to the War Office... for compensation in respect of the premises taken by them. It is with reference, in my judgment, to that position of affairs that the liability, if any, of the [tenant] in respect of the claims made against him in this action must be determined.
>
> ... the defence of impossibility raised by the [tenant] cannot properly be determined by reference only to the terms of the notice to take possession, but must largely turn upon the nature of the taking by the War Office and on the attitude of the [tenant] in relation to the tenancy after that taking was complete.
>
> All that the [tenant was] prevented by the impossibility alleged from doing [during the period of the occupation] was from entering upon the premises for the purpose of carrying out the repairs. It may well be that the cost of effecting the repairs then would have been less than the cost of effecting them when the [landlord] obtained possession. But why on that ground should the [tenant] be released from liability beyond the extent of the difference? I can myself see no reason at all, while I did not gather that any suggestion was made, nor do I think it could properly be made, that liability for non-repair as distinct from the possibility of effecting it was during the period in question in any way superseded as between the [landlord] and the [tenant]."

He held, however, that the covenant to yield up in repair had been discharged, although he gave no reasons for his view. He dealt with the covenant to reinstate in the same way as had Bankes L.J.

Atkin L.J., dissenting, held that the covenants had been frustrated by impossibility of performance. He said:

**18–25**

> "[The obligations to keep in repair] are obligations some of which involve a continuing duty throughout the whole term; others involve the placing of the structure temporarily in the possession of a number of workmen with daily facilities of access... It is... sufficient to say that if performance of a covenant requires the right of access to property, and that right of access is by law taken away, performance of the contract is prima facie rendered impossible. If I covenant to build on a field, the possession of which is lawfully taken from me, it does not

appear necessary for my defence of non-performance that I should also have to prove that I asked the new possessor to be allowed to build on the field and that he refused permission.

[The covenant to yield up] fell to be performed on March 25, 1919. The military were at that time in possession and continued in possession till June . . . I agree [that performance of the covenant was impossible] for reasons which I think apply to the whole of the repairing covenants. It was impossible to surrender the premises to the lessor, and it is perhaps sufficient to say that it becomes therefore immaterial to consider whether if the premises had been surrendered they would have been repaired, maintained, etc. But for the reason I have already given the obligation to repair was excused by legal impossibility."

He went on to hold that the covenant to reinstate on its proper construction could only be performed during the term, and therefore that it too was impossible to perform for the same reasons.

The House of Lords dismissed the tenant's appeal, holding that the covenants had not been discharged. Lord Buckmaster (with whose speech Lords Sumner, Wrenbury and Carson agreed) said with regard to the covenants to repair and yield up in repair:

"It is said that performance had become impossible, and that consequently it must be excused. Impossibility of performance is a phrase that is often lightly and loosely used in connection with contractual obligations. There is no question here of performance having become impossible owing to its prohibition by statute, for no law has prohibited performance, though enjoyment of the premises has been interfered with by legal powers. Further, I entertain grave doubts whether there was any impossibility in fact at all. At any rate, I am satisfied that a terminable occupation by military authorities during an uncertain time, for which compensation may prove to be recoverable, constitutes no answer to the obligations of this repairing covenant. It thus becomes unnecessary to express any opinion about the covenants to insure and to apply the insurance moneys in reinstating the premises."

It is by no means clear from the above passage whether Lord Buckmaster was denying the existence of any principle of frustration by impossibility of performance save in the limited case of performance being prohibited by statute, or whether he was confining himself to saying that, whether or not such a principle did exist, it did not apply on the facts. It is thought that the latter is probably the better view. Lord Atkinson, who gave the only other speech, adopted a different approach:

"Owing to the date at which the fire took place and the fact that the military officers were in occupation on behalf of the Crown till June 4, 1919, I assume it was physically impossible for the [tenant] to have delivered up the possession of the demised premises as he was by the covenant bound to do in good repair and condition at the termination of the lease on March 25, 1919. But the covenant to deliver up in repair was absolute in form, and having regard to the decision in *Brown v Royal Insurance Co. Limited*,[81] I have the very gravest doubt whether the performance of this covenant can be excused by reason of that impossibility."

---

[81] (1859) 120 E.R. 1131. In that case, an insurer who had elected to reinstate was held not to be discharged from his obligation by the fact that in the course of the reinstatement work the premises were demolished as a dangerous structure by the Commissioners of Sewers acting under the Metropolitan Building Act 1855. The effect of this was alleged to be that performance of the obligation to reinstate had become impossible because that obligation only required the insurer to reinstate the premises in their original condition, not to rebuild altogether. Lord Campbell C.J. said: "The defendants undertook to do what was lawful at the time, and has continued to be lawful: that being so, the fact that performance has become impossible is no legal excuse for their not performing it; and they are liable in damages."

With regard to the covenant to reinstate, he agreed with the view of the majority of the Court of Appeal that it could be performed after the end of the lease, and therefore that there had been no impossibility.

In the light of the above it is difficult to do much more than speculate as to how a modern court would approach an argument that a covenant to repair or reinstate has been frustrated by the premises being compulsorily acquired or requisitioned. It is thought that there is no reason in principle why such an argument should not succeed, provided that the facts are such that performance was genuinely impossible, and the degree of impossibility (in terms both of duration and interference with the work) is sufficiently substantial as to strike at the root of the obligation.

## Practical application of the doctrine of discharge by impossibility

It is perhaps not without significance that there is no reported case in which obligations to repair have been held to be discharged by impossibility of performance. It is thought that in practice the cases in which such a defence succeeds are likely to be rare, and to arise out of exceptional facts. Indeed, cases in which the question arises at all are likely to be few and far between, partly because of the widespread modern practice of excepting damage caused by insured risks from the scope of the covenant to repair, and partly because on any view, the tenant will not be discharged from his obligations in respect of periods prior to performance of the obligation becoming impossible, or from the consequences of breaches of those obligations.[82]

18–26

## COVENANTS TO REBUILD OR REINSTATE

### Introductory

Most modern leases impose obligations on one or other party to insure the demised premises, or the building of which they form part, and to rebuild or reinstate in the event of damage or destruction by an insured risk (or lay out insurance moneys in so doing). The law relating to such obligations is strictly speaking not part of the law of dilapidations. However, when a catastrophe occurs, it will generally be necessary in practice to consider both the covenants to repair and the obligations to rebuild or reinstate. For this reason an outline treatment of the latter kind of obligations has been included in this work.

18–27

### Form of the covenant

The covenant may take the form of an unqualified obligation to reinstate or rebuild, or it may be limited to an obligation to expend all insurance moneys received in reinstating or rebuilding. There is an important practical difference

18–28

---

[82] It will be recalled that Denning J.'s primary reason for dismissing the tenant's defence in *Eyre v Johnson* [1946] K.B. 481 was that breaches had been committed prior to the coming into force of the relevant regulation: see para.18–18, above.

between these two types of obligation. Under the former the party insuring takes the risk of the premises being under-insured, or the insurers lawfully refusing to pay up. If either of these occurs, then he must make up the deficiency out of his own moneys. Under the latter the obligation is only to expend insurance moneys in rebuilding or reinstating, so that the party insuring is only liable to rebuild or reinstate to that extent. Where, however, any under-insurance is due to his own breach of covenant in failing to insure in an adequate amount, he may be liable for the difference by way of damages for breach of covenant. Moreover, some leases impose an additional obligation on the party insuring to make up any deficiency out of his own monies.

## TIME FOR PERFORMANCE OF THE OBLIGATION TO EXPEND INSURANCE MONEYS ON REBUILDING OR REINSTATING

### (a)    The general principle

**18–29**    An obligation to expend insurance moneys in reinstating does not fall to be performed until the insurance money has in fact been received.[83] It appears that a similar construction will be given to an obligation to lay out all insurance moneys "to be received", notwithstanding the use of the future tense, so that the covenanting party is not obliged to start the work immediately in anticipation of the insurance moneys being paid subsequently.[84] The party insuring is under an implied obligation to present and prosecute a claim under the policy with all reasonable speed.[85] If, however, payment was legitimately withheld, or proved impossible to obtain (for example, because the company was insolvent) then the duty to reinstate would not arise because the insurance money would never have been received.

The obligation to reinstate is sometimes expressed to arise "forthwith" on receiving the insurance money. This will not generally mean "immediately" in the strict sense of that word, but as soon as reasonably possible.[86] In the absence of words indicating the time for performance, the covenant must be performed within a reasonable time of receiving the insurance money.[87]

### (b)    What is a reasonable time

**18–30**    What is a reasonable time in any particular case will depend on the circumstances. It is thought that these will include the usual practical considerations surrounding a project of the type in question, such as: the

---

[83] *Matthey v Curling* [1922] 2 A.C. 180 at 197, CA and 238, HL; *Re King* [1962] 1 W.L.R. 632 (the point did not arise on appeal: [1963] Ch. 459).
[84] *Matthey v Curling*, above, at 197 (CA) and 238 (HL).
[85] *Vural v Security Archives Ltd* (1989) 60 P. & C.R. 258, in which Knox J. rejected the landlord's argument that the tenant was adequately protected by its right under s.83 of the Fires Prevention (Metropolis) Act 1774 to require the insurers to reinstate. The section is considered in para.18–40, below. See also *Adami v Lincoln Grange Management Ltd* [1998] 1 E.G.L.R. 58 at 59M.
[86] Cf. para.14–08, above.
[87] *Re King* [1963] Ch. 459; *Matthey v Curling*, above; *Farimani v Gates* [1984] 2 E.G.L.R. 66.

obtaining of planning permission and any other necessary consents and permissions; the preparation of plans, working drawings, specifications, bills of quantities and other documents; the seeking of tenders; the selection of a suitable contractor; and other similar matters. Where the party obliged to reinstate is the landlord, he must be mindful that the tenant is suffering probably a far greater loss than himself, so that he should feel serious urgency.[88] Moreover, although the obligation only arises on receipt of the insurance moneys, the reasonableness of the landlord's conduct must be judged on the basis that he will have known for some time that the problem will arise and is ready to take all necessary steps at once.[89]

It appears from the decision of Buckley J. in *Re King*[90] that delays caused by circumstances not in the contemplation of the parties at the date of the lease do not fall to be taken into account. In that case a lease of a factory granted in 1895 for a term of 80 years contained a tenant's covenant to insure and to lay out all insurance moneys received in reinstating or repairing the demised premises. The factory was severely damaged by fire and reduced to a shell. Owing to wartime and post-war restrictions, it could not be rebuilt. The judge held that the covenant imposed an obligation to reinstate within a reasonable time after obtaining the policy money from the insurers. However, he went on to say that what was a reasonable time had to be considered in the light of circumstances as they existed when the lease was entered into. Having observed that this was "long before the sort of difficulties in carrying out building operations which resulted from conditions during the late war were contemplated or thought of by anybody", he went on to hold that the difficulties in obtaining the necessary licences to rebuild the factory were irrelevant to the question of what period of time ought to be regarded as a reasonable time within which to reinstate.

It is by no means clear that the judge's view upon this point is right. Whilst the general principle is that contracts are to be construed by reference to the circumstances existing at the date they are made, this does not mean that the parties are to be denied any power of foresight at all. They may not have foreseen the precise difficulties that in fact arose. Nevertheless, they are quite likely to have foreseen that, in the course of 80 years, there would from time to time exist circumstances preventing the tenant from commencing the work of reinstatement immediately upon receiving the insurance money. That being so, it would have been perfectly reasonable for them to have agreed that the obligation to reinstate should be performed within such time as, having regard to whatever obstacles to the work existed at the material time, should be a reasonable one. It is thought that such a construction is more likely to have accorded with the intentions of the parties as reasonable men than that of the judge.

Personal circumstances will generally be irrelevant in deciding what is a reasonable time. In *Alghussein Establishment v Eton College*[91] the Court of Appeal had to consider an obligation in a development agreement that works would be commenced "so soon as is reasonably practicable". It was held that the

---

[88] *S Turner (Cabinet Works) Ltd v Young* (1955) 165 E.G. 632 (Pearce J.).
[89] *S Turner (Cabinet Works) Ltd v Young*, above.
[90] [1962] 1 W.L.R. 632 (reversed on other grounds: [1963] Ch. 459).
[91] [1988] 1 W.L.R. 587.

particular financial circumstances of the developer, and the question whether in commercial terms it was sensible to start building at any particular time, were irrelevant in deciding when commencement would have been "reasonably practicable".

### (c)   Where the disaster occurs shortly before the end of the lease

**18–31**   Difficulties may arise when the party covenanting to expend insurance money on reinstatement is the tenant, and the fire or other disaster occurs within a short time of the end of the term. The insurance money may not be received until after the term has ended; or there may be insufficient time for performance before the term ends. The question will then arise as to whether the tenant remains liable to do the work even though the lease has expired.

Whilst the answer in each case turns on the proper construction of the lease, it appears that generally speaking the tenant is so liable. Thus, in *Matthey v Curling*[92] a lease contained a tenant's covenant to insure and "to forthwith lay out all moneys to be received in respect of such insurance in rebuilding the same". A fire occurred on February 12, 1919, the lease being due to expire on March 25, 1919. The insurance moneys were not received until after the lease had expired. The tenant argued that, since the obligation did not arise until receipt of the insurance moneys, which had not occurred during the term, the obligation ceased on the expiration of the lease. A majority of the Court of Appeal (Bankes and Younger L.JJ.) held that the tenant remained liable to reinstate, even though that involved entering on the premises after the lease had expired. Atkin L.J. dissented, holding that the obligation could only be performed during the term, although he made it clear that, provided the "activating" event (i.e. receipt of the insurance money) occurred during the term, the fact that the remainder of the term was too short to enable the tenant to do the work did not relieve him of his obligation to pay damages for breach of covenant. He said:

> "If the events upon which the obligation arises occur during the term it seems to me that it matters not that the time for performance is short, even to a degree to make performance physically impossible. From such impossibility the law does not relieve. The lessee's position is precisely the same as in the case of the repairing covenants, in respect of which no one suggests that there would not be a breach though the premises were damaged or destroyed on the last day of the term."

In the House of Lords Lord Atkinson agreed with the view of the majority of the Court of Appeal. He said in his speech:

> "It has been contended that [the tenant] was bound to perform [the covenant to reinstate] before the termination of the lease, which of course was physically impossible. I do not know upon what principle of law this contention is based. The language of the covenant . . . appears to me to be quite inconsistent with any such construction of it. No particular time is definitely fixed within which this covenant must be performed. To hold that such a covenant must be performed while the lease is current would reduce it in many instances to a mere mockery. Dwelling-houses and mansion houses cannot be rebuilt by mere magic, and without that, it would be quite impossible to reinstate them, if they were consumed by fire within perhaps a few months of the end of the term of the leases under which they were respectively held . . .

---

[92] [1922] 2 A.C. 180.

> We have not been referred to any authority establishing that in such a case as this reinstatement must take place within the term of the lease. Nor have I myself been able to find one. Until I have been referred to it, or discovered it, I fear I shall remain of opinion that in the case of an ordinary covenant to reinstate, a covenantor shall in the absence of words expressly or impliedly fixing a time for the performance of his covenant, have what is a reasonable time under all the circumstances of the case for its performance, whether, in the case of a leasehold, that time extends beyond the term or the contrary."

The remaining Law Lords did not express an opinion either way.

If the tenant remains obliged to reinstate after the end of the lease, there would necessarily have to be implied a correlative obligation on the part of the landlord to allow the tenant reasonable facilities to do the work.[93] If the landlord fails or refuses to allow access then the tenant would no longer be obliged to do the work.[94]

## Time for performance of the obligation to expend insurance moneys on rebuilding or reinstating

Where the obligation to reinstate is absolute, it must be performed within a reasonable time of the occurrence of the damage (in the absence of express provision to the contrary).[95] What is reasonable is a question of fact depending on all the circumstances, and reference should be made to the discussion in para.18–30, above.

**18–32**

## What must be rebuilt or reinstated

In most cases the covenant to reinstate will on its proper construction require the reinstatement of the premises in the form in which they existed at the date of the disaster. The obligation will normally be to reinstate "the demised premises", or some similar formulation, and that expression will generally mean the premises in the form in which they are from time to time.[96] It follows that if the premises have been altered or improved since the date of the lease, then they must be reinstated in that state and not in their original form.

**18–33**

In some cases, however, the right construction may be that the obligation to reinstate applies only to the premises in the form in which they were when demised.[97] Thus, in *Loader v Kemp*[98] the premises when demised consisted of two storeys. The landlord covenanted:

> "[I]n case the said messuage or tenement, shop and buildings hereby demised, or any part thereof, be burnt down or damaged by fire, as soon as may be, at his own costs and charges, [to] rebuild and replace the same in the same state as they were in before the happening of such fire"

---

[93] Cf. para.22–32, below.
[94] See *Matthey v Curling*, above (in the Court of Appeal).
[95] Cf. *Farimani v Gates* [1984] 2 E.G.L.R. 66.
[96] See para.7–20 et seq., above.
[97] See para.7–22, above.
[98] (1826) 2 C. & P. 375.

The tenant subsequently added a third storey. The premises were then burnt down. Best C.J. held that the landlord was only obliged to rebuild the premises in the form in which they were at the date of the lease.[99] It is thought, however, that this will rarely be the correct conclusion in modern times, and that clear words will generally be needed to bring it about.

Difficulties sometimes occur in practice in relation to tenant's fixtures. Many insurance provisions are drafted so as to make it clear that the landlord's obligation to insure and reinstate does not extend to tenant's fixtures. In the absence of express provision, the question will depend on the proper construction of the lease as a whole. Given, however, that tenant's fixtures are often installed without the landlord's knowledge or consent, and that they may change from time to time, it is thought that the obligation is likely to be interpreted in the absence of clear words as excluding tenant's fixtures.[100]

## The meaning of "rebuild and reinstate"

**18-34**    Difficulties may arise in practice as to what constitutes performance of the obligation to rebuild and reinstate. One such difficulty is the extent to which the reinstated building must conform to what was there before. It will often be the case, for example, that building methods or materials will have changed since the original building was put up, so that slavish adherence to the original construction would be bad practice if not worse; or that the use of a particular method or material used in the original building will now be unlawful as being contrary to planning or building regulations; or that the planning authority will not allow precise reproduction of the original design. For example, fewer storeys, less site coverage or greater provision of car parking may be required.

The courts have tended to adopt a relatively strict approach to the construction of obligations to reinstate.[101] It appears that whilst exact reproduction of the original will not always be required, nonetheless only immaterial changes are permissible.

### (a)    Changes in materials

**18-35**    In *Camden Theatre v London Scottish Properties Ltd*[102] a lease of a theatre contained a landlord's covenant to insure and to expend all insurance money received in rebuilding and reinstating. A fire occurred which caused extensive smoke damage to the decorations in the auditorium. Certain of the mouldings in the auditorium had originally been decorated with gold leaf. By the time of the

---

[99] His reasoning was that "a landlord would be in a desperate situation, if he were bound to rebuild everything which his tenant may think proper to set up. He might be ruined".

[100] Cf. Ex p. *Gorely* (1864) 4 De D.J. & S. 477 (see para.18–40, below).

[101] See *Camden Theatre v London Scottish Properties Ltd* (Unreported decision of Nicholls J. dated November 30, 1984) and *Vural v Security Archives Ltd* (1990) 60 P. & C.R. 258 (both of which are considered below). For the meaning of "reinstatement" in other contexts, see *Low v Innes* (1864) 4 De G.J. & Sm. 286; *Lidle v War Damage Commission* (1949) L.J.R. 1069; *Schweder v Worthing Gas Light & Coke Co Ltd (No.1)* [1912] 1 Ch. 83; *Anderson v Commercial Union Assurance Co Ltd* (1885) 55 L.J.Q.B. 146.

[102] Unreported decision of Nicholls J. dated November 30, 1984.

fire some of this remained, and some areas had been touched up with gold paint. Following the fire the landlords decorated all the mouldings with gold paint. The judge held that this did not amount to reinstatement and that the tenant was entitled to redecoration in gold leaf despite the element of betterment which this would have involved. He said:

"[The landlords] submitted that reinstate means substantial reinstatement and that slavish adherence to what was there before is not required. [The tenant] submitted that in the case of a decorative finish reinstatement requires the decorations to be put back to the same design, layout and appearance as before, using materials of the same quality and kind. For my part, I doubt whether at bottom there is much difference between these two formulations. The adjective 'same' in [the tenant's] formulation of materials of the same quality and kind must, it seems to me, be read as not excluding immaterial variations in quality and kind, and I did not understand [counsel] to submit otherwise, for he said that common sense was of more assistance than dicta in various authorities dealing with the meaning of the word 'reinstate' in particular textual and factual [contexts]. So understood, [the tenant's] proposition does not seem to me to differ significantly from the rival formulation of 'substantial reinstatement' if one bears in mind that what is substantial is a question of fact and degree."

Later on in his judgment he said:

"I turn to the word 'reinstating' . . . That word, and the phrase 'full reinstatement value' earlier in the sub-clause, appear in the context of a long lease of a building intended to be used as a theatre, club or discotheque with restaurant or as a high-class gambling casino. The object of the [provision] was to secure that following a fire or the occurrence of some other insured risk, the policy money would be used in restoring the building—the use of synonyms cannot be wholly avoided—to its previous condition so that so far as the tenant was concerned it could resume its interrupted use and enjoyment of the property for one of the permitted uses. However, attainment of that object would not require restoration to be exact where exact restoration would obviously be pointless and serve no useful purpose for anyone. To take an extreme example mentioned in the course of argument: if a wall has been decorated several times over a number of years, reinstatement does not require that the successive layers of decoration be reproduced. Moving nearer to the instant case, consider a former church or theatre with mouldings on walls and ceilings decorated with gold leaf which is used by a builder as a warehouse for storing building materials, and suppose that that or a similar use is the only foreseeable use for the building. If the gold leaf in that building were to be obliterated by a fire I do not think that under a general obligation to reinstate the tenant could compel the landlord to redecorate with gold leaf those parts of the mouldings which had managed to survive the warehouse use and had retained their gilding till the fire. Such a course would be pointless, and nonetheless so if the builder genuinely but eccentrically wished to have gold leaf on the walls and ceilings of his warehouse."

In *Vural v Security Archives Ltd*[103] the demised premises consisted of a factory, **18–36** which had a beechwood parquet floor. The landlord covenanted to insure the premises against fire and to expend all moneys received on rebuilding repairing and reinstating the premises. The tenant used the factory for the manufacture of garments, for which either a wooden or a specially coated vinyl floor was important. The factory floor was destroyed by fire. At the time of the fire it was 40 to 50 years old but quite serviceable. The landlord proposed to reinstate the floor by laying heavy duty industrial linoleum. Knox J. held that this did not amount to reinstatement within the meaning of the obligation. In his view, whilst "slavish reconstitution of what was there before is not an inevitable ingredient in reinstatement", nonetheless the relevant question was whether the lino proposed

---

[103] (1989) 60 P. & C.R. 258.

by the landlord was as effective as wood for the floor of a factory in which high quality clothes were manufactured. He went on to say:

> "[F]or a substitute material to be acceptable it has in my judgment in relation to such a utilitarian object as a factory floor to produce as effective a result as the original. If the original material is appreciably more efficient a substitute will not in general constitute reinstatement even though it may be that the substitute is better value for money."

He held on the evidence that the several slight advantages which wood had over lino were just enough to justify the tenant's rejection of lino. In reaching that conclusion he held that the question of value for money was to be ignored

Both decisions emphasise that whilst exact reproduction of the original is not required, departure from the original is only permissible in limited circumstances. The question of when a substitute material may be used is principally one of fact and degree.[104] Where, as in *Camden Theatre v London Scottish Properties Ltd*, the decor of the premises is important to its use, a different material can only be used if exact reproduction of the original would obviously be pointless and serve no useful purpose to anyone. Where, as in *Vural v Security Archives Ltd*, the part of the premises in question is functional, the test is somewhat more flexible in that different material is permissible if the substitute material would be as effective as the original.[105] The question in each case is whether, having regard to all the circumstances, particularly the contemplated use of the premises and the role of the material in question in relation to that use, the substitute material can properly be said to amount to reinstatement.[106]

### (b)   Changes in design

**18–37**   It is thought that broadly the same approach applies in relation to changes in design as applies to the use of different materials. Immaterial changes in design are permissible, but only where the change is such that, having regard to all relevant factors, the new building can properly be said to be a reinstatement of the original. Thus, in *Low v Innes*[107] (a case concerning a covenant to pull down a building and rebuild a new one) Lord Westbury L.C. said:

---

[104] Thus, in *Lidle v War Damage Commission* [1949] L.J.R. 1069 Vaisey J. said: "It is, in my view, impossible to find any answer to the general question of whether, in making good war damage, it is permissible to substitute a different material for the material which was there before—except by replying that sometimes it is, and sometimes it is not. The replacement of stone by brick, wood by steel, tiles by slates, or paving stones by asphalt or gravel, would in some cases be the obvious and sensible and right thing to do; in other cases it would be an abomination or outrage. A hard and fast rule is absolutely out of the question."

[105] See also the example of the warehouse given by Nicholls J. in *Camden Theatre v London Scottish Properties Ltd*, above.

[106] See also *Re De Garis and Rowe's Lease* [1924] V.L.R. 38 (Australia), in which the landlord of a wooden building covenanted to rebuild in the event of destruction by fire. Building in anything except brick or stone was prohibited by a byelaw made after the lease (but under a statute which existed at the date of the lease). It was held, among other things, that the obligation to rebuild did not mean that the original materials had to be used.

[107] (1864) 4 De G.J. & Sm. 286.

"It was argued . . . that this word 'rebuild' involves the obligation of erecting the new house, not only on the same site, but in the same manner and in the same style and shape, and with the same elevation, as the old building. I think it clear that no such conclusion can be derived from the word 'rebuild'."

## Implied obligation to rebuild and reinstate

As a general rule, no covenant to reinstate or expend insurance money on reinstating will be implied merely from the fact that the lease contains a covenant by one party to insure. Thus, in *Lees v Whiteley*[108] a mortgage contained a covenant on the part of the mortgagor to insure but not to reinstate. It was argued that there was an implied covenant to expend the policy money in reinstating. Kindersley V.C., rejecting that contention, said:

**18–38**

"Can I imply [a covenant to apply the policy money in settlement of the mortgage debt or reinstatement of the premises] from the language of the [mortgage]? . . . on examination of the terms of that instrument I am of opinion that I cannot. Were I to do so I would be making a new contract between the parties. It was perfectly competent to the plaintiff to have stipulated that the policy moneys should be applied in liquidation of the mortgage debt or in the restoration of the premises, but he has not done so; and how can I say that the parties intended something which is not stipulated for in this instrument, or make for the plaintiff a better agreement than he thought it necessary to make for himself?"

It is thought that the judge's reasoning is persuasive and accords with the general approach to the implication of terms into contracts.[109] There may, of course, be cases where the language used by the parties makes it clear that they must have intended the party insuring to be under an obligation to use the proceeds of the insurance in rebuilding. Such cases apart, the moneys payable under the insurance policy will belong to the party insuring to do with as he pleases.

The position will be different where the insurance premiums have been paid by the other party, for the inference will then be that the policy was intended to be for the benefit of both parties. This was the case in *Mumford Hotels Ltd v Wheeler*,[110] in which a lease contained a landlord's covenant to keep the demised premises "adequately insured against comprehensive risks"; and a tenant's covenant to pay an insurance rent equal to the amount of the premium expended by the landlord under her covenant to insure. The premises were severely damaged by fire, and the insurers paid out to the landlord a sum in respect of the damage. The landlord argued that in the absence of an express covenant to reinstate she was under no liability to expend any of the insurance money on rebuilding. The tenant contended that there was an implied obligation to reinstate. Harman L.J. identified the true question as being:

---

[108] (1866) L.R. 2 Eq. 143. See also *Sinnott v Bowden* [1912] 2 Ch. 414; *Halifax Building Society v Kneighley* [1931] 2 K.B. 248; *Linden v Staybond Pty Ltd* (1984) 3 B.P.R. 9245.

[109] See paras 1–03 to 1–07, above.

[110] [1964] Ch. 117. See also *Beacon Carpets Ltd v Kirby* [1985] Q.B. 755, discussed at para.18–41, below.

> "[N]ot whether a covenant to reinstate should be implied, but whether the true inference is that Mrs Wheeler is to be treated as insuring for her own benefit or for the joint benefit of herself and the [tenant]."

**18–39** He went on to hold that the landlord was to be treated as having insured for the joint benefit of both parties, and therefore that she was obliged to lay out the insurance money in rebuilding. He said:

> "The strength of the [tenant's] case lies in its obligation to pay the premium, and its right to see that the policy is adequate. Why these provisions if it is to have no interest in the policy moneys? . . . In my judgment the true implication is that Mrs Wheeler's obligation to insure, done as it was at the tenant's expense, was an obligation intended to ensure for the benefit of both parties, and that Mrs Wheeler cannot simply put the money in her pocket and disregard the [tenant's] claim. She must, therefore, if called upon by the [tenant] to do so, use the money as far as it will go towards reinstatement of the property."

It is thought that the above decision is likely to be applied wherever the landlord insures and recovers the premium from the tenant by way of insurance rent. The inference in such a case that the landlord is insuring for the joint benefit of the parties may be strengthened by other indications in the lease, such as a provision conferring on the tenant the right to have a say in the identity of the insurers or the nature of the insured risks, or a provision requiring the tenant's interest to be noted on the policy.[111]

Difficult questions are likely to arise where the tenant covenants to, and does, insure the demised premises, and pays the premiums himself. It is not clear to what extent the principle in *Mumford Hotels Ltd v Wheeler* would apply, since there is no contribution or other act on the part of the landlord from which an intention to insure for his benefit as well could be inferred. However, the fact that the insurance is taken out pursuant to a covenant in the lease might be held to be sufficient, the giving of the covenant being part of the consideration for the grant of the lease, and its presence in the lease being difficult to explain if the landlord were not intended to benefit in some way. Again, the inference would be strengthened if the lease contained other indications that the landlord was intended to benefit from the insurance (such as the exclusion of damage by insured risks from the covenant to repair).

## Statutory right to compel reinstatement

**18–40** Even where the party insuring cannot be directly compelled to spend the insurance money on rebuilding, the other party may be able to bring this about indirectly by exercising his rights under s.83 of the Fires Prevention (Metropolis) Act 1774, which provides as follows:

> "And in order to deter and hinder ill-minded persons from wilfully setting their house or houses or other buildings on fire with a view to gaining to themselves the insurance money, whereby the lives and fortunes of many families may be lost or endangered: Be it further enacted, that it shall and may be lawful to and for the respective governors or directors of the several insurance offices for insuring houses or other buildings against loss by fire, and they are hereby authorised and required, upon the request of any person or persons interested in or

---

[111] See *Adami v Lincoln Grange Management Ltd* [1998] 1 E.G.L.R. 58 at 60D.

entitled unto any house or houses or other buildings which may hereafter be burnt down, demolished or damaged by fire, or upon any grounds of suspicion that the owner or owners, occupier or occupiers, or other person or persons who shall have insured such house or houses or other buildings, have been guilty of fraud, or of wilfully setting their house or houses or other buildings on fire, to, cause the insurance money to be laid out and expended, as far as the same will go, towards rebuilding, reinstating or repairing such house or houses or other buildings[112] so burnt down, demolished or damaged by fire, unless the party or parties claiming such insurance money shall, within sixty days next after his, her or their claim is adjusted, give a sufficient security to the governors or directors of the insurance office where such house or houses or other buildings are insured, that the same insurance money shall be laid out and expended as aforesaid, or unless the said insurance money shall be in that time settled and disposed of to and amongst all the contending parties, to the satisfaction and approbation of such governors and directors of such insurance office respectively."

The Act applies to the whole of England and not just to London.[113] However, it does not apply where the insurance is placed with Lloyd's underwriters, who are not an "insurance office" within the meaning of the section.[114] Neither does it apply where the cause of the loss is an insured peril other than fire.[115]

The insurers are bound to take the steps required by the section upon the happening of one of two events. The first is the making of a request by a person "interested in or entitled unto" the insured property. The second is where the insurers have grounds for suspecting that the owner or occupier or other insured party has been guilty (i) of fraud or (ii) of deliberately setting the insured property on fire. The landlord is clearly a person interested in or entitled to the premises. It is thought that the tenant is likewise included in these words,[116] not only where the subject-matter of the insurance is the demised premises but also where it consists of premises over which the tenant has rights, such as the common parts. In order to exercise the rights conferred by the section, a distinct request must be made to the insurers, before they have settled with the insured, to apply the policy money in rebuilding. Once the policy money has been paid over, it is too late.[117] The non-insuring party cannot himself rebuild first and then make a claim for the policy money.[118]

## Impossibility of rebuilding or reinstating

If the covenant to rebuild or reinstate is impossible to perform, then whether or not the covenant is discharged will be governed by the principles already considered.[119] The application of the insurance money in such circumstances will depend on the proper construction of the terms of the lease. A well-drafted modern lease will contain express provisions dealing with what happens to the insurance money. If there is no express provision, then the question will be

**18–41**

---

[112] This does not include tenant's fixtures: *Ex p. Gorely*, (1864) 4 De D.J. & S. 477.

[113] *Ex p. Gorely* (1864) 4 De G.J. & S. 477; *Sinnott v Bowden* [1912] 2 Ch. 414.

[114] *Portavon Cinema Co Ltd v Price* [1939] 4 All E.R. 601.

[115] *Vural v Security Archives Ltd* (1989) 60 P. & C.R. 258.

[116] *Wimbledon Park Golf Club v Imperial Insurance Co Ltd* (1902) 18 T.L.R. 815.

[117] *Simpson v Scottish Union Insurance Co Ltd* (1863) 1 H. & M. 618.

[118] *Simpson v Scottish Union Insurance Co Ltd*, above.

[119] See paras 18–17 to 18–26, above.

whether the correct inference in all the circumstances is that the parties intended the insurance to be effected for the sole benefit of the party insuring, or for their joint benefit.

In *Re King*[120] the tenant covenanted to insure the demised premises in the joint names of himself and the landlord, to lay out all insurance moneys received in rebuilding or reinstating, and to make up any deficiency out of his own money. Upon reinstatement becoming impossible, it was held by a majority of the Court of Appeal that the insurance moneys belonged to the tenant absolutely. This case was distinguished in *Beacon Carpets Ltd v Kirby*,[121] in which the landlord covenanted to insure the premises in the joint names of the lessor and lessee, and to expend all insurance moneys received in rebuilding or reinstating; and the tenant covenanted to repair, and to pay an insurance rent equal to the amount of the insurance premium expended by the landlord. The premises burnt down, and the insurers duly paid out under the policy. In the event the premises were never rebuilt, the parties eventually agreeing that the lease should be surrendered. The Court of Appeal held that the insurance moneys fell to be divided between the parties in shares proportionate to the value of their respective interests in the premises as at the date of the fire. Whilst each case must inevitably depend on its own facts, it is nonetheless thought that this is likely to be the correct result whenever the respective obligations are divided up in the same, or a similar, way as they were in that case.

## Section 18(1) of the Landlord and Tenant Act 1927

**18–42**   It is probable that a covenant on the part of the tenant to rebuild or reinstate after fire is a covenant to repair for the purposes of s.18(1) of the Landlord and Tenant Act 1927.[122] It would follow that the damages for breach of such an obligation are limited to the amount by which the value of the landlord's reversion has been diminished by the breach. However, a covenant to expend insurance money on reinstating is not within s.18(1).[123]

---

[120] [1963] Ch. 459.

[121] [1985] Q.B. 755. See also *Mumford Hotels Ltd v Wheeler* [1984] Ch. 117, discussed at paras 18–38 to 18–39, above.

[122] *Re King* [1962] 1 W.L.R. 632 (reversed on other grounds [1963] Ch. 459); *Farimani v Gates* [1984] 2 E.G.L.R. 66 per Griffiths L.J. Section 18(1) is considered in Ch.30, below.

[123] *Farimani v Gates*, above.

CHAPTER 19

# THE LANDLORD'S IMPLIED OBLIGATIONS TOWARDS THE TENANT AT COMMON LAW

## INTRODUCTORY

The general principles which govern the implication of terms into contracts have already been considered above.[1] This Chapter deals with the circumstances in which repairing obligations on the part of the landlord are implied at common law (as opposed to statute law), and the extent of those obligations. As will be seen, the general principle is that the landlord is under no implied obligation to repair. The circumstances in which repairing or similar obligations are implied all constitute limited exceptions to that principle.

    In an appropriate case, it may also be necessary to consider whether the landlord is liable in tort (for example, for negligently constructing or carrying out work on the premises[2]). The relevant law is outside the scope of this work and reference should be made to the specialist works on the subject.

19–01

## The general principle

The general principle at common law is that there is no implied covenant on the part of the landlord:

19–02

(1)    that the demised premises are reasonably fit for habitation or occupation[3];

(2)    that the demised premises are reasonably fit for the purpose for which they are let[4];

---

[1] See paras 1–03 to 1–07, above.

[2] The fact that a builder of defective premises is also the landlord will not prevent him from being liable in tort to the tenant or his successors in title if he would otherwise be liable under the general law of negligence: *Rimmer v Liverpool City Council* [1985] Q.B. 1; *Targett v Torfaen Borough Council* [1992] 3 All E.R. 27.

[3] *Hart v Windsor* (1844) 12 M. & W. 68; *Lynch v Thorne* [1956] 1 All E.R. 744; *Sleafer v Lambeth Borough Council* [1960] 1 Q.B. 43; *Duke of Westminster v Guild* [1985] Q.B. 688, approving a statement to this effect in *Woodfall: Landlord and Tenant*; *Tennant Radiant Heat Ltd v Warrington Development Corp* [1988] 1 E.G.L.R. 41; *Southwark LBC v Mills* [2001] 1 A.C. 1; *Lee v Leeds City Council* [2002] 1 W.L.R. 1488.

[4] *Sutton v Temple* (1843) 12 M. & W. 52; *Hart v Windsor* (1844) 12 M. & W. 68; *Manchester Bonded Warehouse v Carr* (1880) 5 C.P.D. 507; *Bottomley v Bannister*, [1932] 1 K.B. 458; *Edler v Auerbach* [1950] 1 K.B. 359 at 374; *Duke of Westminster v Guild*, above; *Southwark LBC v Mills*, above; *Lee v Leeds City Council*, above. See also *Gilbanks v Vancouver City* [1944] 3 W.W.R. 47 (Canada).

(3)    that the landlord will do any repairs either to the demised premises[5] or to the building of which they form part[6];

(4)    that the demised premises will last for the term of the lease.[7]

The general principle has recently been reaffirmed by the House of Lords in *Southwark LBC v Mills*,[8] in which Lord Millett, having referred to *Carstairs v Taylor*[9] and *Kiddle v City Business Properties Ltd*,[10] said in his speech:

> "The doctrine does not depend on fictions, such as the ability of the tenant to inspect the property before taking the lease. It is simply a consequence of the general rule of English law which accords autonomy to contracting parties. In the absence of statutory intervention, the parties are free to let and take a lease of poorly constructed premises and to allocate the cost of putting them in order between themselves as they see fit. The principle applies whether the complaint relates to the state and condition of the demised premises themselves or, as in the cases cited, of other parts of the building in which the demised premises are located."

One aspect of the principle is that the landlord is not liable in his capacity as landlord for defects in the premises which make them unfit for occupation or dangerous, even where he knows of the existence of such defects.[11] Thus in *Robbins v Jones*[12] Erle C.J. said:

> "A landlord who lets a house in a dangerous state is not liable to the tenant's customers or guests for accidents happening during the term: for, fraud apart, there is no law against letting a tumble-down house, and the tenant's remedy is upon his contract, if any."

The above passage was approved by the House of Lords in the leading case of *Cavalier v Pope*.[13] It has been said that the principle is to be kept in close confinement.[14] However, it was held in *McNerny v Lambeth Borough Council*[15]

---

[5] *Colebeck v The Girdlers Co* (1876) 1 Q.B.D. 234; *Ayling v Wade* [1961] 2 Q.B. 228 at 234; *Duke of Westminster v Guild*, above; *Southwark LBC v Mills*, above; *Lee v Leeds City Council*, above; *Carbure Property Ltd v Brile Property Ltd* [2002] VSC 272 (Australia) (in which the Supreme Court of Victoria refused to imply into a lease of a guest house an obligation on the part of the landlord to repair and maintain the structure during the term). Per Bankes L.J. in *Cockburn v Smith* [1924] 2 K.B. 119: "I want to make it plain at the outset that this is not a letting of a whole house, where, without an express covenant or a statutory obligation to repair the landlords would clearly be under no obligation to repair any part of the demised premises whether the required repairs were structural or internal and whether they had or not had notice of the want of repair."
[6] *Southward LBC v Mills*, above, per Lord Millett; *Gavin v Community Housing Association* [2013] EWCA Civ 580.
[7] *Arden v Pullen* (1842) 10 M. & W. 321; *Gott v Gandy* (1853) 2 E. & B. 845.
[8] [2001] 1 A.C. 1.
[9] (1871) L.R. 6 Exch. 217 at 222.
[10] [1942] 1 K.B. 269 ("[The plaintiff] takes the property as he finds it and must put up with the consequences": per Lord Goddard C.J. at 274–275).
[11] *Robbins v Jones* (1863) 15 C.B. (N.S.) 221; *Davis v Foots* [1940] 1 K.B. 116; *Cavalier v Pope* [1906] A.C. 428; *Cheater v Cater* [1918] 1 K.B. 247; *McNerny v Lambeth Borough Council* (1989) 21 H.L.R. 188; *Southwark LBC v Mills* [2001] 1 A.C. 1; *Jackson v J H Watson Property Investment* [2008] 1 E.G.L.R. 33.
[12] Above.
[13] [1906] A.C. 428.
[14] *Rimmer v Liverpool City Council* [1985] Q.B. 1.
[15] Above.

that the principle remains good law in the case of a "bare" landlord, that is to say, a landlord who let the premises without also being the builder.

## EXCEPTIONS

There are the following exceptions to the general principle:                     **19–03**

(1)   where an obligation to repair can be implied in accordance with the ordinary principles applicable to implied terms;
(2)   where the landlord retains ancillary property in his own possession and control;
(3)   where the letting is of a furnished house;
(4)   where the letting is of premises in the course of completion;
(5)   where the right granted is a licence as opposed to a lease.

These are considered in turn below.

## THE FIRST EXCEPTION: IMPLIED OBLIGATIONS TO REPAIR

The principles applicable to the implication of terms into contracts have already     **19–04**
been considered above.[16] Those principles apply as much to leases as they do to other types of contract.[17] In practice, special facts are likely to be required before the court will be prepared to imply a repairing covenant into a lease.[18] In many, probably most, cases the lease will contain sufficient express provisions relating to repair for the correct inference to be that the parties intended it to constitute a comprehensive code, leaving no room for the implication of further terms.[19]

In *Hafton Properties Ltd v Camp*[20] a lease of a flat contained a covenant on the part of a management company to carry out repairs and maintenance but no similar covenant on the part of the landlord. It further provided that if the company went into liquidation the landlord would be entitled (but not obliged) to undertake the company's obligations. The tenant argued that a term was to be implied into the lease to the effect that if the company failed to observe its obligations then the landlord would perform them for the benefit of the tenant. The argument failed. H.H. Judge Fox-Andrews QC said in the course of giving judgment:

> "Where it is sought to raise an implied term one matter to which the court should have regard is whether the lease provides a comprehensive code for the carrying out of repairs and the payment of them. The more comprehensive the code the less room there is for the implication of a term."

---

[16]  See paras 1–03 to 1–07, above.
[17]  *Liverpool City Council v Irwin* [1977] A.C. 239; *Barrett v Lounova (1982) Ltd* [1990] 1 Q.B. 348.
[18]  *Duke of Westminster v Guild* [1985] Q.B. 688, per Slade L.J.
[19]  *Duke of Westminster v Guild*, above; *Gordon v Selico Co Ltd* [1986] 1 E.G.L.R. 71; *Hafton Properties Ltd v Camp* [1994] 1 E.G.L.R. 67; *Adami v Lincoln Grange Management Ltd* [1998] 1 E.G.L.R. 58; *Lee v Leeds City Council* [2002] 1 W.L.R. 1488; *Reger International v Tiree* [2006] 3 E.G.L.R. 131. See also *Cowan v Factor* [1948] I.R. 128.
[20]  Above.

No implied term was necessary because the tenant had the right to enforce compliance by the company with its obligations, and even if the company went into liquidation, the tenant had a right to apply for a receiver and manager.

**19–05**    Likewise, in *Adami v Lincoln Grange Management Ltd*[21] the Court of Appeal rejected the tenant's argument that a long lease of a maisonette and garage contained an implied covenant by the landlord to repair the structure. Sir John Vinelott said:

> "The lease contains an elaborate scheme under which exceptional damage to the structure is to be covered by insurance effected in the joint names of the lessor and the lessee and maintained at the expense of the lessee; similar obligations are to be imposed upon the lessee of every other maisonette or flat in the block. The lessor is given power to enlarge the scope of the policy beyond fire and damage by aircraft, so as to enable the insurance to be extended at the expense of the lessee if it becomes apparent that damage to the structure may result from other causes ... In so far as damage to the structure results from an insured risk, there is simply no ground for importing any implied obligation to do more than lay out any insurance moneys coming into the hands of the lessor, in making good that damage (any deficiency in the insurance moneys being made good by the lessees).
>
> More generally, I can see no ground for importing any obligation on the part of the lessor to carry out works of repair to the block from causes which are not covered by an insurance policy effected pursuant to the terms of the lease ... in particular damage which might result from gradual deterioration of the structure during the term of the lease."

In *Lee v Leeds City Council*[22] two tenancies of council houses contained, respectively, the landlord's covenant to keep in repair the structure and exterior of the dwelling-house implied by s.11 of the Landlord and Tenant Act 1985,[23] and an express landlord's obligation to the same effect. Both houses suffered from condensation, but remedying the underlying causes was not within the ambit of the landlord's obligations because there was no disrepair.[24] It was argued that there should be implied into the tenancies (among other things) an implied obligation on the part of the landlord to keep the dwelling in good condition. The Court of Appeal rejected that argument. The tenancies already contained express or implied obligations to repair and to imply anything further would be to go beyond "the limits of permissible judicial creativity".

In *Janet Reger International v Tiree*[25] the court declined to imply into a lease of a ground-floor shop and basement, which contained an express covenant on the part of the landlord to use reasonable endeavours to maintain, repair and renew the structure, a further obligation on the part of the landlord to remedy any defective part of the structure that caused damage to part of the demised premises that the tenant was obliged to repair under its covenant.[26]

In *Gavin v Community Housing Association*[27] the claimant was the tenant of commercial premises on the ground floor and basement of a building, the upper parts of which had been converted into, and let, as residential flats. The tenant covenanted to put and keep the demised premises in good and substantial repair,

---

[21] [1998] 1 E.G.L.R. 58.
[22] [2002] 1 W.L.R. 1488.
[23] See Ch.20, below.
[24] See Ch.8, above.
[25] [2006] 3 E.G.L.R. 131.
[26] See further on this case para.19–17, below.
[27] [2013] EWCA Civ 580.

decoration and condition ands to decorate them periodically. There was no corresponding covenant by the landlord to repair the retained parts of the building. Its only express covenants were a covenant for quiet enjoyment, and a covenant to insure the demised premises and the development, and to lay out the insurance monies in rebuilding, repairing or otherwise reinstating the demised premises in the event of destruction or damage by an insured risk. The demised premises were damaged on a number of occasions by ingress of water or sewage from the retained parts of the building. It was held in the Court of Appeal that no obligation on the part of the landlord to keep the retained parts in repair, whether absolute in nature or dependent on negligence and notice, was to be implied.[28]

Even where the lease contains no terms relating to repair, the right inference is likely to be that the parties intended there to be no liability for repairs. Thus in *Demetriou v Robert Andrews (Estate Agencies) Ltd*[29] a weekly tenancy of premises intended to be used for the business of subletting rooms was granted to one of several partners. It contained no express repairing obligations on either party. The Court of Appeal allowed the landlord's appeal from the decision of the county court judge who had held that there was to be implied an obligation on the part of the landlord to do structural and external repairs. In his judgment Stuart-Smith L.J. pointed out that:

**19–06**

> "[I]t is a phenomenon, certainly known at common law, that there may be situations in which there is no repairing obligation imposed either expressly or impliedly on anyone in relation to a lease."[30]

A claim to a different implied term failed in *Habinteg Housing Association v James*,[31] in which it was argued that the landlords of a housing estate were under an implied duty to a tenant of a dwelling to treat the estate on a block basis to eradicate an infestation of cockroaches. The implied term was alleged to be "to take reasonable care to abate an infestation arising on the estate which could not be abated other than by the landlord taking timeous action in respect of all or any group of dwellings on the estate". The Court of Appeal held that no such term was to be implied. It lacked clarity of expression; it was not so obvious as to go without saying; and the agreement was enforceable without it.

The fact that the provisions of the lease contemplate that the landlord will do repairs, and confer express rights on him to enter the demised premises for that purpose, will not generally give rise to an implied repairing obligation on his part.[32] Similarly, the fact that the landlord has done repairs from time to time will not generally give rise to any implied obligation to go on doing them.[33] However, it has been suggested that the presence of a tenant's covenant to reside in the

---

[28] See further para.19–20, below.

[29] (1990) 62 P. & C.R. 536.

[30] See also *Ayling v Wade* [1961] 2 Q.B. 228, in which the same point is made by Danckwerts L.J. at 234.

[31] (1994) 27 H.L.R. 299.

[32] *Duke of Westminster v Guild*, above, per Slade L.J.

[33] *London Hospital Board of Governors v Jacobs* [1956] 2 All E.R. 603; *Sleafer v Lambeth Borough Council* [1960] 1 Q.B. 43; *Demetriou v Robert Andrews (Estate Agencies) Ltd (No.1)* (1990) 62 P. & C.R. 536. However, it may be that in special circumstances the landlord would be estopped from denying that he had assumed a liability to repair: see para.1–17, above.

premises by implication requires the landlord to do such repairs as may make it possible for the tenant to perform that obligation.[34]

**19–07**   In all the above cases, the attempt to imply a repairing obligation on the part of the landlord failed. However, the courts have been prepared to imply such an obligation in two circumstances:

(a)   where the lease is silent as to the maintenance of essential means of access;
(b)   where the obligation is implied as a correlative obligation to an express obligation of the tenant.

These are considered in turn below.

## Essential means of access

### (a)   The general principle

**19–08**   As a general principle, a landlord who retains in his own possession means of access or facilities which are essential to the proper enjoyment of the demised premises will prima facie be liable to take reasonable care to keep them in a state of reasonable repair and efficiency. Thus, in *Dunster v Hollis*[35] the only means of access to the demised flats was a common staircase, and Lush J. implied an obligation on the part of the landlord to take reasonable care to keep the steps reasonably safe.

The leading case is *Liverpool City Council v Irwin*,[36] in which a maisonette on the ninth and tenth floors of a tower block was demised under a written tenancy agreement. Access was provided by a staircase and two electric lifts. There was also an internal rubbish chute through which the tenant could discharge refuse for collection at ground level. The tenant's complaints, which were accepted by the trial judge, were that there was continual failure of the lifts, lack of lighting on the stairs, dangerous conditions on the staircase and frequent blockage of the chute. The tenancy agreement imposed obligations and restrictions on the tenant but was silent as to any obligations on the landlord. It was common ground that there was to be implied an easement for the tenants and their licensees to use the stairs, a right in the nature of an easement to use the lifts, and an easement to use the rubbish chutes.

The House of Lords held that repairing obligations on the part of the landlord in relation to the common parts were to be implied. Lord Wilberforce's speech contains the following passage:

"In my opinion, such obligation should be read into the contract as the nature of the contract itself implicitly requires, no more, no less: a test, in other words, of necessity. The relationship accepted by the corporation is that of landlord and tenant: the tenant accepts obligations

---

[34] *Sleafer v Lambeth Borough Council* [1960] 1 Q.B. 43 per Wilmer L.J. at 63; *Adami v Lincoln Grange Management Ltd* [1998] 1 E.G.L.R. 58 at 60L. But see *Lee v Leeds City Council* [2002] 1 W.L.R. 1488, considered in para.19–17, below.
[35] [1918] 2 K.B. 795.
[36] [1977] A.C. 239.

accordingly, in relation *inter alia* to the stairs, the lifts and the chutes. All these are not just facilities, or conveniences provided at discretion: they are essentials of the tenancy without which life in the dwellings, as a tenant, is not possible. To leave the landlord free of contractual obligation as regards these matters, and subject only to administrative or political pressure, is, in my opinion, inconsistent totally with the nature of this relationship. The subject matter of the lease (high rise blocks) and the relationship created by the tenancy demand, of their nature, some contractual obligation on the landlord."

Lord Cross, having referred to the general principle relating to easements (that the grantor is under no obligation to keep the subject matter in repair), said in a passage which appears to be of general application to common parts: **19–09**

"[M]ust it follow that the same principle must be applied to the case where a landlord lets off parts of his property to a number of different tenants retaining in his ownership 'common parts'—halls, staircases, corridors and so on—which are used by all the tenants? I think that it would be contrary to common sense to press the general principle so far. In such a case I think that the implication should be the other way and that, instead of the landlord being under no obligation to keep the common parts in repair and such facilities as lifts and chutes in working order unless he has expressly contracted to do so, he should—at all events in the case of ordinary commercial lettings—be under some obligations to keep the common parts in repair and the facilities in working order unless he has expressly excluded any such obligation."

In *Duke of Westminster v Guild*[37] the Court of Appeal regarded *Liverpool City Council v Irwin*[38] as laying down a prima facie rule applicable to all such cases, the implied landlord's repairing obligation being a "legal incident of the contract".[39] The principle is not confined to local authorities,[40] and there is no reason why it should not include commercial as well as residential lettings.[41] It depends for its application, however, on the tenancy being apparently incomplete. Hence, depending on the facts, it may be more difficult to apply where the tenancy contains detailed obligations on the part of both parties, but is silent as to the common parts. It may then be argued that the parties did not intend the landlord to be under any liability in respect of common parts, the tenant's remedy in the event of disrepair being to carry out any necessary work himself. It is thought that such an argument would only be likely to succeed on relatively special facts.[42]

In *King v South Northamptonshire District Council*[43] the demised premises consisted of a terraced house which had a front and rear access, the latter being from a footpath over which the tenant had a right of way. The tenancy agreement imposed obligations on the tenant but none on the landlord. The Court of Appeal implied an obligation on the part of the landlord to maintain the path. Mann L.J., with whom Sir George Waller agreed, approached the matter on the basis that: **19–10**

---

[37] [1985] Q.B. 688.
[38] [1977] A.C. 239.
[39] i.e. a term implied by law: see para.1–08, above.
[40] *Liverpool City Council v Irwin*, above, per Lord Cross at 259–260.
[41] See the passage from the speech of Lord Cross set out above.
[42] See also para.19–18 et seq., below.
[43] [1992] 1 E.G.L.R. 53.

"[T]he expressed terms of the tenancy, as derived from the conditions of tenancy, were incomplete. They were incomplete because they lacked any obligation upon the landlord at all. In order to give the arrangement a necessary bilateral character, the landlord's obligations have to be derived by implication of law."

The landlord's contention that the rear access was not sufficiently essential or necessary for a repairing obligation to be implied was rejected, on the footing that the rear access was for the removal of refuse and the delivery of coal and the like, and the house could not be enjoyed or function in accordance with its design without it.

Where the terms of the letting expressly include the use of a lift, but are silent as to any obligations concerning the lift, the landlord will generally be under a duty to provide a working lift.[44] Where the tenancy does not expressly confer the right to use a lift, but the lift is an essential means of access, the landlord will be under a duty to take reasonable care to keep it in working order.[45]

### (b)  The extent of the obligation to be implied

**19–11**  The implied obligation may take one of three forms: (a) an absolute obligation to keep the means of access reasonably safe; (b) an obligation to take reasonable care to keep the access in a reasonably safe condition; or (c) an obligation to take reasonable care to avoid exposing the tenant to a concealed danger or a trap of which he has no notice or warning.[46] Prima facie, the appropriate obligation will be (b). Thus, in *Dunster v Hollis*[47] Lush J. held that the landlord was under an implied obligation to take reasonable care to keep steps leading to the demised premises reasonably safe.[48] In *Liverpool City Council v Irwin*[49] the House of Lords rejected the tenant's argument that the implied obligation should be an absolute obligation to repair, holding that it was confined to taking reasonable care to keep the common parts in a state of reasonable repair and efficiency. Lord Wilberforce's formulation was as follows:

"It remains to define the standard ... if, as I think, the test of the existence of the term is necessity the standard must surely not exceed what is necessary having regard to the circumstances. To imply an absolute obligation to repair would go beyond what is a necessary legal incident and would indeed be unreasonable. An obligation to take reasonable care to keep in repair and usability is what fits the requirements of the case. Such a definition

---

[44] *De Meza v Ve-Ri-Best Manufacturing Co Ltd* (1952) 160 E.G. 364. It may be that, following *Liverpool City Council v Irwin*, the duty would be held to be to take reasonable steps to provide a working lift: see para.19–11, below.
[45] *Liverpool City Council v Irwin* [1977] A.C. 239. See also *Karaggianis v Maltown Pty Ltd* (1979) 21 S.A.S.R. 381 (Australia) (implied obligation on landlord of premises on sixth floor of a building to maintain and operate the lifts and escalators in substantially the same state and to the same extent as they were when the lease was executed).
[46] *Dunster v Hollis* [1918] 2 K.B. 795, per Lush J. at 796.
[47] Above.
[48] See also *MacNeill v Hi-Rise Development Ltd* [1974] 3 W.W.R. 296 (Canada) (landlord under implied duty to use reasonable care to keep the means of access in a reasonably safe condition, not merely to warn of hidden dangers).
[49] [1977] A.C. 239. The facts are set out in paras 19–08 to 19–09, above.

involves—and I think rightly—recognition that the tenants themselves have their responsibilities. What it is reasonable to expect of a landlord has a clear relation to what a reasonable set of tenants would do for themselves."

In some cases, however, the Court may be prepared to imply an absolute obligation to repair.[50] It is thought that this will only be done in exceptional circumstances.

The nature of an obligation to take reasonable care is considered in paras 19–19 to 19–22, below.

## Correlative obligations

Where a contract imposes an obligation on one party but is silent as to the obligations of the other party, the court may in appropriate circumstances imply an obligation on that other party correlative to the express obligation. The relevant test is whether it is necessary to imply a correlative obligation to make the contract work.[51] Repairing obligations on the part of the landlord may arise as correlative obligations in the following circumstances:

**19–12**

(1) where the tenant is obliged to pay for the cost of work carried out by the landlord, in which case the landlord may be under a correlative obligation to carry out that work;

(2) where the tenant is liable to carry out repairs but that obligation cannot be performed unless a correlative obligation on the part of the landlord to repair is implied.

These are considered in turn.

### (a) Where the tenant covenants to pay for the cost of works carried out by the landlord

Where one party expressly agrees to pay to the other the cost of performing a particular service, there may be a correlative obligation on that other party to provide the service. Thus, in *Barnes v City of London Real Property Co Ltd*[52] a lease reserved a fixed weekly rent for the cleaning of the premises by a housekeeper. It was held that the landlord was under a correlative obligation to provide a housekeeper to clean the premises. Likewise, in *Murphy v Hurly*[53] the

**19–13**

---

[50] See *King v South Northamptonshire District Council* [1992] 1 E.G.L.R. 53, in which the obligation implied by the judge at first instance, whose decision was upheld by the Court of Appeal, was to repair the footpath. The facts are set out in para.19–10, above. However, no argument appears to have been addressed to the Court on the extent of the obligation to be implied, and it may be that on the facts nothing turned on the distinction. See also *Barrett v Lounova (1982) Ltd* [1990] 1 Q.B. 348, considered in paras 19–15 to 19–16, below.

[51] *Duke of Westminster v Guild* [1985] Q.B. 688.

[52] [1918] 2 Ch. 18.

[53] [1922] 1 A.C. 369.

rent for certain holdings had been fixed and agreed on the basis that the landlords would keep a sea wall in repair. It was held that the landlords were obliged to keep the wall in repair.[54]

However, the fact that the landlord is entitled to recover the cost of a particular item does not automatically mean that he is under a correlative obligation to provide it.[55] Thus, in *Russell v Laimond Properties Ltd*,[56] a lease of a flat entitled the landlord to recover the cost of providing porterage services and maintenance staff, and of providing, maintaining and repairing a flat or other suitable residence for such staff as might from time to time be employed. It was held that the landlord was under no obligation to provide a resident porter. An important factual distinction between this case and *Barnes* is that in the latter, the tenant was liable to pay a fixed sum per week for the housekeeper come what may, whereas in *Russell* the obligation to pay only arose if a resident porter was provided.

In two cases, the courts have considered whether an obligation on the part of the tenant to pay for repairs carried out by the landlord gives rise to a correlative obligation on the landlord to repair. In *Edmonton Corp v Knowles*,[57] the tenant was obliged to pay to the landlord a sum in respect of the cost of redecorating the exterior of the property in every third year of the term. It was held that there was a correlative obligation on the landlord to carry out the redecoration.

The opposite conclusion was reached in *Duke of Westminster v Guild*.[58] That case concerned a drain, part of which ran beneath the demised premises and part of which ran beneath the landlord's adjoining property. The tenant covenanted (a) to repair the demised premises (including that part of the drain under the demised premises); (b) to pay the cost of repairs carried out to the demised premises by the landlords on the tenant's default; and (c) to pay to the landlords the fair proportion of the cost of repairing certain specified common items, including the drain. The drain became defective, and the question was whether the landlords were under any obligation to repair it. One of the tenant's arguments was that a correlative obligation to repair the drain was to be implied by reason of the express obligation to pay the cost of repairs.

**19–14**     The argument was rejected by the Court of Appeal. Slade L.J., giving the judgment of the court, held that the correct test was one of necessity, and there were the following four factors which pointed against any implied term: (a) the lease contained a number of careful and elaborate provisions relating to repairing obligations, and if the parties had intended the landlords to be under the suggested liability, prima facie the lease would have said so; (b) if the landlords were under an obligation to repair the drain, they would also have been under a similar obligation to repair the other items specified in the clause, and these would be obligations of an onerous and extensive nature; (c) the implied term would conflict with the tenant's express repairing obligation because a number of

---

[54] See also *Brikom Investments Ltd v Seaford* [1981] 1 W.L.R. 863, in which a similar result was arrived at by applying the principles of estoppel: see para.1–15, above.
[55] *Russell v Laimond Properties Ltd* [1984] 1 E.G.L.R. 37.
[56] Above.
[57] [1962] 60 L.G.R. 124.
[58] [1985] Q.B. 688.

the items mentioned in the clause, including part of the drain, formed part of the demised premises which the tenant had covenanted to repair; and (d) the implied term was not necessary to make the scheme of the lease a workable one. There was already a perfectly workable scheme, namely (i) the tenant was obliged to repair that part of the drain which was part of the demise, (ii) if he failed to do so, the landlords had the right to enter and repair it and charge the tenant with the cost, (iii) the landlords could, if they wanted, repair their part of the drain and charge the tenant with the cost, and (iv) if the landlords' part of the drain became out of repair, then the tenant had the right to enter and repair it by virtue of the principle that the easement to use the drain carried with it such ancillary rights as are reasonably necessary for its use and enjoyment. The court distinguished *Edmonton Corp v Knowles* on the ground that in the case before it, the tenant only had to pay if the landlord did the work, whereas in *Edmonton Corp v Knowles* the tenant had to pay whether the landlord did the work or not.

The position as a result of these two cases seems to be if what must be paid is a regular fixed sum in respect of work (for example, £100 per quarter in respect of the cost to the landlord of keeping the roof in repair) irrespective of whether such work is done, then a correlative obligation to do the work may be relatively easy to imply. If, however, the obligation is only to pay for the cost of particular work as and when it is carried out, a corresponding obligation to do the work may be harder to imply, particularly where the lease is an apparently complete bargain and the implied obligation is not necessary to make it work.

### (b) Where the tenant's repairing obligation cannot be performed unless a correlative obligation on the part of the landlord is implied

As a general principle, where an obligation of one party cannot be performed without something being done by the other party, a correlative obligation on the part of that other party to do the thing in question will be implied. The principle was formulated by Cockburn C.J. in *Churchward v R.* as follows[59]:

**19–15**

> "I entirely concur ... that although a contract may appear on the face of it to bind and be obligatory on one party, yet there are occasions on which you must imply—although the contract may be silent—corresponding and correlative obligations on the part of the other party in whose favour alone the contract may appear to be drawn up. Where the act done by the party binding himself can only be done upon something of a corresponding character being done by the opposite party, you would there imply a corresponding obligation to do the things necessary for the completion of the contract."

In *Barrett v Lounova (1982) Ltd*[60] the Court of Appeal implied a landlord's obligation to repair the exterior as correlative to a tenant's obligation to repair the interior. In that case a house was demised in 1941 for a term of one year and thereafter on a monthly tenancy. The tenant covenanted:

> "To do all inside repairs (if any) now required and to keep and at the expiration of the tenancy to leave the inside of the said premises and fixtures in good repair order and condition but fair wear and tear to be allowed at the end of the tenancy."

---

[59] [1865] L.R. 1 Q.B. 173.
[60] [1990] 1 Q.B. 348.

There was no landlord's covenant to repair the exterior. The Court of Appeal accepted the tenant's argument that an obligation to this effect should be implied. Kerr L.J., who gave the leading judgment, found the question "difficult and borderline". However, he held that an obligation to keep the outside in repair had to be imposed on someone in order to make the agreement workable, because (a) it was obvious that sooner or later the tenant's covenant to repair the inside could no longer be complied with unless the outside was kept in repair, and (b) the covenant imposed on the tenant was intended to remain enforceable throughout the tenancy, and would not cease to be enforceable if the outside fell into disrepair. In his view, there were therefore three possibilities: (a) the tenant was obliged to repair the outside as well as the inside to such extent as might be necessary to enable him to perform his covenant: however, this would be "unbusinesslike and unrealistic" in the case of a tenancy which was to become a monthly tenancy, and it would also be wrong to imply a covenant relating to the exterior when there was an express covenant relating to the interior; (b) a joint obligation to repair the exterior: that was "obviously unworkable"; and (c) an obligation on the landlord, which was "the only solution which makes business sense". Swinton Thomas J. took the view that:

> "[I]f the parties had been asked, in April 1941, whether such a term should be included in this particular tenancy agreement, which provides that the tenant shall be responsible for internal repairs, they would immediately and without hesitation have agreed that it should be so included."

**19–16** Two questions arise in relation to this decision. The first is whether the facts justified the implication of any term at all. The passage from the judgment of Cockburn C.J. in *Churchward v R.*[61] suggests that a correlative obligation on the part of one party should only be implied where the express obligation on the part of the other party cannot be performed without it. It is difficult to see that this was the case in *Barrett*. On the face of it, the covenant to repair the interior could still have been performed even though the state of the exterior might have made repairs to the interior more expensive and the necessity for them more frequent. Moreover, since the tenancy was for a year followed by a monthly tenancy, the tenant was not locked into performance of his covenant for a long time, but would be able to give notice to quit and leave if performance of the covenant became too onerous. In these circumstances it is thought that the tenancy was not unworkable without the implied term. In any event, as was pointed out by Sir John Vinelott in *Adami v Lincoln Grange Management Ltd*,[62] the cases in which correlative obligations have been implied were cases in which the tenant had agreed to pay for the work, and an obligation to repair the interior is not in this sense correlative to an obligation to repair the exterior.

The second question is whether, even if it was right to imply a term of some kind, the term implied by the Court of Appeal went further than was justified. On the face of it, what was implied was an absolute repairing covenant (although the contrary has been suggested[63]). If so, it is thought that it went further than was

---

[61] Above.
[62] [1998] 1 E.G.L.R. 58 at 60M.
[63] *Gavin v Community Housing Association* [2013] EWCA Civ 580 at [38].

necessary. The general principle which appears from *Liverpool City Council v Irwin*[64] is that the court will only imply such repairing obligation as is necessary to make the contract work. In that case the House of Lords rejected an absolute obligation to repair in favour of an obligation to take reasonable care.[65] It is thought that the most that it was necessary to imply in *Barrett* was an obligation on the landlord to take reasonable care to ensure that the exterior did not get into such a state as to increase what would otherwise be the burden of the tenant's obligation to repair the interior.[66]

*Barrett v Lounova (1982) Ltd* was distinguished in *Adami v Lincoln Grange Management Ltd*,[67] *Lee v Leeds City Council*[68] and *Gavin v Community Housing Association*.[69] In the first of these, Sir John Vinelott (with whom Hutchison and Butler-Sloss L.JJ. agreed) said that Barrett was to be taken as decided on its own special facts.[70] However, in *Holding & Barnes Ltd v Hill House Hammond Ltd*[71] Neuberger J. (at first instance) thought that the decision:

> "does seem to me at least to underline the fact that the court is, as it were, reluctant to conclude that a scheme of repairing obligations should leave open the obligation with regard to repairing the exterior."

In *Lee v Leeds City Council*[72] two tenancies of Council houses had been granted.　**19–17**
One contained the landlord's covenant to keep in repair the structure and exterior of the dwelling house implied by s.11 of the Landlord and Tenant Act 1985,[73] and the other an express landlord's obligation to the same effect. Both houses suffered from condensation, but remedying the underlying causes was not within the ambit of the landlord's obligations because there was no disrepair.[74] It was argued that there should be implied into the tenancies (among other things) an obligation on the part of the landlord to keep the dwelling in a condition which enabled the tenants to perform their obligations under the tenancy (which included, in the case of one tenant, an obligation to use the premises as her only or main home, and in the case of both tenants, an obligation to keep the interior of the dwelling clean and in a reasonable state of decoration).

The Court of Appeal rejected that argument. Chadwick L.J. (with whom Tuckey L.J. and Sir Murray Stuart-Smith agreed) regarded the principle that "there are circumstances in which it will be appropriate to impose on a landlord, on whom the obligation is not in terms imposed by the lease, an obligation to repair in order to match a correlative obligation expressly imposed on the tenant" as "not, I think, in doubt". However, he did not think that any further terms were

---

[64] [1977] A.C. 239.
[65] See para.19–11, above.
[66] Cf. the implied obligation in relation to retained parts: see para.19–18 et seq., below.
[67] [1998] 1 E.G.L.R. 58.
[68] [2002] 1 W.L.R. 1488.
[69] [2013] EWCA Civ 580 at [38].
[70] This has been said to be "a polite way of saying that it was wrong": see Lewison, *The Interpretation of Contracts*, 5th edn (London: Sweet & Maxwell, 2011), at para.6.14, fn.228.
[71] [2000] L. & T.R. 428 (the point did not arise on appeal: [2002] L. & T.R. 7).
[72] [2002] 1 W.L.R. 1488.
[73] See Ch.20, below.
[74] See Ch.8, above.

to be implied. His reasoning was essentially threefold. First, (unlike *Barrett*) both tenancies contained covenants to repair on the part of the landlord. The tenants' obligations were "to be performed in the context that the landlord is responsible for exterior repair". Second, s.8 of the Landlord and Tenant Act 1985 already implies a term as to fitness for habitation, but only in cases where the premises are let at a very low rent.[75] Since Parliament could not have overlooked the possibility that there will or may be cases where premises which are not fit for habitation are let for use as a home, it was to be assumed that Parliament had accepted in such cases that it was not necessary to impose on the landlord an obligation to ensure that the defects which lead to that condition are remedied and that the problem could and should be dealt with under the Environmental Protection Act 1990.[76] Third, an obligation to remedy design defects which led to excessive condensation and mould was not to be regarded as a necessary correlative to the tenant's qualified obligations in respect of internal decorative repair. In that respect:

"The tenant's obligations must be conditioned by the nature of the premises. If the premises suffer from condensation and mould by reason of some inherent design defect, then the tenant cannot be required to do more by way of decoration than is reasonable in those circumstances. To hold that the landlord is obliged to put the premises into a state in which they are free from condensation so that the tenant can decorate them would be to impose on the landlord an obligation which goes far beyond anything that can properly be regarded as correlative to the tenant's obligations."

*Lee* was applied in *Janet Reger International v Tiree*,[77] in which a lease of a ground-floor shop and basement contained a covenant on the part of the tenant to repair the demised premises, and a covenant by the landlord to use reasonable endeavours to maintain, repair and renew the structure. The basement suffered from damp caused by a defectively installed damp-proof membrane in the floor. The remedial works did not fall within the landlord's repairing covenant because there was no relevant state of disrepair.[78] The tenant argued that there was to be implied into the lease an obligation on the part of the landlord to remedy any defective part of the structure that causes damage to part of the demised premises that the tenant was obliged to repair under its covenant. The court refused to imply any such obligation. None of the tests for the implication of a term were satisfied. The term contended for: (i) was not reasonable and equitable, because it turned the landlord's right (under another provision of the lease) to make alterations and improvements into an obligation; (ii) contradicted the express terms of the lease, because some of the remedial work fell within the tenant's covenant and the suggested term therefore transferred work falling within the tenant's covenant to the landlord's covenant; (iii) was not necessary to give business efficacy to the lease; and (iv) was not obvious.

---

[75] See para.20–02 et seq., below.
[76] See para.20–67, below.
[77] [2006] 3 E.G.L.R. 131.
[78] See para.8–01 et seq., above.

## THE SECOND EXCEPTION: RETAINED PARTS

### The general principle

The landlord of a multi-occupied building owes a duty to take reasonable care to ensure that parts retained by him do not cause damage to the tenant or the demised premises. The general principle is as follows:

> "Where the lessor retains in his possession and control something ancillary to the premises demised, such as a roof or staircase, the maintenance of which in proper repair is necessary for the protection of the demised premises or the safe enjoyment of them by the tenant, the lessor is under an obligation to take reasonable care that the premises retained in his occupation and control are not in such a condition as to cause damage to the tenant or to the premises demised."[79]

**19–18**

Thus, in *Cockburn v Smith*[80] the demised premises consisted of the top flat in a block, the landlord retaining in his own possession and control the common roof of the block and the guttering. The landlord gave certain limited express covenants in relation to some of the common parts of the block, but none in relation to the roof and gutters. Due to blockages and corrosion in the guttering, the main walls of the flat became wet, and the damp affected various rooms in the flat. The landlord had notice of the defects in the guttering, but was dilatory in carrying out the necessary work. The Court of Appeal held that he was liable for damages.[81]

The principle has also been applied to means of access retained by the landlord.[82] It may apply even where the cause of the damage to the tenant's property is partly the tenant's own failure to comply with his repairing obligations.[83] However, it does not apply where the damage to the tenant's property is caused by a defect in construction that existed prior to the grant of the lease.[84]

### Nature of the obligation

The principle only applies where the defect in the retained part has resulted in damage. In other words, the obligation concerns not the maintenance of the retained part itself, but only the effect which a failure to maintain it may have on

**19–19**

---

[79] Woodfall, *Landlord and Tenant*, 28th edn (London: Sweet & Maxwell, 1978) which was expressly approved by the Court of Appeal in *Duke of Westminster v Guild* [1985] 1 Q.B. 688.

[80] [1924] 2 K.B. 119.

[81] See also *Carstairs v Taylor* (1871) L.R. 6 Ex. 217; *Blake v Woolf* [1898] 2 Q.B. 426; *Hargroves & Co v Hartopp* [1905] 1 K.B. 472; *Martins Camera Corner Pty Ltd v Hotel Mayfair Ltd* [1976] 2 N.S.W.L.R. 15 (NSW Sup. Ct.).

[82] *Dunster v Hollis* [1918] 2 K.B. 795. See para.19–08, above.

[83] *Tennant Radiant Heat Ltd v Warrington Development Corp* [1988] 1 E.G.L.R. 41.

[84] *Jackson v JH Watson Property Investment* [2008] 1 E.G.L.R. 33 (in which the landlord was held not liable for damage by water ingress caused to tenant's flat by defective concrete laying in the adjoining lightwell, which was present prior to the grant of the lease. The obligation could not be relied on "to impose what is, in effect, an obligation to put right faulty construction work by [the landlord's] predecessor in title.").

the tenant or the demised premises. Provided no damage is caused, it is no breach of the obligation for the landlord to allow the retained part to become out of repair.

This distinction appears clearly from the decision of the Court of Appeal in *Duke of Westminster v Guild*.[85] In that case the demised premises were served by a drain, part of which ran beneath the premises and part of which ran beneath the landlord's adjoining premises. The landlord's part of the drain became blocked, and the blockage prevented water from draining away from the premises. The tenant contended that the landlord was liable by virtue of the principle discussed above. The Court of Appeal rejected his claim. Slade L.J., giving the judgment of the court, said:

> "This is not a case … where there has been an escape of some dangerous, noxious or unwelcome substance from the landlord's premises to the demised premises. The situation in the present case is quite different. Here the essence of the tenant's complaint is that because of the lack of repair of the … drain, he has been prevented from discharging noxious water from his own premises on to the landlord's premises through the … drain. It is the water from the tenant's own premises which has caused the demised premises damage."

It was held in *Gavin v Community Housing Association*[86] that the obligation arises in contract as an implied term of the tenancy, rather than as an independent duty owed in tort. However, it was said in the same case that the precise juristic basis of liability may not matter in cases where the parties have a contractual relationship under the terms of the lease, because in such a case, whether the duty arises in tort or in contract, the court still has to consider whether the express scheme of repair or insurance imposed by the lease excludes any other form of liability which the law might otherwise impose.[87]

The duty can therefore be excluded or modified by express agreement. Likewise, it will be excluded where the express terms of the lease show that the parties did not intend the landlord to be under any, or any further, liability in relation to retained property. Thus, in *Gordon v Selico Co Ltd*[88] the tenant's argument that the principle applied was rejected because, having regard to the scheme for repair laid down by the lease, there was no room for implying any further terms. Slade L.J. said in the course of his judgment:

> "The repair and maintenance scheme provided by this lease is a very cumbersome one and we agree with the learned judge that, even if the lessors and their agents were duly to carry out their obligations, the scheme might not always suffice to give the lessees necessary and timely protection … Nevertheless, on a reading of the lease, we feel little doubt that it was intended, by all parties, to provide a comprehensive code in regard to repair and maintenance of the block. We are by no means satisfied that the implication of any further terms in this respect is necessary to give the lease business efficacy, or that the lessor, assuming it to have been a reasonable person, would have agreed without hesitation to the insertion of the suggested additional implied terms relating to the maintenance and repair of the block."

**19–20** In *Duke of Westminster v Guild*, the facts of which are set out above, one of the Court's reasons for rejecting the tenant's argument that the landlords were under

---

[85] [1985] Q.B. 688.
[86] [2013] EWCA Civ 580 at [31].
[87] [2013] EWCA Civ 580 at [31].
[88] (1986) 18 H.L.R. 219.

an implied obligation in respect of the drain was that the lease contained a number of careful and elaborate provisions relating to repairs.

In *Gavin v Community Housing Association*[89] (the facts of which are set out at para.19–05, above) the implied duty was held in the Court of Appeal to have been excluded by the existence of what was described as a comprehensive scheme under which the tenant covenanted to repair the demised premises, and the landlord covenanted to insure the demised premises and the building of which they formed part and to lay out the insurance monies in rebuilding, repairing or otherwise reinstating the demised premises in the event of destruction or damage by an insured risk.

By contrast, in *Cockburn v Smith*[90] the principle was held to apply in relation to a common roof, notwithstanding an express obligation on the part of the landlord to repair the entrance hall, staircases, passages and landings of the block. The Court of Appeal rejected the argument that this excluded any implied contractual duty in relation to the roof on the ground that the express term related only to parts of the block which the tenant had rights to use under the terms of the tenancy, whereas no such rights were granted in respect of the roof and gutters. Bankes L.J. said:

> "[T]he roof of the building, the means of excluding rain and water and of keeping the flat habitable, is not among the premises expressly or impliedly demised or granted. In my opinion, express agreements concerning premises demised or granted do not exclude tacit agreements concerning matters which are neither demised nor granted, and I cannot think either party contemplated that because the landlords had agreed to keep the entrance hall, staircases, passages and landings sufficiently lighted and in good repair, they should therefore be relieved of all duty to take reasonable care that the roof and gutters should not be in such a state as to render the demised premises uninhabitable."

## The obligation is to take reasonable care

The obligation is not an absolute duty to repair but a more limited duty to take reasonable care to see that the condition of the retained part does not cause damage to the tenant or the demised premises. It is based on negligence and notice.[91] It has been said to correspond in scope to the landlord's obligation to repair defects in the demised premises themselves which arises when facts come to his attention which would put a reasonable landlord on inquiry as to whether works of repair are needed.[92] It follows that the landlord will not be in breach unless it can be shown that reasonable care on his part could have prevented the damage.

**19–21**

In *Carstairs v Taylor*[93] the plaintiff was the tenant of the ground floor of a warehouse, and the landlord occupied the upper part. Water from the roof was collected by gutters into a wooden box, and thence via a pipe into a drain. The gutters and box were inspected periodically by a person employed by the landlord, and were last inspected on April 18. A rat gnawed a hole in the box

---

[89] Above, at [42-44].
[90] [1924] 2 K.B. 119.
[91] *Gavin v Community Housing Association* [2013] EWCA Civ 580 at [32].
[92] Ibid., at [35]. For a discussion of the obligation referred to, see para.22–16 et seq., below.
[93] (1871) L.R. 6 Ex. 217.

between that date and April 22, when a heavy storm occurred. Water passed through the hole in the box into the warehouse and damaged the plaintiff's goods. The court held that the landlord was not liable for the damage. Martin B. said:

> "[T]he defendant was under a liability to use reasonable care in keeping the roof secure, but he cannot be held responsible for what no reasonable care and vigilance would have provided against …
> … He certainly cannot be considered guilty of negligence, for he caused the roof to be examined periodically, and it was, in fact, examined and found secure only four days before the occurrence complained of. He has acted with care, and performed the whole of the duty that was cast upon him."

By contrast in *Cockburn v Smith*[94] the landlord was held to be liable in circumstances where he had been given express notice of the appearance of damp in the plaintiff's flat in October, but did not carry out any inspection until December, and did not complete the work to the roof until the beginning of the following February.

**19–22**   In *Southwark Borough Council v Long*[95] a local authority landlord covenanted to "take reasonable steps to keep the estate and common parts tidy". The Court of Appeal held that the obligation had not been satisfied by employing contractors, since there was no adequate system for monitoring the contractors' performance of their functions. Nor, where the lack of cleanliness consisted of the misuse by tenants of a common rubbish chute, was the duty performed by reminding tenants of the hours in which they were permitted to use the chute, since a large number of tenants could be expected to ignore the advice. The fact that the landlords provided low-cost public housing was relevant when interpreting its obligation, but basic standards of cleanliness could not be compromised, and the obligation could not be construed as excusing the landlords, on the ground of lack of funds, from taking steps which would otherwise be reasonable.

Whether the landlord has taken reasonable steps to keep retained parts in an appropriate condition is a question of fact which will depend upon the circumstances of each case. Relevant considerations will include: whether the landlord carried out such inspections and routine maintenance as often and as thoroughly as might reasonably have been expected of him; whether the defect which caused the damage would have been reasonably discoverable upon inspection; whether the landlord was aware of the defect, or ought in all the circumstances to have been aware of it; whether the landlord acted reasonably in entrusting performance of his obligation to agents or by employing reputable independent contractors, and if so whether he took reasonable steps to satisfy himself that they were doing their job; and whether the damage occurred at a time when the landlord ought reasonably to have discovered and remedied the defect.

---

[94] [1924] 2 K.B. 119. The facts are set out in para.19–10 above.
[95] [2002] 3 E.G.L.R. 37.

## THE THIRD EXCEPTION: FURNISHED HOUSES

### The general principle

A letting of a furnished house contains an implied undertaking by the landlord that the premises are fit for habitation at the commencement of the tenancy.[96] It was explained thus by Kelly C.B. in *Wilson v Finch-Hatton*[97]:

> "There is an implied condition that a furnished house shall be in a good and tenantable condition, and reasonably fit for occupation from the very day on which the tenancy is dated to begin, and that where such a house is in such a condition that there is either great discomfort or danger to health in entering and dwelling in it, then the intending tenant is entitled to repudiate the contract altogether."

19–23

The obligation is a condition of the tenancy. If it is unfulfilled on the day when the tenancy is to begin, the tenant may rescind and quit.[98] There is, however, no warranty that a furnished house will remain in habitable condition throughout the term of the letting,[99] nor is there any duty to inform the tenant of subsequent defects.[100] The fact that the tenancy contains an express tenant's covenant to repair will not necessarily prevent the implied term arising.[101] The implied term does not apply to unfurnished flats or houses, even if newly decorated such that the tenant is expected to move in immediately.[102]

### Circumstances amounting to a breach of the implied obligation

The question whether the premises are reasonably fit for habitation is one of fact and degree. It is clear from the cases that substantial discomfort or actual danger to health is required before the landlord is in breach of the implied term. In *Smith v Marable*[103] Parke B. said:

> "[I]f the demised premises are incumbered with a nuisance of so serious a nature that no person can reasonably be expected to live in them, the tenant is at liberty to throw them up."

19–24

---

[96] *Wilson v Finch-Hatton* (1877) 2 Ex. D. 336; *Powel v Chester* (1885) 52 L.T. 722; *Collins v Hopkins* [1923] 2 K.B. 617. In *Smith v Marable* (1843) 11 M. & W. 5, Parke B. based his decision on the wider (and incorrect) principle that there is an implied condition in a lease of every house that it is fit for habitation. However, the letting in that case was of a furnished house and his decision was correct on its facts: see *Hart v Windsor* (1844) 12 M. & W. 68. See also *Christie v Platt* [1921] 2 K.B. 17.

[97] Above.

[98] *Wilson v Finch-Hatton*, above; *Collins v Hopkins*, above.

[99] *Sarson v Roberts* [1895] 2 Q.B. 395.

[100] *Sarson v Roberts*, above.

[101] In *Wilson v Finch-Hatton*, above, the tenancy contained an express landlord's covenant to repair. The landlord's argument that this had the effect of excluding the implied term was rejected by the Court of Exchequer (see per Kelly C.B. at 343 and per Pollock B. at 345).

[102] *McNerny v London Borough of Lambeth* (1989) 21 H.L.R. 188.

[103] (1843) 11 M. & W. 5.

Likewise, in *Wilson v Finch-Hatton*[104] Kelly C.B. referred to the principle as coming into play where:

"[T]he house is in such a condition that there is either great discomfort or danger to health in entering and dwelling in it."

In *Collins v Hopkins*[105] McCardie J. said:

"What is the meaning of 'fit for habitation'? The meaning of the phrase must vary with the circumstances to which it is applied. In the case of unclean furniture or defective drains or a nuisance by vermin the matter is not, as a rule, one of difficulty. The eye or the nostrils can detect the fault and measure its extent."

**19–25**  Examples of circumstances held to have constituted a breach of the implied undertaking include infestation by bugs[106] and defective drains and filth in the cellar.[107] Ordinary wants of repair, which can be easily remedied, are not a breach of the implied term.[108] Infection by measles[109] and recent occupation by a person suffering from pulmonary tuberculosis[110] have also been held to amount to breaches of the undertaking. The test in relation to infectious diseases was stated by McCardie J. in *Collins v Hopkins*[111] as follows:

"[A] tenant [cannot] renounce his contract because of mere apprehension of risk or through mere dislike to the premises through the fact, *e.g.*, that a person has died upon the premises of smallpox or scarlet fever. He must show more than mere apprehension or dislike. In my view, the question in such a case … is this: was there an actual and appreciable risk to the tenant, his family or household, by entering and occupying the house in which the infectious disorder had occurred? If the risk be serious, no one, I think, could doubt that the tenant may renounce. But in dealing with bacilli which may mean illness and death, I think further that an appreciable measure of actual risk justifies the tenant in throwing up his contract."

However, having regard to advances in medicine, it may be that these cases would be decided differently today.

Further reference should be made to para.20–07 et seq., below, in which the meaning of "fit for human habitation" in s.9 of the Landlord and Tenant Act 1985 is considered.

---

[104] (1877) 2 Ex. D. 336.
[105] [1923] 2 K.B. 617.
[106] *Smith v Marable*, above.
[107] *Wilson v Finch-Hatton*, above; *Charsley v Jones* (1889) 5 T.L.R. 412; *Harrison v Malet* (1886) 3 T.L.R. 58.
[108] *Maclean v Currie* (1884) C. & E. 361 (cracked and fallen ceiling plaster).
[109] *Bird v Lord Greville* (1884) C. & E. 317.
[110] *Collins v Hopkins* [1923] 2 K.B. 617.
[111] Above.

## Possible limitations on the principle

It is to be noted that the decided cases in which the implied term has been held to         **19–26**
exist all concerned lettings of furnished houses or rooms for short periods.[112] In
*Wilson v Finch-Hatton*,[113] Kelly C.B. identified the question to be answered in
the following terms:

> "The question we have to determine is whether, on an agreement of this nature, which is an
> agreement for the letting and hiring of a house, in what is considered a fashionable district, at
> a high rent for three months at the height of the season, if the house prove not merely not
> habitable and not reasonably fit for occupation, but in some respect so unsuitable for the
> accommodation of those who intend to occupy it, that they could not reside in it, even for one
> night, without danger to their health, whether … in such a case the hirer … is at liberty to
> consider the agreement at an end, to throw the house up altogether, and to resist all demands
> for rent."

He went on to explain the reason for implying a term as to fitness for
habitation:

> "It is contended on behalf of the [landlord] that there is no implied warranty or condition that a
> furnished house shall be fit for the purpose for which it is let; but all the cases cited are cases
> of agreements for the letting and hiring of real property. Now the circumstances in which
> furnished houses are, and those in which real property is, demised, differ very greatly. Where
> real property, such as a house and lands, is taken by a tenant in a state so dilapidated as to
> require a large expenditure of money to put it into repair, to hold that the contract contained an
> implied condition that the lessor should put such premises into repair, would be clearly
> contrary to the intention of the parties. When, however, a person takes a furnished house for a
> brief period of time it is clear that he expects to find it reasonably fit for occupation from the
> very day on which he intends to enter, and the lessor is well aware that this is the view
> entertained by the tenant. If indeed this were not so, what limit could be imposed to the time
> during which the tenant might be kept out of possession, and how long would he have to wait
> while the value of his tenancy was daily diminishing?"

Pollock B. said in the same case:

> "If this were the case of an agreement for the letting of real property, the well established rules
> of law would apply, and they would force us to hold that the tenant could not succeed in this
> case; but although in the case of a furnished house many of the incidents which attach to a
> demise of realty may be applicable, inasmuch as rent does in a sense, issue out of the realty,
> still the rent to be paid for a furnished house such as this is not merely rent for the use of the
> realty, but a sum paid for the accommodation afforded by the use of the house, with all its
> appurtenances and contents, during the particular period of three months for which it is taken."

The above passages suggest that the principle only applies to lettings of furnished         **19–27**
accommodation for relatively short periods. This is consistent with *Chester v
Powell*,[114] in which Bacon V.C. limited the application of the principle to lettings
of furnished apartments at the seaside or for temporary accommodation only. It is
questionable to what extent a modern court would be prepared to imply a term of
fitness for habitation into a letting of furnished premises for a substantial term,

---

[112] For example, *Smith v Marable* (1843) 11 M. & W. 5 (five or six weeks); *Wilson v Finch-Hatton*
(1877) 2 Ex. D. 336 (three months); *Collins v Hopkins* [1923] 2 K.B. 617 (26 weeks).
[113] Above.
[114] (1885) 52 L.T. 722.

particularly where the tenancy contains express repairing obligations on the part of the tenant. It is thought that the principle does not apply automatically to every letting of furnished premises, but only to lettings where the circumstances show clearly that a fundamental part of the bargain was that the premises would be fit for immediate occupation on the first day of the term.

## THE FOURTH EXCEPTION: LETTING OF PREMISES IN THE COURSE OF COMPLETION

### The general principle

**19–28**   A lease of a house entered into whilst the house is in the course of completion contains an implied covenant on the part of the landlord that it will be fit for habitation when completed.[115] In *Perry v Sharon Development Co Ltd*[116] Romer L.J. formulated the general rule as follows:

> "[I]n the case of a sale of a completed house, there is to be implied on the part of the vendor no warranty as to the house being in any particular condition. The same rule would apply in the case of an uncompleted house, which is the subject matter of a sale, where the structure stands at the time of the sale. Where, however, the contract is for the sale of a house when completed, there is an implied contract on the part of the vendor, in the absence of there being any express contract as to the way in which the house is to be completed, that the house shall be completed in such a way that it is fit for human habitation."

The reason for the rule was set out by MacKinnon L.J. in the same case:

> "[T]he contract is not merely a contract to sell, but also a contract to do building work, and, insofar as it is a contract to do building work it is only natural and proper that there should be an implied undertaking that the building work should be done properly."

The principle does not apply where the agreement contains an express term dealing with the way in which the premises are to be completed, for the express term will then oust the implied one.[117] Furthermore, the principle only applies where the agreement between the parties expressly or impliedly contemplates that the house will be finished by the landlord. No term will be implied where the house is complete at the date of the agreement,[118] or where the work is to be completed by the tenant. Whether the house is to be regarded as in the course of construction for the purposes of the rule is a question of fact. *Perry v Sharon Development Co Ltd*[119] concerned an agreement for the purchase of a house "erected or in the course of erection", the purchase to be completed on a specified date or "so soon thereafter as the premises shall be completely finished and ready for occupation". At the time of the agreement the house lacked water taps, baths,

---

[115] *Miller v Cannon Hill Estates Ltd* [1931] 2 K.B. 113; *Perry v Sharon Development Co Ltd* [1937] 4 All E.R. 390; *Jennings v Tavener* [1955] 2 All E.R. 769; *Lynch v Thorne* [1956] 1 All E.R. 744; *Hancock v B W Brazier (Anerley)* [1966] 1 W.L.R. 1317. These cases concerned freehold sales but it is thought that there is no reason why the same principle should not apply to lettings.

[116] Above.

[117] *Lynch v Thorne*, above.

[118] *Hoskins v Woodham* [1938] 1 All E.R. 692.

[119] [1937] 4 All E.R. 390.

grates, an electric meter and a lavatory seat, some of the plastering was incomplete, and no decorating had been done. It was held that the construction of the house was sufficiently incomplete for the principle to apply. Where the principle applies, the implied obligation is not limited to work carried out after the agreement but includes work already carried out by the time the agreement is entered into.[120]

It is thought that the implied covenant is not limited to dwelling-houses. There seems no reason in principle why leases of commercial premises in the course of erection, where the parties intend that the work should be finished by the landlord, should not contain a similar implied covenant on the part of the landlord that on completion of the work the premises will be reasonably fit for their contemplated use by the tenant.

## What amounts to a breach

What constitutes a breach of the implied term is a question of fact. An example of **19–29** a case where a breach was held to have been committed is *Jennings v Tavener*,[121] which concerned a bungalow built by the vendor. After it had been completed cracks began to appear in the structure. These were caused by the withdrawal of moisture from the site by the roots of poplar trees in an adjoining cemetery. The vendor had failed to construct the foundations in such a way that this would not happen. He was held liable under the implied covenant that the bungalow would be fit for habitation when completed.

## THE FIFTH EXCEPTION: LICENCES

## Implied term as to fitness for purpose

Although licences are strictly outside the scope of this work, it is right to note that **19–30** in certain circumstances the courts may be prepared to imply terms as to fitness into contractual licences that would probably not be implied had the interest granted been a lease. Thus, in *Wettern Electric Ltd v Welsh Development Agency*[122] a licence of a factory unit was granted for 12 months. The unit had been built on the instructions of the licensor shortly before the licence was granted. The purpose of the licence was to enable the licensees to carry on and expand their business while their existing factory was being enlarged. Shortly after the grant of the licence serious structural defects began to appear, and six months later the unit had become so dangerous that it had to be vacated. Judge Newey QC held that a term should be implied into the licence that the premises were of sound construction and reasonably suitable for the purposes required by the licensee. This should be contrasted with *Morris-Thomas v Petticoat Lane*

---

[120] *Perry v Sharon Development Co Ltd*, above, per Romer L.J. at 395A; *Hancock v B.M. Brazier (Anerley) Ltd* [1966] 1 W.L.R. 1317.
[121] [1955] 2 All E.R. 769.
[122] [1983] Q.B. 796.

*Rentals Ltd*,[123] in which a licence of a former oven was granted to enable the licensee to store antiques, and the Court of Appeal refused to imply a term that the oven should be fit for the sale and storage at all times of antiques and other items.

---

[123] (1987) 53 P. & C.R. 238.

CHAPTER 20

# THE LANDLORD'S IMPLIED OBLIGATIONS TOWARDS THE TENANT UNDER STATUTE

## INTRODUCTORY

For reasons of public policy, statute has intervened in the relationship between landlords and tenants of certain sorts of property in defined circumstances by imposing on the landlord statutory obligations to repair. Contracting out of these obligations is either forbidden, or is permitted only in limited circumstances. The statutory obligations concerning certain dwelling houses, which were formerly contained in various Housing Acts, have now been consolidated in the Landlord and Tenant Act 1985.

**20–01**

## SECTION 8 OF THE LANDLORD AND TENANT ACT 1985: LETTINGS OF HOUSES AT A LOW RENT[1]

### When the section applies

Section 8 of the 1985 Act is printed in Appendix II, below. It applies where:

**20–02**

(1)    there is a contract for the letting of a house for human habitation[2];
(2)    the annual rent does not exceed the statutory limit[3];
(3)    the letting is not for a term of three years or more (the lease not being determinable at the option of either party before the expiration of three years) on terms that the tenant puts the premises into a condition reasonably fit for human habitation.[4]

These will now be considered in turn.

### (a)    A contract for the letting of a house for human habitation

The letting must be for residential purposes, although it does not appear to be necessary that the intended residential occupier should be the tenant himself.[5]

**20–03**

---

[1] For the legislative history of s.8, see *Lee v Leeds City Council* [2002] 1 W.L.R. 1488.
[2] Landlord and Tenant Act 1985 s.8(1).
[3] 1985 Act ss.8(3)(a) and (4).
[4] 1985 Act ss.8(3)(b) and (5).
[5] This is suggested by s.8(2) of the Act, which confers on the landlord a right of entry on giving 24 hours' written notice to the "tenant or occupier".

The letting may be oral.[6] Notwithstanding dicta to the contrary,[7] it is thought that the section applies to a statutory tenancy under the Rent Act 1977, since the statutory implied term would be imported into the statutory tenancy by virtue of s.3(1) of that Act.

"House" includes a part of a house, and any yard, garden, outhouses and appurtenances belonging to the house or usually enjoyed with it.[8] There is no statutory definition of "house" but it is thought that any building which as a matter of ordinary language can reasonably be called a house would be included.[9] Thus, the section would apply to a flat in a converted house. It is probable that it would also apply to living accommodation above a shop, whether or not the building was originally built as a house and later converted to a shop, or was purpose-built with living accommodation.[10] It is thought, however, that a purpose-built tower block would not constitute a house, so that a letting of a flat within it would not fall within the section.[11]

### (b)    The rent must not exceed the statutory limit

**20–04**    The statutory rent limits are as shown in the following table:[12]

| Date of making of contract | Rent limit |
| --- | --- |
| Before July 31, 1923 | In London: £40 |
| | Elsewhere: £26 or £16 |
| | (see Note 1.) |
| On or after July 31, 1923 and before July 31, 1957 | In London: £40 |
| | Elsewhere: £26 |
| On or after July 31, 1957 | In London: £80 |
| | Elsewhere: £52 |

**Notes**

1.    The applicable figure for contracts made before July 31, 1923, is £26 in the case of premises situated in a borough or urban district which at the date of

---

[6] *Rousou v Photi* [1940] 2 K.B. 379.

[7] See *Strood Estates Ltd v Gregory* [1936] 2 K.B. 605, per Sir Boyd Merriman P.

[8] Landlord and Tenant Act 1985 s.8(6).

[9] Cf. s.2(1) of the Leasehold Reform Act 1967, by virtue of which "house" includes "any building designed or adapted for living in and reasonably so called". See *Day v Hosebay Ltd* [2012] 1 W.L.R. 2884 (Supreme Court).

[10] Cf. *Lake v Bennett* [1970] 1 Q.B. 663 and *Tandon v Trustees of Spurgeon's Homes* [1982] A.C. 755.

[11] Cf. *Magnohard Ltd v Earl Cadogan* [2013] 1 W.L.R. 24.

[12] The table is taken verbatim from s.8(4) of the Act.

the contract had according to the last published census a population of 50,000 or more. In the case of a house situated elsewhere, the figure is £16.
2.	The references to "London" are, in relation to contracts made before April 1, 1965, to the administrative county of London and, in relation to contracts made on or after that date, to Greater London exclusive of the outer London boroughs.

The table does not in terms say that the figures are annual figures, but it has never been suggested that anything else is meant. However, the fact that the rent is something other than an annual rent (for example, a weekly rent) does not prevent the section applying.[13] "Rent" means the total sum payable under the tenancy, and no deduction is to be made in respect of rates or other outgoings which the landlord may have agreed to pay.[14] It was argued in *Rousou v Photi*[15] that in the case of a weekly rent it would not be right to take a multiplier of 52 in order to arrive at an annual equivalent, because allowance would have to be made for periods when the house is empty. The Court of Appeal declined to decide the point, although it made it clear that the onus of establishing a multiplier other than 52 would be on the tenant. However, in *Whitcombe v Pollock*[16] it was held that the correct multiplier where the rent was payable weekly was 52.

It is not clear to what extent "rent" is intended to include service charges. This is of importance in relation to long leases at nominal ground rents, which commonly include service charge provisions. If, for the purposes of s.8, rent excludes service charges, then a number of such leases will be within the section. It seems unlikely that this was the intention of Parliament. At common law, rent properly so called would not include service charges. However, for the purposes of the low rent provisions of the Rent Act 1977,[17] "rent" has been held to mean "not rent in the strict sense, but the total payment under the instrument of letting",[18] so that a separate sum payable by way of service charge is included.[19] It is thought that the same must be the case in relation to s.8.[20]

---

[13] *Rousou v Photi* [1940] 1 K.B. 299 (Atkinson J.). The point that the section does not apply at all where the rent is not an annual rent was left open in the Court of Appeal ([1940] 2 K.B. 379, where the decision of Atkinson J. was reversed on another point), although Sir Wilfred Greene M.R. foresaw "difficulties in the way of taking that view", and saw no reason to differ from the view taken by Atkinson J.

[14] *Rousou v Photi* [1940] 2 K.B. 379, CA. *Jones v Nelson* [1938] 2 All E.R. 171 must be treated as overruled.

[15] Above.

[16] [1956] J.P.L. 896 (a decision of the Liverpool Court of Passage). See, however, the Irish case of *Kirkpatrick v Watson* [1943] Ir. Jur. Rep. 4 (not cited in *Whitcombe v Pollock*) in which it was held that the annual equivalent of a weekly rent of 10s. is £26 1s. 5d.

[17] Rent Act 1977 s.5(1).

[18] *Wilkes v Goodwin* [1923] 2 K.B. 86, per Younger L.J. at 105.

[19] *Property Holding Co Ltd v Clark* [1948] 1 K.B. 630.

[20] This is supported by the decision in *Rousou v Photi*, above, to the effect that "rent" means the actual sum payable by the tenant, irrespective of whether it includes rates.

### (c)   Lettings outside the section

**20–05**  The section does not apply where the house is let for a term of three years or more (the lease not being determinable at the option of either party before the expiration of three years) upon terms that the tenant puts the premises into a condition reasonably fit for human habitation.[21] It is thought that the term would be measured from the date on which the tenancy is actually granted and not from any earlier date from which the term is expressed to commence.[22] The reference to an option is probably to an unfettered option.[23] Thus, for example, an option for either party to determine the lease in the event of the death of the landlord would not count.[24]

## What terms are implied

**20–06**  Where s.8 applies, the following terms are implied:

(1)   a condition that the house is fit for human habitation at the commencement of the tenancy[25];

(2)   an undertaking that the house will be kept by the landlord fit for human habitation during the tenancy.[26]

Contracting out is not permitted.[27]

## The meaning of "fit for human habitation"

**20–07**  The Act contains a statutory definition of what is meant by fitness for human habitation.[28] However, the statutory implied terms as to fitness for human habitation first made their appearance in the 19th century,[29] but the statutory definition did not appear until 1957.[30] Prior to then, the courts had been left to work out for themselves what constituted unfitness for human habitation. It is not thought that the basic standard laid down by the courts has been altered, but cases decided prior to 1957 must be read subject to the limitation that no statutory definition then existed.

---

[21] Landlord and Tenant Act 1985 s.8(5).
[22] See *Bradshaw v Pawley* [1980] 1 W.L.R. 10 and the cases there cited. See also para.20–19 below.
[23] Cf. *Parker v O'Connor* [1974] 1 W.L.R. 1160 (a decision on a similar provision in s.12(2)(b) of the Act, discussed in para.20–19, below).
[24] See *Parker v O'Connor*, above.
[25] Landlord and Tenant Act 1985 s.8(1)(a).
[26] 1985 Act s.8(1)(b).
[27] 1985 Act s.8(1), by virtue of which the terms implied by subs.(1) are implied "notwithstanding any stipulation to the contrary".
[28] 1985 Act s.10. See para.20–08, below.
[29] See *Summers v Salford Corp* [1943] A.C. 283 at 285 for a list of the relevant 19th-century statutes.
[30] Housing Act 1957 s.4(1). The requirement to have regard to internal arrangement was added by the Housing Act 1969 s.71.

### (a)    The statutory definition

In determining for the purposes of the Act whether a house is unfit for human     **20–08**
habitation, regard must be had to its condition in respect of the following matters:

(1)    repair;
(2)    stability;
(3)    freedom from damp;
(4)    internal arrangement;
(5)    natural lighting;
(6)    ventilation;
(7)    water supply;
(8)    drainage and sanitary conveniences;
(9)    facilities for preparation and cooking of food and for the disposal of waste
       water.[31]

However, not every defect in one or more of the above respects will render the
house unfit for human habitation. It will be so unfit if, and only if, it is so far
defective in one or more of those matters that it is not reasonably suitable for
occupation in that condition.[32] In considering whether the house is unfit, the
correct approach is to consider whether the defects, taken in the round, mean that
the premises are not reasonably suitable for occupation.[33]

### (b)    Decisions on fitness for human habitation[34]

The basic standard laid down by the courts appears from the following passage     **20–09**
from the judgment of Salter J. in *Jones v Geen*[35]:

> "[T]he standard of repair ... is ... a humble standard. It is only required that the place must be
> decently fit for human beings to live in."

In *Summers v Salford Corp*[36] a sash cord in the only window in one of the two
bedrooms in a four-roomed house broke and the window jammed. Two months
later, when the tenant was cleaning the window, the remaining cord broke, and
the upper sash fell, crushing her hands between the two sashes and trapping her
for 20–30 minutes before she was released. She lost the use of her left hand, and

---

[31] Landlord and Tenant Act 1985 s.10.
[32] 1985 Act s.10.
[33] *Wyse v Secretary of State for the Environment* [1984] J.P.L. 256.
[34] Reference should also be made to the cases decided under s.1 of the Defective Premises Act 1972
(which imposes on a person taking on work for or in connection with the provision of a dwelling a
duty to see that the work which he takes on is done in a workmanlike or, as the case may be,
professional manner, with proper materials and so that as regards that work the dwelling will be fit for
habitation when completed): see, for example, *Bole v Huntsbuild* [2009] EWHC 483 (TCC) and
[2009] EWCA Civ 1146 (Court of Appeal); *Harrison v Shepherd Homes* [2011[ EWCA 1811 (on
appeal: [2012] EWCA Civ 904).
[35] [1925] 1 K.B. 659.
[36] [1943] A.C. 283.

her general health suffered seriously. The House of Lords, reversing the Court of Appeal, held that the house was unfit for human habitation, so that the landlord was liable. Lord Atkin said:

> "The test of the obligation cannot simply be whether, with the disrepair complained of, the tenant can live in the house ... It must not be measured by the magnitude of the repairs required. A burst or leaking pipe, a displaced slate or tile, a stopped drain, a rotten stair tread, may each of them until repair make a house unfit to live in, though each of them may be quickly and cheaply repaired."

He went on to quote from his dissenting judgment in *Morgan v Liverpool Corp*:[37]

> "If the state of repair of a house is such that by ordinary use damage may naturally be caused to the occupier, either in respect of personal injury to life or limb or injury to health, then the house is not in all respects reasonably fit for human habitation."

In holding that the broken sash cord constituted a breach of the obligation he said:

> "[T]he breaking of one sash cord necessarily involved the strong possibility that its fellow cord, especially with the extra strain imposed on it would also break, with the further certainty of danger to anyone handling the window at the time of the break and with the further certainty that until repair that window must either remain permanently closed or permanently open. Either event would prevent that room from being reasonably fit for occupation, and, as this room was one of only two bedrooms, it appears to me clear that until repair the whole house would properly be described as unfit for occupation by a working class family."

A fall of plaster from the ceiling has been held to constitute unfitness for human habitation,[38] and so has a defective lavatory and guttering.[39] Occasional invasion by rats from outside has been held not to be a breach, but the contrary might have been the case if the house was infested in the sense that the rats bred there, were regularly there and, as it were, formed part of the house.[40] A defective hot water system has been held not to amount to unfitness where there was an alternative method of heating water in kettles.[41] It was held in the Scottish case of *Todd v Clapperton*[42] that, applying Lord Atkin's test in *Summers v Salford Corp*,[43] a house was not in all respects reasonably fit for human habitation for the purposes of the condition implied by s.113 and para.1(2) of Sch.10 to the Housing (Scotland) Act 1987, because the state of a pane of glass in an internal door was such that ordinary use, such as opening the door by pushing on the pane

---

[37] [1927] 2 K.B. 131. The majority in that case held that a broken sash cord did not cause the house to be other than "in all respects reasonably fit for human habitation".

[38] *Walker v Hobbs* (1889) 23 Q.B.D. 458; *Fisher v Walters* [1926] 2 K.B. 315; *Porter v Jones* (1942) 112 L.J.K.B. 173.

[39] *Horrex v Pidwell* [1958] C.L.Y. 1461.

[40] *Stanton v Southwick* [1920] 2 K.B. 642. This decision was criticised by Lord Wright in *Summers v Salford Corp*, above.

[41] *Daly v Elstree RDC* [1948] 2 All E.R. 13.

[42] [2009] CSOH 112.

[43] See above.

or seeking to stop the closing of the door by putting one's hand onto the pane, would be likely to cause the pane to break and cause injury to the person in so doing.

### (c)   To what extent the standard differs from an obligation to repair

The standard of fitness for human habitation is lower than that imposed by an ordinary obligation to repair.[44] It follows that where the tenant has covenanted to repair, he is liable to carry out any repairs over and above those necessary to comply with the fitness for human habitation standard.[45] An obligation to repair may be more extensive than the statutory obligation, because the existence of defects requiring repair is irrelevant for the purposes of s.8 as long as the house is reasonably fit for human habitation, whereas an obligation to repair may require the remedying of a defect even though it does not render the house unfit for habitation. On the other hand, the statutory obligation imposes standards, for example as to "internal arrangement", which have little if anything to do with repair. To that extent liability under the section may be more extensive than under a covenant to repair. However, a covenant to keep premises in "habitable" repair may impose no higher standard than the statutory obligation.[46]

**20–10**

### Limitations on the section

Two limitations on the obligations implied by s.8 should be noted. First, it does not apply to common parts not demised.[47] Second, it does not apply where the house cannot be made fit for human habitation at reasonable expense.[48] It does not therefore oblige the landlord to "keep a ruinous house fit for habitation whatever the cost".[49]

**20–11**

---

[44] *Jones v Geen* [1925] 1 K.B. 659.

[45] *Jones v Green*, above. In that case the tenant covenanted to "keep and leave the said premises and fixtures in good and tenantable repair state and condition (fair wear and tear only excepted)". The Divisional Court held that the standard imposed by this covenant was higher than that imposed on the landlord by the statutory implied covenant, with the result that the tenant remained liable to carry out any repairs over and above those required by the statute.

[46] See *Summers v Salford Corp*, [1943] A.C. 283, per Lord Atkin at 289–290.

[47] *Dunster v Hollis* [1918] 2 K.B. 795 (external steps leading to common entrance of house let in rooms).

[48] *Buswell v Goodwin* [1971] 1 W.L.R. 92, in which Widgery L.J. (with whom Karminski and Davies L.JJ. agreed) described a concession by counsel to this effect as "entirely right" (at 97). For the meaning of capable of being made fit for human habitation at reasonable expense reference, see *Kenny v Kingston upon Thames Borough Council* (1985) 17 H.L.R. 344 and the other decisions under what became (until its repeal) s.206 of the Housing Act 1985.

[49] *Buswell v Goodwin*, above, per Widgery L.J. at 97.

## Requirement of notice

20–12    The landlord is not liable under the section until he has notice of the relevant defect.[50] His obligation is then to carry out the necessary work within a reasonable time.[51] Thus, in *Porter v Jones*[52] the landlord was held liable when a defective ceiling fell eight months after the tenant had given him notice of it. By contrast, in *Morgan v Liverpool Corp*[53] the landlord was held not liable where a sash cord broke without warning.

The requirement of notice only applies in relation to the implied undertaking to keep the house fit for human habitation during the term, and not to the implied condition that the house will be so fit at the commencement of the tenancy. The reasoning of the cases in which the requirement as to notice has been held to exist clearly would not apply to the latter.[54] In the Scottish case of *Todd v Clapperton*,[55] the landlord was held to be liable under the condition implied into the lease by s.113 and para.1(2) of Sch.10 to the Housing (Scotland) Act 1987 that the house was, at the commencement of the tenancy, in all respects reasonably fit for human habitation even though the relevant defect was latent and not discoverable by reasonable inspection.

What constitutes notice is discussed in Ch.22, paras 22–05 to 22–12, below.

## Rights of entry

20–13    The landlord, or any person authorised by him in writing, has the right at reasonable times of the day, on giving 24 hours' notice in writing to the tenant or occupier, to enter the premises for the purpose of viewing their state and condition.[56] The notice must be in writing, and may be given either to the tenant or the occupier. It is thought that the 24-hour period will not start to run until the notice is actually received by the intended recipient.[57] The statute does not confer any express right to enter to carry out repairs within the landlord's obligation, but such a right would be implied in any event.[58]

## Remedies for breach

20–14    The tenant has the same remedies for breach of the statutory obligations as he would have had they taken the form of an express covenant by the landlord.[59] The obligation to ensure that the house is fit for human habitation at the

---

[50] *Morgan v Liverpool Corp* [1927] 2 K.B. 131. The correctness of this decision was left open by the House of Lords in *Summers v Salford Corp* [1943] A.C. 283, but it was approved by the House in *McCarrick v Liverpool Corp* [1947] A.C. 219. See also *O'Brien v Robinson* [1973] A.C. 912.

[51] See para.22–15, below.

[52] (1942) 112 L.J.K.B. 173.

[53] Above.

[54] See para.22–03 below.

[55] [2009] CSOH 112.

[56] Landlord and Tenant Act 1985 s.8(2).

[57] Cf. *Sun Alliance & London Assurance Co Ltd v Hayman* [1975] 1 W.L.R. 177.

[58] See para.22–33 below.

[59] For the available remedies, see Ch.28 below.

commencement of the tenancy is implied as a condition of the tenancy,[60] so that if the obligation is broken, the tenant is entitled to repudiate the tenancy in addition to claiming damages from the landlord.[61] The statute does not confer any right of action upon any person other than the tenant.[62] However, other persons may now have a remedy under the Defective Premises Act 1972.[63]

Failure by the landlord to keep the house fit for human habitation may result in a demolition or closing order being made under Pt 9 of the Housing Act 1985. Neither the Rent Act 1977 nor the Housing Act 1988 would then prevent the landlord from obtaining possession,[64] notwithstanding the fact that he would or might be relying on his own wrong.[65] If the condition of the premises which led to the making of the demolition or closing order arose because of breaches by the landlord of his statutory obligations under s.8, then the tenant's damages would include a sum to reflect the loss of his tenancy.[66]

## Agricultural workers

The provisions of s.8 apply where, under a contract of employment of a worker employed in agriculture, the provision of a house[67] for his occupation forms part of his remuneration and the only reason why s.8 does not otherwise apply is that the house is not let to him.[68] In that event the statutory implied condition and undertaking are implied as part of his contract of employment, notwithstanding any stipulation to the contrary, and the provisions of the section apply with the substitution of "employer" for "landlord" and such other modifications as may be necessary.[69] However, this does not affect any obligation of a person other than the employer to repair the house or any remedy for enforcing such obligation.[70]

20–15

## Present-day application of the section

The low rent limits under s.8 mean that it is virtually never encountered in practice nowadays. In *Quick v Taff-Ely Borough Council*[71] Lawton L.J. said in relation to s.6 of the Housing Act 1957 (the immediate statutory predecessor of s.8 of the 1985 Act):

20–16

---

[60] Landlord and Tenant Act 1985 s.8(1)(b).

[61] *Walker v Hobbs & Co Ltd* (1889) 23 Q.B.D. 458; cf. *Smith v Marable* (1843) 11 M. & W. 5.

[62] *Middleton v Hall* (1914) 108 L.T. 804; *Cameron v Young* 1908 S.C. (KH.L.) 7; *Ryall v Kidwell* [1914] 3 K.B. 135.

[63] See para.20–49 et seq., below.

[64] Housing Act 1985 ss.270(3) and 276.

[65] *Buswell v Goodwin* [1971] 1 W.L.R. 92.

[66] *John Waterer Sons & Crisp Ltd v Huggins* (1931) 47 T.L.R. 305, in which the tenant's claim for damages to reflect the loss of security of tenure under the Rent Acts failed because his tenancy had begun before the Acts.

[67] The definition is the same as that discussed in para.20–03, above: see Landlord and Tenant Act 1985 s.9(3).

[68] 1985 Act s.9(1).

[69] 1985 Act s.9(1).

[70] 1985 Act s.9(1).

[71] [1986] Q.B. 809.

"When I read the papers in this case I was surprised to find that the plaintiff had not based his claim on an allegation that at all material times the house let to him by the council had not been fit for human habitation. The uncontradicted evidence, accepted by the trial judge, showed that furniture, furnishings and clothes had rotted because of damp and the sitting room could not be used because of the smell of damp. I was even more surprised to be told by counsel that the provisions of the Housing Act 1957, as amended by the London Government Act 1963, did not apply to the plaintiff's house. By section 6 of the Act of 1957, on the letting of a house at specified low rent, a covenant is implied that the landlord will keep it in a condition fit for human habitation. For most of the time the plaintiff was in occupation of the house let to him by the council it is arguable that it was not fit for human habitation. Unfortunately, the figures which were fixed as being low rents have not been changed for over twenty years. In 1965 a low rent outside central Greater London was one not exceeding £52 per annum. The present day equivalent of that figure, when inflation is taken into account, is well over £312. The plaintiff's rent of £6.75 per week in 1976 was well above the statutory figure. This case would seem to indicate that a new definition of a low rent is needed."

Parliament's failure to update the statutory rent limits has been commented on by other judges. Thus, in *McNerny v Lambeth LBC*[72] Dillon L.J. said:

"The limits [in the 1957 Act] ... are far below the normal rents for a council house or flat ... and Parliament has conspicuously refrained from updating the limits in the 1985 Landlord and Tenant Acts."

In *Issa v Hackney LBC*[73] Brooke L.J. described the statutorily implied covenant as a "completely dead letter". In *Lee v Leeds City Council*[74] Chadwick L.J., having referred to the fact that the original rent limits were retained when s.6 of the Housing Act 1957 was re-enacted in the Landlord and Tenant Act 1985, said:

"The effect is that the rent limits are now far below the average rents for local authority housing—and even further below the average rents for comparable housing in the private sector ... But that must be taken to reflect the legislative intention at the time of the 1985 re-enactment. [75]"

It is noteworthy that the last reported case on s.8 was decided in 1970.[76]

## SECTION 11 OF THE LANDLORD AND TENANT ACT 1985: SHORT LEASES OF DWELLING-HOUSES

### Application of the section

**20–17**    Section 11 of the 1985 Act is printed in Appendix II, below. It applies to (a) a lease of a dwelling-house, (b) which is granted on or after October 24, 1961 for a term of less than seven years.[77] Both of these will be considered in turn.

---

[72] (1988) 21 H.L.R. 188.
[73] [1997] 1 W.L.R. 956.
[74] [2002] 1 W.L.R. 1488.
[75] See also *Southwark Borough Council v Mills* [2001] 1 A.C. 1.
[76] *Buswell v Goodwin* [1971] 1 W.L.R. 92.
[77] Landlord and Tenant Act 1985 s.13(1).

### (a)   A lease of a dwelling-house

This means a lease by which a building or part of a building is let wholly or **20–18**
mainly as a private residence, and "dwelling-house" means that building or part
of a building.[78] This definition focuses on the purpose of the letting, as opposed
to the physical nature of the demised premises. The fact that the premises are a
house is irrelevant if they are let for purposes other than those of a private
residence (for example, business purposes). Whilst the position is not clear, it is
thought that the reference to a letting as a private residence is not to be read in the
plural, so that the section does not apply to a lease of a building let for use as
more than one private residence.[79] This seems consistent with the policy of the
Act, which was to ensure that residential tenants for short terms should not be
liable for major repairs. It seems unlikely that the section was intended to apply,
for example, to a commercial landlord who takes a lease of a building containing
a number of habitable units for the purpose of letting them off. The argument to
the contrary is that the section was intended to ensure that major repairs are
carried out by a person with a long-term interest in the building. It is thought,
however, that there is no good reason to construe the section as interfering with
contracts any more than is necessary to protect tenants of single dwelling-houses.
A lease granted in the circumstances set out in the example given above would be
likely to contain a full repairing covenant, and the rent would have been
negotiated by reference to that liability. It is difficult to see why the section
should be construed as applying to override a bargain made in those
circumstances. Such a construction would not, of course, affect the position of the
sub-tenants of the individual units, because the section would still apply as
between the tenant under the lease and those sub-tenants.

### (b)   Granted on or after October 24, 1961, for a term of less than seven years

In determining whether a term is less than seven years any part of the term which **20–19**
falls before the grant is disregarded.[80] The period of less than seven years is
therefore measured from the date on which the tenancy is granted and not the date
(if earlier) from which the term is expressed to run.[81] Thus, for example, a
tenancy granted on April 1, 1989, for a term of seven-and-a-half years from June
24, 1988, is within the Act. However, where the lease is granted in pursuance of
an agreement for lease, it appears that the term will be treated as commencing on

---

[78] 1985 Act s.16(b).
[79] Cf. *Horford Investments Ltd v Lambert* [1976] Ch. 39 and *St Catherine's College v Dorling* [1980]
1 W.L.R. 66 (both cases on the meaning of "let as a separate dwelling" in s.1 of the Rent Act 1977).
See, however, *Heron Maple House v Central Estates* [2002] 1 E.G.L.R. 35 and *Oakfern Properties v
Ruddy* [2006] EWCA Civ 1389, in which it was held that a person may be "the tenant of a dwelling"
for the purposes of the provisions of ss.18 to 30 of the Landlord and Tenant Act 1985 relating to
service charges even though his tenancy includes other property or more than one dwelling.
[80] Landlord and Tenant Act 1985 s.13(2)(a).
[81] See *Bradshaw v Pawley* [1980] 1 W.L.R. 10 for a full discussion of the distinction between the date
on which a tenancy takes effect and the date from which the term is expressed to run.

the date specified in the agreement. Thus, in *Brikom Investments Ltd v Seaford*[82] the tenant was allowed into possession on November 1, 1969, under a lease to be granted for seven years from that date. The lease was not executed by the landlord until later. The Court of Appeal held that the section did not apply. Where the term is a discontinuous period (for example, a specified week each year for a period of years, as is usually the case with timeshare agreements), the length is to be calculated by adding together the discontinuous periods.[83] Thus, a timeshare lease for 80 periods of one week in each year for 80 years creates a term of 80 weeks not 80 years.[84]

A lease which is determinable at the option of the landlord before the expiration of seven years from the commencement of the term is treated as a lease for less than seven years.[85] However, the option must be an unfettered one, so that an option which is only exercisable on the happening of a certain event, such as the death of the landlord, does not bring the lease within the section.[86] A lease (other than one containing an unfettered option on the part of the landlord to determine the term within the first seven years) is not to be treated as a lease for less than seven years if it confers on the tenant an option for renewal for a term which, together with the original term, amounts to seven years or more.[87]

The landlord may be estopped from denying that he is liable under the section. Thus, in *Brikom Investments Ltd v Seaford*,[88] the section did not apply because the term was for seven years. However, a fair rent had been registered, and demanded and accepted, on the basis that the landlords were liable under the section. The Court of Appeal held that so long as the increased rent was claimed by the landlords, they were estopped from denying liability under the section. In order to be released from this liability, they would have to apply to have the registration corrected so as to reflect the true position.

## Exceptions

### (a)   Successive tenancies

20–20    Section 11 does not apply to a new lease granted to an existing tenant,[89] or a former tenant still in possession,[90] where the previous lease[91] was not a lease to which s.11 applied (and, if that lease was granted before October 24, 1961, it

---

[82] [1981] 1 W.L.R. 863.

[83] *Cottage Holiday Associates Ltd v Customs & Excise Commissioners* [1983] Q.B. 735.

[84] *Cottage Holiday Associates Ltd v Customs & Excise Commissioners*, above.

[85] Landlord and Tenant Act s.13(2)(b).

[86] *Parker v O'Connor* [1974] 1 W.L.R. 1160, in which the Court of Appeal held that the words "is determinable" are not to be read as "is (or may become) determinable".

[87] Landlord and Tenant Act 1985 s.13(2)(c).

[88] [1981] 1 W.L.R. 863.

[89] This means a person who is when, or immediately before, the new lease is granted, the lessee under another lease of the dwelling-house: Landlord and Tenant Act 1985 s.14(2).

[90] This means a person who (a) was the lessee under another lease of the dwelling-house which terminated at some time before the new lease was granted, and (b) between the termination of that lease and the grant of the new lease was continuously in possession of the dwelling-house or of the rents and profits of the dwelling-house: 1985 Act s.14(2).

[91] i.e. the lease referred to in the preceding two footnotes.

would not have been a lease to which s.11 applied if granted after that date). Some examples may help to make this clear:

(1)  In 1984 T. was granted a lease for three years. On its expiry he was granted a further lease for five years. Section 11 applies to the new lease;
(2)  In 1959 T. was granted a lease for three years. On its expiry he was granted a new lease for six years. Section 11 applies to the new lease because, although the previous lease was not one to which s.11 applied (because it was granted before October 24, 1961), nonetheless it would have been such a lease if granted after that date;
(3)  T. held a lease for eight years granted on January 1, 1961. On its expiry he was granted a further lease for three years. Section 11 does not apply to the new lease, because the previous lease, having been granted before October 24, 1961, was not one to which s.11 applied, and it would not have been within the section had it been granted after that date because it was not for a term of less than seven years.

The section does not apply to a new lease granted to an existing tenant,[92] or a former tenant still in possession,[93] if the new lease is a tenancy to which Pt II of the Landlord and Tenant Act 1954 applies, and the previous lease[94] (1) either is such a tenancy, or (2) would be such a tenancy but for s.28 of the 1954 Act.[95] It is noteworthy that s.11 is therefore capable of applying to the first in a line of business tenancies to which Pt II of the 1954 Act applies, although it would have to be shown that the tenancy was a "lease of a dwelling-house".[96] The section is therefore only likely to apply to a business tenancy in very exceptional circumstances.

### (b)  Tenancies to which the section does not apply

The section does not apply to the following tenancies:

20–21

(1)  a lease of a dwelling house which is a tenancy of an agricultural holding within the Agricultural Holdings Act 1986 and in relation to which that Act applies, or a farm business tenancy within the Agricultural Tenancies Act 1995;[97]
(2)  a tenancy granted by the Crown (including a government department);[98]
(3)  a tenancy granted on or after October 3, 1980, to any of the following bodies:[99]
    (a)  a local authority;
    (b)  a National Park authority;

---

[92] See above.
[93] Above.
[94] Above.
[95] Landlord and Tenant Act 1985 s.32(2).
[96] See para.20–18, above.
[97] Landlord and Tenant Act 1985 s.14(3).
[98] *Department of Transport v Egoroff* (1986) 18 H.L.R. 326.
[99] Landlord and Tenant Act 1985 s.14(4) (as amended).

(c)    a new town corporation;

(d)    an urban development corporation;

(e)    the Development Board for Rural Wales;

(f)    a registered social landlord;

(g)    a co-operative housing association;

(h)    an educational institution or other body specified, or of a class specified, by regulations under s.8 of the Rent Act 1977 or para.8 of Sch.1 to the Housing Act 1988 (bodies making student lettings);

(4)    a tenancy granted on or after October 3, 1980, to:

(a)    Her Majesty in right of the Crown (unless the lease is under the management of the Crown Estate Commissioners);

(b)    a government department or a person holding in trust for Her Majesty for the purposes of a government department;[100]

(5)    a tenancy granted on or after January 15, 1989 to a housing action trust established under Pt III of the Housing Act 1988 unless the tenancy was entered into pursuant to a contract made before that date;[101]

(6)    a contracted-out tenancy.[102]

## Terms implied in the case of tenancies entered into before January 15, 1989[103]

**20–22**    Where the tenancy is entered into before January 15, 1989, (or entered into after that date pursuant to a contract made before that date), the following covenants on the part of the landlord are implied:

(a)    to keep in repair the structure and exterior of the dwelling-house (including drains, gutters and external pipes);[104]

(b)    to keep in repair and proper working order the installations in the dwelling-house for the supply of water, gas and electricity and for sanitation (including basins, sinks, baths and sanitary conveniences, but not other fixtures, fittings and appliances for making use of the supply of water, gas and electricity);[105]

(c)    to keep in repair and proper working order the installations in the dwelling-house for space heating and for heating water.[106]

The meaning of these various expressions is considered below.

The onus of proving that the landlord has committed breaches of the statutory obligation is on the tenant.[107]

---

[100] 1985 Act s.14(5).

[101] 1985 Act s.14(4) as amended by the Housing Act 1988 s.116(3) and (4).

[102] See para.20–45, below.

[103] For additional terms implied into tenancies entered into on or after January 15, 1989, see para.20–31 et seq., below.

[104] Landlord and Tenant Act 1985 s.11(1)(a).

[105] 1985 Act s.11(1)(b).

[106] 1985 Act s.11(1)(c).

[107] *Foster v Day* (1969) 208 E.G. 495.

### (a) "to keep in repair"

The implied statutory obligation to keep in repair only arises once there is **20–23** disrepair, i.e. where the subject-matter of the obligation (the structure and exterior of the dwelling-house and the other items in respect of which the obligation arises) has suffered damage or deterioration.[108] The landlord is not obliged to remedy a lack of amenity or inefficiency resulting from a design defect which has not resulted in any relevant disrepair. Thus, the landlord is not obliged to remedy a design defect which has not caused damage to the structure and exterior of the dwelling-house even if the defect has made the premises unsuitable for occupation.[109] It has been held that this principle is not incompatible with the tenant's Convention Rights.[110]

In *Southwark London Borough Council v McIntosh*[111] the premises included a cupboard containing hot pipes which the tenant used for drying clothes. This led to condensation which in turn caused problems of damp both in the cupboard and elsewhere in the flat. At first instance the judge held the landlords liable for breach of the statutorily implied covenant on the ground that they had failed to warn the tenant not to use the cupboard for drying clothes. Lightman J., on appeal, described this as a "totally untenable proposition".[112]

However, once disrepair has occurred, the landlord may (depending on the circumstances) be obliged to remedy the design defect as part of the repairs. But he will not be liable to carry out works which go beyond repair as a matter of fact and degree.[113]

The extent of the obligations imposed by a covenant to keep in repair are considered in detail in Chs 7 to 11 and 14, above, to which further reference should be made.

### (b) "the structure and exterior of the dwelling-house"

In *Campden Hill Towers Ltd v Gardner*[114] it was held by the Court of Appeal that **20–24** where the dwelling-house forms part of a larger building, then the subject-matter of the implied covenant is the structure and exterior of the dwelling-house and not that of the building as a whole. However, it is not necessarily limited to what has been demised. It extends to anything which in the ordinary use of words can be regarded as part of the structure or exterior of the dwelling-house, whether or not included in the demise.[115] Megaw L.J., who gave the leading judgment, explained the principle as follows:

---

[108] *Quick v Taff-Ely Borough Council* [1986] Q.B. 809. See Ch.8, above.
[109] *Quick v Taff-Ely Borough Council*, above; *Lee v Leeds City Council* [2002] 1 W.L.R. 1488.
[110] *Lee v Leeds City Council*, above. See further on Human Rights para.20–68 et seq., below.
[111] [2002] 1 E.G.L.R. 25.
[112] See further on this case para.8–03, above.
[113] *McDougall v Easington District Council* (1989) 21 H.L.R. 310. See Ch.11, above.
[114] [1987] Q.B. 823.
[115] But note that where the tenancy is entered into on or after January 15, 1989 (unless it is entered into pursuant to a contract made before that date), the obligation is wider and extends to any part of the building in which the lessor has an estate or interest: see paras 20–31 to 20–32, below.

"Anything which, in the ordinary use of words, would be regarded as part of the structure, or of the exterior, of the particular 'dwelling-house', regarded as a separate part of the building, would be within the scope of [the obligation]. Thus, the exclusion by the words of ... the underlease of 'any part of the outside walls' would not have the effect of taking outside the operation of [the obligation] that which, in the ordinary use of language, would be regarded as the exterior wall of the flat—an essential part of the flat, as a dwelling-house: that part of the outside wall of the block of flats which constitutes a wall of the flat. The [obligation] applies to the outside wall or walls of the flat; the outside of inner party walls of the flat; the outer side of horizontal divisions between [the flat] and flats above and below; the structural framework and beams directly supporting floors, ceilings and walls of the flat."

The decision was followed in *Douglas-Scott v Scorgie*,[116] which concerned a top-floor flat in a block. The roof of the block did not form part of the demise. The Court of Appeal unanimously allowed an appeal from an assistant recorder, who had held that the roof of the block was not part of the "structure and exterior of the dwelling-house" for the purposes of s.11. Slade L.J. said:

"Following [the *Campden Hill* case] the crucial question to which the assistant recorder should have directed his mind was, in my opinion, whether the roof of the premises would, in the ordinary use of words, be regarded as part of the structure or exterior of the ... top floor flat, when that flat is regarded as a separate part of the [block]. [117]"

**20–25** The meaning of "structure" was considered in *Irvine v Moran*.[118] Having rejected the suggestion that the structure consisted of the entire dwelling-house or the entire constructed building, Mr Recorder Thayne Forbes, QC, sitting as a deputy judge of the Queen's Bench Division, continued as follows:

"... I have come to the view that the structure of the dwellinghouse consists of those elements of the overall dwelling house which give it its essential appearance, stability and shape. The expression does not extend to the many and various ways in which the dwellinghouse will be fitted out, equipped, decorated and generally made to be habitable. I am not persuaded by [counsel for the landlord] that one should limit the expression "the structure of the dwellinghouse to those aspects of the dwellinghouse which are load bearing in the sense that that sort of expression is used by professional consulting engineers and the like; but what I do feel is, as regards the words "structure of the dwellinghouse", that in order to be part of the structure of the dwellinghouse a particular element must be a material or significant element in the overall construction. To some extent, in every case there will be a degree of fact to be gone into to decide whether or not something is or is not part of the structure of the dwellinghouse. It is not easy to think of an overall explanation of the meaning of those words which will be applicable in every case and I deliberately decline to attempt such a definition. I am content for the purposes of this case to say that I accept [counsel's] submission that "structure of the dwellinghouse" has a more limited meaning than the overall building itself and that it is addressed to those essential elements of the dwellinghouse which are material to its overall construction.
    That I think is as far as I am able to go."

In *Grand v Gill*[119] the Court of Appeal accepted the above passage as providing a good working definition of "structure" for the purposes of the statute.[120]

---

[116] [1984] 1 W.L.R. 716.
[117] See further para.7–32, above.
[118] [1991] 1 E.G.L.R. 261.
[119] [2011] EWCA Civ 554.
[120] See further paras 7–34 to 7–38 above.

Where the dwelling-house is a flat, the structure and exterior will include the outside wall or walls of the flat; the outside of inner party walls of the flat; the outer side of horizontal divisions between the flat and flats above and below; and the structural framework and beams directly supporting floors, ceilings and walls of the flat.[121] Where the dwelling-house is on the top floor of a block of flats, the structure and exterior may also include the roof. Thus, in *Douglas-Scott v Scorgie*[122] Slade L.J. said:

> "I can see no reason in principle why the roof above [a top floor flat] should not be capable in some circumstances of falling within the scope of [the obligation] ... To take the simplest case by way of example, if the ceiling and roof of a particular top floor dwelling all formed part of one flat, inseparable, structural unit, it would seem to me prima facie that in the ordinary use of words, the roof and ceiling would be regarded as part of the structure or exterior of that dwelling, as much as its outside walls, inner party walls and so forth. On the other hand, I do not think one can go so far as to say that the roof, or part of the roof, which lies above any so-called top floor flat necessarily will fall within [the obligation]. Borderline cases, for example, might arise where one found a void space or an uninhabited loft between the flat and the roof. Everything must depend on the particular facts of the case."

Also included in the structure and exterior for the purposes of the implied obligation are windows (including frames, sash cords and essential window furniture) and external doors.[123] Decorations are not within the obligation,[124] and neither is door furniture.[125]

Prior to the decision of the Court of Appeal in *Grand v Gill*,[126] the question whether internal plaster is to be regarded as part of the structure for the purposes of s.20 gave rise to a difference of approach in the authorities. In *Irvine v Moran*[127] the deputy judge held that internal plaster is not within the obligation, on the ground that it is "more in the nature of a decorative finish and is not part of the essential material elements that go to make up the structure of the dwelling-house". However, concessions to the contrary were accepted by the court in *Quick v Taff-Ely Borough Council*[128] and *Staves v Leeds City Council*,[129] and in *Hussein v Mehlman*,[130] Mr Stephen Sedley QC (sitting as an assistant recorder) described a submission that the bedroom ceiling was not part of the structure as "untenable". He went on to say:

**20–26**

> "The object of section 11(1)(a) is to place upon the lessor the obligation to maintain the fabric of the building in a safe and habitable condition. A house—at least a 1930s London suburban semi-detached house—without plaster on its ceiling is not a complete house and is certainly not safe or habitable."

---

[121] *Campden Hill Towers Ltd v Gardner*, above. The relevant passage from the judgment of Megaw L.J. is set out above.
[122] [1984] 1 W.L.R. 716.
[123] *Irvine v Moran* [1991 1 E.G.L.R. 261; *Sheffield City Council v Oliver* (Lands Tribunal) LRZ/146/2007.
[124] *Quick v Taff-Ely*, above; *Irvine v Moran*, above.
[125] *Irvine v Moran*, above.
[126] [2011] EWCA Civ 554.
[127] Above.
[128] [1986] Q.B. 809 at 820B and 822G.
[129] (1990) 23 H.L.R. 107.
[130] [1992] 2 E.G.L.R. 27.

The question was left open in *Niazi Services Ltd v van der Loo*.[131] However, it was definitively resolved in *Grand v Gill*,[132] in which the Court of Appeal held that plaster finish on a wall or ceiling is part of the "structure" for the purposes of the statute.[133]

**20–27**  "Exterior" was held in *Brown v Liverpool Corp*[134] to include steps and a flagstone path which were the only means of access to the dwelling-house. Sachs L.J. identified the question as being:

> "[W]hether …. the seven feet approach with the steps at the end of it really was part of the exterior of the terrace building or whether that seven feet pathway and the steps down into it were simply part of a means of traversing a garden. That seems to me …. to be a question of degree and a very close run thing at that ….. it seems to me that ….. [the county court judge] was entitled to come to the conclusion which he reached on this question of fact, *i.e.*, that in all the circumstances the steps formed part of the building."

*Brown* was distinguished in *Hopwood v Cannock Chase District Council*,[135] in which the ordinary means of access to the dwelling-house was from the front, and the landlord was held not liable in respect of a rear yard.[136] Likewise, in *King v South Northamptonshire District Council*[137] it was held that a path running along the rear of terraced houses was not part of the exterior of one of them. In *Irvine v Moran*[138] it was held that a separate garage and separate gates were not part of the exterior of the dwelling-house.[139] In *Cresswell v Sandwell Metropolitan Borough Council*[140] it was held in the county court that outbuildings (comprising a garden shed, coal store and WC) let with a dwelling house were not part of the structure and exterior of the dwelling-house.

### (c)  "to keep in … proper working order"[141]

**20–28**  The obligation imposed by s.11 in relation to the installations to which it applies is not only to keep them in repair but also to keep them in proper working order. An installation is not in proper working order if it does not properly perform its intended function. The fact that the installation is in no worse a state than it was in at the date of the lease is irrelevant. Thus, in *Liverpool City Council v Irwin*[142] Lord Edmund-Davies said:

---

[131] [2004] 1 E.G.L.R. 62.
[132] [2011] EWCA Civ 554.
[133] See further para.7–36, above.
[134] [1969] 3 All E.R. 1345. See further paras 7–41 to 7–43, above.
[135] [1975] 1 W.L.R. 373.
[136] See also *McAuley v Bristol City Council* [1990] 2 Q.B. 134, in which it was conceded that the obligation did not apply in respect of a concrete step forming part of a flight of steps running up the centre of the garden away from the house.
[137] [1992] 1 E.G.L.R. 53.
[138] [1991] 1 E.G.L.R. 261.
[139] It was conceded by the tenant that the driveway, gardens and grounds were not within the obligation.
[140] [2001] 1 C.L. 141.
[141] See further para.13–15, above.
[142] [1977] A.C. 239.

"It is clear that [the] section .... imposes an *absolute* [judge's emphasis] duty upon the landlord 'to keep in repair and proper working order the installations in the dwelling-house'. It can be said that the opening words ('to keep .....') apparently limit the landlord's obligation to preserving the *existing* [judge's emphasis] plant in its original state and create no obligation to improve plant which was, by its very design, at all times defective and inefficient. But the phrase has to be read as a whole, and as I think, it presupposes that at the inception of the letting the installation was 'in proper working order', and that if its design was such that it did not work 'properly' the landlord is in breach."

In that case, a WC cistern overflowed and flooded the floor every time the WC was used. This was probably due to bad design. The House of Lords held that the landlord was nevertheless in breach, on the ground that the cistern was not in proper working order.

The fact that the reason the installation does not work properly is because of bad design, construction or installation is equally irrelevant. Thus, in *O'Connor v Old Etonian Housing Association Ltd*,[143] Lord Phillips M.R. (giving the judgment of the Court of Appeal) said (distinguishing the cases in which it had been held that an obligation to repair does not, of itself, require the covenantor to remedy defects in design or construction[144]):

"There is an obvious distinction between the duty to keep 'in repair' and the duty to keep 'in proper working order' .... An installation cannot be said to be in proper working order if, by reason of a defect in construction or design, it is incapable of working properly."

In principle, therefore, the statutory obligation to keep in proper working order imposes a wider duty than an obligation to repair and keep in repair. Thus, in *Langham Estate Management Ltd v Hardy*[145] H.H. Judge Hazel Marshall QC said:

"a landlord's covenant to 'keep in proper working order' or to 'maintain' is likely to be wider in its scope than a covenant to 'repair', although even this will depend upon the true construction of the covenant in its context. This point is particularly relevant to plant, machinery, equipment and installations. 'Repair' involves remedying a state of disrepair that has arisen, and the obligation does not arise until it has. 'Keep in proper working order', and possibly merely 'maintain', may well require proactive preventative maintenance work, or carrying out adjustments or general servicing before any actual fault develops or a want of repair exists. The covenant to 'keep in proper working order', in particular, may also require the remedying of design or construction defects, which are not wants of repair. This is because such a covenant means ensuring that the relevant installations perform their intended functions 'in a proper, safe and reliable manner' (see *Ultraworth Ltd v General Accident Fire & Life Assurance* Corporation *plc* [2000] 2 E.G.L.R. 115) or, to put it more simply, that they 'work properly': see *O'Connor v Old Etonian Housing Association Ltd* [2002] 1 E.G.L.R. 38."

However, the statutorily implied obligation is related to the physical or mechanical condition of the installation as such and requires that it shall be capable of working properly as an installation.[146] Thus, in *Wycombe Health Authority v Barnett*[147] the Court of Appeal held that the landlord was not in

**20–29**

---

[143] [2002] Ch. 295.
[144] See para.20–23, above, and see also Ch.8, above.
[145] [2008] 3 E.G.L.R. 125 at [62].
[146] *Wycombe Health Authority v Barnett* (1982) 5 H.L.R. 84; *O'Connor v Old Etonian Housing Association* [2002] Ch. 295.
[147] Above.

breach when an unlagged rising mains waterpipe cracked in freezing conditions when the water in it turned to ice. It was said in the same case that an electricity installation would not cease to be in proper working order merely because a fuse blows, although the position would be different if the wiring had deteriorated to such an extent as to cause short circuits. *Wycombe* was followed in *Payne v Rhymney Valley DC*,[148] in which the Court of Appeal again held that the statutorily implied obligation did not oblige the landlord to lag the water system in the tenant's flat. The tenant's argument that *Wycombe* was to be distinguished, on the ground that the house in that case was old, whereas the flat in question was part of a block of flats built in the 1970s in a notoriously cold location, and a modern landlord would have ensured that the water system was properly insulated, was rejected.

In *O'Connor v Old Etonian Housing Association Ltd*[149] the assumed facts were that the landlord had, prior to the commencement of the relevant tenancies, replaced the pipework with smaller bore pipes. Those pipes carried water to the top floor flats successfully for some years, but then (the water pressure having fallen) failed to do so for some six years until the water authority constructed a new pumping station. The judge at first instance held that the landlords were not in breach of the obligation implied by s.11 to keep the specified installations "in proper working order". His decision was reversed by Blackburne J., who held that the obligation in question was an obligation to ensure that the pipes were physically or mechanically capable of supplying water to the flats. The Court of Appeal allowed the landlord's appeal, holding that (i) the obligation obliged the landlord to ensure, at the commencement of the tenancy, that the installations were so designed and constructed as to be capable of performing their functions; (ii) an installation is in proper working order if it is able to function under the conditions of supply that it is reasonable to anticipate will prevail; and (iii) where, once the tenancy has commenced, a variation occurs to the supply that could not reasonably have been anticipated but which requires some alteration to the installation if the installation is to continue to function properly, the question whether the landlord is obliged to make that change depends on the circumstances and no hard and fast rule can be laid down. If it is introduced in a manner and subject to conditions in which it is reasonable to expect customers to modify their installations to accommodate the change, business efficacy may require the landlord to make the necessary modifications. If, however, the change is unforeseen, and is likely to be short lived, the cost of modifying the necessary installations may be disproportionate. The Court of Appeal did not make any finding on the question of breach because the assumed facts were not sufficient to enable a conclusion to be reached.

*O'Connor* was distinguished in *Southwark London Borough Council v Long*.[150] In that case, a tenancy of a council flat contained a covenant by the landlord that "facilities for the collection of refuse .... shall be kept in proper working order". The flat was next door to a large bin into which ran a rubbish chute that upper-floor tenants accessed by way of hoppers in the landing walls.

---

[148] Unreported decision of the Court of Appeal dated October 18, 1989.
[149] [2002] Ch. 295.
[150] [2002] 3 E.G.L.R. 37.

The chute could not accommodate large bin bags, so that noise was caused by tenants attempting to force bags into it, and the bin was often full so that smelly bags accumulated beside it. The Court of Appeal held that the landlord was not obliged to install new facilities. The system had not been inadequate at the beginning of the tenancy, and the landlord was not obliged to provide a system that was adequate in all circumstances as they existed from time to time.

Reference should also be made to reg.36 of the Gas Safety (Installation and Use) Regulations 1998,[151] which imposes on landlords of residential premises held under certain types of lease or a licence strict duties in relation to the maintenance and checking of gas fittings and flues and associated duties.[152]

### (d) "Installations"

Section 11 applies to the installations in the dwelling-house for the supply of water, gas and electricity and for sanitation (including basins, sinks, baths and sanitary conveniences, but not other fixtures, fittings and appliances for making use of the supply of water, gas and electricity) and for space heating and for heating water. This requires a distinction be drawn between installations for the supply of services, for sanitation and for heating, which fall within the obligation, and other installations which consume what is supplied, such as cookers and refrigerators, which are outside the obligation, even though they may be included in the tenancy. **20–30**

A further distinction is to be drawn between the specified installations in the dwelling-house and those elsewhere in the building. The obligation does not apply to the latter, even though they may be necessary for the proper functioning of the former.[153] It follows that a common boiler in the basement of a block of flats would not fall within the obligation, although the radiators and pipework in the individual flats would. However, the Housing Act 1988 has altered the position in the case of tenancies of part only of a building entered into on or after January 15, 1989, or pursuant to a contract made before that date.[154]

## Further terms implied into tenancies granted on or after January 15, 1989

The Housing Act 1988 made certain amendments to s.11 as originally enacted.[155] The amendments do not apply in relation to leases entered into before January 15, 1989, or pursuant to a contract made before that date.[156] Their effect is that where the dwelling-house forms part only of a building then: **20–31**

---

[151] SI 1998/2451.
[152] See para.20–67, below.
[153] *Campden Hill Towers Ltd v Gardner* [1977] Q.B. 823.
[154] See para.20–31 et seq., below.
[155] Housing Act 1988 s.116.
[156] Housing Act 1988 s.116(4).

(a)   the implied covenant to keep in repair the structure and exterior is extended to the structure and exterior of any part of the building in which the landlord has an estate or interest;[157]

(b)   the implied covenant to keep in repair and proper working order the specified installations in the dwelling-house extends to any installation which, directly or indirectly, serves the dwelling-house and which either (i) forms part of any part of a building in which the landlord has an estate or interest, or (ii) is owned by the landlord or under his control.[158]

The landlord is not required to carry out any works or repairs by virtue of (a) or (b) above unless the disrepair (or failure to maintain in working order) is such as to affect the lessee's enjoyment of the dwelling-house or of any common parts[159] which the tenant, as such, is entitled to use.[160]

**20–32**   The effect of the amendments is to remove some of the potential difficulties caused by the interpretation of the unamended s.11 by the Court of Appeal in *Campden Hill Towers Ltd v Gardner*.[161] However, the extended obligations do not apply where the landlord has no estate or interest in the part of the building of which the structure or exterior is in disrepair. Nor do they apply where the relevant installation is neither in a building in which the landlord has an estate or interest nor is owned or controlled by the landlord. In *Niazi Services Ltd v van der Loo*[162] the tenant had a series of annual tenancies of a flat on the top floor of a four-storey building. His landlord was himself a tenant of the flat under a long headlease which did not include any other part of the building. The judge at first instance held the landlord liable under s.11 for (among other things) poor water pressure in the flat (which resulted from a larger take-off pipe having been installed elsewhere in the building as part of works being carried out to the restaurant on the ground floor and basement) and a failure of the lighting in the common parts. The Court of Appeal allowed the landlord's appeal. The landlord did not have any estate or interest in the relevant parts of the building. It was not enough to show that he may have had an estate or interest in the installation itself. Jacob L.J. said:

"[T]he critical question is not whether [the landlord] had an estate or interest in the building of which the defective section of the installation forms part, but whether it had an estate or interest in *that part of* the building of which it formed part. It is not sufficient that [the landlord] had an estate or interest in any part of the building; it had to have an estate or interest in any part of the building of which the defective section of the installation formed part. The implied covenant did not extend to installations located in parts of a building in which the lessor did not have an estate or interest, even if the lessor had an estate or interest in other parts of the same building. Parliament has decided that, in relation to installations that are not owned or controlled by the lessor, the implied covenant should be confined to installations that are in those parts of a building in which the lessor does have an estate or interest."

---

[157] Landlord and Tenant Act 1985 s.11(1A).
[158] 1985 Act s.11(1A).
[159] "Common parts", in relation to any building or part of a building, includes the structure and exterior of that building or part and any common facilities within it: 1985 Act s.11(1B) (applying Landlord and Tenant Act 1987 s.60(1)).
[160] Landlord and Tenant Act 1985 s.11(1A).
[161] [1977] Q.B. 823. See para.20–24, above.
[162] [2004] 1 W.L.R. 1254.

… This interpretation is consistent with the scheme under section 11(1A)(a) in relation to repairs to the structure and exterior. Under para (a), a lessor's extended liability is limited to the obligation to keep in repair the structure and exterior of any part of the building in which it has an estate or interest. In the present case, Niazi had no estate or interest in any part of the building except the top-floor flat. Thus, if Mr van der Loo had suffered damage as a result of some structural disrepair in the lower part of the building, he would have no redress against Niazi under the statute.

We recognise that this construction means that there will be cases where a sublessor will have the benefit of the covenant implied by section 11(1A) from the head lessor in circumstances where the sublessee has no corresponding benefit from the sublessor. But this is inherent in the statutory scheme. It is clear that such a mismatch may arise in relation to the covenant that arises under section 11(1A)(a). Thus, if freeholder X grants a lease of a flat on the top floor of a building to Y, and damage is caused to the flat by the disrepair of part of the building that has not been included in the demise, say the roof, Y will be able to claim damages for breach of the covenant implied by section 11(1A)(a). If Y has sublet the flat to Z, Z will not be able to claim damages from Y for breach of the implied covenant, because Y has no interest or estate in the part of the building that is in disrepair.

It might be thought that this produces an unsatisfactory state of affairs. One solution is for the sublessee to ensure that the terms of the sublease secure for him all the rights that the sublessor enjoys as against the head lessor under the headlease. It may be that parliament would wish to consider whether such a term should be implied. But, at present, it is not."

Where in order to comply with the extended obligation, the landlord needs to carry out works or repairs otherwise than in, or to an installation in, the dwelling-house, and he does not have a sufficient right in the part of the building or the installation concerned to enable him to carry out the required works or repairs, then in any proceedings relating to a failure to comply with the landlord's repairing covenant, so far as it requires him to carry out the works or repairs in question, it is a defence for the landlord to prove that he used all reasonable endeavours to obtain, but was unable to obtain, such rights as would be adequate to enable him to carry out the works or repairs.[163] The purpose of this is to protect a landlord who has the requisite estate or interest in the relevant part of the building for the implied obligation to arise, but who has granted some intermediate interest which prevents him from carrying out the work without the consent of the holder of that interest.[164] The duty on such a landlord is to use all reasonable endeavours to obtain the necessary rights. He is not liable if he is then unable to obtain those rights.

## Exclusions

The covenants implied by s.11 (including that section as amended by the Housing Act 1988) do not require the landlord:

**20–33**

(a)  to carry out works or repairs for which the tenant is liable by virtue of his duty to use the premises in a tenant-like manner, or for which the tenant would be so liable but for an express covenant on his part;[165]

---

[163] Landlord and Tenant Act 1985 s.11(3A).
[164] See *Niazi Services Ltd v Van der Loo* [2004] 1 W.L.R. 1254.
[165] 1985 Act s.11(2)(a).

(b)   to rebuild or reinstate the premises[166] in the case of destruction or damage by fire, or by tempest, flood or other inevitable accident;[167]

(c)   to keep in repair or maintain anything which the tenant is entitled to remove from the dwelling-house.[168]

Each of these requires discussion.

### (a)   The duty of tenant-like user

20–34    The duty of tenant-like user is discussed elsewhere.[169] The effect of this exclusion is that works which would fall to be carried out by the tenant pursuant to that duty are excluded from the landlord's obligation, whether the tenant's duty arises by implication (as it usually does) or by virtue of an express covenant.

### (b)   Damage by catastrophes

20–35    At common law a repairing covenant obliges the covenantor to rebuild or reinstate following damage by fire or other catastrophe.[170] The effect of this exclusion is therefore to lessen the obligation that would otherwise have existed if the landlord's covenant had been entered into at common law.

### (c)   Things which the tenant is entitled to remove

20–36    The tenant's rights of removal extend to all chattels within his ownership and certain types of fixtures installed by him.[171] Anything which he is entitled to remove is excluded from the landlord's implied covenant. Thus, for example, the landlord would not be liable to repair an electric fire brought into the premises by the tenant. The position would be different if the fire had been included in the tenancy as a landlord's fixture.

### Implied precondition of notice

20–37    The implied repairing covenant is subject to a precondition that notice is required before liability arises.[172] This applies even where the defect is latent, i.e. it could not have been discovered by the tenant.[173] Thus, in the leading case of *O'Brien v Robinson*,[174] a bedroom ceiling collapsed and fell on the tenant. The landlord was held not liable for breach of the implied covenant on the ground that insufficient

---

[166]   The remainder of the section uses the word "dwelling-house", but it is doubtful whether anything turns on the distinction.

[167]   Landlord and Tenant Act 1985 s.11(2)(b). On the meaning of "accident" see *Saviane v Stauffer Chemical Co (Australia) Pty Ltd* [1974] 1 N.S.W.L.R. 665 (Australia).

[168]   Landlord and Tenant Act 1985 s.11(2)(c).

[169]   See para.21–03 et seq., below.

[170]   See para.18–11 et seq., above.

[171]   See para.25–23 et seq., below.

[172]   *O'Brien v Robinson* [1973] A.C. 912; *McGreal v Wake* (1984) 13 H.L.R. 107.

[173]   *O'Brien v Robinson*, above.

[174]   Above.

notice of the defect had been given by the tenant even though, prior to the collapse, no defects in the ceiling were visible. Once notice has been given,[175] then the landlord has a reasonable time in which to carry out the work. No breach of covenant is committed if he remedies the defect within that time.[176]

As a result of the interpretation of the unamended s.11 in *Campden Hill Towers Ltd v Gardner*,[177] and of the amendments made to the section by the Housing Act 1988,[178] the landlord's statutorily implied repairing obligations are capable of applying to parts of the building or installations which are not part of the demised premises (for example, a common roof above the demised flat or a common central heating boiler). At common law no notice is required to make a landlord liable for defects to parts of the building within his own possession and control.[179] It is not entirely clear whether notice would nonetheless be held to be required under s.11. The defective ceiling in *O'Brien v Robinson*[180] was part of the demised premises, so that the House of Lords did not have to consider what the position would have been in relation to defects to other parts of the building. However, in reaching its decision, the House clearly regarded itself as applying the common law rules as to notice.[181] Moreover, *Murphy v Hurly*[182] (in which the common law rule that no notice is required in respect of premises retained by the landlord in his own possession and control was applied) was referred to without disapproval.

Notwithstanding the above, it is thought that the principle in *O'Brien v Robinson* is of general application to all cases falling within the covenants implied by s.11, whether in its amended or unamended form. The following considerations would appear to support such a construction:

(1) Cases within the unamended s.11 in which the landlord's obligations extend to parts of the building which are not part of the demise will, by virtue of the decision in *Campden Hill Towers Ltd v Gardner*,[183] be limited to parts which are physically contiguous to the demised premises. By virtue of the same decision, the installations to which the obligations apply will be limited to those within the dwelling-house. In practice the first person to know of disrepair either to the relevant parts or installations is likely to be the tenant. It follows that the reasoning underlying the principle that notice is required still holds good in such cases.

(2) Although the application of the amended s.11 extends to parts of the building and installations which are physically distant from the demised premises, liability only arises where the relevant disrepair is such as to affect the tenant's enjoyment of the dwelling-house or any common parts

---

[175] The nature of the notice required is discussed in paras 22–05 to 22–13, below.
[176] See para.22–15, below.
[177] [1977] Q.B. 823. See para.20–24, above.
[178] See para.20–31, above.
[179] See para.22–15, below.
[180] [1973] A.C. 912.
[181] See in particular the speech of Lord Diplock at 927.
[182] [1922] 1 A.C. 369.
[183] Above.

which he is entitled to use under the terms of the tenancy.[184] It follows that, again, the tenant is likely to be the first person to become aware of the existence of defects falling within the landlord's obligations. This is particularly so where the landlord has not retained possession or control of the relevant part of the building or installation,[185] although it may be that in such a case notice would be required even at common law.[186]

(3)     There is nothing in the speeches in *O'Brien v Robinson*[187] to indicate that the House regarded itself as doing anything other than laying down a rule of general application in relation to s.11.

20–38     If the above is correct, then in all cases within the unamended and the amended s.11 notice of the defect will be required before the landlord's liability arises.

It has been held that the obligation imposed by s.11(1)(b) to keep in repair and proper working order the specified installations in the dwelling-house does not impose on the landlord any greater duty to make inquiries, and so obtain notice of a relevant defect, than does the obligation imposed by s.11(1)(a) to keep in repair the structure and exterior of the dwelling-house.[188]

As to what constitutes notice, reference should be made to Ch.22, below.

## The standard of repair

20–39     In determining the standard of repair under the implied repairing obligations, regard is to be had to the age, character and prospective life of the dwelling-house and the locality in which it is situated.[189] The requirement to have regard to the age, character and locality of the dwelling-house accords with the decisions at common law on the appropriate standard of repair.[190] The requirement to have regard to the prospective life of the dwelling-house has been considered by the Court of Appeal in two cases.

In *London Borough of Newham v Patel*[191] a house scheduled for redevelopment was let to the plaintiff. It suffered from various defects to the roof, walls, floors and guttering, and was damp and ill-ventilated. Following complaints from the plaintiff, the public health inspector reported to the council that the house had originally been classified as unfit for human habitation, and that it remained so. The council took the view that the house should be left uninhabited until it was possible to carry out full redevelopment. It offered alternative accommodation to the plaintiff which he refused. The county court judge found that the council was not in breach of the covenants implied by s.11, and his decision was upheld by the Court of Appeal. In the course of his judgment Templeman L.J. said:

---

[184] See para.20–31, above.
[185] A situation contemplated by s.11(3A): see para.20–32, above.
[186] i.e. because the subject matter of the covenant is not within the landlord's possession or control. See para.22–15, below.
[187] [1973] A.C. 912.
[188] *Sykes v Harry* [2001] Q.B. 1014. See further paras 22–05 to 22–08, below.
[189] Landlord and Tenant Act 1985 s.11(3).
[190] See Ch.9, above.
[191] (1978) 13 H.L.R. 77, CA.

"The prospective life of the dwelling-house affected the duty of the council under [section 11] and they were not bound to carry out repairs which would be wholly useless."

Ormrod L.J. said:

"[T]he terms of [the section] were almost, but significantly not entirely, in line with common law decisions relating to the construction of covenants for repair ... the crucially important addition was the phrase 'prospective life of the dwelling-house' ... that was an exceedingly important qualification. If the prospective life of the dwelling-house, as in this case, was short, then it was perfectly proper, sensible and reasonable to adjust the landlord's obligation accordingly and not to seek to impose a construction on the statute which could only be described as pedantic."

The case is noteworthy because the court appears to have taken the view that, because the prospective life of the house was short, the landlord was in effect relieved from any liability to repair at all.

The above decision was distinguished in *McClean v Liverpool City Council*[192] on the ground that there was no evidence that the dwelling-house in question was at the end of its useful life, whereas in *Patel* the court had found that the repair would be wholly useless. Nourse L.J. referred to a note of the evidence of the tenant's surveyor to the effect that "When look at property life property extremely limited", and said:

**20–40**

"It seems to me that, construing the answer as favourably as is possible to the defendant council, it does not show that this is a case where the property was actually at the end of its life. Because it has a limited life, that does not mean that if it is put into a proper state of repair, it will not have some form of life, albeit only for a matter of a few years."

In *Dame Margaret Hungerford Charity Trustees v Beazeley*[193] the landlords carried out running repairs to an old roof as and when they were notified of a problem. The county court judge held that this was sufficient to comply with the implied statutory obligation even though it was highly desirable that the roof should be replaced. The Court of Appeal declined to interfere with his decision. The question whether the roof had been kept in repair to the necessary standard was one that he had been entitled to decide in favour of the landlord on the basis that the method adopted had been adequate in practice and that the consequential detriment to the inhabitants of the house had been minimal.

The standard of repair is no higher in the case of a local authority landlord than a private sector landlord.[194]

## Burden of proof

The onus of proving a breach of the implied covenant is on the tenant.[195]

**20–41**

---

[192] [1987] 2 E.G.L.R. 56.
[193] [1993] 2 E.G.L.R. 144.
[194] *Wainwright v Leeds City Council* [1984] 1 E.G.L.R. 67.
[195] *Foster v Day* (1969) 208 E.G. 495.

## Rights of entry

**20–42**    Where s.11 applies, there is also implied a covenant by the tenant that the lessor, or any person authorised by him in writing, may at reasonable times of the day and on giving 24 hours' notice in writing to the occupier, enter the demised premises for the purpose of viewing their condition and state of repair.[196] The section confers no express right of entry to carry out work but there is an implied obligation on the tenant to allow the landlord to enter and occupy in order to effect repairs required by the section.[197] The right does not involve a further obligation to give the landlord exclusive occupation unless this is essential for the execution of the repairs, nor does it involve an obligation to give him access to all parts of the house at the same time unless again this is essential.[198]

## Where the tenant covenants to do works which fall within the landlord's implied covenant

**20–43**    Covenants by the tenant to repair the premises[199] (including a covenant to put in repair or deliver up in repair, to paint, point or render, to pay money in lieu of repairs by the tenant, or to pay money on account of repairs by the landlord[200]) are of no effect in so far as they relate to matters which would be the landlord's liability under s.11 (including the amended s.11) except so far as they impose on the tenant[201]:

(a)    a liability to carry out works or repairs for which the tenant is liable by virtue of his duty to use the premises in a tenant-like manner, or would be so liable but for an express covenant on his part;[202]

(b)    a liability to keep in repair or maintain anything which the tenant is entitled to remove from the dwelling-house.[203]

It follows that the tenant cannot be obliged, in whatever guise, to carry out repairs for which the landlord is liable under his implied repairing covenant. Thus, a covenant to paint and decorate the exterior of the dwelling-house is of no effect, because this inevitably involves a degree of protection against the elements and the processes of rot and the like, and is part and parcel of the process of keeping the exterior in repair.[204] However, an obligation to carry out purely decorative internal painting will not be invalidated unless the painting is also required for the purposes of keeping the interior in repair.[205]

---

[196] Landlord and Tenant Act 1985 s.11(6).
[197] See *McGreal v Wake* (1984) 13 H.L.R. 107, and see para.22–32, below.
[198] *McGreal v Wake*, above. See paras 22–43 and 22–44, below.
[199] This must refer to both the dwelling-house and any premises of which it forms a part.
[200] Landlord and Tenant Act 1985 s.11(5).
[201] Landlord and Tenant Act 1985 s.11(4).
[202] See para.21–03 et seq., below.
[203] See para.25–23 et seq., below.
[204] *Irvine v Moran* [1991] 1 E.G.L.R. 261. See further Ch.15, above.
[205] *Irvine v Moran*, above.

Similarly, the tenant cannot be obliged to contribute towards the cost of repairs     **20–44**
falling within the implied covenant. It follows that a service charge in respect of
the cost of works falling within the landlord's liability under the section will be of
no effect. The cost to the landlord of complying with his obligations can only be
recovered by being reflected in the rent.

However, there is nothing to prevent the imposition of a service charge in
respect of other works. Suppose, for example, that the tenant has a flat in a block
forming part of an estate of four blocks, all owned by the same landlord. On the
face of it, a service charge requiring him to contribute to the cost of repairing the
structure and exterior of all four blocks would be valid as regards all the blocks
bar his own. If his tenancy had been granted before January 15, 1989,[206] the
service charge would be also valid as regards repairs to his own block save for the
structure and exterior of, and installations in, his own flat. It is difficult to see the
policy behind this distinction, and it may be that it has simply been overlooked by
Parliament.

## Contracting out

The county court may by order made with the consent of the parties authorise the     **20–45**
inclusion in a lease, or in an agreement collateral to a lease, of provisions
excluding or modifying in relation to the lease the provisions of s.11 with respect
to the repairing obligations of the parties, if it appears to the court that it is
reasonable to do so, having regard to all the circumstances of the case, including
the other terms and conditions of the lease.[207] In the absence of such authorisation
any covenant, whether contained in the lease or any collateral document, is void
in so far as it purports:

(1)    to exclude or limit the obligations of the landlord or the immunities of the
       tenant under s.11; or
(2)    to authorise any forfeiture or impose on the tenant any penalty, disability or
       obligation in the event of his enforcing or relying upon those obligations or
       immunities.[208]

It is difficult to know how the court would be likely to approach an application
for an order excluding or modifying the section. The court is required to be
satisfied that it would be reasonable to authorise the exclusion or modification,
and regard must be had to all relevant circumstances including the other terms of
the lease. The court's power under what was formerly s.38(4) of the Landlord and
Tenant Act 1954[209] to authorise an agreement excluding the security of tenure
provisions conferred by the Act was generally exercised in favour of granting the
order "when [the agreement] is made by business people, properly advised by

---

[206] So that s.11 applies in its unamended form: see para.20–22 et seq., above.
[207] Landlord and Tenant Act 1985 s.12(2).
[208] 1985 Act s.12(1)(a).
[209] Prior to its repeal by the Regulatory Reform (Business Tenancies) (England and Wales) Order
2003.

their lawyers. The court has no material on which to refuse it".[210] In relation to the 1954 Act in its then form, however, the purpose of the requirement for the court's authorisation was not to empower or entitle it to consider the fairness of the bargain but to enable it to satisfy itself that the tenant understood that he was foregoing the protection of the Act,[211] and there was no express requirement that the court be satisfied that it would be reasonable to grant the order. Given the differences in the statutory provisions, and the fact that s.11 relates to residential premises where the consequences of disrepair may be more serious and there may be less equality of bargaining power than in the case of business premises, it is thought that the court's role in relation to s.11 is likely to be much wider. In particular, it is difficult to see how it can decide whether it would be reasonable to make the order without considering the fairness of the bargain. Accordingly, it is thought that, whilst the fact that the parties have agreed is an important factor, the court is unlikely to grant the order unless it is satisfied first, that there exists an acceptable scheme for repairs, and second, that the tenant has received adequate consideration for giving up his s.11 rights.

## Right to Manage ("RTM") Companies

**20–46**     Where the right to manage premises has been acquired by a right to manage a company under Pt 2 of the Commonhold and Leasehold Reform Act 2002, the following provisions apply:[212]

(1)     the obligations imposed on the landlord by s.11 are, so far as relating to any lease of any flat or other unit contained in the premises, instead obligations of the RTM company;

(2)     the RTM company owes to any person who is in occupation of any such flat or unit the same obligations as would be imposed on it under s.11 if that person were a lessee under a lease of the flat or other unit;

(3)     but (1) and (2) above do not apply to an obligation to the extent that it relates to a matter concerning only the flat or other unit concerned;

(4)     the obligations imposed on the RTM company by (1) above in relation to any lease are owed to the lessor (as well as the lessee);

(5)     subsections (3A) to (5) of s.11 have effect[213] with the modifications that are appropriate in consequence of (1) to (3) above;

(6)     the references in s.11(6)[214] include the RTM company and a person who is in occupation of the relevant flat or other unit otherwise than under a lease has, in relation to the flat or other unit, the same obligation as that imposed on a lessee by s.11(6);

(7)     the restriction on contracting out in s.12(1)(a)[215] includes the RTM company.

---

[210] *Hagee (London) Ltd v AB Erikson & Larsen* [1976] Q.B. 209, per Lord Denning M.R.
[211] *Receiver of Metropolitan Police v Palacegate Properties Ltd* [2000] 1 E.G.L.R. 63.
[212] Commonhold and Leasehold Reform Act 2002 s.102 and Sch.7 para.3.
[213] See paras 20–32 and 20–43, above.
[214] See para.20–42, above.
[215] See para.20–45, above.

## Remedies for breach of the obligation

The various remedies available to the tenant for breach of the obligation implied by s.11 are considered in Ch.33, below.

**20–47**

## Res judicata

The principle of res judicata, which prevents a claimant from relitigating a matter which has already been determined against him in previous proceedings, applies to claims for breach of the implied covenant under s.11 of the 1985 Act. In *Onwuama v Ealing LBC*[216] the tenant brought proceedings against her landlord for breach of the implied obligation in relation to damp. In December 2005 the judge held that the damp was not caused by any breach of the obligation. The tenant then brought fresh proceedings against the landlord alleging that the damp was caused by a breach of the implied obligation. Her claim was struck out. Teare J. said:

**20–48**

> "15. Counsel stressed that the landlord's duty to keep premises in repair is a continuing duty. That is correct. The duty existed before December 2005 and continued after December 2005. But to the extent that the Claimant seeks to rely upon dampness which existed not only after but also before December 2005 she will be confronted by the decision in the first action that the cause of that dampness was not a breach of duty by the landlord.
>
> 16. It was further submitted that 'if the judgment were to stand the Claimant could never require the landlord to remedy dampness in the walls or floors of the premises no matter how caused. The cause of damp regardless of evidence to the contrary would always be deemed to be condensation.' This submission fails to understand the decision of [the judge in the first claim]. If there develops some *new* cause of damp in the flat caused by a want of repair then the Claimant can of course allege and prove that. What she cannot do is allege that the cause of the damp which was the subject of complaint in the first action was other than as found by [the judge in the first claim].
> ....
> 18. Towards the end of his reply counsel suggested that it is not possible to say that the entirety of the claim relates to damp which developed before December 2005. He pointed out that damp grows or extends and that he should be permitted to claim in so far as the damp extended or worsened after December 2005. Although this suggestion was made following questions by me I do not consider that it can assist the Claimant. The finding in respect of which the judge found there was an issue estoppel was as to the cause of the damp. Thus even if the claimant's pleaded case had been expressly limited to the extent to which the pre-December 2005 damp had worsened post-December 2005 she would be estopped from contending that that damp had been caused other than as found by [the court in the first action]."

## SECTION 4 OF THE DEFECTIVE PREMISES ACT 1972

## Introductory

Section 4 of the 1972 Act is printed in Appendix II, below. It applies where premises are let under a tenancy which puts on the landlord an obligation to the tenant for the maintenance or repair of the premises.[217] In such a case, the

**20–49**

---

[216] [2008] EWHC 1704 (Q.B.).
[217] See paras 20–50 to 20–54, below.

landlord owes a duty to all persons who might reasonably be expected to be affected by defects in the state of the premises, including the tenant, a duty to take such care as is reasonable in all the circumstances to see that they are reasonably safe from personal injury or damage to property caused by a relevant defect (as defined).[218] The duty is owed if the landlord knows or ought to know of the relevant defect.[219] The section also applies where the landlord is not under an obligation to repair but is entitled to enter the premises to carry out repairs.[220]

Where the right to manage premises has been acquired by an RTM company, the duty under the Act is owed by the RTM company with effect from the acquisition date.[221]

The main importance of s.4 is in relation to the landlord's liability to persons other than the tenant in respect of defects in the demised premises. As such it is outside the scope of this work, which is concerned only with liability as between landlord and tenant. However, s.4 may in some circumstances impose liability on the landlord to the tenant for defects in the demised premises, and it is in this context that it is dealt with in this Chapter.

## Application of the section

**20–50**   Certain of the expressions used in s.4 require further consideration.

### (a)   Premises

**20–51**   There is no requirement that the subject-matter of the letting must be a dwelling-house, from which it follows that the Act applies equally to business or other premises. It was held by the Court of Appeal in *Smith v Bradford Metropolitan Council*[222] that "premises" means the whole of the premises let, both land and buildings. The premises in that case were held to include a patio at the rear of a council house. However, the expression does not include premises which are not part of the letting, such as common parts.

### (b)   Let under a tenancy

**20–52**   "Tenancy" means:

(1)   a tenancy created either immediately or derivatively out of the freehold, whether by a lease or underlease, by an agreement for lease or underlease or by a tenancy agreement, but not including a mortgage term or any interest arising in favour of a mortgagor by his attorning tenant to his mortgagee;[223]

---

[218] See paras 20–55 to 20–57, below.
[219] See para.20–56, below.
[220] See para.20–58, below.
[221] Commonhold and Leasehold Reform Act 2002 ss.102, 181 and Sch.7, para.2.
[222] (1982) 44 P. & C.R. 171.
[223] Defective Premises Act 1972 s.6(1)(a); *King v South Northamptonshire District Council* [1992] 1 E.G.L.R. 53.

(2)    a tenancy at will or a tenancy on sufferance;[224]
(3)    a tenancy, whether or not constituting a tenancy at common law, created by
       or in pursuance of any enactment.[225]

In addition, the section applies to a right of occupation given by contract or
any enactment and not amounting to a tenancy.[226] It therefore applies to licences
as well as tenancies provided that a right of occupation is thereby conferred. It is
thought that a statutory tenancy under the Rent Act 1977 would be included by
virtue either of this or of (c) above.

### (c)    An obligation to the tenant

The obligation does not have to be express, and includes an obligation arising by          **20–53**
implication at common law or under statute.[227] An example would be the implied
landlord's repairing covenant imposed by s.11 of the Landlord and Tenant Act
1985.[228]

### (d)    For the maintenance or repair of the premises

It is thought that the reference to an obligation for the maintenance or repair of          **20–54**
the premises (i.e. the demised premises)[229] is likely to be construed as including
any obligation which can properly be described as an obligation to maintain or
repair even if those words are not expressly used. However, the section is "clearly
directed to maintenance or repair", so that an obligation to keep the premises in
good condition, to the extent that it imposes a duty over and above repair, will not
engage the section.[230]

## To whom the duty imposed by the section is owed

The duty imposed by the section is owed to all persons who might reasonably be          **20–55**
expected to be affected by defects in the state of the premises.[231] This includes
the tenant himself.[232]

## When the duty arises

The duty is owed where:          **20–56**

---

[224] Defective Premises Act 1972 s.6(1)(b).
[225] Defective Premises Act 1972 s.6(1)(c).
[226] Defective Premises Act 1972 s.4(6).
[227] Defective Premises Act 1972 s.4(5).
[228] This is considered in para.20–17 et seq., above.
[229] See para.20–51, above.
[230] *Alker v Collingwood Housing Association* [2007] 2 E.G.L.R. 43 per Carnwath L.J. at [21] to [23].
See para.20–56, below, where this case is further considered.
[231] Defective Premises Act 1972 s.4(2).
[232] *Smith v Bradford Metropolitan Council* (1982) 44 P. & C.R. 171; *McDonagh v Kent Area Health
Authority* (1984) 134 N.L.J. 567; *Barrett v Lounova (1982) Ltd* [1990] 1 Q.B. 348; *McAuley v Bristol
City Council* [1990] 2 Q.B. 134; *Sykes v Harry* [2001] Q.B. 1014.

(1)    there is a "relevant defect"; and
(2)    either:
    (a)    the landlord knows of the relevant defect (whether as a result of being notified by the tenant or otherwise); or
    (b)    the landlord ought in all the circumstances to have known of the relevant defect.[233]

"Relevant defect" means a defect in the state of the premises (i.e. the demised premises[234]) existing at or after "the material time",[235] and arising from, or continuing because of, an act or omission by the landlord which constitutes or would if he had had notice of the defect, have constituted a failure by him to carry out his obligation to the tenant for the maintenance or repair of the premises.[236]

A defect can therefore only amount to a relevant defect if the landlord is (or could by notice be made) liable to remedy it pursuant to his obligation to maintain or repair the premises. Where that is not the case, there is no liability under the section. Thus, in *Alker v Collingwood Housing Association*[237] the landlord covenanted to keep the demised property (a house) in good condition and to repair and maintain, among other parts, external doors. The house had a front door with a ribbed glass panel which was not safety glass but ordinary annealed glass. The tenant suffered serious injuries when she accidentally put her hand through the panel. She claimed damages against the landlord under s.4. The Court of Appeal held that the replacement of the glass panel was not within the landlord's obligation. It was not in disrepair and there had been no failure to maintain it. Laws L.J. (with whom Carnwath and Moore-Bick L.JJ. agreed) said in his judgment:

> "No doubt, the two concepts [i.e. repair and maintain] overlap. Neither of them, however, can, in my judgment, possibly be said to encompass or to include a duty or obligation to make safe. Moreover, a duty to keep 'in good condition', the words used here, even if it encompasses a duty to put into good condition, again cannot encompass a duty to put in safe condition.
> …. [The tenant's case] would extend the scope of the duty arising under section 4 to an extent unjustified by the section's language or by any policy considerations to which the court might reasonably have regard. It would transform section 4 from a statutory embodiment of the landlord's repairing covenant intended to protect persons, not only the tenant, against the effects of wants of repair or maintenance into something else altogether; in effect, a statutory warranty that the premises are reasonably safe."

In *Boldack v East Lindsey District Council*[238] the claimant was injured when a paving slab, which had been leaning against the outside wall of the house, fell onto his foot. It was argued that removal of the slab amounted to work of maintenance, and that maintenance was within the scope of an express right of

---

[233] Defective Premises Act 1972 s.4(2).
[234] See para.20–51, above.
[235] "Material time" means: (1) January 1, 1974, where the tenancy commenced before that date; and (2) otherwise the earliest of (a) the time when the tenancy commences, (b) the time when the tenancy agreement is entered into, and (c) the time when possession is taken of the premises in contemplation of the letting: Defective Premises Act 1972 s.4(3).
[236] Defective Premises Act 1972 s.4(3).
[237] [2007] 2 E.G.L.R. 43.
[238] (1999) 31 H.L.R. 41.

entry for the purpose of carrying out repairs. The Court of Appeal held that removing the slab was not maintenance "any more than it would be if the object was ... a bucket".

In *Drysdale v Hedges*,[239] the landlord of a terraced house covenanted to provide and maintain the structure and exterior of the property in good repair. The claimant tenant was injured when she slipped on the stone front steps leading to the premises. The steps were slippery from a combination of paint and wet, and the wall at the side of the steps was not sufficiently high and/or was not fitted with a guardrail or handrail to stop someone falling down to basement level. The paint had been applied by the landlord, and its effect had been to increase the slipperiness of the steps. It was held that neither the low and unguarded wall nor the presence of the paint on the steps amounted to a relevant defect.

The section modifies the common law requirement of actual notice,[240] so that the landlord is liable even where he did not actually know of the defect if in all the circumstances he should have known of it.[241] Thus, in *Sykes v Harry*[242] the landlord had prior to the start of the tenancy installed a gas fire but subsequently took no steps to get it serviced. The tenant suffered carbon monoxide poisoning as a result of defects in the fire. At first instance the judge held that the landlord was not liable because he had no knowledge of the actual defect that had caused the injury. The Court of Appeal allowed the tenant's appeal. The gas fire had replaced an earlier installation in respect of which the landlord had received notice of a dangerous gas explosion from the Gas Board in relation to an escape of gas from the governor. The landlord was well aware of the importance of regular servicing of the fire and of the risk of defects developing if servicing did not take place. He was also aware that the fire had never been serviced. He had been "put on inquiry that there was a real risk that [the relevant defects] had occurred". Accordingly, by his failure to service the gas fire, or otherwise to take steps to check or make appropriate inquiries of the tenant as to the servicing and/or state of the gas fire during the eight-year period before the tenant's accident, the landlord had failed in his duty to take such care as was reasonable in all the circumstances to see that the tenant was reasonably safe from injury. However, the Court of Appeal declined to disturb the judge's assessment of contributory negligence at 80 per cent.

## The duty imposed by the section

The duty imposed by the section is a duty to take such care as is reasonable in all the circumstances to see that the persons to whom the duty is owed[243] are reasonably safe from (a) personal injury, or (b) damage to their property caused by a "relevant defect"[244] of which the landlord knows (whether as a result of

**20–57**

---

[239] [2012] 162 N.L.J. 1056.
[240] See para.22–05, below.
[241] For a case in which it was held on the facts that the landlord ought to have known of a relevant defect, see *Clarke v Taff Ely BC* (1980) 10 H.L.R. 44 (collapse of rotten floorboards).
[242] [2001] Q.B. 1014.
[243] See para.20–55, above.
[244] See para.20–56, above.

being notified by the tenant or otherwise) or of which he ought to have known.[245] "Personal injury" includes any disease and any impairment of a person's physical or mental condition.[246] It would not therefore include ordinary discomfort or inconvenience resulting from disrepair, unless this has resulted in disease or impairment of the tenant's mental condition.

The duty imposed by the section is in addition to any duty owed by the landlord apart from the section.[247] It follows that where the landlord is under an express or implied repairing obligation, then the tenant has the benefit of both that and the statutory duty. However, the latter duty will generally be less extensive in several respects than that imposed by a repairing covenant. First, it does not impose an absolute duty to carry out repairs but only a qualified duty to take reasonable care.[248] Second, defects which do not cause personal injury or damage to property are outside the scope of the duty. Thus, for example, there would be no duty to remedy defective pointing unless it is so defective that it results in water penetration which in turn causes personal injury or damage to property. Third, the duty only applies in relation to the demised premises, and not to any common parts.[249]

As a result of the above, where the landlord is under a contractual obligation to the tenant to repair, the tenant will in most cases be better off under that obligation than under s.4. The only circumstances in which the tenant would be better off relying on the section is where he cannot establish a breach of the contractual obligation, because he cannot show that the landlord had actual knowledge of the defect.[250] If he can show that the landlord nonetheless ought in all the circumstances to have known of the defect, then he may be able to establish a breach of duty under the Act.[251] Cases such as this apart, however, "the statutory protection for those in occupation of defective premises is geared to the landlord's obligation to repair the premises, and goes no wider than the repair covenant".[252]

## Where the landlord has a right of entry to carry out repairs

**20–58** By s.4(4) of the Act, the duty imposed by s.4(1) also applies where the landlord is entitled, but not obliged, to enter to carry out repairs. It is here that its principal importance as between landlord and tenant lies, since (as has already been noted) where the tenancy contains a contractual obligation to repair on the part of the landlord, the tenant will in most cases be better off under that obligation and will not need to rely on s.4.[253]

---

[245] Defective Premises Act 1972 s.4(1) and (2).
[246] Defective Premises Act 1972 s.6(1).
[247] Defective Premises Act 1972 s.6(2).
[248] For a discussion of the duty to take reasonable care, see paras 19–21 to 19–22, above.
[249] See para.20–51, above.
[250] See para.22–05, below.
[251] See *Sykes v Harry* [2001] Q.B. 1014 (in which the tenant failed to establish a breach of the obligation implied by s.11 of the Landlord and Tenant Act 1985 but succeeded in establishing liability under the 1972 Act). The facts are set out in para.20–56, above.
[252] *McNerny v Lambeth London Borough Council* (1998) 21 H.L.R. 188 per Dillon L.J. at 193.
[253] See para.20–57, above.

Section 4(4) applies where the tenancy expressly or impliedly gives the landlord the right to enter the premises to carry out any description of maintenance or repair of the premises. In such a case, as from the time when the landlord first is, or by notice or otherwise can put himself, in a position to exercise the right and so long as he is or can put himself in that position, he is treated for the purposes of s.4(1) to (3) only (but for no other purpose) as if he were under an obligation to the tenant for that description of repair or maintenance which he has a right to carry out. In *Lee v Leeds City Council*[254] Chadwick L.J. described s.4(4) as introducing a "statutory hypothesis", and explained its effect as follows:

> "A landlord who is not otherwise under an obligation to carry out works of maintenance or repair of a particular description is to be treated—for the purposes of sections 4(1) and (3) but for no other purpose—as if he were under an obligation to carry out works of maintenance or repair of that description if the terms of the tenancy (expressly or impliedly) give him 'the right to enter the premises to carry out [that] description of maintenance or repair of the premises'. So, for example, a landlord who is not otherwise under an obligation to carry out works of repair and maintenance to the garden but who has a right to enter for the purpose of carrying out such works if he chooses will be treated—for the purposes of section 4(1) and (3) of the Act—as if he were under an obligation to carry out such works; with the consequence that he owes a duty to take reasonable care to see that the tenant or other person who might reasonably be expected to be affected by defects in the state of the garden is reasonably safe from personal injury caused by such a defect arising from lack of repair or maintenance …
> … Section 4(4) of the Act requires the landlord to be treated, for the purposes of subsection (1) and (3), as if he were under an obligation to the tenant for maintenance or repair of the premises where the tenancy 'expressly or impliedly gives the landlord the right to enter the premises to carry out any description of maintenance or repair of the premises.' In those circumstances the scope and extent of the deemed obligation is commensurate with the scope and extent of the right to enter."

However, no duty is owed to the tenant in respect of any defect in the state of the **20–59** premises arising from, or continuing because of, a failure to carry out an obligation expressly imposed on the tenant by the tenancy.[255]

It has been said that there is no warrant for a wide construction of the provision, given that it applies to all landlords, not merely to local authorities, and can operate so as to impose a substantial burden upon a landlord in respect of premises under the immediate control of the tenant and in respect of which the landlord has assumed no contractual obligation.[256]

Certain of the above matters require further discussion.

### (a)  A right to enter the premises to carry out any description of maintenance or repair

An express right of entry on the part of the landlord to carry out repairs for which **20–60** neither party assumes a contractual liability is relatively uncommon in leases. Where a right of entry on the part of the landlord exists, it is usually either ancillary to the landlord's obligation to repair[257] (in which case the tenancy is

---

254 [2002] 1 W.L.R. 1488.
255 Defective Premises Act 1972 s.4(4).
256 *McAuley v Bristol City Council* [1992] Q.B. 134, per Ralph Gibson L.J.
257 See para.22–32 et seq., below.

within s.4 anyway), or it is a right to carry out work for which the tenant is liable (in which case no duty is owed to the tenant). However some tenancies (usually local authority lettings) contain an express right of entry on the part of the landlord unaccompanied by any obligation by either party to repair. In such cases the question whether s.4 applies is one of construction of the right to see if it entitles the landlord to enter to repair the defect in question.

In some cases the right will be expressly conferred for the purpose of carrying out repairs. The only question is then whether it extends to the part of the premises in question. Thus, in *Smith v Bradford Metropolitan Council*,[258] the tenancy agreement provided that "the tenant shall ... give the Council officers agents contractors and workmen reasonable facilities for inspecting the premises and their state of repair and for carrying out repairs." The Court of Appeal held that this provision, properly construed, gave the landlord the right to repair a concrete yard at the rear of the property, and therefore that s.4 applied.

In other cases, however, the right may be more general, and the question will be what repairs, if any, is the landlord entitled to enter to carry out. Thus, in *McAuley v Bristol City Council*[259] a weekly tenancy of a council house contained an obligation by the landlord to maintain the structure and exterior of the property in good repair; an obligation by the tenant to keep the premises, including the garden, in a clean and orderly condition; and a provision requiring the tenant to give the council's agents and workmen access to the premises "for any purpose which may from time to time be required by the council". The Court of Appeal held that, properly construed, the express right of entry was limited to purposes which the landlord could lawfully carry out, as between it and the tenant (such as the repair of the structure and exterior pursuant to the express obligation). It was held that a right to enter to repair defects likely to cause personal injury was to be implied,[260] and therefore that the landlord was liable under s.4 when the tenant broke her ankle on an unstable step in the garden.

20–61    In order to trigger liability under s.4, the right of entry must be derived from an existing tenancy: a right of entry in a previous tenancy agreement is not sufficient.[261] Moreover, the only right of entry which is relevant for the purposes of s.4(4) is a right of entry to carry out maintenance or repairs. A right of entry to carry out other work (such as improvement works or other works which do not amount to repairs) does not trigger the deemed liability.[262]

Where there is no express right of entry, the question will be whether a right to enter to carry out repairs can be implied. This is discussed elsewhere.[263]

---

[258] (1982) 44 P. & C.R. 171.
[259] [1992] Q.B. 134.
[260] See further para.22–36, below.
[261] *Boldack v East Lindsey District Council* (1999) 31 H.L.R. 41.
[262] *Lee v Leeds City Council* [2002] 1 W.L.R. 1488; *Dunn v Bradford Metropolitan District Council* [2002] 3 E.G.L.R. 104.
[263] See para.22–30 et seq., below.

## (b)    The duty

Where, in accordance with the above principles, the landlord has an express or    **20–62**
implied right of entry to carry out maintenance or repairs, he is treated as if he
were under an obligation to the tenant for such maintenance and repairs as he is
entitled to enter to carry out.[264] This is for the purposes of s.4 only, and not for
any other purpose,[265] so that the tenant does not acquire a deemed cause of action
in contract. The effect is to give the tenant the same rights and remedies under s.4
as he would have had if the tenancy contained an express or implied landlord's
repairing obligation. The deemed obligation only arises, however, as from the
time when the landlord first is, or by notice can put himself, in a position to
exercise his right of entry, and it lasts only for so long as he is or can put himself
in that position.[266]

The landlord cannot be made liable under s.4 in respect of a failure to carry out
works which are not works of repair or maintenance even where he has a right of
entry to carry out such works.[267] No deemed liability under s.4(4) therefore arises
where the defect which has caused the injury or damage is not a defect arising
from a want of repair (for example, it is a design defect which has not resulted in
disrepair). Thus, in *Lee v Leeds City Council*[268] works to remedy an inherent
design defect which had given rise to excessive condensation and mould, but
which (by virtue of the decision in *Quick v Taff Ely Borough Council*[269]) was not
itself disrepair, were held not to be within the words "any description of
maintenance or repair of the premises", so that a right on the part of the landlord
to enter to carry out those works did not give rise to a deemed duty under s.4(4).

## (c)    Defects for which the tenant is responsible

The landlord does not owe the tenant any duty under the deemed obligation in    **20–63**
respect of any defect in the state of the premises arising from, or continuing
because of, a failure to carry out an obligation expressly imposed on the tenant by
the tenancy.[270] It follows that the tenant cannot rely on the deemed obligation in
so far as the defect is the result of his own breach of covenant. This would not
stop third parties from relying on s.4 as against the landlord, although the
landlord would in turn have a right to damages against the tenant for breach of his
covenant. It is to be noted that the deeming provision refers only to express
obligations on the part of the tenant. Although an obligation imposed on the
tenant by statute is included,[271] an implied obligation arising at common law,
such as the implied duty of tenant-like user,[272] is apparently excluded. In practice

---

[264] Defective Premises Act 1972 s.4(4).
[265] Defective Premises Act 1972 s.4(4).
[266] Defective Premises Act 1972 s.4(4).
[267] *Lee v Leeds City Council* [2002] 1 W.L.R. 1488; *Dunn v Bradford Metropolitan District Council* [2002] 3 E.G.L.R. 104.
[268] Above.
[269] [1986] Q.B. 809. See Ch.8, above.
[270] This includes a statutory obligation: Defective Premises Act 1972 s.4(5).
[271] Defective Premises Act 1972 s.4(4).
[272] See para.21–03 et seq., below.

this would be unlikely to matter because any claim by the tenant based on breach of the landlord's duty would, insofar as it related to defects falling within the implied covenant, be met by a counterclaim by the landlord for breach of the tenant's implied covenant, so that in principle the damages would cancel each other out.

## Contracting out

**20–64** Any term of any agreement which purports to exclude or restrict, or has the effect of excluding or restricting, the operation of s.4, or any liability arising by virtue of any such provision, is void.[273] Contracting out is not therefore permitted under any guise.

## Remedies for breach of the duty

**20–65** The principal remedy for breach of the duty imposed by the section is damages, which are discussed elsewhere.[274] However, in appropriate circumstances the tenant will also be entitled to a mandatory injunction to oblige the landlord to carry out remedial works which he is obliged to carry out under the section.[275]

## THE OCCUPIERS' LIABILITY ACT 1957

## The Occupiers' Liability Act 1957

**20–66** The Occupiers' Liability Act 1957 imposes a duty of care on the occupier of premises. Its principal importance is in relation to the liability of landlord or tenant to third parties as opposed to their liability to each other. As between landlord and tenant, however, the Act may be relevant in relation to common parts, and it is for this reason that a brief treatment of it has been included. For a more detailed treatment, reference should be made to specialist textbooks on the law of tort.

An occupier is someone who has "a sufficient degree of control over premises to put him under a duty of care towards those who came lawfully on to the premises".[276] Where a landlord lets premises to a tenant, he is regarded as parting with all control over them. He does not retain any degree of control, even though he has undertaken to repair the structure. But where he lets parts of a building and retains other parts, he is regarded as retaining control over the parts which are not

---

[273] Defective Premises Act 1972 s.6(3).
[274] See para.33–15 et seq., below. For cases on damages under the 1972 Act, see *Bayoumi v Protim Services Ltd* [1996] E.G.C.S. 187 and *Smith v Drumm* [1996] E.G.C.S. 192.
[275] See *Barrett v Lounova (1982) Ltd* [1990] 1 Q.B. 348.
[276] *Wheat v E. Lacon & Co Ltd* [1966] A.C. 552.

demised.[277] In such a case he will be the occupier for the purposes of the 1957 Act. Thus, a landlord has been held to be the occupier of a staircase in a block of flats.[278]

Where, in accordance with the above, the landlord is the occupier of any part of a building, he owes to all persons who constitute his visitors the "common duty of care".[279] It is probable that a tenant lawfully using the common parts would constitute a visitor for this purpose. The common duty of care is a duty to take such care as in all the circumstances of the case is reasonable to see that the visitor will be reasonably safe in using the premises for the purposes for which he is invited or permitted by the occupier to be there.[280] The Act sets out a number of matters to which regard is to be had in determining the degree of care required of the occupier, and whether the duty of care has been discharged.[281] The common duty of care does not impose on the occupier any obligation to a visitor in respect of risks willingly accepted as his by the visitor.[282] Where there is an obvious danger and the occupier has posted notices warning of the danger, he will not be liable to incur further costs to prevent visitors from such danger.[283] The Act does not prevent the landlord from excluding his liability to the tenant.[284]

An example of an unsuccessful claim under the Act by a tenant is *Irving v London County Council*,[285] in which the plaintiff was the tenant of a flat on the third floor of a block of flats, and the landlords retained possession and control of a common staircase. The lighting for this was controlled by a time switch, which malfunctioned. The plaintiff fell on the staircase whilst using it at night, and was injured. Her claim failed on the ground that the landlord was under no duty to keep the staircase lit at all hours of darkness. By contrast, the claim succeeded in *Alexander v Freshwater Properties*,[286] in which the claimant's index finger was caught in the front door of a block of flats, and the landlord had failed to take such steps as it reasonably ought to have taken to ensure that the door could be safely closed without the risk of injury.

---

[277] *Wheat v E. Lacon & Co Ltd*, above, per Lord Denning M.R.

[278] *Miller v Hancock* [1893] 2 Q.B. 177; *Fairman v Perpetual Investment Building Society* [1923] A.C. 74.

[279] Occupiers' Liability Act 1957 s.2.

[280] Occupiers' Liability Act 1957 s.2(2).

[281] Occupiers' Liability Act 1957 s.2(3) and (4).

[282] Occupiers' Liability Act 1957 s.2(5).

[283] *Tomlinson v Congleton Borough Council* [2003] 3 All E.R. 1122.

[284] The common duty of care is only owed in so far as the occupier is free to and does extend, restrict, modify or exclude his duty to any visitors by agreement or otherwise: Occupiers' Liability Act 1957 s.2(1). The Act contains no provision preventing the landlord from excluding liability to the tenant: see, e.g. *Akerib v Booth* [1960] 1 W.L.R. 454. It is probable that the Unfair Contract Terms Act 1977 would not apply to an exclusion of liability contained in a lease: see *Electricity Supply Nominees Ltd v IAF Group Ltd* [1993] 1 W.L.R. 1059.

[285] (1965) 109 S.J. 157.

[286] [2012] EWCA Civ 1048.

PUBLIC STATUTES

## Liability under public statutes

**20–67**     Liability for defective premises may arise under public statutes in a variety of ways. For example, (a) a number of duties are imposed on landlords by the various health and safety statutes;[287] (b) a wide variety of powers and duties for dealing with defective premises are conferred on local authorities by the Building Act 1984,[288] the Housing Act 1985[289] and the Environmental Protection Act 1990;[290] (c) a landlord of a house in multiple occupation is liable to observe the provisions of the management code set out in the Management of Houses in Multiple Occupation (England) Regulations 2006[291] made under the provisions of Pt XI of the Housing Act 1985; and (d) a landlord of premises occupied, whether exclusively or not, for residential purposes under certain types of lease or a licence is liable to observe reg.36 of the Gas Safety (Installation and Use) Regulations 1998,[292] which imposes strict duties in relation to the maintenance and checking of gas fittings and flues and associated duties. These various provisions are outside the scope of this work, and reference should be made to specialist books on the subject.

## THE HUMAN RIGHTS ACT 1998

**20–68**     The Human Rights Act 1998 is of potential relevance to the law of dilapidations in two principal ways.

First, the effect of s.3 of the Act is that in so far as it is possible to do so, primary legislation and subordinate legislation (whenever enacted) must be read and given effect to in a way which is compatible with the Convention Rights.[293] The section therefore applies to the various statutes considered above (and elsewhere in this work). Thus, it was argued in *Lee v Leeds City Council*[294] that

---

[287] For example, the Factories Act 1961; the Offices, Shops and Railway Premises Act 1963; and the Health and Safety etc. Act 1974 and the regulations made thereunder. In *Westminster City Council v Select Management Ltd* [1985] 1 W.L.R. 576, it was held that for the purposes of the 1974 Act, "non-domestic premises" include the common parts of a block of flats, with the result that the landlord owed a duty under s.4(1) of the Act to persons who came to repair the lifts and electrical installations to ensure that the common parts were safe and without risk to health. It was therefore held that improvement notices served by the local authority on the managing agents of the block requiring work to the lifts and electrical installations had been validly served.

[288] Ss.76 to 83.

[289] Housing Act 1985 Pt VI.

[290] Environmental Protection Act 1990 Pt III.

[291] SI 2006/372 (as amended by the Houses in Multiple Occupation (Management) (England) Regulations 2009 (SI 2009/724)).

[292] SI 1998/2451.

[293] The Convention means the Convention for the Protection of Human Rights and Fundamental Freedoms agreed by the Council of Europe on November 4, 1950 as it has effect for the time being in relation to the UK. The Convention Rights means the rights and fundamental freedoms set out in (a) Arts 2 to 12 and 14 of the Convention, (b) Arts 1 to 3 of the First Protocol and (c) Arts 1 and 2 of the Sixth Protocol, as read with arts 16 to 18 of the Convention. The Convention Rights are set out in Sch.1 to the 1998 Act.

[294] [2002] 1 W.L.R. 1488.

s.3 required the court to re-interpret s.11 of the Landlord and Tenant Act 1985 as imposing on the landlord a liability to keep the premises fit for human habitation, notwithstanding the decision of the Court of Appeal in *Quick v Taff-Ely BC*[295] to the effect that, in the absence of disrepair, the section does not impose liability to remedy design defects even though the dwelling is unfit for habitation.[296] The Court of Appeal rejected the argument on the ground that the obligations imposed by s.11, as interpreted in *Quick*, were not incompatible with Convention Rights.

The second way in which the Human Rights Act may be relevant to the law of dilapidations concerns cases involving public authorities.[297] Section 6(1) provides that it is unlawful for a public authority to act[298] in a way which is incompatible with a Convention Right. The Convention Right likely to be of most relevance to the law of dilapidations is art.8 of Sch.1 to the 1998 Act, which is headed "Right to respect for private and family life" and which provides:

> "1. Everyone has the right to respect for his private and family life, his home and his correspondence.
>    There shall be no interference by a public authority with the exercise of this right except such as is in accordance with the law and is necessary in a democratic society in the interests of national security, public safety or the economic well-being of the country, for the prevention of disorder or crime, for the protection of health or morals, or for the protection of the rights and freedoms of others."

Article 8 is capable in principle of imposing positive as well as negative obligations.[299] The effect of s.6(1) is therefore to impose on a local authority landlord an obligation to take steps to ensure that the condition of a dwelling-house which it has let for social housing is such that the tenant's Convention Rights under art.8 is not infringed.[300] Severe environmental pollution may amount to an infringement of art.8. Thus, in *Lopez Ostra v Spain*[301] a waste treatment plant began operating without a licence and the consequent fumes, noise and smells adversely affected the health of nearby residents. It was held that the state had infringed art.8 by failing to exercise its powers to prevent the nuisance and protect the applicant's home. In appropriate circumstances, therefore, a failure on the part of a public authority to repair premises may amount to an infringement of the tenant's art.8 rights. But this is likely to be the case only in exceptional circumstances. In *Lee v Leeds City Council*[302] the Court of Appeal held that the existence of condensation and consequent mould growth did not infringe the tenants' art.8 rights. Chadwick L.J. (with whom Tuckey L.J. and Sir Murray Stuart-Smith agreed) said:

**20–69**

---

[295] [1986] Q.B. 809.
[296] See Ch.8, above.
[297] A public authority includes a court or tribunal, and persons certain whose functions are functions of a public nature: Human Rights Act 1998 s.6(3).
[298] An "act" includes a failure to act: Human Rights Act 1998 s.6(6).
[299] See *Guerra v Italy* (1998) 26 E.H.R.R. 357 at [58] and *Lee v Leeds City Council*, above.
[300] *Lee v Leeds City Council*, above.
[301] (1994) 20 E.H.R.R. 277. See also *Guerra v Italy*, above.
[302] Above.

"The steps which a public authority will be required to take in order to ensure compliance with Article 8—that is, to ensure 'respect' for private and family life—must be determined, in each case, by having due regard to the needs and resources of the community and of individuals. And, in striking the balance between the resources of a local housing authority (and the need to meet other claims upon those resources) and the needs of the individual tenant, regard must be had to the observation of Lord Hoffmann in *Southwark BC v. Tanner* [as to the need 'to show a proper sensitivity to the limits of permissible judicial creativity' in the field of social housing responsibilities; a field which is 'so very much a matter for the allocation of resources in accordance with democratically determined priorities']. That observation is as pertinent in the present case as it was in the context to which it was addressed—the implication of a contractual term at common law. I find no support in the Strasbourg jurisprudence—or in the jurisprudence which has been developing in these courts since the advent of the 1998 Act—for the proposition that section 6, in conjunction with Article 8, imposes some general and unqualified obligation on local authorities in relation to the condition of their housing stock.

That is not to say that there will never be cases in which a local authority, as the landlord of a dwelling house let for the purposes of social housing which is unfit for human habitation or in a state prejudicial to health, will be in breach of the positive duty inherent in respect for private and family life which is imposed by section 6 of the 1998 Act and Article 8 in Schedule 1 to that Act. But it has not been shown that there has been any breach of duty in the cases which are the subject of these appeals."

If the court were to find that a public authority has acted, or is proposing to act, in a manner which is unlawful under s.6(1), it may grant such relief or remedy (including damages), or make such order, within its powers as it considers just and appropriate.[303]

The detailed provisions of the 1998 Act, and the general law relating to human rights, are outside the scope of this work. For a more definitive treatment, reference should be made to the appropriate specialist works.

---

[303] Human Rights Act 1998 s.8(1).

CHAPTER 21

# IMPLIED OBLIGATIONS AND DUTIES OF THE TENANT TO THE LANDLORD

## INTRODUCTORY

In practice, landlord's repairing obligations are omitted from leases much more often than are tenant's repairing obligations, and virtually all modern leases contain some form of express tenant's repairing and decorating obligation. Nevertheless, there will be a residual number of cases where for whatever reason (perhaps because the tenancy was the result of an informal oral agreement) there will be no express tenant's repairing obligations, and the landlord will need to resort to such implied obligations and duties as may exist.     **21–01**

The principles applicable to the implication of repairing and other obligations on the part of the tenant are the same as those considered in Ch.19, above, in relation to the implication of landlord's obligations. In general terms, subject to what follows, a tenant is under no implied obligation to repair the demised premises during the term or to yield them up in repair at the end of the term. Thus, in the New Zealand case of *BP Oil New Zealand v Ports of Auckland*[1] the demised land had become contaminated by spills and leaks from stored petroleum products. The relevant leases contained covenants on the part of the tenant to keep all buildings and structures on the demised land in good order, condition and repair. Rodney Hansen J. held (among other things) that no term was to be implied into the leases that the tenant would not commit waste against the reversion by causing or allowing the land to become contaminated.

However, a tenant is or may be subject to the following implied obligations or duties:     **21–02**

(1)   the obligation on all tenants to use the demised premises in a tenant-like manner[2];

(2)   the obligation on a yearly tenant to keep the demised premises wind and watertight, which is suggested in some of the cases but whose existence as an obligation separate from (1) above is doubtful[3];

(3)   the obligation on all tenants not to commit voluntary (or commissive) waste[4];

---

[1] [2004] 2 N.Z.L.R. 208. See further on this case para.21–16, below.
[2] See para.21–03 et seq., below.
[3] See paras 21–10 and 21–11 below.
[4] See para.21–12 et seq., below.

(4)   the possible obligation on a tenant for a fixed term not to commit permissive waste.[5]

These are considered below in turn.

## THE DUTY OF TENANT-LIKE USER

### The implied obligation to use the premises in a tenant-like manner

**21–03**    The duty of tenant-like user is implied into all tenancies. It is not an obligation to repair but an obligation as to the tenant's conduct and user of the premises.[6] It was defined by Denning L.J. in the leading case of *Warren v Keen*[7] in the following terms:

> "[The tenant] must take proper care of the place. He must, if he is going away for the winter, turn off the water and empty the boiler. He must clean the chimneys, where necessary, and also the windows. He must mend the electric light when it fuses. He must unstop the sink when it is blocked by his waste. In short, he must do the little jobs about the place which a reasonable tenant would do. In addition, he must, of course, not damage the house wilfully or negligently; and he must see that his family and guests do not damage it: and if they do, he must repair it. But apart from such things, if the house falls into disrepair through fair wear and tear or lapse of time, or for any reason not caused by him, then the tenant is not liable to repair it. >[8]"

As is apparent from this passage, the obligation extends to damage caused by the tenant's family and guests as well as by him.[9]

The obligation is a continuing one. Not only is the tenant obliged to use the premises in a tenant-like manner throughout the term, but he is also under a continuing duty to remedy matters which amount to a breach of that obligation and to yield up the premises at the end of the term with any such breaches remedied.[10] It follows that the Limitation Act will not afford a defence where the failure to use in a tenant-like manner occurred more than six years before the action brought, provided that the action is brought within six years of the end of the term.[11]

### Express duty of tenant-like user

**21–04**    Written tenancy agreements of residential premises often impose on the tenant an express duty of tenant-like user. In such cases, the scope of the duty is a question of construction of the lease having regard to the admissible factual background known to both parties when it was granted.

---

[5] See para.21–19 et seq., below.

[6] *Regis Property Co Ltd v Dudley* [1959] A.C. 370, per Lord Denning at 407.

[7] [1954] 1 Q.B. 15.

[8] See further *Regis Property Co Ltd v Dudley*, above, at 407, in which the same judge dealt with the position of a tenant under a tenancy agreement which contains no express terms as to repairs.

[9] See *Regis Property Co Ltd v Dudley*, above, at 409.

[10] *Marsden v Edward Heyes Ltd* [1927] 1 K.B. 1, esp. per Atkin L.J. at 8.

[11] *Marsden v Edward Heyes Ltd*, above.

In *Langham Estate Management Ltd v Hardy*,[12] a high-class residential property was let at a high rent under a lease containing (among other things) (i) a covenant by the tenant to use the property in a tenant-like manner; (ii) various other covenants on the part of the tenant relating to the upkeep and use of the property and contents; and (iii) obligations on the part of the landlord to put and keep in repair and maintain the structure and exterior of the property, and to repair and keep in proper working order specified installations therein. The last of these was subject to a proviso that the tenant would "indemnify the Landlord in respect of the cost of repairs to such installations or items resulting from misuse of the same however and by whomsoever caused". H.H. Judge Marshall QC explained the scope of the tenant's covenant for tenant-like user as follows:

"[77]   Although accepting that with a high-class letting high standards are appropriate, [counsel for the landlord] ... submitted that this is a two-way street, and a landlord letting a high-class property to high-class standards is entitled to expect high-class standards from the tenant as well. This affects what is to be expected under the tenant's covenant to use the property in a 'tenant–like manner' and, indeed, other covenants ....

[78]   Based upon [that part of the judgment of Denning L.J. in *Warren v Keen* that the tenant must 'do the little jobs about the place which a reasonable tenant would do'[13]] [counsel for the landlord] submitted that the scope of the tenant's covenant to use in a tenant-like manner varies according to the nature of the property. Replacing ordinary standard batteries and light bulbs in a modest council house translates into replacing fancy and sophisticated batteries and light bulbs in a fancy and sophisticated country house.

[79]   Furthermore, since the property is a large English country house clearly designed for use and occupation by a household with live-in staff—and, indeed, the lease itself expressly mentions staff—the landlords were entitled to expect and assume that the tenant or other occupier would have such staff, who would be able to perform the small tasks involved in looking after such a property in a tenant-like manner. He submitted that this meant staff with a sufficient command of English to be able to read and follow instruction manuals for the systems and appliances and follow oral instructions from contractors or installers. The staff could reasonably, he submitted, be expected to include someone with the skills of a handyman, to do any slightly more heavy duty or practical jobs. The [tenants] apparently brought neither. He further submitted that this was all the more so in this case where the tenant was itself a property management company. In my judgment, though, this latter proposition can go no further than [counsel's] lowest position, namely that this would certainly mean that no *lower* standard than otherwise would apply in this case.

[80]   As I understood [counsel for the tenant's] position, he disagreed with [counsel for the landlord's submissions] largely on the basis that these were contrary to the relative apportionment, which he had argued for, of responsibilities between landlord and tenant, imposing these on the landlords rather than the tenant. This tended to reduce any positive content of the tenant's covenant to use in a tenant–like manner, largely confining it (it would seem) to the duty to notify the landlords of any defect, down to a dripping tap or the failure of a remote control for the television, and then waiting for it to be fixed.

[81]   I prefer [counsel for the landlord's] submissions. The draftsman of this lease was plainly aware of a potential conflict between the scope of a tenant's covenant to use in a tenant-like manner that, as the well-known quotation above shows, includes a duty to do acts that could be argued to be 'maintenance', and an express covenant by a landlord to maintain. The first proviso to clause 4(v) shows that that clause was not intended to displace the obligation of the tenant. The drafting of the proviso does not assist as to exactly *what* the content of the tenant's covenant to use in a tenant-like manner was thought to be, merely preserving it whatever it was. I find that it was

---

[12]   [2008] 3 E.G.L.R. 125.
[13]   The passage is set out at para.21–03, above.

therefore the general scope of such a covenant at common law, since that would apply to the facts of this case absent any landlord's covenant that might be argued to affect it. The difference is perhaps between specifically focused periodic maintenance work, which is the landlord's responsibility, and general cleaning and care, which is the tenant's responsibility, but which may well involve positive actions.

[82] I find, therefore, that the appropriate 'little jobs' (to use Denning LJ's phrase) that a reasonable occupier and, hence, a reasonable tenant would expect to do himself with regard to this kind of property were intended to remain the responsibility of the tenant. In so far as it might not be expected that the occupier of a property of this grandeur and quality would personally do such jobs, it would be expected that such a person would have staff with the appropriate skills to do so on his behalf.

[83] I again find support for this view in the contemplation [in the lease] that the landlords should give the tenant seven days' notice of an appointment to do work within their maintenance obligation. This clearly suggests that the jobs being envisaged were more significant than five-minute matters such as changing a battery, mending a fuse or tightening a washer."

There may be cases where an express covenant will be construed as imposing what is, in effect, a duty of tenant-like user on the tenant, even though the obligation is worded in different terms. An example is *Firstcross Ltd v Teasdale*,[14] in which a tenancy agreement of a furnished flat contained the following tenant's covenant:

"1(n) To keep the Flat and the said fixtures fittings appurtenances and items at all times in good and tenantable condition throughout the said term (allowing only for reasonable use thereof and damage by accidental fire) and not to cut maim or injure the same or any part thereof nor to make any alteration or addition thereto."

Clause 8 contained a further provision that:

"If any damage shall be done to the Flat, passages, landings, stairs, passenger or service lifts or entrance hall by the carrying in or removal of goods to or from the Flat, the Tenant shall pay for making good the same also for any damage done to other tenants of the Building."

It was argued by the landlord that the tenant's obligation was to put the flat into tenantable repair and decoration. McNeill J. rejected this. Having quoted the passage from the judgment of Denning L.J. in *Warren v Keen*[15] set out above,[16] he said:

"That seems to me to be an apt description of the sense of clause 1(n) of the relevant agreement. The obligation there placed on the tenant seems to conform precisely with those illustrations of the duty set out by Lord Denning in the passage to which I have just referred. Also, the words of exemption seem to me to accord with those illustrations because the tenant, under this agreement, is not to be liable for conditions which arise through reasonable use of the premises as tenant; nor through damage by accidental fire and he has put on him under clause 8 … a specific obligation which, in my view, it would not have been necessary to impose if there were a general obligation, under clause 1(n), to put and keep in tenantable repair."

14 [1983] 1 E.G.L.R. 87.
15 [1954] 1 Q.B. 15.
16 See para.21–03, above.

## The extent of the duty

The tenant's duty was summarised by Denning L.J. in *Warren v Keen*[17] as being to do "the little jobs about the place which a reasonable tenant would do". Examples of the sort of jobs that this encompasses are given in the passage from Denning L.J.'s judgment set out above.[18] Essentially, the tenant's duty is to take reasonable steps to look after the demised premises, but beyond this he is not liable for disrepair however occurring. The facts of *Warren v Keen* illustrate the difference between the duty of tenant-like user and the obligation imposed by a full repairing covenant. The house in question suffered from the following defects: the internal plaster on certain walls was damp, and stained and perished in parts; the rendering on the front wall was cracked and broken in parts; the window sills of one window were not weatherproof, and the joints and paintwork were decayed; and there was a leak in the hot-water boiler. The Court of Appeal held that the tenant (who was a statutory tenant under the Rent Act, having been a weekly tenant) was not liable for any of these defects under the implied duty of tenant-like user. The tenant would clearly have been liable had the tenancy contained a full repairing covenant.

21–05

An example of conduct which was not sufficiently unreasonable to amount to a breach of duty of tenant-like user is to be found in *Wycombe Health Authority v Barnett*.[19] A house was let on a service tenancy to a district nurse. The mains water supply passed via a pipe, from a stopcock in the kitchen (by means of which the supply could be turned off) to the attic where it joined a cistern. The pipe was unlagged. The house was heated by a gas boiler in the living room and a storage heater in the hall which were inadequate to keep the house comfortably warm in the coldest parts of winter. The tenant left the house intending to be away for one night but was in fact away for two nights. During her absence the temperature fell to six or seven degrees below zero at times. The mains water pipe burst, and serious damage was caused to an upstairs and a downstairs ceiling. The landlord contended that the tenant should have turned off the water at the stopcock before going away, as part of her duty of tenant-like user. He succeeded before the county court judge, who held that:

21–06

"[T]he tenant who leaves home during winter, even for quite a short period, must, if he leaves the premises unheated, take the fairly elementary precaution of emptying the water system."

The Court of Appeal allowed the tenant's appeal. Watkins L.J. said:

"I am not persuaded that a tenant, in order to behave in a tenant-like manner, can reasonably be expected inevitably to lag an internal water pipe as a precaution against the vicissitudes of freezing temperatures. Nor do I regard the obligation of the tenant to extend to always keeping the house heated as a further or alternative precaution. Furthermore, a tenant is not in my view to be expected, even in cold weather, inevitably to turn off a stopcock and drain the water system when leaving the house, though knowing that it would thereafter be unheated and the pipes were unlagged.

---

[17] [1954] 1 Q.B. 15.
[18] See para.21–03, above.
[19] [1982] 2 E.G.L.R. 35. See also on this case *Payne v Rhymney Valley DC* (Unreported decision of the Court of Appeal dated October 18, 1989).

What precaution including lagging, heating and turning off water a tenant can be expected to take in order to be found to have behaved in a tenant-like manner in cold climatic conditions must depend upon the circumstances obtaining at the relevant time, including the severity of cold weather conditions within the house and the length of any contemplated absence from the house … It seems to me extremely unlikely that, during [the time the tenant was away], rather less than three full days, although the weather became a few degrees colder, she or any other reasonable person in her position would have appreciated that there was a risk of the water pipes in her home freezing in her absence. I cannot, therefore, agree with the learned judge, that she acted unreasonably in leaving the house unoccupied without draining the water system and turning the water off at the stopcock. The weather would have had to have been appreciably colder in all the circumstances to lead me to such a conclusion."

**21–07**     It follows that what amounts to tenant-like user primarily depends on what sort of behaviour is reasonable in the particular circumstances. The result in *Barnett* might well have been different had the temperature been such that it would have been obvious to the tenant that the pipe would freeze unless drained. The decision in that case can be contrasted with the Scottish case of *Mickel v McCoard*.[20] In that case the tenant left the premises for a month in the middle of winter without either turning off the water and draining the systems, or informing the landlord of his absence, and was held liable for damage caused by the bursting of pipes owing to frost. The Court of Session held that he owed a duty to the landlord to use a reasonable degree of diligence in preserving the house during his absence, and that there had been a breach of that duty.

In *Langham Estate Management Ltd v Hardy*,[21] a covenant to use the property in a tenant-like manner contained in a lease of a high-class residential property at a high rent was held to be broken by the tenant's failure to clean out a garden fountain; clean a kitchen extractor hood; clear a blocked drain in a bedroom shower; replace failed batteries in the TV remote control; clean exhaust and oil marks on the garage floor and walls caused by the tenant's cars; and clear a blocked garage drain. It was further held that manually setting the entrance gates of the property to the open position, thereby preventing them from working properly, was also a breach of the covenant. However, the tenant was not required to remove moss from the drive, unless and until the moss either became dangerous or caused some other impediment to the convenient use of the premises or the functioning of its facilities.

The importation of fleas and bugs into the premises by the tenant has been held to be a breach of the implied obligation of tenant-like user.[22]

## Voluntary waste

**21–08**     Whilst the duty not to commit voluntary waste[23] is a duty owed in tort,[24] it appears that it is also part of the implied contractual obligation of tenant-like user.[25] It is noteworthy that in *Marsden v Edward Heyes Ltd*[26] all three members

---

[20] 1913 S.C. 1036.
[21] [2008] 3 E.G.L.R. 125. See further on this case para.21–04, above.
[22] *Shaw v Anthony* (1939) E.G. 342.
[23] See para.21–12 et seq., below.
[24] *Defries v Milne* [1913] 1 Ch. 98.
[25] *Whitham v Kershaw* (1886) 16 Q.B.D. 613, per Lord Esher M.R. at 616; *Marsden v Edward Heyes Ltd* [1927] 2 K.B. 1; *Warren v Keen*, above.

of the Court of Appeal treated the obligation not to commit voluntary waste as part of the implied obligation to use in a tenant-like manner. Atkin L.J. said in the course of his judgment:

> "[T]here is an obligation upon the tenant to use the premises in a tenant-like or, which is the same thing, a husband-like manner. It follows that he is under a continuing obligation to repair acts which would amount to voluntary waste and which involve a breach of the obligation to use the premises in a husband-like manner. It is clear that these tenants, by entirely altering the character of the premises, did acts amounting to voluntary waste and to a breach of this obligation. [27]"

The principal consequence of this is that where the lease contains a proviso for re-entry entitling the landlord to forfeit for breach of the terms of the tenancy (as it usually will do), then the landlord will be able to forfeit if the tenant commits voluntary waste. This remedy would not be available if the duty not to commit voluntary waste were owed in tort only. The co-existence of liability in tort, however, remains of importance to the extent that the implied obligation of tenant-like user may yield to an express repairing obligation.[28] In that event, the tenant may thereby be relieved of any implied contractual obligation not to commit voluntary waste. However, he would remain liable in tort, since it appears that the tortious obligation not to commit voluntary waste is not excluded by an express repairing covenant.[29]

## Where there is an express covenant to repair

Where there is an express tenant's covenant to repair, then in most cases the landlord will not need to rely upon the implied duty of tenant-like user. Consequently, the question whether the landlord may still sue in the alternative upon the implied obligation will largely be academic in practice. It is, however, a question discussed in the authorities, and it is conceivable that there will still be cases where it may be relevant.

**21–09**

The general principle is that the existence of an express term precludes the implication of any term dealing with the same subject-matter.[30] However, there is a conflict of authority on whether the implied duty of tenant-like user is excluded by an express obligation to repair. It was held in *Standen v Christmas*[31] that an express tenant's covenant to keep the interior of the premises in tenantable repair had the effect of excluding the implied obligation to use in a tenant-like manner. However, in *Regis Property Co Ltd v Dudley*[32] Lord Denning said of the obligation to use in a tenant-like manner that it was a separate and distinct

---

[26] The facts are set out in para.21–15 below.
[27] See also the passages from the judgments of Bankes and Scrutton L.JJ. set out in para.21–15, below.
[28] See para.21–09, below.
[29] See para.21–17, below.
[30] See para.1–07, above.
[31] (1847) 10 Q.B. 135. It was necessary to rely on the implied obligation because the landlord was an assignee of the reversion and he was not entitled (under the law as it then stood) to sue upon the express repairing covenant given to the original landlord.
[32] [1959] A.C. 370.

obligation from that imposed by a covenant to repair, giving rise to separate and distinct remedies. He doubted whether *Standen v Christmas* was correctly decided. His reasoning was that the tenant's obligations not to commit voluntary waste and to use in a tenant-like manner are not obligations to repair at all but:

> "[O]bligations as to his conduct, and user of the premises, and so long as they are fulfilled, as they ought to be, no question of repair arises. It is true, of course, that if the tenant breaks those obligations . ... he must execute repairs or else pay damages. But in doing so he is not fulfilling an obligation to repair under the terms of his tenancy, express or implied. He is only remedying his own breaches of his common law obligations as to conduct and user. These obligations are altogether separate and distinct from those imposed by a covenant to repair and give rise to separate and distinct remedies."

This reasoning is persuasive. It seems wrong in principle that (to take one of the examples of tenant-like user given in *Warren v Keen*[33]) the tenant should be under no liability, if he is going away for the winter, to turn off the water and empty the boiler merely because his tenancy contains an express repairing covenant. However, Lord Denning's views on the point were clearly obiter, and none of the other Law Lords expressed a view. The correct view is thought to be that an express covenant to repair will exclude the implied duty of tenant-like user only if the correct inference in all the circumstances is that the parties did not intend the tenant to be under any further liability.[34]

## THE OBLIGATION TO KEEP THE DEMISED PREMISES WIND AND WATERTIGHT

### Introductory

**21–10**  Several authorities contain a suggestion that a tenant from year to year is under an implied obligation to keep the demised premises wind and watertight.[35] However, none of them throws any light upon precisely what the obligation involves, and in particular to what extent, if any, it differs from the implied obligation already discussed. The possible existence of the obligation was considered in *Warren v Keen*,[36] in which the Court of Appeal held that it did not apply to a weekly tenant, whatever may be the position in relation to a tenant from year to year.

It is thought that the obligation either does not exist, or if it does, then it adds nothing to the implied obligation to use in a tenant-like manner. It is noteworthy that the Court of Appeal in *Warren v Keen*[37] appears to have been extremely doubtful as to whether a separate obligation to keep wind and watertight exists even in the case of a yearly tenant. Somervell L.J. said:

---

[33] See para.21–03, above.
[34] Cf. *BP Oil New Zealand v Ports of Auckland* [2004] 2 N.Z.L.R. 208 (Australia), considered at para.21–01, above, and para.21–17, below.
[35] *Auworth v Johnson* (1832) 5 C. & P. 239; *Leach v Thomas* (1835) 7 C. & P. 327; *Wedd v Porter* [1916] 2 K.B. 91 at 100.
[36] [1954] 1 Q.B. 15.
[37] Above.

"[T]he researches of counsel have failed to discover any case which throws light on the scope of that obligation, in other words, any case where a tenant has been held liable for failure to keep wind and water tight where the damage would not be covered by the obligation not to commit voluntary waste or the obligation to use the premises and land in a tenant-like manner. So whether there is an additional obligation of a limited kind with regard to repairs in the case of a tenant from year to year remains at any rate in a state of some doubt."

He went on to describe the meaning of "to keep the house wind and watertight" as "obscure". Denning L.J. said:

"[I]t is very difficult to know what 'wind and watertight' means. I asked counsel whether there was any case to be found in the books where a tenant had been held liable for breach of that obligation. I wanted to see what sort of thing it had been held to cover. But there was no such case to be found. In the absence of it, I think that the expression 'wind and watertight' is of doubtful value and should be avoided. It is better to keep to the simple obligation 'to use the premises in a tenant-like manner'."

This passage strongly suggests that Denning L.J. regarded the obligation to keep wind and watertight and the obligation to use in a tenant-like manner as one and the same thing.

**21–11**

Furthermore, it appears that the obligation to keep wind and watertight, to the extent that it exists at all, is subject to an exception in the case of defects caused by fair wear and tear. Thus, in *Warren v Keen*[38] Somervell L.J. held, as an alternative ground for his decision, that the defects in that case[39] could not be covered by the obligation to keep wind and watertight even if one existed. Having said that he was prepared to assume, without deciding, that there was a:

"[M]inor, but so far indefinite obligation, on a tenant from year to year to do certain minor repairs necessary to keep premises wind and watertight."

He went on to say that:

"It seems to me clear that the damage here was due to decay of the walls, and there is no suggestion that that was due to any other cause than fair wear and tear. Here is no suggestion that the tenant started knocking the walls about or anything of that sort, but in the course of time they had become cracked and presumably required re-pointing, because water was seeping in through the cracks which had appeared. The same would appear to have applied to the wood of the window sills. That may have been due not only to age but also to the positive failure to have the external woodwork re-painted every three years, or whatever is the normal time. Those would be both matters which in my opinion could not on any construction come under this formula of keeping the building wind and watertight, having regard to the principles which are to be found in the cases with regard to the implied liability of a tenant from year to year."

The judgment of Romer L.J. contains a passage to the same effect.

There is no reported modern authority since *Warren v Keen* in which the question of a separate obligation to keep wind and watertight has been either considered or argued. It is thought that those cases in which the expression "wind and watertight" is used were not intending to lay down an obligation any more onerous than the implied obligation to use in a tenant-like manner. The latter may on occasion require the tenant to effect minor repairs necessary to keep out the

---

[38] Above.
[39] See para.21–05, above.

rain, for example, mending a window that one of his children has broken. It would not, however, require the tenant to carry out all repairs necessary to keep the demised premises wind and weatherproof. He would not, for example, be under any obligation to repoint.[40] It is thought that the suggested obligation to keep wind and watertight, when properly analysed, goes no further than this.

## THE OBLIGATION NOT TO COMMIT VOLUNTARY WASTE

### The meaning of "voluntary waste"

21–12    Voluntary (or commissive) waste means the deliberate or negligent commission of an act which damages the demised premises. However, an act will not generally constitute voluntary waste unless it results in damage to the landlord's reversion.[41] It follows that minor or trivial damage will generally not amount to waste. An omission, as opposed to a positive act, can hardly ever, and perhaps never, constitute voluntary waste.[42]

### Damage caused to the demised premises

21–13    In principle, anything which damages the demised premises so as to cause damage to the reversion constitutes voluntary waste. Examples of acts falling under this head include pulling the demised premises down,[43] breaking windows or doors,[44] removing landlord's fixtures[45] and removing tenant's fixtures[46] without making good damage to the structure thereby caused.[47] However, removing fixtures without making good matters of mere decoration does not amount to waste.[48] Likewise, failure to fill screw holes or nail holes where the fixture has been screwed or nailed to a wall may be de miminis.[49]

The extent to which damage caused in the course of installing fixtures amounts to waste is unclear. In *Mancetter Developments Ltd v Garmanson*[50] the tenants of industrial premises cut holes in the outside walls of the building in

---

[40] *Warren v Keen*, above.

[41] *Doe d. Grubb v Burlington* (1833) 5 B. & Ad. 507, per Denham C.J.; *Mancetter Developments Ltd v Garmanson* [1986] 1 All E.R. 449.

[42] *Doe d. Grubb v Burlington*, above, per Denham C.J.; *Mancetter Developments Ltd v Garmanson*, above. However, removing trade fixtures which the tenant is entitled to remove constitutes waste if the tenant does not make good damage caused when the fixtures were installed: see para.21–12, below.

[43] *Manchester Bonded Warehouse Ltd v Carr* (1880) 5 C.P.D. 507.

[44] *Ferguson v Anon* 2 Esp. 590; *Warren v Keen* [1954] 1 Q.B. 15, per Denning L.J. at 21.

[45] *Mancetter Developments Ltd v Garmanson*, above.

[46] See para.25–24 et seq., below.

[47] *Mancetter Developments Ltd v Garmanson*, above, from which it appears that the person removing the fixtures commits waste if he does not make good (i) damage caused in the course of removal, and (ii) damage caused when the fixtures were originally installed (for example, holes for pipes to run through). Insofar as the liability to make good is a liability in waste, it is that of the person removing the fixtures and not of the person who installed them: see per Dillon L.J.

[48] *Re De Falbe* [1901] 1 Ch. 523 at 542; *Mancetter Developments Ltd v Garmanson*, above.

[49] *Mancetter Developments Ltd v Garmanson*, above, per Dillon L.J. at 454f.

[50] [1986] 1 All E.R. 449.

order to install trade fixtures. A subsequent occupier removed the fixtures without making good the holes. One of the questions discussed in the judgments in the Court of Appeal was whether in making the holes the tenants had committed waste. Sir George Waller thought they had, because they had done a spoil or destruction to the building. Kerr L.J. disagreed. His reasoning was as follows:

"[The premises] were used for a chemical business … and it is an overwhelmingly probable inference that in making these holes [the tenants] were not acting so inconsistently with the terms of their lease that they could be said thereby to have acted in an untenantlike manner. One can test this by asking oneself whether [the landlords] could possibly have sued [the tenants] for the tort of waste there and then, as soon as the holes had been made. In my view, the answer would clearly be in the negative. It would have been held that although the fabric of the premises had been damaged, there was no act of waste, since the interference with the fabric of the premises did not go so far as to have this effect in the circumstances."

It is thought that this reasoning is to be preferred, and that damage caused in the course of installing trade fixtures will not generally constitute waste, unless the circumstances are such that the tenant has gone beyond what is reasonably contemplated by the lease. However, when the fixtures are removed, the tenant commits waste if he does not make good both that damage and any additional damage caused in the course of removal.[51]

## Alterations

Alterations which result in a substantial alteration in the character of the demised premises amount to voluntary waste.[52] Apart from this, however, an alteration does not constitute waste. Thus in *West Ham Central Charity Board v East London Waterworks Ltd*[53] Buckley J. said:     **21–14**

"If the permanent character of the property demised is not substantially altered, as for instance, by the conversion of pasture land into plough land, by breaking up ancient meadows, or the like I conceive that the law is that it is not now waste for the tenant to do things which within the covenants and conditions of his lease he is not precluded from doing. Within those covenants and conditions he may use his holding as he pleases."

In *Hyman v Rose*[54] Earl Loreburn L.C. formulated the correct approach as follows:

"It is a question of fact whether such an act changes the nature of the thing demised, and regard must be had to the user of the demised premises which is permissible under the lease."

An example of this type of waste occurred in *Marsden v Edward Heyes Ltd.*[55] The original demised premises consisted of a shop with residential premises above. The ground floor contained the shop and a kitchen, separated from each other by a partition wall, and both with fireplaces. On the first floor, which was     **21–15**

---

[51] *Mancetter Developments Ltd v Garmanson*, above.
[52] *West Ham Central Charity Board v East London Waterworks Co Ltd* [1900] 1 Ch. 624; *Hyman v Rose* [1912] A.C. 623; *Marsden v Edward Heyes Limited* [1927] 2 K.B. 1.
[53] Above.
[54] Above.
[55] [1927] 2 K.B. 1.

reached by a staircase, were two bedrooms, separated from each other by a partition wall. Both had fireplaces. The tenant removed both partition walls, all the fireplaces, the staircase, and the windows and doors at the back of the premises. He turned the ground floor into one large shop, and the first floor into a loft, approached by a ladder in place of the original staircase. The Court of Appeal held that the tenant had committed voluntary waste. Bankes L.J. said:

> "[The tenant] must deliver up premises of the same character as those which were demised to him; for example, a tenant who takes a dwelling-house cannot at the end of the tenancy yield up a storehouse, or a stable, or cowhouse, however elaborately constructed. But it is not necessary to further define the obligation, because it cannot be contended that a tenant from year to year, who completely alters the premises, does not commit a breach of his implied obligation in respect of the premises."

Scrutton L.J. said:

> "To use premises in a tenant-like manner means at any rate that a tenant will not make such structural alterations in the premises as will change their character. If a dwelling-house is let and something which is not a dwelling-house is delivered up, the contract to deliver up in a tenant-like condition is broken."

Similarly the dumping of large quantities of hard and soft rubbish so as to raise the level of the land by about 10ft has been held to be voluntary waste.[56] A case going the other way was *Hyman v Rose*,[57] in which the conversion of a chapel into a cinema, which involved the removal of iron railings, the opening of a new door, and internal alterations, was held not to constitute waste.[58]

## Damage caused in the course of ordinary and reasonable use

**21–16**  Damage to the demised premises caused in the course of the reasonable and proper use of them for the purposes for which they were let is not waste. Thus, in *Saner v Bilton (No.1)*[59] a newly built grain warehouse was let for 15 years. The tenant used it for storing grain in a reasonable and proper way. A beam supporting one of the floors broke, and the external walls sank and bulged outwards, necessitating substantial repairs including underpinning. Fry J. held that the tenant had not committed waste. His decision was approved by the Court of Appeal in *Manchester Bonded Warehouse Ltd v Carr*.[60] In that case certain floors in a warehouse were let for seven years, and were then sub-let. One of the sub-tenants stored a large amount of flour on one of the floors, and overloaded it, as a result of which the entire building collapsed. The landlord argued that the tenant was liable for the cost of reconstruction because the overloading of the premises amounted to waste. Lord Coleridge C.J., giving the judgment of the Court, said:

---

[56] *West Ham Central Charity Board v East London Waterworks Ltd* [1900] 1 Ch. 624.
[57] [1912] A.C. 623.
[58] It was also held not to amount to a breach of the covenant to repair: see para.18–04, above.
[59] (1878) 7 Ch. D. 815.
[60] (1880) 5 C.P.D. 507.

"The question in these cases is whether it is the tenant's duty to ascertain what he can do with safety to the property, or whether he is not entitled to assume that it is fit to be used for the purposes for which it is let and for which it is apparently fit. We are of the opinion that the latter is the true view, and that, in the absence of an express agreement to that effect, a tenant is not liable for the destruction of the property let to him if such destruction is in fact due to nothing more than a reasonable use of the property, and any use of it is in our opinion reasonable provided it is for a purpose for which the property was intended to be used, and provided the mode and extent of the user was apparently proper, having regard to the nature of the property and to what the tenant knew of it and to what as an ordinary business man he ought to have known of it. To hold a tenant liable for the destruction of the property by its reasonable use as above explained, would be to hold him liable for latent faults and defects in the property demised. We are of opinion that he is not liable for such faults and defects, in the absence of some express agreement on his part imposing such liability upon him."

He went on to deal with where the onus of proof lies in such cases:

"We are, however, of opinion, that prima facie a tenant is bound to restore the property demised to him, and that if such property is destroyed by the acts of himself or his under-tenants, the presumption is against him, and he must in order to exonerate himself show that the destruction was owing to causes for which he was not responsible."

The case was sent back to the jury to decide whether the loading of the warehouse was reasonable or unreasonable, having regard to whether there was any reason for supposing that what was stored was:

"[T]oo heavy in kind or quantity for its apparent strength or for its strength as known to the [tenant], or as he ought as a business man to have known of it."

## Where there is an express repairing covenant

The obligation not to commit voluntary waste is a duty in tort.[61] It has been held **21–17** in a series of cases that the landlord's remedy for voluntary waste is unaffected by the fact that the tenancy also contains an express tenant's repairing covenant.[62] In *Mancetter Developments Ltd v Garmanson*,[63] Dillon L.J. said in the course of his judgment that where the relevant damage is covered by an express covenant, the landlord has an election whether to sue in tort for waste or in contract on the covenant. However, Kerr L.J. doubted, without expressing a concluded opinion, that alternative claims in tort or contract would be permitted in the majority of cases.[64]

---

[61] Although it is also part of the implied duty of tenant-like user: see para.21–08, above.

[62] *Kinlyside v Thornton* (1776) 2 W. Bl. 1111; *Mayor of London v Hedger* (1810) 18 Ves. 355; *Marker v Kenrick* (1853) 13 C.B. 188; *Defries v Milne* [1913] 1 Ch. 98 at 108; *Marsden v Edward Heyes Ltd* [1927] 2 K.B. 1, per Bankes L.J. at 5–6; *BP Oil New Zealand v Ports of Auckland* [2004] 2 N.Z.L.R. 208 (New Zealand).

[63] [1986 1 All E.R. 449.

[64] Kerr L.J. supported his view by reference to *Jones v Hill* (1817) 7 Taunt. 392, in which Gibbs C.J. said (at 395) that "Waste can only lie for that which would be waste if there were no stipulation respecting it … ". It is thought, however, that when read in the context of the facts of that case, what Gibbs C.J. meant was that the presence of an express covenant to repair cannot affect the question whether or not particular defects constitute waste, and not that alternative claims are not possible. It is noteworthy that *Kinlyside v Thornton*, above, which is a direct authority in favour of the view that a claim in waste is not excluded by an express covenant, was cited in argument, and there is nothing in the short judgment to indicate that the court in *Jones v Hill* regarded itself as not following it. It is fair

In the New Zealand case of *BP Oil New Zealand v Ports of Auckland*,[65] the demised land had become contaminated by spills and leaks from stored petroleum products. The relevant leases contained covenants on the part of the tenant to keep all buildings and structures on the demised land in good order, condition and repair. Rodney Hansen J. held that (i) no term was to be implied into the leases that the tenant would not commit waste against the reversion by causing or allowing the land to become contaminated, but (ii) the repairing covenants did not exclude liability in tort for waste, with the result that the tenant was liable for injury to the land resulting from its acts or omissions, excluding damage resulting from reasonable use. He said:

> "[The tenant] submitted that the doctrine of waste has been excluded by the terms of the leases, in particular, the exclusion of land from the obligation to repair. I found the terms of the repair clauses to demonstrate an intention to exclude [the covenant to repair implied under s.106(b) of the Property Act 1952], but it is clear that different considerations apply when exclusion of liability for waste is concerned. The former concerns an obligation to repair, whereas the doctrine of waste, though including an obligation to repair, is founded on a duty not to cause damage. The existence of an express covenant to repair is insufficient by itself to exclude liability for voluntary or permissive waste."

One reason why the distinction between liability in tort for voluntary waste and liability in contract for breach of the repairing covenant may be of importance in practice is that, where waste is committed by a limited company, a director who gave the relevant instructions for the commission of waste may be personally liable to the landlord even though he is not a guarantor under the lease.[66] By contrast, the only person liable for breach of a repairing covenant is the tenant under the lease at the relevant time and anyone else in the chain of title who is also liable.[67]

## Remedies for voluntary waste

21–18 Insofar as the obligation not to commit voluntary waste is an implied obligation of the tenancy,[68] the landlord has all the usual remedies available for breach of covenant. These are dealt with elsewhere.[69] Insofar as the tenant is liable in tort, the landlord's remedies comprise an injunction to restrain the commission or continuance of voluntary waste,[70] and damages. The measure of damages for waste is the amount by which the value of the landlord's reversion has been

---

to say, however, that the view of Kerr L.J. is consistent with the modern approach to the imposition of liability in tort where contractual liability exists as well: see *Tai Hing Cotton Mill v Liu Chong Hing Bank (No.1)* [1986] A.C. 80.
[65] [2004] 2 N.Z.L.R. 208. See further on this case paras 12–40 and 12–42, above.
[66] *Mancetter Developments Ltd v Garmanson* [1986] 1 All E.R. 449.
[67] See Ch.3, above.
[68] See para.21–08, above.
[69] See Chs 26 to 32, below.
[70] See, for example, *Douglas v Wiggins* (1815) 1 Johns. Ch. R. (Amer.) 435 (injunction granted to restrain the making of material alterations to a house); *Smyth v Carter* (1853) 18 Beav. 78 (injunction granted to restrain tenant from pulling down house and building another); *Brocklesbury v Munn* [1870] W.N. 42 (injunction granted to restrain removal of plate glass windows).

diminished by the waste.[71] This will not necessarily equate to the cost of the necessary works, particularly where the lease still has some years left to run.[72] It has been said that in a very gross case, "vindictive damages" may be given.[73]

## THE OBLIGATION NOT TO COMMIT PERMISSIVE WASTE

### The meaning of "permissive waste"

Voluntary waste is commissive, i.e. it involves the doing of an act which damages or otherwise alters the premises.[74] By contrast, permissive waste means allowing damage to occur to the premises through failure to act. In *Davies v Davies*[75] Kekewich J. defined permissive waste as:

21–19

> "[A]llowing waste which has not come about by [the tenant's] own acts, but comes about by a revolution, or by wear and tear, or by the action of the elements, or in any other way not being his own act."

Permissive waste includes allowing buildings to deteriorate by failure to repair.[76] There are therefore obvious similarities between permissive waste and the liability imposed by a tenant's repairing covenant. There is, however, the important difference that the obligation not to commit permissive waste appears to be limited to the doing of that which is necessary to preserve the premises in the condition they were in at the date of the lease,[77] whereas a covenant to repair may well require the carrying out of works which put the premises into a better condition than they were in when demised.[78] The distinction may go further than this, in that it is at least possible that the tenant will only be liable for permissive waste if the condition of the premises has deteriorated since the date of the lease to such a substantial extent that there has been a change in their character. If this is right, then the difference between permissive waste and the liability imposed by a covenant to repair is even more marked.

### Liability for permissive waste

The following classes of tenant are not liable for permissive waste:

21–20

---

[71] *Whitham v Kershaw* (1886) 16 Q.B.D. 613.

[72] *Whitham v Kershaw*, above.

[73] *Whitham v Kershaw*, above, per Bowen L.J. Use of the expression "vindictive damages" as a synonym for "aggravated" or "exemplary" damages has been criticised: see in particular the speech of Lord Hailsham of St Marylebone L.C. in *Broome v Cassell & Co Ltd (No.1)* [1972] A.C. 1027, where the principles upon which such damages may be awarded are authoritatively discussed.

[74] See para.21–12, above.

[75] (1888) 38 Ch. D. 499.

[76] *Herne v Benbow* (1813) 4 Taunt. 764; *Powys v Blagrave* (1854) 4 De G. M. & G. 448.

[77] See *Jones v Hill* (1817) 2 Taunt. 392, and see also the thorough examination of liability for permissive waste conducted by the court in *Dayani v Bromley LBC (No.1)* [1999] 3 E.G.L.R. 144.

[78] See para.9–21, above.

(1)   tenants at will;[79]
(2)   weekly tenants;[80]
(3)   yearly tenants.[81]

It is thought that by analogy with the above, any other type of periodic tenant, for example, a quarterly tenant, is likewise not liable for permissive waste.

The position regarding a tenant for a fixed term is more difficult. At common law tenants under leases were not liable for waste, the reason being that their interest in the land arose by agreement with the landlord who therefore had the opportunity to impose express obligations relating to the condition of the premises if he wished.[82] However, by s.2 of the Statute of Marlborough 1267 it is provided that:

> "[A]lso farmers, during their terms, shall not make waste, sale or exile of house, woods, men, or of anything belonging to the tenements that they have to farm, without special licence had by writing of covenant, making mention that they may do it; which thing if they do, and thereof be convicted, they shall yield full damage, and shall be punished by amerciament grievously."

**21–21**   The reference to "farmers" has been interpreted as being to tenants for a term of years, i.e. fixed-term tenancies.[83] The question, which has been much debated, is whether the reference in the statute to waste includes permissive waste, or whether it is limited to voluntary waste only. Sir Edward Coke regarded permissive waste as included, saying of s.2 that:

> "To do, or make waste, in legal understanding in this place includes as well permissive waste, which is waste by reason of omission or not doing, as for want of reparation, as waste by reason of commission, as to cut down timber, trees, of prostrate houses or the like; and the same word hath the Statute of Gloucester … and yet it is understood as well of passive as of active waste, for he that suffereth a house to decay, which he ought to repair, doth the waste.[84]"

However, in *Avis v Newman*[85] (a case on the liability of a tenant for life under a settlement) Kay J. said that the words of Sir Edward Coke only included permissive waste where there was an obligation to repair, and that a tenant for life was not liable for permissive waste.

The question whether a tenant for years is liable for permissive waste was left open by the court in *Jones v Hill*.[86] It was suggested in argument in *Harnett v Maitland*[87] that the section does not include permissive waste,[88] but the point was

[79] *Countess of Shrewsbury's Case* (1600) 5 Co. Rep. 136; *Panton v Isham* (1701) 3 Lev 359; *Gibson v Wells* (1805) 1 Bos. & P.N.R. 290; *Harnett v Maitland* (1847) 16 M. & W. 257; *Blackmore v White* [1899] 1 Q.B. 293, per Lord Russell of Killowen C.J. at 299–300.
[80] *Warren v Keen* [1954] 1 Q.B. 15.
[81] *Torriano v Young* (1833) 6 C. & P. 8.
[82] *Countess of Shrewsbury's Case*, above.
[83] *Woodhouse v Walker* (1880) 5 Q.B.D. 404. See also *Dayani v Bromley LBC (No.1)* [1999] 3 E.G.L.R. 144 at 145J.
[84] 2 Inst. 145.
[85] (1889) 41 Ch. D. 532.
[86] (1817) 7 Taunt. 392.
[87] (1847) 16 M. & W. 257.
[88] Ibid., at p.259.

not finally decided, the plaintiff's case being dismissed on a pleading point. However, the judgment of Parke B. (with whom the others concurred) contains a strong indication that a tenant for years is liable for permissive waste. The same judge went on to hold in the subsequent case of *Yellowly v Gower*[89] that a tenant for years is liable for permissive waste. In that case a settlement conferred on the tenant for life power to grant leases on condition that the lessee was not exempted from liability for waste. The tenant for life granted a lease for a fixed term containing a landlord's covenant to repair. It was contended that the lease was void as being outside the terms of the power on the ground, among others, that the landlord's covenant to repair amounted to an implied release of the lessee from liability for permissive waste. This contention succeeded. The question whether a tenant for years was liable for permissive waste arose because Parke B., giving the judgment of the court, took the view that the landlord's covenant would not amount to an implied release if the lessee was not liable for permissive waste anyway. The relevant passage from his judgment is as follows:

> "A doubt has been stated indeed in a note to 2 Saund. 252b, whether a tenant for years is liable for permissive waste, and if he were not, then a covenant by the landlord to repair would not amount to an implied permission to the tenant to omit to repair. These doubts arise from three cases in the Common Pleas: *Gibson v. Wells*,[90] *Herne v. Bembow*,[91] *Jones v. Hill*.[92] Upon examining these cases, none of which appears to be well reported, the Court seems to have contemplated the case only of a tenant at will in the first two cases, and in the last no such proposition is stated, that a tenant for years is not liable for permissive waste. We conceive that there is no doubt of the liability of tenants for terms of years, for they are clearly put on the same footing as tenants for life, both to voluntary and permissive waste by Lord Coke, 1 Inst. 53, *Harnett v. Maitland*,[93] though the degree of repairs required for a tenant from year to year, by modern decisions, is much limited. This being so, the covenant by the lessor to do the repairs implies an exemption of the lessee."

However, the decision is not wholly satisfactory as an authority, because it is not clear to what extent the contrary was argued.

The question whether a tenant for years is liable for permissive waste was again left open by the court in *Woodhouse v Walker*.[94] The point was expressly argued in *Davies v Davies*[95] in which the question again arose in the context of whether a lease granted under a power was void because it exempted the lessee from liability for permissive waste. Kekewich J. held, following *Yellowly v Gower*,[96] that a tenant for years is liable for permissive waste, and therefore that the lease was void. However, in *Warren v Keen*[97] Denning L.J. began his judgment by saying:

---

[89] (1855) 11 Exch. 274.
[90] (1805) 1 Bos. & P.N.R. 290.
[91] (1813) 4 Taunt. 764.
[92] (1817) 7 Taunt. 392.
[93] (1847) 16 M. & W. 257.
[94] (1888) 5 Q.B.D. 404.
[95] (1888) 38 Ch. D. 499.
[96] (1855) 11 Exch. 274.
[97] [1954] 1 Q.B. 15.

> "Apart from express contract, a tenant owes no duty to the landlord to keep the premises in repair. The only duty of the tenant is to use the premises in a husband-like, or what is the same thing, a tenant-like manner."

Although the case was concerned only with a weekly tenant, the above statement of principle is unqualified, and suggests that Denning L.J. did not regard liability for permissive waste as part of the modern law.[98]

Nonetheless, in *Dayani v Bromley LBC (No.1)*[99] Judge Havery QC, having undertaken a thorough review of the many ancient authorities, concluded on the basis of those authorities that a tenant for years is liable for permissive waste. He would, he said, be "flying in the face of overwhelming authority" if he were to hold that the Statute of Marlborough does not provide a remedy against a tenant for years for permissive waste.

**21–22** The law as it stands at present is therefore that a tenant for a fixed term is liable for permissive waste. However, it is questionable whether this is correct. First, so far as concerns the Statute of Marlborough, it can be said that (i) the words "make" waste, sale or exile point to positive acts only; (ii) the special licence spoken of in the section points to positive acts only, being inappropriate to a mere omission to repair; and (iii) it is unreasonable to suppose that the Statute of Gloucester[100] would have prescribed so harsh a penalty as forfeiture and treble damages for such mere omission.[101] Second, there seems no sound reason of policy or fairness why a tenant who has not undertaken any express repairing liability should nonetheless be liable for the carrying out of repairs over and above those required by the implied obligation to use in a tenant-like manner. The general rule in the case of a landlord is that no repairing liability will ordinarily be implied in the absence of an express covenant,[102] and it is difficult to see why the position should be any different in the case of a tenant. Third, periodic tenants are not liable for permissive waste,[103] and the difference between a periodic tenant and a tenant for a fixed term has been much reduced in modern times by the incidence of statutory protection. It is no longer the case in practice that a periodic tenant can be turned out at short notice. There would therefore appear to be no real justification for distinguishing between tenants for fixed terms and other tenants when it comes to permissive waste.

---

[98] See also *Regis Property Co Ltd v Dudley* [1959] A.C. 370 at 407, where the same judge set out his view as to the liability of a tenant under a tenancy agreement which contains no express terms as to repairs.

[99] [1999] 3 E.G.L.R. 144.

[100] The Statute of Gloucester provided a civil remedy for waste. It was repealed by the Civil Procedure Acts Repeal Act 1879.

[101] These points are taken from *Woodfall: Landlord and Tenant*, 28th edn (London: Sweet & Maxwell), Vol.I, para.13.124. However, they were considered and rejected by the court in *Dayani v Bromley LBC (No.1)* [1999] 3 E.G.L.R. 144.

[102] See para.19–02, above.

[103] See para.21–20, above.

## Contrary indications

It should be noted that under the Statute of Marlborough there is no liability for waste where there is a "special licence had by writing of covenant". It is thought that the court would be likely to give this a wide construction so as to include anything which indicates that the parties did not intend the tenant to be liable for permissive waste. A landlord's covenant to repair the demised premises would no doubt be held to exclude any liability the tenant might otherwise have for permissive waste,[104] and it may well be that an express tenant's covenant to repair would also have this effect.[105]

**21–23**

## Remedies for permissive waste

As has been seen, it is only tenants for fixed terms who may be liable for permissive waste,[106] and any such liability arises under the terms of the Statute of Marlborough and not under the lease. It follows that a proviso in the usual form entitling the landlord to re-enter in the event of breach of covenant would not permit forfeiture for permissive waste, because the obligation not to commit permissive waste is not an obligation under the lease (unless of course the lease contains an express covenant not to commit waste).

**21–24**

It is not clear in what circumstances the court would be prepared to grant an injunction restraining permissive waste (which would in effect be a mandatory injunction to carry out works). It has been held that such an injunction should not be granted against a tenant for life.[107] In the case of a tenant for years, the relevant considerations would probably be the same as those applicable to the grant of specific performance of a tenant's repairing covenant. These are dealt with elsewhere.[108] The measure of damages for waste is the amount by which the value of the landlord's reversion has been diminished owing to the waste.[109]

---

[104] See *Yellowly v Gower* (1855) 11 Exch. 274.

[105] Note, however, that the lease in *Dayani v Bromley LBC (No.1)* [1999] 3 E.G.L.R. 144 (see para.21–21, above) contained an express tenant's repairing covenant but this does not seem to have been relied on as excluding liability for permissive waste.

[106] See paras 21–20 to 21–22, above.

[107] *Powys v Blagrave* (1854) 4 De G.M. & G. 448. See the discussion in *Dayani v Bromley LBC (No.1)*, above, esp. at 152D–E.

[108] See paras 33–07 to 33–14, below.

[109] See para.21–18, above.

CHAPTER 22

# CONSIDERATIONS AFFECTING THE PERFORMANCE OF LANDLORD'S OBLIGATIONS TO REPAIR

## INTRODUCTORY

### Landlords' covenants

The principles applicable to the construction of landlords' covenants to repair do not generally differ from those applicable to tenants' covenants.[1] Thus, for example, the fact and degree test[2] applies to a landlord's covenant, so that the landlord is not liable to carry out work which goes beyond repair.[3] However, there are a number of considerations which affect the performance of landlords' obligations which do not arise in the case of tenants' obligations. In this Chapter the following are considered:

**22–01**

(1)  when the landlord's obligation must be performed;[4]
(2)  the landlord's rights of entry to carry out repairs;[5]
(3)  the obligation to make good damage caused in the course of carrying out repairs.[6]

## WHEN THE LANDLORD'S OBLIGATION MUST BE PERFORMED

### The importance of identifying when the landlord is in breach

In the case of a tenant's covenant to repair, it will rarely be necessary to ask precisely when the obligation falls to be performed.[7] However, in the case of a landlord's obligation, the question of exactly when the landlord is in breach of covenant will usually be important in order to decide whether and to what extent the landlord is liable for damage suffered by the tenant by reason of disrepair. In *McGreal v Wake*[8] Lord Donaldson M.R. drew attention to the result of late performance of the landlord's repairing obligation on the occupying tenant:

**22–02**

---

[1]  See para.4–33, above.
[2]  See Ch.11, above.
[3]  See, for example, *Pembery v Lamdin* [1940] 2 All E.R. 434.
[4]  See para.22–02 et seq., below.
[5]  See para.22–25 et seq., below.
[6]  See para.22–47 et seq., below.
[7]  See para.23–02, below.
[8]  (1984) 13 H.L.R. 107.

"A landlord's covenant to repair involves two different elements—a duty to do repairs and a duty to do them at a particular time. Late performance may cause loss and damage to the tenant in that he has to live in unrepaired premises whereas, if the duty had been performed timeously, he would have been living in repaired accommodation."

The landlord will not be liable for loss and damage resulting from disrepair unless he was in breach of covenant at the time it occurred. It follows that it is necessary to be able to identify the point in time at which the landlord is in breach.

## Where the relevant defect is the demised premises[9]

22–03    As a general principle, a covenant to keep premises in repair obliges the covenantor to keep them in repair at all times.[10] However, this principle is subject to an exception in cases where the defect occurs in the demised premises themselves.[11] In such a case, the landlord's obligation is subject to an implied precondition that he is not liable until he has notice of the disrepair.[12] The same principle applies to obligations to repair which are implied by statute.[13] The rule has been described as "unfortunate" because it "penalises the conscientious landlord and rewards the absentee".[14] However, it has been clearly established by two decisions of the House of Lords.[15]

The reason for implying the term was explained by Bramwell B. in *Makin v Watkinson*[16] as follows:

---

[9]  The equivalent paragraph in the Third Edition of this work was cited with approval by H.H. Judge Marshall QC in *Langham Estate Management Ltd v Hardy* [2008] 3 E.G.L.R. 125 at [58].

[10]  *British Telecommunications Plc v Sun Life Assurance Society Plc* [1996] Ch. 69. See para.22–19, below.

[11]  *British Telecommunications Plc v Sun Life Assurance Society Plc*, above.

[12]  *Moore v Clark* (1813) 5 Taunt. 90; *Makin v Watkinson* (1870) L.R. 6 Exch. 25; *London & South Western Railway Co Ltd v Flower* (1875) 1 C.P.D. 77; *Manchester Bonded Warehouse Ltd v Carr* (1880) 5 C.P.D. 507; *Hugall v M'Lean* (1885) 35 L.T.N.S. 94; *Tredway v Machin* (1904) 91 L.T. 310; *Torrens v Walker* [1906] Ch. 166; *Griffin v Pillet* [1926] 1 K.B. 17; *British Telecommunications Plc v Sun Life Assurance Society Plc*, above, per Nourse L.J. at 74G; *Austin v Bonney* [1998] Q ConvR 60,082 (Supreme Court of Queensland); *Earle v Charalambous* [2007] H.L.R. 8; *Langham Estate Management Ltd v Hardy*, above.

[13]  *Morgan v Liverpool Corp* [1927] 2 K.B. 131; *McCarrick v Liverpool Corp* [1947] A.C. 219; *O'Brien v Robinson* [1973] A.C. 912. The first two were concerned with the statutory predecessor of s.8 of the Landlord and Tenant Act 1985 (see para.20–02 et seq., above), and the third with the statutory predecessor of s.11 of the same Act (see para.20–17 et seq., above). However, in all these cases the court was applying what it regarded as the principle at common law, on the basis that since the effect of the statute was to imply a term into the contract, the landlord's duty to repair was contractual in nature (see particularly *Morgan v Liverpool Corp*, above, per Lord Hanworth M.R. at 141; *McCarrick v Liverpool Corp*, per Lord Porter at 224, Lord Simmonds (with whom Lords Thankerton and Macmillan concurred) at 227–228 and Lord Uthwatt at 230–231; *O'Brien v Robinson*, per Lord Diplock at 927 making the same point, and explaining the ratio decidendi of *Morgan* and *McCarrick* in this way).

[14]  *McGreal v Wake* (1984) 13 H.L.R. 107, per Lord Donaldson M.R. at 1254.

[15]  *McCarrick v Liverpool Corp*, above; *O'Brien v Robinson* [1973] A.C. 912.

[16]  (1870) L.R. 6 Exch. 25.

"I have the strongest objection to interpolate words into a contract, and think we ought never to do so unless there is some cogent and almost irresistible reason for it, arising from the absurdity of the contract if it is read without them. Does such a reason exist here? I think it does. I think that we are irresistibly driven to say that the parties cannot have intended so preposterous a covenant as that the defendant should keep in repair that of which he has no means of ascertaining the condition. The lessee is in possession; he can say to the lessor: 'You shall not come on the premises without lawful cause'; and to come for the purpose of looking into the state of the premises would not be a lawful cause. If the lessor comes to repair when no repair is needed he will be a trespasser; if he does not come, he will, according to the plaintiff's contention, be liable to an action on the covenant if repair is needed, and will be liable, not only to the cost of repair, but consequential damage for injury to chattels caused by want of the repairs he had no opportunity of effecting. This is so preposterous that we ought to hold that the parties intended the covenant to be read with the qualification suggested."

The same point was made by Collins M.R. in *Tredway v Machin*[17]:  **22–04**

"[The] rule rests upon the principle that the landlord is not the occupier of the premises, and has no means of knowing what is the condition of the premises unless he is told, because he has no right of access to the demised premises, whereas the occupier has the best means of knowing of any want of repair."

It follows from the above that notice is not required where the subject-matter of the covenant is not part of the demised premises.[18]

The requirement of notice applies notwithstanding the fact that:

(1)   the landlord has the right to enter and view the state of repair;[19]
(2)   the defect in question existed at the date of the lease;[20]
(3)   the defect is latent as opposed to patent, i.e. it is one which the tenant did not know and could not have discovered by reasonable examination.[21]

Once notice has been given, however, then the landlord's duty to repair arises, and no new notice is required if he then carries out the repairs to an unreasonable standard.[22]

## Actual notice required

In general, actual, as opposed to constructive, notice is required before the  **22–05**
landlord is liable. The fact that the landlord has the opportunity of finding out about the relevant disrepair is not enough unless it is shown that he has actual knowledge of such information as would put a reasonable man on inquiry that

---

[17]   (1904) 91 L.T. 310.

[18]   See para.22–16 et seq., below.

[19]   *Hugall v M'Lean* (1885) 35 L.T. (N.S.) 94; *Torrens v Walker* [1906] Ch. 166; *Morgan v Liverpool Corp* [1927] 2 K.B. 131 (esp. per Atkin L.J. at 151 and Lawrence L.J. at 153); *McCarrick v Liverpool Corp* [1947] A.C. 219 (esp. per Lord Porter at 224–226 and Lord Simmonds at 228–229).

[20]   *Uniproducts (Manchester) Ltd v Rose Furnishers Ltd* [1956] 1 W.L.R. 45; *Langham Estate Management Ltd v Hardy* [2008] 3 E.G.L.R. 125 at [59].

[21]   *Morgan v Liverpool Corp*, above; *McCarrick v Liverpool Corp*, above; *O'Brien v Robinson* [1973] A.C. 912. Although these cases were decided in relation to obligations implied by statute, it seems clear that the same would be the case at common law: see fn.13, above.

[22]   *Pembery v Lamdin* [1940] 2 All E.R. 434, per Slesser L.J. at 439.

repairs are needed.[23] Thus in *Hugall v M'Lean*[24] a landlord was held not liable for damage caused by flooding from defective drains notwithstanding the fact that at the date of the flood he did not know, but "had the means of knowing" that the drains were defective. Similarly, in *Uniproducts (Manchester) Ltd v Rose Furnishers Ltd*[25] Glyn-Jones J. said:

> "[Counsel for the tenant] …. as I think, quite rightly—conceded that it was not enough for him to show …. that the landlord had the means of knowledge, but that nothing short of actual knowledge would take the place of notice …. to say that [the landlords] failed to make the inquiry which, perhaps, they should have made, is not to say that [they] had actual knowledge of the defect, which any sort of proper examination would have revealed."

In *Dinefwr Borough Council v Jones*[26] an official of the local authority landlord inspected the premises and noticed certain items of disrepair but not others. Bush J. said:

> "[Counsel for the tenant] has sought to …. say that …. the local authority should be notionally saddled with notice of matters which [the official] had not himself seen, but which an immediate inspection would have disclosed. I do not accept that submission ….I think the local authority in this case are affected only by the actual notice of those matters which [the official] observed when he went to the premises."

It should be noted, however, that even where the landlord does not have actual notice of the defect, he may nevertheless be liable under s.4 of the Defective Premises Act 1972.[27]

## Sufficiency of notice

**22–06**   Notice need not be in any particular form.[28] Nor is it necessary that the landlord should be given notice of the exact degree or extent of the disrepair. It is enough if he is given such information as would put a reasonable man on inquiry that repairs are needed.[29] Thus, in *O'Brien v Robinson*[30] Lord Diplock formulated one of the questions in the appeal as being: "whether what the tenant said to the landlord …. would have put a reasonable landlord upon enquiry as to whether works of repair were needed at that time". In *British Telecommunications Plc v*

---

[23] See para.22–06, below.
[24] (1885) 35 L.T.N.S. 94.
[25] [1956] 1 W.L.R. 45.
[26] (1987) 19 H.L.R. 445.
[27] This is because the duty imposed by s.4 is owed "if the landlord knows (whether as a result of being notified by the tenant or otherwise) or if he ought in all the circumstances to have known of the relevant defect." See the discussion in *Sykes v Harry* [2001] Q.B. 1014 at [17–23], and see para.20–56 et seq., above.
[28] *Holding & Barnes v Hill House Hammond* (unreported decision of Neuberger J. dated March 17, 2000). Note that this was the trial of the action following the judge's determination of a preliminary issue concerning the meaning of the landlord's repairing covenant (reported at [2000] L. & T.R 428) and prior to the decision of the Court of Appeal allowing the tenant's cross-appeal (reported at [20002] 2 P. & C. R. 11 and considered in para.4–09, above).
[29] *Griffin v Pillet* [1926] 1 K.B. 17; *O'Brien v Robinson* [1973] A.C. 912; *Hall v Howard* (1988) 57 P. & C.R. 226; *British Telecommunications Plc v Sun Life Assurance Society Plc* [1996] Ch. 69.
[30] [1973] A.C. 912.

*Sun Life Assurance Society Plc*[31] Nourse L.J. said that the landlord is in breach only when he "has information about the existence of the defect such as would put a reasonable landlord on inquiry as to whether works of repair are needed and he has failed to carry out the necessary works with reasonable expedition thereafter".

The fact that the relevant information was given for a purpose other than complaining about disrepair does not prevent it from constituting sufficient notice.[32] Thus, for example, a repairs notice served on the landlord by a local authority constitutes sufficient notice of the defects to which it refers.[33] However, a counterclaim in proceedings cannot amount to sufficient notice for the purpose of a claim in those proceedings.[34]

**22–07**

Examples of cases where the landlord was held to have had sufficient information are:

(1) *Porter v Jones*,[35] where the tenant gave the landlord notice of a bulge in the ceiling. The ceiling collapsed 18 months later, and the landlord was held liable.

(2) *Griffin v Pillet*,[36] in which the lessee wrote to the lessor on April 2, that "the steps to the front door want attention" and the lessor's builders reported to the lessor on April 8, that "the front steps are in a dangerous condition, and being so defective we have put the matter in hand". On April 14, the steps collapsed, and the lessee was injured. Holding the lessor liable, Wright J. said:

> "In my opinion the notice [in the letter of April 2] was sufficient to put the lessor upon enquiry and to impose upon him the obligation of taking the necessary steps to remedy the defect."

(3) *Sheldon v West Bromwich Corp*.[37] The landlords were aware that a water tank was discoloured through corrosion. They were held liable when the tank subsequently burst, even though the expert evidence indicated that corrosion of itself would not normally require immediate works to be carried out, unless accompanied by the "weeping" of water droplets from the tank, and there was no evidence of any such weeping. Stephenson L.J., giving the judgment of the court, was:

---

[31] [1996] Ch. 69.

[32] *Dinefwr Borough Council v Jones* (1987) 19 H.L.R. 445; *Hall v Howard* (1988) 57 P. & C.R. 226; *McGreal v Wake* (1984) 13 H.L.R. 107.

[33] *McGreal v Wake*, above.

[34] *Al Hassani v Merrigan* (1988) 20 H.L.R. 238. This is because there is no cause of action at the date the counterclaim is brought. However, if the landlord fails to repair after service of the counterclaim, then the counterclaim would constitute sufficient notice for the purposes of a claim based on that failure, but such claim would have to be made in later proceedings.

[35] (1942) 112 L.J.K.B. 173.

[36] [1926] 1 K.B. 17.

[37] (1973) 25 P. & C.R. 360. See Blackburne J.'s analysis of this case in *Fluor Daniel Properties Ltd v Shortlands Investments Ltd* [2000] 2 E.G.L.R. 103.

> "[P]repared to accept, in the language of Lord Diplock in *O'Brien v. Robinson*[38] that the landlord's obligation to start carrying out the works does not arise until he has information about the existence of a defect in the premises such as would put a reasonable man upon inquiry as to whether works of repair are needed."

(4) *Dinefwr Borough Council v Jones.*[39] The local authority landlord requested the district valuer to inspect and value the premises in connection with the tenant's application to buy under the Housing Act 1980. The district valuer's report to the chief executive of the local authority stated that his valuation reflected certain items of disrepair. The Court of Appeal held that the report constituted sufficient notice to the local authority of the disrepair even though it had been prepared for a different purpose.

(5) *Hall v Howard,*[40] in which a surveyor was instructed by the tenant of a house to prepare a valuation report because the tenant wished to purchase the reversion from the landlords. The report described the structural condition of the premises, and set out a list of works of repair or improvement which the surveyor thought necessary. It was subsequently sent to the landlords. The Court of Appeal held that, although served for the immediate purpose of aiding the tenant in his bid for the reversion, the report would have alerted a reasonable landlord to the necessity for repairs falling within the landlord's repairing covenant.

**22–08**   Insufficient notice was held to have been given in the following cases:

(1) *O'Brien v Robinson,*[41] in which the tenant complained to the landlord in the early part of 1965 that the tenants of the upstairs flat were causing nuisance by having late night parties, and that he "could not get any sleep at night through banging and jumping upstairs and if there was not something done, … the ceiling would eventually fall down". He further complained that if something were not done about the parties " … probably the ceiling would fall down". The nuisance stopped shortly afterwards, and no defects in the ceiling were or became visible. The ceiling subsequently collapsed and fell on the tenant on November 26, 1968. The House of Lords held that insufficient notice had been given to fix the landlord with liability. The principal ground for the decision appears to have been that no one at the time of the complaints thought there was any need to take any action in relation to the ceiling, and the effect of the complaint was not that the ceiling was already defective, but that it might become so if nothing was done about the parties.

(2) *Al Hassani v Merrigan,*[42] in which the tenant's solicitors wrote the following letter to the landlord's solicitors on March 7, 1986:

> "There are considerable repairs which require immediate attention. Your client's agent has been notified of these matters on countless occasions. The electricity needs immediate

---

[38] [1973] A.C. 912.
[39] (1987) 17 H.L.R. 445.
[40] (1988) 57 P. & C.R. 226.
[41] Above.
[42] (1988) 20 H.L.R. 238.

attention, the bath has been unusable for a considerable period of time ... Our clients will obtain estimates from reputable firms and then submit them to your client. Your client will have the opportunity of either arranging for the firms to carry out the work himself or our clients will carry out the work and then deduct it from any rent due."

Parker L.J., giving the judgment of the court, was prepared to accept that:

"[A] notice of want of repair need not specify the precise nature or degree of want of repair ... if [the contents of the letter] were sufficient to put the [landlord] on enquiry, and I think they were, the [landlord's] obligation would normally have been to attend and inspect and thereafter carry out such repairs as were necessary."

However, the letter was insufficient because it:

"[E]xpressly stated that the [tenant] would be ascertaining what was necessary and submit estimates ... [The landlord] was being specifically told that he would be told what was necessary in due course, and that he could then either do it or have the cost deducted from the rent."

(3)    *Brewer v Andrews*,[43] in which neither generalised oral complaints to the landlord's agents nor the sending of a schedule itemising numerous repair works carried out by the tenants were held to constitute sufficient notice of disrepair for the purposes of s.11 of the Landlord and Tenant Act 1985.[44]

In *Holding & Barnes v Hill House Hammond*[45] the tenant's case was that notice of disrepair had been given to the landlord in the course of a telephone conversation. Neuberger J. found against it on the facts.

## From whom notice must come

The early authorities are not consistent on whether the notice must come from the tenant himself, or whether it is sufficient if the landlord has knowledge of the disrepair from some other source. In *Hugall v M'Lean*[46] Brett M.R. said:

**22–09**

"I doubt whether, if the landlord had notice *aliunde*, he would be liable, but it is not necessary to decide this."

*Torrens v Walker*[47] contains an obiter dictum by Warrington J. to the like effect. However, in *Griffin v Pillet*[48] Wright J. said that if a landlord acquired actual knowledge of a defect, as he might do if his builders were on the premises doing other work, he would not be:

---

[43] [1997] E.G.C.S. 19.

[44] See para.20–17 et seq., above.

[45] Unreported decision of Neuberger J. dated March 17, 2000. Note that this was the trial of the action following the judge's determination of a preliminary issue concerning the meaning of the landlord's repairing covenant (reported at [2000] L. & T.R 428) and prior to the decision of the Court of Appeal allowing the tenant's cross-appeal (reported at [20002] 2 P. & C. R. 11 and considered in para.4–09, above).

[46] (1885) 35 L.T.N.S. 94.

[47] [1906] 2 Ch. 166.

[48] [1926] 1 K.B. 17.

"[E]ntitled to defend himself in an action for breach of covenant for not doing those repairs merely on the ground that he had no actual notice from the lessee."

Similar views were expressed obiter by Lord Sumner in *Murphy v Hurly*,[49] and by Lord Uthwatt in *McCarrick v Liverpool Corp*.[50] Similarly, in *Uniproducts (Manchester) Ltd v Rose (Furnishers) Ltd*[51] Glyn-Jones J. said that:

"I do not think that anything short of proof by the tenant of actual knowledge by the landlord can relieve him of the necessity of proving that he gave notice to the landlord before he can hold the landlord liable for breach of covenant to repair."

The same view was expressed by Lord Morris of Borth-y-Gest in *O'Brien v Robinson*[52] where, without finally deciding the point, he said:

"The purpose of the notice is to impart knowledge that the moment for action under a covenant to repair has or may have arisen. If a lessor who is under an obligation to keep premises in repair acquires knowledge that there is a state of disrepair which may be dangerous, then, even if such knowledge is not shared by the lessee, I would consider that there arises an obligation on the part of the lessor to take appropriate action."

**22–10**    Thus, in *McGreal v Wake*[53] a repairs notice served on the landlord by the local authority was held to constitute sufficient notice. In *Dinefwr Borough Council v Jones*[54] Bush J., giving the leading judgment, said:

"[N]otice need not necessarily come from the tenant, actual notice will suffice—and I would add to that, from some responsible source."

In *Hall v Howard*[55] the Court of Appeal proceeded on the basis that it was not in issue that notice need not come from the tenant provided that it comes from some responsible source. Similarly, in *Sykes v Harry*[56] it was said in the Court of Appeal that it is not necessary that the landlord's acquisition of knowledge of a defect should come from notice or information supplied by the tenant himself.

The balance of modern authority is therefore strongly in favour of the view that notice need not come from the tenant, provided that it is from a sufficiently reliable source for it to be reasonable to expect the landlord to act upon it. This is consistent with the decision of the Court of Appeal in *Princes House v Distinctive Clubs*,[57] in which it was held that a landlord's entitlement to notice under an express provision was capable of being unilaterally waived by the landlord and, on the facts, could not be relied on by him on in circumstances where he knew of the need for repair and had informed the tenant of his intention to carry out the works. It is therefore thought that the above dicta in *Hugall v M'Lean* and *Torrens v Walker* do not correctly represent the law.

---

[49] [1922] 1 A.C. 369.
[50] [1947] A.C. 219.
[51] [1956] 1 W.L.R. 45.
[52] [1973] A.C. 912.
[53] (1984) 13 H.L.R. 107.
[54] (1987) 19 H.L.R. 445.
[55] (1988) 57 P. & C.R. 226.
[56] [2001] Q.B. 1014 at 1021D.
[57] [2007] 2 E.G.L.R. 75. See para.22–23, below, where this case is further considered.

It should be noted that the duty under s.4 of the Defective Premises Act 1972[58] is owed once the landlord knows of a relevant defect, "whether as the result of being notified by the tenant or otherwise".[59]

## To whom notice must be given

It is thought that the ordinary rules of agency apply to the giving of notice of disrepair under the implied term. It follows that notice can be given to any person (i) who is actually authorised by the landlord to receive it; or (ii) who has been held out by the landlord as having been authorised to receive it; or (iii) whose duty it is to report disrepair to the landlord.[60] Thus, in the Australian case of *Austin v Bonney*[61] the landlord's brother, who lived in the same block as the tenant and collected the rent every week, was held to be the landlord's agent for the purpose of receiving notice of disrepair.

    In *Dinefwr Borough Council v Jones*[62] a point arose concerning the giving of notice to the wrong department of the landlord council. The tenancy agreement required all complaints to be made to "The Chief Housing and Environmental Health Officer, Town Hall, Ammanford". The local authority subsequently reorganised itself, and a tenant's handbook was issued which stated that repairs may be reported by "personal visits to the Architectural Services Department, Town Hall, Ammanford ... or The Municipal Offices, Crescent Road, Llandeilo ... by telephone or letter." An official of the Housing and Environmental Health Department visited the premises in order to ascertain their condition of cleanliness. He was informed by the tenant of certain items of disrepair, and he advised her to list them and send the list to the Architectural Services Department. She did not do so. The Court of Appeal held that the knowledge of the official was nonetheless to be attributed to the local authority, the former being "an official of the council who had expertise and who was capable of assessing the state of repair".

**22–11**

## Where there is a change of landlord

It is not clear whether an assignee of the reversion would be bound by a notice of disrepair given to his predecessor, or whether he must be given a new notice before he becomes liable to repair. In *Birkin v Guardweald*[63] the Official Referee held that an assignee of the reversion was not liable until notice had been given to it of the relevant defect, and it had been given a reasonable time in which to carry out the works (even though the assignor had been given notice and was in breach at the date of the assignment). The Court of Appeal refused (for procedural reasons) to allow the point to be argued on appeal. It is thought, however, that the

**22–12**

---

[58] See para.20–49 et seq., above.
[59] Defective Premises Act 1972 s.4(2).
[60] For a discussion of the principle, see *Metropolitan Properties Co Ltd v Cordery* (1979) 39 P. & C.R. 10.
[61] [1998] Q ConvR 60, 082 (Supreme Court of Queensland).
[62] (1987) 19 H.L.R. 445.
[63] (1997) 29 H.L.R. 908.

Official Referee's view was wrong. Once notice has been given, the landlord's liability is triggered. It is difficult to see why, in principle, a new landlord should not be bound by the notice in the same way as he would be bound by, for example, a notice to quit. Moreover, the tenant may be unaware for some time that there has been a change of landlord, but the new landlord will generally have been able to inquire of the existing landlord, prior to the transfer, whether any notices of disrepair have been served. In these circumstances, the better view is that it is for the new landlord to take the risk of notices to repair having been served and not complied with prior to the transfer, rather than for the tenant to take the risk that the process of getting the work done may have to be re-started each time there is a change of landlord.

## The burden of proving notice

22–13    The burden of proving (on the ordinary civil standard of a balance of probabilities) that the landlord has been given sufficient notice of the relevant disrepair is on the tenant.[64]

## Time for performance once notice is given

22–14    Once the landlord has notice of the need for repairs, he has a reasonable time in which to carry out the work. He does not commit a breach of covenant until the expiry of that time.[65] Thus, in *Morris v Liverpool City Council*[66] the tenant's claim failed because the landlord had not unreasonably delayed in carrying out the work. In the Australian case of *Austin v Bonney*[67] the tenant was injured by falling down defective internal stairs. A majority of the court held that there was no sufficient evidence to establish exactly when notice of the defective nature of the stairs had been given by the tenant, and it could not safely be inferred that a reasonable time had elapsed in which to carry out the repairs. However, if the landlord, on being given notice, denies liability for the repairs, then he may be in breach of covenant before the expiry of a reasonable time, so that if the tenant then carries out the work, he will be entitled to recover the cost as damages.[68]

Even where the landlord is already on notice of a want of repair at the date when the tenancy commences, it is nonetheless in breach of covenant only after a reasonable time for the remedying of the disrepair has elapsed after the commencement of the term.[69] In such a case, however, where the term of the

---

[64] *Holding & Barnes v Hill House Hammond* (unreported decision of Neuberger J. dated March 17, 2000). Note that this was the trial of the action following the judge's determination of a preliminary issue concerning the meaning of the landlord's repairing covenant (reported at [2000] L. & T.R 428) and prior to the decision of the Court of Appeal allowing the tenant's cross-appeal (reported at [20002] 2 P. & C. R. 11 and considered in para.4–09, above).

[65] *Green v Eales* (1841) 2 Q.B. 255; *O'Brien v Robinson* [1973] A.C. 912; *Calabar Properties Ltd v Stitcher* [1984] 1 W.L.R. 287, per Griffiths L.J. at 298.

[66] [1988] 1 E.G.L.R. 47.

[67] [1998] Q ConvR 60, 082 (Supreme Court of Queensland).

[68] *Green v Eales*, above.

[69] *Langham Estate Management Ltd v Hardy* [2008] 3 E.G.L.R. 125 at [60].

tenancy commences after the date on which the tenancy agreement is executed, the reasonable time runs from the date of the agreement, not the date on which the term of the tenancy commences.[70]

What is a reasonable time will depend upon all the circumstances.[71] It is thought that it will generally include a reasonable period in which to ascertain precisely what is wrong; to take advice if necessary; to prepare any necessary documentation in connection with the remedial work (such as specifications or bills of quantities); to select and instruct a builder; and (where reasonable) consult and co-operate with those tenants who will be affected by the work with a view to carrying it out so as to cause as little inconvenience as possible.[72] It is thought that if the work is going to be the subject of a service charge, a reasonable time would also include (save in cases of urgency) the time necessary for serving statutory consultation notices under s.20 and 20ZA of the Landlord and Tenant Act 1985 (as amended).

The equivalent paragraph to the above in the Third Edition of this work[73] was described by Carnwath L.J. (with whom Moses L.J. and the Chancellor agreed) in *Earle v Charalambous*[74] as a "helpful discussion". He went on to say:

"The authors suggest that what is a reasonable time will depend on the circumstances, but is likely to include time to find out what is wrong, to take the necessary advice, to prepare specifications, and to select and instruct a builder. Where the cost is to be recovered through service charges time may also need to be allowed for the statutory consultation procedure. Although we have had no argument on the point, in principle this approach seems to me to be correct once it is accepted that the date of notice is the starting point."

In *Langham Estate Management Ltd v Hardy*,[75] which concerned a letting of a high-class residential property at a high level of rent, the tenant contended that a reasonable time was to be judged solely on an objective view of how long it would be reasonable for the tenant to have to suffer the existence of the fault, which view would be stringent in the context of such a property. HHJ Marshall QC disagreed. She said:

"[69]   I reject [counsel's] approach. First, for example, it would involve the landlord carrying, or contracting with its agent to carry, a whole raft of spare components for systems in the property on the off–chance of their being required. This goes beyond the duties of a landlord, which is to get on reasonably promptly with obtaining any spares actually required to be ordered and installed. Second, it would make the landlord the guarantor of any contractor's performance in respects that are quite outside its control or anticipation. In my judgment, such a burden is not implicit in a landlord's repairing (etc) covenant. Each incident must be considered on its own facts."

---

[70]   *Langham Estate Management Ltd v Hardy*, above, at [61].
[71]   See *McGreal v Wake* (1984) 13 H.L.R. 107, in which it was held that a period of eight weeks from the date on which the landlord acquired knowledge of the defects was reasonable.
[72]   See, in relation to this last, *Princes House v Distinctive Clubs* [2007] 2 E.G.L.R. 75, in which the landlord covenanted to use all reasonable endeavours to maintain, repair and redecorate a block, and the judge at first instance held that it was reasonable for him to consult the convenience of his tenants and, in particular, to have regard to the convenience of the immediately subjacent tenant. This part of his judgment was referred to in the Court of Appeal without disapproval: see per Chadwick L.J. at [15].
[73]   At para.22–13 of the Third Edition.
[74]   [2007] H.L.R. 8.
[75]   [2008] 3 E.G.L.R. 125.

She went on to hold that a "good working test" is as follows:

"[71]   …. Looking at what actually happened, does it appear that an owner–occupier whose objective was to get the relevant repair (or other) work carried out as quickly as reasonably practicable after discovering that it was needed could, or would, have achieved this materially more quickly than in fact happened? This seems to me both to take account of the actual circumstances while also giving due weight to the fact that the landlord has an obligation to put the tenant's interest in having the repair done ahead of any conflicting interest of its own that might cause a delay. This might arise if, for example, the landlord wanted to defer doing works so as to be able to do other works at the same time, or if it wanted to try the least expensive possibilities for eliminating a fault before more expensive ones were resorted to, or if it wanted to delay in order to make an insurance claim. A landlord is not, in my judgment, entitled to put its own interests in saving money, or not disturbing the original perfection of finishes, ahead of the tenant's interest in having the fault located and rectified within a reasonable time (according to the nature and effect of the fault). This does not mean that it cannot give any weight to its own interests, but it does mean that it will be in breach of covenant if doing so causes it to exceed a reasonable time for the repair in all the circumstances."

The judge further held that the circumstances of the letting did not imply a "room-service" standard of attendance by the landlord such as that expected in a five star hotel apartment. She said:

"[51]   Fourth, and however [the tenant] may have viewed the matter, [the tenant] was not taking the equivalent of a 5-star hotel apartment, but was renting a house for ordinary residential occupation in the normal way of life. The level of maintenance and attentiveness required to deliver the expected guest experience at a top-class hotel is not the same as that required to fulfil the repair and maintenance obligations of the landlord of a rented house. In a hotel, the 'household' is run by the hotelier, and a cohort of people is employed to enable instant attention to guest requirements and the constant, and hopefully unobtrusive, upkeep of the premises and its installations. In a residential letting, the 'household' is the tenant's. The landlord's obligation is simply to respond reasonably to carry out the covenanted works of repair and maintenance to the property when things require attention, they being works that would otherwise fall to be carried out by the owner-occupier in the course of normal living.

[52]   The level of rent makes no difference to this fundamental distinction. The high rent in this case arose from the particular size, quality, location and features of the property, and did not in itself imply a 'room service' standard of attention from the landlords. Neither does calling the letting a 'commercial' transaction make any difference. The terms of the tenancy agreement, on their true construction, define the scope of the landlord's (and tenant's) obligations, and not whether the landlord is in the business of letting out residences or is merely letting out his own residence while he has no use for it."

The emphasis in the judge's "good working test" on the landlord's obligation "to put the tenant's interest in having the repair done ahead of any conflicting interest of its own that might cause a delay" suggests that the fact that the work can more cheaply or conveniently (for the landlord) be done either at a different time of year, or as part of a larger programme, will generally be irrelevant. It is thought that this is correct in principle.

However, the fact that doing the work at a particular time would be inconvenient for the tenant may be relevant to what is a reasonable time. Thus, in the above case, the judge went on to find that the landlord was not in breach of covenant in relation to the maintenance of a functioning uplighter system around an outdoor swimming pool during the summer months, because the only effective method of repair was as part of a complete rebuilding of the pool surround, and the tenant would have objected to such work being done during the summer use of the pool. However, the landlord's failure to get on with the works in the winter was held to be unreasonable.

Where the defect is potentially dangerous, or will continue to cause damage if left unattended, temporary repairs may be required to stabilise the situation before more permanent works can be effected. Thus, in *Griffin v Pillet*[76] Wright J. said:

> "[T]he lessor in my judgment was not liable for breach of covenant until he had been able to ascertain the nature of the repairs required. This he knew by April 8, and I think he acted at his peril if he did not at once remedy the non-repair, either by temporary measures, if the permanent repairs could not be immediately effected, or by doing the permanent repairs if this was practicable. If he did not do this he committed a breach of covenant."

**22–15**

Thus, for example, a staircase which is found to be suffering from severe dry rot may need immediate support to prevent its collapse even though proper repair work cannot be carried out until the extent and effect of the outbreak has been properly investigated.

Once the landlord's right of entry to carry out the work has arisen,[77] he will not be in breach of covenant by failing to do the work if the tenant refuses access.[78] If the tenant then carries out the work himself, he will not be entitled to recover the cost from the landlord as damages.[79]

## Where the relevant defect is not in the demised premises

The requirement of notice only applies where the facts are such that it would be unreasonable to expect the landlord to be able to perform his covenant unless he is given notice that repairs are needed. Lord Buckmaster made this clear in *Murphy v Hurly*[80]:

**22–16**

> "The principle upon which notice is required to be given to a lessor requiring him to repair demised premises in accordance with his covenant before proceedings are taken to obtain damages for the breach is not inherent in the relationship of landlord and tenant. The doctrine depends upon the actual facts existing in each case and upon the consideration whether the circumstances are such that knowledge of what may be required to be done to comply with the covenant cannot reasonably be supposed to be possessed by the one party while it is by the other. If these are the conditions, it is so unreasonable to render the ignorant party liable for something which the party with knowledge has never asked him to do that it is assumed the covenant implies a condition as to notice being precedent to liability."

It follows that no notice is required where the subject-matter of the landlord's covenant is not part of the demised premises but remains in the landlord's possession and control.[81] Thus, in *Bishop v Consolidated London Properties*

---

[76] [1926] 1 K.B. 17.
[77] See para.22–25 et seq., below.
[78] *Granada Theatres Ltd v Freehold Investment (Leytonstone) Ltd* [1959] 1 Ch. 592.
[79] *Granada Theatres Ltd v Freehold Investment (Leytonstone) Ltd*, above.
[80] [1922] 1 A.C. 369.
[81] *Melles & Co v Holme* [1918] 2 K.B. 100; *Murphy v Hurley*, above; *Bishop v Consolidated London Properties Ltd* (1933) 102 L.J.K.B. 257; *Minchburn v Peck* (1987) 20 H.L.R. 392; *Loria v Hammer*

*Ltd*[82] the landlords let a flat in a block and covenanted expressly to keep the exterior of the premises and all parts of the block not subject to that or any other letting in good repair. A dead pigeon caused an obstruction in a downfall overflow pipe above the flat, and it and the tenant's furniture were consequently damaged by flooding. The landlords had no notice of the defect, but were nonetheless held liable for breach of covenant. In *Loria v Hammer*[83] Mr John Lindsay QC (sitting as a deputy judge of the Chancery Division) said:

> "[T]he reason why notice is a prerequisite in cases where a lessee is in occupation of the relevant parts is, that being so, a landlord has no means of knowing of the defect until he is told of it. That reason plainly cannot apply when the want of repair is of parts retained by a landlord who can obtain access to them. The reason for the rule thus not existing, neither should the rule apply."

**22–17**  Notice may not be required even where the landlord has not retained legal possession of the subject-matter of his covenant, provided that he has retained control of it. Thus, in *Murphy v Hurly*[84] the landlord covenanted to repair a seawall which was necessary for the protection of the demised premises from the sea. It was not clear whether or not the wall was on land forming part of the demise, but in any event the landlord was intended to retain it in his own control. The House of Lords held that no notice was required to make him liable. It follows that whilst the fact that the subject-matter of the obligation is part of the demised premises will usually suffice to bring the requirement of notice into operation, this will not always be the case.

## Time for performance where no notice is required

**22–18**  Where the landlord's liability is dependent on notice, he has a reasonable time from the giving of notice in which to carry out the work.[85] Where no notice is required, the question is whether the landlord is in breach of covenant as soon as a defect occurs, or whether, even when a defect has occurred, he is not in breach until he has had a reasonable time in which to remedy it. Put another way, the question is whether the covenant amounts to an absolute obligation to ensure that the premises are at all times in repair, or whether the obligation is to remedy disrepair within a reasonable time of it occurring. The distinction is of particular importance where the defect manifests itself suddenly and without warning. For example, a roof may be in a proper state of repair but unusually high winds during the night result in tiles blowing off, with the consequence that water enters the tenant's demise and damages decorations. If the covenant is a warranty that the roof will never be out of repair, the landlord is liable for the damage caused. If it is an obligation to put right the disrepair, the landlord is not liable for the

---

[1989] 2 E.G.L.R. 249; *British Telecommunications Plc v Sun Life Assurance Society Plc* [1996] Ch. 69 (from which it appears that the requirement of notice in cases where the defect occurs in the demised premises themselves is properly to be regarded as an exception to the general principle that a covenant to keep premises in the repair obliges the covenantor to keep them in repair at all times).

[82] Above.
[83] [1989] 2 E.G.L.R. 249.
[84] [1922] 1 A.C. 369.
[85] See para.22–14, above.

damage, although (i) he must replace the tiles, and (ii) he is liable for any further damage caused by his failure to replace the tiles within a reasonable time.

The nature of the distinction has been noted by Lord Diplock in *O'Brien v Robinson*,[86] where he said:

"At the root of any analysis of the landlord's obligations under a repairing covenant lies the initial question whether it is an undertaking by the landlord to prevent the premises ever getting out of repair during the continuance of the tenancy or whether it is an undertaking to do work of repair upon the premises from time to time as and when they have become out of repair. If it is the former, the breach occurs as soon as the premises are in fact out of repair and continues until he has put them back into repair. If it is the latter, there is involved the subsidiary question as to the time at which the landlord's obligation to do the necessary work of repair first arises. Until that time arrives there can be no breach of the obligation; nor can there be any breach thereafter if the landlord then carries out the necessary work of repair with reasonable expedition."

The statutory obligation which he was there considering[87] was one which (as the House held) arose only on notice, and was therefore necessarily within the latter kind of obligation. Lord Diplock accordingly did not give any definite answer to the question whether in the case of an obligation to repair which is not dependent on notice "the breach occurs as soon as the premises are out of repair and continues until he has put them back into repair". In two cases at first instance an affirmative answer has been given to this question.[88] However, the matter has now been settled by the decision of the Court of Appeal in *British Telecommunications Plc v Sun Life Assurance Society Plc*.[89] That case concerned a lease of two floors of an office block. The landlord covenanted to perform the tenant's covenants in the head lease, one of which was "from time to time and at all times during the said term to uphold, maintain, cleanse and keep in complete good and substantial repair and condition" the demised premises (i.e. the whole block). In the summer of 1986 a bulge appeared in the brick cladding forming part of the external walls and main structure of the building, the cause of the defect being the poor fixing of the cladding to the inner wall. The part of the building affected by the bulge was not part of the premises demised to the tenant. The question was whether the landlord was in breach as soon as the bulge appeared or only on the expiration of a reasonable period after its appearance. The Court of Appeal held that liability arose as soon as the bulge appeared. Nourse L.J., who gave the leading judgment, said:

**22–19**

"The general rule is that a covenant to keep premises in repair obliges the covenantor to keep them in repair at all times, so that there is a breach of the obligation immediately a defect occurs. There is an exception where the obligation is the landlord's and the defect occurs in the demised premises themselves, in which case he is in breach only when he has information about the existence of the defect such as would have put a reasonable landlord on inquiry as to whether works of repair are needed and he has failed to carry out the necessary works with reasonable expedition thereafter."

---

[86] [1973] A.C. 912.
[87] The statutory predecessor of s.11 of the Landlord and Tenant Act 1985: see para.20–17, above.
[88] *Bishop v Consolidated London Properties Ltd* (1933) 102 L.J.K.B. 257 and *Loria v Hammer* [1989] 2 E.G.L.R. 249.
[89] [1996] Ch. 69.

*British Telecommunications* has been followed and applied in a number of subsequent cases. In *Passley v Wandsworth LBC*[90] the plaintiff was the tenant of a flat on the top floor of a block. There were frozen pipes on the roof between February 7 and February 14, on which date there was a sudden thaw and a pipe burst. The plaintiff's flat was badly flooded. There was no evidence that the pipe was (before it froze and burst) otherwise than in good condition and repair and in compliance with the landlord's implied obligation under s.11 of the Landlord and Tenant Act 1985.[91] It was held by the Court of Appeal that the landlord was liable for damage suffered by the tenant as a result of the flooding. In *Ladsky v TSB Bank*[92] the Court of Appeal rejected an argument that the facts justified reading the relevant covenant (an obligation to keep mortgaged property in good repair and condition) as importing an obligation to remedy any disrepair within a reasonable time of being informed of its existence. In *Bavage v Southwark LBC*[93] a central sewage stack running down from the roof of a block of flats and serving all the apartments within the block was damaged by vandals, and the plaintiff's flat was flooded with raw sewage. It was held that the landlord was liable for the damage notwithstanding the absence of notice.

**22–20**   The general rule is therefore now clear: where the covenant is to keep premises other than the demised premises in repair there is "a breach of the obligation immediately a defect occurs".[94] However, a number of points remain to be considered.

First, Nourse L.J. said at the end of his judgment:

> "I express no concluded view as to the case where a defect is caused by an occurrence wholly outside the landlord's control. Suppose, for example, that the roof in *Melles & Co. v. Holme*[95] had been damaged by a branch from a tree standing on neighbouring property not in the possession or control of the landlords and that rainwater had found its way down into the plaintiff's rooms by that means ... On reflection and provisionally, I can see no reason why such a case should not, for reasons similar to those expressed in *Makin v. Watkinson*[96] be made the subject of a further exception to the general rule. That point will have to be decided if and when it arises for decision."

Nourse L.J.'s example of the fallen tree branch suggests that what he had in mind by "an occurrence wholly outside the landlord's control" was a case where the event giving rise to the damage originates not on land retained by the landlord in his own possession and control but on land in the possession and control of a third party. This is consistent with the decision in *Bavage v Southwark LBC*,[97] in which the county court declined to apply the exception in circumstances where the event which gave rise to the flooding of the tenant's flat occurred entirely on

---

[90]  (1998) 30 H.L.R. 165, CA.
[91]  See para.20–17 et seq., above.
[92]  (1997) 64 P. & C.R. 372.
[93]  [1998] C.L.Y. 3623.
[94]  *Passley v Wandsworth LBC* (1998) 30 H.L.R. 165 per Hobhouse L.J. at 171. In *Princes House v Distinctive Clubs* [2007] 2 E.G.L.R. 75, it was said in the Court of Appeal (at [19]) that an express provision for the giving of notice by the tenant had been included to protect the landlord from what would otherwise be the consequences of the *British Telecommunications* principle.
[95]  [1918] 2 K.B. 100.
[96]  (1870) L.R. 6 Ex. 25.
[97]  [1998] C.L.Y. 3623. The facts are summarised in para.22–19, above.

land which was within the possession and control of the landlord, even though the damage was caused by vandals. Examples of cases where the exception might apply (assuming it to exist at all[98]) might therefore be damage caused by a lorry careering off the highway, a falling telegraph pole or a collapsing building on adjoining land owned and occupied by a third party. In such cases, the landlord presumably only becomes liable once he has such information as would put a reasonable landlord on inquiry that repairs are needed, and he fails to carry out the works within a reasonable time.

In *Passley v Wandsworth LBC*[99] Hobhouse L.J. appears to have doubted whether the exception exists at all. He referred in his judgment to the relevant part of *British Telecommunications* in the following terms:

**22–21**

> "The example Nourse L.J. gave was where a tree, standing on neighbouring property not in the possession or control of the landlord, fell and damaged the roof of the relevant property as a result of which rainwater reached the parts occupied by the relevant tenant. In my judgment this is simply a question of causation. In principle what causes the defect is not relevant unless it be a fault of the tenant or a fault of the landlord. If there is such an actionable fault, then different and additional questions of liability might arise. But where it is not suggested by either party that the defect was caused by the fault of one of the parties to the lease, then the cause becomes irrelevant. The only relevant consideration is whether or not there is in existence a defect at a given moment in time. If there is a defect, then the breach of covenant has, as Nourse L.J. said, occurred at that time. In my judgment it is not then relevant to ask questions about what caused the defect. The question is simply whether in the ordinary use of language there was at a given point of time a defect in the relevant part of the premises, or (to say the same thing but in different words) whether there was at any moment of time a state of disrepair of the premises. It is that factual situation which gives rise to the obligation and the breach of covenant by the landlord."

The actual decision in *Passley* was that even if the general rule does not apply where the defect is caused by an occurrence wholly outside the landlord's control, the defect in question (a pipe which froze and then burst) was not so caused. Sir John Balcombe (with whom Kennedy L.J. agreed) was "wholly unconvinced that what happened here was indeed wholly outside the landlord's control ... Severe weather in this country is not so uncommon an occurrence that it cannot be foreseen and suitable precautions taken".

Second, the covenant in *British Telecommunications Plc v Sun Life Assurance Society Plc* was to keep the premises in repair. It is not clear to what extent the position would be different in relation to a covenant simply "to repair". At the end of his judgment Nourse L.J. said:

> "[Counsel for the tenant] was disposed to accept that the position might be different in a case where the landlord's obligation was not to keep the premises in repair but simply to repair them. Having confined myself to the former obligation, I say nothing about the latter, which is in any event, as I believe, a rarity in modern leases and tenancy agreements."

The distinction can be justified on the basis that an obligation to "keep" in repair as a matter of language requires the landlord to ensure that the premises are in repair at all times, whereas an obligation "to repair" connotes the carrying out

---

[98] See below.
[99] (1998) 30 H.L.R. 165.

of the operation of repair, which cannot be done until disrepair occurs.[100] On this basis, the landlord cannot be in breach of the latter obligation until a defect has occurred and he has failed to repair it. Such a construction might be supported by the inclusion in the covenant of expressions such as "as and when necessary". The argument the other way is that obligations to repair and to keep in repair have generally been treated in the authorities as meaning much the same thing, and the above approach results in fairly fine distinctions of language leading to potentially very different consequences.

**22–22**     Third, the consequence of the landlord being in breach as soon as a defect occurs is that he will be liable for all foreseeable damage caused to the tenant as a result of the defect even if he was unaware of it. It may be, however, that if the tenant is aware of the defect but does not notify the landlord, he will be held to have failed to mitigate his loss.[101]

Fourth, the rule in *British Telecommunications* may be capable of operating oppressively where the premises comprise a block of flats and compliance with the landlord's repairing obligation is funded by service charges. In such a case, the landlord's ability to pay for repairs as and when necessary may be dependent on prompt payment of interim service charges, and in addition he may need to comply with the prescribed statutory consultation procedure[102] before carrying out the works so as to be able to recover the cost. If, in such a case, he fails to carry out the remedial works promptly, he may find himself liable for damages even though it would not necessarily have been reasonable to expect him to attend to the defect immediately. A point along these lines was made in *Earle v Charalambous*[103] by Carnwath L.J. (with whom Moses L.J. and the Chancellor agreed), in the following passage:

> "The *BT* case, and the earlier cases relied on it, were not concerned with the modern statutory and contractual framework governing residential leases. The lessor's repairing obligation, in a case such as the present, is not free-standing, but is in practice linked to the obligation of the lessees to contribute to the costs so incurred. (Indeed the lessor may be a company owned by the lessees, with no separate assets of its own.) The link is made expressly in the present lease, where the lessor's repairing obligation is 'subject to contribution and payment by the lessee as hereinbefore provided' (cl 4(3)). (It is unnecessary to consider the precise effect of that qualification, which seems open to debate.) To protect lessees, there is an elaborate statutory framework to ensure that they are consulted in advance on major works. In a future case, it may have to be considered whether the 'general rule' as laid down by *BT* requires some modification to take account of the practicalities of the modern relationship of residential lessors and lessees."

It remains to be seen to what extent this invitation will be taken up in future cases.

Fifth, it is not clear to what extent the rule in *British Telecommunications* applies where the disrepair is to parts of the building which are let to another tenant, as opposed to a part within the landlord's exclusive possession and control. In principle, it is thought that, as between the landlord and the tenant who

---

[100] See *Lurcott v Wakeley* [1911] 1 K.B. 905, per Fletcher Moulton L.J. (considered in para.4–29, above).
[101] See *Minchburn v Peck* (1988) 20 H.L.R. 392. See further para.33–37, below.
[102] See the Landlord and Tenant Act 1985 (as amended) s.20 and 20ZA.
[103] [2007] H.L.R. 8.

suffers damage, the landlord is liable as soon as the disrepair occurs, and it is up to him so to arrange his affairs with the tenant of the part in question so that he can carry out periodic inspections for disrepair. It may be, however, that this would qualify as "an occurrence wholly outside the landlord's control" within the ambit of the possible exception to the general rule considered above.

Last, landlord's repairing covenants are sometimes made subject to an express proviso that the landlord is not liable until he has had notice of the disrepair.[104] Such a provision would prevent the principle in *British Telecommunications* from applying.

## Contractual provisions relating to the giving of notice

Some leases expressly provide for the giving of notice before the landlord's liability to repair (or for failure to repair) arises.[105] Where this is the case, the operation of the provision is a matter of construction. However, it is thought that, provided sufficiently clear words were used, there is no reason why such a provision should not have effect. The provisions of the Unfair Contract Terms Act 1977 would not apply.[106]

**22–23**

In *Masterton Licensing Trust v Finco*[107] (a New Zealand case), the landlord of a small shop on the ground floor of a three storey building covenanted to "keep and maintain in good and tenantable weatherproof wear and condition the roof and outer walls" of the shop, subject to a proviso that "the Owner shall not be liable for any damage caused by any failure so to keep and maintain in good and tenantable repair until after the expiry of one (1) month from the date or respective dates on which the Tenant shall have given notice to the Owner of any such want of repair to the Owner". A downpipe on the roof of the building was partially or substantially blocked by pigeon debris, and water backed up over the roof during a storm, escaped over the flashing of the roof guttering and flowed into the shop down the inside walls. It was held by the New Zealand Court of Appeal that on the proper construction of the clause, the proviso covered the same ground as, and was co-extensive with, the obligation, with the result that the landlord was not liable because no notice had been given.

The landlord may waive his entitlement to notice under an express requirement of this kind if he unequivocally communicates to the tenant an intention not to rely on it. Thus, in *Princes House v Distinctive Clubs*[108] a lease of basement premises contained a covenant by the landlord to use all reasonable endeavours to maintain, repair and decorate the block, together with a further provision in the following terms:

---

[104] See para.22–23, below.
[105] See, for example, the proviso to the landlord's repairing covenant in *Credit Suisse v Beegas Nominees Ltd* [1994] 4 All E.R. 803 and (more fully) [1994] 1 E.G.L.R. 76 (set out in para.4–29, above).
[106] Cf. *Electricity Supply Nominees v IAF Group* [1993] 2 E.G.L.R. 95. See further para.33–43, fn.40, below.
[107] [1957] N.Z.L.R. 1137.
[108] [2007] 2 E.G.L.R. 75.

"The Landlord will not be liable to the Tenant in respect of any failure by the Landlord to perform or provide the services ... unless and until the Tenant has notified the Landlord of such failure and the Landlord has failed within a reasonable time to remedy the same."

In the Court of Appeal Chadwick L.J. (with whom Dyson and Thomas L.JJ. agreed) said of this:

"The protection under [the clause] takes two forms. First, the landlords' liability for failure to repair does not arise until the tenant has notified the landlords of that failure. Second, the landlords' liability for failure to repair does not arise until the landlords have failed, within a reasonable time, to remedy that failure. However, although those two conditions are cumulative in the sense that both must be satisfied before the landlords are liable to the tenant for breach of covenant there is no basis for a construction that links the determination of what is a reasonable time to the giving of notice by the tenant. What is a reasonable time depends upon all the circumstances, including the fact, if it be so, that the landlords have known of the need for repair before and independently of any notice given by the tenant."

He went on to hold that, since the provision had been included for the protection of the landlords (because without it, their liability to repair would arise as soon as the relevant premises were defective, whether or not they were aware of it[109]), the landlords could unilaterally waive the benefit of the provision and, on the facts, had done so by writing to the tenant informing it of their intention to carry out the relevant works in the following year. They had thereby indicated to the tenant that they did not intend to rely on the need for notice under the relevant provision before carrying out their obligation to repair. The court further held that, on the facts, the landlord had failed to use all reasonable endeavours to carry out the works by December 2003 (which was, by virtue of the existence of a service charge cap, the material date).

## The nature of the landlord's obligation once liability to repair has arisen

22–24    Unless the relevant covenant limits the landlord's obligation to using his best or reasonable endeavours, his duty under the covenant is absolute in nature. Where his liability arises only on receiving notice,[110] he must remedy the defect within a reasonable time of being notified of it, and he is in breach if he does not. Where the general principle in *British Telecommunications Plc v Sun Life Assurance Society Plc*[111] applies, he must do whatever is necessary to ensure that no disrepair occurs, and he is in breach once a disrepair is shown to exist. In neither case, as a general principle, can he avoid liability by showing that he used his best efforts to prevent or (as the case may be) to remedy the relevant disrepair. Nor, as a general rule, can he escape liability by showing that he bona fide employed competent contractors to carry out the work, if those contractors have not done it, or not done it properly.[112]

---

[109] See para.22–24, below.
[110] See paras 22–03 to 22–14, above.
[111] [1996] Ch. 69. See paras 22–19 to 22–22, above.
[112] *Nokes v Gibbon* (1856) 3 Drew 681; *Adams Furniture Co Limited v Johar Investments Ltd* [1961] 26 D.L.R. (2nd) 380 (Canada).

## THE LANDLORD'S RIGHTS OF ENTRY TO CARRY OUT WORKS

### Introductory

The landlord does not need a right of entry to carry out works where the subject-matter of the covenant is in his own possession or control. However, where the subject-matter is or includes premises which are in the tenant's possession, then an express or implied right of entry is necessary before he can enter and carry out work. In practice the need for an appropriate right of entry is often overlooked, and landlords frequently (and erroneously[113]) assume that such a right exists merely by virtue of their reversionary interest.

22–25

The landlord's potential liability under s.4 of the Defective Premises Act 1972[114] is a further reason why it is important to know what rights of entry he may have to carry out repairs.

### Express rights of entry

Most well-drafted modern leases will reserve express rights of entry into the demised premises in some or all of the following situations:

22–26

(1)  for the purpose of inspecting the demised premises, either generally or specifically to see whether the covenant to repair is being complied with;

(2)  for the purpose of carrying out repairs to the demised premises when the tenant has failed to do so in breach of covenant. Such a provision may take a number of different forms. Common to most forms is a provision entitling the landlord to enter and inspect the premises to see whether or not the covenant to repair is being complied with; to prepare and serve on the tenant a notice specifying any disrepair; a covenant by the tenant to remedy the defects in the notice within a specified time; and a provision entitling the landlord, in the event of the tenant failing to carry out the work, to enter the premises, carry out the work himself and recover the cost of it from the tenant[115];

(3)  for the purpose of carrying out of repairs or alterations to adjoining premises.

It is not usual to find an express right of entry in respect of repairs which the landlord has covenanted to do, because that is adequately covered by the right which is implied in such circumstances at common law.[116]

The scope of an express right of entry is a question of construction. In *Yeomans Row Management Ltd v Bodentien-Meyrick*[117] a tenancy of a dwelling-house contained a provision obliging the tenant to permit the landlords:

---

[113]  See para.22–30, below.

[114]  See para.20–49 et seq., above.

[115]  See para.14–11, above.

[116]  See para.22–32, below.

[117]  [2002] 2 E.G.L.R. 39.

"[T]o execute any repairs or work to the inside or outside of the said flat and also for the purpose of executing any repairs or work to or in connection with any flats above or below or adjoining the said flat to enter upon the said flat or any part thereof with or without any necessary tools or appliances."

The landlord wished to enter the flat to carry out various improvements. The Court of Appeal held that, having regard to the other terms of the lease, the right of entry on its proper construction was limited to the carrying out of repairs or works akin to repairs and did not extend to the carrying out of improvements.

In *Risegold Ltd v Escala Ltd*[118] a deed of transfer conferred an express right to enter "upon such part of the yard at the rear of [the adjoining property] as is necessary for the purpose of carrying out any maintenance repair rebuilding or renewal to [the property]". The transferor's successor in title proposed to demolish the existing single storey warehouse/industrial structures on the property and build a five/six storey block containing commercial units on the ground floor and 24 flats on the upper floors. It could not do so without entering the adjoining property to do various things, such as erecting a fence and scaffolding and oversailing a tower crane. It was held at first instance that "rebuilding or renewal" did not cover replacing what was there with something different in kind, with the result that the purpose for which entry was required fell outside the scope of the right of entry. The Court of Appeal allowed the developer's appeal. Mummery L.J., with whom Keen and Arden L.J. agreed, said that broadly construed the provision would permit entry onto the adjoining property in order to preserve existing buildings on the property, or to pull down the buildings on the property and (a) to put up no new buildings in their place, or (b) to put up buildings similar to the demolished buildings, or (c) to put up different buildings in the place of the demolished buildings.

In *Beaufort Park Residents Management Ltd v Sabahipour*,[119] a lease of a flat contained a tenant's covenant:

"To co-operate at all times with the Lessor and all others interested in Beaufort Park in all measures necessary for repairing maintaining and upholding Beaufort Park and in particular and without prejudice to the generality of the foregoing to permit the Lessor and its Surveyors or Agents with or without workmen and others at all reasonable times to enter upon the flat for the purpose of examining the state and condition thereof ... "

The company secretary of the landlord sought access to inspect the premises following complaints by the tenant of leaky pipes. The tenant refused access but said that he was willing for someone else to inspect. It was held that the company secretary was an agent of the landlord and entitled to access under the covenant. It was not open to the tenant to dictate who carried out the inspection. So long as the person seeking access fell within the definition of being the lessor, its surveyor or its agent, and so long as the purpose of entry was for "examining the state and condition" of the flat, the tenant was obliged to permit entry by that person.

---

[118] [2008] EWCA Civ 1180.
[119] [2012] 1 E.G.L.R. 53.

## Express conditions as to notice and time

The landlord must comply with any express conditions to which the right of entry **22–27** is subject (such as the giving of prior notice or the time at which entry may take place). Failure to comply may render the entry or proposed entry unlawful, in which case the tenant will be entitled either to an injunction restraining the entry, or, if the entry has already occurred, damages for trespass. Common conditions are that a specified period of advance notice must be given (sometimes it is stipulated that this must be in writing), and that the landlord will only be entitled to access either at specified times, or at reasonable times. It has been held that a right of entry "at a convenient time" does not require the tenant to give access on a Sunday.[120]

## Where there are no express conditions as to notice or time

Sometimes a right of entry will be reserved without any express provisions as to **22–28** advance notice or the time at which the right may be exercised. In such cases the question will arise as to whether any such provisions ought to be implied. Whilst each case will depend on its own facts, it is thought that the court would be likely to imply into a right of access which on the face of it is unlimited a term that, save in cases of emergency, the right is only exercisable on the giving of such notice to the tenant as would reasonably enable him to afford access. If such a term were not implied, the unlimited right of entry would entitle the landlord to appear at the premises at any hour of the day or night without any form of prior notice. It seems unlikely that this is what reasonable parties would have intended. However, whether the implied term would go any further than this is unclear. In particular, it is unclear to what extent the court would be prepared to imply a term that the notice must be of a sufficient length to enable the tenant to grant access at a time convenient to him. However, each case will turn on its own facts.

Where the purpose for which the landlord is entitled to enter is not merely to view the premises but also to carry out work, then it may be that the court would be more ready to imply limitations on the times at which he can enter. In such a case thoughtless exercise of the right may well cause major inconvenience and disruption to the tenant. It is thought that the court, whilst giving weight to any bona fide requirement by the landlord to carry out work in the way in which he thought most suitable, would not ignore the legitimate interests of the tenant. However, whatever term is to be implied, it is not thought that it would extend to cases of genuine emergency, where the landlord's right of entry could be exercised without any form of prior notice.

It was argued in *Janet Reger International v Tiree*[121] that there was to be implied into a lease of a ground-floor shop and basement an obligation on the part of the landlord in the following terms:

---

[120] *Earl of Kent's Case* (1588) Gouldsb. 76. One can only speculate as to whether modern attitudes to Sunday observance would affect this ancient authority.
[121] [2006] 3 E.G.L.R. 131 at [74] to [76]. See para.1–07, above, where the facts are set out.

> "If any part of the Retained Parts is in need of remedial works which the Landlord is not obliged to but may carry out under the terms of this lease then the Landlord must, within a reasonable time or upon request, inform the Tenant whether, and if so, when and how it intends to carry out the works."

The court rejected the suggested implication on the ground that it was not necessary.

## The scope of the right

**22–29**   The extent to which an express right of entry entitles the landlord to do more than just inspect those parts of the premises that are visible depends on the proper construction of the particular provision. In some cases the provision will expressly entitle the landlord to expose parts of the premises (for example, exposing structural steelwork by removing concrete cladding); to carry out tests (for example, drain tests); to install and maintain monitoring devices (for example, glass telltales); and to remove and take away samples of materials for testing (for example, samples of concrete). In other cases, the right will be less explicit, and it will be necessary to decide how far it was intended to go. The question is one of construction in each case. However, in two cases the courts have adopted a relatively restrictive approach to the scope of the right.

In the Scottish case of *Possfund Custodial Trustee v Kwik-Fit Properties Ltd*[122] a lease of premises previously been used as a garage, which contained underground tanks formerly used for the storage of fuel, contained the following tenant's covenant:

> "To permit the Landlord and its agents at all reasonable times with or without workmen on giving forty eight hours' written notice (except in emergency) to the Tenant to enter upon the Premises generally to inspect and examine the same, to view the state of repair and condition thereof and to take a schedule of the Landlords' fixtures and of any wants of compliance by the Tenant with its obligations hereunder."

The landlord gave notice to the tenant that it required access to carry out environmental investigations. A method statement was subsequently provided, which was summarised by Lord Reed in his judgment as follows:

> "It stated that the purpose of the proposed investigation was to assess the significance of any potential environmental liability associated with any soil and groundwater contamination that might be present. The investigation would involve several stages. It would first be necessary to carry out a service-avoidance exercise and a ground-penetrating radar survey, in order to identify the exact location of the underground storage tanks, other subsurface structures and live services. This would take up to two days to complete. Drilling works would then be carried out. These would involve drilling five shallow boreholes, to a depth of approximately 6m beneath the surface, in order to collect groundwater samples from shallow perched groundwater likely to be present within made ground or shallow deposits. Four of these boreholes would be drilled around the underground storage tanks in the eastern part of the forecourt of the premises. The fifth of the shallow boreholes would be drilled in the western part of the forecourt. There would, in addition, be a single deep borehole to a depth of approximately 30m beneath the surface in order to collect groundwater samples from the major aquifer within the underlying sandstone. The drilling works would take up to four days to complete. Each borehole would be installed as a 50mm diameter land gas and groundwater

---

[122] [2009] 1 E.G.L.R. 39 (Court of Session, Inner House).

> monitoring well finished with a traffic-strength cover flush with the surface. Approximately 15 soil samples would be collected at various depths and submitted to a laboratory for chemical analysis. Groundwater samples would also be collected and analysed, and land gas concentrations would be monitored. The monitoring would begin at least two days after the completion of the drilling works. A skip would be provided to collect waste arising from the drilling. A representative of Delta Simons would be present for around four days to oversee the drilling works, record observations and collect samples. Cones, barriers and signs would be used to cordon off the areas of the works."

The court held that the proposed investigation did not fall within the covenant. By contrast with other relevant provisions in the lease, the clause did not impose on the landlord an obligation to proceed in such a way as to cause the least practicable disturbance to the tenant, nor was there any obligation to make good any damage caused. Although not conclusive, this strongly suggested that it had not been envisaged or intended that the exercise of the landlord's right of inspection would cause any material disturbance to the tenant or result in any material damage to the premises. The lease contained other pointers to the same conclusion. Had the parties intended that the landlord should be able to interfere with the tenant's possession of the premises to the extent of carrying out intrusive investigations lasting several days, a clearer indication to that effect would have been expected in the lease.

As to the precise limits of the right conferred by cl.3.11, Lord Reed said:

> "It is unnecessary for the purposes of the present case to decide the precise limits of the inspection and examination permitted by these words: whether, for example, the reference in clause 3.11 to 'workmen' implies, as the Lord Ordinary considered, that the landlord is entitled to uncover parts of the premises, for example, by lifting floorboards. The word 'view' suggests, however, that clause 3.11 is concerned with matters that are observable (as distinct, for example, from matters that require the removal of cores and other samples for laboratory analysis). This is consistent with the absence of any requirement to minimise disturbance or to make good damage. "

Much the same conclusion was reached by Sharp J. in *Heronslea (Mill Hill) v Kwik-Fit Properties Ltd.*[123] In that case, a lease of premises which had formerly been used as a petrol station contained (in para.13 of Sch.4) the following tenant's covenant:

> "Upon reasonable prior written notice (except in an emergency when no notice need be given) the Tenant shall permit the Landlord and those authorized by it at all times to enter (and remain unobstructed on) the Premises for the purpose of:
> 13.1.1  inspecting the Premises for any purpose, or
> 13.1.2  making surveys or drawings of the Premises or
> 13.1.3  complying with the Landlord's obligations under this Lease or with any other Legal Obligations of the Landlord.
>    Provided that the Landlord shall cause as little interference and disturbance as is practicable and shall make good any damage caused forthwith and to the reasonable satisfaction of the Tenant."

The landlord sought entry for the purposes of carrying out an environmental investigation survey, which would involve the drilling of 13 boreholes, 12 to a depth of 5m and one at 20m, and the taking of samples. The deep borehole would be drilled using a cable percussion rig over a 5 sq m working area. The shallower

---

[123] [2009] Env. L.R. 28.

holes would be drilled using a smaller rig. Each of the smaller holes would require a 4 sq m rig. The survey would take two days to complete.

Sharp J. upheld the decision of the county court judge that the proposed investigation was not a "survey" within para.13.1.2. The dictionary definition of that word at the time the lease was granted in 2000 ("the process of surveying a tract of ground, coast-line, or any part of the earth's surface; the determination of its form, extent, and other particulars, so as to be able to delineate or describe it accurately and in detail; also, a plan or description thus obtained") did not cover the type of activities the landlord wished to carry out. The use of the preposition "on" together with the words which followed the word "survey" itself ("and drawings") suggested that "survey" in the context meant a survey of (rather than under) the land and of the buildings on the land (in contrast with the clause dealing with hazardous waste, where the parties had provided specifically for what was or was not to be placed "under" the premises). The provisions of the lease relating to environmental matters suggested that the parties had intended to let sleeping dogs lie as regards contamination until shortly before the expiry of the lease, when it was the tenant's obligation, not that of the landlord, to carry out environmental investigations. The covenant for quiet enjoyment would be significantly undermined if the landlord had the right to enter the premises, and conduct whatever could be described as a survey, including a geological survey, no matter how intrusive, no matter what disruption was caused to the tenant's business and however long such activities might take. Much clearer words would have been used if that had been the intention. A reasonable person, having all the background knowledge which would reasonably have been available to the parties in the situation in which they were at the time the lease was executed, would not have thought that para.13.1.2 entitled the landlord to enter the premises for the purpose of drilling boreholes and taking samples.

## The general principle where no express right of entry is reserved

**22–30**    One of the fundamental characteristics of a lease is that it confers on the tenant the right to exclusive possession of the demised premises, i.e. a right to exclude from the premises all other persons including the landlord. One consequence of this is that the landlord has no right merely by virtue of his position as landlord to enter the premises for any purpose whatsoever. Accordingly, unless the tenant consents, or one of the exceptions discussed below applies, he has no right to enter in order, for example, to inspect the condition of the premises, or to carry out repairs, however bad the condition of the premises may be, and however much his interest may be jeopardised by the tenant's failure to repair.[124]

---

[124] *Barker v Barker* (1829) 3 C. & P. 557; *Neale v Wylie* (1824) 3 B. & C. 533; *Doe d. Worcester School Trustees v Rowlands* (1841) 9 C. & P. 734; *Stocker v Planet Building Society* (1879) 27 W.R. 877; *Regional Properties Co Ltd v City of London Real Property Co Ltd* [1981] 1 E.G.L.R. 33; *Akram v Adam* [2003] H.L.R. 28.

The facts of *Stocker v Planet Building Society*[125] afford a dramatic illustration of the principle in operation. The building society let a number of houses on a lease containing a tenant's covenant to repair and a proviso for forfeiture in the event of breach, but no express right for the landlord to enter and repair in the event of the tenant's default. The demised houses were in disrepair. The society itself held under a head lease which was liable to forfeiture on account of the disrepair. The tenant failed to carry out any repairs, and the society (having apparently obtained permission from weekly tenants, to whom some of the houses were sub-let) began to carry out repairs and gave notice to the tenant that it intended to charge him with the cost. The tenant thereupon issued proceedings for an injunction to restrain the society from continuing with the works. The Court of Appeal unanimously found in the tenant's favour. James L.J. said:

> "Where a reversioner has granted a lease with no power of re-entry reserved on breach of a covenant to repair, can he give himself the right to enter and do repairs? It is a plain invasion of the rights of property. He has no more right than any stranger has. There is no excuse in point of law for what has been done. As a matter of law, according to the present legal rights in this country, there is no right in a reversioner to go in and do necessary repairs."

Brett L.J. added that it was "one of the clearest cases I ever heard".

Where the demised premises are sub-let, the rule will apply as between head tenant and sub-tenant in the same way as between head landlord and head tenant. The sub-tenant would be the person entitled to actual physical possession of the demised premises. It follows from this that a consent to entry given by the sub-tenant to the head landlord would bind the head tenant, who would have no right (in the absence of an express provision in the sub-tenancy prohibiting the sub-tenant from giving consent) to restrain the head landlord from entering. In the light of this, it may perhaps be asked why the society in *Stocker v Planet Building Society*[126] did not succeed on the ground that permission to enter had been given by the sub-tenants. The explanation is by no means clear from the report, the point not being mentioned at all in any of the judgments. However, James L.J. is reported as having interjected in argument that: "A weekly tenant has no right to let [the society] interfere with the structure of the property". The correct inference from this may be that what the society wished to repair, namely, the structure of the houses, was not included in the premises demised under any of the sub-lettings.

**22–31**

A more modern illustration of the operation of the rule is *Regional Properties Ltd v City of London Real Property Co Ltd.*[127] In that case two parts of a substantial office block were demised under two separate leases to two different tenants. By the first lease the landlords demised the second to top floors (but excluding the roof and common parts). In this lease the landlords covenanted, among other things, to repair the roof. By the second lease they demised the remainder of the building including the roof and common parts. The second lease

---

[125] Above. The suggestion made by Holroyd J. in *Colley v Streeton* (1823) 2 B. & C. 273 at 280, to the effect that the landlord would have an implied right of entry to carry out repairs in order to protect his head lease from forfeiture, must be taken as incorrect.

[126] Above.

[127] Above.

contained a covenant by the tenants to keep the premises (including the roof) in repair, but did not include any express right of entry in favour of the landlords if the tenants should default. The roof fell into disrepair, and water penetration badly affected the upper floors, to the great annoyance of the occupying sub-tenants who put pressure on the tenants under the first lease, and through them, the landlords, to get it repaired. The landlords were unwilling, for commercial reasons, to forfeit the second lease on the ground of disrepair, and the tenants of the roof were equally unwilling either to carry out the works, or to let anybody else do them. The tenants of the roof sought an injunction preventing the landlords from entering to do the repairs. The tenants of the rest of the building sought an order entitling them to enter on the roof so as to repair it and thereby put an end to the damage being caused to their sub-tenants. Oliver J. granted the order sought by the tenants of the roof, saying:

> "I find the case substantially indistinguishable from the *Stocker* case … and, despite a note in *Woodfall* to the effect that the result of that case might be different today, I am not at all sure that I see why. No reason is given, and the mere fact that a hundred years has passed, and that property rights are perhaps less carefully protected by the law than heretofore, does not, I think, justify me in declining to follow a decision of a strong and unanimous Court of Appeal."

The general principle therefore remains good law. However, there are a number of exceptions, which are considered below.

## Implied licence to enter to carry out repairs which the landlord has covenanted to carry out

22–32    At common law a covenant to repair carries with it an implied right to enter the premises and remain there for a reasonable time for the purpose of complying with the covenant.[128] Thus, in *Edmonton Corporation v WM Knowles & Son*[129] the tenant covenanted to pay to the landlord the cost of painting the exterior of the premises every three years. The landlord was held to be under a correlative obligation to carry out the painting,[130] and to have an implied licence to enter the premises for that purpose.

The right of entry must be exercised reasonably. The landlord must give the tenant notice of his intention to exercise his right,[131] and sufficient information as to the nature and extent of the proposed work.[132] The tenant is entitled to know the general nature and purpose of the work to be performed, and to have such information as would enable him to judge whether the proposed repairs would be likely to fulfil their purpose.[133] However, the tenant is not entitled to a detailed

---

[128] *Saner v Bilton (No.1)* (1878) 7 Ch. D. 815; *Granada Theatres Ltd v Freehold Investment (Leytonstone) Ltd* [1959] Ch. 592, per Jenkins L.J. at 608; *McGreal v Wake* (1984) 13 H.L.R. 107. See also *Wood v Tirrell* (1577) Cary 59.
[129] (1962) 60 L.G.R. 124.
[130] See para.19–13, above.
[131] *Granada Theatres Ltd v Freehold Investments (Leytonstone) Ltd*, above.
[132] Ibid.
[133] Ibid., per Ormrod L.J. at 613.

specification of the works.[134] If the landlord gives sufficient notice, and the tenant refuses access, then the landlord is not in breach of his covenant for so long as such refusal continues.[135]

The exercise by the landlord of his implied right of entry to carry out repairs which he is obliged to carry out will not amount to a breach of his covenant for quiet enjoyment, provided that he acts reasonably in all the circumstances. Thus, in *Goldmile Properties Ltd v Lechouritis*[136] a lease of premises used as a restaurant contained covenants by the landlord for quiet enjoyment and to repair (among other things) the external walls of the building. The landlord carried out works to the external walls using scaffolding. The presence of the scaffolding and the building dust resulting from the works disrupted the tenant's restaurant business. The landlord had taken all reasonable steps to avoid causing unnecessary disturbance to the tenant. The Court of Appeal held that the landlord was not in breach of its covenant for quiet enjoyment.

## Other implied rights of entry

The principles applicable to the implication of a right of entry to carry out repairs are the same as those applicable to the implication of a repairing obligation on the landlord.[137] It follows that a right of entry will not be implied unless it satisfies the tests necessary for the implication of terms into contracts.[138] In general, it must be shown that such implication is necessary to give effect to what the parties obviously intended. It is not enough to show that such implication would be reasonable. Moreover, the express terms of the tenancy may show that no further rights of entry were intended. Thus, in *Plough Investments Ltd v Manchester City Council*[139] Scott J. refused to imply into a lease, which already contained detailed and specific rights of entry, a further right of entry into the demised premises for the purposes of carrying out repairs to the exterior.

**22–33**

## Periodic tenancies

In a series of cases it has been held that a right to enter and repair defects liable to cause personal injury is to be implied into a weekly tenancy of a dwelling-house.

In the leading case of *Mint v Good*[140] the claimant (not the tenant) was injured by the collapse of a wall which separated a highway, on which it abutted, from the forecourt of a house owned by the defendant. The house was let on a weekly tenancy. No express right of entry to carry out repairs was reserved by the defendant. The Court of Appeal held that a right was to be implied, so that the defendant was liable to the plaintiff in nuisance. In the course of his judgment Somervell L.J. said:

**22–34**

---

[134] Ibid.
[135] Ibid.
[136] [2003] 1 E.G.L.R. 60.
[137] *McAuley v Bristol City Council* [1992] Q.B. 134, per Ralph Gibson L.J.
[138] See para.1–03 et seq., above.
[139] [1989] 1 E.G.L.R. 244.
[140] [1951] 1 K.B. 517.

"The question ... here is whether, in the circumstances, a right to enter on and view the premises and do necessary repairs is to be implied. I would have said that there is no term which would be more easily and more necessarily implied by law in a tenancy of this kind than a right in the landlord to enter, to examine the premises, and to do necessary repairs. It must be in the contemplation of both parties to a weekly tenancy that the tenant will not be called on to do repairs, although the Rent Restriction Acts have rather altered the position. Both sides must contemplate as the basis of the contract that the house will be kept in a reasonable and habitable condition by the landlord and not by the tenant, and, although the landlord does not bind himself to do so, both sides contemplate that he will have the right to enter and look after his property by doing repairs."

22–35 The above passage suggests that an unqualified right to enter to carry out any type of repair is to be implied into a weekly tenancy. The same is suggested by *Smith v Bradford Metropolitan Council*,[141] in which the concrete surface of a rear yard was in disrepair and in a potentially dangerous state. The claimant fell and broke his leg. The Court of Appeal held that an express condition of the weekly tenancy, on its proper construction, entitled the landlord to enter and carry out repairs to the yard, so that the landlord was liable under s.4 of the Defective Premises Act 1972.[142] However, Donaldson L.J. and Sir David Cairns held in the alternative that the landlord had an implied right of entry. Donaldson L.J. said:

"[E]ven if I am wrong in thinking that condition 6(ii) can and should be held ... to include [the concrete yard], I would hold that there must be an implied right in [the landlords] to repair any part of their property which they wish to repair, and to enter the demised premises for that purpose."

Sir David Cairns said:

"I am of opinion that [the landlords] would have the right to enter to repair any part of the garden if they chose."

However, it is to be noted that in both cases the court was concerned with defects which had caused personal injury, and indeed, the defect in *Mint v Good* was a public nuisance. The actual decision in each case was that the landlord had the right to enter and remedy the particular defect in question. In neither case was the court concerned with whether the landlord had the right to enter and carry out any wider class of repairs.

22–36 Both cases were considered and explained in *McAuley v Bristol City Council*.[143] In that case, a weekly tenancy of a council house contained an obligation by the landlord to maintain the structure and exterior of the property in good repair; an obligation by the tenant to keep the premises, including the garden, in a clean and orderly condition; and a provision requiring the tenant to give the council's agents and workmen access to the premises "for any purpose which may from time to time be required by the council". The tenant broke her ankle when a defective step in the garden (which was not part of the structure and exterior) moved and caused her to lose her footing. The Court of Appeal held that, properly construed, the express right of entry was limited to purposes which the council

---

[141] (1982) 44 P. & C.R. 171.
[142] See para.20–49 et seq., above.
[143] [1992] Q.B. 134.

could lawfully carry out, as between it and the tenant (such as the repair of the structure and exterior pursuant to the express obligation). The question was therefore whether a right to repair the garden could be implied. It was held that a limited right to enter the premises to repair any defects which might cause injury could be implied. Ralph Gibson L.J. said:

"A reasonable tenant could not sensibly object to such a right. If [the landlords] became aware of a dangerous defect in the steps of a steep garden, as in this case, and asked the tenant for access to repair it, in the interest of all persons who might reasonably be expected to be affected by the defect, the court could, in my judgment, properly require the tenant to allow such access upon the basis of an implied right in [the landlords] to do the work."

The court treated *Mint v Good*[144] and *Smith v Bradford Metropolitan City Council*[145] as decisions in which, on the facts, the implication of a right of entry was necessary to give business efficacy to the tenancy, and not as laying down a general principle that such a right is automatically to be implied into every weekly tenancy.

On the authority of the above decisions, it is thought that, save in exceptional circumstances, any implied right of entry in a weekly tenancy of a dwelling-house is likely to be limited to the repair of defects which may cause personal injury. It is not clear to what extent the same is true in relation to periodic tenancies other than weekly tenancies, but it is thought that there is no reason in principle why the position should be any different.

## Tenancies of council houses

In *Lee v Leeds City Council*[146] secure tenancies of council houses contained express rights on the part of the local authority landlord to enter the premises to carry out repairs. The houses suffered from excessive condensation and mould. The relevant remedial works were not works of repair within the rights of entry because there was no relevant damage.[147] One question was whether the landlord had an implied right of entry in order to carry out the such works. Chadwick L.J. said:

22–37

"[T]here is an element of unreality in question whether the tenancy agreements give the landlord the right to enter the premises in order to remedy the inherent defects in design which are the cause of the excessive condensation and mould. There can be no doubt that, if the landlords were willing to carry out the works, the tenants would be eager for the works to be done. But ... that is not the test. The question is whether the landlord could insist on carrying out the works against the wishes of the tenant.

In the light of the decision of this court in the *McAuley* case[148] I would give an affirmative answer to that question; at least to the extent that the remedial works were required to remedy defects which were a danger to health. It seems to me that, having regard to the obligations to abate statutory nuisance, that may be imposed by a magistrates' court on a landlord by section

---

[144] [1951] 1 K.B. 517.
[145] (1982) 44 P. & C.R. 171.
[146] [2002] 1 W.L.R. 1488.
[147] See generally Ch.8, above.
[148] See para.22–36, above.

82 of the Environmental Protection Act 1990, it is necessary to imply a right in a local authority, where it is the landlord, to enter and do the works which are required for that purpose."

It appears from the above that the position in respect of tenancies of council houses will ordinarily be the same as that in relation to weekly tenancies, namely, that there is an implied a right of entry to remedy defects which might cause injury.

## Rights of entry under statute

### (a)    The Landlord and Tenant Act 1985

**22–38**    Rights of entry to inspect the condition of the demised premises are implied into tenancies in respect of which the landlord is under the obligations imposed by ss.8 and 11 of the Landlord and Tenant Act 1985. These are discussed elsewhere.[149]

### (b)    Regulated tenancies under the Rent Act 1977

**22–39**    Section 148 of the Rent Act 1977 makes it a condition of a protected tenancy of a dwelling-house that the tenant shall afford to the landlord access to the dwelling-house and all reasonable facilities for executing therein "any repairs which the landlord is entitled to execute". Section 3(2) contains an identical provision in relation to statutory tenancies, although this is not strictly necessary because the obligation under s.148 would be imported into the statutory tenancy anyway by virtue of s.3(1).

It is unclear precisely what "entitled to execute" is intended to encompass. On the face of it, it means "has a right to execute", so that the section only operates in respect of repairs which the landlord has some right to carry out. This would appear to exclude the argument that the sections extend to repairs which the landlord wishes to carry out even though he has neither a right nor an obligation to do so.

Both sections apply only to "the dwelling-house". This must refer to the dwelling-house which is the subject of the tenancy, i.e. the dwelling-house referred to in ss.1 and 2 of the Act. The right of entry is to execute repairs "therein" i.e. in the dwelling-house. It therefore appears that the right only arises in relation to repairs to the demised premises and not any adjoining property. If this is correct, then the landlord would not be entitled under either section to enter the premises to repair, say, the common roof which is not included in the demise of the particular flat into which entry is required.[150] However, it may be that the court would give a purposive construction to the expression "dwelling-house",

---

[149] See para.20–42, above.
[150] This is suggested by the county court case of *Tinckham Estate Ltd v Merrick* (1951) 158 E.G. 589.

and construe it as extending to other parts of the building which can properly be regarded as being part of the dwelling-house even though they are technically not included in the demise.[151]

Rights of entry to carry out works specified in an application for various grants are contained in s.116 of the 1977 Act.[152]

### (c)  Assured tenancies

Section 16 of the Housing Act 1988 contains a right of entry in identical terms to that contained in ss.3(1) and 148 of the Rent Act 1977.[153]

**22–40**

### (d)  The Access to Neighbouring Land Act 1992

The Access to Neighbouring Land Act 1992 confers on the court jurisdiction to make an access order permitting a person to enter adjoining or adjacent land belonging to another for the purpose of carrying out works. The works must be to land other than that onto which entry is required, so that the Act will not assist a landlord who wishes to enter the demised premises for the purpose of carrying out works to them. However, it will avail him where access onto the demised premises is needed in order to carry out work to other land or premises. The detailed provisions of the Act are outside the scope of this work, and reference should be made to the Act itself.

**22–41**

### (e)  Other statutory rights of entry

Many statutes which provide for the carrying out of works confer rights of entry for that purpose. Examples are the London Buildings Acts (Amendment) Act 1939[154]; the Building Act 1984[155]; and the Housing Act 1985.

**22–42**

## Where the work cannot be carried out unless the tenant vacates

The nature of the work which the landlord has a right of entry to carry out may be such that it is necessary, or at least highly desirable, that the tenant should move out whilst it is being done. The questions in such cases are, first, whether the landlord can compel the tenant to move out, and second, whether, if the tenant moves, the landlord is liable to compensate him for loss of use of the premises whilst the work is being done. These questions are interrelated.

**22–43**

A distinction must be drawn between that which is strictly necessary in order to enable the landlord to fulfil his obligation, and that which arises from his desire to discharge his obligation as quickly and economically as possible. In the former case, the tenant is obliged to move out, and the landlord is under no liability to compensate him for any resulting loss. In the leading case of *Saner v*

---

[151]  Cf. *Campden Hill Towers Ltd v Gardner* [1977] 1 Q.B. 823.
[152]  See *Akram v Adam* [2003] H.L.R. 28.
[153]  See para.22–39, above.
[154]  London Buildings Acts (Amendment) Act 1939 ss.53 and 141.
[155]  Buildings Act 1984 s.98.

*Bilton (No.1)*[156] the landlord was under an express obligation to carry out extensive works of repair to the demised premises, which were used as a warehouse. Whilst the works were being carried out, the tenant was unable to store goods in any part of the warehouse for four months or more. He claimed an abatement of rent. Dismissing his claim, Fry J. said:

> "It is to be borne in mind that there is an express covenant that the lessor shall keep in good repair and condition the main walls and the main timbers. I have construed that covenant to mean that he shall put them into good condition if necessary, and in my judgment that covenant carries with it an implied licence to the lessor to enter upon the premises of the lessee, and to occupy them for a reasonable time to do that which he has covenanted to do, and which he has not only covenanted to do, but which he has a right to do, because he has an interest in being allowed to perform his covenant. It is said that the time occupied was unreasonable, but of that I have no evidence. It is further said that the construction of the covenant, as carrying with it an implied licence to enter, is inconsistent with the lessor's covenant for quiet enjoyment. I do not think it is, and for this reason, that the covenant for quiet enjoyment, if read as absolutely unqualified, is as inconsistent with an entry on the warehouse for a single moment as it is with an occupation for a month or a year. The mere sending of a man in to do the repairs would be a technical breach of the covenant, if it was construed as absolute and unconditional. But that, in my opinion, is a thing which the plaintiff has a clear right to do, for otherwise he could not perform that which he has covenanted to do. Therefore I think the covenant for quiet enjoyment must be read as subject to the licence which I have held to be implied in the covenant to repair."

This principle was expressly approved by the Court of Appeal in *McGreal v Wake*.[157]

**22–44** However, the position is different where it is not necessary for the landlord to have exclusive occupation of the premises to carry out the work. In such a case, the landlord has no right to require the tenant to vacate. In *McGreal v Wake*[158] Sir John Donaldson M.R. explained the position as follows:

> "However, it does seem to us that this right to enter and occupy must be limited to that which is strictly necessary in order to do the work of repair. The obligation to allow the landlord to enter and occupy in order to effect repairs does not seem to us to involve a further obligation to give the landlord exclusive occupation unless this is essential for the execution of the repairs. Nor does it involve an obligation to give him access to all parts of the house at the same time unless again this is essential."

It follows that the landlord in such a situation has a choice. If he wishes, he can do the work round the tenant. If he does so, he has no claim against the tenant for any additional expense thereby incurred, and the tenant has no claim against him for disturbance, unless this is reasonably avoidable. Alternatively, he can seek to persuade the tenant to move out for the duration of the works, in which case he may have to agree to pay for alternative accommodation, storage charges for furniture, removal expenses and the like.[159] In *McGreal v Wake*[160] Sir John Donaldson M.R. said of the landlord in that case:

---

[156] (1878) 7 Ch. D. 815.
[157] (1984) 13 H.L.R. 107.
[158] Above.
[159] See *Campbell v Daramola* (1974) 235 E.G. 687.
[160] Above.

"He could have asked the tenant to move out, but if this was not essential—and it does not seem to have been—he could not have compelled her to do so. He would have had to make the same choice as that which confronted the tenant—pay more for getting the work done in circumstances in which the contractors could tackle only one room at a time and had to protect the plaintiff's furniture and carpets or pay less and meet the plaintiff's expenses."

Whether in any particular case a landlord will simply rely upon his strict rights or reach an agreement as to compensation will no doubt depend upon how much extra it will cost to do the works with the tenant in occupation, and the level of compensation being sought by the tenant.

## Disturbance caused in the course of the works

Express rights of entry will sometimes provide that the landlord is to cause no more disturbance than is reasonably necessary, or some similar formulation. However, even where this is not spelt out, it will be implied. It is inherent in a right to carry out repairs that some degree of unavoidable disturbance may thereby be caused to the tenant. The tenant has no more entitlement to be compensated for such disturbance than he has for having to give up possession during the works.[161] However, if the landlord carries out the works in an unreasonable way and thereby causes unnecessary disturbance to the tenant, then he goes beyond his right of entry and is liable to the tenant for damages for breach of the covenant for quiet enjoyment or trespass.[162]

**22–45**

## Enforcement of rights of entry

The usual way of enforcing a right of entry is by means of an injunction requiring the tenant to give access or restraining him from preventing the landlord from entering. The grant or refusal of an injunction is a matter for the court's discretion.[163]

**22–46**

## DAMAGE CAUSED IN THE COURSE OF ENTERING OR CARRYING OUT REPAIRS

### Damage caused in the course of carrying out repairs

The performance of a landlord's obligation to repair may result in damage being caused to parts of the premises which are not themselves part of the subject-matter of the covenant. For example, the landlord may be responsible for the repair of the wiring in a residential flat, while the tenant is responsible for the repair and decoration of the interior. If it should be necessary wholly to rewire the

**22–47**

---

[161] See paras 22–43 to 22–44, above, and see *Goldmile Properties Ltd v Lechouritis* [2003] 1 E.G.L.R. 60 (considered in para.22–32, above).

[162] Cf. *Goldmile Properties Ltd v Lechouritis*, above (considered in para.22–32, above).

[163] In *Minja Properties Ltd v Cussins Property Group Ltd* [1998] 2 E.G.L.R. 52 an injunction was granted requiring the tenant to allow the landlord access to carry out disputed repair works to window frames. See further para.12–37, above.

flat, then there may be damage to the decorations and perhaps to the internal walls, even assuming that the work is carried out in a proper and workmanlike fashion. The question will then arise as to who is to pay for making good this damage.

## The general principle

**22–48**    The general principle is that the landlord's obligation to effect repairs carries with it an obligation to make good any consequential damage to the demised premises.[164] Thus, in *McGreal v Wake*[165] the landlords were held liable (i) to make good damage to decorations caused in course of carrying out repair works, and (ii) to clear up debris and clean up following the completion of the works. The rule is part of the duty of the landlord under his covenant to repair; it is not just a head of damage recoverable from a landlord who fails to perform his repairing obligation.[166] The fact that the tenant is under an obligation to redecorate does not affect the operation of the rule.[167]

## What making good is required

**22–49**    The landlord's duty in general terms is to make good the damage caused. It was said in *Bradley v Chorley Borough Council*[168] that "what work can reasonably be required of the landlord will depend upon the facts of each particular case."

The most important factor will be the condition of the premises prior to the work. Prima facie, the landlord must restore what was there before. But it may be, for example, that the existing wallpaper was already so damaged before the work starts that the work in fact causes no consequential damage,[169] or that the condition of the wallpaper was so poor that it will be reasonable to make good by painting the wall with emulsion.[170]

One problem which may arise in practice is the question of betterment. In practical terms, it may only be possible to make good the damage by giving the tenant better decorations than he had before. Where this is the case, the landlord remains obliged to remedy the damage, and it is just the tenant's good luck.[171] Thus, if in the course of the works, the landlord damages the paintwork on part of a wall, his obligation to make good may require him not only to repaint that part, but also to repaint the rest of the wall if it is not possible to repaint the damaged part in such a way as to achieve a reasonable match.

---

[164] *McGreal v Wake* (1984) 13 H.L.R. 107; *Bradley v Chorley Borough Council* (1985) 17 H.L.R. 305; *McDougall v Easington District Council* (1989) 58 P. & C.R. 201.
[165] See fn.48 above.
[166] *Bradley v Chorley Borough Council*, above.
[167] Ibid.
[168] Above.
[169] Ibid., at 309.
[170] Ibid., above, at 309.
[171] *McGreal v Wake*, above, *Bradley v Chorley Borough Council*, above, at 308.

## Express provisions

Express rights of entry to carry out repairs are often subject to a condition that the **22–50** landlord shall make good any damage caused in the exercise of the right, or some similar formulation. It is thought that such a condition would generally be construed as a cross covenant on the part of the landlord rather than a condition of the right to enter. It would follow that failure to observe it would not render the entry unlawful ab initio, but the tenant would be entitled to damages if the landlord fails to make good damage caused.[172]

The scope of the provision is a matter of construction. Thus, in *Crofts v Haldane*[173] the relevant provision was limited to making good damage to adjoining premises. By contrast, in *Greg v Planque*[174] the words "making good all damage thereby occasioned" were held to be wide enough to include not only damage to the premises but also damage to the tenant's trading stock. In assessing damages regard must be had to whether the tenant took all reasonable precautions to minimise the amount of damage.[175]

---

[172] See *Greg v Planque* [1936] 1 K.B. 669.
[173] (1867) L.R. 2 Q.B. 194.
[174] [1936] 1 K.B. 669.
[175] Above.

CHAPTER 23

## CONSIDERATIONS AFFECTING THE PERFORMANCE OF TENANTS' OBLIGATIONS TO REPAIR

### INTRODUCTORY

## Tenants' covenants to repair

A number of considerations are particular to the performance of tenants' repairing    **23–01**
covenants. This Chapter is concerned with the following:

(1)    when the tenant's obligation to repair must be performed[1];
(2)    the extent to which the tenant is liable to repair damage to the demised premises which results from the state of adjoining premises for which the tenant is not liable[2];
(3)    the tenant's rights of entry into retained or adjoining parts[3];
(4)    the tenant's liability for defects occurring to the demised premises after the end of the term.[4]

### WHEN THE TENANT'S OBLIGATION MUST BE PERFORMED

## Introductory

In practice it will not usually be important to know precisely when the tenant's    **23–02**
obligation must be performed. That is because defects occurring in the demised premises during the term will not generally cause any immediate loss or damage to the landlord, and disrepair occurring at or near the end of the term will be covered by the covenant to yield up.[5] However, there are a number of possible situations where it may be necessary to know when the tenant's obligation falls to be performed. The first is where the landlord forfeits the lease for disrepair. If the tenant can show that he was not in breach as regards a particular defect at the time the s.146 notice was served, he will have a defence as regards that item.[6] The second is where an option to renew or determine the lease is made

---

[1]  See para.23–02 et seq., below.
[2]  See para.23–04 et seq., below.
[3]  See para.23–09 et seq., below.
[4]  See para.23–18 et seq., below.
[5]  See para.14–05, above.
[6]  See para.27–12 et seq., below.

conditional on performance of the covenants.[7] If defects can be shown to have existed at the relevant date,[8] then it will be material to consider whether the tenant was at that time in breach as regards those defects.[9] The third is where defects in the demised premises cause damage to adjoining property owned by the landlord. Whether the landlord can recover for such damage will depend in part on whether the tenant's liability to repair the defect in question had arisen by the time the damage occurred. The fourth is where compliance or non-compliance with the repairing obligations is relevant to the rental value of premises for the purposes of rent review.[10]

## Time for performance

23–03     A tenant's covenant to keep the demised premises in repair imposes a continuing duty to repair,[11] so that the covenantor is in breach as soon as the premises are out of repair. In *British Telecommunications Plc v Sun Life Assurance Society Plc*[12] Nourse L.J. stated the correct principle to be as follows:

> "The general rule is that a covenant to keep premises in repair obliges the covenantor to keep them in repair at all times, so that there is a breach of the obligation immediately a defect occurs. There is an exception where the obligation is the landlord's and the defect occurs in the demised premises themselves, in which case he is in breach only when he has information about the existence of the defect such as would put a reasonable landlord on inquiry as to whether works of repair are needed and he has failed to carry out the necessary works with reasonable expedition thereafter."

Reference should be made to para.22–16 et seq., above, in which the principle is further considered. Although *British Telecommunications* concerned a landlord's covenant, the principle applies equally to tenants, so that a tenant who has covenanted to keep premises in repair is in breach as soon as a defect occurs.[13]

One area in which this may be of importance in practice is where the lease contains a tenant's option to break or renew, which is made conditional upon compliance with the tenant's covenants at the relevant date.[14] Thus, in *West Middlesex Golf Club Ltd v Ealing Borough Council*[15] the question was whether the tenant was, at the date of expiry of a notice exercising an option to renew the lease, in breach of its covenants to repair and keep in repair the demised premises. The judge proceeded on the footing that no breach occurred until (i) a defect requiring repair had occurred, and (ii) the tenant had a reasonable time in

---

[7]  See para.35–13 et seq., below.
[8]  Usually, but not always, the expiry of the tenant's notice exercising the option.
[9]  This was the issue in *West Middlesex Golf Club Ltd v Ealing Borough Council* (1994) 68 P. & C.R. 461. See para.23–03, below.
[10]  Since the position must be looked at as the valuation date: see para.35–08 et seq., below.
[11]  See para.14–03, above.
[12]  [1996] Ch. 69.
[13]  *Gibson Investments Ltd v Chesterton Plc (No.1)* [2002] 2 P. & C.R. 32.
[14]  See para.35–13, below.
[15]  (1994) 68 P. & C.R. 461.

which to remedy the defect. It is thought that this approach can no longer stand, following the decision in *British Telecommunications*.

## DEFECTS IN THE DEMISED PREMISES CAUSED BY THE DEFECTIVE STATE OF ADJOINING PREMISES

### Introductory

Defects in the subject-matter of the tenant's repairing obligation may occur as a result of the defective state of adjoining premises for which the tenant is not responsible. For example, the demised premises may consist of the top floor of a building but the roof may be excluded from the demise. If the roof leaks, and the resulting water penetration damages the interior of the premises, the resulting defects will prima facie fall to be repaired by the tenant under his covenant to repair the interior. The questions in such cases will be, first, whether the tenant is obliged to repair the damage to the interior, and second, whether he has any recourse against whoever is responsible for, or in possession of, the roof.

**23–04**

### Where the damage is caused by the landlord's breach of covenant to repair adjoining premises

Where the damage to the demised premises results from the landlord's breach of covenant in failing to repair adjoining premises, the tenant will generally have a claim against the landlord for damages for breach of covenant. There are three possible ways of looking at the tenant's liability as regards repairing the damage to the demised premises:

**23–05**

(1)    The tenant simply acquires a right of action against his landlord, and can include in his claim for damages not merely those losses which have been suffered in the ordinary way as a result of the landlord's breach but also the full cost of complying with his own obligation.[16] No term needs to be implied if this is the correct analysis of the position. It is to be noted, however, that on this approach, the tenant's right of action takes effect as a claim or counterclaim; it does not of itself relieve the tenant from liability to remedy the consequences of the landlord's breach;

(2)    A term is to be implied, in order to give proper effect to the scheme of interrelated obligations in the lease, that the tenant's obligation to repair is suspended or qualified for such time as the landlord remains in continuing breach of his obligation to repair;

(3)    The tenant's covenant, either as a matter of construction or by virtue of an implied term to that effect, does not require the remedying of defects which are caused solely or substantially by the landlord's own breach.

---

[16]    See para.33–25, below.

The approach in (1) is supported to some extent by the decision of the Court of Appeal in *Granada Theatres Ltd v Freehold Investment (Leytonstone) Ltd.*[17] In that case the lease contained a covenant on the part of the tenants to keep the demised premises in good and substantial repair and condition but excluding "structural repairs of a substantial nature to the main walls roofs foundations or main drains". The landlords covenanted to repair maintain and keep the main structure of the building in good structural repair and condition. The tenants claimed damages from the landlords for alleged breaches of their repairing covenant. One of the defences put forward by the landlords was that:

> "[T]he alleged breaches of the landlords' repairing covenant are no more than an accumulation of individual breaches of the lessees' repairing covenant, and, consequently, that the tenants here cannot recover. It is said that, in view of their liability under the covenant for the individual wants of repair making up the totality of disrepair, they must be liable for the totality of disrepair made up of those individual items, and that can be expressed as a set-off or cross-claim for an amount sufficing to wipe out the claim under the landlords' covenant."

Jenkins L.J. (with whom the other members of the Court agreed on this point without adding anything of their own) dealt with this "interesting point" on three grounds. The first concerned the fact that the tenants were recent assignees, and the second was a pleading point. The Lord Justice then added:

> "Finally, it seems to me, if this point were otherwise sound, it could only operate by way of counterclaim; each side would have their claim to damages for breach of covenant, and if one of them wanted to pursue his claim after a claim had been made against him by the opposite party, I should have thought his proper course would have been to do so by an appropriate counterclaim in the action, and, as I understand it, there is no question of any such counterclaim here."

It should be noted, however, that the point was not argued as an implied term but was expressly put as being at most a "set-off or cross-claim for an amount sufficing to wipe out the claim under the landlords' covenant".

**23–06**    Further support for (1) is to be derived from the judgment of Lord Donaldson M.R. in *Bradley v Chorley Borough Council*,[18] when he said that in some circumstances:

> "[F]ailure by one party to fulfil his obligations which are concurrent or related to the obligations of the other party, may well be taken into consideration under a head of damages, but I really do not understand what principle of law the learned judge was applying [when he said in his judgment: 'If the plaintiff (tenant) has any right to require the defendants (landlords) to re-decorate he has, in my view, forfeited those rights because of his complete failure to carry out his own obligation to decorate the interior or even any part thereof'].[19]"

However, *Colebeck v The Girdlers Co*[20] suggests that in some circumstances breach by the landlord may relieve the tenant from the obligation to repair. The

---

[17] [1959] 1 W.L.R. 570.

[18] (1985) 17 H.L.R. 305.

[19] See also *Kelly v Moulds* (1863) 22 U.C.R. 467 (Canada), in which the same view was taken, namely, that the fact that the defects were caused by the landlord was no defence to an action on the tenant's covenant to repair, but gave rise to a cross-claim only.

[20] (1876) 1 Q.B.D. 234.

actual decision in that case was that the landlord was under no implied liability to support and maintain a wall. But Mellor J., giving the judgment of the court, suggested that:

> "[I]t might be an answer to an action for non-repair by the [landlord] against the [tenant] that the repair had been rendered impossible by the neglect of some precedent obligation on the part of the [landlord]."

There is also the decision of Sankey J. in *Citron v Cohen*.[21] In that case the question was whether the tenant was liable to repair damage caused by the escape of water from an outside pipe (as to which the landlord may or may not have been liable) where his own obligation was limited to the good repair of the interior of the premises, "reasonable wear and tear" excepted. In holding that the tenant was not liable Sankey J. said:

> "I think that the position is that, though there may have been no obligation [on the landlord] they were his pipes, and if he did not go and do it [i.e. repair it when given notice of defects] I do not think he can stand by and then compel the tenant to repair the mischief which it has caused, for it would be enhancing the burden under the covenant."

The decision is inadequately reported, and a number of important points are unclear (not least the question of how far the "fair wear and tear" exception was decisive). Nonetheless, as far as it goes, it supports the view that a tenant is not responsible for the consequences of acts of omission or commission by the landlord which increase his burden under his covenant.[22]

It is thought that the correct analysis will generally be (1) above, i.e. that the tenant is not relieved of his duty to repair the damage to the demised premises, but he has a claim against the landlord for the reasonable expenses thereby incurred. In certain circumstances, however, it may be that the court would adopt (2) above, i.e. that the tenant's duty to repair the damage is suspended until the landlord has repaired the defect giving rise to the problem. Thus, for example, if the ceiling (for which the tenant is responsible) has fallen in because of leaks through the roof (arising from the landlord's breach) it is hardly sensible for the tenant to set about repairing and redecorating the ceiling until the roof is repaired. This is supported by the general approach in *Barrett v Lounova (1982) Ltd*[23] (in which the court implied a landlord's obligation to repair the exterior as a correlative obligation to the tenant's covenant to repair the interior).

**23–07**

It is thought that (3) above is unlikely to be correct, at least in the ordinary case. It requires the implication of a term much wider than is necessary. Once the landlord has remedied the defect causing the damage, it does not offend notions of fairness or impair the business efficacy of the contract that the tenant should then be required to perform his covenant and remedy the damage.

Where an item which the tenant is responsible for keeping in repair is out of repair and there is a dispute as to whether its disrepair was caused by the

---

[21] (1920) 36 T.L.R. 560.
[22] See also *Howe v Botwood* [1913] 2 K.B. 387.
[23] [1990] 1 Q.B. 348. See however the criticisms of that case made in paras 19–15 to 19–17, above.

landlord's breach of his repairing covenant, the onus is on the tenant to establish that that is the case (by reference to the normal civil burden of proof).[24]

Thus far it has been assumed that the landlord has covenanted to repair the adjoining premises. It is thought that in general the position would be the same where, although he has not covenanted to repair the adjoining premises, nonetheless he has retained possession of them and so is liable in tort for nuisance.

## Where the damage is caused by the state of adjoining premises for which the landlord is not responsible

23–08    Where the damage to the demised premises results from the defective state of adjoining premises for which the landlord is not responsible, the tenant will ordinarily be liable to repair such damage in the same way as he would if it had resulted, for example, from exceptionally bad weather. Whilst he may have a claim in tort against the owner or occupier of the adjoining premises, there is no reason why, as between him and the landlord, he should not be liable to perform his covenant.

It may be, however, that in certain circumstances the state of adjoining property in the possession or control of the landlord may operate to qualify what would otherwise be the tenant's obligation. For example, the demised premises may consist of a basement with insufficient damp-proofing to the perimeter walls. It may be unreasonable to expect a tenant, who has covenanted to repair the interior only (the landlord giving no covenant in respect of the exterior), to keep the internal plaster on such walls in a proper state of repair at all times because this is likely to involve him in repeated and costly work. Depending on the facts, it may be appropriate to construe the tenant's obligation as only requiring him to do what he reasonably can in the circumstances. That this is the correct approach in some cases is suggested by *Lee v Leeds City Council*,[25] in which it was argued that there was to be implied into tenancies of council houses an obligation on the part of the landlord to remedy design defects which had resulted in excessive condensation and mould but which did not themselves constitute disrepair for the purposes of the landlord's implied repairing obligation under s.11 of the Landlord and Tenant Act 1985.[26] This was said to be a necessary correlative obligation to the tenant's limited obligations in respect of internal decorative repair. In rejecting that argument, Chadwick L.J. said:

> "If the premises suffer from condensation and mould by reason of some inherent design defect, then the tenant cannot be required to do more by way of decoration than is reasonable in those circumstances. To hold that the landlord is obliged to put the premises into a state in which

---

[24] *Holding & Barnes v Hill House Hammond* (unreported decision of Neuberger J. dated March 17, 2000) (note that this was the trial of the action following the judge's determination of a preliminary issue concerning the meaning of the landlord's repairing covenant (reported at [2000] L. & T.R 428) and prior to the decision of the Court of Appeal (reported at [2002] 2 P. & C. R. 11 and considered in para.4–09, above) allowing the tenant's cross-appeal on the preliminary issue).

[25] [2002] 1 W.L.R. 1488.

[26] See para.20–17 et seq., above.

they are free from condensation so that the tenant can decorate them would be to impose on the landlord an obligation which goes far beyond anything that can properly be regarded as correlative to the tenant's obligations."

## RIGHTS OF ENTRY

### Introductory

The existence and extent of the tenant's rights of entry on adjoining property will become relevant where its condition is such that it is causing, or may in the future cause, damage to the demised premises, or where such entry is necessary in order to carry out work to the demised premises.

23–09

### Express rights of entry

Leases often confer on tenants express rights of entry onto retained premises in so far as this may be necessary to perform the tenant's repairing covenant, or in order to repair or lay service conduits. However, it is comparatively rare for a lease to confer an express right of entry onto retained premises in order to repair those premises. Where there is no such right, the tenant will have to rely upon one of the rights considered below.

23–10

### The general principle in the absence of an express right

The general principle governing a tenant's right to enter upon premises belonging to his landlord is the same as that applicable to a landlord's right to enter the demised premises, namely, that, in the absence of consent or one of the established exceptions, there is no such right.[27] It follows that a tenant entering in such circumstances commits a trespass from which he may be restrained by injunction (and for which he may be liable in damages). Thus, in *Metropolitan Properties Ltd v Wilson*[28] leases of flats in a block contained covenants on the part of the landlord to maintain, repair, redecorate and renew the structure of the building and the common parts. There had been a long history of complaints by a number of tenants about the state of repair and decoration of the internal common parts and the exterior of the block. The landlord had prepared a scheme of works and was putting it in hand. A number of tenants objected to the proposed works on the grounds of standard and cost. Without the landlord's consent, they commenced to undertake their own works to the common parts and erected scaffolding on part of the exterior. Etherton J. granted an injunction restraining them from carrying out works to the common parts and requiring the scaffolding to be removed. He held on the facts that there was no prospect of a court at trial holding that the tenants had an implied licence to do as they had done.

23–11

---

[27] *Regional Properties Ltd v City of London Real Property Co Ltd* [1981] 1 E.G.L.R. 33. See para.22–30, above.
[28] [2003] L. & T.R. 15.

## Where the landlord is in breach of covenant to repair the adjoining premises

**23–12**     Where the landlord is in breach of covenant to repair retained parts, one possible course open to the tenant is to apply for an injunction requiring the landlord to carry out the necessary works.[29] However, where the work is urgently required, the tenant may not be able to wait until the trial of his application for an injunction, and the case may not be clear enough for an interim mandatory injunction.[30] Another course may be to apply for the appointment of a receiver or manager,[31] but this may be too cumbersome a procedure where all that is required is a simple repair. In such a case the most practical course may be for the tenant to enter the premises and carry out the work himself. The question is whether he has an implied right to do so. The authorities differ in their approach to this.

In *Regional Properties Co Ltd v City of London Real Property Co Ltd*[32] (the facts of which are set out elsewhere[33]) the tenant of the second to seventh floors of the building sought an injunction restraining the tenant of the roof from preventing him from entering and repairing the roof. The lease of the second to seventh floors contained a landlord's covenant to repair the roof, but the landlord was not in possession of the roof, having demised it to the tenants of the roof. The tenants of the second to seventh floors argued that they had an implied right to enter the roof on the following grounds: first, the principle is that if the landlord fails to repair in breach of covenant, the tenant is entitled to do the work and deduct the cost from the rent[34]; second, it must therefore follow that the tenant has an implied right to enter for this purpose; and third, such right binds all persons claiming under the landlord, including the tenant of the roof in that case. Oliver J. had no hesitation in rejecting this line of argument, describing it as a "total non sequitur", and inconsistent with the decision in *Stocker v Planet Building Society*.[35]

However, it was suggested in *Loria v Hammer*[36] that in certain circumstances a tenant may have an implied licence to enter upon retained premises to carry out work which the landlord should have done. In that case a long lease of a flat contained a landlord's covenant to maintain and keep in good and substantial repair and condition, among other things, the roof. It also conferred on the tenant the right to shelter and protection from other parts of the building. The flat roof of an extension over the flat fell into disrepair and the landlord failed to carry out the necessary work. The tenant carried out the remedial work herself and claimed the cost from the landlord by way of damages for breach of his repairing obligation. It was argued that the tenant's entry was a trespass and therefore that she had no right of recovery. Mr John Lindsay QC (sitting as a deputy judge of the Chancery

---

[29] See para.33–07 et seq., below.
[30] See *Parker v London Borough of Camden* [1986] 1 Ch. 162; *Loria v Hammer* [1989] 2 E.G.L.R. 249; and see para.33–13, below.
[31] See paras 33–51 et seq., below.
[32] [1981] 1 E.G.L.R. 33.
[33] See para.22–31, above.
[34] See para.33–41 et seq., below.
[35] (1879) 27 W.R. 877. See paras 22–30 to 22–31, above.
[36] [1989] 2 E.G.L.R. 249.

Division) rejected this argument, suggesting that in appropriate cases a tenant may have an implied licence to enter upon retained parts and carry out work which the landlord should have done. However, he did not find it necessary finally to decide the point because he held that, even if there had been a trespass, that of itself would not bar recovery of the cost of the work.

It is thought that *Loria v Hammer*, whilst a helpful indication of how the court might approach the matter in particular factual circumstances, cannot be regarded as a conclusive authority on the point. First, it does not appear that *Regional Properties Co Ltd v City of London Real Property Co Ltd*[37] was cited to the judge. Second, the suggestion as to the possible existence of an implied licence was obiter only. Nonetheless, the practical consequences of holding that no implied right of entry exists are very unsatisfactory from the tenant's point of view. His only remedy for disrepair which is adversely affecting his occupation and use will be to commence proceedings for specific performance of the landlord's covenant or get a manager appointed.[38] Neither of these are satisfactory where the work is urgently required. Given this, it is thought that the court may well be persuaded to hold in an appropriate case that the tenant has an implied right of entry in order to remedy breaches of the landlord's repairing covenant.[39] It is to be noted, however, that in *Metropolitan Properties Ltd v Wilson*[40] the court held on the facts that there was no prospect of a court at trial holding that the tenants had an implied licence to enter the retained premises and carry out the works.                                       **23–13**

## Right of entry to abate a nuisance

Where the defect in the retained or adjoining premises constitutes a common law nuisance, the tenant is entitled to enter to abate it.[41] This was one of the grounds on which the tenant of the second to seventh floors in *Regional Properties Co Ltd v City of London Real Property Co Ltd*[42] based his claim to be allowed to enter to repair the roof, i.e. that the condition of the roof amounted to a nuisance which he had a right to enter to abate. Oliver J. rejected this on the ground that the condition of the roof did not amount to a nuisance in the legal sense. However, in *Abbahall Ltd v Smee*[43] (which concerned a three-storey building of which the upper flat and roof were a "flying freehold") it was accepted (and the Court of Appeal agreed) that the owner of the upper part owed a duty of care to the owner of the ground floor to do what was reasonable in the circumstances to prevent or minimise the known risk of damage or injury to the owner of the ground floor or his property, the ground floor owner being under a duty to pay half of the cost of any necessary works. It was held that it was open to the ground floor owner to                                       **23–14**

---

[37] [1981] 1 E.G.L.R. 33.
[38] See Ch.33, below.
[39] Cf. *Abbahall Ltd v Smee* [2003] 2 E.G.L.R. 66.
[40] [2003] L. & T.R. 15. See para.23–11, above, in which the facts are set out.
[41] For a full discussion of this principle, reference should be made to one of the standard textbooks on tort (for example, *Clerk & Lindsell on Torts*, 19th edn (London: Sweet & Maxwell, 2005).
[42] [1981] 1 E.G.L.R. 33. See para.23–12, above.
[43] [2003] 2 E.G.L.R. 66.

seek an injunction giving it access to the relevant part of the property in order to carry out any necessary works. On this basis, where the landlord owes an implied obligation in respect of retained parts,[44] it is thought that the tenant will have a corresponding right to enter such parts in order to carry out any works required to remedy matters amounting to a breach of duty.

## Right of entry to preserve easements

**23–15**    The holder of an easement has a correlative right to enter upon the servient tenement to do whatever is necessary in order to preserve his right.[45] It follows that a tenant entitled to an easement over adjoining property belonging to his landlord has a right to enter and do what is required in order to maintain it. Such right will include an entitlement to carry out any necessary work. It may be that this is the better explanation of *Loria v Hammer*,[46] i.e. that the tenant was entitled to enter and repair in order to preserve the right of shelter and protection expressly conferred by the lease.

The principal problem in practice is likely to be deciding whether or not an easement in fact exists. Sometimes the answer to this will be obvious, either from the wording of the lease itself, or from the surrounding circumstances. For example, a lease of a flat may confer express rights of support from adjoining and subjacent premises; or the existence of a right of way through a particular part of a building may be safely assumed from the fact that this is the only available access to the demised premises and has always been used as such. On other occasions, however, it may be more difficult to decide whether the tenant is entitled to an easement. This is particularly so where the easement claimed consists of a right of shelter. The law does not generally recognise the existence of a right to shelter from the elements, such as is provided by a roof or outside walls.[47] Thus, in *Phipps v Pears*[48] Lord Denning M.R. (with whom the other two members of the court agreed) said:

> "Every man is entitled to pull down his house if he likes. If it exposes your house to the weather, that is your misfortune. It is no wrong on his part .... There is no such easement known to the law as an easement to be protected from the weather. The only way for an owner to protect himself is by getting a covenant from his neighbour that he will not pull down his house ... "

**23–16**    However, that case concerned adjoining buildings, and the right claimed was to have the wall of one house protected from the weather by the other house. It is strongly arguable that the same would not apply where (i) the right claimed is to have one part of a building sheltered by another part, and (ii) the specific purpose of the other part is to protect the first part from the weather and nothing else. The point arose in *Regional Properties Co Ltd v City of London Real Property Co*

---

[44] See para.19–18, above.
[45] *Jones v Pritchard* [1908] 1 Ch. 630; *Bond v Nottingham Corp* [1940] Ch. 429; *Liverpool City Council v Irwin* [1977] A.C. 239; *Duke of Westminster v Guild* [1985] Q.B. 688.
[46] [1989] 2 E.G.L.R. 249 (see esp. counsel's argument at 259F–G). See para.23–12, above.
[47] Although long residential leases commonly confer express rights of shelter; see, for example, the lease in *Loria v Hammer*, above.
[48] [1965] 1 Q.B. 76.

*Ltd*,[49] in which the tenant of the second to seventh floors alleged that he had an easement of shelter in relation to the roof of the building. Oliver J., while not deciding the point, was prepared to hold that it was seriously arguable, and raised "a very difficult question of law". He added in relation to *Phipps v Pears*:

> "I have the strongest suspicion that the somewhat wide expressions used by the Master of the Rolls might not have been formulated having in mind the sort of position that one has here."

However, subsequent cases have proceeded on the footing that *Phipps v Pears* correctly represents the law[50] (albeit that "matters have been transformed by ... developments in the law of nuisance and negligence"[51]).

Nonetheless, there are strong arguments in favour of a right of shelter being capable of existing as an easement, at least in relation to the different parts of multi-occupied buildings. A right of support, which is by no means dissimilar in nature, is a well-recognised species of easement, and it is not easy to see any relevant distinction between a right of support in relation to the floor joists of a flat, and an easement of shelter in relation to its outside walls. In both cases the right claimed prevents the servient owner from doing anything which causes the thing in question to cease fulfilling the function for which it was designed. It seems anomalous if the former can exist as an easement but the latter not. Given that "the category of servitudes and easements must alter and expand with the changes that take place in the circumstances of mankind",[52] it may be that the now widespread practice of living in flats would be held to justify the admission of a right of shelter as an easement known to the law. In any event, even if an express right of shelter cannot take effect as an easement properly so-called, there seems no reason in principle why it cannot be construed as a contractual provision which takes effect to prevent the landlord from depriving the demised premises of the intended shelter and entitles the tenant to enter the relevant premises and carry out any work necessary to protect his demise.

## The Access to Neighbouring Land Act 1992

The Access to Neighbouring Land Act 1992 confers on the court jurisdiction to make an access order permitting a person to enter adjoining or adjacent land belonging to another for the purpose of carrying out works. The works must be to land other than that onto which entry is required, so that the Act will not assist a tenant who wishes to enter land owned by the landlord for the purpose of carrying out works to it. However, it will avail him where access onto the landlord's

23–17

---

[49] [1981] 1 E.G.L.R. 33.

[50] *Giltrap v Busely* (1970) 21 N.I.L.Q. 342; *Marchant v Capital & Counties Property Co Ltd* [1982] 2 E.G.L.R. 152 (reversed on other grounds [1983] 2 E.G.L.R. 156); *Bradburn v Lindsay* [1983] 2 All E.R. 408; *Rees v Skerret* [2001] 1 W.L.R. 1541. It was held in the last mentioned that an owner of a terraced house who demolishes his property owes a positive duty to the owner of the adjoining property to take reasonable steps to provide weather proofing for the exposed dividing wall. This negates to a large extent the practical effect of *Phipps v Pears*. The position may also be different in the case of a party wall within s.38 of the Law of Property Act 1925: see *Gale on Easements*, 18th edn (London: Sweet & Maxwell), para.11–03.

[51] *Abbahall Ltd v Smee* [2003] 2 E.G.L.R. 66 per Chadwick L.J. at [9].

[52] *Dyce v Lady James Hay* (1852) 1 Macq. 305 per Lord St Leonards at 312–313.

premises is needed in order to carry out work to the demised premises. The detailed provisions of the Act are outside the scope of this work, and reference should be made to the Act itself.[53]

## DEFECTS OCCURRING AFTER THE END OF THE TERM

### The general principle

**23–18**     In the absence of express provision to the contrary, the tenant's contractual obligations to repair and decorate the demised premises, whether during or at the end of the term, do not impose any liability to repair defects which only come into existence after the end of the term. Thus, in *Associated Deliveries Ltd v Harrison*[54] an underlease was forfeited by the service of proceedings for forfeiture in October 1979, but the sub-tenant remained in possession until November 1980. By that time the premises were in a very much worse condition than they had been at the date of service of the writ; this was partly due to the passage of time and continuing deterioration without any repairs having been effected, but it was more due to vandalism by third parties. The Court of Appeal held that the correct date for assessing damages against the sub-tenant was the date of forfeiture, and therefore that the cost of the subsequent defects were not recoverable by his landlord under the repairing covenants.

The general principle is, however, subject to two exceptions in the case of damage resulting from previous disrepair, and damage caused by the commission of a tort.

### Damage caused by previous disrepair

**23–19**     Damage may occur after the term has ended as a direct result of the tenant's failure to repair during the term. For example, the roof may be defective and leaking when the lease terminates, and consequent water damage may be caused to the interior after the lease has ended. It is thought that the position would then be as follows. The tenant would not be liable to repair the further damage, because it only came into existence after the covenant to repair ceased to operate. However, at common law, the landlord would be entitled to include in his damages claim a claim for the cost of remedying such further damage as was foreseeably likely to occur as a result of the tenant's failure to deliver up in repair.[55] This would be subject to the principle that the landlord must take reasonable steps to mitigate his loss. The landlord would therefore be under a duty to take reasonable steps once the term has ended to prevent as best he can

---

[53] The Act is discussed in *Woodfall: Landlord and Tenant* (London: Sweet & Maxwell), Vol.I, Ch.15, s.3.

[54] (1984) 50 P. & C.R. 91.

[55] Cf. the New Zealand case of *BP Oil New Zealand v Ports of Auckland* [2004] 2 N.Z.L.R. 208 (considered in paras 12–40 and 12–42, above), in which the tenant was held liable for consequential damage caused as a result of breaches of covenant to repair which was a reasonably foreseeable consequence of such breaches. The measure of damages at common law for breach of a tenant's covenant to repair is considered in Ch.29, below.

any further damage occurring as a result of the then existing defects. In the example given above, this might necessitate temporary covering of the roof by tarpaulins, pending the carrying out of more permanent repairs. It is thought that s.18(1) of the Landlord and Tenant Act 1927[56] would not necessarily exclude the landlord's claim for the cost of remedying further damage, because the valuation of the premises in their existing state would presumably reflect the possibility of further damage arising before the purchaser has a chance to carry out the necessary remedial works. In such a case, the diminution in the value of the reversion owing to the tenant's breaches of covenant will, in principle, include an amount attributable to the cost of remedying further damage which will inevitably occur after the term date as a result of the tenant's breaches at that date.

## Liability in tort

In *Associated Deliveries Ltd v Harrison*[57] Dillon L.J., having held that the tenant was not liable under his covenant for damage occurring after the end of the term, went on to say:

23–20

> "I would feel troubled at this conclusion if indeed there were no other remedy available to a landlord for deterioration of the premises or other ills suffered while a lessee remained in occupation during the twilight period before an order for possession under the writ claiming possession could be obtained and enforced. But ... in appropriate proceedings it seems to me that the landlord could well have a very adequate remedy in a claim for damages for wrongful occupation of the land ... the authorities seem to indicate that in appropriately constituted proceedings the damages recoverable could extend beyond mere payment for the use and occupation of land, to include any loss within the ordinary rules of remoteness of damage which the plaintiff has suffered from being denied possession of the property and so unable to secure and occupy the property for his own purposes."

Accordingly, whilst the landlord cannot claim the cost of remedying post-lease defects as damages for breach of the tenant's covenant to repair, nonetheless he may be able to recover it by way of damages for trespass, where he can show that it was the reasonably foreseeable consequence of the tenant's failure to deliver up possession at the end of the term. It may also be that a similar claim could be made under the express or implied covenant to deliver up vacant possession at the end of the term.[58] In addition, in appropriate circumstances, the landlord may also have a claim for damages for voluntary waste.[59]

---

[56] See Ch.30, below.
[57] (1984) 50 P. & C.R. 91.
[58] See para.14–06, above. The advantage of this would be that the claim could be made against any person in the chain of title who is liable under the covenant to deliver up. This could include sureties: *Associated Deliveries Ltd v Harrison* (1984) 50 P. & C.R. 91. By contrast, a claim in trespass would be limited to those persons actually in possession.
[59] See para.21–12 to 21–13, above.

CHAPTER 24

## SUB-LEASES

### INTRODUCTORY

## Covenants to repair in sub-leases

The basic principles governing the operation of repairing covenants are the same between head tenant and sub-tenant as they are between head tenant and head landlord. However, repairing obligations in sub-leases may give rise to difficulties of construction and enforcement which do not arise where the immediate landlord is the freeholder. The following are dealt with in this Chapter:

**24–01**

(1)    covenants in sub-leases (whether by tenant or sub-tenant) to perform repairing covenants in the head lease[1];
(2)    the proper construction of repairing covenants in sub-leases which are in identical, or very similar, terms to the repairing covenants in the head lease[2];
(3)    liability to repair as between head landlord and sub-tenant.[3]
(4)    Claims by the tenant against the sub-tenant.[4]

### COVENANTS TO PERFORM THE REPAIRING COVENANTS IN THE HEAD LEASE

## Introductory

Sub-leases often contain express covenants by one or other party to perform the covenants in the head lease. Where the covenant is given by the sub-tenant, it will usually be limited to performing such covenants insofar as they relate to the sub-let premises. Where the covenant is given by the head tenant, it will generally be either an unqualified obligation to perform the covenants of the head lease, or an obligation to perform those covenants insofar as they are not the liability of the tenant under the sub-lease. In addition, the head tenant may expressly covenant to indemnify the sub-tenant against breaches of the covenants in the head lease.

**24–02**

---

[1]  See para.24–02 et seq., below.
[2]  See para.24–07, below.
[3]  See para.24–08 et seq., below.
[4]  See para.24–13 et seq., below.

## Construction of the covenant

**24–03**     In some cases it may be unclear to what extent the covenants in the head lease have been incorporated in the sub-lease. The answer in any given case will depend on the proper construction of the relevant provisions. In *Hornby v Cardwell*[5] a sub-lease was granted on terms which provided that "this letting shall be subject in all respects to the terms of [the head lease] and the covenants and stipulations contained therein". In the Court of Appeal, Brett and Cotton L.JJ. treated this as a covenant by the sub-tenant to perform the repairing covenants in the head lease, and to indemnify the tenant against the consequences of not performing those covenants. They held that the tenant was therefore entitled to recover from the sub-tenant the costs of proceedings brought by the head landlord which had been reasonably defended by the tenant.[6]

## Independent obligation or covenant of indemnity

**24–04**     A further question which may arise is whether the obligation to perform the covenants in the head lease takes effect as an independent obligation, or whether it only takes effect in the event of the head landlord taking action against the tenant for non-repair. The answer will depend on the proper construction of the particular covenant. In *Ayling v Wade*[7] an underlease contained a covenant on the part of the landlord (who was himself a tenant under a head lease) to:

> "pay the rent reserved by and to observe the covenants contained in the lease, under which the landlord holds the demised premises, and to keep the tenant indemnified against the same."

The sub-let premises were damaged by water coming in through a defective skylight in the flat roof, and the sub-tenant claimed damages from the head tenant on the ground that there had been a breach of the above covenant. The head tenant contended that the covenant was to be construed as one of indemnity only, its purpose being to protect the sub-tenant against forfeiture of the head lease for disrepair, so that the head tenant would not be liable until steps had been taken against him by the superior landlord to forfeit the head lease. The Court of Appeal rejected this contention, holding that the covenant was an independent covenant to repair, and that the head tenant was liable for breach. The court was plainly impressed by the argument that if the head tenant's contention were correct, then the first half of the covenant (to observe the covenants in the head lease) added nothing to the second half (to indemnify the sub-tenant).

---

[5] (1881) 8 Q.B.D. 329.

[6] The decision that costs were recoverable should be contrasted with *Penley v Watts* (1841) 7 M. & W. 601; *Walker v Hatton* (1842) 10 M. & W. 249; *Logan v Hall* (1847) 4 C.B. 598; *Clare v Dobson* [1911] 1 K.B. 35; and *Lloyds Bank Ltd v Lake* [1961] 1 W.L.R. 884, in all of which the tenant's costs of defending proceedings brought by the head landlord were held to be irrecoverable on the ground that the repairing covenants in the sub-lease did not amount to a covenant of indemnity. These cases are considered in para.24–15, below.

[7] [1961] 2 Q.B. 228.

In *Yorkbrook Investments Ltd v Batten*[8] a sub-lease of a flat contained a covenant on the part of the head tenant in the following terms:

> "That the Lessor will during the said term pay the rent reserved by the Head Lease and will observe and perform the covenants on the part of the Lessee therein contained save in so far as the same are herein comprised and on the part of the Lessee to be observed and performed."

The judge at first instance held that this constituted an indemnity, and therefore that it did not come into operation until the head landlord served a s.146 notice on the head tenant for breach of the obligation to repair in the head lease. However, it was conceded in the Court of Appeal, on the authority of *Ayling v Wade*,[9] that the covenant created an independent obligation and not a mere covenant of indemnity.

## Performance of the covenant

Where the covenant on its proper construction requires the covenanting party to perform the repairing covenants in the head lease, then he must carry out whatever work is required by those covenants. This may have important consequences where the covenanting party is the sub-tenant, particularly where the sub-lease is a short term created out of a long head lease. First, the sub-tenant will have to repair to whatever is the appropriate standard under the head lease.[10] This may involve incurring greater expense than would have been required under a repairing covenant in the sub-lease, even one worded in exactly the same way as the repairing covenant in the head lease.[11] Second, the sub-tenant will have to carry out whatever work falls within the meaning of repair under the head lease,[12] even though this may be more extensive than would have been the case under a repairing covenant in the sub-lease.

**24–05**

## Covenant of indemnity

A sub-tenant's covenant to indemnify the head tenant against breaches of the repairing covenants in the head lease will oblige him to pay the head tenant's reasonable costs of defending proceedings brought against him by the head landlord.[13]

**24–06**

---

[8]  [1985] 2 E.G.L.R. 100.

[9]  Above.

[10]  See Ch.9, above.

[11]  See para.24–07, below.

[12]  See Ch.11, above.

[13]  *Hornby v Cardwell* (1881) 8 Q.B.D. 329; *Penley v Watts*(1841) 7 M. & W. 601; *Walker v Hatton* (1842) 10 M. & W. 249; *Logan v Hall* (1847) 4 C.B. 598; *Clare v Dobson* [1911] 1 K.B. 35; *Lloyds Bank Ltd v Lake* [1961] 1 W.L.R. 884. It was held in all but the first of these cases that the head tenant's costs were irrecoverable because the covenant was not, on its proper construction, a covenant of indemnity.

THE CONSTRUCTION OF REPAIRING COVENANTS IN SUB-LEASES

## Identical words

**24–07**  Where the repairing obligations in the sub-lease are worded differently to those in the head lease, the former must be construed as separate provisions in their own right. However, draftsmen of sub-leases frequently insert repairing covenants which are the same, word-for-word, as those in the head lease, in an attempt to ensure that the totality of the head tenant's liability for repairs can be passed on to the sub-tenant. Nonetheless, as a general principle, even identical words will not necessarily mean that the sub-tenant will be liable for precisely the same works as the head tenant. This is because the correct interpretation of the covenant in each case will depend upon, among other things, the dates when the lease and sub-lease were granted.[14] This applies in relation both to the standard of repair contemplated by the covenant,[15] and to the extent to which the covenant requires the carrying out of major works.[16]

The leading case is *Walker v Hatton*,[17] in which a lease for 21 years was granted on May 10, 1828, and a sub-lease of the same premises was granted on June 15, 1830, for the term of the head lease less 10 days. Both contained repairing covenants in identical terms. The head landlord sued the head tenant for disrepair and recovered damages and costs. The head tenant then sued the sub-tenant, and the question arose as to whether the damages payable by the latter should include (i) the head landlord's costs of the proceedings against the head tenant which the head tenant had been ordered to pay, and (ii) the head tenant's costs of defending those proceedings. It was held that the sub-tenant was not liable. Parke B. based his judgment on the fact that the covenants in the two leases were different in their operation, so that the costs in question were not the necessary consequence of the sub-tenant's breaches. He said:

> "Although the covenants contained in the sub-lease are, with the exception of that relating to painting, the same in language as those contained in the original lease, yet they are different in substance; the periods at which the leases were granted being different. It is now perfectly well settled, that a general covenant to repair must be construed to have reference to the condition of the premises at the time when the covenant begins to operate; and as the one lease was granted in 1828, and the other in 1830, allowing an interval of two years, it is clear that the covenants would not have the same effect, but would vary substantially in their operation."

*Walker v Hatton* has been followed in a number of subsequent cases.[18] In one of them,[19] Lord Coleridge C.J. said:

---

[14]  *Walker v Hatton* (1842) 10 M. & W. 249. See also the cases cited in fn.18, below.
[15]  See Ch.9, above.
[16]  See Ch.11, above.
[17]  Above.
[18]  *Logan v Hall* (1847) 4 C.B. 598; *Williams v Williams* (1874) L.R. 9 C.P. 659; *Clare v Dobson* [1911] 1 K.B. 35. See also *Penley v Watts* (1841) 7 M. & W. 601. These cases should be contrasted with *Hornby v Cardwell* (1881) 8 Q.B.D. 329, in which the relevant covenant was held to be a covenant for indemnity: see para.24–06, above. See further para.24–15 et seq., below.
[19]  *Clare v Dobson*, above.

"The mere fact that the covenants in the two leases run in the same terms does not carry with it the inference, where the leases are of different dates, that the covenants bear the same obligations ... Indeed where, as here, the sub-lease recognises the existence of the head lease, the presumption is that the sub-lessee undertook only the limited liability imposed upon him by the covenants in the sub-lease."

In *Fitzpatrick v Exel Holdings*[20] a head lease was granted in 1979 for 25 years containing a full tenant's repairing covenant. An underlease was subsequently granted in 1997 for just over six years containing a covenant to repair on the part of the sub-tenant subject to the proviso that:

"the Tenant shall not be liable to put or keep the premises in a better state of repair or condition than that now existing and as evidenced by a Schedule of Condition of even date herewith and signed on behalf of the parties hereto, but subject always to the overriding provisions of [the covenant to decorate]."

A sub-underlease was then granted in 2003 for just over 18 months, which contained a covenant to repair on the part of the sub-undertenant in substantially the same terms, save that the proviso was that:

"the Tenant [i.e. the sub-undertenant] shall not be liable to put or keep the premises in a better state of repair or condition than as evidenced by a Schedule of Condition annexed to [the sub-lease] but subject always to the overriding provisions of [the covenant to decorate]."

The words "than that now existing" in the proviso in the sub-lease were therefore omitted in the sub-underlease.

The issue which arose was whether, and if so to what extent the sub-undertenant's liability under the sub-underlease was less than that of the sub-tenant's liability to the head tenant, by reason of the differences in the dates on which the two leases were granted and the length of the terms. The judge held that it was. He took *Walker v Hatton* as authority for the proposition that:

"if two leases are in the same terms but are of different dates, the repairing covenants in the leases do not impose the same obligation because one must also have regard to the starting point of those obligations, namely the condition of the premises before the commencement of the lease."

He accepted that the question was ultimately one of construction, but he held that on the proper construction of the sub-underlease, the sub-undertenant had not agreed to assume the same repairing obligations as the undertenant. He answered an agreed preliminary issue as follows:

"The repairing obligations of [the sub-undertenant] under the sub-underlease are not identical in nature and extent to those contained in the underlease. [The sub-undertenant] will not be liable for (a) the cost of putting the premises into a better general condition and state of repair than they were understood to be in at the date of commencement of its lease on 7 April 2003; (b) the cost of work which would go beyond repair in regard to the length of the sub-underlease."

It follows that the covenants in the sub-lease may impose a different and lesser liability to those in the head lease, notwithstanding that the same words are used,

---

[20] Unreported decision of Mr Recorder Michael Black QC, sitting as a judge of the Technology and Construction Court, July 16, 2008.

particularly where the sub-lease was granted some time after the head lease and/or is for a different term. As a matter of drafting, an identical liability on the sub-tenant can only be achieved by an express covenant to perform the covenants of the head lease in terms which make it clear that the liability intended to be imposed is the same as that which the tenant has in relation to the head landlord.[21]

## LIABILITY AS BETWEEN HEAD LANDLORD AND SUB-TENANT

### No privity of contract as between head landlord and sub-tenant

24–08    Since the head lease and the sub-lease constitute separate contracts, there is no privity of contract between the head landlord and the sub-tenant entitling the one to sue the other on the covenants in the head lease or the sub-lease.[22] However, it is common for leases to contain a provision to the effect that any person to whom a sub-tenancy is granted must enter into a direct covenant with the head landlord to observe and perform the tenant's covenants in the head lease so far as they relate to the sub-let premises. A direct covenant of this kind is usually given in the relevant licence to sub-let (where one is required), but may also be given by way of a separate deed. The effect is to create privity of contract between the head landlord and the sub-tenant and to entitle the former to enforce against the latter those of the tenant's covenants in the head lease which the sub-tenant covenants to perform.

A direct covenant to comply with the terms of the head lease may on its proper construction extend to a period during which the sub-tenancy continues under Pt II of the Landlord and Tenant Act 1954.[23]

### Where the head tenancy is an old tenancy

24–09    The distinction between old tenancies granted before the date on which the Landlord and Tenant (Covenants) Act 1995 came into force (January 1, 1996) and new tenancies granted on or after that date is dealt with in Ch.3, above. Where the head tenancy is an old tenancy, the general principle is that neither the head landlord nor the sub-tenant can sue the other on the covenants in the head lease or the sub-tenancy, because there is no privity of estate between them.[24] To this rule there are the following exceptions or possible exceptions:

(1)    In certain circumstances, the head landlord may be entitled, under the rule in *Tulk v Moxhay*,[25] to enforce a restrictive (i.e. negative) covenant in the head lease directly against a sub-tenant.[26] A positive covenant to repair or

---

[21] See para.24–03, above.

[22] See, however, the Contracts (Rights of Third Parties) Act 1999, considered in para.24–12, below.

[23] *GMS Syndicate Ltd v Gary Elliott Ltd* [1981] 1 W.L.R. 478.

[24] *Holford v Hatch* (1779) 1 Doug. 183; *Mackusick v Carmichael* [1917] 2 K.B. 581.

[25] (1848) 2 Ph. 774.

[26] For this purpose the head landlord's reversion is regarded as a sufficient interest to found an action: *Hall v Ewin* (1888) L.R. 37 Ch. D. 74; *John v Holmes* [1900] 1 Ch. 188; *Regent Oil Co Ltd v J. A.*

decorate in the head lease is not a restrictive covenant for this purpose. However, it may be that covenants in the head lease against alterations and additions would be enforceable directly against the sub-tenant by virtue of this principle.[27] It should be noted that the head landlord's remedies will be equitable only, i.e. an injunction and/or damages under s.50 of the Senior Courts Act 1981; he will not be entitled to damages at common law.

(2)   The sub-tenant may be able to sue the original head landlord on the head landlord's repairing covenants in the head lease by virtue of s.78 of the Law of Property Act 1925.[28]

(3)   Where the head lease is extinguished, the parties may come into a direct legal relationship with each other in one of the ways considered in para.24–11, below.

In *Amsprop Trading Ltd v Harris Distribution Ltd*[29] a sub-lease was surrendered to the head tenant, following which the head landlord forfeited the head lease. The head landlord claimed to be entitled to enforce certain covenants in the sub-lease against the sub-tenant by virtue of s.56 of the Law of Property Act 1925. Neuberger J. dismissed his claim on the ground that it is not enough for s.56 to apply that the covenant is made for the benefit of a third party: it must purport to be made with him.[30] It follows that the head landlord could only have enforced the covenant if it had been made on its face not only with the head tenant but also with the head landlord, even though the latter was not a party to the sub-lease.[31]

---

Gregory (Hatch End) Ltd [1966] Ch. 402. See generally *Megarry and Wade: The Law of Real Property*, 8th edn (London: Sweet & Maxwell, 2012), para.32–045.

[27] Cf. *Langevad v Chiswick Quay Freeholds Ltd* [1999] 1 E.G.L.R. 61.

[28] See *Smith and Snipes Hall Farm Ltd v River Douglas Catchment Board* [1949] 2 K.B. 500; *Williams v Unit Construction Co Ltd* (1951) 19 Conv. 962 (both decisions of the Court of Appeal). It was held in those cases that a contract entered into by the landlord with a third party to keep, respectively, a riverbank and a road in repair could be enforced by a tenant deriving title under the third party, notwithstanding that he was not a party to the contract. These cases have been criticised on the ground that s.78 was intended to be a word-saving provision only, and was not intended to effect a change in the substantive law. However, this criticism of the section was rejected by the Court of Appeal in *Federated Homes Ltd v Mill Lodge Properties Ltd* [1980] 1 W.L.R. 594. It should be noted that *South of England Dairies Ltd v Baker* [1906] 2 Ch. 631, in which it was held that the sub-tenant cannot sue the head landlord on the head landlord's covenants in the head lease, was decided before the relevant change in the law.

[29] [1997] 1 W.L.R. 1025.

[30] See further on this case para.14–12, above. See also the Contracts (Rights of Third Parties) Act 1999, considered in para.24–12, below.

[31] On the facts, however, the head landlord's action would have failed anyway, because the sub-tenant in question was an assignee of the original sub-tenant, and there was no privity of contract or estate between the head landlord and the assignee: see [1997] 1 W.L.R. 1025 at 1034.

## Where the head tenancy is a new tenancy

**24–10**   In the case of new tenancies to which the Landlord and Tenant (Covenants) Act 1995 applies,[32] any landlord or tenant covenant[33] of a tenancy which is restrictive of user is, as well as being capable of enforcement against an assignee, capable of being enforced against any other person who is the owner or occupier of any demised premises[34] to which the covenant relates, even though there is no express provision in the tenancy to that effect.[35] However, this does not operate in the case of a covenant which is expressed (in whatever terms) to be personal to any person, to make the covenant enforceable by or (as the case may be) against any other person, or to make a covenant enforceable against any person if, apart from the section, it would not be enforceable against him by reason of its not having been registered under the Land Registration Act 2002 or the Land Charges Act 1972.[36] The effect of these provisions, where they apply, is that covenants restrictive of user in the head tenancy may be enforced by the head landlord against the sub-tenant and vice versa.

A covenant to repair is not a covenant restrictive of user. It may perhaps be, however, that a covenant against the making of alterations or additions is capable of being included.[37]

## Where the head tenancy ends or is extinguished

**24–11**   Where the head tenancy ends, the head landlord and the sub-tenant may come under a direct liability to each other in one of the following ways:

(1)   Where the head lease is surrendered during the currency of the sub-lease, the head landlord will become the direct landlord of the sub-tenant, and will have as against him the same rights and obligations regarding repairs as the head tenant had against the sub-tenant.[38] This is so even where the sub-tenancy was created in breach of covenant and the head landlord was unaware of it when accepting the surrender of the head lease.[39]

(2)   The sub-tenant may have the benefit of some statutory provision which confers upon him security of tenure.[40] In such a case the terms on which he will hold over will be those contained in the sub-lease, so that the head landlord will become liable under, and entitled to enforce, those terms.

---

[32] For the distinction between old and new tenancies, see para.3–02, above.

[33] See para.3–19, above.

[34] This means any premises demised by the tenancy containing the relevant covenant, and not other premises demised by the same landlord under a different lease: *Oceanic Village Ltd v United Attractions Ltd* [2000] Ch.234.

[35] Landlord and Tenant (Covenants) Act 1995 s.3(5). The Act is considered in Ch.3, above.

[36] Landlord and Tenant (Covenants) Act 1995 s.3(6).

[37] Cf. *Langevad v Chiswick Quay Freeholds Ltd* [1999] 1 E.G.L.R. 61 at 62K.

[38] Law of Property Act 1925 s.139.

[39] *Parker v Jones* [1910] 2 K.B. 32.

[40] For example, Landlord and Tenant Act 1954 s.65(2); Rent Act 1977 s.137; Housing Act 1988 s.18(1).

However, where the sub-tenant applies for a new tenancy under Pt II of the Landlord and Tenant 1954, the court has power to order the new tenancy to contain different terms to the old.[41]

(3)     At common law, where the head lease is forfeited, the sub-tenancy (being a derivative interest) ends automatically. The sub-tenant's principal right in such a case is to apply for a vesting order under s.146(4) of the Law of Property Act 1925, which (if granted) takes effect as a new lease granted by the head landlord.[42] A vesting order is only likely to be granted on terms that the sub-tenant remedies the head tenant's breaches of covenant, and where these include failure to repair, the sub-tenant may have to carry out the work as a condition of obtaining the order.[43] In this way the head landlord may be able indirectly to enforce the head tenant's repairing covenants against the sub-tenant.

In *Twogates Properties Ltd v Birmingham Midshires Building Society*,[44] the head landlord was held to have no right of action for damages for disrepair against a sub-tenant whose lease had been forfeited by the head tenant during the subsistence of the head tenancy and prior to the surrender of that head tenancy. It was held that the covenants to repair were extinguished when the sub-tenancy was forfeited, and there was no continuing estate under the underlease in respect of which ss.139 and 141 of the Law of Property Act 1925 could operate.

## The Contracts (Rights of Third Parties) Act 1999

The effect of the Contracts (Rights of Third Parties) Act 1999 is that a person who is not a party to a contract may in his own right and in his own name enforce a term of it if (a) the contract expressly provides that he may, or (b) the term purports to confer a benefit on him[45] (but the latter does not apply if, on a proper construction of the contract, it appears that the parties did not intend the term to be enforceable by the third party[46]). The third party must be expressly identified in the contract by name, as a member of a class or as answering a particular description, but he need not be in existence when the contract is entered into.[47] The third party cannot enforce the contract other than subject to and in accordance with any relevant terms of the contract.[48] The third party is entitled to any remedy that would have been available to him if he had been a party to the contract, and the rules relating to damages, injunctions, specific performance and other relief apply accordingly.[49]

**24–12**

---

[41]  See para.35–06, below.

[42]  See para.27–86, below. The sub-tenant is also entitled in principle to apply for relief under s.146(2). If granted, relief would operate to restore the head lease as well as the sub-tenancy. In practice, however, such applications are only made in special cases.

[43]  See para.27–87, below.

[44]  (1998) 75 P. & C.R. 380.

[45]  Contracts (Rights of Third Parties) Act 1999 s.1(1).

[46]  Contracts (Rights of Third Parties) Act 1999 s.1(2).

[47]  Contracts (Rights of Third Parties) Act 1999 s.1(3).

[48]  Contracts (Rights of Third Parties) Act 1999 s.1(4).

[49]  Contracts (Rights of Third Parties) Act 1999 s.1(5).

The Act applies only to contracts entered into six months or more after the date on which it came into force (November 11, 1999) so that it is only leases granted on or after May 11, 2000 that are affected.[50]

A detailed consideration of the provisions of the Act is outside the scope of this work, and reference should be made to the Act itself.[51] However, the effect of the Act, where it applies, may be to entitle the head landlord and the sub-tenant to enforce against each other provisions in the head lease or the sub-tenancy even though no privity of contract exists.

## CLAIMS BY THE TENANT AGAINST THE SUB-TENANT

### Claims for damages

24–13    The principles applicable to claims for damages by the head tenant against a sub-tenant for breach of the repairing covenants, or other covenants relevant to dilapidations, in the sub-lease are the same as those which apply to claims by the head landlord against the head tenant, and reference should be made to the discussion in Chs 29 to 32, below.

For the purposes of the first limb of s,18(1) of the Landlord and Tenant Act 1927, the reversion to be valued is the head tenant's leasehold interest. However, the fact that this may be nominal does not mean that the damages recoverable from the sub-tenant will necessarily be nominal, because the tenant's liability to the head landlord under the terms of the head lease is one of the factors to be taken into account when valuing the tenant's interest. [52]

### Where the head lease is forfeited

24–14    Where, as a result of the sub-tenant's breaches, the head landlord forfeits the head lease, the head tenant may thereby lose a valuable asset. It appears, however, that in the absence of a covenant of indemnity in the sub-tenancy, the head tenant will not be entitled to recover from the sub-tenant damages representing the value of the lost interest.[53]

The fact that the head lease is forfeited for reasons unconnected with disrepair will not prevent the head tenant from recovering damages from the sub-tenant for breach of a covenant to repair in the sub-tenancy. Thus, in *Davies v Underwood*[54] the head lease was forfeited for non-payment of rent, and the head landlord recovered possession against the head tenant and the sub-tenant. The head tenant brought proceedings against the sub-tenant for breach of the repairing covenants in the sub-tenancy. The sub-tenant argued that the head tenant had suffered no loss: his reversion had come to an end by his own act, and could not have been

---

[50] Contracts (Rights of Third Parties) Act 1999 s.10.

[51] A helpful discussion of the Act is to found in "The Contracts (Rights of Third Parties) Act 1999 and its Implications for Property Transactions", a lecture given on June 19, 2000 by Dr. Charles Harpum and Professor Andrew Burrows as part of the 25th series of Blundell Lectures.

[52] See further paras 30–44 to 30–45, below.

[53] *Clow v Brogden* (1840) 2 Scott N.R. 303; *Logan v Hall* (1847) 4 C.B. 598.

[54] (1857) 2 H. & N. 570.

sold for anything at all. This argument was rejected on the ground that the head tenant was liable to the head landlord for disrepair notwithstanding the forfeiture, and was accordingly entitled to recover his loss from the sub-tenant.[55]

## The costs of defending proceedings brought by the head landlord

Costs incurred by the head tenant in defending proceedings brought against him by the head landlord are only recoverable from the sub-tenant if the sub-tenancy contains a covenant of indemnity. In the absence of such a covenant, such sums will not generally be recoverable as damages for breach of the sub-tenant's covenants to repair.[56] The reason given in the authorities is that even where the covenants in the head lease and the sub-lease are identical, their effect will generally be different;[57] accordingly, the costs in question are not the necessary consequence of the sub-tenant's breach. It is thought that this reasoning is open to question in modern times. It may be that a better reason would be that where the sub-tenant has no notice of the existence or terms of the head lease, such costs will be too remote.[58] In any event, such costs would only be recoverable if they formed part of the diminution in the value of the head lease as a result of the disrepair.

24–15

Where the sub-tenancy contains a covenant to perform the covenants of the head lease, any costs incurred or payable by the head tenant in proceedings brought by the head landlord, which have been reasonably defended by the head tenant, are recoverable from the sub-tenant.[59]

## Sums paid by the head tenant in settlement of the head landlord's claim against him

It is common to find either that the head lease and the sub-lease contain the same, or similar repairing covenants, or that the sub-lease contains a covenant that the sub-tenant will perform the repairing covenants in the head lease and indemnify the head tenant against any claim by the head landlord. Where the head landlord brings a dilapidations claim against the head tenant, and the head tenant settles it for a money payment, the question may arise as to what extent the head tenant is entitled to recover from the sub-tenant the sum so paid.

24–16

The general principle is that where (i) A has a claim against B for damages for breach of contract, (ii) the facts also give rise to a claim for damages against A by C, and (iii) A settles C's claim, A is entitled to recover from B the amount paid in settlement to C without having to prove that A was liable to C, provided that the settlement between A and C was caused by B's breach of contract and was not too

---

[55] See further paras 30–44 and 30–45, below.
[56] *Penley v Watts* (1841) 7 M. & W. 601; *Walker v Hatton* (1842) 10 M. & W. 249; *Logan v Hall* (1847) 4 C.B. 598; *Pontifex v Foord* (1884) 12 Q.B.D. 152; *Ebbetts v Conquest* [1895] 2 Ch. 377 at 382 (affirmed [1896] A.C. 490); *Clare v Dobson* [1911]1 K.B. 35; *Lloyds Bank Ltd v Lake*, above. See further para.24–07, above.
[57] See para.24–07, above.
[58] The reason given in *Lloyds Bank Ltd v Lake*, above.
[59] *Hornby v Cardwell* (1881) 8 Q.B.D. 329. See paras 24–03 to 24–06, above.

remote.[60] The same applies where B has agreed to indemnify A against C's claim. A claim by C which is not sufficiently strong to be taken seriously does not satisfy this test, nor does a settlement in an amount which is unreasonable in relation to the strength of C's claim.[61] However, it is still necessary for A to prove that B is liable to him (on a claim based on breach of contract) or that the circumstances triggering B's liability to indemnify have come about.[62]

It would appear to follow from this that in the circumstances set out above, the head tenant would prima facie be entitled to recover from the sub-tenant the amount paid to the head landlord without having to prove that he was liable to the head landlord, provided that the above conditions are satisfied, i.e. that (i) the sub-tenant was liable to him for damages or an indemnity under the covenants in the sub-lease, (ii) the settlement with the head landlord was caused by the sub-tenant's breach of contract, or was within the scope of the sub-tenant's indemnity, and (ii) such settlement was not too remote. However, where the head tenant's claim against the sub-tenant arises under the repairing covenants in the sub-lease, difficult questions may arise in practice as to the application of the above principles where those covenants impose a different, and lesser, liability than the covenants in the head lease and/or where the head landlord's claim is settled for a global figure which includes sums attributable to disrepair items for which the sub-tenant is not liable. Moreover, the amount recoverable from the sub-tenant would (where the head tenant's claim arises out of breaches of the repairing obligations in the sub-lease) be subject to the operation of s.18(1) of the Landlord and Tenant Act 1927.[63]

---

[60] *Biggin v & Co. v Permanite* [1951] 2 K.B. 314; *Siemens Building Technology FE v Supershield* [2009] 2 All E.R. Comm 900 (not affected on appeal at [2010] 1 Lloyd's Rep 349).
[61] *Siemens Building Technology FE v Supershield*, above.
[62] Ibid.
[63] See Ch.30, below.

CHAPTER 25

**FIXTURES**

INTRODUCTORY

## Objects in or on premises

In most cases of leasehold premises, articles of various kinds will have been **25-01** affixed to, or brought onto, the demised premises, either by the landlord before the grant of the lease, or by the tenant afterwards. These can range from substantial installations such as lifts and boilers at one end of the scale to items such as desks and carpets at the other. Where they are provided by the landlord, no difficulty will generally arise in classifying and treating them for the purposes of the law of dilapidations. They will be part of the demised premises from the outset, and either they will form part of the subject-matter of the general covenant to repair, or the lease will contain specific covenants providing for how they are to be dealt with. Items provided by the tenant generally give rise to greater difficulty. The sort of questions which arise in practice will include: the extent to which such items are subject to the covenants to keep in repair during the term and to yield up in repair at the end of the term; whether they can be removed by the tenant at the end of the term, or whether they must be left behind as part of the demised premises; how far the tenant is liable if he causes damage to the demised premises when removing them; and whether the tenant is obliged to remove them so that he is liable if he fails to do so.

The correct answer to the above questions will depend on the legal nature of the object in question. For the purposes of the law of dilapidations, an item affixed to the demised property (whether by landlord or tenant) may be:

(1) an integral part of the demised land or building;
(2) a fixture (which may in turn be either a landlord's fixture or a tenant's fixture);
(3) a chattel.[1]

These are considered in turn below.

---

[1] See the threefold classification in *Elitestone Ltd v Morris* [1997] 1 W.L.R. 687 at 691G.

## Integral parts of the demised property

**25–02**  An item affixed to the demised land or building, either in the course of construction or afterwards, so as to become an integral part of it is not a fixture. Thus, in *Boswell v Crucible Steel Co*[2] plate glass windows which to a large extent formed the walls of a warehouse and office building were held not to be landlord's fixtures within the meaning of a repairing covenant. Scrutton L.J. said:

> "[I]t seems to me clear that [the expression 'landlord's fixtures'] cannot include a thing which forms part of the original structure of the building. It must be regarded as confined to things which have been brought into the house and affixed to the freehold after the structure is completed. If these windows could be treated as landlord's fixtures, the whole house would be a landlord's fixture."

Atkin L.J. said:

> "A fixture, as that term is used in connection with a house, means something which has been affixed to the freehold as accessory to the house. It does not include things which were made part of the house itself in the course of its construction. And the expression 'landlord's fixtures', as I understand it, covers all those chattels which have been so affixed by way of addition to the original structure, and were so affixed either by the landlord, or if by the tenant, under circumstances in which they were not removable by him. As these windows were part of the original structure, representing the walls of the house, so that without them there would be nothing that could be described as a warehouse at all, they cannot come under the head of landlord's fixtures. If they could, every brick used in the building would be a landlord's fixture."

Likewise, in *Elitestone v Morris*,[3] Lord Lloyd said:

> "In ordinary language one thinks of a fixture as being something fixed to a building. One would not ordinarily think of the building itself as a fixture."

The above does not mean, however, that just because something can be called a "building", it cannot for that reason be a tenant's fixture: that is particularly so in relation to buildings which are prefabricated and then assembled on site and which can later be taken apart and re-erected elsewhere.[4]

## Fixtures

**25–03**  A fixture is anything which has been affixed to the demised land or building in such a way that it has lost its chattel nature but has not become an integral part of the land or building.[5] Fixtures may be sub-divided into landlord's fixtures and tenant's fixtures.

---

[2] [1925] 1 K.B. 119.
[3] [1997] 1 W.L.R. 687.
[4] *Peel Land & Property (Port No.3) v TS Sheerness Steel* [2013] EWHC 1658 (Ch.) at [67].
[5] See further para.25–07 et seq., below.

## Landlord's fixtures[6]

A landlord's fixture is a fixture which cannot be removed by the tenant, either because it was present when the lease was granted or because, although it was affixed by the tenant, the circumstances are such that he has no right to remove it.[7]

**25–04**

## Tenant's fixtures

A tenant's fixture is a fixture which is removable by the tenant.[8]

**25–05**

## Chattels

A chattel is anything which is neither an integral part of the demised property nor a fixture.

**25–06**

## "Fittings"

The expression "fixtures and fittings" is a common one. However, the word "fittings" has no separate legal meaning, and is best avoided. Where it appears in a lease, its meaning will depend on the proper construction of the lease as a whole. Depending on the context, its meaning may be limited to fixtures properly so-called, or it may include chattels which have not become fixtures.

**25–07**

## WHEN AN OBJECT CEASES TO BE A CHATTEL AND BECOMES A FIXTURE

## Introductory

The general principle at common law is that anything attached to land becomes part of it (*quicquid plantatur solo, solo cedit*).[9] However, the law has developed away from a strict application of this rule,[10] and not every object affixed to the demised premises will be held to have lost its chattel nature. The question is primarily one of fact, and depends in particular on the degree of annexation (i.e. whether and to what extent the item is attached to the demised property),[11] and the purpose of annexation (i.e. the purpose for which the item was affixed).[12] Of these, the second is the more important in the modern law.[13]

**25–08**

---

[6] See further on the meaning of this expression para.7–56, above.

[7] See para.25–24 et seq., below.

[8] See para.25–25 et seq., below.

[9] See para.7–20, above.

[10] *Re De Falbe* [1901] 1 Ch. 523, per Vaughan Williams L.J. at 534; *Berkley v Poulett* [1977] 1 E.G.L.R. 86.

[11] See para.25–09, below.

[12] See para.25–10, below.

[13] See para.25–10, below.

There are a large number of decided cases on the question of what is or is not a fixture.[14] They are not always consistent with each other, and whilst they may be helpful in showing the application of the relevant principles to particular facts, it is important to bear in mind that the question whether an item has ceased to be a chattel is ultimately one of fact in each case, and decided cases cannot be decisive of the status of a particular item. Moreover, many of the cases were decided in or before the last century, and the particular facts must be carefully studied before seeking to apply the reasoning to modern situations where different methods of fixing and removing articles are concerned. The cases cited in the following passages of text should be approached with this warning in mind.

## The degree of annexation

**25–09**  Where an item has been attached or connected in some way to the land or building, there is a rebuttable presumption that it has become a fixture. In *Holland v Hodgson*[15] Blackburn J. summarised the position as follows:

> "Perhaps the true rule is, that articles not otherwise attached to the land than by their own weight are not to be considered as part of the land, unless the circumstances are such as to show that they were intended to be part of the land, the onus of showing that they were so intended lying on those who assert that they have ceased to be chattels, and that, on the contrary, an article which is affixed to the land even slightly is to be considered as part of the land, unless the circumstances are such as to show that it was intended all along to continue a chattel, the onus lying on those who contend it is a chattel."

The same point was made by Joyce J. in *Lyon v London City & Midland Bank*[16]

> "No doubt a chattel on being attached to the soil or to a building prima facie becomes a fixture, but the presumption may be rebutted by shewing that the annexation is incomplete, so that the chattel can be easily removed without injury to itself or to the premises to which it is attached, and that the annexation is merely for a temporary purpose and for the more complete enjoyment and use of the chattel as a chattel."

A relatively slight degree of annexation may be required in order to raise the inference that an item has lost its chattel nature. In general, however, the more firmly the item has been fixed, the more likely it is to be held to be a fixture (or an integral part of the land). In particular, if the extent of the attachment is such that the object cannot be removed without doing great damage either to the land or building to which it is attached, or to the item itself, there will be strong presumption in favour of it having lost its chattel nature. Thus, in *Hellawell v Eastwood*[17] Parke B. said that the relevant consideration was:

---

[14] A full discussion of these is outside the scope of this work, and reference should be made to *Woodfall: Landlord and Tenant* (London: Sweet & Maxwell), Vol.I, Ch.13, s.5.
[15] (1872) L.R. 7 C.P. 328.
[16] [1903] 2 K.B. 135.
[17] (1851) 6 Ex. 295.

"[T]he mode of annexation to the soil or fabric of the house, and the extent to which it is united to them, whether it can easily be removed, *integre, salve, et commode*, or not, without injury to itself or the fabric of the building."

And in *Berkeley v Poulett*[18] Scarman L.J. said:

"[I]f an object cannot be removed without serious damage to, or destruction of, some part of the realty, the case for its having become a fixture is a strong one."

It follows that objects resting on their own weight will prima facie remain chattels. Thus, it has been held that a prefabricated greenhouse, which was bolted to a concrete plinth which came with it and which lay on the ground under its own weight, was not a fixture.[19] On the same principle, sheds and barns resting on their own weight may remain chattels.[20] The fact that the structure rests on ground which has been prepared to receive it, or on a base let into the ground, does not automatically mean it ceases to be a chattel,[21] but there may come a point when it has been so firmly entrenched that it will be held to have become a fixture.[22] However, the fact that an item is not attached in any way to the ground is not decisive against it being a fixture if there can be demonstrated an intention to make it part of the land. For example, dry stone walling may be a fixture, even though the blocks of stone rest on the ground by their own weight only.[23]

## The purpose of annexation

Whilst the degree of annexation will be important, the consideration of principal importance will be the purpose of annexation, i.e. the intention with which the object was fixed.[24] Such intention must be inferred objectively from the circumstances of the case,[25] and direct evidence of the intention of the party who affixed the item is not admissible.[26] In *Elitestone Ltd v Morris*[27] Lord Clyde said:

**25–10**

---

[18] [1977] 1 E.G.L.R. 86.
[19] *Deen v Andrews* (1986) 52 P. & C.R. 17; *H.E. Dibble v Moore* [1970] 2 Q.B. 181.
[20] *Penton v Robart* (1801) 4 Esp. 33; *Wansborough v Maton* (1836) 4 A. & E. 884; *Mears v Callender* [1901] 2 Ch. 388.
[21] *Re Richards, Ex p. Astbury* (1869) L.R. 4 Ch. App. 630, per Giffard L.J. at 638 ("The preparation of the soil does not make the machine a fixture, nor does the fact of its being put into the receptacle so prepared for it make it a fixture.").
[22] See, for example, *Provincial Bill Posting Co v Low Moor Iron Co* [1909] 2 K.B. 344 (advertising hoarding fixed in the ground so firmly that it could not be removed save by digging held to be a fixture).
[23] *Holland v Hodgson* (1872) L. R. 7 C. P. 328, per Blackburn J. The relevant part of his judgment is set out in para.25–10, below.
[24] *Berkeley v Poulett* [1977] 1 E.G.L.R. 86 per Scarman L.J. at 89; *Hamp v Bygrave* [1983] 1 E.G.L.R. 174 per Boreham J. at 177; *Botham v TSB Bank Plc* [1996] E.G.C.S. 149.
[25] *Re De Falbe* [1901] 1 Ch. 523; *Botham v TSB Plc*, above.
[26] *Hobson v Gorringe* [1897] 1 Ch. 182; *Elitestone Ltd v Morris* [1997] 1 W.L.R. 687; *Melluish (Inspector of Taxes) v BMI (No.3) Ltd* [1996] A.C. 454; *Botham v TSB Plc*, above, per Scott V.C; *Peel Land & Property (Port No. 3) v TS Sheerness Steel* [2013] EWHC 1658 (Ch.) at [37].
[27] Above.

"It is important to observe that intention in this context is to be assessed objectively not subjectively. Indeed it may be that the use of the word intention is misleading. It is the purpose which the object is serving which has to be regarded, not the purpose of the person who put it there."

The result of regard being had to the purpose of annexation may be that articles of the same type, fixed in much the same way, will be held to have become fixtures in one set of circumstances but not in another. Thus, for example, cinema seats fixed to the floor were held to be fixtures where they were intended to be permanently fixed,[28] but to remain chattels when they were hired for only 12 weeks and fixed for a temporary purpose.[29]

In *Holland v Hodgson*[30] the question was whether looms attached to the floor of a mill constituted fixtures (for the purposes of a dispute between the mortgagee of the land and the mortgagee of the looms). It was held that they were fixtures. Blackburn J., giving the judgment of the Court of Exchequer Chamber court, said:

"There is no doubt that the general maxim of the law is, that what is annexed to the land becomes part of the land; but it is very difficult, if not impossible, to say with precision what constitutes an annexation sufficient for this purpose. It is a question which must depend on the circumstances of each case, and mainly on two circumstances, as indicating the intention, viz., the degree of annexation and the object of the annexation. When the article in question is no further attached to the land, then by its own weight it is generally to be considered a mere chattel; see *Wiltshear v Cottrell*, and the cases there cited. But even in such a case, if the intention is apparent to make the articles part of the land, they do become part of the land: see *D'Eyncourt v Gregory*. Thus blocks of stone placed one on the top of another without any mortar or cement for the purpose of forming a dry stone wall would become part of the land, though the same stones, if deposited in a builder's yard and for convenience sake stacked on the top of each other in the form of a wall, would remain chattels.

On the other hand, an article may be very firmly fixed to the land, and yet the circumstances may be such as to show that it was never intended to be part of the land, and then it does not become part of the land. The anchor of a large ship must be very firmly fixed in the ground in order to bear the strain of the cable, yet no one could suppose that it became part of the land, even though it should chance that the shipowner was also the owner of the fee of the spot where the anchor was dropped. An anchor similarly fixed in the soil for the purpose of bearing the strain of the chain of a suspension bridge would be part of the land.

Perhaps the true rule is, that articles not otherwise attached to the land than by their own weight are not to be considered as part of the land, unless the circumstances are such as to show that they were intended to be part of the land, the onus of showing that they were so intended lying on those who assert that they have ceased to be chattels, and that, on the contrary, an article which is affixed to the land even slightly is to be considered as part of the land, unless the circumstances are such as to show that it was intended all along to continue a chattel, the onus lying on those who contend that it is a chattel. This last proposition seems to be in effect the basis of the judgment of the Court of Common Pleas delivered by Maule, J., in *Wilde v Waters*. This, however, only removes the difficulty one step, for it still remains a question in each case whether the circumstances are sufficient to satisfy the onus. In some cases, such as the anchor of the ship or the ordinary instance given of a carpet nailed to the floor of a room, the nature of the thing sufficiently shows it is only fastened as a chattel temporarily, and not affixed permanently as part of the land. But ordinary trade or tenant fixtures which are put up with the intention that they should be removed by the tenant (and so are put up for a purpose in one sense only temporary, and certainly not for the purpose of improving the reversionary interest of the landlord) have always been considered as part of the land, though severable by the tenant. In most, if not all, of such cases the reason why the

---

[28] *Vaudeville Electric Cinema v Muriset* [1923] 2 Ch. 74.
[29] *Lyon & Co v London City & Midland Bank* [1903] 2 K.B. 135.
[30] (1872) L.R. 7 C. P. 328.

articles are considered fixtures is probably ... that the tenant indicates by the mode in which he puts them up that he regards them as attached to the property during his interest in the property."

The fact that the looms were put up with the intention of being removed by the tenant and not for the purpose of improving the premises did not therefore prevent them from being fixtures. However, a different approach appears to have been adopted by the Court of Appeal in *Botham v TSB Plc*,[31] in which the question was whether various functional items which had been installed in a flat were, as between the mortgagor of the flat and the mortgagee bank, fixtures subject to the bank's mortgage. Roch L.J., with whom Scott V.C. and Henry L.J. agreed, said in the course of his judgment: **25–11**

> "The test, in the case of an item which has been attached to the building in some way other than simply by its own weight, seems to be the purpose of the item and the purpose of the link between the item and the building. If the item, viewed objectively, is intended to be permanent and to afford a lasting improvement to the building, the thing will have become a fixture. If the attachment is temporary and is no more than is necessary for the item to be used and enjoyed, then it will remain a chattel. Some indicators can be identified. For example, if the item is ornamental and the attachment is simply to enable the item to be displayed and enjoyed as an adornment that will often indicate that this item is a chattel. Obvious examples are pictures. But this will not be the result in every case: for example ornamental tiles on the walls of kitchens and bathrooms. The ability to remove an item or its attachment from the building without damaging the fabric of the building is another indicator. The same item may in some areas be a chattel and in others a fixture. For example a cooker will, if free-standing and connected to the building only by an electric flex, be a chattel. But it may be otherwise if the cooker is a split level cooker with the hob set into a work surface and the oven forming part of one of the cabinets in the kitchen .... [T]he type of person who instals or attaches the item to the land can be a further indicator. Thus items installed by a builder, *e.g.* the wall tiles, will probably be fixtures, whereas items installed by *e.g.* a carpet contractor or curtain supplier or by the occupier of the building himself or herself may well not be."

The court held that the following were fixtures:

(a)  bathroom fittings (towel rails, soap dishes, lavatory roll holders and fittings on baths and basins, namely, taps, plugs and shower heads) which were (per Roch L.J.) "not there ... to be enjoyed for themselves, but they are there as accessories which enable the room to be used and enjoyed as a bathroom. Viewed objectively, they were intended to be permanent and to afford a lasting improvement to the property". It was, however, (per Scott V.C.) "possible that a Victorian bath, standing on its four short legs and connected by appropriate plumbing to the water system and drainage system, might retain its identity as a chattel");

(b)  mirrors and marble panels on the walls in the fitted bathroom;

(c)  kitchen units and work surfaces, including a fitted sink.

The following were held not to have become fixtures:

(a)  fitted carpets, cut to size and held in place by gripper rods[32];

(b)  curtains and blinds;

---

[31]  [1996] E.G.C.S. 149.
[32]  See further paras 25–16 to 25–17, below.

(c) light fittings which were not merely lamp shades but were lights fixed to the walls or ceilings[33];

(d) decorative gas flame effect fires, which were connected to the building only by a gas pipe;

(e) kitchen white goods, comprising a gas hob, extractor fan unit, a wall fitting (holding a cordless electric carving knife, spare blade and rechargeable torch), a freezer fitted under the worktop, an oven fitted into the kitchen units, an integrated dishwasher, an integrated washing machine and dryer, and a refrigerator fitted under the work top. These were manufactured to standard sizes, were fitted into standard sized holes and were easily disconnected and removed.

**25–12**  The approach of Roch L.J. in *Botham* distinguishes between whether the article was intended to be permanently fixed as part of the property, or whether it was attached for the temporary enjoyment or use of the article as an article. On the face of it, this differs from the approach taken in *Holland v Hodgson* and the other cases on trade machinery, where it was held that a machine fixed to the floor was a fixture, even where it was easily removable.[34] It might be said that the purpose of annexation in those cases was the better use of the machine during the term, not the permanent improvement of the property, so that if Roch L.J.'s approach is correct, it ought to have been held that the machine remained a chattel. The possible existence of a different approach as between trade machinery and domestic items is to some extent supported by the judgment of Scott V.C. in *Botham*, in which he said:

"There is, I think, some danger in applying too literally tests formulated for the purpose of decisions regarding machinery in factories to cases regarding articles in residences. There is a danger, also, in applying too literally tests formulated for the purpose of decisions regarding articles of ornamental value only to cases regarding articles whose prime function is utilitarian
...
The issue whether functional articles in a house or flat, such as those with which we are concerned in this case, have become fixtures depends, in my opinion, on the intention with which they were brought into the flat and fixed in position. That there must be some degree of affixing is obvious. It has been suggested that it may, in some cases, suffice that the affixing is no more substantial than the placing of an electric plug in an electric point in the wall. I would reject that suggestion. I do not think that an item of electrical equipment e.g. a dishwasher, a refrigerator, a deep freeze or a washing machine, affixed, if that is an apt word, by no more than a plug in an electric point, could ever be held to have become a fixture.
Assuming, however, that the functional article in question has been affixed to the land or building in a sufficiently substantial manner to enable a contention that it has become a fixture to be conceptually possible, the critical question will be that of intention."

---

[33] See further para.25–19, below.
[34] For example, *Hobson v Gorringe* [1897] 1 Ch. 182; *Reynolds v Ashby & Son* [1903] 1 K.B. 87 (Court of Appeal) and [1904] A.C. 466 (House of Lords); *Crossley Bros v Lee* [1908] 1 K.B. 86; *Pole-Carew v Western Counties & General Manure Co Ltd* [1920] 2 Ch. 97; *Smith v City Petroleum Co* [1940] 1 All E.R. 260. See para.25–20, below.

# Particular articles

## (a) Partitions

Partitions of whatever construction are virtually always fixed to the building in some way or other. It is thought that any substantial connection between the partition and the structure of the building is likely to lead to the conclusion that the partition has lost its chattel nature. For example, a stud wall which is constructed of plasterboard on wooden studs, the studs being fixed to the walls of the building and to the floor, will generally be either a fixture or an integral part of the demised property. However, it may be that free-standing demountable partitions, fixed only by brackets and screws, would, in an appropriate case, be held to remain chattels.[35]

**25–13**

In practice, something may turn on the extent to which a partition is realistically capable of being removed and used elsewhere. If it is, then, depending on the precise facts, it may be easier to conclude that it has not ceased to be a chattel. If, on the other hand, it is of such a nature that either it cannot be removed without destroying it, or if removed it would be effectively useless elsewhere, then it is very likely to be held to have lost its chattel nature.

In the New Zealand case of *Short v Kirkpatrick*[36] partitions which had been solidly affixed to the concrete floor by means of ramset pins, and nailed at the top to ceilings were held to be tenant's fixtures.

## (b) Suspended ceilings

Suspended ceilings are installed in most modern office buildings. They generally consist of ceiling tiles or panels laid on a metal grid, which is suspended from the structure overhead by wires or rods, which are themselves attached to the structure via bolts. It is thought that, in most cases, a suspended ceiling is likely to be a fixture and not a chattel.

**25–14**

## (c) Raised floors

Modern purpose-built office buildings generally include raised floor systems, which usually comprise removable floor panels supported on pedestals, which are glued or bolted to the underlying floor screed. It is thought that in the majority of cases, a raised floor will be a fixture and not a chattel.

**25–15**

## (d) Carpets

A carpet which rests on the floor without being attached in any way will generally remain a chattel. Nor will the fact that a carpet is nailed to the floor make it a fixture. Thus, in *Holland v Hodgson*[37] Blackburn J. said:

**25–16**

---

[35] Cf. *Horwich v Symond* (1915) 84 L.J.K.B. 1083, considered in para.25–21, below.
[36] [1982] 2 N.Z.L.R. 358.
[37] (1872) L.R. 7 C.P. 328.

> "[In] the ordinary instance ... of a carpet nailed to the floor of a room, the nature of the thing sufficiently shows it is only fastened as a chattel temporarily, and not permanently affixed to the freehold."

Likewise, in *Lyon v London & Midland Bank*[38] Joyce J., holding that cinema seats were not fixtures, said:

> "The mode of annexation of these chairs to the freehold is analogous rather to the mode in which a carpet is fastened to a floor rather than to the mode in which engines, boilers, and heavy machinery are affixed to the freehold, and moreover the purpose of the annexation is only temporary."

And in *Horwich v Symond*[39] Buckley L.J. said:

> "The mere fact of some annexation to the freehold is not enough to convert a chattel into realty. That is shewn by the case of carpets, which are certainly not fixtures."

**25–17**    In *Young v Dalgety*[40] carpeting had been fixed to gripper rods which were fixed to the screeded floor with pins which were themselves attached to the carpets. The judge at first instance held that the carpets were fixtures, and the Court of Appeal were prepared to assume (without deciding) that he was right. However, in *Botham v TSB Plc*[41] fitted carpets in a flat, cut to size and kept in place by gripper rods, were held by the Court of Appeal not to be fixtures. Scott V.C. said in the course of his judgment:

> "Carpets, whether or not fitted, and curtains lack that quality of permanency that is to be expected of articles that have become in the eye of the law part of the realty. In *Young v. Dalgety* Mervyn Davies J. said that he 'inclined to the view' that fitted carpeting installed in 19 Hanover Square was a fixture ... The case went to the Court of Appeal on another point. For my part I very much doubt whether fitted carpeting could ever be held to be a fixture. It is relatively easy to take up fitted carpeting. A leaky radiator often necessitates that a carpet be taken up to allow the floor underneath to dry out. There will be many other reasons why a fitted carpet may be taken up. No damage at all to the structure of the building will be caused. Fitted carpets do not become part of the floor itself, and do not, in my judgment, become fixtures."

In the Australian case of *Palumberi v Palumberi*[42] it was held on special facts that carpets laid on runners, which could be removed simply by lifting them off the runners, were fixtures.

The question is one of fact in every case. The above authorities suggest, however, that carpets, whether or not fitted, are unlikely to be held to have become fixtures unless some more permanent method of attachment, such as adhesive, is used.

---

[38] [1903] 2 K.B. 135.
[39] (1915) 84 L.J.K.B. 1083.
[40] [1987] 1 E.G.L.R. 116.
[41] [1996] E.G.C.S. 149.
[42] [1986] N.S.W. Conv.R. 55–287. See also *Westpac Banking Corp v Rabaiov* [1991] A.N.Z. Conv.R. 560.

## (e)  Carpet tiles

The carpets in many modern office buildings comprise carpet tiles, which are **25–18** generally fixed to the floor screed or (where there is a raised floor) floor panels by some form of adhesive. It is thought that in most cases, carpet tiles of this type will be fixtures and not chattels. Thus, in *Botham v TSB Plc*[43] Roch L.J. thought that:

> "There may be cases where carpeting or carpet squares are stuck to a concrete screed in such a way as to make them part of the floor and thus fixtures."

## (f)  Lights and light fittings

Ordinary light bulbs will generally remain chattels. Thus, it has been held that **25–19** light bulbs fixed by bayonet fixings into lamp brackets were not fixtures.[44]

Where light fittings have been fixed to the building, the question whether they have become fixtures will depend on the facts. In *Young v Dalgety*[45] lights comprising fluorescent tubes in glass boxes fixed securely to the plaster of the ceiling were held by the judge at first instance to be fixtures, and the Court of Appeal was prepared to assume, without deciding, that he was right. However, in *Botham v TSB Plc*,[46] light fittings in a flat which were not merely lamp shades but were lights attached to walls and ceilings were (with the exception of two light fittings recessed into ceilings, which were conceded to be fixtures) held to be chattels and not fixtures. The judgments of Roch L.J. and Scott V.C. make it clear that it is possible for light fittings to be so incorporated into a wall or ceiling as to become fixtures. On the facts, however, there was no admissible evidence to justify a conclusion that the light fittings in question had become fixtures. One test adopted by Roch L.J. was to ask whether the light fittings were shown by the evidence to be "part of the electrical installation in the flat".

## (g)  Plant and equipment

Plant resting on its own weight will generally remain a chattel by virtue of the **25–20** principles already discussed.[47] Conversely, plant which has been affixed to the land or building will generally become a fixture. Where machinery has become a fixture by virtue of this principle, then individual parts of it are likewise fixtures, even though removable,[48] and even though removed for repair.[49] However, inessential parts[50] and unfitted spare parts[51] will remain chattels. Difficult questions may arise in practice to the correct classification of complex plant, and

---

[43] [1996] E.G.C.S. 149.
[44] *British Economical Lamp Co Ltd v Empire, Mile End* (1913) 29 T.L.R. 386.
[45] [1987] 1 E.G.L.R. 116.
[46] [1996] E.G.C.S. 149. See para.25–11, above.
[47] See paras 25–08 to 25–12, above.
[48] *Sheffield & South Yorkshire Permanent Benefit Society v Harrison* (1884) 15 Q.B.D. 358.
[49] *Liford's Case* (1614) 11 Co. Rep. 46b, 50a, 50b.
[50] *Jordan v May* [1947] K.B. 427 (generator fixed by bolts held to be a fixture, but storage batteries attached to it by wires held to remain chattels).
[51] *Re Richards, Ex p. Astbury* (1866) L.R. 4 Ch. App. 630.

in particular whether it, or its component parts or some of them, are properly to be regarded as integral parts of the building in which the plant is situated or whether they are chattels or fixtures, and if fixtures, removable tenant's fixtures.[52]

In the Australian case of *Pan Australian Credits (SA) Pty Ltd v Kolim Pty Ltd*,[53] it was held, as between mortgagor and mortgagee, that two air conditioning units were fixtures. The units were installed in a well on the roof of a convention centre; they were fastened by bolts into a fitting in the concrete floor of the well; they were connected to a switchboard by electric cables with flexible conduit; and they were attached to steel ducting which entered the ceiling of the premises and communicated with vents fitted into holes in the ceiling. The whole equipment—units, ducting and vents—constituted a single working system. Matheson J. held that the equipment "was attached in the ways it was, not for the better enjoyment of the equipment as equipment, but for the better enjoyment of the Convention Centre. The nature of the equipment when installed made it essentially part of the Convention Centre."

In the Australian case of *Macrocom v City West Centre*,[54] a satellite dish fixed to the roof of a building, which was supported by a specially constructed structural steel framework underneath the roof and bolted to a framework which was itself bolted to the roof, was held by the New South Wales Supreme Court to be (as between the owner of the building and the owner of the dish) a fixture and not a chattel. The judge said:

> "Its position on the roof, its weight, the fact that additional steel support to the roof was necessary prior to its installation and the way in which it is connected to the building, would leave any outside observer to consider it part of the building and to assume that was the intention."

The judge further commented that, had the issue arisen as between landlord and tenant, he would have held the dish to be a tenant's fixture.

A further issue arose in the same case in relation to transmit equipment in the floor below, to which the dish was connected. The equipment was placed in racks which were bolted or plugged to the floor. Component parts in the racks were held there by small screws or bolts which could easily be removed and the component parts then slid in and out of the racks subject to disconnection from the cables. The judge held that transmit equipment components remained chattels. He said:

> "The rack is not part of the claim. The components slide in and out of the rack; the degree of annexation with screwbolts is slight. The hard wired cabling is perhaps the strongest indication either way, but while it is not as simple as a plug to power, to an electrician it presents no difficulties to hook up. The components can be used with a different satellite dish."

He continued:

---

[52] See for example *Pole-Carew v Western Counties & General Manure* [1920] 2 Ch. 97 and *Peel Land & Property (Port No. 3) v TS Sheerness Steel* [2013] EWHC 1658 (Ch.) (which concerned the correct classification of numerous items of complex plant forming part of the Sheerness steel works).
[53] [1981] 27 S.A.S.R. 353.
[54] [2001] NSWSC 374.

"It is of course necessary to consider whether the transmit equipment is part of an integrated system comprising the satellite dish, the transmission equipment and the equipment which was on the first floor, including the modular equipment Any high grade television type facilities in a building may require an aerial for their effective operation. That aerial may well be a fixture, but that does not necessarily make the television components fixtures, although together they may be thought of an [sic] integrated. There is no doubt that the dish will operate successfully with other transmission components. Had the equipment become redundant I have no doubt that the plaintiff was entitled to replace it with the most recent technology and to take the old parts away. That, I consider, would not have depended upon some special rights to remove tenants' fixtures. These matters are matters of degree, and usually little is gained by comparing the facts in one case with the facts in another. I find the transmit equipment not part of the building."

Similarly, in *NH Dunn Pty Ltd v L.M. Ericsson Pty Ltd*[55] it was held that a PABX (private automatic branch telephone exchange) switchboard remained a chattel and had not become a fixture.

### (h)   Shop fittings

The extent to which shop fittings will have become fixtures will depend on the proper application of the principles already considered. In most cases, however, it is thought that shop fittings will remain chattels. Thus, in *Horwich v Symond*[56] various fittings in a chemists shop, comprising a counter and showcase, a bottle rack, a cupboard and "13ft chemist fittings etc.", all of which were held in position by two nails or a single screw, were held not to have become fixtures. Buckley L.J. said:

25–21

"The question whether these articles were so fixed that they ought to be treated as annexed to the freehold, or were merely chattels is, as I have said, a pure question of fact. The mere fact of some annexation to the freehold is not enough to convert a chattel into realty. That is shewn by the case of carpets, which are certainly not fixtures; and the same principle seems to apply to a shop counter which stands on the floor not as a fixture, but as a chattel with a certain amount of fixing to keep it steady."

Likewise, in *Gibson Lea Interiors Ltd v Makro Self Service Ltd*[57] a variety of shop fittings items installed in cash and carry wholesalers stores, including counters and display gondolas which had been fixed to the walls or floors to ensure that they did not move, were held not to have become fixtures.

### (i)   Buildings and structures

In many, if not most, cases it will be obvious, as a matter of common sense, that a building or structure erected by the tenant has become either an integral part of the demised property, or a fixture. Equally, in other cases, it will be obvious that the item remains a chattel (for example, a Portakabin or a mobile home). In some cases, however, the nature of the building may be such that the question whether

25–22

---

[55] (1979) 2 B.P.R. 9241.
[56] (1915) 84 L.J.K.B. 1083.
[57] [2001] B.L.R. 407.

it is a fixture will be more difficult. The fact that it rests only on its own weight will not be decisive in favour of its being a chattel.[58]

In *Elitestone Ltd v Morris*[59] a chalet or bungalow was built on a site. It rested on concrete foundation blocks in the ground. It could not be taken down and re-erected elsewhere: it could only be removed by a process of demolition. The House of Lords held that it had ceased to be a chattel. Lord Lloyd (with whom Lords Browne-Wilkinson, Nolan and Nicholls agreed) approached the matter in the following way:

> "In the case of a house, the answer is as much a matter of common sense as precise analysis. A house which is constructed in such a way as to be removable, whether as a unit or in sections, may well remain a chattel, even though it is connected temporarily to mains services such as water and electricity. But a house which is constructed in such a way that it cannot be removed at all, save by destruction, cannot have been intended to remain a chattel. It must have been intended to form part of the realty."

It is thought that this statement of general principle can usefully be applied not only to separate structures but also to additions or alterations to existing structures (for example, the installation of a mezzanine floor into a warehouse).

In *Wessex Reserve Forces & Cadets Association v White*,[60] two large huts attached to the ground were held to be fixtures; a stone shed was agreed to be part of the land; and a Portakabin, a pre-fabricated domestic-type garden shed and a sectional pre-cast concrete building with a felt covered roof on a concrete slab were all held to be chattels.

In *Mew v Tristmire Ltd*[61] houseboats, once capable of floating, had been placed clear of the tide on wooden platforms supported by wooden piles driven into, and in some cases cemented into, the bed of the harbour. When originally put on the platforms, they could have been lifted off by crane and floated to a new location, but they had deteriorated to the extent that they could only be lifted off by the use of a crane with an extensive supporting cradle. It was held that they remained chattels and had not become part of the land.

## RIGHTS OF REMOVAL

### Chattels

**25–23**    Articles belonging to the tenant which have retained their chattel nature are removable by him at any time, assuming that there is no special provision in the lease requiring, for example, the demised premises to be furnished or equipped at all times for some particular purpose. Once the term ends, the tenant is liable to remove all chattels brought on to the demised premises by him during the tenancy. Failure to do so is a breach of the express or implied obligation to deliver up possession, for which the landlord is entitled to damages.[62] The

---

[58]  See paras 25–08 to 25–12, above.
[59]  [1997] 1 W.L.R. 687.
[60]  [2005] 3 E.G.L.R. 127 (the point did not arise on appeal: [2006] 2 P. & C. R. 3).
[61]  [2011] EWCA Civ 912.
[62]  See para.14–06, above.

ordinary measure of damages would be the cost of removing and disposing of the items. The statutory ceiling imposed by s.18(1) of the Landlord and Tenant Act 1927 would not apply.[63]

## Tenant's fixtures and landlord's fixtures[64]

Articles which have become fixtures in accordance with the principles considered above[65] are subdivided into "tenant's fixtures" and "landlord's fixtures". A tenant's fixture is an article which has become a fixture but which is removable by the tenant. A landlord's fixture is a fixture which is not removable by the tenant.[66] Neither category includes items which have become an integral part of the building such that they cannot properly be called "fixtures" at all.[67]

**25–24**

## Tenant's fixtures

Three conditions must be satisfied for a fixture to be capable of being a tenant's (i.e. removable) fixture.

**25–25**

### (a)  It must have been affixed by or on behalf of the tenant

It is of the essence of a tenant's fixture that it was affixed by the tenant and not by the landlord. However, it is thought that, provided the article was affixed on behalf of the tenant, it does not matter that it was not affixed by the tenant himself. For example, it is not uncommon to find that the tenant is a holding company which is part of a group, and that trade fixtures have been affixed by a subsidiary or other group company which trades from the premises. It is thought that such fixtures would nonetheless constitute (as between the tenant and the landlord) tenant's fixtures, since the only legal right which the trading company would have to affix articles to the premises would be through the tenant.

**25–26**

In practice, fixtures (particularly those put in as part of fitting out works in shops and offices) are often installed prior to, and in anticipation of, the grant of the lease. Where a specifically enforceable agreement for lease exists, there will be no difficulty because the tenant will already be tenant of the premises in equity.[68] The position is less clear where the tenant is at the time no more than a licensee. However, it is thought that articles affixed in anticipation of the grant of the lease, by or on behalf of the person who is to be the tenant, would not be

---

[63] See Ch.30, below.

[64] The corresponding paragraph, and those following, in the Second Edition of this work were referred to by H.H. Judge Cooke in *Indiana Investments v Taylor* [2004] 3 E.G.L.R. 63 as a "convenient summary of known authority".

[65] See para.25–08 et seq., above.

[66] The expression "landlord's fixture" has no particular significance in the law relating to fixtures, save to denote items which are not tenant's fixtures. However, it is an expression which sometimes appears in repairing covenants, and in that context it is discussed in para.7–56, above.

[67] See para.25–02, above.

[68] Under the principle in *Walsh v Lonsdale* (1882) 21 Ch. D. 9.

prevented from being tenant's fixtures merely because the lease had not then been granted.[69] This seems more consistent with the policy underlying tenant's fixtures[70] than does the contrary view.

### (b)   It must belong to one of the recognised categories of tenant's fixture

**25–27**   The three recognised categories of tenant's fixture are (i) trade fixtures; (ii) ornamental and domestic fixtures; and (iii) agricultural fixtures.

The first is a broad category comprising anything which has been attached by the tenant in order to enable him to carry on his trade or business in the premises. The policy underlying this category is the promotion of the commercial interests of the country, by encouraging business tenants to fit out and equip their premises for the purposes of their trade in the knowledge that they will be able, if they wish, to remove what they have installed before they leave.[71]

Examples from the cases are machinery,[72] public house fittings[73] and petrol pumps.[74] Shop fittings in retail premises are likely to fall within this category, as are fixtures comprising items such as of air conditioning units, partitions, suspended ceilings and shelving in office premises.

Examples of articles in the second category are ornamental panelling,[75] bookcases screwed to the walls[76] and garden ornaments.[77] The third category is outside the scope of this work.

### (c)   Objectively regarded, it must have been affixed with the intention of removing it as and when the tenant so wished

**25–28**   A number of separate tests as to when a fixture is a tenant's fixture have been propounded in the cases and textbooks, and these are discussed below. It is possible, however, that all of them are aspects of one overriding test, namely, the object and purpose of annexation. This has already been considered above in relation to whether an object has become a fixture at all, but it may be that it is also applies in relation to whether a fixture is removable as a tenant's fixture. This is suggested by *Spyer v Phillipson*,[78] which concerned ornamental panelling affixed by the tenant. The issue was not whether it retained its chattel nature but

---

[69] Cf. *Hambros Bank Executor & Trustee Co Ltd v Superdrug Stores Ltd* [1985] 1 E.G.L.R. 99. It is thought that the reasoning in cases such as *Brett v Brett Essex Golf Club* [1986] 1 E.G.L.R. 154 (where the question was whether a building erected under a previous lease was or was not an "improvement" for rent review purposes) is not applicable to the question being considered here.
[70] See para.25–27, below.
[71] *Poole's Case* (1703) 1 Salk. 368; *Penton v Robart* [1801] 2 East 88 at 90; *Woodfall: Landlord and Tenant* (London: Sweet & Maxwell), Vol.I, para.13.142.
[72] *Lawton v Lawton* (1743) 3 Atk. 13
[73] *Elliott v Bishop* (1854) 10 Exch. 496.
[74] *Smith v City Petroleum Co Ltd* [1940] 1 All E.R. 260.
[75] *Spyer v Phillipson* [1931] 2 Ch. 183.
[76] *Birch v Dawson* (1834) 2 A. & E. 37.
[77] *Hamp v Bygrave* [1983] 1 E.G.L.R. 174.
[78] [1931] 2 Ch. 183.

whether, having been affixed so as to lose its chattel nature, it was removable by the tenant or not.[79] On that issue, Lord Hanworth M.R. said in the course of his judgment:

"The question we have to determine in this case is, do the facts which are before us compel the inference that this panelling was fixed, so that the removal of it was no longer contemplated; that the panelling had been finally made an integral part of the dwelling rooms; or is the right inference that the panelling had been put up with the intention on the part of the tenant of removing it as and when he was minded so to do, and that the affixing of the panelling was only for the purpose of the complete enjoyment by the tenant of that expensive panelling?

... I ask myself the question: is there any evidence such as to compel one to come to the conclusion that this expensive panelling was put up some ten or dozen years before the expiration of the lease in order that the value of the flat might be enhanced for the benefit of the landlord, rather than put up for the purpose of the enjoyment of those ornaments by the tenant himself?"

At first instance, Luxmoore J. had quoted a passage from Parke B.'s judgment in *Hellawell v Eastwood*[80] as follows:                           **25–29**

"This is a question of fact depending on the circumstances of each case, and principally on two considerations: first the mode of annexation to the soil or fabric of the house, and the extent to which it is united to them, whether it can easily be removed *integre salve et commode* or not without injury to itself or the fabric of the building; secondly, on the object and purpose of the annexation, whether it was for the permanent and substantial improvement of the dwelling .... or merely for a temporary purpose and the more complete enjoyment and use of it as a chattel."

In the Court of Appeal Romer L.J. quoted Luxmoore J.'s comment on the above passage as follows:

"I think in fact that these are not two considerations, but really only one consideration: what was the object and purpose of the annexation?; and that among the matters which have to be considered in coming to a conclusion in answer to that question, what was the object and purpose of the annexation, are first the mode of annexation, and secondly, what would happen if the mode of annexation were severed, and it is sought to take the particular things away."

Romer L.J. continued as follows:

"Speaking for myself, I think that is a correct statement of the law. So long as the article can be removed without doing irreparable damage to the demised premises I do not think that either the method of annexation or the degree of annexation, or the quantum of damage that would be done to the article itself or to the demised premises by its removal, has really any bearing upon the question of the tenant's rights to remove, except insofar as they throw light on the question of the intention with which the chattel was affixed by him to the demised premises."

It is to be noted, however, that (as Morgan J. pointed out in *Peel Land & Property (Port No.3) v TS Sheerness Steel*[81]) *Hellawell v Eastwood*, was concerned with the difference between a chattel and a fixture, and not with the different question of whether an admitted fixture is nonetheless removable as a tenant's fixture. Nonetheless, the above passages suggest that the overriding

---

[79] See esp. Luxmoore J. at 198 and Lord Hanworth M.R. at 201.
[80] (1851) 6 Ex. 295 at 312.
[81] [2013] EWHC 1658 (Ch.) at [62].

question (to be approached objectively[82]) is whether the object was affixed with the intention of removing it at some time should the tenant so wish, or whether it was intended that it should become a permanent part of the premises. If that is right the various tests which follow are properly to be regarded as aspects of that overriding question and not as conclusive in their own right.

### (i) The object must not have lost its essential chattel nature on being affixed

**25–30**  An item which when affixed becomes an integral part of the demised land or building is not a tenant's fixture.[83] Thus, for example, neither a permanent new building on the demised land nor a permanent addition to the existing demised building (for example, an additional floor or a new roof) would be tenant's fixtures. In *New Zealand Government Property Corp v HM&S Ltd*[84] Lord Denning M.R. said:

> "The term 'tenant's fixtures', for present purposes, means those fixtures which the tenant himself fixed into the premises for the purpose of his trade, that is for the business of the theatre, but which do not become part of the structure itself. Instances are the seats for the stalls, or auditorium, which are fixed by the screws or bolts to the floor, wall brackets for lights which are screwed on to the wall, electric transformers fixed on to the floor, and so forth. Whereas 'landlord's fixtures' for present purposes means those fixtures which the tenant himself fixes into the premises so that they become part of the structure itself .... Instances are improvements made by the tenant by putting in new doors or windows in place of those that were there before, or a new frontage or a new safety curtain. These improvements become part of the structure itself. The tenant cannot remove them when his term comes to an end."

Thus, in *Pole-Carew v Western Counties & General Manure*[85] it was held that industrial plant had been so integrated into the demised building that it was to be regarded as part of it.

However, it does not follow that everything that can be called a "building" must necessarily be excluded from being a tenant's fixture: that is particularly so in relation to buildings which are prefabricated and then assembled on site and which can later be taken apart and re-erected elsewhere.[86]

### (ii)  The object must be of such a nature that it can reasonably be removed without losing its utility and value

**25–31**  As a general rule, it must be possible to set up the article again and use it in another place.[87] But the fact that it may need to be dismantled in order to be removed does not matter.[88] Thus, in *Webb v Frank Bevis Ltd*[89] a shed made of corrugated iron fixed to timber posts, which was capable of being removed in

---

[82] See para.25–10, above.
[83] Such an item is not a "fixture" at all: see para.25–02, above.
[84] [1982] Q.B. 1145.
[85] [1920] 2 Ch. 97.
[86] *Peel Land & Property (Port No. 3) v TS Sheerness Steel* [2013] EWHC 1658 (Ch.) at [67].
[87] *Whitehead v Bennett* (1858) 27 L.J. Ch. 474.
[88] Ibid.; *Webb v Frank Bevis Ltd* [1940] 1 All E.R. 247.
[89] Above.

sections, was held to be removable. However, the concrete base to which it was fixed (by means of the posts being bolted to iron straps fixed in the base) was held to be irremovable. Likewise, in *Wessex Reserve Forces & Cadets Association v White*[90] the superstructure of two large huts, but not the foundations, were held to be tenant's fixtures. However, articles which cannot be removed without destroying them (such as built-in cupboards and some types of partition) will generally be irremovable.

It is not relevant to ask whether the second hand value of the removed item will be greater or less than the market value of the item, sold as scrap. The question whether the item, when severed, will retain its essential utility and value must be given the same answer whether it is asked just after the item is annexed or many years later, so that the market value of the item when it is about to be severed cannot be the basis of the distinction between what is removable and what is not.[91]

## (iii) The object must be capable of being removed without excessive damage to the fabric of the land or building to which it was attached

It must be possible to remove the article without causing undue damage to the premises. However, the fact that removal of the article will cause minor damage to the premises does not matter. Thus, in *Young v Dalgety Plc*[92] light fittings were held to be removable even though this would cause some damage to the plaster, this being described by Fox L.J. as " … a minor matter, being easily remedied". Damage to decorative finishes as opposed to the fabric or structure of the property appears not to be relevant.[93] Whether the nature of the damage is such as to render a fixture incapable of removal is in every case a question of fact and degree. Where what is in issue is the removal of plant, the question is whether the relevant item can be removed without causing substantial irreparable damage to the premises, not whether the premises will be able to function on their own absent the removed item of plant.[94]

In the Canadian case of *Westana Leasing Corp v The Lord Finn 2000 Ltd*,[95] items installed in a restaurant under an equipment lease, which included an exhaust unit, fan and fire suppression system, were held by the Provincial Court of Alberta not to be tenant's fixtures, because removal would have caused structural damage costing more than $5,000 to repair. A similar conclusion was reached by the Supreme Court of Nova Scotia in *Frank Georges Island Investments v Ocean Farmers*[96] in relation to a house and twine shed, which had been installed to enable the tenant to conduct its aquaculture business (although a buoy shed and outhouse were both held to be tenant's fixtures).

**25–32**

---

[90] [2005] 3 E.G.L.R. 127 (on appeal: [2006] 2 P. & C. R. 3).
[91] *Peel Land & Property (Port No. 3) v TS Sheerness Steel*[2013] EWHC 1658 (Ch.) at [66].
[92] [1987] 1 E.G.L.R. 116.
[93] *Spyer v Phillipson* [1931] 2 Ch. 183.
[94] *Peel Land & Property (Port No. 3) v TS Sheerness Steel*, above, at [65].
[95] [2005] ABPC 139.
[96] (2000) Carswell 563 A.P.R. 201.

## Fixtures installed pursuant to an agreement with the landlord

**25–33**    The fact that the tenant is obliged to install fixtures under an agreement with the landlord does not of itself prevent such fixtures from being tenant's fixtures, and therefore removable, unless the agreement expressly or impliedly abrogates the right of removal.[97]

## Fixtures installed to replace landlord's fixtures

**25–34**    Fixtures installed by the tenant to replace fixtures belonging to the landlord are not removable.[98] Thus, for example, where an office building is demised with light fittings belonging to the landlord, and the tenant replaces them with his own, the replacement light fittings will not generally be removable.

## Contractual restrictions on the right to remove tenant's fixtures

**25–35**    The right to remove fixtures may be excluded or restricted by the terms of the lease. For example, the lease may expressly require the tenant to deliver up the demised premises at the end of the term "together with all tenant's fixtures". This would have the effect of preventing the tenant from removing tenant's fixtures at the end of the term. Conversely, the lease will sometimes make it clear that there is no obligation to deliver up tenant's fixtures. For example, the covenant to yield up may be qualified by such words as "excluding tenant's fixtures" or similar words. Often, however, the covenant to yield up will be unclear. It may, for example, require the tenant to deliver up the demised premises "together with all fixtures" or some similar formulation. In such cases the question whether the right of removal has been excluded is a question of construction of the covenant in the context of the lease as a whole, and the following general principles apply.

There is a presumption of construction that the parties did not intend to exclude the tenant's entitlement to remove tenant's fixtures.[99] Thus, in *Lambourn v McLellan*[100] Vaughan Williams L.J. said:

> "[I]f the landlord wishes to restrict his tenant's ordinary right to remove trade machinery or fixtures attached to the demised premises … the landlord must say so in plain language. If the language used leaves matters doubtful, the ordinary right of the tenant to remove trade fixtures will not be affected.[101]"

Thus, if the covenant to deliver up is reasonably capable of being construed as limited to landlord's fixtures alone, then the fact that an obligation to deliver up

---

[97] *Mowats Ltd v Hudson Bros Ltd* (1911) 105 L.T. 400; *Young v Dalgety Plc* [1987] 1 E.G.L.R. 116; *Peel Land & Property (Port No.3) v TS Sheerness Steel* [2013] EWHC 1658 (Ch.) at [155], [158].

[98] *Sunderland v Newton* (1830) 3 Sim. 450.

[99] *Peel Land & Property (Port No.3) v TS Sheerness Steel*, above, at [169].

[100] [1903] 2 Ch. 268.

[101] See also *Duke of Beaufort v Bates* (1862) 3 De G. F. & J. 381 at 390; *Re British Red Ash Collieries Ltd* [1920] 1 Ch. 326.

landlord's fixtures would be superfluous (because the tenant would be liable to do this anyway) does not prevent the covenant being construed as referring to landlord's fixtures only.[102]

However, the presumption will yield to clear words showing that the parties intended to exclude the right of removal. In *Leschallas v Woolf*[103] Parker J. held that a covenant requiring the tenant to deliver up the demised premises "with all and singular the fixtures and articles belonging thereto" was sufficient to include tenant's fixtures, with the result that the right of removal was lost. It should be noted that the lease in question was for 70 years and obliged the tenant to lay out £200 in putting up a substantial dwelling on the demised land. The tenant would have had to deliver up the dwelling at the end of the lease even though he had built it, and there was nothing obviously unfair in requiring him to deliver up fixtures within the dwelling as well. Parker J. said in the course of his judgment:

25–36

> "[I]t is difficult to see how the house covenanted to be built could have been made fit for habitation in accordance with the covenant without affixing things, such as, for example, fire grates, which might under some circumstances be tenant's fixtures; and it is impossible to say at this distance of time (the lease having been granted in 1851) what things in the nature of fixtures were provided by means of the £200 which the lessee covenanted should be expended in erecting and completing the house fit for habitation. The object of the covenant may thus very well have been—and, indeed, I have come to the conclusion that it was—to prevent difficulties arising on these points by making the obligation to deliver up in repair extend not only to landlord's fixtures, but to all fixtures on the premises of whatsoever nature they might be."

In *Re British Red Ash Collieries Ltd*[104] a covenant in a mining lease provided that:

> "[A]t the end or sooner determination of the term all erections, fences and fixed machinery in the demised seams or on the surface of the said premises shall be left in good repair and condition by the lessees."

The Court of Appeal held that the right to remove all fixed machinery, including trade fixtures, had been excluded.[105]

Similarly, a covenant to repair and yield up in repair all buildings erected on the premises during the term has been held to prevent the removal of buildings which amount to trade fixtures.[106]

By contrast, in *Peel Land & Property (Port No.3) v TS Sheerness Steel*[107] a covenant in a lease for 125 years of a steel works not "to erect make or maintain or suffer to be erected made or maintained any building erection alterations or improvements nor to make or suffer to be made any change or addition whatsoever in or to the said premises save in connection with the use of the said

---

[102] *Bishop v Elliott* (1855) 11 Ex. 113; *Dumergue v Rumsey* (1863) 33 L.J. (Ex.) 88; *Leschallas v Woolf* [1908] 1 Ch. 641.

[103] [1908] 1 Ch. 641 (unaffected on this point by *New Zealand Government Property Corp v HM&S Ltd* [1982] Q.B. 1145).

[104] [1920] 1 Ch. 326.

[105] See also *Thresher v East London Waterworks Co Ltd* (1824) 2 B. & C. 608 (covenant to repair erections and buildings held to prohibit removal of brick lime kiln).

[106] *Naylor v Collinge* (1807) 1 Taunt. 19; *Thresher v East London Waterworks Co Ltd*, above.

[107] [2013] EWHC 1658 (Ch.).

premises for such industrial purpose as may from time to time be approved by the Lessors under [the user clause]" was held, in the context of the lease as a whole, not to be sufficiently clear to have the effect of excluding the tenant's right to remover tenant's fixtures.

Older leases sometimes contain a covenant to deliver up the demised premises together with a long list of specified articles, followed by general words such as "together with all other fixtures". Whether or not this has the effect of excluding the right to remove trade fixtures is a question of construction of the particular covenant. Where the particular items are landlord's fixtures, the ejusdem generis rule[108] is likely to be applied to restrict the general words to landlord's fixtures. Thus, in *Bishop v Elliott*[109] a covenant to deliver up at the end of the term the demised premises "together with all locks, keys, bars, bolts, marble and other chimney pieces, foot paces, slabs and other fixtures and articles in the nature of fixtures which should at any time during the term be fixed or fastened to the said demised premises" was held not to include tenant's fixtures.[110] In other cases, however, the correct conclusion may be that the general words were intended to extend to all fixtures of whatever nature.[111]

## Time during which tenant's fixtures may be removed

**25–37**  Once it is established that the item in question is a tenant's fixture, then the tenant has a right to remove it during the tenancy. That right continues for such time as the tenant continues in possession of the demised premises as tenant, whether or not under the same tenancy.[112] Particular points arise, however, out of the different circumstances in which the tenancy may come to an end.

### (a)  Forfeiture

**25–38**  Technically, the lease is forfeit from the date of peaceable re-entry or the date of service of the claim form, depending on which method the landlord employs.[113] However, in the case of forfeiture by proceedings, the tenant has at least until judgment for possession to remove fixtures.[114] It may be that his right continues for such time thereafter as he remains in possession of the premises,[115] or for a reasonable time thereafter (by analogy with the position where unreasonably

---

[108] See para.4–16, above.

[109] (1855) 11 Ex. 113.

[110] See also *Dumergue v Rumsey* 33 L.J. (Ex.) 88; *Lambourn v McLellan* [1903] 2 Ch. 268.

[111] See *Wilson v Whately* (1860) 1 J. & H. 436, in which the listed items were not limited to things which were obviously landlord's fixtures.

[112] *New Zealand Government Property Corp v H. M. & S. Ltd* [1982] Q.B. 1145.

[113] See paras 27–74 to 27–76, below.

[114] *Fitzherbert v Shaw* (1789) 1 Hy. Bl. 258; *Heap v Barton* (1852) 12 C.B. 274.

[115] See *Penton v Robart* (1801) 2 East 88, per Lord Kenyon at 91: "Here the defendant did no more than he had a right to do; he was in fact still in possession of the premises at the time the things were taken away, and therefore there is no pretence to say that he had abandoned his right to them". See, however, the note on this case in *Woodfall: Landlord and Tenant* (London: Sweet & Maxwell), Vol.I, Ch.13, s.5.

short notice is given).[116] It has been held that where the tenancy is forfeited by peaceable re-entry, the right to remove fixtures is lost.[117] In either case, the right to remove fixtures would, of course, revive if relief from forfeiture were to be granted.

### (b) Surrender

Where the tenancy is surrendered and the tenant vacates without removing his fixtures, he will generally have lost the right of removal. Where following the surrender he remains in possession under a new tenancy, then whether he has lost the right to remove his fixtures is a question of construction of the deed of surrender. If the deed is silent, or where the surrender is by operation of law, the right of removal will be carried forward into the new tenancy. In *New Zealand Government Property Corp v HM&S Ltd*[118] Dunn L.J. summarised the law as follows:

25–39

> "I believe the true rule at common law to be that a tenant has the right to remove tenant's fixtures so long as he is in possession as a tenant, whether by holding over, or as a statutory tenant under the Rent Acts, or on an extension of a lease of business premises under Part II of the Landlord and Tenant Act 1954 .... If the tenant surrenders his lease and vacates the premises without removing the tenant's fixtures, then he is held to have abandoned them. But if he surrenders his lease, either expressly or by operation of law, and remains in possession under a new lease, it is a question of construction of the instrument of surrender whether or not he has also given up his right to remove his fixtures. If nothing is said, then the common law rule applies, and he retains his right to remove the fixtures so long as he is in possession as a tenant."

It was held in that case that the grant of a new tenancy did not result in the tenant losing the right to remove trade fixtures installed under the previous tenancy.

### (c) Expiry by effluxion of time

Where a fixed-term tenancy ends and the tenant vacates without removing his fixtures, the right of removal is lost.[119] If the tenant remains in possession on sufferance, it is probable that his right survives for the period for which he holds over.[120] If he holds over as tenant under statute, for example, as a statutory tenant under the Rent Act 1977 or on a continuation tenancy under Pt II of the Landlord and Tenant Act 1954, his right of removal survives for the period of holding over.

25–40

### (d) Notice to quit

Where the tenancy is terminated by notice to quit, the right of removal ends on the expiry of the notice. However, where the length of notice required to

25–41

---

[116] See para.25–41, below.
[117] *Re Palmiero* [1999] 3 E.G.L.R. 27 (Mr Registrar Jaques) applying *Pugh v Arton* (1869) LR 8 Eq. 626.
[118] [1982] Q.B. 1145.
[119] *Lee v Risdon* (1816) 7 Taunt. 188; *Lyde v Russell* (1830) 1 B. & Ad. 394.
[120] *Leader v Homewood* (1858) 5 C.B.N.S. 546.

determine it is too short to allow the fixtures to be removed, the right of removal would appear to extend for a reasonable time after the tenancy has ended.[121] The same is true where the tenancy is a tenancy at will.[122] If the tenant holds over under statute, the right survives for the period of holding over.

## Assignment of the right of removal

**25–42**     The right to remove tenant's fixtures can be assigned to a third party along with the tenant's interest in the fixtures themselves.[123] In such a case the third party may enter the premises to remove the fixtures.[124]

## Whether the tenant is obliged to remove tenant's fixtures

**25–43**     The question whether or not the tenant is liable (as opposed to entitled) to remove tenant's fixtures at the end of the lease frequently occurs in practice in dilapidations cases. This is usually because the presence of the relevant fixtures detracts from the value of the premises on the term date. For example, a failure to remove shop fittings from retail premises, or partitioning, specialist air conditioning or computer installations from an office building, may make the premises less attractive to an incoming tenant who wishes to fit out the building to his own specification. In such a case, the landlord will have no choice other than to remove the fixtures at his own expense, or run the risk of a potential loss of value. For this reason, schedules of dilapidation frequently require the outgoing tenant to remove his fixtures and fittings.

Fitting out work which consists of chattels causes no difficulty, because the tenant is liable to remove chattels by virtue of the express or implied covenant to deliver up.[125] However, the position regarding fitting out work which consists of tenant's fixtures is more difficult, and is not covered by direct authority.

The general principle was said in *Never-Stop Railway (Wembley) Ltd v British Empire Exhibition (1924) Inc*[126] to be that, absent express agreement, the tenant is under no obligation to remove anything that has become part of the demised premises on quitting the premises at the end of the term. In that case, a licence had been granted to construct and operate a railway line, and the issue was whether the licensee was under an implied obligation to remove the railway and associated structures following the determination of the licence. Lawrence J. held that no such obligation was to be implied. He said:

> "[Counsel] contended as a proposition of law that, apart from any express or implied agreement, if a freeholder grants to A. a licence to occupy part of his land for a purpose involving the erection on such land of a building for A.'s sole use during the currency of the licence, then, at the termination of the licence, A. is bound not only to remove himself and all

[121] *Smith v City Petroleum Co Ltd* [1940] 1 All E.R. 260.
[122] *Re Roberts* (1878) 10 Ch. D. 100.
[123] *Cumberland Union Banking Co v Maryport Hematite Iron & Steel Co Ltd (No.2)* [1892] 1 Ch. 415; *Mancetter Developments Ltd v Garmanson Ltd (No.2)* [1986] 1 All E.R. 449.
[124] *Saint v Pilley* (1875) L.R. 10 Exch. 137.
[125] See para.14–06, above.
[126] [1926] 1 Ch. 877.

his goods and chattels from the land, but also to take down and remove the building which he has erected. No authority in support of any such general proposition was produced; and, in the absence of any such authority, I decline to accept it as sound. In the case of landlord and tenant, it is well settled that, in the absence of an agreement to the contrary, any building erected by the tenant upon the demised land immediately becomes part of the land itself, and at the expiration of the lease reverts to the landlord. In such a case, unless the building has been erected in contravention of some stipulation in the lease, the landlord obviously has no right to compel the tenant to take it down and remove it. The relationship of licensor and licensee which existed here seems to me to present an a fortiori case."

If, therefore, tenant's fixtures are, unless and until removed, part of the demised premises, the tenant cannot be under any obligation to remove them when the lease ends. The relevant distinction between a fixture and chattel is that a fixture has become part of the land and a chattel has not.[127] It seems clear that a tenant's fixture is simply a species of fixture, so that it is, until removed, part of the land.[128] Thus, in *Elitestone v Morris*[129] Lord Lloyd said of tenant's fixtures that they are:

" ... fixtures in the full sense of the word (and therefore part of the realty)."

Likewise, in *Legal & General Assurance Society Ltd v Expeditors International (UK) Ltd*[130] Lewison J. said:

" ... in my judgment the premises will include anything which in law has become part of the premises by annexation. A fixture installed by the tenant for the purposes of his trade become part of the premises as soon as it is installed, although the tenant retains a right to sever the fixture on termination of the tenancy."

On this basis, the tenant is not obliged to remove his fixtures when the lease ends. It is thought that this is the correct analysis.[131]

Nonetheless, an obligation to remove tenant's fixtures may arise in a variety of ways, as follows.

    **25–44**

### (a)  *Express obligation to remove*

A well-drafted modern lease may contain an express obligation to remove tenant's fixtures at the end of the term. Alternatively, such an obligation may be found in a licence for alterations. Where this is the case, the tenant must remove

    **25–45**

---

[127] See para.25–01 to 25–06, above; *Crossley Bros Ltd v Lee* [1908] 1 K.B. 86; and see generally *Megarry and Wade: The Law of Real Property*, 8th edn (London: Sweet & Maxwell, 2012), Ch.23.
[128] *Gibson v Hammersmith & City Railway Co Ltd* (1863) 2 Drew & Sim. 603; *Bain v Brand* (1876) 1 App. Cas. 762; *Crossley Bros Ltd v Lee*, above; *Elitestone v Morris* [1997] 1 W.L.R. 687; *Megarry and Wade: The Law of Real Property*, 8th edn (London: Sweet & Maxwell, 2012), para.23–012. *Re Hulse* [1905] 1 Ch. 406 contains (at 411) a dictum to the effect that tenant's fixtures do not become part of the freehold but this is not thought to be the correct analysis.
[129] [1997] 1 W.L.R. 687 at 691.
[130] [2007] 1 P. & C. R. 5 at [32] (on appeal: [2007] 2 P. & C. R. 10).
[131] The same view is expressed in *Woodfall: Landlord and Tenant* (London: Sweet & Maxwell), Vol.I, para.13.148, and *Megarry and Wade: The Law of Real Property*, 8th edn (London: Sweet & Maxwell, 2012), para.23–012.

his fixtures, and failure to do so will render him liable for damages. In an appropriate case, the damages will be assessed by reference to the reasonable cost of removing the fixtures.[132]

### (b) Express obligation to deliver up possession

**25–46**  Most commercial leases will contain, in one form or another, an obligation to deliver up the premises at the end of the term. Such obligation may expressly exclude tenant's fixtures (for example, the obligation may be to yield up the demised premises "excluding tenant's fixtures" or some similar formulation). It is sometimes argued that, by implication, this is to be read as imposing on the tenant a positive obligation to remove tenant's fixtures. Whilst each case will depend on its own facts, it is not thought that this will usually be the correct construction. The better view is that such exclusions are inserted simply to make it clear that the obligation to deliver up does not affect the tenant's ordinary right to remove his fixtures, not that he is positively obliged to exercise that right.[133]

### (c) Express obligation to deliver up in good and tenantable condition

**25–47**  An obligation to deliver up the premises in good and tenantable condition may be held to require the removal of redundant fixtures. Thus, in *Shortlands Investments Ltd v Cargill*[134] the tenant of office premises covenanted to keep the interior of the premises and the landlord's fixtures properly cleansed and in good and tenantable repair and condition and to yield up the premises in that condition. H.H. Judge Bowsher QC held that he was liable to remove the following redundant items installed during the term:

(1)  Clips fixed to a heating unit to hold cables installed by the tenant but which had since been removed. The tenant argued that the clips were in good condition and therefore that there was no disrepair. The judge rejected that contention on the ground that the heating unit was a landlord's fixture, and leaving it with redundant clips affixed to it was not leaving it in good and tenantable repair and condition.

(2)  Ventilation ducts installed to serve equipment which had since been removed. The judge held the tenant liable without giving reasons.

(3)  Halon gas fire extinguishers which had been installed by the tenant as ancillary to other fire protection equipment which the tenant had since removed. The tenant argued it was under no obligation to remove the extinguishers. The judge rejected that argument on the grounds that: the equipment left behind was incomplete; it would not be acceptable to an incoming tenant; the question was not "was the equipment left in good and tenantable condition", but "were the premises as a whole delivered up in good and tenantable condition", as to which the answer was no, because the

---

[132]  See paras 32–10 to 32–12, below.
[133]  See further paras 25–35 and 25–36, above.
[134]  [1995] 1 E.G.L.R. 51.

premises were delivered up with some redundant equipment which would have to be removed to make the premises usable.

It might perhaps be objected that the judge's approach was too wide, on the basis that a covenant to yield up in good and tenantable condition is primarily concerned with the making good of defects in the subject-matter of the covenant, and not with the removal of any part of that subject-matter.[135] Nonetheless, it seems wrong in principle that the tenant should be able with impunity to leave behind items which he himself has caused to become redundant or incomplete or unusable by removing the remainder of the installation of which they were originally part. It can be said that, in such a case, (i) the subject matter of the covenant, regarded as a whole, is properly to be regarded as being physically defective, because redundant items have been affixed to, and made part of, it, and (ii) the appropriate remedial work is to remove the items in question so as to restore the subject matter to good and tenantable condition. It is thought that the decision in *Shortlands* can be justified on this basis.

In the Australian case of *Wincant Pty Ltd v South Australia*,[136] the tenant, with the landlord's consent and prior to taking occupation, carried out substantial fit out works, including the installation of partitioning. The lease contained a covenant at the end of the term peaceably to yield up to the landlord the premises in good and substantial repair and condition reasonable wear and tear excepted together with (among other things) all improvements and additions made to the premises and all landlord's fixtures. The tenant failed to remove any of the works on vacating. The premises had been let as open space, and the works would have to be removed before the premises could be re-let. It was held by the Supreme Court of South Australia that no general obligation to remove fixtures could be implied. However, the majority (Matheson J. and Doyle C.J., Olsson J. dissenting) held that the covenant to yield up obliged the tenant to deliver up the premises in good repair having regard to the condition in which they were when possession was taken. The effect of the presence of the works was that the premises were not in such repair, so that the tenant was in breach. This goes considerably further than *Shortlands*, and it is doubtful to what extent it would be followed in England. Given (among other things) the principle that an obligation to repair is concerned with the making good of physical damage,[137] it is not easy to see how an obligation to deliver up in repair can properly be interpreted as requiring the removal of lawfully installed fixtures, at least where they have not become redundant in the sense considered above. Thus, for example, in *Commercial Union Life Assurance Co Ltd v Label Ink Ltd*[138] H.H. Judge Rich QC (sitting as a Deputy High Court Judge) said that he did not see how the presence of certain shelves and cupboard units in a workshop, which were said to be an unauthorised alteration or addition, could be classified as a disrepair.

---

[135] See paras 8–12 to 8–14, above.
[136] [1997] 69 S.A.S.R. 126.
[137] See Ch.8, above.
[138] [2001] L. & T.R. 29. Note that the question of disrepair arose in that case in the context of whether or not the tenant had complied with a condition precedent in a break option, and the judge's construction of the condition precedent was subsequently disapproved by the Court of Appeal in *Fitzroy House Epworth Street (No.1) v The Financial Times* [2006] 2 E.G.L.R. 13.

## (d)   Implied term

**25–48**   The principles applicable to implied terms are considered in Ch.1, above. In most cases, it is thought that it will be difficult to imply a term that the tenant is obliged to remove tenant's fixtures at the end of the lease. Thus, in *Never-Stop Railway (Wembley) Ltd v British Empire Exhibition (1924) Inc*[139] Lawrence J., in rejecting the argument that a licensee was under an implied obligation to remove a railway and associated structures erected by him during the course of the licence, said:

> "The absence of any express agreement [for the removal of the items] is, in my opinion, not without significance. If it had been the intention of the parties that the plaintiffs should be obliged to remove the erections and other structures, I should have expected that the agreements would have contained some provision …. that at the expiration or sooner determination of the agreements the plaintiffs should take down and remove the erections and other structures, and restore and make good the sites thereof to the satisfaction of the defendants …. I am of opinion that no such implication as the defendants desire the Court to make can fairly be made merely from the terms of the written agreements. …. The mere fact that the defendants do not desire to retain or make use of the erections and other structures, does not, in my judgment, afford any reason for making the desired implication."

The claim based on an implied term likewise failed in the Australian case of *Wincant Pty Ltd v South Australia.*[140]

## (e)   Where the fixture was installed in breach of covenant

**25–49**   In some cases, tenant's fixtures will have been installed in breach of covenant (for example, the covenant against alterations). In that event, the tenant may be liable in an appropriate case to pay damages equating to the cost of removal. However, it should be noted that the relevant breach will usually consist not in failing to remove the fixtures but in putting them up in the first place. If so, the limitation period will start to run when the fixtures are installed, with the result that by the time the lease ends, the landlord's right of action may be statute-barred.[141] The position would be different if the covenant to deliver up were to be construed as requiring the premises to be yielded up at the end of the term with any unlawful alterations removed, because the relevant breach would not occur until the end of the term and time would not start to run until then.

## Exercise of the right of removal

**25–50**   The tenant must make good any damage caused to the premises as the result of (i) installing tenant's fixtures, and (ii) removing them. It was said in *Foley v Addenbroke*[142] that the tenant must leave the premises in such a state as would be most useful and beneficial to the lessors or those who might next take the premises and must not leave the premises in such a state as not to be conveniently applicable to the same purpose. This was interpreted by Dillon L.J. in *Mancetter*

[139] [1926] 1 Ch. 877. See para.25–43 above, in which the relevant facts are set out.
[140] Above.
[141] See para.26–18, below.
[142] (1844) 13 M. & W. 174.

*Developments Ltd v Garmanson Ltd*[143] as meaning that the tenant must make good the premises to the extent of their being left in a reasonable condition. Sir George Waller in the same case formulated the duty as being "to restore the realty to its condition before the original lease was granted". In that case the tenant had installed extractor fans and pipes for use in its chemical business, and in the course of installing them, cut holes in the outside walls of the premises. It was held that when the fixtures were removed there was a duty to fill in the holes. The court rejected an argument that the duty was limited to making good any extra damage caused by the removal. It is not clear, however, to what extent the duty extends to redecorating after removal,[144] or to matters which are de minimis, such as the filling of screw holes or nail holes.[145]

Failure to make good after removal will generally constitute a breach of the covenants to repair and yield up in repair. It also constitutes the tort of waste.[146] In *Mancetter Developments Ltd v Garmanson Ltd*[147] Dillon L.J. analysed the duty as follows:

"[T]he liability to make good the damage is a condition of the tenant's right to remove tenant's fixtures; therefore removal of the fixtures without making good the damage, being in excess of the tenant's right of removal, is waste, actionable in tort, just as much as removal by the tenant of a landlord's fixture which the tenant has no right to remove is waste."

It is not clear whether an action for waste will lie against the tenant where there is a parallel right of action in contract on the covenant to repair and yield up in repair.[148] However, it sometimes happens that fixtures are removed by a person who is not the tenant, for example, a mortgagee or a purchaser of the tenant's business including its trade fixtures. Failure to make good on the part of such person will likewise constitute waste, and this will be the landlord's only remedy against him because, not being the tenant, he is not liable on the covenants to repair and yield up in repair.[149] The tenant will nonetheless remain liable on his covenants, so that the landlord will have a right of action against both.

## Wrongful removal of fixtures

Removal of a fixture which the tenant is not entitled to remove constitutes (a) waste,[150] and (b) (depending on the circumstances) breach of the covenants to repair and yield up.[151] Depending on the precise terms of the covenant, it may also amount to a breach of the covenant against alterations. In addition, the taking away and disposal of a fixture which has been unlawfully severed constitutes unlawful interference with goods.

The landlord's remedies are as follows:

**25–51**

---

[143] [1986] 1 All E.R. 449.
[144] See *Re De Falbe* [1901] Ch. 523; *Spyer v Phillipson* [1931] 2 Ch. 183.
[145] *Mancetter Developments Ltd v Garmanson Ltd*, above, per Dillon L.J. at 454.
[146] See para.21–12 et seq., above.
[147] Above.
[148] See para.21–17, above.
[149] See the facts of *Mancetter Developments Ltd v Garmanson Ltd*, above.
[150] See para.21–12 et seq., above.
[151] See para.18–02 et seq., above.

(1)　Where he discovers the proposed removal before it occurs, he may be entitled to an injunction prohibiting removal;[152]

(2)　Even after severance and removal the item remains the landlord's property. It follows that he may be entitled to an injunction requiring the tenant to return it. Where the tenancy is still in being he may even be entitled to a mandatory injunction requiring the tenant to reinstate the item;[153]

(3)　Damages. It has been held that these are to be assessed by reference to the value of the fixtures in their severed state and not as part of the premises.[154] However, it is thought that in an appropriate case there is no reason why damages should not reflect the diminution in the value of the premises as a result of the removal of the item.

## LIABILITY TO REPAIR FIXTURES

### During the term

**25–52**　An article which has become a fixture (whether or not it is removable by the tenant as a tenants fixture) is part of the demised premises for as long as it remains affixed to the property.[155] It follows from this that a covenant to repair "the demised premises", or some similar formulation embracing the totality of what has been demised, will ordinarily apply to all fixtures, including tenant's fixtures.[156] The tenant could, of course, put an end to his obligation to repair a tenant's fixture during the term by removing it. However, there may well be practical reasons why it would not suit him to do this, and it is not thought that the existence of this possible anomaly casts any serious doubt on the proposition that the covenant to repair applies until the article is removed. Given that the fixture will become the landlord's property if the right of removal is not exercised, there is no reason why the parties should not have intended it to be kept in repair unless and until removed.

The above is subject to any indication to the contrary in the lease. For example, the covenant to repair might be expressed to apply to "the demised premises including any landlord's fixtures". This may be construed as excluding tenant's fixtures.[157] Problems may arise where the covenant, when properly construed, applies only to the original demised buildings. Whilst it will not extend to separate new buildings put up during the term, the extent to which it applies to fixtures subsequently attached to the demised buildings may well involve difficult questions of construction.[158]

---

[152] *Sunderland v Newton* (1830) 3 Sim. 450.

[153] *Phillips v Lamdin* [1949] 2 K.B. 33 (from which it appears that an injunction requiring reinstatement will only be granted where damages would not be an adequate remedy, for example where (as in that case) the item in question (an Adam door) cannot be replaced with an equivalent).

[154] *McGregor v High* (1870) 21 L.T. 803; *Barff v Probyn* (1895) 64 L.J. Q.B. 557.

[155] See para.25–43, above.

[156] Cf. *Wincant Pty Ltd v South Australia* [1997] 69 S.A.S.R. 126 (Australia). See further paras 7–20 to 7–22, above.

[157] *New Zealand Government Property Corp v HM&S Ltd* [1982] Q.B. 1145, per Lord Denning M.R. at 1155; *Ocean Accident & Guarantee Corp v Next Plc* [1996] 2 E.G.L.R. 84.

[158] See *Field v Curnick* [1926] 2 K.B. 374.

The covenant to repair imposed on the landlord by s.11 of the Landlord and Tenant Act 1985 in short leases of dwelling-houses[159] does not apply to anything which the lessee is entitled to remove from the dwelling-house.[160] This would clearly include both tenant's fixtures and chattels owned by the tenant.

## At the end of the term

The principles are the same as those considered in para.25–52, above. The covenant to yield up in repair would not, of course, apply to tenant's fixtures in respect of which the right of removal has been lawfully exercised. However, tenant's fixtures left in situ at the end of the term after the tenant has vacated form part of the premises yielded up, so that (subject to any indications to the contrary in the lease) the tenant would be in breach of covenant if they were not in a proper state of repair.

**25–53**

A contrary decision was reached in *Simmons v Dresden*[161] on a somewhat unusually-worded obligation. The tenant covenanted:

> "[A]t the expiration or sooner determination of the said term quietly to yield up the demised premises .... together with all additions and improvements thereto and all fixtures which during the said term may be affixed or fastened to or upon the demised premises (Tenant's or trade fixtures only excepted Provided always that the same shall be removed prior to the termination date and any damage caused by the removal thereof shall forthwith be made good) and any partitions fixtures and fittings which are not upon the demised premises at the date hereof shall be removed and any damage made good should the Landlord so require and if the Tenant shall not have complied with this clause at the expiry or sooner determination of the said term then the Landlord shall carry out the works and recover the costs of so doing from the Tenant."

H.H. Judge Seymour QC held that, on the proper construction of this provision, the landlord's sole remedy in respect of any partitions, fixtures or fittings not upon the premises at the date of the demise which he required to be removed and which were not removed was to remove them himself and recoup the cost of so doing from the tenants. If he did not exercise his option to require the removal of such items, no other obligation on the part of the tenants, such as to repair what was not removed, arose in substitution. Whilst this may have been the correct construction on the wording of the particular covenant in question, it is thought that the right view will usually be that items which have become part of the demised premises will become subject to the obligation to yield up in repair in the same way as the remainder of the premises.

---

[159] See para.20–17 et seq., above.
[160] Landlord and Tenant Act 1985 s.11(2)(c).
[161] [2004] EWHC 993 (TCC).

A SUGGESTED APPROACH TO ITEMS LEFT BEHIND ON, OR REMOVED
FROM, THE PREMISES AT THE END OF THE TENANCY

## Items left at the end of the tenancy

**25–54**    It frequently happens that at the end of the term the tenant vacates the demised premises leaving a number of items behind. These may range from the sort of rubbish usually associated with moving out (such as broken furniture or discarded files) to fixtures installed during the term, such as partitioning or light fittings. The following approach may help to determine the landlord's rights and remedies in respect of such items:

(1)   Is the item (a) a chattel, or (b) a fixture?
(2)   If the item is a chattel, then:
    (i)    it remains the property of the tenant;
    (ii)   if it has any value, the landlord may owe the tenant a duty to take reasonable care of it;[162]
    (iii)  the landlord has a right of action for breach of the express or implied covenant to deliver up with vacant possession.[163] The damages will include, where appropriate, the cost of removing the item.
(3)   If the item is a fixture, then:
    (i)    it becomes the property of the landlord;
    (ii)   depending upon the terms of the covenant to repair and yield up in repair, the tenant will generally be liable to deliver it up in repair;[164]
    (iii)  in the absence of express or implied provision to the contrary (either in the lease or any relevant licence for alterations) the tenant will usually not have been liable to remove it[165];
    (iv)   if the original installation of the item amounted to a breach of covenant (for example, the covenant against alterations), then (subject to the limitation period not having expired[166]) the landlord will have a right of action for breach of the covenant in question, and the damages may, where appropriate, include the cost of removal and making good.

## Items removed by the end of the tenancy

**25–55**    The converse to the above occurs where the tenant vacates the demised premises at the end of the tenancy taking with him items which the landlord would prefer him to have left behind. The following approach may assist in determining whether the tenant was entitled remove the item:

(1)   Is the item (a) a chattel, or (b) a fixture?

---

[162]  Cf. *Mitchell v Ealing LBC* [1979] Q.B. 1; Torts (Interference with Goods) Act 1977.
[163]  See para.14–06, above.
[164]  See para.25–52, above.
[165]  See paras 25–43 to 25–48, above.
[166]  See para.26–18, below.

(2)   If the item is a chattel, then it is removable in the absence of an express obligation to leave it behind.

(3)   If the item is a fixture, is it a tenant's fixture? This is to be answered by reference to the principles in para.25–24 et seq., above. If it is a tenant's fixture then it is removable in the absence of an express provision to the contrary.

(4)   If the item is a fixture but not a tenant's fixture it was not removable. The landlord's remedies are set out in para.25–51, above.

CHAPTER 26

# THE LANDLORD'S REMEDIES FOR BREACH OF COVENANT ON THE PART OF THE TENANT

## INTRODUCTORY

Once it is established that the tenant is in breach of covenant, it will be necessary    **26–01**
to consider carefully what remedies are open to the landlord, and which of them
is the appropriate one to use in the particular circumstances. In choosing between
them, it will be important to identify at an early stage the object sought to be
achieved by enforcing the covenant, and to select whatever remedy is most likely
to achieve that object. For example, where the overwhelming need is to get
certain urgent work done, and to argue afterwards about who is responsible, the
appropriate remedy will not be the same as where the landlord can afford to await
the result of litigation. Equally important will be the practicalities, such as
whether the tenant is solvent, and what his response to a particular course of
action is likely to be.

The purpose of this Chapter is to summarise the various remedies, and the
advantages and disadvantages of each, so as to enable a decision to be made as to
which to adopt in any given set of circumstances. Each remedy is then considered
in detail in the subsequent Chapters.

## REMEDIES DURING THE TERM

### The available remedies

The remedies available to the landlord in the event of a breach by the tenant of    **26–02**
his repairing obligations during the term are: (a) forfeiture; (b) damages; (c) to
enter, carry out the remedial works, and then claim the cost from the tenant; and
(d) specific performance of the tenant's repairing obligation.

### (a)    Forfeiture[1]

The effect of forfeiture is (subject to the court's power to grant relief) to bring the    **26–03**
term to a premature end. Its advantages are as follows:

(1)    As a general principle, relief is likely to be granted only on condition that
the tenant carries out the necessary remedial works within a time set by the

---

[1] See Ch.27, below.

[593]

court. If the tenant complies with the condition, the landlord will have succeeded in getting the works done at the tenant's expense;

(2) If the tenant does not apply for relief, or fails to comply with the conditions on which it is granted, the landlord will recover possession of the premises earlier than he would have done had the lease continued until its contractual term date. If market conditions for reletting are favourable, this will be to his advantage; and

(3) If the landlord recovers possession, damages for breach of the tenant's repairing obligations will be assessed by reference to the diminution in the value of the landlord's interest in the premises (as at the date of forfeiture) with vacant possession, as opposed to subject to the lease. This is likely to make a considerable difference to the amount recoverable.

**26–04** The disadvantages of forfeiture are as follows:

(1) It requires the prior service of a notice under s.146 of the Law of Property Act 1925, followed by a reasonable time for the tenant to carry out the necessary works;

(2) Where the Leasehold Property (Repairs) Act 1938 applies, and the tenant serves the requisite counter-notice, the leave of the court must be obtained before forfeiting;

(3) As a result of (1) and (2) above, there may be considerable delays before the landlord can forfeit;

(4) Relief from forfeiture, if granted, will relate back to the date of forfeiture. Accordingly, if the tenant applies for relief, there may be a long period in which it will not be known whether or not the lease has ended. This may give rise to problems in relation to such matters as collection of rent and enforcement of the other covenants in that period; and

(5) Forfeiture once effected is irrevocable. The tenant cannot be compelled to apply for relief. If he decides not to apply for relief, the landlord will have empty premises on his hands, and will have lost the benefit of the tenant's covenants. If market conditions are unfavourable, the landlord faces the prospect of a lengthy void before he can relet.

### (b)   Damages[2]

**26–05** A claim for damages alone during the term is not common. If successful, it results in the landlord receiving a sum of money in respect of the breach. However, there are the following disadvantages:

(1) Where the Leasehold Property (Repairs) Act 1938 applies, a s.146 notice must be served, and if the tenant serves a counter-notice, the leave of the court must be obtained before commencing the action;

(2) The measure of damages is limited to the amount by which the value of the landlord's reversion subject to the lease has been diminished by the

---

[2] See para.28–16 et seq. below.

breaches. Where the lease still has some time to run, it may be very difficult to establish a substantial, or indeed any, diminution;

(3)   Any damages awarded must be credited to the tenant in any claim for damages at the end of the term; and

(4)   The work does not get done.

### (c)   Carrying out the necessary remedial works and recovering the cost from the tenant[3]

This remedy is not available unless there is an express term in the lease entitling the landlord to enter, carry out the work, and recover the cost from the tenant (commonly now called a *"Jervis v Harris"* clause[4]). Where the lease contains such a provision, the advantages of using it are as follows:

**26–06**

(1)   The landlord has control over the carrying out of the work;

(2)   The work gets done without the need for lengthy litigation, which may be an extremely important consideration where the work is urgently required; and

(3)   The landlord recovers the cost of the work without needing to prove that the value of his reversion has been diminished.

The disadvantages are:

**26–07**

(1)   The tenant may refuse to allow access, in which case the landlord will have to apply for an injunction requiring the tenant to permit him to enter and carry out the work;

(2)   Even where the tenant is prepared to afford access in principle, there may be difficulties in agreeing appropriate times, working hours, and facilities (such as the provision of electricity for the landlord's contractors);

(3)   If the landlord's right of entry has not arisen for some reason (for example, because the requisite notice under the lease has not been given or is invalid, or because there are no breaches), his entry will be a trespass, and the tenant will be entitled to damages in respect of the disruption suffered;

(4)   The landlord must spend the money before being able to recover it;

(5)   It is probable that a term would be implied into the lease to the effect that the cost of the work must be reasonable. If so, then there will be much scope for the tenant to argue that the landlord's claim for the cost of the work is excessive.

### (d)   Specific performance of the tenant's repairing obligation[5]

Specific performance of the tenant's repairing obligation takes the form of an order by the court requiring the tenant to carry out the remedial work or such part of it as is specified in the order. The advantages of such an order are that:

**26–08**

---

[3]   See para.28–32 et seq. below.
[4]   After the Court of Appeal case of the same name: see para.28–39, below.
[5]   See para.28–02 et seq. below.

(1)   It gets the work done at the tenant's expense; and
(2)   If the tenant fails to comply with the order, he is in contempt of court, and is liable to be imprisoned or to have his assets sequestrated.

The disadvantages of specific performance are:

(1)   Unless the work can be convincingly shown to be urgent for some reason, specific performance is unlikely to be granted on an interim application, so that the landlord may have to wait for the trial before obtaining an order; and
(2)   The remedy is discretionary, and is not available as of right. The landlord will have to show a legitimate interest in having the covenant performed, and he may also have to show that the other remedies available to him are inadequate, or that he has good reasons for not pursuing them.

## Combining remedies

### (a)   Forfeiture

**26–09**   Forfeiture may be combined with a claim for damages, and it is usual for a landlord who forfeits by proceedings to claim damages in the proceedings in addition to seeking possession. Forfeiture cannot be combined with entering the premises and carrying out the work under an express right to that effect. If the landlord has already entered the premises and carried out the work, the right to forfeit for the disrepair[6] will have been waived,[7] and if he has not already done so, then he cannot do so once the lease has been forfeited, because the lease will have ended. A claim for specific performance is likewise inconsistent with an election to forfeit, and the inclusion of such a claim in a forfeiture action will prevent the action from being an effective forfeiture.[8]

### (b)   Damages

**26–10**   A claim for damages may be combined with a claim for forfeiture or a claim for specific performance. There is no reason in principle why a landlord who enters the premises, carries out the work and then sues for the cost cannot not at the same time bring a claim for damages, but it will only be in exceptional circumstances that he will have suffered loss over and above the cost of the work.

---

[6] But not any subsequent right to forfeit which arises by reason of the tenant's failure to pay for the works under a covenant to that effect.
[7] *Doe d. Rutzen v Lewis* (1836) 5 A. & E. 277. See para.27–05 et seq. below.
[8] *Calabar Properties v Seagull Autos* [1969] 1 Ch. 451.

## (c)  Entry to carry out the work followed by a claim for the cost

Apart from the possible addition of a claim for damages, this remedy stands alone. Any right of forfeiture for the disrepair will be waived, and (assuming the landlord to have done all the work) there will be nothing in respect of which specific performance could be ordered.

26–11

## (d)  Specific performance

A claim for specific performance may be combined with a claim for damages. No claim can be made for forfeiture. Specific performance cannot be combined with the remedy of entering, carrying out the work and claiming the cost from the tenant. If the landlord were already to have employed such remedy, there would be nothing which the tenant could be ordered to do; alternatively, if, having sought specific performance, the landlord were then to enter, carry out the work, and then claim the cost, his application for specific performance would have to be abandoned.

26–12

## The choice of remedy during the term

The advantages and disadvantages of each remedy, or combination of remedies, must be carefully weighed having regard to the particular facts of each case. The most important decision the landlord will need to make is whether or not to forfeit the lease. Given the fact that the tenant cannot be compelled to apply for relief, a landlord who forfeits must be prepared for the premises to be vacated. The extent to which this will be attractive will depend on the particular circumstances and the state of the market at the relevant time. If the landlord decides not to forfeit, the decision between the remaining remedies will again depend on the particular facts.

26–13

## REMEDIES AT THE END OF THE TERM

## Damages are the only remedy

Once the lease has ended, the only remedy is an action for damages.[9] Since the lease ceases to exist on the term date, forfeiture is no longer relevant. Similarly, the tenant's liability under the covenants ceases on the term date (save with regard to breaches existing at or before that date), so that performance of the covenants can no longer be specifically enforced. Any express provision entitling the landlord to enter, carry out repair works and recover the cost from the tenant would likewise no longer apply after the term date. It is important for the landlord to bear this in mind when deciding upon his strategy when the lease is approaching its end. If he decides to wait until the lease has ended, his only course will be to bring proceedings for damages.

26–14

---

[9]  See Chs 29 to 32, below.

## MODIFICATIONS OR SUSPENSION OF REMEDIES

### War damage

**26–15** Obligations to repair on the part of both landlord and tenant are modified or suspended in the case of war damage.[10] An obligation to repair, whether express or implied, and whether contained in a lease or a collateral agreement, does not extend to making good war damage.[11] Where, as a result of war damage, compliance with a covenant to repair is impracticable, or only practicable at an unreasonable cost, or of no substantial advantage to the person entitled to the benefit of the obligation, the obligation is suspended until the war damage is made good.[12]

Where an obligation to repair is modified or suspended, or an obligation to make good war damage is extinguished, then all rights and remedies arising out of non-fulfilment of the obligation, including all rights against a guarantor, are modified or suspended or extinguished accordingly.[13] Contracting out is not permitted.[14]

### Requisitioning

**26–16** No remedy for breach of a repairing covenant may be enforced in respect of damage occurring during a period in which premises are requisitioned under emergency powers.[15] However, the tenant remains liable for previous want of repair in so far as it continues during the period of requisitioning.[16]

### Long residential leases

**26–17** A tenant under a long tenancy to which Pt I of the Landlord and Tenant Act 1954 applies is entitled to limited relief from performance of his covenants, including covenants to repair and decorate.[17] These provisions are outside the scope of this work, and reference should be made to specialist textbooks on the subject.

---

[10] Landlord and Tenant (War Damage) Act 1939. See also Landlord and Tenant (War Damage) (Amendment) Act 1941; War Damage Act 1943. For the detailed provisions, reference should be made to the Acts themselves.

[11] Landlord and Tenant (War Damage) Act 1939 s.1.

[12] Landlord and Tenant (War Damage) Act 1939 s.1(2).

[13] Landlord and Tenant (War Damage) Act 1939 s.1(4).

[14] Landlord and Tenant (War Damage) Act 1939 s.21; Landlord and Tenant (War Damage) (Amendment) Act 1941 s.11.

[15] Landlord and Tenant (Requisitioned Land) Act 1944 s.1(1). For the provisions in detail, reference should be made to the Act itself.

[16] *Smiley v Townshend* [1950] 2 K.B. 311. For the effect of requisitioning on the tenant's liability for damages, see para.30–43, below. See also para.18–23 et seq. above.

[17] Landlord and Tenant Act 1954 s.16.

LIMITATION

## The limitation period

Where the obligation to repair is contained in a lease under seal, the relevant    **26–18**
period of limitation is twelve years from the date of the breach.[18] Where the lease
is not under seal, the relevant period is six years from the date of the breach.[19]
Where the covenant is to repair or keep in repair during the term, a fresh breach
occurs every day that the premises are out of repair.[20] The same is true where the
relevant breach is the complete destruction of the demised buildings and their
replacement with something different.[21] A breach of the covenant to yield up the
premises at the end of the term occurs on the last day of the term only, and the
relevant period of limitation starts to run on that day.

---

[18] Limitation Act 1980 s.8(1).
[19] Limitation Act 1980 s.5.
[20] *Maddock v Mallet* (1860) 12 C.L.R. 173; *Granada Theatres Limited v Freehold Investments (Leytonstone) Limited* [1959] Ch. 592 at 608; *Re King* [1962] 1 W.L.R. 632 (reversed on other grounds, [1963] Ch. 459); *Marshall v Bradford MDC* [2002] H.L.R. 20.
[21] *Maddock v Mallet*, above.

CHAPTER 27

**FORFEITURE**

INTRODUCTORY

## The nature of forfeiture

Forfeiture is the process whereby the landlord exercises a right under the lease to terminate it in the event of a default by the tenant, or the happening of a specified event, such as the tenant's bankruptcy. Its effect is to bring the lease, and any sub-leases derived out of it, to an end. The landlord becomes entitled to sue upon those covenants which come into effect at the termination of the lease, including the covenant to yield up in repair. Forfeiture is subject to a number of procedural restrictions, of which the most important are those imposed by s.146 of the Law of Property Act 1925 and the Leasehold Property (Repairs) Act 1938, both of which are considered below.[1] The tenant has the right to apply for relief from forfeiture,[2] and any sub-tenant has the right to apply for a vesting order under s.146(4) of the Law of Property Act 1925.[3]

27–01

## Advantages and disadvantages of forfeiture

The principal advantage of forfeiture is that the landlord will generally succeed in obtaining one or more of three things, namely possession of the premises, performance of the covenant to repair at no cost to himself, or damages. This is because, in the normal case, relief will only be granted on condition that the tenant carries out at least the more important of the works required in order to put the premises into proper repair. If the tenant obtains relief by complying with this condition, the landlord will have succeeded in getting the covenant performed at no cost to himself. If the tenant fails to get relief, the landlord will (i) recover possession, and (ii) be entitled to damages for breach of the covenant to yield up in repair. Those damages will be assessed on the basis that the lease has ended, and are therefore more likely to be substantial than would be the case if the term was still running.[4]

27–02

---

[1] See para.27–12 et seq. and 27–31 et seq., below.
[2] See para.27–77 et seq., below.
[3] See para.27–86 et seq., below.
[4] See Chs 29 to 32, below.

The principal disadvantage of forfeiture is that, once effected, it is irrevocable.[5] The tenant cannot be compelled to apply for relief. It follows that forfeiture will not be the right remedy if the landlord does not want vacant possession, unless he is confident that the tenant will apply for relief and comply with any conditions subject to which it is granted. A second potential disadvantage of forfeiture is that relief if granted relates back to the date of forfeiture. It follows that where the tenant applies for relief, it will not be known whether the lease has ended until the determination of the tenant's application. Until this has happened the landlord cannot enforce the repairing and other covenants of the lease. Forfeiture may therefore have estate management consequences which the landlord will have to bear in mind before deciding whether or not to forfeit.

## CONDITIONS PRECEDENT TO FORFEITURE AT COMMON LAW

### There must be a proviso for re-entry or forfeiture clause

27–03    A lease cannot be forfeited for breach of covenant unless it contains an express provision (called a proviso for re-entry or forfeiture clause) entitling the landlord to bring it to an end in the event of the tenant committing a breach of his obligations under the lease. A well-drafted lease will always contain such a provision. Its scope is a matter of construction, and in cases of doubt it is to be construed against the landlord.[6] The form of proviso for re-entry usually to be found will extend on its proper construction to breaches of all express and implied[7] obligations under the lease.

### There must be a breach of the tenant's obligations under the lease

27–04    The right of forfeiture will not arise unless the tenant has committed a breach of the relevant obligations under the lease. In practice, before contemplating forfeiture for disrepair, the landlord through his surveyor will generally have inspected the premises and compiled a schedule of dilapidations, and will have satisfied himself, with the benefit of legal advice if necessary, that breaches of covenant exist of a sufficiently serious nature to justify forfeiture.

### The right to forfeit for the breach must not have been waived

27–05    The occurrence of a breach entitling the landlord to forfeit gives him a right of election. He is not obliged to forfeit. But if he elects to treat the lease as continuing to exist, he waives the right to forfeit. Waiver of this type occurs where the landlord, with knowledge of the breach, does some unequivocal act

---

[5] See, for example, *GS Fashions Ltd v B & Q Plc* [1995] 1 E.G.L.R. 62 (landlord not entitled to contend that lease had not been forfeited following service of writ for forfeiture and defence admitting forfeiture).

[6] *Creery v Summersell & Flowerdew & Co* [1949] Ch. 751.

[7] Cf. *Doe d. Rains v Kneller* (1829) 4 C. & P. 3.

which recognises the continued existence of the lease.[8] It is well established that accepting rent due is such an act (and so also may be demanding rent due[9]). However, in cases other than those involving an acceptance of or demand for rent, the court is free to look at all the circumstances of the case to consider whether the act said to be a waiver is so unequivocal that, when considered objectively, it could only be regarded as having been done consistently with the continued existence of the tenancy.[10]

A breach of a covenant to repair is a continuing breach, in the sense that a fresh breach occurs every day the premises are out of repair.[11] It follows that an act of waiver with knowledge of the breach will waive the landlord's right to forfeit for disrepair up to the date of the act in question, but it will not affect the right to forfeit for that disrepair in so far as it remains in existence after the date of waiver.[12]

A right to forfeit for breach of a covenant to repair after notice is not waived by the landlord giving the tenant further time in which to do the work (although the right is suspended for that period),[13] or by acceptance of rent pending compliance with the notice.[14] It may also be that it is not waived by acceptance of rent after the notice has expired.[15]

## Acceptance of rent after service of section 146 notice

Where the landlord serves a s.146 notice for breach of the covenant to repair, and subsequently accepts rent, he does not need to serve a fresh notice before forfeiting, provided that the condition of the premises remains the same (or gets worse).[16] Thus, in *Penton v Barnett*[17] the landlord served a notice under s.14(1) of the Conveyancing Act 1881[18] on September 22, 1896, requiring the tenant to execute the repairs specified in the notice within three months. The tenant failed to comply with the notice. On January 14, 1897, the landlord began proceedings for forfeiture. On that date the premises were in the same state of disrepair as at the time of the notice. The landlord also claimed in the proceedings the quarter's rent due in arrears on December 25, 1896. The tenant argued that by claiming rent

**27–06**

---

[8] *Central Estates (Belgravia) Ltd v Woolgar (No.2)* [1972] 1 W.L.R. 1048. See generally Woodfall *Landlord and Tenant* (London: Sweet & Maxwell) Vol.I, at para.17.092 et seq.

[9] This was assumed to be correct in *Expert Clothing Service & Sales Ltd v Hillgate House Ltd* [1986] Ch. 340. However, the point was left open by the Court of Appeal in *Greenwood Reversions Ltd v World Environment Foundation Ltd* [2009] L.& T.R. 2.

[10] *Expert Clothing Service & Sales Ltd v Hillgate House Ltd*, above.

[11] *Doe d. Baker v Jones* (1850) 5 Exch. 498; *Coward v Gregory* (1866) L.R. 2 C.P. 153; *Spoor v Green* (1874) L.R. 9 Ex. 99, per Bramwell B. at 111. See further para.26–18, above.

[12] *Doe d. Hemmings v Durnford* (1832) 2 C. & J. 667; *Doe d. Baker v Jones*, above; *Bennett v Herring* (1857) 3 C.B. (N.S.) 370; *New River Co Ltd v Crumpton* [1917] 1 K.B. 762.

[13] *Doe d. Rankin v Brindley* (1832) 4 B. & Ad. 84.

[14] *Doe d. Rankin v Brindley*, above; *Doe d. Baker v Jones*, above.

[15] *Fryett d. Harris v Jeffreys* (1795) 1 Esp. 393. This seems unsound.

[16] *Penton v Barnett* [1898] 1 Q.B. 276; *Farimani v Gates* [1984] 2 E.G.L.R. 66; *Greenwich LBC v Discreet Selling Estates Ltd* [1990] 2 E.G.L.R. 65. For a detailed discussion of s.146 notices, see para.27–12 et seq., below.

[17] Above.

[18] The statutory predecessor of the Law of Property Act 1925 s.146.

due after the notice the landlord had waived the right to forfeit for the breaches specified in the notice and that a fresh notice was required.[19] His argument was rejected on the ground that the breaches specified in the notice continued between December 25, 1896, and January 14, 1897, and the landlord was entitled to forfeit for those breaches without a new notice.

The same principle applies where the condition of the premises has deteriorated following the service of the notice.[20] Thus, in *Greenwich LBC v Discreet Selling Estates Ltd*[21] s.146 notices in respect of breaches of the covenant to repair were served on July 20, 1983. On September 23, 1983, the landlord applied for leave under the Leasehold Property (Repairs) Act 1938 to commence proceedings for forfeiture. Leave was granted on January 16, 1985. The landlord continued to demand and accept rent up to and including the rent due on March 25, 1985. On April 16, 1985, the landlord began forfeiture proceedings. Between July 1983 and April 1985 some minimal repairs were done but otherwise the notices were not complied with, and there was probably further deterioration during the period. The Court of Appeal held that no new notice was necessary. Staughton L.J. said in the course of his judgment:

> "If, as [counsel] submits is the case, the *ratio* of [*Penton v Barnett*] is that the previous notice is still sufficient in the case of a continuing breach where the condition of the premises remains the same, that must also be the law where the condition of the premises has been allowed to get worse. It is said that the landlord might allow months or years to pass by without giving any further notice and then suddenly seek to forfeit the premises, to the surprise of the tenant, relying on his old notice long ago. In such a case the long delay would no doubt be taken into account in exercising the discretion to grant relief against forfeiture, or it may be that some doctrine of acquiescence or estoppel at common law or equity would come to the aid of the tenant."

27–07    It should be noted, however, that where entirely new breaches have occurred since the date of service of the first notice, a second notice will be necessary if the landlord wishes to rely on the new breaches, whether or not rent is accepted in the meantime, because the new breaches will not have been specified in the first notice. The extent to which a particular defect is properly to be regarded as a new breach requiring a new notice, as opposed to a breach already specified in the first notice which has further deteriorated since that notice was served (in which case no new notice is necessary), is a question of fact and degree in each case.

The position is less clear where the tenant carries out some, but not all, of the work specified in the notice, and the landlord then accepts rent. It is thought that by virtue of the principle in *Penton v Barnett* the landlord will not be prevented from forfeiting in respect of the unremedied breaches. This accords with *New River Co Ltd v Crumpton*,[22] in which the landlord served a notice on the tenant on December 11, 1914 specifying breaches of the covenant to repair by reference to a schedule which contained a long list of items. The tenant remedied three of the

---

[19] It appears to have been assumed that claiming the rent in the proceedings was capable of amounting to a waiver. This does not represent the modern law: see *Canas Property Co Ltd v KL Television Services Ltd* [1970] 2 Q.B. 433, in which it was said that the writ for possession should claim rent up to the date of service and mesne profits thereafter.

[20] *Greenwich LBC v Discreet Selling Estates Ltd*, above.

[21] [1990] 2 E.G.L.R. 65.

[22] [1917] 1 K.B. 762.

items but no others. The landlord continued to accept rent until that due on December 25, 1915. On March 22, 1916 the landlord commenced a forfeiture action. Rowlatt J. held that no new notice was required. His reasoning appears from the following passage from his judgment:

> "[T]he present case admittedly differs from that of *Penton v Barnett* in this respect, that here the tenant had done some partial repairs in obedience to the notice, and therefore the physical condition of the premises was to that extent altered. But what I think the Court of Appeal meant to hold was that the condition of the premises at the time of action brought must be such that the notice shall still be applicable, that is to say, that there shall still be certain of the repairs specified in the schedule which to the knowledge of the tenant are still unexecuted. Here the tenant had done only three items out of a long list of required repairs. She knew what she was required to do and what she had left undone, and that, in my opinion, is enough."

However, a different result was reached in *Guillemard v Silverthorne*.[23] In that case some repairs had been done since the notice,[24] and the landlord accepted rent. Ridley J. held that a new notice was necessary. It has been suggested that the difference in result between the two cases arises wholly from the different facts.[25] However, it is thought that they are difficult to reconcile.[26]

It is difficult to see any basis for distinguishing between the case where the tenant carries out some but very few of the repairs required by the notice, and the case where he carries out many, but not all, of those repairs. It is thought that in each case acceptance of rent does not prevent the landlord from forfeiting for those breaches that remain unremedied. This is consistent with the approach of Rowlatt J. in *New River Co Ltd v Crumpton*,[27] and with the following passage from the judgment of Staughton L.J. in *Greenwich LBC v Discreet Selling Estates Ltd*[28]:     **27–08**

> "It seems to me that a notice under section 146 asserts not only that the tenant is presently in breach but also that he will continue to be in breach unless and until he carries out the repairs required. It must necessarily assert that, if the landlord is to be able to rely at the trial on further delay which will have occurred up to the commencement of proceedings. In those circumstances I see no practical need for any fresh notice if a landlord wishes to rely on that continuing breach as a ground of forfeiture in the future and no legal reason why a fresh notice should be required in respect of the same defects."

## Waiver in practice

For the above reasons the law relating to waiver is generally irrelevant in the case of forfeiture for breach of the covenant to repair. However, it is suggested that there are a number of reasons why it is good practice not to demand or accept rent in respect of the rental period in which forfeiture is to be effected (whether by the commencement of proceedings or by physical re-entry). First, where rent is payable in advance, the tenant may argue that acceptance of rent waives the right     **27–09**

---

[23] (1908) 99 L.T. 584.
[24] It is not clear from the report to what extent the notice was complied with.
[25] *Greenwich LBC v Discreet Selling Estates Ltd* [1990] 2 E.G.L.R. 65 at 68A.
[26] This seems to have been the view of Rowlatt J. himself in *New River Co Ltd v Crumpton* [1917] 1 K.B. 762 (at 766).
[27] Above.
[28] [1990] 2 E.G.L.R. 65.

to forfeit not only for breaches occurring up to the date of acceptance but also for the remainder of the period in respect of which the rent is payable. Whilst it is not thought that such an argument would succeed,[29] there is no point in taking the risk of the tenant running it and thereby delaying the proceedings whilst a preliminary point is litigated. Second, the principle that acceptance of rent after the service of a s.146 notice does not prevent the landlord from forfeiting without a further notice was described by the Court of Appeal in *Farimani v Gates*[30] as "puzzling and surprising". However, the Court regarded itself as bound by the earlier decision of the Court of Appeal in *Penton v Barnett*.[31] The possibility of that case being held in the Supreme Court to have been wrongly decided, or of the court distinguishing it where the facts are different, cannot therefore be ruled out.

A landlord who is concerned to maintain his income flow will not be unduly prejudiced by refusing rent for the rental period in which forfeiture is effected. The arrears of rent can be claimed in the proceedings, and if they remain unpaid after the commencement of proceedings, the landlord can make an application in the proceedings under CPR Pt 25 for an interim payment representing the arrears.[32]

## Waiver by service of notice to repair

27–10   Where the lease contains a general covenant to repair and a covenant to repair defects specified in a notice given by the landlord, the landlord is entitled to forfeit for breach of the former without giving notice under the latter, since the two covenants are separate and distinct.[33] However, a notice to repair given under the covenant to repair on notice will waive any right to forfeit for breach of the general covenant during the period of the notice.[34] Thus, in *Doe d. Morecraft v Meux*[35] a lease contained a general covenant to repair and a covenant to repair defects specified in a notice given by the landlord within three months of the notice. The landlord gave notice to repair "within three months". The notice was construed as having been given under the covenant to repair on notice, with the result that the landlord was not entitled to forfeit for breach of the general covenant during the period of the notice. Where, however, the notice on its true construction is not given under the covenant to repair on notice, then the right to forfeit for breach of the general covenant is unaffected.[36] Thus, in *Few v*

---

[29] It is thought that acceptance of rent will only waive the right to forfeit for breaches existing on the date when the rent is due. Nonetheless, in *Segal Securities Ltd v Thoseby* [1963] 1 Q.B. 887, Sachs J. suggested that, as regards continuing breaches, the acceptance of rent in advance waives breaches then existing for such period as the landlord definitely knows they will continue (at 901). It might be argued on the basis of this that where the landlord knows perfectly well that the tenant is not going to do the repairs, then the right to forfeit is waived for the whole of the period in respect of which the rent is accepted.

[30] [1984] 2 E.G.L.R. 66.

[31] [1898] 1 Q.B. 276. See para.27–07, above.

[32] See CPR Pt 25.7(1)(d).

[33] *Baylis v Le Gros* (1858) 4 C.B. (N.S.) 537.

[34] *Doe d. Morecraft v Meux* (1825) 4 B. & C. 606; *Doe d. Rutzen v Lewis* (1836) 5 A. & E. 277.

[35] Above.

[36] *Doe d. Goatley v Paine* (1810) 2 Camp. 520; *Few v Perkins* (1867) L.R. 2 Ex. 92.

*Perkins*[37] the landlord served a notice to repair "in accordance with the covenants" of the lease. It was held that the notice on its proper construction was not a notice under the covenant to repair on notice, so that the landlord was entitled to forfeit for breach of the general covenant within the three-month period.

Notwithstanding the above, it was held in *Cove v Smith*[38] that a s.146 notice relating to breaches of the general covenant may be served during the currency of a notice to repair given under the covenant to repair on notice. In that case the landlord served on the tenant on May 23, 1885, a notice to repair the premises within three months under the covenant to repair on notice. He then served a notice under s.14(1) of the Conveyancing Act 1881[39] in respect of breaches of the general covenant on June 6, 1885, before the end of the three months. The tenant argued that the effect of the notice under the covenant to repair on notice was to suspend the general covenant until expiry of the notice. This was rejected by Wills J. In reaching his decision, the judge appears to have relied on the fact that the second notice was only served after the tenant showed that he did not intend to do anything in response to the first. It may be that the decision can be justified on the basis that the first notice ceased to be a waiver of the right to forfeit for breach of the general covenant once the tenant had made it clear that he was not going to comply with the notice.

Many modern leases contain covenants to repair on notice which entitle the landlord to enter the premises and carry out the remedial work if the tenant fails to comply with the notice. Where the landlord exercises this right, and carries out the work, the right to forfeit for the disrepair which existed before he entered will have been waived.[40] An alternative analysis may be that the breaches are remedied by the carrying out of the work.[41]

## "Once-and-for-all" breaches

Waiver of a "once-and-for-all" breach deprives the landlord of the right to forfeit for that breach forever. Breach of a specific covenant to put into repair is a once-and-for-all breach.[42] The general covenant to repair is not to be regarded as a covenant to put into repair for this purpose merely because of the principle that the obligation to keep in repair involves an obligation to put into repair.[43] Breach of a covenant to expend insurance moneys in reinstating after fire is also a once-and-for-all breach,[44] and so also is a breach of a covenant against alterations and a breach of a covenant to build by a certain date.

**27–11**

---

[37] Above.

[38] (1886) 2 T.L.R. 778.

[39] The statutory predecessor of the Law of Property Act 1925 s.146.

[40] *Doe d. Rutzen v Lewis* (1836) 5 A. & E. 277.

[41] See *S.E.D.A.C. Investments Ltd v Tanner* [1982] 1 W.L.R. 1342, discussed at paras 27–45 to 27–46 below.

[42] *Coward v Gregory* (1866) L.R. 2 C.P. 153.

[43] See paras 9–21 to 9–22, above.

[44] *Farimani v Gates* [1984] 2 E.G.L.R. 66.

In *Stephens v Junior Army & Navy Stores Ltd*[45] the tenant covenanted to erect buildings by a certain date and to keep them in repair when erected. No buildings were erected by that date, nor by the date when the matter came before the court on the landlord's claim for forfeiture and damages. It was held that breach of the covenant to erect the buildings was a once-and-for-all breach, and that acceptance of rent after the specified date waived the right to forfeit for that breach.

In *First Penthouse Ltd v Channel Hotels & Properties (UK) Ltd*[46] it was held that breach of a covenant to carry out a development project as expeditiously as possible was a once and for all breach which arose when the time for completion expired.

## THE S.146 NOTICE

### Introductory

27–12    A right of re-entry or forfeiture for breach of covenant is not enforceable by action or otherwise[47] unless and until the landlord serves on the tenant a notice:

(a)    specifying the particular breach complained of;
(b)    if the breach is capable of remedy, requiring the tenant to remedy it;
(c)    requiring the tenant to make compensation in money for the breach;

and the tenant fails, within a reasonable time thereafter, to remedy the breach and to make reasonable compensation in money, to the satisfaction of the landlord, for the breach.[48]

The notice is universally referred to as a "s.146 notice". Service of a valid notice is a condition precedent to forfeiture for breach of a tenant's repairing covenant in every case. Failure to serve one will render the forfeiture null and void.[49] Where the landlord forfeits by physical re-entry[50] without having served a notice, his entry will be a trespass, with the result that he will be liable to the tenant in damages. Where the landlord forfeits by the issue and service of proceedings, the lack of a valid notice will render those proceedings a nullity in so far as they claim forfeiture, with the result that the landlord will be liable to pay the tenant's costs. It is therefore of the utmost importance to ensure that a valid notice is served.

There are additional requirements relating to the s.146 notice where the Leasehold Property (Repairs) Act 1938 applies.[51]

---

[45] [1914] 2 Ch. 516.
[46] [2004] L. & T. R. 27.
[47] The statutory restriction therefore applies to forfeiture by peaceable re-entry as well as by proceedings: see *Fox v Jolly* [1916] A.C. 1 at 8.
[48] Law of Property Act 1925 s.146(1).
[49] *Fox v Jolly*, above.
[50] See para.27–75, below.
[51] See para.27–31 et seq., below.

## Construction of the notice[52]

At common law, a contractual notice, even if it contains errors, will be valid if it is:

> "[S]ufficiently clear and unambiguous to leave a reasonable recipient in no reasonable doubt as to how and when [it is] intended to operate.[53]"

The same approach applies to the construction of a s.146 notice.[54] The test is an objective one, in that the question is not how the actual recipient understood the notice, but how a reasonable recipient would have understood it.[55] However, even applying this approach, a s.146 notice has to specify the right breach, and if it does not, it will be invalid.[56]

## Contents of the notice

Section 146(1) of the 1925 Act provides that the notice must (i) specify the particular breach complained of; (ii) if the breach is capable of remedy, require the tenant to remedy the breach; and (iii) in any case require the tenant to make compensation in money for the breach.

It is necessary to examine these three elements in turn.

### "Specifying the particular breach complained of"[57]

#### (a)    The breach not the remedial work

What must be specified is the breach, and not what the tenant is required to do to remedy it. Care must be taken to identify what precisely is the breach in relation to any particular covenant. A breach of a covenant to repair consists of the existence of an unremedied defect.[58] The tenant must be informed of the particular condition of the premises which he is to remedy,[59] but he does not have to be told what he has to do to remedy it. Thus, in *Fox v Jolly*[60] Lord Buckmaster L.C. said in his speech:

> "I can find nowhere in the section the obligation of telling the tenant what it is that he must do. All that the landlord is bound to do is to state particulars of the breaches of covenants of which he complains and call upon the lessee to remedy them. The means by which the breach is to be remedied is a matter for the lessee and not for the lessor. In many cases specification of the

27–13

27–14

27–15

---

[52] See further para.27–36, below.
[53] *Mannai Investment Co Ltd v Eagle Star Assurance Co Ltd* [1997] A.C. 749.
[54] *Akici v L R Butlin Ltd* [2006] 1 W.L.R. 201 at [53–54].
[55] *Mannai Investment Co Ltd v Eagle Star Assurance Co Ltd*, above; *Havant International Holdings v Lionsgate (H) Investment* [2000] L. & T.R. 297.
[56] *Akici v L R Butlin Ltd*, above, at [54].
[57] See further para.36–18 et seq., below.
[58] See *Penton v Barnett* [1898] 1 Q.B. 276, per Collins L.J. at 281 ("The expression 'breach' means the neglect to deal with the condition of the premises ....").
[59] *Penton v Barnett*, above, per Collins L.J. at 281.
[60] [1916] A.C. 1, applied in *Adagio Properties Ltd v Ansari* [1998] 2 E.G.L.R. 69.

breach will itself suggest the only possible remedy. For example, complaint that a covenant to paint or to paper has been broken can only be met by painting and papering. But it does not follow that this is always so. A particular covenant to keep the roof watertight, if broken, would be sufficiently defined by reference to the covenant, a statement that the roof had not been kept watertight, and that the tenant was required to remedy the omission; the means by which this could be accomplished would be for the tenant to determine."

In the same case Lord Sumner said:

"[I]t was argued that the landlord should not only tell the tenant what to do but how to do it. There is nothing of that kind in the section. The legal standard of repair, which the covenant requires, is a matter of law, and the tenant is taken to know it; the practical way of effecting the repair is not to be dictated by the landlord, but to be recommended by a builder."

It follows that a schedule of dilapidations which does no more than set out a list of remedial work without identifying the defect alleged to constitute the disrepair runs the risk of being held to be insufficient. In many cases, of course, the nature of the breach (i.e. the defect) will be clear from the work required. An example might be a requirement to "replace defective cement pointing between ridge tiles on main roof", from which it is reasonably clear that the pointing in question is alleged to be defective. However, in other cases the nature of the breach may be unclear. For example, "carry out underpinning to left flank wall" does not indicate what is wrong with the wall. A second danger with such a schedule is that the remedial work specified by the landlord's surveyor may be found to be too extensive or not appropriate. An example might be a schedule which requires the tenant to replace the roof, when all that needs to be done is localised patching. The tenant might well argue that a notice which incorporated such a schedule was defective.

**27–16**   For the above reasons a schedule of dilapidations which is prepared for the purpose of being annexed to a s.146 notice must specify the individual items of disrepair which are alleged to constitute breaches of the relevant covenants. Provided that this is done, there is no reason why the schedule should not also set out, in another column, the remedial work which the landlord's surveyor believes is necessary in each case. This has the considerable advantage of making it clear to the tenant from the outset what work the landlord says should be done. Use of the form of schedule of dilapidations annexed to the *Pre-Action Protocol for Claims for Damages in relation to the Physical State of Commercial Property at the Termination of a Tenancy*, which came into force on January 1, 2012, is highly recommended.[61] The appropriate form of schedule is further considered in para.36–18 et seq., below.

The notice does not need to refer expressly either to s.146, or to the covenant in question, provided that it adequately identifies the breach.[62]

---

[61] Save that column 5 of the form of schedule provides for the landlord's costings, and there is no need to include this at the s.146 notice stage. The Pre-Action Protocol is fully considered in Ch.37, below, and printed in Appendix 3, below.

[62] *Van Haarlem v Kasner* (1992) 64 P. & C.R. 214.

## (b)  Degree of particularity required

The notice must inform the tenant with reasonable particularity of the breaches of **27–17**
which the landlord complains. A notice which really only says "perform the
covenants", albeit over and over again, is bad.[63] The notice must specify the
breach with sufficient particularity fairly to tell him what he is required to
remedy.[64] In *Fletcher v Nokes*[65] North J. said in the course of his judgment:

> "[T]he landlord need [not] go through every room in the house and point out every defect. But
> the notice ought to be so distinct as to direct the attention of the tenant to the particular things
> of which the landlord complains, so that the tenant may have an opportunity of remedying
> them before an action to enforce a forfeiture of the lease is brought against him.[66]"

In deciding whether the breaches are adequately particularised, it is
permissible in an appropriate case to take into account the fact that the tenant is
likely to be reasonably familiar with the premises. Thus, a statement might be
sufficient to draw his attention to the things of which the landlord complains,
which might be insufficient in the case of a stranger who had never seen the
premises.[67]

In *Fox v Jolly*[68] the demised premises consisted of six houses. The s.146
notice alleged that the covenant to repair had been broken, and that the particular
breaches complained of were committing or allowing the dilapidations mentioned
in the schedule annexed to the notice. The schedule set out repairs under the
general headings of "external", "internal" and "generally". In most cases the
repairs were specified without reference to the individual houses, but in a few
cases individual houses were specified. The House of Lords held that the notice
was good. By contrast, in *Fletcher v Nokes*,[69] where the demised premises again
consisted of six houses, the notice stated that "you have broken the covenants for
repairing the inside and outside of the houses . . . and I require you to repair the
said houses in accordance with the said covenants forthwith . . ." and was held to
be bad. Likewise, in *Gregory v Serle*[70] a notice, the relevant part of which was
"you have committed breaches of the covenants contained in the said lease. First,
that you have not kept the said premises well and sufficiently repaired, and the
party and other walls thereof", was held to be bad. In *Adagio Properties Ltd v
Ansari*[71] a notice which alleged a breach of a covenant against alterations by
"making alterations so as to divide Flat 17 Poynders Court into two separate
studio flats without permission" was held to be a good notice. Wall L.J.
commented that the judge at first instance (who had held the notice to be invalid
because the landlord had not specified the individual alterations complained of)

---

[63] *Fox v Jolly* [1916] 1 A.C. 1 per Lord Sumner at 20.
[64] *Fox v Jolly*, per Lord Parmoor at 22.
[65] [1897] 1 Ch. 271.
[66] This approach was followed by Kekewich J. in *Gregory v Serle* [1898] 1 Ch. 652, and accepted as
correct in *Fox v Jolly* [1916] 1 A.C. 1.
[67] *Fox v Jolly*, above, per Lord Atkinson at 18.
[68] Above.
[69] [1897] 1 Ch. 271.
[70] [1898] 1 Ch. 652.
[71] [1998] 2 E.G.L.R. 69.

had "confused the duty to specify the particular breach complained of, which the landlord is obliged to do, and giving particulars of the breach complained of, which he is not obliged to do".

The extent to which a defect must be particularised in the notice will depend on the facts of each case. The surveyor who prepares the schedule should aim to identify the defect with sufficient particularity that a reasonable tenant would be clear what needs to be attended to. Provided this is done, the fact that the defect is identified in a fairly general way will not matter. For example, "structural disrepair on first floor" would not usually be adequate, because it fails to give the tenant sufficient information as to the whereabouts or nature of the defect of which the landlord complains. By contrast, "slipped or missing tiles on main roof" would ordinarily be sufficient, even though the tenant must find out for himself how many tiles are slipped or missing and whereabouts on the roof they are.

### (c)    Requirements to inspect and carry out work

27–18    Schedules of dilapidation often require the tenant to inspect a particular part of the premises and repair any defect found to exist. This is frequently done where the surveyor preparing the schedule is unable to inspect for himself (perhaps because the part of the premises is inaccessible), or where ascertaining the condition of the part in question requires the carrying out of specialist tests (for example, the electrical system). Thus, for example, it is common to find requirements such as "arrange for drains test and carry out any work found to be necessary". Requirements of this sort run the risk of being held to be bad on the footing that they fail to specify a defect and, therefore, a breach. It is thought that in many cases such requirements will be bad for this reason. However, where it is implicit that a defect exists, then a requirement of this type may be good, even though it leaves it up to the tenant to find out precisely what is wrong.

Thus, in *Fox v Jolly*[72] the s.146 notice contained, among others, the following two items:

> "Examine repair and reinstate all broken or loose tiles to main and w.c. roofs.
>     Examine and repair and put in good sanitary condition all sinks cisterns water closets supply and waste pipes ball valves and taps and all drains and gullies and flush out the same."

It was argued that these were a request to survey, not a request to repair, and therefore that they were bad. The House of Lords rejected the argument. Lord Buckmaster L.C. said:

> "Both these clauses would, in my opinion, have been perfectly good if the word 'examine' were omitted; and I cannot see that its introduction vitiates the rest of the clause."

Lord Sumner said:

---

[72] [1916] 1 A.C. 1.

"It must, however, often be the case that nothing more is practicable than to name some part of the premises and say examine and repair it where necessary. The actual defects may be undiscoverable till actual work has begun, yet the evidence of their reality may be there. Often no description would identify the brick or the slate or the patch of wall or the piece of wood which needs repair. The remedy is to go and see."

It is thought that the relevant distinction in general terms is between a notice which expressly or by implication identifies a defect of which there is some evidence, albeit that the tenant is required to discover the details for himself, and one which does not specify any defect but requires the tenant to investigate the condition of the premises for himself. The former will be good, the latter bad.

### (d)   Reservation of rights in respect of future disrepair

A statement in a notice to the general effect that the landlord's rights are reserved in respect of other disrepair found to be necessary does not invalidate the notice.[73] Thus, in *Fox v Jolly*[74] a s.146 notice ended as follows:

**27–19**

"Well and substantially repair uphold maintain and put the premises in thoroughly good repair and condition and note that the completion of the items mentioned in this schedule does not excuse the execution of other repairs if found necessary."

The tenant's argument that the entire notice was thereby bad was rejected by the House of Lords.

Likewise, in *Greenwich LBC v Discreet Selling Estates Ltd*[75] the inclusion in the schedule of a statement that "This schedule is an interim one and does not represent the full extent of the tenant's liability under the covenants in the lease" was held not to invalidate the notice.

### (e)   Inadequately specified breaches

It is thought that, as a general rule, a s.146 notice which specifies a number of breaches, and is bad as regards some because they are inadequately specified, will still be good as regards the remainder. However, in *Gregory v Serle*[76] a s.146 notice which alleged breaches of the covenants to repair, to decorate the outside, and to decorate the inside, failed sufficiently to specify breaches of the covenant to repair, and Kekewich J. held that the entire notice was bad, even though the breaches of the decorating covenants were adequately specified. *Gregory v Serle* was considered in *Fox v Jolly*,[77] but the point did not arise for decision. However, Lord Buckmaster L.C. said in relation to it:

**27–20**

"[I]t does not necessarily follow that imperfect description of the breach of one covenant would take away from [the landlord] the right to re-enter for breach of the other covenants which had been sufficiently described."

---

[73] *Fox v Jolly*, above; *Greenwich LBC v Discreet Selling Estates Ltd* [1990] 2 E.G.L.R. 65.
[74] Above.
[75] Above.
[76] [1898] 1 Ch. 652.
[77] [1916] A.C. 1.

Lord Atkinson went somewhat further:

"Each breach working a forfeiture must be taken by itself, and the statement in the notice dealing with it be taken by itself. If these two combined would have entitled the landlord to enforce the forfeiture if they stood alone, no other breach being complained of or referred to in the notice, then in my view he would still be entitled to enforce the forfeiture and recover possession, though many other breaches should be complained of in reference to which the notice given was defective .... In my opinion, [the notice in question] was sufficiently clear and specific to satisfy the requirements of the statute in respect to several of the breaches. If that be so, then the fact that the notice is too vague in reference to some other of the breaches mentioned, even if true, does not I think, vitiate the notice *in toto*, or afford a defence to the [landlord's] action."

It is therefore thought that *Gregory v Serle* would be held to have been wrongly decided on this point.

### (f)    Non-existent breaches or covenants

**27–21**    Where more than one breach is alleged in a notice, failure to prove one does not render the notice invalid in relation to those breaches which are proved.[78] A reference in a notice to a non-existent covenant does not invalidate a notice which is otherwise good.[79] However, in *Guillemard v Silverthorne*[80] a notice referred to two non-existent covenants, and set out particulars of breaches which might have been referable to those covenants or might have been referable to covenants which actually existed. The notice was held to be bad.

### (g)    Failure to comply with the Leasehold Property (Repairs) Act 1938

**27–22**    It has been suggested that a s.146 notice which specifies both breaches of covenant within the Leasehold Property (Repairs) Act 1938 and other breaches not falling within that Act, and which is defective as regards the former because it does not comply with the requirements of the 1938 Act, may nonetheless be good as regards the latter.[81] It is thought that the suggestion is correct.

## "If the breach is capable of remedy, requiring the lessee to remedy the breach"

**27–23**    This requirement is fundamental to the purpose of a s.146 notice, which is to give the tenant an opportunity to put right the breaches before his lease is forfeited. Breaches of a covenant to repair or decorate are capable of remedy,[82] so that this

---

[78] *Pannell v City of London Brewery* [1900] 1 Ch. 496; *Blewett v Blewett* [1936] 2 All E.R. 188.

[79] *Silvester v Ostrowska* [1959] 1 W.L.R. 1060 (notice in respect of breaches of covenant to repair not invalidated by allegation of non-existent breach of covenant not to sub-let).

[80] (1908) 99 L.T. 584.

[81] *Starrokate Ltd v Burry* [1983] 1 E.G.L.R. 56.

[82] Indeed, it has been suggested that most breaches are, as a matter of practicality, capable of remedy on the basis that a landlord may be compensated in money and that the distinction drawn in some cases as to negative and positive breaches is overly technical: *Akici v L.R. Butlin Ltd* [2006] 1 E.G.L.R. 34. Accordingly, even a covenant to repair within a particular time frame ought in principle to be capable of remedy.

requirement must be complied with in relation to any s.146 notice served for failure to repair or decorate. A notice which fails to comply with this requirement would be bad.

It is common practice for the notice to specify a time within which the breach must be remedied. However, the statute does not require this. All that it requires is that a reasonable time to remedy the breach must elapse between service of the notice and the exercise of the right of forfeiture.[83] It is thought that it is not good practice to specify a time in the notice. If the time so specified is held to have been unreasonably short, the notice may thereby be invalidated. If the notice specifies a period which is over-generous, it must be at least arguable that the landlord cannot forfeit before the expiry of the period specified, since he will have lulled the tenant into a false sense of security as to the time within which he must remedy his breach.[84] If, on the other hand, no time is specified at all, the worst that can happen is that the court finds that the forfeiture proceedings were started before the expiry of a reasonable time. The proceedings will then be premature, but the notice on which they were based will not be invalidated, with the result that the landlord can issue fresh proceedings without serving a new notice.

However, there is often a very good practical reason for specifying a time for compliance, namely, to inject a sense of urgency into the notice, and to ensure that the tenant gets on with the work as soon as possible. There is no reason why, in order to achieve this, the landlord cannot set out in a covering letter the period that he regards as a reasonable time for complying with the notice, and state that he intends to forfeit the lease if the works have not been carried out within that time. This will have the desired effect of drawing to the tenant's attention the time within which the landlord expects to see the works carried out, but there will be no danger of the notice itself being invalidated. A suggested form of notice and covering letter are set out in Appendix 1, below.

## "In any case, requiring the lessee to make compensation in money for the breach"

Despite the apparently mandatory wording of this provision it has been held that the notice need not require the tenant to make compensation in money if the landlord does not want compensation.[85] Nonetheless it is good practice to include the statutory requirement in the notice. If the landlord is entitled to the compensation required by the notice, then the tenant must pay it or face forfeiture even though he has carried out the works.[86] If the notice does not require compensation, then the tenant will be able to avoid forfeiture simply by doing the work.

27–24

---

[83] *Billson v Residential Apartments Ltd (No.1)* [1992] 1 A.C. 494, per Browne-Wilkinson V.C. (the decision was reversed by the House of Lords ([1992] 1 A.C. 494) but this point is not affected).

[84] Cf. *Doe d. Morecraft v Meux* (1825) 4 B. & C. 606.

[85] *Lock v Pearce* [1893] 2 Ch. 271; *Civil Service Co-Operative Society v McGrigor's Trustee* [1923] 2 Ch. 347; *Rugby School (Governors) v Tannahill* [1935] 1 K.B. 87; *Egerton v Esplanade Hotels (London) Ltd* [1947] 2 All E.R. 88; *Hoffmann v Fineberg* [1949] Ch. 245.

[86] See para.27–30, below.

"Compensation" appears to mean the same as "damages", so that the landlord is only entitled to require compensated for such losses as could properly be made the subject-matter of an action for damages for breach of covenant.[87] Thus, the costs and expenses incurred by the landlord in relation to the preparation of the schedule of dilapidations and the service of the s.146 notice cannot be claimed as compensation.[88] It is not clear whether the notice must require payment of a figure, or whether it is enough if the notice does no more than follow the statutory language by requiring the tenant to make compensation in money for the breaches. The latter is the practice, but there are undoubtedly arguments in favour of the former. Given that the tenant is unlikely to know what, if any, loss the landlord has suffered, and that the consequence of not making reasonable compensation is that the landlord's right of forfeiture remains even where the work has been done,[89] there is something to be said for the view that if the landlord alleges he has suffered loss, then it is for him to specify in his notice the amount which he requires. It is probable, however, that a notice which merely requires compensation without naming a figure would be held to be valid.

In practice, any loss suffered by the landlord as a result of the disrepair will nearly always disappear when the works have been done. However, this will not always be the case. It might be, for example, that the disrepair has resulted in the landlord becoming liable to pay damages to third parties under the Defective Premises Act 1972,[90] or a lower rent being achieved on a letting of adjacent premises also belonging to the landlord. In neither case will the doing of the work fully compensate the landlord for his loss. In such cases the landlord should consider including a claim for compensation in the s.146 notice.

It is not clear whether a failure to claim compensation in the notice will preclude the landlord thereafter from claiming damages for the breaches. It is thought, however, that it would not have this effect. The s.146 notice is not a statutory prerequisite to a damages claim (unless the Leasehold Property (Repairs) Act 1938 applies[91]), so that the landlord could claim damages without any notice. It is difficult to see why that right should be taken away by the service of a s.146 notice in which no claim for compensation is made.

## On whom the notice must be served

27–25    The s.146 notice must be served on "the lessee". This means the tenant under the lease which it is desired to forfeit. Where there are joint tenants the notice must be served on all.[92] Where the lease has been assigned the notice must be served on the assignee in whom the lease is vested at the relevant time, and not the original tenant or (if there have been successive assignments) any earlier

---

[87] *Skinners Company v Knight* [1891] 2 Q.B. 542. It presumably follows from this that any sum which would be irrecoverable by virtue of s.18(1) of the Landlord and Tenant Act 1927 (see Ch.30, below) cannot be made the subject of a claim for compensation.
[88] *Skinners Company v Knight* above. This is further discussed in para.3–06, below.
[89] See para.27–30, below.
[90] See para.20–49 et seq., above.
[91] See para.27–31 et seq., below.
[92] *Blewett v Blewett* [1936] 2 All E.R. 188.

assignee.[93] This remains the case even where the assignment is unlawful since even an unlawful assignment vests the lease in the assignee.[94] It should be noted, however, that where the lease is registered at the Land Registry and the assignee has not been registered as the proprietor, the assignor may remain the person on whom the notice should be served.[95] Where the notice has been validly served on the tenant for the time being, it does not need to be re-served on a subsequent assignee.[96] The notice does not need to be served on the tenant's mortgagees[97] or on any sub-tenant.[98]

The notice need not be addressed to the lessee by name. It may be addressed to "the lessee" by that designation, without his name, or generally to the persons interested without any name, and notwithstanding that any person to be affected by the notice is absent, under disability, unborn or unascertained.[99] It is common practice to address the notice to "AB Limited or other the lessee of the premises known as …".

## Service of the notice[100]

Section 196 of the Law of Property Act 1925 provides for service on the tenant by one or more of the following methods:

(1)    by being left at the tenant's last known place of abode or business in the United Kingdom.[101] It is sufficient to leave the notice at a place that is the furthest that member of the public or a postman can go to communicate to the tenant, so that a notice which is put into the letterbox of a house containing flats and bed sitting rooms will be validly served on the tenant of one of the bed sitting rooms.[102]

27–26

---

[93]  *Cusack-Smith v Gold* [1958] 1 W.L.R. 611.

[94]  *Old Grovebury Manor Farm v W. Seymour Plant & Sales Ltd (No.2)* [1979] 1 W.L.R. 1397.

[95]  Cf. *Brown & Root Technology Ltd v Sun Alliance & London Insurance Co Ltd* (1998) 75 P. & C.R. 223.

[96]  *Kanda v Church Commissioners for England* [1958] 1 Q.B. 332.

[97]  *Egerton v Jones* [1939] 2 K.B. 702; *Church Commissioners for England v Ve-Ri-Best Manufacturing Co Ltd* [1957] 1 Q.B. 238; *Smith v Spaul* [2003] 1 E.G.L.R. 70.

[98]  Although the definition of "lessee" in s.146(5)(b) includes "an original or derivative under-lessee, and the persons deriving title under a lessee", it is thought that this means only that the section applies as between tenant and sub-tenant in the same way as it does between landlord and tenant, and not that the landlord is required to serve notice on the sub-tenant in addition to the head tenant. The express reference in s.146(4) to "under-lessee" seems to support the argument that s.146(1) is only dealing with the person who is the direct tenant of the landlord serving the notice. It is noteworthy that the mortgagee in *Egerton v Jones*, above, (who was held not to be entitled to notice) was a mortgagee by sub-demise. As Lord Goddard C.J. pointed out in *Church Commissioners for England v Ve-Ri-Best Manufacturing Ltd*, above, the necessity is to serve "*the* lessee" (the emphasis is that of the judge), and the decision in that case (that a mortgagee by legal charge, although a "lessee" within s.146(5)(b), was not entitled to notice) likewise supports the view that notice need not be served on a sub-tenant.

[99]  Law of Property Act 1925 s.196(2).

[100]  Note that additional requirements are imposed by s.18(2) of the Landlord and Tenant Act 1927 in the case of forfeiture for breach of a covenant to keep or put premises in repair: see para.27–27, below.

[101]  Law of Property Act 1925 s.196(3).

[102]  *Henry Smith's Charity Trustees v Kyriakou* [1989] 2 E.G.L.R. 110.

(2)   by being affixed or left for the tenant on the premises or any house or building comprised in the lease.[103] It is sufficient to affix the notice to the door of the demised premises.[104] It is also sufficient to insert or put the notice through the letter box.[105] The fact that the landlord knows that the tenant is unlikely to get the notice does not prevent it from being validly served under this provision.[106] A notice is also properly served under this provision if it is left with some person on the demised premises and there are reasonable grounds for supposing that that person will, if possible, pass it on to the tenant;[107]

(3)   by being sent by post in a registered letter addressed to the tenant by name at his last known place of abode or business in the United Kingdom,[108] if the letter is not returned through the post office undelivered.[109] Service is deemed to be effected at the time at which the letter would in the ordinary course be delivered.[110] Recorded delivery may be used instead of a registered letter.[111] Provided the landlord proves on a balance of probabilities that the letter containing the notice was properly addressed, prepaid and sent in one of these ways, and that it has not been returned through the post office undelivered, it will have been properly served even though the tenant never gets it.[112]

It is generally thought that the methods of service provided for by s.196 are not mandatory, so that whatever means of service is adopted, it will be sufficient if the landlord proves that the tenant has in fact received the notice. However, in a case where the lease expressly incorporated the provisions as to notices

---

[103] Law of Property Act 1925 s.196(3).

[104] *Cusack-Smith v Gold* [1958] 1 W.L.R. 611.

[105] *Van Haarlam v Kasner* (1992) 64 P. & C.R. 214; *Kinch v Bullard* [1999] 1 W.L.R. 423.

[106] *Van Haarlam v Kasner*, above; *Blunden v Frogmore Investments Ltd* [2002] 2 E.G.L.R. 29 per Robert Walker L.J.

[107] *Cannon Brewery Ltd v Signal Press Ltd* (1928) 44 T.L.R. 486; *Newborough v Jones* [1975] Ch. 90.

[108] This means the last place of which the landlord knew as the place of abode or business of the tenant even if the tenant has in fact moved: *Price v West London Building Society* [1964] 1 W.L.R. 616. Where the tenant is a limited company then its registered office may be its last known place of business even where the landlord corresponds with the tenant's managing agents at a different address: *National Westminster Bank Ltd v Betchworth Investments Ltd* [1975] 1 E.G.L.R. 57.

[109] Law of Property Act 1925 s.196(4).

[110] Law of Property Act 1925, s.196(4). This is so even where there is no available recipient: *WX Investments Ltd v Begg* [2002] 1 W.L.R. 2849, in which Patten J. said: "The date of such delivery is governed by what the court finds to have been the time when delivery in the ordinary course of post would take place, but this is judged by normal practice and expectations, not by the circumstances and whims of the addressee at the time".

[111] Recorded Delivery Service Act 1962.

[112] *Re No.88, Berkeley Road, N.W.9* [1971] Ch. 648; *Chiswell v Griffon Land Estates Ltd* [1975] 1 W.L.R. 1181; *Italica Holdings SA v Bayadea* [1985] 1 E.G.L.R. 70; *Galinski v McHugh* (1989) 57 P. & C.R. 359; *Wandsworth LBC v Attwell* [1996] 1 E.G.L.R. 57 at 58; *Railtrack Plc v Gojra* [1998] 1 E.G.L.R. 63; *Kinch v Bullard* [1999] 1 W.L.R. 423; *Commercial Union Life Assurance Co Ltd v Moustafa* [1999] L. & T.R. 489; *Blunden v Frogmore Investments Ltd*, above; *Beanby Estates Ltd v Egg Stores (Stamford Hill) Ltd* [2004] 3 All E.R. 184; *C A Webber (Transport) v Railtrack* [2004] 1 W.L.R. 320. Most of these cases were decisions under s.23 of the Landlord and Tenant 1954, but it is thought that the same applies to s.196(4) of the 1925 Act. See, however, s.18(2) of the Landlord and Tenant Act 1927, considered in para.27–27, below.

contained in s.196, it was held that service by email was insufficient, on the ground that one of the methods of service required by s.196 had to be used.[113] This seems unsound, at least as regards s.196 itself: it seems tolerably clear that s.196 was intended to provide a method of service which the person wishing to serve a notice can safely adopt if he wishes to avoid disputes as to whether it was actually received, not to enable someone who has in fact received a notice to dispute that it has been validly served on him.[114]

Service of a s.146 notice on an agent of the tenant who is duly authorised,[115] or held out as being authorised,[116] to receive it will be good service. It should be remembered, however, that unless he is expressly authorised to do so, a solicitor or surveyor does not generally have authority to receive a s.146 notice on behalf of his client.[117] Nor will an implied authority to accept service arise merely because the solicitor is instructed under a retainer creating a duty to pass the notice on to the recipient.[118] Likewise, service on a company in the same group as the tenant will not be good service unless that company has been authorised, or held out as authorised, to accept service on the tenant's behalf.[119]

## Additional requirements in the case of forfeiture for breach of covenant to keep or put premises in repair

Additional requirements are imposed by s.18(2)of the Landlord and Tenant Act 1927 where the breach relied on is a breach of a covenant or agreement to keep or put premises in repair (whether express or implied and whether general or specific). The sub-section is to be construed as one with s.146.[120]. It provides that a right of re-entry or forfeiture for such breach shall not be enforceable, whether by action or otherwise,[121] unless the landlord proves[122] the following:

**27–27**

(1)    that the fact that a s.146 notice has been served on the tenant was known to:

---

[113] E.ON UK Plc v Gilesports Ltd [2012] EWHC 2172 (Ch.) at [54].
[114] Cf. Stylo Shoes Ltd v Prices Tailors Ltd [1960] Ch. 396 (a case under s.23(1) of the Landlord and Tenant Act 1927); Pulleng v Curran (1982) 44 P. & C. R.. 58.
[115] Westway Homes Ltd v Moores [1991] 2 E.G.L.R. 193; Yenula Properties Ltd v Naidu [2003] H.L.R. 18.
[116] Galinski v McHugh, above (notice under s.4 of the Landlord and Tenant Act 1954 on tenant's solicitors held good where the tenant had informed the landlord that his solicitor had full authority to act for him and to accept service of the notice).
[117] Saffron Walden Second Benefit Society v Rayner (1880) 14 Ch. D. 406; Re Munro [1981] 1 W.L.R. 1358; Glen International v Triplerose [2007] 2 E.G.L.R. 81.
[118] Von Essen Hotels 5 v Vaughan [2007] EWCA Civ 1349 per Mummery L.J. at [44]; Glen International v Triplerose, above.
[119] Townsend Carriers Ltd v Pfizer (1977) 33 P. & C.R. 361; Midland Oak Construction Ltd v BBA Group Ltd (unreported decision of the Court of Appeal dated February 15, 1983, noted in Reynolds and Featherstonhaugh, Handbook of Rent Review). See also Lemmerbell Ltd v Britannia LAS Direct Ltd [1998] 3 E.G.L.R. 67; Havant International Holdings v Lionsgate (H) Investment [1999] L. & T.R. 297; Procter & Gamble Technical Centres Ltd v Brixton Plc [2003] 2 E.G.L.R. 24.
[120] Landlord and Tenant Act 1927 s.18(2).
[121] The subsection therefore applies to forfeiture by peaceable re-entry as well as by proceedings.
[122] It is thought that "proves" must have its ordinary meaning of proof in the civil sense, i.e. proof of a balance of probabilities. Cf. Associated British Ports v C.H. Bailey Plc [1990] 2 A.C. 703 (see paras 27–57 to 27–59, below); Calladine-Smith v Saveorder Ltd [2011] EWHC 2501 (Ch.).

(a)    the tenant; or

(b)    an undertenant holding under an underlease which reserved a nominal reversion only to the tenant; or

(c)    the person who last paid the rent due under the lease either on his own behalf or as agent for the tenant or undertenant;

(2)    that a time reasonably sufficient to enable the repairs to be executed has elapsed since the time when the fact of the service of the notice came to the knowledge of any of the above. What is a reasonable time is considered below.[123]

The subsection further provides that where the s.146 notice has been served by registered post or recorded delivery addressed to a person at his last known place of abode[124] in the United Kingdom, then for the purposes of s.18(2) that person is deemed, unless the contrary is proved,[125] to have had knowledge of the fact that the notice has been served as from the time at which the letter would have been delivered in the ordinary course of post. It is suggested that it is good practice always to serve the notice by recorded delivery or registered post, in addition to any other method used, in order to take advantage of the deeming provision.

The subsection does not require the landlord to prove any more than that the fact of service of the s.146 notice was known to any of the specified persons. It does not appear to be necessary to show that any of those persons were aware of the contents of the notice, or even that any of them saw the notice. Nor does the sub-section restrict the way in which the requisite knowledge may be acquired, so that being told orally by a third party would presumably suffice.

### Reasonable time in which to remedy breach

**27–28**    A reasonable time in which to remedy the breaches must elapse between the date of service of the notice and the time when the right of forfeiture is exercised.[126] Where the landlord forfeits for breach of a covenant to keep or put in repair, the time is measured from the date on which the fact of service of the s.146 notice came to the knowledge of any of the persons specified in s.18(2) of the Landlord and Tenant Act 1927.[127] The time must be sufficient to enable all the breaches specified in the notice to be remedied,[128] so that the landlord cannot forfeit until a reasonable time for doing all the repairs in the notice has elapsed.

---

[123] See para.27–28, below.

[124] The deeming provision does not expressly refer to the last known place of business, in contrast to s.196(3) of the Law of Property Act 1925. However, "place of abode" in s.23 of the same Act has been construed as including the place of business of the person to be served: *Stylo Shoes Ltd v Prices Tailors Ltd* [1960] Ch. 396; *Price v West London Investment Building Society* [1964] 1 W.L.R. 616; *Italica Holdings Ltd v Bayadea* [1985] 1 E.G.L.R. 70.

[125] It is thought that this requires the court to make findings of fact on the balance of probabilities on the evidence before it, and that it is not enough for the tenant simply to assert that he did not have the requisite knowledge: Cf. *Calladine-Smith v Saveorder Ltd* [2011] EWHC 2501 (Ch.) (a case on the meaning of "unless the contrary is proved" in s.7 of the Interpretation Act 1978).

[126] Law of Property Act 1925 s.146(1).

[127] See para.27–27, above.

[128] *Hopley v Tarvin Parish Council* (1910) 74 J.P. 209; *Kent v Conniff* (decision of Slade J. on May 21, 1952, not reported on this point).

What is a reasonable time to remedy disrepair is a question of fact, and will vary according to the circumstances of each case. It has been said that generally a period of three months is thought to be adequate but there are no hard and fast rules and all will depend on what is required to be done.[129] The court must look at the period following the s.146 notice, but in deciding what is a reasonable time, it is permissible to take into account the fact that the schedule of dilapidations served with the s.146 notice was sent to the tenant at an earlier time.[130] In *Bhojwani v Kingsley Investment Trust Ltd*[131] the schedule of dilapidations specified cracked brickwork and subsided foundations, and required the tenant to "investigate reasons for subsidence and carry out all repairs necessary, i.e. underpinning existing foundations and re-building wall." The schedule was sent to the tenant in early February 1990. It was then served together with a s.146 notice on March 16, 1990. The landlord forfeited by peaceable re-entry on May 15, 1990. It was held that a reasonable time had not elapsed.

In considering what is a reasonable time, relevant matters will include: the need to instruct a surveyor and for the surveyor to carry out proper investigations[132]; any need to take advice from solicitors as to the extent of the tenant's obligations[133]; any need to draw up plans and specifications, to go out to tender and to compare prices[134]; the availability of suitable contractors; the existence of suitable weather conditions for the carrying out of the works; and the fact that the tenant may be trading whilst the work is being carried out.[135] The landlord should always take advice from his surveyor as to what a reasonable time would be, and the surveyor in giving his advice should ensure that the time is realistic having regard to what has to be done and the contingencies that may occur. The consequences of proceeding before a reasonable time has elapsed will be that the forfeiture will be premature. Any proceedings will therefore be liable to be struck out, and where the forfeiture is effected by physical re-entry, the entry will constitute a trespass for which the landlord will be liable to the tenant in damages. It is suggested that it is therefore good practice to err on the side of caution and to allow plenty of time.

In *Penton v Barnett*[136] a lease contained a covenant to repair and a covenant to **27–29** repair within three months after notice. The landlord served a notice under s.14(1) of the Conveyancing Act 1881[137] requiring the repairs specified in the schedule to be executed within three months. Ridley L.J. said of this in his judgment:

"It cannot be doubted that the time indicated by the notice was a reasonable time, for it is the time specified in one of the covenants to repair contained in the lease."

---

[129] *Bhojwani v Kingsley Investment Trust Ltd* [1992] 2 E.G.L.R. 70, per Mr. Thomas Morison, QC sitting as a deputy judge of the Chancery Division.
[130] *Bhojwani v Kingsley Investment Trust Ltd*, above.
[131] Ibid.
[132] Ibid.
[133] Ibid.
[134] Ibid.
[135] Ibid.
[136] [1898] 1 Q.B. 276.
[137] The statutory predecessor of s.146.

It is thought that this is unsound insofar as it suggests that the obligation in the lease to repair within three months after notice was conclusive that the same period was reasonable for the purpose of the statute. What is a reasonable time depends on all the circumstances at the relevant time, and the fact that a particular period has been agreed for one purpose does not mean that the parties intended to agree it for another. However, it may be that the presence in the lease of an obligation to repair within a specified period of notice is material from which the court could infer, in the absence of any other evidence either way, that the same period is reasonable for the purposes of s.146.

Where the tenant's actions make it clear that he has no intention of complying with the notice, then the landlord is entitled to forfeit before the expiry of what would otherwise be a reasonable time.[138]

## Failure to make reasonable compensation in money

27–30    Even where the tenant carries out the work specified in the s.146 notice, the landlord remains entitled to forfeit unless the tenant, within a reasonable time from the date of service of the notice, makes reasonable compensation in money, to the satisfaction of the landlord, for the breach.[139] The meaning of reasonable compensation has already been considered.[140] This requirement will only be relevant where (a) the s.146 notice requires the tenant to make compensation, and (b) the landlord is entitled to compensation, i.e. the breach has caused him loss which cannot be compensated for by the works being carried out. Hence, it is unlikely to be of practical importance in most cases.

## THE LEASEHOLD PROPERTY (REPAIRS) ACT 1938

### Introductory

27–31    Where it applies, the Leasehold Property (Repairs) Act 1938 operates to impose a bar on forfeiture and claims for damages for breach of repairing covenants until certain conditions have been fulfilled. The scheme of the Act, where it applies, is as follows:

(1)    the landlord must serve on the tenant a s.146 notice containing the information prescribed by the Act;

(2)    the tenant has the right within 28 days of the service of the landlord's notice to serve on the landlord counter-notice claiming the benefit of the Act;

(3)    if the tenant fails to serve counter-notice within the 28-day period, the Act ceases to apply in relation to the breaches specified in the notice, and the landlord is free to forfeit or sue for damages provided that he would otherwise have the right to do so;

---

[138] *Billson v Residential Apartments Ltd (No.1)* [1992] 1 A.C. 494, per Browne-Wilkinson V.C. (the decision was reversed by the House of Lords ([1992] 1 A.C. 494) but this point is unaffected)
[139] Law of Property Act 1925 s.146(1).
[140] See para.27–24, above.

(4) if the tenant serves counter-notice within the 28-day period, the landlord cannot either forfeit or begin an action for damages without the leave of the court;

(5) the court will only grant leave if (i) the landlord proves one or more of the grounds in s.1(5) of the Act, and (ii) the court is satisfied in the exercise of its discretion that leave ought to be granted. The court has power to grant leave subject to conditions;

(6) the landlord is not entitled to the benefit of s.146(3) of the Law of Property Act 1925 in relation to his solicitor's and surveyor's costs unless he applies for leave and the court so directs.

## Application of the Act

The 1938 Act originally only applied to long leases (of 21 years or more) of small houses (of a rateable value of £100 or less). It was amended by s.51 of the Landlord and Tenant Act 1954, and now applies to any lease[141] of whatever property which fulfils the following conditions:

**27–32**

(1) that it was granted for a term of years certain of not less than seven years.[142] The seven-year period is computed from the date on which the lease is granted and not the date (if earlier) from which the term is expressed to run;[143]

(2) that three years or more of the term remain unexpired at the relevant time;[144]

(3) that the property comprised in the tenancy is neither a tenancy of an agricultural holding in relation to which the Agricultural Holdings Act 1986 applies, nor a farm business tenancy.[145]

The Act as amended applies to tenancies granted, and breaches occurring, before or after the commencement of the 1954 Act.[146] It applies where there is an interest belonging to Her Majesty in right of the Crown or to a government

---

[141] The Act also applies to sub-leases, and agreements for a lease or sub-lease where the tenant or sub-tenant has become entitled to have the lease or sub-lease granted: Leasehold Property (Repairs) Act 1938 s.7(1) (applying Law of Property Act 1925 s.146(5)).

[142] Leasehold Property (Repairs) Act 1938 s.7(1) (as amended by Landlord and Tenant Act 1954 s.51(2)); Landlord and Tenant Act 1954 s.51(1).

[143] Cf. *Cadogan (Earl) v Guinness* [1936] Ch. 515; *Bradshaw v Pawley* [1980] 1 W.L.R. 10.

[144] Leasehold Property (Repairs) Act 1938 s.1(1) and (2); Landlord and Tenant Act 1954 s.51(1) and (6). It is thought that in the case of a tenancy to which Pt II of the Landlord and Tenant Act applies, the reference to the term means the term as originally granted, and not as continued by the Act. If the position were otherwise, the point at which the Act ceases to apply could never be known for certain until after the continuation tenancy has ended. The practical difficulties to which this would give rise strongly suggest that this cannot be the right view.

[145] Landlord and Tenant 1954 s.51(1) (as amended by the Agricultural Tenancies Act 1995 s.40).

[146] Landlord and Tenant Act 1954 s.51(5). The Act as amended does not apply where the s.146 notice was served, or the action for damages begun, before the commencement of the 1954 Act: Landlord and Tenant Act 1954 s.51(5) In such a case the 1938 Act before its amendment by the 1954 Act applies: *National Real Estate Co Ltd v Hassan* [1939] 2 K.B. 61.

department, or held on behalf of Her Majesty for the purposes of a government department, in the same way as it would apply if that interest were not an interest so belonging or held.[147]

The Act applies in relation to covenants to keep or put in repair during the currency of the lease all or any of the property comprised in the lease. However, the fact that a particular obligation is contained in the same clause as an obligation to repair, and that that clause may be compendiously described as "the repairing covenant" does not mean that every obligation contained in the clause constitutes an agreement to keep or put in repair within the meaning of the Act; each obligation in the clause must be given its natural and ordinary meaning.[148] Thus, the Act does not apply to an obligation to cleanse a lavatory even though it is contained in the repairing covenant.[149] However, the Act would apply to cleaning required to be done by the covenant to repair.[150] Likewise, the Act does not apply to a covenant to lay out insurance moneys in rebuilding premises damaged by fire.[151] It is thought that the Act would apply to a breach of a covenant to paint in circumstances where the relevant omission also amounts to a breach of the covenant to repair.[152]

## Exceptions

**27–33**   The Act does not apply to a breach of a covenant or agreement insofar as it imposes on the tenant an obligation to put premises in repair that is to be performed upon the tenant taking possession of the premises or within a reasonable time thereafter.[153] It is thought that this is referring to a specific covenant to carry out works at, or within reasonable time of, the start of the lease, and that it does not include the general covenant to repair the premises during the term of the lease, even though performance of the latter may require the premises first to be put into repair.[154] It is doubtful whether the exception is wide enough to include a covenant in a licence to assign which requires the assignee to carry out works of repair within a specified time after the assignment.

The Act only applies to claims against persons who would be entitled to receive a s.146 notice, namely, the tenant or tenants under the lease at the relevant time. It follows that no leave is required to bring an action for damages against a former tenant who has ceased to have any interest in the premises.[155] No leave is therefore required to bring a claim against an original tenant, or intermediate assignee, after the lease has been assigned. On this basis, it would appear to be

---

[147] Landlord and Tenant Act 1954 s.51(3).
[148] *Starrokate Ltd v Burry* [1983] 1 E.G.L.R. 56, per Dunn L.J.
[149] *Starrokate Ltd v Burry*, above.
[150] See *Greg v Planque* [1936] 1 K.B. 669 (cleaning a flue held to amount to "executing repairs" within the meaning of a provision in the lease which entitled the landlord to enter the demised premises to execute repairs and alterations.)
[151] *Farimani v Gates* [1984] 2 E.G.L.R. 66.
[152] See paras 30–03 and 32–14, below (considering *Latimer v Carney* [2006] 3 E.G.L.R. 13).
[153] Leasehold Property (Repairs) Act 1938 s.3.
[154] See paras 9–21 to 9–22, above.
[155] *Cusack-Smith v Gold* [1958] 1 W.L.R. 611. See also *Baker v Sims* [1959] 1 Q.B. 114 at 129.

open to a landlord to evade the restrictions imposed by the Act on claims for damages by the simple expedient of suing the original tenant rather than the current tenant.[156]

The Act only applies to claims for forfeiture or damages. It does not apply to a claim for a debt. The following are not claims for damages:

(1)  a claim under a covenant to spend a fixed sum per annum on repairs and decoration to the premises or in default to pay to the landlord the difference between that sum and what has been spent[157];

(2)  a claim under a covenant to pay the costs and expenses incurred by the landlord in connection with the preparation and service of a s.146 notice[158];

(3)  a claim for the cost of work under a covenant entitling the landlord to enter the premises and carry out repairs falling within the tenant's repairing liability.[159]

The Act does not apply to a claim for specific performance of the tenant's repairing covenant. It follows that in an appropriate case this would be a way of getting round the requirements of the Act.[160] However, specific performance cannot be used to effectuate or encourage the mischief which the 1938 Act was intended to remedy.[161] The court will be astute to ensure that the landlord is not seeking specific performance simply to harass the tenant, and in so doing, the court may take into account considerations similar to those it must take into account under the 1938 Act.[162]

## Where the Act applies

The consequence of the Act applying is that forfeiture, whether by proceedings or peaceable re-entry,[163] and proceedings for damages, are barred until one of the following has occurred:    **27–34**

(1)  the landlord has served a notice under s.146 of the 1925 Act in the form prescribed by the 1938 Act, and the tenant has failed to serve a counter-notice within the requisite 28-day period. In such a case the Act

---

[156] See the argument of counsel for the defendant in *Cusack-Smith v Gold*, above.

[157] *Moss Empires Ltd v Olympia (Liverpool) Ltd* [1939] A.C. 544.

[158] *Bader Properties Ltd v Linley Property Investments Ltd* (1968) 19 P. & C.R. 620; *Middlegate Properties Ltd v Gidlow-Jackson* (1977) 34 P. & C.R. 4.

[159] *Jervis v Harris* [1996] Ch. 195. See para.28–39, below.

[160] See [1982] Conv. 71 (J. Martin).

[161] *Rainbow Estates Ltd v Tokenhold Ltd* [1999] Ch. 64. See further para.28–08, below.

[162] *Rainbow Estates Ltd v Tokenhold Ltd*, above, at 37G.

[163] Leasehold Property (Repairs) Act 1938 s.1(3), which prohibits proceedings, "whether by action or otherwise", to enforce a right of forfeiture.

imposes no further restrictions on forfeiture.[164] However, an action for damages cannot be commenced until a month after the service of the s.146 notice;[165]

(2)    (where the tenant has served a counter-notice) the landlord has applied for and obtained the leave of the court;

(3)    the Act has ceased to apply because less than three years of the term remain unexpired. Once this point has been reached there is nothing to stop the landlord forfeiting or beginning an action for damages.[166] This is so even where the tenant served counter-notice at a time when the Act did apply and the landlord did not apply for leave, or leave was refused. Thus, in *Baker v Sims*[167] the tenant served a counter-notice at a time when the Act applied. The lease was subsequently surrendered, and the landlord sued the tenant for damages for breach of the covenant to repair during the term. The tenant argued that the action was incompetent because no leave had been obtained. His argument was rejected by the Court of Appeal.

## Contents of the s.146 notice

**27–35**    The notice required by the Act is a notice under s.146 of the Law of Property Act 1925.[168] It must contain a statement in characters not less conspicuous than those used in any other part of the notice to the effect that the lessee is entitled under the 1938 Act to serve on the lessor a counter-notice claiming the benefit of the Act, and a statement in the like characters specifying the time within which, and the manner in which, under the Act a counter-notice may be served, and specifying the name and address of the lessor.[169] A suggested form of notice is given in Appendix 1, below.

### (a)    Approach to construction of notices

**27–36**    The wording of the notice does not need to follow precisely the language of the Act, which must be interpreted in a reasonable way.[170] In *Middlegate Properties Ltd v Messimeris*[171] Lord Denning M.R. said:

> "We have been referred to some of the precedent books. Some give forms with more detail than others. All I would say is that these notices should be construed reasonably. If they tell the tenant with sufficient clearness what the statute requires, they are good."

---

[164] But all other conditions precedent must still be satisfied, such as the expiry of a reasonable time in which to remedy the breaches: see paras 27–03 to 27–30, above.

[165] Leasehold Property (Repairs) Act 1938 s.1(2).

[166] *Dwellings Developments Ltd v Drake* (1954) 163 E.G. 192; *Baker v Sims* [1959] 1 Q.B. 114. These cases concerned the position before the Act was amended by s.51 of the Landlord and Tenant Act 1954, but it is thought that the position is the same in relation to the Act as amended: see *Baker v Sims* at 128.

[167] Above.

[168] See para.27–12 et seq., above.

[169] Leasehold Property (Repairs) Act 1938 s.1(4).

[170] *Middlegate Properties Ltd v Messimeris* [1973] 1 W.L.R. 168; *BL Holdings Ltd v Marcolt Investments Ltd* [1979] 1 E.G.L.R. 97.

[171] Above.

Similarly, in *BL Holdings Ltd v Marcolt Investments Ltd*[172] Brandon L.J. said:

> "It is the substance of the notice that matters, not whether it follows precisely the wording of the sub-section. There is no room for technicality in the matter. On the other hand the application of this principle must not be carried to the point where, because the notice is not expressed in terms which would be clear to an ordinary tenant, the protection which the Act was intended to afford is significantly watered down."

The notice must be construed on the supposition that it is being sent to any reasonable hypothetical tenant, and not necessarily to a tenant or tenant's agent versed in the niceties of the law of landlord and tenant and acquainted with the detailed provisions of the 1938 Act.[173]

The general principles relating to the construction of contractual notices were reviewed and restated by the House of Lords in *Mannai Investment Co Ltd v Eagle Star Assurance Co Ltd*.[174] In that case Lord Steyn held that such notices, even if they contain errors, will be valid if they are:

> "[S]ufficiently clear and unambiguous to leave a reasonable recipient in no reasonable doubt as to how and when they are intended to operate."

The test is an objective one, in that the question is not how the actual recipient understood the notice, but how a reasonable recipient would have understood it.[175] It is thought that a similar approach would be applied to the construction of notices given under the 1938 Act.[176]

## (b)   The statement required by the Act must be in characters not less conspicuous than those used in any other part of the notice

This means that the statement required by the Act must be in characters which are no less readable than the remainder of the notice. In *Middlegate Properties Ltd v Messimeris*[177] the landlord had used a stock form of notice, which had blank spaces at the top right-hand side for inserting details of the premises, the landlord's name and address and the lease. Those details had been filled in using a typeface which was bigger than the duplicated parts of the notice, and blacker in tone. The tenant's contention that the notice was thereby bad was rejected by the Court of Appeal. Lord Denning M.R. said:

**27–37**

> "[T]he part of the notice which informed the tenant of his right to serve a counter-notice and the manner of service was] perfectly legible and easy to read. No one could possibly overlook [it] or be misled in any way. It told the tenant plainly all that the statute required. The statute was aimed at a different mischief altogether—the mischief of putting clauses in small print or on the back which no ordinary person would read. Seeing that this case is not within the mischief, I do not think that we should construe the statute so as to invalidate the notice. We should

---

[172] Above.
[173] Counsel's concession in *BL Holdings Ltd v Marcolt Investments Ltd*, above.
[174] [1997] A.C. 749.
[175] *Mannai Investment Co Ltd v Eagle Star Assurance Co Ltd*, above; *Havant International Holdings v Lionsgate (H) Investment* [2000] L. & T.R. 297.
[176] Cf. *Akici v L R Butlin Ltd* [2006] 1 W.L.R. 201 at [53–54]. See para.27–13, above.
[177] [1973] 1 W.L.R. 168.

construe 'not less conspicuous' so as to mean 'equally readable' or 'equally sufficient' to tell the tenant of his right to give a counter-notice."

## (c) The statement must be to the effect that the lessee is entitled to serve a counter-notice claiming the benefit of the Act

**27–38** The notice must unequivocally inform the tenant of his right to serve a counter-notice. In *BL Holdings Ltd v Marcolt Investments Ltd*[178] a notice which stated that "if you wish to rely upon the provisions of [the 1938 Act], then such notice thereof must be served upon your landlords .... was held to be defective.

## (d) The notice must specify the time within which, and the manner in which, counter-notice may be served

**27–39** The various methods of service are considered in para.27–44, below. If the notice fails to specify any means by which counter-notice may be served, then it is bad.[179] If only one method is specified, then the notice may be good. Thus, in *Middlegate Properties Ltd v Messimeris*[180] the notice did not set out all the ways in which counter-notice could be served, and in particular it did not specify recorded delivery in addition to registered post. It was held to be valid. Lord Denning M.R. said:

> "The tenant says that [the notice] was bad because it only specified registered post and not also recorded delivery service. He points out that under the Recorded Delivery Service Act 1962, recorded delivery is equal to registered post. I think this point is bad also. The statement is sufficient if it specifies one good manner of service. It need not specify all."

This appears to suggest that specifying one good method of service is sufficient in all circumstances. However, in *BL Holdings Ltd v Marcolt Investments Ltd*[181] Stephenson L.J. said of the above passage:

> "It may be that the statement of [Lord Denning M.R.] went too far if it is taken to mean that it is unnecessary for a lessor to specify more than one good manner of service in all circumstances. If, however, the words of the Master of the Rolls are read in relation to the question which was before the court, namely, whether it was necessary to add to a statement that the notice could be left at or sent by registered post 'to our office', a statement that registered post included recorded delivery ... obviously that decision does not go as far as the language of the Master of the Rolls might appear to go."

It may therefore be that there will be circumstances in which specifying only one method of service will not be enough. An example might be where the only method specified is, to the knowledge of the landlord, impractical for the lessee to employ.

---

[178] [1979] 1 E.G.L.R. 97.
[179] *BL Holdings Ltd v Marcolt Investments Ltd* [1979] 1 E.G.L.R. 97.
[180] [1992] 1 E.G.L.R. 61.
[181] Above.

### (e)   The notice must specify the name and address for service of the lessor

A notice which specifies the name and address of the landlord's solicitors is valid if those solicitors are authorised to accept service.[182]

**27–40**

### (f)   Subsequent correspondence

Where the notice is bad, a subsequent letter which incorporates it by reference and makes good the deficiency may constitute a good notice. Thus, in *Sidnell v Wilson*[183] the landlord's notice was bad because it did not contain a statement that the tenant was entitled to serve a counter-notice claiming the benefit of the 1938 Act. However, a subsequent letter which referred to the first notice and contained the information required by the Act was held by the Court of Appeal to be a valid notice.

**27–41**

### (g)   The notice may be addressed to "the lessee"

The notice may be addressed to the lessee by that designation, without his name, or generally to the persons interested, without any name, and notwithstanding that any person to be affected by the notice is absent or under disability.[184]

**27–42**

## On whom the notice must be served

The notice required by the 1938 Act must be served on "the lessee".[185] This expression has the same meaning as it does in s.146 of the Law of Property Act 1925.[186] The person to be served with notice is the person entitled to a s.146 notice, namely the tenant under the lease.[187] No notice need therefore be served on mortgagees or sub-tenants.[188] Once a notice has been served on the person who is the tenant at the time the notice is given, then no further notice need be served if the lease is subsequently assigned.[189]

**27–43**

---

[182] *Middlegate Properties Ltd v Messimeris*, above.
[183] [1966] 2 Q.B. 67.
[184] Leasehold Property (Repairs) Act 1938 s.7(2) (applying Law of Property Act 1925 s.196(2)).
[185] Leasehold Property (Repairs) Act 1938 s.1(1) and (2).
[186] Leasehold Property (Repairs) Act 1938 s.7(1).
[187] *Smith v Spaul* [2003] 1 E.G.L.R. 70.
[188] See para.27–25, above.
[189] *Kanda v Church Commissioners for England* [1958] 1 Q.B. 332.

## Service of the notice

**27–44**    The provisions of s.196 of the Law of Property Act 1925 apply to the service of the landlord's notice.[190] These provisions have already been considered.[191] The provisions of s.18(2) of the Landlord and Tenant Act 1927[192] do not apply to notices under the 1938 Act which are served as a prerequisite only to proceedings for damages.[193] However, where the notice is served as a prerequisite to forfeiture, then the provisions of the subsection apply.

## Where the landlord has already carried out the works

**27–45**    A valid notice under the 1938 Act can only be served in relation to a breach which subsists at the date of the notice. It was held in *SEDAC Investments Ltd v Tanner*[194] that no notice can be served once the remedial work has been carried out, even if this is done by the landlord.

In that case repair work to the front wall of the demised premises was required as a matter of urgency, and the landlord entered and carried out the work himself. He then served a s.146 notice in the form required by the 1938 Act, and applied for leave to commence proceedings to recover the cost of the work from the tenant by way of damages for breach of the repairing covenant in the lease. The tenant contended that the court had no jurisdiction to grant leave, because the landlord's s.146 notice was of no effect, having been served after the breach had already been remedied by the landlord. This contention was upheld by Mr Michael Wheeler QC (sitting as a deputy High Court judge). His reasoning was as follows:

> "The whole scheme of s.1 of the Act of 1938 appears to commence with—and to hinge upon—the service of a valid lessor's s.146 notice: and if, therefore, I am right in holding that a s.146 notice, to be effective, must be served *before* [judge's emphasis] the breach is remedied, I am forced to the conclusion that in a case such as the present, where the lessor remedied the breach before attempting to serve a notice under s.146(1), he has thereby put it out of his power to serve a valid s.146 notice at all, with the result that he has deprived the lessee of his right to serve a counter-notice: and the consequence of this seems inevitably to be that the court has no jurisdiction to give the lessor leave to commence proceedings for damages because the jurisdiction arises … only when (and because) the lessee has served a valid counter-notice."

**27–46**    It is thought that the judge's decision was wrong. First, the carrying out of the remedial work will not always remedy the effects of the breach. For example, the disrepair may have resulted in the landlord having become liable to pay damages to third parties under the Defective Premises Act 1972,[195] or the rental value of adjoining premises may have been diminished. The landlord would therefore have a right of action for damages which would survive the carrying out of the

---

[190]  Leasehold Property (Repairs) Act 1938 s.7(2).
[191]  See para.27–26, above.
[192]  Section 18(2) is considered in para.27–27, above.
[193]  The subsection only applies in relation to the enforcement of a right of re-entry or forfeiture: Landlord and Tenant Act 1927 s.18(2).
[194]  [1982] 1 W.L.R. 1342.
[195]  See para.20–49 et seq., above.

remedial work by the tenant. However, if the judge's conclusion is correct, the landlord loses his right to bring proceedings for damages once the tenant does the work. It is difficult to see that the Act was intended to prohibit claims of this sort.

Second, even if the breach is remedied by the carrying out of the works by the tenant, the same cannot be true where the work is done by the landlord. The tenant's obligation under the repairing covenant is to remedy disrepair at his own expense. If the tenant breaks his obligation by failing to carry out repairs, the breach is not remedied by the same work being done by the landlord, for this is not part of the parties' bargain. In such a case the landlord has remedied not the breach but the state of disrepair which the breach has brought into existence. It is thought that the only relevant effect of the landlord carrying out the work is that the breach becomes incapable of remedy; it does not prevent the landlord from serving a s.146 notice under the Act as a prerequisite to claiming damages.[196]

## Waiver of defective s.146 notice

Defects in a s.146 notice are capable of being waived by the tenant.[197] However, it appears that notwithstanding certain obiter dicta of Lord Denning M.R. in *Sidnell v Wilson*,[198] the service of an unqualified counter-notice under the Act will not normally prevent the tenant from subsequently contending that the landlord's notice is invalid.[199] In order to constitute a waiver something in the nature of an express or implied promise not to rely on the invalidity of the landlord's notice at any future date will usually be required.[200]

27–47

## The tenant's counter-notice

### (a)    Contents

The tenant's counter-notice need do no more than inform the landlord that the tenant claims the benefit of the Leasehold Property (Repairs) Act 1938. The general principles applicable to construction of notices would no doubt apply, so that precise adherence to the statutory language is not essential provided that the notice is sufficiently clear and unambiguous as to leave a reasonable recipient in no reasonable doubt as to what was meant.[201] However, it is possible that a counter-notice which does not specify the name of the lessee by whom it is given

27–48

---

[196] An argument along these lines was addressed to Vinelott J. in *Hamilton v Martell Securities Ltd* [1984] 1 Ch. 266. The judge said that although he could see force in the distinction between remedying a state of disrepair and remedying a breach of covenant, nonetheless he was not persuaded that the decision in *SEDAC Investments Ltd v Tanner* was wrong.
[197] *BL Holdings Ltd v Marcolt Investments Ltd* [1979] 1 E.G.L.R. 97.
[198] [1966] 2 Q.B. 67.
[199] *BL Holdings Ltd v Marcolt Investments Ltd*, above.
[200] Ibid., per Brandon L.J. at 856.
[201] See *Mannai Investment Co Ltd v Eagle Star Assurance Co Ltd* [1997] A.C. 749.

is bad.[202] The notice should therefore state expressly the name of the person by whom, or on whose behalf, it is given. It is not proper for a solicitor who is acting on behalf of a tenant who has received a s.146 notice to refuse to give his client's name.[203] A suggested form of counter-notice is set out in Appendix I, below.

### (b) Time limits

27–49    The counter-notice must be served within 28 days from the date on which the s.146 notice is served or deemed to have been served. The court has no power to extend time.

### (c) By whom the counter-notice must be served

27–50    The counter-notice must either be served by the tenant himself, or on his behalf by some duly authorised agent. But a counter-notice cannot validly be served by a mortgagee, whether he is out of possession[204] or in possession.[205]

### (d) On whom the counter-notice must be served

27–51    The counter-notice should be served either on the landlord, or on any person who has authority to accept service on his behalf.[206] Where, unknown to the tenant, the reversion has changed hands, the tenant is entitled to serve counter-notice on the original landlord until he has received notice that such person has ceased to be the landlord, and notice of the name and address of the new landlord.[207]

### (e) Service

27–52    The provisions of s.196 of the Law of Property Act 1925 apply to the service of the tenant's counter-notice.[208] These provisions have already been considered.[209]

### Effect of failure to serve counter-notice

27–53    If the tenant fails to serve a valid counter-notice in time, the 1938 Act ceases to be relevant. The landlord is entitled to forfeit or bring proceedings for damages without the leave of the court. The fact that the landlord served a s.146 notice on

---

[202] *Pascall v Galinski* [1970] 1 Q.B. 38 per Lord Denning M.R. at 43F. See also *Lemmerbell Ltd v Britannia LAS Direct Ltd* [1998] 3 E.G.L.R. 67; *Havant International Holdings v Lionsgate (H) Investment* [2000] L. & T.R. 297; and *Procter & Gamble Technical Centres Ltd v Brixton Plc* [2003] 2 E.G.L.R. 24.

[203] *Pascall v Galinski*, above.

[204] *Church Commissioners for England v Ve-Ri-Best Manufacturing Co Ltd* [1957] 1 Q.B. 238.

[205] *Smith v Spaul* [2003] 1 E.G.L.R. 70 (criticising *Target Home Loans Ltd v Iza Ltd* [2000] 1 E.G.L.R. 23).

[206] The position of solicitors and others is considered in para.27–26, above.

[207] Landlord and Tenant Act 1954 s.51(4).

[208] Leasehold Property (Repairs) Act 1938 s.7(2).

[209] See para.27–26, above.

a person who was not entitled to notice (for example, a mortgagee or sub-tenant[210]), and that such person has given a counter-notice in time, does not affect this.[211]

## Effect of service of counter-notice

Where the tenant serves a valid counter-notice in time, the landlord cannot forfeit, whether by proceedings or peaceable re-entry, or bring an action for damages otherwise than with the leave of the court.[212] Nor is he entitled to the benefit of s.146(3) of the Law of Property Act 1925[213] unless he applies to the court for leave to take proceedings, in which case the court has power to direct whether and to what extent he is to be entitled to the benefit of s.146(3).[214]

Where the lease has been assigned after the service of the counter-notice, then leave must be sought against the assignee even if leave has already been given against the assignor.[215]

**27–54**

## The application to the court

The appropriate venue and procedure for applying to the court for leave is considered in Ch.36, para.38–06 et seq., below.

It has been held in the county court that the landlord cannot validly make an application for leave under the 1938 Act once he has issued and served forfeiture proceedings for non-payment of rent and those proceedings remain undetermined.[216]

An application under the 1938 Act for leave to commence proceedings for forfeiture is a pending land action within s.17(1) of the Land Charges Act 1972.[217]

**27–55**

### THE GROUNDS ON WHICH LEAVE CAN BE GIVEN

## Introductory

Section 1(5) of the 1938 Act set out five grounds on which leave can be given. They are alternatives, so that it is sufficient if the landlord proves any one.[218]

**27–56**

---

210 See para.27–25, above.
211 *Church Commissioners for England v Ve-Ri-Vest Manufacturing Co Ltd* [1957] 1 Q.B. 238.
212 Leasehold Property (Repairs) Act 1938 s.1(3).
213 See paras 34–11 to 34–12, below.
214 Leasehold Property (Repairs) Act 1938 s.2.
215 *Kanda v Church Commissioners for England* [1958] 1 Q.B. 332.
216 Unreported decision of Recorder Prevezer QC dated September 17, 2005.
217 *Selim Ltd v Bickenhall Engineering Ltd* [1981] 1 W.L.R. 1318. This is not affected by the fact that the application is also for leave to commence proceedings for damages, but Sir Robert Megarry V.C. doubted whether an action for damages for breach of covenant is by itself a pending land action.
218 *Phillips v Price* [1959] 1 Ch. 181; see also *Associated British Ports v C.H. Bailey Plc* [1990] 2 A.C. 703.

## The meaning of "proves"

**27–57**  Prior to the decision of the Court of Appeal in *Sidnell v Wilson*[219] the word "proves" was treated as meaning proof on a balance of probabilities.[220] However, in *Sidnell v Wilson* the Court of Appeal held that the landlord need only show a prima facie or arguable case that the tenant is in breach, i.e. a case which, if believed, would entitle the landlord to succeed. In *Land Securities Plc v Receiver for the Metropolitan Police District*[221] Megarry V.C. held that the decision in *Sidnell v Wilson* applied not only to proof that the tenant is in breach, but also to proof of the grounds in s.1(5) of the Act. The result of these decisions in practice was that it became relatively easy for the landlord to obtain leave under the Act. The court did not generally consider the tenant's evidence but confined its approach to asking itself whether the landlord's evidence, if true, established the landlord's case. The landlord had to show nothing more than "a plausible case which the tenant [was] not permitted to controvert."[222]

However, in *Associated British Ports v C.H. Bailey Plc*[223] the House of Lords held that "proves" means proof on the ordinary civil standard of a balance of probabilities. This applies both to proving that the tenant is in breach of covenant, and to establishing one or more of the grounds in s.1(5) of the Act. As a result, *Sidnell v Wilson*[224] and *Land Securities Plc v Receiver for the Metropolitan Police District*[225] must be regarded as having been overruled on the issue of the burden of proof.

**27–58**  It is thought that the decision in *Associated British Ports v C.H. Bailey Plc*[226] accords with the policy of the 1938 Act, and that its reversal of the previous practice is to be welcomed. However, one of the difficulties to which it gives rise is the possibility of the same question, namely the extent to which the tenant is in breach of covenant, being tried twice: once in the course of proceedings for leave, and (if the landlord gets leave) a second time in the subsequent proceedings for forfeiture or damages. The undesirability of this was the principal reason behind the decision in *Sidnell v Wilson*,[227] and it was urged on the House of Lords as a reason for upholding the previous practice. Lord Templeman dealt with it in the following passage:

> "The battle between landlord and tenant must be fought out at some stage and Parliament has directed that it shall be fought under the Act of 1938 when the landlord seeks leave to pursue his remedies for breach of covenant, leaving only the question of relief to be determined under s.146 of the Act of 1925. If the landlord fails to prove that he is entitled to pursue his remedies, the tenant is entitled, as of right, to a dismissal of the landlord's application under the Act of 1938; the tenant is immediately relieved from the threat of forfeiture implicit in the s.146

---

[219] [1966] 2 Q.B. 67.
[220] *Phillips v Price* [1959] Ch. 181; *Re Metropolitan Film Studios Ltd's Application* [1962] 1 W.L.R. 1315.
[221] [1983] 1 W.L.R. 439.
[222] *Associated British Ports v C.H. Bailey Plc* [1990] 2 A.C. 703, per Lord Templeman.
[223] Above.
[224] [1996] 2 Q.B. 67.
[225] [1983] 1 W.L.R. 439.
[226] Above.
[227] Above.

notice served on him and from the expense and uncertainty of forfeiture proceedings, in which, if there are many allegations of breach of covenant, the tenant must rebut every single allegation of breach or plead for mercy in respect of any breach which is proved. If the landlord, applying under the Act of 1938, proves that the tenant is in breach of his repairing covenant and that the immediate remedying of the breach is necessary, the tenant will know what steps he must take to avoid forfeiture. In an appropriate case, the court, hearing the application under the Act of 1938, can itself specify the breaches which must be remedied and, for example, may in the exercise of the power conferred on the court by s.1(6) of the Act of 1938, adjourn or dismiss the application of the landlord on condition that certain repairs are carried out. Of course, if the landlord and tenant agree that the battle shall be fought in forfeiture proceedings, then leave under the Act of 1938 may be granted by consent without the landlord adducing detailed evidence at that stage. But if the landlord and tenant do not agree, then the landlord must attempt to prove his case under the Act of 1938 and, if he fails to do so, there will be no forfeiture proceedings. If the landlord does prove his case under the Act of 1938, I do not accept that it is necessary or proper that the battle need or should be fought all over again on the hearing of the forfeiture proceedings or that, in practice, additional expense and delay will result. In any event, the Act of 1938 requires that the landlord shall prove his case; the Act of 1925 requires that the tenant shall satisfy the court that he is entitled to relief."

There will be no difficulty where the application for leave is refused, since there will then be no subsequent proceedings. However, where leave is granted, the question will inevitably arise at the trial of the ensuing proceedings as to the nature and extent of the breaches of covenant.[228] The court which granted leave will already have considered this question, at least to the extent of having found on a balance of probabilities that breaches exist of a kind that justify the grant of leave. It is thought that once the court has granted leave, the tenant will be estopped at the subsequent trial from (i) denying that he was in breach at the date of the hearing of the application for leave, and (ii) disputing the existence at the date of the hearing of the application for leave of any specific breaches then found by the court to exist. It follows that, where the state of the premises remains the same between the hearing of the application for leave and the trial of the landlord's action, the question of breach will not usually need to be tried again. Even here, however, difficulties may arise if the court giving leave has not identified in sufficient detail the breaches which it found to exist. In such cases it is not inconceivable that the question of breach would have to be gone into again at trial. In addition, it is thought that it would be open to the parties at trial to show that the state of the premises has changed since the earlier hearing.[229] The tenant will be entitled to prove that he has done all or some of the work. The landlord will be entitled to adduce evidence with a view to showing that the state of the premises has worsened since the hearing for leave, so that existing breaches have become more serious. To this extent also it may be necessary for the court trying the landlord's action to inquire into precisely what breaches the court giving leave found to exist.

27–59

One consequence in practice of the decision in *Associated British Ports v C.H. Bailey Plc* is that leave will be harder to obtain than was previously the case. The ease with which it was possible to obtain leave under the former law resulted in abuse in some cases, the elimination of which is clearly in accordance with the

---

[228] This question will be relevant both to liability and (where the proceedings are for forfeiture) the terms of relief.

[229] See *Onwuama v Ealing LNC* [2008] EWHC 1704 (Q.B.) (a case under s.11 of the Landlord and Tenant Act 1985), considered in para.20–48, above.

policy of the 1938 Act. However, leave is likely to take longer to obtain as well. A contested application may require a full trial, with Scott schedules, experts' reports and cross-examination of witnesses. The result of this may be to discourage landlords with genuine reasons for wanting to enforce repairing covenants from applying for leave. However, this consequence cannot fairly be laid at the door of the decision in *Associated British Ports v C.H. Bailey Plc*: it is the result of the Act itself.

## The date at which the grounds must be established

**27–60**  The question of the date at which the grounds must be proved was considered by Ungoed Thomas J. in *Re Metropolitan Film Studios Ltd's Application*.[230] He pointed out that if the date of the hearing of the application was the relevant date then the tenant would be able to take advantage of delays in the course of the proceedings to carry out the work and thereby defeat the landlord's application. He went on to say:

> "It seems to me that the section should not be so construed as to subject the lessors' vested rights to being automatically barred by action of the lessee subsequent to the issue of the summons."

On the facts before him, however, the question did not arise because the disrepair was substantial, and about 70 per cent of the work remained undone at the date of the hearing.

This suggests that the relevant date is the date of issue of the application. However, the wording of the grounds in s.1(5) of the Act suggests that the relevant date is the date when the court considers the matter, i.e. the date of the hearing. It is thought that this is the better view. The policy of the Act would certainly seem to support this being the correct date. Any injustice to the landlord which results from a change in circumstances since the issue of the application can be dealt with by an appropriate costs order. Where some or all of the grounds (a) to (d) existed at the date of the application but have ceased to exist by the date of the hearing, then it may be that in appropriate circumstances the court would still be able to grant leave under ground (e).

The question of the correct date was considered by Cox J. in *Landmaster Properties Ltd v Thackeray Property Services*,[231] who said that she agreed with the view expressed in the preceding passage in the text[232] and the reasoning that underpins it. She went on to say:

> "The policy of the Act, and the use of the present tense throughout the subsection, seem to me to point to the date of the hearing as being the date at which the section 1(5) grounds must be proved."

---

[230] [1962] 1 W.L.R. 1315.
[231] [2003] 2 E.G.L.R. 30.
[232] Which appeared in the same form in the Second Edition.

## Ground (a): That the immediate remedying of the breach is requisite for preventing substantial diminution in the value of [the landlord's] reversion, or that the value thereof has already been substantially diminished by the breach

Ground (a) is divided into the following two limbs:[233]                                   **27–61**

(1)  that the immediate remedying of the breach in question is requisite for preventing substantial diminution in the value of the landlord's reversion; or
(2)  that the value of the landlord's reversion has already been substantially diminished by the breach.

In each case the reversion in question must be valued subject to the lease, and not with vacant possession. Proving either limb of ground (a) may therefore be difficult where the term has a substantial time left to run.[234] The hypothetical purchaser will have the continuing benefit of the tenant's repairing obligations in the lease, and the level of rent will generally be unaffected by the disrepair because any future rent reviews will be conducted on the express or implied assumption that the premises are in repair. In these circumstances in the majority of cases the disrepair will not have resulted in substantial diminution in the value of the reversion. It is one thing to say that a purchaser would prefer the premises to be in good condition, so that given the choice of two buildings, both held under repairing leases and one in disrepair and the other not, he is likely to opt for the one in good condition. It is another to prove to the satisfaction of the court that he would pay a substantially lower sum for the building in disrepair. There are some cases, however, where it may be reasonably clear that a purchaser would pay less. For example, the strength of the tenant's covenant may be poor. If the disrepair is serious, or if the end of the lease is not that far away, and the repairs are such that they will have to be done before the premises can be relet, then the purchaser may make a substantial discount to reflect the possibility of the tenant neither doing the work nor making any payment of damages in lieu. Another example may be where the disrepair is such that the landlord will suffer damage unless it is remedied immediately, perhaps because it poses a danger to third parties who would have rights of action under the Defective Premises Act 1972.[235] The question of diminution in the value of the reversion during the term is further considered in Ch.30, below.

The question of what is substantial is one of fact and degree. It has been said that:

> "'Substantial' in this connection is not the same as 'not unsubstantial', *i.e.* just enough to avoid the *de minimis* principle. One of the primary meanings of the word is equivalent to considerable, solid or big ... Applying the word in this sense, it must be left to the discretion

---

[233]  See *Re Metropolitan Film Studios Ltd's Application* [1962] 1 W.L.R. 1315 at 1320.
[234]  Thus, in *Sidnell v Wilson* [1966] 2 Q.B. 67 Lord Denning M.R. said that "... in the great majority of dilapidation cases where there is want of repair during the term, leave will not be given: for in most cases the reversion is not diminished much in value by the breach."
[235]  See para.20–49 et seq., above.

of the judge of fact to decide as best he can according to the circumstances of each case … Aristotle pointed out long ago that the degree of precision that is attainable depends on the subject-matter.[236]"

**27–62**  It is thought that it will be relevant to consider not only the amount of the diminution but also the proportion which it bears to the value of the reversion in repair. For example, it is thought that a diminution of £15,000 in relation to a reversion worth £5 million in repair would not generally be substantial; however, the same diminution in relation to a reversion worth £30,000 in repair would clearly be substantial.

Ground (a) was held to be have been proved in *Phillips v Price*,[237] in which Harman J. said:

> "It is admitted that there have been wholesale breaches of the repairing covenants; the landlord says £5,000 worth, and even the first respondent agrees £2,500 worth. No attempt has been made to keep this property in the state in which the tenant is bound to keep it. The first respondent has simply taken his rents and done as little as he could. It seems to me clear that this property in good repair must be worth more than in its present condition. It is said, however, that this is a property in which a compulsory purchase order has been made, and site value only will be paid, and that the same thing would have happened if the property had been kept in first class order throughout the term of the lease. I do not accept that at all. It seems to me ridiculous to say that it would have made no difference if the London County Council surveyors had found that the property was in first class repair, even though the other properties in the road were not. In that case, two things might have happened: either this property might have been excluded from the clearance area, in which case market value would have been paid for it, or some so-called ex-gratia payment might have been payable for it … The question at issue in an action of this sort is damage to the reversion; and the damage to the reversion which in my judgment has to be proved is that there would be a substantial difference between what the London County Council may be made to pay for the property, or the site as it is, and as it ought to be. How much that may be, I have no idea, and I do not propose to interfere with the trial judge by suggesting it."

## Ground (b): that the immediate remedying of the breach is required for giving effect in relation to the premises to the purposes of any enactment, or of any byelaw or other provision having effect under an enactment, or for giving effect to any order of the court or requirement of any authority under any enactment or any such byelaw or other provision as aforesaid

**27–63**  Ground (b) comprises two types of work:

(1)  work which is necessary to comply with statutes, byelaws or provisions having effect under a statute, such as a statutory instrument or regulations made by a body empowered by a statute to make them;

(2)  work which is the subject of a court order or a requirement of a competent authority in the exercise of powers conferred by a statute, byelaw or provision having effect under a statute.

---

[236] *Palser v Grinling* [1948] A.C. 291 (a case on furnished lettings under the Rent Acts).
[237] [1959] 1 Ch. 181.

An example of (1) might be repair works required to comply with the provisions of statutes such as the Offices, Shops and Railway Premises Act 1963 or the Factories Act 1961 or regulations made thereunder. An example of (2) might be works which are the subject of a notice served by the local housing authority under the provisions of the Housing Act 1985. Provided that, as between landlord and tenant, the tenant is liable to carry out the works, it does not seem to matter for the purposes of ground (b) that the person required or liable to carry out the works under the statute or notice in question is the landlord.

## Ground (c): where the lessee is not in occupation of the whole of the premises as respects which the covenant or agreement is proposed to be enforced, that the immediate remedying of the breach is required in the interests of the occupier of those premises or of part thereof

Ground (c) applies where the premises or part are occupied by a third party who is being adversely affected by the tenant's failure to comply with his repairing obligations. In *Phillips v Price*[238] Harman J. regarded it as self-evident that it would be in the interests of the 12 sub-tenants of flats in the building that the relevant remedial works should be done. In practice ground (c) is most commonly used where part of the premises (such as a flat above a shop) is sub-let to a residential occupier. If s.11 of the Landlord and Tenant Act 1985 applies to the sub-tenancy,[239] the tenant's failure to carry out the works may constitute a breach of his obligations under the sub-tenancy as well as of the repairing covenant in the head lease. In such a case, if the sub-tenant were to obtain a court order requiring the tenant to carry out repairs within the section, the landlord would be able to rely on ground (b) in addition to ground (c).

**27–64**

## Ground (d): that the breach can be immediately remedied at an expense that is relatively small in comparison with the much greater expense that would probably be occasioned by postponement of the necessary work

Ground (d) can be summarised in the cliché that "a stitch in time saves nine". It is thought that it is primarily directed towards disrepair which, if not checked immediately, will result in damage to other parts of the building. An example might be an attack of dry rot which requires to be eradicated immediately if it is not to spread. However, the ground may also apply where, as a result of rapidly increasing building costs, the same work will, if left, cost considerably more to remedy than would be the case if it were done now. In the exercise of its discretion,[240] the court would no doubt have regard to whether such increases are in fact nominal because they result only from the effects of inflation.

**27–65**

---

[238] [1959] 1 Ch. 181.
[239] See para.20–17 et seq., above.
[240] See paras 27–67 to 27–69, below.

## Ground (e): special circumstances exist which in the opinion of the court render it just and equitable that leave should be given

**27–66**    Ground (e) confers on the court a discretion to grant leave even though the landlord cannot establish any of the other grounds. However, it does not allow the court to give leave whenever it would be just and equitable to do so: there must be special circumstances why leave should be given.[241] In *Phillips v Price*[242] (where the premises consisted of a slum tenement) Harman J. held that neither the existence of a compulsory purchase order, which was said to have been brought about by the tenant's breaches, and under which the compensation would be limited to cleared site value only, nor the fact that the tenant had assigned the lease to a limited company with a view to avoiding liability, constituted "special circumstances" within ground (e).

In *Landmaster Properties Ltd v Thackeray Property Services*[243] the judge at first instance granted leave under grounds (a) and (e) in circumstances where the premises (which the tenant had allowed to become derelict) had been completely destroyed by fire shortly after the date of the landlord's application for leave. Cox J., dismissing the appeal against his decision, held that there had been no evidence before him to support the grant of leave under ground (a), but that he had been entitled to take the view that there were special circumstances justifying the grant of leave under ground (e).

In *Agricullo v Yorkshire Housing*,[244] neither the tenant's admission that the premises were in disrepair nor the fact that if leave were not given, the landlord would be left without a remedy were held to be enough to constitute "special circumstances" for the purposes of ground (e). It was held that:

> "the cases in which leave is to be granted in special circumstances ought, on principle, to be ones in which something out of the ordinary occurs to justify the immediate commencement of proceedings."

## The court's discretion to grant leave

**27–67**    Even where the landlord proves both that there are breaches and that grounds under s.1(5) of the Act exist, the court still has an overriding discretion whether or not to grant leave.[245] In some of the cases under the Act a narrow view has been taken of the discretion. Thus, in *Phillips v Price*[246] Harman J. said:

> "I have a discretion—I am not bound—to give the landlord leave to sue, a discretion which entitles me to give him leave if I think fit; and, in my judgment, he certainly ought to be given leave. After all, the lessee originally covenanted to do all these things, and got possession of the property upon that footing, and exacted the rack rent, paying a ground rent and electing to perform his covenanted obligations. Why should the landlord not be entitled to his covenanted

---

[241] *Phillips v Price* [1959] Ch. 181.
[242] Above.
[243] [2003] 2 E.G.L.R. 30.
[244] [2010] 2 P & CR 11. See further on this case para.34–07, below.
[245] *Phillips v Price*, above; *Re Metropolitan Film Studios Ltd's Application* [1962] 1 W.L.R. 1315; *Land Securities Plc v Receiver for the Metropolitan Police District* [1983] 1 W.L.R. 439.
[246] Above.

rights, whatever they are, because the statute passed with a view to preventing some oppression, which is not clear to me, says that certain things must be proved to the court before such an action is begun? If they are proved, I cannot see why I should interfere further with the freedom of contract which landlords, to some small extent, still do retain."

The above passage was quoted by Ungoed-Thomas J. in *Re Metropolitan Film Studios Ltd's Application.*[247] He went on to say that the discretion under the Act:

"[I]s of an interlocutory nature, not to be exercised to exclude the lessor from his rights … unless the court is clearly convinced that, despite compliance with the requirement specified in the paragraphs of sub-section (5), the application should be refused."

However, a wider approach to the exercise of the discretion was taken by Sir    **27–68**
Robert Megarry V.C. in *Land Securities Plc v Receiver for the Metropolitan Police District,*[248] in which he said that he would have difficulty in agreeing with the view that leave should always be given unless the court was "clearly convinced" that it should not. He pointed out that proceedings for forfeiture and damages are burdensome on tenants, and that the Act of 1938 was plainly passed so as to prevent oppression from the threat of such proceedings. He concluded:

"I would have thought that the discretion of the court was much less fettered than is suggested by subjecting it to the words 'clearly convinced'. The fact that one of the paragraphs of sub-section (5) must have been satisfied before the discretion is opened does of course of itself point towards the landlord being given leave to bring proceedings; but there may be many other factors present which ought to be considered in deciding whether or not to grant leave, including the fact that only prima facie evidence is required under sub-section (5), and I do not see why in balancing all the relevant matters nothing save a clear conviction that leave should be refused should suffice for refusing leave."

He refused leave in the exercise of his discretion on the ground that proceedings for forfeiture would be a pointless exercise in view of the fact that other proceedings raising the same or similar issues were already pending between the same parties.

In *Associated British Ports v C.H. Bailey Plc*[249] Harman J.[250] said of the discretion:

"In my view when the result of the exercise of the discretion is merely to allow steps to be taken which may lead to the grant of a remedy after proper proof of facts, there must be an inclination in favour of the exercise."

It is thought that the wider view expressed in *Land Securities Plc v Receiver for*    **27–69**
*the Metropolitan Police District* is to be preferred, and that the discretion is unfettered. In practice it will no doubt be true in many cases that if the landlord establishes one or more of the grounds, it will then be up to the tenant to put forward reasons why the court should nonetheless refuse leave. It is thought, however, that the exercise of the discretion should be approached free from any presumption either way.

---

[247] Above.
[248] [1983] 1 W.L.R. 439.
[249] [1989] 1 E.G.L.R. 69 (unaffected on this point by the decision in the House of Lords).
[250] Not the same Harman J. who decided *Phillips v Price*, above, but his son.

An example of a case where the discretion would have been exercised against the landlord had the matter got that far is *Ladbroke Hotels Ltd v Sandhu*,[251] in which Robert Walker J. said (obiter) that the fact that commercial premises had been designed and built for a specialised use, which had become totally obsolete, would be a strong reason for the court to decide under the 1938 Act that a tenant ought not to be held liable for substantial repairs to premises which would inevitably have to be substantially reconstructed, if not completely demolished, before long.

In granting or refusing leave, the court may impose such terms and conditions on the landlord or the tenant as it thinks fit.[252] The following are some of the options open to the court:

(1)   to grant leave in respect of some only of the work specified in the schedule of dilapidations. This would be appropriate where the court finds that some of the work in the schedule does not fall within any of the grounds in s.1(5) of the Act, or that even where grounds are made out in relation to all of the work, it would nonetheless be appropriate for some other reason to confine leave to certain specified works only;

(2)   to adjourn or dismiss the landlord's application on condition that specified repairs are carried out[253];

(3)   to grant leave on terms that proceedings are not issued for a specified period so as to give the tenant the opportunity to do the work.

## Fees and costs

**27–70**   Where the tenant serves a counter-notice under the Act, the landlord is not entitled to the benefit of s.146(3) of the Law of Property Act 1925[254] in relation to his costs and expenses, unless he makes an application for leave, in which case the court has power to direct whether and to what extent he is to be so entitled.[255] The Act does not affect the enforceability of contractual provisions in the lease relating to fees and costs.[256]

In *Phillips v Price*[257] a direction was made that the landlord was to get such benefit from s.146(3) as might be decided by judge hearing the proceedings for which leave had been given.

---

[251] [1995] 2 E.G.L.R. 92
[252] Leasehold Property (Repairs) Act 1938 s.1(6).
[253] An option suggested in *Associated British Ports v C.H. Bailey Plc* [1990] 2 A.C. 703 per Lord Templeman.
[254] See paras 34–11 to 34–12, below.
[255] Leasehold Property (Repairs) Act 1938 s.2.
[256] *Bader Properties Ltd v Linley Property Investments Ltd* (1968) 19 P. & C.R. 620; *Middlegate Properties Ltd v Gidlow-Jackson* (1977) 34 P. & C.R. 4.
[257] [1959] Ch. 181.

## OTHER STATUTORY RESTRICTIONS ON FORFEITURE

### War damage

Where under s.1 of the Landlord and Tenant (War Damage) Act 1939 an obligation to repair is modified or suspended, or an obligation to make good war damage as such is extinguished, then any right of forfeiture arising out of the non-fulfilment of the obligation is modified or suspended or extinguished accordingly.[258]

27–71

### Long residential leases

A number of restrictions on forfeiture apply in relation to long residential leases. First, Pt I of the Landlord and Tenant Act 1954 contains restrictions on forfeiture in relation to long tenancies of residential property.[259] Second, where the lease falls within the Leasehold Reform Act 1967, and a claim to acquire the freehold or an extended lease has been made, no proceedings for forfeiture may be brought without the leave of the court.[260] Third, the Commonhold and Leasehold Reform Act 2002 imposes a number of further restrictions on forfeiture.[261] These provisions are outside the scope of this work, and reference should be made to specialist works on the subject.

27–72

### Insolvency

Additional restrictions on forfeiture are imposed by the Insolvency Act 1986. The effect of these is that in a number of cases the landlord is not entitled to forfeit without the leave of the court. These restrictions are outside the scope of this work, and reference should be made to specialist works on the subject.

27–73

## WHAT AMOUNTS TO FORFEITURE?

### How forfeiture is effected

Forfeiture may be effected either by commencing proceedings for possession, or by physical re-entry.

27–74

---

[258] Landlord and Tenant (War Damage) Act 1939 s.1(4). See further para.26–15, above.
[259] Landlord and Tenant Act 1954 s.16.
[260] Leasehold Reform Act 1967 Sch.3 para.4(1). See also the Leasehold Reform, Housing and Urban Development Act 1993 Schs 3 and 12.
[261] Commonhold and Leasehold Reform Act 2002 ss.167–171.

## Forfeiture by peaceable re-entry

**27–75**    Physical re-entry requires an unequivocal act which shows that the landlord intends to exercise the right of forfeiture. The safest method is by changing the locks so that the tenant is excluded. Other possible methods include letting a third party into occupation as tenant, or accepting an existing sub-tenant as tenant under a new tenancy between him and the landlord[262] (but not simply allowing a sub-tenant to remain on the terms of his existing sub-tenancy[263]). It is sensible practice when forfeiting by changing the locks to take photographs of the condition and contents of the premises at the time, so as to prevent subsequent allegations by the tenant that either the premises, or the contents, were damaged in the course of, or after, the entry.

It is unlawful to forfeit other than by proceedings where the premises are let as a dwelling and any person is lawfully residing in them.[264] In practice this means that if there is any possibility of anyone living in the premises, then physical re-entry should not be attempted. Further, it is a criminal offence for a person without lawful authority (which does not include an interest in or right to possession or occupation of any premises) to threaten or use violence for the purpose of securing entry to premises upon which there is (to the knowledge of the person using or threatening violence) someone present who is opposed to the entry (unless the person using or threatening violence is a displaced residential occupier or a protected intending occupier of the premises or is acting on behalf of such an occupier).[265]

The principal advantage of physical re-entry is that it saves the time and expense of proceedings in a case where the tenant has disappeared or is unlikely for some other reason to contest the landlord's claim. The principal disadvantage is that if for some reason the right to forfeit has not arisen (for example, because the s.146 notice is defective, or a reasonable time has not elapsed since it was served), the re-entry will be a trespass for which the landlord will be liable in damages. For this reason, a landlord contemplating forfeiture by physical re-entry should consider very carefully before proceeding whether he is sure that all the common law and statutory preconditions set out above have been complied with.

## Forfeiture by proceedings

**27–76**    Forfeiture by the commencement of proceedings is not effected until the proceedings have been both issued and served: mere issue is not sufficient.[266]

---

[262] *Baylis v Le Gros* (1858) 4 C.B.N.S. 537; *London & County (A. & D.) Ltd v Wilfred Sportsman Ltd* [1971] Ch. 764.

[263] *Ashton v Sobelman* [1987] 1 W.L.R. 177.

[264] Protection from Eviction Act 1977 s.2. The phrase "let as a dwelling" means let as wholly or partly a dwelling, so that the restrictions in the 1977 Act apply where the premises have a mixed business and residential use: *Pirabakaran v Patel* [2006] 3 E.G.L.R. 23.

[265] Criminal Law Act 1977 s.6 (as amended). For the detailed provisions of s.6, reference should be made to specialist works on criminal law.

[266] *Canas Property Co Ltd v K.L. Television Services Ltd* [1970] 2 Q.B. 433.

RELIEF FROM FORFEITURE

## The court's jurisdiction

The court has jurisdiction to grant relief from forfeiture under s.146(2) of the Law **27–77**
of Property Act 1925 (save in certain cases which are of no relevance to the law
of dilapidations). This subsection empowers the court to grant or refuse relief as
the court, having regard to the proceedings and conduct of the parties under
s.146(1) and to all the other circumstances, thinks fit. The discretion thus given to
the court is extremely wide. It is provided that relief may be granted on such
terms, if any, as to costs, expenses, damages, compensation, penalty or otherwise,
including the granting of an injunction to restrain any like breach in the future, as
the court, in the circumstances of each case, thinks fit. There is no residual power
to grant relief under the court's former equitable jurisdiction.[267] It follows that
where for any reason relief is not available under s.146(2) of the 1925 Act then
there is no further right to relief. In appropriate circumstances, the court has
power to grant relief in respect of part only of the demised premises.[268]

## The application for relief

The application for relief may be made either by counterclaim under Pt 20 of the **27–78**
CPR to the landlord's claim for forfeiture, if any, or by a separate claim.[269] It is
preferable to apply in the landlord's claim wherever possible.

Where the lease is vested in joint tenants, then all must apply: relief cannot be
granted to one or some only.[270]

## Time for making the application for relief

The tenant may apply for relief under s.146(2) of the 1925 Act where the landlord **27–79**
"is proceeding" to enforce the right of re-entry.[271] An application may be made as
soon as a s.146 notice has been served.[272] The fact that the landlord has forfeited
by peaceable re-entry does not affect the court's jurisdiction to grant relief, so that
the tenant may still apply even though the landlord is in possession.[273] Where the
landlord forfeits by proceedings, a claim for relief may be made at any time prior
to execution of any order for possession.[274] The discretionary nature of the power
to grant relief should be borne in mind, however, so that the application should be

---

[267] *Official Custodian for Charities v Parway Estates Developments Ltd* [1985] Ch. 151; *Smith v
Metropolitan City Properties Ltd (No.1)* [1986] 1 E.G.L.R. 52; *Billson v Residential Apartments Ltd*
[1992] 1 A.C. 494, CA (reversed by the House of Lords ([1992] 1 A.C. 494) on other grounds).
[268] *G.M.S. Syndicate Ltd v Gary Elliott Ltd* [1982] Ch. 1.
[269] Law of Property Act 1925 s.146(2).
[270] *Fairclough & Sons Ltd v Berliner* [1931] 1 Ch. 60. A judgment for possession against one of two
joint tenants is ineffective: see *Gill v Lewis* [1956] 2 Q.B. 1.
[271] Law of Property Act 1925 s.146(2).
[272] *Pakwood Transport Ltd v 15 Beauchamp Place Ltd* (1978) 36 P. & C.R. 112.
[273] *Billson v Residential Apartments Ltd (No.1)* [1992] 1 A.C. 494.
[274] *Hammersmith and Fulham Borough Council v Top Shop Centres Ltd* [1990] Ch. 237

made promptly where possible. The right to relief is lost once the landlord has obtained and enforced a judgment for possession,[275] even though the lease has not yet been expunged from the charges register of the landlord's title.[276]

## The court's power to grant relief

27–80 Section 146(2) of the 1925 Act confers on the court a complete discretion whether to grant or refuse relief. The court is expressly directed to have regard to "the proceedings and conduct of the parties under the foregoing provisions of this section,[277] and to all the other circumstances." Relief may be granted on such terms, if any, as to costs, expenses, damages, compensation, penalty or otherwise, including the granting of an injunction to restrain any like breach in the future, as it thinks fit.

The fact that the breach is wilful, i.e. deliberate, is relevant in considering whether or not relief should be granted.[278] However, there is no principle to the effect that where the breach is wilful, relief should only be granted in exceptional cases.[279] In exercising its discretion the court will look at all relevant circumstances. Save in exceptional circumstances, relief from forfeiture for breach of a covenant to repair is generally granted, albeit on terms that the tenant does the work. However, relief was refused in *Lordship Lane Property Co Ltd v Honesgran Property Co Ltd*,[280] in which the tenants had promised to carry out the repairs in order to:

> "[D]rag out the matter so that they might continue to receive the profit rentals [from their sub-tenants] without in fact conforming to their obligations."

## Terms of relief

27–81 In the ordinary case, relief from forfeiture for disrepair will usually be granted on terms that the tenant carries out the remedial work within a time scale laid down by the court. However, each case depends on its own facts, and the court has power to grant relief without requiring the tenant to carry out the work. Thus, in *Rose v Hyman*[281] Cozens-Hardy M.R. laid down the following as a general principle in relation to the terms on which relief will be granted:

> "In the first place the applicant must, so far as possible, remedy the breaches alleged in the notice, and pay reasonable compensation for the breaches which cannot be remedied."

---

[275] *Billson v Residential Apartments Ltd (No.1)*, above.
[276] *Abbey National Building Society v Maybeech* [1985] Ch. 190.
[277] This can only be a reference to s.146(1) (considered in para.27–12 et seq., above), which provides that a right of forfeiture shall not be enforceable unless the landlord has served a notice in the specified form and the tenant has failed to comply within a reasonable time.
[278] *Shiloh Spinners Ltd v Harding* [1973] A.C. 691.
[279] *Southern Depot Ltd v British Railways Board* [1990] 2 E.G.L.R. 39, per Morritt J. at 43.
[280] (1962) 182 E.G. 209.
[281] [1911] 2 K.B. 234.

However, in the House of Lords[282] Earl Loreburn said that:

"[T]he discretion given by the section is very wide. The court is to consider all the circumstances and the conduct of the parties. Now it seems to me that when the Act is so expressed to provide a wide discretion, meaning, no doubt, to prevent one man from forfeiting what in fair dealing belongs to someone else, by taking advantage of a breach from which he is not commensurately and irreparably damaged, it is not advisable to lay down any rigid rules for guiding that discretion. I do not doubt that the rules enunciated by the Master of the Rolls in the present case reflect the point of view from which judges would regard an application for relief. But I think it ought to be distinctly understood that there may be cases in which any or all of them may be disregarded. If it were otherwise the free discretion given by the statute would be fettered by limitations which have nowhere been enacted."

In *Associated British Ports v C.H. Bailey Plc*[283] (which concerned a former dry dock which had outlived its usefulness), Lord Templeman, having cited the above passage, said:

"In the present case, therefore, it would be open for a judge in the exercise of the discretion conferred on him by section 146 of the Act of 1925 to grant relief against forfeiture of a lease with nearly 60 years to run without requiring the tenant to spend over £600,000 without substantial benefit to anybody."

It is not, therefore, an inflexible rule that relief can only be granted on terms that the work be done. It is thought, however, that it would only be appropriate to grant relief without requiring the tenant to remedy the breaches where the court is satisfied either that the works will be of no real benefit to any party, or that special circumstances otherwise exist by virtue of which it would be inequitable to make the carrying out of the works a condition of relief. However, there is no reason in principle why the court could not, in an appropriate case, grant relief on terms that some only of the works are carried out, or that the works are carried out at a future date as opposed to forthwith. It is thought that where the Leasehold Property (Repairs) Act 1938 applies, it will generally be appropriate to grant relief on terms that the works are done, because the landlord will already have satisfied the court that leave under that Act ought to be granted.

**27–82**

In principle, there is no reason why the terms on which relief is granted should not include the remedying of breaches other than those specified in the s.146 notice.[284] It may be appropriate to do this where, for example, new breaches have occurred since the date of the notice and, where the Leasehold Property (Repairs) Act 1938 applies,[285] those breaches are of such nature that leave would have been given under that Act if sought. However, a different view may be taken in relation to breaches which the landlord could have, but did not, specify in the notice, particularly where leave under the 1938 Act would have been required and would not have been given.

---

[282] [1912] A.C. 623.

[283] [1990] 2 A.C. 703.

[284] The passage from the judgment of Cozens-Hardy M.R. in *Rose v Hyman* [1911] 2 K.B. 234, set out above, appears to suggest the contrary, but it is thought that this is too narrow a view of the discretion: see the passage from the speech of Earl Loreburn in the House of Lords ([1912] A.C. 623), set out above.

[285] See para.27–31 et seq., above.

Where relief is granted on terms that the tenant carries out work within a specified time, the court has power to extend that time. This remains so even where the order granting relief was a consent order.[286] However, in *Fivecourts v J.R. Leisure Developments Ltd*[287] the court refused to grant further time to a tenant who had failed to comply with a condition for relief in a consent order which required works of repair to be done in accordance with a set timetable. In an exceptional case, the court may vary the terms of relief, even where these were agreed in a consent order, where subsequent events justify doing so.[288]

27–83    Payment of compensation can be made a term of relief. This will generally be appropriate where the breach has caused the landlord damage which cannot be compensated for by the doing of the repairs. An example might be where the disrepair has caused damage to third parties for which the landlord is liable, and has paid damages, under the Defective Premises Act 1972.[289] Payment of the landlord's costs may also be made a term of relief.[290]

It should be noted that there is no power to compel the tenant to comply with the terms on which relief is granted. The effect of the tenant failing to comply is that the lease remains forfeited.

## The effect of the making of an application for relief

27–84    Where the tenant applies for relief, there may be a considerable period of uncertainty before it is known whether or not he will get it. The application for relief will take some time to come to trial, and where relief is granted on terms, the tenant must comply with the terms before he gets relief. During this period it may become necessary to know to what extent the landlord remains able to enforce the covenants in the lease.

Where the lease is forfeited by proceedings, it is not extinguished until judgment is given for possession.[291] The judgment relates back to the commencement of proceedings.[292] Relief from forfeiture likewise relates back to the commencement of proceedings.[293] The position of the tenant in the intervening period between the commencement of proceedings and the grant of relief has been judicially described as "one of very considerable complexity".[294] It is clear that the tenant remains tenant under the lease for certain purposes, for

---

[286]  *Chandless-Chandless v Nicholson* [1942] 2 K.G. 321; *Starside Properties Ltd v Mustapha* [1974] 1 W.L.R. 816.

[287]  [2001] L. & T.R. 5.

[288]  *Ropac v Inntrepreneur Pub Co (CPC) Ltd* [2001] L. & T.R. 10; *Fivecourts v J.R. Leisure Developments Ltd* [2001] L. & T.R. 5.

[289]  See para.20–49 et seq., above.

[290]  See para.34–23, below.

[291]  *Driscoll v Church Commissioners for England* [1957] 1 Q.B. 330, per Denning L.J. at 339–340; *Borzak v Ahmed* [1965] 2 Q.B. 320; *City of Westminster v Ainis* (1975) 29 P. & C.R. 469; *Liverpool Properties Ltd v Oldbridge Investments Ltd* [1985] 2 E.G.L.R. 111; *Ivory Gate Ltd v Spetale* [1998] 2 E.G.L.R. 43; *Maryland Estates Ltd v Bar-Joseph* [1999] 1 W.L.R. 83. It appears from these authorities that whilst the issue and service of the proceedings are conclusive evidence of the landlord's unequivocal election to forfeit, the lease is not actually brought to an end until judgment.

[292]  *Canas Property Co Ltd v K.L. Television Services Ltd* [1970] 2 Q.B. 433.

[293]  *Dendy v Evans* [1910] 1 K.B. 263

[294]  *Liverpool Properties Ltd v Oldbridge Investments Ltd*, above, per Parker L.J. at 1352.

example for the purpose of applying for a new lease under Pt II of the Landlord and Tenant Act 1954.[295] The principles relevant to the law of dilapidations are as follows.

First, the claim for relief is an equitable defence to the claim for forfeiture.[296] It follows that once the tenant has made a bona fide claim for relief and that claim is arguable, the landlord is not entitled to possession until the claim for relief has been dismissed, or the tenant has failed to comply with the conditions on which relief was granted. The landlord is not entitled to summary judgment for possession pending the trial of the claim for relief.[297] The fact that the claim for relief is contested does not make any difference, unless it is not genuine.[298]

Second, the landlord will not be entitled to an interim injunction enforcing the tenant's covenants during the intervening period.[299] The reasoning behind this appears to be that the commencement of proceedings for forfeiture operates as an unequivocal election to determine the lease, and a subsequent claim to enforce the covenants is inconsistent since it necessarily proceeds on the basis that the lease is still subsisting. It should be noted, however, that there is nothing to stop the landlord from enforcing any liability the tenant may have in tort (for example, in nuisance). Further, by virtue of the principle that relief relates back to the commencement of proceedings, once relief is granted then acts or omissions during the intervening period may retrospectively become a breach of covenant.

**27–85**

Third, if the tenant fails to obtain relief, his liability under the repairing covenants ends on the date of forfeiture (the date of service of the claim form, or the date of peaceable re-entry, as the case may be), which becomes the relevant date for the assessment of damages for breach of the tenant's covenant to deliver up in repair.[300]

Where the landlord forfeits by physical re-entry, the position may be simpler. It has been said that the lease is thereby brought to an end, and if any subsequent claim for relief succeeds, there is a new and separate lease on the same terms and conditions as the old.[301] On this basis, it follows that neither landlord nor tenant are entitled to enforce the covenants in the intervening period, and the relevant date for assessing damages for breach of the tenant's covenant to yield up will be the date of the re-entry.

---

[295] *Meadows v Clerical, Medical & General Life Assurance Society Ltd* [1980] 1 All E.R. 454.

[296] *Liverpool Properties Ltd v Oldbridge Investments Ltd*, above.

[297] *Liverpool Properties Ltd v Oldbridge Investments Ltd*, above; *Sambrin Investments Ltd v Taborn* [1990] 1 E.G.L.R. 61. These cases were decided under the former Rules of the Supreme Court, but there is no reason to believe that the position under Pt 24 of the CPR is any different.

[298] *Liverpool Properties Ltd v Oldbridge Investments Ltd*, above, per Parker L.J. at 1353.

[299] *Wheeler v Keeble (1914) Ltd* [1920] 1 Ch. 57. Note that the tenant may nonetheless obtain an interim injunction enforcing the landlord's covenants: *Peninsula Maritime Ltd v Padseal Ltd* [1981] 2 E.G.L.R. 43.

[300] *Associated Deliveries Ltd v Harrison* (1984) 50 P. & C.R. 91. See para.30–07, below.

[301] *Liverpool Properties Ltd v Oldbridge Investments Ltd* [1985] 2 E.G.L.R. 111, per Parker L.J. See however *Ivory Gate Ltd v Spetale* [1998] 2 E.G.L.R. 43 and *Maryland Estates Ltd v Bar-Joseph* [1999] 1 W.L.R. 83.

## Vesting orders in favour of a sub-tenant

**27–86**    Forfeiture of a superior lease brings to an end all derivative sub-leases. The effect of the grant of relief to the head tenant under s.146(2) of the Law of Property Act 1925 is that any sub-lease is automatically restored,[302] so that no separate application on the part of the sub-tenant is necessary. If the head tenant does not apply for, or fails to obtain, relief, then it is necessary for the sub-tenant to take action to protect his position. In appropriate circumstances he may apply for relief under s.146(2),[303] but the more usual course is to apply for a vesting order under s.146(4) of the 1925 Act, under which the court has power to make a vesting order in favour of a sub-tenant of the whole or any part of the property comprised in the head lease. A vesting order takes effect as a new lease and does not operate to restore the former sub-tenancy.[304] One consequence of this is that the grant of a vesting order in favour of a superior sub-tenant does not have the effect of restoring any sub-underleases created out of that sub-tenancy.[305] A sub-tenant lower down the chain cannot therefore rely on a vesting order granted to a sub-tenant higher up but must make his own separate application for a vesting order.

An application for a vesting order can only be made where the lessor "is proceeding" to enforce a right of forfeiture. In this respect the position is the same as that under s.146(2) of the 1925 Act, and reference should be made to para.27–79, above.

## The court's power to grant a vesting order

**27–87**    The court has a complete discretion as to the grant or refusal of a vesting order. The relevant considerations are in many respects similar to those which apply to the grant of relief under s.146(2).[306] However, there is the additional factor that the parties have not previously been in the relationship of landlord and tenant. The court will take into account the fact that the effect of a vesting order will be to impose on the landlord a person whom he did not choose.[307] One result of this is that a vesting order will not generally be made in favour of an unlawful sub-tenant, i.e. one whose sub-tenancy was created in breach of a covenant against sub-letting in the head lease.

The court may vest the property comprised in the head lease or part in the sub-tenant for the whole term of the head lease or part upon such conditions as to execution of any deed or other document, payment of rent, costs, expenses, damages, compensation, giving security, or otherwise, as the court in the circumstances of each case may think fit. Where the head lease has been forfeited for disrepair, a vesting order will usually only be granted on terms that the

---

[302] *Dendy v Evans* [1910] 1 K.B. 263.
[303] See *Escalus Properties Ltd v Robinson* [1996] Q.B. 231.
[304] *Cadogan v Dimovic* [1984] 1 W.L.R. 609; *Official Custodian for Charities v Mackey* [1985] Ch. 168.
[305] *Hammersmith and Fulham Borough Council v Topshops Centres Ltd* [1990] Ch. 237.
[306] These are discussed in para.27–80 et seq., above.
[307] *Creery v Summersell* [1949] Ch. 751.

sub-tenant (a) remedies the disrepair,[308] and (b) undertakes the repairing obligations in the head lease,[309] in each case in relation to the premises to be comprised in the vesting order. In addition the applicant for a vesting order will usually be required to undertake to pay the head landlord's costs of the forfeiture proceedings against the head tenant, save to the extent that such costs are recovered from the head tenant.[310]

In *Hill v Griffin*[311] a sub-tenant of part of the premises let under the head lease applied for a vesting order. The circumstances were such that the court had no power to make a vesting order for more than a monthly tenancy. The head lease contained what was described in the Court of Appeal as a "very wide repairing covenant". The sub-let part was in a bad state of repair. The sub-tenant contended that a vesting order should be made on less onerous terms as to repair than those in the head lease. The county court judge refused a vesting order, and the Court of Appeal held that there were no grounds for interfering with his decision. Slade L.J. said in the course of his judgment:

> "If relief were now to be granted on the terms suggested by [counsel for the tenant], the effect would be to impose upon the landlords a person whom they had never accepted as their own tenant and would be to give them far less extensive rights in relation to repair than they had against [the head tenant]. It does not seem to me that . . . this would be right."

The court has power to make a vesting order in respect of the whole of the property let under the head lease even though the sub-tenancy comprises only part of that property. Problems sometimes occur in practice where the premises have been sub-let in parts, and the landlord's interests would be prejudiced if a number of separate vesting orders were granted to the individual sub-tenants. The landlord may be able to show, for example, that his reversion would be more valuable if the premises were let to a single head tenant on full repairing terms than would be the case if it were subject to separate leases of part, where responsibility for repairs could only sensibly be arranged on the basis of the common parts being repaired by the landlord in return for a service charge. In such a case the court may refuse to make separate vesting orders but make a vesting order of the whole of the premises in favour of the sub-tenants jointly (or one sub-tenant on terms that he grants new sub-leases to the remaining sub-tenants) subject to the same repairing liabilities as the forfeited head lease.

**27–88**

---

[308] *Gray v Bonsall* [1904] 1 K.B. 601, per Romer L.J. at 608; *Official Custodian for Charities v Mackey (No.2)* [1985] 1 W.L.R. 1308 (applicants for vesting orders required to undertake to use their best endeavours to execute agreed works within 15 months).

[309] *Creery v Summersell* [1949] Ch. 751; *Official Custodian for Charities v Mackey (No.2)*, above; *Hill v Griffin* [1987] 1 E.G.L.R. 81. In the first case Harman J. said at 767 that "I think this remains a jurisdiction to be exercised sparingly because it thrusts upon the landlord a person whom he has never accepted as tenant and creates *in invitum* a privity of contract between them. It appears to me that I ought only to vest the head term in the under-lessees upon the footing that they enter into covenants in all respects the same, or at least as stringent, as the covenants in the head lease".

[310] *Official Custodian for Charities v Mackey (No.2)*, above.

[311] Above.

## RELIEF UNDER S.147 OF THE LAW OF PROPERTY ACT 1925

### Introductory

**27–89**    Section 147 of the Law of Property Act 1925 confers on the court power to grant relief in relation to liability to carry out internal decorative repair. The court's power under the section is wider than its power to grant relief under s.146(2), or a vesting order under s.146(4), in that, in an appropriate case, it may relieve the tenant from liability to perform the covenant altogether. It follows that if he applies in time, the tenant may prevent forfeiture for failure to carry out internal decorations from taking place at all, rather than having to rely on the court's discretion to grant relief once the lease has been forfeited.

### Application for relief under the section

**27–90**    An application for relief under s.147 may be made after a notice is served on a lessee[312] "relating to internal decorative repairs to a house or other building."[313] The service of a s.146 notice specifying internal decorative disrepair would clearly be enough to entitle the tenant to apply under the section, as would a contractual notice under a covenant to repair and decorate on notice. If the court is satisfied that the notice is unreasonable, having regard to all the circumstances of the case (including in particular the length of the tenant's term remaining unexpired), then it may wholly or partially relieve the tenant from liability for the repairs.[314] The section applies notwithstanding any stipulation to the contrary.[315]

### Exceptions

**27–91**    The section does not apply in the following cases:

(1)    where the liability arises under an express covenant or agreement to put the property into a decorative state of repair, and that obligation has never been performed.[316] It is thought that this would include the usual form of covenant to redecorate the interior of the premises at specified intervals throughout the term of the lease;[317]

(2)    to any matter necessary or proper for putting or keeping the property in a sanitary condition, or for the maintenance or preservation of the structure;[318]

---

[312] "Lessee" includes a sub-tenant, a person holding under an agreement for lease, and any person liable to effect the repairs: Law of Property Act 1925 s.147(3).

[313] Law of Property Act 1925 s.147(1).

[314] Law of Property Act 1925 s.147(1).

[315] Law of Property Act 1925 s.147(3).

[316] Law of Property Act 1925 s.147(2)(i).

[317] It is noteworthy that, unlike the similar exception in s.3 of the Leasehold Property (Repairs) Act 1938 (see para.27–33, above) the exception is not confined to obligations which are to be performed on taking possession of the premises, or within a reasonable time thereafter.

[318] Law of Property Act 1925 s.147(2)(ii).

(3)    to any statutory liability to keep a house in all respects reasonably fit for human habitation;[319]

(4)    to any covenant or stipulation to yield up the house or other building in a specified state of repair at the end of the term.[320] The tenant cannot therefore rely on the section when the landlord seeks to enforce the covenant to deliver up at the end of the term.

## Section 147 in practice

Applications under s.147 are rare in practice. It is thought that this is because, first, the scope of the section is considerably cut down by the number of exceptions[321]; second, where the lease is subject to the Leasehold Property (Repairs) Act 1938, it will generally be difficult for the landlord to obtain leave in respect of internal decoration work, so that the landlord's claim may never get beyond that stage; and third, landlords seldom seek to enforce liability for internal decoration without also relying on other breaches outside the section altogether. In practice tenants do not seem to consider it worthwhile making a separate application under s.147 in respect only of the internal decoration. Nonetheless, the section confers a valuable benefit on tenants, and it is suggested that it is good practice for advantage to be taken of it whenever possible.

**27–92**

---

[319] Law of Property Act 1925 s.147(2)(iii).
[320] Law of Property Act 1925 s.147(1), s.147(2)(iv).
[321] See para.27–91, above.

# CHAPTER 28

## OTHER REMEDIES DURING THE TERM

### INTRODUCTORY

### The available remedies

The following remedies during the term are considered in this Chapter: (a) specific performance[1]; (b) damages[2]; (c) entry by the landlord to remedy disrepair where there is no provision in the lease entitling him to do so[3]; and (d) entry by the landlord to remedy disrepair pursuant to a provision in the lease.[4]

**28–01**

### SPECIFIC PERFORMANCE

### The nature of the remedy

At common law, a party who entered into a contract and failed to perform it thereby made himself liable in damages, but could not be compelled by the court to carry out his obligation. The Courts of Equity, recognising that in some cases damages were not an adequate remedy, devised the remedy of specific performance, i.e. an order requiring the party in breach to do what he had promised to do. Like the other equitable remedy to which it bears strong similarities, the mandatory injunction, specific performance is a discretionary remedy, which will only be granted where it appears to the court in all the circumstances to be just and equitable.

**28–02**

### The availability of specific performance to enforce a tenant's repairing covenant

It was formerly thought to be the law that specific performance could not be granted of a tenant's covenant to repair. This view was based on a number of old authorities containing statements to the effect that the court will not ordinarily decree specific performance of a covenant to repair[5] (although on occasions,

**28–03**

---

[1] See para.28–02 et seq., below.
[2] See para.28–16 et seq., below.
[3] See para.28–27 et seq., below.
[4] See para.28–32 et seq., below.
[5] *City of London v Nash* (1747) 3 Atk. 512; *Mosely v Virgin* (1796) 3 Ves. Jun. 184; *Lane v Newdigate* (1804) 10 Ves. Jun. 192; *Hill v Barclay* (1810) 16 Ves. Jun. 402; *Paxton v Newton* (1854) 2 Sm. & G. 437; *Hepburn v Leather* (1884) 50 L.T. 660.

however, the court appears to have got round the rule by granting an injunction[6]). In particular, it was based on *Hill v Barclay*,[7] a decision of Lord Eldon which was treated by Pennycuick V.C. in *Jeune v Queen's Cross Properties Ltd*[8] as an authority laying down the principle that a landlord cannot obtain against his tenant an order for specific performance of a covenant to repair.[9] As recently as 1989 in a New Zealand case, *Greetings Oxford Koala Hotel Pty Ltd v Oxford Square Investments Pty Ltd*,[10] Young J. regarded it as "trite law" that equity would not ordinarily grant specific performance of a covenant to repair or a covenant of a like nature. He went on to hold that:

> "[T]here is a principle which does not go quite so far and that is that, where the landlord has covenanted to repair or maintain some part of the property which is not the subject of the lease and which the tenant is not able to enter onto and repair at his own expense, then in a proper case, the equity court may grant a mandatory order to compel the landlord to carry out the repair or maintenance."

However, he thought there would be room for argument that:

> "[T]here is a wider principle ... namely that these days the court can always grant an injunction or give other equitable relief when justice requires it."

28–04    Earlier editions of this work expressed the view that there is no reason in principle why specific performance should not be granted to compel the performance of a tenant's repairing covenant.[11] It has since been held in *Rainbow Estates Ltd v Tokenhold Ltd*[12] at first instance that specific performance is available in principle.[13] The judge (Mr Lawrence Collins QC, sitting as a deputy judge of the Chancery Division) said in the course of his judgment:

> "In my judgment, a modern law of remedies requires specific performance of a tenant's repairing covenant to be available in appropriate circumstances, and there are no constraints of principle or binding authority against the availability of the remedy."

It is thought that this represents the modern law and would be upheld by an appellate court were the point to be tested on appeal. It is noteworthy that in *Co-Operative Insurance Society Ltd v Argyll Stores (Holdings) Ltd*[14] (in which the House of Lords declined to order specific performance of a covenant to keep

---

[6] See *Lane v Newdigate*, above, in which the plaintiff was the tenant of a mill, the operation of which was being affected by the defendant's failure to repair a canal. Lord Eldon L.C. refused to order the defendant to repair the canal. However, he granted an order restraining the defendant from impeding the plaintiff from navigating the canal for the necessary purposes of the mill, or from using and enjoying the mill, by continuing to keep the canal out of good repair, order or condition. The practical effect of this was much the same as an order directing the defendant to repair the canal.

[7] (1810) 16 Ves. Jun. 402.

[8] [1974] Ch. 97.

[9] Although it is thought that it did not in fact go this far: see the First Edition of this work, para.22–03.

[10] (1989) 18 N.S.W.L.R. 33.

[11] The relevant passage in the Second Edition was quoted by the judge in *Rainbow Estates Ltd v Tokenhold Ltd* [1999] Ch. 64.

[12] Above.

[13] *Rainbow Estates Ltd v Tokenhold Ltd*, above.

[14] [1998] A.C. 1.

premises open for retail trade) Lord Hoffmann, who gave the only speech, distinguished between orders to achieve a result (for example, to erect a building or to repair) and orders to carry on an activity (for example to keep open for trade). This suggests that he thought that specific performance of a tenant's repairing covenant would be available in principle.[15]

## When specific performance is likely to be granted

Specific performance is a discretionary remedy, and a party is not entitled to it as of right. However, the discretion must be exercised judicially and in accordance with settled principles.[16] In *Rainbow Estates Ltd v Tokenhold Ltd*[17] the judge said:

    **28–05**

> "Subject to the overriding need to avoid injustice or oppression, it will be appropriate for the remedy to be available when damages are not an adequate remedy or, in the more modern formulation, when specific performance is the appropriate remedy. This will be particularly important if there is substantial difficulty in the way of the landlord effecting repairs: the landlord may not have a right of access to the property to effect necessary repairs, since (in the absence of contrary agreement) a landlord has no right to enter the premises, and the condition of the premises may be declining."

However, he warned that:

> "[N]ot only is there is great need for caution in granting the remedy against a tenant, but also that it will be a rare case in which the remedy of specific performance will be the appropriate one: in the case of commercial leases, the landlord will normally have the right to forfeit or to enter and do the repairs at the expense of the tenant; in residential cases, the landlord will normally have the right to forfeit in appropriate cases.[18]"

In that case there was evidence of serious disrepair and deterioration of the premises; statutory notices under the Housing Act 1985 and the Environmental Protection Act 1990 had been served; and the landlord had no alternative remedy (there being no right of re-entry or right to enter to carry out works and recover the cost from the tenant). Specific performance was granted.

It is thought that the following general conditions would have to be established before an order for specific performance of a tenant's repairing covenant will be made.

### (a)   *Damages not an adequate remedy*

As a general rule, specific performance will not be granted where damages would be an adequate remedy. Damages for breach of a tenant's repairing covenant

    **28–06**

---

[15] In addition, Lord Hoffmann referred without disapproval to *Jeune v Queen's Cross Properties Ltd* [1974] Ch. 97 (in which an order for specific performance of a landlord's repairing covenant was made).

[16] *Haywood v Cope* (1858) 25 Beav. 140, per Lord Romilly M.R. at 151.

[17] [1998] 2 E.G.L.R. 34.

[18] It is thought that insofar as this passage suggests that specific performance should not be granted where the landlord has a right of forfeiture, it goes too far: see para.28–09, below.

during the term are rarely a satisfactory remedy.[19] They are difficult to assess; the amount awarded may not adequately compensate the landlord for the tenant's failure to repair; and because the breach is a continuing one, a series of actions may be necessary.[20] Accordingly, this requirement is unlikely to prove a problem in most cases.

### (b)   The work must be sufficiently identified

**28–07**   The work which the tenant is to be ordered to carry out must be identified sufficiently for the tenant to know what he has to do, and for the court to know whether he has complied with the order.[21] The landlord must therefore have prepared a schedule of the works which must be "sufficiently certain to be capable of enforcement".[22] It is thought that in general terms the schedule should be sufficiently detailed for a reasonably competent and experienced builder reading it to know what has to be done. Thus, a blanket requirement for the tenant to carry out "all works necessary to put the premises into repair in accordance with the covenants to repair in the lease" will not be sufficient. However, the degree of precision required will vary from case to case. The tenant may be well aware of what needs doing, or the disrepair may be so serious that some form of order is required immediately. Thus, in the Australian case of *Greetings Oxford Koala Hotel Pty Ltd v Oxford Square Investments Pty Ltd*[23] Young J. pointed out that:

> "It has been recognised in the case of interlocutory injunctions, that it is sometimes better to take the risk that the defendant may have some problems in comprehending exactly what the injunction covers, rather than make no injunction at all."

For example, where the defect of which the landlord complains consists of a part of the premises having become dangerous to the public (such as falling masonry), then depending on the precise facts it may be sufficient simply to require the tenant to carry out such work as is necessary to avert the danger.[24] Where the premises are in disrepair but the landlord has no right to inspect to see what exactly is wrong, then the court has power in an appropriate case to order the tenant to permit the landlord's expert to inspect and report on what needs to be done.[25]

---

[19] See para.28–16 et seq., below.

[20] This factor is relevant on the question of whether or not damages would be an adequate remedy: see *Beswick v Beswick* [1968] A.C. 58, HL.

[21] *Morris v Redland Bricks Ltd* [1970] A.C. 652 (a building case); *Flashman v Avenue Properties (St John's Wood) Ltd* (unreported decision dated June 12, 1978), where Templeman J. refused a tenant's application for specific performance of a landlord's repairing obligation on the ground that the necessary works were not sufficiently particularised; *Rainbow Estates Ltd v Tokenhold Ltd* [1999] Ch. 64; *Co-Operative Insurance Society Ltd v Argyll Stores (Holdings) Ltd* [1998] A.C. 1.

[22] *Rainbow Estates Ltd v Tokenhold Ltd* [1999] Ch. 64.

[23] (1989) 18 N.S.W.L.R. 33.

[24] See further paras 33–07 to 33–11, below.

[25] Senior Courts Act 1981 s.33; County Courts Act 1984 s.52(i); CPR rr.25.1 and 25.5; *Parker v Camden LBC* [1986] Ch. 162.

### (c) It is just and equitable in all the circumstances for specific performance to be granted

The court must be satisfied that in all the circumstances it is appropriate to grant specific performance. A number of factors will be relevant under this head.      **28–08**

First, although the Leasehold Property (Repairs) Act 1938[26] does not apply to a claim for specific performance, the court will prevent specific performance being used to effectuate or encourage the mischief which the 1938 Act was intended to remedy. Thus, in *Rainbow Estates Ltd v Tokenhold Ltd*[27] the judge said:

> "Although the court should not use the provisions of section 1(5) of the 1938 Act as if they were applicable, it should be astute to ensure that the landlord is not seeking the decree simply in order to harass the tenant: in so doing, the court may take into account considerations similar to those it must take into account under the 1938 Act.[28]"

Second, the landlord must have a legitimate interest in the covenant to repair being performed. For example, if his real reason for seeking to enforce the covenant is to prevent a proposed assignment of which he disapproves but which he cannot otherwise stop, or to put pressure on the tenant in connection with a forthcoming rent review or lease renewal, then specific performance might well not be granted. It is thought that legitimate reasons for enforcing the covenant would include, for example, the fact that the defective state of the premises is a source of danger to the public; or that it is affecting the value of the landlord's adjoining property, by making it harder to let; or that it is causing damage to other parts of the building occupied by the landlord or other tenants of his; or that the landlord wishes to sell or mortgage his interest in the premises and the disrepair is adversely affecting his chances of doing this on favourable terms.

Third, the balance of hardship must be in favour of granting specific performance.[29] The court must balance the landlord's interest in having the covenant performed against the consequences to the tenant if the order is made. Relevant factors will no doubt include the extent to which the carrying out of the works will involve the tenant in disruption and expenditure.

Fourth, whilst it is not thought that the existence of other possible remedies will      **28–09**
necessarily be fatal to the landlord's prospects of obtaining an order for specific performance nonetheless the fact that the landlord could enforce the covenant in other ways is likely to be relevant to whether the court grants the order. It is thought that the landlord must have sufficient reasons why he cannot or does not wish, for example, to forfeit the lease or to enter the premises and carry out the work under an express provision in the lease entitling him to do so. In *Rainbow Estates Ltd v Tokenhold Ltd*[30] the factors which the court took into account in deciding to grant specific performance included the fact that the leases in question, unusually, contained no right of re-entry, so that the landlord was not

---

[26] See para.27–31 et seq., above.
[27] *Rainbow Estates Ltd v Tokenhold Ltd* [1999] Ch. 64.
[28] *Rainbow Estates Ltd v Tokenhold Ltd*, above.
[29] See, for example, *Posner v Scott-Lewis* [1987] Ch. 25.
[30] [1999] Ch. 64. See para.28–05 et seq., above.

entitled to forfeiture, nor did they entitle the landlord to enter to carry out works and recover the cost from the tenants. However, insofar as that case suggests that specific performance should not be granted where the landlord has a right of forfeiture,[31] it is thought that it goes too far. The effect of forfeiture is to terminate the lease, and the landlord may have good reasons for not wishing to do this (for example, the premises may be over-rented and he does not wish to lose the income stream). If, in such a case, specific performance would otherwise be an appropriate remedy, it seems unfair to deny it on the ground that the landlord could forfeit instead.

Fifth, the tenant must have the legal capacity to carry out the work. The court will not make an order for specific performance which cannot lawfully be carried out. This requirement will not give rise to any difficulty where the tenant is in occupation of the part of the premises to which the works are to be carried out, but the position may be different where the premises are sub-let, or where the works involve entry on land not in the occupation of either landlord or tenant. In both cases, consideration will have to be given to what rights of entry the tenant has against the sub-tenant or the adjoining owner in order to carry out the works.[32]

Last, there must be no other reason why it would be inappropriate or impractical to grant specific performance. An example of a case under this head is *Bowen Investments v Tabcorp Holdings*,[33] in which the Federal Court of Australia held that it would not be appropriate to order the tenant of an office building to reinstate a foyer which it had demolished in breach of covenant. On the facts, the correct date for assessing damages was the expiry date of the original lease on January 31, 2007, but by reason of the grant of a new lease (which was disregarded for the purposes of assessing damages) the tenant's interest would not in reality come to an end until 2012 at the earliest. The court (giving judgment in March 2008) saw:

> "all manner of difficulty in making an order that will not come into effect for many years perhaps at a time when the person who controls [the landlord] may not want the order."

In the Scottish case of *Douglas Shelf Seven Ltd v Cooperative Wholesale Society Ltd,*[34] the landlord brought proceedings for damages for breach of a keep-open clause, and recovered damages for loss of capital value and accrued revenue losses. The landlord then brought further proceedings seeking an order that the tenant carry out the works specified in an interim schedule of dilapidations. The tenant contended that having elected to seek damages in the previous proceedings in respect of the landlord's loss for the remainder of the term on the basis that there would be no further trading from the premises, it was not open to the landlord subsequently to seek specific performance of the repairing covenant during the term (although it was accepted that the repairing obligations would be enforceable in full at the termination of the lease). That argument was rejected by the Outer House of the Court of Session. The previous

---

[31] See the passage in the judgment set out in para.28–05, above.
[32] See para.23–09 et seq., above.
[33] [2008] FCAFC 38. The facts are set out at para.32–11, below.
[34] [2009] CSOH 3.

proceedings were concerned solely with the breach of the keep-open covenant. By electing to seek damages for that breach, the landlord was not disabled or prevented from seeking specific performance of other clauses in the lease.

## Defences to specific performance

A full consideration of the law relating to specific performance is outside the scope of this work.[35] However, those defences which are likely to be of most relevance in the law of dilapidations are as follows.

28–10

### (a)   Delay

As a general rule, a party seeking specific performance must bring his claim promptly and as soon as the nature of the case will permit.[36] Accordingly, depending on the facts, long delay in bringing proceedings may be a defence to specific performance. For example, where the landlord has been aware for a long period of the defective state of which he now complains, and has taken no step to enforce the tenant's repairing obligations, it may be that specific performance would be refused, particularly if the tenant has, in the meantime, altered his position in some way. However, delay is not a defence where circumstances have changed over the period (for example, where the disrepair has grown steadily worse), or where the facts are such that it would be unfair to allow the tenant to rely on the delay.

28–11

### (b)   Hardship

Specific performance may be refused where to grant it would cause hardship to the defendant.[37] However, the circumstances must be "extraordinary and persuasive".[38] To be relevant, hardship either must exist at the date of the lease, or be due in some way to the claimant.[39] As a general rule, the fact that the defendant cannot afford to perform the obligation is not sufficient.[40] Thus, in *Francis v Cowlcliffe*[41] an order for specific performance of a covenant to provide and maintain a lift was made, notwithstanding evidence that the defendant landlord was insolvent and could not afford to perform the covenant without finance from an outside source.[42] It follows that financial inability to do the work will not generally be a defence to a claim for specific performance of a tenant's

28–12

---

[35] Reference should be made to the specialist works on specific performance.
[36] *Eads v Williams* (1854) 4 De G. M. & G. 674.
[37] *Patel v Ali* [1984] Ch. 283.
[38] *Patel v Ali*, above; *Alexander v Lambeth LBC* [2000] C.L.Y. 3931.
[39] *Patel v Ali*, above.
[40] *Nicholas v Ingram* [1958] N.Z.L.R. 972 (New Zealand); *Francis v Cowlcliffe Ltd* (1977) 33 P. & C.R. 368.
[41] Above.
[42] The judge said in the course of his judgment: "It is said that this [i.e. the order for specific performance] will inevitably result in the defendants being wound up. Even if this were so, that does not seem to me to be any reason why the plaintiff should not have her order."

repairing covenant, although in an extreme case it may be that specific performance would be refused under the principle considered in para.28–13, below.

### (c)  Pointlessness and impossibility

28–13    The court will not make an order for specific performance in circumstances where the order would be pointless, or where it would be impossible for the tenant to comply. Thus, the tenant will not be ordered to carry out works which he has no legal right to carry out (for example, because the premises are sub-let and he has no right of entry as against the sub-tenant[43]). Likewise, it is thought that the tenant would not be ordered to carry out repairs where the lease has insufficient time remaining for the work to be completed.

## Interim orders

28–14    The court has power to grant an interim mandatory injunction requiring the carrying out of work pending trial.[44] However, such an order will only be granted in very exceptional cases.[45] It is thought that an order is unlikely to be granted where the only damage being suffered by the landlord is financial in nature and there is no immediate risk to health or safety. However, the court retains an overriding discretion, and there may be cases where a mandatory injunction would be appropriate even where there is no such risk. Where what has to be done is unclear, the court may order the defendant to permit the plaintiff's expert to inspect and report on what needs doing.[46]

In general, an interim order is unlikely to be made unless the work is relatively straightforward. Thus, in *Parker v Camden LBC*[47] Lord Donaldson M.R. said in relation to a broken-down heating system:

> "Where it is merely a question of throwing a switch, the court would without doubt order Camden to throw the switch; and, if it did not do it, would authorise the plaintiffs to do it instead. On the other hand, if it is a question of entirely rebuilding the boiler system, I cannot imagine that any court would make a mandatory injunction to that effect."

Again, however, the question is one for the court's discretion on the facts of each individual case. A summary order for specific performance was made in *Rainbow Estates Ltd v Tokenhold Ltd*,[48] in which the schedule of works relied on by the landlord was unchallenged and was "sufficiently certain to be capable of enforcement".

---

[43] For rights of entry, see paras 22–25 to 22–46 and 23–09 to 23–17 above.

[44] CPR r.25.1; *Parker v Camden LBC* [1986] Ch. 162.

[45] *Parker v Camden LBC*, above. In that case a mandatory injunction was granted where the defendant council were in admitted breach of a covenant to keep in repair boilers in sheltered accommodation, and the breach gave rise to "actual and major discomfort and inconvenience and to a real risk of damage to health".

[46] *Parker v Camden LBC*, above; CPR r.25.1.

[47] Above.

[48] [1999] Ch. 64.

## Remedies for non-compliance

Failure to comply with an order for specific performance is a contempt of court. Where the party in contempt is an individual, he may be committed to prison, or have his assets sequestrated. Where such party is a limited company, the property of the company, or the personal property of any director or other officer, may be sequestrated, and any director or other officer may be committed to prison.[49] In addition, the court may direct that the act required to be done may, so far as practicable, be done by the party who obtained the order, or some other person appointed by the court, at the cost of the disobedient party.[50]

28–15

## DAMAGES DURING THE TERM

### Introductory

This section is concerned with claims for damages while the term of the lease is still running. Reference should also be made to Chs 29 to 32, below, in which damages at the end of the term are considered.

28–16

### The Leasehold Property (Repairs) Act 1938

The Leasehold Property (Repairs) Act 1938[51] applies to actions for damages as well as to actions for forfeiture. It applies where the lease was granted for more than seven years, and three years or more remain unexpired at the commencement of the action for damages. It does not therefore apply where the landlord begins his action in the last three years of the term. Nor does it apply to a breach of covenant in so far as it imposes on the tenant an obligation to put premises in repair that is to be performed upon the tenant taking possession of the premises or within a reasonable time thereafter.[52] Where the Act applies the landlord will have to serve a s.146 notice in the form required by the Act and, if the tenant serves counter-notice within the 28-day period, will need to obtain the leave of the court before commencing proceedings.[53]

28–17

### The measure of damages at common law

The measure of damages at common law for breach of a tenant's covenant to repair during the currency of the term is the amount by which the value of the landlord's reversion has been diminished by reason of the breach.[54] Thus, in *Doe d. Worcester School Trustees v Rowlands*[55] Coleridge J. said:

28–18

---

[49] See CPR rr.81.4(1), (3) and 81.20(1), (3).
[50] CPR r.50.1(3) and Sch.1, RSC O.45 r.8; *Parker v Camden LBC* [1986] Ch. 162.
[51] See para.27–31 et seq., above.
[52] Leasehold Property (Repairs) Act 1938 s.3.
[53] See para.27–34 et seq., above.
[54] *Doe d. Worcester School Trustees v Rowlands* (1841) 9 C. & P. 734; *Turner v Lamb* (1845) 14 M. & W. 412; *Smith v Peat* (1853) 9 Ex. 161; *Atkinson v Beard* (1861) 11 C.P. 245 (Canada); *Coward v*

"[I]n estimating the damages in cases where the lease has a long time to run, it is not fair to take the amount that would be necessary to put the premises into repair as the measure of the damages; for in such cases, when the damages are awarded to the landlord, he is not bound to expend them in repairs, neither can he do so without the tenant's permission to enter on the premises. The true question therefore is—to what extent is the reversion injured by the non-repair of the premises?"

In *Ebbetts v Conquest*[56] in the Court of Appeal Lopes L.J. stated the general rule as follows:

"[T]he measure of damages for breach of the covenant to keep in repair during the currency of the term is the loss which is occasioned to the lessor's reversion—a loss which will be greater or less according as the term of the tenant at the time of the breach has a less or greater time to run."

However, in the House of Lords[57] Lord Herschell, with whom Lords Macnaghten and Morris concurred, said:

"I do not think any hard and fast rule can be laid down as to the damages which may be recovered by the covenantee during the currency of a lease in respect of a breach of a covenant to keep the demised premises in repair. All the circumstances of the case must be taken into consideration, and the damages must be assessed at such a sum as reasonably represents the damage which the covenantee has sustained by the breach of covenant. I quite agree with the criticism to which Lord Holt's view[58] has been subjected[59] if that learned judge intended to lay down that, whatever the circumstances and however long the term had to run, the damages must necessarily be what it would cost to put the premises into repair. On the other hand, I think it would be equally wrong to hold that this could never be the measure of damages, whatever the circumstances and however nearly the term had expired. But in the present case, if the test be applied of inquiring how much the value of the respondents' reversion has been diminished by the breach of covenant, a test for which I understand the appellants to contend, I cannot see that there has been any error in the assessment of damages."

**28–19** It is not clear whether Lord Herschell meant that in some circumstances the cost of the work might be recoverable even though it exceeds the damage to the reversion, or whether he was doing no more than pointing out that in some cases the cost of the work may be a helpful guide to the amount by which the reversion has been damaged. It is thought that the latter is the better view.[60] That the

---

*Gregory* (1866) L.R. 2 C.P. 153; *Mills v East London Union* (1872) L.R. 8 C.P. 79; *Ebbetts v Conquest* [1895] 2 Ch. 377 (affirmed sub nom *Conquest v Ebbetts* [1896] A.C. 490); *Gooderham and Worts v Canadian Broadcasting Corp* [1947] A.C. 66 at 83; *Crewe Services & Investments Corp v Silk* [1998] 2 E.G.L.R. 1.
[55] Above.
[56] Above.
[57] [1896] A.C. 490.
[58] This is a reference to *Vivian v Champion* 2 Ld. Raym. 1125, in which Holt C.J. said: "We always inquire in these cases what it will cost to put the premises in repair and give so much damages, and the plaintiff ought in justice to apply the damages to the repair of the premises."
[59] This is a reference to *Smith v Peat*, above, and *Turner v Lamb*, above.
[60] See *Crewe Services & Investment Corp v Silk* [1998] 2 E.G.L.R. 1, in which Robert Walker L.J., having referred to Lord Herschell's speech, went on to say: "So in this sort of case diminution in the value of the reversion is the test at common law".

damage to the reversion is the correct measure was reaffirmed by Lord Macmillan in *Gooderham & Worts v Canadian Broadcasting Corp*,[61] in which he said:

> "The measure of damages is the diminution in the value of the reversion resulting from the breach, without prejudice to any further claim which the landlord may have at the termination of the tenancy."

Similarly, in *Crewe Services & Investment Corp v Silk*[62] the Court of Appeal held that the correct measure is the diminution in the value of the reversion resulting from the breaches.

## Section 18(1) of the Landlord and Tenant Act 1927

The first limb of s.18(1) of the Landlord and Tenant Act 1927 provides that damages for breach of a covenant to keep or put premises in repair during the currency of a lease shall in no case exceed the amount (if any) by which the value of the landlord's reversion is diminished owing to the breach.[63] This is the same as the common law measure of damages for breach of covenant to repair during the term, so that the subsection has not altered the law.[64]

**28–20**

The diminution in the value of the reversion is arrived at by comparing the value of the landlord's reversion on the assumption that the premises are in the state in which they ought to be, and its value on the assumption that the premises are in their actual state.[65] In each case, the reversion must be valued subject to the lease and with the benefit of any right of action which a purchaser of the reversion would have against the tenant for non-repair.[66] However, it is not always necessary to undertake detailed valuations, and the fact that no valuation evidence is before the court does not necessarily mean that the landlord cannot prove damage to the reversion.[67] Nonetheless:

> "Where a landlord claims damages for breach of a repairing covenant near the beginning or in the middle of the term of a long lease (and on the assumption that he gets leave under the Leasehold Property (Repairs) Act 1938 as amended) he will, if he fails to lead evidence of diminution in the value of the reversion, run a serious risk of the court concluding that there has been no significant diminution. Where a tenant is defending such a claim towards the end of the term of the lease, he will, if he fails to lead evidence that the diminution is much less than the cost of repairs, run a serious risk of the court accepting that cost (or that cost only slightly discounted) as the best evidence of the diminution.[68]"

---

[61] [1947] A.C. 66.
[62] Above.
[63] Reference should be made to Ch.30, below, which contains a detailed discussion of the first limb of s.18(1) in the context of claims for damages at the end of the term.
[64] See *Crewe Services & Investment Corp v Silk*, above, in which Robert Walker L.J. thought that s.18(1) "does not really affect the position".
[65] *Re King* [1962] 1 W.L.R. 632 (reversed on appeal on different grounds: [1963] Ch. 459); *Baroque Investments v Heis* [2012] EWHC 2886 (Ch.) at [17].
[66] *Re King*, above, at 649; *Baroque Investments v Heis*, above, at [17].
[67] See *Crewe Services & Investment Corp v Silk*, above, at 4L to 5C. See further para.30–47, below.
[68] *Crewe Service & Investment Corp v Silk*, above, at 5B.

The second limb of s.18(1) (under which no damages are recoverable if it is shown that the premises, in whatever state of repair they might be, would at or shortly after the termination of the term have been or be pulled down, or such structural alterations made therein as would render valueless the repairs) does not apply to an action for damages for breach of a covenant to keep or put in repair during the term.[69] It follows that the fact that the premises are to be pulled down, or structurally altered, after the end of the term will not of itself afford a defence to a claim for damages during the term. However, it may be highly relevant to the question whether there has been any diminution in the value of the reversion.

## The date of assessment

28–21    The general rule is that damages are assessed as at the date of breach.[70] Clearly, however, the landlord cannot have damages representing the diminution in the value of the reversion on every one of the days that the premises can be shown to have been out of repair. It is thought that the correct approach in most cases will be to value the reversion as at the date of the hearing.[71]

However, assessment at the date of the hearing is not an inflexible rule. In some cases it may be appropriate to value the reversion at an earlier date. Thus, in *Re King*[72] the demised factory burnt down in 1944. In 1953 the landlord began proceedings for damages for breach of the tenant's covenant to keep the premises in repair during the term. In the same year the property was acquired by the London County Council pursuant to a compulsory purchase order. The council went into possession in 1957 and demolished the remainder of the factory. Buckley J. assessed damages as at the last day on which the reversion belonged to the landlord.

In *Baroque Investments v Heis*,[73] the lease had been surrendered on terms which provided for (among other things) the release of the tenant's liability in respect of any breach of covenant "whether arising on or after, but not before, the date of" the surrender. On the same day as the surrender, the landlord relet the premises with an initial rent free period of 19 months. The landlord argued that although the normal rule was that damages for breach of the covenant to keep in repair were to be assessed as at the date of breach, i.e. the day before the surrender, nonetheless (i) the rule ought to be displaced in order more accurately to reflect the loss sustained, and (ii) (in accordance with the principle in *Bwllfa & Merthyr Dare Steam Collieries (1891) v Pontypridd Waterworks Co*[74]) the court was entitled to have regard to the facts that occurred after the relevant date rather than speculate. The Chancellor rejected both contentions. Damages were to be

---

[69] Landlord and Tenant Act 1927 s.18(1); *Re King* [1962] 1 W.L.R. 632.
[70] See paras 32–06 to 32–08, below.
[71] This was done in *Shortridge v Lamplugh* (1702) 2 Ld. Raym. 798 and in *Crewe Services & Investment Corp v Silk* [1998] 2 E.G.L.R. 1. The point was left open in *Gooderham & Worts v Canadian Broadcasting Corp* [1947] A.C. 66.
[72] [1962] 1 W.L.R. 632 (reversed on appeal on different grounds: [1963] Ch. 459).
[73] [2012] EWHC 2886 (Ch.).
[74] [1903] A.C. 426.

assessed by reference to the value of the reversion in and out of repair on the day before the surrender on the assumption that the lease was still continuing,[75] and the *Bwllfa* principle did not apply.

Where the action is begun while the term is still running but the term has expired by the trial, damages are likely to be assessed as at the date of expiry of the lease, that being the last date on which the tenant was liable to repair. Thus, in *Drummond v S & U Stores Ltd*[76] the writ was issued just under two years before the term date of the lease, but the lease had expired by the date of the hearing. Glidewell J. assessed damages as at the term date of the lease.

## The amount of damages recoverable

Whether and to what extent the breaches will have resulted in damage to the landlord's reversion will depend on the facts. An important factor will be the length of term remaining.[77] Thus, "if the lease had 99 years to run, it could not make much difference in the value of the reversion whether the premises are now in repair or not."[78] However:

**28–22**

> "[T]his would not be applicable in all cases [since] there are circumstances in which it might be of the utmost importance to the reversioners that the buildings should be in a proper state of repair.[79]"

Nonetheless, in many cases, particularly where the term still has some time to run, it may be difficult to show that the breaches have resulted in any appreciable damage to the reversion. Since the reversion is valued subject to the lease, the hypothetical purchaser of the landlord's interest will have the full benefit of the rent, the amount of which will be unaffected by the disrepair. If a rent review is due to take place, the tenant will be unable to point to the disrepair in order to obtain a lower rent.[80] Moreover, the purchaser will have the continuing benefit of the tenant's covenant to repair and yield up in repair, and of any right there may be to carry out repairs in default and recover the cost from the tenant.[81] In these circumstances it may be difficult to prove that the effect of the disrepair has been to cause any diminution in the value of the reversion.[82] However, each case will turn on its own facts.

---

[75] The identification of the day before the surrender as the relevant date for assessment would appear to have been a consequence of the particular way the relevant release in the surrender had been drafted, because where a lease has been surrendered, damages would ordinarily be assessed on the basis that the lease has ended and the landlord is in possession. See further para.2–05, above.
[76] [1981] 1 E.G.L.R. 42.
[77] See *Crewe Services & Investment Corp v Silk* [1998] 2 E.G.L.R. 1 at 5B.
[78] *Doe d. Worcester School Trustees v Rowlands* (1841) 9 C. & P. 734, per Coleridge J. at 739. See also *Turner v Lamb* (1845) 14 M. & W. 412, in which Alderson B. commented that the damage for non-repair may surely be very different if the reversion comes to the landlord in six months or in 900 years.
[79] *Ebbetts v Conquest* [1896] A.C. 490, per Lord Herschell at 493.
[80] See para.35–08, below.
[81] *Re King* [1962] 1 W.L.R. 632 (reversed on appeal on different grounds: [1963] Ch. 459).
[82] The corresponding sentence in the Third Edition of this work was cited with approval by the Chancellor in *Baroque Investments v Heis* [2012] EWHC 2886 (Ch.) at [18].

In some cases, however, particularly where the term is nearing its end, there may be a substantial diminution in the value of the reversion as a result of the breaches. Indeed, where the lease has only a short period to go, and the tenant is not entitled to security of tenure, there may be little difference in practice between the damage to the reversion at that time and the damage once the lease has ended.[83] Similarly, if the disrepair is such that the landlord may be liable to third parties under the Defective Premises Act 1972,[84] there may be no difficulty in establishing a substantial diminution in the value of the reversion, even where the lease has some time to go.

In valuing the reversion, account must be taken of any statutory security of tenure to which the tenant may be entitled at the end of the term.[85] For example, the fact that the lease falls within Pt II of the Landlord and Tenant Act 1954, so that the tenant will be entitled to a new tenancy under that Act, may have a considerable bearing on the extent to which any breaches have resulted in damage to the reversion.[86] Prima facie, the new tenancy will contain the same repairing obligations as the current tenancy, and the tenant will be unable to rely on the disrepair to reduce the new rent. These factors may result in the reversion being worth much the same out of repair as it is in repair.[87]

**28-23** In assessing the amount of the diminution, if any, it may be relevant to look at whether the landlord is able and intends to expend his damages on carrying out the works.[88] However, an intention will not necessarily avail the landlord where it would be unreasonable to do the work.[89] Equally, the fact that the landlord cannot carry out the work until the lease ends may be relevant. In *Ebbetts v Conquest*[90] the court dealt with this by taking the cost of the work as at the date of trial and reducing it to such sum as, when invested, would produce a sum equal to that cost at the end of the lease.[91] However, the possibility of inflationary increases in the cost of building work may make this exercise somewhat haphazard, and in any event, a sum arrived at on this basis could only be awarded as damages if it equates to the damage to the reversion (i.e. if such a calculation would be carried out by the notional purchaser of the reversion at the relevant time).

---

[83] See, for example, *Drummond v S & U Stores Ltd* [1981] 1 E.G.L.R. 42, in which a writ for damages was issued just under two years before the term date but damages were assessed as at the date of trial, by which time the lease had expired.
[84] See para.20–49 et seq., above.
[85] See *Family Management Ltd v Gray* [1980] 1 E.G.L.R. 46; *Crown Estate Commissioners v Town Investments Ltd* [1992] E.G.L.R. 61; *Crewe Services & Investment Corp v Silk* [1998] 2 E.G.L.R. 1; and cf. *Pivot Properties Ltd v Secretary of State for the Environment* (1980) 41 P. & C.R. 248. cf. paras 30–31 to 30–35, below.
[86] See *Family Management Ltd v Gray*, above; *Crown Estate Commissioners v Town Investments Ltd*, above.
[87] Cf. paras 30–31 et seq.
[88] See *Crewe Services & Investment Corp v Silk* above, in which the possible significance of the landlord's intention, or lack of it, was considered by the Court of Appeal. See also paras 30–15 to 30–20, below.
[89] *Ruxley Electronics & Construction Ltd v Forsyth* [1996] A.C. 344. See further paras 30–15 to 30–20 and 32–02 to 32–05, below.
[90] [1896] A.C. 490, H.L. (affirming [1985] 2 Ch. 377).
[91] This was also done in *Kent v Conniff* [1953] 1 Q.B. 361 (unreported on this point).

In *Crewe Services & Investment Corp v Silk*[92] a claim for damages for disrepair was brought against a tenant under an agricultural tenancy protected by the Agricultural Holdings Act 1986 (by virtue of which it would continue during the tenant's life unless he gave notice to quit or it was terminated in the circumstances set out in the Act). The landlord claimed just under £35,000, being the cost of the remedial work alleged to be necessary. The county court judge held that just under £14,000 worth of work was necessary and awarded that amount as damages, without hearing evidence as to any diminution in the value of the reversion. The Court of Appeal held that the judge had been wrong to treat the undiscounted cost of repair as a safe guide, particularly given the absence of any finding that the landlord was going to do any repairs itself, but that he had not been bound to award only nominal damages on the basis that no loss had been proved.[93] Doing the best it could on the evidence, it held that the cost of the works was £11,633 and that such figure should be discounted by almost three-quarters so as to arrive at a diminution in the value of the reversion of £3,000.

## Where the landlord is himself a tenant

The fact that the landlord is himself a tenant with repairing liabilities up the chain can be taken into account in deciding whether the disrepair has caused damage to the reversion.[94] Thus, in *Ebbetts v Conquest*[95] a lease was granted for 61 years, and a sub-lease was granted for the original term less 10 days. Both lease and sub-lease contained covenants to repair in identical terms. The premises were out of repair, and the head tenant brought an action for damages against the sub-tenant. At the time when the action was heard there were about three and a half years of the term of the sub-lease remaining. The Official Referee awarded damages by taking what it would cost to put the premises into the covenanted state of repair, and then allowing a rebate to reflect the fact that the lease still had some years to run. His assessment was upheld in the Court of Appeal and the House of Lords. In the latter, Lord Herschell said in his speech:

28–24

> "If the premises were now in good repair, the reversion of the [head tenants] would secure them the improved rent of £100 a year to the end of the term, without any liability of their part, unless it were to the extent to which repairs subsequently became necessary. As matters stand they can only receive this rent subject to the liability of restoring the premises to good repair, so that they may in that condition re-deliver them to their lessor. The difference between these two positions represents the diminution in the value of their reversion owing to the breach of covenant, and on this basis the damages seem to me to have been properly assessed."

The sub-tenant's argument that the head tenant was not bound to expend the damages on repairs, and that owing to the nature of the premises and the changed circumstances of the neighbourhood the freeholder would not want the premises put into repair at the end of the term, was rejected on the ground that:

---

[92] Above.
[93] See further para.30–47, below.
[94] See paras 30–44 to 30–45, below.
[95] [1896] A.C. 490 (affirming [1985] 2 Ch. 377).

"The duty of the appellants as between themselves and the respondents was to fulfil the obligation of the covenant into which they entered, and to keep the premises in repair. If they had done so, the present question would not have arisen. They have broken their covenant, and when sued for the breach they have, in my opinion, no right to demand that a speculative inquiry shall be entered upon as to what may possibly happen and what arrangements may possibly be come to, under the special circumstances of the case, when the superior lease expires by effluxion of time."

It is thought, however, that had there been convincing valuation evidence to the effect that a purchaser of the head lease would not have reduced his bid to take account of the disrepair, the result might have been different.

## Where damages are awarded

**28–25**  Since a covenant to repair imposes a continuing obligation to repair throughout the term,[96] there is no reason in theory why the landlord should not recover damages for breaches in existence at a particular time, and then, if the breaches are not remedied, commence a further action for the same disrepair.[97] It appears that if he does this, he must give credit for the amount of damages recovered in the earlier proceedings. Thus, in *Henderson v Thorn*[98] the landlord had brought proceedings claiming damages for disrepair during the term. The tenant paid a sum of money into court which the landlord accepted, but did not spend on doing the work. At the end of the term the landlord brought a further action for damages, relying on the breaches alleged in the first action and some additional items arising since that action. The tenant argued that the damages should be assessed only in relation to such breaches as had occurred since the first action, and that any breaches which were or could have been included in the claim in the first action should not be taken into account. The argument was rejected on the ground that the damages in the first action represented damages for the diminution in the value of the reversion, whereas the proper measure in the second action was the cost of the works necessary to put the premises into repair at the end of the term (that being at that time the appropriate measure of damages[99]). The court awarded the cost of the works but deducted the sum paid by the tenant in the earlier action.

The same result was reached in *Ebbetts v Conquest*.[100] In that case the tenant had brought an action against a sub-tenant for damages for disrepair three-and-a-half years before the term date of the underlease. He recovered damages assessed by reference to the cost of the work, less a discount for immediate payment.[101] The sum recovered was not spent on repairing the premises. When the sub-tenancy expired the tenant brought a further action for damages against the sub-tenant. Bigham J. held that the tenant was not precluded from recovering damages in the second action, since the questions in the two actions were different: in the first action, the question was the damage to the

---

[96] See para.14–03, above.
[97] See *Coward v Gregory* (1866) L.R. 2 C.P. 153.
[98] [1893] 2 Q.B. 164.
[99] See para.29–04 et seq., below.
[100] (1900) 82 L.T. 560.
[101] See para.28–24, above.

reversion then, whereas the issue in the second was the state of disrepair at the date of the expiry of the sub-lease. However, he held that the sub-tenant was entitled to be credited with the damages he had already paid together with interest at 4 per cent from the date of payment up to the date of termination of the sub-lease.

## Advantages and disadvantages of the remedy

The principal disadvantage of an action for damages during the currency of the lease is that it does not get the work done. Unless he has an appropriate right of entry, the landlord cannot expend his damages in carrying out the work, and the tenant, having paid damages, is unlikely to undertake it himself. Further disadvantages of a claim for damages during the term are the need to overcome the restrictions imposed by the Leasehold Property (Repairs) Act 1938, and the difficulty of proving damage to the reversion. In these circumstances, it will generally be more appropriate to employ another remedy, with which (in an appropriate case[102]) a claim for damages can be combined.

**28–26**

## ENTRY BY THE LANDLORD TO REMEDY DISREPAIR WHEN THERE IS NO EXPRESS PROVISION ENTITLING HIM TO RECOVER THE COST

## Introductory

Most modern leases contain express provisions entitling the landlord to enter to remedy disrepair which is the tenant's liability, and to recover from the tenant the cost of so doing.[103] However, in the absence of any such provision, the landlord has no right to enter the demised premises to carry out works.[104] His entry will constitute a trespass, and probably also a breach of his express or implied covenant for quiet enjoyment, and may be restrained by injunction.[105] This section is concerned with the question whether, if the landlord has no legal right to enter and carry out work which is the tenant's liability but nonetheless does so, he is entitled to recover the cost of that work by way of damages for breach of the tenant's covenant to repair.

**28–27**

## Recovery of the cost

The argument that the cost of the work is irrecoverable is based on the fact that the carrying out of the work will have been unlawful, so that the landlord's claim for the cost arises out of his own trespass. In *Hamilton v Martell Securities Ltd*[106] Vinelott J. said in the course of his judgment:

**28–28**

---

[102] See Ch.26, above.
[103] See paras 14–11 to 14–12, above.
[104] See paras 22–30 to 22–31, above.
[105] See paras 22–30 to 22–31, above.
[106] [1984] Ch. 266.

"[A] lessor who does not reserve the right to enter and remedy a want of repair arising from a breach of the lessee's covenants, and who nonetheless does so is, in law, a trespasser, and it is not obvious that he would be entitled to recover the moneys he has spent as damages for breach of covenant, or that he could rely on the lessee's breach of covenant in allowing the want of repair to arise as founding a claim for damages or for forfeiture, once he himself has remedied the state of disrepair."

However, the point did not arise for decision in that case, and the judge expressed no concluded view on it. Nonetheless the above passage, so far as it goes, is some support for the argument that the cost of the work is irrecoverable.

**28–29**   A case going the other way is *Colley v Streeton*.[107] In that case an underlease contained covenants by the sub-tenant to repair and to repair on notice. The sub-tenant failed to repair, as a result of which the tenant was threatened with forfeiture by the head landlord. The tenant served a notice to repair, and when the sub-tenant failed to comply, the tenant entered the premises without the sub-tenant's consent, carried out the repairs, and sought to recover the cost from the sub-tenant. His claim succeeded. Abbott C.J. and Holroyd J. proceeded on the footing that trespass was no defence to the tenant's claim, although the sub-tenant would have an action in trespass which could be maintained in other proceedings. Holroyd J. in addition thought that the tenant had a right to enter to carry out the work by virtue of the proviso for re-entry.[108] Bayley J. did not expressly refer to the point at all in his short judgment in which he described the case as "free from all doubt".

In the subsequent case of *Williams v Williams*,[109] where the facts were much the same,[110] the tenant's claim for the cost of the work failed on the ground that there was no damage to the reversion.[111] It does not appear from the report that the tenant's entry was with the consent of the sub-tenant, but in any event it was not argued that the tenant's claim was barred because it arose out of his own trespass.

The balance of authority therefore appears to be in favour of the view that the mere fact that the carrying out of the work is unlawful is not of itself a bar to the recovery of damages for breach. It is thought that this is the correct approach. If the landlord's entry has caused damage, the tenant will have a cross-claim in trespass. If not, it is difficult to see why the landlord should not in an appropriate case be entitled to damages in an amount equal to the cost he has incurred in carrying out work which was the tenant's liability.

---

[107] (1823) 2 B. & C. 273. See also *Loria v Hammer* [1989] 2 E.G.L.R. 249 discussed in para.23–12, above.

[108] It is thought that this cannot be correct in the absence of evidence that the tenant entered in order to forfeit the sub-tenancy.

[109] (1874) L.R. 9 C.P. 659. See para.28–31, below.

[110] Save that in *Williams v Williams* the tenant entered before the expiry of the notice to repair, so that his claim was based on the general covenant.

[111] See further on this case para.28–31 below.

## Limitations on the amount of damages recoverable

On the assumption that the landlord is entitled to damages in principle, there **28–30** remain a number of hurdles to be overcome. If the Leasehold Property (Repairs) Act 1938[112] applies, a s.146 notice in the form prescribed by the Act will need to be served. It was held in *SEDAC Investments Ltd v Tanner*[113] that a s.146 notice cannot validly be served after the work has been done, because the breach has by then been remedied. In that case, the court refused leave to a landlord who had entered and carried out repairs falling within the tenant's repairing covenant, and then served a s.146 notice, on the ground that the notice was invalid and the court therefore had no power to grant leave. The correctness of this decision is considered elsewhere.[114] If it is right, the cost of the work will be irrecoverable in cases where the Act applies, unless (i) a s.146 notice complying with the Act is served before the work is done, and (ii) the tenant is given 28 days in which to serve a counter-notice. In many cases, however, this will defeat the whole object of entering and carrying out the work, which is to get it done quickly because it is urgently required.

Where a valid notice is served and the tenant gives the requisite counter-notice, leave under the Act must be obtained before the claim can be brought. If the landlord applies to the court before entering, the tenant may oppose leave on the ground that the landlord is proposing to commit a trespass, and therefore that the court should not exercise its discretion in his favour. If the landlord waits until after he has done the work, he may be in difficulties in establishing any of the statutory grounds. Grounds (a) to (d)[115] all proceed on the footing that the breach remains in existence at the date when the court is asked to give leave. If the reasoning in *SEDAC Investments Ltd v Tanner*[116] is correct, leave may be refused on the basis that the breach no longer exists, and therefore that the grounds do not apply. The landlord would therefore have to rely on ground (e) (special circumstances rendering it just and equitable that leave should be given).[117]

Further, in all cases the amount recoverable will be limited by s.18(1) of the Landlord and Tenant Act 1927[118] to the amount by which the value of the landlord's reversion was diminished by the breach. It will not therefore automatically equate to the cost incurred by the landlord in carrying out the work. There are two potential difficulties resulting from this. First, there is the question whether as a matter of law the value of the reversion can be said to have been diminished at all, given that the landlord has carried out the work. Second, there is the question whether any diminution can in fact be established.

The decision in *Williams v Williams*[119] suggests at first sight that if the landlord **28–31** enters and carries out the work, any damage to the reversion will thereby have

---

[112] See para.27–31 et seq., above.
[113] [1982] 1 W.L.R. 1342.
[114] See paras 27–45 to 27–46, above.
[115] See paras 27–61 to 27–65, above.
[116] Above.
[117] See para.27–66, above.
[118] See para.28–20 et seq., above, and Ch.30, below.
[119] (1874) L.R. 9 C.P. 659.

been eliminated. In that case, the tenant under a head lease sub-let the premises on terms which included covenants by the sub-tenant to repair and to repair on two months' notice. The head landlord served on the tenant a notice to repair under the covenants of the head lease. The tenant served on the sub-tenant a notice to repair within two months under the covenant in the sub-tenancy to repair on notice. Before the two months was up, the tenant entered the premises and carried out the repairs. He did this in order to protect the head lease from forfeiture. He then sought to recover the cost of the work from the sub-tenant as damages. The sub-tenant denied liability for breach of the covenant to repair on notice because the tenant had done the work before the two months were up. Not surprisingly, this argument succeeded. However, the tenant also relied on the general covenant to repair. The sub-tenant admitted breaches of this covenant, but argued that the tenant was only entitled to nominal damages because at the date the action was brought there was no damage to the tenant's reversion, the premises having by then been repaired. This argument also succeeded. The basis of the decision appears to be that the carrying out of the work by the tenant had prevented any damage to the reversion occurring. It is not clear to what extent the fact that the landlord was himself a tenant under a head lease was central to the decision. Lord Coleridge C.J. relied on the fact that the covenants in the sub-lease were different in substance to those in the head lease, and distinguished *Colley v Streeton*[120] on this ground. This suggests that the real ground for his decision might have been that the sub-tenant's failure to do the work did not result in any damage to the tenant's reversion, because the work in question was not necessarily the same as that required under the head lease. However, Brett L.J., who gave the only other judgment, did not mention this point. Moreover, both Lord Coleridge C.J. and Brett L.J. appear to have accepted that the cost of the work could have been recovered by way of damages for breach of the covenant to repair on notice but for the fact that the action had been brought before the notice expired. It is not easy to see why the two covenants should be so different in their operation.

*Williams v Williams* is therefore an unsatisfactory authority. It may be that it is explicable on the basis that the effect of the notice to repair within two months was to waive any liability under the general covenant until the two months were up.[121] In any event, it is not thought that the decision lays down any general principle that where the landlord carries out the work, he thereby eliminates any damage to his reversion so that no damages are recoverable, and insofar as it does, it is thought that it is erroneous. The only reason why there is no damage to the landlord's reversion in such cases is that the landlord has done the work. It is difficult to see any justification in principle for holding that the very act of remedying the breach itself extinguishes the landlord's entitlement to recover the cost thereby incurred as damages. It is thought that the correct analysis is that the issue of damage to the reversion must be looked at immediately prior to the carrying out of the work by the landlord. Even then, however, there may be no

---

[120] (1823) 2 B. & C. 273. See para.28–29, above.

[121] See *McGregor on Damages*, 18th edn, at para.23–76; Foa, *Landlord and Tenant*, 8th edn, p.223. The relationship between the general covenant and the covenant to repair on notice is considered in para.14–10 and para.27–10, above.

diminution. The reversion to be valued is the reversion to the subsisting lease. The landlord will have to show that a purchaser of his interest would have paid less for the premises in disrepair than he would have done had they been in repair. Reference should be made to para.28–20 et seq., above.

## ENTRY BY THE LANDLORD TO REMEDY DISREPAIR PURSUANT TO AN EXPRESS PROVISION ENTITLING HIM TO DO SO

### Introductory

Provisions of this type are extremely common, and have already been considered elsewhere.[122] The usual form of clause confers on the landlord a right to enter and inspect the premises, serve on the tenant a notice requiring him to remedy within a prescribed time any breaches of his repairing obligations found on the inspection, carry out such work if the tenant fails to do so and recover the cost of so doing from the tenant. The extent of the right in any particular case, and the circumstances in which it can be exercised, will obviously depend on the precise terms of the particular clause in question.

**28–32**

### The scope of the clause

Whilst each case turns on the drafting of the provision in question, most clauses of this type apply only to breaches of the tenant's repairing and (in some cases) decorating obligations. Where this is the case, the landlord's right of entry to carry out remedial works will not arise in relation to, for example, the removal of unauthorised alterations. Nor, since it will generally be confined to breaches existing at the relevant time, will it arise in relation to works required by covenants (such as the covenant to yield up) which only come into effect at the end of the term.[123]

**28–33**

Where the landlord's notice relates to or includes a failure to carry out internal decorative repairs, the tenant will have a right to apply for relief under s.147 of the Law of Property Act 1925.[124]

### Contractual conditions precedent

The exercise of the landlord's right is virtually always made subject to various conditions precedent, such as the prior service of a notice specifying the works in question, and the expiry of a prescribed period from the service of the notice without the tenant having done the work. A landlord who fails to observe these may find that his subsequent entry on the premises is held to be a trespass for which he is liable in damages, or that his expenditure on repairs is irrecoverable, or both. It is therefore important to ensure that the notice is properly drafted in

**28–34**

---

[122] See para.14–11 et seq., above.
[123] For the position in relation to further defects found on site in the course of carrying out remedial works in default, see para.28–38, below.
[124] See para.27–89 et seq., above.

accordance with the requirements of the clause; that it is validly served on the tenant; and that the landlord does not enter until after the expiry of the prescribed time.

It should be borne in mind that provisions of this type are likely to be given a restrictive construction by the court. Thus, in *Amsprop Trading Ltd v Harris Distribution Ltd*[125] Neuberger J. construed a provision obliging the tenant to comply with a repairs notice within three months and in default to permit the landlord to enter and carry out the works, and to pay the landlord's costs of the work, as meaning that the tenant's obligation to comply with the notice fell away if the lease ended within the three-month period. He said in the course of his judgment:

> "[A] provision such as [the covenant in question], which gives the landlords substantial powers, and in particular power to carry out work at the tenant's expense, should be construed narrowly rather than widely."

## The notice required

**28–35**    The form and contents of the notice will depend on the particular wording of the clause in question. However, under most forms of clause the notice must specify the relevant disrepair. It must therefore inform the tenant of the particular condition of the premises which he is required to remedy. The degree of precision required in any case will depend on the wording of the clause and the nature of the relevant disrepair. But specifying the remedial works which the landlord says are necessary is not the same thing as specifying the relevant disrepair.[126] In practice, there may be a number of different ways of putting right the disrepair, all of which would amount to compliance with the covenant, and the choice between them is a matter for the tenant.[127] A landlord who serves a notice which sets out the required remedial work runs two risks: first, that the notice will be held to be invalid in relation to the disrepair in question, because the method specified is not an appropriate method, or goes further than the covenant requires; and second, that if the tenant defaults and the landlord decides on site that some other method of repair would be more appropriate, he may be unable to recover the cost because that method was not specified in the notice. For these reasons, a landlord who wishes to suggest that the defect is remedied in some particular way will generally be better advised to do so in a covering letter which does not form part of the formal notice.

It is sometimes argued that the inclusion in the notice of a requirement to remedy a defect which does not fall within the terms of the clause invalidates the whole notice, even in relation to defects which do fall within the clause. Whilst each case will turn on its own facts, it is not thought that this will usually be the correct conclusion. First, it means that once the notice can be shown to include an item not within the clause, the landlord has no right to enter to remedy any of the other defects in the notice, even if that is urgently required. Second, if the above

---

[125] [1997] 1 W.L.R. 1025. See further on this case paras 14–12 and 24–09, above.
[126] See para.27–12 et seq., above, in which the contents of s.146 notices are considered, and see also para.36–22, below.
[127] See para.10–04, above.

argument is right, it means that once the tenant alleges that the notice includes an item outside the clause, the landlord is in an impossible position: either he must serve another notice without that item; or face long delays whilst the point is litigated; or run the risk of going ahead in the knowledge that if the tenant is right, the landlord's entry will (as regards all the works in the notice) be a trespass for which he will be liable in damages. The same is true even where the tenant makes no response to the notice: it may subsequently be shown that the notice contained an impermissible item, in which case the landlord's entry will have been a trespass from the start. The practical effect will be to deprive the landlord of much of the benefit which the clause was intended to give him, and indeed, to turn the clause into a potential trap. Third, the conclusion that a notice which includes impermissible items is nonetheless valid as regards permissible items will not ordinarily result in any injustice to the tenant. If the landlord wrongly specifies something which is not the tenant's liability, the tenant need not do it, and if the landlord then does it, the tenant will have a complete defence to a claim for recovery of the cost and a claim for damages in relation to any disruption attributable to the carrying out of that item. Fourth, the conclusion that the notice is valid notwithstanding the inclusion of defects not within the clause accords with the cases on notices under s.146 of the Law of Property Act 1925, in which it has been held that failure to prove one of the breaches specified in the notice does not render the notice invalid in relation to those breaches which are proved.[128]

For these reasons, it is thought that in most cases the correct view will be that the notice must be looked at on an item-by-item basis, and that the inclusion of items outside the clause will not invalidate the notice in relation to items within it, save perhaps where the impermissible items are so inextricably linked with the permissible items that the whole notice is vitiated.

## The works carried out by the landlord

One question which may arise in practice concerns what method of repair the landlord is entitled to adopt. No difficulty will arise where the relevant defect can only reasonably be repaired in one way. However, where there is more than one way of performing the covenant, the general principle is that the choice between methods is for the tenant. as the covenanting party.[129] It is not immediately obvious what happens where the tenant fails to comply with the notice, and the landlord then enters and remedies the defect. On one view, given that the tenant has been given the opportunity to remedy the defect and has not taken it, the landlord is entitled to select which method of repair to adopt, and his choice cannot be criticised provided he chooses a method which is reasonable in all the circumstances. Such an argument can be supported by reference to the authorities on service charges.[130] The alternative view is that the landlord is limited to the method that is, in cost terms, the most favourable to the tenant, and that if he repairs to any higher standard, he is going outside the terms of his rights of entry

**28–36**

---

[128] See paras 27–19 to 27–21, above.
[129] See paras 10–06 to 10–07, above.
[130] See paras 10–08 to 10–10, above.

and recovery, or at least that the excess is irrecoverable. It is thought that the former is the better view, although in practice the courts are likely to scrutinise carefully the method adopted by the landlord to ensure that it is reasonable in all the circumstances. If this is right, then it is a good reason why a tenant who receives a notice should consider doing the work himself. Other reasons are that he can use contractors and professional advisers of his own choice, negotiate his own prices and terms, and programme the work to suit his own convenience.

Another question which may arise in practice concerns what happens where the landlord carries out works which go beyond the tenant's obligation on any view, but which have the effect of remedying the state of affairs giving rise to the breach. Suppose, for example, that the breach consists of a leaking asphalt roof which requires no more than a few localised patch repairs, but the landlord replaces it in its entirety with a roof of a different construction and design, such works going beyond anything that could reasonably be regarded as a performance of the tenant's covenant. Is the landlord nonetheless entitled to the cost of what he would have had to spend on patch repairs? Whilst the question would ultimately be one of construction, it might well be argued in such a case that if nothing has been done which can fairly be described as repair, then the tenant is not obliged to pay anything. Such an argument might be supported by reference to the decision in *Crane Road Properties v Hundalani*,[131] in which the claimant's claim for half the costs of repairing a road failed where the works actually done were accepted to go far beyond repair, and nothing had been done which could fairly be described as work falling within the obligation to contribute.

## Specifying or remedying some only of the defects

**28–37**    A further question may be the extent to which the landlord can recover under the clause if either his notice specifies some only of the then existing defects in the premises, or, having entered, he remedies only some of the defects specified in the notice.

In *Bruntwood 2000 First Properties Ltd v British Telecom Plc*,[132] a lease of a 1970s office building let for 25 years contained the following provision:

> "provided further that if the Tenant shall fail to leave the demised premises in such condition as aforesaid then and in such case the Landlord may do or effect all such repairs renovations and decorations for which the Tenant shall be liable hereunder and the cost thereof shall be paid by the Tenant to the Landlord on demand and the certificate of the Landlord's Surveyor certifying the cost to the Landlord shall be final and binding on the Tenant and the Tenant will also pay to the Landlord mesne profits at the rate of the rent payable hereunder immediately prior to the said expiration or determination during the period reasonably required for carrying out such work and the amount of such mesne profits shall be added to the cost of carrying out such work as aforesaid save in the case of such delay being attributable to the Landlord."

It was held that the landlord's entitlement to the cost of the work did not arise unless he did all the work for which the tenant was liable. The purpose of the provision was held to be to enable the landlord to avoid any loss caused by the

---

[131] [2006] EWHC 2066 (Ch).
[132] Unreported decision of H.H. Judge Pelling QC, sitting as a High Court Judge, dated December 11, 2008.

tenant's failure to deliver up the premises in repair by carrying out the works himself. It was therefore an alternative to a claim for damages for terminal dilapidations.

It is thought that this reasoning is not applicable to the more usual form of express right of entry to carry out works, which is operable at any time during the term, and whose purpose is to enable the landlord to deal with relevant disrepair whilst the tenant is still in possession. In such a case, it is difficult to see any good reason in principle why the landlord should be compelled to specify in his notice every single defect in the premises at the relevant time, and then, having entered, remedy each and every item of disrepair specified in the notice. In practice, there may (and often will) be only one or two major items of disrepair which are of concern. It would be odd if the clause were to be construed in such a way as to prevent the landlord from targeting such areas without dealing at the same time with what may be numerous items of minor disrepair that are of no concern to anyone. In such a case, an "all or nothing" approach would seem to be in neither party's interests. Accordingly, whilst each case obviously turns on the construction of the particular words used in the light of the relevant admissible background, it is thought that, in the ordinary case, the fact that the landlord's notice relates to some only of the then existing defects or that the landlord undertakes some only of the works specified in the notice will not prevent him from recovering the cost of those works actually carried out.

## Further defects discovered after entry

The landlord's right of entry, once it has arisen, will generally only be to remedy the defects specified in the notice. Prima facie, there is no right to remedy any further defects which are discovered once on site. Depending on the facts, it may be that a defect, the general nature of which is specified in the notice but which is found on site to be more extensive than was first anticipated, would be covered by the notice. However, a new defect, unrelated to anything in the notice, would not be, and it is very doubtful whether a general catch-all in the notice (such as "remedy any other defects found to exist") would be sufficient.[133] It follows that the landlord's inspection prior to serving the notice should be as thorough as is practicable in the circumstances, and careful thought should be given when drafting the notice (or schedule attached to it) to the description of the defects in question.

28–38

## The Leasehold Property (Repairs) Act 1938

There was formerly doubt as to whether the tenant's obligation to pay the cost expended by the landlord in carrying out the works was in truth an obligation to pay damages, so that the provisions of the Leasehold Property (Repairs) Act 1938 applied. Somewhat curiously, the point did not arise for decision until 1983, when McNeill J. held that the Act applies.[134] The following year, Vinelott J. reached the

28–39

---

[133] Cf. para.27–19, above.
[134] *Swallow Securities Ltd v Brand* (1983) 45 P. & C.R. 328.

opposite conclusion,[135] and his decision was followed in two other cases at first instance.[136] Although this settled the point at first instance, it remained uncertain what view an appellate court would take.[137] That uncertainty has been resolved by the decision of the Court of Appeal in *Jervis v Harris*[138] to the effect that the 1938 Act does not apply. The thrust of the court's reasoning is to be found in the following passage from the judgment of Millett L.J.:

> "The tenant's liability to reimburse the landlord for his expenditure on repairs is not a liability in damages for breach of his repairing covenant. The landlord's claim sounds in debt not damages; and it is not a claim to compensation for breach of the tenant's covenant to repair, but for reimbursement of sums actually spent by the landlord in carrying out repairs himself."

The covenant in *Jervis v Harris* was to pay the cost of the works on demand, language which is itself consistent with an obligation in debt. The drafting of most such clauses is to the same general effect. In some cases, however, the cost is expressed to be payable "as liquidated damages" or some similar formulation. If this is to be interpreted literally, it would seem to follow that the 1938 Act would apply. Nonetheless, the substance of such an obligation is the same as that considered in *Jervis v Harris*, in that the liability to pay is triggered not by breach of the tenant's repairing covenant but by the landlord's own expenditure on repairs. It is thought that a court faced with this point would look at the reality of the obligation, and not at the label used by the parties.

## Section 18(1) of the Landlord and Tenant Act 1927

**28–40**   Although *Jervis v Harris*[139] was concerned with the 1938 Act, the effect of the court's decision that the landlord's claim for the cost of the works is a claim in debt not damages is that s.18(1) of the Landlord and Tenant Act 1927[140] does not apply to the landlord's claim. It follows that the landlord does not need to show that the sum claimed equates to the damage to his reversion, or indeed, that the value of his reversion has been damaged at all. This has potentially far-reaching consequences for terminal dilapidations claims. A landlord who waits for the lease to end and then sues on the covenant to yield up must prove damage to the value of his reversion in the ordinary way. But a landlord who chooses instead to invoke a *Jervis v Harris*-type clause in the last year of the term can, in principle, get the work done at the tenant's expense without having to prove any damage to the reversion.

---

[135] *Hamilton v Martell Securities Ltd* [1984] Ch. 266.
[136] *Colchester Estates (Cardiff) Ltd v Carlton Industries Plc* [1986] Ch. 80 and *Elite Investments v T.I. Bainbridge (Silencers) Ltd (No.2)* [1986] 2 E.G.L.R. 43.
[137] See the First Edition of this work, para.22–20.
[138] [1996] Ch. 195.
[139] Above.
[140] See para.28–20, above, and Ch.30, below.

## Implied limitations on the exercise of the right[141]

Although the question of possible statutory limitations on the landlord's rights **28-41**
has been disposed of by *Jervis v Harris*, there remains the question of the extent
to which the court may, in an appropriate case, be prepared to imply limitations
on the circumstances in which the landlord's rights under clauses of this type may
be exercised.

No difficulty arises where the landlord has a legitimate interest in the
remedying of the defects in question.[142] However, cases may arise in practice
where the disrepair has no adverse effect on the value of the landlord's reversion,
and leave under the 1938 Act to forfeit or claim damages would not be given, and
yet the landlord threatens to, or does, enter to carry out remedial works as part of
a some wider strategy (for example, to put pressure on the tenant to agree a rent
review or surrender the residue of a long term at a low rent). The adverse effect
on the tenant will be twofold: not only will he have to pay for works which are
unnecessary, but he will have to suffer the disruption of the landlord coming in to
do them.[143]

A tenant faced with such a situation may argue for the implication of an
appropriate term into the clause, perhaps to the effect that the right can only be
exercised bona fide for the purpose of protecting the landlord's interests.[144] It is
thought, however, that in the ordinary case, such an argument is unlikely to
succeed. Leases containing clauses of this kind are usually lengthy and carefully
drafted documents, so that the presumption that the parties have said all they
intended to say will be particularly strong.[145] It will generally be difficult to say
that a reasonable person, looking at the language of the lease in the light of the
relevant background, would readily understand the parties to have intended the
landlord's rights to be limited in some way. In addition, any implied term would
be difficult to formulate.

Moreover, the courts have generally been sceptical about the possibility of **28-42**
landlords abusing their rights under *Jervis v Harris* clauses. In *Hamilton v
Martell Securities Ltd*[146] it was submitted on behalf of the tenant that possible
abuse by unscrupulous landlords justified the court in holding that the 1938 Act
applied. Vinelott J. regarded the fact that the landlord must initially meet the cost
of carrying out the repairs as a "considerable disincentive" to abuse. The same
view was taken by the Court of Appeal in *Jervis v Harris*,[147] in which Millett L.J.
cited with approval this part of Vinelott J.'s judgment.[148] This emphasises the
distinguishing feature of clauses of this type, which is that the landlord must

---

[141] See paras 1–03 to 1–07, above, where the principles relating to implied terms are considered.
[142] See, for example, the facts of *S.E.D.A.C. Investments Ltd v Tanner* [1982] 1 W.L.R. 1342.
[143] One course open to a tenant in such a situation is to refuse the landlord access to carry out the
works and then resist an application for an injunction on the ground that it would be oppressive and
disproportionate: see *Hammersmith & Fulham LBC v Creska (No.2)* [2000] L. & T.R. 288, considered
in para.26–43, below.
[144] Cf. *Quennell v Maltby* [1979] 1 W.L.R. 318.
[145] See paras 1–06 to 1–07, above.
[146] [1984] Ch. 266.
[147] [1996] Ch. 195.
[148] Above, at 205 B–E.

actually incur the expense of the works himself before his rights of recovery arise. It is thought that in most cases this feature is likely to be conclusive against the existence of implied limitations on the exercise of the right.

This is not necessarily to say, however, that the landlord can remain on the premises for as long as he likes, doing what he likes and spending as much as he likes. First, it is thought that in most cases the court would be ready to imply a term to the effect that the cost of the work must be reasonable in amount, and that the work must be carried out to a reasonable standard, so that the tenant is not liable for any part of the cost which is excessive or which relates to poor quality work.[149] Second, if the landlord remains on the premises for an unreasonably long time, it may well be that he would be liable for damages on the basis that, either on the proper construction of the clause or by virtue of an implied term, his right of entry is only for such period as is reasonable in all the circumstances.[150]

## Where the tenant is not prepared to permit access

**28–43**     Where the tenant refuses access, the landlord's remedy will be to apply for an appropriate injunction. The grant or refusal of an injunction, and any terms imposed on either party, will be a matter for the court's discretion. The court has power to order damages in lieu of an injunction under s.50 of the Senior Courts Act 1981.

In deciding whether to grant an injunction requiring the tenant to allow access, and if so, on what, if any, terms, the court will take all relevant matters into account. These will include the following: the nature and seriousness of the relevant defects; the extent to which there exists a genuine dispute as to whether the works fall within the tenant's obligations and/or the *Jervis v Harris* clause; the landlord's reasons for wanting to carry out the work; the tenant's reasons for refusing access; the likely effect on the tenant of carrying out the works, and in particular, whether it will need to move out or will otherwise be substantially inconvenienced; the likely consequences for the landlord if the works cannot be carried out; the extent of any existing or anticipated damage to the landlord's reversionary interest; any offers made by the tenant; and the tenant's likely solvency at the end of the term as compared to the time at which the application is made. This is not intended to be an exhaustive list, and other factors may be relevant or even decisive depending on the circumstances.

An injunction was refused in *Hammersmith & Fulham LBC v Creska (No.2)*.[151] In that case it had been held in previous proceedings between the parties that the tenant was liable to repair underfloor heating.[152] The landlord gave notice of its wish to enter and carry out the work under a *Jervis v Harris* clause. The tenant made satisfactory proposals in relation to three of the floors in

---

[149] Cf. *Finchbourne v Rodrigues* [1976] 3 All E.R. 581; *Morgan v Stainer* [1993] 2 E.G.L.R. 73; *Crane Road Properties Ltd v Hundalani* [2006] EWHC 2066 (Ch). However, whether a term as to reasonableness is to be implied will depend on all the circumstances, and there may be cases where no such term is appropriate: see the cases on insurance, which are summarised in *Berrycroft Management v Sinclair Gardens Investments Ltd* [1997] 1 E.G.L.R. 47.
[150] Cf. *Goldmile Properties Ltd v Lechouritis* [2003] 1 E.G.L.R. 60.
[151] [2000] L. & T.R. 288.
[152] See para.10–04, above.

the building but declined to repair the system in the ground floor because that floor was used to house the mainframe computer (which required special air conditioning and false flooring), the heating system on that floor was not used and would not be used even if repaired, and it would be disproportionately expensive and disruptive to move the computer. The tenant offered to carry out the necessary repairs at the end of the term and in the meantime to put money into a secured account to cover the cost of the works. The landlord applied for an injunction restraining the tenant from refusing access. It contended that since the breach was of a negative contractual obligation the court had no discretion to refuse an injunction.

Jacob J. declined to grant an injunction. He held, first, that the relevant provision could equally well be regarded as a positive covenant to permit access, and second, that in any event the court had power to refuse an injunction even in the case of a breach of a negative covenant. He referred to *Jaggard v Sawyer*,[153] in which the Court of Appeal applied *Shelfer v City of London Electric Lighting Co Ltd (No.1)*.[154] In that case Lindley L.J. described the following as a good working rule:

> "(1) If the injury to the plaintiff's legal right is small, (2) And is one which is capable of being estimated in money, (3) And is one which can be adequately compensated by a small money payment, (4) And the case is one in which it would be oppressive to the defendant to grant an injunction—then damages in substitution for an injunction may be given.[155]"

The facts of *Hammersmith* were rather unusual. In a straightforward case where the landlord has a legitimate reason for wanting to carry out the work and any resulting inconvenience to the tenant would not be disproportionate, an injunction requiring the tenant to permit access is likely to be granted fairly readily, albeit on terms designed to protect the tenant against excessive or unreasonable disruption. In *Hammersmith*, the judge, having held that the court had jurisdiction to refuse an injunction in the case of breaches of negative covenants, went on to say that:

**28–44**

> "This is not to say that the court will lightly disregard obligations freely entered into. On the contrary; where a party has entered into an obligation freely (a contractual obligation), then it will normally be just and convenient to enforce that obligation. It requires some very special circumstances for the court to say no, it will not, in the exercise of its discretion, enforce that which was undertaken by contract."

Nonetheless, where the landlord's expressed desire to carry out the work will result in oppression and an injunction would be a disproportionate remedy, *Hammersmith* at least serves as a reminder that the court may refuse an injunction in a proper case.

---

[153] [1995] 1 W.L.R. 269.

[154] [1895] 1 Ch. 287.

[155] The *Shelfer* principles continue to be applied by the courts as the starting point in claims for an injunction: see, for example, *Regan v Paul Properties Ltd* [2007] Ch. 135 (in which a mandatory injunction was granted requiring the defendant to demolish premises erected by him in breach of the claimant's rights of light).

## Declaratory relief in advance of entry

**28–45**    In practice, what often happens is that a landlord's notice under a provision of this type is met by the tenant contending that the defects set out in the notice, or the proposed remedial works, or both, are outside the ambit of the clause, such that if the landlord enters and carries out the works, he does so at his own risk and the tenant will contest any subsequent claim for the cost. One possible course open to a landlord in such a case would be to apply to the court, prior to carrying out the work, for appropriate declaratory relief (for example, that the tenant is in breach of covenant to the extent set out in the notice, or that the remedial work proposed by the landlord is the appropriate method of complying with the covenant in preference to the lesser work proposed by the tenant).

A declaration is a discretionary remedy. When considering whether or not to grant a declaration, the court will take into account justice to the claimant, justice to the defendant, whether the declaration would serve a useful purpose and whether there are any other special reasons why or why not the court should grant a declaration.[156] Although the court will not generally be prepared to make a declaration in relation to an academic or hypothetical matter, a declaration which relates to an assertion of a present right, albeit one whose scope or nature may be affected by future events, is not excluded under this principle: what is essential is the existence of a present controversy.[157] In accordance with these principles, it is thought that the court would have power to make a declaration in a case where a dispute arises in relation to a landlord's notice under a provision of this type, notwithstanding the fact that the landlord has not yet entered and carried out the works. Whether it would do so in any particular case, however, would depend on the detailed facts, and in particular the extent to which (i) it is sensibly possible to determine the dispute in advance of the works being undertaken, and/or (ii) the making of a declaration would serve a useful purpose in relation to the dispute.

## Advantages and disadvantages of the remedy

**28–46**    The principal advantage of the type of provision under consideration is that it gives the landlord the right to enter and remedy the disrepair. This may be a very valuable right in itself, particularly if (for example) the property is one unit forming part of a larger complex, and the current disrepair is having a detrimental effect upon the letting value of the remainder of the complex, or where the disrepair creates a source of danger to third parties for which the landlord may be liable. In these sorts of situations the landlord's principal concern is to get the work done, and it is here that a right to go in and do the work is crucial, since otherwise the tenant may be entitled to prevent the landlord from entering.[158] A second advantage is that the landlord will be able to repair the premises to the standard required by the covenant using his own materials and contractors of his choice, and to the satisfaction of his own surveyor.

---

[156] *Financial Services Authority v Rourke* [2002] C.P.Rep. 14.
[157] *British Technology Group Ltd v Boehringer Mannheim Corporation* [2000] EWHC Patents 148 at [18].
[158] See para.22–30, above.

The disadvantages would seem to be as follows. First, there is the need to arrange the practical details of the work, such as access, working hours, protection for the tenant's possessions and a supply of electricity and water for the contractors. Second, there may be arguments as to whether the notice was valid; whether the landlord's entry was premature; whether the defects or the remedial work fell within the terms of the clause; whether the cost was reasonable; whether the work was properly done; and whether the landlord's workmen caused damage to the tenant's possessions. Third, the landlord will have to expend his own money in advance of recovering from the tenant. Fourth, if the right of entry has for any reason not arisen or been exceeded, the landlord may be liable for damages the amount of which may, depending on the facts, be substantial. Last, the inclusion in the lease of a provision of this type may make the landlord liable to third parties under s.4 of the Defective Premises Act 1972.[159]

---

[159] See para.20–49 et seq., above.

CHAPTER 29

# DAMAGES AT THE END OF THE TERM (1): THE COMMON LAW MEASURE OF DAMAGES FOR BREACH OF THE COVENANT TO REPAIR

INTRODUCTORY

## The meaning of "damages"

For the purposes of the law of dilapidations, "damages" may be defined as the monetary compensation payable by a party who is in breach of a repairing or decorating obligation to the other party. Damages are compensatory, that is to say, they are awarded to compensate the innocent party for loss caused by the breach, and not to punish the guilty party for breaking the obligation.[1] Once the term has come to an end, a claim for damages is the only remedy for disrepair.

**29-01**

## Classification of claims for damages at the end of the term

Claims for damages at the end of the term may be divided into two principal categories.

**29-02**

The first comprises claims for damages for breach of a covenant to keep, put or leave premises in repair which are subject to the statutory ceiling on damages imposed by s.18(1) of the Landlord and Tenant Act 1927. For the reasons explained below, it is necessary in relation to such claims to consider first the common law measure of damages and then the operation of s.18(1). The common law measure of damages is considered in this Chapter. Section 18(1) is dealt with in Ch.30, below, and worked valuation examples are provided in Ch.31, below.

The second category comprises claims for damages to which s.18(1) does not apply. Examples are claims for damages for breach of the covenant to decorate,[2] and the covenant against alterations. The measure of damages applicable to such claims is considered in Ch.32, below.

In reality, a terminal dilapidations claim is very likely to include both categories of claim, and the relevant considerations applicable to each will overlap to a considerable degree. In many, perhaps most, cases in practice, the end result will be the same, whether that part of the claim which falls into the

---

[1] See for example *British Westinghouse Electric and Manufacturing Co. Ltd v Underground Electric Railways Co. of London Ltd* [1912] A.C. 673, 688–689 per Viscount Haldane LC (HL).
[2] Other than decoration which is required by the covenant to repair: see paras 15–03 to 15–06, above, and para.30–03, below.

second category is treated separately or not. For that reason, both types of claim are often treated together for the purposes of assessing damages.

## Prerequisites to claims for damages at the end of the term

**29–03**    There are no common law or statutory prerequisites to a claim for damages at the end of the term. For example, no s.146 notice is necessary. However, the landlord should ensure that, if at all possible, he complies with the pre-action Protocol.[3] The Protocol is considered in Ch.37 below, and is reprinted in Appendix III.

## DAMAGES FOR BREACH OF THE COVENANT TO REPAIR AT THE END OF THE TERM

### The common law measure

**29–04**    The common law measure of damages for breach of a covenant to yield up in repair is generally accepted to be (a) the proper cost of putting the premises into repair, and (b) (where appropriate) loss of rent and other losses during the period needed to carry out the repairs. These heads are considered in paras 29–06 to 29–23, below.

### Section 18(1) of the Landlord and Tenant Act 1927

**29–05**    The common law measure is subject to 18(1) of the Landlord and Tenant Act 1927, which provides as follows:

> "(1) Damages for breach of a covenant or agreement to keep or put premises in repair during the currency of a lease, or to leave or put premises in repair at the termination of a lease, whether such covenant or agreement is express or implied, and whether general or specific, shall in no case exceed the amount (if any) by which the value of the reversion (whether immediate or not) is diminished owing to the breach of such covenant or agreement as aforesaid; and in particular no damage shall be recovered for a breach of any such covenant or agreement to leave or put premises in repair at the termination of a lease, if it is shown that the premises, in whatever state of repair they might be, would at or shortly after the termination of the tenancy have been or be pulled down, or such structural alterations made therein as would render valueless the repairs covered by the covenant or agreement."

Section 18(1) is therefore divided into two limbs.[4] The first is to the effect that damages cannot exceed the amount by which the value of the landlord's reversion is diminished by reason of the breach; the second is that no damages are recoverable where the premises are to be pulled down or structural alterations are to be carried out at or shortly after the end of the term.

---

[3] *The Pre-Action Protocol for Claims for Damages in relation to the Physical State of Commercial Property at the Termination of a Tenancy.*
[4] See *Culworth Estates Ltd v Society of Licensed Victuallers* (1991) 62 P. & C.R. 211, per Dillon L.J.

Section 18(1) imposes a limit on the common law measure of damages, but it does not alter the method of assessment.[5] All it does is to limit the amount recoverable. For this reason, it remains necessary to consider the common law measure. It is thought that the correct approach will generally be, first, to consider what would be recoverable at common law; then to establish the amount of the diminution in the value of the reversion; and lastly, insofar as the former exceeds the latter, to reduce the former accordingly. In practice, however, in cases where it is clear that the statutory limit will operate to reduce the amount of damages recoverable, the first stage is sometimes omitted, and the exercise is concerned only with assessing the damage to the reversion.

This chapter is concerned with the damages recoverable at common law. Section 18(1) is considered in Ch.30, below.

## THE COST OF THE WORKS

### The rule in *Joyner v Weeks*

A series of cases in the latter part of the 19th century show that the courts had by then come to regard the common law measure of damages for breach of a covenant to yield up the demised premises in repair at the end of the term as the reasonable cost of the necessary remedial works, irrespective of the extent to which, if at all, that accorded with the landlord's real loss. Examples of cases where that approach was applied are:

**29–06**

(1)   *Inderwick v Leech*,[6] in which before the end of the lease the landlord made up his mind to take down and rebuild the premises and did so after bringing the action;[7]

(2)   *Rawlings v Morgan*,[8] where the landlord had, before the lease expired, orally agreed with third parties that the premises should be pulled down and that a new lease should be granted under which the third parties would spend about £4,000 in erecting new buildings. The condition in which the premises would be at the end of the lease formed no ingredient in the third parties' calculation in making their bargain. Shortly after the lease expired the third parties went into possession, and demolished the demised premises;

(3)   *Morgan v Hardy*,[9] where the premises and the surrounding property had greatly diminished in value since the lease was granted, as a result of which many of the repairs required under the covenant were not suited to the premises and were not necessary for their use and enjoyment. The referee found that the sum required to repair the premises according to the

---

[5] *Hanson v Newman* [1934] Ch. 298, per Luxmoore J. at 300–301 (affirmed on appeal, also at [1934] Ch. 298); *Jones v Herxheimer* [1950] 2 K.B. 106, per Jenkins L.J. at 119; *Crown Estate Commissioners v Town Investments Ltd* [1992] 1 E.G.L.R. 61. See further para.29–08, below.

[6] (1885) 1 T.L.R. 484.

[7] The tenant's defence that because of this the cost of the works should not be recoverable is described by the law reporter, reporting in 1885, as "novel".

[8] (1865) 18 C.B. (N.S.) 776.

[9] (1886) 17 Q.B.D. 770 (affirmed (1886) 35 W.R. 588, CA).

covenant totalled £1,680, and that the cost of doing only the works which were actually required amounted to £1,200. Denman J. held that the landlord was entitled to the full amount of £1,680.

The leading case is the decision of the Court of Appeal in *Joyner v Weeks*.[10] In that case, the landlord brought proceedings for disrepair against the tenant at the end of the lease, claiming £70 which was the cost of making good the dilapidations. Just under two years before the lease was due to end, the landlord had let the demised premises on a reversionary lease to commence on the date when the tenant's lease ended. The new tenant was already the tenant of the premises on either side of the demised premises, and the purpose of the reversionary lease was to enable him to convert the ground floor of the three sets of premises into a single shop. He covenanted (i) to lay out £200 in carrying out alterations, and (ii) to repair. He carried out the alterations, in the course of which he demolished some parts of the demised premises which were out of repair. He spent a further £45 on repairing other parts of the demised premises. The tenant contended that by reason of these matters the landlord had suffered no loss, or alternatively that his loss was limited to £45. He succeeded before the Official Referee, who awarded the landlord nominal damages of a farthing. The Divisional Court reversed the Official Referee, holding that the correct measure of damages was the diminution in the value of the reversion.[11] Wright J., giving the judgment of the court, said:

> "Two measures have been suggested, the first the amount of money which it will cost the lessor to do the repairs, with some allowance for loss of rent or occupation during the time of reparation and with some deduction where proper by reason of substitution of new for old; the second, the diminution of the value of the lessor's estate by reason of the non-repair. In general they will both come to the same thing, and it can seldom be the case that the diminution in value can be more than the cost of repair. It may, however, often be the case that the diminution in value by reason of some or all of the tenant's defaults is much less than the cost of making them good. A part of the structure may have been designed for a purpose which has become obsolete, or a building may for many reasons be found at the end of a term to be as valuable, or nearly as valuable, in a partially as in a completely repaired state. In such cases, which measure is to be preferred? . . . It appears to us that the better measure is the amount of the diminution of value, but not exceeding the cost of doing the repairs (with the addition and deduction above suggested), and that in the cases which appear to adopt the other test it was not intended to decide that the cost of repairing ought to be or can properly be given so far as it exceeds the diminution of value. To give that excess might in effect be to give an unfair kind of specific performance to the great detriment of the lessee without any advantage to the lessor as such; whereas the proper function of a right of action for damages for breach of contract seems to be to make good to the aggrieved party the damages which he has actually sustained."

**29–07**  It is hard to disagree with much of the above. However, the decision of the Divisional Court was reversed by the Court of Appeal, where it was held that the landlord was entitled to recover £75 damages.[12] Lord Esher M.R. said in the course of his judgment:

---

[10] [1891] 2 Q.B. 31.
[11] Above.
[12] Above.

"A series of dicta of learned judges has been referred to, which seem to me to show that for a very long time there has been a constant practice as to the measure of damages in such cases. Such an inveterate practice amounts, in my opinion, to a rule of law. That rule is that, when there is a lease with a covenant to leave the premises in repair at the end of the term, and such covenant is broken, the lessee must pay what the lessor proves to be a reasonable and proper amount for putting the premises into the state of repair in which they ought to have been left. It is not necessary in this case to say that that is an absolute rule applicable under all circumstances; but I confess that I strongly incline to think that it is so. It is a highly convenient rule. It avoids all the subtle refinements with which we have been indulged today, and the extensive and costly inquiries which they would involve. It appears to me to be a simple and business-like rule; and, if I were obliged to decide that point, I am very much inclined to think that I should come to the conclusion that it is an absolute rule. But it is not necessary to determine that point in the present case. The rule that the measure of damages in such cases is the cost of repair, is, I think, at all events, the ordinary rule, which must apply, unless there be something which affects the condition of the property in such a manner as to affect the relation between the lessor and the lessee in respect to it. The question is whether there is any such circumstance in the present case. I think that there clearly is not. The circumstances relied upon by the defendant did not affect the property as regards the relation between the lessor and the lessee in respect to it. They arose from a relation, the result of a contract between the plaintiff and a third person, to which the defendant was no party, and with which he had nothing to do."

Fry L.J. agreed, quoting with approval the statement of Denman J. in *Morgan v Hardy*[13] to the effect that:

"When the reversion has actually fallen in, I can see no reason to doubt that the proper rule is that laid down in *Mayne on Damages*, p. 253: 'Where the action is brought upon the covenant to repair at the end of the term, the damages are such a sum as will put the premises into the state of repair in which the tenant was bound to leave them'."

Continuing, Fry L.J. said:

"That is a rule of law and practice which appears to me to have the sanction of many cases . . . I cannot help observing that the rule so laid down is one of great practical convenience. It is more simple than the inquiry to what extent the reversion is damaged, which appears to me to involve many matters in respect to which the lessor has nothing to say to the lessee. It is much more simple than the rule suggested by the judgment of the court below, *viz.*, that the measure of damages is the amount of the diminution in value of the reversion not exceeding the cost of repairs. That involves the ascertainment of two amounts in order to take the smaller of the two. However exact such a measure of damages may be, there is, as it seems to me, a complexity about it which unfits it for determining affairs as between man and man in a court of law. I think the ordinary prima facie rule is what I have mentioned."

The landlord therefore recovered the cost of the remedial works, even though (i) that was not a cost which he or anyone else either had incurred or would incur, and (ii) it seems very likely that the diminution in the value of his reversion, if indeed there was any, was much lower.

The subsequent decisions proceeded on the basis that *Joyner v Weeks* had **29–08** established a settled principle that the measure of damages at common law was the reasonable cost of the work. Thus, in *Henderson v Thorn*[14] Wills J, giving the judgment of the Divisional Court, said (after referring to *Joyner v Weeks*):

---

[13] (1886) 17 Q.B.D. 770.
[14] [1993] 2 Q.B. 164.

THE COST OF THE WORKS

"An action for breach of covenants to repair and leave in repair is brought at the end of the term, and a large sum of money claimed as damages; it is true that the sum paid by the tenant is often a sum preposterous in relation to the real damage to the landlord: as, where he is going to pull down the premises and is, therefore, not the loser by a penny because they are returned on his hands out of repair. In such a case, the rule of law may amount to putting into the landlord's pocket money far beyond the damage which he has actually suffered; but it must be remembered that there are difficulties on the other side, and that, but for this rule of law, a tenant who has broken his contract might come off better than if he had kept it; a result not to be lightly encouraged. It is not surprising that of these two principles the Court of Appeal has chosen that which they believed to be the workable one, that is, that at the end of the term, no matter how indifferent it may be to the landlord whether his premises are in perfect order or not, yet if the repairing covenants are not performed the landlord is entitled to recover the amount necessary to put them into repair."

Likewise, in *Ebbetts v Conquest*[15] Lopes L.J. set out the principle as follows:

"The general rule with regard to damages in actions of this kind may be stated thus: Where the term has come to an end and the action is on the covenant to leave in repair, the measure of damages is the sum it will take to put the premises into the state of repair in which the tenant ought to leave them according to his covenant."

The judgment of Rigby L.J. was to the same effect:

"[A]s a general rule there is a difference in the assessment of damages in an action for breach of a covenant to yield up in repair brought after the determination of the term, and in an action for breach of a covenant to keep in repair brought during the continuance of the term. In the first case, an arbitrary rule is laid down upon grounds of convenience, that whether or not the lessor in fact loses by the want of repair, he shall be paid the amount which would be necessary to place the premises in good repair. It may happen that a payment of that amount would not induce him to repair—it may be far more to his interest to let the building be pulled down; but these considerations are not taken into account, principally because they depend upon the arrangements which the lessor has made with other persons, with which the lessee has nothing to do at all, as to which in general he will have no information, and as to which at the time he enters into the bargain he can have none."

Lord Esher's formulation of the rule in *Joyner v Weeks* suggests that there may be circumstances which rendered the rule inapplicable.[16] The same can be said of the description of the rule in *Ebbetts v Conquest* as a "general rule". Nonetheless, it would appear that by the end of the 19th century, the rule had come to be regarded as a rule of law of general application.

It was against the above background that s.18(1) of the Landlord and Tenant Act 1927 was enacted. It is to be noted that it did not substitute a new measure of damages for the common law measure. Instead, it prescribed limits on the amount recoverable. It did not therefore interfere with the common law measure as it was then understood to be. Luxmoore J. made this point in *Hanson v Newman*:[17]

---

[15] [1895] 2 Ch. 377 (unaffected on this point by the decision of the House of Lords ([1896] A.C. 490)).
[16] See *Tito v Waddell (No.2)* [1977] Ch. 106 at 329.
[17] [1934] Ch. 298 (affirmed on appeal, also at [1934] Ch. 298). This part of the judge's judgment was cited with approval by Jenkins L.J. in *Jones v Herxheimer* [1950] 2 K.B. 106 at 119.

"Under the law before the Landlord and Tenant Act 1927 was passed, a landlord could recover by way of damages at the termination of his term the actual cost of executing the repairs required to fulfil the covenant. The Landlord and Tenant Act 1927 has not changed the law in that respect; all that it has done is to impose a limit on the amount of those damages."

The purpose of s.18(1) was not therefore to alter the common law rule, but to militate against its rigour. In *Salisbury v Gilmore*[18] Lord Greene M.R. said of the subsection:

"Its broad purpose is not open to doubt. Before it was enacted, a lessor could recover damages from his tenant for breach of a covenant to deliver up in repair notwithstanding that the buildings were going to be pulled down or structurally altered in such a way as to make it useless to perform the covenant. The enforcement of the covenant in such circumstances was regarded as an unjust enrichment of the lessor and the legislature in s.18, sub-s. 1, set itself to remove the injustice."

Likewise, in *Duke of Westminster v Swinton*[19] Denning J. said:

"The position is that in *Joyner v Weeks* it was held by the Court of Appeal that on a breach of covenant to deliver up in repair at the end of the lease, the cost of repairs was the measure of damages in all cases, even though the money was not going to be used on repair, and even though the premises were going to be pulled down next day ... It was in order to remedy *Joyner v Weeks* that s.18 of the Landlord and Tenant Act, 1927, was passed."

## Whether the rule in *Joyner v Weeks* continues to represent the common law

It is doubtful whether *Joyner v Weeks* would be decided the same way today. First, the very inflexibility of the rule is contrary to the basic principle of damages, which is that the claimant is entitled to be compensated for his loss. Second, a different approach applies in relation to all breaches of covenant other than a covenant to repair, where the law is that the cost of the work is recoverable only where it is reasonable to carry it out and not where the expenditure would be out of all proportion to the benefit.[20] Thus, for example, damages for breach of an obligation to reinstate are not automatically measured by reference to the cost of the works.[21] It seems anomalous that a different rule should apply in relation to covenants to repair.

29–09

It was argued in *Shortlands Investments Ltd v Cargill Plc*[22] that there is no such rule of law as that stated by Lord Esher M.R., *Joyner v Weeks* having been decided before the courts became used to dealing with complicated principles of valuation. The Official Referee rejected this, holding that so far as the Court of Appeal expressed itself as stating a rule (and there were limits to the expression of the rule), the rule in *Joyner v Weeks* stands today subject only to s.18(1) of the Landlord and Tenant Act 1927.

---

[18] [1942] 2 K.B. 38.
[19] [1948] 1 K.B. 524.
[20] See in particular *Ruxley Electronics Ltd v Forsyth* [1996] A.C. 344. The common law measure of damages for damages other than for breach of the covenant to repair is considered in Ch.32, below.
[21] See paras 32–10 to 32–12, below.
[22] [1995] 1 E.G.L.R. 51.

In *Latimer v Carney*[23] Arden L.J. said:

"[24] The basic measure of damages for breach of the covenant to repair is the reasonable costs of executing the repairs required to fulfil the covenant: see *Hanson v Newman* [1934] Ch. 298. This general rule is subject to the statutory cap in section 18(1) of the 1927 Act .... It is also subject to general principles of law, including the principle established in *Ruxley Electronics & Construction Limited v Forsyth* [1996] A.C. 344. In that case the House of Lords held that where the expenditure required to be done to an asset to remedy a breach of contract is out of all proportion to the benefit to be obtained, the appropriate measure of damages will be the diminution in value of the asset...

...

[60] ...parliament enacted the cap in section 18(1) to meet the rigour of the measure of damages for breach of the repair covenant at common law. It may be that the courts would not apply the common law measure of damages in all cases today: I would accept the argument of counsel... that, if the common law measure alone were relevant to a landlord's claim, the courts today might, in an appropriate case, adopt the measure of damages in section 18(1) in preference to that which has previously been held to be the measure at common law: see generally *Ruxley*."

This suggests strongly that if s.18(1) had not been enacted, a modern court would almost certainly hold that the common law measure of damages for breach of the covenant to repair at the end of the term is that set out in *Ruxley Electronics & Construction Limited v Forsyth*[24] and not that in *Joyner v Weeks*. That is no doubt correct. It does not follow, however, that the common law measure must now be taken to be that in *Ruxley*. As pointed out above, s.18(1) was clearly enacted on the assumption that *Joyner v Weeks* correctly represented the law. Consistently with this, virtually all of the decided cases on damages for terminal dilapidations have, proceeded, expressly or implicitly, on the basis that the damages recoverable are the lesser of the cost of the works (plus any recoverable loss of rent) and the diminution in the value of the landlord's reversion resulting from the disrepair.[25]

**29–10** Nonetheless, in *PgfII SA v Royal & Sun Alliance Insurance Plc*,[26] H.H. Judge Toulmin QC appears to have treated s.18(1) as having restored the ordinary common law rule of damages, as it should have been understood (i.e. as that set out in *Ruxley*), rather than as having capped the common law measure in *Joyner v Weeks* by reference to the diminution in the value of the reversion. That this was his view is suggested by the following passages in his judgment:

"[34] In relation to the common law assessment of damages there is no tension between Section 18 of the Landlord and Tenant Act 1927 and the common law as expounded in

---

[23] [2006] 3 E.G.L.R. 13 at [60].
[24] [1996] A.C. 344.
[25] See, for example, *Hanson v Newman* [1934] Ch. 298; *Jones v Herxheimer* [1950] 2 K.B. 106; *Jacquin v Holland* [1960] 1 W.L.R. 258; *Shane v Runcorn* [1967] E.G.D. 88; *Crown Estate Commissioners v Town Investments* [1992] 1 E.G.L.R. 61; *Craven (Builders) Ltd v Secretary of State for Health* [2000] 1 E.G.L.R. 128; *Lintott Property Developments v Bower* [2005] All E.R. (D) 454; *Ravengate Estates Ltd. v Horizon Housing Group Ltd.* [2007] EWCA Civ 1368; *Val Dal Footwear Ltd. v Ryman Ltd* [2010] 1 W.L.R. 2015 (CA); *Sunlife Europe Properties Ltd v Tiger Aspect Holdings* [2013] EWHC 463 (TCC); *Hammersmatch Properties (Welwyn) Ltd v Saint-Gobain Ceramics* [2013] EWHC 1161 (TCC).
[26] [2011] 1 P. & C.R. 11.

DAMAGES AT THE END OF THE TERM (1)

> *Ruxley* ... the common law rule is intended to provide a landlord with reasonable compensation for the damage that he suffered. This is appropriate because Parliament has decided that reasonable damages for dilapidations cannot exceed the value of the diminution of the value of the reversion.
>
> ...
>
> [39]   ... I should emphasise the test of reasonableness in relation to common law damages."

It is fair to say that this is, in a sense, a logical extension of the proposition that *Joyner v Weeks* would have been decided differently, if it had been decided after *Ruxley*, since the more authoritative exposition by the House of Lords must be taken to have expressed the law as it should have been expressed by the Court of Appeal in *Joyner v Weeks*. But *Ruxley* was a building contract case, not a dilapidations case, and neither *Joyner v Weeks* nor s.18(1) was referred to by the House of Lords. It is not thought that the judge was correct to rely on *Ruxley* as having, in effect, restated the common law measure of damages for disrepair at the end of the term. For the reasons set out above, s.18(1) was enacted on the assumption that *Joyner v Weeks* correctly stated the position at common law. Its purpose was to cap the amount which would otherwise be assessed on that basis. If (as seems to be suggested in a number of places in the judgment in *PgfII*) it is now necessary to attempt a synthesis between the common law measure of damages and that introduced by s.18(1), there is a real danger that the important distinctions and differences between the two approaches will be lost. Nor does the above passage from Arden L.J.'s judgment in *Latimer v Carney*[27] (to the effect that if the common law measure alone were relevant to a landlord's claim, the court might, in an appropriate case, adopt a different measure of damages to that which has previously been held to be the common law measure), provide any real support for the view that, even though the common law measure does not stand alone, it is now to be taken as being different to that which it has always been understood to be.

The cases which followed *PgfII* have not espoused H.H. Judge Toulmin's view. Thus, in *Sunlife Europe Properties v Tiger Aspect Holdings*,[28] in which *PgfII* was cited, the judge accepted counsel's submission that the measure of the recoverable loss in a terminal dilapidations action is the lower of:

"(1)   The total of (a) the cost of remedying the defects (putting the property back into the covenanted condition), and (b) any rent actually lost and other expenses actually incurred whilst the defects are being remedied; and
(2)   The diminution in the value of the landlord's reversion, as at the term date, caused by the breaches—the statutory cap."

Likewise, the conventional approach to the common law measure was adopted by the court in *Hammersmatch Properties (Welwyn) v Saint-Gobain Ceramics & Plastics*,[29] a case which was also decided after *PgfII*.

---

[27] See above.
[28] Above, at [121].
[29] [2013] EWHC 1161 (TCC).

For the above reasons, it is thought that the common law measure remains that laid down by *Joyner v Weeks*.[30] However, the debate may, in any event, be somewhat academic. Given that damages are capped by reference to the diminution in the value of the landlord's reversion, it is not easy to think of an example of a case where the result is likely to differ according to whether the common law measure of damages is that laid down in *Joyner v Weeks* or that in *Ruxley*. For that to be the case, the amount assessed by reference to *Ruxley* would presumably need to be higher than the reasonable cost of the works but lower than the diminution in the value of the reversion. It is difficult to see that this is ever likely to occur in practice.

## The cost of the works

29–11    The recoverable amount in respect of the cost of the repairs is the reasonable and proper amount necessary for putting the premises into the state in which they ought to have been left by the tenant.[31] The exercise therefore involves, first, identifying the relevant works, and second, arriving at the reasonable and proper cost of those works. The cost of the work will include any necessary ancillary expenses, such as professional fees.[32]

Where the landlord's claim is based on the cost of work actually carried out by him, it will be necessary to consider whether such work properly equates to the work by reference to which damages are to be assessed, or whether it extends beyond this. If the latter is the case, then the sum recoverable will be limited to the cost of the work which is relevant for the purposes of assessing damages.[33] One way of doing this in practice may be to reduce the cost of the work actually carried out so as to reflect any element of betterment. This was done in *Twinmar Holdings v Klarius UK*.[34] The landlord claimed £2,643.40 in respect of the cost of replacing entrance gates and a height barrier which had been removed and so had to be replaced. The original barrier was a rigid structure which was slotted over posts at each end. The original posts remained in place, but the landlord installed new posts and an improved barrier. Edwards-Stuart J. reduced the sum claimed by two thirds to reflect the difference between what the tenant was liable to do and what had in fact been done. Likewise, in *Sunlife Europe Properties v Tiger Aspect Holdings*,[35] a deduction of 50 per cent was made from the cost incurred by the landlord in upgrading basement toilets in order to reflect the work for which the tenant was liable, which was limited to restoring the toilets to a working but utilitarian condition.

---

[30] See further *'Is the Law of Repair in Repair'*, a lecture given by Nicholas Taggart to the RICS Dilapidations Forum Conference 2012 on September 27, 2012, in which the same view is elegantly expressed.

[31] *Joyner v Weeks* [1891] 2 Q.B. 31, per Lord Esher M.R. at 43.

[32] See paras 30–25 and 34–27 et seq., below.

[33] *Soward v Leggatt* (1836) 7 C. & P. 613; *Carmel Southend Ltd v Strachan and Henshaw Ltd* [2007] 3 E.G.L.R. 15; *Sunlife Europe Properties v Tiger Aspect Holdings* [2013] EWHC 463 (TCC) at [43, 45-46].

[34] [2013] EWHC 944 (TCC) at [68-70].

[35] Above, at [121].

## Value added tax

In an appropriate case there must be added to the cost of the work any VAT which **29–12**
the landlord is liable to pay on the repair work and which he cannot reclaim as
input tax. Damages at common law will include VAT either where the landlord
has already done the work[36] and paid VAT, or where there is a realistic possibility
that he will do so in the future, provided that he cannot reclaim it as input tax.[37]
Whether VAT is reclaimable depends on the landlord's own tax position. The
nature of his business may be such that input tax cannot be recovered, or can be
only partially recovered, or he may be unregistered for VAT. The position may
also be affected by whether he has elected to charge VAT on rent.

In *Drummond v S & U Stores Ltd*[38] the landlord was an individual, who was
not registered for VAT. She contended that the cost of the work ought to include
VAT, because she might well wish to do the work, and if she did so, she would
incur VAT which she could not reclaim. The argument for the tenant was that the
landlord was most probably going to relet to a new tenant who would do the work
and who would be registered for VAT, so that VAT could be reclaimed. Glidewell
J. found in favour of the landlord on the ground that:

> "[I]f [counsel for the tenant] is correct it means that, albeit the landlord may very well in fact
> relet the premises, nevertheless the effect of depriving her of value added tax on the damages,
> or as part of the damages, would effectively be to close her other options, that is to say, if she
> changed her mind and decided that she would like to sell the premises and put the money to
> some other use but that she wanted to sell them in lease condition, then she would have to
> incur value added tax and she would not have recovered it as part of her damages."

VAT was also awarded on the cost of the works in *Sun Life Assurance Plc v
Racal Tracs Ltd*.[39]

By contrast, the landlord's claim for VAT failed in *Elite Investments Ltd v T.I.* **29–13**
*Bainbridge (Silencers) Ltd (No.2)*.[40] In that case damages based on the cost of the
work had been awarded at an earlier stage of the proceedings,[41] but the landlord
had still not done the work some eight months later when the matter again came
before the court to determine whether the damages ought to include VAT. Having
considered *Drummond v S & U Stores Ltd*,[42] the judge held that the correct
approach was to look at the evidence as a whole and then determine whether
there was some realistic option on the part of the landlord, even if it was not the
landlord's first choice and perhaps not the probable outcome, that threw the
burden of the VAT on to the landlord. The judge also noted:

---

[36] i.e. the work by reference to which damages are to be assessed: see para.29–14, below.

[37] *Drummond v S & U Stores Ltd* [1981] 1 E.G.L.R. 42.

[38] Above.

[39] [2000] 1 E.G.L.R. 138. The case went to the Court of Appeal on another point ([2001] 1 W.L.R.
1562) but no appeal was brought against the judge's decision on damages.

[40] [1987] 6 E.G.L.R. 43.

[41] *Elite Investments Ltd v T.I. Bainbridge (Silencers) Ltd (No.2)* [1986] 2 E.G.L.R. 43.

[42] Above.

"It is not a matter of assessing the chances as in some cases ... This would be an all or nothing matter, even though it means that if the landlord exercised some other option it would follow that there had been some windfall to the landlord."

He went on to find on the evidence that the landlord had no intention of doing any work on the premises. The claim for VAT therefore failed.

## Where there are several different ways of performing the covenant[43]

29–14    In practice there may be a number of different ways of performing a covenant to repair.[44] For example, it may be equally appropriate to repair a defective roof either by carrying out patching repairs, or by completely replacing it.[45] For the purposes of applying the common law measure, it is necessary to identify what works the tenant must be assumed to have been liable to carry out.

The general principle of damages is that where the defendant has the option of performing the contract in alternative ways, damages must be assessed on the assumption that he will perform it in the way most beneficial to himself and not in that most beneficial to the claimant.[46] The effect of this is that where there are a number of different ways of performing the covenant to repair, damages will, in the ordinary case, be assessed at common law by reference to the cost of the lesser, and cheaper, work. Thus, in *Ultraworth Ltd v General Accident Fire & Life Assurance Co Ltd*[47] it was held that a covenant to repair an air conditioning and heating system could be performed either by (as the landlord contended) substantial renewal or (as the tenant argued) reconditioning, and damages at the end of the term were assessed by reference to the cost of the latter. Likewise, in *Carmel Southend Ltd v Strachan & Henshaw Ltd*[48] the roof of an industrial unit could have been repaired at the expiry of the lease either by patch repairs or by overcladding with new profile metal sheeting, and the court held that damages were to be assessed on the basis of the cost of the lesser work.

29–15    In some cases, however, the effect of the cheaper work may be to produce a better specified building than the more expensive work. For example, it may be more economic to replace an item with its modern equivalent than it will be either to repair it or to procure an exact equivalent of the original. It is thought that, in such a case, the court cannot assume, as a matter of law, that the tenant would have chosen the latter in preference to the former. Thus, in *Durham Tees Valley Airport Ltd v bmibaby Ltd*[49] Patten L.J. said (referring to the reasoning of the majority of the Court of Appeal in *Abrahams v Herbert Reiach*[50]):

---

[43] An earlier version of the corresponding paragraph in the Third Edition of this work was referred to and applied by H.H. Judge Coulson, QC in *Carmel Southend Ltd v Strachan and Henshaw Ltd* [2007] 3 E.G.L.R. 15 at [9].
[44] See paras 10–06 to 10–07, above.
[45] See for example *Murray v Birmingham City Council* [1987] 2 E.G.L.R. 53.
[46] See *McGregor on Damages*, 18th edn, at para.8–093 et seq.
[47] [2000] 2 E.G.L.R. 115.
[48] [2007] 3 E.G.L.R. 15.
[49] [2010] EWCA Civ 485.
[50] [1922] 1 K.B. 477.

"Where there is only a single obligation to be performed it is clear that the majority view was that an assessment of damages should not, as a matter of law, be limited strictly to what was the minimum level of performance permitted under the contract but should extend to a calculation of how the contract would have been performed at the relevant time had it not been repudiated. This will take into account the likely profitability of the contract and any other relevant facts that would have influenced the method of performance."

He concluded:

"The court, in my view has to conduct a factual inquiry as to how the contract would have been performed had it not been repudiated. Its performance is the only counter-factual assumption in the exercise. On the basis of that premise, the court has to look at the relevant economic and other surrounding circumstances to decide on the level of performance which the defendant would have adopted. The judge conducting the assessment must assume that the defendant would not have acted outside the terms of the contract and would have performed it in his own interests having regard to the relevant factors prevailing at the time. But the court is not required to make assumptions that the defaulting part would have acted uncommercially merely in order to spite the claimant. To that extent, the parties are to be assumed to have acted in good faith although with their own commercial interests very much in mind."

On this approach, the court must ask itself, as a matter of fact, how in practice the tenant would have remedied the defect had he elected to do so. That will usually be at the least expense to him. Consistently with this, in *Hammersmatch Properties (Welwyn) v Saint-Gobain Ceramics & Plastics*,[51] Ramsey J. said (referring to *Riverside Property Investments v Blackhawk Automotive*[52] and *Carmel Southend Ltd v Strachan & Henshaw Ltd*[53]):

"Where a reasonable surveyor might advise either repair or replacement, damages are to be assessed by reference to the cost of repair unless replacement would be cheaper."

These cases would suggest that where work which produces a lower specification building will in fact cost more than work which results in a better building (and so is not work which the tenant would realistically be likely to have done had it elected to comply with its obligations) the cheaper, albeit higher specification, work will be the relevant work for the purposes of the common law measure of damages.[54]

It should be noted that the principle referred to above (i.e. that damages are to be assessed by reference to the lesser work) will only apply where the lesser work constitutes a performance of the covenant:[55] if it does not, it is irrelevant for the purposes of assessing damages. Where it applies, the principle is not affected by the fact that the landlord has actually carried out more extensive works; he will not be entitled to the cost of those works if the tenant could have performed the covenant by doing less extensive, and cheaper, work.[56]

---

[51] [2013] EWHC 1161 (TCC).
[52] [2005] 1 E.G.L.R. 114.
[53] Above.
[54] See further para.30–10, below.
[55] See Chs 9 and 10, above.
[56] See *Soward v Leggatt* (1836) 7 C. & P. 613; *Carmel Southend Ltd v Strachan and Henshaw Ltd* [2007] 3 E.G.L.R. 15; *Sunlife Europe Properties v Tiger Aspect Holdings* [2013] EWHC 463 (TCC) at [45–46]. See further para.29–11, above.

The correct application of the above principles may cause difficulties where the covenant to repair is qualified by reference to a schedule of condition. The relevant breach will generally consist of a failure to keep the premises in the state set out in or evidenced by the schedule, but it may not be sensible or economic in practice to restore the premises to that state without "improving" them over and above that state.[57] Consistently with the above cases, it is thought that for the purposes of assessing damages, the remedial work is the "improvement" work, provided that that is the way in which the tenant would have complied with the covenant had he elected to do so.

## Discount for betterment

**29–16**   In many cases it will not be possible to perform the covenant to repair without improving the premises to some degree. Thus, for example, a defective part of the premises may have reached the point at which it is no longer capable of being patch-repaired, so that the covenantor is obliged to replace it. The landlord will therefore get back a new item in place of an old. Moreover, the replacement item may itself have an element of improvement: thus, for example, the only sensible way of repairing a house with a defective wooden door may be to replace the door with a self-sealing aluminium door.[58]

There are suggestions in some of the old authorities that at common law the tenant may be entitled, where appropriate, to a discount from the full cost of the remedial works in order to reflect this factor.[59] Thus, in *Joyner v Weekes*[60] Wright J. described the cost of works measure as being "the amount of money which it will cost the lessor to do the repairs . . . with some deduction where proper by reason of substitution of new for old." However, it is doubtful to what extent this represents the modern law. The general principle of damages is that no deduction for betterment is to be made where it is impossible to put the claimant back into the position he would have been in but for the defendant's breach of contract without giving him something new in place of something old.

The leading modern authority is *Harbutt's "Plasticene" Ltd v Wayne Tank & Pump Co Ltd*,[61] in which the claimant's factory was burnt down as a result of the defendant's breach of contract. The claimant was awarded the cost of rebuilding the factory without any allowance for betterment. The reasoning underlying the decision appears to have been that it was not possible to reinstate the damage without providing a new factory. It is thought that the same principle must apply to cases where it is not possible to perform a covenant to repair without using new materials or otherwise improving the premises. For example, it will not

---

[57]   See para.14–13 et seq., above.

[58]   *Stent v Monmouth District Council* (1987) 19 H.L.R. 269.

[59]   *Yates v Dunster* (1855) 11 Ex. 15; *Joyner v Weeks* [1891] 2 Q.B. 31 (Wright J.). It is thought that *Soward v Leggatt* (1836) 7 C. & P. 613 is not, when properly analysed, a case where a deduction for betterment was made. The better explanation is that the work carried out by the landlord (laying new joists resting on brick supports instead of on the earth) went beyond the work which the tenant was liable to carry out, so that it was irrelevant for the purpose of assessing damages.

[60]   [1891] 2 Q.B. 31.

[61]   [1970] 1 Q.B. 447 (overruled on another point in *Photo Production Ltd v Securicor Transport Ltd* [1980] A.C. 827); *Bacon v Cooper Metals Ltd* [1982] 1 All E.R. 397.

generally be possible to repair a rotten window frame without cutting out the rot and jointing in new wood or, where the rot is serious, replacing the entire frame. In such cases the damages should not be reduced because the landlord is getting back a new frame in place of the old.

The above view accords with the authorities. In *Howe v Botwood*[62] a lease of a dwelling-house contained a covenant on the part of the tenant to pay outgoings, and a covenant by the landlord to keep the exterior in repair. The sanitary authority served notice requiring the landlord to carry out certain work which involved the renewal and reconstruction of a defective outside drain. The landlord carried out the work and claimed from the tenant the cost in so far as it exceeded repair. His claim was rejected on the ground that the tenant's covenant had to be read as being subject to the performance by the landlord of his covenant to repair, and the work was necessary to enable the landlord to perform that covenant. Lord Coleridge C.J. said:

**29–17**

> "In my opinion, if it was physically impossible to execute the work of repair without making these renewals and replacements, then the expense thereof falls upon the landlord under his covenant. I can draw no distinction between what is physically necessary and what is legally necessary to enable the landlord to perform his covenant; and if it was legally necessary for the performance of those repairs in the way in which they were executed, the cost of doing those repairs which were legally necessary for the performance of the landlord's covenant to repair is cast upon the landlord."

Likewise, in *McGreal v Wake*[63] it was held that a landlord is liable to make good decorations after carrying out necessary works of repair, and that if he fails to do so, the tenant's damages are not to be reduced on account of the fact that he is getting new decorations. Sir John Donaldson M.R. said:

> "In some circumstances that may involve a windfall profit to the tenant because it may be impossible to do that without giving him rather better decorations than he had beforehand ... we were referred to *Harbutt's 'Plasticene' Limited v Wayne Tank and Pump Co. Limited* [64] as authority for the proposition that if there is no way in which one can put the other party in the same position as he ought to have been without conferring an additional benefit on him, that is the obligation and it is just his good luck."

In *Graham v The Markets Hotel Pty Ltd*[65] (an Australian case) the tenant dismantled and removed a lavatory, in breach of the covenant to repair. Damages were assessed by reference to the cost of installing a new lavatory, without any deduction for betterment. Latham C.J. said in the course of his judgment:

> "There is a difference between repairing a house and building a new house in place of an old house. It is a question of degree whether rebuilding part of a house does or does not fall within the category of repairing a house. The covenant to repair does not involve the covenantee in an obligation to make improvements, but if he cannot perform his covenant to repair without making improvements, then the expense of making the improvements falls upon him. This is the case whether the necessity arises from physical causes or from legal causes."

---

[62] [1913] 2 K.B. 387.
[63] (1984) 13 H.L.R. 107. See also *Bradley v Chorley Borough Council* (1985) 17 H.L.R. 305.
[64] [1970] 1 Q.B. 447.
[65] (1943) 67 C.L.R. 567.

Similarly, in *Re Zis*[66] (another Australian case) the tenant removed certain bush timber sheep yards, in breach of covenant. The landlord replaced them with pre-cut dressed timber yards. It was argued that damages should be reduced to reflect the fact that the original yards only had one-third of their original life left. Virtue J. rejected this, holding that the landlord was entitled to the full amount. He said:

> "The defendant, I am satisfied, has destroyed these yards and he is bound under the covenants of the lease to replace them. I am satisfied that the only practicable way of replacing them now is by the erection of dressed timber yards of the nature and description suggested by the applicant. In my view, therefore, the applicant's contention is correct, and he is entitled to the cost of replacing these yards and is not liable to any deduction in respect of the increase in value of the yards so erected as against those which existed when the lease commenced.[67]"

The same principle applies where damages for breach of a landlord's obligation to repair are assessed by reference to the cost of making good damage to the demised premises caused by the landlord's breach: in such a case, no deduction for betterment is to be made.[68]

**29–18**     The above is subject to a possible exception where the tenant is obliged under the covenant completely to rebuild the demised premises following total destruction by fire or other catastrophe.[69] In *Yates v Dunster*[70] an old and dilapidated warehouse and small dwelling-house were let for 15 months on terms, the tenant agreeing to "maintain the premises in as good a state as they will be when the agreed repairs by me are done". Shortly after the tenancy began, the premises were destroyed by fire. The cost of rebuilding the premises was £1,635, but when rebuilt they would have been more valuable by £600 than if they had been repaired before the fire. It appears to have been accepted that the tenant's failure to rebuild after the fire constituted a breach of his repairing covenant. It was held that the landlord was only entitled by way of damages to £1,635 less £600. No reasons for the decision are given in the report, although it appears from a reported intervention by Parke B. in argument that the court regarded as relevant the fact that the tenant was only bound to "put the premises in the same state as they would have been, if he had repaired them at the time he took them". A similar result was reached in the Australian case of *Strang v Gray*,[71] in which the demised premises were completely destroyed by fire, and damages for breach of the covenant to repair and yield up in repair were assessed by reference to the cost of rebuilding less an allowance for the increase in value of the premises when rebuilt.

---

[66] [1961] W.A.R. 120. See also *Clowes v Bentley Pty Ltd* [1970] W.A.R. 24 (Australia), in which it was held that no deduction for betterment should be made in assessing damages for breach of a tenant's covenant to repair a hotel.
[67] The judge distinguished his own earlier decision in *Strang v Gray* (1952) 55 W.A.L.R. 9 (see para.29–15, above) on the ground that it was a case of total destruction, to which different considerations applied. p.XXX.
[68] *Calabar Properties Ltd v Stitcher* [1984] 1 W.L.R. 287, per Stephenson L.J.
[69] See Ch.18, above.
[70] (1855) 11 Ex. 15.
[71] (1952) 55 W.A.L.R. 9.

However, it is by no means clear to what extent these cases correctly represent the law. First, on the face of it, they are inconsistent with the general principle set out in *Harbutt's "Plasticene" Ltd v Wayne Tank & Pump Co Ltd*.[72] Second, it is difficult to see any logical distinction between cases where the premises have been completely destroyed, and cases where the defect requiring repair falls short of complete destruction, in relation to which no deduction for betterment is allowed.[73]

## Burden of proof

As a general principle, the burden of proving the common law claim is on the landlord who is making it. Prima facie, therefore, he must show not only that the tenant was in breach of covenant on the term date, but also the nature and reasonable cost of any necessary remedial work. In an appropriate case, however, the court may be prepared to draw appropriate inferences. Thus, in *Sunlife Europe Properties Ltd v Tiger Aspect Holdings Ltd*[74] Edwards-Stuart J. held that: "where the tenant is in breach of his covenant, in the absence of evidence to the contrary the court is entitled to infer that remedial work is necessary to remedy the breach...".

**29–19**

## LOSS OF RENT AND OTHER LOSSES[75]

### Introductory

The damages recoverable at common law are not limited to the reasonable cost of the works. In principle, other losses suffered by reason of the tenant's failure to yield up the premises in repair at the expiry of the lease are also recoverable. The various heads are considered below.

**29–20**

### Loss of rent

Rent which the landlord has lost by reason of being unable to relet the premises during the period reasonably necessary for the carrying out of the repairs is a recoverable head of loss.[76] Thus, in *Joyner v Weekes*[77] Wright J. at first instance described the cost of repair measure as including "some allowance for loss of rent or occupation during the time of reparation".

**29–21**

However, loss of rent will only be awarded where it genuinely represents the landlord's loss, i.e. where he is unable to relet the premises because of the need to

---

[72] [1970] 1 Q.B. 447. See above.
[73] See paras 29–16 to 29–17, above.
[74] [2013] EWHC 463 (TCC) at [46]. See also *Latimer v Carney* [2007] 1 P. & C.R. 13 (CA).
[75] See further on loss of rent and other losses paras 30–26 to 30–28, below.
[76] *Woods v Pope* (1835) 6 C. & P. 782; *Birch v Clifford* (1891) 8 T.L.R. 103; *Drummond v S. & U. Stores Ltd* [1981] 1 E.G.L.R. 42; *Culworth Estates Ltd v Society of Licensed Victuallers* (1991) 62 P. & C.R. 211.
[77] [1891] 2 Q.B. 31.

carry out repairs. There must be a causal connection between the failure to repair and the loss which is claimed.[78] As Mr Recorder Anthony Butcher QC, sitting as a Deputy Official Referee, put it in the unreported case of *Scottish Mutual Assurance Society Ltd v British Telecommunications Plc*[79]:

> "If the loss of rent during the period needed to carry out repairs is to figure as a head of damages in a claim for damages for breach of the obligation to carry out such repairs during the currency of the term of the lease then it is, I consider, an essential prerequisite that it should be demonstrated on the balance of probabilities that the carrying out of those repairs after the end of the term has prevented or will prevent the letting of the premises for that period."

It follows that where the landlord would not have been able to relet the premises any earlier than he has done even if they had been yielded up in repair, loss of rent will not ordinarily be recoverable. Thus, the landlord's claim for loss of rent, insurance rent and service charge failed in *Marchday Group v British Telecommunications*,[80] because there was, on the facts, no reason to suppose that the premises would have been relet any earlier than they had been even if they had been delivered up in full repair. Likewise, in the Australian case of *Alamdo Holdings Property Ltd v Australian Window Furnishings (NSW) Property Ltd*[81] it was held that the landlord had failed to prove that if the tenant had not been in breach of covenant, it would have received rent earlier than it did. The landlord did not discharge that onus merely by showing that some of the works required by an incoming tenant were works that the tenant should have carried out; it was necessary to show that, if those works had been carried out by the end of the lease, the payment of rent would have commenced earlier.

The period over which loss of rent is awarded will depend on how long it would reasonably have taken the landlord to carry out the work. In an appropriate case, this will include the time necessary for preparing plans, specifications and working drawings; putting the work out to tender; analysing tenders; selecting a contractor; and commencing and completing the work.[82] It may be relevant to consider what steps the landlord could reasonably have taken prior to the expiry of the lease.[83] The considerations to be borne in mind in deciding for the purposes of a s.146 notice what is a reasonable time within which to comply with a schedule of dilapidations may be applied by analogy.[84]

---

[78] *PgfII SA v Royal & Sun Alliance Insurance Plc* [2011] 1 P. & C. R. 11 at [70].
[79] Judgment given on March 18, 1994.
[80] [2003] EWHC 2627 (TCC).
[81] [2006] NSWCA 224.
[82] See *Drummond v S. & U. Stores Ltd*, above, in which the evidence was that the period from the time when the tenant was first under notice to carry out works to the time the works could have been completed was between 13 and 16 weeks, and Glidewell J. awarded a quarter's rent.
[83] See *Drummond v S. & U. Stores Ltd*, above.
[84] See paras 27–28 to 27–29, above.

## Service charges, insurance rent and void rates

In principle, service charges and insurance rent which the landlord would **29–22** otherwise have been able to recover from an incoming tenant during the period reasonably necessary for the carrying out of the works, and void rates which he would not have had to pay if he had been able to relet the premises during that period, are also recoverable heads of loss. The applicable principles are similar to those in relation to loss of rent.[85] In relation to service charges, however, care must be taken to identify the landlord's real loss. He cannot recover service charges in relation to services which he has not in fact provided because the premises are empty. He can only recover the proportion applicable to the demised premises of the cost of services which he has actually provided, which he would have been able to recover had he been able to relet the premises during the works period.

## Alternative accommodation

The landlord may intend to occupy the demised premises at the expiry of the **29–23** lease but be unable to do so by reason of the need to carry out the remedial works. It is thought that there is no reason in principle why he should not be entitled to recover any losses thereby incurred, subject obviously to the application of the ordinary principles relating to causation, mitigation and remoteness.[86] This accords with *Joyner v Weekes*,[87] in which Wright J. at first instance referred to the cost of repair measure as including some allowance for "loss of... occupation during the time of reparation". Thus, in *Twinmar Holdings v Klarius UK*,[88] the damages awarded to the landlord for terminal dilapidations included the cost incurred by the landlord in relation to alternative accommodation over the works period, less the amount it would have had to pay in any event.

## DEFENCES

The ordinary principles relating to causation, mitigation and remoteness apply to **29–24** claims for damages for breach of the covenant to repair at the end of the term as they do to any other claim for breach of contract.[89]

In *Sunlife Europe Properties v Tiger Aspect Holdings*[90] the landlord carried out less expensive works than the works by reference to which damages would otherwise have been assessed. Edwards Stuart J. held that the damages receoverable were limited to the cost of the works actually carried out: the tenant was "entitled to take the benefit of the mitigation".

---

[85] See para.29–21, above.
[86] See para.29–24, below.
[87] [1891] 2 Q.B. 31.
[88] [2013] EWHC 944 (TCC) at [82-89].
[89] A detailed discussion of these is outside the scope of this work, and reference should be made to the standard textbooks on the law of contract (for example *Chitty on Contracts* (30th edn), Vol.I, Ch.26).
[90] [2013] EWHC 463 (TCC) at [158].

In the New Zealand case of *BP Oil New Zealand v Ports of Auckland*,[91] the demised land had become contaminated by spills and leaks from stored petroleum products. The leases contained obligations on the part of the tenant to keep all buildings and structures on the demised land in good order, condition and repair. The landlord did not suggest that the covenants created an obligation to remediate the land itself. It argued instead that the tenant was liable for consequential damage caused as a result of breaches of covenant, including contamination resulting from the tenant's failure to repair and maintain storage tanks and ancillary equipment. That argument succeeded before Rodney Hansen J., who held that the tenant was liable for contamination which was a reasonably foreseeable consequence of any breaches of the covenants to repair. It is thought that the position would be the same under English law.

The fact that the landlord has actually carried out more extensive work than was caused by the breach does not of itself prevent him from recovering the cost of such work as would have been necessary to remedy the breach.[92]

---

[91] [2004] 2 N.Z.L.R. 208.
[92] *Sunlife Europe Properties v Tiger Aspect Holdings*, above, at [46].

CHAPTER 30

## DAMAGES AT THE END OF THE TERM (2): S.18(1) OF THE LANDLORD AND TENANT ACT 1927

### INTRODUCTORY

### Section 18(1)

The common law measure of damages for disrepair at the end of the term is considered in Ch.29, above. The amount recoverable is capped by s.18(1) of the Landlord and Tenant Act 1927, which provides as follows:

> "(1) Damages for breach of a covenant or agreement to keep or put premises in repair during the currency of a lease, or to leave or put premises in repair at the termination of a lease, whether such covenant or agreement is express or implied, and whether general or specific, shall in no case exceed the amount (if any) by which the value of the reversion (whether immediate or not) is diminished owing to the breach of such covenant or agreement as aforesaid; and in particular no damage shall be recovered for a breach of any such covenant or agreement to leave or put premises in repair at the termination of a lease, if it is shown that the premises, in whatever state of repair they might be, would at or shortly after the termination of the tenancy have been or be pulled down, or such structural alterations made therein as would render valueless the repairs covered by the covenant or agreement."

Section 18(1) is therefore divided into two limbs.[1] The first is to the effect that damages cannot exceed the amount by which the value of the landlord's reversion is diminished by reason of the breach; the second is that no damages are recoverable where the premises are to be pulled down or structural alterations are to be carried out at or shortly after the end of the term. These are considered in turn below.

### THE FIRST LIMB OF S.18(1)

### The first limb of s.18(1)

The following discussion is concerned with the first limb of s.18(1) of the Landlord and Tenant Act 1927, i.e. that part of it which provides as follows:

> "Damages for breach of a covenant or agreement to keep or put premises in repair during the currency of a lease, or to leave or put premises in repair at the termination of a lease, whether such covenant or agreement is express or implied, and whether general or specific, shall in no

30–01

30–02

---

[1] See *Culworth Estates Ltd v Society of Licensed Victuallers* (1991) 62 P. & C.R. 211, per Dillon L.J.

case exceed the amount (if any) by which the value of the reversion (whether immediate or not) is diminished owing to the breach of such covenant or agreement as aforesaid."

## Application of the first limb

**30–03**   Section 18(1) applies to a covenant or agreement to keep or put premises in repair during the term, or to leave or put premises in repair at the end of the term.[2] It therefore applies to covenants to put into repair; to keep in repair; and to yield up in repair. It is thought that it also applies to covenants of a similar nature, such as covenants to maintain, and covenants to keep in good condition, provided that their effect is in substance the same as a covenant to repair. However, the fact that a particular obligation is contained in "the repairing covenant" does not mean that every obligation contained in the covenant will fall within the section; it will be necessary to give each obligation in the covenant its natural and ordinary meaning.[3] Thus, a covenant to cleanse a lavatory is outside s.18(1),[4] but the subsection applies to cleaning required to be done by the covenant to repair.[5]

It has been held by the Court of Appeal that s.18(1) applies to a claim for damages by reason of the tenant's failure to decorate where such failure constitutes a breach of the covenant to repair, even though that same failure also constitutes a breach of a covenant in the lease to redecorate at periodic intervals.[6] The effect in practice is thought to be that most breaches of the covenant to decorate will be caught by the subsection. In principle, however, a breach of a covenant to decorate, which does not overlap to any material extent with a breach of the covenant to repair, remains outside the subsection, although it seems unlikely that this sort of case will occur very often in practice.

The subsection does not apply to a covenant to expend a specified sum per annum on repairs or in default or pay to the landlord the difference between that sum and what was spent.[7] Nor does it apply where the specified sum is payable pursuant to an option on the part of the landlord to require the tenant to pay the sum in lieu of painting.[8] It is probable that a covenant to reinstate premises after fire falls within s.18(1).[9] However, a covenant to expend insurance money on reinstating is not within the subsection.[10]

In *Irontrain Investments v Ansari*[11] it was held by the county court judge at first instance that s.18(1) has no application to a claim for damages for breach of a repairing obligation made by a landlord in his capacity as lessee, and not in his

---

[2] Landlord and Tenant Act 1927 s.18(1).
[3] *Starrokate Ltd v Burry* [1983] 1 E.G.L.R. 56, per Dunn L.J. (a case on the Leasehold Property (Repairs) Act 1938). See para.4–20 et seq., above.
[4] *Starrokate Ltd v Burry*, above.
[5] See *Greg v Planque* [1936] 1 K.B. 669 (cleaning a flue held to amount to "executing repairs" within the meaning of a provision in the lease which entitled the landlord to enter the demised premises to execute repairs and alterations).
[6] *Latimer v Carney* [2006] 3 E.G.L.R. 13.
[7] *Moss Empires Ltd v Olympia (Liverpool) Ltd* [1939] A.C. 544. See para.30–64, below.
[8] *Plummer v Ramsey* (1934) 78 S.J. 175.
[9] *Re King* [1962] 1 W.L.R. 632 (reversed on other grounds [1963] Ch. 459); *Farimani v Gates* [1984] 2 E.G.L.R. 66, per Griffiths L.J. See para.18–27 et seq., above.
[10] *Farimani v Gates*, above.
[11] [2005] EWCA Civ 1681.

capacity as landlord. The Court of Appeal did not find it necessary to consider the point on appeal, because they found that the defendant tenant was in any event liable in negligence.

## The relationship between the first limb and the common law measure of damages

The effect of the first limb is to impose a statutory ceiling on the amount of damages recoverable.[12] It follows that where the amount recoverable at common law would exceed the diminution in the value of the reversion, the damages are limited to the latter. An illustration of this is given by *Jaquin v Holland*.[13] In that case the landlord spent £19 10s. at the end of the tenancy in putting the premises into a lettable condition, and then relet them at the same rent for which they had been let under the earlier tenancy. The work which was necessary to comply with the tenant's repairing obligation would have cost £91 13s. 6d. according to the tenant's surveyor, and £102 16s. according to the surveyor for the landlord. The diminution in the value of the reversion caused by the breaches of covenant was found by the court to be £50. The tenant contended that the correct amount of damages was £19 10s. The Court of Appeal approached the matter by asking first what was the cost of the work needed to comply with the tenant's covenant (i.e. applying the common law measure). This was not £19 10s., but either £91 13s. 6d. or £102 16s. The court then held that the effect of s.18(1) was that this figure was to be reduced to the amount of the diminution in the value of reversion. The landlord was therefore entitled to £50 by way of damages.

A further illustration is *Shane v Runwell*.[14] The question of whether there was any damage to the reversion was tried in advance of the extent and cost of the works. The sum claimed by the landlords in respect of the cost of the works said to be necessary was over £5,000. Roskill J. held that the maximum damage to the reversion was £3,500, so that "there will, if the claim when ultimately quantified before the Official Referee exceeds £3,500, be a ceiling of that amount upon the defendants' liability".

**30–04**

## The reversion

"The reversion", as that expression is used in the first limb of s.18(1) of the 1927 Act, means the landlord's interest, subject to the lease where the lease still exists, and otherwise in possession.[15] Thus, in *Hanson v Newman*[16] Romer L.J. said:

**30–05**

> "The reversion in [s18(1)], if it be a freehold reversion, means the freehold subject to the lease, and valuing the reversion for the purposes of the section you must value the freehold subject to so much, if any, of the term of the lease as remains in existence."

---

[12] See para.29–08, above.
[13] [1960] 1 W.L.R. 258.
[14] [1967] E.G.D. 88.
[15] *Hanson v Newman* [1934] Ch. 298.
[16] Above.

In *Smiley v Townshend*[17] Denning L.J. said:

> "What has to be considered is the diminution in value of the reversion at the end of the lease; and I take the word 'reversion' to mean the landlord's then interest in the premises ... The question is, therefore, how much was the market value of the landlord's interest diminished at the end of the lease by reason of the disrepair ...?"

Where the landlord has only a leasehold interest, the reversion means that interest.[18] The landlord's interest must be valued subject to any existing sub-tenancies which are binding on the landlord,[19] and also to the interest of any requisitioning authority,[20] but not to any reversionary lease granted by the landlord before the end of the tenancy to take effect immediately thereafter.[21] In the last mentioned case, the reversion must be valued on the assumption that the reversionary lease has not been granted, although the terms of that lease would doubtless be relevant evidence of the value of the reversion on the term date.

Subject to the above, what must be valued is the reversion as it exists at the end of the lease. In *Van Dal Footwear v Ryman*,[22] a building was let to Rymans, which remained in occupation following the expiry of the term under a series of tenancies at will. It was common ground that the repairing obligations under the lease were carried forward into the tenancies at will. One of the purposes of the tenancies at will was to enable Rymans to agree a new lease if they could. In December 2005 and July 2006 they made two offers to the landlord to take a new lease, neither of which was accepted. They vacated on July 28, 2007 leaving the building in disrepair. The judge assessed the cost of the repair works at £135,606. He assessed the diminution in the value of the reversion by reference to a notional sale of the landlord's interest in the building as at July 28, 2007 with and without the repair works done. However, the experts were agreed that in order for the property to have been sold in its actual condition on July 28, 2007, it would have been necessary to have marketed it for six months beforehand. The judge found that during the hypothetical marketing period Ryman would have repeated its offers to take a new lease to a prospective purchaser who would have accepted them, so that the purchase of the reversion and the grant of the new lease would have occurred at the same time. On that basis, the purchaser would have increased its offer for the building in disrepair by 7.4%, which gave rise to a diminution of £48,538.

The Court of Appeal allowed the landlord's appeal. What must be valued is the reversion at the moment when it reverts to the landlord. What the judge had been required to do was to value the bundle of rights that the landlord actually had on the valuation date. On that date the landlord did not have the benefit of an

---

[17] [1950] 2 K.B. 311.

[18] This is considered in para.30–44 et seq., below.

[19] *Jeffs v West London Property Corp Ltd* [1954] J.P.L. 114 (sub-tenants protected by the Rent Act); *Family Management Ltd v Gray* [1980] 1 E.G.L.R. 46; *Crown Estate Commissioners v Town Investments Ltd* [1992] 1 E.G.L.R. 61 (sub-tenancies within Part II of the Landlord and Tenant Act 1954). See para.30–31 et seq., below.

[20] *Smiley v Townshend* [1950] 2 K.B. 311.

[21] *Terroni v Corsini* [1931] 1 Ch. 515; *Hanson v Newman* [1934] Ch. 298, per Lawrence L.J. at 305; *Jaquin v Holland* [1960] 1 W.L.R. 258, per Devlin L.J. at 267; *Smiley v Townshend* above, per Denning L.J.; *Haviland v Long* [1952] 2 Q.B. 80. See para.30–36, below.

[22] [2010] 1 W.L.R. 2015.

agreement for lease with Rymans or even an offer capable of acceptance. The proposition that property must be assumed to have been exposed to the market does not entail reconstructing that hypothetical marketing period: it is no more than an assumption required to enable the valuation to take place. The facts which the judge had taken into account with reference to an entirely notional preceding marketing period were of no relevance to the valuation required by s.18(1) of the 1927 Act. By valuing the reversion with the benefit of an agreement for lease with Rymans, the judge had valued the wrong thing, and the 7.4% uplift on value could not stand. As Lewison J. explained in his judgment:

> "The judge's answer to the hypothetical question that he posed led him to value the reversion on the basis that there was a contract in place for [the tenant] for a new lease. This had the result that the judge did not value the landlord's reversion. He valued the freehold with the benefit of an agreement for lease with [the tenant]. That was not a right that the landlord had, and was not therefore part of the reversion."

Where the lease has been forfeited, the reversion means the landlord's interest without any part of the lease remaining.[23] The tenant is not entitled to a set-off in respect of the value to the landlord of an accelerated reversion.[24]

The position where the landlord is himself a tenant is considered at para.30–44 et seq., below.

## The value of the reversion

A long line of cases, beginning with *Hanson v Newman*,[25] have proceeded on the basis that for the purposes of the first limb of s.18(1), the value of the reversion means its value if sold in the market on the term date.[26] Thus, for example, in *Smiley v Townshend*,[27] Denning L.J. (with whom Bucknill L.J. agreed) identified the question as being "how much was the market value of the landlord's interest diminished at the end of the lease by reason of the disrepair for which the [tenant] was responsible?", and in *Latimer v Carney*,[28] Arden L.J. said that what the court has to do is "to find the difference between the value of the premises in disrepair on the open market and the value that the premises would have had had there been no breach of the covenant to repair". The exercise required by the first limb

**30–06**

---

[23] *Hanson v Newman* [1934] Ch. 298.
[24] Ibid.
[25] [1934] Ch. 298.
[26] See for example *Salisbury v Gilmore* [1942] 2 K.B. 38 per MacKinnon L.J. at 48; *Portman v Latta* [1942] WN 97; *Landeau v Marchbank* [1949] 2 All E.R. 172; *Jones v Herxheimer* [1950] 2 K.B. 106 at 117–119; *Smiley v Townshend* [1950] 2 K.B. 311; *Shane v Runcorn* [1967] EGD 88; *Culworth Estates v Society of Licensed Victuallers* (1991) 62 P. & C. R. 211; *Shortlands Investments v Cargill* [1995] 1 E.G.L.R. 51; *Craven (Builders) v Secretary of State for Health* [2001] 1 E.G.L.R. 128; *Ultraworth v General Accident Fire & Life Assurance Co.* [2000] 2 E.G.L.R. 115; *Latimer v Carney* [2006] 3 E.G.L.R. 13; *Ravengate Estates v Horizon Housing Group* [2007] EWCA Civ 1368 at [21]; *Hammersmatch Properties (Welwyn) Ltd v Saint-Gobain Ceramics & Plastics* [2013] EWHC 1161 (TCC).
[27] [1950] 2 K.B. 311 at 320.
[28] [2006] 3 E.G.L.R. 13 at [25].

is therefore an objective one, to be undertaken by reference to the value of the premises in the market, and not a subjective one, which looks at value to the particular landlord.

However, a limitation on damages by reference to market value will not always produce what might be thought to be a fair result. Suppose, for example, that the owner of a large dwelling-house in which he has lived all his life and to which he wishes to retire, lets it for three years to a tenant on full repairing terms whilst he is posted abroad; and that when he returns at the end of the three years, he finds substantial breaches of covenant which render the house incapable of occupation and which he will need to put right before he can move back in. He may be acting entirely reasonably in wishing to do so. Under the first limb of s.18(1), however, the tenant can escape liability altogether by proving that the most likely buyer of the house, whether in or out of repair, would demolish it and construct a block of flats, so that the defects have caused no diminution in the market value of the house. That might be thought to be rather unfair. It might be said that the purpose of s.18(1) was to militate against the perceived injustice of the common law rule as to damages,[29] the effect of which was that in many cases the landlord was put into a better position than he would have been in if the tenant had complied with his covenant, and that parliament cannot have intended to exclude a claim for the cost of the remedial works where the landlord intends to carry them out and such intention is reasonable in all the circumstances.

Nonetheless, the objective approach is clearly established by the cases, and it has the obvious advantage that the tenant's liability will not vary according to the particular individual circumstances of whoever happens to be his landlord at the end of the term.[30] Perhaps one practical solution to this sort of problem would be to anticipate it by replacing the conventional covenant to yield up in repair with a covenant to pay the costs incurred by the landlord in carrying out repairs at the end of the term, in which event it is thought that s.18(1) would not apply.[31]

### The date of assessment

30–07 The diminution in the value of the reversion is to be assessed as at the date of termination of the lease, when the covenant to yield up in repair takes effect.[32] There is then a "moment of time when the freehold reversion, unencumbered, is vested in the landlord, and the question is: what is the value of the freehold reversion at that time?"[33] This has the important consequence that events occurring after the end of the lease cannot themselves reduce or extinguish the damages, although they may throw light on the value of the reversion on the relevant date. This is considered further in para.30–37 et seq., below.

---

[29] See para.29–06 to 29–08, above.
[30] For a further discussion of this point, see articles in the Estates Gazette on March 21 (Dowding/Cohen) and October 31, 2009 (Taggart/Levy), and "Section 18 Revisited" (a lecture given by Jonathan Gaunt QC and Vivien King on July 8, 2013 as part of the 38th series of Blundell lectures).
[31] See para.30–65, below.
[32] *Hanson v Newman*, above, *Smiley v Townshend*, above; *Associated Deliveries Ltd v Harrison* (1984) 50 P. & C.R. 91.
[33] *Jaquin v Holland* [1960] 1 W.L.R. 258 per Ormerod L.J. at 263.

## Establishing the amount of the diminution

The amount by which the value of the reversion has been diminished by reason of the disrepair is generally to be found by carrying out two valuations of the landlord's interest as at the relevant date, the first on the assumption that the premises were then in the state they would have been in if the tenant had performed his covenant,[34] and the second on the basis that the premises were then in their actual state and condition. The difference between the two figures, if any, represents the damage to the reversion caused by the disrepair.[35] In *Hanson v Newman*[36] Luxmoore J. at first instance explained the correct approach as follows:

**30–08**

> "What the section provides for is that the damages for breach of covenant on the termination of a lease are not to exceed the amount by which the value of the reversion, whether immediate or not, in the premises is diminished owing to the breach of such covenant or agreement; that is, you take the value of the reversion as it is with the breach—the value of the property which has reverted as it is subject to the breach—and you take it as it would be if there were no breach, and you provide that the amount of damage shall not exceed the amount by which the value of the property repaired exceeds the value of the property unrepaired."

Luxmoore J.'s judgment was approved in the Court of Appeal by Lawrence and Romer L.JJ., the former adopting the above passage and saying that he "could not express it better". In *Ravengate Estates Ltd v Horizon Housing Group Ltd*[37] the correct approach was restated by Mann J. as follows:

> "It is important to bear in mind that a section 18(1) exercise involves determining a difference in value. That in turn involves two imaginary sales—one sale of the demised property in proper repair, and one of the property not in repair. The difference between those two values is the diminution in the value of the reversion. One would often expect a section 18(1) exercise to set out each figure, with justifications for each, so that the merits of each figure can be assessed by the judge and the relevant mathematical exercise carried out. In order to ascertain the two sale prices it will usually be necessary to identify the nature of the market and therefore the nature of the purchaser—see the approach of Neuberger J. in *Craven (Builders) Ltd v. Secretary of State for Health* [2000] 1 E.G.L.R. 128."

Precisely how these comparative valuations are to be carried out is, of course, a matter for an expert valuer. It will generally be relevant to consider the following matters, among others:

**30–09**

(1) the sort of person who would be likely to purchase the landlord's interest;

(2) what plans the likely purchaser would have for the property; whether, for example, he would relet the premises, and if so, whether he would (i) do some or all of the works before doing so, or (ii) grant a rent-free period to the incoming tenant in return for the works being done under the new lease,

---

[34] This necessarily involves first identifying what works the tenant should have done. The effect is that, save in exceptional circumstances, the exercise of establishing the breaches and the remedial work must be gone through before the s.18 valuations can be carried out.

[35] *Hanson v Newman* [1934] Ch. 298; *Smiley v Townshend* [1950] 2 K.B. 311; *Jones v Herxheimer* [1950] 2 K.B. 106; Re King [1962] 1 W.L.R. 632 (reversed on appeal on different grounds: [1963] Ch. 459); *Culworth Estates Ltd v Society of Licensed Victuallers* (1991) 62 P. & C.R. 211.

[36] [1934] Ch. 298.

[37] [2007] EWCA Civ 1368.

or (iii) relet at a lower rent without either doing the works or getting them done by the incoming tenant; or whether he would refurbish or redevelop the premises, and if so, to what extent the work which the tenant should have done would still be necessary[38];

(3)    where the purchaser will himself carry out the work, what additional expenses he is likely to incur in doing so, such as loss of rent and service charge, interest on money borrowed, professional fees and VAT.

Having regard to the above, and any other relevant matters, the valuer must then decide what price could have been obtained in the market for the landlord's reversion as at the relevant date on the two hypotheses set out above.

Reference should be made to Ch.31, below, which contains a discussion of the valuer's approach together with a number of worked examples.

## The assumed in-repair state

**30–10**    For the purposes of ascertaining the value of the premises in the condition they would have been in if the tenant had performed his covenant, it is necessary to identify the works which must be assumed to have been carried out. The nature of these, and the quality of the specification for the premises which results from them, may be highly relevant to the general attractiveness of the premises to the market, and the extent of any likely "supersession".[39] It is thought that the correct approach is that the repair works which must be assumed to have been carried out are the same as those by reference to which damages at common law are to be assessed, i.e. they equate to the works the cost of which the landlord would be entitled to recover at common law absent s.18(1). These are considered in Ch.29, above.

A different approach was argued for in *Sunlife Europe Properties v Tiger Aspect Holdings*,[40] in which the tenant contended that the assumed in-repair state for the purposes of the first limb of s.18(1) was the condition the premises would have been in if the tenant had carried out repairs during the term as and when they became necessary. In that case, (so it was argued) the premises would have been left at the end of the term with adequately maintained 1970s plant, although that would have included some replacements – on a like-for-like or nearest equivalent basis – because some of the original base-built items would have had to have been replaced during the term. In the event, however, the judge did not find it necessary to decide the point.

---

[38] For an example of a case where various different types of prospective purchaser were considered, see *Ultraworth Ltd v General Accident Fire & Life Assurance Co Ltd* [2000] 2 E.G.L.R. 115.
[39] See para.30–30, below.
[40] [2013] EWHC 463 (TCC) at [33–35].

## Notional sale as a whole or in parts

In carrying out the valuations required by the subsection, the valuer must assume that the landlord's interest in the entirety of the premises is being notionally sold on the valuation date (i.e. the date of termination of the lease[41]). One question which sometimes arises in practice is whether, in so doing, the valuer must assume a single hypothetical sale of the premises as a whole, or whether, if the circumstances are such that in reality a seller of the premises would be advised to dispose of them in parts in order to obtain the best overall price, it is permissible to assume separate notional sales of parts and then to aggregate the resulting values in order to arrive at the overall value of the premises for the purposes of s.18(1). It is thought that, in principle, the latter is the correct view. If the premises are such that their true value can only be realised by selling them in separate parts, it is difficult to see that anything in s.18(1) precludes the valuer from reflecting that factor in his valuations. However, this is subject to the important proviso that the aggregate subject matter of such sales must include all the premises.[42]

**30–11**

## Where the premises are part of a larger unit

In some cases, the premises to be valued may be part of a larger holding, all of which is owned by the landlord, such that in reality they would only be marketed and sold as part of that larger holding. For example, the freehold interest in a single floor of a multi-storey office building would not in practice be sold separately from the remainder.[43] One question in such cases is the extent to which s.18(1) requires or entitles the valuer to value the premises as part of the larger holding. In some cases, the question may not arise, because it will be obvious that the value of the reversion in the premises has been diminished without the need for valuation evidence. Thus, in *Jones v Herxheimer*[44] there was "no question as a practical matter of a separate sale of the five rooms let to [the tenant] ... separately from the rest of the house", so that the process of valuing the reversion in its repaired and unrepaired state was "a purely hypothetical calculation wholly removed from the practical realities of the matter."[45] In other cases, (for example, where the correct valuation method is by reference to the estimated income the premises will generate in and out of repair) there may be no need to look beyond the premises themselves. In some cases, however, the facts may justify an argument that the true market value of the premises in and out of repair can only properly be arrived at if they are valued as part of a larger unit. A possible objection to this is that the value of the premises may be affected by the state of repair of the remainder of the holding, which is nothing to do with the tenant's

**30–12**

---

[41] See para.30–07, above.

[42] It is thought that this approach is consistent with the decisions of the House of Lords in *Duke of Buccleuch v IRC* [1967] 1 A.C. 506 and *IRC v Gray* [1994] S.T.C. 360, both of which concerned the correct valuation approach for estate duty purposes.

[43] In theory, it might be sold by way of a long lease at a premium, but the price would then depend on the length of the lease and its terms, particularly with regard to repair.

[44] [1950] 2 K.B. 106. See further para.30–15, below.

[45] Above, per Jenkins L.J. at 118.

breaches of covenant. However, in most cases this will not make any real difference in practice, because the relevant condition will be common to both the in-repair and the out-of-repair valuations, so that any effect on value attributable to the inclusion in the notional sale of premises other than the demised premises will affect both valuations equally. As Blackburne J. said in *Mason v TotalFinaElf UK Ltd*[46]:

> "[T]he purpose of the exercise is to isolate the effect on value of the tenant's failure to do the relevant works, from which it follows that the only variable between the two valuations is the works. All other factors are constants."

However, it is conceivable that the effect on value of the condition of the remainder of the holding will not necessarily be the same in both the in-repair and the out-of-repair valuations. Moreover, it will still be necessary to identify that part of the overall price which is attributable to the premises alone, which may in turn require the valuer to look at the values of each part in isolation.

It is thought that each case will depend on its own facts. It may perhaps be going too far to say that the diminution in value must in every case be assessed on the basis that the premises are being sold on their own, whatever artificial assumptions that may involve. However, it is thought that where the premises are assumed to be sold as part of a large unit, it will usually be correct to assume that the existence of the remainder of the holding is as neutral as possible in valuation terms.

## Where there would be no buyer for the premises in reality

30–13    The fact that no buyer for the premises could have been found on the relevant date does not mean that the s.18(1) exercise need not be gone through,[47] or that the damage to the reversion is necessarily nil. This is because "a site does not cease to have a value on [a particular date] merely because it is not instantly realisable on that date."[48] In *Craven (Builders) Ltd v Secretary of State for Health*[49] Neuberger J., having found that there was no buyer for a large former textile mill on the relevant date, held that the court was not thereby relieved of the task of determining what a willing buyer would pay and that the least unlikely buyer would have paid £40,000 less for the premises by reason of the disrepair.

## Where the reversion has a negative value

30–14    Even where the premises are in good repair, the reversion may have a negative value because the nature of the premises and market conditions are such that the owner would have to pay someone to take them. In such a case, the effect of the disrepair may be to increase that negative value. If so, the amount of such

---

[46] [2003] 3 E.G.L.R. 91.
[47] *Shane v Runwell* [1967] E.G.D. 88.
[48] *Shane v Runwell*, above, per Roskill J. at 99.
[49] [2000] 1 E.G.L.R. 128. See further para.30–29 et seq., below.

increase is the diminution for the purposes of s.18(1).[50] In *Shortlands Investments Ltd v Cargill Plc*,[51] the Official Referee said in the course of his judgment:

"At the heart of this case, as it seems to me, is a point of principle which arises out of the implicit assumption of [the tenant's expert and the tenant] that it is impossible to accept that one negative value can be worse or better than another negative value. ... [I]t seems to have been assumed by [the tenant's expert] that once the value of a property gets down to £nil there cannot be any diminution in value. That may be true in many or perhaps most cases of chattels. It is quite a different situation where an owner of a leasehold property has an onerous interest which he wishes to transfer. Such an interest is transferable on the market if not 'saleable'. If one assumes a willing transferor and a willing transferee, there will be a point in negotiations for a payment from the transferor where the parties are willing to do a deal."

It was held on the facts of that case that the value of the landlord's reversion (which was a leasehold interest) assuming the tenant to have complied with its covenants was minus £92,622 and the value of the reversion assuming the premises to be in their actual state and condition was minus £387,943.37, leaving a diminution of £295,321.37.

## Where the landlord has done the remedial works

A number of authorities contain statements to the effect that where the landlord has done the works for which he claims, the cost of the works is prima facie evidence or a very real guide to the damage to the reversion.[52] This has been applied not only where the landlord himself does the work, but also where it is done by an incoming tenant at the landlord's expense (either by direct payment or in the form of a rent reduction).[53]

**30–15**

The leading case is *Jones v Herxheimer*,[54] where the demised premises consisted of five rooms on two floors of a house. The tenant covenanted to deliver up the interior of the rooms in good and tenantable repair. The rooms were in a bad state of decorative repair when the tenant vacated them. The landlord had them redecorated throughout and then relet them. He claimed the cost of the work as damages. At the trial he called on evidence that the cost of the work represented the damage to the reversion. The tenant called a surveyor who said that the repairs in question, which were purely decorative, would not affect the value of the premises. The county court judge found in favour of the landlord, and the tenant appealed. The Court of Appeal dismissed the appeal, holding that there was evidence on which the county court judge could properly have come to the conclusion that the reversion was damaged to the extent of the cost of the works. Jenkins L.J., giving the judgment of the court, referred to a dictum of

---

[50] *Shortlands Investments Ltd v Cargill Plc* [1995] 1 E.G.L.R. 51. See further the cases on the measure of damages between head tenant and sub-tenant, considered in para.30–44 et seq., below.
[51] [1995] 1 E.G.L.R. 51.
[52] *Smiley v Townshend* [1950] 2 K.B. 311; *Drummond v S. & U. Stores Ltd* [1981] 1 E.G.L.R. 42; *Culworth Estates Ltd v Society of Licensed Victuallers* (1991) 62 P. & C.R. 211.
[53] *Drummond v S. & U. Stores Ltd*, above. For the relevance of arrangements between the landlord and an incoming tenant, see para.30–36, below.
[54] [1950] 2 K.B. 106.

Lynskey J. in *Landeau v Marchbank*[55] that "… the fact that repairs are necessary is not itself even prima facie evidence of damage to the value of the reversion." He said:

> "With the passage just quoted, as a general proposition, we are unable to agree. We find nothing in the earlier authorities to justify the conclusion, as a matter of law, that in no case and in no circumstances can the fact that repairs are necessary, and the cost of those repairs, be taken as at least prima facie evidence of damage to the value of the reversion and of the extent of such damage. There must be many cases in which it is in fact quite obvious that the value of the reversion has, by reason of a tenant's failure to do some necessary repair, been damaged precisely to the extent of the proper cost of effecting the repair in question. Nor do we understand the Lords Justices in *Hanson v. Newman*[56] as purporting to lay down an invariable rule of law to the effect that in all cases and in all circumstances the procedure of placing values on the reversion repaired and the reversion unrepaired, and then ascertaining the difference, must necessarily be gone through in order to ascertain the diminution in the value of the reversion attributable to the want of repair."

**30–16** Having referred to the fact that the landlord had carried out the work, he went on to say in an important passage:

> "[I]f there is evidence that the repairs done, being repairs within the covenant, were no more than was reasonably necessary to make the rooms fit for occupation or reletting for residential purposes, we fail to see why the proper cost of those repairs should not be regarded prima facie as representing a diminution in the value of the reversion due to the tenant's breach of covenant, being money which the landlord, acting as an ordinary prudent owner, had to spend on the property owing to the breach, and would not have had to spend but for the breach."

The evidence of the tenant's surveyor as to the capital values of the whole house and of the part let to the tenant was:

> "[B]eside the point. There could be no question as a practical matter of a sale of the five rooms let to the defendant (which, as we have said above, constitute the reversion) separately from the rest of the house. The surveyor's intention was presumably to show that there was no diminution in the value of the reversion according to the calculation prescribed in *Hanson v. Newman*.[57] That calculation is no doubt the right criterion to apply in many if not most cases, and we do not for a moment intend to cast any doubt on its validity as a measure of damages recoverable under section 18, sub-section (1), in cases to which it is appropriate. But we certainly deprecate its introduction as a *sine qua non* into all cases, including a small and simple case like the present concerned with a letting of some of the rooms in a house, where it becomes a purely hypothetical calculation wholly removed from the practical realities of the matter. Nor do we think that the county court judge was necessarily bound to accept the surveyor's assertion in re-examination to the effect that the want of repair did not affect the letting value of the premises, if he was satisfied, on the evidence as a whole, as we think he clearly was, that the repairs … were reasonably necessary to make the five rooms fit, according to ordinary standards, for occupation or re-letting for residential purposes."

**30–17** The important features in *Jones v Herxheimer* were that (i) the landlord had carried out the works; (ii) the works were reasonably necessary to make the premises fit for occupation or re-letting; and (ii) the premises consisted of part only of a house, which was never likely to be the subject of a separate sale. However, it is thought that the principle that the cost of repairs, where executed,

---

[55] [1949] 2 All E.R. 172.
[56] [1934] Ch. 298.
[57] Above. See para.30–08, above.

is prima facie evidence of the damage to the reversion is one of general application. Thus, in *Smiley v Townshend*[58] Denning L.J. said:

> "In cases where it is plain that the repairs are not going to be done by the landlord, the cost of them is little or no guide to the diminution in the value of the reversion, which may be nominal ... But in cases where the repairs have been, or are going to be, done by the landlord, the cost may be a very real guide. That is shown by the recent case of *Jones v. Herxheimer*[59] ... In cases where it is open to question whether the repairs will be done by the landlord ... then the cost may afford a starting figure; but it should be scaled down according to the circumstances, remembering that the real question is: what is the injury to the reversion?"

Lynskey J.'s dictum in *Landeau v Marchbank*[60] was referred to by Singleton L.J., who said that he agreed with it except that:

> "I would substitute the word 'conclusive' for the words 'even prima facie'. Evidence of lack of repair is not conclusive evidence of damage to the value of the reversion; but it may well be, and generally is held to be, prima facie evidence of it.[61]"

The same approach was adopted in *Maddox Properties Ltd v Davis*,[62] in which the demised premises consisted of a flat, and the landlord had expended about £80 in remedying the tenant's disrepair. The assessment of damages was referred to a referee. No direct evidence was adduced that the cost of repairs represented the damage to the reversion. The referee nonetheless concluded that the measure of damage to the reversion was the cost of the work carried out by the landlord, and recommended that such sum be awarded as damages. The county court judge refused to follow the recommendation, on the ground that there was no direct evidence of damage to the reversion, and the referee had not been entitled to draw the inference that there had been. The landlord's appeal was allowed by the Court of Appeal. Cohen L.J. (with whom Asquith and Singleton L.JJ. concurred) said that he agreed with the passage from the judgment of Singleton L.J. in *Smiley v Townshend*[63] set out above. Significantly, he went on to point out that no evidence had been adduced by the tenant to show that the cost of repairs was not a proper basis for arriving at the damage to the reversion.[64]

In *Culworth Estates Ltd v Society of Licensed Victuallers*[65] Dillon L.J. said in the course of his judgment:

**30–18**

> "As Denning L.J. stated in *Smiley v. Townshend* at p. 322, the question to be asked is by what amount, at the end of the lease, was the value of the existing reversion reduced by reason of the lack of repair. He pointed out, on the same page, that in cases where the repairs have been or are going to be done by the landlord, the cost may be a very real guide. That is essentially how the cost of repairs comes into the assessment of damages—as a guide to the diminution in

---

[58] [1950] 2 K.B. 311.
[59] See fn.12 above.
[60] [1949] 2 All E.R. 172. See para.30–15 above.
[61] This was described by Robert Walker L.J. in *Crewe Services & Investment Corp v Silk* [1998] 2 E.G.L.R. 1 as "a fairly major qualification. Singleton L.J. was in substance disapproving of what Lynskey J. had said".
[62] (1950) 155 E.G. 155.
[63] [1950] 2 K.B. 311.
[64] See also *Palmer v Pronk, Davis & Rusby Ltd* [1954] E.G.D. 156, CA.
[65] (1991) 62 P. & C.R. 211.

the value of the reversion. It follows that Denning L.J. was correct in saying, on the same p.322, that 'in cases where it is plain that the repairs are not going to be done by the landlord, the cost of them is little or no guide to the diminution in the value of the reversion, which may be nominal'."

However, the above statements of principle must be read in the light of certain observations in the judgment of Robert Walker L.J. in *Crewe Services & Investment Corp v Silk*[66] (which concerned a claim for damages during the currency of a tenancy of an agricultural holding[67]). In that case there was no evidence that the landlord intended to carry out the remedial work, so that it was "not … necessary to go into the possible significance of an actual intention on the part of the landlord to remedy wants of repair during the currency of a lease or tenancy". However, Robert Walker L.J. went on to say, obiter, that damages must be arrived at by an objective test. He continued as follows:

"What Denning L.J. had to say in *Smiley v. Townshend*[68] was not necessary to the decision. It seems to have received less than the wholehearted acceptance from this court in *Culworth Estates v. Society of Licensed Victuallers*[69] … It should perhaps now be read in the light of what Lord Lloyd said in *Ruxley Electronics & Construction Limited v. Forsyth* [1996] A.C. 344 at p.372C:

'The courts are not normally concerned with what a plaintiff does with his damages. But it does not follow that intention is not relevant to reasonableness, at least in those cases where the plaintiff does not intend to reinstate.'

*Ruxley* was not a landlord and tenant case, but the principle stated by Lord Lloyd seems of general application. However, it is not necessary to reach a concluded view."

**30–19** The decision in *Ruxley* was to the effect that the extent to which damages for breach of an obligation to carry out works are to be assessed by reference to the cost of the works depends on an objective test, namely, whether it would be reasonable in all the circumstances to do the works.[70] The point being made by Robert Walker L.J. is thought to have been that Denning L.J.'s formulation in *Smiley v Townshend* concentrated overmuch on the subjective state of mind or behaviour of the actual landlord as opposed to whether carrying out the works was, looked at objectively, a reasonable course of action in all the circumstances. Nonetheless, in *Latimer v Carney*[71] Arden L.J. (with whom Wilson L.J. agreed) said:

"Although courts are not normally concerned with what a claimant does with its damages, a landlord's conduct in taking steps or not taking steps to remedy a breach of the covenant to repair may throw light on the question of whether the repairs are reasonably necessary and, thus, on the question of whether there was any diminution in value of the reversion as a result of the disrepair."

[66] [1998] 2 E.G.L.R. 1.
[67] The facts are set out in para.28–23, above.
[68] See para.30–17, above.
[69] The passage is set out above.
[70] See further paras 32–03 to 32–05, below.
[71] [2006] 3 E.G.L.R. 13 at [24].

In the light of the above, it is thought that the correct view is as follows. Where the court is satisfied that the landlord has done the work (either himself or through an incoming tenant), the cost of the work prima facie represents the damage to the reversion, and it is for the tenant to show the contrary.[72] This is subject, however, to the important qualification that it must be reasonable to carry out the works. The fact that the landlord has actually done them is material which the court may, depending on the facts, take into account on that issue. But where carrying out the works would be unreasonable in all the circumstances, the cost will be no guide to the diminution in the value of the reversion, and the fact that the landlord has done the works will not assist him. In practice, however, where (i) the landlord has done the work for which he claims, (ii) that course was not obviously unreasonable, and (iii) there are no special circumstances, the tenant may find it difficult to persuade the court that the cost of the works is other than the best guide to the damage to the reversion.

The fact that the landlord has carried out only some of the works for which he claims will not prevent him, in an appropriate case, from recovering a higher figure by way of damages. Thus, in *Jaquin v Holland*[73] the landlord had carried out works to the value of £19 10s but recovered damages of £50 (that being the lesser of the cost of the works for which the tenant was liable and the diminution in the value of the reversion). Conversely, even where the court finds that the landlord intends to do the works for which he claims, the diminution in the value of the reversion may nonetheless be held to be a lower sum. Thus, in *Mason v TotalFinaElf UK Ltd*[74] the landlord had done very few of the works by the date of the trial but intended to carry out the remainder of the works if and to the extent that he was put in funds. Blackburne J. held on the evidence that the diminution in the value of the reversion was £73,500, which was substantially less than the cost of the works (£134,738).

## Where the landlord has not done, but intends to do, the remedial works

In principle, as is shown by the passage from the judgment of Denning L.J. in *Smiley v Townshend*[75] set out above,[76] a genuine intention to do the works may be a guide to the diminution in the value of the reversion. However, this needs to be approached with care. Doing the works is one thing. The landlord has expended his own money without knowing whether his dilapidations claim will succeed or not. An asserted but unperformed intention to do the works may have less force, because the landlord has not laid out any money. Moreover, claims that the landlord would have done the works on the term date but for lack of funding, and that he intends to do them once damages for dilapidations are paid, are easy to make, and difficult to test, and it may be questionable (as it was on the facts

**30–20**

---

[72] The burden of proof under the first limb is considered in para.30–46, below.
[73] [1960] 1 W.L.R. 258.
[74] [2003] 3 E.G.L.R. 91.
[75] [1950] 2 K.B. 311.
[76] At para.30–17.

found in *Ruxley*[77]) whether any such intention will continue once the litigation is over. It is no doubt for that reason that Neuberger J. said in *Craven (Builders) v Secretary of State for Health* that the cost of the works can be prima facie evidence of diminution in value where the landlord *"clearly"* intends to carry out the works.[78]

The underlying question in all cases will be how probative the landlord's state of mind is on the question of the diminution in the value of the reversion. In *Hammersmatch Properties (Welwyn) v Saint-Gobain Ceramics & Plastics*[79] Ramsey J. said:

> "In terms of the intention of [the landlord], it seemed to me that the evidence did not show any clear intention one way or another but was more an approach of keeping options open pending these proceedings in circumstances where, I accept, [the landlord] could not obtain or afford the funding necessary to put the building in repair. I therefore accept [the tenant's] submission that, at least in any sense which is probative of the diminution in value on the term date, [the landlord] did not intend to carry out the dilapidations for which it claims."

## Where the landlord has not done, and will not do, the remedial works

30–21  Where the landlord has not done, and does not intend to do, the works, the cost may be no guide at all to the damage to the reversion.[80] In such a case it will be for the landlord to establish that he has nonetheless suffered a diminution in the value of the reversion. In *Latimer v Carney*[81] Arden L.J. (with whom Wilson L.J. agreed) said:

> "48. The failure to carry out the repairs would clearly be an indication that the repairs were not necessary as the landlords claimed. Put another way, whether sums were actually spent on doing repairs is relevant to the question whether the repairs were necessary or not. If they were not necessary, damage to the reversion could not be inferred from them. But even where the repairs had not been carried out there could be other explanations for the failure that could satisfy the judge that the indication was not well-founded, as where the landlord decides not to repair the property himself but proceeds to sell it at a lower price than he could have obtained if the repairs had been remedied."

As appears from this passage, the fact that the landlord has not done the work does not mean that the damages will necessarily be nominal.[82] Thus, in *Culworth Estates Ltd v Society of Licensed Victuallers*[83] the premises consisted of industrial property which was in disrepair at the expiration of the lease on June 24, 1986. The cost of the remedial works was £175,000 together with £21,875 in respect of professional fees. The landlord did not carry out the work, and never intended to. Instead, in September 1986 the landlord sold the premises for £320,000 to a third

---

[77] [1996] A.C. 344 at 362H–363A.
[78] [2000] 1 E.G.L.R 128 at 131K.
[79] [2013] EWHC 1161 (TCC).
[80] *Smiley v Townshend* [1950] 2 K.B. 311; *Culworth Estates Ltd v Society of Licensed Victuallers* (1991) 62 P. & C.R. 211.
[81] [2006] 3 E.G.L.R. 13.
[82] *Culworth Estates Ltd v Society of Licensed Victuallers*, above; *Crewe Services & Investment Corp v Silk* [1998] 2 E.G.L.R. 1. See further para.36–12, below.
[83] Above.

party, who intended to convert them into workshops. The price of £320,000 represented the value of the premises, in disrepair, for development. The third party did not carry out the repairs or any development. In March 1988 the premises were sold again for £550,000 to the owner of adjoining premises who carried out a subdivision scheme. The judge accepted the evidence of the landlord's valuer that the premises would have had a value for letting or sale as a single unit if they had been in repair in accordance with the lease. He found that the difference between this value and the value of the premises in disrepair at the end of the term (£320,000) greatly exceeded the cost of the works. The judge therefore awarded damages of £227,875, which represented the cost of the works, fees and £31,000 for loss of rent. The Court of Appeal refused to interfere with his finding.

The important point in *Culworth* was that, on the evidence accepted by the judge, the landlord had suffered a loss even though he had not carried out the work. If the premises had been in repair, they would have been worth substantially more than they were worth as a result of the disrepair. Presumably the landlord could have realised that additional value. Since the difference exceeded the cost of repair, the latter figure was awarded. **30–22**

In *Shortlands Investments Ltd v Cargill Plc*[84] the landlord did not do the works for which he claimed but instead marketed the premises after the expiry of the lease, and then relet them slightly over a year later on terms which included the payment to the incoming tenant of a substantial sum to reflect the disrepair for which the outgoing tenant was liable and other disrepair. The Official Referee found that the fact that the premises were in disrepair gave the incoming tenant a bargaining counter which enabled it to demand and obtain a sum specifically for the disrepair. On that basis, he held that the cost of repairs was "the best possible guide" in the assessment of damages.

### The cost of the works

Where the damage to the reversion equates to, or includes, the cost of the works, the relevant cost is the reasonable cost of carrying out those works which the tenant ought to have done.[85] It is likely that in most cases the cost actually incurred by the landlord will be taken as prima facie evidence of the reasonable cost, which it is for the tenant to displace, particularly where the landlord obtained estimates and proceeded on the basis of the lowest. However, it is always open to the tenant to show, if he can, that the cost incurred by the landlord was excessive. **30–23**

Where it can be shown that the likely purchaser of the landlord's reversion would have carried out less work than that claimed by the landlord, the cost which is relevant will be the cost of those works which the purchaser would have done. In such a case the damage to the reversion will not include the cost of the additional work, because that cost will not generally form any part of the reduction in the value of the reversion attributable to the disrepair.

---

[84] [1995] 1 E.G.L.R. 51.
[85] See Ch.29 and para.30–10, above.

## Value added tax[86]

30–24　The position in relation to VAT on the cost of the works has already been noted.[87] The effect of s.18(1) is that VAT will only be recoverable where it forms part of the damage to the reversion. In the cases already considered, the court was in effect proceeding on the assumption that the hypothetical purchaser of the reversion would be in the same position in relation to VAT as was the actual landlord. In theory at least, it may be possible to show that the particular VAT position of the actual landlord would not be shared by the hypothetical purchaser of the reversion. If it can be proved that the hypothetical purchaser of the reversion would be able to reclaim VAT as input tax, it would seem to follow that the diminution in the value of the reversion would not include any element in respect of VAT. It follows that VAT would not be recoverable as part of the damages, even though it has been incurred by the actual landlord. The difficulties of proving such a proposition will, in most cases, be considerable.[88]

## Professional fees

30–25　Where the damage to the reversion equates to, or includes, the cost of the works, professional fees incurred in connection with the work (for example, preparing a specification and working drawings, and supervising the work) will ordinarily be recoverable as well,[89] provided that the work is such that it is reasonable to incur fees. However, the costs of drawing up a schedule of dilapidations may not be recoverable as damages for breach of the repairing covenant.[90] The recovery of fees and costs is considered in Ch.34, below.

## Loss of rent

30–26　The recovery of loss of rent at common law has already been considered.[91] By virtue of the first limb of s.18(1), loss of rent is only recoverable to the extent that it forms part of the damage to the reversion arising from the disrepair.[92] Hence the question in every case will be whether the facts are such that the hypothetical purchaser would reduce what he would otherwise have bid for the reversion by an amount representing loss of rent for some or all of the period necessary for the

---

[86] This paragraph was approved and applied by the judge in *Sun Life Assurance Plc v Racal Tracs Ltd* [2000] 1 E.G.L.R. 138. The case went to the Court of Appeal on another point ([2001] 1 W.L.R. 1562) but no appeal was brought against the judge's decision on damages.

[87] See paras 29–12 to 29–13, above.

[88] It was held in *Sun Life Assurance Plc v Racal Tracs Ltd*, above, that the notional purchaser, like the actual landlord, would not be able to recover VAT, so that VAT should be included as part of the cost of the works.

[89] *Culworth Estates Ltd v Society for Licensed Victuallers* [1990] 2 E.G.L.R. 36, (affirmed (1991) 62 P. & C.R. 211). See para.34–27 et seq., below.

[90] *Maud v Sandars* [1943] 2 All E.R. 783; *Lloyds Bank Ltd v Lake* [1961] 1 W.L.R. 884. See further para.34–05, below.

[91] See para.29–20 et seq., above.

[92] *Hammersmatch Properties (Welwyn) v Saint-Gobain Ceramics & Plastics* [2013] EWHC 1161 (TCC) at [148].

carrying out of the works. Answering this question will generally involve considering what the purchaser would be likely to do with the building, and (if he would do the work) to what extent he would be influenced by any delay in reletting caused by the works.

Loss of rent will generally only be recoverable where there is a causal link between the disrepair and the loss of rent. In a straightforward case where damages are assessed by reference to the cost of the work, and the landlord would have been able to relet the premises immediately but for the works, loss of rent for the period reasonably necessary to carry out the work will generally be recoverable. In such a case the hypothetical purchaser of the reversion would reduce his bid by an amount corresponding to the loss of rent. However, loss of rent may still be recoverable even where the damages are not assessed by reference to the cost of the repair works. For example, where the notional purchaser would assess his bid for the reversion in disrepair by deducting the value of such rent-free period as he would have to give an incoming tenant in return for a covenant to do the work, the damages are likely to include the value of the rent-free period. Similarly, where the notional purchaser would relet the premises without doing the work but at a lower rent than he could have got for the premises in repair, the damages will generally be assessed by reference to the capitalised difference between the two figures.

The position may be different where the state of the market is such that the premises could not be relet in whatever state of repair they may be, or where the repair works can be carried out over the same period as a refurbishment scheme. In such cases, loss of rent will not generally be recoverable because the notional purchaser will not take loss of rent into account in formulating his bid.

In *Firle Investments Ltd v Datapoint International Ltd*[93] the landlord intended after the term date to carry out a refurbishment scheme. The judge said of his claim for loss of rent:

**30–27**

> "It is well established that this may be awarded in appropriate cases but a proper causal connection must be demonstrated. If the landlord would not have been able to re-let the premises even if yielded up in repair or if, as here, the hypothetical purchaser would not have attempted to re-let until after the premises had been refurbished, no rental loss will have been caused by the breach of the repairing covenant unless the extent of the survival items [i.e. those repairs works which would not be negated by the refurbishment] was such that, had they been done, the period reasonably required to carry out the refurbishment would have been reduced. In such circumstances loss of rent over that period might well be a material factor to be taken into account when valuing the reversion. However, in this case, Mr Scarr's oral evidence in chief was that the refurbishment contract would have taken about the same time even if the repairs which, he contended would have survived, had been carried out. Accordingly, in my judgment, no loss of rent component needs to be considered in this case."

Loss of rent was awarded as part of the damages in *Drummond v S. & U. Stores Ltd*[94] and *Culworth Estates Ltd v Society of Licensed Victuallers.*[95]

---

[93] [2000] EWHC 105 (TCC).
[94] [1981] 1 E.G.L.R. 42.
[95] [1990] 2 E.G.L.R. 36 (affirmed (1991) 62 P. & C.R. 211).

## Service charges and void rates

**30–28**   There is no reason in principle why the landlord should not be entitled to recover as damages other heads of financial loss suffered by him through not being able to relet the premises until the repair works have been done. Examples are service charges which the landlord would otherwise have been able to recover from an incoming tenant,[96] and void rates which the landlord would not have had to pay if the premises had been relet to a new occupier. However, as with all other heads of loss, these heads will only be recoverable to the extent that they form part of the damage to the reversion. As with loss of rent, much will turn on what the notional purchaser would do with the premises, and how he would regard any potential loss of service charge or void rates.

## Development value[97]

**30–29**   Where the notional purchaser would be a person intending to redevelop the premises irrespective of their state of repair, the diminution in the value of the reversion may be nil. The purchaser will compute his bid for the premises by reference to their development value, and the state of repair will not generally enter into his calculations.[98] The same may be the case where the purchaser would, irrespective of the state of repair of the premises, carry out such substantial works that the pre-existing state of repair would be irrelevant. Thus, in *Landeau v Marchbank*,[99] the premises were sold by the landlord at the end of the lease for conversion into two flats and two maisonettes at a price that was agreed on all sides to be a good price. Lynskey J. held that no damage to the reversion had been proved.[100] In *Mather v Barclays Bank Plc*[101] the landlord relet the premises after the end of the lease to a third party who covenanted to carry out improvements and substantial works which cost over twice what the repairs would have cost. The value of the premises repaired but unimproved was found to be less than their value in their existing state but improved in the manner contemplated by the new lease. It was held that no damage to the reversion had been proved. In *Ultraworth Ltd v General Accident Fire & Life Assurance Co*

---

[96] Care must be taken to identify the landlord's real loss. He cannot recover service charges in relation to services which he has not in fact provided because the premises are empty. This head of claim is limited to the proportion applicable to the demised premises of services which the landlord has actually provided (such as insurance), and in respect of which he would have been able to recover the cost had he been able to relet the premises. See further para.29–22, above.

[97] Redevelopment value is also relevant in the context of the second limb of s.18(1) of the 1927 Act, which is considered in para.30–48 et seq., below.

[98] Unless he would grant a short-term tenancy pending redevelopment, in which case he might make a deduction for disrepair which affected the prospects of finding a tenant: see below.

[99] [1949] 2 All E.R. 172.

[100] This authority is cited only as an example. The judge's approach, which was that the fact that repairs were necessary was "not in itself even prima facie evidence of damage to the value of the reversion" was subsequently disapproved by the Court of Appeal in *Jones v Herxheimer* [1950]2 K.B. 106, and accepted only in an altered form in *Smiley v Townshend* [1950] 2 K.B. 311: see paras 30–15 to 30–19, above.

[101] [1987] 2 E.G.L.R. 254.

*Ltd*[102] the court held that the likely purchaser of an office building would be a refurbisher, an owner-occupier or a developer and that whichever it was, the disrepair had not resulted in any damage to the value of the reversion.

The same may be true where the notional buyer would change the use of the premises, such that some or all of the disrepair would be irrelevant to what he would pay for them. Thus, in *Smiley v Townshend*,[103] Denning L.J. gave the example of a letting of a house which would be suitable only for use as a warehouse at the end of the term, where decorative repairs would be useless, so that there would be no damage to the reversion by reason of their not being done.

In principle, development value may be reflected in either the value of the premises out of repair, or their value in repair, or both. So, for example, the value of the premises in disrepair may be their site value for redevelopment, but they may have a higher value in repair for reletting. Thus, in *Shane v Runcorn*[104] the court found on the evidence that (i) the investment value of the premises in repair was £11,000; (ii) their site value was £7,500; so that (iii) the diminution in value was £3,500, and the damages were capped at that amount (even though the cost of works claim was higher). Likewise, in *Hammersmatch Properties (Welwyn) v Saint-Gobain Ceramics & Plastics*,[105] the value of a large 1930s office and industrial building in its actual condition was held to be £2.1m, which represented its site value for demolition and development, but its value in repair for letting (following the carrying out of relatively minor conversion works to enable it to be let in parts) was held to be £3m, so that damages were capped at £900,000.

An alternative possibility, where the likely purchaser would be a person intending to redevelop the premises, is that he may do short-term works to enable him to derive an income from the premises pending carrying out his scheme. Thus, in *Craven (Builders) Ltd v Secretary of State for Health*[106] a large former textile mill was left in a bad state of disrepair. The cost of the remedial works was £312,500. The value of the building in its existing state was £245,000. Neuberger J. held that the least unlikely buyer would be a person speculating on a market improvement and prepared to hold the property for two or three years while making up his mind whether to refurbish or whether to carry out a major redevelopment. Such a person, whilst largely indifferent to the execution of repairs, would nevertheless attribute some value to them, if only because they would assist with short lettings. Damages were assessed at £40,000.

It was argued in *PgfII SA v Royal & Sun Alliance Insurance Plc*[107] that "a landlord should not be entitled to recover damages for dilapidations where a property has latent development value which may (or may not) be realised at some stage in the future. As a result there is no diminution in the value of the reversion whatever state the premises are left in". H.H. Judge Toulmin, QC commented "this has not been argued successfully in the 83 years since the [1927] Act has been passed", and that to accord with this submission, the first

---

[102] [2000] 2 E.G.L.R. 115.
[103] [1950] 2 K.B. 311.
[104] [1967] E.G.D. 88.
[105] [2013] EWHC 1161 (TCC).
[106] [2000] 1 E.G.L.R. 128.
[107] [2011] 1 P. & C.R. 11.

limb of s.18(1) would have to read "damages for breach of covenant shall in no case exceed the amount by which the value of the reversion (including its prospective value) is diminished owing to the breach of such covenant". He went on to conclude as follows:

> "[Section 18(1)] was not intended to deal with a case where there is a latent development value which may or may not be realised at some future date. It would be unreasonable if a landlord was told that he could not have the cost of the disrepair of the previous tenant because of a development value which, at the date of termination of the lease, he had no intention of realising."

If by this, the judge was intending to say that, for the purposes of the first limb of s.18(1), the potential of the premises to be redeveloped at some time in the future must be disregarded in carrying out a valuation of the premises unless the landlord has an actual intention to redevelop, then his view is inconsistent with the many authorities decided under s.18(1) in which the reversion has been valued taking into account such value.[108] His view would appear to involve a confusion between the second limb of s.18(1) (which does indeed require an actual intention before it becomes relevant) and the first limb, which requires the landlord's reversion to be valued objectively, on two different bases, by reference to its market value, where any effect on value of any "latent development value" cannot be ignored, even if there is no immediate intention to realise that value. Moreover, the judge's comment was clearly influenced by his earlier holding that the common measure of damages is no longer that set out in *Joyner v Weeks*, a view which it has been suggested elsewhere in this work was erroneous.[109] It is the authors' experience that an assessment of what latent redevelopment value may exist is very commonly undertaken in most cases where the landlord himself has no intention to carry out any particular works.

## Supersession

30–30    A very common type of case in practice occurs where the purchaser would be likely to upgrade the building in such a way that its pre-existing state of repair would remain relevant, but only to a limited extent.[110] An example might be the refurbishment of an office building to bring it up to modern standards where only some of the work which the tenant should have carried out would survive the upgrading works. In such a case, depending on the facts, the diminution in the value of the reversion might well be limited to the cost of those repair works

---

[108] See above.
[109] See para.29–10, above.
[110] This concept is referred to in the RICS Guidance Note "Dilapidations—A Guide to Best Practice", 5th edn, as "supersession".

which would survive the refurbishment.[111] In *Firle Investments Ltd v Datapoint International Ltd*[112] Mr Colin Reese, QC agreed with and adopted the foregoing part of the text,[113] and went on to say:

"78. ... Expressing the essence of the general principle in my own words, I would put it this way: If none of the repairs could realistically be expected to survive the refurbishment or if only such an insignificant proportion could be expected to survive as to fall within the 'de minimis' concept, it is difficult to see how the value of the landlord's interest at the term date would have been in any way diminished by reason of the disrepair. Equally, whenever some not insignificant part or parts of the repairs could realistically be expected to survive the refurbishment, it seems fairly obvious (a) that the value of the landlord's interest at the term date is likely to be to some extent diminished by reason of the disrepair and (b) that the extent of the diminution is likely to be related to the value of the repairs that could realistically be expected to survive ('the survival items') and whatever (if any) reduction in the time required for refurbishment was to be expected if those repairs had been carried out by the tenant before the term date."

He went onto consider how the value of the survival items was to be assessed, and concluded that logically the relevant value was the potential saving to the purchaser under the refurbishment scheme of not having to carry out such items. However, in *Latimer v Carney*[114] Arden L.J. (with whom Wilson L.J. agreed) said that in the above passage the judge had made the proposition "far firmer and more absolute" than the statement in the text, and held that the judge's reformulation must be interpreted as not departing from that statement, so that he is to be taken as having held that "it is *likely* [Arden L.J.'s emphasis] that there is no diminution in value when repair works are superceded by works of refurbishment that would be undertaken by the purchaser". She went on to say:

"38. I would, however, accept that where the repair works which the tenant in breach of a covenant to repair is bound to do will be overtaken by refurbishments which the landlord or a purchaser of the property proposes to do, that indicates that the reversion has a latent development value. The landlord would have to show that the repairs caused damage to the reversion, and this may in the circumstances be difficult. Alternatively he will have to show that the refurbishment would incorporate some of the repairs the former tenant should have carried out, i.e. that specific repairs would 'survive' the refurbishment. The question whether the repairs to be done by the former tenant in any particular case survive may raise difficult issues of fact and judgment, but no specific examples of difficulty have been suggested to us."

This type of situation is often described as "supersession". A recent judicial explanation of this concept is to be found in *Sunlife Europe Properties v Tiger Aspect Holdings*,[115] where Edwards-Stuart J. said:

"Where market conditions at the expiry of the lease require upgrading or refurbishment works to be carried out in order to enable the building to be let to the appropriate type of tenant, a tenant in breach of a repairing covenant is not liable for the costs of any work to remedy the breach to the extent that such work would be rendered abortive by the need to upgrade or refurbish the building (i.e. where there is supersession)."

---

[111] See *Mather v Barclays Bank Ltd* [1987] 2 E.G.L.R. 254 at 261B. For an example of a case where the damages equated to the cost of the "survival" items, see *Ravengate Estates v Horizon Group* [2007] EWCA Civ 1368.
[112] [2000] EWHC 105 (TCC).
[113] In the First Edition at para.23–24.
[114] [2006] 3 E.G.L.R. 13
[115] Above, at [46].

In *Shortlands Investments Ltd v Cargill Plc*[116] it was argued on behalf of the tenant that no damage to the value of the landlord's reversion had been caused, because any incoming tenant would undertake a modern fit-out (for example, he would replace the existing rectangular ceiling tiles with square tiles, regardless of their state of cleanliness or repair), and (more narrowly) any incoming tenant would remove the partitions and thereby damage ceilings and carpets such that they would have to be replaced anyway. In fact, the tenant to whom the premises were relet after the expiry of the lease had them fitted out to a very expensive and lavish standard (including the replacement of ceiling tiles), but the Official Referee found that as at the term date no one could have been expected to foresee that a future tenant would fit out to that standard. He rejected both arguments on the facts. By contrast, in *Ravengate Estates v Horizon Housing Group*[117] the premises were ripe for redevelopment, such that any potential purchaser would have carried out a development which would have rendered otiose most of the repairs claimed by the landlord. The diminution in the value of the reversion was assessed by reference to the amount which the buyer would have required to be deducted from the purchase price in respect of the cost of remedying those items of disrepair that would have survived a redevelopment.

## Where the premises are sub-let on the relevant date

30–31    The premises must be valued subject to any sub-tenancies subsisting on the term date of the lease which will become binding on the landlord.[118] The hypothetical purchaser's bid for the reversion in and out of repair must therefore be assessed on the assumption that he will become the landlord of the sub-tenants. This may have important consequences in relation to whether there has been any damage to the reversion.

### (a)    Where the sub-tenancies contain repairing obligations on the part of the landlord

30–32    Where the purchaser will become liable as against the sub-tenant to carry out some or all of the repairs, he may take a more serious view of the disrepair than he otherwise would. For example, the sub-tenancy may contain an express landlord's repairing covenant in relation to parts of the demised premises, or common parts. Or, where the sub-let premises comprise a dwelling, the sub-tenant may be entitled to the benefit of the implied repairing covenant in s.11 of the Landlord and Tenant Act 1985.[119] Even if s.11 does not apply, the state of repair may nonetheless be such that the local authority may exercise its powers

---

[116] [1995] 1 E.G.L.R. 51.

[117] [2007] EWCA Civ 1368.

[118] *Jeffs v West London Property Corp Ltd* [1954] J.P.L. 114 (residential sub-tenant protected by the Rent Act); *Family Management Ltd v Gray* [1980] 1 E.G.L.R. 46; *Crown Estate Commissioners v Town Investments Ltd* [1992] 1 E.G.L.R. 61 (business sub-tenants holding over under the Landlord and Tenant Act 1954). For the circumstances in which sub-tenancies may become binding on the head landlord, see para.24–11 et seq., above.

[119] See para.20–17 et seq., above.

under the Housing Act 1985 to compel the landlord to carry out the necessary work. In each of these cases, the purchaser of the reversion is likely to formulate his bid for the premises in their unrepaired state on the basis that he will have to carry out at least that work which he will become liable, as against the sub-tenant or the local authority, to carry out.

### (b) Where the premises are occupied by sub-tenants entitled to the protection of Part II of the Landlord and Tenant Act 1954

The fact that the premises are occupied on the relevant date by sub-tenants under tenancies to which Part II of the Landlord and Tenant Act 1954 applies must be taken into account in assessing the damage to the reversion. There will be two important consequences for the purposes of the valuation. First, the sub-tenant will become the direct tenant of the landlord upon the expiry of the head tenancy.[120] The landlord will therefore become entitled to the benefit of any obligations to repair or pay service charges in the sub-tenancy, and he will likewise be obliged to perform any landlord's covenants in the sub-tenancy to repair or provide services. Second, the sub-tenant will be entitled to a new tenancy under the 1954 Act. The new lease will prima facie be on the same terms (including repairing covenants and service charge obligations) as the existing tenancy. The new rent will be fixed by the court without taking into account any disrepair which is attributable to the sub-tenant's breaches of the repairing covenants in the current tenancies.[121]

**30–33**

The effect of the above may be to reduce or extinguish what would otherwise be the damage to the reversion. Thus, for example, if the sub-tenancies contain comprehensive service charge obligations on the part of the sub-tenants, by virtue of which the landlord will be able to recover the entire cost of the repair work, the damage to the reversion may be nil.[122]

The leading case is *Family Management Ltd v Gray*.[123] In that case the premises were sub-let to sub-tenants under full repairing leases, and the disrepair which was the subject of the landlord's action against the head tenant was due to breaches by the sub-tenants of their repairing covenants. They had by the term date of the head lease applied for new tenancies under the Act. It was "almost certain" that they would renew, and they did in fact subsequently take new 20-year leases. Both sides approached the question of whether there had been any diminution in the value of the landlord's reversion attributable to the head tenant's disrepair by looking at the difference between the rental value of the premises in repair and their value out of repair. The Court of Appeal held that there was no difference, because the reversion had to be valued subject to the rights of the sub-tenants to renew, and they could not, when renewing, pray in aid their own breaches of covenant in order to reduce the rent.

---

[120] Landlord and Tenant Act 1954 s.65.

[121] The corresponding paragraph in the Third Edition of this work was cited with approval by the Court of Appeal in *Lyndendown v Vitamol* [2007] 3 E.G.L.R. 11 at [3].

[122] In practice, however, the notional purchaser of the reversion may reduce his bid to allow for the risk that the cost will not be recovered in full.

[123] [1980] 1 E.G.L.R. 46.

**30–34**    In *Family Management Ltd v Gray* the repairing covenants in the head lease and the sub-tenancies were the same or similar, and the whole of the premises were sub-let. Where these factors are not present, the position will be different. Thus, in *Crown Estate Commissioners v Town Investments Ltd*[124] the demised premises were on the term date of the head lease occupied as to part by sub-tenants with rights to new tenancies under the 1954 Act, and part was empty. The sub-tenancies contained repairing obligations which did not correspond with those in the head lease. The premises were in disrepair, and the landlord carried out the remedial work after the expiry of the head lease. Some time after the expiry of the head lease the sub-tenants were granted new leases by the landlord for terms commencing on the expiry date of the head lease. The landlord claimed the cost of the repairs from the head tenant by way of damages for breach of the covenants to repair in the head lease. The matter came before the court on the hearing of a preliminary issue on the extent to which *Family Management Ltd v Gray* was distinguishable. It was argued that it could be distinguished on the following four grounds: (1) that the landlord had carried out the repairs; (2) that the service charge covenants in the new leases did not entitle the landlords to recover the cost of the repairs; (3) that the repairing covenants in the head lease did not correspond with those in the sub-tenancies; and (4) that part of the premises was unoccupied at the relevant time.

Mr Recorder Barry Green, QC, sitting as an official referee, rejected the first and second of these distinctions, on the ground that both the carrying out of the repairs, and the grant of new leases containing defective service charge machinery, were events which occurred after the term date of the head lease, and neither were operative or potential as at that date.[125] He accepted the third and fourth distinctions. He therefore held that the liability of the tenant for breach of the repairing obligations in the head lease was extinguished, save that it was open to the landlord to seek to prove at trial that the reversion had been damaged by reason of (1) the non-correspondence between the repairing covenants in the head lease and those in the sub-tenancies, and (2) breaches of the repairing covenant in the head lease in relation to those parts of the premises which were empty at the relevant time.

*Crown Estate Commissioners v Town Investments Ltd* proceeded on the basis that *Family Management Ltd v Gray* was indistinguishable save in the four respects set out above. However, it is thought that *Family Management* is not an authority for the proposition that where the facts as to occupation are the same as in that case (i.e. the premises are occupied on the term date of the head lease by sub-tenants under leases which fall within Pt II of the 1954 Act, and which contain the same or similar repairing covenants as the head lease), there can be no damage to the reversion as a matter of law. The conclusion in that case that there had been no damage to the reversion was based on the evidence, and in particular the virtual certainty that the sub-tenants would renew. Where the notional purchaser of the reversion on the term date of the head lease would take the view that the sub-tenants may not renew, or that they may not be good for the cost of repairs, the position may be different. It is thought that this is a matter of

---

[124] [1992] 1 E.G.L.R. 61.
[125] The relevance of events occurring after the term date is considered in para.30–37 et seq., below.

evidence, not law. Where the disrepair is not particularly serious, and the sub-tenant is a good covenant who is bound to renew, the valuer may conclude that the purchaser would not reduce by very much what he would otherwise have been prepared to pay. Even here, however, there may be force in the argument that the purchaser is likely to bid less to reflect the risk that matters will not turn out as he expects.[126] On the other hand, where the sub-tenant is a poor covenant, who is likely to disappear in the near future, the purchaser may make a substantial reduction from what he would otherwise have paid, particularly where the remedial work is such that it will need to be done before any reletting can take place. It should be noted, however, that it is the position as it would have appeared on the term date of the head lease that is relevant: subsequent events cannot be taken into account.[127]

It is thought that for the above reasons *Family Management Ltd v Gray*,[128] when correctly analysed, is no more than an example of a case where, on the evidence before the court, no diminution was proved, and that it does not preclude a finding that the value of the reversion has been diminished where such finding is justified on the evidence. It is noteworthy that in *Crown Estate Commissioners v Town Investments Ltd*,[129] *Family Management Ltd v Gray* was treated as authority for four propositions, namely, that in valuing a reversion which is not in possession but is subject to continuation tenancies under the 1954 Act, (1) the court must take that fact into account as a reality and not treat the reversion as if it were in possession; (2) the court must take into account all relevant matters relating to the continuation tenancies which may affect the value of the reversion; (3) the court has limited power to admit evidence of matters which arise after the expiry date of the contractual head tenancy; and (4) the court must assume that the rent will be fixed under the 1954 Act on the basis that the premises are in repair, for otherwise the tenant would be taking advantage of his own wrong. It is thought that this analysis is correct. It follows that whether and to what extent the presence of a sub-tenant on the term date affects the value of the landlord's reversion will depend on the evidence in each case. This accords with the approach of the Court of Appeal in *Lyndendown v Vitamol*,[130] in which the question was treated as one of evidence. In that case the tenant under a full repairing lease of premises on an industrial estate sub-let with consent, and the sub-tenant covenanted with the landlord to perform the covenants in the head lease. Prior to the grant of the sub-lease, the tenant's parent company gave an undertaking to the sub-tenant in a side letter that the latter's obligations to repair would be limited to making the property wind and watertight and that any surplus repairs would be carried out at the expense of the parent company. The sub-tenant remained in occupation under the 1954 Act following the expiry of the head lease. The landlord sued the tenant for damages for terminal dilapidations. The landlord accepted that, unless the side letter altered the position, any damage to the reversion was nil or nominal since, as at the term date of the lease, a

**30–35**

---

[126] This argument was not advanced in *Family Management Ltd v Gray* [1980] 1 E.G.L.R. 46.
[127] See para.30–37 et seq., below.
[128] Above.
[129] Above.
[130] [2007] 3 E.G.L.R. 11.

sub-tenant was in occupation, holding under a sub-lease, to which the 1954 Act applied, containing the same or similar repairing covenants, which the landlord could enforce directly by virtue of s.65(2) of the 1954 Act. The judge at first instance accepted the evidence of the tenant's expert that the side letter had no effect on value. The Court of Appeal (citing the view expressed in the Third Edition of this work that the question whether the value of the reversion has been damaged when a sub-tenant is in occupation on the term date is one of evidence[131]) refused to disturb his findings.

## Arrangements made by the landlord with a new tenant[132]

**30–36**   It sometimes happens in practice that after the lease has ended, the landlord relets the premises to a new tenant, or enters into some other arrangement, the result of which is that a third party becomes liable to, or does, put the premises into repair. Such an arrangement cannot in itself affect the damages recoverable from the outgoing tenant.[133] However, it may nonetheless be relevant when considering the extent to which the value of the reversion has been diminished by the disrepair.[134]

The leading case is *Haviland v Long*.[135] In that case, shortly before the lease ended, the landlord relet the premises to a new tenant who agreed to carry out the repairs subject to the landlord undertaking to reimburse to him any sums recovered from the outgoing tenant by way of damages for breach of the covenant to repair. The outgoing tenant argued that the landlord had lost any entitlement to damages because, by virtue of the arrangement with the new tenant, there was no damage to the reversion. The Court of Appeal rejected this, on the ground that at the time the new lease was granted, the landlord had a contingent right to recover damages from the outgoing tenant in the event of there being a breach at the term date, and that right was not lost by reason of the bargain made with the new tenant; that arrangement was *res inter alios acta*, i.e. it was a matter between the landlord and the new tenant, and did not concern the outgoing tenants. The same has been held in relation to a reversionary lease granted by the landlord.[136]

It follows that an arrangement with a new tenant or third party cannot directly affect damages, in the sense that it cannot of itself either afford a defence to the claim, or increase the amount of damages recoverable. Thus, for example, the fact that the landlord has relet the premises to an incoming tenant on terms that the incoming tenant does the work in return for a rent-free period is not conclusive in favour of the damages being the value of the rent-free period. However, an arrangement with a third party may nonetheless be of great relevance when assessing damages. First, where the arrangement is in substance that the remedial

---

[131] The corresponding passage is set out in para.30–34, above.
[132] See further para.30–05, above.
[133] *Haviland v Long* [1952] 2 Q.B. 80; *Drummond v S.& U. Stores Ltd* [1981] 1 E.G.L.R. 42.
[134] See para.30–37, below.
[135] Above.
[136] *Terroni v Corsini* [1931] 1 Ch. 515. See also *Hanson v Newman* [1934] Ch. 298, per Lawrence L.J. at 305; *Jaquin v Holland* [1960] 1 W.L.R. 258, per Devlin L.J. at 267; *Smiley v Townshend* [1950] 2 K.B. 311, per Denning L.J. at 320; *Drummond v S. & U. Stores Ltd* [1981] 1 E.G.L.R. 42.

work will be done by the incoming tenant at the landlord's expense (either by direct payment or by a rent reduction), the carrying out of the work by the new tenant may be treated as the equivalent of the landlord doing the work.[137] The result of this may be that the cost of the work will prima facie be taken to represent the amount of the diminution in the value of the reversion caused by the disrepair.[138] Second, the arrangement may throw light on the value of the reversion at the term date because it may indicate how the market would have dealt with the premises. This is further considered in para.30–37 et seq. below.

## The relevance of events occurring after the term date

The relevant date for assessing damages is the term date of the lease.[139] Events which occur after that date are not directly relevant to the assessment, in the sense that they cannot in themselves reduce or extinguish the damages. However, insofar as they are operative or potential at the term date, they may throw light on the value of the reversion at the relevant date.

**30–37**

Thus, in *Smiley v Townshend*[140] the premises were requisitioned at all relevant times. After the end of the term, when the premises were still requisitioned, the landlord brought proceedings against the tenant for damages for disrepair. It was argued on behalf of the tenant that the proper date for assessing damages was not the end of the lease, but the date when possession actually reverted to the landlord; that, since this time had not yet arrived, the court should look into the future to see what the condition of the premises would be; and that the requisitioning authority might still make good some or all of the disrepair. The Court of Appeal rejected this, holding that the correct date for assessing damages was the term date of the lease. Denning L.J. went on to say in relation to events occurring after the term date:

> "It does not follow, however ... that when you come to apply the proper measure of damage—injury to the reversion—future events and probabilities are to be disregarded: they may have an important bearing on the value of the reversion at the end of the lease ... But in such cases the subsequent event, when it happens, is not in itself sufficient to extinguish the damages. It is only evidence, albeit strong evidence, of the future as it appeared at the end of the lease ... The true view, therefore, is that matters happening subsequently to the end of the lease do not of themselves affect the damages. The only effect of subsequent demolition is that it shows, in retrospect, what was the future when the lease came to an end, and thus throws strong light on the injury to the reversion at that time ... although future events do not in themselves reduce or extinguish the damages, nevertheless they may properly be regarded in so far as they throw light on the value of the reversion at the end of the lease."

In *Family Management Ltd v Gray*[141] Shaw L.J., having referred to the judgment of Denning L.J. in *Smiley v Townshend*, went on to say:

**30–38**

---

[137] *Drummond v S.& U. Stores Ltd*, above.
[138] See paras 30–15 to 30–19, above.
[139] See para.30–07, above.
[140] [1950] 2 K.B. 311.
[141] [1980] 1 E.G.L.R. 46.

"So events which follow upon the determination of the lease but which are independent of any fact or consideration which was either operative or potential at the date when the lease expired cannot affect the determination of the loss to the reversion. As I read the judgment cited it decides that factors which existed, either as operative or potential factors but which had substance and reality at the date when the reversion fell in, were to be considered as having a bearing on the valuation of the loss or damage to the reversion by the failure on the part of the lessee to comply with his covenants under a lease."

It was accordingly held that regard must be had, in assessing the damage to the reversion, to the fact that the premises were on the term date sub-let to sub-tenants who had applied for new tenancies under the Landlord and Tenant Act 1954, and that it was almost certain that new tenancies would be granted.[142] The following passage from the judgment of Shaw L.J. suggests strongly that what was relevant was the position as it appeared at the term date, not the fact that new leases were in due course granted:

"The fact that 20 year leases were granted perhaps does not in itself matter ... but that there were leases in prospect and that there was a right on the part of the sub-lessees to look for new leases, and that the chances were that they would arise by negotiation or be granted by the court was a reality which ought and had to be recognised."

30–39    The same approach was taken in *Crown Estate Commissioners v Town Investments Ltd.*[143] In that case it was held that, in assessing damages where the premises were sub-let on the term date, the court could not take into account (1) the fact that the landlord subsequently carried out the work, and (2) the fact that the new leases subsequently granted to the sub-tenants contained defective service charge machinery by reason of which the landlord would not be able to recover all the costs of the work. The judge's reason was that there was no evidence that either event was operative or potential on the term date. He said in the course of his judgment:

"An example of a future event which might be admissible is this. Suppose that in *Family Management Limited v. Gray*[144] there had been firm evidence that one of the shop tenants was in financial difficulty as at the date of expiry and might well not be able to take up a new lease. If by the date of trial that potentiality had become an actuality and he had not taken up the new lease then that subsequent event would be admissible as corroboration of the evidence of what had previously been only a potentiality.

To vary the example: suppose that there was no such evidence of financial trouble as at the date of expiry of the lease but that by the date of trial the tenant had become insolvent. It seems to me that evidence of the insolvency would be inadmissible because it was not 'operative or potential' at the expiry of the lease *upon the evidence* [judge's emphasis] as at that date. The fact that the seeds of the insolvency very probably existed as at the date of expiry is irrelevant unless there was evidence that as at that date those seeds then existed."

The above authorities were referred to in *Sun Life Assurance Plc v Racal Tracs Ltd,*[145] in which two offers from prospective tenants were received prior to the term date. Mr. Recorder M. Black, QC held that the "limited extent" to which he

---

[142] This case is further considered in paras 30–33 to 30–35, above.
[143] [1992] 1 E.G.L.R. 61.
[144] [1980] 1 E.G.L.R. 46.
[145] [2000] 1 E.G.L.R. 138. The case went to the Court of Appeal ([2001] 1 W.L.R. 1562) on another point but no appeal was brought against the judge's decision on damages.

was permitted to look at events after the term date was as corroboration of the strength of the offers.[146] Likewise, in *Latimer v Carney*[147] Arden L.J. (with whom Wilson L.J. agreed) said that:

> "[S]ubsequent events can be taken into account if they relate to the bases of valuation and thus throw light upon it. Such events would include refurbishment or sale of the premises after the term date."

Reference should also be made to *Baroque Investments v Heis*,[148] in which the lease had been surrendered on terms which provided for (among other things) the release of the tenant's liability in respect of any breach of covenant "whether arising on or after, but not before, the date of" the surrender. On the same day as the surrender, the landlord relet the premises with an initial rent free period of 19 months. The landlord argued that although the normal rule was that damages for breach of the covenant to keep in repair were to be assessed as at the date of breach, i.e. the day before the surrender, nonetheless (i) the rule ought to be displaced in order more accurately to reflect the loss sustained, and (ii) (in accordance with the principle in *Bwllfa & Merthyr Dare Steam Collieries (1891) v Pontypridd Waterworks Co*[149]) the court was entitled to have regard to the facts that occurred after the relevant date rather than speculate. The Chancellor rejected both contentions. Damages were to be assessed by reference to the value of the reversion in and out of repair on the day before the surrender on the assumption that the lease was still continuing,[150] and the *Bwllfa* principle did not apply.

The above statements of principle represent an application in the dilapidations field of the well-known valuation principle that the valuer cannot have regard to matters which could not have been known about on the valuation date. Thus, in *Gaze v Holden*[151] a will granted options to purchase a farm at a value which was to be ascertained by "valuation in the usual way" as at the date of exercise of the option. The question arose as to whether regard could be had to the fact that a lease to which the farm was subject on the valuation date had been surrendered thereafter. Judge Finlay, QC, sitting as a judge of the Chancery Division, held that:

**30–40**

> "'Valuation in the usual way' means taking into account the events which have happened as at the date when the property falls to be valued … and taking into account not only the actualities at that date but the possibilities in relation to all the circumstances; and that the valuer has, as best he can, to form his own judgment as to how these possibilities and the various prospects that there are inherent in the then existing situation affect the valuation of the property as at that date; but that he is not entitled to take into account events which have happened

---

[146] See further *Currys Group Plc v Martin* [1999] 3 E.G.L.R. 165 for a discussion of the circumstances in which evidence of events occurring after the valuation date is helpful or admissible on the question of the market rent of the premises on the relevant date.
[147] [2006] 3 E.G.L.R. 13.
[148] [2012] EWHC 2886 (Ch.).
[149] [1903] A.C. 426.
[150] The identification of the day before the surrender as the relevant date for assessment would appear to have been a consequence of the particular way the relevant release in the surrender had been drafted , because where a lease has been surrendered, damages would ordinarily be assessed on the basis that the lease has ended and the landlord is in possession.
[151] [1983] 1 E.G.L.R. 147.

subsequently and which resolve how these various possibilities and prospects in fact turn out. To do so would be to introduce into the valuation a species of foresight which would not be available to any willing buyer or willing seller entering into a contract as at the date upon which the property falls to be valued."

Nonetheless, in practice, the steps taken by the actual landlord after the expiry of the lease in relation to disrepair may be compelling evidence of the extent to which the reversion has been damaged. An arrangement between the landlord and a third party cannot in itself affect the damages because (i) it is *res inter alios acta*,[152] and (ii) it occurred after the relevant date. However, in the ordinary case, it may afford cogent evidence of the way the hypothetical purchaser would have looked at the reversion on the term date. Thus, in *Mather v Barclays Bank Plc*[153] the court approached the valuation of the premises in their existing state by reference to the terms of the arrangement entered into by the actual landlord with a third party after the expiry of the lease.[154] Similarly, in *Shortlands Investments Ltd v Cargill Plc*[155] the court looked at the circumstances surrounding a reletting after the term date as evidence of the damage to the reversion on the term date. The same approach was taken by the court in *Firle Investments Ltd v Datapoint International Ltd*,[156] in which Mr Colin Reese, QC said:

"In my judgment the refurbishment of Inforex House which was planned, and in due course implemented, affords cogent evidence of the way in which the only realistically contemplatable hypothetical purchaser would have looked at the realistic commercial possibilities of the building at the term date."

30–41    On the same principle, the fact that the actual landlord relets the premises after the term date on terms that the works are done by the incoming tenant in return for a rent-free period, or a discounted rent until the first review, may afford cogent evidence of how the market would have regarded the disrepair. If the notional purchaser would have done the same thing, then he would prima facie have reduced his bid for the premises in disrepair by an amount equal to the value of the rent forgone. The diminution in the value of the reversion will therefore be the value of the lost rent. The same would apply in relation to any other type of transaction undertaken by the landlord after the term date. If, for example, without having done the repairs, he were to sell the premises shortly thereafter, the terms of the sale may be held to afford strong prima facie evidence of the value of the premises in their actual condition at the time.[157]

## Compulsory purchase

30–42    The fact that a compulsory purchase order has been, or will or may be, made in relation to the premises is a factor which must be taken into account in valuing the reversion for the purposes of the first limb of s.18(1). It may result in there

---

[152] See para.30–36, above.
[153] [1987] 2 E.G.L.R. 254.
[154] Above, at 260C.
[155] [1995] 1 E.G.L.R. 51.
[156] [2000] EWHC 105 (TCC).
[157] See *Culworth Estates Ltd v Society of Licensed Victuallers* (1991) 62 P. & C.R. 211.

being no damage to the reversion as a result of the disrepair. Thus, in *London County Freehold and Leasehold Properties Ltd v Wallis-Whiddett*,[158] the London County Council resolved on March 5, 1946, to make a compulsory purchase order in relation to property which included the demised premises. The lease expired on June 24, 1947. The order was made shortly afterwards on August 11, 1947, and confirmed by the Minister of Health on March 5, 1948. The landlords entered into negotiations with the acquiring authority, and on May 11, 1948 agreed a price of £14,000. The property was conveyed to the authority shortly thereafter. The landlords sued the tenants for £1,500, being the cost of repairs required under the lease. Humphreys J. held that the claim failed because there had been no damage to the value of the reversion.

However, the tenant cannot rely on a compulsory purchase order which is only made because of the state of repair of the property, and which would not have been made otherwise. Thus, in *Hibernian Property Co Ltd v Liverpool Corp*[159] a lease containing repairing covenants became vested in a local authority. The authority allowed the premises to fall into disrepair to such an extent that the premises were subsequently included (by the same authority) in a clearance area on the ground that they were unfit for human habitation. The premises were subsequently compulsorily acquired, and the landlord was entitled to site value compensation only. It was held that the authority was not entitled to rely on the first limb of s.18(1), and that the measure of damages was the difference between the value of the premises in repair on the date of notice of entry and site value.

## Requisitioning

If the premises are requisitioned, the relevant date for assessing damages remains the date of termination of the lease.[160] The reversion to be valued is the landlord's interest subject to the requisition.[161] As a result of the Landlord and Tenant (Requisitioned Land) Act 1944,[162] the tenant is not liable for defects occurring during the period of requisitioning. However, he remains liable for defects in existence at the beginning of the requisitioning period.[163] He is entitled to the benefit of any repairs carried out by the requisitioning authority prior to the termination of the lease.[164] Repairs carried out by the authority after the end of the lease are not to be taken into account because they are *res inter alios acta*.[165] However, the possibility of the requisitioning authority carrying out repairs after the end of the lease may be taken into account in valuing the reversion, as may the fact that the landlord will be unable to relet the premises while the requisition remains in force.[166]

**30–43**

---

[158] [1950] W.N. 180.
[159] [1973] 1 W.L.R. 751. This case is further considered in para.30–61, below.
[160] *Smiley v Townshend* [1950] 2 K.B. 311.
[161] Ibid.
[162] See para.20–16, above.
[163] *Smiley v Townshend*, above.
[164] Ibid.
[165] Ibid.
[166] Ibid.

## Where the landlord is himself a tenant[167]

**30–44**  Where the landlord is himself a tenant, the reversion in question means his leasehold interest. The damages recoverable from the sub-tenant will represent the amount by which the value of the head lease has been diminished by reason of the sub-tenant's breaches. It does not follow, however, that because the reversion is nominal, damages will likewise be nominal.[168] The effect of the sub-tenant's breaches may be to convert the reversion into a liability, so that it may have a minus value. Thus, in *Lloyds Bank Ltd v Lake*[169] the Official Referee, Sir Brett Cloutman, QC, said:

> "As a matter of simple logic it will not do to say that because the value of the property in repair is nil, therefore, the value is still nil if it is out of repair due to the breaches of the outgoing tenant. Not at all. The value is minus £X, which is what the tenant must pay someone to take over, first, the fag-end of the lease, and later the last moment of the lease. Certainly, the reversion is only momentary and notional … but this need not prevent it from being valued.[170]"

It follows that, where appropriate, the damage to the reversion will be assessed by reference to what the head tenant would have to pay someone to take an assignment of the head lease.

**30–45**  In *Ebbetts v Conquest*[171] the tenant under a 61-year lease containing repairing covenants sub-let the premises for the remainder of the term of the head lease less 10 days on identical repairing covenants. The tenant brought proceedings against the sub-tenant for damages for disrepair. At the time when the action was heard there were about three-and-a-half years of the term of the sub-lease remaining. The Official Referee awarded damages by taking what it would cost to put the premises into the covenanted state of repair, and then allowing a rebate to reflect the fact that the sub-lease still had some years to run. His assessment was upheld in the Court of Appeal and the House of Lords.[172]

It is not clear to what extent the decision in *Ebbetts v Conquest* turned on the fact that the sub-tenant was aware of the existence and terms of the head lease. All three members of the Court of Appeal relied on this fact.[173] However, Lord Herschell, who gave the only speech in the House of Lords,[174] did not refer to it. It is thought that the fact that the sub-tenant is unaware of the terms of the head lease will not prevent damages for breach of the repairing covenants in the sub-tenancy from being assessed by reference, where appropriate, to the diminution in value of the head lease by reason of the breaches. Thus, in *Lloyds*

---

[167] See further Ch.24, above.
[168] *Clow v Brogden* (1840) 2 M. & G. 39; *Davies v Underwood* (1857) 2 H. & N. 570; *Conquest v Ebbetts* [1896] A.C. 490; *Lloyds Bank Ltd v Lake* [1961] 1 W.L.R. 884.
[169] Above.
[170] See also *Shortlands Investments Ltd v Cargill Plc* [1995]1 E.G.L.R. 51, in which the landlord was itself a tenant holding under a lease with a negative value.
[171] [1896] A.C. 490.
[172] This case is further considered in para.28–24, above.
[173] See [1895] 2 Ch. 377 at 383, 384 and 387.
[174] [1896] A.C. 490.

*Bank Ltd v Lake*[175] the sub-tenant had no notice that his was an underlease, but it was nonetheless held that the measure of damages was the amount by which the value of the head lease had been diminished by reason of the sub-tenant's breaches.

The head tenant's action for damages failed in *Williams v Williams*.[176] In that case the head tenant entered the sub-let premises and carried out the works in order to avoid a forfeiture of the head lease. The works fell within the sub-tenant's liability under the covenant to repair in the sub-tenancy, but the head tenant's claim was dismissed on the ground that there was no damage to the reversion at the date of action brought. This case is considered in para.28–31, above, to which reference should be made. It is thought that insofar as it is inconsistent with the principles set out above, then it was wrongly decided.

## The burden of proof under the first limb of section 18(1)

It has been held that the burden of proving that s.18(1) does not operate to extinguish or reduce the damages recoverable at common law is on the landlord.[177] It is thought that this will only be the case where the landlord has not done, and does not intend to do, the repair works. In such a case, it is for the landlord to prove that the value of the reversion has nonetheless been diminished. Thus, in *Mather v Barclays Bank Plc*[178] new tenants covenanted to carry out improvements and substantial work costing over twice the cost of the repairs. It was held that the burden of proving a diminution in the value of the reversion was on the landlord.[179] However, where the landlord has done the repairs, or intends to do them, it is thought that the burden of proving that the damage to the reversion is less than the cost of the works is on the tenant.[180]

**30–46**

The corresponding paragraph to the above in the First Edition of this work was said by Neuberger J. in *Craven (Builders) Ltd v Secretary of State for Health*[181] accurately to explain the topic. The judge went on to hold that since the landlord had not done the works for which he was claiming, the burden of proving a diminution in the value of the reversion was on him. Likewise, in *Mason v TotalFinaElf UK Ltd*[182] Blackburne J. treated the burden of proof as depending on whether the works had been done but added that this was "subject to any actual valuation evidence before the court".

---

[175] [1961] 1 W.L.R. 884.
[176] (1874) L.R. 9 C.P. 659.
[177] *Crown Estate Commissioners v Town Investments Ltd* [1992] 1 E.G.L.R. 61; *Lintott Pty Developments v Bower* [2005] All E.R. (D) 454.
[178] [1987] 2 E.G.L.R. 254.
[179] *Mather v Barclays Bank Plc*, above, at 261E–F.
[180] See above, and see *Mather v Barclays Bank Plc*, above, at 261E.
[181] [2000] 1 E.G.L.R. 128.
[182] [2003] 3 E.G.L.R. 91.

## The effect of failure to adduce valuation evidence as to the diminution in the value of the reversion

**30–47**   Since the burden of proof under the first limb of s.18(1) is on the landlord,[183] there may be cases in which a failure to adduce satisfactory valuation evidence as to the diminution in the value of the reversion will result in the landlord failing to recover some or all of the sums he claims. Thus, in *Portman v Latta*[184] the demised premises were by the end of the lease unlettable as a private residence, but might have had a use as institutional premises. The landlord's evidence was that the cost of the repairs (£1,042 6s. 10d.) was necessarily the amount by which the value of the reversion had been diminished. However, no evidence was called as to the value of the reversion in repair, so that the court had nothing against which to compare the cost of the works. The judge rejected the landlord's evidence and assessed damages at £650.

However, the fact that the two valuations required by s.18(1) have not been undertaken does not relieve the court from having to consider the existence or otherwise of damage to the reversion, nor does it prevent the court, in appropriate circumstances, from concluding that such damage has occurred. Thus, in *Jones v Herxheimer*[185] the court assessed damages by reference to the cost of the work without specific valuation evidence as to the diminution in the value of the reversion. In *Crewe Services & Investment Corp v Silk*[186] (which concerned a claim for damages during the term) the county court judge had assessed damages by reference to the cost of the remedial work without hearing expert valuation evidence from either side. Robert Walker L.J. said:

> "I am sure that the judge would have been assisted by evidence of the effect of disrepair (caused by a tenant's breaches of covenant) on the value of the freehold interest in the farm if it had been put on the market, subject to and with the benefit of the tenancy, at the date of the hearing.
> ... I am, however, by no means sure that the judge needed evidence, beyond what was before him, for the simple proposition that a tenanted farm in a seriously bad state . is worth less than a tenanted farm where the tenant has complied with all his obligations...
> The true position is ... that general damages are at large, and the judge must do the best he can, just as the jury would have had to do when civil actions were heard by juries ...[187]
> Where a landlord claims damages for breach of a repairing covenant near the beginning or in the middle of the term of a long lease (and on the assumption that he gets leave under the Leasehold Property (Repairs) At 1938 as amended) he will, if he fails to lead evidence of diminution in the value of the reversion, run a serious risk of the court concluding that there has been no significant diminution. Where a tenant is defending such a claim towards the end of the term of the lease he will, if he fails to lead evidence that the diminution is much less than the cost of repairs, run a serious risk of the court accepting that cost (or that cost only slightly discounted) as the best evidence of diminution. In most cases the evidence before the court (even if imperfect and incomplete) will be more important than issues as to the burden of proof."

---

[183]   See para.30–46, above.
[184]   [1942] W.N. 97.
[185]   [1950] 2 K.B. 106. The facts are set out in para.30–15, above.
[186]   [1998] 2 E.G.L.R. 1.
[187]   This part of the judgment was cited and applied by H.H. Judge Reddihough (sitting as a judge of the High Court) in *Lintott Property Developments v Bower* [2005] All E.R. 454.

In *Latimer v Carney*[188] the landlords carried out the repairs for which they claimed, together with other works, in order to relet the premises. At the trial they adduced evidence of the estimated cost of the repairs set out in the schedule of dilapidations but not of the actual cost of the works carried out or of any resulting diminution in the value of the reversion. The judge at first instance dismissed the landlords' claim on the ground that they had failed to prove any damage to the value of the reversion. The Court of Appeal allowed the landlords' appeal. Even in the absence of expert evidence, diminution in the value of the reversion should have been inferred from the fact that the works had to be done before the premises could be relet and from the estimated costs of the repairs. The court awarded the landlord the estimated cost of the work to the roof, which they could show they had carried out, and the estimated cost of the other repairs subject to a discount of 60 per cent to take account of the uncertainty as to the extent to which the relevant disrepair affected the value of the reversion. Arden L.J. (with whom Wilson L.J. agreed) said in the course of her judgment (which contains a valuable discussion of the correct approach in cases where the landlord fails to adduce expert valuation evidence of the diminution in the value of the reversion resulting from the disrepair):

> "25. The effect of section 18 is, in any case where its application is in issue between the parties, to require the court to find the amount of the damage to the value of the reversion of the premises caused by the failure to repair. To do this the court has to find the difference between the value of the premises in disrepair on the open market and the value that the premises would have had if there had been no breach of the covenant to repair. It need not do more than find that this difference was at least as great as the amount claimed against the tenant. In an ideal world, the parties will agree the relevant values or alternatively they will have produced the evidence of a single expert as to those values, or, if the court has given permission for more than one expert, they will produce their experts' evidence together with a joint report from them identifying the differences between their views and the reasons for such differences so that the judge can come to a conclusion as to which expert evidence he prefers. But the failure to adduce expert evidence does not preclude a finding as to those values by other means because in many cases it will be obvious that the disrepair must have caused some damage to the value of the reversion and that the cost of doing the repairs is a reliable guide to the amount of that damage."

It follows that, whilst a failure to adduce valuation evidence as to the occurrence or non-occurrence of diminution in the value of the reversion will not necessarily be fatal, a well-advised party will usually ensure that such evidence is before the court.[189]

## THE SECOND LIMB OF S.18(1)

### The second limb of s.18(1)

The second limb of s.18(1) of the 1927 Act provides as follows:                     **30–48**

---

[188] [2006] 3 E.G.L.R. 13.
[189] In *Latimer v Carney* [2006] 3 E.G.L.R. 13, Arden L.J. quoted the corresponding passage in the Third Edition of this work, saying that it was advice "worth recalling".

"[A]nd in particular no damage shall be recovered for a breach of any such covenant or agreement to leave or put premises in repair at the termination of a lease,[190] if it is shown that the premises, in whatever state of repair they might be, would at or shortly after the termination of the tenancy have been or be pulled down, or such structural alterations made therein as would render valueless the repairs covered by the covenant or agreement."

The second limb was aimed at the injustice which resulted from the common law rule that the cost of the work could be awarded as damages even where the premises were going to be, or had been, demolished or altered.[191] Thus, the broad purpose of the second limb has been said to be[192]:

"[N]ot open to doubt. Before it was enacted, a landlord could recover damages from his tenant for breach of a covenant to deliver up in repair notwithstanding that the buildings were going to be pulled down or structurally altered in such a way as to make it useless to perform the covenant. The enforcement of the covenant in such circumstances was regarded as an unjust enrichment of the lessor and the legislature in section 18, sub-section 1, set itself to remove the injustice."

Notwithstanding the opening words "and in particular", the courts have tended to regard the second limb as a separate part of s.18(1), rather than merely as an example of a particular instance where there would be no damage to the reversion. For example, it was referred to by Lord Greene M.R. in *Salisbury v Gilmore*[193] as "the second branch" of s.18(1).[194] It follows that the second limb must be considered separately from the first, although in practice there may be a degree of overlap.[195]

## Differences between the first and second limbs

30–49    There are two principal differences between the first and second limbs. First, the first limb operates to limit damages. The second, by contrast, has the effect, where it applies, of extinguishing the right to damages altogether. Second, the first limb is objective, in the sense that the position of the actual landlord is immaterial to the question of what damage, if any, has been caused to the value of the reversion. The second limb is subjective, in that it is the state of mind of the actual landlord (or a relevant third party, such as the local authority) that is the relevant consideration.

---

[190] See para.29–20, in which the covenants to which s.18(1) applies are considered.
[191] See paras 29–06 to 29–10, above.
[192] *Salisbury v Gilmore* [1942] 2 K.B. 38.
[193] Above.
[194] Above, at 44. See also *Culworth Estates Ltd v Society of Licensed Victuallers* (1991) 62 P. & C.R. 211, per Dillon L.J.
[195] In *Shortlands Investments Ltd v Cargill Plc* [1995] 1 E.G.L.R. 51 the Official Referee regarded the second limb of s.18(1) as helpful in construing the first limb.

## The relevant date

The relevant date for the application of the second limb is the date of expiry of **30–50**
the lease. Where the lease expires by effluxion of time, the relevant date is the
term date.[196] Where the lease has been forfeited, the relevant date is the date of
the forfeiture.[197] Where the lease has been continued under Pt II of the Landlord
and Tenant Act 1954, the relevant date is the date on which it ends under the
provisions of that Act.

## The operation of the second limb

The second limb applies where, viewing the matter as at the relevant date: **30–51**

(1)     the premises are going to be pulled down on the relevant date; or
(2)     the premises are going to be pulled down shortly after the relevant date; or
(3)     such structural alterations as would render valueless the repairs covered by
        the covenant are going to be made on the relevant date; or
(4)     such structural alterations as would render valueless the repairs covered by
        the covenant are going to be made shortly after that date.[198]

Whether any of these apply is a question of fact. Lord Evershed M.R. put it
thus in *Keats v Graham*[199]:

> "What the court is required by the section to do is to reach a conclusion of fact: Aye or no, were
> these premises going to be pulled down as things were at the date of termination of the
> tenancy?"

It should be noted that it does not have to be the landlord who intends to pull
the premises down, or carry out structural alterations. An intention on the part of
some other relevant party, such as a local authority acting under statutory powers,
is sufficient.[200]

It is thought that the words "shortly after the termination of the tenancy" mean **30–52**
"within a short time after the termination of the tenancy". What is a short time is
a question of fact in each case. What must be asked is whether as at the term date,
having regard to all the circumstances, the relevant demolition or structural
alterations are likely to be carried out within a short time, or whether the period
which will elapse before anything is done is too long for it to be properly

---

[196] *Salisbury v Gilmore* [1942] 2 K.B. 38. See para.30–54, below.
[197] *Lordship Lane Property Co Ltd v Honesgran Property Co Ltd* (1962) E.G. 209. See paras 27–74
to 27–76, above.
[198] See generally *Salisbury v Gilmore*, above; *Keats v Graham* [1960] 1 W.L.R. 30. The second limb
was said by Lord Greene M.R. in the former to be "worded in a way which at first sight appears
crabbed and ungrammatical" (at 44).
[199] Above.
[200] *Salisbury v Gilmore*, above; *Keats v Graham*, above. *Hibernian Property Co Ltd v Liverpool Corp*
[1973] 1 W.L.R. 751 contains a suggestion to the opposite effect, but it is thought that it is incorrect.
Neither of the above cases is referred to in the judgment, although *Salisbury v Gilmore* was cited in
argument.

described as "short". In deciding what constitutes a short time, the fact that no legal entitlement to possession arises until the term date of the tenancy will no doubt be one of the many relevant considerations. Having regard to the policy underlying the second limb,[201] another relevant factor will presumably be the extent to which the time which will elapse before the work is to be done is such as to enable any benefit to be derived from the repair works.

The only two categories of work that qualify under the second limb are demolition and such structural alterations as would render valueless the repairs covered by the covenant. It follows that, where no demolition is to take place, any work that falls short of structural alteration will not bring the second limb into play even though it may render valueless the repairs. The references in the second limb to "the premises" and "the repairs covered by the covenant or agreement" suggest that the second limb will only apply where either the whole of the premises is to be demolished, or the effect of the structural alterations will be to render valueless the entirety of the repairs for which the landlord claims. Thus, in *Firle Investments Ltd v Datapoint International Ltd*[202] it was held that the second limb could not be relied on because repair works to the value of £15,242 would have survived the intended refurbishment.[203]

## The meaning of "structural alterations"

30–53    "Structural alterations" are not defined. In other contexts, a covenant in a lease of a luxury penthouse flat not to make any structural alterations has been held not to prohibit replacing steel external windows and doors with aluminium ones,[204] and for the purposes of Sch.8 to the Housing Act 1974, works amounting to structural alteration, extension or addition have been held to include the installation of a central heating system.[205] In the latter case, "structural" was defined to mean:

> "[S]omething which involves the fabric of the house as opposed to the provision merely of a piece of equipment. It matters not whether the fabric is load bearing or otherwise.[206]"

The following passage from the judgment of Judge White in *Pickering v Phillimore*[207] was quoted with approval[208]:

> "A house is a 'complex unity', particularly a modern house. 'Structural' implies concern with the 'constituent or material' parts of that unity. What are the 'constituent' or 'material' parts? In my judgment in any ordinary sense they involve more than simply the load bearing elements, for example, the four walls, the roof and the foundations. The constituent parts are

---

[201] See para.30–48, above.

[202] [2000] EWHC 105 (TCC).

[203] However, it appears to have been assumed in *Carmel Southend v Strachan & Henshaw* [2007] 3 E.G.L.R. 15 that the second limb of s.18(1) is capable of operating even where some of the repairs will survive the intended work.

[204] *Bent v Highcliff Developments Ltd* (unreported decision of Mr. Nicholas Warren, QC (sitting as a deputy judge of the High Court) dated August 6, 1999).

[205] *Pearlman v Keepers and Governors of Harrow School* [1979] Q.B. 56.

[206] Ibid., per Geoffrey Lane L.J.

[207] Unreported (May 10, 1976).

[208] *Pearlman v Keepers and Governors of Harrow School*, above, per Eveleigh L.J.

more complex than that. [He then suggested a definition of 'structural' as] ... appertaining to the basic fabric and parts of the house as distinguished from its decorations and fittings."

However, "structural alterations" do not include works of repair. In *Carmel Southend v Strachan & Henshaw*,[209] the tenant was liable for patch repairing the roof of an industrial unit by the replacement of the roof lights and a small number of roof sheets. Following the termination of the lease the landlord overclad the roof with new profile metal sheeting. Its claim for the cost of that work failed on the ground that, although the work could properly be described as repair, it went beyond the tenant's liability under the covenant. The tenant argued that the landlord's alternative claim for the cost of the lesser works was to be reduced by stripping out the cost of replacing the roof lights. That work had been superceded by the overcladding, which amounted to a "structural alteration" within the second limb of s.18(1). That argument was rejected. H.H. Judge Coulson, QC said in his judgment:

> "[63] The authorities suggest that the term 'structural alterations' is to be given a wide interpretation: see *Firle Investments Ltd v. Datapoint International Ltd* [2000] EWHC 105 (TCC) and *Pickering v. Phillimore* unreported 10 May 1976. However, these and other authorities all proceed on the (not unreasonable) assumption that the structural alterations are different from the repairs covered by the covenants, and that they are not (as would be the case if [the tenant's arguments were right]) one and the same.
>
> [64] In my judgment, this is the principal reason why the situation here is a long way from the sort of position with which the second limb of section 18 was designed to deal. Here, there was a straight fight between two different remedial schemes, both of which were described by the experts as repairs. I have decided that the lesser scheme was appropriate because it was reasonably and sensibly possible. However, the mere fact that [the landlord] undertook a more extensive and expensive repair scheme does not, in my view, trigger the second limb of section 18.
>
> ...
>
> [66] In addition, to the extent that it is relevant, I am doubtful whether the overcladding could be described as a structural alteration. As I have noted, the experts referred to it as a repair. Moreover, it was suggested that it might be a structural alteration because it imposed a greater loading on the steel frame. However, most repair work involves an increase, to a greater or lesser extent, to the loading imposed on the frame of a building. If that were the only test for a structural alteration, it might be very difficult to identify any work of repair that was not also a structural alteration. Again, that is plainly not what the second limb of section 18 was designed to address."

Subject to the above, it is thought that, having regard to the policy underlying the second limb,[210] the court would be likely to give a relatively wide meaning to "structural alterations", so as to ensure that the tenant does not have to pay damages for disrepair which will not survive works to be carried out on or shortly after the term date.[211]

---

[209] [2007] 3 E.G.L.R. 15. See para.12–09, above, where the facts are set out.
[210] See para.30–48, above.
[211] The corresponding sentence in the Second Edition of this work was adopted by the judge in *Firle Investments Ltd v Datapoint International Ltd* [2000] EWHC 105 (TCC).

## The degree of fixity of intention required

**30–54** An intention (usually, but not always,[212] on the part of the landlord) to pull down or carry out structural alterations must exist before the second limb will apply. Thus, in *Salisbury v Gilmore*[213] Lord Greene M.R. said:

> "[T]he crucial date is the date of termination of the lease. Once that date has passed, the tenant is no longer in a position to fulfil his covenant; and if it is shown that before that date arrives the landlord has decided to pull down the building and that this intention is still existing at that date, the requirements of [the second limb] are, in my opinion, satisfied."

The intention itself must therefore exist as at the term date, albeit that such intention may be to pull down or carry out structural alterations either on the term date or shortly thereafter.

**30–55** The classic definition of what is meant by "intention" in this context is that of Asquith L.J. in *Cunliffe v Goodman*[214]:

> "An 'intention' to my mind connotes a state of affairs which the party intending—I will call him X—does more than merely contemplate: it connotes a state of affairs which, on the contrary, he decides so far as in him lies, to bring about, and which, in point of possibility, he has a reasonable prospect of being able to bring about, by his own act of volition.
>
> X cannot, with any due regard to the English language, be said to 'intend' a result which is wholly beyond the control of his will. He cannot 'intend' that it shall be a fine day tomorrow: at most he can hope or desire or pray that it will. Nor, short of this, can X be said to 'intend' a particular result if its occurrence, though it may be not wholly uninfluenced by X's will, is dependent on so many other influences, accidents and cross-currents of circumstance that, not merely is it quite likely not to be achieved at all, but, if it is achieved, X's volition will have been no more than a minor agency collaborating with, or not thwarted by, the factors which predominately determine its occurrence. If there is a sufficiently formidable succession of fences to be surmounted before the result which X aims at can be achieved, it may well be unmeaning to say that X 'intended' that result."

Contrasting "intention" with "mere contemplation" he went on to say:

> "Not merely is the term 'intention' unsatisfied if the person professing it has too many hurdles to overcome, or too little control of events: it is equally inappropriate if at the material date that person is in effect not deciding to proceed but feeling his way and reserving his decision until he shall be in possession of financial data sufficient to enable him to determine whether the project will be commercially worthwhile."

On the facts of that case the landlord had not formed the necessary intention because:

> "Neither project moved out of the zone of contemplation—out of the sphere of the tentative, the provisional and the exploratory—into the valley of decision."

**30–56** In the same case Singleton L.J. said in the course of his judgment:

---

[212] See para.30–51, above. For the sake of simplicity, the relevant intention is treated in the following discussion as being that of the landlord.
[213] [1942] 2 K.B. 38.
[214] [1950] 2 K.B. 237.

"[T]here must be a decision on the part of the landlord. In one sense an intention to pull down may be the same thing, but it is not so unless it is a clearly formed intention, or a firm intention, in the sense that the landlord has made up his mind. Contemplation by the landlord is clearly not enough."

In his view, the second limb did not apply because:

"On the facts the landlord was contemplating pulling down and rebuilding; and probably she would have done so if she could have obtained approval of a scheme which was attractive commercially. On the other hand, [the local authority] might have inserted, as a term of their approval of a scheme, conditions as to selling price or rents which would have made it unattractive to the landlord."

It is clear from the above passages that "intention" comprises two distinct elements, both of which must be present if the second limb is to apply:

(1)    The landlord must have made up his mind to pull down, or carry out structural alterations. A provisional desire is not enough. He must have reached a definite decision. It does not matter if his decision is revocable, but it is not sufficient if he has not got beyond the stage of contemplating doing the work; and

(2)    There must be a reasonable prospect of the landlord being able to implement his decision. There must not be so many obstructions still to be overcome that he cannot properly be said to "intend" the work. If by the relevant date he has not obtained all necessary planning and other consents, and arranged finance, then it must be shown that he would be likely to be able to overcome these hurdles.

An example of the practical application of these requirements is *Firle Investments Ltd v Datapoint International Ltd*,[215] in which it was held that the landlord had the necessary intention to satisfy the second limb. As at the term date:    **30–57**

"[The landlord] was continuing to press ahead with what was in reality its long contemplated refurbishment plan. Unlike Lady Cunliffe who, prior to the term date, was contemplating an attractive possibility but simply feeling her way and reserving decision, [the landlord] had made a firm decision to refurbish Inforex House; the detail of the scheme had been sufficiently thought through for the purposes of practical commercial decision-making; [the landlord's] decision was naturally subject to possible review/revocation if something unexpected or untoward was to happen but, to borrow the words of Asquith L.J., [the landlord] had moved out of the zone of contemplation into the valley of decision."

Reference should further be made to the numerous cases on the meaning of "intention" in the context of s.30(1)(f) and (g) of the Landlord and Tenant Act 1954.[216]

---

[215] [2000] EWHC 105 (TCC).
[216] See Woodfall, Landlord and Tenant, Vol.2, paras 22.106 to 22.109.

## Subsequent changes of mind

**30–58**   What is relevant is the fate of the building as it appears on the term date. If on that date the landlord has a settled intention to demolish, then the fact that he subsequently changes his mind is irrelevant. Thus, in *Salisbury v Gilmore*,[217] the landlord decided before the lease ended that he would pull down the premises and construct a new building when the lease ended on September 29, 1939. That intention continued to subsist on the term date of the lease, but was not abandoned until October 5, 1939 following the outbreak of the Second World War. The landlord's claim for damages failed, the subsequent change of mind being held by the Court of Appeal to be irrelevant. It is thought that the converse must equally follow, so that if the landlord only forms an intention to demolish after the lease has ended, then the second limb does not prevent him recovering damages.[218]

## Events occurring after the relevant date

**30–59**   Events occurring after the term date of the lease will generally be irrelevant. Thus, in *Keats v Graham*[219] part of the demised premises consisted of a rear extension, for which a temporary planning permission had been granted. The permission expired on April 1, 1956. The landlord's application for an extension was turned down. Three months before the tenancy expired on March 27, 1957, the local authority wrote asking for a written assurance that the extension would be removed within 14 days. In May 1957, after the tenancy expired, the landlord let the premises to another tenant, and in October 1957 he applied for, and was granted, conditional permission to retain the rear extension until December 1, 1962. The Court of Appeal held that evidence of the events which occurred after the relevant date was not admissible, and that, as at the termination of the tenancy, the probabilities were that the premises were going to be pulled down, so that the landlord's claim was excluded by the second limb of s.18(1). Lord Evershed M.R. said in relation to evidence of subsequent events:

> "My own inclination, based on *Salisbury v. Gilmore*,[220] is that, strictly speaking, [evidence of these events was] not admissible. What the court is required by the section to do is to reach a conclusion of fact: Aye or no, were these premises going to be pulled down as things were at the date of termination of the tenancy? No doubt it may be said that, if some matter of fact is doubtful, later events may by reflection clarify and explain what had gone on before."

Sellers L.J. said in the course of his judgment:

---

[217] [1942] 2 K.B. 38.
[218] Cf. *Lordship Lane Property Co Ltd v Honesgran Property Co Ltd* (1962) 182 E.G. 209. Note, however, that the landlord's claim might still be precluded by the first limb of s.18(1) if it could be shown that as at the term date the premises had sufficient redevelopment potential for the site value even in repair to exceed the investment value. See para.30–29, above.
[219] [1960] 1 W.L.R. 30.
[220] [1942] 2 K.B. 38.

"I am inclined to think that in the majority of cases evidence of events after the material date for consideration would be immaterial and therefore inadmissible. Perhaps that ought to be qualified to this extent, that it may be that a future event may cast some light on an uncertain state of mind or an intention at a prior date. But that can very rarely happen. It would not be admissible, I think, to adduce evidence that at a later date than the material date for consideration the building was still standing, because that would not affect the issue for consideration: it would really be a statement as to what in fact had developed. I think that is clear from the nature of the inquiry stated in the section … If one is looking at evidence at a later date it may well be that it indicates a change of intention and does very little, if anything, to assist the inquiry as to what were the probabilities at the time when the lease came to an end."

*Keats v Graham* was followed by Sachs J. in *Lordship Lane Property Co Ltd v Honesgran Property Co Ltd.*[221] In that case the lease was forfeited by issue of proceedings on November 18, 1960. Sachs J. declined to admit evidence that in and after July 1961 the local authority intended to make a compulsory purchase order in relation to property which included the demised premises.

## The meaning of "in whatever state of repair they might be"

The second limb only applies where the premises, "in whatever state of repair they might be", would at or shortly after the termination of the tenancy have been or be pulled down or such structural alterations made as would render valueless the repairs. This means that the landlord must have intended to carry out the relevant demolition or structural alterations irrespective of the condition of the premises, i.e. even if the premises had been yielded up in repair. Thus, for example, a local authority which compulsorily acquires the premises for the purposes of securing and carrying out a redevelopment scheme will be caught by the second limb.[222]

30–60

However, the second limb does not apply where the works would not have been carried out if the premises had been yielded up in repair. Thus, in the Australian case of *Graham v The Markets Hotel Pty Ltd*[223] the tenant of a licensed hotel removed a lavatory, in breach of its covenant to repair. As a consequence the landlord was obliged to install new sanitary accommodation which, because of licensing requirements, involved alterations. The tenant relied on the Australian equivalent of the second limb of s.18(1) of the 1927 Act. His argument was rejected by the High Court of Australia. Latham C.J. said of the second limb:

"These words, in my opinion, are intended to cover a case where, even if the covenant had been fully observed, the premises would have been pulled down or structural alterations would have been made which would have rendered the repairs valueless. That is to say, the words 'in whatever state of repair they might be' mean 'irrespectively of the state of repair in which the premises might be'. In the present case the relevant structural alterations made by the plaintiffs were not made irrespectively of the state of repair in which the premises were left by the defendant. They were rendered necessary by the fact that the defendant had broken his covenant by yielding up the premises without any sanitary accommodation upon them."

---

[221] (1962) 182 E.G. 209.
[222] *Richard Parsons v Bristol CC* [2007] 3 E.G.L.R. 73 at [10].
[223] (1943) 67 C.L.R. 567.

**30–61**    Similarly, where the premises are left in such a bad state of repair that they are compulsorily acquired by the local authority for the purposes of redevelopment, the tenant cannot rely on the second limb. In *Hibernian Property Co Ltd v Liverpool Corp*[224] the tenant was the local authority. The premises were declared unfit for human habitation, and were subsequently included in a clearance area. Had the tenant complied with its repairing covenants, then the property would either have been excluded from the clearance area, or the compensation payable to the landlord would have exceeded what was in fact payable, namely, site value only. The tenant relied on s.18(1), contending that no damages were recoverable. Caulfield J. found in favour of the landlord. His first ground was that, on the facts, it had not been shown that the premises would at or shortly after the termination of the tenancy have been or be pulled down. His second reason was that:

> "I do not ... think that [section 18(1)] is even capable of being construed as enabling a municipal corporation, by its own failure to comply with covenants to repair so that the house has to be demolished, to contend that the second part gives it relief in a claim for damages for breach of covenant ... Can it be the law that a local authority can allow property of which it is the lessee to fall into disrepair in breach of its own covenant, then, having gone through the formalities of compulsory purchase, pay only site value? I do not think that it can be. As I see it, the corporation would be rewarding itself for breach of its own obligation."

In *Lordship Lane Property Co Ltd v Honesgran Property Co Ltd*[225] the premises were designated unfit for human habitation, and the local authority intended to acquire them compulsorily. The result of this would have been that the landlord would have been entitled to site value only by way of compensation. The order had not been made by the date of the trial. Sachs J. found in favour of the landlord on the ground that the intention to make a compulsory purchase order had not existed on the term date of the lease, and evidence of what happened after the lease was inadmissible.[226] However, he also held in the alternative that:

> "[[T]he landlord] would, in my view, be entitled to the same measure of damages even if that evidence were admissible. It is the default of the defendants which has directly caused the position, if it arises, that there will be a compulsory acquisition upon a site value basis, rather than that of a market value basis, and the difference between those two figures is greater than the amount required to repair the premises ... In those circumstances, section 18 of the 1927 Act provides no obstacle to the plaintiffs recovering [the cost of repairs]."

## Service of a s.25 notice specifying ground (f)

**30–62**    It is sometimes argued that a landlord of business premises, who serves on the tenant a s.25 notice stating that he would oppose an application for the grant of a new tenancy on the ground set out in s.30(1)(f) of the Landlord and Tenant Act

---

[224] [1973] 1 W.L.R. 751.

[225] (1962) 182 E.G. 209.

[226] See para.30–59, above.

1954,[227] is thereby prevented from claiming damages for disrepair. However, the position is less clear-cut than this. It may be that in certain circumstances the notice would be held to give rise to an estoppel, although it is doubtful whether the mere service of the notice without more would suffice. All that the notice asserts is that if the tenant applies for a new tenancy, then whoever is the landlord at the time of the hearing will oppose on ground (f). It is thought that for an estoppel to arise, there would need to be some more definite representation that the landlord intended to carry out work the effect of which would be to render valueless any repairs carried out by the tenant. There would also need to be reliance on the representation by the tenant, for example, by vacating the premises in the belief that the landlord intended to redevelop and that no claim for dilapidations would therefore be made.

The notice may also be relevant where the issue is whether the landlord had an intention falling within the second limb of s.18(1) of the 1927 Act. It is thought that the notice on its own would not be conclusive evidence of this, since the relevant date will be the term date and the notice will have been served at least six months before that date. However, it is thought that the notice will constitute some evidence of the requisite intention. The weight to be given to it in any particular case will depend on what other evidence is available and what explanation the landlord puts forward for having served it.

### Burden of proof under the second limb of section 18(1)

The burden of proving that either part of the second limb of s.18(1) applies is on the tenant.[228]

**30–63**

## CONTRACTING OUT OF OR AVOIDING S.18(1)

### Contracting out of s.18(1)

Section 18(1) does not (unlike, for example, s.19 of the same Act) say that it applies "notwithstanding any express provision to the contrary", nor does it contain any express anti-avoidance provisions. However, its purpose was to mitigate against the rigour of the common law measure of damages (as it was then understood),[229] which Parliament clearly regarded as unfair and unsatisfactory.[230] It is expressed in mandatory terms, that is to say, it provides that damages for breach of a repairing covenant "shall in no case" exceed the diminution in the

**30–64**

---

[227] i.e. that the landlord intends on the termination of the current tenancy to demolish or reconstruct the premises comprised in the holding or a substantial part of those premises or to carry out substantial work of construction on the holding or part thereof and that he cannot reasonably do so without obtaining possession of the holding.
[228] *Salisbury v Gilmore* [1942] 2 K.B. 38; *Cunliffe v Goodman* [1950] 2 K.B. 237; *Crown Estate Commissioners v Town Investments Ltd* [1992] 1 E.G.L.R. 61; *P & O Property Holdings Ltd v Secretary of State for the Environment, Transport and the Regions* [2000] 1 P.L.S.C.S. 37 (in which this was common ground).
[229] See paras 29–06 to 29–08, above.
[230] See para.29–08, above.

value of the reversion, and that no damage "shall be recovered" if it is shown that the premises would have been pulled down or structurally altered. Given this, it is not thought that the parties to a lease containing a tenant's repairing covenant can validly contract out of s.18(1) by an express agreement that it shall not apply to a claim for damages for dilapidations under their lease, or that it shall operate in some modified form, or that some other approach to the assessment of damages is to be used.

In *Moss Empires Ltd v Olympia (Liverpool) Ltd*,[231] the tenant covenanted "to expend during each year of the said term on … repairs and decoration a sum of five hundred pounds and at the end of each year of the said term to produce to the lessors evidence of such expenditure or to pay to them at the end of each such year a sum equal to the difference between the amount so expended and five hundred pounds …". The tenant spent less than £500 on repairs in certain years, and the landlord claimed the difference between what had been spent and £500 for each of the relevant years. The tenant contended (among other things) that the landlord's claim was a claim for damages, which fell foul of s.18(1). That claim succeeded (by a majority) in the Court of Appeal but failed in the House of Lords, where it was held that on the proper construction of the covenant, the tenant had been given the alternative of either spending £500 a year on repairs or spending a lesser sum, and paying the difference to the landlord. The landlord's claim for the difference was not a claim for damages but a claim in debt, to which s.18(1) did not apply. It was not suggested in any of the speeches that s.18(1) was anything other than mandatory in its operation.

## Possible methods of avoidance

**30–65**  If the above is correct, it would follow that a straightforward covenant by the tenant to pay the cost of the works required to remedy any breaches of the repairing covenant at the end of the term would be ineffective. However, a claim for the cost of works under a clause which provides that, if the tenant is in breach of his repairing covenants during the term, the landlord may serve notice requiring him to carry out remedial works and (if the tenant does not do so within the stipulated time) the landlord may enter the premises, carry out the works and recover the cost of doing so from the tenant, is not a claim for damages.[232] Section 18(1) does not therefore apply to such a claim.[233] It would therefore be open to the landlord, in principle, to invoke a clause of this type in good time whilst the term subsists so as to avoid any potential difficulties under s.18(1) once the term has ended. Indeed, the authors have experience of at least one property company which instructed its solicitors, acting on the grant of an entire office building, to draft the lease on the basis that all major repairs (excepting only internal decorative repairs) should be the responsibility of the landlord during the term, with an obligation on the tenant to reimburse in full the landlord's costs of doing so. The resulting scheme was very similar to a conventional service charge regime such as would commonly be found in multi-let premises where, as a

---

[231] [1939] A.C. 544.

[232] *Jervis v Harris* [1996] Ch. 195. See further para.28–39, above.

[233] Although the tenant may have various other defences: see para.28–32 et seq., above.

matter of practicality, the landlords undertake the obligation to carry out major works (making individual tenants liable only for the interior of their own premises), the cost of such works being funded through service charges paid on a proportionate basis by all the tenants. Such a scheme (even when applied to a whole building) would be outside the scope of s.18(1), because the tenant undertakes no repairing obligation (and accordingly can never be in breach so as to put any claim against him within s.18(1)) and the claim against the tenant for reimbursement is clearly a claim for debt, not damages.

The usual form of covenant only operates during the term, but there is no obvious reason why the same principle should not apply in relation to works carried out after the lease has ended. If so, a covenant by the tenant to pay the costs incurred by the landlord in carrying out any works necessary to remedy any breaches of the tenant's covenants which are found to exist on the term date ought, in principle, to be effective without the landlord needing to prove any diminution in the value of his reversion.[234] However, the landlord will still need to spend his own money in advance of a decision from the court as to what breaches exist, what remedial works are required, and what costs are justified.[235]

[234] Cf. the form of covenant in *Bruntwood 2000 First Properties Ltd v British Telecom Plc* (unreported decision of H.H. Judge Pelling QC, sitting as a High Court Judge, dated December 11, 2008), considered in para.28–37, above.
[235] See the discussion in 28–32 et seq., above.

[755]

CHAPTER 31

## VALUATIONS UNDER THE FIRST LIMB OF S.18(1) OF THE LANDLORD AND TENANT ACT 1927: WORKED EXAMPLES

### INTRODUCTORY

The limitations imposed by s.18(1) of the Landlord and Tenant Act 1927 on the quantum of damages recoverable for breach of a covenant to repair have already been considered in Ch.30, above. As has been seen, the relevant limitation is that such damages cannot exceed the amount by which the value of the landlord's reversion has been diminished by reason of the breach in question. The object of the valuation exercise is therefore to arrive at the diminution in the value of the landlord's reversion attributable to the tenant's failure to carry out the relevant repair works. Detailed valuations are not always required for this exercise. In some cases it will be obvious that the value of the reversion must have been damaged by an amount at least equal to the cost of the works of repair, and the court may be prepared to proceed without formal valuation evidence of this.[1] In most cases, however, it will be necessary to carry out detailed valuations of the landlord's interest in the premises at the relevant date in and out of repair.

31–01

This Chapter considers the basic approach to s.18(1) valuations, with particular reference to the more common methods by which valuers arrive at capital values for properties in and out of repair. It is not intended to be comprehensive, and reference should be made to the relevant valuation textbooks for a fuller treatment. The discussion is followed by worked examples of the sort of valuations that might be carried out in practice.

### THE BASIC VALUATION APPROACH

#### The two valuations required by s.18(1)

The application of s.18(1) involves two valuations of the landlord's reversionary interest, one on the assumption that the works of repair necessary to satisfy the tenant's obligations have been carried out, and the other (which represents the factual position at the relevant date) on the assumption that those works have not been done. These two valuations will be referred to respectively as the "value in repair" and the "value out of repair". Both involve capital valuations. Since the object of the exercise is to isolate the impact on value of the disrepair, it follows

31–02

---

[1] See paras 30–15 to 30–17 and 30–47, above.

that in all respects other than the disrepair, the valuations must be based on identical assumptions so as to compare like with like.[2] Accordingly, both valuations share the following features:

(1) where the claim is brought following the expiry of the lease, the valuation date is that of termination of the lease; where the claim is made during the term of the lease, the date is that of the hearing;[3]

(2) the subject matter of the valuation is the immediate landlord's reversionary interest in the demised premises;

(3) the market conditions by reference to which the two valuations are carried out are the same although their effect may not be the same as regards both valuations;

(4) external factors affecting the valuation, such as planning constraints and third party rights, are the same although, again, their effect may not be the same for each valuation.

Although the general valuation approach is apparent from the decided cases,[4] s.18(1) does not itself specify any valuation criteria to be adopted by the valuer in valuing the reversion. It is thought that there is no reason in principle why the valuer should not proceed by reference to the definition of market value in the RICS Appraisal and Valuation Manual (the "Red Book")[5] save to the extent that any part of this is excluded by the particular circumstances of the valuation in question.[6]

## Arriving at a capital value

**31–03**     In some cases the valuer may be able to arrive at a capital value by the direct comparison method, i.e. by looking at prices paid for comparable properties in the same condition as the actual or assumed condition of the subject premises and making such adjustments as he considers appropriate. For example, where the premises consist of a house in a residential area it may be relatively straightforward to value in and out of repair by reference to sale prices achieved for similar houses in differing states of repair in the same road or area. However, it is unlikely that such relatively straightforward comparison will be possible in relation to commercial property, although the valuer may nonetheless find the price achieved on an actual sale of the property chronologically close to the

---

[2] As Blackburne J. said in *Mason v. TotalFinaElf UK Limited* [2003] E.G.L.R. 91: "... the purpose of the exercise is to isolate the effect on value of the tenant's failure to do the relevant works, from which it follows that the only variable between the two valuations is the works. All other factors are constants."

[3] See paras 28–21 and 30–07, above. Valuing as at the trial date may present a problem for a valuer preparing his report, since the valuation date is likely to be some time away and may even be unknown at the date of writing the report. In practice, the appropriate course will usually be to adopt the date of the report as the valuation date but to make it clear that the valuer's view may alter if market conditions change between then and the date of the trial.

[4] See para.30–02 et seq. above.

[5] See the current edition dated March 2012, and in particular VS 3.2. See also GN2, GN4 and GN5.

[6] And save that there would appear to be no reason for excluding the bid of a special purchaser.

termination of the lease a helpful guide to the value in repair or the value out of repair, as the case may be. The commonest method in such cases is to assess a capital figure by reference to the estimated income that the premises will generate (a) in repair and (b) out of repair. This involves in each case the following basic steps:

(1)   The valuer assesses the estimated annual rental value ("ERV") of the premises. This is usually done by reference to letting transactions of comparable properties (although in relation to the out of repair valuation, such transactions may not exist or be hard to compare), and is a matter of valuation judgement;

(2)   The valuer then decides what percentage rate of return a purchaser of the premises would require on his investment. This is known as the yield, and is usually assessed by reference to transactions comprising investment sales of comparable properties with comparable interests. Determining the appropriate yield is a matter of judgement and will generally be more subjective than the assessment of rental value. The difficulty may be compounded by the fact that no reliable investment sale comparisons can be found, especially in relation to the out of repair valuation, because most investment transactions will be on the basis that the tenant is liable for repair, and it is often or usually assumed that he has therefore performed his covenants. From the yield is derived the multiplier (the years' purchase) to apply to the ERV (deferred where appropriate) to arrive at the capital value;

(3)   Lastly, the valuer deducts from the resulting capital value figure the fees and costs the hypothetical purchaser would incur in acquiring the premises, as well as those he would be expect to incur disposing of the interest.

In reality, the exercise is invariably more complex, because of the need to reflect such matters as when the income steam will become available, what holding and marketing costs will be incurred until the premises are fully let, and the nature and cost of the works (whether repairs or more extensive works) that can be expected to be carried out and when. These matters will be directly influenced by the expectations and requirements of the market at the relevant time

**31–04**

A critical question in a s.18(1) valuation will often be the extent to which the ERV is affected by the state of repair of the premises. This will depend on market conditions at the valuation date. In addition, the yield which the notional purchaser will require may differ according to the state of repair (unless the disrepair is not significant): the condition of the premises out of repair may be such that the purchaser would regard them as a riskier investment than he would if they were in repair, and he would require a higher yield, with the result that the years' purchase to be applied to the ERV would be lower than that which would be appropriate for a valuation in repair.

## WORKED EXAMPLES

### The assumed facts

**31–05**   The following assumed facts are common to each of the worked examples that follow:

(1)   The building is a self-contained office block built about 20 years ago. The total floor area is 20,000 square feet. There are two passenger lifts. The heating is by means of a central boiler in the basement which serves radiators on each floor. There are outdated suspended ceilings. There are no raised floors and no air conditioning. There is no car parking.

(2)   The building was let under a lease granted for 15 years containing covenants on the part of the tenant to repair and yield up in repair, and to decorate at specified intervals and in the last year of the term (save in Example VI, where each floor was let individually to the same tenant on pro rata full repairing and decorating terms).

(3)   The lease expired on December 25, last year and the tenant vacated on that date.

(4)   The following works are required to comply with the tenant's covenants: the asphalt roof covering needs complete renewal; the exterior needs cleaning; the lift cars, lift machinery and central heating boiler and pipework need overhauling; some wiring and light fittings need to be replaced; some of the toilet fittings need to be replaced; the entire premises need to be redecorated internally; and the individual floors need to be recarpeted.

(5)   The total cost of the works is £225,000 including fees and VAT and the works would take in the order of six months to complete.

(6)   The existing planning use is as offices.

(7)   (Other than in Example V and Example VI), the entire building is vacant on the valuation date.

For the sake of simplicity, (i) the examples omit holding costs (such as finance costs, rates, security and insurance), and purchase, disposal and marketing costs; (ii) it has been assumed that the influence of VAT is neutral; (iii) deferment of income during works and marketing periods has been ignored; and (iv) years' purchase figures are expressed on the basis that rent is receivable annual in arrear (although liability to pay rent quarterly in advance is the norm).

### Comparison with the common law claim

**31–06**   For the reasons already explained elsewhere,[7] the diminution in the value of the reversion resulting from the tenant's breaches constitutes the cap on the amount of damages recoverable: it is not itself the measure. It is necessary in every case where s.18(1) applies to compare the relevant diminution with the amount of

---

[7] See paras 29–05 and 29–08, above.

damages recoverable at common law.[8] The damages recoverable by the landlord are limited to the diminution in the value of the reversion where this is less than the common law figure: otherwise, they are the common law figure. The following worked examples are concerned only with assessing the diminution in the value of the reversion, and the comparison exercise has not been undertaken. It is necessary to remember, however, that in practice it is a necessary part of the exercise of arriving at the overall figure recoverable by the landlord.

## The valuer's approach

In assessing the capital values in and out of repair, the valuer must consider each of the possible courses open to the hypothetical purchaser on the valuation date, and ask himself which the purchaser would be most likely to adopt. Those possibilities are: to do all the works and then relet; to do some only of the works and then relet; to do none of the works and try to relet immediately; to redevelop the premises; to "mothball" the premises (with or without a "soft strip") (i.e. to shut the premises down and await a change in the market[9]); and to carry out works of refurbishment (with or without at the same time doing some or all of the repair and decoration works) and then relet. Some of these may rule themselves out or in without the need for detailed consideration. For example, if the roof is leaking badly, some work may have to be done to it whatever decision is made. Deciding what other works would be undertaken will usually involve carrying out valuations on different assumptions to see which throws up the highest value out of repair (and therefore the lowest diminution). A criticism which is sometimes fairly made of some s.18(1) valuations which arrive at the conclusion that the diminution equates to the cost of the remedial works is that, by proceeding on the assumption that the hypothetical buyer would do the work, they necessarily assume what they set out to prove. In reality, of course, the valuer must first establish (by valuation or otherwise) that the buyer would in fact do some or all of the repair works before he is able to conclude that the cost of such works is relevant to value.

31–07

The following are examples of the way the diminution might be arrived at by the valuer in a wide variety of different market conditions. They are intended as illustrations only: in reality, the position will often be considerably more complicated.

---

[8] The common law measure is considered in Ch.29, above.
[9] See *Craven (Builders) Limited v Secretary of State for Health* [2000] 1 E.G.L.R. 128 (considered in para.30–29, above) in which the least unlikely buyer was found to be a person speculating on a market improvement and prepared to hold the property for two or three years while making up his mind what to do.

## Example I

**31–08** In this example, market conditions are such that in the valuer's view the buyer would carry out the totality of the works before reletting. The ERV in repair is £400,000, three months would have to be allowed for marketing on completion of the works, and a rent-free period of three months would have to be given to secure a letting.

**IN REPAIR**

| | | |
|---|---|---:|
| ERV 20,000 x sq ft £20/ft$^2$ | | £400,000 |
| Years' purchase in perpetuity @ 8% | | 12.5 |
| | | £5,000,000 |

*Less*

| | | |
|---|---|---:|
| Loss of rent during (i) marketing period: | 3 months | |
| Loss of rent during (ii) rent-free period: | 3 months | |
| | 6 months | £200,000 |
| **VALUE IN REPAIR:** | | **£4,800,000** |

**OUT OF REPAIR**

| | | |
|---|---|---:|
| ERV 20,000 sq ft x £20/ft$^2$ | | £400,000 |
| Years' purchase in perpetuity @ 8.25% | | 12.1325 |
| | | £4,853,000 |

*Less*

| | | |
|---|---|---:|
| Cost of works | | £225,000 |
| Loss of rent during (i) works period: | 6 months | |
| Loss of rent during (ii) marketing period: | 3 months | |
| Loss of rent during (iii) rent-free period: | 3 months | |
| | 1 year | £400,000 |
| | | £625,000 |
| **VALUE OUT OF REPAIR** | | **£4,228,000** |
| **DIMINUTION IN VALUE** | | **£572,000** |

## Example II

**31–09** In this example, the valuer's view is that the purchaser would decide that only some of the works affect value. The remainder are not worth doing because they would not result in a sufficiently increased ERV to justify the cost.[10] The buyer

---

[10] Note that in practice the valuer would only be able to arrive at this conclusion by carrying out at least one other valuation to identify the justification.

would spend £50,000 on the works. The ERV on completion of those works is £390,000. The marketing and rent-free periods are as in Example I.

## IN REPAIR

| | | |
|---|---|---|
| ERV 20,000 sq ft x £20.00/ft$^2$ | | £400,000 |
| Years' purchase in perpetuity @ 8% | | 12.5 |
| | | £5,000,000 |

*Less*

| | | |
|---|---|---|
| Loss of rent during (i) marketing period: | 3 months | |
| Loss of rent during (ii) rent-free period: | 3 months | |
| | 6 months | £200,000 |

| | | |
|---|---|---|
| VALUE IN REPAIR: | | £4,800,000 |

## OUT OF REPAIR

| | | |
|---|---|---|
| ERV 20,000 sq ft x £19.50/ft$^2$ | | £390,000 |
| Years' purchase in perpetuity @ 8.25% | | 12.1325 |
| | | £4,731,675 |

*Less*

| | | |
|---|---|---|
| Loss of rent during (i) marketing period: | 3 months | |
| Loss of rent during (ii) rent-free period: | 3 months | |
| Loss of rent during (iii) works period: | 6 months | |
| | 1 year | £390,000 |
| | | £50,000 |
| Cost of works | | £440,000 |

| | | |
|---|---|---|
| VALUE OUT OF REPAIR | | £4,291,675 |
| **DIMINUTION IN VALUE** | | **£508,325** |

## Example III

In this example, the valuer takes the view that the buyer would decide that none of the works would result in an increased ERV, and it is most worthwhile to try to relet the building in its existing state. The ERV in repair is £380,000 p.a., a marketing period of four months would be necessary and a rent-free period of nine months would need to be given to the new tenant. The ERV out of repair is likewise £380,000 p.a., it would take nine months to find a tenant, and the tenant would need to be given a 12-month rent-free period and a break clause after three years to induce him to enter into a letting. The appropriate yield for the premises in repair is 8.25% (producing a years' purchase of 12.1325), whereas that for the

**31–10**

premises out of repair is 9% (giving a multiplier of 11.11). Despite the disrepair, it is assumed for the purposes of the example that the tenant will take a full repairing lease.

**IN REPAIR**

| | | |
|---|---|---|
| ERV 20,000 sq ft x £19.00/ft$^2$ | | £380,000 |
| Years' purchase in perpetuity @ 8.25% | | 12.1325 |
| | | £4,610,350 |

*Less*

| | | |
|---|---|---|
| Loss of rent during (i) marketing period: | 4 months | |
| Loss of rent during (ii) rent-free period: | 9 months | |
| | 1.083 years | £411,540 |

| | | |
|---|---|---|
| VALUE IN REPAIR: | | £4,198,810 |

**OUT OF REPAIR**

| | | |
|---|---|---|
| ERV 20,000 sq ft x £19.00/ft$^2$ | | £380,000 |
| Years' purchase in perpetuity @ 9%[11] | | 11.11 |
| | | £4,221,800 |

*Less*

| | | |
|---|---|---|
| Loss of rent during (i) marketing period: | 9 months | |
| Loss of rent during (ii) rent-free period: | 12 months | |
| | 1.75 years | £665,000 |

| | | |
|---|---|---|
| VALUE OUT OF REPAIR: | | £3,556,800 |

| | | |
|---|---|---|
| **DIMINUTION IN VALUE** | | **£642,010** |

## Example IV

**31–11**    In this example, the valuer considers that the buyer would decide that the course which produces the highest capital value would be to carry out a scheme of refurbishment consisting of stripping out and replacing all mechanical and electrical services, including the existing central heating plant; installing new external cladding and window units; redesigning and refitting the toilets; and installing raised floors, suspended ceilings (with upgraded lighting) and perimeter trunking. Carrying out this scheme would result in approximately 80% of the repair and decoration work being negated. The refurbishment scheme would cost £1m. inclusive of fees but exclusive of VAT and take 12 months to complete; the relevant remaining repair and decoration works would cost an additional £50,000 and take an extra net period of one month to carry out; the ERV on completion of

---

[11] The yield has been increased partly to reflect the disadvantage of the tenant's break clause.

all the works is £600,000 p.a. Three months would need to be allowed for marketing following completion of the works, and a rent-free period of three months would be necessary.

## IN REPAIR

| | | |
|---|---|---:|
| ERV 20,000 sq ft x £30.00/ft² | | £600,0000 |
| Years' purchase in perpetuity @ 7% | | 14.286 |
| | | £8,571,600 |

*Less*

| | | | |
|---|---|---|---:|
| Cost of refurbishment works | | | £1,000,000 |
| Loss of rent during (i) marketing period: | | 3 months | |
| Loss of rent during (ii) rent-free period: | | 3 months | |
| Loss of rent during (iii) works period: | | 12 months | |
| | | 1.5 years | £900,000 |
| | | | £1,900,000 |
| VALUE IN REPAIR | | | £6,671,600 |

## OUT OF REPAIR

| | | |
|---|---|---:|
| ERV 20,000 sq ft x £30.00/ft² | | £600,000 |
| Years' purchase in perpetuity @ 7.5%[12] | | 13.33 |
| | | £7,998,000 |

*Less*

| | |
|---|---:|
| Cost as above: | £1,900,000 |
| Cost of works (of repair): | £50,000 |
| Loss of rent during repair works period (1 month): | £50,000 |
| | £2,000,000 |
| VALUE OUT OF REPAIR | £5,998,000 |
| **DIMINUTION IN VALUE** | **£673,600** |

It is to be noted that in this example the "In repair" valuation is really an "In repair and improved" valuation, and the works of repair which feature in the valuation are only those works which are not negated by the works of improvement. Nonetheless it is considered that this approach complies with s.18(1), assuming always that the underlying facts, and market conditions, justify it.

---

[12] A higher yield is used as the interest out of repair carries a greater risk and is less attractive, which is not fully reflected in the other adjustments. An alternative valuation method would be to undertake a development appraisal which builds in a developer's profit. It is for the valuer to judge when a development appraisal approach is more appropriate. Clearly, the more development-orientated the works, the more likely it will be that such an approach can be justified

## Example V

**31–12**     In this example, two floors of the building are sub-let on terms that the sub-tenants repair and decorate the interior of the sub-let premises and contribute by way of service charge to the cost of repairing and decorating the structure, exterior and common parts. The sub-tenancies continued after the expiry of the head lease under Pt II of the Landlord and Tenant Act 1954, and the sub-tenants have applied for new tenancies. It is assumed for the purposes of this example that it is reasonably likely, though not entirely certain, that both sub-tenants will take new tenancies of the space they occupy at rents which will not be reduced by reason of the disrepair to the sub-let premises.[13] It is also assumed that those new tenancies will be granted nine months after the expiry of the headlease, and in the meantime the sub-tenants will be liable for interim rents totalling £177,500. The valuer takes the view that the hypothetical buyer would carry-out only the repair and decoration works to the vacant floors at a cost of £55,000. He would also carry-out the external repair works at a cost of £90,000, of which £45,000 would be recoverable from the sub-tenants by way of service charge. Such works would not interfere with occupation or marketing. Each set of works would run concurrently, and would take three months to complete. The ERV of the vacant floors is £200,000 p.a. A reasonable marketing period for the vacant floors would be three months following completion of the works, and rent-free periods of three months would be necessary to attract new tenants to take leases each of the vacant floors.

**IN REPAIR**

| | |
|---|---:|
| ERV 20,000 sq ft x £20.00/ft$^2$ | £400,000 |
| Years' purchase in perpetuity @ 8% | 12.5 |
| | £5,000,000 |

*Less*

| | |
|---|---:|
| Interim rent shortfalls (say 10,000 sq ft @ 15% of ERV for 9 months) | |
| | £22,500 |
| | £4,977,500 |

*Less*

Loss of rent during (i) marketing period:   3 months
on half of
building

---

[13] See paras 30–33 to 30–35, above.

| | | |
|---|---|---|
| Loss of rent during (ii) rent-free period: | 3 months on whole building[14] | |
| | 6 months | £150,000 |
| **VALUE IN REPAIR:** | | **£4,827,500** |
| **OUT OF REPAIR** | | |
| ERV 20,000 sq ft x £20,00/ft$^2$ | | £400,000 |
| Years' purchase in perpetuity @ 8.5% | | 11.765 |
| | | £4,706,000 |
| *Less* | | |
| Interim rent shortfalls as above: | | £22,500 |
| Cost of works on vacant floors: | | £55,000 |
| Irrecoverable cost of works to vacant floors: | | £45,000 |
| Loss of rent during marketing and rent free periods as above: | | £150,000 |
| Loss of rent during works period (3 months on half of the building):[15] | | £50,000 |
| | | £322,500 |
| **VALUE OUT OF REPAIR:** | | **£4,383,500** |
| **DIMUNITION IN VALUE** | | **£444,000** |

## Example VI

In this example, each floor was originally let individually to the same tenant co-terminously on pro rata full repairing and decorating terms. At the end of the leases the tenant vacated two floors, having six months before agreed and entered into the renewal of its tenancies on the other two floors on a single lease for a ten year term effective from the expiry of the then existing leases. Since then, the prospects for rental growth have reduced. The new lease included a tenant's break option at the end of the fifth year, and the agreed rent was £220,000 per annum. The hypothetical buyer, in the valuer's view, would carry out repair and decoration works to the vacant floors at a cost of £55,000 but not a further £20,000 that the actual owner intends to spend on brickwork cleaning, as it is considered that this will not add to rental or capital value or aid re-letting in any material way. The hypothetical buyer would also carry out external repair works

31–13

---

[14] This is taken on the whole building as it is assumed that the rents on renewal will include the equivalent of a rent free period, i.e. that they will be in effect headline rents plus a rent-free period. In reality the renewed leases might instead reflect a shorter rent free period (as the occupation already exists) or a net effective rent, by which is meant a rent from day one of the renewed lease diluted to reflect the absence of any rent free period.

[15] This assumes that the sub-tenants are not inconvenienced by the works.

at a cost of £90,000, which would benefit each floor equally. He would also spend a further £100,000 on the internal common parts (which the tenant often complained were in such a state as to be in breach of the landlord's covenant, a point now accepted by the landlord). The works would not interfere with occupation but would take three months in total, the most lengthy being the works to the internal common parts. Marketing in this particular example cannot start until all of the works referred to have been completed, and will then take three months. Rent-free periods of three months will be necessary to attract new tenants. The ERV assuming all works are undertaken is £100,000 per annum per floor.

## IN REPAIR

| | |
|---|---:|
| ERV 10,000 sq ft x £20.00/ft$^2$ | £220,000 |
| Years' purchase in perpetuity@ 8.5%[16] | 11.765 |
| | £2,588,300 |
| | |
| ERV 10,000 sq ft x £20.00/ft$^2$ | £200,000 |
| Years' purchase in perpetuity @ 8% | 12.5 |
| | £2,500,000 |
| | £5,088,300 |

*Less*

| | |
|---|---:|
| Irrecoverable cost of work to internal common parts: | £100,000 |
| Loss of rent during above works period: 3 months on vacant half of the building: | £50,000 |
| Loss of rent during rent free: 3 months on vacant half of building: | £50,000 |
| | £200,000 |
| | |
| VALUE IN REPAIR | £4,888,300 |

## OUT OF REPAIR

| | |
|---|---:|
| ERV 10,000 sq ft x £22.00/ft$^2$ | £220,000 |
| Years' purchase in perpetuity @ 8.5% | 11.765 |
| | £2,588,300 |
| | |
| ERV 10,000 sq ft x £20.00/ft$^2$ | £200,000 |
| Years' purchase in perpetuity @ 8% | 12.5 |
| | £2,500,000 |
| | £5,088,300 |

*Less*

---

[16] In this particular example the valuer, using his judgement, has decided to use a yield of 8.5%, rather than 8% because the renewed leases of the two floors were not an open market transactions, but renewals to an existing occupier (and in that sense a special purchaser) and agreed six months earlier.

| | |
|---|---:|
| Works to vacant floors: | £55,000 |
| Works to exterior (half not recoverable): | £45,000 |
| Irrecoverable cost of work to internal common parts: | £100,000 |
| Loss of rent during works period: | |
| 3 months on vacant half of the building: | £50,000 |
| Loss of rent during rent free: 3 months on vacant half of building: | £50,000 |
| | £300,000 |
| VALUE OUT OF REPAIR | £4,788,300 |
| **DIMINUTION IN VALUE** | **£100,000** |

CHAPTER 32

# DAMAGES AT THE END OF THE TERM (3): BREACHES OF COVENANT OTHER THAN THE COVENANT TO REPAIR

## INTRODUCTORY

The measure of damages for breach of a covenant to repair has been considered in Chs 29 to 31, above. This Chapter is concerned with damages at the end of the term for breach of covenants other than repairing covenants. The particular covenants considered are (i) covenants to reinstate alterations, and (ii) covenants to decorate, but the relevant principles are applicable to a claim for damages for breach of any covenant relevant to dilapidations other than a repairing covenant within s.18(1) (for example, a covenant against alterations, or a covenant to comply with statutes).

**32–01**

## THE COMMON LAW MEASURE OF DAMAGES FOR BREACH OF AN OBLIGATION TO CARRY OUT WORKS

### The general principle

At common law the fundamental object of damages is to compensate the claimant for loss resulting from the defendant's breach of obligation by putting him in the position he would have been in if the breach had not been committed. In *Robinson v Harman*,[1] Parke B. stated the rule as follows:

**32–02**

> "The rule of the common law is that where a party sustains a loss by reason of a breach of contract, he is, so far as money can do it, to be placed in the same situation, with respect to damages, as if the contract had been performed."

There is no rule that damages for breach of an obligation to carry out works are to be assessed in all circumstances by reference to the cost of carrying out those works.[2] The true rule is that the damages recoverable will in all cases depend on what loss the landlord can be said to have suffered. In an appropriate case, that loss will equate to the cost of carrying out the works together with, where appropriate, an allowance for the time they will take to carry out; in others, it will be limited to the damage to the reversion, if any, as a result of the failure to carry out the works; in others it may be nominal or nil.

---

[1] (1848) 1 Exch. 850 at 855.
[2] *Ruxley Electronics & Construction Ltd v Forsyth* [1996] 1 A.C. 344.

## Cost of the works or diminution in value

**32–03**    The principal consideration in deciding whether or not it is appropriate to assess damages by reference to the cost of carrying out the works which the defendant should have done is whether, in all the circumstances, it is reasonable for the claimant to carry out the works. The leading case is the decision of the House of Lords in *Ruxley Electronics & Construction Ltd v Forsyth*.[3] In that case, the claimant had entered into a building contract whereby the contractor agreed to build a swimming pool. The specification provided that the depth of the pool should be 7ft 6in. In fact, due to default of the subcontractor, the pool as built was only 6ft 9in at its deepest point. The trial judge found as a fact that the pool as built was perfectly safe to dive into; that there was no evidence that the shortfall in depth had decreased the value of the pool; that the only practicable method of achieving a pool of the required depth would be to demolish the existing pool and construct a new one at a cost of £21,560; that he was not satisfied that the claimant intended to build a new pool at such cost; that such cost would be wholly disproportionate to the disadvantage of keeping the pool as built; and that it would be unreasonable to carry out the works. The question was whether, on the basis of those findings, the judge had been right to refuse to assess damages on the basis of the cost of the works necessary to reconstruct the pool so as to achieve the depth contracted for. In upholding the decision of the judge, and reversing the Court of Appeal on this point, Lord Lloyd set out the true position as follows:

> "If the court takes the view that it would be unreasonable for the plaintiff to insist on reinstatement, as where, for example, the expense of the work involved would be out of all proportion to the benefit to be obtained, then the plaintiff will be confined to the difference in value."

Lord Mustill said:

> "[T]he test of reasonableness plays a central part in determining the basis of recovery, and will indeed be decisive in a case such as the present when the cost of reinstatement would be wholly disproportionate to the non-monetary loss suffered by the employer."

It was held that the damages were limited to the difference in value irrespective of whether or not the claimant had an intention, given sufficient damages, to reinstate.

**32–04**    *Ruxley* shows that damages are to be assessed by reference to an objective test,[4] namely, whether it would be reasonable in all the circumstances to do the work. However, Lord Jauncey's speech suggests that in some circumstances, there may be a subjective element:

> "[I]n taking reasonableness into account in determining the extent of loss it is reasonableness in relation to the particular contract and not at large. Accordingly, if I contracted for the erection of a folly in my garden which shortly thereafter suffered a total collapse it would be irrelevant

---

[3] [1996] A.C. 344.
[4] See *Crewe Services & Investment Corp v Silk* [1998] 2 E.G.L.R. 1 per Robert Walker L.J.

to the determination of my loss to argue that the erection of such a folly which contributed nothing to the value of my house was a crazy thing to do."

In other words, it may, depending on the facts, be reasonable to carry out the work even though there has been no diminution in the value of the landlord's reversion by reason of the tenant's failure to do it.[5]

Where carrying out the works would be unreasonable in the above sense, the claimant will not be awarded the cost of the works even if he has done them or genuinely intends to do them. In practice, however, whether or not the claimant has done (or intends to do) the works will in most cases be relevant to the overall question of reasonableness. Thus, in *Ruxley* Lord Lloyd said:

> "The courts are not normally concerned with what a plaintiff does with his damages. But it does not follow that intention is not relevant to reasonableness, at least in those cases where the plaintiff does not intend to reinstate."

If the court is satisfied that the works have been or will be done, it may be ready in practice to draw the inference that this is the reasonable course, so that damages will be assessed by reference to the cost incurred or to be incurred.[6] Conversely, where the claimant has not done the work for which he claims and does not intend to do so, the burden may in practice be on him to show why the cost should nonetheless be awarded. Thus, in *Tito v Waddell (No.2)*[7] a claim for damages was brought for breach of an obligation to replant following the use of the land for the removal of phosphate. Megarry V.C. declined to award damages based on the cost of replanting because there was no satisfactory evidence that the claimants intended to replant. Instead damages were awarded based on the diminution in value of the land in question.

**32–05**

Where damages are awarded based on the cost of carrying out the works, they may include, in appropriate circumstances, consequential loss resulting from the breach, such as loss of use of the premises whilst the works are being done.[8]

## The date of assessment

A further aspect which may distinguish the position at common law from that under s.18 of the Landlord and Tenant Act 1927 is the date of assessment. It is well established that the relevant date for the purposes of s.18 is the date the lease ends. The reversion in and out of repair is valued by reference to market conditions prevailing at that date and events occurring thereafter are generally irrelevant.[9] The general principle at common law is that damages for breach of

**32–06**

---

[5] See, for example, *Eyre v Rea* [1947] 1 K.B. 567, in which the cost of reinstatement was awarded as damages even though the premises were more valuable in their existing state. This case is further considered in para.32–10, below. See also the Australian case of *Bowen Investments v Tabcorp Holdings*, considered at para.32–11, below.

[6] Cf. *Radford v De Froberville* [1977] 1 W.L.R. 1262.

[7] [1977] Ch. 106. The judgment contains a helpful discussion of the circumstances in which the cost of the works contacted for is recoverable.

[8] See, for example, *Applegate v Moss* [1971] 1 Q.B. 406.

[9] See Ch.30, above.

contract are assessed as at the date of breach.[10] The effect of the date of breach rule is that (i) where damages are assessed by reference to the cost of the works which the tenant should have carried out at or by the end of the lease, the relevant costs will be assessed by reference to prices in force as at the date when the landlord, acting with all reasonable speed, could first put the works in hand,[11] and (ii) where damages are assessed by reference to the diminution in the value of the reversion, the reversion is valued as at the term date.[12] However, the date of breach rule is not absolute. It is "only a general or basic rule and is subject to many exceptions".[13] If it would produce injustice, the court has power to assess damages at some other date. One situation in which this power may be exercised is where it would be reasonable for the claimant to postpone carrying out the works for some period after the date of breach.

**32–07**     An example of this is *Dodd Properties (Kent) Ltd v Canterbury City Council*.[14] The defendants had caused damage to the claimant's premises in 1968, but had denied liability until shortly before the trial in 1978. It was common ground that damages were to be assessed by reference to the cost of the necessary remedial works, but the question arose as to whether the correct date at which such costs should be assessed was 1970 (the earliest date when it was physically possible to have carried out the works) or 1978 (the date of the trial). The claimants did not carry out the works prior to the trial because (i) this would have resulted in some financial stringency, and (ii) the defendants were denying liability and the claimants took the view that it would not have made commercial sense to carry out the works until they were sure of recovering the cost from the defendants. The judge found that it was reasonable for the claimants to defer the works until the trial. The Court of Appeal held that the cost of the work was to be assessed as at 1978. Megaw L.J. said:

> "The true rule is that, where there is a material difference between the cost of repair at the date of the wrongful act and the cost of repair when the repairs can, having regard to all relevant circumstances, first reasonably be undertaken, it is the latter time by reference to which the cost of repair is to be taken in assessing damages."

Donaldson L.J. stated the position as follows:

> "In the absence of special and extraneous factors, there is no divergence between the interest of a plaintiff and a defendant on the choice of the most propitious moment at which to effect reinstatement. Both wish to achieve the maximum economy, at least so long as the plaintiff is in doubt whether he will be entitled to a full indemnity from the defendant. It follows that, in a case in which a plaintiff has reinstated his property before the hearing, the costs prevailing at the date of that operation which were reasonably incurred by him are prima facie those which are relevant. Equally, in a case in which a plaintiff has *not* [court's emphasis] effected reinstatement by the time of the hearing, there is a prima facie presumption that the costs then prevailing are those which could be adopted in ascertaining the cost of reinstatement. There may indeed be cases in which the court has to estimate costs at some future time as being the reasonable time at which to reinstate. But that is not this case.
> This is, however, only a prima facie approach. It may appear on the evidence that the

---

[10]  See for example *Miliangos v George Frank Textiles Ltd* [1976] A.C. 443 per Lord Wilberforce.
[11]  See *Dodd Properties (Kent) Ltd v Canterbury City Council* [1980] 1 W.L.R. 433.
[12]  Cf. para.30–07, above.
[13]  *Dodd Properties (Kent) Ltd v Canterbury City Council*, above, per Donaldson L.J.
[14]  Above.

plaintiff, acting reasonably, should have undertaken the reinstatement at some earlier date than that in fact adopted or, as the case may be, earlier than the hearing. If so, the relevant costs are those ruling at that earlier date. Whether this is regarded as arising out of the primary measure of damages, i.e. that the relevant time is when the property should have been reinstated, or whether it is regarded as being a reflection of a plaintiff's duty to mitigate his loss, may not matter."

The date of breach rule was also departed from in *Alcoa Minerals of Jamaica Inc v Broderick*,[15] in which the defendant's nuisance had damaged the claimant's house. The claimant was unable to pay for the necessary repairs. Between 1989, when the damage first occurred, and 1994 the cost of the works quadrupled because of inflation. The Privy Council held that there is no absolute rule that where the claimant at the date of breach does not have the funds to repair the damage, his impecuniosity is to be ignored as a matter of law. Treating the question as whether the claimant was in breach of his duty to mitigate, Lord Slynn (giving the judgment of the Board) held that the claimant had behaved reasonably in waiting until money was available from the defendant, and he was entitled to the cost of the work as at 1994.

    32–08

There seems no reason in principle why Megaw L.J.'s "true rule"[16] (that damages are to be assessed as at the date on which the repairs can, having regard to all relevant circumstances, first reasonably be undertaken) should not be equally applicable to the assessment of damages for breach of a tenant's obligation to carry out works where it has been decided that the cost of remedial works is the appropriate measure of damages. If the landlord can satisfy the court that in all the circumstances he acted reasonably in delaying doing the works until the trial, the costs will be assessed by reference to prices in force at the date of trial. However, it has been said that in normal circumstances the date of breach rule will apply where damages are to be assessed by reference to the diminution in the value of the reversion.[17]

## DAMAGES FOR BREACH OF COVENANT TO REINSTATE ALTERATIONS

### Introductory

Obligations to reinstate alterations at the end of the term are considered in Ch.16, above. In some cases the obligation to reinstate is unqualified; in others, it only arises if the landlord so requires. It will generally be the case, either expressly or by necessary implication, that the requirement cannot be made after the term has ended and the tenant has gone out of possession. In practice, damages for breach of the obligation to reinstate frequently form part of dilapidations claims, sometimes a very significant part.

    32–09

---

[15] [2002] 1 A.C. 371.
[16] See para.32–07 above.
[17] See *Dodd Properties (Kent) Ltd v Canterbury City Council* [1980] 1 W.L.R. 433, per Donaldson L.J.

## The measure of damages

**32–10**     Although there are obvious similarities between a covenant to repair and a covenant to reinstate premises at the end of the term, they are not the same. In particular, the latter is not a covenant to put, keep or leave in repair, so that the provisions of s.18(1) of the Landlord and Tenant Act 1927 do not apply to it.[18] The measure of damages is therefore governed by the common law. Whilst (as has been seen[19]) the common law measure of damages for breach of a covenant to leave in repair is the proper cost of the necessary remedial works, there is no analogy between this and a covenant to reinstate alterations.[20] It follows that the damages recoverable for breach of an obligation to reinstate are to be assessed by reference to the principles considered in paras 32–02 to 32–08, above. The question will be what, in all the circumstances, is the landlord's loss, and (where he claims the cost of reinstating) whether reinstatement would be reasonable. There is no rigid rule that damages are the cost of reinstatement.[21] Equally, there is no principle that the cost of reinstatement cannot be given even where that exceeds the damage to the reversion.[22]

In *Eyre v Rea*[23] a lease of a dwelling-house contained covenants not to alter the internal planning of the premises, not to permit the premises to be used otherwise than as a private dwelling-house in one occupation, and not to underlet or part with the possession of any part of the premises. The tenant granted sub-leases of parts of the premises to sub-tenants who, by arrangement with him, converted the premises into five separate flats. The landlord forfeited the lease and claimed damages for the breach. The evidence was that the landlord intended to carry out the works of reconversion for estate management reasons, even though from a purely financial point of view the premises were more valuable as five separate flats. Atkinson J. awarded the cost of the works of reconversion plus loss of rent over the period necessary to carry out the work during which no rent could be earned.

**32–11**     By contrast, in *James v Hutton*[24] only nominal damages were awarded for breach of an obligation to reinstate. In that case the tenant of a shop entered into a licence permitting the erection of a new shop front. The licence contained a covenant by the tenant at the end of the lease (if so required) to restore the premises at the end of the term to the same state as they had been in before the licence was granted. The tenant failed to restore the premises when required to do so at the end of lease. The landlord brought proceedings for damages claiming as

---

[18] Cf. *Eyre v Rea* [1947] 1 K.B. 567 (covenant not to alter the internal planning of the premises). It is noteworthy that in *James v Hutton* [1950] 1 K.B. 9 (covenant to reinstate at the end of the term) no suggestion was made that the measure of damages was affected by s.18(1).
[19] See paras 29–06 to 29–11, above.
[20] *James v Hutton and J. Cook & Sons Ltd*, above.
[21] *Westminster v Swinton* [1948] 1 K.B. 524, per Denning J. at 534.
[22] See *Tito v Waddell (No.2)* [1977] Ch. 106, per Megarry V.C. at 332–334; *Eyre v Rea* [1947] 1 K.B. 567.
[23] Above.
[24] Above.

damages the cost of doing the work. The landlord had not done the work, and there was no evidence that she intended to. Lord Goddard C.J. said in the course of his judgment:

> "What, then, is the measure of damages applicable to the breach of a covenant to restore on request when the only evidence is that there has been no compliance with that request? In our opinion, the general rule as to damages for breach of contract ought to be applied, namely, to ascertain the amount of damage actually suffered...
>
> We see no ground here for assuming that the plaintiff in this case has suffered any damage at all. She has got back a shop, or would have done, if the premises had not been requisitioned, provided with a modern and convenient shop front, and there was no suggestion that the work had not been carried out properly. We do not for one moment suggest that it might not be possible for a lessor in circumstances such as these to give evidence that she or her superior landlords at the end of the term desired to carry on or to let the premises for the purpose of carrying on a business for which the altered shop front would be inappropriate and the old one suitable. In that case she might well say that it is of value to her to have her shop back in its former condition and she would suffer damage, if the lessee's covenant to restore was not carried out, but if it is a mere matter of getting back a shop which has been altered and there is no suggestion that any damage whatever has been caused to the plaintiff thereby, it appears to us that she has suffered no damage by reason of the defendant's failure to comply with her requirements to reinstate."

In the Australian case of *Bowen Investments v Tabcorp Holdings*,[25] an office building was let in 1996 for 10 years from February 1, 1997. The tenant covenanted not without the landlord's approval to "make or permit to be made any substantial alteration or addition to the demised premises". In July 1997, the tenant demolished the foyer (which was brand-new and of high quality) and constructed a new foyer to a different style and design without the landlord's consent. The judge at first instance declined to award damages equal to the cost of reinstatement (except to the extent required to restore the premises to their original lettable area) on the principal ground that there was no diminution in the value of the landlord's reversion.

The Federal Court of Australia allowed the landlord's appeal, holding that the correct measure of damages in the circumstances was the cost of reinstatement. Finkelstein and Gordon J.J. (citing, among other things, Ch.31 of the Third Edition of this work) held the correct measure of damages to be whatever it is reasonable for the wronged party to recover. What is reasonable in a particular case is not to be measured in purely economic terms or solely from the viewpoint of a hypothetical rational economic actor. The landlord's wish to have the foyer restored had not been shown to be unreasonable, and personal preferences of a subjective nature are not irrelevant when choosing the appropriate measure of damage, especially if the claimant's predilections are not excessive or extravagant. All three members of the court (giving judgment in March 2008) treated the date of expiry of the lease on January 31, 2007 as the correct date for assessing damages.[26]

The overall question will be whether reinstatement is reasonable. However, it is thought that in most cases where the landlord has not reinstated, and does not intend to do so, the position will in practice be the same as that under the first

**32–12**

---

[25] [2008] FCAFC 38.
[26] See further paras 32–06 to 32–08, above.

limb of s.18(1) of the 1927 Act, namely, that damages are likely to be assessed on the basis of the diminution in the value of the reversion, if any, caused by the tenant's failure to reinstate. Equally, where the landlord has reinstated, or can satisfy the court that he genuinely intends to do so, damages will equate to the cost of the work together with, where appropriate, loss of rent, and any other relevant losses, unless the court thinks that in doing the work the landlord has acted, or is proposing to act, unreasonably. The fact that the cost of the work exceeds the damage to the reversion will not prevent an award of damages on this basis.[27] However, where the reversion has not been damaged (because the premises are more valuable in their altered state), the court will no doubt examine the landlord's evidence on reinstatement that much more carefully in order to satisfy itself that the cost of reinstatement properly represents what he has lost.

## DAMAGES FOR BREACH OF COVENANT TO DECORATE

### Introductory

32–13    Covenants to decorate are considered in Ch.15, above. As with obligations to reinstate alterations, damages for failure to decorate often form a substantial part of a claim for terminal dilapidations.

### The measure of damages

32–14    An obligation to decorate may arise under the covenant to repair or by virtue of an express covenant to decorate at periodic intervals.[28] It has been held by the Court of Appeal that a claim for damages by reason of the tenant's failure to decorate is subject to the statutory cap on damages imposed by s.18(1) of the Landlord and Tenant Act 1927 where such failure constitutes a breach of the covenant to repair even though that same failure also constitutes a breach of a covenant in the same lease to redecorate at periodic intervals.[29] Section 18(1) does not apply to a claim for damages for failure to carry out pure decoration work which does not fall within the covenant to repair.[30] The measure of damages will therefore be governed by the common law principles discussed above.

## VALUATION EVIDENCE IN NON-REPAIR CASES

### Whether valuation evidence should be adduced

32–15    The question sometimes arises as to whether it is necessary, in cases where the breaches consist of or include non-repair items, to adduce valuation evidence that the value of the landlord's reversion has been diminished by the tenant's failure to carry out those items. It is sometimes asserted that there is no need for such

---

[27] See, e.g. *Eyre v Rea*, above.
[28] See Ch.15, above, where the distinction is explained.
[29] *Latimer v Carney* [2006] 3 E.G.L.R. 13.
[30] See paras 15–08 and 30–03, above.

evidence because s.18(1) of the 1927 Act does not apply. Whilst each case depends on its own facts, it is thought that it will often be appropriate to adduce such evidence. First, even though s.18(1) does not apply, the court may still assess damages by reference to the diminution in value if it thinks that it would be unreasonable to carry out the works.[31] Second, whether or not the breaches have resulted in damage to the value of the reversion may of itself be relevant to whether it would be reasonable for the works to be done and hence whether damages should be assessed by reference to the cost of the works. Third, where the breaches include repair items, it will usually be necessary for valuation evidence to be adduced in any event. If such evidence is limited to the repair items only, it will be necessary to decide what assumptions should be made regarding whether or not the non-repair items have been attended to (since this may affect whether the repair items have caused damage to the value of the reversion), and it is not immediately obvious what those assumptions should be. No difficulty arises, however, if the non-repair items are treated in the same way as the repair items, i.e. the in-repair valuation assumes that the premises are in the condition they would be in if all the remedial works (including non-repair items) had been done, and the out of repair valuation assumes that the premises are in their existing state, i.e. without any of the items having been attended to.

For these reasons, careful consideration should be given to adducing valuation evidence in claims for damages for failure to carry out non-repair works.

---

[31] See above.

# CHAPTER 33

# THE TENANT'S REMEDIES FOR BREACH OF COVENANT ON THE PART OF THE LANDLORD

## THE AVAILABLE REMEDIES

### The available remedies

The following remedies are available to the tenant in the event of a breach by the landlord of his repairing obligations:

33–01

(1)   to seek specific performance of the landlord's obligation to repair[1];
(2)   to claim damages (or counterclaim damages in an action brought by the landlord)[2];
(3)   to carry out the remedial work himself[3];
(4)   to set-off against the rent the damages to which he would be entitled[4];
(5)   where the breach is repudiatory, to accept the repudiation and quit the premises[5];
(6)   to apply for the appointment of a receiver or manager.[6]

There are also remedies provided by various specialised statutory provisions, including housing, environmental and health and safety law.[7]

### The limitation period

Where the landlord's obligation to repair is contained in a lease under seal, the relevant period of limitation is 12 years from the date of the breach.[8] Where the lease is not under seal, the relevant period is six years from the date of the

33–02

---

[1]  See para.33–07, below.
[2]  See para.33–15, below.
[3]  See para.33–40, below.
[4]  See para.33–41, below.
[5]  See para.33–45, below.
[6]  See paras 33–51 and 33–66, below.
[7]  See para.33–68, below.
[8]  Limitation Act 1980 s.8(1).

breach.[9] Where the obligation is to repair or keep in repair during the term, a fresh breach occurs every day that the premises are out of repair.[10]

## War damage

33–03    Obligations to repair on the part of both landlord and tenant are modified or suspended in the case of war damage.[11] This is considered in Ch.26, para.26–15, above.

# THE CHOICE OF REMEDY

## Limitations on the available remedies

33–04    Not all of the remedies set out above are available in every case. For example, specific performance is discretionary; the extent to which a lease can be repudiated is not yet settled beyond doubt; and the right of set-off may have been excluded by agreement. Once the lease has ended, the only remedy for past disrepair is damages, either by means of a separate action or counterclaim, or set-off against past arrears of rent.

## Combining remedies

33–05    Some of the tenant's remedies are cumulative. It is common, for example, for the court to order the landlord to carry out the necessary repair work and at the same time order him to pay damages for his past failure to repair. Other remedies are mutually exclusive. For example, an order for specific performance would be inconsistent with a finding that the lease has come to an end by the tenant accepting the landlord's repudiatory breach. In many cases it will be appropriate to apply for different remedies in the alternative. For example, the tenant might apply for the appointment of a manager under Pt II of the Landlord and Tenant Act 1987 to carry out the necessary repair works and in the alternative for an order of specific performance requiring the landlord to do the work himself.

## Making the choice

33–06    The choice of remedy will depend upon the particular circumstances of each case. It will be necessary to consider carefully what the tenant's objectives are. If the principal objective is to obtain compensation for damage caused by disrepair, the appropriate remedy will be a claim for damages, either by bringing proceedings,

---

[9] Limitation Act 1980 s.5.

[10] *Maddock v Mallet* (1860) 12 I.C.L.R. 173; *Granada Theatres Ltd v Freehold Investment (Leytonstone) Ltd* [1959] Ch. 592; *Re King* [1962] 1 W.L.R. 632 (reversed on other grounds [1963] Ch. 459); *Marshall v Bradford District Council* [2002] H.L.R. 22. See further para.26–18, above.

[11] Landlord and Tenant (War Damage) Act 1939. See also Landlord and Tenant (War Damage) (Amendment) Act 1941; War Damage Act 1943. For the provisions in detail, reference should be made to the Acts themselves.

or by exercising the right of set-off against rent. If, on the other hand, the work is urgently required, then the remedies to be considered will be an application for specific performance, the self-help remedy of the tenant carrying out the work himself and an application for the appointment of a receiver or manager to do the work in place of the landlord. The relative merits of each of these courses will need to be thought about carefully.

The identity of the landlord will always be an important consideration. If the landlord is a substantial public company, or the trustees of a long-established settled estate, there is unlikely to be any problem in obtaining compliance with an order for specific performance and payment of any damages ordered. If, on the other hand, the landlord is a private limited company with no substantial assets, it may not be good for any damages awarded, and an order for specific performance may lead to delays in enforcement and to the ultimate insolvency of the company. In such circumstances consideration may need to be given to self-help remedies, such as the tenant carrying out the work himself, and setting off any damages claim against rent; or an application for the appointment of a receiver or manager to take over performance of the landlord's obligations. Where the landlord is a private landlord, the tenant can complain to the local authority if he believes its powers and duties under housing legislation to be relevant. Where the landlord is itself a local authority, the tenant is deprived of this option since the local authority cannot use its powers against itself, but he has the additional option of complaining to the local ombudsman.

The nature and consequences of the defect will be equally important to consider. If the work is urgent, the prime objective will generally be to get it done as soon as possible. If it is relatively minor, the expense of proceedings may be unjustified, and the tenant may be better advised to exercise a self-help remedy. However, if the work involves extensive work to premises outside the tenant's demise, and the co-operation of other occupiers of the building is likely to be required, then self-help may be impractical, and the tenant's only course will be either an application for specific performance, or an application for the appointment of a receiver or manager to undertake the work. Different considerations may apply where the work is such that the tenant can afford to wait. For example, where the premises are residential, it may be worth seeking to persuade the local authority to intervene under their statutory powers relating to housing, despite the fact that this may be a slow process. Alternatively, it may be appropriate to deduct an appropriate sum from the rent by way of set-off in the hope that the landlord will thereby be prompted into attending to the tenant's complaint.

A third matter to consider in practice will be whether and to what extent the cost of any remedial work will be recoverable from the tenant by way of service charge. If the tenant is likely to end up paying for whatever is done, then depending on the nature of the defect, he may prefer to claim damages only, as opposed to adopting a remedy which is aimed at making the landlord do the work.

## SPECIFIC PERFORMANCE

### Introductory

**33–07**   Specific performance of a tenant's covenant to repair has already been considered.[12] Much of what is said there is equally relevant to specific performance of a landlord's covenant to repair, and reference should be made accordingly.

### The availability of the remedy

**33–08**   The court has jurisdiction in an appropriate case to grant specific performance of a landlord's covenant to repair. Thus, in *Jeune v Queen's Cross Properties Ltd*[13] four flats in a building were let on underleases containing a landlord's covenant to maintain, repair and renew the structure of the building. The landlord failed to reinstate a York stone balcony after its partial collapse. The tenants sought an order that he reinstate it forthwith in the form in which it existed prior to the partial collapse. Pennycuick V.C. granted the order. He said:

> "[I]n common sense and justice, it seems perfectly clear that [specific performance] is the appropriate relief. [The landlord's] repairing covenant requires it to maintain, repair and renew the structure, including the external walls. A mandatory order upon the [landlord] to reinstate the balcony is a much more convenient order than an award of damages leaving it to the individual [tenants] to do the work. There is nothing burdensome or unfair in the order sought."

Having considered whether the court had jurisdiction to grant the order he concluded:

> "I cannot myself see any reason in principle why, in an appropriate case, an order should not be made against a landlord to do some specific work pursuant to his covenant to repair. Obviously, it is a jurisdiction which should be carefully exercised. But in a case such as the present where there has been a plain breach of covenant to repair and there is no doubt at all what is required to be done to remedy the breach, I cannot see why an order for specific performance should not be made."

Similarly, specific performance has been granted of a landlord's obligation to repair a lift.[14]

**33–09**   In the above cases, the part of the building in disrepair was not part of the demised premises. It has been suggested that specific performance cannot be granted of a landlord's covenant to repair the demised premises.[15] However, it is thought that this is unsound, and that the court would order specific performance

---

[12] See para.28–02 et seq., above.

[13] [1974] Ch. 97.

[14] *Francis v Cowlcliffe Ltd* (1976) 33 P. & C.R. 368; *Peninsular Maritime Ltd v Padseal Ltd* [1981] 2 E.G.L.R. 43.

[15] *Granada Theatres Ltd v Freehold Investment (Leytonstone) Ltd* [1959] 1 Ch. 592 (in which Jenkins L.J. said, obiter, of the landlord's covenant in that case to repair the main structure of the demised premises, that it was "clearly not specifically enforceable"); *Greetings Oxford Koala Hotel Pty Ltd v Oxford Square Investments Pty Ltd* (1989) 18 N.S.W.L.R. 33 (Australia).

in an appropriate case. To order the landlord to repair would not be to order him to commit a trespass, since by virtue of his repairing covenant, he would have an implied right to enter.[16]

The distinction is irrelevant where the demised premises consist of a dwelling. In that case the court has power to grant specific performance under s.17 of the Landlord and Tenant Act 1985, which provides that in proceedings in which the tenant of a dwelling alleges a breach on the part of his landlord of a repairing covenant relating to any part of the premises in which the dwelling is comprised, the court may order specific performance of the covenant whether or not the breach relates to a part of the premises let to the tenant and notwithstanding any equitable rule restricting the scope of the remedy.[17] It follows that specific performance may be ordered under the subsection both where the breach relates to the demised dwelling, and where it relates to any part of the premises in which the dwelling is comprised. "Repairing covenant" means a covenant to repair, maintain, renew, construct or replace any property.[18] "Covenant" includes an implied obligation in a lease under seal,[19] and it is thought that it would include an obligation contained in a document made under hand only.[20] A statutory tenant under the Rent Act 1977 is included in the definition of "tenant".[21] The definition of "landlord" includes any person against whom the tenant has a right to enforce a repairing covenant.[22] It follows that specific performance can be ordered where the repairing obligations are undertaken not by the landlord but by a management company or maintenance trustee.

## Establishing a claim to specific performance

Specific performance is a discretionary remedy. The conditions which need to be established before an order for specific performance will be made have already been considered in relation to a tenant's covenant,[23] and the position is broadly the same in relation to specific performance of a landlord's covenant. In most cases the tenant or a sub-tenant will be in occupation of the premises, so that disrepair is likely to cause continuing loss of beneficial enjoyment. The requirement that damages must not be an adequate remedy is therefore unlikely to prove an obstacle in the majority of cases.

33–10

The principal problem in practice may be in compiling a schedule of works of sufficient particularity.[24] For example, in *Flashman v Avenue Properties (St*

---

[16] See para.22–32, above.

[17] Landlord and Tenant Act 1985 s.17(1).

[18] Landlord and Tenant Act 1985 s.17(2)(d).

[19] *Gordon v Selico Co Ltd* [1985] 2 E.G.L.R. 79 (not affected on this point on appeal, [1986] 1 E.G.L.R. 71).

[20] The point was left open in *Gordon v Selico Co Ltd*, above, and did not arise on appeal ([1986] 1 E.G.L.R. 71).

[21] Landlord and Tenant Act 1985 s.17(2)(a).

[22] Landlord and Tenant Act 1985 s.17(2)(c).

[23] See para.28–02 et seq., above.

[24] See *Co-operative Insurance Society Ltd v Argyll Stores (Holdings) Ltd* [1998] A.C. 1 for a discussion of the requirement of precision in any order for specific performance.

*John's Wood) Ltd*[25] Templeman J. refused to order specific performance of a landlord's obligation to keep in good repair the wiring in a residential flat "because I cannot myself, and I do not think anybody can, sit down and write out a list of what exactly the landlord ought to do". Instead he granted a declaration that the landlord was in breach of covenant.

In practice, the tenant may be aware only of the general nature of the disrepair in so far as it has affected his premises, and the ultimate cause of the damage occurring to his premises may be in premises retained by the landlord to which the tenant has no access. Where the tenant is unable to be specific, it is thought that the court may in an appropriate case be prepared to make an order in more general terms than would otherwise be done. If, for example, the roof of an office building leaks, but the tenant of the top floor has no right to go on the roof to find out what is wrong, it may be appropriate to order the landlord to carry out such work as may be necessary to prevent the roof from leaking. Thus, in *Gordon v Selico Co Ltd*[26] the order made by the judge required the defendant landlord of a block of flats at its own expense and without recovery from the plaintiff tenants within eight months "to put the building of which the premises form part into such reasonable condition as not to cause damage to the plaintiffs or to the premises demised by the lease by the incursion of water, the propagation of dry rot, or otherwise", with liberty to the parties to apply for any necessary directions for that purpose, including the settlement of a schedule of necessary works. The judgment was affirmed by the Court of Appeal[27] in the form of an order "for specific performance of the lessor's covenants", with discretion for the detailed working out of the order being given to the Chief Chancery Master. Likewise where the landlord can be taken to be aware of what is required, then a relatively general form of order may suffice. For example, the order in *Jeune v Queen's Cross Properties Ltd*[28] was that the landlord:

> "[D]o forthwith reinstate the York stone balcony situate at the front of the building known as … in the form in which it existed prior to its partial collapse on May 13, 1972."

**33–11**  However, wherever possible, a proper attempt to identify what needs doing should be made. It should be noted that in an appropriate case the court has power to order the landlord to permit the tenant's expert to inspect and report on what needs doing.[29]

There are no statutory restrictions on the enforcement of landlords' repairing covenants comparable to the Leasehold Property (Repairs) Act 1938. The landlord therefore has no statutory protection against frivolous or malicious claims by tenants requiring exact compliance with repairing obligations. It is thought, however, that in practice the discretionary nature of specific performance will be protection enough: in general, the court will only make an order

---

[25] Unreported decision dated June 12, 1978. The reference in the transcript to the landlord's counsel as "Mr Kirk Douglas", the well-known Hollywood actor, is erroneous.

[26] [1985] 2 E.G.L.R. 97 (affirmed at [1986] 1 E.G.L.R. 71).

[27] [1986] 1 E.G.L.R. 71.

[28] [1974] Ch. 97. The facts are set out in para.33–08 above.

[29] Senior Courts Act 1981 s.33; County Courts Act 1984 s.52(i); CPR rr.25.1 and 25.5; *Parker v Camden LBC* [1986] Ch. 162.

where there is a real practical reason why the work must be done, and in other cases, the tenant will be left to his remedy in damages.

## Defences to specific performance

Reference should be made to Ch.28, para.28–10 et seq., above, where the relevant defences to specific performance are considered. It should be noted in particular that financial inability to perform the covenant will not generally be a defence to specific performance.[30] The fact that the tenant is in breach of his obligations under the lease to pay service charges will not prevent specific performance being ordered, at least where the service charges were withheld because of the landlord's breach of covenant.[31]

**33–12**

## Interim orders

The court has power to grant an interim order requiring the landlord to carry out repairs pending trial.[32] However, given that this is a mandatory order, it is only likely to be made in cases where there is a real risk to health and safety.[33]

**33–13**

## Pending land action

A tenant's claim for specific performance of the landlord's repairing covenant is not registrable as a pending land action under the Land Charges Act 1972.[34]

**33–14**

## DAMAGES

## Introductory

A tenant's claim against his landlord for damages for breach of the landlord's repairing covenant is not subject to any statutory limitation such as that imposed on claims against tenants by s.18 of the Landlord and Tenant Act 1927. The measure of damage is therefore governed by the principles of common law. In *Hewitt v Rowlands*[35] Bankes L.J. said:

**33–15**

> "Prima facie the measure of damages for breach of the obligation to repair is the difference in value to the tenant ... between the house in the condition in which it now is and the house in the condition in which it would be if the landlord on receipt of notice had fulfilled its obligation to repair.[36]"

---

[30] *Francis v Cowlcliffe* (1977) 33 P. & C.R. 368.
[31] *Gordon v Selico Co Ltd* [1985] 2 E.G.L.R. 79 (affirmed [1986] 1 E.G.L.R. 71).
[32] CPR r.25.1; *Parker v Camden LBC* [1986] Ch. 162.
[33] *Parker v Camden LBC*, above. See further para.28–14, above.
[34] *Regan & Blackburn Ltd v Rogers* [1985] 1 W.L.R. 870.
[35] (1924) 93 L.J.K.B. 1080.
[36] In *Earle v Charalambous* [2007] H.L.R. 8 Carnwath L.J. regarded Bankes L.J.'s statement of the general principle as "uncontroversial and authoritative".

In *Calabar Properties Ltd v Stitcher*[37] Griffiths L.J. said:

"The object of awarding damages against a landlord for breach of his covenant to repair is not to punish the landlord but, so far as money can, to restore the tenant to the position he would have been in had there been no breach. This object will not be achieved by applying one set of rules to all cases regardless of the particular circumstances of the case. The facts of each must be looked at carefully to see what damage the tenant has suffered and how he may be fairly compensated by a monetary award."

In *Wallace v Manchester City Council*[38] Morritt L.J. set out the relevant principles as follows:

"First, the question in all cases of damages for breach of an obligation to repair is what sum will, so far as money can do it, place the tenant in the position he would have been in if the obligation to repair had been duly performed by the landlord. Second, the answer to that question inevitably involves a comparison of the property as it was for the period when the landlord was in breach of his obligation with what it would have been if the obligation had been performed. Third, for periods when the tenant remained in occupation of the property, notwithstanding the breach of the obligation to repair, the loss to him requiring compensation is the loss of comfort and convenience that results from living in a property that was not in the state of repair it ought to have been if the landlord had performed his obligation: *McCoy & Co. v. Clark; Calabar Properties Limited v. Stitcher*; and *Chiodi v. De Marney*. Fourth, if the tenant does not remain in occupation, but, being entitled to do so, is forced by the landlord's failure to repair to sell or sublet the property, he may recover for the diminution of the price or recoverable rent occasioned by the landlord's failure to perform his covenant to repair: *Calabar Properties Limited v. Stitcher*.
    Obviously, the tenant cannot claim damages in accordance with the third proposition for periods occurring after the date of sale or sublease referred to in the fourth. To that extent, as shown by *Calabar Properties Limited v Stitcher*, those two heads are mutually exclusive."

In *Langham Estate Management Ltd v Hardy*[39] H.H. Judge Marshall, QC summarised the principles to be derived from *Wallace*, and the cases following it, as follows:

"[164] The essential question is:
    What sum will, so far as money can, place the tenant in the position he would have been in if the obligation to repair had been duly performed by the landlord?
    [165] After noting that this inevitably involves a comparison of the property as it should have been with what it in fact was for the period when the landlord was in breach, [Morritt L.J.] then says that for periods when the tenant remained in occupation of the property the loss requiring compensation is "the loss of comfort and convenience" to him that results from living in a property that was not in the state it ought to have been in.
    [166] There are two ways of arriving at a logical figure for the assessment of such damage. One is to put a global figure on the loss and damage suffered; the other is to make an appropriate allowance against the rent paid for the relevant period, usually as a percentage. The former places more emphasis upon valuing the loss suffered and the latter upon valuing the value not received. They ought to amount to the same thing, but one approach may feel more natural than the other, depending upon the facts. It is entirely a matter for the trial judge which approach it is more appropriate to adopt, and it is even permissible to combine the two, although care must be taken to avoid double–counting. It is also advisable to cross–check the result of either approach against the other as a reality check."

---

[37] [1984] 1 W.L.R. 287.
[38] [1998] 3 E.G.L.R. 38 at 42B-D.
[39] [2008] 3 E.G.L.R. 125.

The remainder of this section looks at the various heads of damage to which, depending on the facts, a tenant may be entitled in accordance with the above principles.

## The period in respect of which damages may be claimed

The landlord is liable to pay damages as from the date on which he is in breach of covenant. It should be noted that not every defect falling within the scope of the landlord's covenant to repair will amount without more to a breach of covenant. In many cases, the covenant will be subject to an implied precondition that the landlord is not liable until he has notice of the defect, and once he has notice, he has a reasonable time in which to carry out repairs before he is in breach.[40] In such a case, the tenant may suffer loss during the period between the occurrence of the defect and the time when it is repaired by the landlord, but such loss is not recoverable as damages unless the landlord delays unreasonably in carrying out the work following notice.[41]

**33–16**

## Discomfort and inconvenience

A tenant who does not vacate the premises but continues to occupy them in their unrepaired state is entitled to general damages for the discomfort and inconvenience of occupying premises in disrepair.

**33–17**

The question to be answered in each case is what sum is required to compensate the tenant for the distress and inconvenience experienced because of the landlord's failure to perform his obligation to repair.[42] It was formerly unclear to what extent it is permissible to assess damages under this head by reference to a notional reduction in the rental value of the premises in repair in circumstances where the lease is not held as an investment.[43] However, it is now settled that there is no objection in principle to the use of this approach even where the premises are not so held.[44] Indeed, in many cases, a notional reduction in the rent payable for the premises or (where different) their rental value in repair will be the correct starting point for the assessment of damages for discomfort and inconvenience. However, the tenant is not entitled under this head to recover (by way of an abatement) either the whole or any part of the rent actually paid or payable for the relevant period.[45] Nor is he entitled to separate awards for both

---

[40] See para.22–03 et seq., above.
[41] *Green v Eales* (1841) 2 Q.B. 225; *Calabar Properties Ltd v Stitcher* [1984] 1 W.L.R. 287; *McGreal v Wake* (1984) 13 H.L.R. 107; *Morris v Liverpool City Council* (1988) 20 H.L.R. 498; *Earle v Charalambous* [2007] H.L.R. 8.
[42] *Wallace v Manchester City Council* [1998] 3 E.G.L.R. 38 per Morritt L.J. at 42; *Langham Estate Management Ltd v Hardy* [2008] 3 E.G.L.R. 125; *Grand v Gill* [2011] EWCA Civ 554.
[43] See *Calabar Properties v Stitcher* [1984] 1 W.L.R. 287.
[44] *Wallace v Manchester City Council*, above; *Niazi Services v van der Loo* [2004] 1 W.L.R. 1254; *English Churches Housing Group v Shine* [2004] H.L.R. 42; *Earle v Charalambous*, above; *Grand v Gill, above.*
[45] *Hussein v Mehlman* [1992] 2 E.G.L.R. 287; *Electricity Supply Nominees Ltd v National Magazine Co Ltd* [1999] 1 E.G.L.R. 130.

discomfort and inconvenience and diminution in value, because those are alternative ways of expressing the same concept.[46]

An alternative to the notional reduction in rent approach is to make what Morritt L.J. in *Wallace v Manchester City Council*[47] called a "global award", that is to say, such sum as the court thinks represents proper compensation for the discomfort and inconvenience suffered by the tenant for the relevant period without reference to rent or rental value. In such a case, however, the judge "would be well advised to cross-check his prospective award by reference to the rent payable for the period equivalent to the duration of the landlord's breach of covenant" and thereby "avoid over- or under-assessments through failure to give proper consideration to the period of the landlord's breach of obligation or the nature of the property."[48]

In *Electricity Supply Nominees Ltd v National Magazine Co Ltd*[49] (which concerned commercial premises) H.H. Judge Hicks, QC explained the rationale of the notional reduction in rent approach as follows:

> "[R]ack-rents are some evidence, and often sufficiently good evidence, of the value of fully enjoyed occupation to tenants, in which case consideration of diminution of that value can properly start from there and may often helpfully be approached in terms of its proportional reduction. That is also, as I understand it, the sense in which Morritt L.J. approved a 'notional' reduction in the rent as a means of assessment of damages for disrepair in *Wallace*. The exceptions prove the rule, in the sense of illustrating its underlying rationale and the limits of its proper application, so that neither ground rent (as in the *Calabar Properties*[50] case) nor rents depressed below market levels by statutory intervention (as in *Chiodi v. De Marney*[51]) provide adequate guides to the value of a tenant's beneficial occupation, although, in my experience, even the latter (suitably geared up in the light of local knowledge) may be better than nothing as a starting point in the somewhat rough and ready realities of county court litigation.[52]"

In *Earle v Charalambous*,[53] which concerned a claim by the tenant of a long leasehold flat on the top floor of a building in Islington for damages for breach of the landlord's covenant to repair the roof, Carnwath L.J. (with whom Moses L.J. and Morritt C. agreed) said (rejecting the tenant's argument that damages were to be assessed by reference to levels of past awards for damages and not by reference to market value) said:

> "I do not think that a direct analogy can be drawn with awards in relation to protected periodic tenancies, still less with the 'modest' awards thought appropriate in other areas of the law (see e.g. *Watts v. Morrow* [1991] 1 W.L.R 1421, 1439G). A long-lease of a residential property is not only a home, but is also a valuable property asset. Distress and inconvenience caused by disrepair are not free-standing heads of claim, but are symptomatic of interference with the lessee's enjoyment of that asset. If the lessor's breach of covenant has the effect of depriving

---

[46] *Hussein v Mehlman*, above; *Electricity Supply Nominees Ltd v National Magazine Co Ltd*, above.
[47] [1998] 3 E.G.L.R. 38.
[48] *Wallace v Manchester City Council*, above, per Morritt L.J. at 42.
[49] [1999] 1 E.G.L.R. 130.
[50] [1984] 1 W.L.R. 287.
[51] (1989) 21 H.L.R. 6.
[52] In *Earle v Charalambous* [2007] H.L.R. 8, Carnwath L.J. regarded the whole of H.H. Judge Hicks, QC's judgment as "persuasive" and quoted part of the passage in the text.
[53] Above.

the lessee of that enjoyment, wholly or partially, for a significant period, a notional judgment of the resulting reduction in rental value is likely to be the most appropriate starting point for assessment of damages."

In some cases, it will be appropriate to take the rent actually payable as representative of the rental value of the premises in repair. Thus, in *Niazi Services Ltd v van der Loo*[54] a flat in Chelsea was let at a full market rent of £34,800 per annum. Damages for breach of the landlord's covenant to repair implied by s.11 of the Landlord and Tenant Act 1985[55] were assessed at £48,000, the greater part of which represented a notional reduction of 40 per cent of the rent payable for the relevant period.[56] Likewise, in *Clarke v Lloyds TSB Bank Ltd*[57] (a case relating to commercial premises) the judge based his award of damages on the actual rent passing, because the expert evidence showed that the rental value of the premises in repair was increasing over the relevant period and "the calculation ... based upon the escalating rental values produces an unacceptably large figure representing, as it does, in excess of two years' rent". In other cases, however, (for example, where the premises are let on a long lease at a ground rent[58]) it will be necessary to ignore the rent actually payable and proceed by reference to the rack rental value of the premises in repair.

Expert valuation evidence of the rental value of the premises in repair will be admissible in an appropriate case, although it will not always be necessary.[59] In *Earle v Charalambous*[60] the judge at first instance based his assessment of the rental value of a long leasehold flat in repair on evidence given by the tenant as to researches he had carried out and the judge's own impression of the rental value of a one-bedroom flat of the type in question in that part of London. The Court of Appeal rejected the landlord's contention that there was no proper evidence to support the judge's figure, on the ground that there was no need for other evidence: the tenant was well able to carry out his own researches into rental values of equivalent properties and the judge was entitled to accept his figures in the absence of evidence to the contrary.[61]

**33–18**

Generally, the notional reduction in rental value will not be capable of precise estimation and will be a matter for the judgment for the court, rather than for expert valuation evidence.[62] In an appropriate case, however, expert evidence may be admissible on the amount of the reduction. Thus, in *Electricity Supply Nominees Ltd v National Magazine Co Ltd*[63] H.H. Judge Hicks, QC held that the

---

[54] [2004] 1 W.L.R. 1254.
[55] See para.20–17 et seq., above.
[56] See also *English Churches Housing Group v Shine* [2004] H.L.R. 42.
[57] [2002] 3 E.G.L.R. 93.
[58] See *Elmcroft Developments v Tankersley-Sawyer* [1984] 1 E.G.L.R. 47; *Earle v Charalambous* [2007] H.L.R. 8.
[59] *Earle v Charalambous*, above, at [31].
[60] Above.
[61] Above at [34].
[62] *Wallace v Manchester City Council* [1998] 3 E.G.L.R. 38 per Morritt L.J. at 42; *Earle v Charalambous*, above, at [32].
[63] [1999] 1 E.G.L.R. 130. In *Earle v Charalambous*, above, Carnwath L.J. regarded the whole of H.H. Judge Hicks, QC's judgment as "persuasive".

measure of damages for breach of a landlord's covenant to use reasonable endeavours to provide lift and air conditioning services to office premises was:

"[T]he resulting diminution in value to the tenant of its occupation of the premises for the relevant period, evidence of the rent payable under the lease being admissible (but not conclusive) as to such value had there been no breach, and the evidence of valuation experts being relevant and admissible as to such value following such breaches as may be found."

The notional reduction in rent approach has also been used to assess damages for disrepair in commercial cases. One such example is *Electricity Supply Nominees Ltd v National Magazine Co Ltd.*[64] Another is *Larksworth Investments Ltd v Temple (No.2),*[65] which also concerned office premises. In that case, there was "a visible want of repair, with an effect on the amenity and efficiency of the offices, for an aggregate period of five years". The Court of Appeal, allowing an appeal from an award of £37,500, awarded £25,000. Robert Walker L.J. said:

"It seems to me that some sort of mathematical approach is necessary in this case, even if it is adopted not as a binding principle but simply as a guide or check."

The figure of £25,000 represented, for the five-year period, the whole of the annual rent attributable to two unusable rooms plus an allowance of £2.50 per square foot (against a total rent of approximately £9 per square foot) for the remainder of the premises affected by the breach of covenant.

Likewise, in *Clarke v Lloyds TSB Bank Ltd*[66] damages of £165,000 were awarded for failure to provide adequate air conditioning. The expert evidence was to the effect that premises without air conditioning were worth two-thirds of premises with air conditioning. The damages figure represented one-third of the actual rent passing over the relevant period and then rounded up.

**33–19**  There is no reason in principle why in an appropriate case damages should not exceed the rent payable. Thus, in *Chiodi's v De Marney*[67] a flat was let at the registered rent of £8 per week. The landlord was in breach of covenant to repair for about three-and-a-half years until the tenant moved out of the demised flat. The county court judge awarded general damages for inconvenience and distress at the rate of £30 per week for that period. The landlord appealed, contending that the judge had failed to give sufficient weight to the fact that the recoverable rent was only £8 per week. It was argued that the value of the premises to the tenant could not exceed the recoverable rent, and that the amount of the recoverable rent should provide a guide or test to the maximum award for inconvenience, discomfort and distress. The Court of Appeal dismissed the appeal, holding that the judge had not erred in failing to take account of the rent as a prima facie indication of the level of his award.

However, it has been held, in relation to damages for breach of the landlord's covenant implied by s.11 of the Landlord and Tenant Act, 1985,[68] that damages

---

[64] Above.
[65] [1999] B.L.R. 297.
[66] [2002] 3 E.G.L.R. 93.
[67] (1988) 21 H.L.R. 6.
[68] See para.20–17 et seq., above.

for discomfort and inconvenience should not ordinarily exceed the rent payable. Thus, in *English Churches Housing Group v Shine*,[69] Wall L.J., giving the judgment of the Court of Appeal, said:[70]

> "Whilst we accept that the guidelines helpfully set out by Morritt LJ in *Wallace v. Manchester City Council* are not to be applied in a mechanistic or dogmatic way, and whilst we equally accept that there will be cases in which the level of distress or inconvenience experienced by a tenant may require an award in excess of the level of rent payable, we take the view that the plain interference of Morritt LJ's judgment, and the figures identified in the case itself, demonstrate that if an award of damages for stress and inconvenience arising from a landlord's breach of the implied covenant to repair is to exceed the level of the rental payable, clear reasons need to be given by the court for taking that course, and the facts of the case—notably the conduct of the landlord—must warrant such an award. It must, we think, always be remembered that an award of damages under LTA 1985 section 11 is an award for a breach of contract by the landlord, not for a tort committed by the landlord. It is, accordingly in our judgment logical that the calculation of the award of damages for stress and inconvenience should be related to the fact that the tenant is not getting proper value for the rent, which is being paid for defective premises. Moreover, the reason for the awards being modest is, it seems to us, related to the fact that the tenant in a secure weekly tenancy has the benefit of occupying premises at a rent, which is well below that which the same premises would be likely to command in the open market ... we see nothing in the instant case to take it out of what might be described as the basic rule of thumb that—all other things being equal—the maximum award for damages in the case such as the present should be the rental value of the premises."

The fact that a fair rent has been fixed by the rent officer which takes account of the disrepair does not prevent the tenant from being entitled to damages for breach of the landlord's covenant to repair.[71] However, the fact that the premises have been let at a very low rent on account of the disrepair may be relevant in assessing damages.[72]

Damages for disrepair in residential cases commonly include discomfort and inconvenience suffered by members of the tenant's family.[73] It was suggested in *Electricity Supply Nominees Ltd v National Magazine Co Ltd*[74] that where the tenant is a corporation damages cannot be awarded for inconvenience and discomfort suffered by the tenant's staff and customers.[75] However, in *Credit Suisse v Beegas Nominees Ltd*[76] (in which the landlord's breach of covenant had resulted in water penetration into office premises) Lindsay J. awarded a limited company general damages for inconvenience, saying:

**33–20**

> "I am unconvinced that one can evaluate inconvenience to a tenant in occupation by reference simply to the diminution in prospective letting value to some hypothetical other tenant. General damages are notoriously at large, but doing the best I can to have regard to the inconvenience suffered by staff and customers in these expensive and prestigious premises over the period I have described I fix general damages at £40,000."

---

[69] [2004] H.L.R. 42.
[70] See para.20–17 et seq., above.
[71] *Sturolson & Co v Mauroux* (1988) 20 H.L.R. 332.
[72] *London Borough of Newham v Patel* (1978) 12 H.L.R. 77.
[73] See, e.g. *Calabar Properties Ltd v Stitcher* [1984] 1 W.L.R. 287 (tenant's husband).
[74] [1999] 1 E.G.L.R. 130.
[75] [1999] 1 E.G.L.R. 130 at 134B.
[76] [1994] 4 All E.R. 803 and (more fully) [1994] 1 E.G.L.R. 76.

Similarly, in *Larksworth Investments Ltd v Temple House Ltd (No.2)*[77] the Court of Appeal took into account when assessing damages the fact that parts of the premises were "made less pleasant for use by solicitors, staff and clients, and the general inconvenience and discomfort associated with premises which [counsel] described, not inaptly, as being down at heel".[78]

In *Langham Estate Management Ltd v Hardy*,[79] a company tenant took a letting of a high class residential property for occupation by others. It did not itself occupy the premises. H.H. Judge Marshall QC held that the company was nonetheless entitled to more than merely nominal damages for breach of the landlord's repairing and other covenants. She said:

> "[Counsel's] submission was that in the absence of any direct evidence from the occupier of the actual effect upon it of the loss of amenity caused by any breaches of covenant that I found (as contrasted, I interpose, with argument, often theoretical, made by others on their behalf), the award of damages would be merely the kind of irreducible minimum that is awarded in cases of breaches causing mere inconvenience rather than serious discomfort or damage (such as damp, leaks, water or wind ingress, wood rot or malfunctioning electric circuitry). Such awards, he submitted, were to be measured in hundreds of pounds, not thousands.
>
> I consider that [counsel] was right not to press for nominal damages only. Even though a company in [the tenant's] position may not itself have suffered any damage as a result of a breach of the landlords' covenant, it does so in the sense that it has paid for something that it did not receive. The law does not, in my judgment, permit a landlord to get away with non-performance of its covenant while still being paid on the basis of having performed. The appropriate compensation for the tenant is a payment representing the value of the amenity that it did not receive, and was therefore unable to pass on to its licensee. The assessment then comes back to the third principle of *Wallace*,[80] cited above, but without regard to any particular susceptibilities of the actual occupiers."

In an appropriate case damages may be awarded for inconvenience and discomfort suffered by the tenant during the carrying out of the remedial works.[81] However, such damages are only recoverable to the extent that the works would not have been necessary if the landlord had performed his covenant when he should have done.[82]

**33–21**  The extent of the tenant's use of the premises may be relevant to the correct assessment of damages. However, each case will turn on its own facts. In *McCoy & Co v Clark*[83] Sir David Cairns said in the course of his judgment:

> "It is all very well to say that the [tenant] was not spending a great deal of the day in the flat and that he was using it mainly as a sleeping place. If he had the flat as a sleeping place and was willing to pay £9 per week for the flat for that purpose, then he is entitled to a flat which is comfortable for that purpose, and if it is substantially reduced in the degree of comfort, then I think that what he ought to recover is something proportional to that reduction."

[77] [1999] B.L.R. 297.
[78] Above at 302. See also *Clarke v Lloyds TSB Bank Ltd* [2002] 3 E.G.L.R. 93.
[79] [2008] 3 E.G.L.R. 125
[80] This is a reference to *Wallace v Manchester City Council* [1998] 3 E.G.L.R. 38. The relevant passage from Morritt L.J.'s judgment is set out at para.32–15, above.
[81] See *Televantos v McCulloch* (1991) 23 H.L.R. 412.
[82] See para.33–16, above.
[83] (1984) 13 H.L.R. 87.

However, it has been held that the fact that the tenant is a single man living alone as opposed to a woman with a young family is relevant in assessing damages for general inconvenience.[84]

Where part of the disrepair is due to defects for which the tenant is liable, the damages must be reduced to reflect that fact.[85]

In assessing the likely level of damages for disrepair in residential cases, it is usually helpful to look at the amounts which the courts are currently awarding. Excellent sources of reference for this are *Legal Action, Current Law* and the *Housing Law Reports*, all of which periodically summarise or report cases in which damages have been awarded against residential landlords for disrepair. These afford a very useful guide to the general level of damages currently being awarded by county courts in such cases.

## Other heads of damage

### (a) Ill health

Damages for ill health resulting from the disrepair are recoverable in principle.[86] The fact that the tenant is treated in hospital and makes a substantial recovery quicker than he would have done had he not had treatment will go in reduction of damages.[87] However, the fact that he had a comfortable time in hospital is irrelevant.[88] If he fails to mitigate the effect of the breach on his health, the damages will be reduced accordingly.[89]

**33–22**

### (b) Mental distress and anxiety

Damages for mental distress were awarded in *Chiodi v De Marney*.[90] However, as a general principle damages for mental distress will not be awarded for breach of contract unless the object of the contract is to provide pleasure, relaxation, peace of mind or freedom from molestation.[91] In *Branchett v Beaney*[92] it was held that damages for distress are not recoverable for breach of a covenant for quiet enjoyment, since such a covenant is not of the exceptional type which is considered by the law to have as one of its purposes the provision of peace of mind or freedom from distress. It is difficult to see how an ordinary covenant to

**33–23**

---

[84] *Taylor v Knowsley Borough Council* (1985) 17 H.L.R. 376. In *Electricity Supply Nominees Ltd v National Magazine Co Ltd* [1999] 1 E.G.L.R. 130 Judge Hicks, QC regarded this case as difficult to reconcile with *McCoy & Co v Clark*, above.

[85] *Hewitt v Rowlands* (1924) 93 L.J.K.B. 1080; *Elmcroft Developments Ltd v Tankersley-Sawyer* [1984] 1 E.G.L.R. 47.

[86] *McCoy & Co v Clark* (1984) 13 H.L.R. 87 (pneumonia caused by dampness); *Chiodi v De Marney* [1988] 2 E.G.L.R. 64 (arthritis, colds and influenza).

[87] *McCoy & Co v Clark*, above.

[88] Ibid.

[89] Ibid.

[90] Above.

[91] *Watts v Morrow* [1991] 1 W.L.R. 1421 per Bingham L.J. See generally *McGregor on Damages*, 18th edn, para.3–019 et seq.

[92] [1992] 2 E.G.L.R. 33.

repair differs for these purposes from a covenant for quiet enjoyment. It is therefore thought that damages for mental distress will not ordinarily be recoverable as a separate head of damages for breach of a landlord's covenant to repair. However, stress and depression suffered by the tenant which is no different in kind from that of any tenant in his position may perhaps be reflected in an award of damages for discomfort and inconvenience.[93]

### (c) Damage to personal property

**33–24**  Where the breach has resulted in damage to the tenant's personal property, such as furniture or carpets, then in principle the damages will include the cost of making good the damage or the value of the damaged items.[94]

### (d) Damage to the demised premises

**33–25**  Where the landlord's breach has resulted in damage to the demised premises and the landlord is not liable to repair that damage under his repairing covenant, the damages recoverable by the tenant will in principle include the reasonable cost of making good the damage in question.[95] The overall question will be whether it is reasonable in all the circumstances to do the work.[96] The fact that the tenant is liable for the work under his repairing covenant may, in an appropriate case, be a powerful, albeit not conclusive, reason for saying that it would be reasonable to carry out the work. It is thought, however, that the fact that the tenant is not so liable will not prevent the cost of the work being awarded as damages in an appropriate case.

No deduction for betterment will be made where the damage cannot in practice be remedied save by new work in place of old.[97]

### (e) The cost of carrying out repair work which the landlord should have done

**33–26**  The reasonable cost of carrying out repair work falling within the landlord's repairing obligation is recoverable as damages in an appropriate case.[98] Thus, in

---

[93] *Earle v Charalambous* [2007] H.L.R. 8 at [39].

[94] *Hewitt v Rowlands* (1924) 93 L.J.K.B. 1080 (piano, pictures and a carpet); *McCoy & Co v Clark* (1982) 13 H.L.R. 87 (curtains); *Calabar Properties v Stitcher* [1984] 1 W.L.R. 287; *Chiodi v De Marney, above; Passley v Wandsworth LBC* (1998) 30 H.L.R. 165 (record collection).

[95] *Green v Eales* (1841) 2 Q.B. 225; *Holding & Barnes v Hill House Hammond* (unreported decision of Neuberger J. dated March 17, 2000) (note that this was the trial of the action following the judge's determination of a preliminary issue concerning the meaning of the landlord's repairing covenant (reported at [2000] L. & T.R 428) and prior to the decision of the Court of Appeal (reported at [20002] 2 P. & C. R. 11 and considered in para.4–09, above) allowing the tenant's cross-appeal on the preliminary issue).

[96] Cf. paras 32–02 to 32–05, above.

[97] *Harbutt's "Plasticine" Ltd v Wayne Tank & Pump Co Ltd* [1970] 1 Q.B. 447; *McGreal v Wake* (1984) 13 H.L.R. 107; *Bradley v Chorley Borough Council* (1985) 17 H.L.R. 305; *Calabar Properties Ltd v Stitcher* [1984] 1 W.L.R. 287, per Stephenson L.J. See para.29–16, above.

[98] *Green v Eales* (1841) 2 Q.B. 225; *Hewitt v Rowlands* (1924) 93 L.J.K.B. 1080; *Granada Theatres Ltd v Freehold Investment (Leytonstone) Ltd* [1959] 1 Ch. 592 at 608; *Calabar Properties Ltd v*

*Hewitt v Rowlands*[99] the demised premises consisted of a cottage occupied by a statutory tenant. It suffered from damp, and the gutters and roof were in need of repair. The case was remitted by the Court of Appeal to the Liverpool district registrar to assess damages in accordance with the directions of the court. His task was commented on by Stephenson L.J. in *Calabar Properties Ltd v Stitcher*[100] as follows:

> "What the difference in value to the plaintiff of the statutory tenancy of the cottage repaired and unrepaired may have been was not an easy matter for the registrar to assess, but I suspect he would not have gone far wrong if he had equated it with what the plaintiff might have to spend on performing the landlord's covenant (assuming the landlord would not perform it himself) and substantial general damages for inconvenience and discomfort."

In *Marenco v Jacramel Co Ltd*[101] the tenant occupied on a long lease one of 12 flats in two blocks of flats. The lease contained a covenant by the landlord to keep and maintain the exterior of the flat and the building in good repair and condition, and a covenant by the tenant to pay a proportion of the cost by way of service charge. Various defects existed to the blocks which fell within the landlord's covenant. The cost of the remedial work was £384. The landlords refused to carry out the work until the other tenants had contributed towards the cost of previous works and given security for future contributions. The tenant brought proceedings for damages claiming the cost of the work. The county court judge held that she was entitled to one-twelfth of £384 (£32), on the ground that all the other flats were equally affected by the breaches; since the tenant's service charge contribution was also one-twelfth of the cost of the work, it followed that she was entitled to nothing. The Court of Appeal allowed the tenant's appeal, and awarded her the full cost of the work less the amount of her service charge contribution.

The overall question will be whether it is reasonable in all the circumstances, first, for the work to be done, and second, for it to be done by the tenant.[102] The fact that the tenant has not done the work by the date of the hearing is not conclusive against an award of the cost as damages.[103] However, where the work remains undone by that date, it is thought that the court is unlikely to award damages based on the cost of carrying it out where it is satisfied that the landlord intends to do the work himself, and a fortiori where it has ordered the landlord to do the work.

Where the landlord would have been able to recover the cost of the work under a service charge provision if he had carried it out, and the tenant carries it

---

*Stitcher*, above; *Loria v Hammer* [1989] 2 E.G.L.R. 249; *Holding & Barnes v Hill House Hammond* (unreported decision of Neuberger J. dated March 17, 2000) (note that this was the trial of the action following the judge's determination of a preliminary issue concerning the meaning of the landlord's repairing covenant (reported at [2000] L. & T.R 428) and prior to the decision of the Court of Appeal (reported at [20002] 2 P. & C. R. 11 and considered in para.4–09, above) allowing the tenant's cross-appeal on the preliminary issue). See further para.33–40, below.

[99] Above.

[100] Above.

[101] [1964] E.G.D. 319.

[102] Cf. paras 32–02 to 32–05, above.

[103] *Hewitt v Rowlands*, above; *Marenco v Jacramel Co Ltd*, above.

out, a deduction may be made from the tenant's damages to reflect the amount that the tenant would have had to pay by way of service charge had the landlord done the work.[104]

## Where the tenant vacates the premises for the duration of the works and then returns

33–27     Where the works are sufficiently substantial that the tenant reasonably moves out of the premises for the duration of the works, and then returns, the damages will prima facie be the cost of alternative accommodation, the cost of any consequential redecoration of the interior, and some award for all the unpleasantness of living in the premises as they deteriorated until they became uninhabitable.[105]

### (a) The cost of alternative accommodation

33–28     The cost of alternative accommodation is recoverable in principle if the tenant is obliged to vacate the premises as a result of the landlord's breach of covenant.[106] However, it should be borne in mind that, where liability is dependent on notice and the landlord repairs the defect reasonably promptly after receiving notice of it, he is not in breach[107]; consequently, if the tenant has to move out during the work, he cannot claim the cost of alternative accommodation as damages.[108] If, on the other hand, the landlord unreasonably delays in carrying out the repairs, then he will be in breach, and if the tenant then moves out (assuming he would not otherwise have had to do so), the reasonable costs of alternative accommodation will be recoverable as damages.[109] However, the tenant's real reason for leaving the premises must be the disrepair.[110] It is thought that he would have to give credit for such period as he would have had to move out anyway even if the landlord had performed his covenant when he should have done.

In *Earle v Charalambous*[111] the tenant moved out of the demised flat following the collapse of the kitchen ceiling as a result of the landlord's breaches of covenant and went to live with his parents, where he remained for some 21 months until the repairs had been completed. In the Court of Appeal Carnwath L.J. said:

---

[104] *Marenco v Jacramel Co Ltd*, above; *Loria v Hammer* [1989] 2 E.G.L.R. 249 at 259D.

[105] *Calabar Properties Ltd v Stitcher* [1984] 1 W.L.R. 287, per Griffiths L.J.

[106] *Calabar Properties Ltd v Stitcher*, above; *Earle v Charalambous* [2007] H.L.R. 8; *Alexander v Lambeth LBC* [2000] C.L.Y. 3931.

[107] See para.22–14, above.

[108] *Green v Eales* (1841) 2 Q.B. 225; *Calabar Properties Ltd v Stitcher* [1984] 1 W.L.R. 287, esp. per Griffiths L.J. at 298; *McGreal v Wake* (1984) 13 H.L.R. 107; *Morris v Liverpool City Council* (1988) 20 H.L.R. 498.

[109] *McGreal v Wake*, above; *Calabar Properties Ltd v Stitcher*, above; *Morris v Liverpool City Council*, above.

[110] *Calabar Properties Ltd v Stitcher*, above, per Griffiths L.J.

[111] Above.

"I begin from the position that the lessee was deprived of the entire enjoyment of his property throughout this period. Whether one treats rental value as a measure of that loss, or one looks to the cost of renting equivalent accommodation, that would suggest a potential award of [the rental value for the period in question]. The lessee was able to mitigate his loss by living with his parents for this period, but that does not mean that the compensatable loss is confined to his transport problems. That would leave him with nothing for the loss of enjoyment of his property for almost two years. Not surprisingly perhaps, the precise legal status of his agreement with his parents was open to question. But the judge was entitled to accept it as some indication of his loss. Although his reasoning might have been more clearly expressed, the overall award of just under half the rental value for this period, during which he had no use at all of his property, was a fair estimate of his loss, and is not open to criticism in principle."

The cost of alternative accommodation is only recoverable to the extent that it is reasonable in amount.[112]

### (b) Moving into the alternative accommodation

In an appropriate case, removal costs are recoverable,[113] and so are the costs of storing furniture.[114] In addition, damages are recoverable for the worry and inconvenience of moving into the alternative accommodation.[115]

**33–29**

### (c) Other consequential expenses

Consequential losses which the tenant suffers by reason of having to live elsewhere, such as storage of his possessions and additional travel costs,[116] are recoverable in principle.

**33–30**

### (d) Costs and outgoings in relation to the demised premises

Running costs and outgoings on the demised premises for the period in which the tenant is out of occupation are not generally recoverable. This is because the tenant has to pay outgoings on some property, and the cost of the alternative accommodation prima facie represents the loss which the tenant has suffered by being kept out of the demised premises.[117]

**33–31**

### (e) Consequential redecoration and cleaning up on returning

If the tenant's decorations are damaged in the course of remedial works carried out by the landlord, the landlord will be liable to redecorate.[118] In such a case, any costs incurred by the tenant in redecorating are recoverable as damages for breach of the landlord's obligation. It is thought that redecoration costs would also be recoverable where the landlord is not liable to redecorate under the above principle, but the damage to the decorations arises as a result of his breach of

**33–32**

---

[112] *Earle v Charalambous*, above.
[113] *McGreal v Wake*, above.
[114] Ibid.
[115] *Lubren v Lambeth LBC* (1987) 20 H.L.R. 165.
[116] See *Earle v Charalambous* [2007] H.L.R. 8.
[117] Ibid.
[118] This is considered in para.22–47 et seq., above.

covenant to repair some other part of the premises. The cost of clearing up and cleaning the premises on returning are also recoverable in an appropriate case.[119]

## Service charges

**33–33** Where the landlord is entitled to recover the cost of complying with his repairing obligations by way of service charge, and the effect of the landlord's breach of covenant is that more extensive work is necessary, the tenant will in principle be entitled to damages equal to the additional service charges which he would not have had to pay had the landlord complied with his obligation.[120] Thus, in *Princes House v Distinctive Clubs*[121] the landlord was obliged to use all reasonable endeavours to repair the roof of the block and the tenant was obliged to pay a service charge in respect of the costs reasonably and properly incurred by the landlord in performing that obligation. The service charge was capped for the first five years of the lease (up to December 24, 2003). The roof was in disrepair but in breach of covenant the landlords failed to carry out the remedial works until 2004. It was held that had the landlord complied with its obligations, the works would have been completed prior to December 24, 2003 so that the tenant's service charge contribution would have been subject to the cap. Damages were awarded by reference to the excess service charges paid over and above the cap.

Care must be taken, however, in the formulation of such claims. First, where the landlord in default is a predecessor in title of the present landlord, the latter will only be liable for any additional work becoming necessary as a result of his own failure to repair since becoming landlord: the claim for the balance will have to be made against the predecessor in title responsible.[122] Second, it is thought that the tenant will have to give credit for the use of the money which he would have had to pay by way of service charge had the landlord complied with his obligation when he should have done.[123] Third, where the breach consists of delay in carrying out maintenance work, the right conclusion on the facts may be that much the same work would have been necessary even if the landlord had complied with his obligation at an earlier date.[124]

---

[119] *McGreal v Wake* (1984) 13 H.L.R. 107.

[120] *Continental Property Ventures v White* [2006] 1 E.G.L.R. 85; *Princes House v Distinctive Clubs* (unreported decision of Mr Jonathan Gaunt, QC sitting as a deputy judge of the Chancery Division dated September 25, 2006). However, the fact that repair works are only necessary (or are more extensive that would otherwise have been the case) by reason of a breach of the landlord's repairing obligations does not of itself mean that the cost of such works is unreasonably incurred for the purposes of s.18 of the Landlord and Tenant Act 1985: *Continental Property Ventures v White*, above.

[121] Above.

[122] See Ch.3 above.

[123] Cf. *Marenco v Jacramel Co Ltd* [1964] E.G.D. 319 (considered in para.33–26, above); *Loria v Hammer* [1989] 2 E.G.L.R. 249 at 259D.

[124] See *Postel Properties Ltd v Boots the Chemist* [1996] 2 E.G.L.R. 60.

## Where the tenant has sold the premises or would have done so but for the disrepair

If the tenant assigns the lease before the disrepair has been remedied, the measure **33–34** of damages will be the difference in the price he receives for the premises in their damaged condition and that which they would have fetched in the open market if the landlord had observed his repairing covenant.[125] Where the tenant could have assigned the lease but was prevented from doing so by the disrepair, the damages will include where appropriate the outgoings payable in respect of the premises after the date on which the lease could have been assigned, and a sum to reflect the fact that the tenant will continue to be liable under the lease in the future.[126] Thus, in *Credit Suisse v Beegas Nominees Ltd*[127] a prestigious office building was in disrepair, in breach of the landlord's covenant. Had the landlord carried out the repairs when he should have done, then the tenant could and would have assigned its underlease for a premium of £85,000. As a result of the landlord's breach, the underlease could not be assigned. Lindsay J. awarded by way of damages, among other things: (1) the lost premium of £85,000; (2) the outgoings payable in respect of the premises from the date on which the underlease could have been assigned; (3) rent, insurance and service charges payable by the tenant after the date on which the underlease could have been assigned; and (4) a sum to reflect the fact that the tenant would remain tenant until the expiry of the underlease in 2008 but would be able, as soon as practicable after the repair works had been completed, to sub-underlet at the best rent then obtainable to a sub-tenant of a kind to whom the landlord would be likely to permit a sub-underletting. The landlord's argument in relation to the last of these was that no damages should be given in respect of any period after the hearing because the tenant could always bring fresh proceedings if further loss occurred. However, Lindsay J. held that the loss in question was not loss flowing from future breaches but future losses from a past breach, and therefore that it was recoverable in principle.

In addition, where the disrepair results in the tenant being unable to assign the lease, further consequential losses are recoverable, such as abortive costs incurred in trying to sell the lease,[128] and running costs on the demised premises pending a sale.[129] It would appear, however, that other consequential losses, such as loss of executive time in dealing with the landlord and the local authority in getting the repairs done,[130] and loss of the opportunity to reinvest the proceeds of sale,[131] may be irrecoverable as being too remote.

---

[125] *Calabar Properties Ltd v Stitcher* [1984] 1 W.L.R. 287, per Griffiths L.J. See also *City & Metropolitan Properties Ltd v Greycroft* [1987] 1 W.L.R. 1085.

[126] *Credit Suisse v Beegas Nominees Ltd* [1994] 4 All E.R. 803 and (more fully) [1994] 1 E.G.L.R. 76.

[127] Above.

[128] *City & Metropolitan Properties Ltd v Greycroft Ltd* [1987] 1 W.L.R. 1085; *Credit Suisse v Beegas Nominees Ltd*, above.

[129] *Credit Suisse v Beegas Nominees Ltd*, above.

[130] *City & Metropolitan Properties Ltd v Greycroft*, above.

[131] Ibid.

## Loss of the ability to sub-let

**33–35**  In principle, damages are recoverable for loss suffered by the tenant as a result of being unable to sub-let, or only being able to do so at a reduced rent.[132] Such a claim is subject to the ordinary rules regarding remoteness of damage, so that (in general terms) the loss will only be recoverable if it is of a kind which the landlord, when he entered into the contract containing the obligation to repair, ought to have realised was not unlikely to result from the breach.[133]

Where, at the time he granted the lease, the landlord had actual knowledge that the tenant intended to sub-let, no question of remoteness arises. More commonly, however, the landlord will not have been told that in so many words, and the question will be whether loss of sub-letting is damage of a kind which is too remote. In *Mira v Aylmer Square Investments Ltd*[134] the landlord constructed a number of penthouses on the roofs of blocks of flats in North London. The work was carried out in such a way that the tenants of the flats were held to be entitled to damages for breach of the covenant for quiet enjoyment. The question was whether they could recover as part of those damages sums equal to the rents which they would have been able to obtain by sub-letting their flats. The landlord argued that such loss was too remote. The Court of Appeal rejected that contention. Stuart-Smith L.J., who gave the leading judgment, said:

> "It seems to me that the prospect of that damage occurring was not very unusual and was easily foreseeable. The leases were long leases. They clearly contemplated that there would, or might be, assignments or sublettings. No formality whatever was required for subletting for less than 12 months and there was very little restriction, only the requirement of notice and registration, for subletting for longer than that period or for assignments. Flats of this sort are not infrequently sublet. The tenants may wish to leave them for short periods of time without relinquishing the right to own them completely, wanting to return at some future time.
>
> There are many reasons why a person in that position may wish to sublet. People may prefer that they should have their home occupied rather than left unoccupied at the mercy of burglars and others. They may wish to obtain income to defray expenses of other accommodation or holidays, or for other reasons.
>
> It is clear from the decision in the *Calabar* case that, if a tenant is driven out of possession by breaches of a repairing covenant or breach of a covenant for quiet enjoyment, he can recover the costs of alternative accommodation. If the tenant happens to own other accommodation which he is driven to use, through the landlord's breach, he ought to be able to recover the loss which he actually sustains because he is unable to sublet the flat in question during the time that it is rendered uninhabitable."

The question therefore depends on what is the correct inference in all the circumstances as to what is likely to have been in the reasonable contemplation of the parties when they entered into the lease.

---

[132] *Calabar Properties Ltd v Stitcher* [1984] 1 W.L.R. 287 at 299D; *Mira v Ayler Square Investments Ltd* [1990] 1 E.G.L.R. 45.

[133] A detailed discussion of the law relating to remoteness of damage is outside the scope of this work, and reference should be made to the standard textbooks on the law of contract (for example *Chitty on Contracts*, 31st edn, Vol.I, Ch.26).

[134] [1990] 1 E.G.L.R. 45.

## Loss of profits

The landlord's breach of covenant may result in damage to the demised property, **33–36** or the contents, as a result of which the tenant's business may be adversely affected. For example, water coming through a badly leaking roof of an industrial building may cause damage to the tenant's machines on the top floor, as a result of which he may have to cease production while the machines are repaired, and thereby lose the profit he could have made. In principle, loss of this kind will be recoverable, provided that it was within the contemplation of the parties at the date of the lease that the premises would be used for the purposes of the business of the type in question. In other cases, such loss may be too remote to be recoverable.[135]

In *Electricity Supply Nominees Ltd v National Magazine Co Ltd*[136] it was submitted that loss of profits was a recoverable head of damage in principle. Judge Hicks QC did not feel it necessary to reach a concluded decision, but went on to say:

> "My provisional view is that if contemplated by the parties within the second limb of *Hadley v. Baxendale* (1854) 9 Exch. 341 loss of profit would be recoverable, but as a measure of the diminution in value of the tenancy to the tenant, not in addition to any other measure of that diminution."

In *Hawkins v Woodhall*[137] Arden L.J. (with whom Smith L.J. and Sir Andrew Morritt agreed) said in relation to a claim for damages for loss of profits by a tenant of shop premises:

> "The [tenants] counterclaim damages for breach of the repairing obligation, as I say, in terms of the loss of profit to them through the premises being unsuitable for their business and also for diminution in value of the tenancy. The [tenants] claim damages. Accordingly I have to ask this question: what sum will, so far as money can, place the respondents in the position they would have been in if the obligations to repair had been performed by [the landlord]? The premises had been let for the purpose of carrying on business as a bedding centre. The various versions of the tenancy agreement were written on notepaper headed 'Direct Beds Bedding Centre'. The premises could not be used for that purpose if there was significant water penetration and damp. It was therefore reasonably within the contemplation of both parties that if the disrepair for which the landlord was responsible resulted in the premises being seriously damp, the business of a bedding centre would probably suffer. The judge was satisfied that the decrease in sales was due to defects in the premises ... Accordingly, in these circumstances, as a matter of law a claim lay for loss of profits and for diminution in the value of the tenancy."

However, the court went on to hold (among other things) that (i) the maximum period for which the tenants were entitled to damages was 15 months, which was a reasonable time to enable them to pursue the landlord to do the repairs, give the appropriate notice to terminate the tenancy and find alternative premises[138]; (ii) the tenants had failed to prove the loss of profit because they were unable to show

---

[135] A detailed discussion of the law relating to remoteness of damage is outside the scope of this work, and reference should be made to the standard textbooks on the law of contract (for example *Chitty on Contracts*, 31st edn, Vol.I, Ch.26).
[136] [1999] 1 E.G.L.R. 130.
[137] [2008] EWCA Civ 932.
[138] [2008] EWCA Civ 932 at [45] to [47].

what sales had taken place specifically from the demised premises as opposed to all three of the shops from which the business was carried on[139]; and (iii) no claim could be made by the tenants (who were individuals) in respect of a period after they had transferred the business to a limited company.[140]

## Defences to damages

**33–37**  The ordinary principles relating to causation, mitigation and remoteness apply to claims for damages by tenants for breach of the landlord's repairing obligations as they do to any other claim for breach of contract.[141]

Thus, even where the landlord's liability is not dependent on notice, the damages may be reduced on the ground of failure to mitigate if the tenant fails to report disrepair to the landlord.[142] Unreasonable behaviour which results in substantial delay in the completion of the repair works and substantial additional costs may also constitute a failure to mitigate,[143] as may an unreasonable failure by the tenant to terminate the tenancy and find alternative accommodation elsewhere,[144] and an unreasonable failure by the tenant to carry out the remedial works himself and claim the cost from the landlord.[145] However, where the tenant continues to use a part of the premises which he knows to be in disrepair, and he is then injured by the disrepair, his continued use will not constitute a failure to mitigate provided that it was reasonable.[146]

The tenant may lose his right to damages if he prevents the landlord from entering in order to carry out repairs.[147]

Similarly, the tenant's claim may fail on the ground that the damage claimed is too remote. Thus, in *Berryman v Hounslow LBC*,[148] the landlord failed in breach of covenant to keep the lifts in an 18-storey block of flats in reasonable repair (which the Court of Appeal interpreted as meaning in reasonable working order), such that one lift was out of commission and the other was not working at the relevant time. The claimant, who lived on the fifth floor, made several trips using the stairs to carry up her shopping, with her baby on her hip on each trip. She slipped a disc. The Court of Appeal, dismissing her claim for damages against the

---

[139] Ibid., at [50] to [53].

[140] Ibid., at [39] to [43]. It appears that the tenants were the sole directors and shareholders of the company, so that the conclusion that the company was the appropriate claimant after the business had been transferred to it might be thought to be somewhat technical: see, for example, *Esso Petroleum Co v Mardon* [1976] Q.B. 801.

[141] A detailed discussion of these is outside the scope of this work, and reference should be made to the standard textbooks on the law of contract (for example *Chitty on Contracts*, 31st edn, Vol.I, Ch.26).

[142] *Minchburn v Peck* (1988) 20 H.L.R. 392, in which Bingham L.J. commented: "A landlord or a tenant are contracting parties even though their contract is of a special kind. There is, however, nothing in the contract which excludes the ordinary principle of the law of contract that an injured party cannot recover damage which he could without expense to himself and by straightforward means have avoided."

[143] *English Churches Housing Group v Shine* [2004] H.L.R. 42.

[144] *Hawkins v Woodhall* [2008] EWCA Civ 932 at [46].

[145] *Hawkins v Woodhall*, above, at [45].

[146] *Porter v Jones* [1942] 2 All E.R. 570.

[147] *Granada Theatres Ltd v Freehold Investment (Leytonstone) Ltd* [1959] Ch. 592.

[148] (1998) 30 H.L.R. 567.

landlord, held that whilst it was not unlikely that if the lift was immobile the tenant would walk up the stairs, this did not make a slipped disc a foreseeable consequence of the duty to keep the lift in order. Henry L.J. said:

"The breach to be foreseen is that of an immobile lift. The initial impression that that gives is that an immobile lift is a safe lift because the dangers associated with lifts involve their crashing down. On the other hand, as the lift is the means of access to the flats in this tower block, it is not unlikely that someone discommoded by the fact that the lift is not operational will walk upstairs. Walking upstairs is marginally more dangerous than walking on the flat. But the fact that going upstairs might make you marginally more likely to stumble does not, in my judgment, make an injury arising from such a stumble a foreseeable consequence of the breach of contract to keep the lift in working order."

This case should be contrasted with *Marshall v Rubypoint Ltd*,[149] in which the claimant tenant was held to be entitled to recover damages in respect of loss caused by burglars who had entered through a defective main door which the landlord, in breach of covenant, had failed to repair. The Court of Appeal rejected the landlord's contention that the presence of the internal door to the tenant's flat rendered such loss too remote. Buckley J. said:

**33–38**

"In my judgment, it would have been within the contemplation of the parties that if the front door fell into disrepair and did not provide any real obstacle to a would-be intruder, a burglary was not unlikely. I do not consider the fact that flat C had its own front door alters the position. A burglar, having gained easy access through the main front door would be out of sight of passers-by and feel more secure. He would be unlikely to baulk at the prospect of forcing an internal door."

Likewise, in *Mira v Aylmer Square Investments Ltd*[150] the Court of Appeal rejected the landlord's contention that the loss of sub-rents was too remote to be recoverable as damages for breach of the covenant for quiet enjoyment.

The landlord may also have a defence to a claim for damages for disrepair where it can show that the tenant's breach of contract in failing to pay rent and service charges was the substantial cause of its failure to repair, such that:

(1)   the tenant is liable for damages for non-payment in an amount equal to the landlord's liability for damages; and
(2)   the two claims cancel each other out.[151]

## Pending land action

A tenant's claim for damages for breach of the landlord's repairing covenant is not registrable as a pending land action under the Land Charges Act 1972, even when coupled with a claim for specific performance of the landlord's covenant to repair.[152]

**33–39**

---

[149] [1997] 1 E.G.L.R. 69.
[150] [1990] 1 E.G.L.R. 45. See para.33–35, above.
[151] *Bluestorm v Portvale Holdings* [2004] 2 E.G.L.R. 38.
[152] *Regan & Blackburn Ltd v Rogers* [1985] 1 W.L.R. 870.

## CARRYING OUT THE WORKS

### Right to carry out the works

33–40    Where the landlord's breach of covenant relates to the demised premises themselves, the tenant will have a right to carry out the necessary repairs by virtue of his interest in the premises as tenant, in which case the reasonable cost of carrying out the works will prima facie be recoverable as damages.[153] Where the breach relates to property retained by the landlord, the question whether the tenant has an implied right to enter to remedy the disrepair is less clear.[154] If he has such a licence, the reasonable cost of carrying out the repairs will be recoverable as damages in an appropriate case, but the position may be more difficult if his entry would be a trespass.[155]

## SET-OFF AGAINST RENT

### The nature of set-off

33–41    Where the tenant is entitled to damages for breach of the landlord's repairing covenant, that right can be enforced either by beginning proceedings against the landlord, or by counterclaiming in proceedings brought by the landlord. In addition, however, where the claim amounts to a set-off against rent or other sums due to the landlord, it operates to extinguish the tenant's liability for those sums. The effect of this is that it takes effect as a defence to the landlord's claim as opposed to just a cross-claim.

A right of set-off is superior to a mere right to counterclaim in a number of important ways. First, since it exists independently of any actual legal proceedings, it gives the tenant a simple self-help remedy in the case of breach by the landlord of his repairing obligations. The tenant need not himself initiate proceedings; he can merely withhold rent until such time as he judges that the right of set-off has been exhausted. If the landlord disputes the existence or the amount of the set-off, he must take the initiative, usually by bringing proceedings. Second, because the set-off operates as a defence, the landlord will not normally be entitled to summary judgment for the arrears, except to the extent that it is plain beyond argument that liability for some arrears exists over and above the amount of the claimed set-off.[156] Third, the question of who should pay the costs of any proceedings may depend on whether a set-off exists. Fourth, there may be reasons why a claim against the landlord is of less value than a set-off. For example, if the landlord is in liquidation the tenant would have to prove in respect of any claim for damages, but if the claim takes effect as a set-off the claim is discharged in full through non-payment of the rent. Fifth, the landlord will not be entitled to interest on the arrears of rent under a contractual

---

[153] See para.32–26, above.
[154] See para.23–09 et seq., above.
[155] See para.23–12, above.
[156] See CPR Pt 24. But details of the set-off must be given: see para.33–44, below.

provision in the lease because the arrears will have been extinguished. Last, the landlord is not entitled to distrain for rent in respect of which the tenant has a set-off.[157]

## Availability of set-off

A common law right to set-off against rent sums which the tenant has actually expended in himself carrying out works of repair for which the landlord is liable has long been recognised.[158] However, the equitable right of set-off against rent goes further and extends to unliquidated damages for breach of the landlord's repairing obligations, even where the tenant has not himself carried out the works for which the landlord is liable, provided that the claim arises under the lease itself, or directly from the relationship of landlord and tenant, or pursuant to an agreement for lease.[159] Further, a right of set-off against a previous landlord may be exercised against a new landlord's claim for rent arrears which have been assigned to him by the previous landlord (or which have passed to him under s.141 of the Law of Property Act 1925).[160] However, a claim for unliquidated damages against a previous landlord may not be set-off against a claim by a successor in title for rent arrears falling due after the transfer of the reversion unless the lease specifically provides otherwise.[161] A claim for damages for disrepair against the landlord may not be set-off against a claim for rent or service charges brought by a manager appointed under Pt II of the Landlord and Tenant Act 1927.[162]

The court may refuse to allow an equitable set-off against rent where to permit a set-off would be inequitable because of the conduct of the party seeking a set-off.[163]

**33–42**

---

[157] *Eller v Grovecrest Investments Ltd* [1994] 4 All E.R. 845.

[158] *Taylor v Beal* (1591) Cro. Eliz. 222; *Lee-Parker v Izzet (No.1)* [1971] 1 W.L.R. 1688; *Holding & Barnes v Hill House Hammond* (unreported decision of Neuberger J. dated March 17, 2000) (note that this was the trial of the action following the judge's determination of a preliminary issue concerning the meaning of the landlord's repairing covenant (reported at [2000] L. & T.R 428) and prior to the decision of the Court of Appeal (reported at [20002] 2 P. & C. R. 11 and considered in para.4–09, above) allowing the tenant's cross-appeal on the preliminary issue).

[159] *British Anzani (Felixstowe) v International Marine Management (U.K.) Ltd* [1980] Q.B. 137; *Melville v Grapelodge Developments Ltd* (1980) 39 P. & C.R. 179; *Televantos v McCulloch* (1991) 23 H.L.R. 412; *London Borough of Haringey v Stewart* (1991) 23 H.L.R. 557; *Filross Securities Ltd v Midgeley* [1998] 3 E.G.L.R. 43.

[160] *Muscat v Smith* [2004] 1 W.L.R. 2853. See para.3–15, above.

[161] *Edlington Properties v J.H. Fenner & Co* [2006] 1 W.L.R. 1583.

[162] *Maunder-Taylor v Blaquiere* [2003] 1 W.L.R. 379. See para.33–51 et seq., below.

[163] *Bluestorm v Portuale Holdings* [2004] 2 E.G.L.R. 38 (in which the tenant had by its refusal to pay rent and service charges brought about the very breaches of the repairing covenants of which it complained).

## Exclusion of the right of set-off

**33–43**  It is open to the parties to a contract to agree that the right of set-off shall be excluded.[164] However, clear words must be used. A provision that the rent is to be paid "without any deduction" or "without deduction or abatement" is insufficient, in the absence of any context suggesting the contrary, to operate by implication as an exclusion of the tenant's equitable right of set-off.[165] A covenant to pay the rent by direct debit may exclude the right of set-off.[166]

## Exercise of the right of set-off

**33–44**  There is no formal procedure by which the right of set-off must be exercised, but a prudent tenant will inform the landlord at the earliest appropriate moment of his reason for withholding rent. This may deter the landlord from seeking to recover the rent by proceedings or distress. The tenant whose set-off is based upon an unliquidated claim faces the difficulty that he may be unable exactly to quantify the amount of his claim. If he misjudges the amount, he is exposed to the risk that the landlord will be successful in obtaining judgment for the balance of the arrears, with possible adverse consequences for the tenant, including a liability to pay all or some of the costs. For this reason, it is suggested that an early attempt be made to quantify the amount to which the tenant is entitled, so that rent is not withheld in any greater amount.

Where the tenant relies on a set-off of damages for disrepair as a defence to the landlord's application for summary judgment under CPR Pt 24, he must give proper particulars of his claim. In *Asco Developments Ltd v Gordon*[167] Sir Robert Megarry V.C. is reported as having said that:

> "If a defendant wished to say that summary judgment ought not to be given against him because he had some cross-claim for a greater amount, it was fairly obvious that he must tell the plaintiff and the court what the claim and the amount were, giving enough detail to carry some degree of conviction ... the court must ... refuse to allow tenants who were in arrears with their rent to defeat any claim to judgment under Order 14 by general and unquantified allegations of breaches of repair obligations by their landlords which in many cases might well be imaginative rather than real."

Although this case was decided under the former RSC Ord.14, it is thought that the court would adopt a similar approach in relation to CPR Pt 24.

---

[164] *Gilbert Ash (Northern) Ltd v Modern Engineering (Bristol) Ltd* [1974] A.C. 689.
[165] *Connaught Restaurants Ltd v Indoor Leisure Ltd* [1993] 2 E.G.L.R. 108, overruling *Famous Army Stores Ltd v Meehan* [1993] 1 E.G.L.R. 73; *Edlington Properties Ltd v J.H. Fenner & Co Ltd* [2006] 1 W.L.R. 1583. Note that an exclusion of the right of set-off against rent is not invalidated by the Unfair Contract Terms Act 1977: *Electricity Supply Nominees Ltd v I.A.F. Group Ltd* [1993] 2 E.G.L.R. 95; *Star Rider v Inntrepreneur Pub Co Ltd* [1998] 1 E.G.L.R. 53; *Unchained Growth III Plc v Granby Village (Manchester) Management Co Ltd* [2000] L. & T.R. 186.
[166] *Esso Petroleum v Milton* [1997] 1 W.L.R. 938; *Star Rider v Inntrepreneur Pub Co Ltd* [1998] 1 E.G.L.R. 53; *Gibbs Mew Plc v Gemmell* [1999] 1 E.G.L.R. 43.
[167] [1978] 2 E.G.L.R. 41.

## QUITTING THE PREMISES

### The general principle

As a general principle, the existence even of substantial breaches by the landlord of his repairing obligations does not affect the continued existence of the lease and the tenant's continuing obligations under it.[168] This is so even where the lease is signed on the basis of a written undertaking given by the landlord to carry out repairs.[169] The same is the case where the relevant disrepair is not the liability of either party.[170]

**33–45**

### Where the breach amounts to a repudiation

It is now generally accepted that a lease can, like any other contract, be terminated by the commission by one party of a repudiatory breach which is accepted by the other party.[171] Accordingly, where the landlord's breach of his covenant to repair amount to a repudiatory breach, the tenant is entitled to accept it and thereby put an end to the lease.

**33–46**

However, not every breach will be of this character. It is thought that in order to be repudiatory, the breach must be sufficiently serious as to deprive the tenant of the whole, or substantially the whole, benefit which he entered into the lease to obtain.[172] In *Hussein v Mehlman*,[173] which concerned a letting of a residential flat, the landlord's breaches of the repairing covenants implied by s.11 of the Landlord and Tenant Act 1985 were so serious as to make the premises uninhabitable. The landlord refused to carry out the necessary repairs. The tenant returned the keys to the landlord's agents and vacated the premises. Mr Stephen Sedley, QC, sitting as an assistant recorder, held that the landlord's breaches were repudiatory, and that by vacating the premises and returning the keys, the tenant had accepted the landlord's breaches as putting an end to the lease.

---

[168] *Matthey v Curling* [1922] 2 A.C. 180; *Lee-Parker v Izzet (No.1)* [1971] 1 W.L.R. 1688 at 1693F; *Melville v Grapelodge Developments Ltd* (1978) 39 P. & C.R. 179.

[169] *Hunt v Silk* (1804) 5 East 449; *Surplice v Farnsworth* (1844) 7 Man. & G. 576; *Melville v Grapelodge Developments Ltd*, above.

[170] *Arden v Pullen* (1842) 10 M. & W. 321.

[171] *Hussein v Mehlman* [1992] 2 E.G.L.R. 287; *Nynehead Developments Ltd v RH Fibreboard Containers Ltd* [1999] 1 E.G.L.R. 7 at 12. The proposition was treated as correct without argument by the Court of Appeal in *Chartered Trust Ltd v Davies* [1997] 2 E.G.L.R. 83. In a long line of nineteenth century cases, it was held that a contract of letting could be terminated by the innocent party without notice if the other party failed to fulfil a fundamental term of the contract: *Edwards v Barrington* (1825) Ry. & M. 268; *Collins v Barrow* (1831) M. & Rob. 112; *Izon v Gorton* (1839) 6 Bing N.C. 95; *Arden v Pullen* (1842) 10 M. & W. 321; *Smith v Marrable* (1842) 11 M. & W. 5; and *Wilson v Finch Hatton* (1877) 2 Ex. D. 336 (see further on these cases para.19–23 et seq., above). For a more detailed discussion of termination of leases by breach, see *Megarry & Wade*, 8th edn (London: Sweet & Maxwell, 2012) at para.18–106 et seq.

[172] *Hongkong Fir Shipping Co Ltd v Kawasaki Kisen Kaisha Ltd* [1962] 2 Q.B. 26.

[173] [1992] 2 E.G.L.R. 287.

## FRUSTRATION

**33–47**  A contract is frustrated where, without fault of either party and for which the contract makes no sufficient provision, an event occurs which so significantly changes the nature of the outstanding contractual rights from what the parties could reasonably have contemplated when the contract was made that the contract is discharged.[174] In *National Carriers Ltd v Panalpina (Northern) Ltd*[175] the House of Lords held that the doctrine of frustration is in principle applicable to leases. However, it was held not to apply on the facts of that case, in which a demised warehouse became unusable because of a street closure. It was stressed that the cases in which the facts would justify the conclusion that a lease had been frustrated would be rare. It may be that one such case would be where some vast convulsion of nature destroys the subject-matter of the lease.[176] Cases such as this apart, it is difficult to think of any set of facts which would both constitute a breach by the landlord of its repairing obligations and amount to an event frustrating the lease. If the physical state of premises were ever to result in a lease being frustrated, it is thought likely that the disrepair will be so serious as to fall outside the repairing obligations of either party. Conversely, if the landlord were to remain under an obligation to carry out the necessary remedial works, the doctrine of frustration would not apply because the lease would have made express provision for the frustrating event.

## SPECIAL RIGHTS OF LOCAL AUTHORITY TENANTS

**33–48**  Special rights are conferred on secure tenants of local authorities by the Secure Tenants of Local Housing Authorities (Right to Repair) Regulations 1994[177] as amended by the Secure Tenants of Local Housing Authorities (Right to Repair) (Amendment) Regulations 1994[178] made under s.96 of the Housing Act 1985. The Regulations give such tenants the right to have qualifying repairs carried out, at their landlord's expense, to dwelling-houses of which they are the tenant, and to receive compensation from their landlords if such repairs are not carried out within a prescribed period. The repairs in question are those which remedy a defect specified in column 1 of the Schedule to the Regulations, and will not, in the opinion of the landlord, cost more than £250 to carry out. Those defects include such items as total or partial loss of electric power, water supply, gas supply and space or water heating, blocked or leaking foul drain and soil stack, blocked sink, bath or basin, leaking roof and rotten timber flooring or stair tread. Reference should be made to the Regulations for their detailed provisions. By the Secure Tenants of Local Housing Authorities (Right to Repair) (Amendment) Regulations 1997[179] the Regulations were extended to introductory tenants of local housing authorities.

---

[174] *National Carriers Ltd v Panalpina (Northern) Ltd* [1981] A.C. 675.
[175] Above.
[176] *Cricklewood Property & Investment Co Ltd v Leightons Investment Trust Ltd* [1945] A.C. 221.
[177] SI 1994/133.
[178] SI 1994/844.
[179] SI 1997/73.

## APPOINTMENT OF A RECEIVER

### Jurisdiction

The High Court has a general jurisdiction to appoint a receiver whenever it appears to be just and convenient to do so.[180] In appropriate circumstances the court has power to make an interlocutory order for the appointment of a receiver.[181] An order appointing a receiver may be protected by a caution.[182]

**33–49**

The power to appoint a receiver has been exercised in several cases where the landlord was in breach of the obligation to carry out repairs,[183] both where the landlord could not be found and his obligations to repair were unperformed,[184] and where the landlord was performing some of his duties but neglecting major repairs.[185] The jurisdiction to appoint a receiver is discretionary, but it is more likely to be exercised where the landlord's reversion is long distant and he has no economic interest in carrying out the repairs.[186] The court has power to appoint a receiver where the default is that of a management company and not that of the landlord.[187] However, the power to appoint a receiver will not be exercised where the landlord is a body on whom Parliament has conferred powers and imposed duties and responsibilities of an important kind (such as a local authority charged under the Housing Act 1985 with the duty of maintaining housing accommodation).[188]

There are two important practical limitations on the usefulness of this remedy. First, the receiver will need funds out of which to pay for the necessary repairs. Where the leases provide for the payment of advance service charges, then the terms of the receiver's appointment will usually enable him to collect these in and use them to fund the works. However, where the leases have no such provisions, or those provisions are inadequate, the receiver will need to be put in funds by those appointing him if he is to be able to undertake works. Second, the court has no power to direct that the landlord remunerate the appointed receiver.[189] The receiver will be the agent of the court not the parties, and the court's only power to pay the receiver is its power to permit the receiver to retain money out of the assets of the receivership.[190] Even if the receiver's costs can properly form part of the costs of the litigation in which his appointment is ordered, no order for costs will be made at an interlocutory stage when the rights of the parties have not been finally decided.[191] Accordingly the receiver is unlikely to take office unless he is

---

[180] Senior Courts Act 1981 s.37.
[181] Ibid.
[182] *Clayhope Properties Ltd v Evans* [1986] 1 W.L.R. 1223.
[183] *Hart v Emelkirk* [1983] 1 W.L.R. 1289; *Daiches v Bluelake Investments Ltd* [1985] 2 E.G.L.R. 67; *Blawdziewicz v Diadon Establishment* [1988] 2 E.G.L.R. 52.
[184] *Hart v Emelkirk*, above.
[185] *Daiches v Bluelake Investments Ltd*, above.
[186] *Blawdziewicz v Diadon Establishment*, above.
[187] *Hafton Properties Ltd v Camp* [1994] 1 E.G.L.R. 67.
[188] *Gardner v London Chatham & Dover Railway Co Ltd (No.1)* (1867) L.R. 2 Ch. App. 201; *Parker v Camden LBC* [1986] Ch. 162.
[189] Ibid.
[190] *Clayhope Properties Ltd v Evans*, above.
[191] Ibid.

satisfied that his remuneration can be met out of the assets in respect of which he has been appointed, or he has an enforceable indemnity from a suitable party, such as the tenant or other interested person.

33–50    Where a tenant (in his capacity as such) is in a position to apply under s.24 of the Landlord and Tenant Act 1987 for an order appointing a manager,[192] he may not make an application to the court for it to exercise any jurisdiction existing apart from the 1987 Act to appoint a manager.[193] It follows that in the case of residential premises the court's general power to appoint a receiver is likely to be little used, for in most cases the procedure under the 1987 Act will be available. However, the power remains of potential importance in relation to commercial premises.

## APPOINTMENT OF A MANAGER UNDER PART II OF THE LANDLORD AND TENANT ACT 1987

### Introductory

33–51    Part II of the 1987 Act (which has been amended by the Housing Act 1996 and the Commonhold and Leasehold Reform Act 2002) confers on the First-tier Tribunal (Property Chamber)[194] a statutory power by order (whether interlocutory or final) to appoint a manager in relation to buildings containing flats. However, a tenant (in his capacity as such) cannot apply to the tribunal for it to exercise in relation to any premises any jurisdiction to appoint a receiver or manager in any circumstances on which an application could be made by him for an order under Pt II appointing a manager to act in relation to those premises.[195] It is thought to follow from this that a tenant of premises within Pt II of the 1987 Act cannot apply to the High Court under its discretionary power to appoint a receiver[196] even where he has made an application under Pt II and that application has been refused.

### Who can apply

33–52    An application under Pt II may be made by a tenant of a flat contained in premises to which Pt II applies.[197] Part II applies to premises consisting of the whole or part of a building if the building contains two or more flats.[198] A flat means a separate set of premises, whether or not on the same floor, which:

(1)    forms part of a building, and

---

[192] See para.33–51 et seq.
[193] Landlord and Tenant Act 1987 s.21(6).
[194] The jurisdiction of the leasehold valuation tribunal was transferred to the First-tier Tribunal (Property Chamber) as from July 1, 2013. See the Transfer of Tribunal Functions Order 2013 (SI 2013/1036).
[195] Landlord and Tenant Act 1987 s.21(6).
[196] See paras 33–49 to 33–50, above.
[197] Landlord and Tenant Act 1987 s.21(1).
[198] Landlord and Tenant Act 1987 s.21(2).

(2)   is divided horizontally from some other part of that building, and

(3)   is constructed or adapted for use for the purposes of a dwelling.[199]

An application under Pt II may be made:

(1)   jointly by tenants of two or more flats if they are each entitled to make an application;[200]

(2)   in respect of two or more premises to which Pt II applies;[201]

(3)   where the tenancy of a flat contained in premises to which Pt II applies is held by joint tenants, by any one or more of those tenants.[202]

## Who cannot apply

An application under Pt II of the 1987 Act cannot be made by a tenant under a tenancy to which Pt II of the Landlord and Tenant Act 1954 applies.[203] This covers cases where the flat is occupied by the tenant for the purposes or partly for the purposes of a business carried on by him. However, such a tenant may apply for the appointment of a receiver under the High Court's discretionary power.[204]    **33–53**

## Landlords against whom an application cannot be made

Part II of the 1987 Act does not apply to any premises at a time when the interest of the landlord in the premises is held by certain classes of landlord. These are as follows.    **33–54**

### (a) An exempt landlord[205]

An exempt landlord is a landlord who is one of the following:    **33–55**

(1)   a district, county, county borough, or London borough council, the Common Council of the City of London, the London Fire and Emergency Planning Authority, the Council of the Isles of Scilly, a police authority established under s.3 of the Police Act 1996, the Mayor's Office for Policing and Crime, a joint authority established by Pt IV of the Local Government Act 1985, an economic prosperity board established under s.88 of the Local Democracy, Economic Development and Construction Act 2009, or a combined authority established under s.103 of that Act;

(2)   the Commission for the New Towns or a development corporation established by an order made (or having effect as if made) under the New Towns Act 1981;

---

[199] Landlord and Tenant Act 1987 s.60(1).
[200] Landlord and Tenant Act 1987 s.21(4)(a).
[201] Landlord and Tenant Act 1987 s.21(4)(b).
[202] Landlord and Tenant Act 1987 s.21(5).
[203] Landlord and Tenant Act 1987 s.21(7).
[204] See paras 33–49 to 33–50, above.
[205] Landlord and Tenant Act 1987 s.21(3)(a).

(3) an urban development corporation within the meaning of Pt XVI of the Local Government, Planning and the Land Act 1980;

(4) a housing action trust established under Pt III of the Housing Act 1988;

(5) the Broads Authority;

(6) the Homes and Communities Agency;

(7) a National Park authority;

(8) the Regulator of Social Housing

(9) a housing trust (as defined in s.6 of the Housing Act 1985) which is a charity;

(10) a non-profit private registered provider of social housing;

(11) a registered social landlord;

(12) a fully mutual housing association which is neither a private registered provider of social housing nor registered social landlord ;

(13) a waste disposal authority.[206]

### (b) A resident landlord[207]

**33–56** A landlord of any premises consisting of the whole or part of a building is a resident landlord of those premises at any time if:

(1) the premises are not, and do not form part of, a purpose-built block of flats; and

(2) at that time the landlord occupies a flat contained in the premises as his only or principal residence; and

(3) he has so occupied such a flat throughout a period of not less than 12 months ending with that time.[208]

A purpose-built block of flats means a building which contained as constructed, and contains, two or more flats.[209]

However, Pt II is not prevented from applying to any premises because the interest of the landlord in the premises is held by a resident landlord if at least one-half of the flats contained in the premises are held on long leases which are not tenancies to which Pt II of the Landlord and Tenant Act 1954 applies.[210]

### (c) Charitable land

**33–57** Part II of the 1987 Act does not apply to premises which are included within the functional land of any charity.[211] Functional land of a charity is land occupied by the charity or trustees for it, and wholly or mainly used for charitable purposes.[212]

---

[206] Landlord and Tenant Act 1987 s.58(1) as amended by various statutes and statutory instruments.
[207] Landlord and Tenant Act 1987 s.21(3)(a).
[208] Landlord and Tenant Act 1987 s.58(2).
[209] Landlord and Tenant Act 1987 s.58(3).
[210] Landlord and Tenant Act 1987 s.21(3A).
[211] Landlord and Tenant Act 1987 s.21(3)(b).
[212] Landlord and Tenant Act 1987 s.60(1). "Charity" is further defined in the same sub-section.

## Crown land

Part II of the 1987 Act does not apply to a tenancy from the Crown.[213]                    **33–58**

## Section 22 notice

Before applying for the appointment of a manager, the tenant must serve a                    **33–59**
preliminary notice under s.22 of the 1987 Act.[214] The notice is analogous to a
notice under s.146 of the Law of Property Act 1925 as a preliminary to forfeiture.
Its purpose is to give the landlord the opportunity of remedying the matters
complained of. If the matters complained of are capable of remedy, and the
landlord remedies them within the time specified in the notice, the tenant cannot
apply for the appointment of a manager. It is thought that, save in exceptional
circumstances, disrepair will always be capable of remedy. It follows that where a
s.22 notice is served in relation to disrepair, the landlord will be able to prevent
an application being made under Pt II by carrying out the work within the
specified period.

## Requirements for a valid s.22 notice

The s.22 notice must be in writing and may be sent by post.[215] It must be served                    **33–60**
on the landlord and any person (other than the landlord) by whom obligations
relating to the management of the premises or any part of them are owed to the
tenant under his tenancy.[216] Where a notice is served on the landlord, and his
interest in the relevant premises is subject to a mortgage, he must, as soon as
reasonably practicable after receiving the notice, serve a copy on the
mortgagee.[217] The notice must:[218]

(1)   specify the tenant's name, the address of his flat, and an address in England
      and Wales (which may be the address of his flat) at which any person on
      whom the notice is served may serve notices, including notices in
      proceedings, on him in connection with Pt II;
(2)   state that the tenant intends to make an application for an order under s.24
      of the Act[219] to be made by a leasehold valuation tribunal in respect of such
      premises to which Pt II applies as are specified in the notice, but (if (4)
      below is applicable) that he will not do so if the landlord complies with the
      requirement specified in pursuance of that paragraph;

---

[213] Landlord and Tenant Act 1987 s.56 (as amended by the Commonhold and Leasehold Reform Act 2002).
[214] Landlord and Tenant Act 1987 s.22(1). The tribunal has power to dispense with the requirement for a s.22 notice: see para.32–62, below.
[215] Landlord and Tenant Act 1987 s.54(1).
[216] Landlord and Tenant Act 1987 s.22(1).
[217] Landlord and Tenant Act 1987 s.22(4).
[218] Landlord and Tenant Act 1987 s.22(2).
[219] i.e. an order appointing a manager under Pt II.

(3)   specify the grounds on which the tribunal would be asked to make such an order and the matters that would be relied on by the tenant for the purpose of establishing those grounds. It is thought that the grounds in question are those set out in the Act,[220] whilst the matters relied on are the facts on which the tenant relies to establish the grounds;

(4)   where those matters are capable of being remedied by any person on whom the notice is served, require him within such reasonable period as is specified in the notice, to take steps for the purpose of remedying them as are so specified;

(5)   contain such information (if any) as the Secretary of State may by regulations prescribe.

## Dispensing powers of the tribunal

33–61   The tribunal has power to dispense with the requirement for a s.22 notice.[221] The power may only be exercised if the tribunal is satisfied that it would not be reasonably practicable to serve the notice on the relevant person. When exercising the power, the tribunal may direct that such other notices are served, or such other steps are taken, as it thinks fit. The power may be exercised at the hearing of the application for the appointment of a manager, or at any other time.

Even where the tribunal does not dispense altogether with the requirement for a preliminary notice, it may still, if it thinks fit, make an order appointing a manager even though the period specified in the notice for remedying the matters complained of was not a reasonable period, or the notice failed in some other respect to comply with the requirements in Pt II or in any regulations.[222] This power was exercised by the court[223] in *Howard v Midrome*,[224] in which Warner J. made an order appointing a manager even though (a) the s.22 notice did not in terms contain a statement that the tenant would not apply to the court if the landlord complied with the specified requirements, and (b) the notice specified an unreasonably short period. The latter defect was dispensed with on the ground that the landlord would not have complied anyway.

## Conditions precedent to an application to the tribunal

33–62   Where a s.22 notice has been served on the landlord, no application to a leasehold valuation tribunal for the appointment of a manager can be made unless either (1) the period specified in the notice has expired without the relevant person having taken the steps that he was required to take by the notice, or (2) the matters complained of were not capable of remedy.[225] Where service of a preliminary notice has been dispensed with,[226] no application for the appointment of a

---

[220] See para.33–63, below.
[221] Landlord and Tenant Act 1987 s.22(3).
[222] Landlord and Tenant Act 1987 s.24(7).
[223] At the time the court's powers under Pt II had not been transferred to the tribunal.
[224] [1991] E.G.L.R. 58.
[225] Landlord and Tenant Act 1987 s.23(1)(a).
[226] See para.33–61 above.

manager can be made unless either (1) any notices which the tribunal required to be served have been served and any other steps which it required to be taken have been taken, or (2) no direction was given by the tribunal when making the order dispensing with the requirement for a notice.[227]

## Conditions precedent to the appointment of a manager

An order for the appointment of a manager may only be made where:

33–63

(1)   the tribunal is satisfied that:
    (i)   any relevant person either is in breach of any obligation owed by him to the tenant under his tenancy and relating to the management of the premises in question or any part of them,[228] or (in the case of an obligation dependent on notice) would be in breach of any such obligation but for the fact that it has not been reasonably practicable for the tenant to give him the appropriate notice, and
    (ii)   it is just and convenient to make the order in all the circumstances of the case;
(2)   where the tribunal is satisfied that:
    (i)   unreasonable service charges have been made, or are proposed or likely to be made, and
    (ii)   it is just and convenient to make the order in all the circumstances of the case;
(3)   where the tribunal is satisfied that:
    (i)   unreasonable variable administration charges have been made, or are proposed or likely to be made, and
    (ii)   it is just and convenient to make the order in all the circumstances of the case;
(4)   where the tribunal is satisfied that:
    (i)   any relevant person has failed to comply with any relevant provision of a code of practice approved by the Secretary of State under s.87 of the Leasehold Reform, Housing and Urban Development Act 1993 (codes of management practice), and
    (ii)   it is just and convenient to make the order in all the circumstances of the case;
(5)   where the tribunal is satisfied that other circumstances exist which make it just and convenient for the order to be made.[229]

For the purposes of (2) above, a service charge must be taken to be unreasonable if the amount is unreasonable having regard to the items for which it is payable; if the items for which it is payable are of an unnecessarily high standard; or if the items for which it is payable are of an insufficient standard

---

[227] Landlord and Tenant Act 1987 s.23(1)(b).
[228] This includes the repair, maintenance or insurance of those premises: Landlord and Tenant Act 1987 s.24(11).
[229] Landlord and Tenant Act 1987 s.24(2).

with the result that additional service charges are or may be incurred.[230] "Service charge" means a service charge within the meaning of s.18(1) of the Landlord and Tenant Act 1987 (but does not include service charges payable by the tenant of a dwelling the rent of which is registered under Pt IV of the Rent Act 1977 unless the amount is entered as variable under s.71(4)).[231]

## The powers of the tribunal

**33–64**  An order appointing a manager may be made either at the substantive hearing or at an interlocutory stage pending the hearing.[232] The manager may be appointed to carry out in relation to any premises to which Pt II applies[233] such functions in connection with the management of the premises,[234] or such functions of a receiver, or both as the tribunal thinks fit.[235] The order may be granted subject to such conditions as the tribunal thinks fit, and its operation may be suspended on terms fixed by the tribunal.[236] Thus, for example, the tribunal may make an order appointing a manager but suspend it on terms that the landlord carries out the work within a specified period. The premises in respect of which the order is made may, if the tribunal thinks fit, be more or less extensive that those specified in the tenant's application.[237]

The order may make provision with respect to such matters relating to the exercise by the manager of his functions under the order, and such incidental or ancillary matters, as the tribunal thinks fit.[238] In particular the order may provide for the following:

(1)  for rights and liabilities arising under contracts to which the manager is not a party to become rights and liabilities of the manager;
(2)  for the manager to become entitled to prosecute claims in respect of causes of action (whether contractual or tortious) accruing before or after the date of his appointment;
(3)  for remuneration to be paid to the manager by the landlord, or by the tenants of the premises in respect of which the order is made, or by all or any of those persons. The tribunal's power to order the landlord to remunerate the manager is important, since there is no such power under the High Court's discretionary jurisdiction.[239] However, remuneration by

[230] Landlord and Tenant Act 1987 s.24(2A).
[231] Landlord and Tenant Act 1987 s.24(2A).
[232] Landlord and Tenant Act 1987 s.24(1). An interlocutory order for the appointment of a manager pending trial of the tenant's application for an acquisition order under Pt III of the Act was made by Warner J. in *Howard v Midrome* [1991] 1 E.G.L.R. 58.
[233] This includes amenity land outside the curtilage of the leased building: *Cawsand Fort Management Co. Ltd v Stafford* [2008] 1 W.L.R. 371.
[234] This includes repair, maintenance, improvement and insurance: Landlord and Tenant Act 1987 s.24(11).
[235] Landlord and Tenant Act 1987 s.24(1).
[236] Landlord and Tenant Act 1987 s.24(6).
[237] Landlord and Tenant Act 1987 s.24(3).
[238] Landlord and Tenant Act 1987 s.24(4).
[239] *Clayhope Properties Ltd v Evans* [1988] 1 W.L.R. 358. See paras 33–49 to 33–50, above.

the landlord has been held to be inappropriate where the manager is the alter ego of the tenants and is being appointed only for an interim period until trial[240];

(4)     for the manager's functions to be exercisable by him (subject to the tribunal's power to vary or discharge the order[241]) either during a specified period or without limit of time.[242]

The manager may himself apply to the tribunal for directions.[243]

The Land Charges Act 1972 and the Land Registration Act 2002 apply in relation to an order appointing a manager as they apply in relation to an order appointing a receiver or sequestrator of land.[244] If the order has been protected by an entry under either of those Acts and the order is subsequently varied or discharged,[245] the tribunal may order that such entry be cancelled.[246]

## Variation or discharge of the order

The tribunal may, on the application of any person interested, vary or discharge an order made under Pt II.[247] Such variation or discharge may be either conditional or unconditional.[248] The tribunal must not vary or discharge an order on the application of any relevant person unless it is satisfied that the variation or discharge will not result in a recurrence of the circumstances which led to the order being made, and that it is just and convenient in all the circumstances of the case to vary or discharge the order.[249] However, an order must not be discharged by reason only that the premises in respect of which the order was made have ceased to be premises to which Pt II applies because the interest of the landlord has become vested in an exempt landlord, or a resident landlord, or because the premises have become functional land of a charity.[250]

33–65

## Nature of a manager appointed under Pt II

The nature of a manager appointed under Pt II of the 1987 Act was considered by the Court of Appeal in *Maunder-Taylor v Blaquiere*.[251] It was held that the manager is not "appointed as the manager of the landlord, or even of the landlord's obligations under the lease". Instead, he carries out the functions which he has been appointed to carry out "in his own right as a court-appointed official"

33–66

---

[240] *Howard v Midrome* [1991] 1 E.G.L.R. 58.
[241] This is considered in para.32–66, below.
[242] Landlord and Tenant Act 1987 s.24(5).
[243] Landlord and Tenant Act 1987 s.24(4).
[244] Landlord and Tenant Act 1987 s.24(8).
[245] See para.33–65, below.
[246] Landlord and Tenant Act 1987 s.24(9).
[247] Landlord and Tenant Act 1987 s.24(9).
[248] Landlord and Tenant Act 1987.
[249] Landlord and Tenant Act 1987 s.24(9A).
[250] Landlord and Tenant Act 1987 s.24(10).
[251] [2003] 1 W.L.R. 379.

and "in a capacity independent of the landlord".[252] It was therefore held that the tenant in that case was not entitled to set-off against the manager's claims for service charges a claim for damages against the landlord for failure to repair.

## RIGHT TO MANAGE COMPANIES

33–67     Where the right to manage has been acquired by a right to manage a company under Pt 2 of the Commonhold and Leasehold Reform Act 2002, the relevant provisions of Pt II of the 1987 Act are modified in the manner provided for in the 2002 Act.[253]

## OTHER REMEDIES

### Parts III and IV of the Landlord and Tenant Act 1987

33–68     Part III of the 1987 Act (as amended) enables certain tenants of flats held under long leases compulsorily to acquire their landlord's interest. This is a remedy of last resort, but in appropriate circumstances it may be the most effective way of permanently dealing with a landlord who fails to repair time and time again, or a landlord who has disappeared. Once the tenants have acquired the landlord's interest, it will be open to them to decide amongst themselves what are the most appropriate arrangements for dealing with repairs. They will, of course, be bound by any repairing obligations contained in leases to which the interest acquired is subject.

Part IV of the 1987 Act (as amended) contains provisions enabling any party to a long lease of a flat (including the landlord) to apply for the lease to be varied on the ground that it fails to make satisfactory provision with respect to, among other matters, the repair or maintenance of the flat, the building containing the flat or any land or building which is let to the tenant under the lease or in respect of which rights are conferred on him under it. Whilst this will not deal directly with disrepair, nonetheless it will enable tenants whose leases contain insufficient repairing obligations on the part of the landlord to apply to the court for the leases to be varied so as to impose satisfactory obligations as regards repairs.

The detailed scheme of Pts III and IV is outside the scope of this work, and reference should be made to standard textbooks dealing with the subject.

### Statutory powers and duties under housing, environmental and health and safety law

33–69     A wide variety of powers and duties for dealing with disrepair are available to public authorities under the provisions of the Housing Act 1985, the Housing Act 2004 and the Environmental Protection Act 1990. In many cases it may be more effective for the tenant to require the appropriate authority to take action against

---

[252] [2003] 1 W.L.R. 379 per Aldous L.J. (with whom Tuckey and Longmore L.JJ. agreed).
[253] Commonhold and Leasehold Reform Act 2002 s.102 and Sch.7 para.8.

disrepair under these provisions than for him to take action himself. Further, a number of duties are imposed by the various health and safety statutes.[254] In some cases these are placed upon the occupier, but in many cases they are imposed on the landlord. Breach of the duty may give the tenant a cause of action in tort for breach of statutory duty. These provisions are outside the scope of this work, and reference should be made to specialist works on the subject.

[254] For example, the Factories Act 1961; the Offices, Shops and Railway Premises Act 1963; and the Health and Safety at Work Act 1974 and the regulations made thereunder. In *Westminster City Council v Select Management Ltd* [1985] 1 W.L.R. 576, it was held that for the purposes of the 1974 Act "non-domestic premises" include the common parts of a block of flats, with the result that the landlord owed a duty under s.4(1) of the Act to persons who came to repair the lifts and electrical installations to ensure that the common parts were safe and without risk to health. It was therefore held that improvement notices served by the local authority on the managing agents of the block requiring work to the lifts and electrical installations had been validly served.

CHAPTER 34

# THE RECOVERY OF FEES AND COSTS

## INTRODUCTORY

## Fees and costs in dilapidations claims

The technical nature of the issues raised by any claim for dilapidations means that both landlords and tenants will generally require expert advice, and will incur professional fees in doing so. Expenditure on professional fees can be very considerable, so much so that in some cases, what starts off as a claim over disrepair ends as a dispute over who is to pay the costs incurred in relation to the claim. In virtually all cases, fees and costs incurred by the landlord form a part of the eventual claim. The purpose of this Chapter is to identify the various stages at which fees and costs may be incurred in the course of a dilapidations claim, and to consider the extent to which they may be recovered.

**34–01**

## Stages at which fees and costs are incurred

Whether the claim is made by the landlord against the tenant or vice versa, fees and costs in dilapidations claims are usually incurred at the following stages:

**34–02**

(1)   in preparing and serving a schedule of dilapidations and (in an appropriate case) a s.146 notice;[1]
(2)   in complying with the pre-action requirement of the Civil Procedure Rules, in particular with any applicable pre-action Protocol;[2]
(3)   in the course of litigation to enforce the claim if it is resisted;[3]
(4)   in relation to the works of repair, if these are carried out by the party making the claim.[4]

The recovery of fees and costs at each of these stages is considered in the remainder of this Chapter.

---

[1]   See paras 34–05 to 34–12, below.
[2]   See para.34–13 to 34– 15, below.
[3]   See para.34–22, below.
[4]   See para.34–27, below.

## RICS scale fees

**34–03**   The Royal Institution of Chartered Surveyors previously published a recommended scale of fees in relation to dilapidations (BS7.2.[5]). However, it was thought to be contrary to the principle of fair market competition, and it was abandoned in February 2000 at the behest of the Office of Fair Trading. For details of the former scale fees, reference should be made to the First Edition of this work.

## Apportionment of fees

**34–04**   One difficulty which arises in practice, particularly in relation to surveyor's fees, is in attributing particular parts of an overall bill to one or other of the main heads of costs described above. For example, it would be quite usual for the landlord to employ the same surveyor to prepare the initial schedule of dilapidations, to supervise the remedial works, and to act as expert witness in litigation against the tenant. The surveyor's fees under these various heads will be treated differently as regards whether they can be recovered from the tenant. It is therefore suggested that it is good practice, wherever a claim is likely to become litigious, for bills for professional fees to be broken down appropriately.

COSTS INCURRED IN SERVING A SCHEDULE OF DILAPIDATIONS AND S.146 NOTICE

### Whether the costs of serving a schedule are recoverable as damages

**34–05**   The first step in any dilapidations claim, whether by the landlord or the tenant, and whether during or after the lease has ended, is to identify the existence and extent of the relevant breaches. This is usually done by a building surveyor. Sometimes, a careful inspection alone is enough. On other occasions, the surveyor may need to carry out or arrange for opening up works or tests, or to take samples for analysis. Once his inspections and investigations are complete, the surveyor draws up a schedule of dilapidations or breaches, which is then served on the other party, often by a solicitor. The party at whose behest the schedule is served will be liable in the first instance to pay the surveyor's fees for preparing the schedule and the fees of any solicitor by whom it is served.

There is a conflict of authority on the extent to which such fees are recoverable from the other party as damages for breach of the repairing covenant.

In *Maud v Sandars*[6] the landlord claimed by way of damages £20 in respect of the cost of the schedule of dilapidations. The landlord argued that:

> "[I]t was only due to the fact that the tenant had broken his covenant ... that he had had to incur that expense in order to assess the damages to which he was entitled for the defendant's breach of covenant."

---

[5] *Professional Charges for Building Surveying Services*, published by the Royal Institution of Chartered Surveyors.
[6] [1943] 2 All E.R. 783.

The tenant contended that the sum was not recoverable, because it did not represent damage to the reversion but was a sum which the landlord incurred in order to ascertain the amount he was entitled to claim from the tenant. This argument succeeded before Lewis J., who held that the cost of the schedule was not recoverable.

In *Lloyds Bank Ltd v Lake*,[7] the Senior Official Referee (HH Sir Brett Cloutman V.C., QC) held that he should follow *Maud v Sandars* on this point, saying:

> "In a strictly drawn lease there is often found a specific provision making the lessee liable for [the costs of the schedule of dilapidations], and in such a case the amount is included in the damages (see *Woodfall*, pp.737 and 962); that is precisely because the law and practice are as Lewis J. stated. In this state of the authorities and of the practice, as I know it, I must follow the decision in *Maud v Sandars*, and if a different practice is to be laid down, this must be by the Court of Appeal."

However, in *Pgf II SA v Royal & Sun Alliance Insurance Plc*,[8] H.H. Judge Toulmin QC declined to follow *Maud v Sandars* and awarded damages of £6,000 plus VAT in respect of the landlord's reasonable costs of producing the schedule of dilapidations. He said:

> "I cannot see any reason of principle why a reasonable sum should not be recoverable from a tenant for serving a Schedule of Dilapidations at the end of a lease. The Schedule is required as a direct consequence of the tenant's breach of covenant. The diminution of value only operates as a cap. Lord Lloyd in [*Ruxley Electronics & Construction Ltd v Forsyth*[9]] made it clear that in many cases the cost of repair would be the obvious measure of damage. Lewis J's analysis of general principle cannot survive the more detailed analysis of Lord Lloyd in *Ruxley*...
>
> On my earlier analysis I have found the position is no different in cases under Section 18 of the 1927 Act. I find therefore that in this case the reasonable cost of preparing a Schedule of Dilapidations is the direct consequence of the tenant's breach and is recoverable."

It may be noted in passing that the judge did not refer to the decision of the Court of Appeal in *Skinners Co v Knight*,[10] in which the costs of serving a s.146 notice were held not to be recoverable as damages.[11]

The position is therefore not straightforward. However, in the absence of any definitive appellate authority, the correct view is thought to be that the extent to which the costs of preparing the schedule of dilapidations will be recoverable by way of damages at common law in any particular case will depend on whether such costs can properly be said to have been caused by the breaches of covenant. By definition, a schedule of dilapidations is only prepared where breaches have been found to exist, and its purpose is to set out such breaches and the remedial work the surveyor regards as necessary. The costs of preparing it can properly be said to have been caused by the relevant breaches to the extent that such costs are higher by virtue of the breaches than they would have been if no breaches had been committed. But to the extent that such costs include an element that would

---

[7] [1961] 1 W.L.R. 884.
[8] [2011] 1 P. & C. R. 11.
[9] [1996] AC 344. See further on this case para.32–03, above.
[10] [1891] 2 Q.B. 542.
[11] See para.34–06, below.

have been incurred in any event (i.e. the relevant party would have been liable to pay a fee to the surveyor for inspecting the premises even if his inspection had revealed nothing), it may well be that such element is irrecoverable, because it was not incurred as a consequence of the breaches: it was incurred in ascertaining whether any breaches had occurred, and it would have been payable even if no breaches had been found.

The position is complicated by the statutory limitation on damages for breach of a covenant to repair imposed by s.18(1) of the Landlord and Tenant Act 1927, by virtue of which damages cannot exceed the amount by which the value of the landlord's reversion is diminished owing to such breach.[12] In valuing the reversion out of repair, it must obviously be assumed that the premises are vacant, and that the hypothetical purchaser already knows the extent of the disrepair (because if he does not possess this knowledge, the exercise of deciding how much less, if any, he would pay for the reversion by reason of the disrepair cannot sensibly be done). It is therefore difficult to see how the costs of preparing a schedule of dilapidations could ever form any part of the damage to the reversion. However, since s.18(1) is only a cap on damages, that would not matter in practice in a case where the diminution in value exceeds the landlord's common law claim, including (if otherwise recoverable) the costs of serving the schedule of dilapidations.

## Costs of serving a s.146 notice

34–06     In *Skinners Co v Knight*[13] the jury found that the premises were in disrepair when the landlord served a notice under the then equivalent of s.146 of the Law of Property Act 1925. However, they were unable to reach a verdict as to whether the disrepair had been remedied by the date the landlord re-entered. The landlord claimed that he was nonetheless entitled to judgment on the basis that the tenant had failed to make "compensation" in money as required by the statute, because he had failed to pay the landlord's solicitor's and surveyor's fees and the costs of serving the notice. The Court of Appeal held that the "compensation" referred to in the statute was to be equated with "damages", and that the expenses:

> "[A]rise not from the breach of covenant, but solely from the fetter which the wisdom of the legislature has imposed on the enforcement of the cause of action arising from the breach."

On the current state of the law, therefore, the costs of preparing and serving a s.146 notice are not recoverable as damages. It is no doubt because of this that leases almost invariably contain express covenants providing for the tenant to pay such costs.[14]

---

[12]  See Ch.30 above.
[13]  Above.
[14]  See para.34–07, below.

## Express covenants to pay the landlord's costs of s.146 notices or proceedings under s.146[15]

As noted above, leases almost always contain an express covenant on the part of **34–07** the tenant to pay the landlord's costs of preparing and serving a notice under s.146, or incurred in proceedings under s.146, or some similar formulation. The proper construction of such provisions will depend on the particular circumstances of each case.

Where the s.146 notice is served with a schedule of dilapidations, it is thought that in the ordinary case, the costs of the schedule will be recoverable as part of the costs of the notice. Thus, in *Johnsey Estates (1990) v The Secretary of State for the Environment*,[16] a covenant by the tenant to:

> "[P]ay all expenses (including solicitors costs and surveyors fees) incurred by the Landlord incidental to the preparation and service of a notice under [s.146] notwithstanding forfeiture is avoided otherwise than by relief granted by the court"

was held to extend to the costs of preparing and serving a schedule of dilapidations served with the notice and referred to in it (although not a report that was not so served or referred to).

The practice is sometimes encountered of serving a notice and accompanying schedule in the last few weeks of the term, in order to enable the landlord to claim the costs of the schedule of dilapidations under a provision of this type. In such cases, there is usually no possibility of forfeiture, because the term will expire before a reasonable time to carry out the work has elapsed. It is thought that in such a case the costs of the notice and schedule are unlikely to be recoverable. The correct construction of such provisions will usually be that they are only intended to apply where the notice is served as a genuine prerequisite to forfeiture, and not where the sole purpose of the notice is to recover costs. Thus, in *Johnsey Estates (1990) v The Secretary of State for the Environment*[17] the landlord served on the tenant a s.146 notice together with a schedule of dilapidations three days before the term was due to expire pursuant to a tenant's break notice. The landlord's claim for the costs of the notice and schedule was rejected on the ground that, since the tenant had already served a break notice and the three days remaining before the end of the term was insufficient to enable the remedial works to be carried out, the s.146 notice could not have been intended to be a genuine s.146 notice and was a sham. The same view was taken in *Lintott Property Developments v Bower*,[18] in which the relevant s.146 notice had been served a month prior to the date on which the lease would expire by effluxion of time.

---

[15] See further paras 34–24 to 34–26, below.
[16] Unreported decision of H.H. Judge Moseley, QC (sitting as an Official Referee in the Technology and Construction Court) dated August 6, 1999. The point did not arise on appeal at [2001] 2 E.G.L.R. 128.
[17] Above. The relevant covenant is set out above. The point did not arise on appeal at [2001] 2 E.G.L.R. 128.
[18] [2005] All E.R. (D) 454.

A common form of provision is a covenant on the part of the tenant to pay the costs and expenses incurred by the landlord "in or in contemplation of any proceedings under s.146 of the Law of Property Act 1925 whether or not relief from forfeiture is obtained from the court", or some similar formulation.

In *Fairview Investments Ltd v Sharma*,[19] the tenant covenanted to pay all expenses "under section 146 of the Law of Property Act 1925 or incurred in contemplation of or in proceedings under sections 146 or 147 of that Act". Chadwick L.J. (with whom Thorpe L.J. agreed) regarded the covenant as requiring the lessee to pay (1) the lessor's costs in relation to the preparation and service of a section 146 notice; (2) the costs incurred by the lessor after notice and in contemplation of proceedings to enforce the right of re-entry (i.e. contemplated possession proceedings); and (3) the costs of proceedings actually commenced (i.e. actual possession proceedings). In *Forcelux v Binnie*[20], the Court of Appeal held that a covenant to pay "all costs charges and expenses (including legal costs ...) which may be incurred by the Lessor in or in contemplation of any steps or proceedings under sections 146 or 147" extended as a matter of construction to the landlord's costs of possession proceedings brought to enforce a right of re-entry following a notice under section 146(1), the costs of an application to set aside a possession order made in those proceedings and the costs of the lessee's application for relief from forfeiture (although the landlord's claim for costs was rejected in the exercise of the Court's discretion[21]). In *Pertemps Group Ltd v Crosher & James*,[22] it was held in the county court that a covenant to pay all reasonable expenses, including solicitors' costs and surveyors' fees, properly incurred by the landlord incidental to the preparation and service of a notice under s.146 of the Law of Property Act 1925 was capable of extending to the landlord's surveyor's fees for attending the property to discuss the works and progress following service of a s.146 notice and schedule of dilapidations.

In *Agricullo v Yorkshire Housing*,[23] a lease of business premises was granted in 2001 for 29 years on terms which included a tenant's repairing covenant. Clause 9.3 provided as follows:

> "The Tenant shall pay to the Landlord, on demand, and on an indemnity basis, the fees, costs and expenses charged, incurred or payable to the Landlord, and its advisors or bailiffs in connection with any steps taken in or in contemplation of, or in relation to, any proceedings under section 146 or 147 of the Law of Property Act 1925 or the Leasehold Property (Repairs) Act 1938, including the preparation and service of all notices, and even if forfeiture is avoided (unless it is relief granted by the court)"

The roof was in disrepair. In February 2003 the landlord served a s.146 notice in the form required by the Leasehold Property (Repairs) Act 1938. The tenant served a counter-notice. The tenant ultimately carried out the works between February and July 2005. The landlord issued proceedings claiming (among other things) solicitors' and surveyors' costs incurred in dealing with matters arising

---

[19] Unreported decision of the Court of Appeal dated October 14, 1999.
[20] [2010] H.L.R. 20.
[21] See para.33–25, below.
[22] [1997] 7 C.L. 489.
[23] [2010] 2 P & CR 11

from the tenant's breaches of covenant from the date of the counter-notice until completion of the repairs. It argued that the relevant costs fell within clause 9.3, so that its claim was in debt and the Leasehold Property (Repairs) Act 1938 Act did not therefore apply.[24] That argument was rejected by the Court of Appeal. The costs were not attributable to steps taken "in or in contemplation of, or in relation to, any proceedings under section 146". Proceedings under s.146 are proceedings for the forfeiture of the lease. No such proceedings had been taken nor could they have been taken without the Court's leave under the 1938 Act. The costs had been incurred in relation to persuading the tenant to do the work and ensuring that the work was properly done. That process was consensual. The fact that the work undertaken by the tenant was an alternative to forfeiture proceedings and due in part to the threat of such proceedings was not enough. Once the tenant served counter-notice, the landlord could have applied for leave, in which case it could have recovered its costs as costs in those proceedings, or it could have carried out the works itself under a *Jervis v Harris* clause, in which case it could have recovered the costs as a debt under that clause. But its election to deal with the problem by negotiation took the steps subsequently taken by its solicitors and surveyors on its behalf outside clause 9.3.

## Wider forms of express covenant[25]

The form of covenant considered above is limited to costs incurred in connection with forfeiture proceedings. However, many modern leases contain covenants to pay the landlord's costs which are not so limited. Such covenants take a number of forms. An example in a dilapidations context is *Riverside Property Investments Ltd v Blackhawk Automotive*,[26] in which the lease contained covenants by the tenant to pay "all proper costs and expenses (including solicitors costs and surveyors fees) incurred by the Lessor in or incidental to the preparation and service of any notice or schedule relating to dilapidations and whether or not the same is served before or after the expiration of the said term" (Clause 22(b)); and "all costs and expenses incurred by the Lessor in or in connection with the enforcement of any of the Lessee's covenants and conditions herein contained whether during the currency of or after the termination of the said term" (Clause 22(c)). The landlord claimed various costs in connection with a terminal dilapidations claim. H.H. Judge Coulson, QC held that the following principles were to be applied in considering such claim:

34–08

"*Principles relevant to costs claims*
    [81] Principle 1
    In order to be recoverable under clause 22(b), the item of cost or expenditure must be incidental to the preparation and service of any notice or dilapidations schedule. If the reason why the item of cost or expense was incurred was unconnected with the preparation of a dilapidations schedule, such as the proposed early surrender of the lease, it does not seem to me that it can be recoverable under clause 22(b) of the lease.
    [82] Principle 2
    The costs and expenses recoverable under clause 22(c) are those incurred in connection

---

[24] See para.27–31 et seq., above.
[25] See further paras 34–24 to 34–26, below.
[26] [2005] 1 E.G.L.R. 114 (TCC).

with the enforcement of the repairing covenants. Accordingly, the work for which the cost or expense is claimed must be work that is connected to attempts by [the landlord] to compel [the tenant] to perform those covenants. That must mean, in practice, that the work related to the collection of information or advice that was then passed on to [the tenant] in an attempt to get it to comply with the covenants. Thus, items of work that were performed on behalf of [the landlord] that went, say, to the preparation of reports that were never passed on to [the tenant] and about which it was therefore ignorant, cannot be costs incurred in connection with the enforcement of the covenant."

The judge further held that the cost of in-house services was recoverable in principle (subject to proper evidence of causation and loss), provided that proper records of the time expended had been kept so that the claim could be quantified.[27] He went on to consider (and reject in large measure) a large number of heads of cost claimed by the landlord. His judgment on this aspect provides a useful illustration of the way in which claims for costs in dilapidations claims under express provisions in leases are approached in practice.

## The amount recoverable under an express provision[28]

**34–09**     The amount recoverable under an express covenant to pay the landlord's costs will depend on the proper construction of the covenant. In general, the tenant will prima facie be liable to pay the whole amount incurred.[29] However, it is thought that there will generally be an implied term to the effect that the fees and costs must be reasonable in amount.[30] In practice this is unlikely to cause any difficulty for the landlord, provided that he can demonstrate that his surveyor's or solicitor's bill is reasonably in line with what would be charged for the same work by a firm of equivalent standing.

It is sometimes mistakenly argued that the presence of a covenant by the tenant to pay the landlord's surveyor's or solicitor's fees has the effect that, as against the professional adviser in question, the tenant is liable to pay the fees and the landlord is not. This is not the case. Such a covenant operates only as between landlord and tenant, and does not affect the position between the landlord and the relevant adviser. The landlord remains contractually bound to pay the adviser's fees whether or not he recovers them from the tenant. Some advisers may agree to postpone payment until the landlord has recovered the amount from the tenant, but there is no obligation to do this unless the adviser has agreed to act on this basis. It also follows that the adviser has no right to recover his fees from the tenant, although the tenant may sometimes pay him directly as a matter of convenience.

The restrictions imposed by the Leasehold Property (Repairs) Act 1938 do not apply to a claim for fees and costs under an express covenant of the sort under

---

[27]  Above, at [87].

[28]  See further paras 34–24 to 34–26, below.

[29]  See para.34–25, below.

[30]  See *Riverside Property Investments Ltd v Blackhawk Automotive* [2005] 1 E.G.L.R. 114 at [85](iv) and [86](v). See also (in a service charge context) *Finchbourne v Rodrigues* [1976] 3 All E.R. 581; *Plough Investments Ltd v Manchester City Council* [1989] 1 E.G.L.R. 244; *Holding & Management Ltd v Property Holding & Investment Trust Plc* [1989] 1 W.L.R. 1313; and *Morgan v Stainer* [1993] 2 E.G.L.R. 73.

consideration.[31] This is because the claim is for a debt and not for damages.[32] For the same reason the claim is not subject to s.18(1) of the Landlord and Tenant Act 1927.[33]

## Payment of the landlord's costs as a condition of relief from forfeiture

The court's discretionary power to make payment of the landlords costs a condition of granting relief from forfeiture is considered elsewhere.[34] The fact that the landlord's costs of the schedule of dilapidations are not recoverable as damages does not prevent the court from making the payment of those costs a condition of the grant of relief from forfeiture.[35]     **34–10**

## Section 146(3) of the Law of Property Act 1925

Section 146(3) provides that the landlord:     **34–11**

> "[S]hall be entitled to recover as a debt due to him from a lessee, and in addition to damages (if any), all reasonable costs and expenses properly incurred by the lessor in the employment of a solicitor and surveyor or value, or otherwise, in reference to any breach giving rise to a right of re-entry or forfeiture which, at the request of the lessee, is waived by the lessor, or from which the lessee is relieved under the provisions of this Act."

The subsection therefore only applies where (a) there is a breach; (b) the breach gives rise to a right of forfeiture; and (c) either the forfeiture is waived by the landlord at the request of the tenant, or the tenant is granted relief from forfeiture under the provisions of s.146. The landlord cannot therefore rely on the subsection where:

(1)    his surveyor inspects the premises and finds no breaches of covenant;
(2)    the tenant, on receipt of the s.146 notice, remedies the breach himself;[36]
(3)    the tenant does not apply for, or is refused, relief from forfeiture.

The reference to the breach being "waived … at the request of the lessee" is somewhat curious. It appears to be limited to the case where the tenant asks the landlord not to forfeit for the breach and the landlord agrees. It does not apply where the right to forfeit is waived other than at the request of the tenant, for example, by acceptance of rent with knowledge of the breach,[37] which cannot sensibly be categorised as waiver at the tenant's request. The rationale behind this seems to be that the landlord should not be deterred from agreeing to waive his right to forfeit by the fact that he will thereby lose his costs.

---

[31] *Bader Properties Ltd v Linley Property Investments Ltd* (1968) 19 P. & C.R. 620.
[32] Ibid.
[33] *Middlegate Properties Ltd v Gidlow-Jackson* (1977) 34 P. & C.R. 4.
[34] See para.34–23, below.
[35] *Bridge v Quick* (1892) 61 L.J.Q.B. 375.
[36] *Nind v Nineteenth Century Building Society* [1894] 2 Q.B. 226.
[37] See para.27–05 et seq., above.

The costs and expenses which are recoverable are limited to reasonable costs properly incurred. It follows that it is open to the tenant to challenge the landlord's claim for costs both on the ground that the amount is excessive, and on the ground that the costs in question should never have been incurred at all. In both cases it is thought that the court is likely to approach the matter by asking itself whether a reasonable landlord in the position of the actual landlord would have incurred the costs that the actual landlord in fact incurred.

**34–12**   The effect of s.146(3), where it applies, is to create a statutory debt. If the tenant fails to pay, the landlord's remedies are limited to those applicable to the enforcement of a debt. They would not include forfeiture, since the liability to pay is not made an implied obligation under the lease, with the result that the proviso for re-entry would not apply. However, where the lease contains a covenant to comply with statutes, it might be argued that failure to pay the statutory debt amounted to a breach of such covenant entitling the landlord to forfeiture.

In cases where the Leasehold Property (Repairs) Act 1938 applies,[38] and the tenant serves a counter-notice claiming the benefit of the Act, the landlord will only be entitled to the benefit of s.146(3) if he applies for leave under the Act to forfeit or commence proceedings for damages[39] and the court makes a direction that he is to be entitled to the benefit of the subsection.[40] In practice, where the court grants leave under the 1938 Act, it usually makes a direction at the same time either that the landlord is to have the benefit of s.146(3) or that the landlord is to have such benefit to the extent that the judge who hears the proceedings for which leave is given thinks is appropriate.[41]

## COSTS INCURRED IN COMPLYING WITH A PRE-ACTION PROTOCOL

### Pre-action protocols

**34–13**   There are two pre-action protocols in dilapidations cases: the Pre-Action Protocol for Claims for Damages in Relation to the Physical State of Commercial Property at the Termination of a Tenancy (the Dilapidations Protocol), and the Pre-Action Protocol for Housing Disrepair Cases. Both are considered in Ch.37, below. Failure to comply with a pre-action protocol may result in costs and other sanctions against the party in default. Thus, CPR r.44.2(5)(a) includes, as one example of conduct which is relevant to the exercise of the court's discretion as to costs, "the extent to which the parties followed the Practice Direction (Pre-Action Conduct) or any relevant pre-action protocol", and para.4.6 of the Practice Direction (Pre-Action Conduct) sets out various possible consequences (as to payment of costs and interest) which may result from non-compliance.

---

[38] See para.27–31 et seq., above.
[39] Leasehold Property (Repairs) Act 1938 s.2.
[40] Leasehold Property (Repairs) Act 1938 s.2.
[41] See for example *Phillips v Price* [1959] Ch. 181.

## Where the claim is settled without litigation

Where a claim is settled following the use of the appropriate protocol, the agreed terms are likely to provide for whether and to what extent either party is entitled to be paid by the other its costs of complying with the protocol. In the absence of agreement, there is no legal entitlement to recover costs incurred in complying with a pre-action protocol where the dispute is settled before proceedings are brought.[42] However, where one party agrees as part of the settlement to pay the other a reasonable sum in relation to costs (but the amount is not agreed), the court has power to settle the amount.[43]

**34–14**

Paragraph 3.7 of the Pre-Action Protocol for Housing Disrepair Cases[44] provides that if the tenant's claim is settled without litigation on terms which justify bringing it, the landlord will pay the tenant's out-of-pocket expenses (which is defined to mean expenses incurred in a small track claim as a result of the claim, such as loss of earnings and experts' fees). However, the court has no power to enforce payment of the tenant' expenses. Thus, *Birmingham CC v Lee*,[45] Hughes L.J., giving the judgment of the Court of Appeal, said:

> "[the Protocol] proceeds upon the assumption (or hope) that the parties will settle if there is an early exchange of claim and response and that that settlement will include the claimant's reasonable costs if his claim was justified. Whilst that may be the assumption, or hope, the protocol itself has no coercive power as to costs, and if there is no legal action, there is no court to compel payment of the costs which are anticipated by paragraph 3.7."

## Where the claim is litigated

Where the claim is not settled and the matter proceeds to litigation, the position as regards the costs of complying with a pre-action protocol would appear to be as follows. First, for the purposes of s.51 of the Senior Courts Act 1981 (which provides that the "costs of and incidental to" proceedings are in the discretion of the court) costs incurred by a party in complying with a pre-action protocol are capable of being "costs of and incidental to" any proceedings which are begun if the protocol procedure fails to lead to a settlement.[46] Consistently with this, CPR r.44.2(6)(d) expressly confers on the court power to order a party to pay costs incurred before proceedings have begun, which is wide enough to include (in an appropriate case) the costs of complying with the relevant pre-action protocol. Second, whether or not a particular item of pre-action protocol costs can properly be described as having been incurred "incidental" to the proceedings will be a matter of fact.[47] Third, unless the circumstances are exceptional and thereby give rise to some sort of unreasonable conduct, costs incurred by a defendant at the stage of a pre-action protocol in dealing with and responding to issues which are subsequently dropped from the action when proceedings are commenced cannot

**34–15**

---

[42] See the *White Book*, Vol.1 at para.C1A–016.
[43] See the *White Book*, Vol.1 at para.C1A–016.
[44] This is printed in Appendix III, below, and considered in Ch.37, below.
[45] [2009] H.L.R. 20.
[46] *McGlinn v Waltham Contractors* [2005] 3 All E.R. 1126 (H.H. Judge Coulson, QC) at [6] to [9].
[47] Ibid., at [9].

be costs "incidental" to those proceedings and are not recoverable as part of the costs of those proceedings.[48] It would seem to follow that if the landlord's schedule of dilapidations at the protocol stage includes, say, 100 items, but the landlord is persuaded to withdraw 10 of them so that the subsequent claim only relates to the remaining 90, the costs incurred by the landlord in relation to the 10 abandoned items are not recoverable in the litigation. Cases of this kind apart, however, a successful party who recovers his costs can ordinarily expect to recover costs reasonably incurred in complying with a pre-action protocol, save where the court thinks that in all the circumstances some different order would be appropriate.[49]

In *Birmingham CC v Lee*[50], the Court of Appeal held that where a tenant serves a letter of claim under the Pre-Action Protocol for Housing Disrepair Cases and the landlord then carries out the repairs, with the result that the tenant's subsequent claim for consequential damage is allocated to the small claims track, the tenant is entitled to its pre-allocation costs up to the date the repairs were completed on the fast track scale, because, up to that point, the tenant had a claim for specific performance which would have been allocated to the fast track. Hughes L.J., giving the judgment of the Court of Appeal, said:

> "The tenant who has a justifiable claim for disrepair needs legal assistance in advancing it. He must initiate it in accordance with the protocol. If the effect of the claim is to get the work done, then providing that the landlord was liable for the disrepair the tenant ought to recover the reasonable costs of achieving that result."

## COSTS INCURRED IN LITIGATION

### Introductory

**34–16**    The costs of issuing and serving proceedings and costs incurred in the litigation thereafter are recoverable as part of the costs of the litigation if the court so orders. These include not only solicitor's and counsel's fees but also surveyor's fees for preparing a Scott Schedule, advising on the claim, preparing experts' reports and giving evidence in court.

### The general principle

**34–17**    The court has a complete discretion as to who pays the costs of litigation.[51] However, that discretion must be exercised judicially and in accordance with settled principles. The overriding general principle is that "costs follow the

---

[48]   Ibid., at [10] to [16].
[49]   See *Callery v Gray (No.1)* [2001] 3 All E.R. 833, in which Lord Woolf said at [54] that "Where an action is commenced and a costs order is then obtained, the costs awarded will include costs reasonably incurred in complying with a pre-action protocol".
[50]   [2009] H.L.R. 15.
[51]   Senior Courts Act 1981 s.51; CPR Pt 44, especially r.44.2.

event", that is to say that the unsuccessful party pays the successful party's costs.[52] In *Lewis v Haverfordwest Rural District Council*[53] Lord Goddard C.J. stated the rule as follows:

> "There is a settled practice of the courts that in the absence of special circumstances a successful litigant should receive his costs, and that it is necessary to show some grounds for exercising the discretion of refusing an order which would give them to him, and the discretion must be judicially exercised."

Although this was a statement of the practice prior to the CPR, it remains accurate in general terms. Thus, CPR r.44.2(2) provides that if the court decides to make an order about costs, the general rule is that the unsuccessful party will be ordered to pay the costs of the successful party, but the court may make a different order. The general rule therefore remains that costs follow the event.

CPR r.44.2(4) provides that in deciding what (if any) order to make about costs, the court will have regard to all the circumstances, including-

(1) the conduct of all the parties. By CPR r.44.2(5) "conduct" includes:
   (a) conduct before, as well as during, the proceedings, and in particular the extent to which the parties followed the Practice Direction (Pre-Action Conduct) or any relevant pre-action protocol,
   (b) whether it was reasonable for a party to raise, pursue or contest a particular allegation or issue,
   (c) the manner in which a party has pursued or defended his case or a particular allegation or issue,
   (d) whether a claimant who has succeeded in his claim, in whole or in part, exaggerated his claim;
(2) whether a party has succeeded on part of his case, even if he has not been wholly successful;
(3) any payment into court or admissible offer to settle made by a party which is drawn to the court's attention, and which is not an offer to which costs consequences under CPR Pt 36 apply.[54]

(1)(b) and (d) of the above will be of particular relevance to dilapidations claims. They enable the court to reflect, where appropriate, the relative success and failure of each party by making (for example) orders for costs on an issue-by-issue basis or by awarding the party who has been successful overall only a proportion of his costs. It is no longer the case that a party who fails on some issues and therefore succeeds on part only of his case can necessarily expect to recover all his costs simply because he has recovered more than was offered or admitted by the other party, particularly if the court thinks that he has exaggerated his claim.[55]

---

[52] CPR r.44.2(2) which, however, specifically qualifies its expression of the general rule by noting that "the court may make a different order".
[53] [1953] 1 W.L.R. 1486.
[54] See paras 34–19 to 34–21, below.
[55] See para.34–22 below, where this is further considered.

In *Business Environment Bow Lane v Deanwater Estates (No.2)*[56] (in which a landlord who had substantially failed in his claim for damages for terminal dilapidations was ordered to pay the tenant's costs on an indemnity basis[57]) H.H. Judge Toulmin, QC said of (1)(d) above:

> "The effect of exaggerating a claim may be to prevent parties having realistic discussions at an early stage to resolve a dispute or prevent a successful mediation. In such cases the result of the exaggeration may be to prevent a settlement of the dispute at an early stage. Similarly, if a case is not merely exaggerated but is put on a wholly unsustainable basis, it may prevent an early settlement. It may also prevent a defendant from being able to assess realistically the value of the Claimant's case and make an appropriate Part 36 offer. This will be particularly the case when only the Claimant is able in the first instance to evaluate its own losses. In appropriate cases the Defendant should not be left at such a disadvantage. The situation may, of course, be different if the Defendant is in a position at an early stage fully to evaluate the Claimant's case."

## Detailed assessment of costs

**34–18**    A party who is awarded his costs against the other party will not generally recover everything he has spent. The amount recoverable is either summarily assessed by the court (in short cases) or is the subject of "detailed assessment" under CPR Pt 47.[58] Costs are assessed on the standard basis or on the indemnity basis as the court may decide, but the court will not in either case allow costs which have been unreasonably incurred or are unreasonable in amount.[59] On an assessment of costs on the standard basis the court will only allow costs which are proportionate to the matters in issue and will resolve any doubts which it may have as to whether the costs were reasonably and proportionately incurred or were reasonable and proportionate in amount in favour of the paying party.[60] On an assessment on the indemnity basis any doubts as to whether costs were reasonably incurred or reasonable in amount are to be resolved in favour of the receiving party.[61] The factors to be taken into account in deciding the amount of costs are set out in CPR 44.4, by virtue of which the court must have regard to (among other things) the conduct of all the parties, the amount or value of any money or property involved, the importance of the matter to all the parties, the particular complexity of the matter or the difficulty or novelty of the questions raised, the skill, effort, specialised knowledge and responsibility involved, the time spent on the case, the place where and the circumstances in which work or any part of it was done, and the receiving party's last approved or agreed budget.[62]

An order for indemnity costs will generally only be made where the facts of the case and/or the conduct of the parties is such as to take the situation away

---

[56] [2008] 3 E.G.L.R. 105.
[57] See para.34–22, below, where this case is further considered.
[58] CPR r.44.6.
[59] CPR r.44.3(1).
[60] CPR r.44.3(2). For the meaning of "proportionate", see CPR 44.3(5).
[61] CPR r.44.3(3).
[62] CPR 44.4(3).

from the norm.[63] Such an order was made in *Business Environment Bow Lane v Deanwater Estates (No.2)*,[64] in which the landlord's claim for damages for terminal dilapidations was substantially unsuccessful and it had persisted in advancing a claim which was not genuine and which it knew or ought to have known was unsustainable.[65]

The assessment of costs which are payable under a contract is dealt with in para.34–26, below.

## Part 36 offers

CPR Pt 36 and the accompanying Practice Directions contain provisions enabling **34–19** each party to make a written offer to settle (a "Pt 36 offer") intended to protect him in respect of costs in the event of the offer not being accepted and the litigation going ahead. Pt 36 provides only for the making of written offers, and the former practice of making payments into court no longer applies. The detailed provisions of Pt 36 are outside the scope of this work, but the following is a summary.

Any Pt 36 offer must be in writing and comply with certain prescribed formalities, one of which is that (unless it is made less than 21 days before the start of the trial) it must specify a period of not less than 21 days within which the defendant will be liable for the claimant's costs in accordance with CPR 36.10 if the offer is accepted.[66] A Pt 36 offer may be made at any time, including before the commencement of proceedings.[67] A Pt 36 offer which offers to pay or accept a sum of money will be treated as inclusive of all interest until the expiry of the period specified in it or (if the offer was made less than 21 days before the start of the trial) a date 21 days after the date the offer was made.[68] Before the expiry of "the relevant period" (which means, in the case of an offer made not less than 21 days before trial, the period specified in the offer or such longer period as the parties agree, and otherwise means the period up to the end of the trial or such other period as the court determines) a Pt 36 offer may be withdrawn or its terms changed to be less advantageous to the offeree only if the court gives permission.[69] After the expiry of the relevant period (and provided that the offer has not been accepted) the offeror may (by written notice served on the offeree) withdraw the offer or change its terms to be less advantageous without the court's permission.[70] Subject to certain exceptions which are not relevant for these purposes, a Pt 36 offer by a defendant to pay a sum of money in settlement of a claim must be an offer to pay a single sum of money, and an offer which includes

---

[63] *Excelsior Commercial and Industrial Holdings v Salisbury Hamer Johnson* [2002] EWCA Civ 879. See the *White Book*, Vol.1, at para.44.4.3 where the relevant cases are considered in detail.
[64] [2008] 3 E.G.L.R. 105.
[65] See para.34–22, below, where this case is further considered. A preliminary issue of liability had earlier gone to the Court of Appeal: see para.1–10, above.
[66] CPR r.36.2(2).
[67] CPR r.36.3(2)(a).
[68] CPR r.36.3(3).
[69] CPR r.36.3(5).
[70] CPR r.36.3(6) and (7).

an offer to pay all or part of the sum, if accepted, at a later date than 14 days following the date of acceptance will not be treated as a Pt 36 offer unless it is accepted.[71]

The offeree may, within seven days of a Pt 36 offer being made, request the offeror to clarify the offer, and if the offeror fails to do so within seven days of receiving the request, the offeree may (unless the trial has started) apply for an order that he does so. If the court makes such an order, it must specify the date on which the Pt 36 offer is to be treated as having been made.[72]

Save in certain circumstances, a Pt 36 offer may be accepted (by serving written notice of acceptance on the offeror) at any time (whether or not the offeree has subsequently made a different offer) unless the offeror serves notice of withdrawal on the offeree.[73] However, the court's permission to accept a Pt 36 offer is required where (among other things) the trial has started.[74] Where the court gives permission, it will (unless the parties have agreed costs) make an order dealing with costs and may order that the costs consequences of acceptance of a Pt 36 offer set out in CPR 36.10 apply.[75] Unless the parties agree, a Pt 36 offer may not be accepted after the end of the trial but before judgment is handed down.[76]

**34–20**  Where a Pt 36 offer is accepted within the relevant period, the claimant will be entitled to his costs up to the date on which notice of acceptance is served on the offeror.[77] Where a defendant's Pt 36 offer relates to part only of the claim and at the time of serving notice of acceptance the claimant abandons the balance of the claim, the claimant will be entitled to his costs up to the date of serving notice of acceptance unless the court otherwise orders.[78] In each case, costs will be assessed on the standard basis.[79] Where a Pt 36 offer made less than 21 days before the start of trial is accepted or where a Pt 36 offer is accepted after expiry of the relevant period, the court will make an order as to costs if the parties do not agree liability for costs, and (where the offer is accepted after expiry of the relevant period) unless the court orders otherwise, the claimant will be entitled to his costs up to the date on which the relevant period expired and the offeree will be liable for the offeror's costs for the period from the date of expiry of the relevant period to the date of acceptance.[80]

Where a Pt 36 offer is accepted and relates to the whole claim, the claim will be stayed upon the terms of the offer.[81] Where a Pt 36 offer which relates to part only of the claim is accepted, the claim will be stayed as to that part on the terms of the offer and (subject to CPR r.36.10(2)[82]) the court must decide the liability

---

[71] CPR r.36.4.
[72] CPR r.36.8.
[73] CPR r.36.9(2).
[74] CPR r.36.9(3).
[75] CPR r.36.9(4).
[76] CPR r.36.9(5).
[77] CPR r.36.10(1).
[78] CPR r.36.10(2).
[79] CPR r.36.10(3).
[80] CPR r.36.10(4) and (5).
[81] CPR r.36.11(1).
[82] See above.

for costs unless the parties have agreed costs.[83] The court's power to enforce the terms of the Pt 36 offer and to deal with any question of costs relating to the proceedings is unaffected by any stay.[84] Unless the parties otherwise agree in writing, where a defendant's Pt 36 offer that is or includes an offer to pay a sum of money is accepted, the sum must be paid to the offeree within 14 days of the date of the acceptance, and if it is not paid within that period or such other period as is agreed, the offeree may enter judgment for the unpaid sum.[85] Where any other Pt 36 offer is accepted, a party who alleges that it has not been honoured may apply to enforce its terms without starting a new claim.[86] Special provisions apply where the claimant wishes to accept a Pt 36 offer made by one or more but not all of a number of defendants.[87]

Where a Pt 36 offer is made but not accepted, the costs consequences following judgment are set out in CPR r.36.14. They may be summarised as follows:

(1)    Where a claimant fails to obtain a judgment more advantageous than a defendant's Pt 36 offer, the court will, unless it is unjust to do so, order that the defendant is entitled to his costs from the date on which the relevant period expired, and interest on those costs;

(2)    Where judgment against the defendant is at least as advantageous to the claimant as the proposals contained in a claimant's Pt 36 offer, the court will, unless it considers it unjust to do so, order that the claimant is entitled to (i) interest on the whole or any part of a sum of money (excluding interest) awarded at a rate not exceeding 10 per cent above base rate for some or all of the period starting with the date on which the relevant period expired; (ii) his costs on an indemnity basis from the date on which he relevant period expired; (iii) interest on those costs at a rate not exceeding 10 per cent above base rate; and (iv) an additional amount not exceeding £75,000 calculated by applying a prescribed percentage to an amount which is (a) where the claim is or includes a monetary claim, the sum awarded to the claimant by the court, (b) where the claim is only a non-monetary claim, the sum awarded to the claimant by the court in terms of costs;[88]

(3)    For the above purposes, in relation to any money claim or money element of a claim, "more advantageous" means better in money terms by any amount, and "at least as advantageous" is to be construed accordingly;[89]

(4)    In considering whether it would be unjust to make the above orders, the court will take into account all the circumstances of the case including (i)

---

[83] CPR r.36.11(3).

[84] CPR r. 36.11(5)

[85] CPR r.36.11(6) and (7).

[86] CPR r.36.11(8).

[87] CPR r.36.12.

[88] Where the sum awarded is up to £500,000, the prescribed percentage is 10 percent of the amount awarded. Where the sum awarded is above £500,000 up to £1,000,000, the prescribed percentage is 10% of the first £500,000 and 5% of any amount above that figure.

[89] This reverses the effect of the decision of the Court of Appeal in *Carver v BAA* [2009] 1 W.L.R. 113. It is now longer open to the court, when deciding whether one party has beaten the other side's Pt.36 offer, to undertake "a wide-ranging review of all the facts and circumstances of the case in

the terms of any Pt 36 offer; (ii) the stage in the proceedings when any Pt 36 offer was made, including in particular how long before the trial started the offer was made; (iii) the information available to the parties at the time when the Pt 36 offer was made; and (iv) the conduct of the parties with regard to the giving or refusing to give information for the purposes of enabling the offer to be made or evaluated;

(5)    The above provisions do not apply to a Pt 36 offer that has been withdrawn or one that has been changed so that its terms are less advantageous to the offeree, and the offeree has beaten the less advantageous offer, or one that was made less than 21 days before trial, unless the court has abridged the relevant period.

Pt 36 does not prevent a party from making an offer to settle in whatever way he chooses, but if that offer is not made in accordance with Pt 36, it will not have the costs consequences specified in Pt 36.[90] It is therefore better, where possible, to use the Pt 36 procedure.

A Pt 36 offer is treated as "without prejudice save as to costs", and (subject to certain exceptions) the fact that it has been made must not be communicated to the trial judge until the case has been decided.[91]

**34–21**    The importance of an early assessment of the prospects by both parties is obvious. The party faced with the claim must give careful consideration to the question of making a Pt 36 offer as early as possible and, in particular, whether he should accept any offer made by the claimant. The costs consequences of not making an offer soon enough or in a sufficient amount are likely to be considerable, and the consequence of not accepting a claimant's Pt 36 offer (if made at a realistic level) may be draconian. If the claim is one where the claimant is bound to recover something, and the only real issue is how much (a situation which occurs frequently where the claim is brought by the landlord for damages for terminal dilapidations), then the defendant may be at risk of having to pay all the costs even if the claimant recovers less than he claims.[92] Similarly the party making the claim must make a realistic assessment of his prospects of "beating" any Pt 36 offer which has been made. It is worth remembering that even in very substantial dilapidations actions the risk of having to pay the other side's costs at the end of the day can sometimes assume a greater financial significance than the amount of damages in issue.

---

deciding whether the judgment, which is the fruit of the litigation, was worth the fight" (per Ward L.J.). The only relevant factor now is how the judgment compares in money terms with the amount offered.
[90] CPR r.36.1(2). However, the court must still consider any such offer (provided it is otherwise admissible) in deciding what order to make about costs: CPR 44.2(4)(c).
[91] CPR r.36.13(1) and (2).
[92] See para.34–22, below.

## Costs in dilapidations cases

In some cases, there will be a single issue in a dilapidations claim (for example, **34–22** whether or not a roof needs replacement), and one or other party will be successful in relation to it. In that event, save where the successful party has behaved unreasonably in some way (and subject to any relevant Pt 36 offers), the effect of the general rule explained above is likely to be that such party will get his costs of the action. In other cases, there may be a number of different issues, and either there may be no clear overall "winner", or the party who has "won" may nonetheless have lost on important issues along the way. An example which often occurs in practice concerns claims by landlords for damages for terminal dilapidations. Such claims will generally include a large number of allegations of individual breaches of covenant. Some may be agreed by the trial, but others may remain in issue and have to be decided by the court. In addition to questions of liability for disrepair, there may be other substantial issues, such as (for example) whether and if so to what extent the tenant is liable to remove items installed during the lease, the extent of any diminution in the value of the landlord's reversion and whether and if so to what extent the landlord is entitled to the costs of the schedule of dilapidations under a contractual provision of the sort considered above. The outcome is very often that the landlord recovers less (sometimes much less) than the total amount of his claim.

On one view, the landlord in such a case ought to be awarded his costs. He can say that he has had to come to court to recover the amount awarded, and it was always open to the tenant to make an appropriate offer. But the tenant can say that the landlord failed on part of his claim, so that it would be unjust for him to recover all his costs. Each case will depend on its own facts. In general terms, however, where the landlord has recovered a substantial sum, and the tenant has failed to make any relevant Pt.36 offer, the starting position is likely to be that the landlord ought to be awarded his costs. An example is *PgfII SA v Royal & Sun Alliance Plc*,[93] in which the landlord's claim for terminal dilapidations in its pre-action Protocol letter was for just under £3.5m; its Pt 36 offer was £1.75m. and it recovered £735,749.40. The tenant's expert's cladding scheme had been preferred to that of the landlord's expert. The tenant was nonetheless ordered to pay the whole of the landlord's costs on the standard basis. However, where the claim includes one or more discrete and substantial items on which the landlord has failed altogether, or where he has otherwise acted unreasonably in relation to the litigation, the right costs order may well be either to award him only a proportion of his costs or to award costs on an issue-by-issue basis (i.e. to make different costs orders in relation to different issues). Four examples from dilapidations cases may be given. In *Johnsey Estates (1990) Ltd v Secretary of State for the Environment, Transport and the Regions*,[94] the landlord was ordered to pay the tenant's costs of a particular issue on which it had failed, namely, a claim to recover the costs of preparing and serving a s.146 notice. In *Craven (Builders) Ltd v Secretary of State for Health*,[95] Neuberger J. deprived the

---

[93] [2010] EWHC 1981 (TCC).
[94] [2001] 2 E.G.L.R. 128.
[95] [2001] 1 E.G.L.R. 128.

landlord of a proportion of its costs (5 per cent) because it had raised and then abandoned an issue that the tenancy had continued after a certain date. In *Firle Investments v Datapoint International*,[96] the landlord was deprived of 30 per cent of its costs in relation to a particular period because it had pursued matters which it should have abandoned.

In *Hammersmatch Properties (Welwyn) Ltd v Saint-Gobain Ceramics & Plastics Ltd*[97] the landlord's costs were reduced by 20 per cent to reflect the fact that additional costs had been incurred in relation to the issue of whether it intended to carry out the remedial works, on which it had been unsuccessful, and also the fact that the tenant had succeeded on various issues arising out of the schedule of dilapidations.

Where the landlord's claim has substantially failed, he may be ordered to pay all the tenant's costs even though he has succeeded in recovering a small amount.[98] Thus, in *Business Environment Bow Lane v Deanwater Estates (No.2)*,[99] the landlord served a schedule of dilapidations in April 2005 setting out a claim for in excess of £550,000. Proceedings were issued in February 2006 claiming £246,572.80 for the cost of the works, £52,975.14 for professional fees and £115,384.62 for loss of rent (making a total of £414,932.56). The Particulars of Claim included an incorrect allegation that the works had been carried out, which had been verified by a statement of truth signed by the landlord's solicitor. The tenant's response to the Scott Schedule indicated that it accepted liability only for two items in the total sum of £1,073.50. In February 2008 the landlord made a Pt 36 offer agreeing to accept that sum, provided that its costs were paid. The tenant declined to pay the landlord's costs. The parties then agreed that judgment should be entered for the landlord for £1,073.50 and that the issue of costs should be determined by the court at a hearing. The landlord argued that it ought to be awarded its costs because it had recovered a sum which was not de minimis and the tenant could have made an earlier Pt 36 offer to safeguard its position. H.H. Judge Toulmin QC rejected that argument, and ordered the landlord to pay the whole of the tenant's costs on an indemnity basis. On the question of who was to be regarded as the winner, he said:

> " This case was put on the basis that the Defendant was liable to pay as dilapidations the cost of the very substantial internal remedial works carried out to the property under the terms of the lease. In the end, the Claimant was forced to concede that the work which was carried out was, except for a trivial sum, not referable to dilapidations but to the Claimant's wholesale refurbishment of the building as offices. Equally in relation to external works the Claimant claimed for very substantial works which were not in fact carried out. The Claimant's dilapidation schedules which were produced by their expert bore, therefore, no relation to the position which they were forced to concede shortly before the trial took place. It is clear therefore that the Claimant lost on the issue of dilapidations. I conclude that in this litigation there was a clear winner and loser and that the Claimant was the clear loser and should realistically have realised that this was the result."

[96] [2001] EWCA Civ 1106. See below, in which the relevant part of the judgment is set out.
[97] [2013] EWHC 2227 (TCC)/
[98] A fortiori where he recovers only nominal damages and does not obtain anything else of value to him: see *Anglo-Cyprian Trade Agencies Ltd v Paphos Wine Industries Ltd* [1951] 1 All E.R. 873; *Alltrans Express Ltd v CVA Holdings Ltd* [1984] 1 W.L.R. 394.
[99] [2008] 3 E.G.L.R. 105

On the question of indemnity costs, he said:

"In my view the Claimant both before and after the institution of proceedings acted in a way which took this case out of the norm. It represented to the Defendant both before and after the start of the litigation that it had a very substantial dilapidations claim. The Claimant knew what work it intended to carry out from the time when it made its initial claim for over £500,000 for dilapidations. The scope of the work was no doubt refined in the summer of 2005 and during the tendering stage. This claim was persisted in at the time of the service of the Particulars of Claim. The Statement of Truth, made on its behalf on the claim form and in the Statement of Claim attested to the fact that this was a genuine claim for dilapidations and that the work claimed for had been carried out. Any proper investigation of this claim both before the Particulars of Claim were served and afterwards, would have revealed (a) that the external works had not been carried out, and (b) that this was indeed not a genuine claim for dilapidations. Even in the Schedule of Dilapidations served on 7 December 2007 the Claimant persisted in a substantial claim which it knew or ought to have known was unsustainable. In these circumstances the appropriate order is that the Claimant pay the Defendant's costs other than those subject of the order of the Court of Appeal on an indemnity basis."[100]

The landlord in the above case had accepted the sum offered in the tenant's Pt 36 offer. But what happens where the landlord in a claim for damages for terminal dilapidations does not accept the tenant's Pt 36 offer but then goes on to beat it only by a small margin?

Under the former practice, a claimant who recovered more than the amount paid into court could generally expect to recover all his costs. Thus, in *Johnsey Estates (1990) Ltd v Secretary of State for the Environment, Transport and the Regions*,[101] the landlord claimed damages for terminal dilapidations together with interest from the date of the expiry of the lease on June 24, 1994. Its initial contention was that the diminution in the value of the reversion was £1.25 million. The tenant contended that the diminution was £150,000, and on September 25, 1996 paid £200,000 into court. Following the exchange of valuer's reports, the landlord's valuer reduced his diminution figure to £1.025 million, and the tenant's valuer increased his figure to £200,000. On February 19, 1999 the tenant paid a further £250,000 into court, making a total of £450,000 in all. The judge at trial held that the diminution in value was £200,000, and awarded that sum plus interest of £36,000, making a total of £236,000 in all. Accordingly, the landlord recovered more than the first payment in on September 25, 1996 but less than the second payment in on February 19, 1999. The judge made the following costs orders (among others): (i) he awarded the landlord its costs up to the date of

---

[100] The defendant tenant's contention that the landlord's claim for damages for dilapidations was precluded by a collateral contract had been tried as a preliminary issue. The tenant had failed in the Court of Appeal (see para.1–10, above) and had been ordered to pay the landlord's costs of the preliminary issue. Following H.H. Judge Toulmin's judgment in relation to the costs of the action, the landlord's costs of the preliminary issue in the Court of Appeal were subsequently assessed by a Master at nil, on the ground that they were not reasonably incurred, because they had been incurred in an action in which the landlord sought an exaggerated sum that should never have been claimed. Mann J. (sitting with Master Campbell and Mr. Simon Kenny as assessors) allowed the landlord's appeal, on the basis that the Court of Appeal's order had been intended to deal with the costs of the preliminary issue as a discrete set of costs, which were to be paid by the tenant to the landlord irrespective of the fate of the action, and the Master should have assessed the costs of the preliminary issue by reference to their reasonableness and propriety within that issue, and not by reference to the ultimate fate of the action, no matter how misconceived it might have been: see *Business Environment Bow Lane v Deanwater Estates* [2009] 3 E.G.L.R. 21.
[101] [2001] 2 E.G.L.R. 128.

the first payment in; (ii) he ordered the landlord to pay the tenant's costs of the diminution in value issue from the date of the first payment in to the date of the second payment in; and (iii) he ordered the landlord to pay all the tenant's costs from the date of the second payment in. The landlord appealed, contending that since it had recovered more than the amount of the first payment in, it should have been given its costs up to the date of the second payment in. The Court of Appeal allowed the appeal, and ordered the tenant to pay the landlord's costs of the diminution in value issue between the date of the first and second payments in.

Much the same approach was taken in *Firle Investments v Datapoint International*,[102] in which the landlord claimed damages for terminal dilapidations of £385,000 and recovered £53,695.25 following a four-day trial in March 2000. On December 17, 1999 the tenant paid £35,000 into court. On March 1, 2000 the landlord made a claimant's Pt 36 offer of £135,000. The tenant then paid a further £15,000 into court on March 10, 1999, some 10 days before the date of trial. The result was therefore that the amount recovered exceeded the amount paid in by something in excess of £3,500. The trial judge awarded the landlord one-third of its costs up to the date of the second payment in, and 15 per cent thereafter. The Court of Appeal allowed the landlord's appeal, substituting an order that the landlord should get all of its costs up to the second payment in and (because the landlord had unsuccessfully pursued certain matters at trial) and 70 per cent of its costs thereafter. Schiemann L.J. said in his judgment:

"17. ... [I]t seems to me that the judge was clearly in error in relation to the period up to 10th March 2000. The claimant succeeded by a substantial amount so far as the offers which were on the table were concerned. The defendant could have made a payment in and therefore in principle the claimant is entitled to its costs. This is not a case where there were clear separate issues on some of which the claimant won and others lost if issues be taken as matters which had to be proved by one side or the other in detail for the points to succeed. As it seems to me up to 10th March the position ought to be that the claimant gets its costs in full as opposed merely to one-third of its costs which was the view of the judge. That difference, as it seems to me, is such as entitles this court to interfere.

18. The position, thereafter, is a little bit more difficult. That is because the judge points out in the course of his long judgments various matters in which the claimant persisted right until the end in asserting as regards its intentions which it should not have persisted in asserting. No one now knows precisely what effect that had on the trial. It is not suggested that that as such determined the defendant's attitude as to payment in, but it undoubtedly will have lengthened the trial. Further, the claimant's actions as revealed in its correspondence undoubtedly were, one might almost say, such as to warn the defendant off the course and make it seem most unlikely that further negotiations could be pursued. For my part I would regard that latter point as a relatively small point although in principle it must be right that this court will encourage parties to negotiate without putting their own positions in an extreme manner. As I say for my part I am not persuaded entirely that the attitude adopted by Mr Hutchins' clients in respect to some matters was an attitude which was unreasonable for them to adopt even though the judge did not, in the event, accept that part of the evidence. It is often the case that in a case there will be a hundred or more sub-issues on some of which one party does less well than he hoped, and the other party does less well than he hoped.

19. However the various factors which the judge did indicate were ones in the investigation of which time was taken at the trial, which do, as it seems to me, given that that is the view that the judge formed, entitle the defendants to say that the claimants should not have all their costs in relation to the period after 10th March. I do not claim to have approached this in anything like a scientific way, but it seems to me that the figure adopted by the learned judge

---

[102] [2001] EWCA Civ 1106.

of 15 per cent is quite wrong in principle, but if one acknowledges that there is some force in some of the points that he make, a figure which entitles the claimants to recover 70 per cent of their costs is closer to the sort of thing that ought to have been ordered."

In *Hammersmatch Properties (Welwyn) Ltd v Saint-Gobain Ceramics & Plastics Ltd*[103] the landlord's claim for damages for terminal dilapidations was for in excess of £7.6m at the time of service of its first schedule of dilapidations. By the time the proceedings were commenced, its claim had reduced to in excess of £4.4m plus continuing loss of rent and insurance rent at a combined annual rate of £752,498.40. The tenant made a Pt 36 offer of £500,000, followed by a further Pt 36 offer of £1m. The landlord made a Pt 36 offer of £3.2m. The Court awarded damages of £900,000 plus the agreed cost of the schedule of dilapidations (£20,320.40) which, together with interest to the date of judgment, came to £1,058,768.00. As at the last date for acceptance of the tenant's second Pt 36 offer, the total sum awarded (including interest up to that date) amounted to £1,003,637.90, which was only £3,637.90 more than the tenant's offer. The tenant sought a proportion of its costs, relying on CPR r.44.2(4)(c) (which provides that in deciding what costs order to make, the court must have regard to "any admissible offer to settle made by a party which is drawn to the court's attention, and which is not an offer to which costs consequences under Part 36 apply").[104] Ramsey J. held that whilst CPR r.44.2(4)(c) would clearly apply "where there is an open offer made for more than is recovered or an offer purportedly under Part 36 for a sum in excess of the sum recovered but where, for some reason it does not have the Part 36 costs consequences", it should not alter the costs consequences in a case where the tenant had made a Pt 36 offer which was too low and there had been no unreasonable refusal to negotiate that could have been taken into account under CPR r.44.2(4).[105] However, he reduced the landlord's costs by 20 per cent to reflect the fact that additional costs had been incurred in relation to the issue of whether the landlord intended to carry out the remedial works (on which it had been unsuccessful), and also the fact that the tenant had succeeded on various issues arising out of the schedule of dilapidations.

The above authorities show that where the landlord beats the tenant's Pt 36 offer by a small amount, he is nonetheless likely to recover all of his costs, even where his claim is for a very much larger amount. However, the position may be different where he has unreasonably refused to negotiate, or his claim is exaggerated or has been substantially unsuccessful (as in *Business Environment Bow Lane v Deanwater Estates (No.2)*[106]), or that he has acted unreasonably in relation to aspects of the litigation (as in *Firle v Datapoint*[107] and *Hammersmatch Properties (Welwyn) Ltd v Saint-Gobain Ceramics & Plastics Ltd*[108]).

---

[103] [2013] EWHC 2227 (TCC).
[104] See para.34.17, above.
[105] See para.34.17, above.
[106] [2008] 3 E.G.L.R. 105. See above.
[107] Above.
[108] Above.

## Payment of costs as a condition of relief from forfeiture

**34–23**     The general principle as regards relief from forfeiture is that the landlord is prima facie entitled to be put into the position in which he would have been had there been no forfeiture.[109] In applying that principle, payment of the landlord's costs is frequently made a condition of relief from forfeiture.[110] The general rule is that such costs ought to be awarded on an indemnity basis.[111] However, the court retains an overall discretion, and a different order may be made where the landlord has acted unreasonably or failed on some issues. Moreover, where the landlord has unreasonably opposed the grant of relief, he may be ordered to pay the tenant's costs on the standard basis, and the tenant will be able to set those costs off against what he would otherwise be required to pay to the lessor as a term of obtaining relief from forfeiture.[112]

## Contractual provisions relating to costs of litigation[113]

**34–24**     Some modern leases contain comprehensive provisions under which the tenant is obliged to pay the landlord's costs of litigation in connection with breaches of covenant. Two questions commonly arise in relation to such provisions: (i) the costs to which the landlord is entitled; and (ii) whether and to what extent such provisions are relevant when the court is deciding what costs order to make.

### (a)    The landlord's entitlement

**34–25**     The extent of the landlord's entitlement to his costs of litigation under a contractual provision is a question of construction of the particular provision.

In *Drummond v S & U Stores Ltd*[114] Glidewell J. construed a covenant requiring the tenant to pay to the landlord all costs, charges and expenses incurred by the landlord in or in contemplation of any proceedings in respect of the lease under ss.146 and 147 of the Law of Property Act 1925 as entitling the landlord to costs on a solicitor and client (i.e. indemnity[115]) basis, rather than on the standard basis.[116] Likewise, in *Church Commissioners for England v Ibrahim*[117] an obligation in a tenancy of a flat to "pay and compensate the Landlords fully for

---

[109] *Egerton v Jones* [1939] 2 K.B. 702.

[110] Or the grant of a vesting order: see *Official Custodian for Charities v Mackey (No.2)* [1985] 1 W.L.R. 1308.

[111] *Bland v Ingrams Estates Ltd (No.2)* [2002] Ch. 177 at [14]; *Patel v K&J Restaurants Ltd* [2010] EWCA Civ 1211 at [104] (not following a dictum of Lord Templeman in *Billson v Residential Apartments Ltd (No. 1)* [1992] A.C. 494). The indemnity basis is considered in para.34–18, above.

[112] *Howard v Fanshawe* [1895] 2 Ch. 581; *Abbey National Building Society v Maybeech* [1985] Ch. 190; *Bland v Ingrams Estates Ltd (No.2)* above, at [14].

[113] See further paras 34–07 to 34–09, above.

[114] [1981] 1 E.G.L.R. 42.

[115] It is thought that the judge must have meant the solicitor and own client basis (i.e. the costs which the landlord would have to pay his own solicitor), rather than the old "solicitor and client" basis, which became the common fund basis, and is now the standard basis.

[116] See para.34–18, above, in which the difference between the standard basis and the indemnity basis is explained.

[117] [1997] 1 E.G.L.R. 13.

any costs expense loss or damage incurred or suffered by the Landlords as a consequence of any breach of the agreements on the part of the Tenant in this Agreement and to indemnify the Landlords from and against all actions claims and liabilities in that respect" was held by the Court of Appeal to entitle the landlords to costs on an indemnity basis. The argument that the provision was limited to payment of costs on the standard basis was said not to attribute meaning to the words "fully for any costs" or the later words "to indemnify" in the clause.[118]

However, a different result was reached in *Primeridge v Jean Muir*,[119] in which a tenant's covenant to pay the landlord all proper costs, charges and expenses incurred in connection with any breach of covenant by, or the recovery of arrears of rent from, the tenant, was construed as entitling the landlord to costs on the standard basis only. It was said that such a provision will not be construed as entitling the landlord to costs on an indemnity basis unless it plainly and unambiguously so provides.[120]

A contractual provision entitling the landlord to recover costs of litigation will not ordinarily entitle him to recover costs that have been unreasonably incurred.[121] Nor is it likely to be construed as entitling the landlord, as against the other party to the litigation, to recover costs over and above those awarded by the court.[122] Thus, in *Holding & Management Ltd v Property Holding & Investment Trust Plc*[123] the judge at first instance made no order as to costs in proceedings between a maintenance trustee and various tenants. The maintenance trustee claimed to be reimbursed its costs by virtue of a contractual provision in the lease. In the Court of Appeal Nicholls L.J. said:

"The effect of the plaintiff's claim to reimbursement is this. The plaintiff brought proceedings against the tenants. At the conclusion the judge decided that, as between the plaintiff and the tenants, there should be no order as to costs; each party should bear its own costs of the proceedings. On the plaintiff's argument that still leaves the plaintiff entitled to require the self-same tenants to pay its costs, by including those costs in the following year's maintenance

---

[118] Cf. *Bank of Baroda v Panessar* [1987] Ch. 335, in which the court construed a provision in a guarantee relating to "all costs charges and expenses which you may incur in enforcing or obtaining payment of the sums of money due to you from the principal" as entitling the creditor to costs on an indemnity basis.
[119] [1992] 1 E.G.L.R. 273.
[120] See further *Re Adelphi Hotel (Brighton) Ltd* [1953] 1 W.L.R. 955, in which a provision in a mortgage to the effect that the security extended to "all costs, charges and expenses incurred or paid [by the mortgagee] in relation to the negotiation for, and preparation, completion, realisation and enforcement of this security" was held to entitle the mortgagee to the costs of enforcing the security only on what is now the standard basis.
[121] *Holding & Management Ltd v Property Holding & Investment Trust Plc* [1989] 1 W.L.R. 1313; *Morgan v Stainer* [1993] 2 E.G.L.R. 73.
[122] *Cotterell v Stratton* (1874) L.R. 17 Eq. 543; *ANZ Banking Group (New Zealand) Ltd v Gibson* [1981] 2 N.Z.L.R. 513 (New Zealand); *Bank of Baroda v Pannessar* [1987] Ch. 335 at 355E; *Holding & Management Ltd v Property Holding & Investment Trust Plc*, above; *Morgan v Stainer* [1993] 2 E.G.L.R. 73. See, however, *Drummond v S & U Stores Ltd* [1981] 1 E.G.L.R. 42, in which the judge held that insofar as any part of any costs falling within a contractual provision relating to costs was not recoverable as costs in the action, then the landlord was entitled to recover it under the provision. Reference should also be made to s.20C of the Landlord and Tenant Act 1985, which confers on tenants of dwellings a right of challenge in relation to the inclusion in service charges of costs incurred or to be incurred in proceedings.
[123] Above.

provision which the tenants are contractually bound to pay. This is indeed a case seeking to get through the back door what has been refused at the front. The contention has, I think, only to be spelled out for its unattractiveness and unreasonableness to become apparent."

### (b)    The making of costs orders by the court

**34–26**    It has been held that whilst the making of an order for the payment of costs by one party to another party is always a discretionary order, where there is a contractual right to the costs, the discretion should ordinarily be exercised so as to reflect that contractual right.[124] In *Church Commissioners for England v Ibrahim*[125] Roch L.J. explained the correct approach as follows:

> "The recorder is, in my view, correct that parties to litigation cannot tie the hands of the court on the question of costs by agreement whether that agreement is one made after the commencement of proceedings or in the contract, breach of the terms of which gives rise to the proceedings. The court's power to decide by whom costs should be paid could probably not be fettered by a prior contract between the parties to the effect that a successful litigant should have to pay costs to an unsuccessful litigant. Clearly it would be contrary to the public interest that the court should be deprived of the powers given under section 51(6) [of the Supreme Court Act 1981] to disallow wasted costs. Further, section 51(8) requires the person responsible for determining the amount of costs to take account of the factor there mentioned if it exists and that duty placed on that person cannot, in my view, be abrogated by a term in the contract. Whether the court's discretion to decide by whom the costs of proceedings should be paid could be fettered by a contractual agreement made before the litigation is started is a more difficult question which does not arise in this appeal.
>
> Having made these observations, in my judgment, the statements of principle in [*Gomba Holdings (UK) Ltd v Minories Finance Ltd (No.2*[126])] are not confined to mortgage cases and have a wider application. The successful litigant's contractual rights to recover the costs of any proceedings to enforce his primary contractual rights is a highly relevant factor when it comes to making a costs order. He is not, in my view, to be deprived of his contractual rights to costs where he has claimed them unless there is good reason to do so and that applies both to the making of a costs order in his favour and to the extent that costs are to be paid to him. Indeed I would adopt the citation in the *Gomba Holdings* case from the judgment of Vinelott J which appears at p. 193A, namely:
>
>> 'If the parties have agreed the basis of taxation it would, I think, be an improper exercise of the court's discretion to direct the taxation on some other basis, unless satisfied that there had been some conduct on the part of the mortgagee disentitling him to costs or to costs on the agreed basis.'
>
> A good reason for depriving a successful litigant to part of the costs to which the contractual term would entitle him would be that that part of the costs came within the definition of wasted costs in section 51(7), that is to say they were costs incurred by him as a result of improper, unreasonable or negligent conduct on his part or that of his legal or other representatives. There may well be other sufficient reasons for interfering with the basis of taxation."

The general rule that the court's discretion should ordinarily be exercised so as to reflect a contractual right to costs was departed from in *Forcelux v Binnie*.[127] Warren J. (with whom Ward and Jacob L.JJ. agreed) said:

---

[124] *Gomba Holdings (UK) Ltd v Minories Finance Ltd (No.2)* [1993] Ch. 171; *Church Commissioners for England v Ibrahim* [1997] 1 E.G.L.R. 13.
[125] Above.
[126] Above.
[127] [2010] H.L.R. 20. See further on this case, para.34–07, above.

"[Counsel] accepts the jurisdiction of the court to make a different order notwithstanding the contractual position, but submits that the general principle is that the discretion should be exercised in line with the contract … I do not dissent in any way from the proposition that the general principle is as he states. But the general principle is not a rule of law and it may well be that in a particular case, or even in a class of case, the court's discretion should be used to override the contractual right.

    For example, if a lessor loses a piece of litigation at first instance which it was reasonable for him to fight, it might be wrong to deprive him of a contractual right to costs. But if he goes on to appeal the decision against him and loses the appeal, then it is not obvious to me that the general rule should be that the discretion should be exercised in accordance with the contractual right; or if it is the general rule, then the court should be willing to depart from it quite readily."

It follows that where the lease on its true construction obliges the tenant to pay the landlord's costs on an indemnity basis and the landlord is successful in the litigation, the court will ordinarily order the tenant to pay the landlord's costs on an indemnity basis. However, the position may be different where the landlord is not the successful party or he has otherwise conducted the litigation unreasonably.

CPR r.44.5 deals with the assessment of costs which are payable under a contract.[128] Where the court assesses (whether by summary or detailed assessment) costs which are payable by the paying party to the receiving party under the terms of a contract, the costs payable under those terms are, unless the contract expressly provides otherwise, to be presumed to be costs which have been reasonably incurred and are reasonable in amount, and the court will assess them accordingly.[129] These presumptions are rebuttable, and PD 44 sets out circumstances where the court may order otherwise.[130] It should be noted that CPR r.44.5 only applies where the court is assessing costs payable under a contract: it does not require the court to make an assessment of such costs. The question whether the court's discretion to award costs should be exercised in accordance with the contract therefore remains governed by the principles set out above.

## COSTS INCURRED IN CARRYING OUT WORKS OF REPAIR

### Introductory

The costs incurred by one party in carrying out repair work falling within the liability of the other party may be recoverable, either by way of damages,[131] or (where the works are done by the landlord) under an express provision in the lease entitling him to enter and carry out work falling within the tenant's liability.[132] The question in such cases is the extent to which fees and costs incurred in preparing for and carrying out the work will be recoverable in addition to the cost of the work itself.

**34–27**

---

[128] For the assessment of costs, see para.34–18, above.
[129] CPR r.44.5(1).
[130] CPR r.44.5(2).
[131] See Chs 28 to 33 above.
[132] See para.14–11 et seq. and para.28–32 et seq., above.

## Specification and supervision fees

**34–28**    Where the costs of carrying out repair work are recoverable, then in principle professional fees incurred in connection with preparing the specification for, and supervising, the work will be recoverable as well.[133] It must be shown that the nature of the work and the other relevant circumstances are such that a reasonable and prudent person would incur such fees, and the fees will be limited to a reasonable amount. Further, where the claim is made by a landlord and is for damages representing the cost of the work, the provisions of s.18(1) of the Landlord and Tenant Act 1927 must be taken into account.[134] If the diminution in the value of the reversion does not include specification or supervision fees (perhaps because the work is sufficiently minor in relation to the premises as a whole that the hypothetical purchaser of the reversion would make no allowance for fees), then the damages recoverable will be limited accordingly.

## Advisory, testing and exploratory work

**34–29**    In an appropriate case, the cost of professional advice as to the extent of the necessary remedial work will be recoverable as part of the cost of the work, and so also will the cost of testing and exploratory work where this is a necessary part of specifying and carrying out the works necessary to remedy disrepair which is known to exist. For example, where the disrepair consists of a known outbreak of dry rot, it is thought that the cost of remedial work may properly include the necessary opening up works to establish the extent of the outbreak, and hence the extent of the necessary remedial works. However, such costs must be carefully distinguished from the costs of general investigations and advice as to whether disrepair exists at all. Costs in the latter category will not generally form part of the cost of the remedial works. Thus, in *Plough Investments Ltd v Manchester City Council*[135] a lease entitled the landlord to recover "the cost of carrying out repairs". Scott J. held that a distinction was to be drawn between, on the one hand, general advice as to the condition of the building and, on the other hand, specific advice as to the means of remedying a specific state of disrepair, the former being within the covenant but the latter not. Accordingly, the cost of a full structural survey and report was not recoverable, but the cost of a detailed specification of the work necessary to remedy defective windows, parapet walls and cracked bricks and blocks would have been, provided that it did not go beyond what was reasonably necessary to remedy the disrepair.

Likewise, in *Commercial Union Life Assurance Co Ltd v Label Ink Ltd*[136] H.H.J Rich, QC (sitting as a Deputy High Court Judge) held in the absence of any evidence that four gas-fired heaters were defective, the cost of testing them was

---

[133]  See for example *Culworth v Society of Licensed Victuallers* [1990] 2 E.G.L.R. 36 (affirmed (1991) 62 P. & C.R. 211) (professional fees of 12.5 per cent added to agreed cost of repair works).
[134]  See Ch.30, above.
[135]  [1989] 1 E.G.L.R. 244.
[136]  [2001] L. & T.R. 29. Note that the question of disrepair arose in that case in the context of whether or not the tenant had complied with a condition precedent in a break option, and the judge's construction of the condition precedent was subsequently disapproved by the Court of Appeal in *Fitzroy House Epworth Street (No.1) v Financial Times* [2006] 2 E.G.L.R. 13.

not recoverable as damages for breach of a tenant's covenant at all material times to keep the demised premises in good and substantial repair and condition.

# CHAPTER 35

# DILAPIDATIONS QUESTIONS ARISING IN RELATED FIELDS

## INTRODUCTORY

This Chapter is concerned with a number of property law fields in which dilapidations questions may arise or be relevant. It is concerned only with the dilapidations aspects of these areas and not, save where unavoidable, with the substantive law applicable, for which reference must be made to the standard works on the subject.

**35–01**

Dilapidations aspects relevant to the following areas are considered: (a) the renewal of business tenancies under Pt II of the Landlord and Tenant Act 1954[1]; (b) rent reviews[2]; and (c) options to renew and determine leases.[3]

## THE RENEWAL OF BUSINESS TENANCIES UNDER PT II OF THE LANDLORD AND TENANT ACT 1954[4]

### Introductory

Part II of the Landlord and Tenant Act 1954 provides for the continuation and renewal of business tenancies. In general, the law of dilapidations will affect the landlord and tenant of business premises in the following ways:

**35–02**

(1) during the early years of the contractual term, when the possible continuation and renewal of the tenancy lie far in the future, their relationship is governed by the general principles of the law of dilapidations, which are considered elsewhere in this work;

(2) as the business tenancy draws towards its close, and during such period as it may be continued by the 1954 Act, the general law continues to apply but important practical questions arise as to the way in which the repairing obligations are to be enforced[5];

---

[1] See para.35–02 et seq., below.
[2] See para.35–08 et seq., below.
[3] See para.35–13 et seq., below.
[4] For an authoritative treatment of the law relating to business tenancies, see Reynolds and Clark, *Renewal of Business Tenancies*, 4th edn.
[5] See paras 35–03 to 35–04, below.

(3) if the tenant applies for a new tenancy under the Act, the landlord may seek to oppose on the ground of breach by the tenant of his repairing obligations[6];

(4) either separately or in relation to such a ground of opposition, the landlord may seek to have a term included in any new tenancy to be granted which would require the tenant immediately to carry out a specific schedule of works[7];

(5) the terms which the court will include in any new tenancy to be granted will usually contain obligations as to repair[8];

(6) the existence of, and responsibility for, disrepair of the premises during such period as the current tenancy is being continued may affect the amount of interim rent payable by the tenant to the landlord[9];

(7) the physical condition of the premises, both actual and assumed, and the future obligations of parties as to repair, may affect the amount of rent payable during any new tenancy granted by the court.[10]

## Enforcement of the repairing covenants as the business tenancy nears its end

35–03 In most cases, it will be as a business tenancy approaches the end of its contractual term that the question of enforcement of the tenant's repairing obligations will become most relevant. The effect of the Act is that a business tenancy to which the Act applies cannot come to an end unless terminated in accordance with the provisions of the Act.[11] The result is that a business tenancy will be continued under the Act following the original contractual term date unless and until terminated in one of the ways provided for by the Act. However, this does not of itself deprive the landlord of his normal remedies for disrepair, including forfeiture, which is a method of termination expressly preserved by the Act[12]. Nor, it is thought, will the landlord's right of forfeiture or damages be restricted by the provisions of the Leasehold Property (Repairs) Act 1938 if less than three years of the original contractual term remain unexpired, even if the tenancy is one which potentially may be continued by the operation of the 1954 Act.[13] However, the procedural restrictions imposed by s.146 of the Law of Property Act 1925 will continue to apply,[14] and the tenant will still have the right to apply for relief from forfeiture.[15]

---

[6] See para.35–05, below.
[7] See para.35–06, below.
[8] See para.35–06, below.
[9] Under ss.24A–24D of the 1954 Act as amended by the Regulatory Reform (Business Tenancies) (England and Wales) Order 2003.
[10] See para.35–07, below.
[11] Landlord and Tenant Act 1954 s.24(1).
[12] Landlord and Tenant Act 1954 s.24(2).
[13] The 1938 Act is considered in para.27–31 et seq., above. See para.27–32 fn.144, above.
[14] s.146 is considered in para.27–12 et seq., above.
[15] This is considered in para.27–77 et seq., above.

## Forfeiture

A number of tactical considerations apply in relation to forfeiting a tenancy which is being continued, or is shortly to be continued, under the Act. The effect of forfeiture is to determine the lease.[16] Since an application for a new tenancy may only be made in respect of a subsisting tenancy to which the Act applies,[17] the effect of forfeiture is to put an end to the right of either party to make or continue such an application. However, if the tenant obtains relief an application may thereafter be made or pursued. Once the tenant has applied for relief, his application will not be struck out by reason of the forfeiture, at least where there is a possibility of his obtaining relief.[18] One obvious effect, therefore, of the landlord seeking to forfeit the tenancy will be to delay the progress of the application, since further steps in the application are likely to be halted pending disposal of the forfeiture proceedings. It will often not be in the landlord's best interests to do this. Moreover, as a general principle, relief from forfeiture for disrepair will generally be granted on terms that the tenant remedies such of the breaches as the court thinks ought to be remedied,[19] whereas the court may still refuse a new tenancy under ground (a) even where the tenant agrees to carry out the whole of the remedial work.[20] Even where the court is prepared to exercise its discretion under ground (a) in favour of the tenant on terms that he agrees to the inclusion in the new tenancy of a schedule of works, it is very difficult to see that any such schedule would be any less onerous than the works which would be made a condition of relief: indeed, the converse is likely to be the case, given that the forfeiture relates to a relatively short and transient continuing interest, whereas the new tenancy will be for a longer term. In the rare case where the breaches are so severe that the landlord would be justified in asking the court to refuse relief altogether, the facts of the case would make it almost inevitable that the court would, in any event, refuse the tenant a new tenancy, assuming that the landlord had specified the appropriate ground of opposition.[21] But if relief were to be granted on condition that the tenant carries out the remedial works and the tenant were to comply with that condition, it would be considerably harder for the landlord then to persuade the court that a new tenancy should nonetheless be refused under ground (a).[22]

It follows that once a business tenancy is approaching its end, it will generally only be advisable for the landlord to seek to enforce his repairing obligations by forfeiture where (a) he has good reasons for wishing to delay the hearing of the application for a new tenancy, or (b) there is a real likelihood that the terms which the court would impose would prevent the tenant obtaining relief, or (c) the

**35–04**

---

[16] See para.27–01, above.
[17] Landlord and Tenant Act 1954 s.24(1).
[18] See *Meadows v Clerical Medical & General Life Assurance Society Ltd* [1981] Ch. 70.
[19] See para.27–81 et seq., above.
[20] See para.35–05, below.
[21] See para.35–05, below.
[22] See *Betty's Cafes v Phillips Furnishing Stores (No.1)* [1959] A.C. 20, in which Lord Keith suggested (at 46) that the court when exercising its discretion under grounds (a) to (c) might take account of the fact that the tenant had purged past breaches by the time the matter came before the court.

landlord wishes to regain possession but has failed to specify a ground of opposition such as to enable him successfully to oppose the application for a new tenancy, or (d) the landlord has specified one of the grounds of opposition[23] which would entitle the tenant to claim compensation under s.37 of the 1954 Act.[24]

## Opposing the grant of a new tenancy on the ground of disrepair

**35–05**    The grounds on which the landlord may oppose an application for a new tenancy under section 30(1) of the 1954 Act include the following (commonly known as ground (a)):

> "(a) Where under the current tenancy the tenant has any obligations as respects the repair and maintenance of the holding, that the tenant ought not to be granted a new tenancy in view of the state of repair of the holding, being a state resulting from the tenant's failure to comply with the said obligations."[25]

The reference to obligations "under the current tenancy" is thought to be wide enough to include implied as well as express obligations. It is to be noted that what is relevant is the state of repair of "the holding". The holding is not necessarily the entirety of the premises comprised in the current tenancy, but only such part as is occupied by the tenant as at the date of the hearing.[26] It follows that there may be breaches of the repairing obligations of the current tenancy which cannot be relied upon under ground (a). For example, the tenancy might be of a ground-floor shop with a residential upper part which is no longer occupied by the end of the tenancy, so that it no longer forms part of the "holding" for the purposes of the Act. The landlord would not then be able to rely on disrepair in relation to that part to oppose the tenant's application under ground (a). This point is of real importance in practice, given that the most serious disrepair will generally be likely to exist in relation to those parts of the premises which are not occupied. A landlord who wishes to oppose in such circumstances should specify in addition to ground (a), ground (c) which allows him to oppose on the grounds of "other substantial breaches by [the tenant] of his obligations under the current tenancy …". This would seem to apply to breaches of the repairing obligations under the current tenancy relating to parts of the premises other than "the holding".

The words "ought not", which appear in both grounds (a) and (c), confer on the court a discretion whether or not to grant a new tenancy once the grounds have been made out. In exercising this discretion the court can look at all the circumstances in connection with the breach relied upon and at the conduct of the tenant as a whole in regard to his obligations under the tenancy.[27] In *Lyons v*

---

[23] i.e. under Landlord and Tenant Act 1954 s.30(1)(e), (f) or (g).

[24] In order to succeed in his claim for compensation the tenant probably has to keep his tenancy subsisting (i.e. unforfeited), at least up to its contractual expiry date—consider in particular s.37(1) of the 1954 Act.

[25] Landlord and Tenant Act 1954 s.30(1)(a).

[26] Landlord and Tenant Act 1954 s.23(3).

[27] *Eichner v Midland Bank Executory and Trustee Company Ltd* [1970] 1 W.L.R. 1120.

*Central Commercial Properties London Ltd*[28] serious breaches had accrued without any attempt by the tenant to remedy them, because he was hoping to assign his interest once he had obtained a new tenancy under the Act to a company which would undertake a substantial reconstruction of the premises. The Court of Appeal dismissed an appeal from the judge's refusal to grant a new tenancy, the arrangement with the third party being held to be extraneous and irrelevant. However, in exercising its discretion the court will take into account the tenant's willingness to accept an obligation in the new tenancy to carry out an agreed schedule of repairs forthwith upon the grant of the new tenancy.[29] It has not been expressly decided whether such a covenant would take effect subject to the provisions of the Leasehold Property (Repairs) Act 1938,[30] but it is thought that the Act would not apply because the covenant imposes on the tenant "an obligation to put premises in repair that is to be performed upon the lessee taking possession of the premises or within a reasonable time thereafter" within the meaning of s.3 of the 1938 Act.[31] However, a contrary argument might be based upon the fact that a tenant being granted a new tenancy under the 1954 Act is already in possession.

The relevant date for the purposes of deciding whether ground (a) applies is the date of the hearing.[32] However, in exercising its discretion the court may look at the position both at the date of the landlord's s.25 notice and the date of the hearing.[33]

## The terms of the new tenancy as to repair

The terms of the new tenancy are such as may be agreed between landlord and tenant or, in default of agreement, determined by the court; and in determining the terms, the court must have regard to the terms of the new tenancy and to all relevant circumstances.[34] In *O'May v City of London Real Property Co Ltd*[35] the House of Lords laid down guidelines as to the way in which that discretion is to be exercised. In that case, the current tenancy was a lease of part of a modern office building under which the landlord covenanted to repair the exterior, plant and common parts of the building and the tenants covenanted to keep in repair the part demised to them. There was no obligation on the tenants to contribute by way of service charge to the cost of the landlords performing their obligations. When the tenants applied for a new tenancy under the 1954 Act the landlord sought to introduce new comprehensive service charge provisions; it was argued that the tenants would be adequately compensated by a suitable reduction in the amount of rent. Rejecting the landlords' proposal, the House of Lords emphasised that the court must begin by considering the terms of the current tenancy, which

35–06

---

[28] [1958] 1 W.L.R. 869.
[29] Cf. *Nihad v Chain* [1956] 167 E.G. 139 (a county court decision).
[30] The Act is considered in para.27–31 et seq., above.
[31] See para.27–33, above.
[32] See *Betty's Cafes v Phillips Furnishing Stores (No.1)* [1959] A.C. 20.
[33] *Betty's Cafes v Phillips Furnishing Stores (No.1)*, above per Viscount Simonds at 36, Lord Morton at 42 and Lord Keith at 46–47.
[34] Landlord and Tenant Act 1954 s.35.
[35] [1983] 2 A.C. 726.

had been freely agreed between the landlords and the tenants, the onus being on the party seeking to alter those terms to show that this was justified in terms of essential justice and fairness. The landlords had failed to show that it was fair to the tenants that they should be asked to accept a transfer of responsibility for what might be major repairs in return for a relatively small reduction in their rent. It was emphasised that, subject to this, the discretion of the Court was of the widest possible kind, having regard to the almost infinitely varying circumstances of individual leases, properties, businesses and parties involved in business tenancies all over the country.

In many cases, the approach laid down in *O'May* will prevent landlords from shifting major repairing burdens from themselves to their tenants. However, it is not to be supposed that the terms of the current tenancy relating to repairs will be duplicated in the new tenancy in every case. In an appropriate case, the court will order a new tenancy at an exclusive rent, with the tenant's contribution to repairs covered by a separate service charge, even where that is not the case under the current tenancy.[36]

Difficulties may sometimes occur where the parties to the renewal of a sub-lease are the freeholder and the sub-tenant (the intermediate tenant having dropped out of the picture), and the terms of the expired head lease contained an obligation on the part of the lessee to keep the premises in full repair, while the terms of the sub-lease imposed no repairing obligations on the sub-tenant or only limited obligations, such as an obligation to repair the interior. The landlord can argue that it should not be disadvantaged by losing the tenant's full repairing covenant which had been the basis of the bargain between it and its tenant. The sub-tenant can say in reply that the terms of "the current tenancy", that is to say the sub-tenancy being renewed, placed the repairing obligations upon the landlord, not the tenant. Quite how the court would resolve this argument would depend on the detailed facts, although the *O'May* principle would appear to favour the sub-tenant, who might also be able to argue in an appropriate case that the freeholder had forfeited his right to object by having failed to control the terms upon which the sub-lease had been granted.

## The rent payable under the new tenancy

**35–07**    The rent payable under the new tenancy is that at which, having regard to the terms of the tenancy (other than those relating to rent), the holding might reasonably be expected to be let in the open market by a willing lessor, subject to certain disregards.[37]

---

[36] Examples are *Hyams v Titan Properties Ltd* [1972] 24 P. & C.R. 359 and *Edwards & Walkden (Norfolk) Ltd v The Mayor and Commonalty and Citizens of the City of London* [2012] EWHC 2527 (Ch). See further on terms as to repairs and service charges *Bullen v Goodland* 105 S.J. 231; *Leslie & Goodwin Investments Ltd v Prudential Assurance Co Ltd* [1987] 2 E.G.L.R. 395; *Boots the Chemist Ltd v Pinkland Ltd* [1992] 2 E.G.L.R. 98; *Amarjee v Barrowfen Properties Ltd* [1993] 2 E.G.L.R. 133; and *Davy's of London (Wine Merchants) v The Mayor Commonalty and Citizens of the City of London* (unreported decision noted in Reynolds and Clark, *Renewal of Business Tenancies*, 4th edn, at para.8–52).
[37] Landlord and Tenant Act 1954 s.34(1).

There are two principal ways in which the repairing obligations as between landlord and tenant may affect the amount of the new rent. First, the new rent must be assessed on the assumption that the tenant's repairing obligations under the current tenancy have been complied with as at the date of grant of the new tenancy.[38] The reason is that if the premises are in a state of substantial disrepair due to the tenant's own default, it would be allowing him to benefit from his own wrong if the rent were to be depressed on that account. The same reasoning does not apply to the landlord's obligations to repair. If those obligations have not been performed, then that is something which can be taken into account as a potentially depressing effect on the rent.[39] The second effect arises from the terms of the new tenancy (which may or may not be the same as those of the current tenancy), because the rent is to be fixed "having regard to the terms of the tenancy". The terms of the repairing obligations may affect the rent at which the premises might reasonably be expected to be let in the market.[40] For example, in *Norwich Union Life Assurance Society Ltd v British Railways Board*[41] (a rent review case) the presence in the lease of an exceptionally onerous repairing covenant was held by an arbitrator to justify a discount of 27.5 per cent from the open-market rent derived from comparable transactions upon less onerous terms. Likewise in *O'May v City of London Real Property Co Ltd*[42] it was agreed between the valuers that if the tenant were to assume responsibility by way of service charge for a proportion of the cost of structural repairs, then a (comparatively modest) deduction from the rent otherwise payable would be appropriate.

## RENT REVIEWS

### Introductory

Commercial leases granted for terms of over five years invariably contain provision for rent review at periodic intervals (usually, but not always, every five years). The review clause will generally provide for the reviewed rent to be assessed by reference to a notional letting of the premises on the review date between a hypothetical willing landlord and willing tenant for a specified notional term (usually, but not always, the unexpired residue of the actual term as at the review date) on the same terms as the actual lease. Prima facie, the reviewed rent will be affected both by the state of repair of the premises on the review date and by the terms of the lease as regards repair. These are considered below.

**35–08**

---

[38] *Family Management Ltd v Gray* [1980] 1 E.G.L.R. 46.
[39] *Fawke v Viscount Chelsea* [1980] Q.B. 441.
[40] See further para.35–12, below.
[41] [1987] 2 E.G.L.R. 137. See further on this case para.35–12, below.
[42] [1983] 2 A.C. 726. See further on this case para.35–06, above.

## Effect of the state of repair

**35–09**  The state of repair of the premises being notionally let may have a substantial effect on the amount of rent which the hypothetical willing parties would agree. Prima facie, the premises must be valued in the condition in which they exist at the review date.[43] If they then suffer from some physical defect, the valuer will have to consider whether, and by what amount, that defect would reduce their market value. For example, in *Civil Aviation Authority v Langford*[44] the structural condition of a newly erected office building was such that it was held to have only a nominal value for rating purposes.

However, the prima facie task of the valuer to value the premises as they stand may be varied by express or implied assumptions to the contrary. Two of the most common are (i) an assumption as to compliance with repairing covenants, and (ii) a disregard of tenant's improvements. These are considered below.

## Assumption as to compliance with covenants

**35–10**  Rent review clauses often contain an express assumption the effect of which is that the valuer must assume that the tenant's repairing and decorating covenants have been complied with as at the review date. Even where there is no such provision, one will be implied, since otherwise the tenant would be benefiting from his own wrong by paying a rent which was lower than it would have been if he had complied with his covenants.[45] There is no reported case dealing expressly with whether the converse assumption (that the landlord has complied with his repairing covenants) is to be implied, but it is thought that there will generally be no justification for doing so.[46] The likely effect of such an assumption would be to increase the rent payable by the tenant, so that an implication along these lines would result in the landlord benefiting from his own wrong. The presence in the lease of an express assumption that the tenant has complied with his covenants would make it even more difficult for the landlord to argue that an assumption ought to be implied that he has complied with his obligations.[47] Nonetheless, rent review clauses sometimes (though not often) include an express assumption that the landlord has complied with his repairing obligations, in which case the valuer must value on the assumption that the premises are in the state they would have been in if the landlord had complied with his repairing covenants even if that is not in fact the case. The tenant's redress will lie in the other remedies which he will have under the lease in respect of the landlord's breaches.[48] For example, the presence of such an assumption in the rent-review clause may be a cogent reason in favour of granting to the tenant the discretionary remedy of specific performance of the landlord's obligation with a view to ensuring that the

---

[43]  See *Ponsford v H.M.S. Aerosols Ltd* [1979] A.C. 63.

[44]  (1978) 248 E.G. 947

[45]  *Harmsworth Pension Funds Trustees Ltd v Charringtons Industrial Holdings Ltd* (1985) 49 P. & C.R. 297; *Secretary of State for the Environment v Euston Centre Investments Ltd* [1994] N.P.C. 130.

[46]  Cf. *Fawke v Viscount Chelsea* [1980] Q.B. 441.

[47]  See para.1–06 et seq., above.

[48]  These are considered in Ch.33, above.

premises are in fact fully repaired as at the relevant rent-review date.[49] If the tenant decides to claim damages he will be able to point to the fact that the rent which he is in fact paying is calculated on the basis of full repair, whereas the premises as he enjoys them are in disrepair. In an appropriate case general damages for loss of use, inconvenience and discomfort may be calculated by reference to the difference.[50]

Where the review clause contains an express or implied assumption as to compliance with covenants, and there is an admitted defect requiring repair, questions sometimes arise as to how that defect must be assumed to have been repaired as at the review date. Where only one method will satisfy the covenant,[51] that method must be assumed. However, where the defect can reasonably be repaired in more than one way, it appears that the method which is most favourable to the tenant must be assumed.[52]

## Disregard of improvements

Most rent review clauses contain, in one form or another, a provision requiring the valuer to disregard (or disregard the effect on rent of) improvements carried out by the tenant other than pursuant to an obligation to the landlord. Questions frequently arise in practice as to the inter-relationship between this and the assumption of compliance with covenants considered in para.35–10, above. There is no difficulty where the work carried out is obviously an improvement and not a repair (for example, the installation of a mezzanine floor in a warehouse). Nor is there any difficulty where the relevant disrepair can only reasonably and sensibly be remedied by introducing some element of betterment. For example, a roof may have got to the point where it is so defective that nothing short of complete replacement will suffice. In that event, the tenant will ordinarily be obliged to replace the roof under his repairing obligation.[53] The result may be to "improve" the premises but the disregard will not be engaged because the work will have been carried out under an obligation. The new roof must be rentalised. But the facts may be such that the defective state of the roof could reasonably and properly be dealt with in one of several different ways, for example, by patch repairs, over-sheeting or complete replacement. The tenant may decide, for commercial reasons connected with his future occupation, to take the third option. He will then argue that the work was an improvement because it went further than was necessary. The landlord will say that it was a repair because its effect was to eliminate the defect.

In principle, two views are possible in such cases. The first is that the work actually carried out must be disregarded as an improvement, and the rent must

35–11

---

[49] See para.33–07 et seq., above.
[50] See para.33–15 et seq., above.
[51] See Ch.9, above.
[52] See *Land Securities Plc v Westminster City Council (No.2)* [1995] 1 E.G.L.R. 245, in which the rent was fixed on the assumption that running repairs as opposed to complete replacement had been carried out to certain air conditioning plant. See also *Ladbroke Hotels Ltd v Sandhu* [1995] 2 E.G.L.R. 92 and *Secretary of State for the Environment v Euston Centre Investments Ltd* [1994] N.P.C. 130, both of which concerned dilapidations questions arising in a rent-review context.
[53] See para.12–06 et seq., above.

then be fixed on the assumption that the premises are in the condition they would have been in if the minimum work reasonably necessary to perform the covenant had been carried out. This can be justified on the following grounds: (i) the rent would have been fixed on this basis if the tenant had done nothing,[54] and he ought not to be in any worse position because he has chosen to go further than he need to; (ii) it results in the rent being fixed by reference to the state of affairs which would have resulted from performance of the bargain and not something more; and (iii) since the work was not carried out pursuant to an obligation, it is not excluded from the disregard on that account.

The alternative view is that the work must be rentalised provided that it can still properly be described as repair within the covenant (i.e. it does not go beyond repair as a matter of fact and degree[55]). This can be justified on the basis that (i) since the work was a repair it cannot at one and the same time have been an improvement, and (ii) since this was the way in which the tenant chose to perform his repairing obligation, it must be taken to have been carried out pursuant to an obligation to the landlord and thus excluded from the disregard for that additional reason. This view can be said to accord with the decision of H.H. Judge Rich, QC in *Gibson v Chesterton (No.2)*,[56] in which the judge held that work which remedies an existing state of disrepair but which exceeds what the tenant was obliged to do is nonetheless not an improvement for the purposes of the disregard unless it creates something which is "recognisably different from what would result from merely remedying such state, and the difference has a significant effect upon letting value". There is much to be said for this view, but it can be criticised on the ground that it gives rise to the anomaly that a tenant who has failed to comply with his obligations at all is in a better position on review than a conscientious tenant who has done more than was strictly necessary. That can be said to be wrong in principle.

## Valuation effect of repairing covenants imported into the notional lease

35–12    Rent-review clauses are commonly (though not invariably) drafted in terms which require the valuer to assume that the new lease which is being granted contains the same covenants as are contained in the actual lease. The terms of those covenants may affect the amount of rent which the notional willing parties would agree. For example, in most cases, a tenant would be willing to pay more rent for a lease which imposed upon him only an interior repairing obligation without a service charge provision, than he would be for a lease on full repairing terms, or a lease under which he was required to pay for the cost of the performance by the landlord of his obligations by way of service charge. Whether this is in fact so in any particular case, and if so, what is the amount of the differential, will be a matter of valuation. Where there are plenty of comparable transactions upon the same basis as that required by the rent-review clause, the

---

[54] See para.35–10, above.
[55] See Ch.11, above.
[56] [2003] EWHC 1255. The facts and the relevant part of the judge's judgment are set out in para.10–13, above.

valuer will no doubt be able to value directly. Where all or most of the comparables are upon a different basis as to repair the valuer may feel it necessary to make an upwards or downwards adjustment as the case may be.

A striking example of a downward adjustment is to be found in the case of *Norwich Union Life Assurance Society Ltd v British Railways Board*.[57] In that case, a lease granted in 1968 demised an office building for a term of 150 years, with rent reviews every 21 years. The tenant covenanted "to keep the demised premises in good and substantial repair and condition and when necessary to rebuild, reconstruct or replace the same and in such repair and condition to yield up the same at the expiration or sooner determination of the term." On the first review, the question of the amount of rent went to arbitration. The arbitrator found as a fact that the building suffered from defects, and held that the lease imposed a liability far beyond that contemplated in an ordinary full repairing covenant. Basing himself on comparable transactions relating to properties let on ordinary full repairing terms, he made a downward adjustment of 27.5 per cent. Whilst this does not, of course, amount to anything more than an example of the effect of an onerous covenant on particular facts, it illustrates the degree to which repairing obligations may influence the value of the lease in an appropriate case.

## OPTIONS TO RENEW AND TO DETERMINE LEASES

### Introductory

A tenant's option to determine or renew a lease is often made conditional on the covenants of the lease having been performed at the material time. In such cases, compliance is a condition precedent to the valid exercise of the option.[58] The law of dilapidations becomes relevant in connection with the exercise of such options because, as the decided cases show, it is the covenant to repair which most often gives rise to difficulties in fulfilment of the condition precedent.

**35–13**

### The operative date

The date or dates on which the condition must be satisfied is a question of construction of the lease. In some cases the relevant date will be the date of service of the notice exercising the option[59]; in others, it is sufficient if the condition is satisfied when the notice expires.[60] A formulation commonly found is a requirement that the tenant shall have performed the covenants "up to" the relevant date. This will generally be construed as meaning not that the tenant must never have committed any breaches throughout the term, but only that there

**35–14**

---

[57] [1987] 2 E.G.L.R. 137.
[58] *Porter v Shephard* 6 T.R. 665; *Greville v Parker* [1910] A.C. 335; *Finch v Underwood* (1876) 2 Ch.D. 310; *Bastin v Bidwell* (1881) 18 Ch. D. 238; *Simons v Associated Furnishers*, above; *West Country Cleaners Ltd v Saly* [1966] 1 W.L.R. 1485; *Bass Holdings Ltd v Morton Music Ltd* [1988] Ch. 493; *Bairstow Eves (Securities) Ltd v Ripley* (1993) 65 P. & C.R 220; *Trane (United Kingdom) Ltd v Provident Mutual Life Assurance Co Ltd* [1995] 1 E.G.L.R. 33.
[59] *Finch v Underwood*, above; *Robinson v Thames Mead Park Estates Ltd* [1947] Ch. 334.
[60] *Simons v Associated Furnishers Ltd* above; *West Country Cleaners Ltd v Saly*, above.

be no subsisting breaches (as opposed to spent breaches) at the relevant date.[61] The reasons were explained by Kerr L.J. in *Bass Holdings Ltd v Morton Music Ltd*[62] as follows:

> "First, it must be accepted that absolute and precise compliance by the tenant with every single covenant throughout the period of the lease prior to the operative date is virtually impossible of attainment. If this were required as a condition precedent, then the option would in practice be worthless or merely at the mercy of the landlord. Therefore the parties cannot have intended that the absence of spent breaches should be a condition precedent. Secondly, however, it is natural and sensible that the landlord should require the tenant not to be in breach of any covenant on the operative date and that all outstanding claims for breach of covenant should have been previously satisfied, so that the lease is then effectively clear. The proviso is therefore to be construed as intended to apply to subsisting breaches, with the result that the relevant condition precedent is the absence of any subsisting breach."

A subsisting breach is a breach in respect of which the landlord has a subsisting cause of action.[63] A breach which is otherwise spent will not be treated as subsisting merely because the landlord still has a cause of action for nominal damages.[64] However, a subsisting breach (such as a failure to paint in the last year of the term) cannot be excluded on the ground that only nominal damages are recoverable.[65] The application of these principles to breaches of the covenant to repair during the term will generally be straightforward. Such breaches will be regarded as spent if the repairs have been done by the operative date. However, if the breaches have caused the landlord loss and damage which survives the carrying out of the work (such as liability to third parties under the Defective Premises Act 1972[66]), it may be that the breaches will remain subsisting for these purposes until the tenant has paid any damages to which the landlord is entitled.

In *West Middlesex Golf Club Ltd v Ealing LBC*[67] various representatives of the tenants carried out a tour of inspection of the relevant parts of the premises immediately prior to service of the relevant notice, and satisfied themselves that there were no subsisting breaches. The judge accepted this evidence and held that the condition precedent had been fulfilled at the material date, notwithstanding evidence that an inspection on behalf of the landlords some days later had revealed various disrepairs. The correctness of this approach (which is similar to that adopted in *Trane (UK) Ltd v Provident Mutual Life Assurance Co Ltd*[68]) must be reconsidered in the light of the decision of the Court of Appeal in *British Telecommunications Plc v Sun Life Assurance Society Ltd*,[69] from which it appears that in most cases where a tenant has covenanted to keep premises in repair he will be in breach as soon as the breach manifests itself (not on the expiry of a reasonable time thereafter). It may be, however that the same result could be reached in an appropriate case by way of construction of the option

---

[61] *Bass Holdings Ltd v Morton Music Ltd*, above.
[62] Above.
[63] *Bass Holdings Ltd v Morton Music Ltd*, above; *Bairstow Eves (Securities) Ltd v Ripley*, above.
[64] *Bairstow Eves (Securities) Ltd v Ripley*, above.
[65] Ibid.
[66] This is considered in para.20–49 et seq., above.
[67] [1993] 68 P. & C.R. 461.
[68] [1995] 1 E.G.L.R. 33.
[69] [1996] Ch. 69. See para.22–18 et seq., above.

clause. It may also be that the position would be different where the relevant obligation is to repair (as opposed to keep in repair).[70]

It has been suggested that an option to renew which is conditional on the tenant having "reasonably performed and observed [the tenant's covenants] … up to the termination of the tenancy hereby created" would entitle the court to look at the conduct of the tenants throughout the term and not just the position on the break date.[71]

## Strict compliance required

Unless the relevant condition is qualified in some way,[72] it must be strictly complied with. There is no doctrine to the effect that trivial or minor breaches do not defeat the option.[73] Thus, the option has been defeated by the existence on the operative date of trifling repairs[74]; and by a failure to paint in the last year of the term.[75] However, the covenant to repair will not ordinarily be construed as requiring the tenant to keep the premises in perfect physical order as opposed to substantial repair.[76] It follows that the existence of physical defects on the operative date will not necessarily amount to breaches of covenant. It should also be noted that, insofar as the tenant has a reasonable time from the occurrence of disrepair in which to remedy it before he is in breach,[77] the existence on the operative date of a defect will not amount to a breach if it occurred very recently and the tenant has not yet had a reasonable time in which to repair it.[78] However, once a breach of covenant is found to exist on the material date, the option will have been defeated, notwithstanding the fact that the breach is minor, or that the landlord has suffered no damage.

**35–15**

## Condition requiring material compliance

In *Commercial Union Life Assurance Co Ltd v Label Ink Ltd*[79] a tenant's option to determine was made conditional on there not being any "material" breach of covenant. H.H. Judge Rich QC (sitting as a deputy High, Court judge) held that a breach was material if, but only if, having regard to all the circumstances, and to the proper efforts of the tenant to comply with his covenants, as well as the

**35–16**

---

[70] *British Telecommunications Plc v Sun Life Assurance Society Ltd*, above.
[71] *Bassett v Whitely* (1982) 45 P. & C.R. 87 per Griffiths L.J. at 92.
[72] See below.
[73] *Finch v Underwood* (1876) 2 Ch. D. 310; *West Country Cleaners (Falmouth) Ltd v Saly* [1966] 1 W.L.R. 1485; *Quirkco Investments Ltd v Aspray Transport Ltd* [2012] L.& T.R. 12.
[74] *Finch v Underwood*, above; *Kitney v Greater London Properties Ltd* (1984) 272 E.G. 786.
[75] *West Country Cleaners (Falmouth) Ltd v Saly*, above; *Bairstow Eves (Securities) Ltd v Ripley* (1993) 65 P. & C.R. 220.
[76] See Ch.9, above, in which the standard of repair is considered.
[77] See para.23–03 above.
[78] *West Middlesex Golf Club v Ealing LBC* [1993] 68 P. & C.R. 461. Sed quaere: see para.23–03, above.
[79] [2001] L. & T.R. 29.

adverse effect on the landlord of any failure to do so, it will be fair and reasonable to refuse the tenant the privilege which the lease grants (in that case, an option to determine).

However, that test was disapproved by the Court of Appeal in *Fitzroy House Epworth Street (No.1) v Financial Times*,[80] in which a tenant's right to break was only exercisable if the tenant had "materially" complied with its obligations. The Court of Appeal further rejected the landlord's argument that the insertion of "material" was intended to exclude only those beaches which were trivial or trifling. The correct test was held to be that materiality is to be assessed by reference to the ability of the landlord to relet or sell the property without delay or additional expenditure. The Court of Appeal further held that the test is an objective one, with the result that the following facts found by the judge at first instance (and relied on by him) were not relevant: (i) that the tenant had taken all reasonable steps to put and keep the premises in repair, had spent nearly £1 million for that purpose and had followed professional advice as to what was required; (ii) that the tenant made all reasonable efforts to secure the landlord's agreement as to what was needed to ensure compliance and would have incorporated any reasonable requirement of the landlord into its remedial programme if asked; (iii) that the landlord unreasonably declined to involve itself in the tenant's attempts to agree a remedial programme and adopted an attitude of waiting and seeing whether it could catch the tenant out on a technicality so as to prevent it from determining the lease because the market was soft; and (iv) that it would be most unreasonable to the tenant if it was unable to determine the lease and it would also be most unreasonable if the landlord, given its behaviour, was unable to prevent such determination from occurring. However, the judge below had also found that (a) the number, nature and value of the outstanding defects was insubstantial; (b) the outstanding defects had no effect on the landlord's ability to obtain a further tenant nor on any terms that it could reasonably expect to negotiate, and in particular, the defects would not have deterred prospective tenants nor have led to a longer rent-free period or to a lower rent being agreed; (c) each breach was, in itself, either minor or trivial, and when taken together the breaches still amounted to minor or trivial breaches; (d) what was left was a residual but limited number of limited breaches at the conclusion of the tenant's repair programme; and (e) the limited nature of the remaining breaches was such that the overall damage to the reversion was negligible or nil and there were no recoverable damages, or only trivial damages. The Court of Appeal held that in the light of those findings, the tenant had materially complied with its obligations.

*Fitzroy House Epworth Street (No.1) v Financial Times*[81] was applied by Mr B Livesey QC, sitting as a deputy judge of the High Court, in *Mourant Property Trust v Fusion Electronic (UK)*.[82] In that case it was common ground between the experts that an incoming tenant would require compensation for the outstanding disrepair in the form of a rent-free period. The judge preferred the evidence of the landlord's expert to the effect that a rent-free period of three and a half months

---

[80] [2006] 2 E.G.L.R. 13.
[81] Above.
[82] [2009] EWHC 3659 (Ch)

would have to be given in respect of one of the units and a period of four months in respect of the other. On that basis he held that the breaches were material. He further rejected an argument advanced on behalf of the tenant that, in determining whether there had been material compliance, the court was entitled to take into account the fact that the landlord held a security deposit in the form of a bond worth some £29,000 at the date of the breach. Whether there was a material breach or not could only be determined by the nature and extent of the disrepair and the effect it would have on the lettability of the premises, in accordance with the test in *Fitzroy House*.

## Condition requiring substantial compliance

It was said in *Fitzroy House Epworth Street (No.1) v Financial Times*[83] that the words "substantial" and "material", depending on the context, are interchangeable.[84] On that basis, the test set out in the preceding paragraph is equally applicable to conditions requiring substantial as opposed to material compliance with covenants.

**35–17**

## Condition requiring reasonable compliance

As with conditions requiring material or substantial performance, the general rule that the covenants must be performed to the letter does not apply to a condition which requires "reasonable" performance of the covenants.[85] However, there is no authoritative judicial exposition of what is meant by "reasonable". In *Fitzroy House Epworth Street (No.1) v Financial Times*[86] it was said in the Court of Appeal that the word "reasonable" connotes a different test from "material" or "substantial",[87] but the test was not further explained. It is thought that such a condition requires the tenant to show that he has done what a reasonable tenant would have done in the circumstances, reasonableness being a question of fact in each case.[88] In carrying out that exercise, it may be that the court could have regard to at least some of the considerations held in *Fitzroy House Epworth Street (No.1) v Financial Times*[89] to be irrelevant in the context of a condition requiring "material" performance.[90]

Two cases may be contrasted. In *Gardner v Blaxill*[91] it was held that outstanding breaches of the repairing covenants did not defeat an option the exercise of which was conditional on the tenant having "reasonably" fulfilled his

**35–18**

---

[83] Above.
[84] Above, at [36].
[85] *Gardner v Blaxill* [1960] 1 W.L.R. 752; *Bassett v Whitely* (1982) 45 P. & C.R. 87; *Stretch v West Dorset D.C.* [1996] E.G.C.S. 76; *Reed Personnel Services Plc v American Express Ltd* [1997] 1 E.G.L.R. 229.
[86] Above.
[87] Above, at [36].
[88] See *Gardner v Blaxill*, above.
[89] Above.
[90] See para.35–16, above.
[91] Above.

covenants. By contrast, in *Reed Personnel Services Plc v American Express Ltd*[92] it was held that the covenants to repair and decorate had not been reasonably performed. Jacob J. gave various examples of what reasonable performance might consist of. One was that where the covenant requires two coats of paint, one might be enough; another was that where the covenant obliges the tenant to re-carpet at the end of the lease, it might not be necessary to do so where the carpet is in perfectly good condition.

## Options to break and options to renew

35–19    Where the pre-condition requires that the tenant's covenants should have been strictly complied with, there is no difference for the purposes of the above between an option to break and an option to renew.[93] However, where the pre-condition requires only that the tenant's covenants should have been reasonably complied with, it appears that there may be a difference, and that some breaches may be regarded as more serious where the tenant is leaving than when he is renewing.[94]

## Practical considerations for tenants

35–20    A tenant who has undertaken full or substantial repairing obligations under the lease will have particular difficulties in fulfilling a strict and unqualified condition precedent, because, as Nicholls L.J. put it in *Bass Holdings Ltd v Morton Music Ltd:*[95]

> "However diligent or even punctilious a tenant may be in carrying out his obligations under his lease, in [leases of buildings containing a full range of repairing and other covenants by a tenant] there will in practice inevitably be occasions when there will be outstanding some dilapidations which would, strictly, constitute breaches of the repairing or decorating covenants."

In practice, there will in most cases be at least some subsisting breaches of the repairing and decorating covenants of a lease at any one time. The difficulty in complying with the condition precedent will be compounded by the practical consideration that it is often more expensive and troublesome for the tenant fully to perform his repairing and decorating covenants than it is to reach a mutually acceptable financial settlement with the landlord (although negotiating this is often left until after the operative date has passed, by which time the tenant has lost much of his bargaining power). A tenant will be particularly inclined to take this attitude where the effect of the exercise of the option is that he is to be granted a lengthy new term (thus postponing the immediate importance to the landlord in practical terms of having the premises repaired), or even to acquire the freehold (where the landlord would have no continuing interest in the state of

---

[92] [1997] 1 E.G.L.R. 229.
[93] *Bass Holdings Ltd v Morton Music Ltd*, above; *Reed Personnel Services Ltd v American Express Ltd*, above, at 230D.
[94] *Reed Personnel Services Ltd v American Express Ltd* above, at 230K–L.
[95] [1988] Ch. 493.

repair of the premises if (as is usual) the formula for assessing the price to be paid assumed full repair). Furthermore, covenants to repair often pose difficulties of interpretation and, even where their meaning is clear, it may be a matter of differing expert opinion as to whether or not they have been fulfilled in particular circumstances.

However, the problem is not intractable. First, the tenant must be aware at an **35–21** early stage of the need to comply with the condition, and seek appropriate advice upon the interpretation of his repairing and other obligations under the lease. In addition to the repairing obligations, consideration must be given to the obligation to decorate in the last year of the term, to the covenant against alterations, and to any reinstatement obligations in a licence. Second, he should seek surveying advice well before the relevant time period as to what works ought to be carried out in order to comply with the covenants. Where the advice is that another surveyor might require a higher standard of repair, then it will be as well to err on the side of caution. Third, an attempt should be made to agree a schedule of works with the landlord, or even to agree that, in return for a cash payment, the repairing obligations will be taken to have been fulfilled for the purposes of exercise of the option.[96] Fourth, the tenant should ensure that the works are carried out in good time by trustworthy contractors and under competent supervision. The landlord's surveyor should be asked to inspect the completed works, and to state whether or not he is satisfied with them. The landlord cannot, of course, be forced to co-operate at any of these stages, but it is suggested that if this procedure has been gone through the court will not be eager to assist the landlord in discovering some breach that has been overlooked so as to defeat the option. Thus, in *Finch v Underwood*[97] Mellish L.J. said:

> "In a case like this, if a tenant wishes to claim the benefit of such a covenant he should send in his surveyor to see what repairs are needed and should effect the repairs which the surveyor certifies to be requisite. The court would be inclined to give credit to a survey thus honestly made, and would lean towards holding the condition precedent to have been complied with."

The above passage was explained by the Court of Appeal in *Fitzroy House Epworth Street (No.1) v Financial Times*[98] as meaning that in the circumstances postulated by Mellish L.J., the court would be likely to accept the evidence of the tenant's surveyor to the effect that the covenant had been duly performed by the material time.

---

[96] Although care should be taken to ensure that any such agreement is binding.
[97] (1876) 2 Ch. D. 310.
[98] [2006] 2 E.G.L.R. 13 at [9].

# CHAPTER 36

## DILAPIDATIONS CLAIMS IN PRACTICE

### INTRODUCTORY

Only a small number of dilapidations cases are tried each year; even fewer **36–01**
feature in the law reports. This is despite the fact that the number of potential
claims must annually be tens of thousands, since almost every lease or tenancy of
any description of property is likely to impose an obligation to repair upon the
tenant or the landlord or both, and in many cases those obligations will not have
been fully complied with. One reason for this is that although landlords and
tenants are normally well aware of the potential for such claims, they generally
recognise that the problems are essentially practical ones which ought ideally to
be settled by negotiation rather than litigation. They will be reinforced in this
attitude by the advice of their surveyors, which will essentially be common-sense
advice concentrated more on the commercial realities than the legal niceties of
the situation.

The Woolf reforms (which introduced the Civil Procedure Rules ("CPR")),
with their emphasis on settling cases out of court whenever possible, together
with the Pre-Action Protocol for Housing Disrepair Cases and the Pre-Action
Protocol for Claims for Damages in Relation to the Physical State of Commercial
Property at Termination of a Tenancy (the Dilapidations Protocol), are likely to
make the number of dilapidations claims which result in court proceedings even
smaller. These two Protocols are considered in Ch.37, below.

### MATTERS TO BE TAKEN INTO ACCOUNT BY THE LANDLORD WHEN CONSIDERING MAKING A CLAIM FOR DILAPIDATIONS

#### Events prompting a claim

A number of occurrences may prompt the landlord into active consideration of **36–02**
the possibility of bringing a claim for dilapidations against his tenant. The
attitude which he will take to the possibility of pursuing a claim will be
influenced by the nature of the event which prompts it. These events include the
following.

#### (a)  Disrepair becoming apparent on inspection

Many landlords, especially those who own large estates or property portfolios, **36–03**
regularly inspect their tenanted properties. In the course of such inspections the

surveyor may do no more than note for record purposes what he has observed, or he may discuss informally with the tenant certain particular items which he would like to be attended to. Where significant items of disrepair are apparent, which are actually or potentially the cause of damage to the reversion, the surveyor may advise the landlord to consider some kind of formal action. This may be appropriate, for example, where the dilapidated condition or shabby appearance of the property is detrimentally affecting the standing of other properties owned by the landlord in the locality. In such a case, the landlord might decide to take formal action even in the case of relatively trivial or cosmetic disrepairs, in the interest of a higher policy of good estate management. Similarly, the inspection might reveal disrepairs which, although comparatively trivial, might lead to much greater problems in the future. Obvious examples include disrepairs to the roof of a building which, if not immediately remedied, might lead to an outbreak of dry rot or to other serious damage to the fabric.

### (b)  Assignment of reversion

36–04    When the lease has a substantial number of years to run, the landlord will ordinarily not be particularly concerned about the theoretical effect on the value of his reversion even of quite significant disrepairs. The reason is that the theoretical diminution in the value of his reversion is only a "paper" loss. On the other hand, if the landlord wishes to sell his reversion or to raise substantial finance on it, the paper loss may become a reality. He may thus wish to take effective action to force the tenant to comply with his covenants.

### (c)  Proposed assignment of term

36–05    Some landlords use the occasion of an application by the tenant for consent to assign the residue of the term as an opportunity to compel compliance with the repairing covenants. Such landlords will seek to make it a condition of their consent that either the assignor or the assignee carries out a specified programme of works. Whether such a requirement is lawful depends upon the terms of the alienation covenant, read in conjunction with s.19 of the Landlord and Tenant Act 1927.[1] The use of this tactic by landlords involves them in a greater element of risk since the passing of the Landlord and Tenant Act 1988 which gives the tenant the right to sue for damages if consent is withheld unreasonably.

### (d)  Emergencies

36–06    Sometimes there will be an unforeseen failure of part of the structure of the building which the landlord, either of his own volition or under compulsion from some statutory authority, wishes to have remedied as a matter of urgency. The landlord's concern in such cases will not be so much to prevent damage to its reversion as to avoid the potential civil liability to third parties injured as a result

---

[1] See Woodfall, *Landlord and Tenant* (London: Sweet & Maxwell), Vol.I, para.11.146, in which the cases dealing with refusal by landlords to consent to assignments where breaches of the repairing covenants of the lease exist are discussed.

of the disrepair, and the criminal sanctions which might follow a failure to remedy it. An example is *SEDAC Investments Ltd v Tanner*,[2] where the ironical result of the landlord's prompt action in himself repairing a dangerous structure for which the tenant was liable was that the tenant was relieved from liability to pay for it.

### (e)   Complaints

Quite apart from the case of emergencies, active consideration of a claim to enforce the repairing covenants may be prompted by complaints, either from statutory authorities, or from adjoining occupiers, or from sub-tenants in the building. The landlord's attitude in such situations will be governed by the extent of his liabilities under statute, his exposure to claims for damages by third parties or even moral considerations, where the tenant is neglecting its responsibilities towards sub-tenants who are in a relatively weak bargaining position.

**36–07**

### (f)   Rent reviews

Although almost all rent reviews are conducted upon the assumption that the tenant's repairing covenants have been complied with,[3] some landlords believe that the full potential of the property will not be apparent to the arbitrator or independent expert if the premises are in poor repair or decorative condition when he makes his inspection. Thus an imminent rent review may be a reason for seeking compliance with the repairing obligations of the lease.

**36–08**

### (g)   Imminent expiry of the term

The most common situation in which the landlord will actively start to consider his remedies against the tenant for breach of the repairing obligation arises as the term comes to its end. The reasons for this are obvious. So long as a substantial term remains unexpired, the actual damage suffered by the landlord to his reversion is likely to be a "paper" loss only, or at least difficult to quantify. Further, most leases will originally have been subject to the procedural restrictions on the enforcement of the repairing covenants imposed by the Leasehold Property (Repairs) Act 1938, which applies up to the point when less than three years of the term remain unexpired.[4] If the premises are yielded up at the end of the term in disrepair, however, the landlord will in many cases suffer a real loss, and that loss can be quantified. The practical result in most cases will be that the landlord has difficulty in reletting or otherwise disposing of the premises, or has himself to finance a programme of works, or has to give an incoming tenant an extended rent free period to reflect the disrepair. This immediate prospect of sustaining financial loss or incurring substantial expenditure or loss naturally concentrates the landlord's attention upon forcing the tenant to make compensation for that loss or to underwrite that expenditure. If the tenant is likely

**36–09**

---

[2] [1982] 1 W.L.R 1342. This case is further considered in paras 27–45 to 27–46, above.
[3] See para.35–10, above.
[4] See para.27–31 et seq., above.

to seek to renew his lease under the Landlord and Tenant Act 1954 Pt II, the landlord may wish to oppose the application on the ground of disrepair, or to ensure that the terms of any new tenancy provide that a suitable programme of works be undertaken by the tenant within a specified period of the commencement of the new term.[5]

## Deciding whether to bring a claim

**36–10**  Whether the landlord decides to take any action depends partly on the event which prompts his consideration of the claim, partly on the nature of the remedies available to him, and partly on his overall assessment of the benefits of making a claim weighed against the costs and risks of doing so.

The procedures introduced by the Civil Procedure Rules[6] reflect the policy that litigation should be seen as a last resort, to be invoked only when all attempts at compromise have failed. To that end, the Dilapidations Protocol requires a number of steps to be taken with a view to formulating, clarifying and settling commercial dilapidation claims by way of Alternative Dispute Resolution or otherwise. Its procedures must be observed as an essential precursor to the start of proceedings, failing which sanctions for non-compliance will apply. The Pre-Action Protocol for Housing Disrepair Cases is framed in terms which reflect the practical reality that such claims are almost inevitably brought by tenants against landlords, rather than vice versa, and requires similar measures to be undertaken. These two approved Protocols are discussed in more detail in Ch.37, below.

Sometimes, as in the case of emergencies or a claim for damages at the end of the term, the landlord will have very little option other than to make a claim. In other cases, the risks may very well outweigh the advantages. In all cases, however, the landlord should carefully review the information which he has, and consider whether more is necessary before he can decide how best to proceed. He may already be in possession of sufficient information to enable him to decide whether to make a claim. He may have had notice of a specific disrepair, and it may be clear what is necessary in order to remedy it. He will of course have in his possession the lease and any relevant licences to alter or deeds of variation, and he should always carefully check, with the advice of his surveyor and solicitor if necessary, that the matters complained of fall within the tenant's obligations. There may be documents such as a schedule of condition or schedules of dilapidations compiled on earlier occasions which throw light upon the matter. In an appropriate case, it may also be worth seeking to locate any correspondence relating to the condition of the premises which came into existence before the lease, or has taken place since its grant, and (in relation to a claim involving defective mechanical and electrical services) taking steps to obtain service records and the results of any inspections carried out by or on behalf of insurers.

---

[5] See paras 35–05 and 35–06, above.
[6] See Ch.37, below.

## Relevant considerations

In deciding whether to bring a claim, the landlord will wish to consider, among **36–11** other things, the range of remedies available to him and what they would achieve[7]; the likely cost of instructing his surveyor to take matters further by inspecting the premises, perhaps with a view to preparing a full schedule of dilapidations, and the prospects of recovering those costs from the tenant[8]; whether the tenant is likely to be solvent; whether the time is right to bring a claim, or whether the prospects of success and the commercial advantages might be greater if the claim were to be left over to a later date; how long it is likely to take before the claim is resolved; and (most importantly of all) what he is ultimately seeking to achieve. He will also need to bear in mind both the need to comply with any relevant Protocol, and the fact that the costs of so complying will not necessarily be recoverable under the lease or as litigation costs.[9] It may be desirable in some cases to set matters in motion at an early stage, so that if necessary a formal claim can be lodged immediately upon the expiry of the lease without the need to carry out further essential preparatory work.

## Whether the landlord should do the works before bringing a claim for terminal dilapidations

One of the most difficult practical decisions in connection with a proposed claim **36–12** for dilapidations at the end of the term is whether or not to do the work before making the claim. There are several advantages in doing the work. First, further defects for which the tenant is liable may be exposed which would not otherwise have come to light until after the claim has been brought and settled. There will generally be no reason why these defects cannot be added to any schedule already served on the tenant. Second, once the work has been done, the cost incurred by the landlord may be held to afford strong evidence of the damage to the reversion caused by the disrepair, and it will be for the tenant to disprove this.[10] Third, if the tenant fails to instruct a surveyor to inspect the premises before the works are done (despite having been invited by the landlord to do so), then any surveyor he subsequently instructs will be at the considerable disadvantage of not having seen for himself the extent of the disrepair in respect of which the landlord claims. Fourth, if the landlord does not do the work, the tenant is likely to rely on this in negotiations or litigation as evidence either that the alleged defects are not sufficiently serious as to require remedy, or that any which do exist have not resulted in any damage to the reversion. Fifth, depending on the state of the market, doing the work may improve the prospects of finding a tenant or increase the rental value of the premises, or both.

However, there will be other considerations which may tell against doing the work. First, there is the landlord's tax position, which may dictate a particular course. Second, the landlord may not be able to afford to do the work until his

---

[7] See Ch.26, above.
[8] Recovery of professional fees is considered in Ch.34, above.
[9] See para.34–13 et seq., above.
[10] See paras 30–15 to 30–22, above.

claim against the tenant is settled. Third, there is the fact that the landlord will have to incur the cost of the work, and there will generally be little point in doing this unless it will result in some benefit, either in terms of increasing the chances of finding a new tenant, or increasing the rental value, or in some other way. If the state of the market is such that doing the work would result in no benefit, the landlord may prefer to wait until the market improves before taking any step.

The fact that the landlord does not do the work is not necessarily fatal to his prospects of recovering damages in an amount equal to the cost of the work.[11] However, he will need to explain what his reason was for not doing the work. If it was because he cannot afford to do the work, and he can satisfy the court that once he is put in funds by the tenant, the work will be done, the fact that he has not done the work may lose some or all of its significance. If, on the other hand, the reason is that the state of the market cannot justify doing the work at present (because for example, no new tenant could be found whether or not the building is in repair or there is a possibility that redevelopment will be the better option once the market improves), this is bound to have some effect in practice on the landlord's claim. Precisely what the effect will be depends on the expert evidence at trial as to what, if any, damage to the reversion has been suffered.

## Action by landlord where the works are to be done

**36–13**    If the works are to be done before the claim is brought, the landlord should ensure that the tenant is given an opportunity to inspect the building before the works are commenced. If the schedule of dilapidations has not already been served, then it should be served under cover of an open letter stating that the landlord intends to commence the remedial work on such and such a date; that the tenant and his surveyor are free to inspect the building at any time before that date; and that if the tenant wishes to inspect, then he or his surveyor should contact the landlord to arrange a convenient time. A letter in this form will prevent it being subsequently alleged that the works were done in order to cover up the fact that the landlord's schedule was exaggerated. If the tenant does not take the opportunity to inspect, photographs of the defects should be taken so as to prove, if necessary, that they existed and to illustrate their extent and seriousness. If further defects are discovered once the work has been started, and they are to be the subject of a claim, then the tenant should be given a similar opportunity to inspect them before they are remedied and similar steps should be taken as are described above so as to be able to prove these further details.

---

[11] See paras 30–21 to 30–22, above.

INSPECTION BY THE LANDLORD'S SURVEYOR[12]

## Assembling the information

As has been pointed out, the landlord's surveyor will already be in possession of **36–14** a certain amount of information which will be useful on his inspection. In particular the lease, lease plans, deeds of variation and any schedule of condition or previous schedules of dilapidation should be carefully analysed. Depending on the purpose of the inspection, the surveyor may also wish to familiarise himself with any licences for alteration, since he will wish to make a note of any unauthorised works which may require to be removed or subsequently be made the subject of a claim for damages. The licences may also contain reinstatement clauses in the case of authorised alterations. Part of the surveyor's task may be to consider whether or not it is in the landlord's interest to require reinstatement. Often the obligation to reinstate lapses unless the landlord has served notice requiring reinstatement by a certain date, and in any event any such requirement is normally to be exercised before expiry of the term.[13] Where the landlord is entitled under the terms of the relevant reinstatement provision to "pick and choose" which works of alteration he wishes to be reinstated and which to be left, care will have to be taken to make this choice in the landlord's best interests, and to communicate the decision to the tenant as required by the relevant provision.

## Rights of entry[14]

Where the lease is still in existence, the surveyor must satisfy himself that there is **36–15** a right of entry for inspection purposes. He must take note of any requirements (such as the giving of prior notice), any restrictions upon the times when he may enter, and the purposes for which such entry is permitted. Normally the lease will contain a general right to enter and view the state of repair, which will in most cases be sufficient to allow the landlord's surveyor to carry out his inspection. Sometimes, the surveyor will wish to carry out exploratory works involving interference with the demised premises in order to investigate whether certain defects exist and, if they do exist, how serious they are. Such works may not be permitted by the terms of the lease,[15] in which case they can therefore only be carried out if the tenant consents. Where the exploratory work is of such a nature as to cause damage to the premises or disruption to his business, the tenant may well insist upon an undertaking by the landlord that the premises will be made good or suitable compensation paid. Often clauses which permit entry to carry out such works make express provision for this. The surveyor should bear this in mind in deciding upon and carrying out such works.

---

[12] See also the RICS Guidance Note, *Dilapidations*, 6th edn, ss.4 and 5, which contain helpful practical guidance on assembling information and inspecting.

[13] See paras 16–05 to 16–06, above.

[14] See generally Ch.22, para.22–25 et seq., above.

[15] See para.22–29, above.

## Assistance

**36–16**    The surveyor will need to consider what assistance he may need in the course of his inspection and what equipment he is likely to require. For example, where extensive opening up work is to be undertaken, a builder may be needed. In some cases it may be necessary to call upon other professionals, for example structural engineers, or electrical and mechanical engineers, to undertake part of the survey.

## The inspection

**36–17**    As well as carrying out his prime task, namely the compilation of the schedule of dilapidations, the surveyor should note any other matters which might be relevant to future litigation. For example, if he inspects premises which are being used by the tenant for some industrial process, he may observe damage which that process is causing to the fabric of the building. This may be relevant to a subsequent claim where the cause of the damage and responsibility for it is in issue. It is always useful to take photographs. This is particularly so if the matter ends in litigation, because the necessary remedial works may have been carried out, thus destroying the evidence of the defects, or an issue may arise as to how far the premises have deteriorated further between the date of expiry of the lease and the matter coming on for trial. In some cases, it may be appropriate to take samples, perhaps of deteriorated building materials or rotten timber; the surveyor should of course first check his entitlement to do so. In the course of his inspection the surveyor should make a careful note of what he sees. This may be in written form or on a tape recording which is subsequently transcribed. In either case the notes should be retained even after they have been incorporated in a formal schedule of dilapidations in case points of detail need to be checked or verified at some later stage.

## THE SCHEDULE OF DILAPIDATIONS[16]

## Interim and final schedules

**36–18**    Surveyors sometimes distinguish between what are called "interim schedules" and "final schedules". Unfortunately, the term "interim schedule" is used in a variety of senses. First, it may indicate that the surveyor has not purported to take a full and complete survey, but has merely contented himself with noting the major items of concern. Second, it may indicate simply that it is a schedule which is compiled during the term of the lease, and not one which is intended to found the basis for any claim for damages when the premises are yielded up. Such an "interim schedule" may be just as full as a "final schedule", although its purpose

---

[16] See also the RICS Guidance Note, *Dilapidations*, 6th edn, s.6, which contains helpful practical guidance on preparing a Schedule of Dilapidations and includes (as Appendix B) an example of a schedule of dilapidations. The Dilapidations Protocol (reprinted in Appendix 3, below) also contains (at Annex B) a form of schedule of dilapidations if prepared by a surveyor and (at Annex C) a form of schedule of dilapidations if prepared by a landlord.

is different. Third, it may mean that the items noted are those which in the surveyor's opinion require to be done even if a new lease is granted to the tenant as a result of negotiations with the landlord or as a result of an order of the court under Pt II of the Landlord and Tenant Act 1954: such a schedule is "interim" in the sense that it aims at a standard lower than that necessary fully to comply with the tenant's repairing obligations. Fourth, the surveyor may compile an "interim schedule" in the expectation that it can be used to support the issue of proceedings claiming damages immediately upon the expiry of the term, but that, once the landlord has possession and is able to carry out a fuller inspection unhampered by the tenant's rights of continuing occupation, the interim schedule will be replaced for the purposes of the litigation by a fuller "final schedule". In view of this confusion in the terminology, it is not proposed to adopt it in this Chapter.

## The purpose of the schedule

The purpose for which the schedule is prepared will influence its contents. The landlord may have gone no further than to decide that it is desirable to have a brief schedule drawn up so that he can decide what future action to take, if any. Alternatively, and more commonly, the purpose of the schedule may be to form the basis of a notice to the tenant to carry out certain work, in default of which the landlord will carry out the work at the tenant's expense; or to be served together with a s.146 notice; or to form the basis for a claim for terminal dilapidations; or to indicate to a contractor at some future date what are the works which are required to be carried out. **36–19**

## The form of the schedule

The surveyor should choose a form of schedule which is suitable to the subject-matter. If it relates to comparatively small premises, such as one floor of an office building, it may be no more than a miscellaneous list of various categories of disrepair. In the case of a larger building, it is usual to deal with structural elements separately, identifying the particular wall, roof, chimney stack, etc. which is being referred to. The particular parts of the building are then set out on a room-by-room or floor-by-floor basis and finally items relating to common parts, lifts or general items such as electrics and drains are dealt with as separate categories. **36–20**

It will generally be good practice to identify, in relation to each alleged breach, the particular provision of the lease or other document (such as a licence to alter) said to have been broken; the physical state of affairs alleged to constitute the breach;[17] and the remedial work said to be necessary.[18] The surveyor will also need to consider whether it is necessary or appropriate to include costings. In some cases (for example, where the schedule is intended to be served with a s.146

---

[17] See para.35–22, below.
[18] These matters are obligatory in cases to which the Dilapidations Protocol applies: see para.36–21 and 37–10, below.

notice) there may be no need for a priced schedule. In other cases (for example, where the schedule is to be served as part of a formal claim under the Dilapidations Protocol) costings will be necessary.

Clearly, there can be no single right way of preparing a schedule: the golden rule is that it must give the tenant proper particulars of the landlord's case, and be easily understood, precise and free from ambiguity.

## The form of schedule required under the Dilapidations Protocol[19]

**36–21**    The Dilapidations Protocol applies to claims for terminal dilapidations in relation to commercial property. It is printed in full in Appendix III, below. It provides for a schedule to be sent to the tenant in the form attached at either Annex B, which should be used where the schedule is prepared by a surveyor,[20] or Annex C, which should be used where the schedule is prepared by the landlord. The form of schedule in each case is substantively the same. It must set out what the landlord considers to be the breaches, the works required to be done to remedy those breaches and, if relevant, the landlord's costings.[21] Those matters must be set out in column form, the columns comprising (i) the item number; (ii) the clause of the lease or other document relied on; (iii) the breach complained of; (iv) the remedial works required; and (v) the landlord's costings. The breaches should be divided into relevant categories (for example, repair, reinstatement, redecoration, etc.), which should be listed separately in the schedule and (where appropriate) identify any notices served by the landlord requiring reinstatement works to be undertaken.[22]

The schedule must be endorsed either by the landlord, or where it is prepared by a surveyor, by the landlord's surveyor; where the latter is the case, the surveyor must have regard to the principles laid down in the RICS Guidance Note on Dilapidations.[23] The schedule should confirm that in the opinion of the landlord or his surveyor: (i) all the works set out in the schedule are reasonably required to remedy the breaches which the landlord considers to have been committed; (ii) where endorsed by the landlord, full account has been take of its intentions for the property; (iii) where endorsed by the landlord's surveyor, full account has been taken of the landlord's intentions for the property, as advised by the landlord; and (iv) the costings, if any, are reasonable.[24]

The schedule must be sent within a reasonable time: what is reasonable will vary from case to case, but will generally be within 56 days after the termination of the tenancy.[25] The schedule may be served before the termination of the tenancy, but if so, the landlord should either confirm at the end of the tenancy that the situation remains as in the earlier schedule or serve a further schedule within

---

[19] The Dilapidations Protocol is dealt with in detail in Ch.37, below.
[20] "Surveyor" encompasses reference to any other suitably qualified person: Dilapidations Protocol para.1.3.
[21] Dilapidations Protocol para.3.1.
[22] Dilapidations Protocol para.3.2.
[23] Dilapidations Protocol para.3.5. See further paras 37–10 to 37–12, below.
[24] Dilapidations Protocol para.3.6.
[25] Dilapidations Protocol para.3.3.

a reasonable time.[26] If possible, the schedule should also be sent electronically to enable the tenant's comments to be incorporated in the one document.[27]

## The schedule must set out the breaches

The schedule of dilapidations must identify the breaches of covenant which the landlord relies on. By "breaches" is meant the relevant defects in the subject matter of the covenant which are asserted to constitute breaches by the tenant of his repairing or other relevant obligations.[28]

**36–22**

Sometimes, a schedule is drawn up in the form of a schedule of works; that is to say, the document does not indicate what is wrong with the building but only what, in the opinion of the landlord's surveyor, is necessary to put it right. It is suggested that this practice is undesirable. The use of such a schedule may invalidate a contractual notice to remedy disrepair under a covenant to repair on notice which requires the landlord to serve a schedule "of wants of repair found to exist at the premises in contravention of the tenant's covenants", as opposed to a list of works which the landlord wishes to be carried out.[29] A similar point can be made in relation to s.146 of the Law of Property Act 1925 which requires the landlord to "specify the breach complained of": the breach is the existence of the actual disrepairs, not the failure to carry out certain specified works.[30] Furthermore, service of a schedule in this form involves a confusion of two separate stages in the five-part approach to liability set out earlier in this work,[31] because it elides the nature of the deterioration of the subject-matter of the covenant with the works necessary to remedy that deteriorated state. This is potentially dangerous, because there will often be more than one way in which particular defects could be remedied. For example, where the wall of a building is damp, with the result that the plaster is in a defective condition, the landlord's surveyor might specify in the schedule: "install damp-proof course at base of main flank wall". It might be argued that the tenant would be within his rights in ignoring this item altogether if the proper performance of his covenant could be achieved without him inserting a damp-proof course, even if there were lesser works (not specified in the schedule) which he should have done to remedy the defect. The schedule should therefore specify the respects in which the premises are dilapidated. Once this has been done, there is no reason why the surveyor should not also indicate what, in his opinion, is the appropriate form of remedial work which should be undertaken in order to remedy the defect.[32]

Sometimes schedules served by landlords purport to require tenants to carry out their own tests and inspections in order to determine whether defects exist. A commonly found example is "test all drains throughout the building". In the absence of some specific stipulation in the lease, the tenant is under no obligation

---

[26] Dilapidations Protocol para.3.4.
[27] Dilapidations Protocol para.3.7.
[28] See Ch.8, above.
[29] See para.28–35, above.
[30] See paras 27–15 to 27–16, above.
[31] See Chs 6 to 11, above.
[32] Note that in cases to which the Dilapidations Protocol applies, it is obligatory for the schedule to identify both the breaches and the remedial work: see para.36–21, above, and para.37–10, below.

to carry out such tests on behalf of the landlord, and these items are accordingly meaningless: if there is something wrong with the drains or the electrics which requires to be remedied, the landlord's surveyor should find this out for himself (if necessary, arranging for specialist tests or reports) and specify the results of his investigations in the schedule. If, however, the schedule properly specifies a defect, then in an appropriate case, it may be permissible to require the tenant to inspect for himself and do what is necessary.[33]

Many schedules include a general "sweep up provision", such as "generally carry out all works necessary to comply with the covenants in the lease". Since this does not specify any particular breaches nor require any particular works to be carried out, it serves no substantive purpose, although it does make it clear that the tenant should not rely on the schedule as necessarily intended to be comprehensive or as relieving him from the need to carry out any other repairs required by the lease. In addition, it is generally good practice to indicate at the foot of a schedule that the landlord reserves the right to serve a further schedule in respect of any further breaches of covenant which may be found to have occurred.[34] This will preserve his position in the event that defects are subsequently discovered, for example after a full test of the electrical system, or in the course of carrying out remedial works.

## MATTERS TO BE CONSIDERED BY THE TENANT WHEN FACED WITH A CLAIM FOR DILAPIDATIONS

### General considerations

36–23  The tenant's position differs from that of the landlord in that, at the early stages at least, he is likely to take a passive rather than an active role. This does not mean, however, that he should simply do nothing and await the service of a schedule of dilapidations; there is much that he himself can do to minimise his liability and to put himself into a position to bring negotiations with the landlord to a successful conclusion. Some of the many matters which he will wish to consider are discussed below. It should also be noted that, where it applies, the Dilapidations Protocol requires the tenant to take an active role in assessing for himself, and agreeing with the landlord, the likely extent of liability and quantum.[35]

### An early compromise with the landlord

36–24  It may be appropriate in many cases for tenants to seek to reach agreement with their landlords as to how the question of dilapidations should be dealt with well before matters come to a head. Whether the tenant intends to yield up possession or to seek renewal under the Landlord and Tenant Act 1954, he might find it to his advantage to suggest that the landlord's and tenant's surveyors meet on the premises at an early stage in order to attempt to agree a joint schedule of

---

[33] See para.27–18, above.
[34] See para.27–19, above.
[35] See Ch.37, below.

dilapidations. Once this has been done it would be for the landlord and the tenant to negotiate an agreement whereby some or all of the identified items were done by the tenant, or were to be left to be done by the landlord at an agreed price paid by the tenant or subject to an agreed contribution from the tenant, or the whole matter might be settled by payment of a lump sum from tenant to landlord with no obligation on either party actually to carry out any works. Such a solution has the merit of simplicity and certainty, but is surprisingly seldom adopted in practice, perhaps because neither landlord nor tenant has the will to reach a fair compromise until the pressures of actual or potential litigation are brought to bear. It also has the disadvantage for the landlord that he is being asked to settle at a time before he has possession and possibly therefore before he knows the full extent of the works which he will have to do; and the tenant may feel that he is yielding at too early a stage any possibility of arguing that the value of the landlord's reversion has not been damaged by any disrepair, or that the landlord intends to redevelop or refurbish the premises in such a way as would eliminate or reduce the tenant's liability. Nonetheless, as between certain kinds of parties, and in respect of certain kinds of premises, such as those which have been newly built, this form of early compromise has much to commend it.

## Compliance with the covenants

The tenant could, of course, avoid the possibility of a claim for dilapidations by ensuring that the premises are at all times kept, and are yielded up, in full compliance with the tenant's obligations. Where the tenant is under a full repairing obligation this is easier said than done. First, there can be no certainty that the tenant's view of what is necessary in order to comply with his covenants will correspond with that of the landlord, so that unless the tenant either complies fully with a schedule served on him by the landlord or with an agreed compromise schedule, the possibility of future litigation will still be present. Second, if a major programme of works is necessary, most tenants will find it inconvenient and disruptive to have it carried out whilst they remain in possession. They will therefore have the alternatives of putting up with the disruption or moving out of all or part of the premises while the works are done. This is likely to suit a tenant only where he has decided to wind up his business, and either has already found alternative accommodation or could conveniently do so in sufficient time to enable the works to be completed between the date when he vacates the premises and the expiry of the term. Third, by simply doing the works the tenant gives up any possibility of relying on s.18 of the Landlord and Tenant Act 1927.

Nonetheless, the advantages to the tenant of doing the work should not be overlooked. First, the tenant will have control over the carrying out of the works and the expenditure of money and can choose his own contractors. This may have the effect that he can do the work more quickly and cheaply than the landlord. Second, if he takes appropriate professional advice, and makes a bona fide attempt to comply with his covenants, then the onus on the landlord of proving breaches on the term date may, in practice, to be a heavy one. Third, if a claim by the landlord can be forestalled, the tenant is likely to save a considerable amount

**36–25**

in professional fees. By contrast, if he does not do the work but instead pays the cost by way of damages, then he may end up having to pay the landlord's surveyor's fees as well as those of his own surveyor. Fourth, the tenant will avoid liability for interest.[36]

In making his decision, the tenant will need to take into account his tax position, and the taxation consequences of adopting a particular course.

## The effect of the disrepair on the value of the landlord's reversion

**36–26** The tenant must consider the extent to which, if he fails to do the work, the value of the landlord's reversion will thereby be damaged. This will involve considering, among other things, the present and future state of the market; the extent to which disrepair will affect the landlord's ability to relet the premises, or their rental value; and the likelihood or otherwise of refurbishment or redevelopment of the premises. In all cases, therefore, where the claim for dilapidations is likely to be substantial the tenant should take advice as to the likely future of the building. The landlord himself may already have given the tenant some ammunition, perhaps by applying for planning permission, or serving a notice on the tenant under s.25 of the Landlord and Tenant Act 1954 specifying ground (f) of s.30(1), thus indicating the landlord's intention to carry out substantial works to the premises. In other cases, quite apart from any intentions which the landlord may have, the tenant may receive valuation advice to the effect that the diminution in value of the landlord's reversion is likely to be substantially less than the probable cost of complying with a schedule of dilapidations.

## The tenant's future plans

**36–27** The tenant should consider his potential liability for dilapidations as part of his overall business strategy. There may be cases where the premises are suitable for the tenant but the consequence of remaining in occupation and seeking to renew his tenancy under the 1954 Act would be a substantial dilapidations liability. If he were to move out instead, it might be that the landlord would decide that the premises should be redeveloped, thus eliminating the tenant's liability. Or the landlord might be anxious to regain possession and therefore be prepared to concede a waiver of the tenant's dilapidations liability in return for an early surrender. There may be cases where it would suit the tenant to move premises but the inevitable result of giving up possession would be a large bill for dilapidations. In such circumstances the tenant might be better advised to renew his lease, perhaps on the basis that he would only be required to carry out certain essential repairs as opposed to a full schedule, and then assign his renewed lease, taking suitable indemnities from the assignee as to liability for the eventual dilapidations claim.

---

[36] See para.38–36 et seq., below.

## Whether the bill can be passed to third parties

Sometimes there will be other parties who are potentially liable to indemnify the tenant against part or all of the landlord's claim. An obvious example is where the whole of the premises are sub-let on repairing covenants at least as onerous as those of the tenant's own lease. In such a case, assuming the sub-tenant to be solvent, the tenant should endeavour to bring it into the negotiations as soon as possible. Where the sub-tenant in such a case intends to renew his sub-lease of the whole premises under the 1954 Act, holding directly from the landlord, then the tenant's liability for dilapidations may be eliminated entirely.[37] However, in practice, the position is unlikely to be so clear-cut. In particular, questions of considerable legal and practical complexity may arise where the premises are only partly sub-let; where some only of the sub-tenants have rights under the 1954 Act; where the sub-tenants have no repairing liability as such, but are bound to make service charge contributions; or where the terms of the various sub-tenancies differ as to liability for repairs and service charge contributions.

**36–28**

A common situation in practice occurs where the building is sub-let on sub-tenancies containing service charge provisions, and the head landlord makes a claim for dilapidations against the head tenant shortly before the head tenancy is due to expire. Insofar as the work falls within the service charge provisions, the head tenant will generally only be able to recover the cost from the sub-tenants if he carries it out before (a) his head tenancy has ended, and (b) the relevant sub-tenancy has ended. In practice, by the time the head landlord's claim is made, it may be too late for the head tenant to recover the cost of the work under the service charge provisions.[38] The existence of this possibility is a good reason for considering well in advance of the term date of the head lease whether and to what extent repair works should be carried out.

## Weighing up the costs

In considering all the above matters the tenant is seeking to minimise the amount of money which it will have to pay either to the landlord or to its own contractors in respect of the dilapidated condition of the premises. The tenant should include in this calculation all associated costs including the fees which it may have to pay to its own professional advisers. It should also bear in mind that the landlord may have heads of claim in addition to the basic cost of works, principally interest and loss of rent. It will also be relevant to consider the tax implications of a particular course of action.

**36–29**

---

[37] See paras 30–31 to 30–35, above.

[38] However, the fact that the head landlord may himself be able to recover the cost of the work from sub-tenants whose sub-tenancies continue after the end of the head tenancy under the 1954 Act will be relevant in assessing the extent to which the value of the head landlord's reversion has been diminished: see paras 30–31 to 30–35, above.

## Evidence

**36–30** Where the tenant intends to yield up the premises in circumstances where it is likely that a claim for dilapidations will be made, he should ensure that he has sufficient evidence of the state of the premises to deal with that claim. In some cases he may be justified in asking his own surveyor to compile a schedule of condition even if the landlord has not taken any steps towards the compilation of a schedule of dilapidations. Photographs are always useful. The evidence should, as nearly as possible, reflect the position as at the date when the premises are to be yielded up, rather than several months in advance, or several months later.

## NEGOTIATION AND COMPROMISE

## Introductory

**36–31** Most dilapidations claims are settled by agreement. The practical impact of the relevant Protocols will doubtless lead to an even greater number of settlements.[39] Whilst the art of successful negotiation is indefinable, this section suggests a number of ways in which landlord or tenant may manoeuvre himself into the most favourable position.

## Assessing the position

**36–32** A successful negotiator must always take a realistic view of the strengths and weaknesses of his position and of those of the other party. In a dilapidations case this will involve an assessment of the relevant legal principles and of the expert evidence, including the expert evidence of the other party if that is known. Often, however, negotiations will start at a stage when the whole picture has not fully emerged. It may appear likely that further investigations will reveal the existence of new items of disrepair or that further exploratory tests may show that certain remedial works are not in fact necessary. There may even be a relevant leading case pending before the courts which, if decided one way, may have an effect upon the legal merits. The negotiator should always try to keep one eye open on such future possibilities, either favourable or adverse, so that he can seek to reach agreement at the time which suits him best.

Quite apart from the merits of the claim itself, the negotiations may be significantly affected by the commercial pressures bearing upon landlord or tenant. The landlord may have difficulty in raising the finance necessary to carry out the works and run the litigation, yet may be receiving no income from the property in the meantime. This may make him ready to settle at a lower figure than might otherwise be justified. Similarly if the tenant's parent company were negotiating to sell its shareholding, it might be to its advantage to settle an outstanding dilapidations claim for a cash payment rather than to seek to persuade its purchaser to buy the shares subject to the outstanding litigation. Often the existence of these pressures will not be public knowledge and can only

---

[39] See Ch.37, below.

be a matter of speculation by the negotiator; on other occasions, they may have been the subject of public announcements or press comment, of which the negotiator ought to be aware. In some cases the solvency of the tenant will be a major factor, and the landlord may be better advised to settle for a lesser sum if that would avoid pushing the tenant into bankruptcy. Where parties other than the landlord and tenant have rights or liabilities, the negotiator should make a judgment as to whether his position is strengthened or weakened by their participation in the negotiations.

## The psychology of litigation

One reason why most dilapidations claims are settled without proceedings being issued by the landlord is that the threat of litigation with all its attendant costs and risks is itself a potent factor leading to a compromise solution. It does not follow, however, that it is always best for the landlord to threaten immediate litigation as a spur to compromise. Often such threats tend to have the opposite effect; the tenant may feel that his own investigations and consideration of the situation have not yet been completed, and that an early threat of litigation by the landlord suggests that the landlord has something to fear from these being continued. Thus, threats and their implementation may make him take a more entrenched position. On the other hand, if negotiations have been dragging on for months without any real progress being made, the issue of proceedings might be thought by the landlord to be essential to give them a new urgency. The potential liability for costs will thus become a more immediate fear, since once battle is joined, there will be solicitors and counsel to pay. In addition to these considerations, the use of the relevant Protocol will, in most cases, considerably assist the process of compromise by formalising pre-litigation discussions.[40] In particular, the structures set out in the Protocols ought to make it easier for landlord and tenant to exchange views and information at a relatively early stage without feeling that they are prejudicing their respective positions.

**36–33**

## Terminal dilapidations claims

The outcome of many, perhaps most, claims for damages for terminal dilapidations is that the landlord will receive an award of damages but not at the full figure which he claims. This highlights a considerable advantage which the landlord has, at least at the early stages of such litigation. If he has a valid claim and he complies with the various procedures set out in the Dilapidations Protocol, he can be reasonably confident of having his costs of litigation paid by the tenant unless an offer under Pt 36 of the Civil Procedure Rules[41] has been made or he has otherwise conducted himself unreasonably.[42] The effect of this is that, at least at the outset, the costs pressure upon the tenant will generally be greater than that

**36–34**

---

[40] See Ch.37, below.
[41] See paras 34–19 to 34–21, above.
[42] See paras 34–17 and 34–22, above. This does not apply, of course, where the tenant is legally aided. Nor will it necessarily apply in relation to the costs of issues or claims on which the landlord is ultimately unsuccessful: see ibid.

upon the landlord, and this pressure can be increased if the landlord takes advantage of the procedure introduced under Pt 36 of the Civil Procedure Rules which allows a claimant to make a formal offer to settle, with severe consequences for the defendant if the claimant subsequently does better than his offer.[43] It is therefore essential for the tenant to neutralise this advantage by making a realistic Pt 36 offer as soon as he can possibly do so. When this has been done, both parties are at risk as to costs; whether the balance is tilted against landlord or tenant depends upon how likely the eventual award of damages is to exceed the amount offered. Therefore the making of a Pt 36 offer should be regarded by negotiators on both sides as being a real opportunity to settle the case. Even if the landlord thinks that the offer is on the low side, it may be an appropriate time for him to make a counter-offer on the high side, and then open "without prejudice" negotiations to see if a compromise can be agreed. Both parties should always bear in mind that the considerable amount of work involved in preparing a terminal dilapidations claim for trial will always make costs a significant factor and that, if costs are allowed to build up to an excessive level, this may of itself make it impossible for either side to settle.

## "WITHOUT PREJUDICE" AND "SUBJECT TO CONTRACT"

### "Without prejudice"

36–35     The effect of a document or conversation being "without prejudice" is that, in the ordinary case, neither party is entitled to reveal to the court either its existence or its contents. The rule is not absolute, in that without prejudice material may be referred to and relied on in certain exceptional circumstances (for example, where the fact that there were negotiations is relevant to an application to dismiss for want of prosecution, or where the question is whether a party has acted reasonably to mitigate his loss).[44] Absent any of these, however, material which is properly without prejudice is absolutely privileged. It is sometimes mistakenly said that the without prejudice nature of a document or conversation may be "waived" by one of the parties. This is incorrect. It is not open to one party to reveal without prejudice material without the consent of the other. However, once a binding agreement is reached, then (i) the negotiations cease to be without prejudice, and may be relied on to establish the agreement, and (ii) where the agreement is in writing, objective facts communicated between the parties in the course of the negotiations are admissible in order to construe it.[45]

The without prejudice rule does not depend for its application on there being an express or implied threat of litigation underlying the negotiations or some proximity in time to the litigation eventually begun: the crucial consideration is whether in the course of the negotiations the parties contemplated or might

---

[43] See para.34–19 to 34–21, above.
[44] For the exceptions to the rule, see the judgment of Robert Walker L.J. in *Unilever Plc v Procter & Gamble Co Ltd*. [2000] 1 W.L.R. 2436; *Savings and Investment Bank v Fincken* [2004] 1 All E.R. 1125; *Oceanbulk Shipping & Trading SA v TMT Asia Ltd* [2011] 1 A.C. 662.
[45] *Oceanbulk Shipping & Trading SA v TMT Asia Ltd*, above.

reasonably have contemplated litigation if they could not agree.[46] The rule is "founded on the public policy of encouraging litigants to settle their differences rather than litigate them to a finish".[47] It extends to negotiations concerning earlier proceedings involving an issue which remains unresolved[48]. An opening offer in a negotiation can be "without prejudice" even though there may not at that stage be any dispute.[49] The failure to use the words "without prejudice" expressly will not matter, since as soon as it appears that the discussions or correspondence were part of an attempt to compromise, the court will generally be prepared to infer that they were without prejudice.[50] Accordingly, once it is clear that there is an impending dilapidations dispute, as where the landlord has complained about dilapidations or has caused a schedule to be served or has served a s.146 notice, all discussions between landlord and tenant with a view to compromising the dispute are likely to be taken in law to be on a "without prejudice" basis, unless it is specifically agreed by the parties to the contrary. Nonetheless, where negotiations are taking place, it is generally good practice to mark all correspondence "without prejudice" and to agree that all discussions are on a "without prejudice" basis, even though this may not be strictly necessary, since it will avoid any argument on the point.

Sometimes expressions such as "off the record" or "confidential" are used. These have no specific legal meaning, but their use may indicate that the discussions were intended to be without prejudice.

## "Subject to contract"

The parties can also specify that their discussions are on a "subject to contract" **36–36** basis, that is to say that they are not of themselves capable of constituting a binding agreement unless that agreement is recorded in a formal contract. Making negotiations "subject to contract" has the advantage (and disadvantage) that either party is entitled to change its mind and revert to its original position at any time up to the signing of a formal contract, even if there is apparent agreement on all outstanding matters. In most cases, the risks of being bound from inadvertence are probably greater than the risks of losing a favourable compromise, so it will probably be best in most cases for negotiations to be made "subject to contract".

It should be noted that the terms "without prejudice" and "subject to contract" should not be regarded as interchangeable; their purpose and effect is entirely different, particularly in that "without prejudice" negotiations can lead to a binding agreement whereas "subject to contract" negotiations cannot, short of a formal contract.

---

[46] *Barnetson v Framlingham Group* [2007] 1 W.LR. 2443.
[47] *Rush & Tompkins v GLC* [1989] A.C. 1280 per Lord Griffiths at 1299. See further on the public policy underlying the rule *Chocoladefabriken Lindt & Sprungli A.B. v The Nestle Co Ltd* [1978] R.P.C. 287 and *Bradford & Bingley v Rashid* [2006] 1 W.L.R. 2066.
[48] *Ofulue v Bossert* [2009] 1 A.C. 990
[49] *South Shropshire District Council v Amos* [1986] 1 W.L.R. 1271.
[50] Ibid.

CHAPTER 37

# PRE-ACTION CONDUCT AND PROTOCOLS FOR DILAPIDATIONS CLAIMS

## INTRODUCTORY

## The civil justice reforms

The Woolf Reforms which introduced the Civil Procedure Rules ("CPR") placed particular emphasis on pre-action conduct, with a view to encouraging parties to negotiate as soon as litigation becomes a possibility, and to make realistic offers to settle. The principal themes were that litigation is to be viewed as a last resort, so that parties should consider alternatives to litigation before starting proceedings;[1] that parties are expected to adopt a "cards on the table" approach by disclosing their case in outline in letters of claim and response, and by exchanging information, including key documents; that parties are expected to behave in a proportionate manner by applying cost-benefit principles to disputes before starting proceedings and to conduct litigation in the light of that analysis; and that the issues should be defined and narrowed before proceedings are issued so that the case can be properly managed from an early stage.[2] The main means chosen for implementing this approach was the introduction of rules governing "Pre-Action Conduct", and, in particular areas, "Pre-Action Protocols", which lay down the ways in which parties to a dispute which may end up in litigation should conduct themselves. The sanction which was devised to ensure compliance with the general rules of pre-action conduct or the more specific rules laid down in any relevant Protocol was the introduction of the principle that regard would be had to compliance or non-compliance in the exercise of the court's case management powers and when making orders as to costs.

37–01

## The Practice Direction—Pre-Action Conduct

The aim of the Practice Direction—Pre-Action Conduct is to enable parties to settle the issue between them without the need to start proceedings, and to support the efficient management by the court and the parties of proceedings that

37–02

---

[1] For a discussion of the relevant alternatives in dilapidations claims, see Ch.39, below.
[2] The *White Book*, Vol.1, para.C1A–002.

cannot be avoided.[3] These aims are to be achieved by encouraging the parties to (i) exchange information about the issue, and (ii) consider using a form of Alternative Dispute Resolution.[4]

The Practice Direction goes on to describe the approach of the courts to compliance and non-compliance with the Practice Direction or a relevant pre-action Protocol. It refers to CPR r.3.1(4) and (5) and CPR r.3.9(1)(e), which entitle the court to take into account compliance or non-compliance with any relevant protocol when giving directions for the management of claims, and further entitle the court to order a party which has failed to comply without good reason to pay a sum into court, and to CPR r.44.3(5)(a), which includes within the conduct relevant to the exercise of the discretion as to costs "conduct before, as well as during proceedings and in particular the extent to which the parties followed any relevant pre-action protocols".[5] It provides that the court will expect the parties to have complied with the Practice Direction and any relevant pre-action Protocol; that the court may ask the parties to explain what steps were taken to comply prior to the start of the claim; and that where there has been a failure of compliance by a party, the court may ask that party to provide an explanation.[6]

When considering compliance the court will:

(1) be concerned about whether the parties have complied in substance with the relevant principles and requirements and is not likely to be concerned with minor or technical shortcomings;
(2) consider the proportionality of the steps taken compared to the size and importance of the matter;
(3) take account of the urgency of the matter. Where a matter is urgent (for example, an application for an injunction) the court will expect the parties to comply only to the extent that it is reasonable to do so.[7]

Examples are given of cases where a party may be found to have failed to comply, namely by (i) not having provided sufficient information to enable the other party to understand the issues; (ii) not having acted within a time limit set out in a relevant pre-action Protocol, or, where no specific time limit applies, within a reasonable period; (iii) having unreasonably refused to consider Alternative Dispute Resolution; or (iv) without good reason, not having disclosed documents requested to be disclosed.[8]

The Practice Direction then spells out the sanctions which may be applied for non-compliance with the Practice Direction or a relevant pre-action Protocol. It provides that in deciding whether to impose sanctions, the court will look at the overall effect of non-compliance on the other party.[9] If the court is of the opinion that there has been non-compliance, the sanctions which it may impose include

---

[3] Practice Direction—Pre-Action Conduct para.1.1.
[4] Practice Direction—Pre-Action Conduct para.1.2.
[5] Practice Direction—Pre-Action Conduct para.4.1. See para.34–13 et seq., above.
[6] Practice Direction—Pre-Action Conduct para.4.2.
[7] Practice Direction—Pre-Action Conduct para.4.3.
[8] Practice Direction—Pre-Action Conduct para.4.4.
[9] Practice Direction—Pre-Action Conduct para.4.5.

(i) staying the proceedings until steps have been taken which ought to have been taken; (ii) an order that the party at fault pays the costs, or part of the costs, of the other party; (iii) an order that the party at fault pays those costs on an indemnity basis; (iv) if the party at fault is the claimant in whose favour an order for the payment of a sum of money is subsequently made, an order that the claimant is deprived of interest on all or part of that sum, and/or interest is awarded at a lower rate than would otherwise have been awarded; and (v) if the party at fault is the defendant, and an order for the payment of a sum of money is subsequently made in favour of the claimant, an order that the defendant pay interest on all or part of that sum at a higher rate than would otherwise have been awarded.[10]

## The relevant pre-action Protocols

The two pre-action Protocols which are applicable to dilapidations claims are the Pre-Action Protocol for Claims for Damages in Relation to the Physical State of Commercial Property at the Termination of a Tenancy (the Dilapidations Protocol), which came into force on January 1, 2012, and the Pre-Action Protocol for Housing Disrepair Cases (the Housing Disrepair Protocol), which came into force in 2003. Both are printed in full, with Annexes, in Appendix III. The Dilapidations Protocol is considered in paras 37–08 to 37–24, below, and the Housing Disrepair Protocol in paras 37–25 to 37–32, below.      **37–03**

The following general comments as to the differences between the scope and application of the two Protocols should be borne in mind. The Housing Disrepair Protocol is concerned with residential property only, and deals with disrepair for which the landlord is responsible under the terms of the tenancy. It therefore proceeds upon the basis that it will be the tenant who is the claimant. It is in the nature of such claims that they will most commonly arise during the course of the tenancy, not at its end, and that the tenant's remedy will not be limited to a claim for damages only, but may also require works to be done. The Dilapidations Protocol, by contrast, being directed towards claims for damages in relation to commercial property at the end of the tenancy, proceeds upon the basis that the claimant will be the landlord, claiming damages for breach of the tenant's obligations under the lease at the end of the term. It is recognised in the Housing Disrepair Protocol that the potential claimant, being the tenant, may not have the professional advice of a solicitor or a surveyor, and most of the forms are drafted on the basis of alternative variants making provision for this. The tone, and degree of detail, to be found in the two Protocols also reflects the expectation that the Housing Disrepair Protocol will normally be used in relatively small cases, where the claimant may be a lay person, with relatively little knowledge of the law and practice of dilapidations. By contrast, the Dilapidations Protocol is written in a way more appropriate to the more sophisticated property owner or occupier likely to be involved in a dispute concerning commercial property.

---

[10] Practice Direction—Pre-Action Conduct para.4.6.

## Cases not subject to a pre-action Protocol

**37–04**   Many claims relating to dilapidations will not fall within the scope of either Protocol. Examples are a landlord's claim during the term for specific performance, forfeiture or the cost of works carried out under a *Jervis v Harris* clause, or a claim by a commercial tenant for damages for breach of the landlord's repairing obligations. Such cases are dealt with in paras 36–33 to 36–34, below.

## Disclosure

**37–05**   In many cases, the appropriate pre-action conduct will involve one or both parties in providing documents to the other. It is provided by the Practice Direction— Pre-Action Conduct that, save where a relevant pre-action protocol contains its own provisions about the topic, documents provided by one party to another in the course of complying with the Practice Direction or any relevant pre-action Protocol must not be used for any purpose other than resolving the matter, unless the disclosing party agrees in writing.[11] Accordingly, if no settlement results, neither party can, in any ensuing litigation, rely on or otherwise make use of any document disclosed by the other party in the course of complying with the Practice Direction or either of the two relevant Protocols, unless that other party agrees in writing. Instead, such document will have to be obtained through the process of disclosure in the proceedings (assuming it to be otherwise disclosable).

## Experts

**37–06**   In all cases where the evidence of an expert is necessary (save where a relevant pre-action protocol contains its own provisions about the topic), the parties must consider how best to minimise expense.[12] Guidance on instructing experts is set out in Annex C to the Practice Direction—Pre-Action Conduct.

## What is required is substantial compliance

**37–07**   What is required is compliance in substance with the relevant principles and requirements of the Practice Direction and any relevant pre-action Protocol: the court is not likely to be concerned with minor or technical shortcomings.[13] Nor will it allow the process to be used as a weapon or so as to confer an unfair tactical advantage on one side.

In *Orange Personal Communications Services Ltd v Hoare Lea*[14] Akenhead J. made the following general observations:

---

[11]   Practice Direction—Pre-Action Conduct paras 9.1 and 9.2.
[12]   Practice Direction—Pre-Action Conduct paras 9.1 and 9.4.
[13]   Practice Direction—Pre-Action Conduct para.4.3(1).
[14]   [2008] EWHC 223 (TCC) at [31].

"(a) The overriding objective (in CPR Part 1) is concerned with saving expense, proportionality, expedition and fairness; the Court's resources are a factor. This objective whilst concerned with justice justifies a pragmatic approach by the Court to achieve the objective. The overriding objective is recognised even within the Protocol as having a material application.

(b) The Court is given very wide powers to manage cases in CPR Part 3 and elsewhere so as to achieve or further the overriding objective.

(c) The Court should avoid the slavish application of individual rules, practice directions or Protocols if such application undermines the overriding objective.

(d) Anecdotal information about the effectiveness of the Pre-Action Protocol process in the [Technology and Construction Court] is mixed. It is recognised as being effective both in settling disputes before they even arrive in the Court and narrowing issues but also as being costly on occasion and enabling parties to delay matters without taking matters very much further forward.

(e) Whilst the norm must be that parties to litigation do comply with the Protocol requirements, the Court must ultimately look at non-compliances in a pragmatic and commercially realistic way. Non-compliances can always be compensated by way of costs orders."

In *T J. Brent v Black & Veatch Consulting*,[15] an order for costs was refused where the defendant had substantially complied with the relevant Protocol. Akenhead J. said in his judgment:

"... in substance, the Defendant was very well aware, before these proceedings commenced, what the nature of the claim was against it. It did not know every detail. It did not know because the Claimants themselves did not know precisely what amount was to be claimed, but it knew in substance and it was able to deal with it in substance. The Defendant was able to work out what its defences were in some detail. The Defendant was given every opportunity to attend meetings to discuss matters and to settle the disputes. The Court should be slow to allow the rules to be used in those circumstances for one party to obtain a tactical or costs advantage where in substance the principles of the Protocol have been complied with."

## THE DILAPIDATIONS PROTOCOL[16]

## Application of the Protocol

The Dilapidations Protocol applies to commercial property situated in England and Wales. It relates to claims for damages for dilapidations against tenants at the termination of a tenancy.[17]    **37–08**

The parties are not released from compliance with the Protocol simply because they have not sought professional advice from a surveyor. In such a case, they should still, so far as is reasonably possible, comply with the Protocol.[18]

References in the Protocol to a surveyor include reference to any other suitably qualified person.[19]

---

[15] [2008] EWHC 1497 (TCC) at [45].
[16] The Dilapidations Protocol is printed in full, with Annexes, in Appendix III, below.
[17] Dilapidations Protocol para.1.1.
[18] Dilapidations Protocol para.1.3.
[19] Dilapidations Protocol para.1.3.

## Objectives of the Protocol

**37–09**    The Protocol sets out the conduct that the court would normally expect prospective parties to follow prior to the commencement of proceedings: it establishes a reasonable process and timetable for the exchange of relevant information, and sets standards for the content and quality of schedules and "Quantified Demands" and, in particular, the conduct of pre-action negotiations.[20] Its objectives are (i) to encourage the exchange of early and full information about the dispute; (ii) to enable the parties to avoid litigation by agreeing a settlement of the dispute before proceedings are started; and (iii) to support the efficient management of proceedings where litigation cannot be avoided.[21] A flow chart is attached at Annex A showing each of the stages that parties are expected to undertake before the commencement of proceedings.

The court, in considering any sanctions to impose for non-compliance, will (among other things) be concerned about whether the parties have complied in substance with the relevant principles and requirements of the Protocol, and is not likely to be concerned with minor or technical shortcomings.[22]

## The schedule

**37–10**    The landlord must send the tenant a schedule in the form attached at either Annex B or Annex C.[23] The form of schedule at Annex B must be used where the schedule is prepared by a surveyor, and that at Annex C where the schedule is prepared by the landlord. In each case, the schedule must set out what the landlord considers to be the breaches, the works required to be done to remedy those breaches and, if relevant, the landlord's costings.[24] Those matters must be set out in column form, the columns comprising (i) the item number; (ii) the clause of the lease or other document relied on; (iii) the breach complained of; (iv) the remedial works required; and (v) the landlord's costings. The breaches should be divided into relevant categories (for example, repair, reinstatement, redecoration, etc.), which should be listed separately in the schedule and (where appropriate) identify any notices served by the landlord requiring reinstatement works to be undertaken.[25]

The schedule must include a statement that it contains the true views of the landlord or (as the case may be) the surveyor employed by the landlord to prepare the schedule.[26]

The schedule must be sent within a reasonable time: what is reasonable will vary from case to case, but will generally be within 56 days after the termination of the tenancy.[27] A schedule may be served before the termination of the tenancy,

---

[20] Dilapidations Protocol para.1.2.
[21] Dilapidations Protocol para.2.1.
[22] Dilapidations Protocol para.1.5 (referring to paras 4.3 to 4.5 of the Practice Direction—Pre-Action Conduct). See para.37–07, above.
[23] Dilapidations Protocol para.3.1.
[24] Dilapidations Protocol para.3.1.
[25] Dilapidations Protocol para.3.2.
[26] See the forms of schedule at Annexes B and C. See further paras 37–11 to 37–12, below.
[27] Dilapidations Protocol para.3.3.

but if so, the landlord should either confirm at the end of the tenancy that the situation remains as in the earlier schedule or serve a further schedule within a reasonable time.[28] Wherever possible, the schedule should also be sent electronically to enable the tenant's comments to be incorporated in the one document.[29]

## Endorsement

The schedule must be endorsed either by the landlord, or where it is prepared by a surveyor, by the landlord's surveyor.[30] The required endorsement must confirm that in the opinion of the landlord or his surveyor: (i) all the works set out in the schedule are reasonably required to remedy the breaches which the landlord considers to have been committed; (ii) where endorsed by the landlord, full account has been taken of its intentions for the property; (iii) where endorsed by the landlord's surveyor, full account has been taken of the landlord's intentions for the property, as advised by the landlord; and (iv) the costings, if any, are reasonable.[31]

**37–11**

It is clear that the purpose of requiring the endorsement, together with the references in the body of the schedule to the schedule containing "the true views of" the landlord or the landlord's surveyor (as the case may be),[32] is to fulfil a similar role to that of a Statement of Truth in formal court pleadings. It emphasises that items are not to be included in the schedule without a full and proper consideration of whether those items can be justified.

Where the schedule has been prepared by the landlord's surveyor, then in endorsing the schedule he must have regard to the principles laid down in the RICS Guidance Note on Dilapidations.[33] The relevant Guidance Note[34] includes the following statements of particular relevance:-

> "1.1.5 Often, after a surveyor has advised his or her client, a document is sent or disclosed to the other party to the lease, to third parties, or to a court or tribunal. That document can be held out as the product of the surveyor applying his or her training, knowledge and expertise to the matter. The surveyor, while complying with his or her client's instructions, should ensure that any such document does not contain statements or assertions that the surveyor knows, or ought to know, are not true or properly sustainable or arguable.
>
> 1.1.6 Surveyors should not allow their professional standards to be compromised in order to advance clients' cases. Surveyors should not allow a document that contains statements or assertions that they know, or ought to know, are not true or properly sustainable or arguable to be sent bearing their name or the name of their firm. A surveyor should give proper advice even though the client might choose to ignore it."[35]

---

[28] Dilapidations Protocol para.3.4. See further para.36–15, below.
[29] Dilapidations Protocol para.3.7.
[30] Dilapidations Protocol para.3.5.
[31] Dilapidations Protocol para.3.6.
[32] See the forms of schedule at Annexes B and C.
[33] Dilapidations Protocol para.3.5.
[34] RICS Guidance Note Dilapidations, 6th edition.
[35] Para.7.5.3 of the Guidance Note states that, before giving the endorsement required by the Dilapidations Protocol, the surveyor should consider the guidance set out in these paragraphs.

In *PgfII SA v Royal & Sun Alliance Insurance*[36] the landlord served a schedule of dilapidations prior to the term date which did not contain the surveyor's endorsement required by an earlier version of the Protocol, although a later version of the schedule did include the endorsement. It was held that the failure was a technicality, and that no costs sanction should be applied.

## "The landlord's intentions for the property"

**37–12**  As noted above, where the schedule is endorsed by the landlord, it must include confirmation that full account has been taken of his intentions for the property, and where the schedule is endorsed by the landlord's surveyor, the latter must confirm that in his opinion full account has been taken of the landlord's intentions for the property, as advised by the landlord.[37] A number of points arise out of this requirement.

First, whilst the landlord or, as the case may be, his surveyor must take account of the landlord's intentions for the property when preparing the schedule, and include an endorsement to that effect in the schedule, there is no requirement to state or otherwise identify what the landlord's intentions for the property in fact are. This part of the Protocol may be contrasted with the subsequent provision that where the tenant or his surveyor consider that any items in the schedule or Quantified Demand are likely to be superseded by works to be carried out by the landlord or are likely to be superseded by the landlord's intentions for the property, this must be stated in the Response, and "particulars should be given of the material on which the tenant or tenant's surveyor relies" and "the items to which this view is relevant should be identified".[38]

Second, where the schedule is prepared by the landlord's surveyor, he must take full account of the landlord's intentions for the property "as advised by the landlord". The surveyor must therefore take the landlord's instructions as to his intentions for the property. On the face of it, however, the Protocol does not require the surveyor to undertake any further investigations into the landlord's intentions, or to form any independent opinion of his own as to whether, for example, the landlord's intentions are feasible or reasonable or accord with what a well-advised landlord would do.[39] This part of the Protocol may be contrasted with the subsequent provisions relating to the tenant's Response, under which the tenant or his surveyor are required to confirm that account has been taken of what the tenant, or the tenant's surveyor, "reasonably believes to be the landlord's intentions for the property".

Third, it is not immediately obvious why, in any event, the Protocol requires the landlord's intentions to be taken into account in preparing the schedule. The purpose of the schedule is to set out the landlord's common law claim, that is to

[36] [2010] EWHC 1981 (TCC).
[37] Dilapidations Protocol para.3.6.
[38] Dilapidations Protocol para.5.6.
[39] Note, however, the requirement for the surveyor to have regard to the principles laid down in the RICS Guidance Note on Dilapidations, which include a professional obligation on the surveyor to ensure that the schedule does not contain statements or assertions that the surveyor knows, or ought to know, are not true or properly sustainable or arguable: see para.36–11, above.

say, what breaches the landlord says have been committed, what remedial works he says are necessary and what he says those works will cost. In principle, the common law claim must be identified before it is possible to inquire into the diminution in the value of the reversion for the purposes of the exercise required by s.18(1) of the Landlord and Tenant Act.[40] But the actual landlord's intentions are not relevant to his common law claim. They are only relevant to s.18(1), and even then, as regards the first limb, only evidentially, not directly.[41] Moreover, one possible consequence of the requirement for the schedule to take account of the actual landlord's intentions is that it will exclude items which will be superseded by non-repair works which the actual landlord intends to carry out. But those items are properly part of the common law claim, and their exclusion at the schedule stage may lead to difficulty when applying s.18(1) (because, for example, the hypothetical buyer's intentions would, for whatever reason, be different to those of the actual landlord). For this reason, this part of the Protocol can be said with some force to confuse (i) the landlord's common law claim with the matters which will become relevant under s.18(1), and (ii) the actual landlord's intentions with those of the hypothetical buyer of the reversion.

Fourth, the Protocol does not explain what it means by "intentions". If, however, one purpose of requiring the landlord's intentions for the property to be specifically addressed is because this is relevant to the second limb of s 18(1) of the Landlord and Tenant Act 1927,[42] then it presumably follows that, for this purpose at least, "intentions" is used in the same sense as in the second limb of s.18(1) of the Landlord and Tenant Act 1927, i.e. as referring to:

> "… a state of affairs which the party intending … does more than merely contemplate: it connotes a state of affairs which, on the contrary, he decides so far as in him lies, to bring about, and which, in point of possibility, he has a reasonable prospect of being able to bring about, by his own act of volition."[43]

In other words, by "the landlord's intentions", the Protocol is not referring to something which the landlord is considering or exploring as a possibility. It means something which he has made up his mind to do.[44]

Last, following on from the last point, the Protocol proceeds on the implicit assumption that the landlord will have identified his intentions for the property by the time the schedule is served. In practice, however, that will often not be the case. There may be a variety of possible options for the property, and the landlord may not yet have decided which to pursue. In many cases, the property will be on the market and the landlord may be waiting to see what, if any, offers emerge. In such cases, it cannot sensibly be said that the landlord has any intentions for the property, at least in the sense of having made a final decision as to what to do. Quite how the landlord or his surveyor should deal with cases of this sort will depend on the detailed facts. However, one possible approach would simply be to

---

[40] See Ch.30, above.
[41] See paras 30–20 to 30–21, above.
[42] See para.30–48 et seq., above.
[43] *Cunliffe v Goodman* [1950] 2 K.B. 237.
[44] See further paras 30–54 to 30–57, below.

omit this part of the endorsement on the basis that the landlord has no relevant "intentions for the property" of which account can be taken in preparing the schedule.

## Quantified Demand

**37–13**   The Protocol provides for the sending to the tenant of a Quantified Demand, which must be sent within the same timescale for sending the schedule.[45] It does not have the same status as a statement of case in court proceedings.[46]

The Quantified Demand must (i) set out clearly all aspects of the dispute, and set out and substantiate the monetary sum sought as damages in respect of the breaches in the schedule as well as any other items of loss for which damages are sought, and whether VAT applies; (ii) confirm that the landlord and/or his surveyor will attend a meeting or meetings;[47] and (iii) specify a date (being a reasonable time) by which the tenant should respond, which will usually be within 56 days after sending the Quantified Demand.[48]

Where the monetary sum claimed is based on the cost of works, it must be fully quantified and substantiated by either an invoice or a detailed estimate.[49] Where the sum claimed includes other losses, they must be set out in detail, substantiated and fully quantified, and the landlord must explain the legal basis on which they are claimed, for example, whether they are sought as part of the damages claim or under some express or implied provision of the lease.[50] Obvious examples would be a claim for loss of rent, insurance rent and service charges, a claim for empty rates or a claim for the costs of preparing the schedule of dilapidations. In many cases, it will not be possible to set out or substantiate an actual figure, in which case the correct course will ordinarily be to include an estimated or provisional figure and explain how it has been arrived at.

The figures set out in the Quantified Demand must be restricted to the landlord's likely loss, which is not necessarily the same as the cost of works to remedy the breaches.[51] Nor should the Quantified Demand include items of works that are likely to be superseded by the landlord's intentions for the property.[52] These two provisions require a careful consideration by the landlord or his surveyor of the question whether or not a pure "cost of works" basis is appropriate, or whether the claim is capped at a lesser amount by reason of s.18(1) of the Landlord and Tenant Act 1927, and the related question of the extent to which, if at all, the landlord has "intentions for the property" which would be likely, if implemented, to supersede the works in the schedule.[53]

---

[45] Dilapidations Protocol para.4.2.3.
[46] Dilapidations Protocol para.4.1.
[47] See para.36–17, below.
[48] Dilapidations Protocol para.4.2.
[49] Dilapidations Protocol para.4.3.
[50] Dilapidations Protocol para.4.4.
[51] Dilapidations Protocol para.4.5.
[52] Dilapidations Protocol para.4.6. See para.36–12, above.
[53] See Ch.30, above.

Where the Quantified Demand is prepared by the landlord's surveyor, then he must have regard to the principles laid down in the RICS Guidance Note on Dilapidations.[54]

## Tenant's Response

The tenant must respond to the Quantified Demand within a reasonable time, which will usually be 56 days after the landlord sends the Quantified Demand.[55] The Response does not have the same status as a defence in court proceedings.[56] Where appropriate, the tenant must respond using the schedule provided by the landlord, and the Response should be in sufficient detail to enable the landlord to understand clearly the tenant's views on each item.[57]

**37–14**

The Response must be endorsed by the tenant or, where it is prepared by a surveyor, by his surveyor: in the latter case, the surveyor must have regard to the principles laid down in the RICS Guidance Note on Dilapidations.[58] The endorsement should confirm that in the tenant's or the tenant's surveyor's opinion (i) the works detailed in the Response are all that were reasonably required for the tenant to remedy the alleged breaches of its covenants or obligations; (ii) any costs set out in the Response are reasonably payable for such works; and (iii) account has been taken of what the tenant, or tenant's surveyor, reasonably believes to be the landlord's intentions for the property.[59] The significance of the requirement for this endorsement is the same as that already discussed in relation to the parallel requirement for an endorsement in the landlord's schedule.[60]

If the tenant or his surveyor considers that any items in the schedule or Quantified Demand are likely to be superseded by works to be carried out by the landlord or are likely to be superseded by the landlord's intentions for the property, then this should be stated in the Response, with particulars of the material relied upon and the items to which the alleged supersession is relevant.[61]

Perhaps surprisingly, the Protocol does not specifically require the Response to set out the tenant's detailed case in relation to any of the matters set out in the Quantified Demand other than those set out in the landlord's schedule. However, it is thought that, where possible, appropriate details of the tenant's case in relation to any such matters should be given. For example, where the Quantified Demand includes a claim for loss of rent, but the tenant's view is that market conditions are such that no rent would be lost while the works are carried out, or that the landlord has over-estimated the likely length of the works or the appropriate rental rate, then the tenant should say so in his Response. Such a "cards on the table" approach would seem to be entirely consistent with the underlying policy and objectives both of the Dilapidations Protocol itself and of the Practice Direction—Pre-Action Conduct.

---

[54] Dilapidations Protocol para.4.7. See para.36–11, above.
[55] Dilapidations Protocol para.5.2.
[56] Dilapidations Protocol para.5.1.
[57] Dilapidations Protocol paras 3.7, 5.3.
[58] Dilapidations Protocol para.5.4. See para.36–11, above.
[59] Dilapidations Protocol para.5.5.
[60] See para.36–12, above.
[61] Dilapidations Protocol para.5.6.

## Service of a schedule prior to lease expiry

**37–15**   As noted above, the Protocol provides that a schedule may be served before the termination of the tenancy, but if so, the landlord must either confirm at the end of the tenancy that the situation remains as in the earlier schedule or serve a further schedule within a reasonable time.[62] In practice, landlords often arrange for their surveyor to inspect the premises and draw up a terminal schedule of dilapidations in the last few months before the lease expires. Such schedule is then served on the tenant, again before the lease ends. The question may then arise as to whether such schedule must be in the form required by the Protocol, and whether it must be accompanied by a Quantified Demand.

The answer is that, strictly speaking, the schedule need only comply with the Protocol, and be served with a Quantified Demand, if it is intended formally to set in motion the Protocol process (although that does not, of course, mean that it will not ordinarily be good practice for the schedule to be in the form required by the Protocol).

That in turn raises the question of when it will be appropriate to initiate the Protocol procedure. The answer in any given case will depend on the particular circumstances. Sometimes, a schedule drawn up prior to lease expiry will have been prepared at a time when the tenant was still in occupation, such that it will be necessary to re-inspect the premises and draw up a more comprehensive schedule at lease expiry. In such a case, it is likely to be potentially wasteful of time and costs to initiate the Protocol process prior to lease expiry (because, for example, the tenant may carry out some or all of the works; further defects may occur in the course of the tenant vacating; the landlord's further inspection at lease expiry may reveal significant further defects; or there may be developments in the market which affect the landlord's intentions for the property). Nonetheless, the service of the prior schedule may well enable the Protocol process, when and if initiated, to run more efficiently and smoothly, because the tenant will have been given advance warning of the landlord's likely claim so as to enable him to consider his position, carry out any works he wishes and be ready to deal with a more formal claim at lease expiry. In such a case, however, it may be sensible for the landlord to make it clear that he is not thereby intending to initiate the Protocol procedure, and that a further schedule and Quantified Demand will follow at lease expiry.

There may be other cases, however, where the Protocol process can properly be initiated prior to lease expiry. For example, the premises may be vacant, such that the landlord's surveyor has had a full opportunity to inspect and carry out any necessary tests etc. In such a case, the landlord may want to move matters along as fast as reasonably possible. In such a case, it is not thought that there is any reason in principle why the landlord cannot initiate the Protocol process prior to the lease ending, although he would, of course, have to confirm at lease expiry that the situation remains as stated in the schedule (or serve a further schedule). Depending on the facts, it may be reasonable in such a case for the tenant to delay serving the Response until after such confirmation has been received.

---

[62] Dilapidations Protocol para.3.4.

## Disclosure of documents

The Protocol provides for the disclosure of documents. This will generally be limited to the documents required to be enclosed with the Quantified Demand and the Response (which clearly falls short of full disclosure of all relevant documents which would need to be disclosed during the litigation process), but the parties can agree that further disclosure can be given.[63] Documents provided by one party to another in the course of complying with the Practice Direction or the Dilapidations Protocol cannot be used for any purpose other than resolving the matter, unless the disclosing party agrees in writing.[64]

    The Protocol refers to the possibility of making an application for pre-action disclosure under CPR 31 if the parties disagree about some aspect of the disclosure process, but goes on to provide that the parties should assist each other and avoid the need for such an application.[65]

**37–16**

## Negotiations

The Protocol encourages the landlord and the tenant and/or their respective surveyors to meet before the tenant is required to respond to the Quantified Demand, and it further provides that they should generally meet within 28 days after the tenant sends its Response.[66] Such meetings are without prejudice,[67] and the parties should seek to agree as many of the items as possible.[68]

**37–17**

## Alternative Dispute Resolution

The Protocol requires the parties to consider whether some form of Alternative Dispute Resolution[69] would be more suitable than litigation, and if so, to agree which form to adopt.[70] It goes on to warn parties that they may be required by the court to provide evidence that alternative means of resolving their dispute were considered; that the courts take the view that litigation should be a last resort, and that claims should not be issued prematurely when a settlement is still actively being explored; and that the court will take into account the extent of the parties' compliance with the Protocol when making orders about who should pay costs.[71]

    The Protocol expressly recognises that no party can or should be forced to mediate or enter into any form of ADR.[72]

**37–18**

---

[63] Dilapidations Protocol para.6.1.
[64] Practice Direction—Pre-Action Conduct paras 9.1 and 9.2.
[65] Dilapidations Protocol para.6.1.
[66] Dilapidations Protocol para.7.1.
[67] See further para.36–24, below.
[68] Dilapidations Protocol para.7.1.
[69] Alternatives to Litigation are discussed in detail in Ch.39, below.
[70] Dilapidations Protocol para.8.1.
[71] Dilapidations Protocol para.8.1.
[72] Dilapidations Protocol para.8.3.

## Quantification of the landlord's loss

**37–19**    Prior to issuing proceedings, the landlord must quantify his loss by providing to the tenant a detailed breakdown of the issues and consequential losses based on (i) a formal diminution valuation; or (ii) an account of the actual expenditure; or (iii) (where it has carried out some but not all remedial action), a combination of both; unless, in all the circumstances, it would be unreasonable to do so.[73] Any formal diminution valuation should be prepared by a valuer.[74] The reference to a "formal" diminution valuation, or an "account" of actual expenditure, emphasises that a degree of precision and formality is required, presumably so that the tenant is able to take a realistic view of the exact quantification of its liability enabling it to make an appropriate offer of settlement and/or take steps to protect its position as to costs by making a formal offer under CPR Pt 36.[75]

Where the landlord has not carried out all the works specified in the schedule but intends to carry out some or all of them, he must (i) identify which works he intends to carry out; (ii) state when he intends to do such works; (iii) state what steps he has taken towards getting such proposed works done (for example, preparing a specification or bills of quantities or inviting tenders); and (iv) clearly show the scope of such proposed works to enable any effect on the dilapidations claim to be identified.[76]

## Diminution valuations[77]

**37–20**    Where the landlord has not carried out all the works specified in the schedule, and either (i) he intends to carry out some or all of them, or (ii) he does not intend to carry out some or all of them, then he should provide a formal diminution valuation unless, in all the circumstances, it would be reasonable not to.[78] This assumes that the landlord will have a settled intention one way or the other.[79] In practice, his state of mind may be more fluid: for example, he may be marketing the premises for sale or re-letting and he may be waiting to see what offers are forthcoming before finally making up his mind. Nevertheless, it is thought that in the ordinary case it will generally be in accordance with the underlying objectives of the Protocol for the landlord to provide a valuation.

Where the tenant relies on a defence on the basis of diminution, it must state its case for so doing, and provide a diminution valuation to the landlord within a reasonable time, which will generally be within 56 days after the landlord sends to the tenant the detailed breakdown of issues and losses referred to in the preceding paragraph.[80]

One potential practical difficulty with these provisions is that, where diminution valuations are provided, each party's valuation will generally be

---

[73] Dilapidations Protocol para.9.1.
[74] Dilapidations Protocol para.9.2.
[75] See para.34–19 et seq., above.
[76] Dilapidations Protocol para.9.3.
[77] See Ch.30, above.
[78] Dilapidations Protocol para.9.4.
[79] Cf. para.36–12, above.
[80] Dilapidations Protocol paras 9.5 and 9.6.

based on the assumption that the appropriate remedial works are those for which that party contends. For this reason, where, as is almost always the case, the parties substantially disagree on the extent of liability, the valuations will not necessarily advance matters much further. What appears to be a large difference of opinion between the valuers may, on analysis, turn out to be a difference as regards the extent of the remedial work. It is therefore suggested that if possible, each valuer should provide a valuation based on the remedial works contended for by the other party as well as the party instructing him. In an appropriate case, that will enable the parties to see whether the real difference between them relates to the amount of any diminution in value, or whether (as is frequently the case) what really divides them is the extent of liability.

## Stock take

Finally, the Protocol provides for a "stock take" in circumstances where the procedure set out in the Protocol has not resolved the dispute. They should undertake a further review of their respective positions, and should consider the state of the papers and the evidence in order to see if proceedings can be avoided and, at the least, narrow the issues between them.[81] This underlines yet again the objectives underlying the Dilapidations Protocol.     37–21

## Costs

The Dilapidations Protocol makes no provision for payment by either party of the other party's costs.[82] Costs are therefore a matter for negotiation. However, if court proceedings ensue, the costs of complying with the Dilapidations Protocol may be recoverable as part of the costs of the litigation.[83]     37–22

## Sub-tenants

The Dilapidations Protocol does not expressly deal with what happens where the tenant wishes to pass on the claim, in whole or in part, to sub-tenants. However, the Protocol applies as between tenant and sub-tenant in the same way as it does between landlord and tenant, so that in principle, the tenant must comply with the Protocol before he commences any proceedings against a sub-tenant. In such a case, however, the steps required by the Protocol may have to be tailored to reflect the fact that the tenant is himself a defendant to an existing claim by the head landlord.     37–23

Where a third party is brought into an existing action without having been involved in the previous Protocol procedures, there are two conflicting considerations: on the one hand, the new party should not be deprived of the benefits of the Protocol; on the other hand, it is desirable, if possible, that the

---

[81] Dilapidations Protocol para.10.
[82] Contrast the Housing Disrepair Protocol: see para.37–31, below.
[83] See paras 34–13 to 34–15, above.

existing trial timetable should be maintained.[84] In an appropriate case, it may be right to stay the proceedings to enable compliance with the Protocol in relation to the third party.[85] Where costs and time would have been saved had the Protocol process been followed, the claimant may be ordered to pay the third party's costs up to the stage which compliance with the Protocol would have achieved.[86]

## Admissibility in court proceedings

37–24    One question which may arise in practice is the extent to which it is open to one of the parties to rely in subsequent court proceedings on something done or said by the other in the course of complying with the Protocol.

The Practice Direction—Pre-Action Conduct provides in terms that documents provided by one party to another in the course of complying with the Practice Direction or any relevant pre-action Protocol must not be used for any purpose other than resolving the matter, unless the disclosing party agrees in writing.[87] The Dilapidations Protocol itself provides that any meetings between the parties are without prejudice.[88] Accordingly, if court proceedings ensue, it is not open to a party either (i) to make any use of documents previously provided by the other party in the course of compliance (save with that other's written agreement), or (ii) to rely on something said or done by the other party in any meeting held in the course of compliance (save to the extent that any such meeting is agreed to be open). The Dilapidations Protocol does not expressly deal with the status of any of the remaining steps required to be taken by way of compliance, that is to say, the landlord's schedule and Quantified Demand, the tenant's Response, the landlord's quantification of loss and any formal diminution valuations provided by either party to the other. However, it is thought that these documents can be referred to in court proceedings in the same way as, for example, a conventional letter before action or any other open pre-action correspondence. That view is consistent with (i) the express provision in the Protocol that the Quantified Demand and the Tenant's Response are not intended to have the same status as a statement of case or defence in proceedings[89] (which is presumably aimed at preventing parties being held to them in subsequent court proceedings in circumstances where that would not be reasonable or appropriate), and (ii) the express provision that meetings are without prejudice,[90] coupled with the absence of any corresponding provision in relation to any other step required by the Protocol. It therefore seems probable that, for example, it would be open to the parties to rely in any subsequent court proceedings on something said in any formal diminution valuation served on behalf of the other party.

---

[84] *Alfred McAlpine Capital Projects Ltd v SIAC Construction (UK) Ltd* [2006] B.L.R. 139.

[85] See *Alfred McAlpine Capital Projects Ltd v SIAC Construction (UK) Ltd*, above, at [39–41], where the relevant considerations are considered; *Orange Personal Communications Services Ltd v Hoare Lea* [2008] EWHC 223 (TCC) at [28].

[86] See *Daejan Investments Ltd v Park West Club Ltd* [2004] BLR 223; *Orange Personal Communications Services Ltd v Hoare Lea*, above, at [26].

[87] Practice Direction—Pre-Action Conduct paras 9.1 and 9.2.

[88] Dilapidations Protocol para.7.1. See para.37–17, above.

[89] Dilapidations Protocol paras 4.1 and 5.1.

[90] Dilapidations Protocol para.7.1.

## THE HOUSING DISREPAIR PROTOCOL[91]

### Scope of Protocol

The Pre-Action Protocol for Housing Disrepair Cases (the Housing Disrepair Protocol) covers claims by any person with a disrepair claim, including tenants' lessees and members of the tenant's family.[92] A "disrepair claim" is a civil claim arising out of the condition of residential premises (other than a claim which originates as a counterclaim or set-off in other proceedings), and may include a related personal injury claim.[93] The types of claim which the Protocol is intended to cover include those brought under s.11 of the Landlord and Tenant Act 1985,[94] s.4 of the Defective Premises Act 1972,[95] common law nuisance and negligence and those brought under the express terms of a tenancy agreement or lease (but not claims under s.82 of the Environmental Protection Act 1990).[96]

37–25

While the Dilapidations Protocol is expressly confined to claims arising at the termination of the lease, those covered by the Housing Disrepair Protocol are much more likely to arise during the currency of the tenancy, and the tenant's objective is therefore likely to be to persuade or compel the landlord to carry out necessary repairs as much as to be paid damages for losses suffered. The quantum of claim is likely to be less than in many commercial cases, and will, in a typical case, include compensation for inconvenience and/or distress suffered because of the condition of the property, and special damages such as loss of, or damage to, specific items such as clothes, carpets, curtains, wallpaper, bedding or extra electricity costs.[97] Since there may be a number of cases where the tenant is represented neither by a solicitor nor a surveyor, the Housing Disrepair Protocol is couched in language more accessible to lay people than is the Dilapidations Protocol.

### Early Notification Letter[98]

In order to avoid delay in notifying the landlord, the Protocol provides for the sending, where appropriate, of an "Early Notification Letter", which notifies the landlord of the claim in advance of the Letter of Claim.[99] This is intended to be a helpful tool, but it may not be necessary in every case. Examples of cases where it might be appropriate are where a repair is urgent, or where there is likely to be some delay before enough details are available to make a claim. Notwithstanding this, even the Early Notification Letter should contain details of the defects, in the form of a schedule, if appropriate; details of notification to the landlord of the

37–26

---

[91] The Protocol is printed in full, together with Annexes, in Appendix III, below.
[92] Housing Disrepair Protocol para.3.1(c).
[93] Housing Disrepair Protocol para.3.1(a).
[94] See para.20–17 et seq.,, above.
[95] See para.20–49 et seq., above.
[96] Housing Disrepair Protocol para.3.1(b).
[97] See the definition of "Damages" and "Special Damages", in the Glossary at para.4.10 of the Housing Disrepair Protocol, where such heads of damage are specifically referred to.
[98] See Housing Disrepair Protocol para.3.2
[99] See para.37–27, below.

defects or some other reason for believing that the landlord has notice thereof; proposals as to an expert; and disclosure of relevant documents.

## Letter of Claim[100]

37–27    The next step which is envisaged is a Letter of Claim by the tenant, which covers much the same ground as the Early Notification Letter, but which should also include a statement of "the effect of the defects on the tenant and special damages".

## Forms of Letter

37–28    Specimen Early Notification Letters and Letters of Claim are set out in Annexes to the Housing Disrepair Protocol in alternative versions covering the situation where the tenant's solicitor is writing on his behalf, and those where it is the tenant himself who is writing.

## Landlord's response[101]

37–29    Whether the tenant has sent an Early Notification Letter or a Letter of Claim, the landlord should reply within 20 working days. The landlord's response should include copies of all relevant records or documents, a response to the tenant's proposals for instructing an expert, and a statement as to:

(i)     whether liability is admitted and, if so, in respect of which defects, and, if liability is disputed, the reasons for this;
(ii)    any point as to lack of notice or any difficulty in gaining access;
(iii)   a full schedule of intended works including anticipated start and completion dates and a timetable for the works;
(iv)    any offer of compensation;
(v)     any offer in respect of costs.

It is expressly noted in paragraph 3.5.3 that failure to respond within the time limit (namely 20 working days of the relevant letter) will be a breach of the Protocol. Clearly these stipulations as to what the response should contain are designed (in a suitable case) to encourage the landlord to make an early offer to settle the claim.

---

[100] See Housing Disrepair Protocol para.3.3.
[101] See Housing Disrepair Protocol para.3.5

## Experts[102]

The Protocol makes detailed provisions as to the role which experts may play in cases to which it applies, including the appointment of a single joint expert, or a joint inspection by experts instructed by each party. Clearly, it is envisaged that, in many such cases, there will be a degree of agreement between experts (or a decision of an agreed joint expert) sufficient to lead to a resolution of most or all of the issues between the parties.

**37–30**

## Costs[103]

If the tenant's claim is settled without litigation on terms which justify bringing it, the landlord must pay the tenant's out-of-pocket expenses (which is defined to mean expenses incurred in a small track claim as a result of the claim, such as loss of earnings and experts' fees). A Statement of Costs Form is attached at Appendix F to inform the landlord of the costs of the claim.

**37–31**

However, the court has no power to enforce payment of the tenant' expenses in such a case. Thus, *Birmingham CC v Lee*,[104] Hughes L.J., giving the judgment of the Court of Appeal, said:

> "[the Protocol] proceeds upon the assumption (or hope) that the parties will settle if there is an early exchange of claim and response and that that settlement will include the claimant's reasonable costs if his claim was justified. Whilst that may be the assumption, or hope, the protocol itself has no coercive power as to costs, and if there is no legal action, there is no court to compel payment of the costs which are anticipated by paragraph 3.7."

In that case, the tenant served a letter of claim under the Protocol, and the landlord then carried out the repairs, with the result that the tenant's subsequent claim for consequential damage was allocated to the small claims track. The Court of Appeal held that the tenant was entitled to its pre-allocation costs up to the date the repairs were completed on the fast track scale, because, up to that point, the tenant had a claim for specific performance which would have been allocated to the fast track. Hughes L.J. said:

> "The tenant who has a justifiable claim for disrepair needs legal assistance in advancing it. He must initiate it in accordance with the protocol. If the effect of the claim is to get the work done, then providing that the landlord was liable for the disrepair the tenant ought to recover the reasonable costs of achieving that result."

---

[102] See Housing Disrepair Protocol para.3.6.
[103] See Housing Disrepair Protocol para.3.7.
[104] [2009] H.L.R. 20.

## Guidance Notes[105]

**37–32**  As well as the Protocol itself, there are extensive Guidance Notes, where additional points are made in relation to many of the matters covered by the Protocol, including practical points such as relevant addresses, the Glossary of relevant terms, and matters such as a "Contact Point" to whom the tenant should address correspondence.

## CASES NOT SUBJECT TO A PRE-ACTION PROTOCOL

### Introductory

**37–33**  As pointed out above, many claims relating to dilapidations (such as a landlord's claim during the term for specific performance, forfeiture or the cost of works carried out under a *Jervis v Harris* clause, or a claim by a commercial tenant for damages for breach of the landlord's repairing obligations) will not be subject to either of the two relevant Protocols. The principles governing pre-action conduct which apply in such cases are as follows.

### Pre-action conduct

**37–34**  Unless the circumstances make it inappropriate, the parties should, before starting proceedings, (i) exchange sufficient information about the matter to allow them to understand each other's position and make informed decisions about settlement and how to proceed; and (ii) make appropriate attempts to resolve the matter without starting proceedings, and in particular, consider the use of an appropriate form of ADR to do so.[106] The parties must act in a reasonable and proportionate manner in all dealings with one another; in particular, the costs incurred must be proportionate to the complexity of the matter and any money at stake.[107] The parties are not to use the Practice Direction as a tactical device to secure an unfair advantage for one party or to generate unnecessary costs.[108]

Before starting proceedings, (i) the claimant should set out the details of the matter in writing by sending a letter before claim to the defendant; and (ii) the defendant should give a full written response within a reasonable period, preceded, if appropriate, by a written acknowledgement of the letter of claim.[109] A reasonable period of time will vary depending on the circumstances, but as a general guide, (i) the defendant should send a letter of acknowledgement within 14 days of receipt of the letter of claim (if a full response has not been sent within that period); (ii) where the matter is straightforward, a full response should normally be provided within 14 days; (iii) where the matter requires the involvement of an insurer or other third party, or where there are issues about

---

[105]  See Housing Disrepair Protocol paras 4.1 to 4.9.
[106]  Practice Direction—Pre-Action Conduct para.6.1.
[107]  Practice Direction—Pre-Action Conduct para.6.2.
[108]  Practice Direction—Pre-Action Conduct para.6.2.
[109]  Practice Direction—Pre-Action Conduct para.7.1.

evidence, then a full response should normally be provided within 30 days; (iv) where the matter is particularly complex, for example requiring specialist advice, then a period of longer than 30 days may be appropriate; and (v) a period of longer than 90 days in which to provide a full response will only be considered reasonable in exceptional circumstances.[110]

Detailed guidance on pre-action procedure is set out in Annex A to the Practice Direction—Pre-Action Conduct, which contains detailed provisions in relation to the claimant's letter before claim, the defendant's acknowledgement of the letter before claim, the defendant's full response, the claimant's reply and taking stock. Adopting the procedure in Annex A is likely to satisfy the court in most circumstances where no pre-action Protocol applies and where the claimant does not follow any statutory or other formal pre-action procedure.[111]

Annex B to the Practice Direction—Pre-Action Conduct sets out the specific information that should be provided in a debt claim by a claimant who is a business against a defendant who is an individual.

---

[110] Practice Direction—Pre-Action Conduct para.7.2.
[111] Practice Direction—Pre-Action Conduct para.7.3.

# CHAPTER 38

# DILAPIDATIONS CLAIMS UNDER THE CIVIL PROCEDURE RULES

## INTRODUCTORY

The practice and procedure of civil litigation under the Civil Procedure Rules **38–01** ("the CPR") is outside the scope of this work, and reference should be made to the *White Book* and other specialist works on the subject. This Chapter is confined to some of the more important aspects of litigation under the CPR which are of particular relevance to dilapidations claims.

## Before starting proceedings

Even before the CPR greatly increased the significance of what passed between **38–02** the parties before the issue of proceedings, it was always considered to be courteous and sometimes to be essential for the intending claimant to write a "letter before action". This term was used to describe a letter notifying the proposed defendant that the prospective claimant intended to commence proceedings against him but would not do so if the defendant was prepared to satisfy the claim, by making a payment or carrying out works, as the case might be. Its purpose was to give the proposed defendant one last chance to avoid proceedings, and it had an added significance in that it generally marked the point from which the expenses of pursuing the claim could be recovered as costs in the proceedings. The CPR, one of the most important aims of which was to reduce the number of claims which went to the courts, place great emphasis on the steps which the parties should take in order to settle their differences *before* proceedings are issued. The prescribed pre-action conduct and relevant Protocols are dealt with in Ch.37, above.

## JURISDICTION

One welcome reform introduced by the CPR was the abolition, for most **38–03** purposes, of the distinctions between those claims which were within the jurisdiction of the High Court and those which were within the jurisdiction of the county court. Questions as to which court is the more appropriate still remain, but such questions are largely dealt with by the process of transfer from one court to another, rather than by formal limits on jurisdiction. One exception may be claims for leave under the Leasehold Property (Repairs) Act 1938.[1] Subject to

---

[1] See para.38–05 et seq., below.

this, the case management of dilapidations claims will be treated in the same way as other civil proceedings under the CPR, and matters such as allocation to the fast track or the multi-track will be judged according to the CPR criteria. One particular feature of dilapidations claims which should be noted is that, because of their inherent technical complexity, they are particularly suited to be tried in the Technology and Construction Court.

## The Technology and Construction Court

**38–04**    The judges of the Technology and Construction Court ("the TCC"), who were formerly known as "Official Referees", are judges who specialise in certain types of case, including those which involve defective buildings or building work. Their special expertise in the detailed and technical nature of the issues arising in such cases makes them ideally suited to trying many types of dilapidations case. Even before the CPR, these courts had developed special procedures and directions suitable for complex cases, of which the parties could take advantage. As from March 25, 2002 procedure in the TCC has been governed by Pt 60 of the CPR and the Practice Direction "Technology and Construction Court Claims" supplementing Pt 60. The second edition of the Technology and Construction Court Guide was published on October 3, 2005, and revised for the second time with effect from October 1, 2010. Reference should be made to these sources for their detailed terms. There now follows a brief summary.

A claim may be brought as "a TCC claim" if it involves issues or questions which are technically complex or a trial by a TCC judge is desirable. Examples given in the Practice Direction of claims which it may be appropriate to bring as TCC claims include "(g) claims between landlord and tenant for breach of a repairing covenant".[2] TCC claims must be issued in the High Court or one of the county courts specified in the Practice Direction, namely Birmingham, Bristol, Cardiff, Central London, Chester, Exeter, Leeds, Liverpool, Manchester, Mold, Newcastle and Nottingham. If a claim is issued in the High Court outside London, it is preferable to issue it in one of the District Registries in which a TCC judge will usually be available, namely Birmingham, Bristol, Cardiff, Chester, Exeter, Leeds, Liverpool, Manchester, Mold, Newcastle and Nottingham. If it is intended to issue a TCC claim any application before the claim form is issued should be made to a TCC judge.[3] There is provision for transfer of proceedings started in a court where no TCC judge is available to one where such a judge would be available.[4] The court will assign the claim to a named TCC judge who will have the primary responsibility for the case management of that claim[5]. All documents relating to the claim must be marked with the words "Technology and Construction Court" and the name of the assigned TCC judge[6]. Applications

---

[2] Practice Direction to Pt 60, para.2.1.
[3] Practice Direction to Pt 60, para.4.1.
[4] Practice Direction to Pt 60, para.5.1.
[5] Practice Direction to Pt 60, para.6.1.
[6] Practice Direction to Pt 60, para.6.2.

should normally be made to the assigned TCC judge[7]. Detailed provisions are made for case management conferences, pre-trial reviews, listing and trial[8].

## THE LEASEHOLD PROPERTY (REPAIRS) ACT 1938

### The 1938 Act

The substantive provisions of the Leasehold Property (Repairs) Act 1938 are considered in detail in Ch.27, para.27–31 et seq., above.

**38–05**

### The appropriate court

Section 6 of the 1938 Act provides that the appropriate court in which an application for leave should be made is the county court, unless the proceedings by action for which leave may be given "would have to be taken in a court other than the county court", in which case the application should be made to that other court. This is subject to s.24 of the County Courts Act 1984, which provides that if the parties agree, by a memorandum signed by them or their respective legal representatives or agents, that a county court specified in the memorandum shall have jurisdiction in proceedings under (among other statutes) the 1938 Act, that court shall have jurisdiction to hear and determine the proceedings. In any event, however, as a result of the changes made by the CPR (and earlier changes made by the Courts and Legal Services Act 1990 and the High Court and County Courts Jurisdiction Order 1991), there is now no case in which proceedings for either forfeiture or damages or both "would have to be taken" in the High Court: such proceedings may be taken in either court. It would seem to follow that an application for leave under the Act must be brought in the county court, and that the High Court no longer has jurisdiction to grant leave.[9] The point is of less importance than it was formerly, since there is no longer any difference in procedure as between the High Court and the county court in any relevant respect, but if proceedings are started in the wrong court and subsequently need to be transferred, this may result in delay and additional cost.

**38–06**

The claim must be started in the county court for the district in which the land is situated.[10]

---

[7] Practice Direction to Pt 60, para.7.1.
[8] Practice Direction to Pt 60, paras 8, 9, 10, 11.
[9] See further the Practice Direction to CPR r.56.2.(2), which provides that a landlord and tenant claim (which includes a claim under the 1938 Act) must normally be brought in the county court.
[10] CPR r.56.2(1). This is expressed to be subject to para.(2), which provides that a claim may be started in the High Court if the claimant files with his claim form a certificate stating the reasons for bringing the claim in that court, verified by a statement of truth. However, it seems unlikely that para.(2) has effect in relation to claims under the 1938 Act because of the provisions of s.6 of the Act: see above.

## Making the application

**38–07**     The procedure for making an application under the 1938 Act is governed by the Practice Direction to CPR Pt 56.[11] The application must be made by way of proceedings under CPR Pt 8. The claimant must file any written evidence on which he intends to rely when he files his claim form and serve it on the defendant with the claim form.[12] Normally, this evidence will be in the form of witness statements, but in addition the claimant can rely upon the matters set out in the claim form as evidence, provided it is verified by a statement of truth.[13] The ordinary rules of evidence will apply, so that, for example, any reliance upon hearsay evidence will be subject to the restrictions and safeguards imposed by the Civil Evidence Act 1995, and expert evidence can only be relied upon if permitted by the court under the procedures described in para.38–20 et seq., below. The defendant is required to acknowledge service within 14 days after service of the claim form, and to serve at the same time any written evidence upon which he intends to rely.[14] This is a very short time within which to prepare the necessary evidence, particularly if expert evidence is to be relied upon, or if there is a dispute about the detail of the schedule of dilapidations, and in practice a defendant may well have to seek the court's permission to serve evidence outside the time limit. The claimant may serve further written evidence in reply within 14 days of service of the defendant's acknowledgement of service.[15] The court may require or permit a party to give oral evidence at the hearing and may give directions requiring the attendance for cross-examination of a witness who has given written evidence.[16]

The court may give directions immediately after a CPR Pt 8 claim form is issued, either on the application of a party or on its own initiative.[17] The court may on the hearing date proceed to hear the case and dispose of the claim or give case management directions.[18] Any directions sought from the court in proceedings under the 1938 Act will, in almost all cases, need to include permission to the parties under CPR Pt 35 to rely on expert evidence.

## The landlord's evidence in support

**38–08**     Following the decision of the House of Lords in *Associated British Ports v C.H. Bailey Plc*,[19] it will be necessary for the landlord to prove his case for leave on the ordinary standard of a balance of probabilities.[20] This extends to all aspects of

---

[11] Somewhat curiously, the Practice Direction does not in terms refer to the 1938 Act, although Pt 56 itself does: see r.56.1(1). However, the Practice Direction would nonetheless appear to apply to claims under the Act: see the *White Book*, Vol.1 at para.56PD.2.

[12] CPR r.8.5(1) and (2).

[13] CPR r.8.5(7).

[14] CPR r.8.3(1) and 8.5(3).

[15] CPR r.8.5(5).

[16] CPR r.8.6(2) and (3).

[17] Practice Direction 8A, para.6.1.

[18] Practice Direction 8A, para.8.1.

[19] [1990] 2 A.C. 703.

[20] See paras 27–57 to 27–59, above.

his case, including the service and validity of the s.146 notice; the existence of breaches of covenant; the existence of grounds under s.1(5) of the Act; and any matters on which the landlord relies to show that the discretion should be exercised in his favour. It is therefore necessary to assemble the written evidence in relation to an application for leave with care, particularly where it is known that the application will be opposed. Under the previous procedures, affidavits were often relied upon which failed to explain adequately the true nature of the grounds and supporting facts upon which the application was based. Thus, in *Land Securities Plc v Receiver for the Metropolitan Police District*,[21] Megarry V.C. criticised the landlord's evidence in the following terms:

> "The evidence is not impressive. Expressions of opinion by a chartered surveyor which do little more than apply to the building something of the language of paragraphs (a) (b) and (e) [of s.1(5) of the 1938 Act] and wind up with a watered down version of (e), obviously leave a good deal to be desired."

Following the decision in *Associated British Ports v C.H. Bailey Plc*[22] it is now even more important that the written evidence adduced on behalf of the landlord sets out the landlord's case fully.

In practice, much of what the landlord needs to prove (such as the lease, the s.146 notice and the counter-notice) is likely to be common ground between the parties. However, in the absence of agreement, the landlord must adduce evidence to prove all of the following:

**38–09**

(1)   the lease. A copy should be attached to the claim form or exhibited to the relevant witness statement, and the original of the counterpart should be available at the hearing;

(2)   (if the landlord is not the original landlord), the vesting of the reversion in the landlord. Where the title is registered, this can be done by exhibiting to the relevant witness statement office copies of the land or charge certificate showing that the landlord is registered as proprietor. If the title is unregistered, then the landlord will need to exhibit the relevant conveyances showing the devolution of title from the original landlord to him;

(3)   (if the tenant is not the original tenant), the vesting of the lease in the tenant. Sometimes the landlord may have a copy of the instrument effecting the assignment, in which case this can be exhibited. If not, then evidence that the tenant has paid rent on his own account to the landlord will generally be taken as sufficient prima facie evidence that the lease has been assigned to the tenant. This inference would be strengthened by production of a licence to assign permitting the assignment of the lease to the tenant;

(4)   service of a valid s.146 notice containing the information prescribed by the Act. Where the notice has been formally acknowledged or service is admitted it will not normally be necessary to prove this. Where strict proof is for some reason required, the evidence to be adduced will depend on how the notice was served. If it was served by post, then a witness statement should be obtained from the person who prepared and posted it, and (where

---

[21] [1983] 1 W.L.R. 439.
[22] [1990] 2 A.C. 723. See paras 25–57 to 27–59, above.

recorded delivery was used) the certificate of posting should be exhibited. If it was served by being affixed to the premises, then the person who did this will need to put in a witness statement;

(5)     service of a counter-notice. The notice should be exhibited to the relevant witness statement;

(6)     the existence of breaches of the covenant to repair. This must be done by the evidence of the surveyor who prepared the schedule of dilapidations, together with any other relevant witnesses (such as the landlord or his managing agents) who can give admissible evidence in relation to the breaches;

(7)     the existence of one or more grounds under s.1(5) of the 1938 Act. This will be done by adducing expert evidence, which may be that of a building surveyor, valuer, engineer or other appropriate expert or a combination of these;

(8)     the existence of any facts on which the landlord relies to show that the court's discretion should be exercised in his favour. How this is to be done will depend on what is to be proved.

## The tenant's evidence

**38–10**     Where the application is defended, the live issues are likely to be the existence of the breaches; the existence of grounds under s.1(5); and whether the discretion should be exercised in the landlord's favour. The tenant's evidence will need to address all of these.

## Hearsay evidence

**38–11**     In the absence of agreement, hearsay evidence will only be admissible subject to the restrictions and safeguards imposed by the Civil Evidence Act 1995, which makes hearsay evidence admissible but provides that the court must take its hearsay nature into account in deciding what weight to give to it. Evidence of a particular fact should ideally be given by a person who has personal knowledge of it. The same is true, in principle, of matters of expert opinion. If, for example, the schedule of dilapidations incorporates a report by a specialist lift engineer, then the evidence ought, ideally, to include a witness statement from the engineer verifying his report. Similarly, if the landlord's surveyor relies on what the works will cost to carry out, his costings must either represent his own opinion (albeit arrived at after discussion with another expert), or if they do not, a witness statement should be put in from the person who provided them. Likewise, any facts relating to comparables relied on by either surveyor in any valuation in relation to ground (a) must be strictly proved if they cannot be agreed, otherwise they can only be put in evidence subject to the restrictions and safeguards of the Civil Evidence Act 1995.

## Expert evidence

Expert evidence is considered in para.38–20 et seq., below. Applications for leave
under the 1938 Act may involve more than one expert on each side. Thus, for
example, it will nearly always be necessary to call a surveyor to deal with the
existence of breaches. Sometimes, depending on his level of expertise and the
complexity of the issues, the same surveyor will be able to deal with what the
works are likely to cost, any matters of valuation under ground (a), and any other
grounds relied on. In other cases, however, it may be necessary to call a quantity
surveyor to deal with costings, and a valuer to deal with the valuation issues
under ground (a). If there are substantial issues as to the condition of services,
then an electrical and mechanical engineer may be needed as well. The court is,
of course, likely to use its case management powers to limit the number of
experts to that which is strictly necessary.

**38–12**

## SUMMARY JUDGMENT UNDER PT 24 OF THE CIVIL PROCEDURE RULES

## Summary judgment

Under Pt 24 of the CPR the court may give summary judgment against a claimant
or defendant on the whole of a claim or on a particular issue if it considers that
the claimant has no real prospect of succeeding on the claim or issue, or that the
defendant has no real prospect of successfully defending the claim or issue, and
that there is no other reason why the case or issue should be disposed of at a
trial[23]. One important respect in which Pt 24 departs from the former RSC Ord.14
is the ability which it gives to a *defendant* to apply for summary judgment, but it
is thought that summary judgment will rarely be given in favour of a defendant in
a dilapidations claim (except, perhaps, where the defendant relies upon the
second limb of s.18(1) of the Landlord and Tenant Act 1927[24]). Applications by a
claimant are most likely to be for judgment for damages to be determined by the
court at a further hearing since, although liability may be clear, the quantum of
the claim is still likely to be in dispute. If judgment is given on this basis the
amount of damages will be decided by the court at a subsequent hearing.

**38–13**

## Procedure under Pt 24

An application for summary judgment is made by an application notice before the
master or district judge. To the extent that it is necessary to support an application
by evidence, this can either be contained in the claim form itself or in the
application notice, supported by the appropriate statement of truth, or in a witness
statement served with the application. The application notice or evidence must
identify concisely any point of law or provision in a document on which the
applicant relies and/or state that the application is made because the applicant
believes that on the evidence the respondent has no real prospect of succeeding

**38–14**

---

[23] CPR r.24.2
[24] See para.30–48 et seq., above.

on the claim or issue or (as the case may be) of successfully defending the claim or issue to which the application relates and that the applicant knows of no other reason why the disposal of the claim or issue should await trial.[25]

## Summary judgment in dilapidations cases

**38–15**     In practice, the most common sort of application for summary judgment in dilapidations proceedings is likely to be a landlord's application for summary judgment on liability, leaving all questions as to damages to be determined at a further hearing. Such an application can appropriately be made where it is plain that there exist at least some items of disrepair for which the defendant is liable. In such cases, the claimant will argue that even if one breach can be shown to exist, he must be entitled to judgment in his favour. There are two arguments against this, one technical and one practical. First, it can be argued that technically the mere proof of breaches is not sufficient to entitle the claimant to damages to be determined. He will also have to prove that the existence of the proved breach or breaches has caused a diminution in the value of his reversion, since otherwise he will not be entitled to any damages at all, not even nominal damages, by virtue of the provisions of s.18(1) of the Landlord and Tenant Act 1927. Accordingly, it can be said that mere proof of breach does not entitle the claimant to anything; on the contrary, if it should turn out that the breaches have caused no diminution in the reversion his claim should be dismissed with costs. While this argument may be successful in a case where only a very small number of breaches can definitely be proved, it is less likely to prevail where it is obvious that there are a large number of items for which the defendant is responsible. In such a case, the court may conclude that it is sufficiently clear that some diminution has been caused for judgment on liability to be appropriate. The second argument against the making of such an order is essentially practical. If the court orders damages to be determined at a later hearing, it will not generally make any specific findings as to what breaches exist. It follows that whoever subsequently determines the amount of damages will in effect be trying the question of what breaches existed all over again. Even if the court finds that a particular breach exists at the hearing of the application for summary judgment, the nature of that breach will have to be gone into again on the determination of damages, because it will often be relevant at that stage to consider what is the appropriate remedial work. For example, the court may find on the application for summary judgment that the roof covering is defective. That will be sufficient to establish a breach, but in order to determine damages, it will be necessary to enquire whether the covenant requires the roof covering to be replaced in its entirety, or whether localised patch repairs will do. It is thought that for these reasons, summary judgment will often be an unnecessary extra step which achieves nothing other than to delay final judgment and to increase costs.

An added complication arises where the landlord's claim is not for damages at the expiry of the term but for forfeiture of the lease and damages. In such a case it is likely that the tenant will be counterclaiming for relief from forfeiture.

---

[25] Practice Direction to CPR r.24 para.2(3).

Provided that this counterclaim is bona fide and has at least some prospect of success, the court cannot make an order for possession under Pt 24 pending the trial of the counterclaim.[26] The court hearing the application for relief will have to decide what are the items of disrepair for which the defendant is liable, how serious those breaches are, the circumstances in which the breaches arose and whether the defendant ought to be granted relief upon terms that he carry out a specific schedule of works. This is an investigation into essentially the same matters which would have to be investigated on the determination of damages. Thus it would be necessary to ensure that the application for relief and the determination were heard by the same court as part of the same hearing.

It is therefore thought that in many cases where the landlord seeks summary judgment for damages to be determined, the court ought properly to conclude that there is an "other compelling reason why the case or issue should be disposed of at a trial" within the meaning of CPR r.24.2(b). In such a case, it seems that the court should dismiss the application (since the court will no longer follow its former practice of giving leave to defend). If the court takes the view that the application for summary judgment has served no useful purpose it is likely to order the claimant to pay the costs.    **38–16**

In any event, for the reasons considered above, in most cases there will be little to be gained by an application for summary judgment for damages to be determined, save possibly a dent in the tenant's morale by having lost the first round. Moreover, judgment for damages to be determined carries with it the risk that further items of disrepair, for which the tenant is liable, may be discovered after judgment. Once judgment has been given, the existing proceedings cannot be amended to add the new breaches. At best, the landlord will have to begin new proceedings. At worst, the new proceedings may be struck out under CPR r.3.4(2)(b) as being an abuse of process, because the landlord should have included all the breaches in the previous proceedings.[27]

A tenant against whom judgment for damages to be determined is given should ensure that the order makes clear that he is, on the subsequent determination, entitled to dispute the individual items in the schedule. If he does not do this, it may be argued on the determination that the effect of the judgment was that he cannot dispute anything in the schedule.

THE SCOTT SCHEDULE

## The Scott Schedule

As well as the usual pleadings which are commonly encountered in civil litigation generally, dilapidations claims normally involve a special form of pleading known as a "Scott Schedule". This is named after George Alexander Scott, who was an Official Referee from 1920 to 1933. The nature of the disputes referred to the Official Referees (now the Technology and Construction Court)    **38–17**

---

[26] By analogy with the position under RSC O.14: *Liverpool Properties Ltd v Oldbridge* [1985] 2 E.G.L.R. 111; *Sambrin Investments Ltd v Taborn* [1990] 1 E.G.L.R. 61.

[27] See para.1–18, above.

involved them in deciding a large number of facts on an item-by-item basis, and the traditional forms of pleading proved cumbersome in dealing with such disputes. Scott's invention was a form of pleading which brought both parties' cases in relation to each of the disputed items together in tabular format in a single document, which could easily be referred to by counsel, witnesses and the judge, throughout the trial. It is settled practice for the judge of the TCC, as successor to the Official Referees, to order that a Scott Schedule be prepared.[28] Such a direction may also be made, where it is appropriate, by any court.

The initial burden of preparing the Schedule is on the claimant. He must prepare a document setting out under appropriate headings his case in relation to liability and quantum on an item-by-item basis. Where appropriate, this can be based on the schedule of dilapidations prepared by his surveyor. A recommended form of Scott Schedule and an example of a completed Scott Schedule are contained in the RICS Guidance Note on Dilapidations.[29] These provide for the following columns:

(1)  an item number for ease of reference;
(2)  the number of the clause alleged to have been broken;
(3)  the breach complained of;
(4)  the remedial works required;
(5)  the tenant's comments;
(6)  the landlord's comments;
(7)  the landlord's costing of the landlord's items;
(8)  the tenant's costing of the works admitted or suggested by the tenant.

In most cases, it will be appropriate that the Scott Schedule be prepared in the above format. However, the form of schedule chosen will need to reflect the nature of the dispute and the likely issues, so that a degree of flexibility will be required in practice, so that more columns (or the same columns in a different order) may be desirable.

**38–18**  It is important that the defendant pleads his case properly in the Scott Schedule. The purpose of the Schedule is to enable both sides to know what the issues are. A bare denial of liability for a particular item does not advance matters. For example, where the claimant pleads in column (3) that "the roof covering is torn or holed over approximately 60 per cent of its total area", the defendant's case may be (a) that the roof is not torn or holed at all as alleged; or (b) that the roof is torn or holed, but not to the extent alleged by the claimant. The defendant should make clear which of these is his case.

A final column is then left blank. Although traditionally regarded as being the column which the judge will fill in for the purpose of his judgment, it will in practice start to be filled in during the trial itself as items are agreed, admitted or deleted. It should be emphasised that the Scott Schedule is designed to encapsulate the parties' respective cases in relation to the detailed items of claim, and is taken to be without prejudice to any defence of a general nature which has

---

[28] See the Case Management Directions Form which is Appendix B to Practice Direction 60—Technology and Construction Court Claims.
[29] RICS Guidance Note (6th edn) s.7.16 and Appendices C and D.

been raised in relation to liability or quantum. Thus, by admitting that items of disrepair existed and that remedial works were necessary to put them right at a certain cost, the defendant is not thereby admitting that they were his liability under his covenants (assuming some general defence as to liability to have been pleaded), nor that the cost of remedying the defects is the appropriate quantification of the claimant's loss if any. These general defences should be raised in the defence in the ordinary way and need not be repeated in the Scott Schedule (although it may be prudent to state expressly at the start of the tenant's comments what reservations are being made).

As well as saving much time during the trial itself, the Scott Schedule also serves to concentrate the parties' minds at a relatively early stage upon the exact nature of their detailed cases, and the nature and importance of the issues which divide them. The preparation of the Schedule at an early stage will thus give both parties an opportunity to narrow the differences between them, and may assist them to reach a realistic compromise. In all save the simplest cases, therefore, it is recommended that an order should be sought as soon as practicable for the preparation of a Scott Schedule.

## DISCLOSURE IN DILAPIDATIONS CASES

## Disclosure

Disclosure is the procedure by which the court enables one party to litigation to obtain the right to inspect and, if he desires, to have copies of documents in the control of the other party. In dilapidations cases, it is probably of the most significance in relation to issues arising under s.18(1) of the Landlord and Tenant Act 1927, and in particular whether the landlord intended to redevelop the premises following the termination of the lease. In such a case disclosure will enable the tenant to see not merely those documents which were available to the public at the relevant time, such as planning applications, but also internal memoranda and other documents evidencing the landlord's private thinking on the matter.

**38–19**

Under CPR Pt 31, a party has a duty to make a reasonable search for documents which adversely affect his own case or adversely affect or support another party's case and to make and serve on the other parties a list of those documents. The party must also include in the list any other documents on which he relies. The disclosing party must then permit the other parties to inspect the documents in the list, except where there is a right to withhold inspection, or where it is considered that it would be disproportionate to the issues in the case to allow disclosure of those documents. A right to withhold a document most commonly arises where a successful claim for privilege can be made. Documents which contain advice from legal advisers on legal matters are absolutely privileged, but this does not apply to other advice from non-legal advisers. Thus, if a landlord were to take the advice of counsel some months before the expiry of the lease as to his prospects of obtaining planning permission for a redevelopment, his instructions to his solicitor, the solicitor's instructions to counsel, and counsel's opinion would all be privileged. But other advice which the same landlord had obtained in relation to the proposed development, for example from a valuation surveyor as to the viability of the scheme, would not be privileged. Another head of privilege which may be relevant in such cases is the head of privilege protecting from disclosure documents which came into existence with the predominant purpose of being used in the preparation of actual or contemplated litigation. The exact boundaries of this privilege are ill-defined. It is thought that it would not generally extend to the notes by a building surveyor in the course of his initial inspection of premises with a view to compiling a schedule of dilapidations, but that it would cover his notes made on a subsequent visit for the purposes of pricing a Scott Schedule. It would not cover a valuation of the demised premises carried out for the purposes of a general valuation of the landlord's portfolio, even if the valuer took into account the state of repair of the demised premises, but it would cover a report prepared by the same valuer for the purposes of countering the tenant's contention that there had been no diminution to the landlord's reversion.

## EXPERT EVIDENCE

### Admissibility of opinion evidence

**38–20**
As a general rule, a witness is only entitled to give evidence of facts: he is not entitled to express his opinion. However, an exception to this is made in the case of expert witnesses, who are entitled to give opinion evidence in relation to the matters the court has to decide. Indeed the whole point of calling an expert is to provide the court with evidence of a person who is equipped by his training and experience to form an opinion on the matter.

By virtue of CPR r.35.4, no party may call an expert or put in evidence an expert's report without the court's permission. An application for permission must provide an estimate of the costs of the expert, identify the field of the expertise to be relied upon and the issues which the expert evidence will address and (if practicable) identify the expert. The permission, if granted, will then relate only to the identified field and/or expert. Generally, the expert evidence will be given in the form of a written report and (except in a fast-track case) the expert will normally be directed to attend the hearing, where he is liable to be cross-examined on his report.

The circumstances in which permission will be given for expert evidence to be adduced are as follows[30]:

"When considering whether to give permission for the parties to rely on expert evidence and whether that evidence should be from a single joint expert the court will take into account all the circumstances in particular, whether:
(a)    it is proportionate to have separate experts for each party on a particular issue with reference to—
(i)    the amount in dispute; and
(ii)    the importance to the parties; and
(iii)    the complexity of the issue;

---

[30] CPR Pt 35 PD para.7

(b)    the instruction of a single joint expert is likely to assist the parties and the court to resolve the issue more speedily and in a more cost-effective way than separately instructed experts;

(c)    expert evidence is to be given on the issue of liability, causation or quantum;

(d)    the expert evidence falls within a substantially established area of knowledge which is unlikely to be in dispute or there is likely to be a range of expert opinion;

(e)    a party has already instructed an expert on the issue in question and whether or not that was done in compliance with any practice direction or relevant pre-action protocol;

(f)    questions put in accordance with rule 35.6 are likely to remove the need for the other party to instruct an expert if one party has already instructed an expert;

(g)    questions put to a single joint expert may not conclusively deal with all issues that may require testing prior to trial;

(h)    a conference may be required with the legal representatives, experts and other witnesses which may make instruction of a single joint expert impractical; and

(i)    a claim to privilege makes the instruction of any expert as a single joint expert inappropriate."

The court will usually give appropriate directions in relation to expert evidence in the exercise of its case management powers, but it may (and often will) do so in response to a specific application made by a party. Part 35 of the CPR contains detailed provisions with regard to experts and assessors, which are expanded in the Practice Direction supplementing Pt 35 and the Protocol for the Instruction of Experts to give Evidence in Civil Claims published in June 2005 and amended in October 2009. The following note appearing at the start of the Practice Direction explains the purpose of Pt 35:

> "Part 35 is intended to limit the use of oral expert evidence to that which is reasonably required. In addition, where possible, matters requiring expert evidence should be dealt with by only one expert. Experts and those instructing them are expected to have regard to the guidance contained in the Protocol for the Instruction of Experts to give Evidence in Civil Claims annexed to this practice direction. (Further guidance on experts is contained in Annex C to the Practice Direction (Pre-Action Conduct))."

In *Field v Leeds City Council*[31] the county court judge had refused permission to the defendant council to call as an expert witness one of its employees, who had, as a member for 10 years of the claims investigation section, been involved in looking into disrepair matters for the council. The Court of Appeal held that there was no objection in principle to a person employed by one of the parties being called as an expert by that party, provided he was properly qualified. The court noted, however, that it was important that such a person should have full knowledge of the requirements for an expert to give evidence in court and that he should be fully familiar with the need for objectivity.[32]

**38–21**

## The duties and responsibilities of expert witnesses

In recent years the courts and some of the professional bodies to which expert witnesses belong have increasingly emphasised that the primary function, and duty, of an expert witness is to assist the court on matters within his expertise. In

**38–22**

---

[31] [2000] 1 E.G.L.R. 54.

[32] See also *Admiral Management Services Ltd v Para-Protect Europe Ltd* [2001] 1 W.L.R. 2722, in which *Field v Leeds City Council*, above, was followed and applied by the Court of Appeal.

*National Justice Compania Naviera SA v Prudential Assurance Co Ltd (No.1)*[33]
Cresswell J. set out seven propositions relevant to the performance by expert
witnesses of this duty. These propositions were much quoted in the textbooks,[34]
in the course of court proceedings and in various reported judgments. The Royal
Institution of Chartered Surveyors also broke new ground by publishing a
Practice Statement and Guidance Note for Surveyors Acting as Expert Witnesses.
The Practice Statement had three striking features. First, it required members of
the RICS who accepted an appointment to act as expert witness to draw to the
attention of their lay clients, at the time the instructions were accepted, that the
Practice Statement applied. Second, it made compliance with the Practice
Statement a requirement of professional conduct for members of the RICS in
performing the function of an expert witness, so that a failure to comply would
amount to a disciplinary offence. Finally, it required a member, in the body of any
expert report which he compiled in the capacity of a witness, to set out his duties
under the Practice Statement and to confirm that he had complied with them. This
served to bring the Practice Statement to the attention of the courts and other
tribunals in which such evidence was given, as well as reminding the witness,
each time he prepared such a report, of his duties. The most recent edition of this
Practice Statement was published with effect from January 1, 2009, and a recent
second addendum is now available.

The same concern to emphasise that the primary duty of the expert witness is
to the court and not to his client underlies the similar provisions incorporated in
CPR r.35.10, which requires an expert's report (i) to comply with the
requirements set out in Practice Direction 35 (para.3.3 of which requires an
expert's report to be verified by a statement of truth in a prescribed form),[35] and
(ii) to state at the end that the expert understands and has complied with his duty
to the court. This echoes the similar declaration required by the RICS Practice
Statement.

To the same effect is para.2 of Practice Direction 35, which sets out the
following general requirements for expert evidence as follows:

"**2.1** Expert evidence should be the independent product of the expert uninfluenced by the
pressures of litigation.
**2.2** Experts should assist the court by providing objective, unbiased opinions on matters
within their expertise, and should not assume the role of an advocate.
**2.3** Experts should consider all material facts, including those which might detract from
their opinions.
**2.4** Experts should make it clear—
(a)     when a question or issue falls outside their expertise; and
(b)     when they are not able to reach a definite opinion, for example because they have
insufficient information.
**2.5** If, after producing a report, an expert's view changes on any material matter, such
change of view should be communicated to all the parties without delay, and when appropriate
to the court."

---

[33] [1993] 2 E.G.L.R. 183.
[34] See, for example, in the First Edition of this work, where the seven propositions were quoted in
full. Since these propositions have now largely been subsumed in the relevant provisions of the CPR
it has not been thought appropriate to quote them again here.
[35] See para.38–33 to 38–44, below.

The Protocol for the Instruction of Experts to give Evidence in Civil Claims, published by the Civil Justice Council in July 2005, and amended in October 2009, for the guidance of experts and those who instruct them, neatly encapsulates the relevant principles as follows:

> "Experts always owe a duty to exercise reasonable skill and care to those instructing them, and to comply with any relevant professional code of ethics. However when they are instructed to prepare evidence for the purpose of civil proceedings … they have an overriding duty to help the court on matters within their expertise … This duty overrides any obligation to the person instructing or paying them. Experts must not serve the exclusive interest of those who retain them … Experts should provide opinions which are independent, regardless of the pressures of litigation. In this context a useful test of 'independence ' is that the expert would express the same opinion if given the same instructions by an opposing party. Experts should not take it upon themselves to promote the point of view of the party instructing them or engage in the role of advocates.[36]"

## Single joint experts

An important and controversial innovation introduced by the CPR is the court's power under r.35.7 to direct, where two or more parties wish to submit expert evidence on a particular issue, that the evidence on that issue is to be given by one expert only. The introduction to Practice Direction 35 states that where possible matters requiring expert evidence should be dealt with by only one expert. The provisions relating to single joint experts are set out in para.7.[37] Those parties who wish to submit expert evidence are referred to as "the instructing parties".[38] The identity of the single joint expert may be agreed by the instructing parties but, if they cannot agree, the court itself may select the expert from a list prepared or identified by the instructing parties or direct that the expert be selected in some other manner.

**38–23**

In *Peet v Mid-Kent Area NHS Trust*[39] Lord Woolf C.J. made certain comments of a general nature with regard to the role of the single joint expert. He said:

> "As we will see when we come to the framework which is provided by the Civil Procedure Rules, the Rules permit the Court to require the parties to use a single expert. This is not a matter of choice for the parties. In the absence of special circumstances I consider that the appropriate way that the power should be exercised is to require a single expert rather than an expert for each party. It is only by so doing that control can be exercised over the costs involved."

Later, he added:

---

[36] See s.4 of the Protocol for the Instruction of Experts.
[37] See para.38–20, above.
[38] The significance of the reference to "the instructing parties" is that, in a case where there are more than two parties, not all parties may wish to rely upon expert evidence. Those parties which do not wish to do so are not required to instruct the joint expert and can challenge his evidence in the same way as they could challenge any other expert evidence put before the court, but they will not, of course, have any expert evidence of their own upon which they can rely.
[39] [2001] EWCA Civ 1703; [2002] 1 W.L.R. 210.

"In relation to Part 35.7 I would emphasise that the power of the court to direct that the evidence be given by a single joint expert is unrestricted. The court has a wide discretion and that discretion has to be used in order to further the overriding principles set out in Part 1 of CPR."

**38–24** Referring to the framework provided by the Rules, Lord Woolf M.R. stressed that it was "designed to provide a flexible framework", and that "there will always be cases which require special treatment because of particular issues which arise thereunder." Nonetheless, he stated, "in general the Rules should cater satisfactorily for the great majority of situations where expert evidence ... is required."

Where a direction for a single joint expert has been made, r.35.8 permits each instructing party to give instructions to the expert a copy of which must be sent to the other instructing parties. The court may give directions about the payment of the expert's fees and expenses and any inspection, examination or experiments which the expert wishes to carry out. The court can, before an expert is instructed, limit the amount that can be paid by way of fees and expenses to the expert and order the instructing parties to pay that amount into court. Unless the court otherwise directs, the instructing parties are jointly and severally liable for the payment of the expert's fees and expenses.

**38–25** Rule 35.6 permits a party to put written questions to another party's expert[40] and also permits a party[41] to put written questions about his report to a single joint expert.

Neither the CPR nor the Practice Direction gives explicit guidance as to what is to happen once the single joint expert has reported.[42] However, a number of decided cases have somewhat clarified the procedures. In *Peet v Mid Kent Area Healthcare NHS Trust*[43] Lord Woolf C.J. quoted a passage from the *White Book* which said:

"If a single joint expert is called to give oral evidence at trial it is submitted, although the rule and the Practice Direction do not make this clear, that both parties will have the opportunity to cross-examine him or her, but with a degree of restraint given that the expert has been instructed by the parties."

Lord Woolf observed:

"That paragraph may be applicable in some cases, but it certainly should not be regarded as being of general application. I summarise my reasons for so saying. The starting point is: unless there is reason for not having a single expert, there should only be a single expert. If there is no reason which justifies more evidence than that from a single expert on any particular topic, then again in the normal way the report prepared by the single expert should be the evidence in the case on the issues covered by the expert's report. In the normal way,

---

[40] This is dealt with in more detail in paras 38–29 to 38–30, below.
[41] The right is not, apparently, confined to "the instructing parties" nor are the instructing parties themselves prevented from making use of this procedure.
[42] However, it must be borne in mind that the provisions of the CPR as to experts generally apply equally to a single joint expert, who may thus, for example, make a written request for directions to assist him in carrying out his function as an expert under r.35.14(1). Such directions could include a requirement for the parties to provide information to the single joint expert, by analogy with the provisions of r.35.9.
[43] [2001] EWCA Civ 1703. [2002] 1 W.L.R. 210

therefore, there should be no need for that report to be amplified or tested by cross-examination. If it needs amplification, or if it should be subject to cross-examination, the court has a discretion to allow that to happen. The court may permit that to happen either prior to the hearing or at the hearing. But the assumption should be that the single joint expert's report is the evidence. Any amplification or cross-examination should be restricted as far as possible. Equally, where the parties agree that there should be a single joint expert, and a single joint expert produces a report, it is possible for the court to permit a party to instruct his or her own expert and for the expert to be called at the hearing. However, there must be good reason for that course to be adopted ... if there is an issue which requires cross-examination, or requires additional evidence, that is one thing. But the court should seek to avoid that situation arising, otherwise the objectives of having a single expert will in many situations be defeated."

Lord Woolf's general approach was applied by the Court of Appeal in *Popek v National Westminster Bank Plc*,[44] in which the court upheld a decision by the judge to strike out a claim, where the single joint expert's report demonstrated that there had been no breach of duty on the part of the defendant. The Court of Appeal held that the judge had not been in error in depriving the claimant of the opportunity of putting his version of facts to the expert by way of cross-examination. However, it is to be noted that, in that case, the claimant had not taken the opportunity at an earlier stage to put his disputed version in questions to the single joint expert.

**38–26**

The reluctance to allow extensive cross-examination of a single joint expert exhibited by these decisions must not, however, be pressed too far, since in some cases even where a joint expert has reported, a right to cross-examine and make submissions may be indispensable in the interests of justice, as appears from the decision of Neuberger J. in *Layland v Fairview New Homes Plc*.[45] In that case a valuer had been appointed as single joint expert to assess the amount of diminution in the value of a flat which the claimants claimed had suffered as a result of the grant of planning permission to build an incinerator and power plant on nearby land. The expert concluded that there was no diminution in value and the defendants accordingly applied for summary judgment. Neuberger J. held that, in order to resist summary judgment dismissing the claim under Pt 24, the claimants had to establish that they had a real prospect of successfully challenging the single joint expert's conclusion. Provided there was a prospect of the expert through cross-examination, or the court, through submissions, being persuaded to a different conclusion than that supported by the single joint expert's report, the claim could not be dismissed on the basis of the expert's view. Since there were points which could be put to the expert and accepted by him or by the court and since the court could not properly reject those points without hearing how the single joint expert dealt with them, it would not be right to grant summary judgment dismissing the claim. Although the claimants' case on diminution looked weak and speculative and even if successful was unlikely to result in a large award, it could not fairly be said to stand no realistic chance of success.

---

[44] [2002] EWCA Civ 42.
[45] [2002] EWHC 1350 (Ch).

**38–27**    In *Pattison v Cosgrove*[46] a single joint expert had been appointed in a boundary dispute to report on various issues including the position of the boundary and whether certain works of excavation had undermined certain structures. Having received the single joint expert's report, both parties put further questions to the single joint expert. Subsequently one of the parties applied to the court for permission to call another expert. This was refused. On appeal, Neuberger J. allowed the application. He said:

> "Although it would be wrong to pretend that this is an exhaustive list, the factors to be taken into account when considering an application to permit a further expert to be called are these. First, the nature of the issue or issues; secondly, the number of issues between the parties; thirdly, the reason the new expert is wanted; fourthly, the amount at stake and, if it is not purely money, the nature of the issues at stake and their importance; fifthly, the effect of permitting one party to call further expert evidence on the conduct of the trial; sixthly, the delay, if any, in making the application; seventhly, any delay that the instructing and calling of the new expert will cause; eighthly, any other special features of the case; and, finally and in a sense all embracing, the overall justice to the parties in the context of the litigation."[47]

**38–28**    It should be noted that the single joint expert is not appointed by the court to advise it or to present evidence to it.[48] It follows that the report of the single joint expert is evidence available to each of the instructing parties which that party may or may not decide to put in evidence. It seems that the party putting in the evidence would then be bound by it and could not dispute it by, for example, cross-examining the single joint expert. Where questions have been put to the single joint expert by a party under r.35.6, his answers will be treated as part of his report by virtue of r.35.6(3). It is thus likely that, in a typical case, where there has been a direction for a single joint expert, the report will consist of the expert's original report together with answers to such questions as the parties have chosen to put to him. If one of the instructing parties is entirely content with the result of this process, he will put the report in evidence and make it part of his case. If all of the parties take this course the expert's report will become agreed evidence. If one of the instructing parties is not happy with the report of the single joint expert (including his replies to any questions which that party has submitted) that party may decide not to put the report in evidence. His problem will then be that he has no evidence of his own on this particular issue, unless he is able to persuade the court that, notwithstanding the fact that a direction for a single joint expert has been made, it would be appropriate for him to have permission to instruct his own expert dealing with that particular issue. A party which has not put the report of the single joint expert in evidence as part of his case (whether or not he is one of the "instructing parties") would be entitled to seek a direction that the single joint expert is to give evidence, and to cross-examine him. Although that party might well have the benefit of advice from his own expert in the relevant discipline on that particular issue, which could form the basis for cross-examination, that expert could not be called (unless the court has given permission).

---

[46] [2001] C.P. Rep. 68.
[47] See further on the circumstances in which a party will be allowed to instruct a new expert, *Daniels v Walker* [2000] 1 W.L.R. 1382 and *Peet v Mid Kent Healthcare NHS Trust* [2002] 1 W.L.R. 210.
[48] The appointment of an assessor under Pt 35 is quite distinct—see r.35.15 and paras 10.1 to 10.4 of the Practice Direction *Experts and Assessors*, which govern this procedure.

Even at the time of writing (July 2013) it remains unclear how often the court will make a direction for a single joint expert in dilapidations cases; and whether such experts will be directed on the issue of what breaches exist, what remedial works are required, what is the proper pricing of those works, what damage (if any) has been caused to the landlord's reversion, or in relation to all these issues. The authors' impression is that joint experts are not appointed in dilapidations claims with any great frequency in major claims in the TCC, although it may be that such appointments are more readily made, in the interests of proportionality, in smaller claims in the County Court.

Neither the CPR nor the Practice Direction require the court to give any special status to the evidence of a single joint expert. In practice, of course, the opinion of a single joint expert, chosen by more than one party (or by some process directed by the court), instructed by those parties and having been subjected to questioning by those parties, is likely to be considered by the court as being especially authoritative, quite apart from the fact, in most cases where a joint expert has been appointed, there will be no other expert evidence on that particular issue.

## Written questions to experts

CPR r.35.6 allows each party to put to an expert instructed by another party or to a single joint expert written questions about his report. Such questions may be put once only, must be put within 28 days of service of the expert's report and must be for the purpose only of clarification of the report (unless the court gives permission or the other party agrees).   **38–29**

It is important to note that the answers to such questions become part of the evidence of the expert who has provided the answers, that is to say they become part of the evidence being relied upon by the party who has instructed the expert. Accordingly, the party who has asked the question can (if the answer supports his case) accept that part of the evidence but retains the right (where the answer does not support his case) to cross-examine the expert upon it and (to the extent that the directions given permit this) call evidence to contradict or undermine the answer given. Thus it seems that the right to ask questions can usefully be used both (a) to obtain the expert's confirmation that he accepts certain points upon which the questioning party wishes to rely but also (b) to expose for cross-examination a view of the expert which is thought to be vulnerable to attack. The power to put such questions may also draw out useful background material, such as whether there are particular matters upon which the expert has relied in order to support particular conclusions already stated in his report.

Tactically, the party putting the questions will have to consider to what extent the points which he might raise can be more effectively dealt with in cross-examination and to what extent he wishes the other party's expert to set out in advance of cross-examination his answer to the question.

Where a party has put a written question to an expert and the expert does not answer that question, the court is entitled under CPR r.35.6(4) to order that the party who instructed the expert may not rely upon his evidence and/or that the party may not recover the fees and expenses of that expert from any other party.   **38–30**

## Discussions between experts

**38–31**  CPR r.35.12 provides that the court may, at any stage, direct a discussion between experts for the purpose of requiring them to (a) identify and discuss the expert issues in the proceedings, and (b) where possible, reach agreed opinion on those issues. The court may specify the issues which the experts must discuss and may direct that, following a discussion, the experts must prepare a statement for the court showing (a) those issues on which they agree and (b) those issues on which they disagree and a summary of their reasons for disagreeing. Practice Direction 35 contains the following further provisions in relation to discussions between experts:

> "**9.1** Unless directed by the court discussions between experts are not mandatory. Parties must consider, with their experts, at an early stage, whether there is likely to be any useful purpose in holding an experts' discussion and if so when.
>
> **9.2** The purpose of discussions between experts is not for experts to settle cases but to agree and narrow issues and in particular to identify:
> (i)   the extent of the agreement between them;
> (ii)  the points of and short reasons for any disagreement;
> (iii) action, if any, which may be taken to resolve any outstanding points of disagreement; and
> (iv)  any further material issues not raised and the extent to which these issues are agreed.
>
> **9.3** Where the experts are to meet, the parties must discuss and if possible agree whether an agenda is necessary, and if so attempt to agree one that helps the experts to focus on the issues which need to be discussed. The agenda must not be in the form of leading questions or hostile in tone.
>
> **9.4** Unless ordered by the court, or agreed by all parties, and the experts, neither the parties nor their legal representatives may attend experts' discussions.
>
> **9.5** If the legal representatives do attend—
> (i)   they should not normally intervene in the discussion, except to answer questions put to them by the experts or to advise on the law; and
> (ii)  the experts may if they so wish hold part of their discussions in the absence of the legal representatives.
>
> **9.6** A statement must be prepared by the experts dealing with paragraphs 9.2(i)–(iv) above. Individual copies of the statements must be signed by the experts at the conclusion of the discussion, or as soon thereafter as practicable, and in any event within 7 days. Copies of the statements must be provided to the parties no later than 14 days after signing.
>
> **9.7** Experts must give their own opinions to assist the court and do not require the authority of the parties to sign a joint statement.
>
> **9.8** If an expert significantly alters an opinion, the joint statement must include a note or addendum by that expert explaining the change of opinion."

The procedure under CPR r.35 conforms to the well-established principle that the experts' overriding duty is to the court. Thus, in *Robin Ellis Ltd v Malwright Ltd*[49] (decided under the former Rules of the Supreme Court) the Official Referee, Judge Bowsher, QC, pointed out that it is not for the parties to tell the experts what opinions they are allowed to hold, and that the duty owed to the court by the experts is to express in their agreement the views which they themselves honestly hold.

The effect of paras 9.4 and 9.5 of Practice Direction 35 is that neither the parties nor their legal representatives are entitled to attend experts' discussions, unless the court otherwise orders or the parties and the experts agree, and if legal

---

[49] [1999] B.L.R. 81.

representatives do attend, (i) their role will normally be limited to answering questions put to them by the experts or advising on the law, and (ii) the experts are entitled, if they wish, to hold part of their discussions without the legal representatives present. Moreover, by paras 9.6 and 9.7, the joint statement must be signed at the conclusion of the discussion, or as soon thereafter as practicable, and in any event within 7 days, and the experts do not need their clients' authority to sign a joint statement. The combined effect of these provisions is to minimise the involvement of lawyers in the process of experts' meetings. In particular, it is no longer open to a party to instruct an expert to attend an experts' meeting on terms that he has no authority to sign a joint statement until it is approved by that party's solicitor.

Experts will sometimes be able to reach agreement to such an extent that their attendance at trial can be dispensed with. For example, the respective building surveyors may be able to agree on what work should have been done and what it would have cost, leaving the question of damage to the reversion as the only live issue at trial. Even where complete agreement on a substantive issue does not prove possible, the experts will often be able to reach agreement in relation to matters which would otherwise take up time at trial. For example, valuers should in most cases be able to agree on matters such as floor areas and the details of their respective comparables, and building surveyors who differ on what work is required should nonetheless be able to agree on the cost of the work for which each contends.

Echoing the previous provision to the effect that the meeting between experts should be on a "without prejudice" basis, CPR r.35.12(4) provides that the content of the discussions between experts shall not be referred to at the trial unless the parties agree.

During the discussions, the experts should make a proper attempt to identify and narrow the issues on which they differ. If an expert is persuaded by his opposite number that his view on a particular matter is wrong, he will be unable to write a report expressing that view, and he ought instead to set out, as an agreed matter, the view to which he has now come in the joint statement for the court. CPR r.35.12(5) provides that, where experts reach agreement on an issue during their discussions, the agreement shall not bind the parties unless the parties expressly agree to be bound by the agreement. However, this does not, of course, release the expert from his duty to the court as to the truthfulness of his evidence, so that, in practice, where an expert has reached agreement with his opposite number, the party instructing him will usually have little option but to agree its inclusion in the statement. However, in *Stallwood v David and Adamson*[50] the circumstances in which an expert witness for the claimant changed his opinion to the detriment of the claimant's case were held to be such as to entitle the claimant to call a second expert.

**38–32**

The rules clearly envisage an attempt in good faith by both experts to discuss the issues, to narrow the differences between them, and to record what common ground exists. For example, it would not be compliance with the rules for an expert to attend discussions and inform his opposite number that he has no

---

[50] [2006] EWHC 2600 (Q.B.); [2007] R.T.R. 11.

instructions to discuss anything but he is prepared to listen to what is said to him. Similarly, the meeting should not generally be used to discuss settlement of the action, because there will then be a danger that the expert will confuse his duty to the court with his duty to his client to obtain the best possible settlement. Consistently with this, para.9.2 of Practice Direction 35 provides in terms that the purpose of discussions between experts is not for them to settle cases.

The power to direct discussions may be exercised by the court "at any stage", but the most advantageous time for such discussions will normally be after the experts have had time to carry out research and to formulate personal views, but before reports are exchanged, enabling those reports to be written on the basis of the areas of agreement and disagreement identified at the meeting. Often, a further meeting after exchange of reports may be useful if the result of exchange is further to clarify the nature of the matters in difference.

## Contents of experts' reports[51]

**38–33** CPR r.35.10(1) requires an expert's report to comply with the requirements set out in Practice Direction 35. CPR 35.10(2) requires the expert to state at the end of his report that he understands and has complied with his duty to the court. CPR 35.10(3) requires the report to state the substance of all material instructions, whether written or oral, on the basis of which the report was written. By virtue of r.35.10(4), these instructions are not to be privileged against disclosure, although the court will not order disclosure of any specific document or permit any questioning in court by the other party in relation to those instructions unless the court has reasonable grounds to consider that the statement of the substance of the instructions is inaccurate or incomplete.[52]

Paragraph 3 of Practice Direction 35 provides as follows:

"**3.1** An expert's report should be addressed to the court and not to the party from whom the expert has received instructions.

**3.2** An expert's report must:

(1). give details of the expert's qualifications;

(2). give details of any literature or other material which has been relied on in making the report;

(3). contain a statement setting out the substance of all facts and instructions which are material to the opinions expressed in the report or upon which those opinions are based;

(4). make clear which of the facts stated in the report are within the expert's own knowledge;

(5). say who carried out any examination, measurement, test or experiment which the expert has used for the report, give the qualifications of that person, and say whether or not the test or experiment has been carried out under the expert's supervision;

(6). where there is a range of opinion on the matters dealt with in the report—
(a). summarise the range of opinions; and
(b). give reasons for the expert's own opinion;

(7). contain a summary of the conclusions reached;

(8). if the expert is not able to give an opinion without qualification, state the qualification; and

---

[51] Reference should also be made to the RICS Practice Statement and Guidance Note for Surveyors acting as Expert Witnesses.

[52] As to disclosure in dilapidations cases, see para.38–19 above.

(9).    contain a statement that the expert—
    (a)    understands his duty to the court, and has complied with that duty; and
    (b)    is aware of the requirements of Part 35, this practice direction and the Protocol
        for Instruction of Experts to give Evidence in Civil Claims.
**3.3** An expert's report must be verified by a statement of truth in the following form—

'I confirm that I have made clear which facts and matters referred to in this report are within my own knowledge and which are not. Those that are within my own knowledge I confirm to be true. The opinions I have expressed represent my true and complete professional opinions on the matters to which they refer.'"

The requirement in para.3.2(6) that where "there is a range of opinion on the matters dealt with in the report", the report should summarise the range of opinions, and give reason for the expert's own opinion (which echoes CPR35.10(3)), appears to be addressed to issues of practice or principle on which there is a known and acknowledged range of opinion between experts in the field. It is not thought to mean that on every occasion on which an expert thinks that another expert might disagree with him on a particular point, he is required to say so and go on to say what view that other expert might hold.

Subject to these particular provisions, the contents of an expert's report will, of course, vary from case to case. Some general points can, however, be made.     **38–34**

First, the report should always come from a named individual, rather than from a firm or company. Expert evidence is personal, in the sense that the opinions expressed in the report must be the personal opinion of an individual, and that individual may be called upon to give oral evidence and be cross-examined in due course. It follows that the report should for the most part be written in the first person singular rather than the first person plural.

Second, the report must demonstrate the witness' credentials to be considered an expert and, in order to explain the nature of his particular expertise, the report should contain a statement not merely of his formal qualifications but also something about his career and the nature of his practical experience. Once again, it is the expert's personal qualification to give expert evidence, not that of his firm, which is in point.

Third, in dilapidations cases the expert's evidence will almost always be based upon what he has observed upon his inspection of the premises, as well as other matters. He should give the dates of these inspections and, where appropriate, explain the reason for each visit, and what he observed on each occasion.

Fourth, the expert may wish to make particular points about the physical nature of the subject-matter of his inspection. He will have to decide whether the best means of conveying this to the court is by a verbal description or by reference to location plans, or photographs or a combination of some or all of these.

Fifth, the expert's opinion is likely to be based upon detailed data assembled from a variety of sources. In order that the court can understand this, and rule upon the admissibility of certain parts of the evidence if necessary, it should be made clear in the body of the report what is the source and nature of the information being relied upon. Sometimes the expert will simply be setting out or referring to something of which he has first-hand knowledge, such as a schedule of dilapidations referred to by the building surveyor who drew it up. Sometimes the expert will be referring to information of a factual nature supplied by third parties; for example the expert valuer may refer to details of comparable transactions supplied to him by other agents. Sometimes the data will be of a more generalised nature, such as statistical surveys, analyses of market trends or indices of building costs.

Last, having thus demonstrated the material, factual and otherwise, upon which he evidence is based, the expert should set out clearly the conclusions which he has reached. He should also set out in as much detail as he considers appropriate the method and line of reasoning which has led him to his conclusions.

**38–35**    Throughout his report, the expert must bear in mind that he is required to be objective, and to express his honest opinion. He must not put forward arguments which he does not believe in, and he must not express opinions which he does not in fact hold. He should avoid giving any impression of having "descended into the arena". Where there is a point that can fairly be made against him, he should acknowledge it and say why it does not cause him to change his views. He should aim for a balanced and fair assessment of the subject-matter of his report.

## INTEREST

### Interest

**38–36**    The court has power to award simple interest at such rate as the court thinks fit or as may be prescribed on all or any part of a debt or damages in respect of which judgment is given, or payment is made before judgment, for all or any part of the period between the date when the cause of action arose and the date of payment or judgment, whichever is the earlier.[53] Interest may be calculated at different rates in respect of different periods.[54] The court cannot award interest on arrears of contractual interest.[55]

The purpose of an award of interest is not to punish the defendant but to compensate the claimant for being kept out of his money.[56] It follows that, whilst the court retains an overriding discretion not to award interest, in practice interest is awarded relatively readily, particularly where the parties are commercial parties.

Where damages are awarded for disrepair, interest will generally be awarded from the date on which the cause of action arose until the date of judgment. Thus, interest on damages for failure to yield up in repair will run from the term date of the lease until the date of judgment. This fact must be borne in mind by tenants who are considering making a Pt 36 offer.[57]

The rate of interest is within the court's discretion. However, a relevant factor in a dilapidations claim between commercial parties is likely to be the rate which

---

[53]  Senior Courts Act 1981 s.35A; County Courts Act 1984 s.69(1).
[54]  Senior Courts Act 1981 s.35A(6); County Courts Act 1984 s.69(5).
[55]  Senior Courts Act 1981 s.35A(4); County Courts Act 1984 s.69(4).
[56]  *London, Chatham & Dover Railway Co Ltd v South Eastern Railway Co Ltd* [1893] A.C. 429 per Lord Herschell at 437.
[57]  See CPR r.36.3(3). See further on Pt 36 offers paras 34–19 to 34–21, above.

the claimant would have had to pay to borrow the sum awarded in the judgment.[58] In practice, interest is likely to be awarded at a stated per cent above base rate.

In *Johnsey Estates (1990) Ltd v Secretary of State for the Environment, Transport and the Regions*[59] the diminution in the value of the reversion was held to be £200,000. Interest was awarded on that sum from the term date of the lease.

**38–37**

In *Craven (Builders) Ltd v Secretary of State for Health*[60] the diminution in the value of the reversion was assessed at £40,000. The tenant accepted that prima facie interest should be payable from the term date but argued that the landlord should be deprived of two and a half years' interest because it had delayed, in breach of a court order to set down, in bringing the action on for trial. Neuberger J. rejected that contention on the principal ground that he was not satisfied that the landlord was substantially to blame or that there had been any unreasonable delay. He added that if the delay had been after the Civil Procedure Rules had come into force and if he had been satisfied that the delay was not merely failure to obey court orders but was due to the landlord delaying in some way or another, then he would have deprived the landlord of some interest, and he might even have done so even if it had not been established that it was the landlord's fault.

In *Grand v Gill*[61] the tenant succeeded in recovering damages for breach of the landlord's implied repairing covenant under s.11 of the Landlord and Tenant Act 1985. Interest was awarded at 2 per cent from a later date than the date of the issue of the claim to reflect the fact that the damages awarded included a material element of compensation in respect of a period subsequent to the issue of the claim.

In *Pgf II SA v Royal & Sun Alliance Insurance Plc*[62] interest was awarded on damages for terminal dilapidations at the rate which the landlord had to pay to finance a refurbishment carried out after the term date of the lease, which was 3 per cent over LIBOR (the London Inter-Bank Offered Rate). The judge rejected a submission, based on a statement in *McGregor on Damages*,[63] that the appropriate rate was one per cent over base rate.

In *Twinmar Holdings v Klarius UK*[64] interest was awarded on damages for terminal dilapidations from the date of termination of the lease at 3 per cent over base rate.

It should be noted that interest can only be awarded on money claimed in proceedings.[65] There is no power to award interest where the defendant discharges his liability for the debt or damages before the claimant commences proceedings. This fact should be borne in mind by tenants who are liable to pay the cost of work carried out by the landlord under a covenant allowing him to enter and carry out remedial work at the tenant's expense. If the debt is paid

---

[58] Cf. *Claymore Services Ltd v Nautilus Properties Ltd* [2007] B.L.R. 452 at 461, in which Jackson J. reviewed the authorities; *Pgf II SA v Royal & Sun Alliance Insurance Plc* [2010] EWHC 1459 (TCC).
[59] [2001] 2 E.G.L.R. 128.
[60] [2001] 1 E.G.L.R. 128.
[61] [2011] EWCA Civ 554.
[62] Above.
[63] 18th edn at para.15–116.
[64] [2013] EWHC 944 (TCC).
[65] Senior Courts Act 1981 s.35A(3); County Courts Act 1984 s.69(3).

before the landlord commences proceedings, then (absent a contractual interest clause in the lease) there will be no liability for interest. If, on the other hand, the debt is paid shortly after proceedings have been brought, then the landlord will be entitled to ask for interest to be awarded in relation to the period beginning on the date when the liability to pay arose. Where the defendant is an original tenant, then interest may be awarded from the date of the assignee's default, even though the original tenant was unaware of the default at the time.[66] However, the court may be persuaded to adopt a more realistic approach and award interest only from the date on which the defendant first became aware of the assignee's default.[67]

## Offers to settle

**38–38** It should be noted that CPR Pt 36 contains provisions entitling the court to award interest in circumstances where a Pt 36 offer is made and not accepted, and the relevant party fails to do any better at trial. These provisions are considered at para.34–19 et seq., above.

---

[66] See *Allied London Investments Ltd v Hambro Life Assurance Co Ltd (No.2)* [1985] 1 E.G.L.R.45.
[67] *Estates Gazette Ltd v Benjamin Restaurants Ltd* [1994] 1 W.L.R. 1528.

# CHAPTER 39

## ALTERNATIVES TO LITIGATION

### INTRODUCTORY

Most dilapidations disputes are resolved by agreement. The positive encouragement given to the use of alternative dispute resolution by the CPR and the relevant Protocols[1] has increased the number of claims resolved in this way, and that trend is likely to continue. In many cases, it will be possible for the parties or their advisers to reach agreement between themselves without the need to involve any third party. In other cases, it will be possible to reach agreement only after an early neutral evaluation[2] and/or a mediation.[3] If agreement cannot be reached, it will be necessary to consider the appropriate forum for resolving the dispute. The general practice in the past has been for the claiming party to institute proceedings in court. However, litigation is not always the best way of resolving a dilapidations dispute. Other possibilities are arbitration[4] or expert determination.[5] These have a number of potential advantages when compared with litigation, and consideration should always be given to whether one or other would be the better way of having the claim determined.

**39–01**

### THE COURT'S APPROACH

One of the principal objectives of the CPR is to encourage the settlement of disputes by the use of alternative dispute resolution (ADR). The court's duty under the CPR to further the overriding objective by actively managing cases includes (among other things) (i) encouraging the parties to use an ADR procedure if the court considers that appropriate and facilitating the use of such procedure, and (ii) helping the parties to settle the whole or part of the case.[6] The

**39–02**

---

[1] See para.37–02, below.
[2] See para.37–03, below.
[3] See para.37–04, below.
[4] See para.37–05 et seq., below.
[5] See para.37–07, below.
[6] CPR r.1.4(2). Note, however, that the court's power does not include ordering reluctant parties to use ADR as opposed to encouraging and facilitating them to do so. In *Halsey v Milton Keynes General NHS Trust* [2004] 4 All E.R. 920 the Court of Appeal said that even if, contrary to its view, the court has jurisdiction to order unwilling parties to refer their disputes to mediation, it was difficult to conceive of circumstances in which it would be appropriate to exercise it. It was said that "it is one thing to encourage the parties to agree to mediation, even to encourage them in the strongest terms. It is another to order them to do so. It seems to us that to oblige truly unwilling parties to refer their disputes to mediation would be to impose an unacceptable obstruction on their right of access to the court".

powers available to the court include (at the request of the parties or of its own initiative) directing a stay of proceedings for the purposes of enabling the parties to try to settle the case by ADR or other means, and to extend the stay until such date or for such period as it considers appropriate.[7] Both the Chancery Guide and the Queen's Bench Guide provide that parties are encouraged to use ADR (such as, but not confined to, mediation and conciliation) as a possible means of resolving disputes or particular issues, and go on to point out that the settlement of disputes by ADR can significantly reduce costs, save parties the delay of litigation, enable parties to settle their disputes while preserving their existing commercial relationships and provide a wider range of solutions than those offered in litigation.[8]

Consistently with this, the Pre-Action Protocol for Claims for Damages in Relation to the Physical State of Commercial Property at the Termination of a Tenancy (the Dilapidations Protocol) requires the parties to consider whether some form of ADR procedure would be more suitable than litigation, pointing out that the courts take the view that litigation should be a last resort and that claims should not be issued prematurely when a settlement is still actively being explored.[9] A similar position is taken in the Pre-Action Protocol for Housing Disrepair Cases.[10] Both Protocols are considered in Ch.37, above.

An unreasonable failure by one party to take part in ADR may be taken into account by the court when deciding what costs order to make and may, depending on the circumstances, be a reason for depriving that party of some or all of its costs even though it has been successful in the litigation. The leading case is *Halsey v Milton Keynes General NHS Trust*,[11] in which the Court of Appeal held that a departure from the general rule that the unsuccessful party will be ordered to pay the costs of the successful party[12] is not justified unless it is shown (the burden being on the unsuccessful party) that the successful party acted unreasonably in refusing to agree to ADR. It was further held that in deciding whether such party has acted unreasonably, the court must bear in mind the advantages of ADR over the court process, although there is no presumption in favour of mediation: the question must be determined having regard to all the circumstances of the case, which include (but are not limited to) the following: (i) the nature of the dispute; (ii) the merits of the case; (iii) the extent to which other settlement methods had been attempted; (iv) whether the costs of ADR were disproportionately high; (v) whether any delay in setting up and attending the ADR would have been prejudicial; and (vi) whether the ADR had a reasonable prospect of success. Within these parameters, reasonableness is a question of fact in each case.[13] A party who agrees to mediation but then takes an unreasonable position in the mediation is in the same position as one who unreasonably refuses to mediate.[14]

---

[7] See generally CPR r.26.4 and the Practice Direction to CPR Pt 26.

[8] Chancery Guide, Ch.17; Queen's Bench Guide, para.6.6.

[9] The Dilapidations Protocol, para.8.1.

[10] The Pre-Action Protocol for Housing Disrepair Cases, para.4.1.

[11] [2004] 4 All E.R. 920.

[12] CPR r.44.3(2).

[13] The relevant cases are considered in the *White Book*, Vol.1, at para.44.3.13.

[14] *Earl of Malmesbury v Strutt & Parker* [2008] EWHC 424.

## EARLY NEUTRAL EVALUATION

An early neutral evaluation (ENE) is a without prejudice, non-binding, early **39–03**
evaluation of the dispute or of particular issues by a neutral third party (who may,
where the dispute has already reached the courts, be a judge). The purpose is to
give the parties some idea of the strengths and weaknesses of their respective
cases and of the likely reaction of the court to the various arguments. The
evaluator's assessment may enable them to compromise their dispute entirely or
to agree particular facts or issues with a view to shortening the trial.

ENE is specifically referred to in the Technology and Construction Court
Guide,[15] which provides (among other things) that an ENE may be carried out by
any appropriately qualified person, whose opinion is likely to be respected by the
parties; that in an appropriate case and with the consent of the parties, a TCC
judge may provide an ENE either in respect of the full case or of particular issues
arising within it; and that such an ENE will not, save with the agreement of the
parties, be binding on the parties.[16] Where the parties wish the ENE to be carried
out by the court, the assigned judge may choose to do the ENE himself, in which
case he will take no further part in the proceedings once he has produced the ENE
unless the parties otherwise agree, or he may select another available TCC judge
to undertake the ENE.[17] The judge undertaking the ENE will give directions for
the preparation and conduct of the ENE, which may include a stay of the
substantive proceedings.[18] The ENE may be carried out entirely on paper or there
may be a hearing with or without evidence.[19] The parties should agree whether
the entire ENE procedure is to be without prejudice, or whether it can be referred
to at any subsequent trial or hearing.[20]

Although the relevant part of the Technology and Construction Court Guide
obviously only applies to claims which are before that court, there is no reason in
principle why the ENE procedure cannot be used in relation to a dilapidations
dispute which has not yet reached the stage of litigation. It is thought that this
may be particularly helpful where settlement of the claim is being held up by a
few key sticking points, such as (for example) the meaning of a particular clause
in the lease or the extent to which the tenant is liable for a particular item or items
in the schedule of dilapidations.

The evaluator may be appointed either by agreement or by an appointing body
(such as CEDR or the RICS). His identity will obviously depend on the
circumstances, but in dilapidations cases he will generally be a lawyer, surveyor
or engineer experienced in the relevant field. It will usually be advisable to enter
into a written ENE agreement providing for, among other things, the appointment
of the evaluator, the confidential and without prejudice nature of the process, the
procedure to be followed, the form and content of the evaluation and liability for

---

[15] Technology and Construction Court Guide, s.7.5. See also the Admiralty & Commercial Courts Guide, s.G.2.
[16] Technology and Construction Court Guide, s.7.5.1.
[17] Technology and Construction Court Guide, s.7.5.3.
[18] Technology and Construction Court Guide, s.7.5.4.
[19] Technology and Construction Court Guide, s.7.5.4.
[20] Technology and Construction Court Guide, s.7.5.4.

and payment of the evaluator's fees. A helpful model form is available from the Centre for Effective Dispute Resolution (CEDR) at *http://www.cedr.com/about_ us/modeldocs* [Accessed July 30, 2013].

The authors' experience is that ENE is seldom used in cases involving dilapidations claims, but it is thought that the procedure is one which, in principle at least, might be usefully be employed more often than appears to be the case at present.

## MEDIATION

**39–04**     A mediation is a facilitated negotiation assisted by an independent third party. The mediator's role is not to adjudicate on the rights and wrongs of the dispute but to help the parties to resolve their differences. Like an ENE, a mediation can only be undertaken by agreement between the parties. It will generally be advisable for the parties to enter into a written mediation agreement. Helpful model forms are available from the Centre for Effective Dispute Resolution (CEDR) at *http://www.cedr.com/about_us/modeldocs* [Accessed July 30, 2013]. The procedure at a mediation is flexible, and it is up to the parties to decide, either in advance or with the mediator's assistance, what form the mediation should take (for example, whether there should be an exchange of written mediation statements and/or the making of short opening statements, and whether it would be appropriate at any point for the parties or their advisers to meet face to face or whether the negotiations are best conducted via the mediator throughout the process).

In principle, mediation is well suited to the resolution of contested dilapidations claims, particularly claims for damages where it is clear that the claiming party is entitled to something and the only question is how much. In many such claims, particularly ones involving a large number of disputed items of alleged disrepair, the costs of going to court may well outweigh the value of the claim, and it will be in both parties' interests to settle at an early stage. In such cases, a skilled mediator may be able to bring about a settlement which the parties could not have achieved on their own. Moreover, (as with any negotiation) any such settlement need not be confined to the remedies available to the court. There may be other matters which are of commercial importance to the parties but which neither could achieve through the ordinary litigation process. One of the advantages of mediation is that it enables all such matters to be dealt with as part of the overall negotiation process.

As with ENE, the mediator may be appointed either by agreement or by an appointing body, and the choice will depend on the particular circumstances. However, it will generally be appropriate to appoint a person who is not only a qualified mediator but who also has some experience of dilapidations work.

## ARBITRATION[21]

An arbitrator is an independent third party who is appointed by or at the behest of the parties to decide their dispute in the same way as would a judge. However, whereas litigation is the resolution of disputes in the courts established by the state, and is thus a public process, arbitration is based on the agreement of the parties (with limited intervention by the state in the public interest through legislation, principally the Arbitration Act 1996), and is, in this sense, private. It follows that any resort to arbitration to resolve a dispute must start with an arbitration agreement. In the context of dilapidations disputes, such an agreement may sometimes be found in a clause in the lease, giving either party the right to refer to arbitration any disputes arising under the lease. In practice, however, such clauses are, in practice, rarely encountered in leases in a form wide enough to embrace the typical dilapidations dispute (as opposed to a more limited arbitration clause aimed at a particular subject-matter such as service charges, where arbitration clauses are more common, or rent review, where provision for determination by arbitration is widespread). In the absence of such a clause, arbitration will only be possible if the parties agree (for the purposes of their immediate dispute) that it is to be referred to arbitration. Provided that such an agreement is in writing (as is required by s.5 of the 1996 Act) it will be enforceable by either party. If there is an arbitration clause in the lease or if a specific agreement to arbitrate as just described exists, then if the other party seeks instead to resort to litigation a stay can be obtained from the court under s.9 of the 1996 Act.

The arbitrator should be a person who is qualified to understand the issues arising in the particular dispute referred to him. Indeed, one of the advantages of arbitration is that it enables the parties to select a person with specialist knowledge and experience of the relevant area. Often, the parties will be able to agree on a named person (in which case they should take the precaution of finding out from that person, in advance, that he is willing and able to accept the appointment). That will generally be preferable, since it gives the parties the maximum control over the identity of the person who is to decide their dispute. If they cannot agree and the arbitration arises under an arbitration clause in the lease, the clause will usually provide that in default of agreement on his identity, the arbitrator is to be appointed by a third party (often the President of the Royal Institution of Chartered Surveyors (RICS) or of the Law Society) on the application of either party. If no appointment procedures are set out in the lease, or if for some reason those which are set out fail to operate, the 1996 Act provides a "fall back" appointment procedure in the event of the parties being unable to agree on the appointee.[22] If the arbitration arises under a specific arbitration agreement for the purposes of an existing dilapidations dispute, the parties will be able either to specify a named individual in their agreement, or (if they are unable

39–05

---

[21] For a detailed treatment of the law relating to arbitration, see *Russell on Arbitration* (23rd edn) 2007.
[22] Arbitration Act 1996 ss.18 and 27.

ARBITRATION

to do that) to provide for the arbitrator to be appointed by an identified appointing body (for example, the President of the RICS under the RICS scheme considered in para.37–08, below).

Once appointed, the arbitrator will give directions for a speedy and cost-effective resolution of the dispute under s.34 of the 1996 Act. There is considerable flexibility in the range of available procedures. The arbitration may be conducted wholly in writing or there may be an oral hearing. The arbitrator may be given power to "take the initiative in ascertaining the facts and the law".[23] The strict rules of evidence may or may not apply.[24] Procedural matters may either be agreed by the parties or (in the absence of agreement) determined by the arbitrator in accordance with his general duty under s.33 to act fairly and impartially between the parties, giving each party a reasonable opportunity of putting forward his case and dealing with that of his opponent, and adopting procedures suitable to the circumstances of the particular case, avoiding unnecessary delay and expense, so as to provide a fair means for the resolution of the matter falling to be determined. Although this bears some superficial resemblance to litigation procedures under the CPR, the important difference is that the parties are given control of most aspects of arbitration proceedings (save in case of disagreement between them, where the arbitrator is to decide) while under the CPR the court's case management powers override the wishes of the parties as to how the proceedings should progress.

The arbitrator must produce a written award, which must deal with all the matters referred to him, including interest[25] and costs.[26] It is enforceable as if it were a judgment of the court.[27] The award must contain reasons (unless it is an agreed award or the parties have agreed to dispense with reasons).[28]

There is a limited right of appeal on questions of law arising out of the award (which may be excluded altogether by agreement).[29] The court also has a limited supervisory role, allowing it to correct procedural irregularities, but only in the particular circumstances set out in s.68 of the 1996 Act.

39–06    In the context of a typical dilapidations dispute, the principal advantages of arbitration over litigation are twofold.

First, the right to choose a specific person to decide the dispute enables the parties to have the matter resolved by a person from an appropriate discipline who is thought for some particular reason to be a more suitable tribunal than a judge. That may be a significant advantage where the dispute involves complex technical issues. For example, where the dispute concerns the extent to which an air conditioning installation in an office building at the end of the lease was defective and required replacement, it would be open to the parties to appoint a mechanical and electrical engineer as arbitrator. The arbitrator's power to appoint

[23] Arbitration Act 1996 s.34(2)(g).
[24] Arbitration Act 1996 s.34(2)(f).
[25] Arbitration Act 1996 s.49.
[26] Arbitration Act 1996 ss.59 to 65. It is common practice for the arbitrator to make an award determining the substantive issues which is final on all matters save costs and then, if the parties cannot agree between themselves who should pay the costs, a final award as to costs.
[27] Arbitration Act 1996 s.66.
[28] Arbitration Act 1996 s.52(4).
[29] Arbitration Act 1996 s.69.

a legal or other assessor to assist him under s.37 means that the parties are not confined to a single discipline.[30] For example, where the dispute involves matters of law, a surveyor arbitrator might appoint a lawyer to assist him,[31] or where the dispute involves both liability and quantum, a building surveyor arbitrator might appoint a valuer as assessor.[32]

The second advantage of arbitration is that the dispute is likely to be resolved more speedily. That is partly because the arbitrator is able to streamline the procedures to meet the requirements of the particular dispute (although that is perhaps less of a difference since the advent of the CPR), and also because the arbitrator is, in general terms, at the parties' disposal, whereas a judge has public duties towards other litigants with the result that a comparable case in court is unlikely to be tried within the timescale which could be achieved at arbitration.

However, arbitration also has disadvantages when compared with litigation. One has already been referred to above, namely, the limited nature of the right of appeal (although that may be of less importance in relation to disputes which turn, as do most dilapidations disputes, on questions of fact or expert opinion). A further disadvantage is that the parties must pay the arbitrator's fees, and that of any assessor whom he may appoint. In a dilapidations case, where the complexity of the issues may require a lot of time to be devoted by the arbitrator and assessor, the additional costs burden may be quite considerable. In addition, where a lengthy hearing is involved, the costs of hiring a suitable venue must also be borne in mind. By comparison, the court fees payable in respect of a comparable dispute being resolved by litigation are relatively insignificant.

Nonetheless, arbitration can be a highly effective and speedy way of resolving a dilapidations dispute. It is frequently used in relation to valuation disputes, in which context it has worked extremely well. Its use in dilapidations disputes has historically been more limited, but there is no reason in principle why that should be so. Nor does an arbitrator have to be appointed in relation to the entire dispute. There is no reason why he cannot be appointed to resolve a particular issue, or group of issues. A good example of a case where this might be appropriate is a terminal dilapidations claim where, although the schedule consists of a large number of items, the real dispute concerns one particular substantial and highly contentious item (such as the roof). In such a case, it may well be appropriate to appoint an arbitrator to resolve that single issue in the expectation that once this has happened, it will be possible to settle the remainder of the claim without difficulty.

---

[30] Although the final decision on all matters is that of the arbitrator alone, not the assessor, who is only there to advise him.

[31] A course which is often taken in complex rent review disputes.

[32] An alternative would be to appoint several arbitrators, each from different disciplines.

## EXPERT DETERMINATION[33]

**39–07**   Like arbitration, an expert determination involves the dispute being decided by an independent third party, rather than by the courts. As with an arbitrator, there is no reason why an expert cannot be appointed to resolve a particular issue, or group of issues, as opposed to the entire claim. Likewise, as with an arbitrator, there is no reason why the parties cannot refer to the decision of an expert questions which involve construction or other questions of law as well as questions of fact or expert opinion.[34]

However, there are important differences between arbitration and expert determination.[35] Principal among these are that (i) whereas an arbitrator acts on the evidence and arguments put before him by the parties in the same way as a judge, an expert must decide the matter referred to him according to his own knowledge and experience, and he is not bound by the material adduced by the parties; (ii) an expert's powers and duties derive from the agreement under which he is appointed and there is no statutory equivalent of the Arbitration Act 1996;[36] (iii) there is no right of appeal against an expert's determination (although the determination will not bind the parties if the expert has departed from his instructions to a material extent[37]); and (iv) an expert is liable to the parties for negligence whereas an arbitrator is not.

It is thought that expert determination may be less a suitable dispute resolution method than arbitration for determining a dilapidations claim where substantial issues and sums of money are involved. This is because such a dispute will generally be so complex that it cannot generally be safely entrusted to the decision of a third party without the benefit of hearing and weighing and adjudicating upon the various points put forward by the opposing parties. However, expert determination is likely to be very well suited to the determination either of disputes where the issues are straightforward or the sums at stake are relatively low, or of particular issues which the parties cannot agree and the resolution of which is likely to facilitate an overall settlement of the entire claim.

## RICS SCHEME

**39–08**   The Dispute Resolution Service of the Royal Institution of Chartered Surveyors maintains a panel of surveyors specialising in dilapidations who are available for appointment as arbitrators or independent experts to resolve dilapidations

---

[33] For a detailed treatment of the law relating to expert determinations, see Kendall, Freedman and Farrell, *Expert Determination*, 4th edn (London: Sweet & Maxwell, 2008).

[34] *Nikko Hotels (UK) Ltd v MEPC Plc* [1991] 2 E.G.L.R. 103 (doubting an obiter dictum in *Re Davstone Estates' Leases*); *Brown v GIO Insurance* [1998] Lloyd's Rep. I.R. 201. See Kendall, Freedman & Farrell, *Expert Determination*, 4th edn (London: Sweet & Maxwell, 2008) at para.11.5 et seq.

[35] For a full discussion, see Kendall, Freedman and Farrell, *Expert Determination*, para.1.12 and Ch.16.

[36] So, for example, the expert cannot award interest or costs unless specifically empowered to do so.

[37] See *Jones v Sherwood Computer Services* [1992] 1 W.L.R. 277 and *Veba Oil Supply & Trading GmbH v Petrograde Inc* [2002] 1 All E.R. 703.

disputes, or particular issues in such disputes. In many cases, of course, the parties will be able to agree on a suitable appointee without the need to use the scheme. But where agreement cannot be reached, it is thought that the scheme provides an excellent way of appointing an arbitrator or independent expert with appropriate specialist knowledge and experience of dilapidations work. An application form can be obtained from the RICS Dispute Resolution Service at Surveyor Court, Westwood Way, Coventry CV4 8JE (quoting reference DRS2D) or can be downloaded at *http://www.rics.org/uk* [Accessed July 30, 2013].

CHAPTER 40

## PROPOSALS FOR REFORM

### INTRODUCTORY

### Piecemeal development

The law of dilapidations is derived essentially from the common law, as opposed    **40–01**
to statute. Like many other areas of the English common law, it has developed
somewhat sporadically and on a case-by-case basis. There are very few statutes
of universal application, and those that there are have generally been enacted by
way of a response to the perceived unfairness of the common law in a particular
area.[1] Other statutory interventions have taken place in the residential field, but
these have not followed any coherent scheme, and in at least one area[2] reform is
long overdue.[3]
  A good example of the piecemeal and uneven development of the law is the
availability of specific performance as a means of enforcing repairing obligations.
For centuries, it was believed that the remedy was simply not available,[4] certainly
in relation to the enforcement of a tenant's covenant and possibly also in relation
to a landlord's covenant.[5] However, in 1974 an order for specific performance of
a landlord's covenant was made in relation to the reinstatement of a partially
collapsed balcony.[6] In the same year jurisdiction to grant specific performance of
a landlord's covenant in favour of a tenant of a dwelling was finally conferred by
statute.[7] Nonetheless, considerable uncertainty remained regarding the availability of the remedy in relation to a tenant's covenant.[8] In March 1996 the Law
Commission recommended that the court should be given a general power to
decree specific performance of repairing obligations, whether of landlord or
tenant.[9] That recommendation has still not been implemented, but in 1998 the

---

[1] For example, s.18(1) of the Landlord and Tenant Act 1927, and the Leasehold Property (Repairs)
Act 1938.
[2] Namely, the covenant for fitness for habitation implied by s.8 of the Landlord and Tenant Act 1985,
the rent limits of which are so low that the section has fallen completely into disuse.
[3] See para.20–16, above.
[4] See para.28–03, above.
[5] See *Jeune v Queen's Cross Properties Ltd* [1974] 1 Ch. 97 at 99G.
[6] *Jeune v Queen's Cross Properties Ltd*, above. See further para.33–08, above.
[7] Housing Act 1974 s.125, now re-enacted in the Landlord and Tenant Act 1985 s.17. See further
para.33–08, above.
[8] See the Third Edition of this work, para.22–03.
[9] See para.40–04, below.

High Court decided at first instance that power to order specific performance of a tenant's repairing covenant exists anyway.[10]

The uneven development of the law itself has tended to be matched by a deeply conservative approach to the drafting of dilapidations obligations in leases. With some exceptions, draftsmen have tended to stick to the old tried and tested formulae (such as the traditional obligation to repair and keep in repair). These have generally concentrated on the technical operations to be carried out to the premises (for example, to repair and decorate) rather than the state in which the premises are to be kept (for example, in such condition that they are fit for occupation for the purposes for which they are being let).[11] The consequence has been that in some cases the relevant obligation has been held not to have been broken even thought the premises are clearly unusable (for example, because there is no "disrepair",[12] or because the relevant work goes beyond "repair" properly so-called[13]).

**40–02**  The result of the above is that in a number of areas the law of dilapidations does not provide the sort of comprehensive solution to modern problems which a more structured and radical approach might have provided. These deficiencies are perhaps more marked in their effect in the residential field, but they are by no means limited to that field.

## The Law Commission's view

**40–03**  In March 1996 the Law Commission published a report entitled *Landlord and Tenant: Responsibility for the State and Condition of Property*.[14] The report contains a useful summary and discussion of many aspects of the existing law, and sets out proposals for reform. The introduction concludes, by reference to the decisions in *Quick v Taff-Ely Borough Council*[15] and *Habinteg Housing Association v James*,[16] that there are "serious shortcomings in the law which governs the repair and maintenance of leasehold property". The report was published prior to the decision of the House of Lords in *Southwark Borough Council v Mills*,[17] in which the House reaffirmed the general rule that the landlord gives no implied covenant with regard to the condition of the property being let, and held that two tenants of council flats had no remedy at common law for substantial interference by noise resulting from the lack of sound proofing. It is a safe assumption that the decision would have been regarded by the Commission as further support for its views on the need for reform.

---

[10] *Rainbow Estates Ltd v Tokenhold* [1999] Ch. 64. See further paras 28–04 and 28–05, above.
[11] Although see the discussion of covenants to keep in good condition in paras 4–29 and 4–30, 8–12 to 8–14, 9–41 and 9–42 and 11–46, above.
[12] As in *Post Office v Aquarius Properties Ltd* [1987] 1 All E.R. 1055. See para.8–02, above.
[13] See Ch.11, above.
[14] Law Com. No.238.
[15] [1986] Q.B. 809. See para.8–01, above.
[16] (1994) 27 H.L.R. 299. See para.19–06, above.
[17] [2001] 1 A.C. 1. See para.19–02, above.

## THE LAW COMMISSION REPORT

### The principal recommendations

Reference should be made to the report itself for the full details of the proposals. The following is a summary of its principal recommendations:

40–04

(1)    that in the absence of express agreement as to the allocation of liability for repairs there should be implied into every lease (other than a lease of a dwelling-house for a term of less than seven years, a lease of an agricultural holding, a farm business tenancy and an oral lease) a covenant that the landlord should keep the premises and any associated premises in repair. The standard of repair should be that which is appropriate having regard to the age, character and prospective life of the premises and to their locality. This is a potentially far-reaching proposal, the effect of which would be to alter fundamentally the existing law;[18]

(2)    that, subject to certain exceptions, there should be implied into every lease of a dwelling-house for a term of less than seven years, under which the dwelling-house is let wholly or mainly for human habitation, a covenant by the landlord that the dwelling-house is fit for human habitation at the commencement of the lease, and that the landlord will keep it fit for human habitation during the lease (but the landlord is not liable under the implied covenant if the property cannot be made fit for human habitation at reasonable expense). The criteria for fitness are the same as those applied in s.604 of the Housing Act 1985. One important effect of this proposal would be to shift the focus away from the remedying of physical defects (which is the position under the existing statutorily implied term[19]) to the doing of whatever is necessary to make the dwelling fit for human habitation, irrespective of whether the cause of the unfitness is disrepair properly so-called. It is thought that the proposed term would render the landlord liable, for example, to eliminate dampness resulting from condensation caused by faulty building design,[20] and to install appropriate sound proofing;[21]

(3)    that a court should have power to decree specific performance of a repairing obligation in any lease or tenancy, and that the remedy should be available to a landlord, a tenant or any other party to the lease in respect of a breach of a repairing obligation by the other party notwithstanding any equitable rule restricting the scope of the remedy. Given the position which the common law has now arrived at,[22] it is perhaps doubtful whether this proposal is needed any longer;

---

[18] For the existing law where the tenancy contains no express obligation on either party as to repairs, see para.19–02, above.

[19] i.e. under the Landlord and Tenant Act 1985 s.11. See further para.20–17 et seq., above.

[20] The carrying out of works necessary to prevent dampness caused by condensation is not, in the absence of disrepair, within the landlord's covenant implied by s.11 of the Landlord and Tenant Act 1985. See further para.8–01, above.

[21] See the facts of *Southwark Borough Council v Mills* [2001] 1 A.C. 1.

[22] See paras 28–04 and 33–08, above.

(4)    that the law of waste should no longer apply to a tenant holding under a lease, a tenant at will, a tenant at sufferance or a licensee;

(5)    that the covenant for tenant-like user should be abolished;

(6)    that there should be an implied statutory covenant or duty by which any tenant or licensee would undertake to take proper care of the premises let to him or of which he was in possession or occupation and any common parts, to make good any damage wilfully done or caused to such premises by him or any other person lawfully in occupation or visiting the premises, and not to carry out any alterations or works the actual or probable result of which is to destroy or alter the character of the premises to the detriment of the interest of the landlord or licensor, the parties to be free to exclude or modify such covenant or duty by express agreement.

## IMPLEMENTATION OF THE REPORT

**40–05**    In *Habinteg Housing Association v James*[23] Staughton L.J. said in relation to the problem in that case (an alleged infestation of cockroaches on a housing estate which the landlord was not liable to do anything about[24]):

> "We are told that the Law Commission has been considering such a problem. It is to be hoped that they will recommend a solution. What is more, it is hoped that if they do, Parliament will carry it out. Judges and lawyers are sometimes reproached when the law does not produce the right result. There are occasions when the reproach should be directed elsewhere."

In *Issa v Hackney LBC*[25] (which was decided shortly after the publication of the Law Commission report) Brooke L.J. said:

> "Parliament has now had the Law Commission's report for over six months. The resolution of this injustice lies in decisions being taken about the allocation and distribution of public sector finance to the health service and to local government which are for ministers and Parliament and not for judges to take in our constitutional scheme of things."

In *Lee v Leeds City Council*[26] Chadwick L.J. commented on the recommendation in the report that there should be an implied term as to fitness for habitation[27] in the following terms:

> "Parliament has not found time to give effect to that recommendation. At the least, it has not done so directly. Unless, as the appellants contend, the solution to the problem can be found in the provisions of the Human Rights Act 1998, the position remains 'that there continues to exist a class of case where a serious wrong continues to be without a remedy in the civil courts'."

Notwithstanding this considerable judicial encouragement, the Law Commission report has not been implemented to date, and given the passage of time since its publication, it must now be doubtful whether that will ever happen.

---

[23] (1994) 27 H.L.R. 299.
[24] See para.19–06, above.
[25] [1997] 1 W.L.R. 956.
[26] [2002] 1 W.L.R. 1488.
[27] See para.40–04, above.

# FORMS AND PRECEDENTS

This section contains a selection of forms and precedents for use in a variety of different situations. They should be regarded as no more than suggestions to be adapted as appropriate having regard to the facts of each individual case.

## 1. Section 146 Notice—Leasehold Property (Repairs) Act 1938 not applying

To A.B. Limited or other the lessee of the premises known as ....... pursuant to a lease dated ....... made between (1) C.D. Limited and (2) E.F. Limited

We, G.H. & Co., of ........, solicitors and agents for your lessor, I.J. Limited, hereby give you notice as follows:

1. In the above mentioned lease the lessee covenanted as follows:

   *[set out verbatim the covenants relied on]*

2. The above mentioned covenants have been broken and the particular breaches complained of are that there exist the defects, wants of repair and dilapidations set out in the Schedule of Dilapidations served herewith which you have failed to remedy.

3. We hereby require you to remedy all the aforesaid breaches in so far as they are capable of remedy and to make compensation in money therefor to I.J. Limited.

4. If you fail to comply with this notice within a reasonable time then it is the intention of I.J. Limited to forfeit the above mentioned lease and to claim damages for breach of covenant.

Dated .......

Signed .......

## 2. Section 146 Notice—Leasehold Property (Repairs) Act 1938 applying

To A.B. Limited or other the lessee of the premises known as ....... pursuant to a lease dated ....... made between (1) C.D. Limited and (2) E.F. Limited

We, G.H. & Co., of ......., solicitors and agents for your lessor, I.J. Limited, hereby give you notice as follows:

1. In the above mentioned lease the lessee covenanted as follows:

   [*set out verbatim the covenants relied on*]

2. The above mentioned covenants have been broken and the particular breaches complained of are that there exist the defects, wants of repair and dilapidations set out in the Schedule of Dilapidations served herewith which you have failed to remedy.

3. We hereby require you to remedy all the aforesaid breaches in so far as they are capable of remedy and to make compensation in money therefor to I.J. Limited.

4. If you fail to comply with this notice within a reasonable time then it is the intention of I.J. Limited to forfeit the above mentioned lease and to claim damages for breach of covenant.

5. You are entitled under the provisions of the Leasehold Property (Repairs) Act 1938 to serve on the lessor a counter-notice claiming the benefit of that Act.

6. Such counter-notice must be served within 28 days from the date of service of this notice upon you.

7. Such counter-notice may be served in any of the following ways:
   (1) by handing it to the lessor personally;
   (2) by leaving it at the last known place of abode or business in the United Kingdom of the lessor;
   (3) By sending it by post in a registered letter or by the recorded delivery service addressed to the lessor by name at such last known place of abode or business in the United Kingdom if the letter is not returned by the postal operator (within the meaning of the Postal Services Act 2011) concerned undelivered; and service in this manner shall be deemed to be made at the time at which the letter would in the ordinary course of post be delivered.

8. The name and address for service of the lessor is:

Dated .......

Signed .......

## 3. Letter from landlord's solicitor accompanying section 146 notice

[date]

Dear Sir,

[address of premises]

We act as solicitors on behalf of your landlord I.J. Limited. We enclose by way of service upon you a notice under section 146 of the Law of Property Act 1925 together with the Schedule of Dilapidations referred to in it.

You will note from the notice that you are required to remedy the breaches specified in it, and that if you fail to remedy those breaches within a reasonable time then it is the intention of A.B. Limited to forfeit your lease and claim damages for breach of covenant. We are instructed that I.J. Limited, having taken the advice of its surveyors, considers that a reasonable time for remedying the breaches would be three months from the date on which you receive this letter. Accordingly, if you fail to remedy the breaches within that period, then E.F. Limited will take such action against you as it may be advised. Please note that the terms of this letter do not form part of, and are not to be taken as incorporated in, the section 146 notice.

Please acknowledge receipt of this letter and its enclosures.

Yours faithfully, *etc.*

## 4. Counter-notice claiming the benefit of the 1938 Act

TO I.J. Limited or other the lessor of the premises known as ....... pursuant to a lease dated ....... made between (1) C.D. Limited and (2) E.F. Limited

We, K.L. & Co., of ......., solicitors and agents for your lessee, A.B. Limited, hereby give you notice that the said A.B. Limited hereby claims the benefit of the Leasehold Property (Repairs) Act 1938.

Dated .......

Signed .......

**5. Notice to repair pursuant to covenant to repair on notice**

TO A.B. Limited or other the lessee of the premises known as ....... pursuant to a lease dated ....... made between (1) C.D. Limited and (2) E.F. Limited

We, G.H. & Co., of ......., solicitors and agents for your lessor, I.J. Limited, hereby give you notice as follows:

1. In the above mentioned lease the lessee covenanted as follows:

   [*set out verbatim the covenants relied on*]

2. The defects, wants of repair and dilapidations shown in the Schedule of Dilapidations served herewith now exist at the demised premises.

3. You are hereby required, pursuant to clause ....... of the above mentioned lease, to remedy the said defects, wants of repair and dilapidations within [*set out time specified in clause*].

4. If you fail to comply with paragraph 3 above then the lessor will enter the demised premises and carry out the necessary remedial works pursuant to the said clause and the cost thereof will become recoverable from you in the manner therein specified.

Dated .......

Signed .......

## 6. Notice requiring access pursuant to provision in lease

TO A.B. Limited or the lessee of the premises known as ....... pursuant to a lease dated ....... made between (1) C.D. Limited and (2) E.F. Limited

We, G.H. & Co., of ......., solicitors and agents for your lessor, I.J. Limited, hereby give you notice pursuant to clause ....... of the above mentioned lease that access is required for the purposes mentioned in the said clause on [*specify date and time of day, complying with any express requirements of the clause*].

Dated .......

Signed .......

Court Forms

## 7. Part 8 claim by landlord for leave under the 1938 Act to commence proceedings for forfeiture and damages

IN THE NONESUCH COUNTY COURT

Claim No. 04123

BETWEEN:

A.B. LIMITED

Claimant

AND

C.D. LIMITED

Defendant

DETAILS OF CLAIM

1. This is a claim under the Leasehold Property (Repairs) Act 1938 ("the Act") and is made under Part 8 of the Civil Procedure Rules.

2. The remedies which the Claimant seeks are as follows:

(1) An order pursuant to section 1(3) of the Act that the Claimant have leave to commence proceedings against the Defendant for (a) forfeiture of the lease referred to in paragraph 2 below on the ground of the Defendant's breaches of its repairing obligations thereunder, and (b) damages for such breach.

(2) An order pursuant to section 2 of the Act that the Claimant do have the benefit of section 146 (3) of the Law of Property Act 1925 in relation to the reasonable costs and expenses incurred by the Claimant in reference to such breaches.

(3) An order that the Defendant do pay the Claimant's costs of these proceedings to be assessed if not agreed.

3. The legal basis on which the Claimant claims the above remedies is as follows:

(1) The Claimant is the freehold owner of the premises known as 14 and 14A, High Street, Nonesuch ("the premises").

(2) By a lease dated 5th February 2006 made between (1) E.F. Limited and (2) G.H. Limited ("the lease") the premises were demised for a term of ten years from 25th December 2005 at the initial yearly rent of £75,000 (subject to review) and otherwise subject to the covenants on the part of the tenant therein contained.

(3) The Claimant will refer to the lease at the trial for its full terms and true effect.

(4) On or about 1st April 2006 the reversion immediately expectant upon the determination of the lease became vested in the Claimant.

(5) On or about 19th July 2007 the term of the lease was assigned to and became vested in the Defendant.

(6) By clause 2(7) of the lease the tenant covenanted throughout the term to repair the premises and keep the same in good and tenantable repair and condition.

(7) In breach of the said covenants the Defendant has failed to repair the premises and keep the same in good and tenantable repair and condition. Full particulars of the said breaches and of the work necessary to remedy the same are contained in the Schedule of Dilapidations which is Exhibit "JK1" to the Witness Statement of Mr James Kirk which is served herewith.

(8) Clause 4 of the lease contained a proviso for re-entry in the event of, among other things, the tenant failing to perform and observe its covenants therein.

(9) On 1st December 2011 the Claimant by its solicitors served on the Defendant a notice pursuant to section 146 of the Law of Property Act 1925 and section 1 of the Act specifying the aforesaid breaches and requiring the same to be remedied.

(10) By a counter-notice served on the Claimant on or about 14th December 2011 the Defendant by its solicitors claimed the benefit of the Act.

(11) The immediate remedying of the breaches is requisite for preventing substantial diminution in the value of the Claimant's reversion. Further or alternatively the value of the Claimant's reversion has already been substantially diminished by the said breaches.

(12) Further:

(1) the said immediate remedying of the breaches marked with the letter "A" in the right hand column of the Schedule of Dilapidations served herewith is requisite for giving effect in relation to the ground floor of the premises to the purposes of section 16 of the Offices Shops and Railway Premises Act 1963; and

(2) the immediate remedying of the breaches marked with the letter "B" in the right hand column of the said Schedule is requisite for giving effect in relation to the first floor of the premises to an improvement notice served on the Defendant by the Nonesuch District Council pursuant to the provisions of section 12 of the Housing Act 2004.

(13) Further, the Respondent is not in occupation of the whole of the premises having sub-let the flat on the first floor thereof to Mr and Mrs Jones and the immediate remedying of those breaches marked with the letter "C" in the right hand column of the said Schedule is required in their interests.

(14) Further, the breaches can be immediately remedied at an expense that is relatively small in comparison with the much greater expense that would probably be occasioned by the postponement of the necessary work.

(15) Further, special circumstances exist which render it just and equitable that leave should be given.

## PARTICULARS OF SPECIAL CIRCUMSTANCES

(1) The Claimant wishes to charge his freehold interest in the premises as security for a loan but has been unable to do so because of the Defendant's said breaches;

(2) The first floor of the premises is unfit for human habitation and the Claimant has on numerous occasions received complaints in respect thereof both from the said Mr and Mrs Jones and from the Nonesuch District Council;

(3) If the repairs notice served on the Defendant is not complied with then the Nonesuch District Council may do the work themselves in which event the amount expended by them together with interest will be a charge on the premises.

(16) By reason of the matters aforesaid the grounds set out in section 1(5)(a) to (e) (inclusive) of the Act exist in relation to the premises and the Claimant is accordingly entitled to the relief sought herein.

### [STATEMENT OF TRUTH]

**8. Particulars of Claim by landlord for forfeiture and damages**

IN THE HIGH COURT OF JUSTICE

QUEEN'S BENCH DIVISION

Claim No.

BETWEEN:

A.B. LIMITED

Claimant

AND

C.D. LIMITED

Defendant

PARTICULARS OF CLAIM

1. The Claimant is the freehold owner and entitled to possession of the premises known as Unit 4, Export Trading Estate, Nonesuch ("the premises").

2. By a lease dated 21st May 2000 made between (1) E.F. Limited and (2) G.H. Limited ("the lease") the premises were demised for a term of twenty one years from 25th March 2000 at the initial yearly rent of £21,500 (subject to review) and otherwise subject to the covenants on the part of the tenant therein contained. A copy of the lease is attached.

3. The Claimant will refer to the lease at the trial for its full terms and true effect.

4. On or about 1st April 2001 the reversion immediately expectant upon the determination of the lease became vested in the Claimant.

5. On or about 23rd June 2002 the term of the lease was assigned to and became vested in the Defendant.

6. The said yearly rent was increased to £81,000 with effect from 25th March 2010 pursuant to the rent review provisions contained in the Third Schedule to the lease.

7. In the lease the tenant covenanted as follows:

(1) By clause 2(13), throughout the term to keep the premises in good and tenantable repair and condition;

(2) By clause 2(14), to decorate the exterior of the premises in every third year of the term;

(3) By clause 2(15), to decorate the interior of the premises in every seventh year of the term.

8. In breach of the said covenants the Defendant:

(1) has failed to keep the premises in good and tenantable repair and condition;

(2) has failed to decorate the exterior of the premises in the ninth year of the term;

(3) has failed to decorate the interior of the premises in the seventh year of the term.

Full particulars of the said breaches and of the works necessary to remedy the same are contained in the Schedule of Dilapidations served herewith.

9. Clause 4 of the lease contained a proviso for re-entry in the event of, among other things, the tenant failing to perform and observe the covenants on its part therein contained.

10. On 1st December 2011 the Claimant by its solicitors served on the Defendant a notice pursuant to the provisions of section 146 of the Law of Property Act 1925 specifying the aforesaid breaches and requiring the same to be remedied.

11. By a counter-notice served on the Claimant on or about 14th December 2011 the Defendant claimed the benefit of the Leasehold Property (Repairs) Act 1938.

12. The Defendant failed to remedy the said breaches within a reasonable time from the date of service upon him of the notice referred to in paragraph 10 above or at all.

13. By an order made on 1st June 2012 in proceedings between the Claimant and the Defendant in the Nonesuch County Court under case number 041234 District Judge Rainbow granted to the Plaintiff leave pursuant to the aforesaid Act to commence proceedings against the Defendant for forfeiture of the lease and damages for breach of covenant.

14. By reason of the matters aforesaid the Claimant is entitled and by the issue and service of these proceedings hereby does forfeit the lease.

15. The Defendant's said breaches of covenant have caused the Claimant loss and damage.

## PARTICULARS

Cost of works necessary to remedy defects as shown in the said Schedule £25,100.00

Professional fees in supervising said works £3,102.00

Value Added Tax on above £4,935.35

Loss of rent during period reasonably necessary for the carrying out of the works (£81,000 per annum for 3 months) £20,250

TOTAL £60,637.35

16. The Claimant will contend so far as necessary that the above costs represent the damage to its reversion resulting from the said breaches.

17. The Defendant remains in occupation of the premises.

18. The rental value of the premises at the date hereof is not less than £81,000 per annum.

19. The Claimant's claim does not relate to residential premises.

20. The Claimant does not know of any person entitled to claim relief against forfeiture as underlessee (including a mortgagee) under section 146(4) of the Law of Property Act 1925 or in accordance with section 38 of the Senior Courts Act 1981.

21. The Claimant is entitled to and claims interest on all sums recovered herein pursuant to section 35A of the Senior Courts Act 1981 for such period and at such rate as this Honourable Court shall consider to be just and equitable.

And the Claimant claims:

  (1) Possession of the premises
  (2) Damages for breach of covenant;
  (3) Mesne profits from the date of service of these proceedings until possession shall be delivered up;
  (4) Interest under paragraph 21 above.

### [STATEMENT OF TRUTH]

**9. Defence and counterclaim by tenant for relief under section 147 of the Law of Property Act 1925 and relief from forfeiture**

IN THE HIGH COURT OF JUSTICE

QUEEN'S BENCH DIVISION

Claim No.

BETWEEN:

A.B. LIMITED

Claimant

AND

C.D. LIMITED

Defendant

DEFENCE AND COUNTERCLAIM

1. In this Defence and Counterclaim:
    (1) references to paragraph numbers are to the corresponding paragraph number in the Particulars of Claim; and
    (2) the definitions in the Particulars of Claim are adopted.

DEFENCE

2. Save that it is denied that the Claimant is entitled to possession of the premises the Defendant otherwise admits paragraphs 1 to 7 (inclusive). The Defendant will likewise refer to the lease at the trial for its full terms and true effect.

3. The Defendant admits that in breach of covenant it has allowed certain defects to accrue and remain unremedied as indicated on the annotated Schedule referred to in Paragraph 6 hereof. Save as aforesaid paragraph 8(1) is denied.

4. The Defendant denies paragraph 8(2). The Defendant decorated the exterior of the premises in accordance with clause 2(14) of the lease between about January and March 2008.

5. The Defendant admits that in breach of covenant it failed to decorate the interior of the premises in the seventh year of the term.

6. Save as aforesaid the Defendant denies paragraph 8. In particular it is denied that the Schedule of Dilapidations therein referred to accurately identifies such defects as then existed or now exist. The Defendant's detailed case in relation to each alleged defect is indicated on the annotated copy of the said Schedule which is served herewith.

7. The Defendant admits paragraphs 9 to 11 (inclusive).

8. The Defendant denies paragraph 12.

9. The Defendant admits paragraph 13.

10. The Defendant denies each and every allegation in paragraphs 14 to 16 (inclusive).

11. The Defendant will rely on section 18(1) of the Landlord and Tenant Act 1927 and will contend that such breaches as have been committed have not resulted in any diminution in the value of the Plaintiff's reversion.

12. The Defendant admits paragraph 17.

13. The Defendant denies paragraph 18.

14. The Defendant admits paragraph 19.

15. The Defendant admits that there is no such person as is referred to in paragraph 20.

16. The Defendant denies that the Claimant is entitled to or ought to be awarded interest as alleged in paragraph 21 or at all.

17. The Defendant denies that the Claimant is entitled to the relief sought or to any relief.

## COUNTERCLAIM

18. The Defendant repeats its Defence.

19. The section 146 notice served on the Defendant by the Claimant relates in part to the Defendant's failure to carry out internal decorative repairs. Such notice was unreasonable and the Defendant is accordingly entitled to and claims relief under the provisions of section 147 of the Law of Property Act 1925.

## PARTICULARS

(1) The premises are and were at all material times in an adequate state of internal decorative repair having regard to their age, character and location and the nature of the business carried on there in by the Defendant;

(2) Such lack of internal decorative repair as may have existed or exist has not resulted and will not result in any damage to any other part of the building containing the premises, nor has the value of the Claimant's reversion been diminished thereby;

(3) Complete redecoration of the interior of the premises would require the premises to be closed down for a period of at least three weeks which would be disruptive to the Defendant's business.

20. Further, the Defendant seeks relief from forfeiture on such terms and conditions as this Honourable Court shall consider to be just and equitable.

And the Defendant counterclaims:

(1) An order pursuant to section 147 of the Law of Property Act 1925 relieving the Defendant from liability to carry out the internal decorative repairs specified in the Claimant's section 146 notice.

(2) Relief from forfeiture.

[STATEMENT OF TRUTH]

**10. Particulars of claim by landlord for specific performance and damages**

IN THE HIGH COURT OF JUSTICE

QUEEN'S BENCH DIVISION

Claim No.

BETWEEN:

A.B. LIMITED

Claimant

AND

I.J. LIMITED

Defendant

PARTICULARS OF CLAIM

1. By a lease dated 4th September 2005 made between (1) K.L. Limited and (2) the Defendant ("the lease") the premises known as Nonesuch House, High Street, Nonesuch ("the premises") were demised for a term of 15 years from 24th June 2005 at the initial yearly rent of £65,000 (subject to review) and otherwise subject to the covenants on the part of the tenant therein contained. A copy of the lease is attached.

2. The Claimant will refer to the lease at the trial for its full terms and true effect.

3. On or about 1st April 2008 the reversion immediately expectant upon the determination of the lease became vested in the Claimant.

4. By clause 3(9) of the lease the tenant covenanted throughout the term to repair the premises and keep the same in good and substantial repair.

5. In breach of the said covenant the Defendant has failed to repair the premises and to keep the same in good and substantial repair.

PARTICULARS

The ornamental stonework on the northern and western elevation of Nonesuch House is cracked, loose and defective, and parts thereof have fallen off. The

969

condition of the said stonework is dangerous to members of the public using the High Street. Full particulars of the works necessary to remedy the defects are set out in the Schedule of Dilapidations which is Exhibit NA1 to the Witness Statement of Mr. Nicholas Allen served herewith.

6. The Claimant has on a number of occasions drawn the aforesaid breaches to the Defendant's attention and requested the Defendant to remedy the same. The Claimant will rely in particular upon the Claimant's solicitors' letter to the Defendant dated 1st June 2011 in which the Defendant was sent the aforesaid Schedule of Dilapidations and requested to carry out the works therein specified.

7. Notwithstanding the aforesaid the Defendant has failed to carry out the works necessary to remedy the said breaches and the Claimant believes that the Defendant will not carry out such works unless ordered to do so by this Honourable Court.

8. By reason of the Defendant's said breaches the Claimant has suffered loss and damage and the value of its reversion has been diminished.

9. The Claimant is entitled to and claims interest on all sums recovered herein pursuant to section 35A of the Senior Courts Act 1981 for such period and at such rate as this Honourable Court shall consider to be just and equitable.

And the Claimant claims:

(1) An order that the Defendant do forthwith carry out or cause to be carried out the works set out in column 3 of the aforesaid Schedule of Dilapidations;
(2) Damages for breach of covenant;
(3) Interest under paragraph 9 above.

[STATEMENT OF TRUTH]

**11. Particulars of claim by landlord for damages at the end of the term**

IN THE HIGH COURT OF JUSTICE

TECHNOLOGY AND CONSTRUCTION COURT

Claim No.

BETWEEN:

A.B. LIMITED

Claimant

AND

O.P. LIMITED

Defendant

PARTICULARS OF CLAIM

1. The Claimant is the freehold owner of the premises known as Unit 9, Export Trading Estate, Nonesuch ("the premises").

2. By a lease dated 15th April 1989 made between (1) Q.R. Limited and (2) the Defendant ("the lease") the premises were demised for a term of twenty one years from 25th March 1989 at the initial yearly rent of £15,000 (subject to review) and otherwise subject to the covenants on the part of the tenant therein contained. A copy of the lease is attached.

3. The Claimant will refer to the lease at the trial for its full terms and true effect.

4. On or about 1st April 2003 the reversion immediately expectant upon the determination of the lease became vested in the Claimant.

5. In the lease the tenant covenanted as follows:

    (1) By clause 2(13), throughout the term to keep the premises in good and tenantable repair and condition;

    (2) By clause 2(14), to decorate the exterior of the premises in every third year of the term and in the last year thereof;

    (3) By clause 2(15), to decorate the interior of the premises in every seventh year of the term and in the last year thereof;

(4) By clause 2(21) at the expiration of the term to yield up the premises to the lessor repaired and decorated in accordance with the foregoing covenants.

6. The said term expired by effluxion of time on 25th March 2010 and the Defendant vacated the premises on or before that date.

7. In breach of the said covenants the Defendant failed to keep the premises in good and tenantable repair and condition during the term; failed to decorate the exterior and interior thereof in the last year of the term; and failed to deliver up possession of the premises at the end of the term repaired and decorated in accordance with the covenants in the lease. Full particulars of the said breaches and of the works necessary to remedy the same are contained in the Schedule of Dilapidations served herewith.

8. The Defendant's said breaches of covenant have caused the Claimant loss and damage.

## PARTICULARS

Cost of works necessary to remedy defects as shown in the said Schedule: £110,000

Professional fees in supervising said works: £13,200

Value Added Tax on above: £21,560

Loss of rent during period reasonably necessary for the carrying out of the works (£110,000 per annum for 3 months): £27,500

TOTAL £172,260

9. The Claimant will contend so far as necessary that the above costs represent the damage to its reversion resulting from the said breaches.

10. By clause 2(24) of the lease the tenant covenanted to pay all costs and expenses (including surveyor's fees) incurred by the lessor in the preparation and service of a schedule of dilapidations during or after the end of the term.

11. The Claimant incurred costs and expenses amounting to £4,993.75 in the preparation and service of the Schedule of Dilapidations referred to in paragraph 7 above.

## PARTICULARS

Fees of S.T. & Co. for preparing schedule: £4,000.00

Fees of U.V. & Co. for serving schedule: £250.00

Value added tax on above: £743.75

Total £4,993.75

12. By reason of the matters aforesaid the Defendant is liable to pay the said sum to the Claimant.

13. The Claimant is entitled to and claims interest on all sums recovered herein pursuant to section 35A of the Senior Courts Act 1981 for such period and at such rate as this Honourable Court shall consider to be just and equitable.

And the Claimant claims:

    (1) Damages for breach of covenant
    (2) £4,993.75 under paragraph 11 above
    (3) Interest under paragraph 13 above.

### [STATEMENT OF TRUTH]

**12. Defence by tenant to landlord's claim for damages at the end of the term**

IN THE HIGH COURT OF JUSTICE

TECHNOLOGY AND CONSTRUCTION COURT

Claim No.

BETWEEN:

A.B. LIMITED

Claimant

AND

O.P. LIMITED

Defendant

DEFENCE

1. The Defendant is unable to admit or deny paragraph 1 of the Particulars of Claim and requires the Claimant to prove it.

2. The Defendant admits paragraphs 2 to 6 (inclusive) of the Particulars of Claim and will likewise refer to the lease at the trial for its full terms and true effect.

3. The Defendant denies each and every allegation in paragraph 7 of the Particulars of Claim. The premises were kept and maintained and yielded up in the state and condition required by the Defendant's said covenants. The Defendant's detailed case is set out in the annotated copy of the said Schedule served herewith.

4. The Defendant denies each and every allegation in paragraph 8 of the Particulars of Claim. In particular it is denied:
   (1) that it is necessary to carry out the works set out in the said Schedule or any of them in order to put the premises into repair.
   (2) that the prices shown in the said Schedule represent, in any event, the reasonable and proper cost of carrying out such works.
   (3) that the Claimant will incur the alleged or any loss of rent by reason of carrying out the said works.
   (4) that the rate of rent pleaded is the open market rental value of the premises during the period in question.

5. Further the Defendant denies that the existence (which is denied) of any defects in the premises for which the Defendant is responsible under its covenants has diminished the value of the Claimant's reversion, and the Defendant will rely so far as necessary on section 18(1) of the Landlord and Tenant Act 1927. Further or alternatively if (which is denied) any such diminution, has been caused it is denied that the same is represented by the cost pleaded in paragraph 8 of the Particulars of Claim. Accordingly paragraph 9 of the Particulars of Claim is denied.

6. The Defendant admits paragraph 10 of the Particulars of Claim.

7. The Defendant is unable to admit or deny any of the allegations in paragraph 11 of the Statement of Claim and requires the Claimant to prove them.

8. The Defendant denies paragraph 12 of the Particulars of Claim. Clause 2(24) of the lease on its true construction only applies to the costs and expenses of a Schedule of Dilapidations in so far as such Schedule sets out breaches of covenant which in fact exist. It is denied that the Schedule referred to in the Particulars of Claim was such a schedule.

9. Further or alternatively clause 2(24) only applies to costs and expenses in so far as the same are reasonable in amount. The sums claimed by the Claimant are unreasonably high.

10. The Defendant denies that the Claimant is entitled to or ought to be awarded interest as alleged in paragraph 13 of the Particulars of Claim or at all.

11. The Defendant denies that the Claimant is entitled to the relief sought or to any relief.

[STATEMENT OF TRUTH]

**13. Particulars of claim by office tenant for damages and specific performance of landlord's covenant to repair**

IN THE HIGH COURT OF JUSTICE

TECHNOLOGY AND CONSTRUCTION COURT

Claim No.

BETWEEN:

W.X. LIMITED

Claimant

AND

Z.Y. LIMITED

Defendant

PARTICULARS OF CLAIM

1. By a lease dated 3rd October 2000 made between (1) A.B. Limited and (2) the Claimant ("the lease") premises comprising the third floor of Office House, Nonesuch ("the premises") were demised for a term of fifteen years from 29th September 2000 at the initial yearly rent of £32,500 (subject to review). A copy of the lease is attached.

2. The Claimant will refer to the lease at the trial for its full terms and true effect.

3. On or about 1st June 2003 the reversion immediately expectant upon the determination of the lease became vested in the Defendant.

4. By clause 3(2) of the lease the lessor covenanted to repair and maintain the structure of Office House and in particular the roof and outside walls thereof.

5. In breach of the said covenant the Defendant has failed to repair and maintain the roof of Office House.

PARTICULARS

The roof covering is defective and leaking in many places. Water has penetrated into the premises on numerous occasions since about October 1998 and such penetration continues at the date hereof. The Defendant has on a number of occasions applied a proprietary sealant to parts of the roof covering but the same has been ineffective to prevent the leaks. The said roof covering requires to be stripped off and replaced.

6. By letters dated 1st January and 4th February 2012 the Claimant requested the Defendant to replace the roof covering but by a letter dated 10th February 2012 the Defendant declined to do so.

7. The Claimant believes that the Defendant will not replace the roof covering unless ordered to do so by this Honourable Court.

8. By reason of the Defendant's said breaches of covenant:

    (1) The Claimant's use and enjoyment of the premises has been substantially interfered with. Since about October 2003 there has been an increasing smell of damp in the premises. Since about the same time damp patches have appeared on the ceilings and walls of the premises. The rooms marked 1, 2 and 4 on the lease plan have been unusable since about 5th December 2003. The Claimant's staff have complained on numerous occasions about the state of the premises. On 3rd March 2004 the managing director's secretary gave notice to leave giving as her reason the appalling state of the premises.

    (2) Damage has been caused to the interior of the premises. Particulars of the work necessary to repair and redecorate the same and the estimated cost thereof are set out in Part I of the Schedule served herewith.

    (3) Damage has been caused to the Claimant's office equipment. Particulars of the items damaged, the nature of the damage and the estimated cost of repairing the damage or (where necessary) replacing the item are set out in Part II of the said Schedule.

9. Accordingly by reason of the Defendant's said breaches the Claimant has suffered loss and damage.

## PARTICULARS OF SPECIAL DAMAGE

Estimated cost of carrying out the works in Part I of the Schedule: £10,000

Estimated cost of repairing or replacing the items in Part II of the Schedule: £12,500

10. The Claimant is entitled to and claims interest on all sums recovered herein pursuant to section 35A of the Senior Courts Act 1981 for such period and at such rate as this Honourable Court shall consider to be just and equitable.

And the Claimant claims:

(1) An order that the Defendant do forthwith replace or cause to be replaced the covering of the roof of Office House;
(2) Damages for breach of covenant;
(3) Interest under paragraph 10 above.

[STATEMENT OF TRUTH]

**14. Particulars of Claim by residential tenant for specific performance of landlord's covenant to repair and damages**

IN THE HIGH COURT OF JUSTICE

IN THE NONESUCH COUNTY COURT

Claim No.

BETWEEN:

### (1) JOHN SMITH

### (2) HELEN SMITH

Claimants

AND

### A.B. LIMITED

Defendant

PARTICULARS OF CLAIM

1. By a written agreement made on or about 1st January 1995 C.D. Limited let to the Claimants the second floor flat known as Flat 3, 17 Villa Street, Nonesuch on a weekly tenancy at the rent of £83.00 per week payable in advance on the Monday of each week. A copy of the agreement is attached.

2. On a day unknown to the Claimants but believed to be in or about March 2000 the reversion immediately expectant on the determination of the said tenancy became vested in the Defendant.

3. By virtue of the provisions of section 11 of the Landlord and Tenant Act 1985 it was an implied term of the said tenancy that the landlord would keep in repair the structure and exterior of the premises (including drains, gutters and external pipes) and would keep in repair and proper working order the installations in the dwelling-house for the supply of water, gas and electricity and for sanitation (including basins, sinks, baths and sanitary conveniences).

4. On 14th November 2007 the First Claimant informed one Michael Smith of the Defendant's managing agents by telephone that water was leaking into the bedroom of the premises every time it rained.

5. By a letter dated 1st March 2010 the Second Claimant informed the Defendant's managing agents that the electrical installation in the premises was faulty, and in particular that (a) the light in the bedroom flickered during and after periods of rain, and (b) the Second Claimant had on two occasions received electric shocks from the power point in the living room.

6. The Claimants have since complained of the aforesaid defects to the Defendant or its managing agents on numerous occasions both by telephone and by letter.

7. In breach of the said term the Defendant has failed to remedy the said defects within a reasonable time of being notified thereof or at all.

8. Further or alternatively the facts and matters set out above constitute breaches on the part of the Defendant of its statutory duty owed to the Claimants under section 4(1) of the Defective Premises Act 1972.

9. Full particulars of the works necessary to remedy the said defects are set out in section D of the report of James Johnson F.R.I.C.S. served herewith. On 23rd April 2010 the Claimants by their solicitors sent a copy of the said report to the Defendant under cover of a letter requesting the Defendant to attend to the said works forthwith but the Defendant has failed to reply to the said letter or carry out any of the said works.

10. The Claimants believe that the Defendant will not remedy the said defects unless ordered to do so by this Honourable Court.

11. As a result of the said defects:

    (1) The Claimants have suffered discomfort, distress and inconvenience. They have been obliged to place buckets under the bedroom ceiling to catch the water every time it rains. The bedroom has smelt of damp increasingly since about December 2004, and there are patches of mould on the ceiling and walls;

    (2) On two occasions, namely 23rd February and 1st March 2009 the Claimants were forced to spend the night in an adjoining hotel because the leaks made it impossible to sleep in the bedroom of the premises;

    (3) The Second Claimant suffers from arthritis and bronchitis both of which have been exacerbated by the dampness in the premises;

    (4) The Claimants have been unable to use the power point in the living room;

    (5) Damage has been caused to the decorations in the bedroom;

    (6) The carpet in the bedroom has had to be thrown away;

    (7) The books, clothing and other possessions listed in the schedule served herewith have been damaged by damp and have had to be thrown away.

12. Accordingly, by reason of the Defendant's said breaches, the Claimants have suffered loss and damage.

## PARTICULARS OF SPECIAL DAMAGE

Cost of hotel accommodation: £117.50

Estimated cost of redecorating bedroom: £500.00

Cost of replacement carpet: £125.00

Cost of replacing items in schedule: £1,000.00

13. The Claimants are entitled to and claim interest on all sums recovered herein pursuant to section 69(1) of the County Courts Act 1984 for such period and at such rate as this Honourable Court shall consider to be just and equitable.

And the Claimants claim:

(1) An order that the Defendant do forthwith carry out or cause to be carried out the works set out in section D of the report served herewith;
(2) Damages;
(3) Interest under paragraph 13 above.

## STATUTORY MATERIAL

### Law of Property Act 1925 c.20

PART V LEASES AND TENANCIES

## 146 Restrictions on and relief against forfeiture of leases and underleases

(1) A right of re-entry of forfeiture under any proviso or stipulation in a lease for a breach of any covenant or condition in the lease shall not be enforceable, by action or otherwise, unless and until the lessor serves on the lessee a notice—

    (a) specifying the particular breach complained of; and

    (b) if the breach is capable of remedy, requiring the lessee to remedy the breach; and

    (c) in any case, requiring the lessee to make compensation in money for the breach;

and the lessee fails, within a reasonable time thereafter, to remedy the breach, if it is capable of remedy, and to make reasonable compensation in money, to the satisfaction of the lessor, for the breach.

(2) Where a lessor is proceeding, by action or otherwise, to enforce such a right of re-entry or forfeiture, the lessee may, in the lessor's action, if any, or in any action brought by himself, apply to the court for relief; and the court may grant or refuse relief, as the court, having regard to the proceedings and conduct of the parties under the foregoing provisions of this section, and to all the other circumstances, thinks fit; and in case of relief may grant it on such terms, if any, as to costs, expenses, damages, compensation, penalty, or otherwise, including the granting of an injunction to restrain any like breach in the future, as the court, in the circumstances of each case, thinks fit.

(3) A lessor shall be entitled to recover as a debt due to him from a lessee, and in addition to damages (if any), all reasonable costs and expenses properly

incurred by the lessor in the employment of a solicitor and surveyor or valuer, or otherwise, in reference to any breach giving rise to a right of re-entry or forfeiture which, at the request of the lessee, is waived by the lessor, or from which the lessee is relieved, under the provisions of this Act.

(4) Where a lessor is proceeding by action or otherwise to enforce a right of re-entry or forfeiture under any covenant, proviso, or stipulation in a lease, or for non-payment of rent, the court may, on application by any person claiming as under-lessee any estate or interest in the property comprised in the lease or any part thereof, either in the lessor's action (if any) or in any action brought by such person for that purpose, make an order vesting, for the whole term of the lease or any less term, the property comprised in the lease or any part thereof in any person entitled as under-lessee to any estate or interest in such property upon such conditions as to execution of any deed or other document, payment of rent, costs, expenses, damages, compensation, giving security, or otherwise, as the court in the circumstances of each case may think fit, but in no case shall any such under-lessee be entitled to require a lease to be granted to him for any longer term than he had under his original sub-lease.

(5) For the purposes of this section—

(a) "Lease" includes an original or derivative under-lease; also an agreement for a lease where the lessee has become entitled to have his lease granted; also a grant at a fee farm rent, or securing a rent by condition;

(b) "Lessee" includes an original or derivative under-lessee, and the persons deriving title under a lessee; also a grantee under any such grant as aforesaid and the persons deriving title under him;

(c) "Lessor" includes an original or derivative under-lessor, and the persons deriving title under a lessor; also a person making such grant as aforesaid and the persons deriving title under him;

(d) "Under-lease" includes an agreement for an under-lease where the under-lessee has become entitled to have his under-lease granted;

(e) "Under-lessee" includes any person deriving title under an under-lessee.

(6) This section applies although the proviso or stipulation under which the right of re-entry or forfeiture accrues is inserted in the lease in pursuance of the directions of any Act of Parliament.

(7) For the purposes of this section a lease limited to continue as long only as the lessee abstains from committing a breach of covenant shall be and take effect as a lease to continue for any longer term for which it could subsist, but determinable by a proviso for re-entry on such a breach.

(8) This section does not extend—

(i) To a covenant or condition against assigning, underletting, parting with the possession, or disposing of the land leased where the breach occurred before the commencement of this Act; or

(ii) In the case of a mining lease, to a covenant or condition for allowing the lessor to have access to or inspect books, accounts, records, weighing machines or other things, or to enter or inspect the mine or the workings thereof.

(9) This section does not apply to a condition for forfeiture on the bankruptcy of the lessee or on taking in execution of the lessee's interest if contained in a lease of—

(a) Agricultural or pastoral land;
(b) Mines or minerals
(c) A house used or intended to be used as a public-house or beershop;
(d) A house let as a dwelling-house, with the use of any furniture, books, works of art, or other chattels not being in the nature of fixtures;
(e) Any property with respect to which the personal qualifications of the tenant are of importance for the preservation of the value or character of the property, or on the ground of neighbourhood to the lessor, or to any person holding under him.

(10) Where a condition of forfeiture on the bankruptcy of the lessee or on taking in execution of the lessee's interest is contained in any lease, other than a lease of any of the classes mentioned in the last sub-section, then—

(a) if the lessee's interest is sold within one year from the bankruptcy or taking in execution, this section applies to the forfeiture condition aforesaid;
(b) if the lessee's interest is not sold before the expiration of that year, this section only applies to the forfeiture condition aforesaid during the first year from the date of the bankruptcy or taking in execution.

(11) This section does not, save as otherwise mentioned, affect the law relating to re-entry or forfeiture or relief in case of non-payment of rent.

(12) This section has effect notwithstanding any stipulation to the contrary.

[(13) The county court has jurisdiction under this section—

[. . . ]¹]²

---

¹ Subject to savings specified in art.12 by High Court and County Courts Jurisdiction Order 1991/724 Sch.1(I) para.1.
² Section 146(13) added by County Courts Act 1984 (c.28) s.148(1), Sch.2 Pt.II para.5 and modified by County Courts Act 1984 (c.28) s.24(2)(c).

**147 Relief against notice to effect decorative repairs**

(1) After a notice is served on a lessee relating to the internal decorative repairs to a house or other building, he may apply to the court for relief, and if, having regard to all the circumstances of the case (including in particular the length of the lessee's term or interest remaining unexpired), the court is satisfied that the notice is unreasonable, it may, by order, wholly or partially relieve the lessee from liability for such repairs.

(2) This section does not apply–

   (i) where the liability arises under an express covenant or agreement to put the property in a decorative state of repair and the covenant or agreement has never been performed;

   (ii) to any matter necessary or proper—

      (a) for putting or keeping the property in a sanitary condition, or

      (b) for the maintenance or preservation of the structure;

   (iii) to any statutory liability to keep a house in all respects reasonably fit for human habitation;

   (iv) to any covenant or stipulation to yield up the house or other building in a specified state of repair at the end of the term.

(3) In this section "lease" includes an underlease and an agreement for a lease, and "lessee" has a corresponding meaning and includes any person liable to effect the repairs.

(4) This section applies whether the notice is served before or after the commencement of this Act, and has effect notwithstanding any stipulation to the contrary.

[(5) The county court has jurisdiction under this section[ ... ]³.]⁴

**Landlord and Tenant Act 1927 c.36**

PART II GENERAL AMENDMENTS OF THE LAW OF LANDLORD AND TENANT

**18 Provisions as to covenants to repair**

(1) Damages for a breach of a covenant or agreement to keep or put premises in repair during the currency of a lease, or to leave or put premises in repair at the

---

³ Words repealed; subject to savings specified in art.12 by High Court and County Courts Jurisdiction Order 1991/724 Sch.1(I) para.1.
⁴ Section 147(5) added by County Courts Act 1984 (c.28) s.148(1), Sch.2 Pt.II para.6 and modified by County Courts Act 1984 (c.28), s.24(2)(c); amended by SI 1990/776 art.4(1)(b).

termination of a lease, whether such covenant or agreement is expressed or implied, and whether general or specific, shall in no case exceed the amount (if any) by which the value of the reversion (whether immediate or not) in the premises is diminished owing to the breach of such covenant or agreement as aforesaid; and in particular no damage shall be recovered for a breach of any such covenant or agreement to leave or put premises in repair at the termination of a lease, if it is shown that the premises, in whatever state of repair they might be, would at or shortly after the termination of the tenancy have been or be pulled down, or such structural alterations made therein as would render valueless the repairs covered by the covenant or agreement.

(2) A right of re-entry or forfeiture for a breach of any such covenant or agreement as aforesaid shall not be enforceable, by action or otherwise, unless the lessor proves that the fact that such a notice as is required by section one hundred and forty-six of the Law of Property Act, 1925, had been served on the lessee was known either—

(a) to the lessee; or
(b) to an under-lessee holding under an under-lease which reserved a nominal reversion only to the lessee; or
(c) to the person who last paid the rent due under the lease either on his own behalf or as agent for the lessee or under-lessee;

and that a time reasonably sufficient to enable the repairs to be executed had elapsed since the time when the fact of the service of the notice came to the knowledge of any such person.

Where a notice has been sent by registered post addressed to a person at his last known place of abode in the United Kingdom, then, for the purposes of this subsection, that person shall be deemed, unless the contrary is proved, to have had knowledge of the fact that the notice had been served as from the time at which the letter would have been delivered in the ordinary course of post.

This subsection shall be construed as one with section one hundred and forty-six of the Law of Property Act, 1925.

(3) This section applies whether the lease was created before or after the commencement of this Act.

## Leasehold Property (Repairs) Act 1938 c.34

### 1 Restriction on enforcement of repairing covenants in long leases of small houses

(1) Where a lessor serves on a lessee under subsection (1) of section one hundred and forty-six of the Law of Property Act, 1925, a notice that relates to a breach of a covenant or agreement to keep or put in repair during the currency of the

lease [all or any of the property comprised in the lease][5], and at the date of the service of the notice [three][6] years or more of the term of the lease remain unexpired, the lessee may within twenty-eight days from that date serve on the lessor a counter-notice to the effect that he claims the benefit of this Act.

(2) A right to damages for a breach of such a covenant as aforesaid shall not be enforceable by action commenced at any time at which [three][7] years or more of the term of the lease remain unexpired unless the lessor has served on the lessee not less than one month before the commencement of the action such a notice as is specified in subsection (1) of section one hundred and forty-six of the Law of Property Act, 1925, and where a notice is served under this subsection, the lessee may, within twenty-eight days from the date of the service thereof, serve on the lessor a counter-notice to the effect that he claims the benefit of this Act.

(3) Where a counter-notice is served by a lessee under this section, then, notwithstanding anything in any enactment or rule of law, no proceedings, by action or otherwise, shall be taken by the lessor for the enforcement of any right of re-entry or forfeiture under any proviso or stipulation in the lease for breach of the covenant or agreement in question, or for damages for breach thereof, otherwise than with the leave of the court.

(4) A notice served under subsection (1) of section one hundred and forty-six of the Law of Property Act, 1925, in the circumstances specified in subsection (1) of this section, and a notice served under subsection (2) of this section shall not be valid unless it contains a statement, in characters not less conspicuous than those used in any other part of the notice, to the effect that the lessee is entitled under this Act to serve on the lessor a counter-notice claiming the benefit of this Act, and a statement in the like characters specifying the time within which, and the manner in which, under this Act a counter-notice may be served and specifying the name and address for service of the lessor.

(5) Leave for the purposes of this section shall not be given unless the lessor proves—

    (a) that the immediate remedying of the breach in question is requisite for preventing substantial diminution in the value of his reversion, or that the value thereof has been substantially diminished by the breach;

    (b) that the immediate remedying of the breach is required for giving effect in relation to the [premises][8] to the purposes of any enactment, or of any byelaw or other provision having effect under an enactment, [or for giving

---

[5] Words substituted by Landlord and Tenant Act 1954 (c.56) s.51(2)(a).
[6] Word substituted by Landlord and Tenant Act 1954 (c.56) s.51(2)(a)(b).
[7] Word substituted by Landlord and Tenant Act 1954 (c.56) s.51(2)(a)(b).
[8] Words substituted by Landlord and Tenant Act 1954 (c.56) s.51(2)(c).

effect to any order of a court or requirement of any authority under any enactment or any such byelaw or other provision as aforesaid][9];

(c) in a case in which the lessee is not in occupation of the whole of the [premises as respects which the covenant or agreement is proposed to be enforced][10], that the immediate remedying of the breach is required in the interests of the occupier of [those premises][11] or of part thereof;

(d) that the breach can be immediately remedied at an expense that is relatively small in comparison with the much greater expense that would probably be occasioned by postponement of the necessary work; or

(e) special circumstances which in the opinion of the court, render it just and equitable that leave should be given.

(6) The court may, in granting or in refusing leave for the purposes of this section, impose such terms and conditions on the lessor or on the lessee as it may think fit.

## 2 Restriction on right to recover expenses of survey, etc.

A lessor on whom a counter-notice is served under the preceding section shall not be entitled to the benefit of subsection (3) of section one hundred and forty-six of the Law of Property Act, 1925, (which relates to costs and expenses incurred by a lessor in reference to breaches of covenant), so far as regards any costs or expenses incurred in reference to the breach in question, unless he makes an application for leave for the purposes of the preceding section, and on such an application the court shall have power to direct whether and to what extent the lessor is to be entitled to the benefit thereof.

## 3 Saving for obligation to repair on taking possession

This Act shall not apply to a breach of a covenant or agreement in so far as it imposes on the lessee an obligation to put [premises ][12] in repair that is to be performed upon the lessee taking possession of the premises or within a reasonable time thereafter.

## 4 [ . . . ][13]

## 5 Application to past breaches

This Act applies to leases created, and to breaches occurring, before or after the commencement of this Act.

---

[9] Words substituted by Landlord and Tenant Act 1954 (c.56) s.51(2)(c).
[10] Words substituted by Landlord and Tenant Act 1954 (c.56) s.51(2)(d).
[11] Words substituted by Landlord and Tenant Act 1954 (c.56) s.51(2)(d).
[12] Word substituted by Landlord and Tenant Act 1954 (c.56) s.51(2)(e).
[13] Repealed by Landlord and Tenant Act 1954 (c.56) s.51(2)(f).

## 6 Court having jurisdiction under this Act

[(1) In this Act the expression "the court" means the county court, except in a case in which any proceedings by action for which leave may be given would have to be taken in a court other than the county court, and means in the said excepted case that other court.][14]

[ . . . ][15]

## 7 Application of certain provisions of 15 & 16 Geo. 5 c. 20

(1) In this Act the expressions "lessor," "lessee" and "lease" have the meanings assigned to them respectively by sections one hundred and forty-six and one hundred and fifty-four of the Law of Property Act, 1925, except that they do not include any reference to such a grant as is mentioned in the said section one hundred and forty-six, or to the person making, or to the grantee under such a grant, or to persons deriving title under such a person; and "lease" means a lease for a term of [seven years or more, not being a lease of an agricultural holding within the meaning of the][16] [Agricultural Holdings Act 1986][17]. [which is a lease in relation to which that Act applies and not being a farm business tenancy within the meaning of the Agricultural Tenancies Act 1995][18]

(2) The provisions of section one hundred and ninety-six of the said Act (which relate to the service of notices) shall extend to notices and counter-notices required or authorised by this Act.

## 8 Short title and extent

(1) This Act may be cited as the Leasehold Property (Repairs) Act, 1938.

(2) This Act shall not extend to Scotland or to Northern Ireland.

## Landlord and Tenant Act 1954 c.56

### PART IV MISCELLANEOUS AND SUPPLEMENTARY

## 51 Extension of Leasehold Property (Repairs) Act 1938

(1) The Leasehold Property (Repairs) Act 1938 (which restricts the enforcement of repairing covenants in long leases of small houses) shall extend to every

---

[14] Section 6(1) modified by County Courts Act 1984 (c.28) s.24(1)(e).
[15] Repealed by County Courts Act 1959 (c.22) Sch.3.
[16] Words substituted by Landlord and Tenant Act 1954 (c.56) s.51(2)(g).
[17] Words substituted by Agricultural Holdings Act 1986 (c.5) ss.99, 100, Sch.13 para.3, Sch.14 para.17.
[18] Words inserted by Agricultural Tenancies Act 1995 (c.8) Sch.1 para.8.

tenancy (whether of a house or of other property, and without regard to rateable value) where the following conditions are fulfilled, that is to say,—

    (a)    that the tenancy was granted for a term of years certain of not less than seven years;

    (b)    that three years or more of the term remain unexpired at the date of the service of the notice of dilapidations or, as the case may be, at the date of commencement of the action for damages; and

    [(c)   that the tenancy is neither a tenancy of an agricultural holding in relation to which the Agricultural Holdings Act 1986 applies nor a farm business tenancy][19]

(2) [ ... ][20]

(3) The said Act of 1938 shall apply where there is an interest belonging to Her Majesty in right of the Crown or to a Government department, or held on behalf of Her Majesty for the purposes of a Government department, in like manner as if that interest were an interest not so belonging or held.

(4) Subsection (2) of section twenty-three of the Landlord and Tenant Act 1927 (which authorises a tenant to serve documents on the person to whom he has been paying rent) shall apply in relation to any counter-notice to be served under the said Act of 1938.

(5) This section shall apply to tenancies granted, and to breaches occurring, before or after the commencement of this Act, except that it shall not apply where the notice of dilapidations was served, or the action for damages begun, before the commencement of this Act.

(6) In this section the expression "notice of dilapidations" means a notice under subsection (1) of section one hundred and forty-six of the Law of Property Act 1925.

## Defective Premises Act 1972 c.35

### 4 Landlord's duty of care in virtue of obligation or right to repair premises demised

(1) Where premises are let under a tenancy which puts on the landlord an obligation to the tenant for the maintenance or repair of the premises, the landlord owes to all persons who might reasonably be expected to be affected by defects in the state of the premises a duty to take such care as is reasonable in all the circumstances to see that they are reasonably safe from personal injury or from damage to their property caused by a relevant defect.

---

[19] Substituted by Agricultural Tenancies Act 1995 (c.8) Sch.1 para.11.
[20] Amends Leasehold (Property Repairs) Act 1938 (c.34).

(2) The said duty is owed if the landlord knows (whether as the result of being notified by the tenant or otherwise) or if he ought in all the circumstances to have known of the relevant defect.

(3) In this section "relevant defect" means a defect in the state of the premises existing at or after the material time and arising from, or continuing because of, an act or omission by the landlord which constitutes or would if he had had notice of the defect, have constituted a failure by him to carry out his obligation to the tenant for the maintenance or repair of the premises; and for the purposes of the foregoing provision "the material time" means—

(a) where the tenancy commenced before this Act, the commencement of this Act; and
(b) in all other cases, the earliest of the following times, that is to say—
  (i) the time when the tenancy commences;
  (ii) the time when the tenancy agreement is entered into;
  (iii) the time when possession is taken of the premises in contemplation of the letting.

(4) Where premises are let under a tenancy which expressly or impliedly gives the landlord the right to enter the premises to carry out any description of maintenance or repair of the premises, then, as from the time when he first is, or by notice or otherwise can put himself, in a position to exercise the right and so long as he is or can put himself in that position, he shall be treated for the purposes of subsection (1) to (3) above (but for no other purpose) as if he were under an obligation to the tenant for that description of maintenance or repair of the premises; but the landlord shall not owe the tenant any duty by virtue of this subsection in respect of any defect in the state of the premises arising from, or continuing because of, a failure to carry out an obligation expressly imposed on the tenant by the tenancy.

(5) For the purposes of this section obligations imposed or rights given by any enactment in virtue of a tenancy shall be treated as imposed or given by the tenancy.

(6) This section applies to a right of occupation given by contract or any enactment and not amounting to a tenancy as if the right were a tenancy, and "tenancy" and cognate expressions shall be construed accordingly.

[ ... ]

**6 Supplemental**

(1) In this Act—

"disposal", in relation to premises, includes a letting, and an assignment or surrender of a tenancy, of the premises and the creation by contract of any other right to occupy the premises, and "dispose" shall be construed accordingly;

"personal injury" includes any disease and any impairment of a person's physical or mental condition;

"tenancy" means—

(a) a tenancy created either immediately or derivatively out of the freehold, whether by a lease or underlease, by an agreement for a lease or underlease or by a tenancy agreement, but not including a mortgage term or any interest arising in favour of a mortgagor by his attorning tenant to his mortgagee; or

(b) a tenancy at will or a tenancy on sufferance; or

(c) a tenancy, whether or not constituting a tenancy at common law, created by or in pursuance of any enactment;

and cognate expressions shall be construed accordingly.

(2) Any duty imposed by or enforceable by virtue of any provision of this Act is in addition to any duty a person may owe apart from that provision.

(3) Any term of an agreement which purports to exclude or restrict, or has the effect of excluding or restricting, the operation of any of the provisions of this Act, or any liability arising by virtue of any such provision, shall be void.

[ ... ]²¹

### Landlord and Tenant Act 1985 c.70

*Implied terms as to fitness for human habitation*

## 8 Implied terms as to fitness for human habitation

(1) In a contract to which this section applies for the letting of a house for human habitation there is implied, notwithstanding any stipulation to the contrary—

(a) a condition that the house is fit for human habitation at the commencement of the tenancy, and

(b) an undertaking that the house will be kept by the landlord fit for human habitation during the tenancy.

(2) The landlord, or a person authorised by him in writing, may at reasonable times of the day, on giving 24 hours' notice in writing to the tenant or occupier,

---

²¹ Original s.6(4) repealed Occupiers' Liability Act 1957 (c.31) s.4.

enter premises to which this section applies for the purposes of viewing their state and condition.

(3) This section applies to a contract if—

    (a)  the rent does not exceed the figure applicable in accordance with subsection (4), and

    (b)  the letting is not on such terms as to the tenant's responsibility as are mentioned in subsection (5).

(4) The rent limit for the application of this section is shown by the following Table, by reference to the date of making of the contract and the situation of the premises:

TABLE

| *Date of making of contract* | *Rent limit* |
| --- | --- |
| Before 31st July 1923. | In London: £40.<br>Elsewhere: £26 or £16 (see Note 1). |
| On or after 31st July 1923 and before 6th July 1957. | In London: £40.<br>Elsewhere: £26. |
| On or after 6th July 1957. | In London: £80.<br>Elsewhere: £52. |

NOTES

1 The applicable figure for contracts made before 31st July 1923 is £26 in the case of premises situated in a borough or urban district which at the date of the contract had according to the last published census a population of 50,000 or more. In the case of a house situated elsewhere, the figure is £16.

2 The references to "London" are, in relation to contracts made before 1st April 1965, to the administrative county of London and, in relation to contracts made on or after that date, to Greater London exclusive of the outer London boroughs.

(5) This section does not apply where a house is let for a term of three years or more (the lease not being determinable at the option of either party before the expiration of three years) upon terms that the tenant puts the premises into a condition reasonably fit for human habitation.

(6) In this section "house" includes—

(a)  a part of a house, and

(b)  any yard, garden, outhouses and appurtenances belonging to the house or usually enjoyed with it.

## 9 Application of s. 8 to certain houses occupied by agricultural workers

(1) Where under the contract of employment of a worker employed in agriculture the provision of a house for his occupation forms part of his remuneration and the provisions of section 8 (implied terms as to fitness for human habitation) are inapplicable by reason only of the house not being let to him—

(a)  there are implied as part of the contract of employment, notwithstanding any stipulation to the contrary, the like condition and undertaking as would be implied under that section if the house were so let, and

(b)  the provisions of that section apply accordingly, with the substitution of "employer" for "landlord" and such other modifications as may be necessary.

(2) This section does not affect any obligation of a person other than the employer to repair a house to which this section applies, or any remedy for enforcing such an obligation.

(3) In this section "house" includes—

(a)  a part of a house, and

(b)  any yard, garden, outhouses and appurtenances belonging to the house or usually enjoyed with it.

## 10 Fitness for human habitation

In determining for the purposes of this Act whether a house is unfit for human habitation, regard shall be had to its condition in respect of the following matters—

repair,
stability,
freedom from damp,
internal arrangement,
natural lighting,
ventilation,
water supply,
drainage and sanitary conveniences,
facilities for preparation and cooking of food and for the disposal of waste water;

and the house shall be regarded as unfit for human habitation if, and only if, it is so far defective in one or more of those matters that it is not reasonably suitable for occupation in that condition.

*Repairing obligations*

## 11 Repairing obligations in short leases

(1) In a lease to which this section applies (as to which, see sections 13 and 14) there is implied a covenant by the lessor—

- (a) to keep in repair the structure and exterior of the dwelling-house (including drains, gutters and external pipes),
- (b) to keep in repair and proper working order the installations in the dwelling-house for the supply of water, gas and electricity and for sanitation (including basins, sinks, baths and sanitary conveniences, but not other fixtures, fittings and appliances for making use of the supply of water, gas or electricity), and
- (c) to keep in repair and proper working order the installations in the dwelling-house for space heating and heating water.

[(1A) If a lease to which this section applies is a lease of a dwelling-house which forms part only of a building, then, subject to subsection (1B), the covenant implied by subsection (1) shall have effect as if—

- (a) the reference in paragraph (a) of that subsection to the dwelling-house included a reference to any part of the building in which the lessor has an estate or interest; and
- (b) any reference in paragraphs (b) and (c) of that subsection to an installation in the dwelling-house included a reference to an installation which, directly or indirectly, serves the dwelling-house and which either—

  - (i) forms part of any part of a building in which the lessor has an estate or interest; or
  - (ii) is owned by the lessor or under his control.

(1B) Nothing in subsection (1A) shall be construed as requiring the lessor to carry out any works or repairs unless the disrepair (or failure to maintain in working order) is such as to affect the lessee's enjoyment of the dwelling-house or of any common parts, as defined in section 60(1) of the Landlord and Tenant Act 1987, which the lessee, as such, is entitled to use.][22]

(2) The covenant implied by subsection (1) ("the lessor's repairing covenant") shall not be construed as requiring the lessor—

- (a) to carry out works or repairs for which the lessee is liable by virtue of his duty to use the premises in a tenant-like manner, or would be so liable but for an express covenant on his part,

---

[22] Sections 11(1A), 11(1B) inserted by Housing Act 1988 (c.50) s.116(1)(4).

    (b)  to rebuild or reinstate the premises in the case of destruction or damage by fire, or by tempest, flood or other inevitable accident, or

    (c)  to keep in repair or maintain anything which the lessee is entitled to remove from the dwelling-house.

(3) In determining the standard of repair required by the lessor's repairing covenant, regard shall be had to the age, character and prospective life of the dwelling-house and the locality in which it is situated.

[(3A) In any case where—

    (a)  the lessor's repairing covenant has effect as mentioned in sub-section (1A), and

    (b)  in order to comply with the covenant the lessor needs to carry out works or repairs otherwise than in, or to an installation in, the dwelling-house, and

    (c)  the lessor does not have a sufficient right in the part of the building or the installation concerned to enable him to carry out the required works or repairs,

then, in any proceedings relating to a failure to comply with the lessor's repairing covenant, so far as it requires the lessor to carry out the works or repairs in question, it shall be a defence for the lessor to prove that he used all reasonable endeavours to obtain, but was unable to obtain, such rights as would be adequate to enable him to carry out the works or repairs.][23]

(4) A covenant by the lessee for the repair of the premises is of no effect so far as it relates to the matters mentioned in subsection (1)(a) to (c), except so far as it imposes on the lessee any of the requirements mentioned is subsection (2)(a) or (c).

(5) The reference in subsection (4) to a covenant by the lessee for the repair of the premises includes a covenant—

    (a)  to put in repair or deliver up in repair,

    (b)  to paint, point or render,

    (c)  to pay money in lieu of repairs by the lessee, or

    (d)  to pay money on account of repairs by the lessor.

(6) In a lease in which the repairing covenant is implied there is also implied a covenant by the lessee that the lessor, or any person authorised by him in writing, may at reasonable times of the day and on giving 24 hours' notice in writing to the occupier, enter the premises comprised in the lease for the purpose of viewing their condition and state of repair.

---

[23] Section 11(3A) inserted by Housing Act 1988 (c.50) s.116(2)(4).

## 12 Restriction on contracting out of s. 11

(1) A covenant or agreement, whether contained in a lease to which section 11 applies or in an agreement collateral to such a lease, is void in so far as it purports—

(a) to exclude or limit the obligations of the lessor or the immunities of the lessee under that section, or
(b) to authorise any forfeiture or impose on the lessee any penalty, disability or obligation in the event of his enforcing or relying upon those obligations or immunities,

unless the inclusion of the provision was authorised by the county court.

(2) The county court may, by order made with the consent of the parties, authorise the inclusion in a lease, or in an agreement collateral to a lease, of provisions excluding or modifying in relation to the lease, the provisions of section 11 with respect to the repairing obligations of the parties if it appears to the court that it is reasonable to do so, having regard to all the circumstances of the case, including the other terms and conditions of the lease.

## 13 Leases to which s. 11 applies: general rule

(1) Section 11 (repairing obligations) applies to a lease of a dwelling-house granted on or after 24th October 1961 for a term of less than seven years.

(2) In determining whether a lease is one to which section 11 applies—

(a) any part of the term which falls before the grant shall be left out of account and the lease shall be treated as a lease for a term commencing with the grant,
(b) a lease which is determinable at the option of the lessor before the expiration of seven years from the commencement of the term shall be treated as a lease for a term of less than seven years, and
(c) a lease (other than a lease to which paragraph (b) applies) shall not be treated as a lease for a term of less than seven years if it confers on the lessee an option for renewal for a term which, together with the original term, amounts to seven years or more.

(3) This section has effect subject to—

section 14 (leases to which section 11 applies: exceptions), and
section 32(2) (provisions not applying to tenancies within Part II of the Landlord and Tenant Act 1954).

## 14 Leases to which s. 11 applies: exceptions

(1) Section 11 (repairing obligations) does not apply to a new lease granted to an existing tenant, or to a former tenant still in possession, if the previous lease was

not a lease to which section 11 applied (and, in the case of a lease granted before 24th October 1961, would not have been if it had been granted on or after that date).

(2) In subsection (1)—

"existing tenant" means a person who is when, or immediately before, the new lease is granted, the lessee under another lease of the dwelling-house;
"former tenant still in possession" means a person who—

(a) was the lessee under another lease of the dwelling-house which terminated at some time before the new lease was granted, and
(b) between the termination of that other lease and the grant of the new lease was continuously in possession of the dwelling-house or of the rents and profits of the dwelling-house; and

"the previous lease" means the other lease referred to in the above definitions.

(3) Section 11 does not apply to a lease of a dwelling-house which is a tenancy of an agricultural holding within the meaning of the [Agricultural Holdings Act 1986][24] [and in relation to which that Act applies or to a farm business tenancy within the meaning of the Agricultural Tenancies Act 1995.][25].

(4) Section 11 does not apply to a lease granted on or after 3rd October 1980 to—

a local authority,
[a National Park authority,][26]
a new town corporation,
an urban development corporation,
the Development Board for Rural Wales,
a [registered social landlord][27],
a co-operative housing association, or
an educational institution or other body specified, or of a class specified, by regulations under section 8 of the Rent Act 1977 [or paragraph 8 of Schedule 1 to the Housing Act 1988][28] (bodies making student lettings)
a housing action trust established under Part III of the Housing Act 1988.

---

[24] Words substituted by Agricultural Holdings Act 1986 (c.5) ss.99, 100, Sch.13 para.3, Sch.14 para.64.
[25] Words inserted by Agricultural Tenancies Act 1995 (c.8) Sch.1 para.31.
[26] Words inserted by Environment Act 1995 (c.25) Sch.10 para.25(1).
[27] Words substituted by Housing Act 1996 (Consequential Provisions) Order 1996/2325 Sch.2 para.16(2).
[28] Words inserted by Local Government and Housing Act 1989 (c.42) s.194(1), Sch.11 para.89.

(5) Section 11 does not apply to a lease granted on or after 3rd October 1980 to—

(a) Her Majesty in right of the Crown (unless the lease is under the management of the Crown Estate Commissioners), or
(b) a government department or a person holding in trust for Her Majesty for the purposes of a government department.

## 15 Jurisdiction of county court

The county court has jurisdiction to make a declaration that section 11 (repairing obligations) applies, or does not apply, to a lease—

(a) whatever the net annual value of the property in question, and
(b) notwithstanding that no other relief is sought than a declaration.

## 16 Meaning of "lease" and related expressions

In sections 11 to 15 (repairing obligations in short leases)—

(a) "lease" does not include a mortgage term;
(b) "lease of a dwelling-house" means a lease by which a building or part of a building is let wholly or mainly as a private residence, and "dwelling-house" means that building or part of a building;
(c) "lessee" and "lessor" mean, respectively, the person for the time being entitled to the term of a lease and to the reversion expectant on it.

## 17 Specific performance of landlord's repairing obligations

(1) In proceedings in which a tenant of a dwelling alleges a breach on the part of his landlord of a repairing covenant relating to any part of the premises in which the dwelling is comprised, the court may order specific performance of the covenant whether or not the breach relates to a part of the premises let to the tenant and notwithstanding any equitable rule restricting the scope of the remedy, whether on the basis of a lack of mutuality or otherwise.

(2) In this section—

(a) "tenant" includes a statutory tenant,
(b) in relation to a statutory tenant the reference to the premises let to him is to the premises of which he is a statutory tenant,
(c) "landlord" in relation to a tenant, includes any person against whom the tenant has a right to enforce a repairing covenant, and
(d) "repairing covenant" means a covenant to repair, maintain, renew, construct or replace any property.

[ ... ]

*Supplementary provisions*

## 35 Application to Isles of Scilly

(1) This Act applies to the Isles of Scilly subject to such exceptions, adaptations and modifications as the Secretary of State may by order direct.

(2) An order shall be made by statutory instrument which shall be subject to annulment in pursuance of a resolution of either House of Parliament.

## 36 Meaning of "lease" and "tenancy" and related expressions

(1) In this Act "lease" and "tenancy" have the same meaning.

(2) Both expressions include—

   (a)  a sub-lease or sub-tenancy, and

   (b)  an agreement for a lease or tenancy (or sub-lease or sub-tenancy).

(3) The expressions "lessor" and "lessee" and "landlord" and "tenant", and references to letting, to the grant of a lease or to covenants or terms, shall be construed accordingly.

## 37 Meaning of "statutory tenant" and related expressions

In this Act—

   (a)  "statutory tenancy" and "statutory tenant" mean a statutory tenancy or statutory tenant within the meaning of the Rent Act 1977 or the Rent (Agriculture) Act 1976; and

   (b)  "landlord", in relation to a statutory tenant, means the person who, apart from the statutory tenancy, would be entitled to possession of the premises.

## 38 Minor definitions

In this Act—

"address" means a person's place of abode or place of business or, in the case of a company, its registered office;

["arbitration agreement", "arbitration proceedings" and "arbitral tribunal" have the same meaning as in Part I of the Arbitration Act 1996; [and "post-dispute arbitration agreement", in relation to any matter, means an arbitration agreement made after a dispute about the matter has arisen;][29]][30]

---

[29] Words inserted subject to savings specified in SI 2004/669 Sch.2 para.6 by Commonhold and Leasehold Reform Act 2002 (c.15) Pt 2 c.5 s.155(2).
[30] Definition inserted subject to savings specified in SI 1997/1851 Sch.1 para.1 by Housing Act 1996 c.52 Pt III c.I s.83(5).

"co-operative housing association" has the same meaning as in the Housing Associations Act 1985;

"dwelling" means a building or part of a building occupied or intended to be occupied as a separate dwelling, together with any yard, garden, outhouses and appurtenances belonging to it or usually enjoyed with it;

"housing association" has the same meaning as in the Housing Associations Act 1985;

"local authority" means a district, county, [county borough][31] or London borough council, the Common Council of the City of London or the Council of the Isles of Scilly and in sections 14(4), 26(1) and 28(6) includes [ . . . ][32] [the Broads Authority][33], a police authority established under [section 3 of the Police Act 1996][34], [the Metropolitan Police Authority][35], [ . . . ][36] a joint authority established by Part IV of the Local Government Act 1985 [, an authority established for an area in England by an order under section 207 of the Local Government and Public Involvement in Health Act 2007 (joint waste authorities)][37] [and the London Fire and Emergency Planning Authority][38];

"local housing authority" has the meaning given by section 1 of the Housing Act 1985;

"new town corporation" means—

(a) a development corporation established by an order made, or treated as made, under the New Towns Act 1981, or

(b) the Homes and Communities Agency so far as exercising its functions in relation to anything transferred (or to be transferred) to them as mentioned in section 52(1)(a) to (d) of the Housing and Regeneration Act 2008, or

(c) the Welsh Ministers so far as exercising functions in relating to anything transferred (or to be transferred) to them as mentioned in section 36(1)(a)(i) to (iii) of the New Towns Act 1981[38a]

"protected tenancy" has the same meaning as in the Rent Act 1977;

["registered social landlord" has the same meaning as in the Housing Act 1985 (see section 5(4) and (5) of that Act);][39]

"restricted contract" has the same meaning as in the Rent Act 1977;

[31] Words inserted by Local Government (Wales) Act 1994 (c.19) Sch.8 para.7.
[32] Words repealed by Education Reform Act 1988 (c.40) ss.231(7), 235(6), 237(2), Sch.13 Pt.I.
[33] Words inserted by Norfolk and Suffolk Broads Act 1988 (c.4) ss.23(2), 27(2), Sch.6 para.26.
[34] Words substituted by Police Act 1996 (c.16) Sch.7(I) para.1(2)(x).
[35] Words added by Greater London Authority Act 1999 (c.29) Sch.27 para.53.
[36] Words repealed by Criminal Justice and Police Act 2001 (c.16) Sch.7(5)(1) para.1.
[37] Words inserted by Local Government and Public Involvement in Health Act 2007 (c.28) Sch.13(2) para.42.
[38] Words added by Greater London Authority Act 1999 (c.29) Sch.29(I) para.44.
[38a] Words substituted by the Housing and Regeneration Act 2008 s.56, Sch.8 para.36: see SI 2008/3068 arts 1(2), 2(1)(w), 3.
[39] Words substituted by Housing Act 1996 (Consequential Provisions) Order 1996/2325 Sch.2 para.16(4).

"urban development corporation" has the same meaning as in Part XVI of the Local Government, Planning and Land Act 1980.

## Landlord and Tenant Act 1987 c.31

PART II APPOINTMENT OF MANAGERS BY THE COURT

### 21 Tenant's right to apply to court for appointment of manager

(1) The tenant of a flat contained in any premises to which this Part applies may, subject to the following provisions of this Part, apply to [the appropriate tribunal][40] for an order under section 24 appointing a manager to act in relation to those premises.

(2) Subject to subsection (3), this Part applies to premises consisting of the whole or part of a building if the building or part contains two or more flats.

(3) This Part does not apply to any such premises at a time when—

(a)  the interest of the landlord in the premises is held by an exempt landlord or a resident landlord, or
(b)  the premises are included within the functional land of any charity.

[(3A) But this Part is not prevented from applying to any premises because the interest of the landlord in the premises is held by a resident landlord if at least one-half of the flats contained in the premises are held on long leases which are not tenancies to which Part 2 of the Landlord and Tenant Act 1954 (c.56) applies.][41]

(4) An application for an order under section 24 may be made—

(a)  jointly by tenants of two or more flats if they are each entitled to make such an application by virtue of this section, and
(b)  in respect of two or more premises to which this Part applies;

and, in relation to any such joint application as is mentioned in paragraph (a), references in this Part to a single tenant shall be construed accordingly.

(5) Where the tenancy of a flat contained in any such premises is held by joint tenants, an application for an order under section 24 in respect of those premises may be made by any one or more of those tenants.

---

[40] The jurisdiction of the leasehold valuation tribunal was transferred to the First-tier Tribunal (Property Chamber) as of July 1, 2013: see the Transfer of Tribunal Functions Order 2013 (SI 2013/1036).
[41] Added by Commonhold and Leasehold Reform Act 2002 (c.15) Pt 2 c.5 s.161.

(6) An application to the court for it to exercise in relation to any premises [any jurisdiction][42] to appoint a receiver or manager shall not be made by a tenant (in his capacity as such) in any circumstances in which an application could be made by him for an order under section 24 appointing a manager to act in relation to those premises.

(7) References in this Part to a tenant do not include references to a tenant under a tenancy to which Part II of the Landlord and Tenant Act 1954 applies.

## 22 Preliminary notice by tenant

(1) Before an application for an order under section 24 is made in respect of any premises to which this Part applies by a tenant of a flat contained in those premises, a notice under this section must (subject to subsection (3)) be served [by the tenant on—][43]

    [(i)  the landlord, and
    (ii)  any person (other than the landlord) by whom obligations relating to the management of the premises or any part of them are owed to the tenant under his tenancy.][44]

(2) A notice under this section must—

    (a)  specify the tenant's name, the address of his flat and an address in England and Wales (which may be the address of his flat) at which [any person on whom the notice is served][45] may serve notices, including notices in proceedings, on him in connection with this Part;
    (b)  state that the tenant intends to make an application for an order under section 24 to be made by [the appropriate tribunal][46] in respect of such premises to which this Part applies as are specified in the notice, but (if paragraph (d) is applicable) that he will not do so if the [requirement specified in pursuance of that paragraph is complied with][47];
    (c)  specify the grounds on which the court would be asked to make such an order and the matters that would be relied on by the tenant for the purpose of establishing those grounds;
    (d)  where those matters are capable of being remedied by [any person on whom the notice is served, require him][48], within such reasonable period as is specified in the notice, to take such steps for the purpose of remedying them as are so specified; and

---

[42] Words substituted by Housing Act 1996 (c.52) Pt III c.I s.86(2).
[43] Modified by Commonhold and Leasehold Reform Act 2002 (c.15) Pt 2 c.5 s.160(2).
[44] Modified by Commonhold and Leasehold Reform Act 2002 (c.15) Pt 2 c.5 s.160(2).
[45] Modified by Commonhold and Leasehold Reform Act 2002 (c.15) Pt 2 c.5 s.160(2).
[46] See SI 2013/1036.
[47] Modified by Commonhold and Leasehold Reform Act 2002 (c.15) Pt 2 c.5 s.160(2).
[48] Modified by Commonhold and Leasehold Reform Act 2002 (c.15) Pt 2 c.5 s.160(2).

    (e)  contain such information (if any) as the Secretary of State may by regulations prescribe.

(3) [the appropriate tribunal][49] may (whether on the hearing of an application for an order under section 24 or not) by order dispense with the requirement to serve a notice under this section [on a person][50] in a case where it is satisfied that it would not be reasonably practicable to serve such a notice on the [person][51], but [a leasehold valuation tribunal][52] may, when doing so, direct that such other notices are served, or such other steps are taken, as it thinks fit.

(4) In a case where—

    (a)  a notice under this section has been served on the landlord, and (b) his interest in the premises specified in pursuance of subsection (2)(b) is subject to a mortgage, the landlord shall, as soon as is reasonably practicable after receiving the notice, serve on the mortgagee a copy of the notice.[ . . . ][53]

## 23 Application to court for appointment of manager

(1) No application for an order under section 24 shall be made to [the appropriate tribunal][54] unless—

    (a)  in a case where a notice has been served under section 22, either—

        (i)  the period specified in pursuance of paragraph (d) of subsection (2) of that section has expired without the person required to take steps in pursuance of that paragraph having taken them, or
        (ii)  that paragraph was not applicable in the circumstances of the case; or

    (b)  in a case where the requirement to serve such a notice has been dispensed with by an order under subsection (3) of that section, either—

        (i)  any notices required to be served, and any other steps required to be taken, by virtue of the order have been served or (as the case may be) taken, or
        (ii)  no direction was given by the court when making the order.

(2) [ . . . ][55]

---

[49] See SI 2013/1036.
[50] Modified by Commonhold and Leasehold Reform Act 2002 (c.15) Pt 2 c.5 s.160(2).
[51] Modified by Commonhold and Leasehold Reform Act 2002 (c.15) Pt 2 c.5 s.160(2).
[52] Words substituted by Housing Act 1996 (c.52) Pt III c.I s.86(2).
[53] Modified by Commonhold and Leasehold Reform Act 2002 (c.15) Pt 2 c.5 s.160(2).
[54] As from July 1, 2013 the jurisdiction of the leasehold tribunal has been transferred to the First-tier Tribunals (Property Chamber): see SI 2013/1036.
[55] Repealed by Commonhold and Leasehold Reform Act 2002 (c.15) Sch.14 para.1.

## 24 Appointment of manager

(1) [The appropriate tribunal][56] may, on an application for an order under this section, by order (whether interlocutory or final) appoint a manager to carry out in relation to any premises to which this Part applies—

    (a)  such functions in connection with the management of the premises, or

    (b)  such functions of a receiver,

or both, as the court thinks fit.

(2) [The appropriate tribunal][57] may only make an order under this section in the following circumstances, namely—

    (a)   where the court is satisfied—

        (i)  that [any relevant person][58] either is in breach of any obligation owed by him to the tenant under his tenancy and relating to the management of the premises in question or any part of them or (in the case of an obligation dependent on notice) would be in breach of any such obligation but for the fact that it has not been reasonably practicable for the tenant to give him the appropriate notice, and

        [ . . . ][59]

      (iii)  that it is just and convenient to make the order in all the circumstances of the case; or

   [(ab)  where the court is satisfied—

        (i)  that unreasonable service charges have been made, or are proposed or likely to be made, and

       (ii)  that it is just and convenient to make the order in all the circumstances of the case;

  (aba)  where the tribunal is satisfied—

        (i)  that unreasonable variable administration charges have been made, or are proposed or likely to be made, and

       (ii)  that it is just and convenient to make the order in all the circumstances of the case;

   (ac)  where the court is satisfied—

        (i)  that [any relevant person][60] has failed to comply with any relevant provision of a code of practice approved by the Secretary of State

---

[56] See above.
[57] See above.
[58] Modified by Commonhold and Leasehold Reform Act 2002 (c.15) Pt 2 c.5 s.160(4).
[59] Repealed by Housing Act 1996 (c.52) Pt III c.I s.85(2).
[60] Modified by Commonhold and Leasehold Reform Act 2002 (c.15) Pt 2 c.5 s.160(4).

under section 87 of the Leasehold Reform, Housing and Urban Development Act 1993 (codes of management practice); and

(ii) that it is just and convenient to make the order in all the circumstances of the case;][61]

(b)  where the court is satisfied that other circumstances exist which make it just and convenient for the order to be made.

[(2ZA) In this section "relevant person" means a person—

(a) on whom a notice has been served under section 22, or
(b) in the case of whom the requirement to serve a notice under that section has been dispensed with by an order under subsection (3) of that section.][62]

[(2A) For the purposes of subsection (2)(ab) a service charge shall be taken to be unreasonable—

(a) if the amount is unreasonable having regard to the items for which it is payable,
(b) if the items for which it is payable are of an unnecessarily high standard, or
(c) if the items for which it is payable are of an insufficient standard with the result that additional service charges are or may be incurred.

In that provision and this subsection "service charge" means a service charge within the meaning of section (18)(1) of the Landlord and Tenant Act 1985, other than one excluded from that section by section 27 of that Act (rent of dwelling registered and not entered as variable).][63]

(2B) In subsection (2)(aba) "variable administration charge" has the meaning given by paragraph 1 of Schedule 11 to the Commonhold and Leasehold Reform Act 2002.

(3) The premises in respect of which an order is made under this section may, if the court thinks fit, be either more or less extensive than the premises specified in the application on which the order is made.

(4) An order under this section may make provision with respect to—

(a) such matters relating to the exercise by the manager of his functions under the order, and
(b) such incidental or ancillary matters,

---

[61] Added by Housing Act 1996 (c.52) Pt III c.I s.85(3).
[62] Modified by Commonhold and Leasehold Reform Act 2002 (c.15) Pt 2 c.5 s.160(4).
[63] Added by Housing Act 1996 (c.52) Pt III c.I s.85(4).

as the court thinks fit; and, on any subsequent application made for the purpose by the manager, the court may give him directions with respect to any such matters.

(5) Without prejudice to the generality of subsection (4), an order under this section may provide—

> (a) for rights and liabilities arising under contracts to which the manager is not a party to become rights and liabilities of the manager;
>
> (b) for the manager to be entitled to prosecute claims in respect of causes of action (whether contractual or tortious) accruing before or after the date of his appointment;
>
> (c) for remuneration to be paid to the manager by any relevant person, or by the tenants of the premises in respect of which the order is made or by all or any of those persons;
>
> (d) for the manager's functions to be exercisable by him (subject to subsection (9)) either during a specified period or without limit of time.

(6) Any such order may be granted subject to such conditions as the court thinks fit, and in particular its operation may be suspended on terms fixed by the court.

(7) In a case where an application for an order under this section was preceded by the service of a notice under section 22, the court may, if it thinks fit, make such an order notwithstanding—

> (a) that any period specified in the notice in pursuance of subsection (2)(d)of that section was not a reasonable period, or
>
> (b) that the notice failed in any other respect to comply with any requirement contained in subsection (2) of that section or in any regulations applying to the notice under section 54(3).

(8) The Land Charges Act 1972 and the [Land Registration Act 2002][64] shall apply in relation to an order made under this section as they apply in relation to an order appointing a receiver or sequestrator of land.

(9) [The appropriate tribunal][65] may, on the application of any person interested, vary or discharge (whether conditionally or unconditionally) an order made under this section; and if the order has been protected by an entry registered under the Land Charges Act 1972 or the Land Registration Act 2002, the court may by order direct that the entry shall be cancelled.

---

[64] Words substituted by Land Registration Act 2002 (c.9) Sch.11 para.20.
[65] See above.

[(9A) The [tribunal][66] shall not vary or discharge an order under subsection (9) on the application of [any relevant person][67] unless it is satisfied—

(a) that the variation or discharge of the order will not result in a recurrence of the circumstances which led to the order being made, and

(b) that it is just and convenient in all the circumstances of the case to vary or discharge the order.][68]

(10) An order made under this section shall not be discharged by the appropriate tribunal by reason only that, by virtue of section 21(3), the premises in respect of which the order was made have ceased to be premises to which this Part applies.

(11) References in this [Part][69] to the management of any premises include references to the repair, maintenance, improvement or insurance of those premises.

**24A–24B.** [ ... ][70]

PART III COMPULSORY ACQUISITION BY TENANTS OF THEIR LANDLORD'S INTEREST

## 25 Compulsory acquisition of landlord's interest by qualifying tenants

(1) This Part has effect for the purpose of enabling qualifying tenants of flats contained in any premises to which this Part applies to make an application to the court for an order providing for a person nominated by them to acquire their landlord's interest in the premises without his consent; and any such order is referred to in this Part as "an acquisition order".

(2) Subject to subsections (4) and (5), this Part applies to premises if—

(a) they consist of the whole or part of a building; and

(b) they contain two or more flats held by tenants of the landlord who are qualifying tenants; and

(c) [the total number of flats held by such tenants is not less than two-thirds of the total number of flats contained in the premises][71].

(3) [ ... ][72]

---

[66] Substituted by Commonhold and Leasehold Reform Act 2002 (c.15) Sch.13 para.9.
[67] Modified by Commonhold and Leasehold Reform Act 2002 (c.15) Pt 2 c.5 s.160(4).
[68] Added by Housing Act 1996 (c.52) Pt III c.I s.85(6).
[69] Modified by Commonhold and Leasehold Reform Act 2002 (c.15) Pt 2 c.5 s.160(4).
[70] Repealed by Commonhold and Leasehold Reform Act 2002 (c.15) Sch.14 para.1.
[71] Substituted by Leasehold Reform, Housing and Urban Development Act 1993 (c.28) Pt I c.VI s.85(2)(a).
[72] Repealed by Leasehold Reform, Housing and Urban Development Act 1993 (c.28) Pt I c.VI s.85(2)(b).

(4) This Part does not apply to premises falling within subsection (2) if—

    (a)  any part or parts of the premises is or are occupied or intended to be occupied otherwise than for residential purposes; and

    (b)  the internal floor area of that part or those parts (taken together) exceeds 50 per cent. of the internal floor area of the premises (taken as a whole);

and for the purposes of this subsection the internal floor area of any common parts shall be disregarded.

(5) This Part also does not apply to any such premises at a time when—

    (a)  the interest of the landlord in the premises is held by an exempt landlord or a resident landlord, or

    (b)  the premises are included within the functional land of any charity.

(6) The Secretary of State may by order substitute for the percentage for the time being specified in subsection (4)(b) such other percentage as is specified in the order.

## 26 Qualifying tenants

(1) Subject to subsections (2) and (3), a person is a qualifying tenant of a flat for the purposes of this Part if he is the tenant of the flat under a long lease other than one constituting a tenancy to which Part II of the Landlord and Tenant Act 1954 applies.

(2) A person is not to be regarded as being a qualifying tenant of a flat contained in any particular premises consisting of the whole or part of a building if [by virtue of one or more long leases none of which constitutes a tenancy to which Part II of the Landlord and Tenant Act 1954 applies, he is the tenant not only of the flat in question but also of at least two other flats contained in those premises][73]

(3) A tenant of a flat under a long lease whose landlord is a qualifying tenant of that flat is not to be regarded as being a qualifying tenant of that flat.

[(4) For the purposes of subsection (2) any tenant of a flat contained in the premises in question who is a body corporate shall be treated as the tenant of any other flat so contained and let to an associated company, as defined in section 20(1).][74]

---

[73] Words substituted by Housing Act 1988 (c.50), s.119 Sch.13 para.4(1).
[74] Section 26(4)inserted by Housing Act 1988 (c.50) s.119 Sch.13 para.4(2).

## 27 Preliminary notice by tenants

(1) Before an application for an acquisition order is made in respect of any premises to which this Part applies, a notice under this section must (subject to subsection (3)) be served on the landlord by qualifying tenants of the flats contained in the premises who, at the date when it is served, constitute the requisite majority of such tenants.

(2) A notice under this section must—

(a)  specify the names of the qualifying tenants by whom it is served, the addresses of their flats and the name and the address in England and Wales of a person on whom the landlord may serve notices (including notices in proceedings) in connection with this Part instead of serving them on those tenants;

(b)  state that those tenants intend to make an application for an acquisition order to be made by the court in respect of such premises to which this Part applies as are specified in the notice, but (if paragraph (d) is applicable) that they will not do so if the landlord complies with the requirement specified in pursuance of that paragraph;

(c)  specify the grounds on which the court would be asked to make such an order and the matters that would be relied on by the tenants for the purpose of establishing those grounds;

(d)  where those matters are capable of being remedied by the landlord, require the landlord, within such reasonable period as is specified in the notice, to take such steps for the purpose of remedying them as are so specified; and

(e)  contain such information (if any) as the Secretary of State may by regulations prescribe.

(3) The court may by order dispense with the requirement to serve a notice under this section in a case where it is satisfied that it would not be reasonably practicable to serve such a notice on the landlord, but the court may, when doing so, direct that such other notices are served, or such other steps are taken, as it thinks fit.

(4) Any reference in this Part to the requisite majority of qualifying tenants of the flats contained in any premises is a reference to qualifying tenants of the flats so contained with [not less than two-thirds][75] of the available votes; and for the purposes of this subsection—

(a)  the total number of available votes shall correspond to the total number of those flats for the time being let to qualifying tenants; and

(b)  there shall be one available vote in respect of each of the flats so let which shall be attributed to the qualifying tenant to whom it is let.

---

[75] Words substituted by Leasehold Reform, Housing and Urban Development Act 1993 (c.28) Pt I c.VI s.85(3).

(5) Nothing in this Part shall be construed as requiring the persons constituting any such majority in any one context to be the same as the persons constituting any such majority in any other context.

## 28 Applications for acquisition orders

(1) An application for an acquisition order in respect of any premises to which this Part applies must be made by qualifying tenants of the flats contained in the premises who, at the date when it is made, constitute the requisite majority of such tenants.

(2) No such application shall be made to the court unless—

(a) in a case where a notice has been served under section 27, either—

    (i) the period specified in pursuance of paragraph (d) of subsection (2) of that section has expired without the landlord having taken the steps that he was required to take in pursuance of that provision, or

    (ii) that paragraph was not applicable in the circumstances of the case; or

(b) in a case where the requirement to serve such a notice has been dispensed with by an order under subsection (3) of that section, either—

    (i) any notices required to be served, and any other steps required to be taken, by virtue of the order have been served or (as the case may be) taken, or

    (ii) no direction was given by the court when making the order.

(3) An application for an acquisition order may, subject to the preceding provisions of this Part, be made in respect of two or more premises to which this Part applies.

(4) Rules of court shall make provision—

(a) for requiring notice of an application for an acquisition order in respect of any premises to be served on such descriptions of persons as may be specified in the rules; and

(b) for enabling persons served with any such notice to be joined as parties to the proceedings.

(5) The Land Charges Act 1972 and the [Land Registration Act 2002][76] shall apply in relation to an application for an acquisition order as they apply in relation to other pending land actions.

---

[76] Words substituted by Land Registration Act 2002 (c.9) Sch.11 para.20.

(6) [ . . . ]⁷⁷

## 29 Conditions for making acquisition orders

(1) The court may, on an application for an acquisition order, make such an order in respect of any premises if—

(a)  the court is satisfied—

    (i)  that those premises were, at the date of service on the landlord of the notice (if any) under section 27 and on the date when the application was made, premises to which this Part applies, and

    (ii)  that they have not ceased to be such premises since the date when the application was made, and

(b)  either of the conditions specified in subsections (2) and (3) is fulfilled with respect to those premises, and

(c)  the court considers it appropriate to make the order in the circumstances of the case.

(2) The first of the conditions referred to in subsection (1)(b) is that the court is satisfied—

(a)  that the landlord either is in breach of any obligation owed by him to the applicants under their leases and relating to the [ . . . ]⁷⁸ management of the premises in question, or any part of them, or (in the case of an obligation dependent on notice) would be in breach of any such obligation but for the fact that it has not been reasonably practicable for the tenant to give him the appropriate notice, and

(b)  that the circumstances by virtue of which he is (or would be) in breach of any such obligation are likely to continue, [ . . . ]⁷⁹

(c)  [ . . . ]⁸⁰

[(2A) The reference in subsection (2) to the management of any premises includes a reference to the repair, maintenance, improvement or insurance of those premises.]⁸¹

(3) The second of those conditions is that, both at the date when the application was made and throughout the period of [two years]⁸² immediately preceding that

---

⁷⁷ Repealed by Land Registration Act 2002 (c.9) Sch.13 para.1.
⁷⁸ Modified by Commonhold and Leasehold Reform Act 2002 (c.15) Sch.9 para.9.
⁷⁹ Words repealed by Leasehold Reform, Housing and Urban Development Act 1993 (c.28) Pt I c.VI s.85(4).
⁸⁰ Words repealed by Leasehold Reform, Housing and Urban Development Act 1993 (c.28) Pt I c.VI s.85(4).
⁸¹ Modified by Commonhold and Leasehold Reform Act 2002 (c.15) Sch.9 para.9.
⁸² Words substituted subject to savings specified in SI 1996/2212 Sch.1 para.1 by Housing Act 1996 (c.52) Pt III c.I s.88.

date, there was in force an appointment under Part II of a person to act as manager in relation to the premises in question [which was made by reason of an act or omission on the part of the landlord][83].

(4) An acquisition order may, if the court thinks fit—

(a) include any yard, garden, outhouse or appurtenance belonging to, or usually enjoyed with, the premises specified in the application on which the order is made;
(b) exclude any part of the premises so specified.

(5) Where—

(a) the premises in respect of which an application for an acquisition order is made consist of part only of more extensive premises in which the landlord has an interest, and
(b) it appears to the court that the landlord's interest in the latter premises is not reasonably capable of being severed, either in the manner contemplated by the application or in any manner authorised by virtue of subsection (4)(b),

then, notwithstanding that paragraphs (a) and (b) of subsection (1) apply, the court shall not make an acquisition order on the application.

(6) In a case where an application for an acquisition order was preceded by the service of a notice under section 27, the court may, if it thinks fit, make such an order notwithstanding—

(a) that any period specified in the notice in pursuance of subsection (2)(d) of that section was not a reasonable period, or
(b) that the notice failed in any other respect to comply with any requirement contained in subsection (2) of that section or in any regulations applying to the notice under section 54(3).

(7) Where any premises are premises to which this Part applies at the time when an application for an acquisition order is made in respect of them, then, for the purposes of this section and the following provisions of this Part, they shall not cease to be such premises by reason only that—

(a) the interest of the landlord in them subsequently becomes held by an exempt landlord or a resident landlord, or
(b) they subsequently become included within the functional land of any charity.

---

[83] Words inserted by Commonhold and Leasehold Reform Act 2002 (c.15) Pt 2 c.5 s.160(5).

## 30 Content of acquisition orders

(1) Where an acquisition order is made by the court, the order shall (except in a case falling within section 33(1)) provide for the nominated person to be entitled to acquire the landlord's interest in the premises specified in the order on such terms as may be determined—

    (a)  by agreement between the landlord and the qualifying tenants in whose favour the order is made, or

    (b)  in default of agreement, by a rent assessment committee under section 31.

(2) An acquisition order may be granted subject to such conditions as the court thinks fit, and in particular its operation may be suspended on terms fixed by the court.

(3) References in this Part, in relation to an acquisition order, to the nominated person are references to such person or persons as may be nominated for the purposes of this Part by the persons applying for the order.

(4) Those persons must secure that the nominated person is joined as a party to the application, and no further nomination of a person for the purposes of this Part shall be made by them after the order is made (whether in addition to, or in substitution for, the existing nominated person) except with the approval of the court.

(5) Where the landlord is, by virtue of any covenant, condition or other obligation, precluded from disposing of his interest in the premises in respect of which an acquisition order has been made unless the consent of some other person is obtained—

    (a)  he shall use his best endeavours to secure that the consent of that person to that disposal is obtained and, if it appears to him that that person is obliged not to withhold his consent unreasonably but has nevertheless so withheld it, shall institute proceedings for a declaration to that effect; but

    (b)  if—

        (i)  the landlord has discharged any duty imposed on him by paragraph (a), and

        (ii)  the consent of that person has been withheld, and

        (iii)  no such declaration has been made,

the order shall cease to have effect.

(6) The Land Charges Act 1972 and the [Land Registration Act 2002][84] shall apply in relation to an acquisition order as they apply in relation to an order

---

[84] Words substituted by Land Registration Act 2002 (c.9) Sch.11 para.20.

affecting land made by the court for the purpose of enforcing a judgment or recognisance.

## 31 Determination of terms by rent assessment committees

(1) [The appropriate tribunal][85] shall have jurisdiction to determine the terms on which the landlord's interest in the premises specified in an acquisition order may be acquired by the nominated person to the extent that those terms have not been determined by agreement between the landlord and either—

    (a)  the qualifying tenants in whose favour the order was made, or

    (b)  the nominated person;

and (subject to subsection (2)) [the tribunal][86] shall determine any such terms on the basis of what appears to them to be fair and reasonable.

(2) Where an application is made under this section for to determine the consideration payable for the acquisition of a landlord's interest in any premises, [the tribunal]1 shall do so by determining an amount equal to the amount which, in their opinion, that interest might be expected to realise if sold on the open market by a willing seller on the appropriate terms and on the assumption that none of the tenants of the landlord of any premises comprised in those premises was buying or seeking to buy that interest.

(3) In subsection (2) "the appropriate terms" means all of the terms to which the acquisition of the landlord's interest in pursuance of the order is to be subject (whether determined by agreement as mentioned in subsection (1) or on an application under this section) apart from those relating to the consideration payable.

(4) On any application under this section the interests of the qualifying tenants in whose favour the acquisition order was made shall be represented by the nominated person, and accordingly the parties to any such application shall not include those tenants.

(5) [ . . . ][87]

(6) Nothing in this section shall be construed as authorising [the appropriate tribunal][88] to determine any terms dealing with matters in relation to which provision is made by section 32 or 33.

---

[85] Words substituted by the Transfer of Tribunal Functions Order 2013 (SI 2013/1036).

[86] Words substituted subject to savings specified in SI 1996/2212 Sch.1 para.2 by Housing Act 1996 (c.52) Sch.6(IV) para.5(b).

[87] Words substituted subject to savings specified in SI 1996/2212 Sch.1 para.2 by Housing Act 1996 (c.52) Sch.6(IV) para.5(b).

[88] Words substituted by the Transfer of Tribunal Functions Order 2013 (SI 2013/1036).

## 32 Discharge of existing mortgages

(1) Where the landlord's interest in any premises is acquired in pursuance of an acquisition order, the instrument by virtue of which it is so acquired shall (subject to subsection (2) and Part II of Schedule 1) operate to discharge the premises from any charge on that interest to secure the payment of money or the performance of any other obligation by the landlord or any other person.

(2) Subsection (1) does not apply to any such charge if—

(a)  it has been agreed between the landlord and either—

(i)  the qualifying tenants in whose favour the order was made, or
(ii)  the nominated person,

that the landlord's interest should be acquired subject to the charge, or

(b)  the court is satisfied, whether on the application for the order or on an application made by the person entitled to the benefit of the charge, that in the exceptional circumstances of the case it would be fair and reasonable that the landlord's interest should be so acquired, and orders accordingly.

(3) This section and Part II of Schedule 1 shall apply, with any necessary modifications, to mortgages and liens as they apply to charges; but nothing in those provisions shall apply to a rentcharge.

## 33 Acquisition order where landlord cannot be found

(1) Where an acquisition order is made by the court in a case where the landlord cannot be found, or his identity cannot be ascertained, the order shall provide for the landlord's interest in the premises specified in the order to vest in the nominated person on the following terms, namely—

(a)  such terms as to payment as are specified in subsection (2), and
(b)  such other terms as the court thinks fit, being terms which, in the opinion of the court, correspond so far as possible to those on which the interest might be expected to be transferred if it were being transferred by the landlord.

(2) The terms as to payment referred to in subsection (1)(a) are terms requiring the payment into court of—

(a)  such amount as a surveyor selected by the President of the Lands Tribunal may certify to be in his opinion the amount which the landlord's interest might be expected to realise if sold as mentioned in section 31(2); and
(b)  any amounts or estimated amounts remaining due to the landlord from any tenants of his of any premises comprised in the premises in respect of which the order is made, being amounts or estimated amounts determined

by the court as being due from those persons under the terms of their leases.

(3) Where any amount or amounts required by virtue of subsection (2) to be paid into court are so paid, the landlord's interest shall, by virtue of this section, vest in the nominated person in accordance with the order.

## 34 Discharge of acquisition order and withdrawal by tenants

(1) If, on an application by a landlord in respect of whose interest an acquisition order has been made, the court is satisfied—

   (a) that the nominated person has had a reasonable time within which to effect the acquisition of that interest in pursuance of the order but has not done so, or
   (b) that the number of qualifying tenants of flats contained in the premises in question who desire to proceed with the acquisition of the landlord's interest is less than the requisite majority of qualifying tenants of the flats contained in those premises, or
   (c) that the premises in question have ceased to be premises to which this Part applies,

the court may discharge the order.

(2) Where—

   (a) a notice is served on the landlord by the qualifying tenants by whom a notice has been served under section 27 or (as the case may be) by whom an application has been made for an acquisition order, or by the person nominated for the purposes of this Part by any such tenants, and
   (b) the notice indicates an intention no longer to proceed with the acquisition of the landlord's interest in the premises in question,

the landlord may (except in a case where subsection (4) applies) recover under this subsection any costs reasonably incurred by him in connection with the disposal by him of that interest down to the time when the notice is served; and, if the notice is served after the making of an acquisition order, that order shall cease to have effect.

(3) If (whether before or after the making of an acquisition order) the nominated person becomes aware—

   (a) that the number of qualifying tenants of flats contained in the premises in question who desire to proceed with the acquisition of the landlord's interest is less than the requisite majority of qualifying tenants of the flats contained in those premises, or
   (b) that those premises have ceased to be premises to which this Part applies,

he shall forthwith serve on the landlord a notice indicating an intention no longer to proceed with the acquisition of that interest, and subsection (2) shall apply accordingly.

(4) If, at any time when any proceedings taken under or by virtue of this Part are pending before the court or the Upper Tribunal[88a]—

   (a)  such a notice as is mentioned in subsection (2) or (3) is served on the landlord, or

   (b)  the nominated person indicates that he is no longer willing to act in the matter and nobody is nominated for the purposes of this Part in his place, or

   (c)  the number of qualifying tenants of flats contained in the premises in question who desire to proceed with the acquisition of the landlord's interest falls below the requisite majority of qualifying tenants of the flats contained in those premises, or

   (d)  those premises cease to be premises to which this Part applies,

or if the court discharges an acquisition order under subsection (1), the landlord may recover such costs incurred by him in connection with the disposal by him of his interest in those premises as the court or (as the case may be) the Tribunal may determine.

(5) The costs that may be recovered by the landlord under subsection (2) or (4) include costs incurred by him in connection with any proceedings under this Part (other than proceedings before a rent assessment committee).

(6) Any liability for costs arising under this section shall be the joint and several liability of the following persons, namely—

   (a)  where the liability arises before the making of an application for an acquisition order, the tenants by whom a notice was served under section 27, or

   (b)  where the liability arises after the making of such an application, the tenants by whom the application was made,

together with (in either case) any person nominated by those tenants for the purposes of this Part.

(7) In relation to any time when a tenant falling within paragraph (a) or (b) of subsection (6) has ceased to have vested in him the interest under his lease, that paragraph shall be construed as applying instead to the person who is for the time being the successor in title to that interest.

---

[88a] See the Transfer of Tribunal Functions (Lands Tribunal and Miscellaneous Amendments) Order 2009 (SI 2009/1307).

(8) Nothing in this section shall be construed as authorising the court to discharge an acquisition order where the landlord's interest has already been acquired in pursuance of the order.

(9) If—

(a)  an acquisition order is discharged, or ceases to have effect, by virtue of any provision of this Part, and
(b)  the order has been protected by an entry registered under the Land Charges Act 1972 or the [Land Registration Act 2002][89],

the court may by order direct that that entry shall be cancelled.

PART IV VARIATION OF LEASES

Applications relating to flats

**35 Application by party to lease for variation of lease**

(1) Any party to a long lease of a flat may make an application to [the appropriate tribunal][90] for an order varying the lease in such manner as is specified in the application.

(2) The grounds on which any such application may be made are that the lease fails to make satisfactory provision with respect to one or more of the following matters, namely—

(a)  the repair or maintenance of—

(i)  the flat in question, or
(ii)  the building containing the flat, or
(iii)  any land or building which is let to the tenant under the lease or in respect of which rights are conferred on him under it;

(b)  the insurance of the building containing the flat or of any such land or building as is mentioned in paragraph (a)(iii);
(c)  the repair or maintenance of any installations (whether they are in the same building as the flat or not) which are reasonably necessary to ensure that occupiers of the flat enjoy a reasonable standard of accommodation;
(d)  the provision or maintenance of any services which are reasonably necessary to ensure that occupiers of the flat enjoy a reasonable standard of accommodation (whether they are services connected with any such installations or not, and whether they are services provided for the

---

[89] Words substituted by Land Registration Act 2002 (c.9) Sch.11 para.20.
[90] Words substituted by the Transfer of Tribunal Functions Order 2013 (SI 2013/1036).

benefit of those occupiers or services provided for the benefit of the occupiers of a number of flats including that flat);

(e) the recovery by one party to the lease from another party to it of expenditure incurred or to be incurred by him, or on his behalf, for the benefit of that other party or of a number of persons who include that other party;

(f) the computation of a service charge payable under the lease[;][91]

[(g) such other matters as may be prescribed by regulations made by the Secretary of State][92].

(3) For the purposes of subsection (2)(c) and (d) the factors for determining, in relation to the occupiers of a flat, what is a reasonable standard of accommodation may include—

(a) factors relating to the safety and security of the flat and its occupiers and of any common parts of the building containing the flat; and

(b) other factors relating to the condition of any such common parts.

[(3A) For the purposes of subsection (2)(e) the factors for determining, in relation to a service charge payable under a lease, whether the lease makes satisfactory provision include whether it makes provision for an amount to be payable (by way of interest or otherwise) in respect of a failure to pay the service charge by the due date.][93]

(4) For the purposes of subsection (2)(f) a lease fails to make satisfactory provision with respect to the computation of a service charge payable under it if—

(a) it provides for any such charge to be a proportion of expenditure incurred, or to be incurred, by or on behalf of the landlord or a superior landlord; and

(b) other tenants of the landlord are also liable under their leases to pay by way of service charges proportions of any such expenditure; and

(c) the aggregate of the amounts that would, in any particular case, be payable by reference to the proportions referred to in paragraphs (a) and (b) would [either exceed or be less than][94] the whole of any such expenditure.

(5) [Procedure regulations under Schedule 12 to the Commonhold and Leasehold Reform Act 2002 and Tribunal Procedure Rules][95] shall make provision—

---

[91] Modified by Commonhold and Leasehold Reform Act 2002 (c.15) Pt 2 c.5 s.162.
[92] Modified by Commonhold and Leasehold Reform Act 2002 (c.15) Pt 2 c.5 s.162.
[93] Modified by Commonhold and Leasehold Reform Act 2002 (c.15) Pt 2 c.5 s.162.
[94] Words substituted by Leasehold Reform, Housing and Urban Development Act 1993 (c.28) Pt I c.VI s.86 and added by the Transfer of Tribunal Functions Order 2013 (SI 2013/1036).
[95] Modified by Commonhold and Leasehold Reform Act 2002 (c.15) Pt 2 c.5 s.163(2).

(a)  for requiring notice of any application under this Part to be served by the person making the application, and by any respondent to the application, on any person who the applicant, or (as the case may be) the respondent, knows or has reason to believe is likely to be affected by any variation specified in the application, and

(b)  for enabling persons served with any such notice to be joined as parties to the proceedings.

[(6) For the purposes of this Part a long lease shall not be regarded as a long lease of a flat if—

(a)  the demised premises consist of or include three or more flats contained in the same building; or

(b)  the lease constitutes a tenancy to which Part II of the Landlord and Tenant Act 1954 applies.][96]

(8) In this section "service charge" has the meaning given by section (18)(1) of the 1985 Act.[ ... ][97]

(9) For the purposes of this section and sections 36 to 39, "appropriate tribunal" means—

(a)  if one or more of the long leases concerned relates to property in England, the First-tier Tribunal or, where determined by or under Tribunal Procedure Rules, the Upper Tribunal; and

(b)  if one or more of the long leases relates to property in Wales, a leasehold valuation tribunal.[97a]

## 36 Application by respondent for variation of other leases

(1) Where an application ("the original application") is made under section 35 by any party to a lease, any other party to the lease may make an application to the [tribunal][98] asking it, in the event of its deciding to make an order effecting any variation of the lease in pursuance of the original application, to make an order which effects a corresponding variation of each of such one or more other leases as are specified in the application.

(2) Any lease so specified—

(a)  must be a long lease of a flat under which the landlord is the same person as the landlord under the lease specified in the original application; but

---

[96] Section 35(6)(7) substituted by Housing Act 1988 (c.50) s.119 Sch.13 para.5.
[97] Modified by Commonhold and Leasehold Reform Act 2002 (c.15) Pt 2 c.5 s.163(2).
[97a] Modified by the Transfer of Tribunal Functions Order 2013 (SI 2013/1036).
[98] Word substituted by Commonhold and Leasehold Reform Act 2002 (c.15) Pt 2 c.5 s.163(3).

(b)  need not be a lease of a flat which is in the same building as the flat let under that lease, nor a lease drafted in terms identical to those of that lease.

(3) The grounds on which an application may be made under this section are—

(a)  that each of the leases specified in the application fails to make satisfactory provision with respect to the matter or matters specified in the original application; and
(b)  that, if any variation is effected in pursuance of the original application, it would be in the interests of the person making the application under this section, or in the interests of the other persons who are parties to the leases specified in that application, to have all of the leases in question (that is to say, the ones specified in that application together with the one specified in the original application) varied to the same effect.

## 37 Application by majority of parties for variation of leases

(1) Subject to the following provisions of this section, an application may be made to [the appropriate tribunal][99] in respect of two or more leases for an order varying each of those leases in such manner as is specified in the application.

(2) Those leases must be long leases of flats under which the landlord is the same person, but they need not be leases of flats which are in the same building, nor leases which are drafted in identical terms.

(3) The grounds on which an application may be made under this section are that the object to be achieved by the variation cannot be satisfactorily achieved unless all the leases are varied to the same effect.

(4) An application under this section in respect of any leases may be made by the landlord or any of the tenants under the leases.

(5) Any such application shall only be made if—

(a)  in a case where the application is in respect of less than nine leases, all, or all but one, of the parties concerned consent to it; or
(b)  in a case where the application is in respect of more than eight leases, it is not opposed for any reason by more than 10 per cent. of the total number of the parties concerned and at least 75 per cent. of that number consent to it.

(6) For the purposes of subsection (5)—

---

[99] Words substituted by the Transfer of Tribunal Functions Order 2013 (SI 2013/1036).

(a) in the case of each lease in respect of which the application is made, the tenant under the lease shall constitute one of the parties concerned (so that in determining the total number of the parties concerned a person who is the tenant under a number of such leases shall be regarded as constituting a corresponding number of the parties concerned); and

(b) the landlord shall also constitute one of the parties concerned.[ . . . ][100]

*Orders varying leases*

## 38 Orders [ . . . ][101] varying leases

(1) If, on an application under section 35, the grounds on which the application was made are established to the satisfaction of the [tribunal][102], the [tribunal][103] may (subject to subsections (6) and (7)) make an order varying the lease specified in the application in such manner as is specified in the order.

(2) If—

(a) an application under section 36 was made in connection with that application, and

(b) the grounds set out in subsection (3) of that section are established to the satisfaction of the [tribunal][104] with respect to the leases specified in the application under section 36,

the [tribunal][105] may (subject to subsections (6) and (7)) also make an order varying each of those leases in such manner as is specified in the order.

(3) If, on an application under section 37, the grounds set out in subsection (3) of that section are established to the satisfaction of the [tribunal][106] with respect to the leases specified in the application, the tribunal may (subject to subsections (6) and (7)) make an order varying each of those leases in such manner as is specified in the order.

(4) The variation specified in an order under subsection (1) or (2) may be either the variation specified in the relevant application under section 35 or 36 or such other variation as the tribunal thinks fit.

(5) If the grounds referred to in subsection (2) or (3) (as the case may be) are established to the satisfaction of the [tribunal][107] with respect to some but not all

---

[100] Words substituted by Commonhold and Leasehold Reform Act 2002 (c.15) Pt 2 c.5 s.163(4).
[101] Words repealed subject to savings specified in SI 2004/669 Sch.2 para.12 by Commonhold and Leasehold Reform Act 2002 (c.15) Sch.14 para.1.
[102] Modified by Commonhold and Leasehold Reform Act 2002 (c.15) Pt 2 c.5 s.163(5).
[103] Modified by Commonhold and Leasehold Reform Act 2002 (c.15) Pt 2 c.5 s.163(5).
[104] Modified by Commonhold and Leasehold Reform Act 2002 (c.15) Pt 2 c.5 s.163(5).
[105] Modified by Commonhold and Leasehold Reform Act 2002 (c.15) Pt 2 c.5 s.163(5).
[106] Modified by Commonhold and Leasehold Reform Act 2002 (c.15) Pt 2 c.5 s.163(5).
[107] Modified by Commonhold and Leasehold Reform Act 2002 (c.15) Pt 2 c.5 s.163(5).

of the leases specified in the application, the power to make an order under that subsection shall extend to those leases only.

(6) [A tribunal][108] shall not make an order under this section effecting any variation of a lease if it appears to the [tribunal]—

(a) that the variation would be likely substantially to prejudice—

    (i) any respondent to the application, or

    (ii) any person who is not a party to the application,

and that an award under subsection (10) would not afford him adequate compensation, or

(b) that for any other reason it would not be reasonable in the circumstances for the variation to be effected.

(7) [A tribunal][109] shall not, on an application relating to the provision to be made by a lease with respect to insurance, make an order under this section effecting any variation of the lease—

(a) which terminates any existing right of the landlord under its terms to nominate an insurer for insurance purposes; or

(b) which requires the landlord to nominate a number of insurers from which the tenant would be entitled to select an insurer for those purposes; or

(c) which, in a case where the lease requires the tenant to effect insurance with a specified insurer, requires the tenant to effect insurance otherwise than with another specified insurer.

(8) [A tribunal][110] may, instead of making an order varying a lease in such manner as is specified in the order, make an order directing the parties to the lease to vary it in such manner as is so specified; and accordingly any reference in this Part (however expressed) to an order which effects any variation of a lease or to any variation effected by an order shall include a reference to an order which directs the parties to a lease to effect a variation of it or (as the case may be) a reference to any variation effected in pursuance of such an order.

(9) [A tribunal][111] may by order direct that a memorandum of any variation of a lease effected by an order under this section shall be endorsed on such documents as are specified in the order.

(10) Where [a tribunal][112] makes an order under this section varying a lease [the tribunal] may, if it thinks fit, make an order providing for any party to the lease

---

[108] Modified by Commonhold and Leasehold Reform Act 2002 (c.15) Pt 2 c.5 s.163(5).
[109] Modified by Commonhold and Leasehold Reform Act 2002 (c.15) Pt 2 c.5 s.163(5).
[110] Modified by Commonhold and Leasehold Reform Act 2002 (c.15) Pt 2 c.5 s.163(5).
[111] Modified by Commonhold and Leasehold Reform Act 2002 (c.15) Pt 2 c.5 s.163(5).
[112] Modified by Commonhold and Leasehold Reform Act 2002 (c.15) Pt 2 c.5 s.163(5).

to pay, to any other party to the lease or to any other person, compensation in respect of any loss or disadvantage that [the tribunal] considers he is likely to suffer as a result of the variation.

## 39 Effect of orders varying leases: applications by third parties

(1) Any variation effected by an order under section 38 shall be binding not only on the parties to the lease for the time being but also on other persons (including any predecessors in title of those parties), whether or not they were parties to the proceedings in which the order was made or were served with a notice by virtue of section 35(5).

(2) Without prejudice to the generality of subsection (1), any variation effected by any such order shall be binding on any surety who has guaranteed the performance of any obligation varied by the order; and the surety shall accordingly be taken to have guaranteed the performance of that obligation as so varied.

(3) Where any such order has been made and a person was, by virtue of section 35(5), required to be served with a notice relating to the proceedings in which it was made, but he was not so served, he may—

    (a) bring an action for damages for breach of statutory duty against the person by whom any such notice was so required to be served in respect of that person's failure to serve it;

    (b) apply to [the appropriate tribunal][113] for the cancellation or modification of the variation in question.

(4) [A tribunal][1] may, on an application under subsection (3)(b) with respect to any variation of a lease—

    (a) by order cancel that variation or modify it in such manner as is specified in the order, or

    (b) make such an order as is mentioned in section 38(10) in favour of the person making the application,

as it thinks fit.

(5) Where a variation is cancelled or modified under paragraph (a) of subsection (4)—

    (a) the cancellation or modification shall take effect as from the date of the making of the order under that paragraph or as from such later date as may be specified in the order, and

---

[113] Modified by the Transfer of Tribunal Functions Order 2013 (SI 2013/1036).

(b) the [tribunal]¹¹⁴ may by order direct that a memorandum of the cancellation or modification shall be endorsed on such documents as are specified in the order;

and, in a case where a variation is so modified, subsections (1) and (2) above shall, as from the date when the modification takes effect, apply to the variation as modified.

*Applications relating to dwellings other than flats*

## 40 Application for variation of insurance provisions of lease of dwelling other than a flat

(1) Any party to a long lease of a dwelling may make an application to [the appropriate tribunal]¹¹⁵ for an order varying the lease, in such manner as is specified in the application, on the grounds that the lease fails to make satisfactory provision with respect to any matter relating to the insurance of the dwelling, including the recovery of the costs of such insurance.

(2) Sections 36 and 38 shall apply to an application under subsection (1) subject to the modifications specified in subsection (3).

(3) Those modifications are as follows—

(a) in section 36—

(i) in subsection (1), the reference to section 35 shall be read as a reference to subsection (1) above, and
(ii) in subsection (2), any reference to a flat shall be read as a reference to a dwelling; and

(b) in section 38—

(i) any reference to an application under section 35 shall be read as a reference to an application under subsection (1) above, and
(ii) any reference to an application under section 36 shall be read as a reference to an application under section 36 as applied by subsection (2) above.

[(4) For the purpose of this section, a long lease shall not be regarded as a long lease of a dwelling if—

(a) the demised premises consist of three or more dwellings; or
(b) the lease constitutes a tenancy to which Part II of the Landlord and Tenant Act 1954 applies.

---

¹¹⁴ Modified by Commonhold and Leasehold Reform Act 2002 (c.15) Pt 2 c.5 s.163(6).
¹¹⁵ Words substituted by the Transfer of Tribunal Functions Order 2013 (SI 2013/1036).

(4A) Without prejudice to subsection (4), an application under sub-section (1) may not be made by a person who is a tenant under a long lease of a dwelling if, by virtue of that lease and one or more other long leases of dwellings, he is also a tenant from the same landlord of at least two other dwellings.

(4B) For the purposes of subsection (4A), any tenant of a dwelling who is a body corporate shall be treated as a tenant of any other dwelling held from the same landlord which is let under a long lease to an associated company, as defined in section 20(1).][116]

(5) In this section "dwelling" means a dwelling other than a flat.[ ... ][117]

(6) For the purposes of subsection (1), "appropriate tribunal" means—

   (a)  if one or more of the dwellings concerned is in England, the First-tier Tribunal or, where determined by or under Tribunal Procedure Rules, the Upper Tribunal; and

   (b)  if one or more of the dwellings concerned is in Wales, a leasehold valuation tribunal.[118]

---

[116] Substituted by Housing Act 1988 (c.50) s.119 Sch.13 para.6.
[117] Words substituted by Commonhold and Leasehold Reform Act 2002 (c.15) Pt 2 c.5 s.163(7).
[118] Words inserted by the Transfer of Tribunal Functions Order 2013 (SI 2013/1036).

# PROTOCOLS

PRE-ACTION PROTOCOL FOR CLAIMS FOR DAMAGES IN RELATION TO THE
PHYSICAL STATE OF COMMERCIAL PROPERTY AT TERMINATION OF A TENANCY
(THE "DILAPIDATIONS PROTOCOL")

## 1. Introduction

1.1 This protocol applies to commercial property situated in England and Wales. It relates to claims for damages for dilapidations against tenants at the termination of a tenancy. These are generally referred to as terminal dilapidations claims. There is a separate Pre-Action Protocol for Housing Disrepair cases.

1.2 This protocol sets out conduct that the court would normally expect prospective parties to follow prior to the commencement of proceedings. It establishes a reasonable process and timetable for the exchange of information relevant to a dispute, sets standards for the content and quality of schedules and Quantified Demands and, in particular, the conduct of pre-action negotiations.

1.3 If the landlord or tenant does not seek professional advice from a surveyor they should still, in so far as reasonably possible, fully comply with the terms of this protocol. In this protocol 'surveyor' is intended to encompass reference to any other suitably qualified person.

1.4 This protocol does not define 'dilapidations', 'repair', 'reinstatement' or 'redecoration.' Work to property which may be required will depend on the contractual terms of the lease and any other relevant documents.

1.5 Where the court considers non-compliance, and the sanctions to impose where it has occurred, it will, amongst other things, be concerned about whether the parties have complied in substance with the relevant principles and requirements and is not likely to be concerned with minor or technical shortcomings (see paragraphs 4.3 to 4.5 of the Practice Direction on Pre-Action Conduct).

## 2. Overview of Protocol—General Aim

2.1 The protocol's objectives are:

2.1.1 to encourage the exchange of early and full information about the dispute;

2.1.2 to enable the parties to avoid litigation by agreeing a settlement of the dispute before proceedings are commenced; and
2.1.3 to support the efficient management of proceedings where litigation cannot be avoided.

2.2 A flow chart is attached at Annex A, which shows each of the stages that the parties are expected to undertake before the commencement of proceedings.

## THE PROTOCOL

### 3. The schedule of dilapidations (schedule)

3.1 The landlord should send the tenant a schedule in the form attached at either Annex B or C. It should set out what the landlord considers to be the breaches, the works required to be done to remedy those breaches and, if relevant, the landlord's costings.
3.2 Breaches should be separated into relevant categories e.g. repair, reinstatement, redecoration etc. They should be listed separately in the schedule and should (where appropriate) identify any notices served by the landlord requiring reinstatement works to be undertaken.
3.3 Schedules should be sent within a reasonable time.
What is a reasonable time will vary from case to case, but will generally be within 56 days after the termination of the tenancy.
3.4 The landlord may send a schedule before termination of the tenancy. However, if it does so, at the termination of the tenancy the landlord should:

3.4.1 confirm that the situation remains as stated in the schedule; or
3.4.2 send a further schedule within a reasonable time.

3.5 The schedule should be endorsed either by the landlord, or where it is prepared by a surveyor, by the landlord's surveyor. If the schedule has been prepared by the landlord's surveyor, then in endorsing the schedule, the surveyor should have regard to the principles laid down in the Royal Institution of Chartered Surveyors' Guidance Note on Dilapidations.
3.6 The endorsement should confirm that in the landlord's or the landlord's surveyor's opinion:

3.6.1 all the works set out in the schedule are reasonably required to remedy breaches referred to in paragraph 3.1 above;
3.6.2 where endorsed by the landlord, full account has been taken of its intentions for the property;
3.6.3 where endorsed by the landlord's surveyor, full account has been taken of the landlord's intentions for the property, as advised by the landlord; and
3.6.4 the costings, if any, are reasonable.

3.7 Wherever possible the schedule should be sent electronically to enable the tenant's comments to be incorporated in one document.

## 4. Quantified Demand

4.1 The Quantified Demand is not intended to have the same status as a statement of case in proceedings.

4.2 The Quantified Demand should:

> 4.2.1 set out clearly all aspects of the dispute, and set out and substantiate the monetary sum sought as damages in respect of the breaches detailed in the schedule as well as any other items of loss for which damages are sought. It should also set out whether VAT applies;
>
> 4.2.2 confirm that the landlord and/or its surveyor will attend a meeting or meetings as proposed under section 7 below;
>
> 4.2.3 be sent within the same timescale for sending the tenant a schedule (see paragraph 3.3 above); and
>
> 4.2.4 specify a date (being a reasonable time) by which the tenant should respond. This will usually be within 56 days after sending the Quantified Demand.

4.3 Where the monetary sum sought is based on the cost of works, it should be fully quantified and substantiated by either an invoice or a detailed estimate.

4.4 If the Quantified Demand includes any other losses, they must be set out in detail, substantiated and fully quantified. The landlord should explain the legal basis for the recovery of losses, e.g. whether they are sought as part of the damages claim or under some express or implied provision of the lease.

4.5 The figures set out in the Quantified Demand should be restricted to the landlord's likely loss. This is not necessarily the same as the cost of works to remedy the breaches.

4.6 The Quantified Demand should not include items of work that are likely to be superseded by the landlord's intentions for the property.

4.7 If the landlord's surveyor prepares the Quantified Demand, the surveyor should have regard to the principles laid down in the Royal Institution of Chartered Surveyors' Guidance Note on Dilapidations.

## 5. The Response

5.1 The Response is not intended to have the same status as a defence in proceedings.

5.2 The tenant should respond to the Quantified Demand within a reasonable time. This will usually be within 56 days after the landlord sends the Quantified Demand.

5.3 Where appropriate, the tenant should respond using the schedule provided by the landlord. The Response should be set out in sufficient detail to enable the landlord to understand clearly the tenant's views on each item.

5.4 The Response should be endorsed either by the tenant or, where it is prepared by a surveyor, by the tenant's surveyor. In endorsing the schedule, the tenant's surveyor should have regard to the principles laid down in the Royal Institution of Chartered Surveyors' Guidance Note on Dilapidations.

5.5 The endorsement should confirm that in the tenant's or tenant's surveyor's opinion:

> 5.5.1 the works detailed in the Response are all that were reasonably required for the tenant to remedy the alleged breaches of its covenants or obligations;
>
> 5.5.2 any costs set out in the Response are reasonably payable for such works; and
>
> 5.5.3 account has been taken of what the tenant, or tenant's surveyor, reasonably believes to be the landlord's intentions for the property.

5.6 If the tenant or tenant's surveyor considers that any items in the schedule or Quantified Demand are likely to be superseded by works to be carried out by the landlord or are likely to be superseded by the landlord's intentions for the property then:

> 5.6.1 this should be stated in the Response;
>
> 5.6.2 particulars should be given of the material on which the tenant or tenant's surveyor relies; and
>
> 5.6.3 the items to which this view is relevant should be identified.

## 6. Disclosure of Documents

6.1 Disclosure will generally be limited to the documents required to be enclosed with the Quantified Demand and the tenant's Response. The parties can agree that further disclosure may be given. If either or both of the parties consider that further disclosure should be given but there is disagreement about some aspect of that process, they may be able to make an application for pre-action disclosure under CPR 31. Parties should assist each other and avoid the necessity for such an application.

## 7. Negotiations

7.1 The landlord and tenant and/or their respective surveyors are encouraged to meet before the tenant is required to respond to the Quantified Demand and should generally meet within 28 days after the tenant sends the Response. The meetings will be without-prejudice and the parties should seek to agree as many of the items in dispute as possible.

## 8. Alternative Dispute Resolution

8.1 The parties should consider whether some form of alternative dispute resolution procedure would be more suitable than litigation, and if so, endeavour to agree which form to adopt. Both the landlord and the tenant may be required by the court to provide evidence that alternative means of resolving their dispute were considered. The courts take the view that litigation should be a last resort, and that claims should not be issued prematurely when a settlement is still actively being explored. Parties are warned that the court will take into account the extent of the parties' compliance with this protocol when making orders about who should pay costs (see CPR rule 44.3(4) and (5)(a)).

8.2 Information on mediation and other forms of alternative dispute resolution may be found through the following: www.justice.gov.uk/guidance/mediation/index.htm. The Royal Institute of Chartered Surveyors (www.rics.org) and Property Litigation Association (www.pla.org.uk) websites also list a number of experienced mediators.

8.3 It is expressly recognised that no party can or should be forced to mediate or enter into any form of alternative dispute resolution.

## 9. Quantification of Loss

9.1 Prior to issuing proceedings, the landlord should quantify its loss by providing to the tenant a detailed breakdown of the issues and consequential losses based on either a formal diminution valuation or an account of the actual expenditure or, where it has carried out some but not all remedial action, a combination of both; unless, in all the circumstances, it would be unreasonable to do so.

9.2 If a formal diminution valuation is produced, it should be prepared by a valuer.

9.3 If the landlord has not carried out all the works specified in the schedule but intends to carry out some or all of them, the landlord must:

> 9.3.1 identify which works it intends to carry out;
> 9.3.2 state when it intends to do such proposed works;
> 9.3.3 state what steps it has taken towards getting such proposed works done, e.g. preparing a specification or bills of quantities or inviting tenders; and
> 9.3.4 clearly show the scope of such proposed works to enable any effect on the dilapidations claim to be identified.

9.4 In a case falling within paragraph 9.3, or in a case where the landlord has not carried out all the works specified in the schedule, and does not intend to carry out some or all of the works so specified, then it should provide a formal diminution valuation unless, in all the circumstances, it would be reasonable not to.

9.5 If the tenant relies on a defence on the basis of diminution, it must state its case for so doing and provide a diminution valuation to the landlord.

9.6 The tenant's diminution valuation shall be sent to the landlord within a reasonable time. A "reasonable time" will vary from case to case but generally will be within 56 days after the landlord sends the tenant a detailed breakdown of issues and losses under paragraph 9.1.

## 10. Stocktake

10. Where the procedure set out in this protocol has not resolved the dispute between the landlord and tenant, they should undertake a further review of their respective positions. The parties should consider the state of the papers and the evidence in order to see if proceedings can be avoided and, at the least, narrow the issues between them.

## Annex A

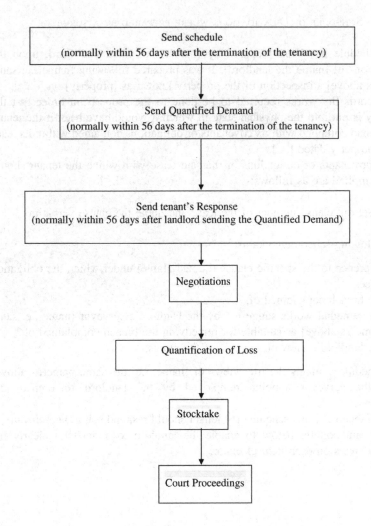

Send schedule
(normally within 56 days after the termination of the tenancy)

Send Quantified Demand
(normally within 56 days after the termination of the tenancy)

Send tenant's Response
(normally within 56 days after landlord sending the Quantified Demand)

Negotiations

Quantification of Loss

Stocktake

Court Proceedings

NB:
1. The provisions of this Protocol should be adopted in respect of each of the stages detailed in this flowchart.
2. The parties should consider throughout this process whether alternative dispute resolution would assist in settling the dispute.

## ANNEX B

### SCHEDULE OF DILAPIDATIONS WHERE PREPARED BY A SURVEYOR

This schedule has been prepared by [name, individual and firm], upon the instructions of [name the landlord]. It was prepared following [name i.e. same name as above]'s inspection of the property known as [property] on [date].

It records the works required to be done to the property in order that the property is put into the physical state in which it would have been if the tenant [name] had complied with its covenants or obligations contained within its lease of the property dated [    ].

The covenants or obligations of the said lease with which the tenant should have complied are as follows:-

[Set out clause number of the lease and quote the clause verbatim].

The following schedule contains:

- reference to the specific clause (quoted above) under which the obligation arises,
- the breach complained of,
- the remedial works suggested by the landlord's surveyor [name i.e. same name as above] as suitable for remedying the breach complained of,
- the landlord's view on the cost of the works.

The schedule contains the true views of [name, i.e. the same name as above] being the surveyor appointed/employed by the landlord to prepare the schedule.

Upon receipt of this schedule the tenant should respond using this schedule in the relevant column below to enable the landlord to understand clearly the tenant's views on each item of claim.

| 1 | 2 | 3 | 4 | 5 |
|---|---|---|---|---|
| Item No. | Clause No. | Breach complained of | Remedial works required | Landlord's costings |
| | | | | |
| | | | | |
| | | | | |
| | | | | |
| | | | | |
| | | | | |
| | | | | |
| | | | | |

**ENDORSEMENT**

I [name, i.e. the same name as above] confirm that in my opinion:

- all the works set out in the schedule are reasonably required to remedy breaches complained of;
- full account has been taken of the landlord's intentions for the property, as advised by the landlord; and
- the costings, if any, are reasonable.

DATED
SIGNED

[..............................]

[......................................]

[Name and address of surveyor appointed by landlord]

APPENDIX THREE

ANNEX C

SCHEDULE OF DILAPIDATIONS WHERE PREPARED BY THE LANDLORD

This schedule has been prepared by [name of landlord][[name of person preparing schedule if landlord is not an individual] on behalf of the landlord]. It was prepared following [name i.e. same name as above]'s inspection of the property known as [property] on [date].

It records the works required to be done to the property in order that the property is put into the physical state in which it would have been if the tenant [name] had complied with its covenants or obligations contained within its lease of the property dated [   ].

The covenants or obligations of the said lease with which the tenant should have complied are as follows:-

[Set out clause number of the lease and quote the clause verbatim].

The following schedule contains:

- reference to the specific clause (quoted above) under which the obligation arises,
- the breach complained of,
- the remedial works suggested by the landlord as suitable for remedying the breach complained of,
- the landlord's view on the cost of the works.

The schedule contains the true views of the landlord.

Upon receipt of this schedule the tenant should respond using this schedule in the relevant column below to enable the landlord to understand clearly the tenant's views on each item of claim.

| 1 | 2 | 3 | 4 | 5 |
|---|---|---|---|---|
| Item No. | Clause No. | Breach complained of | Remedial works required | Landlord's costings |
| | | | | |
| | | | | |
| | | | | |
| | | | | |
| | | | | |
| | | | | |
| | | | | |
| | | | | |
| | | | | |

**ENDORSEMENT**

I [name, i.e. the same name as above] confirm that in my opinion:

- all the works set out in the schedule are reasonably required to remedy breaches complained of;
- full account has been taken of [my] [the landlord's] intentions for the property; and
- the costings, if any, are reasonable.

DATED [.....................................................]

SIGNED

[.....................................................]
[Name of the person signing and address of landlord]

PRE-ACTION PROTOCOL FOR HOUSING DISREPAIR CASES

## [PREPARED BY THE HOUSING DISREPAIR PROTOCOL WORKING PARTY]

### 1 Introduction

Following a review of the problems of civil housing disrepair claims, Lord Woolf recommended in his final Access to Justice Report in July 1996 that there should be a Pre-action Protocol.

The Protocol, which covers claims in England and Wales, is intended to encourage the exchange of information between parties at an early stage and to provide a clear framework within which parties in a housing disrepair claim can attempt to achieve an early and appropriate resolution of the issues. An attempt has been made to draft the Protocol in plain English and to keep the contents straightforward in order to make the Protocol accessible and easy to use by all, including those representing themselves.

The Protocol embraces the spirit of the Woolf Reforms to the Civil Justice System. As Lord Woolf noted, landlords and tenants have a common interest in maintaining housing stock in good condition. It is generally common ground that in principle court action should be treated as a last resort, and it is hoped that the Protocol will lead to the avoidance of unnecessary litigation. Before using the Protocol tenants should therefore ensure that the landlord is aware of the disrepair. Tenants should also consider whether other options for having repairs carried out and/or obtaining compensation are more appropriate. Examples of other options are set out in paragraph 4.1(b).

Should a claim proceed to litigation, the court will expect all parties to have complied with the Protocol as far as possible. The court has the power to order parties who have unreasonably failed to comply with the Protocol to pay costs or be subject to other sanctions.

### 2 Aims of the Protocol

The Practice Direction on Protocols in the Civil Procedure Rules provides that the objectives of pre-action Protocols, are:

(1) *to encourage the exchange of early and full information about the prospective legal claim,*
(2) *to enable parties to avoid litigation by agreeing a settlement of the claim before the commencement of proceedings,*
(3) *to support the efficient management of proceedings where litigation cannot be avoided.*

The specific aims of this Protocol are:

- To avoid unnecessary litigation
- To promote the speedy and appropriate carrying out of any repairs which are the landlord's responsibility

- To ensure that tenants receive any compensation to which they are entitled as speedily as possible
- To promote good pre-litigation practice, including the early exchange of information and to give guidance about the instruction of experts
- To keep the costs of resolving disputes down.

## 3 Protocol

When using this Protocol, please refer to the **Guidance Notes** in paragraph 4.

### 3.1 Definitions

For the purposes of this Protocol:

(a) A disrepair claim is a civil claim arising from the condition of residential premises and may include a related personal injury claim. (See paragraphs 4.4 (c), (d) and (e) of the Guidance Notes.) It does not include disrepair claims which originate as counterclaims or set-offs in other proceedings.

(b) The types of claim which this Protocol is intended to cover include those brought under Section 11 of the Landlord and Tenant Act 1985, Section 4 of the Defective Premises Act 1972, common law nuisance and negligence, and those brought under the express terms of a tenancy agreement or lease. It does not cover claims brought under Section 82 of the Environmental Protection Act 1990 (which are heard in the Magistrates' Court).

(c) This protocol covers claims by any person with a disrepair claim as referred to in paragraphs (a) and (b) above, including tenants, lessees and members of the tenant's family. The use of the term 'tenant' in this protocol is intended to cover all such people. (See also paragraph 4.4(e).)

### 3.2 Early Notification Letter

(a) Notice of the claim should be given to the landlord as soon as possible. In order to avoid delay in notifying the landlord it may be appropriate to send a letter notifying the landlord of the claim (Early Notification Letter) before sending a letter setting out the full details of the claim (Letter of Claim). An Early Notification letter is intended to be a helpful tool, but it will not be necessary in every case. It might be appropriate where, for example, a repair is urgent or there is likely to be some delay before enough details are available to make a claim. The Early Notification Letter to the landlord should give the following information:

(i) tenant's name, the address of the property, tenant's address if different, tenant's telephone number and when access is available

    (ii) details of the defects, including any defects outstanding, in the form of a schedule, if appropriate. Attached at Annex G of paragraph 5 is a specimen schedule which can be used to inform the landlord of the disrepair

    (iii) details of any notification previously given to the landlord of the need for repair or information as to why the tenant believes that the landlord has knowledge of the need for repair

    (iv) proposed expert (see paragraph 3.6)

    (v) proposed letter of instruction to expert (see Annex C of paragraph 5)

    (vi) tenant's disclosure of such relevant documents as are readily available.

(b) The Early Notification Letter should also request the following disclosure from the landlord:

All relevant records or documents including:

    (i) copy of tenancy agreement including tenancy conditions

    (ii) documents or computerised records relating to notice given, disrepair reported, inspection reports or repair works to the property.

(c) The Early Notification Letter should include the authorisation for release of the information (except in a case where the tenant is acting in person).

(d) Specimen Early Notification Letters are attached at Annex A of paragraph 5. They may be suitably adapted as appropriate.

## 3.3 Letter of Claim

(a) The tenant should send to the landlord a Letter of Claim at the earliest reasonable opportunity. The Letter of Claim should contain the following details (if they have not already been provided in an Early Notification Letter):

    (i) tenant's name, the address of the property, tenant's address if different, the tenant's telephone number and when access is available

    (ii) details of the defects, including any defects outstanding, in the form of a schedule, if appropriate. Attached at Annex G of paragraph 5 is a specimen schedule which can be used to inform the landlord of the disrepair

    (iii) history of the defects, including attempts to rectify them

    (iv) details of any notification previously given to the landlord of the need for repair or information as to why the tenant believes that the landlord has knowledge of the need for repair

    (v) the effect of the defects on the tenant (see paragraphs 4.4 (c), (d) and (e) regarding personal injury claims)

    (vi) details of any special damages (see form attached at Annex E of paragraph 5 and definition of 'special damages' at paragraph 4.10)

(vii) proposed expert (see paragraph 3.6)

(viii) proposed letter of instruction to the expert (See Annex C of paragraph 5)

(ix) tenant's disclosure of relevant documents.

(b) If not already requested in an Early Notification Letter, the Letter of Claim should also request the following disclosure from the landlord: All relevant records or documents including:

    (i) copy of tenancy agreement including tenancy conditions

    (ii) tenancy file

    (iii) documents relating to notice given, disrepair reported, inspection reports or requirements to the property

    (iv) computerised records.

(c) If not requested in an Early Notification Letter, the Letter of Claim should also include the authorisation for release of the information (except in a case where the tenant is acting in person).

(d) Specimen Letters of Claim are attached at Annex B of paragraph 5. It will be seen that there are different versions depending on whether or not an Early Notification Letter has been sent. The letters may be suitably adapted as appropriate.

### 3.4 Limitation Period

The procedures in this Protocol do not extend statutory limitation periods. If a limitation period is about to expire, the tenant may need to issue proceedings immediately unless the landlord confirms that they will not rely on limitation as a defence in subsequent proceedings. (See paragraph 4.8 for guidance about the limitation period, and paragraph 4.10 for a definition of 'limitation period'.) Alternatively the tenant can ask the landlord to agree to extend the limitation period.

### 3.5 Landlord's Response

### 3.5.1 Response to First Letter

The landlord should normally reply within 20 working days of the date of receipt of the first letter from the tenant i.e. the Early Notification Letter or the Letter of Claim if no Early Notification Letter is sent. (See paragraph 4.10 for a definition of 'working days'). The Landlord's response to the first letter, whether an Early Notification letter or a Letter of Claim, should include the following:

*Disclosure*

(a) All relevant records or documents including:

    (i) copy of tenancy agreement including tenancy conditions

(ii) documents or computerised records relating to notice given, disrepair reported, inspection reports or requirements to the property.

*Expert*

(b) A response to the tenant's proposals for instructing an expert including:

(i) whether or not the proposed single joint expert is agreed
(ii) whether the letter of instruction is agreed
(iii) if the single joint expert is agreed but with separate instructions, a copy of the letter of instruction
(iv) if the appointment of a single joint expert is not agreed, whether the landlord agrees to a joint inspection.

### 3.5.2 Response to Letter of Claim

(a) The landlord's response to the tenant's Letter of Claim should include:

(i) whether liability is admitted and if so, in respect of which defects. If liability is disputed in respect of some or all of the defects, the reasons for this
(ii) any point which the landlord wishes to make regarding lack of notice of the repair or regarding any difficulty in gaining access
(iii) a full schedule of intended works including anticipated start and completion dates and a timetable for the works
(iv) any offer of compensation
(v) any offer in respect of costs
(vi) the information set out at 3.5.1(a) and (b), if it has not already been provided.

(b) On receipt of the Letter of Claim (whether or not an Early Notification Letter was sent), the landlord may provide a response to the issues set out at paragraph (a) above either:

(i) within 20 working days of the date of receipt of the Letter of Claim (see paragraph 4.10 for a definition of 'working days') or
(ii) within 20 working days of the date of receipt of the report of the single joint expert (see paragraph 3.6(h)) or date of receipt of the experts' agreed schedule following a joint inspection (see paragraph 3.6(g)).

### 3.5.3 If Landlord does not Respond

(a) If no response is received from the landlord to the Early Notification Letter within 20 working days, the tenant should send a Letter of Claim giving as many of the details outlined at paragraph 3.3 as possible, on the basis of the information the tenant has to hand.

(b) Failure to respond within the time limits set out in paragraphs 3.5.1 and 3.5.2, or at all, to the Early Notification Letter or the Letter of Claim will be a breach of the Protocol. (See paragraphs 4.7(a) and (b) regarding time limits and the power of the court if the Protocol is breached).

## 3.6 Experts

### General

See Paragraph 4.6 for guidance regarding the use of experts.

(a) Tenants should remember that in some cases it might not be necessary to instruct an expert to provide evidence of disrepair, for example, if the only issue relates to the level of any damages claimed. It may be advisable to take photographs of any defects before and after works, and consideration should be given to the use of video footage, particularly if an expert has not been instructed.

(b) The expert should be instructed to report on all items of disrepair which the landlord ought reasonably to know about, or which the expert ought reasonably to report on. The expert should be asked to provide a schedule of works, an estimate of the costs of repair, and to list any urgent works.

(c) Information is given at paragraph 4.6(a) about obtaining lists of independent experts who can be instructed in disrepair cases.

### Single Joint Expert

(d) If the landlord does not raise an objection to the proposed expert or letter of instruction within 20 working days of the date of receipt of the Early Notification Letter or Letter of Claim, the expert should be instructed as a single joint expert, using the tenant's proposed letter of instruction. Attached at Annex C of paragraph 5 are specimen letters of instruction to an expert. Alternatively, if the parties cannot agree joint instructions, the landlord and tenant should send their own separate instructions to the single joint expert. If sending separate instructions, the landlord should send the tenant a copy of the landlord's letter of instruction with their response to the first letter. (The tenant has already forwarded the proposed letter of instruction to the landlord).

### Joint Inspection

(e) If it is not possible to reach agreement to instruct a single joint expert, even with separate instructions, the parties should attempt to arrange a joint inspection, i.e. an inspection by different experts instructed by each party to take place at the same time. If the landlord wishes to send their own expert to a joint inspection, they should inform both the tenant's expert and the tenant's solicitor. If the landlord instructs their own expert to inspect then the tenant can also instruct their own expert. It will be for the court to decide subsequently, if proceedings are issued, whether or not either party has acted reasonably.

*Time Limits*

(f) Whether a single joint expert or a joint inspection is used, the property should be inspected within 20 working days of the date that the landlord responds to the tenant's first letter.

(g) If there is a joint inspection, the experts should produce an agreed schedule of works detailing:

(i) the defects and required works which are agreed and a timetable for the agreed works

(ii) the areas of disagreement and the reasons for disagreement.

The agreed schedule should be sent to both the landlord and the tenant within 10 working days of the joint inspection.

(h) If there is a single joint expert, a copy of the report should be sent to both the landlord and the tenant within 10 working days of the inspection. Either party can ask relevant questions of the expert.

(i) At Annex D of paragraph 5 are flowcharts showing the time limits in the Protocol.

*Urgent Cases*

(j) The Protocol does not prevent a tenant from instructing an expert at an earlier stage if this is considered necessary for reasons of urgency, and the landlord should give access in such cases. Appropriate cases may include:

(i) where the tenant reasonably considers that there is a significant risk to health and safety

(ii) where the tenant is seeking an interim injunction

(iii) where it is necessary to preserve evidence.

*Access*

(k) Tenants must give reasonable access to the landlord for inspection and repair in line with the tenancy agreement. The landlord should give reasonable notice of the need for access, except in the case of an emergency. The landlord must give access to common parts as appropriate, eg. for the inspection of a shared heating system.

*Costs*

(l) Terms of appointment should be agreed at the outset and should include:

  (i) the basis of the expert's charges (either daily or hourly rates and an estimate of the time likely to be required, or a fee for the services);

  (ii) any travelling expenses and other relevant expenses;

  (iii) rates for attendance at court should this become necessary, and provisions for payment on late notice of cancellation of a court hearing;

  (iv) time for delivery of report;

  (v) time for making payment;

  (vi) whether fees are to be paid by a third party; and

  (vii) arrangements for dealing with questions for experts and discussions between experts and for providing for the cost involved.

(m) If a single joint expert is instructed, each party will pay one half of the cost of the report. If a joint inspection is carried out, each party will pay the full cost of the report from their own expert. (See paragraph 3.7).

(n) The expert should send separately and directly to both parties answers to any questions asked.

### 3.7 Costs

(a) If the tenant's claim is settled without litigation on terms which justify bringing it, the landlord will pay the tenant's reasonable costs or out of pocket expenses. (See paragraph 4.10 for a definition of 'costs' and 'out of pocket expenses'.)

(b) Attached at Annex F of paragraph 5 is a Statement of Costs Form which can be used to inform the landlord of the costs of the claim.

### 4 GUIDANCE NOTES

### 4.1 Alternative Dispute Resolution

(a) The parties should consider whether some form of alternative dispute resolution procedure (see paragraph 4.10 for a definition of alternative dispute resolution) would be more suitable than litigation, and if so, endeavour to agree which form to adopt. Both the Claimant and Defendant may be required by the Court to provide evidence that alternative means of resolving their dispute were considered. The Courts take the view that litigation should be a last resort, and that claims should not be issued prematurely when a settlement is still actively being explored. Parties are warned that if the protocol is not followed (including this paragraph) then the Court must have regard to such conduct when determining costs.

(b) It is not practicable in this protocol to address in detail how the parties might decide which method to adopt to resolve their particular dispute. However, summarised below are some of the options for resolving disputes without litigation:

- Discussion and negotiation.
- Early neutral evaluation by an independent third party (for example, a lawyer experienced in the field of housing disrepair or an individual experienced in the subject matter of the claim).
- Mediation—a form of facilitated negotiation assisted by an independent neutral party.
- Other options in respect of the following specific categories:

   (i) For council tenants:

   - local authority repairs, complaints and/or arbitration procedures.
   - the Right to Repair Scheme. The scheme is only suitable for small, urgent repairs of less than £250 in value.

   Information and leaflets about the scheme in England can be obtained from the Department for Communities and Local Government, Eland House, Bressenden Place, London SW1E 5DU. Tel: 020 7944 3672 (http://www.communities.gov.uk/index.asp?id=1152130).
   Information about the scheme in Wales can be obtained from the National Assembly for Wales, Cathays Park, Cardiff, CF10 3NQ. Tel. 029 2082 5111.

   - Commission for Local Administration in England. Tel. 0845 602 1983.
   - the Local Government Ombudsman for Wales. Tel. 01656 661325.

   (ii) For tenants of social landlords who are not council tenants, and for tenants of qualifying private landlords:

   - In England, the Independent Housing Ombudsman. 3rd Floor, Norman House, 105–109 Strand, London WC2R 0AA. Tel 020 7836 3630.
   In Wales, the National Assembly for Wales, Cathays Park, Cardiff CF10 3NQ. Tel. 029 2082 5111.

   - Local authority environmental health officers.

   (iii) For private tenants:

● Local authority environmental health officers.

(c) The Legal Services Commission has published a booklet on 'Alternatives to Court', CLS Direct Information Leaflet 23 (www.clsdirect.org.uk/legalhelp/leaflet23.jsp), which lists a number of organisations that provide alternative dispute resolution services.

(d) *It is expressly recognised that no party can or should be forced to mediate or enter into any form of ADR.*

(e) *Information about repair rights generally is available free of charge from the following web pages: www.shelter.org.uk/housingadvice/index.asp and www.legalservices.gov.uk/leaflets/cls/index.htm.*

(f) *The former Department for Transport, Local Government and the Regions issued Good Practice Guidance on Housing Disrepair Legal Obligations in January 2002. Copies of the Guidance (ISBN 185112523X) can be obtained from Communities and Local Government Publications, PO Box 236, Wetherby LS23 7NB. Tel: 0870 1226 236. Fax: 0870 1226 237. Textphone: 0870 1207 405. E-mail: communities@two ten.com. (free to download from the Communities and Local Government website at http://www.communities.gov.uk/index.asp?id=1502470). A summary, Housing Research Summary No. 154, is available free on the Communities and Local Government website at the following link http://www.communities.gov.uk/index.asp?id=1155697. Hard copies are no longer available. The Communities and Local Government website http://www.communities.gov.uk/index.asp?id=1150232 is a general source of information for landlords and tenants.*

## 4.2 Scope of the Protocol

(a) This Protocol is intended to apply to all civil law claims which include a claim for disrepair, but not to counterclaims or set-offs in disrepair claims, which originate as other proceedings. (See paragraph 4.10 for an explanation of 'counterclaim' and 'set-off'.) In cases which involve a counterclaim or set-off, the landlord and tenant will still be expected to act reasonably in exchanging information and trying to settle the case at an early stage.

(b) In practice, most disrepair cases will have a value of more than £1,000 but less than £15,000 and so are likely to be allocated to the fast track if they come to court. (See paragraph 4.10 for an explanation of 'the fast track'.) The Protocol is aimed at this type of case. The need to keep costs down is especially important in claims of lower value. The approach of the Protocol is however, equally appropriate to all claims and the Protocol should also be followed in small track and multi-track claims. (See paragraph 4.10 for an explanation of 'small claims track' and 'multi-track'.) The court will expect to see reasonable pre-action behaviour applied in all cases.

## 4.3 Early Notification Letter

(a) The Early Notification Letter is not intended to replace the direct reporting of defects to the landlord at an early stage, using any procedure the landlord may have established. The Protocol is for use in those cases where, despite the landlord's knowledge of the disrepair, the matter remains unresolved.

(b) It is recognised that disrepair cases can range from straightforward to highly complex, and that it is not always possible to obtain detailed information at an early stage. In order to avoid unnecessary delay and to ensure that notice of the claim is given to the landlord at the earliest possible opportunity, the Protocol suggests the use of two letters in some cases; an Early Notification Letter and a later Letter of Claim. (See paragraph 3.2(a) and Annexes A & B of paragraph 5.)

(c) A copy of the Protocol need only be sent to the landlord if the tenant has reason to believe that the landlord will not have access to the Protocol e.g. because the landlord is an individual or small organisation. If in doubt, a copy should be sent.

## 4.4 Letters of Claim and landlord's response

(a) Letters of Claim and a landlord's response are not intended to have the same status as a statement of case in court proceedings. Matters may come to light after the Letter of Claim has been sent, or after the landlord has responded, which could mean that the case of one or both parties is presented slightly differently than in the Letters of Claim or in the landlord's response. It would be inconsistent with the spirit of the Protocol to seek to capitalise on this in the proceedings, provided that there was no intention to mislead. In particular, advantage should not be taken regarding discrepancies relating to the general details of notice given in the Early Notification Letter.

(b) See paragraph 4.3(c) regarding the sending of a copy of the Protocol by the tenant to the landlord.

*Cases with a Personal Injury Element*

(c) Housing disrepair claims may contain a personal injury element. This should be set out in the Letter of Claim, as should a clear indication of the identities of all persons who plan to make a personal injury claim.

(d) There is also a Personal Injury Protocol. This Protocol should be followed for that part of the disrepair claim which forms a personal injury claim, unless it is insufficient to warrant separate procedures and would therefore be dealt with only as part of the disrepair claim and evidenced by a General Practitioner's letter. The Personal Injury Protocol should be followed for any claim which requires expert evidence other than a

General Practitioner's letter. If the disrepair claim is urgent, it would be reasonable to pursue separate disrepair and personal injury claims, which could then be case managed or consolidated at a later date.

(e) Paragraph 3.3(a)(v) refers to the effect of the defects on 'the tenant'. This should be taken to include all persons who have a personal injury claim. The details of any such claim and of all likely claimants should be set out in the Letter of Claim.

## 4.5 Disclosure of documents

(a) When giving disclosure, the landlord should copy all relevant documents. In housing disrepair claims, this includes any and all documents relating in particular to the disrepair and to notice given by the tenant to the landlord of the disrepair. Notice is often given by personal attendance at the landlord's office, and copies of any notes of meetings and oral discussions should also be copied, along with other relevant documents. Documents regarding rent arrears or tenants' disputes will not normally be relevant.

(b) The aim of the early disclosure of documents by the landlord is not to encourage 'fishing expeditions' by the tenant, but to promote an early exchange of relevant information to help in clarifying or resolving issues in dispute. The tenant should assist by identifying the particular categories of documents, which they consider relevant.

(c) The 20 working days time limit specified in paragraph 3.5 runs from the date of receipt of either letter. Receipt of the letter is deemed to have taken place two days after the date of the letter. If necessary, a written request for extra time should be made by the landlord to the tenant. Should a case come to court, the court will decide whether the parties have acted reasonably, and whether any sanctions, including costs orders, are appropriate. The principles regarding time limits are referred to again at paragraph 4.7.

(d) Nothing in the Protocol restricts the right of the tenant to look personally at their file or to request a copy of the whole file. Neither is the landlord prevented from sending to the tenant a copy of the whole file, should the landlord wish.

## 4.6 Experts

(a) Information about independent experts can be obtained from:

  (i) The Chartered Institute of Environmental Health, Chadwick Court, 15 Hatfields, London SE1 8DJ Tel: 020 7928 6006. Ask for a copy of the Consultants and Trainers Directory;

  (ii) The Law Society, 113 Chancery Lane, London WC2A 1PL, Tel: 020 7831 0344. Refer to the Society's Expert Witness Directory; and

(iii) The Royal Institution of Chartered Surveyors, 12 Great George Street, Parliament Square, London SW1P 3AD, Tel: 0845 304 4111. Ask for a copy of the relevant regional directory.

(b) The Protocol encourages the use of a single joint expert. In order to make it less likely that a second expert will be necessary, the Protocol provides for the landlord to forward their own instructions directly to the single joint expert if they cannot agree joint instructions. Both parties can ask relevant questions of the expert. If the parties cannot agree on a single joint expert, either with joint or separate instructions, the Protocol suggests a joint inspection by each party's expert.

(c) The specimen letters at Annexes A and B of paragraph 5 ask for reasons to be given as to why the landlord objects to the expert proposed by the tenant. Should a case come to court, it will be for the court to decide whether the parties have acted reasonably and whether the costs of more than one expert should be recoverable.

(d) Parties should bear in mind that it may not always be necessary to obtain expert evidence of disrepair, and in view of this, the Protocol encourages the use of photos before and after works, and if appropriate, video evidence.

(e) Parties are reminded that the Civil Procedure Rules provide that expert evidence should be restricted to that which is necessary and that the court's permission is required to use an expert's report. The court may limit the amount of experts' fees and expenses recoverable from another party.

(f) When instructing an expert, regard should be had to any approved Code of Guidance for Experts and whether a copy of the Protocol should be sent to the expert.

## 4.7 Time limits

(a) The time scales given in the Protocol are long stops and every attempt should be made to comply with the Protocol as soon as possible. If parties are able to comply earlier than the time scales provided, they should do so.

(b) Time limits in the Protocol may be changed by agreement. However, it should always be borne in mind that the court will expect an explanation as to why the Protocol has not been followed or has been varied and breaches of the Protocol may lead to costs or other orders being made by the court.

## 4.8 Limitation period

(a) In cases where the limitation period will shortly expire, the tenant should ask in the first letter for an extension of the limitation period. The extension requested should be only so long as is necessary to avoid the cost of starting court proceedings.

(b) It will be for the court to decide whether refusal to grant the request is reasonable and whether any sanctions, including costs orders, are appropriate.

## 4.9 Contact point

Where a landlord is not an individual, a person should be designated to act as a point of contact for the tenant as soon as possible after the landlord receives the first letter from the tenant and (if one is involved) their solicitor. The appointee's name and contact details should be sent to the tenant and their solicitor as soon as possible after the appointment is made.

## 4.10 Glossary

| | |
|---|---|
| **Alternative Dispute Resolution** | Mediation, or other dispute resolution method, which seeks to settle disputes without the need for court proceedings. |
| **Costs** | Legal fees or, in a small track claim, out of pocket expenses incurred as a result of a claim. (See Out of Pocket Expenses below.) |
| **Counterclaim** | A claim that either party makes in response to an initial claim by the other. |
| **Damages** | Money obtained as the result of a claim to compensate for inconvenience and/or distress suffered because of the condition of the property. (See also Special Damages below.) |
| **Defect/Disrepair** | A fault or problem with a property, for which the landlord is responsible. |
| **Disclosure** | The making available by one party to the other of documentation relevant to the claim. |
| **Fast Track/Multi Track/ Small Claims Track** | Cases which proceed to court will be allocated to separate tracks depending on their value. The separate tracks have different rules and procedures. Housing cases worth between £1,000–£15,000 where there is a claim for works to be done will usually be allocated to |

the fast track. Housing cases where the costs of the repairs and/or the damages do not exceed £1,000 will usually be dealt with on the small claims track. Cases over £15,000 will usually be allocated to the multi track.

**Joint Inspection**

An inspection of a property carried out at the same time by one expert instructed by the tenant and by one expert instructed by the landlord.

**Limitation Period**

The time limit after which a legal action cannot be started. In most housing cases it is six years. In personal injury cases it is three years.

**Litigation**

A court case or court proceedings. The taking of legal action by someone.

**Notice**

Notification of a disrepair, either directly by the tenant in writing or orally to the landlord or his employee, or indirectly, by inspection of the property by the landlord or his employee.

**Out of Pocket Expenses**

Expenses incurred in a small track claims as a result of the claim, such as loss of earnings and experts' fees.

**Protocol**

A code or procedure—in this case for dealing with housing disrepair.

**Set-off**

Where one party agrees with the other's claim or part of it, but sets up one which counterbalances it.

**Single Joint Expert**

An expert who is instructed by both the tenant and the landlord, either with joint or separate instructions.

**Special Damages**

Compensation for loss of or damage to specific items e.g. clothes, carpets, curtains, wallpaper, bedding or extra electricity costs.

**Tenant**

Someone who rents land (including property) owned by another. (See also the definition at paragraph 3.1(c).)

**Third Party**                    Someone other than the landlord or tenant.

**Working Days**                   All days other than Saturdays, Sundays and
                                   bank holidays.

## 5 ANNEXES

**SPECIMEN LETTERS**

It will be noted that the attached specimen letters are in pairs for use by solicitors
and by tenants acting in person respectively.

It is emphasised that they may be suitably adapted as appropriate.

The letters, with the paragraph of the Protocol to which each one relates, are
as follows:

**Annex A**

Early Notification Letter (see paragraph 3.2.)

**Annex B**

Letter of Claim (see paragraph 3.3.)
Note: There are two versions of this:

(a)  for use where an Early Notification Letter has been sent;
(b)  for other cases.

**Annex C**

Letter of Instruction to Expert (see paragraph 3.6.)

**Annex D**

Early Notification Letter Flowchart

**Annex E**

Special Damages Form

**Annex F**

Statement of Costs

**Annex G**

Schedule

## A EARLY NOTIFICATION LETTER

EARLY NOTIFICATION LETTER

**(i) LETTER FROM SOLICITOR**

**To Landlord**

**Dear Sirs,**

### RE: TENANT'S NAME AND ADDRESS OF PROPERTY

We are instructed by your above named tenant. (*Include a sentence stating how the case is being funded.*) We are using the Housing Disrepair Protocol. *We enclose a copy of the Protocol for your information.\**

Repairs

Your tenant complains of the following defects at the property (*set out nature of defects*).

*We enclose a schedule, which sets out the disrepair in each room.\**

You received notice of the defects as follows: (*list details of notice relied on*).

Please arrange to inspect the property as soon as possible. Access will be available on the following dates and times:- (*list dates and times as appropriate*)

Please let us know what repairs you propose to carry out and the anticipated date for completion of the works.

Disclosure

Please also provide within 20 working days of receipt of this letter, the following: -

All relevant records or documents including:-

(i)     copy of tenancy agreement including tenancy conditions

(ii)    documents or computerised records relating to notice given, disrepair reported, inspection reports or repair works to the property.

We enclose a signed authority from our clients for you to release this information to ourselves.

We also enclose copies of the following relevant documents from our client:-

Expert

If agreement is not reached about the carrying out of repairs within 20 working days of this letter, we propose to jointly instruct a single joint expert *(insert expert's name and address)* to carry out an inspection of the property and provide a report. We enclose a copy of their CV, plus a draft letter of instruction. Please let us know if you agree to his/her appointment. If you object, please let us know your reasons within 20 working days.

If you do not object to the expert being instructed as a single joint expert, but wish to provide your own instructions, you should send those directly to *(insert expert's name)* within 20 working days of this letter. Please send to ourselves a copy of your letter of instruction. If you do not agree to a single joint expert, we will instruct *(insert expert's name)* to inspect the property in any event. In those circumstances, if you wish to instruct your expert to attend at the same time, please let ourselves and *(insert expert's name)* know within 20 working days of this letter.

Claim

Our client's disrepair claim requires further investigation. We will write to you as soon as possible with further details of the history of the defects and of notice relied on, along with details of our client's claim for general and special damages.


Yours faithfully,

*\* Delete as appropriate*

APPENDIX THREE

**(ii) LETTER FROM TENANT**

**To Landlord**

**Dear**

<h2 style="text-align:center">RE: YOUR NAME AND ADDRESS OF PROPERTY</h2>

I write regarding disrepair at the above address. I am using the Housing Disrepair Protocol. *I enclose a copy of the Protocol for your information.*\*

<u>Repairs</u>

The following defects exist at the property *(set out nature of defects)*.

*I enclose a schedule which sets out the disrepair in each room.*\*

Please arrange to inspect the property as soon as possible. Access will be available on the following dates and times:- *(list dates and time as appropriate)*

You received notice of the defects as follows: *(list details of notice relied on)*.

Please let me know what repairs you propose to carry out and the anticipated date for completion of the works.

<u>Disclosure</u>

Please also provide within 20 working days of receipt of this letter, the following: -

All relevant records or documents including:-

(i)     copy of tenancy agreement including tenancy conditions

(ii)    documents or computerised records relating to notice given, disrepair reported, inspection reports or repair works to the property.

I also enclose copies of the following relevant documents:- *(list documents enclosed)*

<u>Expert</u>

If agreement is not reached about the carrying out of repairs within 20 working days, I propose that we jointly instruct a single joint expert *(insert expert's name and address)* to carry out an inspection of the property and provide a report. I enclose a copy of their CV, plus a draft letter of instruction. Please let me know if you agree to his/her appointment. If you object, please let me know your reasons within 20 working days.

If you do not object to the expert being appointed as a single joint expert but wish to provide your own instructions, you should send those directly to *(insert expert's name)* within 20 working days. Please send a copy of your letter of instruction to me. If you do not agree to a single joint expert I will instruct *(insert expert's name)* to inspect the property in any event. In those circumstances if you wish your expert to attend at the same time, please let me and *(insert expert's name)* know within 20 working days.

Claim

I will write to you as soon as possible with further details of the history of the defects and of notice relied on, along with details of my claim for general and special damages.


Yours sincerely,


*\* Delete as appropriate*

## B LETTER OF CLAIM

**LETTER OF CLAIM**

*(a)* ***For use where an Early Notification Letter has been sent (as set out in Annex A).***

**(i)   LETTER FROM SOLICITOR**

**To Landlord**

**Dear Sirs,**

**RE: TENANT'S NAME AND ADDRESS OF PROPERTY**

We write further to our letter of (*insert date*) regarding our client's housing disrepair claim. We have now taken full instructions from our client.

Repairs

The history of the disrepair is as follows:-(*set out history of defects*).

*I enclose a schedule which sets out the disrepair in each room.* \*

You received notice of the defects as follows (*list details of notice relied on*).

The defects at the property are causing (*set out the effects of the disrepair on the client and their family, including any personal injury element. Specify if there will be any other additional claimant*).

Please forward to us within 20 working days of receipt of this letter a full schedule of works together with the anticipated date for completion of the works proposed.

Claim

We take the view that you are in breach of your repairing obligations. Please provide us with your proposals for compensation. (*Alternatively, set out suggestions for general damages i.e. £x for x years*). *Our client also requires compensation for special damages, and we attach a schedule of the special damages claimed.* \*

Yours faithfully,

*\* Delete as appropriate*

**(ii)    LETTER FROM TENANT**

**To Landlord**

**Dear**

**RE: YOUR NAME AND ADDRESS OF PROPERTY**

I write further to my letter of (*insert date*) regarding my housing disrepair claim. I am now able to provide you with further details.

Repairs

The history of the disrepair is as follows:-(*set out history of defects*).

You received notice of the defects as follows (*list details of notice relied on*).

The defects at the property are causing (*set out the effects of the disrepair on you and your family, including any personal injury element. Specify if there will be any other additional claimant*).

Please forward to me within 20 working days of receipt of this letter a full schedule of works together with the anticipated date for completion of the works proposed.

Claim

I take the view that you are in breach of your repairing obligations. Please provide me with your proposals for compensation. (*Alternatively, set out suggestions for general damages i.e. £x for x years*). I also require compensation for special damages, and I attach a schedule of the special damages claimed. *

Yours sincerely,

* *Delete as appropriate*

*(b)* **For use where an Early Notification Letter has <u>NOT</u> been sent.**

**(i)   LETTER FROM SOLICITOR**

**To Landlord**

**Dear Sirs,**

**RE: TENANT'S NAME AND ADDRESS OF PROPERTY**

We are instructed by your above named tenant. (*Insert a sentence stating how the case is being funded.*)  We are using the Housing Disrepair Protocol. *We enclose a copy of the Protocol for your information.* *

<u>Repairs</u>

Your tenant complains of the following defects at the property (*set out nature and history of defects*).

*We enclose a schedule which sets out the disrepair in each room.* *

You received notice of the defects as follows (*list details of notice relied on*).

The defects at the property are causing (*set out the effects of the disrepair on the client and their family, including any personal injury element, specifying if there are any additional claimants*).

<u>Disclosure</u>

Please provide within 20 working days of receipt of this letter a full schedule of the works you propose to carry out to remedy the above defects and the anticipated date for completion of the works.

Please also provide within 20 working days of this letter the following: -

All relevant records or documents including:-

|      |                                                                                                                  |
|------|------------------------------------------------------------------------------------------------------------------|
| (i)  | copy of tenancy agreement including tenancy conditions                                                           |
| (ii) | tenancy file                                                                                                     |
| (iii)| documents relating to notice given, disrepair reported, inspection reports or repair works to the property.      |
| (iv) | computerised records                                                                                             |

We enclose a signed authority from our clients for you to release this information to ourselves.

We also enclose copies of the following relevant documents:-  (*list documents enclosed*)

Expert

If agreement is not reached about the carrying out of repairs within 20 working days of receipt of this letter, we propose to jointly instruct a single joint expert (*insert expert's name and address*) to carry out an inspection of the property and provide a report. We enclose a copy of their CV, plus a draft letter of instruction. Please let me know if you agree to his/her appointment. If you object, please let me know your reasons within 20 working days.

If you do not object to the expert being instructed a single joint expert, but wish to provide your own instructions, you should send those directly to (*insert expert's name*) within 20 working days. Please send to ourselves a copy of your letter of instruction to ourselves. If you do not agree to a single joint expert, we will instruct (*insert expert's name*) to inspect the property in any event. In those circumstances, if you wish to instruct your expert to attend at the same time please let ourselves and (*insert expert's name*) know within 20 working days.

Claim

We take the view that you are in breach of your repairing obligations. Please provide us with your proposals for compensation. *(Alternatively, set out suggestions for general damages i.e. £x for x years). Our client also requires compensation for the special damages, and we attach a schedule of the special damages claimed.*\*

Yours faithfully,

\* *Delete as appropriate*

**(ii)  LETTER FROM TENANT**

**To Landlord**

**Dear**

**RE: YOUR NAME AND ADDRESS OF PROPERTY**

I write regarding the disrepair at the above address. I am using the Housing Disrepair Protocol. *I enclose a copy of the Protocol for your information.\**

Repairs

The property has the following defects (*set out nature and history of defects*).

*I enclose a schedule which sets out the disrepair in each room.\**

You received notice of the defects as follows (*list details of notice relied on*).

The defects at the property are causing (*set out the effects of the disrepair on you and your family, including any personal injury element, specifying if there are any additional claimants*).

Please provide within 20 working days of receipt of this letter a full schedule of the works you propose to carry out to remedy the above defects and the anticipated date for completion of the works.

Disclosure

Please also provide within 20 working days of receipt of this letter the following: -

All relevant records or documents including:-

       (i)     copy of tenancy agreement including tenancy conditions

       (ii)    tenancy file

       (iii)   documents relating to notice given, disrepair reported, inspection reports or repair works to the property

       (iv)   computerised records.

I also enclose copies of the following relevant documents:-  (*list documents enclosed*).

Expert

If agreement is not reached about the carrying out of repairs within 20 working days of receipt of this letter, I propose that we jointly instruct a single joint expert *(insert expert's name and address)* to carry out an inspection of the property and provide a report. I enclose a copy of their CV, plus a draft letter of instruction. Please let me know if you agree to his/her appointment. If you object, please let me know your reasons within 20 working days.

If you do not object to the expert being instructed as a single joint expert, but wish to provide your own instructions, you should send those directly to *(insert expert's name)* within 20 working days. Please also send a copy of the letter of instruction to me. If you do not agree to a single joint expert, I will instruct *(insert expert's name)* to inspect the property in any event. In those circumstances, if you wish to instruct your expert to attend at the same time please let me and *(insert expert's name)* know within 20 working days.

Claim

I take the view that you are in breach of your repairing obligations. Please provide me with your proposals for compensation. *(Alternatively, set out suggestions for general damages i.e. £x for x years).* I also require compensation for special damages, and I attach a schedule of the special damages claimed.*

Yours sincerely,

*\* Delete as appropriate*

## C   LETTER OF INSTRUCTION TO EXPERT

### LETTER OF INSTRUCTION TO EXPERT

(i)     LETTER FROM SOLICITOR

Dear

### RE: TENANT'S NAME AND ADDRESS OF PROPERTY

We act for the above named in connection with a housing disrepair claim at the above property. We are using the Housing Disrepair Protocol. *We enclose a copy of the Protocol for your information.\**

Please carry out an inspection of the above property by (date)\*\* and provide a report covering the following points:-

(a)     whether you agree that the defects are as claimed

(b)     whether any of the defects is structural

(c)     the cause of the defect(s)

(d)     the age, character and prospective life of the property.

Access will be available on the following dates and times:-  (list dates and times as appropriate)

*You are instructed as a single joint expert / The landlord is (landlord's name and details) / The landlord will be providing you with their own instructions direct / The landlord will contact you to confirm that their expert will attend at the same time as you to carry out a joint inspection.\**

Please provide the report within 10 working days of the inspection. Please contact us immediately if there are any works which require an interim injunction.

If the case proceeds to court, the report may be used in evidence.  In order to comply with court rules we would be grateful if you would insert above your signature a statement that the contents are true to the best of your knowledge and belief.  We refer you to part 35 of the Civil Procedure Rules which specifies experts' responsibilities, the contents of any report, and the statements experts must sign.

*Insert details as to cost and payment.*

Yours sincerely,

\*       *Delete as appropriate*
\*\*      *The date to be inserted should be 20 working days from the date of the letter, in accordance with paragraph 3.6(f) of the Protocol.*

(ii)    **LETTER FROM TENANT**

Dear

**RE: YOUR NAME AND ADDRESS OF PROPERTY**

I am currently in dispute with my landlord about disrepair at the above property. I am using the Housing Disrepair Protocol. *I enclose a copy of the Protocol for your information.*\*

Please carry out an inspection of the above property by (*date*)\*\* and provide a report covering the following points:-

(a)    whether you agree that the defects are as claimed

(b)    whether any of the defects is structural

(c)    the cause of the defect(s)

(d)    the age, character and prospective life of the property.

Access will be available on the following dates and times:-  (list dates and times as appropriate)

*You are instructed as a single joint expert / The landlord is (landlord's name and details) / The landlord will be providing you with their own instructions direct / The landlord will contact you to confirm that their expert will attend at the same time as you to carry out a joint inspection.*\*

Please provide the report within 10 working days of the inspection.  Please contact me immediately if there are any works which require an interim injunction.

If the case proceeds to court, the report may be used in evidence.  In order to comply with court rules I would be grateful if you would insert above your signature a statement that the contents are true to the best of your knowledge and belief. I refer you to part 35 of the Civil Procedure Rules which specifies experts' responsibilities, the contents of any report, and the statements experts must sign.

*Insert details as to cost and payment.*

Yours sincerely,

\*       *Delete as appropriate*
\*\*     *The date to be inserted should be 20 working days from the date of the letter, in accordance with paragraph 3.6(f) of the Protocol.*

## D   EARLY NOTIFICATION LETTER FLOWCHART

# Early Notification Letter Flowchart

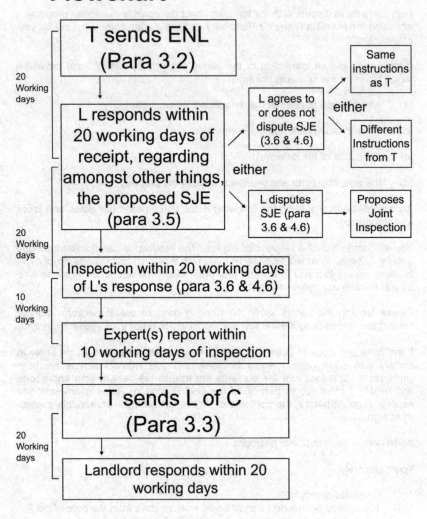

# Letter of Claim Flowchart

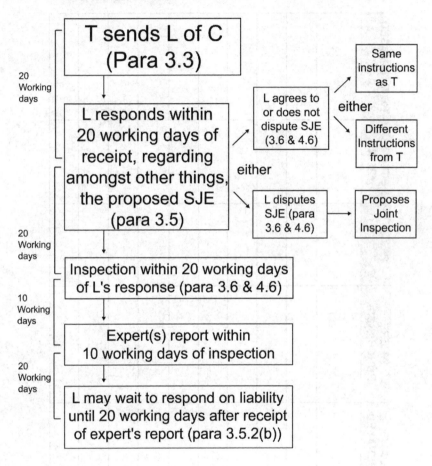

# E SPECIAL DAMAGES FORM

## SPECIAL DAMAGES FORM

| ITEM | DATE PURCHASED | WHERE PURCHASED | PRICE | RECEIPTS – YES/NO | HOW DAMAGED |
|------|----------------|-----------------|-------|-------------------|-------------|
| 1 |  |  |  |  |  |
| 2 |  |  |  |  |  |
| 3 |  |  |  |  |  |
| 4 |  |  |  |  |  |
| 5 |  |  |  |  |  |
| 6 |  |  |  |  |  |
| 7 |  |  |  |  |  |
| 8 |  |  |  |  |  |
| 9 |  |  |  |  |  |
| 10 |  |  |  |  |  |

## F STATEMENT OF COSTS

# Statement of Costs
# (summary assessment)

**Judge/Master**

| In the | |
|---|---|
| | **Court** |
| **Case Reference** | |

**Case Title**

**[Party]'s Statement of Costs for the hearing on** *(date)*                    **(interim application/fast track trial)**

Description of fee earners*

    (a) *(name) (grade) (hourly rate claimed)*

    (b) *(name) (grade) (hourly rate claimed)*

Attendances on                    *(party)*

| | | | | |
|---|---|---|---|---|
| (a) *(number)* | hours at £ | | £ | 0.00 |
| (b) *(number)* | hours at £ | | £ | 0.00 |

Attendances on opponents

| | | | | |
|---|---|---|---|---|
| (a) *(number)* | hours at £ | | £ | 0.00 |
| (b) *(number)* | hours at £ | | £ | 0.00 |

Attendance on others

| | | | | |
|---|---|---|---|---|
| (a) *(number)* | hours at £ | | £ | 0.00 |
| (b) *(number)* | hours at £ | | £ | 0.00 |

Site inspections etc

| | | | | |
|---|---|---|---|---|
| (a) *(number)* | hours at £ | | £ | 0.00 |
| (b) *(number)* | hours at £ | | £ | 0.00 |

Work done on negotiations

| | | | | |
|---|---|---|---|---|
| (a) *(number)* | hours at £ | | £ | 0.00 |
| (b) *(number)* | hours at £ | | £ | 0.00 |

Other work, not covered above

| | | | | |
|---|---|---|---|---|
| (a) *(number)* | hours at £ | | £ | 0.00 |
| (b) *(number)* | hours at £ | | £ | 0.00 |

Work done on documents

| | | | | |
|---|---|---|---|---|
| (a) *(number)* | hours at £ | | £ | 0.00 |
| (b) *(number)* | hours at £ | | £ | 0.00 |

Attendance at hearing

| | | | | |
|---|---|---|---|---|
| (a) *(number)* | hours at £ | | £ | 0.00 |
| (b) *(number)* | hours at £ | | £ | 0.00 |
| (a) *(number)* | hours travel and waiting at £ | | £ | 0.00 |
| (b) *(number)* | hours travel and waiting at £ | | £ | 0.00 |

                                       **Sub Total £**     0.00

> **IMPORTANT: This form has been revised to show the four grades of fee earner which have been agreed between the Supreme Court Costs Office and the Law Society and with the concurrence of the Head of Civil Justice. It is being introduced in advance of the formal amendment in the December update to the Civil Procedure Rules. THIS MESSAGE WILL NOT PRINT OUT.**

**N260** Statement of Costs (summary assessment) (10.01)                    *Printed on behalf of The Court Service*

## Appendix Three

**Brought forward £** `0.00`

Counsel's fees *(name) (year of call)* [_____]

        Fee for [advice/conference/documents]      £ [_____]

        Fee for hearing      £ [_____]

Other expenses

        [court fees]      £ [_____]

        Others      £ [_____]

        *(give brief description)*

        **Total**      £ `0.00`

        Amount of VAT claimed

                on solicitors and counsel's fees      £ [_____]

                on other expenses      £ [_____]

        **Grand Total**      £ `0.00`

The costs estimated above do not exceed the costs which the *(party)* [_____]
is liable to pay in respect of the work which this estimate covers.

Dated [_____]      Signed [_____]

                                    Name of firm of solicitors
[partner] for the *(party)* [_____]

---

\* 4 grades of fee earner are suggested:

(A) Solicitors with over eight years post qualification experience including at least eight years litigation experience.

(B) Solicitors and legal executives with over four years post qualification experience including at least four years litigation experience.

(C) Other solicitors and legal executives and fee earners of equivalent experience.

(D) Trainee solicitors, para legals and other fee earners.

"Legal Executive" means a Fellow of the Institute of Legal Executives. Those who are not Fellows of the Institute are not entitled to call themselves legal executives and in principle are therefore not entitled to the same hourly rate as a legal executive.

In respect of each fee earner communications should be treated as attendances and routine communications should be claimed at one tenth of the hourly rate.

# G SCHEDULE

Schedule
Disrepair Protocol
## TENANT

| | Item Number | Room (tick where appropriate) | Disrepair (identify briefly) | Notice given (How was the landlord made aware of the problem) | Inconvenience suffered (How has the disrepair affected you) |
|---|---|---|---|---|---|
| Exterior of premises, roof and access Comment: | | | | | |
| Entrance, hall and storage Comment: | | | | | |
| Living room (s) Comment: | | | | | |
| Kitchen Comment: | | | | | |
| Bathroom Comment: | | | | | |
| Bedroom 1 Comment: | | | | | |
| Bedroom 2 Comment: | | | | | |
| Bedroom 3 Comment: | | | | | |
| Other Comment | | | | | |

# INDEX

This index has been prepared using Sweet and Maxwell's Legal Taxonomy. Main index entries conform to keywords provided by the Legal Taxonomy except where references to specific documents or non-standard terms (denoted by quotation marks) have been included. These keywords provide a means of identifying similar concepts in other Sweet and Maxwell publications and online services to which keywords from the Legal Taxonomy have been applied. Readers may find some minor differences between terms used in the text and those which appear in the index. Suggestions to *sweetandmaxwell.taxonomy@thomson.com*.

**All references are to paragraph number**

**Abuse of process**
  claims
    differing issues, 1–18
    failure to raise, 1–18
  public interest, 1–18
  res judicata, 1–18
  right to fair trial, 1–18
  subsequent claims, 1–18
**Access**
  *see also* **Powers of entry**; **Rights of re-entry**
  absolute obligation, 19–11
  common parts, 19–08—19–09, 19–11, 19–18
  concealed dangers, 19–11
  easements, 19–09
  essential means of access, 19–07—19–11
  footpaths, 19–10, 20–27
  implied obligation, 19–07
  lifts, 19–08, 19–10
  precedent, App 1
  reasonable care, 19–11
  reasonable repair and efficiency, 19–08
  staircases, 19–08, 20–27
**Adjoining premises**
  introduction, 23–04
  repair covenants
    landlords' breach of covenant, 23–05—23–07
    premises not landlord's responsibility, 23–08
    tenant's liability, 23–04—23–05, 23–08
    tenant's right of action, 23–05
  rights of entry
    abatement, 23–14
    absence of express right, 23–11
    easements, 23–15—23–16
    express rights, 23–10
    introduction, 23–09
    landlords' breach of covenant, 23–12

    statutory compliance, 23–17
**"Age character and locality of premises"**
  standard of repair, 9–13—9–17
**Agricultural holdings**
  housing provision, 20–15
**Airspace**
  advertising signs, 7–07
  flats, 7–07
  maisonettes, 7–07
  ownership, 7–07
  roof profiles, 7–07
**Alterations**
  interpretation of lease, 7–20, 7–24—7–25
  notice
    form of notice, 16–04
    oral notice, 16–04
    precondition to liability, 16–03
    reasonableness, 16–07
    timing, 16–05—16–06
    valid notice, 16–03
    void for uncertainty, 16–04
  premises
    annexation, 7–20
    attachments, 7–20
    land subject to lease, 7–20
    lease of messuage, 7–20
  reinstatement
    absolute obligations, 16–02
    consent to alterations, 16–01
    damages, 16–12
    deeds of licence, 16–01
    express terms, 5–07, 14–39
    landlord otherwise requires, 16–08
    partial reinstatement, 16–10
    reinstatement on notice, 16–03—16–07
    scope of obligation, 16–09

# INDEX

# INDEX

# INDEX